# Full-Circle Learning

## MyLab™: Learning Full Circle for Marketing, Management, Business Communication, Intro to Business, and MIS

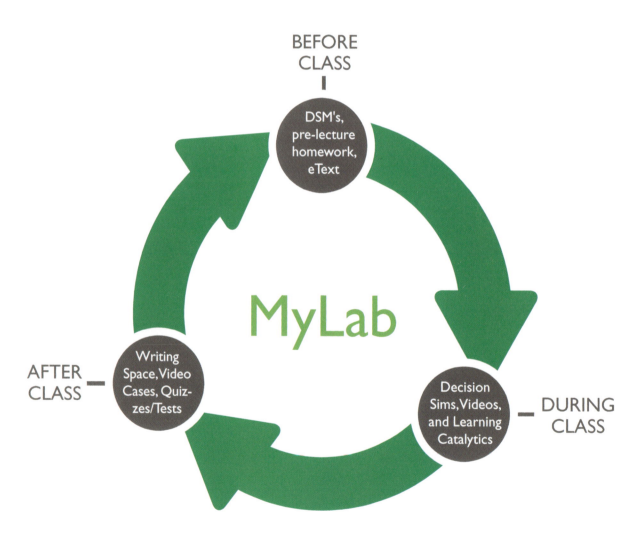

BEFORE CLASS

DSM's, pre-lecture homework, eText

MyLab

DURING CLASS

Decision Sims, Videos, and Learning Catalytics

AFTER CLASS

Writing Space, Video Cases, Quizzes/Tests

# MyMarketingLab™: Improves Student Engagement Before, During, and After Class

**Prep and Engagement**

- **Video exercises** – engaging videos that bring business concepts to life and explore business topics related to the theory students are learning in class. Quizzes then assess students' comprehension of the concepts covered in each video.

- **Learning Catalytics** – a "bring your own device" student engagement, assessment, and classroom intelligence system helps instructors analyze students' critical-thinking skills during lecture.

- **Dynamic Study Modules (DSMs)** – through adaptive learning, students get personalized guidance where and when they need it most, creating greater engagement, improving knowledge retention, and supporting subject-matter mastery. Also available on mobile devices.

- **Business Today** – bring current events alive in your classroom with videos, discussion questions, and author blogs. Be sure to check back often, this section changes daily.

- **Decision-making simulations** – place your students in the role of a key decision-maker. The simulation will change and branch based on the decisions students make, providing a variation of scenario paths. Upon completion of each simulation, students receive a grade, as well as a detailed report of the choices they made during the simulation and the associated consequences of those decisions.

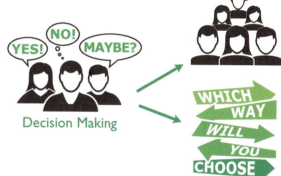

**Decision Making**

WHICH WAY WILL YOU CHOOSE

**Critical Thinking**

turnitin

- **Writing Space** – better writers make great learners—who perform better in their courses. Providing a single location to develop and assess concept mastery and critical thinking, the Writing Space offers automatic graded, assisted graded, and create your own writing assignments, allowing you to exchange personalized feedback with students quickly and easily.

  Writing Space can also check students' work for improper citation or plagiarism by comparing it against the world's most accurate text comparison database available from **Turnitin**.

- **Additional Features** – included with the MyLab are a powerful homework and test manager, robust gradebook tracking, comprehensive online course content, and easily scalable and shareable content.

http://www.pearsonmylabandmastering.com

**PEARSON**

# Marketing Management

**15**

## PHILIP KOTLER
Northwestern University

## KEVIN LANE KELLER
Dartmouth College

**PEARSON**

Boston   Columbus   Indianapolis   New York   San Francisco   Amsterdam   Cape Town
Dubai   London   Madrid   Milan   Munich   Paris   Montréal   Toronto
Delhi   Mexico City   São Paulo   Sydney   Hong Kong   Seoul   Singapore   Taipei   Tokyo

**Vice President, Business Publishing:** Donna Battista
**Editor-in-Chief:** Stephanie Wall
**Acquisitions Editor:** Mark Gaffney
**Development Editor:** Elisa Adams
**Program Manager Team Lead:** Ashley Santora
**Program Manager:** Jennifer Collins
**Editorial Assistant:** Daniel Petrino
**Vice President, Product Marketing:** Maggie Moylan
**Director of Marketing, Digital Services and Products:** Jeanette Koskinas
**Executive Product Marketing Manager:** Anne Fahlgren
**Field Marketing Manager:** Lenny Ann Raper
**Senior Strategic Marketing Manager:** Erin Gardner
**Project Manager Team Lead:** Judy Leale
**Project Manager:** Becca Groves
**Operations Specialist:** Carol Melville
**Creative Director:** Blair Brown

**Senior Art Director:** Janet Slowik
**Interior and Cover Designer:** Integra Software Services Pvt Ltd.
**Vice President, Director of Digital Strategy & Assessment:** Paul Gentile
**Manager of Learning Applications:** Paul Deluca
**Digital Editor:** Brian Surette
**Digital Studio Manager:** Diane Lombardo
**Digital Studio Project Manager:** Robin Lazrus
**Digital Studio Project Manager:** Alana Coles
**Digital Studio Project Manager:** Monique Lawrence
**Digital Studio Project Manager:** Regina DaSilva
**Full-Service Project Management and Composition:** Integra Software Services Pvt Ltd.
**Printer/Binder:** LSC Communications
**Cover Printer:** Phoenix Color/Hagerstown
**Text Font:** Minion Pro 9.5/11.5

**Library of Congress Cataloging-in-Publication Data**
Kotler, Philip.
  Marketing management/Philip Kotler, Kevin Lane Keller.—15e [edition].
    pages cm
  ISBN 978-0-13-385646-0 (student edition)
  1. Marketing—Management.  I. Keller, Kevin Lane, 1956-  II. Title.
  HF5415.13.K64 2016
  658.8—dc23
                       2014023870

4   17

ISBN 10:    0-13-385646-1
ISBN 13: 978-0-13-385646-0

This book is dedicated to my wife and best friend, Nancy, with love.

**—PK**

This book is dedicated to my wife, Punam, and my two daughters,

Carolyn and Allison, with much love and thanks.

**—KLK**

# About the Authors

Philip Kotler

**Philip Kotler** *is one of the world's leading authorities on marketing. He is the S. C. Johnson & Son Distinguished Professor of International Marketing at the Kellogg School of Management, Northwestern University. He received his master's degree at the University of Chicago and his Ph.D. at MIT, both in economics. He did postdoctoral work in mathematics at Harvard University and in behavioral science at the University of Chicago.*

*Dr. Kotler is the coauthor of* Principles of Marketing *and* Marketing: An Introduction. *His* Strategic Marketing for Nonprofit Organizations, *now in its seventh edition, is the best seller in that specialized area.* Dr. Kotler's *other books include* Marketing Models; The New Competition; Marketing Professional Services; Strategic Marketing for Educational Institutions; Marketing for Health Care Organizations; Marketing Congregations; High Visibility; Social Marketing; Marketing Places; The Marketing of Nations; Marketing for Hospitality and Tourism; Standing Room Only—Strategies for Marketing the Performing Arts; Museum Strategy and Marketing; Marketing Moves; Kotler on Marketing; Lateral Marketing; Winning at Innovation; Ten Deadly Marketing Sins; Chaotics; Marketing Your Way to Growth; Winning Global Markets; *and* Corporate Social Responsibility.

*In addition, he has published more than 150 articles in leading journals, including the* Harvard Business Review, Sloan Management Review, Business Horizons, California Management Review, *the* Journal of Marketing, *the* Journal of Marketing Research, Management Science, *the* Journal of Business Strategy, *and* Futurist. *He is the only three-time winner of the coveted Alpha Kappa Psi award for the best annual article published in the* Journal of Marketing.

*Professor Kotler was the first recipient of the American Marketing Association's (AMA) Distinguished Marketing Educator Award (1985). The European Association of Marketing Consultants and Sales Trainers awarded him their Prize for Marketing Excellence. He was chosen as the Leader in Marketing Thought by the Academic Members of the AMA in a 1975 survey. He also received the 1978 Paul Converse Award of the AMA, honoring his original contribution to marketing. In 1995, the Sales and Marketing Executives International (SMEI) named him Marketer of the Year. In 2002, Professor Kotler received the Distinguished Educator Award from the Academy of Marketing Science. In 2013, he received the William L. Wilkie "Marketing for a Better World" Award and subsequently received the Sheth Foundation Medal for Exceptional Contribution to Marketing Scholarship and Practice. In 2014, he was inducted in the Marketing Hall of Fame.*

*He has received honorary doctoral degrees from Stockholm University, the University of Zurich, Athens University of Economics and Business, DePaul University, the Cracow School of Business and Economics, Groupe H.E.C. in Paris, the Budapest School of Economic Science and Public Administration, the University of Economics and Business Administration in Vienna, and Plekhanov Russian Academy of Economics. Professor Kotler has been a consultant to many major U.S. and foreign companies, including IBM, General Electric, AT&T, Honeywell, Bank of America, Merck, SAS Airlines, Michelin, and others in the areas of marketing strategy and planning, marketing organization, and international marketing.*

*He has been Chairman of the College of Marketing of the Institute of Management Sciences, a Director of the American Marketing Association, a Trustee of the Marketing Science Institute, a Director of the MAC Group, a member of the Yankelovich Advisory Board, and a member of the Copernicus Advisory Board. He was a member of the Board of Governors of the School of the Art Institute of Chicago and a member of the Advisory Board of the Drucker Foundation. He has traveled extensively throughout Europe, Asia, and South America, advising and lecturing to many companies about global marketing opportunities.*

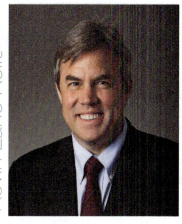

**Kevin Lane Keller** *is the E. B. Osborn Professor of Marketing at the Tuck School of Business at Dartmouth College. Professor Keller has degrees from Cornell, Carnegie-Mellon, and Duke universities. At Dartmouth, he teaches MBA courses on marketing management and strategic brand management and lectures in executive programs on those topics.*

*Previously, Professor Keller was on the faculty at Stanford University, where he also served as the head of the marketing group. Additionally, he has been on the faculty at the University of California at Berkeley and the University of North Carolina at Chapel Hill, has been a visiting professor at Duke University and the Australian Graduate School of Management, and has two years of industry experience as Marketing Consultant for Bank of America.*

*Professor Keller's general area of expertise lies in marketing strategy and planning and branding. His specific research interest is in how understanding theories and concepts related to consumer behavior can improve marketing strategies. His research has been published in three of the major marketing journals: the* Journal of Marketing, *the* Journal of Marketing Research, *and the* Journal of Consumer Research. *He also has served on the Editorial Review Boards of those journals. With more than 90 published papers, his research has been widely cited and has received numerous awards.*

*Actively involved with industry, he has worked on a host of different types of marketing projects. He has served as a long-term consultant and advisor to marketers for some of the world's most successful brands, including Accenture, American Express, Disney, Ford, Intel, Levi Strauss, Procter & Gamble, and Samsung. Additional brand consulting activities have been with other top companies such as Allstate, Beiersdorf (Nivea), BlueCross BlueShield, Campbell, Colgate, Eli Lilly, ExxonMobil, General Mills, GfK, Goodyear, Hasbro, Intuit, Johnson & Johnson, Kodak, L.L.Bean, Mayo Clinic, MTV, Nordstrom, Ocean Spray, Red Hat, SAB Miller, Shell Oil, Starbucks, Unilever, and Young & Rubicam. He has also served as an academic trustee for the Marketing Science Institute and served as their Executive Director from July 1, 2013, to July 1, 2015.*

*A popular and highly sought-after speaker, he has made speeches and conducted marketing seminars to top executives in a variety of forums. Some of his senior management and marketing training clients have included include such diverse business organizations as Cisco, Coca-Cola, Deutsche Telekom, ExxonMobil, GE, Google, IBM, Macy's, Microsoft, Nestle, Novartis, Pepsico, SC Johnson and Wyeth. He has lectured all over the world, from Seoul to Johannesburg, from Sydney to Stockholm, and from Sao Paulo to Mumbai. He has served as keynote speaker at conferences with hundreds to thousands of participants.*

*Professor Keller is currently conducting a variety of studies that address strategies to build, measure, and manage brand equity. His textbook on those subjects,* Strategic Brand Management, *in its fourth edition, has been adopted at top business schools and leading firms around the world and has been heralded as the "bible of branding."*

*An avid sports, music, and film enthusiast, in his so-called spare time, he has helped to manage and market, as well as serve as executive producer for, one of Australia's great rock-and-roll treasures, The Church, as well as American power-pop legends Tommy Keene and Dwight Twilley. He also serves on the Board of Directors for The Doug Flutie, Jr. Foundation for Autism, the Lebanon Opera House, and the Montshire Museum of Science. Professor Keller lives in Etna, NH, with his wife, Punam (also a Tuck marketing professor), and his two daughters, Carolyn and Allison.*

# Brief Contents

# Contents

# Preface

## What's New in the 15th Edition

The 15th edition of *Marketing Management* is a landmark entry in the long successful history of the market leader. With the 15th edition, great care was taken to provide an introductory guide to marketing management that truly reflects the modern realities of marketing. In doing so, classic concepts, guidelines, and examples were retained while new ones were added as appropriate. Three broad forces—globalization, technology, and social responsibility—were identified as critical to the success of modern marketing programs. These three topics are evident all through the text.

As has been the case for a number of editions now, the overriding goal of the revision for the 15th edition of *Marketing Management* was to create as comprehensive, current, and engaging a MBA marketing textbook as possible. Where appropriate, new material was added, old material was updated, and no longer relevant or necessary material was deleted.

Even though marketing is changing in many significant ways these days, many core elements remain, and we feel strongly that a balanced approach of classic and contemporary approaches and perspectives is the way to go. *Marketing Management,* 15th edition, allows those instructors who have used the 14th edition to build on what they have learned and done while at the same time offering a text that is unsurpassed in breadth, depth, and relevance for students experiencing *Marketing Management* for the first time.

The successful across-chapter reorganization into eight parts that began with the 12th edition of *Marketing Management* has largely been preserved, although several adjustments have been made to improve student understanding, as described below. Many of the favorably received within-chapter features that have been introduced through the years, such as topical chapter openers, in-text boxes highlighting noteworthy companies or issues, and the Marketing Insight and Marketing Memo boxes that provide in-depth conceptual and practical commentary, have been retained.

Significant changes to the 15th edition include:

- Brand-new opening vignettes for each chapter set the stage for the chapter material to follow. By covering topical brands or companies, the vignettes are great classroom discussion starters.
- Almost half of the in-text boxes are new. These boxes provide vivid illustrations of chapter concepts using actual companies and situations. The boxes cover a variety of products, services, and markets, and many have accompanying illustrations in the form of ads or product shots.
- Each end-of-chapter section now includes two expanded Marketing Excellence mini-cases highlighting innovative, insightful marketing accomplishments by leading organizations. Each case includes questions that promote classroom discussion and student analysis.
- The global chapter (8, previously Chapter 21) has been moved into Part 3 on Connecting with Customers and the new products chapter (15, previously Chapter 20) has been moved into Part 5 on Creating Value. The positioning and brand chapters (10 and 11) have been switched to allow for the conventional STP sequencing. These moves permit richer coverage of the topics and better align with many instructors' teaching strategy.
- A new chapter (21) titled Managing Digital Communications: Online, Social Media, and Mobile has been added to better highlight that important topic. Significant attention is paid throughout the text to what a new section in Chapter 1 calls "the digital revolution."
- The concluding chapter (23) has been retitled "Managing a Holistic Marketing Organization for the Long Run" and addresses corporate social responsibility, business ethics, and sustainability, among other topics.
- Chapter 12 (previously Chapter 11) has been retitled "Addressing Competition and Driving Growth" to acknowledge the importance of growth to an organization.

## What Is *Marketing Management* All About?

*Marketing Management* is the leading marketing text because its content and organization consistently reflect changes in marketing theory and practice. The very first edition of *Marketing Management*, published in 1967, introduced the concept that companies must be customer and market driven. But there was little mention of what have now become fundamental topics such as segmentation, targeting, and positioning. Concepts such as brand equity, customer value analysis, database marketing, e-commerce, value networks, hybrid channels, supply chain management, and integrated marketing communications were not even part of the marketing vocabulary then. *Marketing Management* continues to reflect the changes in the marketing discipline over the past almost 50 years.

Firms now sell goods and services through a variety of direct and indirect channels. Mass advertising is not nearly as effective as it was, so marketers are exploring new forms of communication, such as experiential, entertainment, and viral marketing. Customers are telling companies what types of product or services they want and when, where, and how they want to buy them. They are increasingly reporting to other consumers what they think of specific companies and products—using e-mail, blogs, podcasts, and other digital media to do so. Company messages are becoming a smaller fraction of the total "conversation" about products and services.

In response, companies have shifted gears from managing product portfolios to managing *customer* portfolios, compiling databases on individual customers so they can understand them better and construct individualized offerings and messages. They are doing less product and service standardization and more niching and customization. They are replacing monologues with customer dialogues. They are improving their methods of measuring customer profitability and customer lifetime value. They are intent on measuring the return on their marketing investment and its impact on shareholder value. They are also concerned with the ethical and social implications of their marketing decisions.

As companies change, so does their marketing organization. Marketing is no longer a company department charged with a limited number of tasks—it is a company-wide undertaking. It drives the company's vision, mission, and strategic planning. Marketing includes decisions like whom the company wants as its customers, which of their needs to satisfy, what products and services to offer, what prices to set, what communications to send and receive, what channels of distribution to use, and what partnerships to develop. Marketing succeeds only when all departments work together to achieve goals: when engineering designs the right products; finance furnishes the required funds; purchasing buys high-quality materials; production makes high-quality products on time; and accounting measures the profitability of different customers, products, and areas.

To address all these different shifts, good marketers are practicing holistic marketing. *Holistic marketing* is the development, design, and implementation of marketing programs, processes, and activities that recognize the breadth and interdependencies of today's marketing environment. Four key dimensions of holistic marketing are:

1. *Internal marketing*—ensuring everyone in the organization embraces appropriate marketing principles, especially senior management.

2. *Integrated marketing*—ensuring that multiple means of creating, delivering, and communicating value are employed and combined in the best way.

3. *Relationship marketing*—having rich, multifaceted relationships with customers, channel members, and other marketing partners.

4. *Performance marketing*—understanding returns to the business from marketing activities and programs, as well as addressing broader concerns and their legal, ethical, social, and environmental effects.

These four dimensions are woven throughout the book and at times spelled out explicitly. The text is organized to specifically address the following eight tasks that constitute modern marketing management in the 21st century:

1. Developing marketing strategies and plans
2. Capturing marketing insights
3. Connecting with customers
4. Building strong brands
5. Creating value
6. Delivering value
7. Communicating value
8. Conducting marketing responsibly for long-term success

# What Makes *Marketing Management* the Marketing Leader?

Marketing is of interest to everyone, whether they are marketing goods, services, properties, persons, places, events, information, ideas, or organizations. As it has maintained its respected position among students, educators, and businesspeople, *Marketing Management* has kept up to date and contemporary. Students (and instructors) feel that the book is talking directly to them in terms of both content and delivery.

*Marketing Management* owes its marketplace success to its ability to maximize three dimensions that characterize the best marketing texts—depth, breadth, and relevance—as measured by the following criteria:

- **Depth.** Does the book have solid academic grounding? Does it contain important theoretical concepts, models, and frameworks? Does it provide conceptual guidance to solve practical problems?
- **Breadth.** Does the book cover all the right topics? Does it provide the proper amount of emphasis on those topics?
- **Relevance.** Does the book engage the reader? Is it interesting to read? Does it have lots of compelling examples?

The 15th edition builds on the fundamental strengths of past editions that collectively distinguish it from all other marketing management texts:

- **Managerial orientation.** The book focuses on the major decisions that marketing managers and top management face in their efforts to harmonize the organization's objectives, capabilities, and resources with marketplace needs and opportunities.
- **Analytical approach.** *Marketing Management* presents conceptual tools and frameworks for analyzing recurring problems in marketing management. Cases and examples illustrate effective marketing principles, strategies, and practices.
- **Multidisciplinary perspective.** The book draws on the rich findings of various scientific disciplines—economics, behavioral science, management theory, and mathematics—for fundamental concepts and tools directly applicable to marketing challenges.
- **Universal applications.** The book applies strategic thinking to the complete spectrum of marketing: products, services, persons, places, information, ideas, and causes; consumer and business markets; profit and nonprofit organizations; domestic and foreign companies; small and large firms; manufacturing and intermediary businesses; and low- and high-tech industries.
- **Comprehensive and balanced coverage.** *Marketing Management* covers all the topics an informed marketing manager needs to understand to execute strategic, tactical, and administrative marketing.

# Instructor Resources

At the Instructor Resource Center, www.pearsonhighered.com/irc, instructors can easily register to gain access to a variety of instructor resources available with this text in downloadable format. If assistance is needed, our dedicated technical support team is ready to help with the media supplements that accompany this text. Visit http://247.pearsoned.com for answers to frequently asked questions and toll-free user support phone numbers.

The following supplements are available with this text:

- **Instructor's Resource Manual**
- **Test Bank**
- **TestGen® Computerized Test Bank**
- **PowerPoint Presentation**
- **Instructor Video Library**
- **Image Library**

# Acknowledgments

The 15th edition bears the imprint of many people. *From Phil Kotler:* My colleagues and associates at the Kellogg School of Management at Northwestern University continue to have an important impact on my thinking: Nidhi Agrawal, Eric T. Anderson, James C. Anderson, Robert C. Blattberg, Miguel C. Brendl, Bobby J. Calder, Gregory S. Carpenter, Alex Chernev, Anne T. Coughlan, David Gal, Kent Grayson, Karsten Hansen, Dipak C. Jain, Lakshman Krishnamurti, Angela Lee, Vincent Nijs, Yi Qian, Mohanbir S. Sawhney, Louis W. Stern, Brian Sternthal, Alice M. Tybout, and Andris A. Zoltners. I also want to thank the S. C. Johnson Family for the generous support of my chair at the Kellogg School. Completing the Northwestern team are my former Deans, Donald P. Jacobs and Dipak Jain and my current Dean, Sally Blount, for providing generous support for my research and writing.

Several former faculty members of the marketing department had a great influence on my thinking: Steuart Henderson Britt, Richard M. Clewett, Ralph Westfall, Harper W. Boyd, Sidney J. Levy, John Sherry, and John Hauser. I also want to acknowledge Gary Armstrong for our work on *Principles of Marketing*.

I am indebted to the following coauthors of international editions of *Marketing Management* and *Principles of Marketing* who have taught me a great deal as we worked together to adapt marketing management thinking to the problems of different nations:

- Swee-Hoon Ang and Siew-Meng Leong, National University of Singapore
- Chin-Tiong Tan, Singapore Management University
- Friedhelm W. Bliemel, Universitat Kaiserslautern (Germany)
- Linden Brown; Stewart Adam, Deakin University; Suzan Burton: Macquarie Graduate School of Management, and Sara Denize, University of Western Sydney (Australia)
- Bernard Dubois, Groupe HEC School of Management (France) and Delphine Manceau, ESCP-EAP European School of Management
- John Saunders, Loughborough University and Veronica Wong, Warwick University (United Kingdom)
- Jacob Hornick, Tel Aviv University (Israel)
- Walter Giorgio Scott, Universita Cattolica del Sacro Cuore (Italy)
- Peggy Cunningham, Queen's University (Canada)

I also want to acknowledge how much I have learned from working with coauthors on more specialized marketing subjects: Alan Andreasen, Christer Asplund, Paul N. Bloom, John Bowen, Roberta C. Clarke, Karen Fox, David Gertner, Michael Hamlin, Thomas Hayes, Donald Haider, Hooi Den Hua, Dipak Jain, Somkid Jatusripitak, Hermawan Kartajaya, Milton Kotler, Neil Kotler, Nancy Lee, Sandra Liu, Suvit Maesincee, James Maken, Waldemar Pfoertsch, Gustave Rath, Irving Rein, Eduardo Roberto, Joanne Scheff, Norman Shawchuck, Joel Shalowitz, Ben Shields, Francois Simon, Robert Stevens, Martin Stoller, Fernando Trias de Bes, Bruce Wrenn, and David Young.

My overriding debt continues to be to my lovely wife, Nancy, who provided me with the time, support, and inspiration needed to prepare this edition. It is truly our book.

*From Kevin Lane Keller:* I continually benefit from the wisdom of my marketing colleagues at Tuck—Punam Keller, Scott Neslin, Kusum Ailawadi, Praveen Kopalle, Peter Golder, Ellie Kyung, Yaniv Dover, Eesha Sharma, Fred Webster, Gert Assmus, and John Farley—as well as the leadership of Dean Paul Danos. I also gratefully acknowledge the invaluable research and teaching contributions from my faculty colleagues and collaborators through the years. I owe a considerable debt of gratitude to Duke University's Jim Bettman and Rick Staelin for helping to get my academic career started and serving as positive role models to this day. I am also appreciative of all that I have learned from working with many industry executives who have generously shared their insights and experiences. With this 15th edition, I received some extremely helpful research assistance from a talented group of Dartmouth undergraduate RAs—Caroline Buck, James Carlson, Ryan Galloway, Jack Heise, Jeff Keller, Jill Lyon, Richard Newsome-White, Rahul Raina, and Cameron Woodworth, —who were as accurate, thorough, dependable, and cheerful as you could possibly imagine. Alison Pearson provided superb administrative support. Finally, I give special thanks to Punam, my wife, and Carolyn and Allison, my daughters, who make it all happen and make it all worthwhile.

We are indebted to the following colleagues at other universities who reviewed this new edition:

- Jennifer Barr, Richard Stockton College
- Lawrence Kenneth Duke, Drexel University LeBow College of Business
- Barbara S. Faries, Mission College, Santa Clara, CA
- William E. Fillner, Hiram College
- Frank J. Franzak, Virginia Commonwealth University
- Robert Galka, De Paul University
- Albert N. Greco, Fordham University
- John A. Hobbs, University of Oklahoma
- Brian Larson, Widener University
- Anthony Racka, Oakland Community College, Auburn
- Hills, MI
- Jamie Ressler, Palm Beach Atlantic University
- James E. Shapiro, University of New Haven
- George David Shows, Louisiana Tech University

We would also like to thank colleagues who have reviewed previous editions of *Marketing Management*:

Homero Aguirre, TAMIU

Alan Au, University of Hong Kong

Hiram Barksdale, University of Georgia

Boris Becker, Oregon State University

Sandy Becker, Rutgers University

Parimal Bhagat, Indiana University of Pennsylvania

Sunil Bhatla, Case Western Reserve University

Michael Bruce, Anderson University

Frederic Brunel, Boston University

John Burnett, University of Denver

Lisa Cain, University of California at Berkeley and Mills College

Surjit Chhabra, DePaul University

Yun Chu, Frostburg State University

Dennis Clayson, University of Northern Iowa

Bob Cline, University of Iowa

Brent Cunningham, Jacksonville State University

Hugh Daubek, Purdue University

John Deighton, University of Chicago

Kathleen Dominick, Rider University

Tad Duffy, Golden Gate University

Mohan Dutta, Purdue University

Barbara Dyer, University of North Carolina at Greensboro

Jackkie Eastman, Valdosta State University

Steve Edison, University of Arkansas–Little Rock

Alton Erdem, University of Houston at Clear Lake

Elizabeth Evans, Concordia University

Barb Finer, Suffolk University

Chic Fojtik, Pepperdine University

Renee Foster, Delta State University

Ralph Gaedeke, California State University, Sacramento

Robert Galka, De Paul University

Betsy Gelb, University of Houston at Clear Lake

Dennis Gensch, University of Wisconsin, Milwaukee

David Georgoff, Florida Atlantic University

Rashi Glazer, University of California, Berkeley

Bill Gray, Keller Graduate School of Management

Barbara Gross, California State University at Northridge

Lewis Hershey, Fayetteville State University

Thomas Hewett, Kaplan University

Mary Higby, University of Detroit–Mercy

Arun Jain, State University of New York, Buffalo

Michelle Kunz, Morehead State University

Eric Langer, Johns Hopkins University

Even Lanseng, Norwegian School of Management

Ron Lennon, Barry University

Michael Lodato, California Lutheran University

Henry Loehr, Pfeiffer University–Charlotte

Bart Macchiette, Plymouth University

Susan Mann, Bluefield State College

Charles Martin, Wichita State University

H. Lee Matthews, Ohio State University

Paul McDevitt, University of Illinois at Springfield

Mary Ann McGrath, Loyola University, Chicago

John McKeever, University of Houston

Kenneth P. Mead, Central Connecticut State University

Henry Metzner, University of Missouri, Rolla

Robert Mika, Monmouth University

Mark Mitchell, Coastal Carolina University

Francis Mulhern, Northwestern University

Pat Murphy, University of Notre Dame

Jim Murrow, Drury College

Zhou Nan, University of Hong Kong

Nicholas Nugent, Boston College

Nnamdi Osakwe, Bryant & Stratton College

Donald Outland, University of Texas, Austin

Albert Page, University of Illinois, Chicago

Young-Hoon Park, Cornell University

Koen Pauwels, Dartmouth College

Lisa Klein Pearo, Cornell University

Keith Penney, Webster University

Patricia Perry, University of Alabama

Mike Powell, North Georgia College and State University

Hank Pruden, Golden Gate University

Christopher Puto, Arizona State University

Abe Qstin, Lakeland University

Lopo Rego, University of Iowa

Richard Rexeisen, University of St. Thomas

William Rice, California State University–Fresno

Scott D. Roberts, Northern Arizona University

Bill Robinson, Purdue University

Robert Roe, University of Wyoming

Jan Napoleon Saykiewicz, Duquesne University

Larry Schramm, Oakland University

Alex Sharland, Hofstra University

Dean Siewers, Rochester Institute of Technology

Anusorn Singhapakdi, Old Dominion University

Jim Skertich, Upper Iowa University

Allen Smith, Florida Atlantic University

Joe Spencer, Anderson University

Mark Spriggs, University of St. Thomas

Nancy Stephens, Arizona State University

Michael Swenso, Brigham Young University, Marriott School

Thomas Tellefsen, The College of Staten Island–CUNY

Daniel Turner, University of Washington

Sean Valentine, University of Wyoming

Ann Veeck, West Michigan University

R. Venkatesh, University of Pittsburgh

Edward Volchok, Stevens Institute of Management

D. J. Wasmer, St. Mary-of-the-Woods College

Zac Williams, Mississippi State University

Greg Wood, Canisius College

Kevin Zeng Zhou, University of Hong Kong

A warm welcome and many thanks to the following people who contributed to the global case studies developed for the 14th edition:

Mairead Brady, Trinity College

John R. Brooks, Jr., Houston Baptist University

Sylvain Charlebois, University of Regina

Geoffrey da Silva, Temasek Business School

Malcolm Goodman, Durham University

Torben Hansen, Copenhagen Business School

Abraham Koshy, Sanjeev Tripathi, and Abhishek, Indian Institute of Management Ahmedabad

Peter Ling, Edith Cowan University

Marianne Marando, Seneca College

Lu Taihong, Sun Yat-Sen University

The talented staff at Pearson deserves praise for their role in shaping the 15th edition. We want to thank our editor, Mark Gaffney, for his contribution to this revision, as well as our program manager, Jennifer M. Collins. We also want to thank our project manager, Becca Groves, for making sure everything was moving along and falling into place in such a personable way, both with regard to the book and supplements. We benefited greatly from the superb editorial help of Elisa Adams, who lent her considerable talents as a development editor to this edition. We also thank our marketing managers, Anne Fahlgren and Lenny Ann Raper. Certainly, we are grateful for the editorial support provided by Daniel Petrino. Lastly, we'd like to thank the following MyLab contributors: Susan C. Schanne, School of Management, Eastern Michigan University, and Barbara S. Faries, MBA, Mission College, Santa Clara.

## Philip Kotler

S. C. Johnson Distinguished Professor of International Marketing,
Kellogg School of Management,
Northwestern University,
Evanston, Illinois

## Kevin Lane Keller

E. B. Osborn Professor of Marketing,
Tuck School of Business,
Dartmouth College,
Hanover, New Hampshire

# In This Chapter, We Will Address the Following **Questions**

1. Why is marketing important? (p. 3)

2. What is the scope of marketing? (p. 5)

3. What are some core marketing concepts? (p. 9)

4. What forces are defining the new marketing realities? (p. 13)

5. What new capabilities have these forces given consumers and companies? (p. 16)

6. What does a holistic marketing philosophy include? (p. 20)

7. What tasks are necessary for successful marketing management? (p. 27)

Unilever is fundamentally changing how it is doing its marketing, including putting more emphasis on developing markets.

*Source: Bloomberg via Getty Images*

# 1 Defining Marketing for the New Realities

**Formally and informally, people and organizations engage in a vast number of activities** we can call marketing. In the face of a digital revolution and other major changes in the business environment, good marketing today is both increasingly vital and radically new. Consider Unilever.[1]

*Under the leadership of ex-P&G marketing executive Paul Polman and marketing whiz Keith Weed, Unilever is steering in an aggressive new direction. Its new marketing model "Crafting Brands for Life" establishes social, economic, and product missions for each brand, including Dove, Ben & Jerry's, Lifebuoy, and Knorr. Polman states, "I have a vision of all of our brands being a force for good, with each having over a billion fans or more to help drive change." One part of* the mission, for instance, is sustainability—specifically, to halve its ecological footprint while doubling revenues. To improve advertising and marketing communications, it aims to strike a balance between "magic" and "logic," doubling marketing training expenditures and emphasizing ad research. To better understand the digital world, CMO Weed took 26 top marketing executives to Silicon Valley to visit Google, Facebook, and Hulu and led a similar group to visit Hollywood executives at Disney and Universal. Unilever has set its sights on developing and emerging (D&E) markets, hoping to grow 15 percent to 20 percent annually in China and to draw 70 percent to 75 percent of business from D&E markets by 2020. The company has also adopted "reverse innovation" by applying branding and packaging innovations from developing markets to recession-hit developed markets. In Spain, it now sells Surf detergent in five-wash packs. In Greece, it offers mashed potatoes and mayonnaise in small packages.

**Good marketing is no accident.** It is both an art and a science, and it results from careful planning and execution using state-of-the-art tools and techniques. In this book, we describe how skillful marketers are updating classic practices and inventing new ones to find creative, practical solutions to new marketing realities. In the first chapter, we lay our foundation by reviewing important marketing concepts, tools, frameworks, and issues.

# The Value of Marketing

Finance, operations, accounting, and other business functions won't really matter without sufficient demand for products and services so the firm can make a profit. In other words, there must be a top line for there to be a bottom line. Thus, financial success often depends on marketing ability. Marketing's value extends to society as a whole. It has helped introduce new or enhanced products that ease or enrich people's lives. Successful marketing builds demand for products and services, which, in turn, creates jobs. By contributing to the bottom line, successful marketing also allows firms to more fully engage in socially responsible activities.[2]

## MARKETING DECISION MAKING

CEOs recognize that marketing builds strong brands and a loyal customer base, intangible assets that contribute heavily to the value of a firm.[3] Many firms, even service and nonprofit, now have a chief marketing officer (CMO) to put marketing on a more equal footing with other C-level executives such as the chief financial officer (CFO) or chief information officer (CIO).[4]

In an Internet-fueled environment where consumers, competition, technology, and economic forces change rapidly and consequences quickly multiply, marketers must choose features, prices, and markets and decide how much to spend on advertising, sales, and online and mobile marketing. Meanwhile, the economic downturn that began globally in 2008 and the sluggish recovery since have brought budget cuts and intense pressure to make every marketing dollar count.

There is little margin for error in marketing. Just a short time ago, MySpace, Yahoo!, Blockbuster, and Barnes & Noble were admired leaders in their industries. What a difference a few years can make! Each of these brands has been completely overtaken by an upstart challenger—Facebook, Google, Netflix, and Amazon—and they now struggle, sometimes unsuccessfully, for mere survival. Firms must constantly move forward. At greatest risk are those that fail to carefully monitor their customers and competitors, continuously improve their value offerings and marketing strategies, or satisfy their employees, stockholders, suppliers, and channel partners in the process.

## WINNING MARKETING

Skillful marketing is a never-ending pursuit, but some businesses are adapting and thriving in these changing times. Consider American Express. [5]

**AMERICAN EXPRESS: SMALL BUSINESS SATURDAY**  Launched in 2010 via radio and TV ads, social media, and PR, American Express's Small Business Saturday program encouraged people to shop at smaller, local retailers on the Saturday after Thanksgiving. Among businesses that participated, sales rose 28 percent. In 2012, American Express provided social media marketing kits, e-mail templates, and signage to help spread the word. More than 350 small business organizations supported the initiative, more than 3 million users "liked" the Small Business Saturday Facebook page, and 213,000 related tweets were posted on Twitter. President Obama tweeted, "Today, support small businesses in your community by shopping at your favorite store" and took his daughters to local bookstores. American Express cardholders got a $25 rebate for shopping at local, independent stores on Small Business Saturday. The company reported a roughly 21 percent increase in transactions for both 2011 and 2012 due to the program.

Other top marketers are following suit. Using a Web-only campaign, BMW claimed a $110 million revenue gain for its 1-series. More than 3 million people saw a five-video teaser campaign, and 20,000 gave their contact details. BMW also targeted influential bloggers and used feedback from social media as input to styling and sales forecasts.[6]

Even business-to-business firms are getting into the action. Corning has struggled transcending its reputation as sellers of Pyrex cookware—a business it sold more than a decade ago—to its current status as makers of highly engineered specialty glass and ceramic products. To expand the vision on Wall Street as a company with a rich portfolio, Corning created a YouTube video, "A Day Made of Glass…Made Possible by Corning." Unconventionally long but beautifully put together, within three weeks it attracted more than a million views. Much of the social conversation it created revolved around themes of glass, product toughness, and hope for the future—exactly what Corning wanted.[7]

American Express' Small Business Saturday has struck a chord with consumers, including TV celebrity Katie Couric.

Source: WireImage for American Express

# The Scope of Marketing

To be a marketer, you need to understand what marketing is, how it works, who does it, and what is marketed.

## WHAT IS MARKETING?

**Marketing** is about identifying and meeting human and social needs. One of the shortest good definitions of marketing is "meeting needs profitably." When Google recognized that people needed to more effectively and efficiently access information on the Internet, it created a powerful search engine that organized and prioritized queries. When IKEA noticed that people wanted good furnishings at substantially lower prices, it created knock-down furniture. These two firms demonstrated marketing savvy and turned a private or social need into a profitable business opportunity.

The American Marketing Association offers the following formal definition: *Marketing is the activity, set of institutions, and processes for creating, communicating, delivering, and exchanging offerings that have value for customers, clients, partners, and society at large.*[8] Coping with these exchange processes calls for a considerable amount of work and skill. *Marketing management* takes place when at least one party to a potential exchange thinks about the means of achieving desired responses from other parties. Thus, we see **marketing management** as *the art and science of choosing target markets and getting, keeping, and growing customers through creating, delivering, and communicating superior customer value.*

We can distinguish between a social and a managerial definition of marketing. A social definition shows the role marketing plays in society; for example, one marketer has said that marketing's role is to "deliver a higher standard of living." Here is a social definition that serves our purpose: *Marketing is a societal process by which individuals and groups obtain what they need and want through creating, offering, and freely exchanging products and services of value with others.* Cocreation of value among consumers and with businesses and the importance of value creation and sharing have become important themes in the development of modern marketing thought.[9]

Managers sometimes think of marketing as "the art of selling products," but many people are surprised when they hear that selling is *not* the most important part of marketing! Selling is only the tip of the marketing iceberg. Peter Drucker, famed management theorist, put it this way:[10]

> There will always, one can assume, be need for some selling. But the aim of marketing is to make selling superfluous. The aim of marketing is to know and understand the customer so well that the product or service fits him and sells itself. Ideally, marketing should result in a customer who is ready to buy. All that should be needed then is to make the product or service available.

When Nintendo designed its Wii game system, when Apple launched its iPad tablet computer, and when Toyota introduced its Prius hybrid automobile, these manufacturers were swamped with orders because they had designed the right product, based on careful marketing homework about consumers, competition, and all the external factors that affect cost and demand.

## WHAT IS MARKETED?

Marketers market 10 main types of entities: goods, services, events, experiences, persons, places, properties, organizations, information, and ideas. Let's take a quick look at these categories.

GOODS  Physical goods constitute the bulk of most countries' production and marketing efforts. Each year, U.S. companies market billions of fresh, canned, bagged, and frozen food products and millions of cars, refrigerators, televisions, machines, and other mainstays of a modern economy.

SERVICES  As economies advance, a growing proportion of their activities focuses on the production of services. The U.S. economy today produces a services-to-goods mix of roughly two-thirds to one-third.[11] Services include the work of airlines, hotels, car rental firms, barbers and beauticians, maintenance and repair people, and accountants, bankers, lawyers, engineers, doctors, software programmers, and management consultants. Many market offerings mix goods and services, such as a fast-food meal.

EVENTS  Marketers promote time-based events, such as major trade shows, artistic performances, and company anniversaries. Global sporting events such as the Olympics and the World Cup are promoted aggressively to companies and fans. Local events include craft fairs, bookstore readings, and farmer's markets.

EXPERIENCES  By orchestrating several services and goods, a firm can create, stage, and market experiences. Walt Disney World's Magic Kingdom lets customers visit a fairy kingdom, a pirate ship, or a haunted house.

The pageantry of the Olympics, shown here in Sochi, Russia, adds to its marketability.

*Source: © McClatchy-Tribune Information Services /Alamy*

Customized experiences include a week at a baseball camp with retired baseball greats, a four-day rock and roll fantasy camp, and a climb up Mount Everest.

**PERSONS** Artists, musicians, CEOs, physicians, high-profile lawyers and financiers, and other professionals often get help from marketers.[12] Many athletes and entertainers have done a masterful job of marketing themselves—NFL quarterback Peyton Manning, talk show veteran Oprah Winfrey, and rock and roll legends The Rolling Stones. Management consultant Tom Peters, himself a master at self-branding, has advised each person to become a "brand."

**PLACES** Cities, states, regions, and whole nations compete to attract tourists, residents, factories, and company headquarters.[13] Place marketers include economic development specialists, real estate agents, commercial banks, local business associations, and advertising and public relations agencies. The Las Vegas Convention & Visitors Authority has met with much success with its provocative ad campaign "What Happens Here, Stays Here," portraying Las Vegas as "an adult playground."

**PROPERTIES** Properties are intangible rights of ownership to either real property (real estate) or financial property (stocks and bonds). They are bought and sold, and these exchanges require marketing. Real estate agents work for property owners or sellers, or they buy and sell residential or commercial real estate. Investment companies and banks market securities to both institutional and individual investors.

**ORGANIZATIONS** Museums, performing arts organizations, corporations, and nonprofits all use marketing to boost their public images and compete for audiences and funds. Some universities have created chief marketing officer (CMO) positions to better manage their school identity and image, via everything from admission brochures and Twitter feeds to brand strategy.[14]

Oprah Winfrey has built a personal brand worth billions which she has used across many lines of business.

*Source: Chris Pizzello/Invision/AP*

**INFORMATION** Information is essentially what books, schools, and universities produce, market, and distribute at a price to parents, students, and communities. Firms make business decisions using information supplied by organizations like Thomson Reuters: "We combine industry expertise with innovative technology to deliver critical information to leading decision makers in the financial, legal, tax and accounting, healthcare, science and media markets, powered by the world's most trusted news organization."[15]

**IDEAS** Every market offering includes a basic idea. Charles Revson of Revlon once observed: "In the factory we make cosmetics; in the drugstore we sell hope." Products and services are platforms for delivering some idea or benefit. Social marketers promote such ideas as "Friends Don't Let Friends Drive Drunk" and "A Mind Is a Terrible Thing to Waste."

## WHO MARKETS?

**MARKETERS AND PROSPECTS** A **marketer** is someone who seeks a response—attention, a purchase, a vote, a donation—from another party, called the **prospect**. If two parties are seeking to sell something to each other, we call them both marketers.

Marketers are skilled at stimulating demand for their products, but that's a limited view of what they do. They also seek to influence the level, timing, and composition of demand to meet the organization's objectives. Eight demand states are possible:

1. *Negative demand*—Consumers dislike the product and may even pay to avoid it.
2. *Nonexistent demand*—Consumers may be unaware of or uninterested in the product.
3. *Latent demand*—Consumers may share a strong need that cannot be satisfied by an existing product.
4. *Declining demand*—Consumers begin to buy the product less frequently or not at all.
5. *Irregular demand*—Consumer purchases vary on a seasonal, monthly, weekly, daily, or even hourly basis.
6. *Full demand*—Consumers are adequately buying all products put into the marketplace.
7. *Overfull demand*—More consumers would like to buy the product than can be satisfied.
8. *Unwholesome demand*—Consumers may be attracted to products that have undesirable social consequences.

In each case, marketers must identify the underlying cause(s) of the demand state and determine a plan of action to shift demand to a more desired state.

**MARKETS** Traditionally, a "market" was a physical place where buyers and sellers gathered to buy and sell goods. Economists describe a *market* as a collection of buyers and sellers who transact over a particular product or product class (such as the housing market or the grain market).

Five basic markets and their connecting flows are shown in Figure 1.1. Manufacturers go to resource markets (raw material markets, labor markets, money markets), buy resources and turn them into goods and services, and sell finished products to intermediaries, who sell them to consumers. Consumers sell their labor and receive money with which they pay for goods and services. The government collects tax revenues to buy goods from resource,

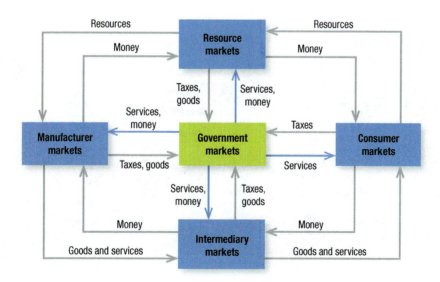

| Fig. 1.1 |

Structure of Flows in a Modern Exchange Economy

**| Fig. 1.2 |**

A Simple Marketing System

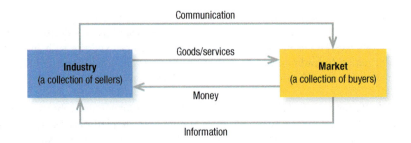

manufacturer, and intermediary markets and uses these goods and services to provide public services. Each nation's economy, and the global economy, consists of interacting sets of markets linked through exchange processes.

Marketers view sellers as the industry and use the term **market** to describe customer groups. They talk about need markets (the diet-seeking market), product markets (the shoe market), demographic markets (the "millennium" youth market), geographic markets (the Chinese market), or voter markets, labor markets, and donor markets.

Figure 1.2 shows how sellers and buyers are connected by four flows. Sellers send goods and services and communications such as ads and direct mail to the market; in return they receive money and information such as customer attitudes and sales data. The inner loop shows an exchange of money for goods and services; the outer loop shows an exchange of information.

**KEY CUSTOMER MARKETS**  Consider the following key customer markets: consumer, business, global, and nonprofit.

***Consumer Markets***  Companies selling mass consumer goods and services such as juices, cosmetics, athletic shoes, and air travel establish a strong brand image by developing a superior product or service, ensuring its availability, and backing it with engaging communications and reliable performance.

***Business Markets***  Companies selling business goods and services often face well-informed professional buyers skilled at evaluating competitive offerings. Advertising and Web sites can play a role, but the sales force, the price, and the seller's reputation may play a greater one.

***Global Markets***  Companies in the global marketplace navigate cultural, language, legal, and political differences while deciding which countries to enter, how to enter each (as exporter, licenser, joint venture partner, contract manufacturer, or solo manufacturer), how to adapt product and service features to each country, how to set prices, and how to communicate in different cultures.

***Nonprofit and Governmental Markets***  Companies selling to nonprofit organizations with limited purchasing power such as churches, universities, charitable organizations, and government agencies need to price carefully. Much government purchasing requires bids; buyers often focus on practical solutions and favor the lowest bid, other things equal.[16]

Governments are a key customer market for many companies.

# Core Marketing Concepts

To understand the marketing function, we need to understand the following core set of concepts (see Table 1.1).

## NEEDS, WANTS, AND DEMANDS

*Needs* are the basic human requirements such as for air, food, water, clothing, and shelter. Humans also have strong needs for recreation, education, and entertainment. These needs become *wants* when directed to specific objects that might satisfy the need. A U.S. consumer needs food but may want a Chicago-style "deep-dish" pizza and a craft beer. A person in Afghanistan needs food but may want rice, lamb, and carrots. Our wants are shaped by our society.

*Demands* are wants for specific products backed by an ability to pay. Many people want a Mercedes; only a few can buy one. Companies must measure not only how many people want their product, but also how many are willing and able to buy it.

These distinctions shed light on the criticism that "marketers get people to buy things they don't want." Marketers do not create needs: Needs pre-exist marketers. Marketers might promote the idea that a Mercedes satisfies a person's need for social status. They do not, however, create the need for social status.

Some customers have needs of which they are not fully conscious or cannot articulate. What does the customer mean in asking for a "powerful" lawn mower or a "peaceful" hotel? The marketer must probe further. We can distinguish five types of needs:

1. Stated needs (The customer wants an inexpensive car.)
2. Real needs (The customer wants a car whose operating cost, not initial price, is low.)
3. Unstated needs (The customer expects good service from the dealer.)
4. Delight needs (The customer would like the dealer to include an onboard GPS system.)
5. Secret needs (The customer wants friends to see him or her as a savvy consumer.)

Responding only to the stated need may shortchange the customer.[17] Consumers did not know much about tablet computers when they were first introduced, but Apple worked hard to shape consumer perceptions of them. To gain an edge, companies must help customers learn what they want.

## TARGET MARKETS, POSITIONING, AND SEGMENTATION

Not everyone likes the same cereal, restaurant, university, or movie. Marketers therefore identify distinct segments of buyers by identifying demographic, psychographic, and behavioral differences between them. They then decide which segment(s) present the greatest opportunities. For each of these *target markets,* the firm develops a *market*

| TABLE 1.1 | Core Marketing Concepts |
|---|---|
| Needs, Wants, and Demands | |
| Target Markets, Positioning, and Segmentation | |
| Offerings and Brands | |
| Marketing Channels | |
| Paid, Owned, and Earned Media | |
| Impressions and Engagement | |
| Value and Satisfaction | |
| Supply Chain | |
| Competition | |
| Marketing Environment | |

*offering* that it *positions* in target buyers' minds as delivering some key benefit(s). Volvo develops its cars for the buyer to whom safety is a major concern, positioning them as the safest a customer can buy. Porsche targets buyers who seek pleasure and excitement in driving and want to make a statement about their wheels.

## OFFERINGS AND BRANDS

Companies address customer needs by putting forth a **value proposition**, a set of benefits that satisfy those needs. The intangible value proposition is made physical by an *offering*, which can be a combination of products, services, information, and experiences.

A *brand* is an offering from a known source. A brand name such as Apple carries many different kinds of associations in people's minds that make up its image: creative, innovative, easy-to-use, fun, cool, iPod, iPhone, and iPad to name just a few. All companies strive to build a brand image with as many strong, favorable, and unique brand associations as possible.

## MARKETING CHANNELS

To reach a target market, the marketer uses three kinds of marketing channels. *Communication channels* deliver and receive messages from target buyers and include newspapers, magazines, radio, television, mail, telephone, smart phone, billboards, posters, fliers, CDs, audiotapes, and the Internet. Beyond these, firms communicate through the look of their retail stores and Web sites and other media, adding dialogue channels such as e-mail, blogs, text messages, and URLs to familiar monologue channels such as ads.

*Distribution channels* help display, sell, or deliver the physical product or service(s) to the buyer or user. These channels may be direct via the Internet, mail, or mobile phone or telephone or indirect with distributors, wholesalers, retailers, and agents as intermediaries.

To carry out transactions with potential buyers, the marketer also uses *service channels* that include warehouses, transportation companies, banks, and insurance companies. Marketers clearly face a design challenge in choosing the best mix of communication, distribution, and service channels for their offerings.

## PAID, OWNED, AND EARNED MEDIA

The rise of digital media gives marketers a host of new ways to interact with consumers and customers. We can group communication options into three categories.[18] *Paid media* include TV, magazine and display ads, paid search, and sponsorships, all of which allow marketers to show their ad or brand for a fee. *Owned media* are communication channels marketers actually own, like a company or brand brochure, Web site, blog, Facebook page, or Twitter account. *Earned media* are streams in which consumers, the press, or other outsiders voluntarily communicate something about the brand via word of mouth, buzz, or viral marketing methods. The emergence of earned media has allowed some companies, such as Chipotle, to reduce paid media expenditures.[19]

**CHIPOTLE**   One of the fastest-growing restaurant chains over the last decade, Chipotle is committed to fresh food. The company supports family farms and sources sustainable ingredients from local growers who behave responsibly toward animals and the environment. It has over 1,600 stores and over 1.7 million social media fans—yet spends next to nothing on traditional paid media. Instead Chipotle engages customers through Facebook, Twitter, and other social media via its grassroots "Food With Integrity" digital strategy which puts the focus on what it sells and where it comes from. As CMO Mark Crumpacker notes, "Typically, fast-food marketing is a game of trying to obscure the truth. The more people know about most fast-food companies, the less likely they'd want to be a customer." YouTube videos with country legend Willie Nelson and indie rocker Karen O from the Yeah Yeah Yeahs musically made Chipotle's case against processed foods and the industrialization of family farms.

## IMPRESSIONS AND ENGAGEMENT

Marketers now think of three "screens" or means to reach consumers: TV, Internet, and mobile. Surprisingly, the rise of digital options did not initially depress the amount of TV viewing, in part because, as one Nielsen study found, three of five consumers use two screens at once.[20]

Chipotle found marketplace success with little paid media, focusing on social media to tell its story of "Food With Integrity."

*Impressions,* which occur when consumers view a communication, are a useful metric for tracking the scope or breadth of a communication's reach that can also be compared across all communication types. The downside is that impressions don't provide any insight into the results of viewing the communication.

*Engagement* is the extent of a customer's attention and active involvement with a communication. It reflects a much more active response than a mere impression and is more likely to create value for the firm. Some online measures of engagements are Facebook "likes," Twitter tweets, comments on a blog or Web site, and sharing of video or other content. Engagement can extend to personal experiences that augment or transform a firm's products and services.

## VALUE AND SATISFACTION

The buyer chooses the offerings he or she perceives to deliver the most *value,* the sum of the tangible and intangible benefits and costs. Value, a central marketing concept, is primarily a combination of quality, service, and price (qsp), called the *customer value triad.* Value perceptions increase with quality and service but decrease with price.

We can think of marketing as the identification, creation, communication, delivery, and monitoring of customer value. *Satisfaction* reflects a person's judgment of a product's perceived performance in relationship to expectations. If performance falls short of expectations, the customer is disappointed. If it matches expectations, the customer is satisfied. If it exceeds them, the customer is delighted.

## SUPPLY CHAIN

The supply chain is a channel stretching from raw materials to components to finished products carried to final buyers. As Figure 1.3 shows, the supply chain for coffee may start with Ethiopian farmers who plant, tend, and pick the coffee beans and sell their harvest. If sold through a Fair Trade cooperative, the coffee is washed, dried, and packaged for shipment by an Alternative Trading Organization (ATO) that pays a minimum of $1.26 a pound. The ATO transports the coffee to the developed world where it can sell it directly or via retail channels. Each company in the chain captures only a certain percentage of the total value generated by the supply chain's value delivery system. When a company acquires competitors or expands upstream or downstream, its aim is to capture a higher percentage of supply chain value.

Problems with a supply chain can be damaging or even fatal for a business. When Johnson & Johnson ran into manufacturing problems with its consumer products unit (which makes Tylenol and other products), it hired away from Bayer AG a top executive known for her skill at fixing consumer and supply chain problems.[21]

| **Fig. 1.3** |

The Supply Chain
for Coffee

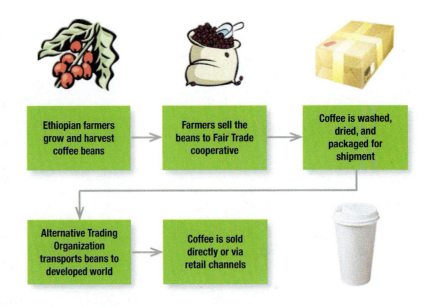

## COMPETITION

Competition includes all the actual and potential rival offerings and substitutes a buyer might consider. An automobile manufacturer can buy steel from U.S. Steel in the United States, from a foreign firm in Japan or Korea, or from a mini-mill such as Nucor at a cost savings, or it can buy aluminum parts from Alcoa to reduce the car's weight or engineered plastics from Saudi Basic Industries Corporation (SABIC) instead of steel. Clearly, U.S. Steel is more likely to be hurt by substitute products than by other integrated steel companies and would be defining its competition too narrowly if it didn't recognize this.

## MARKETING ENVIRONMENT

The marketing environment consists of the task environment and the broad environment. The *task environment* includes the actors engaged in producing, distributing, and promoting the offering. These are the company, suppliers, distributors, dealers, and target customers. In the supplier group are material suppliers and service suppliers, such as marketing research agencies, advertising agencies, banking and insurance companies, transportation companies, and telecommunications companies. Distributors and dealers include agents, brokers, manufacturer representatives, and others who facilitate finding and selling to customers.

The *broad environment* consists of six components: demographic environment, economic environment, social-cultural environment, natural environment, technological environment, and political-legal environment. Marketers must pay close attention to the trends and developments in these and adjust their marketing strategies as needed. New opportunities are constantly emerging that await the right marketing savvy and ingenuity. Consider Pinterest.[22]

**PINTEREST** One of the fastest-growing social media sites ever—its surpassed 10 million monthly unique U.S. visitors in January 2012 and *doubled* that just four months later—Pinterest is a visual bookmarking tool that lets users collect and share images of projects or products on digital scrapbooks or "pinboards." Especially popular with women planning weddings, saving recipes, and designing kitchen upgrades, Pinterest has driven more traffic to websites in a month than Twitter, Google+, LinkedIn, and YouTube combined. Part of its appeal is its unique customizable grid of images. Pinterest's sweet spot is that users are often in a shopping mindset; one study showed almost 70% of online purchasers who found a product via Pinterest went on to buy, compared to 40% for Facebook. Brands from Dell and Mercedes-Benz to Peanut Butter & Co. and Zombie SAK are integrating the site into their social media strategies. Nevertheless, Pinterest is still exploring how to best monetize its business venture.

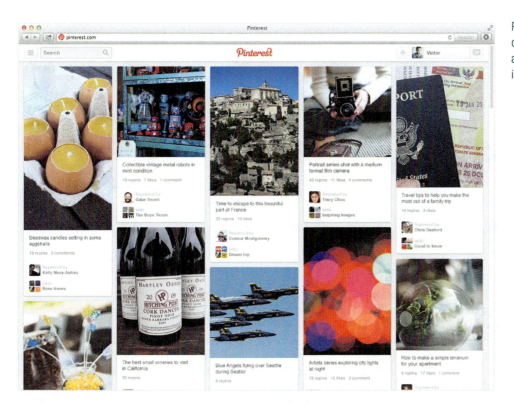

Pinterest has tapped into consumer desire to collect and share personally relevant images online.

# The New Marketing Realities

The marketplace is dramatically different from even 10 years ago, with new marketing behaviors, opportunities, and challenges emerging. In this book we focus on three transformative forces: technology, globalization, and social responsibility.

## TECHNOLOGY

The pace of change and the scale of technological achievement can be staggering. The number of mobile phones in India recently exceeded 500 million, Facebook's monthly users passed 1 billion, and more than half of African urban residents were able to access the Internet monthly.[23]

With the rapid rise of e-commerce, the mobile Internet, and Web penetration in emerging markets, the Boston Consulting Group believes brand marketers must enhance their "digital balance sheets." [24] Massive amounts of information and data about almost everything are now available to consumers and marketers. In fact, technology research specialists Gartner predicts that by 2017, CMOs will spend more time on information technology (IT) than chief information officers (CIOs). Aetna's CMO and CIO have already collaborated successfully for years, launching new products and services including iTriage, a popular health app for the iPhone. With iTriage, users can research ailments, find nearby physicians, and learn about prescribed medicines.[25]

Procter & Gamble (P&G) is determined to stay ahead of technology trends.[26]

**P&G** P&G uses the latest Web-based tools in all 80 countries where it sells products: ubiquitous high-speed networking, data visualization, and high-speed analysis of multiple information streams. In 40 locations worldwide, a massive business sphere can display real-time market share, profits, and prices by country, region, brand, and product. Tide laundry detergent has a dedicated "news desk" that monitors social media chatter and joins in when relevant. When Tide was used to clean up a nasty fuel spill in a NASCAR race, the brand ran social media ads with real news footage within 72 hours. P&G looks at a wide range of technology applications. One pilot study showed that field salespeople increased revenue 1.5 percent merely by using iPads to show store customers the layouts of different floor displays.

When Tide was used to clean a fuel spill at a NASCAR, P&G quickly spread the word on social media.

Source: Getty Images for NASCAR

The old credo "information is power" is giving way to the new idea that "sharing information is power."[27] Software giant SAP's online community numbers more than 2 million customers, partners, and others. Once a year, 100 are chosen to contribute ideas to product development.[28]

At the other end of the size spectrum, by running Facebook ads offering a free cut, shampoo, and hot towel treatment to new customers in exchange for name, phone number, e-mail address, and preferred social network, The Gent's Place barbershop in Frisco, TX, has picked up 5,000 clients. Its average marketing cost for each was $10.13, which it quickly recoups from repeat purchases.[29]

Even traditional marketing activities are profoundly affected by technology. To improve sales force effectiveness, drug maker Roche decided to issues iPads to its entire sales team. Though the company had a sophisticated customer relationship management (CRM) software system before, it still depended on sales reps to accurately input data in a timely fashion, which unfortunately did not always happen. With iPads, however, sales teams can do real-time data entry, improving the quality of the data entered while freeing up time for other tasks.[30]

## GLOBALIZATION

The world has become a smaller place. New transportation, shipping, and communication technologies have made it easier for us to know the rest of the world, to travel, to buy and sell anywhere. By 2025, annual consumption in emerging markets will total $30 trillion and contribute more than 70 percent of global GDP growth.[31] A staggering 56 percent of global financial services consumption is forecast to come from emerging markets by 2050, up from 18 percent in 2010.

Demographic trends favor developing markets such as India, Pakistan, and Egypt, with populations whose median age is below 25. In terms of growth of the middle class, defined as earning more than $3,000 per year, the Philippines, China, and Peru are the three fastest-growing countries.[32]

Globalization has made countries increasingly multicultural. U.S. minorities have much economic clout, and their buying power is growing faster than that of the general population. According to the University of Georgia's Terry College of Business minority buying report, the combined buying power of U.S. racial minorities (African Americans, Asians, and Native Americans) is projected to rise from $1.6 trillion in 2010 to $2.1 trillion in 2015, accounting for 15 percent of the nation's total. The buying power of U.S. Hispanics will rise from $1 trillion in 2010 to $1.5 trillion in 2015, nearly 11 percent of the nation's total. One survey found that 87 percent of companies planned to increase or maintain multicultural media budgets.[33]

Globalization changes innovation and product development as companies take ideas and lessons from one country and apply them to another. After years of little success with its premium ultrasound scanners in the Chinese market, GE successfully developed a portable, ultra-low-cost version that addressed the country's unique market needs. Later, it began to successfully sell the product throughout the developed world for use in ambulances and operating rooms where existing models were too big.[34]

## SOCIAL RESPONSIBILITY

Poverty, pollution, water shortages, climate change, wars, and wealth concentration demand our attention. The private sector is taking some responsibility for improving living conditions, and firms all over the world have elevated the role of corporate social responsibility.

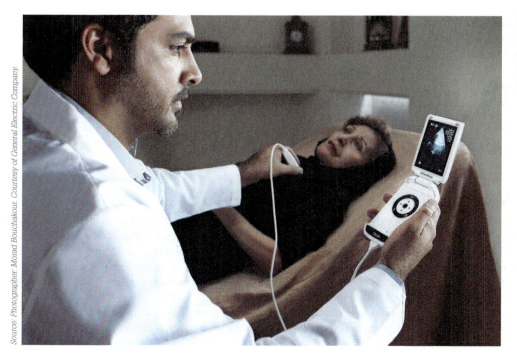

Source: Photographer Morad Bouchakour. Courtesy of General Electric Company.

Product introduced into developing markets, such as GE's portable ultrasound scanner, are finding success in developed markets too.

Because marketing's effects extend to society as a whole, marketers must consider the ethical, environmental, legal, and social context of their activities.[35] "Marketing Insight: Getting to Marketing 3.0" describes how companies need to change to do that.

The organization's task is thus to determine the needs, wants, and interests of target markets and satisfy them more effectively and efficiently than competitors while preserving or enhancing consumers' and society's long-term well-being.

---

**marketing insight**

## Getting to Marketing 3.0

Philip Kotler, Hermawan Kartayaya, and Iwan Setiawan believe today's customers want marketers to treat them as whole human beings and acknowledge that their needs extend beyond pure consumerism. Successful marketing is thus distinguished by its human or emotional element. A third wave of thinking, values-driven and heralded as "Marketing 3.0," has moved us beyond the product-centric and consumer-centric models of the past, these authors say. Its three central trends are increased consumer participation and collaborative marketing, globalization, and and the rise of a creative society.

- We live with sustained technological development—low-cost Internet, cheap computers and mobile phones, open source services and systems. Expressive and collaborative social media, such as Facebook and Wikipedia, have changed the way marketers operate and interact with consumers.

- Culturally relevant brands can have far-reaching effects. A cultural brand might position itself as a national or local alternative to a global brand with poor environmental standards, for instance.

- Creative people are increasingly the backbone of developed economies. Marketing can now help companies tap into creativity and spirituality by instilling marketing values in corporate culture, vision, and mission.

These authors believe the future of marketing will be horizontal: consumer-to-consumer. They feel the recent economic downturn has not fostered trust in the marketplace and that customers now increasingly turn to one another for credible advice and information when selecting products.

**Sources:** Philip Kotler, Hermawan Kartajaya, and Iwan Setiawan, *Marketing 3.0: From Products to Customers to the Human Spirit* (Hoboken, NJ: Wiley, 2010); Michael Krauss, "Evolution of an Academic: Kotler on Marketing 3.0," *Marketing News*, January 30, 2011; Vivek Kaul, "Beyond Advertising: Philip Kotler Remains One of the Most Influential Marketing Thinkers," *The Economic Times*, February 29, 2012. For more stimulating related ideas, see also Jim Stengel, *Grow: How Ideals Power Growth and Profit at the World's Greatest Companies* (New York: Crown, 2011).

As goods become more commoditized and consumers grow more socially conscious, some companies—including The Body Shop, Timberland, and Patagonia—incorporate social responsibility as a way to differentiate themselves from competitors, build consumer preference, and achieve notable sales and profit gains.[36]

# A Dramatically Changed Marketplace

These three forces—technology, globalization, and social responsibility—have dramatically changed the marketplace, bringing consumers *and* companies new capabilities. The marketplace is also being transformed by changes in channel structure and heightened competition.

## NEW CONSUMER CAPABILITIES

Social media is an explosive worldwide phenomenon. In Germany, the percentage of consumers over 65 accessing the Internet increased from 24 percent to 33 percent from 2011 to 2012; most belonged to a social media service. The number of Germans browsing the Web wirelessly increased to 29 million in 2012 and was expected to hit 60 million in 2016. More than 10 percent of Germans were using tablets to access the Internet in 2012. Almost two-thirds of German companies surveyed in 2012 reported positive payback to their social media activities (Facebook, Twitter, social media newsrooms, customer feedback communities).[37]

Empowerment is not just about technology, though. Consumers are willing to move to another brand if they think they are not being treated right or do not like what they are seeing, as Progressive Insurance found out.[38]

**PROGRESSIVE INSURANCE**  Kate Fisher, a Progressive customer, was killed by an underinsured driver who ran a red light. Her family felt they had to sue the driver for negligence to prompt Progressive to make up what the driver could not pay. Matt Fisher, Kate's brother, was furious when Progressive actively participated in the negligent driver's legal defense. His Tumblr post, "My Sister Paid Progressive Insurance to Defend Her Killer in Court," was picked up by media outlets and sparked public outrage on Progressive's Facebook and Twitter pages. More than 1,000 customers reported dropping Progressive, and many more said they would not do business with the company. Although Progressive felt it had defensible business reasons for its actions, critics were enraged by its awkward responses, like: "We fully investigated this claim and relevant background and feel we properly handled the claim within our contractual obligations." After a few tumultuous days, Progressive reportedly settled with the Fishers for tens of thousands of dollars more than the $76,000 they had sought.

Expanded information, communication, and mobility enable customers to make better choices and share their preferences and opinions with others around the world. Table 1.2 summarizes some of the new consumer capabilities we outline next.

- *Consumers can use the Internet as a powerful information and purchasing aid.* From the home, office, or mobile phone, they can compare product prices and features, consult user reviews, and order goods online

| TABLE 1.2 | New Consumer Capabilities |
|---|---|
| Can use the Internet as a powerful information and purchasing aid | |
| Can search, communicate, and purchase on the move | |
| Can tap into social media to share opinions and express loyalty | |
| Can actively interact with companies | |
| Can reject marketing they find inappropriate | |

from anywhere in the world 24 hours a day, seven days a week, bypassing limited local offerings and realizing significant price savings. They can also engage in "showrooming": comparing products in stores but buying online.[39] Because consumers and other constituents can in fact track down virtually any kind of company information, firms now realize that transparency in corporate words and actions is of paramount importance.

- *Consumers can search, communicate, and purchase on the move.* Consumers increasingly integrate smart phones and tablets into their daily lives. One study found the majority of European smart phone owners use their devices to research products and make purchases.[40] There is one cell phone for every two people on the planet—and 10 times more cell phones are produced globally each day than babies are born. Telecommunications is one of the world's trillion-dollar industries, along with tourism, military, food, and automobiles.[41]

- *Consumers can tap into social media to share opinions and express loyalty.* Personal connections and user-generated content thrive on social media such as Facebook, Flickr, Wikipedia, and YouTube. Sites like Dogster for dog lovers, TripAdvisor for travelers, and Moterus for bikers bring together consumers with a common interest. At CarSpace.com, auto enthusiasts talk about chrome rims, the latest BMW model, and where to find a great local mechanic.

- *Consumers can actively interact with companies.* Consumers see their favorite companies as workshops from which to draw out the offerings they want. By opting in or out of lists, they can receive marketing and sales-related communications, discounts, coupons, and other special deals. With smart phones, they can scan barcodes and QR (Quick Response) codes to access a brand's Web site and other information.[42]

- *Consumers can reject marketing they find inappropriate.* Some customers today may see fewer product differences and feel less brand loyal. Others may become more price- and quality-sensitive in their search for value. Almost two-thirds of consumers in one survey reported that they disliked advertising.[43] For these and other reasons, consumers can be less tolerant about undesired marketing. They can choose to screen out online messages, skip commercials with their DVRs, and avoid marketing appeals through the mail or over the phone.

## NEW COMPANY CAPABILITIES

At the same time, globalization, social responsibility, and technology have also generated a new set of capabilities to help companies cope and respond (see Table 1.3).

- *Companies can use the Internet as a powerful information and sales channel, including for individually differentiated goods.* A Web site can list products and services, history, business philosophy, job opportunities, and other information of interest to consumers worldwide. Solo Cup marketers note that linking their storefronts to their Web site and Facebook page makes it easier for consumers to buy Solo paper cups and plates while engaging with the brand online.[44] Thanks to advances in factory customization, computer technology, and database marketing software, companies can allow customers to buy M&M candies with their names on

| TABLE 1.3 | New Company Capabilities |
|---|---|
| Can use the Internet as a powerful information and sales channel, including for individually differentiated goods | |
| Can collect fuller and richer information about markets, customers, prospects, and competitors | |
| Can reach customers quickly and efficiently via social media and mobile marketing, sending targeted ads, coupons, and information | |
| Can improve purchasing, recruiting, training, and internal and external communications | |
| Can improve cost efficiency | |

Many different products, such as M&Ms, can now be customized by consumers.

them, Wheaties boxes or Jones soda cans with their picture on the front, and Heinz ketchup bottles with customized messages.[45]

- *Companies can collect fuller and richer information about markets, customers, prospects, and competitors.* Marketers can conduct fresh marketing research by using the Internet to arrange focus groups, send out questionnaires, and gather primary data in several other ways. They can assemble information about individual customers' purchases, preferences, demographics, and profitability. The drugstore chain CVS uses loyalty-card data to better understand what consumers purchase, the frequency of store visits, and other buying preferences. Its ExtraCare program supports 69 million shoppers in more than 7,300 stores. Eighty-two percent of CVS's front store (non-pharmacy) sales go through the ExtraCare program.[46]

- *Companies can reach consumers quickly and efficiently via social media and mobile marketing, sending targeted ads, coupons, and information.* GPS technology can pinpoint consumers' exact location, letting marketers send them messages at the mall with wish-list reminders and coupons or offers good only that day. Location-based advertising is attractive because it reaches consumers closer to the point of sale. Social media and buzz are also powerful. Over a two-year period, Dell took in more than $2 million in U.S. revenue from coupons provided through Twitter and another $1 million from people who started at Twitter and bought a new computer on Dell's Web site. By mid-2012, the @DellOutlet Twitter account had more than 1.6 million followers.[47] Word-of-mouth marketing agency BzzAgent recruited 600,000 consumers who voluntarily join promotional programs for products and services they deem worth talking about.

- *Companies can improve purchasing, recruiting, training, and internal and external communications.* Firms can recruit new employees online, and many have Internet training products for their employees, dealers, and agents. Blogging has waned as companies embrace social media. "We want to be where our customers are," said Bank of America after dropping its blog in favor of Facebook and Twitter.[48] Farmers Insurance uses specialized software to help its 15,000 agents nationwide maintain their own Facebook pages.[49] Via intranets and databases, employees can query one another, seek advice, and exchange information. Seeking a single online employee portal that transcended business units, General Motors launched a platform called mySocrates in 2006 to carry announcements, news, links, and historical information. GM credits the portal with $17.4 million in cost savings to date.[50] Popular hybrid Twitter/Facebook-type products designed especially for business employees have been introduced by Salesforce.com, IBM, and several start-ups.[51]

- *Companies can improve their cost efficiency.* Corporate buyers can achieve substantial savings by using the Internet to compare sellers' prices and purchase materials at auction or by posting their own terms in reverse auctions. Companies can improve logistics and operations to reap substantial cost savings while improving accuracy and service quality. Small businesses can especially unleash the power of the Internet. Physicians operating a small practice can use Facebook-like services such as Doximity to connect with referring physicians and specialists.[52]

## CHANGING CHANNELS

One of the reasons consumers have more choices is that channels of distribution have changed as a result of retail transformation and disintermediation.

- *Retail transformation.* Store-based retailers face competition from catalog houses; direct-mail firms; newspaper, magazine, and TV direct-to-customer ads; home shopping TV; and e-commerce. In response, entrepreneurial retailers are building entertainment into their stores with coffee bars, demonstrations, and performances, marketing an "experience" rather than a product assortment.
- *Disintermediation.* Early dot-coms such as Amazon.com, E*TRADE, and others successfully created *disintermediation* in the delivery of products and services by intervening in the traditional flow of goods. In response, traditional companies engaged in *reintermediation* and became "brick-and-click" retailers, adding online services to their offerings. Some with plentiful resources and established brand names became stronger contenders than pure-click firms.

## HEIGHTENED COMPETITION

While globalization has created intense competition among domestic and foreign brands, the rise of private labels and mega-brands and a trend toward deregulation and privatization have also increased competition.

- *Private labels.* Brand manufacturers are further buffeted by powerful retailers that market their own store brands, increasingly indistinguishable from any other type of brand.
- *Mega-brands.* Many strong brands have become mega-brands and extended into related product categories, including new opportunities at the intersection of two or more industries. Computing, telecommunications, and consumer electronics are converging, with Apple and Samsung releasing a stream of state-of-the-art devices from MP3 players to LCD TVs to fully loaded smart phones.
- *Deregulation.* Many countries have deregulated industries to create greater competition and growth opportunities. In the United States, laws restricting financial services, telecommunications, and electric utilities have all been loosened in the spirit of greater competition.
- *Privatization.* Many countries have converted public companies to private ownership and management to increase their efficiency. The telecommunications industry has seen much privatization in countries such as Australia, France, Germany, Italy, Turkey, and Japan.[53]

# Marketing in Practice

Given the new marketing realities, organizations are challenging their marketers to find the best balance of old and new and to provide demonstrable evidence of success. "Marketing Memo: Reinventing Marketing at Coca-Cola" describes some of the many different ways that that top marketing organization has changed.

## MARKETING BALANCE

Companies must always move forward, innovating products and services, staying in touch with customer needs, and seeking new advantages rather than relying on past strengths. India's Hindustan Unilever asks all staff members—not just marketers—to obtain a "consumer license" to work on its brands, which requires spending 50 hours of face time with shoppers. As one senior executive noted, "Our consumers are moving faster than marketers do; whether in terms of rural or urban changes or the way they consume media and entertainment."[54]

Moving forward especially means incorporating the Internet and digital efforts into marketing plans. Marketers must balance increased spending on search advertising, social media, e-mails, and text messages with appropriate spending on traditional marketing communications. But they must do so in tough economic times, when accountability has become a top priority and returns on investment are expected from every marketing activity. The ideal is retaining winning practices from the past while adding fresh approaches that reflect the new marketing realities.[55]

*Source: Associated Press*

Coca-Cola reinforces its message of happiness with special promotional "Hug Me" vending machines which dispense free product.

## MARKETING ACCOUNTABILITY

Marketers are increasingly asked to justify their investments in financial and profitability terms, as well as in terms of building the brand and growing the customer base. Organizations recognize that much of their market value comes from intangible assets, particularly brands, customer base, employees, distributor and supplier relations, and intellectual capital. They are thus applying more metrics—brand equity, customer lifetime value, return on marketing investment (ROMI)—to understand and measure their marketing and business performance and a broader variety of financial measures to assess the direct and indirect value their marketing efforts create.

## MARKETING IN THE ORGANIZATION

As the late David Packard of Hewlett-Packard observed, "Marketing is far too important to leave to the marketing department." Increasingly, marketing is *not* done only by the marketing department; every employee has an impact on the customer. Marketers now must properly manage all possible touch points: store layouts, package designs, product functions, employee training, and shipping and logistics. To create a strong marketing organization, marketers must think like executives in other departments, and executives in other departments must think more like marketers. Interdepartmental teamwork that includes marketers is needed to manage key processes like production innovation, new-business development, customer acquisition and retention, and order fulfillment.

# Company Orientation toward the Marketplace

Given these new marketing realities, what philosophy should guide a company's marketing efforts? Let's first review the evolution of marketing philosophies.

## THE PRODUCTION CONCEPT

The **production concept** is one of the oldest concepts in business. It holds that consumers prefer products that are widely available and inexpensive. Managers of production-oriented businesses concentrate on achieving high production efficiency, low costs, and mass distribution. This orientation has made sense in developing countries such as China, where the largest PC manufacturer, Legend (principal owner of Lenovo Group), and domestic appliances giant Haier have taken advantage of the country's huge and inexpensive labor pool to dominate the market. Marketers also use the production concept when they want to expand the market.

## THE PRODUCT CONCEPT

The **product concept** proposes that consumers favor products offering the most quality, performance, or innovative features. However, managers are sometimes caught in a love affair with their products. They might commit the "better-mousetrap" fallacy, believing a better product will by itself lead people to beat a path to their door. As many start-ups have learned the hard way, a new or improved product will not necessarily be successful unless it's priced, distributed, advertised, and sold properly.

## THE SELLING CONCEPT

The **selling concept** holds that consumers and businesses, if left alone, won't buy enough of the organization's products. It is practiced most aggressively with unsought goods—goods buyers don't normally think of buying such as insurance and cemetery plots—and when firms with overcapacity aim to sell what they make, rather than make what the market wants. Marketing based on hard selling is risky. It assumes customers coaxed into buying a product not only won't return or bad-mouth it or complain to consumer organizations but might even buy it again.

## THE MARKETING CONCEPT

The **marketing concept** emerged in the mid-1950s as a customer-centered, sense-and-respond philosophy. The job is to find not the right customers for your products, but the right products for your customers. Dell doesn't prepare a PC or laptop for its target market. Rather, it provides product platforms on which each person customizes the features he or she desires in the machine.

The marketing concept holds that the key to achieving organizational goals is being more effective than competitors in creating, delivering, and communicating superior customer value to your target markets. Harvard's Theodore Levitt drew a perceptive contrast between the selling and marketing concepts: [56]

> Selling focuses on the needs of the seller; marketing on the needs of the buyer. Selling is preoccupied with the seller's need to convert his product into cash; marketing with the idea of satisfying the needs of the customer by means of the product and the whole cluster of things associated with creating, delivering, and finally consuming it.

## THE HOLISTIC MARKETING CONCEPT

Without question, the trends and forces that have defined the new marketing realities in the first years of the 21st century are leading business firms to embrace a new set of beliefs and practices. The **holistic marketing** concept is based on the development, design, and implementation of marketing programs, processes, and activities that recognize their breadth and interdependencies. Holistic marketing acknowledges that everything matters in marketing—and that a broad, integrated perspective is often necessary.

Holistic marketing thus recognizes and reconciles the scope and complexities of marketing activities. Figure 1.4 provides a schematic overview of four broad components characterizing holistic marketing: relationship marketing, integrated marketing, internal marketing, and performance marketing. We'll examine these major themes throughout this book.

**RELATIONSHIP MARKETING** Increasingly, a key goal of marketing is to develop deep, enduring relationships with people and organizations that directly or indirectly affect the success of the firm's marketing activities. **Relationship marketing** aims to build mutually satisfying long-term relationships with key constituents in order to earn and retain their business.

Four key constituents for relationship marketing are customers, employees, marketing partners (channels, suppliers, distributors, dealers, agencies), and members of the financial community (shareholders, investors, analysts). Marketers must create prosperity among all these constituents and balance the returns to all key stakeholders. To develop strong relationships with them requires understanding their capabilities and resources, needs, goals, and desires.

**| Fig. 1.4 |**

Holistic Marketing
Dimensions

The ultimate outcome of relationship marketing is a unique company asset called a **marketing network**, consisting of the company and its supporting stakeholders—customers, employees, suppliers, distributors, retailers, and others—with whom it has built mutually profitable business relationships. The operating principle is simple: build an effective network of relationships with key stakeholders, and profits will follow. Thus more companies are choosing to own brands rather than physical assets, and they are subcontracting activities to firms that can do them better and more cheaply while retaining core activities at home.

Companies are also shaping separate offers, services, and messages to *individual customers,* based on information about their past transactions, demographics, psychographics, and media and distribution preferences. By focusing on their most profitable customers, products, and channels, these firms hope to achieve profitable growth, capturing a larger share of each customer's expenditures by building high customer loyalty. They estimate individual customer lifetime value and design their market offerings and prices to make a profit over the customer's lifetime.

Marketing must skillfully conduct not only customer relationship management (CRM), but partner relationship management (PRM) as well. Companies are deepening their partnering arrangements with key suppliers and distributors, seeing them as partners in delivering value to final customers so everybody benefits. IBM is a business-to-business powerhouse that has learned the value of strong customer bonds.[57]

**IBM** Having celebrated its 100th corporate anniversary in 2011, IBM is a remarkable survivor that has maintained market leadership for decades in the challenging technology industry. The company has managed to successfully evolve its business and seamlessly update the focus of its products and services numerous times in its history—from mainframes to PCs to its current emphasis on cloud computing, "big data," and IT services. Part of the reason is that IBM's well-trained sales force and service organization offer real value to customers by staying close to them and fully understanding their requirements. IBM often even cocreates products with customers; with the state of New York it developed a method for detecting tax evasion that reportedly saved taxpayers $1.6 billion over a seven-year period. As famed Harvard Business School professor Rosabeth Moss Kanter has noted, "IBM is not a technology company but a company solving problems using technology."

**INTEGRATED MARKETING** Integrated marketing occurs when the marketer devises marketing activities and assembles marketing programs to create, communicate, and deliver value for consumers such that "the whole is greater than the sum of its parts." Two key themes are that (1) many different marketing activities can create, communicate, and deliver value and (2) marketers should design and implement any one marketing activity with all other activities in mind. When a hospital buys an MRI machine from General Electric's

Medical Systems division, for instance, it expects good installation, maintenance, and training services to go with the purchase.

The company must develop an integrated channel strategy. It should assess each channel option for its direct effect on product sales and brand equity, as well as its indirect effect through interactions with other channel options.

All company communications also must be integrated so communication options reinforce and complement each other. A marketer might selectively employ television, radio, and print advertising, public relations and events, and PR and Web site communications so each contributes on its own and improves the effectiveness of the others. Each must also deliver a consistent brand message at every contact. Consider this award-winning campaign for Iceland.[58]

**ICELAND**   Already reeling from some of the biggest losses in the global financial crisis in 2008, Iceland faced more misfortune when dormant volcano Eyjafjallajökull unexpectedly erupted in April 2010. Its enormous plumes of ash created the largest air-travel disruption since World War II, resulting in a wave of negative press and bad feelings throughout Europe and elsewhere. With tourism generating around 20 percent of the country's foreign exchange and bookings plummeting, government and tourism officials decided to launch "Inspired by Iceland." This campaign was based on the insight that 80 percent of visitors to Iceland recommend the destination to friends and family. The country's own citizens were recruited to tell their stories and encourage others to join in via a Web site or Twitter, Facebook, and Vimeo. Celebrities such as Yoko Ono and Eric Clapton shared their experiences, and live concerts generated PR. Real-time Web cams across the country showed that the country was not ash-covered but green. The campaign was wildly successful—22.5 million stories were created by people all over the world—and ensuing bookings were dramatically above forecasts.

**INTERNAL MARKETING**  **Internal marketing**, an element of holistic marketing, is the task of hiring, training, and motivating able employees who want to serve customers well. Smart marketers recognize that marketing activities within the company can be as important—or even more important—than those directed outside the company. It makes no sense to promise excellent service before the company's staff is ready to provide it.

Marketing succeeds only when all departments work together to achieve customer goals (see Table 1.4): when engineering designs the right products, finance furnishes the right amount of funding, purchasing buys the right materials, production makes the right products in the right time horizon, and accounting measures profitability

Iceland's fully integrated modern tourism campaign helped to halt a slide in visitors to the country.

| TABLE I.4 | Assessing Which Company Departments Are Customer-Minded |
|---|---|

**R&D**

- They spend time meeting customers and listening to their problems.
- They welcome the involvement of marketing, manufacturing, and other departments to each new project.
- They benchmark competitors' products and seek "best of class" solutions.
- They solicit customer reactions and suggestions as the project progresses.
- They continuously improve and refine the product on the basis of market feedback.

**Purchasing**

- They proactively search for the best suppliers.
- They build long-term relationships with fewer but more reliable, high-quality suppliers.
- They don't compromise quality for price savings.

**Manufacturing**

- They invite customers to visit and tour their plants.
- They visit customer plants.
- They willingly work overtime to meet promised delivery schedules.
- They continuously search for ways to produce goods faster and/or at lower cost.
- They continuously improve product quality, aiming for zero defects.
- They meet customer requirements for "customization" where possible.

**Marketing**

- They study customer needs and wants in well-defined market segments.
- They allocate marketing effort in relation to the long-run profit potential of the targeted segments.
- They develop winning offers for each target segment.
- They measure company image and customer satisfaction on a continuous basis.
- They continuously gather and evaluate ideas for new products, product improvements, and services.
- They urge all company departments and employees to be customer centered.

**Sales**

- They have specialized knowledge of the customer's industry.
- They strive to give the customer "the best solution."
- They make only promises that they can keep.
- They feed back customers' needs and ideas to those in charge of product development.
- They serve the same customers for a long period of time.

**Logistics**

- They set a high standard for service delivery time and meet this standard consistently.
- They operate a knowledgeable and friendly customer service department that can answer questions, handle complaints, and resolve problems in a satisfactory and timely manner.

**Accounting**

- They prepare periodic "profitability" reports by product, market segment, geographic areas (regions, sales territories), order sizes, channels, and individual customers.
- They prepare invoices tailored to customer needs and answer customer queries courteously and quickly.

**Finance**

- They understand and support marketing expenditures (e.g., image advertising) that produce long-term customer preference and loyalty.
- They tailor the financial package to the customer's financial requirements.
- They make quick decisions on customer creditworthiness.

**Public Relations**

- They send out favorable news about the company and "damage control" unfavorable news.
- They act as an internal customer and public advocate for better company policies and practices.

**Source:** © Philip Kotler, *Kotler on Marketing* (New York: Free Press, 1999), pp. 21–22. Reprinted with permission of The Free Press, a Division of Simon & Schuster Adult Publishing Group. Copyright © 1999 by Philip Kotler. All rights reserved.

in the right ways. Such interdepartmental harmony can only truly coalesce, however, when senior management clearly communicates a vision of how the company's marketing orientation and philosophy serve customers. The following example highlights some of the potential challenge in integrating marketing:

> The marketing vice president of a major European airline wants to increase the airline's traffic share. His strategy is to build up customer satisfaction by providing better food, cleaner cabins, better-trained cabin crews, and lower fares, yet he has no authority in these matters. The catering department chooses food that keeps food costs down; the maintenance department uses inexpensive cleaning services; the human resources department hires people without regard to whether they are naturally friendly; the finance department sets the fares. Because these departments generally take a cost or production point of view, the vice president of marketing is stymied in his efforts to create an integrated marketing program.

Internal marketing requires vertical alignment with senior management and horizontal alignment with other departments so everyone understands, appreciates, and supports the marketing effort.

**PERFORMANCE MARKETING** **Performance marketing** requires understanding the financial and nonfinancial returns to business and society from marketing activities and programs. As noted previously, top marketers are increasingly going beyond sales revenue to examine the marketing scorecard and interpret what is happening to market share, customer loss rate, customer satisfaction, product quality, and other measures. They are also considering the legal, ethical, social, and environmental effects of marketing activities and programs.

When they founded Ben & Jerry's, Ben Cohen and Jerry Greenfield embraced the performance marketing concept by dividing the traditional financial bottom line into a "double bottom line" that also measured the environmental impact of their products and processes. That later expanded into a "triple bottom line" to represent the social impacts, negative and positive, of the firm's entire range of business activities.

Many firms have failed to live up to their legal and ethical responsibilites, and consumers are demanding more responsible behavior.[59] One research study reported that at least one-third of consumers around the world believed that banks, insurance providers, and packaged-food companies should be subject to stricter regulation.[60]

# Updating the Four Ps

Many years ago, McCarthy classified various marketing activities into *marketing-mix* tools of four broad kinds, which he called *the four Ps* of marketing: product, price, place, and promotion.[61] The marketing variables under each P are shown in Figure 1.5.

A complementary view of the four Ps can be found in Marketing Insight: Understanding the 4 As of Marketing,"

Given the breadth, complexity, and richness of marketing, however—as exemplified by holistic marketing—clearly these four Ps are not the whole story anymore. If we update them to reflect the holistic marketing

| **Fig. 1.5** |

The Four
P Components of
the Marketing Mix

**marketing insight**

# Understanding the 4 As of Marketing

According to Jagdish Sheth and Rajendra Sisodia, poor management as a consequence of not knowing what drives consumers is behind the majority of marketing failures. The authors make the case that consumer knowledge is a much more reliable route to success. Their customer-centric marketing management framework emphasizes what they believe are the most important consumer values—acceptability, affordability, accessibility, and awareness—which they dub the four As.

### Acceptability

*Acceptability* is the extent to which a firm's total product offering exceeds customer expectations. The authors assert that Acceptability is the dominant component in the framework and that design, in turn, is at the root of acceptability. Functional aspects of design can be boosted by, for instance, enhancing the core benefit or increasing reliability of the product; psychological acceptability can be improved with changes to brand image, packing and design, and positioning.

### Affordability

*Affordability* is the extent to which customers in the target market are able and willing to pay the product's price. It has two dimensions: economic (ability to pay) and psychological (willingness to pay). Acceptability combined with affordability determines the product's value proposition. When Peachtree Software lowered the price of its accounting software from $5000 to $199 and started charging for customer support, sales demand increased enormously.

### Accessibility

*Accessibility*, the extent to which customers are able to readily acquire the product, has two dimensions: availability and convenience. Successful companies develop innovative ways to deliver both, as on-line shoe retailer Zappos does with excellent customer service and return policies and its tracking of up-to-the-minute information about warehouse stock, brands, and styles.

### Awareness

*Awareness* is the extent to which customers are informed regarding the product's characteristics, persuaded to try it, and reminded to repurchase. It has two dimensions: brand awareness and product knowledge. Sheth and Sisodia say awareness is ripest for improvement because most companies are either ineffectual or inefficient at developing it. For instance, properly done advertising can be incredibly powerful, but word-of-mouth marketing and co-marketing can more effectively reach potential customers.

Sheth and Sisodia base the 4 As framework on the four distinctive roles a consumer plays in the marketplace—seeker, buyer, payer, and user. A fifth consumer role—evangelizer—captures the fact that consumers often recommend products to others and are increasingly critical with the advent of the Internet and social media platforms.

Note that we can easily relate the 4 As to the traditional 4 Ps. Marketers set the product (which mainly influences acceptability), the price (which mainly influences affordability), the place (which mainly influences accessibility), and promotion (which mainly influences awareness).

**Sources:** Jagdish N. Sheth and Rajendra Sisodia, *The 4 A's of Marketing: Creating Value for Customer, Company and Society* (New York: Routledge, 2012); "New Rules: Jagdish Sheth Outlines 4A's of Marketing," *The Financial Express*, April 6, 2004; "Industry Leaders Discuss Marketing for Not for Profit Organizations @ BIMTECH Marketing Summit," www.mbauniverse.com, May 1, 2012.

concept, we arrive at a more representative set that encompasses modern marketing realities: people, processes, programs, and performance, as in Figure 1.6.

*People* reflects, in part, internal marketing and the fact that employees are critical to marketing success. Marketing will only be as good as the people inside the organization. It also reflects the fact that marketers must view consumers as people to understand their lives more broadly, and not just as shoppers who consume products and services.

*Processes* reflects all the creativity, discipline, and structure brought to marketing management. Marketers must avoid ad hoc planning and decision making and ensure that state-of-the-art marketing ideas and concepts play an

**| Fig. 1.6 |**

**The Evolution of Marketing Management**

| Marketing Mix Four Ps |
|---|
| Product |
| Place |
| Promotion |
| Price |

| Modern Marketing Management Four Ps |
|---|
| People |
| Processes |
| Programs |
| Performance |

appropriate role in all they do, including creating mutually beneficial long-term relationships and imaginatively generating insights and breakthrough products, services, and marketing activities.

*Programs* reflects all the firm's consumer-directed activities. It encompasses the old four Ps as well as a range of other marketing activities that might not fit as neatly into the old view of marketing. Regardless of whether they are online or offline, traditional or nontraditional, these activities must be integrated such that their whole is greater than the sum of their parts and they accomplish multiple objectives for the firm.

We define *performance* as in holistic marketing, to capture the range of possible outcome measures that have financial and nonfinancial implications (profitability as well as brand and customer equity) and implications beyond the company itself (social responsibility, legal, ethical, and the environment).

Finally, these new four Ps actually apply to *all* disciplines within the company, and by thinking this way, managers more closely align themselves with the rest of the company.

# Marketing Management Tasks

Figure 1.7 summarizes the three major market forces, two key market outcomes, and four fundamental pillars of holistic marketing that help to capture the new marketing realities. With these concepts in place, we can identify a specific set of tasks that make up successful marketing management and marketing leadership. We'll use the following situation to illustrate these tasks in the context of the plan of the book. (The "Marketing Memo: Marketers' Frequently Asked Questions" is a good checklist for the questions marketing managers ask, all of which we examine in this book.)

> Zeus Inc. (name disguised) operates in several industries, including chemicals, cameras, and film. The company is organized into SBUs. Corporate management is considering what to do with its Atlas camera division, which produces a range of professional quality 35mm and consumer-friendly digital cameras. Although Zeus has a sizable share and is producing revenue, the 35mm market is rapidly declining at an accelerating rate. In the much faster-growing digital camera segment, Zeus faces strong competition and has been slow to gain sales. Zeus's corporate management wants Atlas's marketing group to produce a strong turnaround plan for the division.

## DEVELOPING MARKETING STRATEGIES AND PLANS

The first task facing Atlas is to identify its potential long-run opportunities, given its market experience and core competencies (see Chapter 2). Atlas can design its cameras with better features. It can make a line of digital video cameras, or it can use its core competency in optics to design a line of binoculars and telescopes. Whichever direction it chooses, it must develop concrete marketing plans that specify the marketing strategy and tactics going forward.

**The New Marketing Realities**

| Fig. 1.7 |

## The New Marketing Realities

## CAPTURING MARKETING INSIGHTS

Atlas needs a reliable marketing information system to closely monitor its marketing environment so it can continually assess market potential and forecast demand. Its microenvironment consists of all the players who affect its ability to produce and sell cameras—suppliers, marketing intermediaries, customers, and competitors. Its macroenvironment includes demographic, economic, physical, technological, political-legal, and social-cultural forces that affect sales and profits (see Chapter 3).

Atlas also needs a dependable marketing research system. To transform strategy into programs, marketing managers must make basic decisions about their expenditures, activities, and budget allocations. They may use sales-response functions that show how the amount of money spent in each application will affect sales and profits (see Chapter 4).

## CONNECTING WITH CUSTOMERS

Atlas must consider how to best create value for its chosen target markets and develop strong, profitable, long-term relationships with customers (see Chapter 5). To do so, it needs to understand consumer markets (see Chapter 6). Who buys cameras, and why? What features and prices are they looking for, and where do they shop? Atlas also sells 35mm cameras to business markets, including large corporations, professional firms, retailers, and government agencies (see Chapter 7), where purchasing agents or buying committees make the decisions. Atlas needs to gain a full understanding of how organizational buyers buy. It needs a sales force well trained in presenting product benefits. Atlas must also take into account changing global opportunities and challenges (see Chapter 8).

## BUILDING STRONG BRANDS

Atlas will not want to market to all possible customers. It must divide the market into major market segments, evaluate each one, and target those it can best serve (see Chapter 9). Suppose Atlas decides to focus on the consumer market and develop a positioning strategy (see Chapter 10). Should it position itself as the "Cadillac" brand, offering superior cameras at a premium price with excellent service and strong advertising? Should it build a simple, low-priced camera aimed at more price-conscious consumers? Or something in between? Atlas must understand the strengths and weaknesses of the Zeus brand as customers see it (see Chapter 11). Is its 35mm film heritage a handicap in the digital camera market?

Atlas must consider growth strategies while also paying close attention to competitors (see Chapter 12), anticipating their moves and knowing how to react quickly and decisively. It may want to initiate some surprise moves, in which case it needs to anticipate how its competitors will respond.

---

### marketing memo | Marketers' Frequently Asked Questions

1. How can we spot and choose the right market segment(s)?
2. How can we differentiate our offerings?
3. How should we respond to customers who buy on price?
4. How can we compete against lower-cost, lower-price competitors?
5. How far can we go in customizing our offering for each customer?
6. How can we grow our business?
7. How can we build stronger brands?
8. How can we reduce the cost of customer acquisition?
9. How can we keep our customers loyal longer?
10. How can we tell which customers are more important?
11. How can we measure the payback from different types of marketing communications?
12. How can we improve sales force productivity?
13. How can we establish multiple channels and yet manage channel conflict?
14. How can we get the other company departments to be more customer-oriented?

## CREATING VALUE

At the heart of the marketing program is the product—the firm's tangible offering to the market, which includes the product quality, design, features, and packaging (see Chapter 13). To gain a competitive advantage, Atlas may provide leasing, delivery, repair, and training as part of its product offering (see Chapter 14). Based on its product positioning, Atlas must initiate new-product development, testing, and launching as part of its long-term view (see Chapter 15).

A critical marketing decision relates to price (see Chapter 16). Atlas must decide on wholesale and retail prices, discounts, allowances, and credit terms. Its price should match well with the offer's perceived value; otherwise, buyers will turn to competitors' products.

## DELIVERING VALUE

Atlas must also determine how to properly deliver to the target market the value embodied in its products and services. Channel activities include those the company undertakes to make the product accessible and available to target customers (see Chapter 17). Atlas must identify, recruit, and link various marketing facilitators to supply its products and services efficiently to the target market. It must understand the various types of retailers, wholesalers, and physical-distribution firms and how they make their decisions (see Chapter 18).

## COMMUNICATING VALUE

Atlas must also adequately communicate to the target market the value embodied by its products and services. It will need an integrated marketing communication program that maximizes the individual and collective contribution of all communication activities (see Chapter 19). Atlas needs to set up mass communication programs consisting of advertising, sales promotion, events, and public relations (see Chapter 21). It also has to tap into online, social media, and mobile options to reach consumers whenever and wherever it may be appropriate (see Chapter 20). Atlas also needs to plan more personal communications, in the form of direct and database marketing, as well as hire, train, and motivate salespeople (see Chapter 22).

## CONDUCTING MARKETING RESPONSIBLY FOR LONG-TERM SUCCESS

Finally, Atlas must build a marketing organization capable of responsibly implementing the marketing plan (see Chapter 23). Because surprises and disappointments can occur as marketing plans unfold, Atlas will need feedback and control to understand the efficiency and effectiveness of its marketing activities and how it can improve them.

# Summary

1. Marketing is an organizational function and a set of processes for creating, communicating, and delivering value to customers and for managing customer relationships in ways that benefit the organization and its stakeholders. Marketing management is the art and science of choosing target markets and getting, keeping, and growing customers through creating, delivering, and communicating superior customer value.

2. Marketers are skilled at managing demand: They seek to influence its level, timing, and composition for goods, services, events, experiences, persons, places, properties, organizations, information, and ideas. They also operate in four different marketplaces: consumer, business, global, and nonprofit.

3. Marketing is not done only by the marketing department. It needs to affect every aspect of the customer experience. To create a strong marketing organization, marketers must think like executives in other departments, and executives in other departments must think more like marketers.

4. Today's marketplace is fundamentally different as a result of major societal forces that have resulted in many new consumer and company capabilities. In particular, technology, globalization, and social responsibility have created new opportunities and challenges and significantly changed marketing management. Companies seek the right balance of tried-and-true methods with breakthrough new approaches to achieve marketing excellence.

5. There are five competing concepts under which organizations can choose to conduct their business: the production concept, the product concept, the sell-

ing concept, the marketing concept, and the holistic marketing concept. The first three are of limited use today.

6. The holistic marketing concept is based on the development, design, and implementation of marketing programs, processes, and activities that recognize their breadth and interdependencies. Holistic marketing recognizes that everything matters in marketing and that a broad, integrated perspective is often necessary. Four

components of holistic marketing are relationship marketing, integrated marketing, internal marketing, and performance marketing.

7. The set of tasks necessary for successful marketing management includes developing marketing strategies and plans, capturing marketing insights, connecting with customers, building strong brands, creating, delivering, and communicating value, and creating long-term growth.

---

## MyMarketingLab

Go to **mymktlab.com** to complete the problems marked with this icon ⭐ as well as for additional Auto-graded and Assisted-graded writing questions.

---

# Applications

---

## Marketing Debate
### Does Marketing Create or Satisfy Needs?

Marketing has often been defined in terms of satisfying customers' needs and wants. Critics, however, maintain that marketing goes beyond that and creates needs and wants that did not exist before. They feel marketers encourage consumers to spend more money than they should on goods and services they do not really need.

**Take a position:** Marketing shapes consumer needs and wants versus Marketing merely reflects the needs and wants of consumers.

## Marketing Discussion
### Shifts in Marketing

⭐ Consider the three key forces driving the new marketing realities. How are they likely to change in the future? What other major trends or forces might affect marketing?

---

## Marketing Excellence

### >> Nike

Nike hit the ground running in 1962. Originally known as Blue Ribbon Sports, the company focused on providing high-quality running shoes designed for athletes by athletes. Founder Philip Knight believed high-tech shoes for runners could be manufactured at competitive prices if imported from abroad. Nike's commitment to designing innovative footwear for serious athletes helped build a cult following among U.S. consumers.

Nike believed in a "pyramid of influence" where the preferences of a small percentage of top athletes influenced the product and brand choices of others. Nike's marketing campaigns have always featured accomplished athletes. For example, runner Steve Prefontaine,

the company's first spokesperson, had an irreverent attitude that matched Nike's spirit.

In 1985, Nike signed up then-rookie guard Michael Jordan as a spokesperson. Jordan was still an up-and-comer, but he personified superior performance. Nike's bet paid off—the Air Jordan line of basketball shoes flew off the shelves and revenues hit more than $100 million in the first year alone. As one reporter stated, "Few marketers have so reliably been able to identify and sign athletes who transcend their sports to such great effect."

In 1988, Nike aired the first ads in its $20 million "Just Do It" ad campaign. The campaign, which ultimately featured 12 TV spots in all, subtly challenged a generation of athletic enthusiasts to chase their goals. It was a natural manifestation of Nike's attitude of self-empowerment through sports.

As Nike began expanding overseas, the company learned that its U.S.-style ads were seen as too aggressive in Europe, Asia, and South America. Nike realized it had to "authenticate" its brand in other countries, so it focused on soccer (called football outside the United States) and became active as a sponsor of youth leagues, local clubs, and national teams. However, for Nike to build authenticity among the soccer audience, consumers had to see professional athletes using its product, especially athletes who won.

Nike's big break came in 1994 when the Brazilian team (the only national team for which Nike had any real sponsorship) won the World Cup. That victory transformed Nike's international image from a sneaker company into a brand that represented emotion, allegiance, and identification. Nike's new alliance with soccer helped propel the brand's growth internationally. In 2003, overseas revenues surpassed U.S. revenues for the first time, and in 2007, Nike acquired Umbro, a British maker of soccer-related footwear, apparel, and equipment. The acquisition made Nike the sole supplier to more than 100 professional soccer teams around the world and boosted Nike's international presence and authenticity in soccer. The company sold Umbro in 2012 for $225 million.

In recent years, Nike's international efforts have been focused on emerging markets. During the 2008 Summer Olympics in Beijing, Nike honed in on China and developed an aggressive marketing strategy that countered Adidas's sponsorship of the Olympic Games. Nike received special permission from the International Olympic Committee to run Nike ads featuring Olympic athletes during the games. In addition, Nike sponsored several teams and athletes, including most of the Chinese teams. This aggressive sponsorship strategy helped ignite sales in the Asian region by 15 percent.

In addition to expanding overseas, Nike has successfully expanded its brand into many sports and athletic categories, including footwear, apparel, and equipment. Nike continues to partner with high-profile and influential athletes, coaches, teams, and leagues to build credibility in these categories. For example, Nike aligned with tennis stars Maria Sharapova, Roger Federer, and Rafael Nadal to push its line of tennis clothing and gear. Some called the famous 2008 Wimbledon match between Roger Federer and Rafael Nadal—both dressed in swooshes from head to toe—a five-hour Nike commercial valued at $10.6 million.

To promote its line of basketball shoes and apparel, Nike has partnered with basketball superstars such as Kobe Bryant and LeBron James. In golf, Nike's swoosh appears on many golfers but most famously on Tiger Woods. In the years since Nike first partnered with Woods, Nike Golf has grown into a $523 million business and literally changed the way golfers dress and play today. Tiger's powerful influence on the game and his Nike-emblazoned style has turned the greens at the majors into "golf's fashion runway."

Nike is the biggest sponsor of athletes in the world and plans to spend more than $3 billion in athletic endorsements between 2012 and 2017. The company also has a history of standing by its athletes, such as Tiger Woods and Kobe Bryant, even as they struggle with personal problems. It severed its relationship with Lance Armstrong in 2012, however, after strong evidence showed that the cyclist doped during his time as an athlete and while competing during all Tour de Frances. Nike released a statement explaining, "Nike does not condone the use of illegal performance enhancing drugs in any manner." Prior to the scandal, the company had helped develop Armstrong's LIVESTRONG campaign to raise funds for cancer. It designed, manufactured, and sold more than 80 million yellow LIVESTRONG bracelets, netting $500 million for the Lance Armstrong Foundation.

While Nike's athletic endorsements help inspire and reach consumers, its most recent innovations in technology have resulted in more loyal and emotionally connected consumers. For example, Nike's lead in the running category has grown to 60 percent market share thanks to its revolutionary running application and community called Nike+ (plus). Nike+ allows runners to engage in the ultimate running experience by seeing their real-time pace, distance, and route and by giving them coaching tips and online sharing capabilities. Nike expanded Nike+ to focus on key growth areas like basketball and exercise and recently launched Nike+ Basketball, Nike+ Kinect, and Nike+Fuelband, a bracelet/app that tracks daily activities.

Like many companies, Nike is trying to make its company and products more eco-friendly. However, unlike many companies, it does not promote these efforts. One brand consultant explained, "Nike has always been about winning. How is sustainability relevant to its brand?" Nike executives agree that promoting an eco-friendly message would distract from its slick high-tech image, so efforts like recycling old shoes into new shoes are kept quiet.

As a result of its successful expansion across geographic markets and product categories, Nike is the top athletic apparel and footwear manufacturer in the world. In 2014, revenues exceeded $27 billion, and Nike dominated the athletic footwear market with 31 percent market share globally and 50 percent market share in the United States. Swooshes abound on everything from wristwatches to skateboards to swimming caps. The firm's long-term strategy, however, is focused on running, basketball, football/soccer, men's training, women's training, and action sports.

**Questions**

1. What are the pros, cons, and risks associated with Nike's core marketing strategy?

2. If you were Adidas, how would you compete with Nike?

**Sources:** Justin Ewers and Tim Smart, "A Designer Swooshes In," *U.S. News & World Report*, January 26, 2004, p. 12; "Corporate Media Executive of the Year," *Delaney Report*, January 12,

2004, p. 1; Barbara Lippert, "Game Changers: Inside the Three Greatest Ad Campaigns of the Past Three Decades," *Adweek*, November 17, 2008; "10 Top Nontraditional Campaigns," *Advertising Age*, December 22, 2003, p. 24; Chris Zook and James Allen, "Growth Outside the Core," *Harvard Business Review*, December 2003, p. 66; Jeremy Mullman, "NIKE; What Slowdown? Swoosh Rides Games to New High," *Advertising Age*, October 20, 2008, p. 34; Allison Kaplan, "Look Just Like Tiger (until You Swing)," *America's Intelligence Wire*, August 9, 2009; Reena Jana and Burt Helm, "Nike Goes Green, Very Quietly," *BusinessWeek*, June 22, 2009; Emily Jane Fox and Chris Isidore, "Nike Ends Contracts with Armstrong," *CNNMoney.com*, October 17, 2012; Nike Annual Report 2012.

## Marketing Excellence

### >> Google

In 1998, two Stanford University PhD students, Larry Page and Sergey Brin, founded a search engine company and named it Google. The name plays on the number *googol*—1 followed by 100 zeroes—and refers to the massive quantity of data available online that the company helps users find. Google's corporate mission is "To organize the world's information and make it universally accessible and useful." As such, the company focuses first and foremost on creating the perfect search engine. Google search works because it uses the millions of links on other Web sites to help determine which sites offer the most valuable content. The company has become the worldwide market leader for search engines through its strategic business focus and constant product innovation.

Google creates and distributes its products for free, which in turn has attracted a host of online advertisers seeking targeted advertising space. About 96 percent of its revenues come from online advertising, which means that creating new advertising space is critical to the company's growth. Google sells advertising space on its search pages through a program called AdWords, which is linked to specific keywords. Hundreds of thousands of companies use AdWords by buying "search ads," little text-based boxes shown alongside relevant search results that advertisers pay for only when users click on them. Google also runs an advertising program called AdSense, which allows any Web site to display targeted Google ads relevant to the content of its site. Web site publishers earn money every time their visitors click on these ads.

In addition to offering prime online real estate for advertisers, Google adds value by providing tools so businesses can better target their ads and understand the effectiveness of their marketing. Google Analytics, for example, is free to Google's advertisers and provides a custom report detailing how Internet users found the site, what ads they saw and/or clicked on, how they behaved on the site, and how much traffic was generated.

With its ability to deploy data that enable up-to-the-minute improvements in a Web marketing program, Google supports a style of marketing in which the advertising resources and budget can be constantly monitored and optimized. Google calls this approach "marketing asset management," implying that advertising should be managed like assets in a portfolio depending on the market conditions. Rather than following a marketing plan developed months in advance, companies use the real-time data collected on their campaigns to optimize the campaign's effectiveness and be more responsive to the market.

Since its launch, Google has expanded far beyond its search capabilities with numerous other products, applications, and tools that benefit both consumers and businesses. The goal behind each product was to help users find information they need and to help them get things done better, faster, and easier than before. Today, Google's wide range of products and services fall into the following categories: Web (Web Search, iGoogle, Google Chrome), Mobile (Mobile, Search for Mobile, Maps for Mobile), Media (Picasa, Google Play, Youtube.com, which Google acquired in 2006 for $1.65 billion), Geo (Earth, Maps), Home & Office (Docs, Gmail, Calendar), Social (Google+, Blogger), Specialized Search (Patents, Finance, Scholarly Papers), and Innovation.

As the world becomes more mobile, Google is betting big in the mobile category. In 2008, Google launched Android, a mobile operating system that went head to head with Apple's iPhone. The biggest differentiation between the two was that Android was free, open sourced, and backed by a multimillion-dollar investment. That meant Google wanted its partners to help build and design Android over the years. The investment paid off, and by 2010, Android became the number-one mobile operating system in the market.

As Google expanded into mobile technology, it quickly became the leader in mobile advertising with 75 percent market share for search ads and approximately 50 percent market share for all mobile ads. In 2012, Google entered the mobile device category when it purchased Motorola and launched the Nexus 7, a sleek tablet that competed directly with the iPad and Kindle. As Google looks toward the future, the company wants to offer the ultimate mobile solution—Google mobile devices along with mobile services so users can use all Google all the time.

Google's ultimate goal is to reach as many people as possible on the Web—whether by PC or by mobile devices. The more users on the Web, the more advertising Google can sell. Google's new products not only accomplish this goal but also make the Web a more personalized experience.

Google has enjoyed great success as a company and a brand in its short lifetime. From the beginning, it has strived to be one of the "good guys" in the corporate world, supporting a touchy-feely work environment, strong ethics, and a famous founding credo: "Don't be evil." Google currently holds a 67 percent market share for core searches in the United States, significantly greater than Microsoft's 17 percent and Yahoo!'s 15 percent market shares. Globally, Google holds a more dominant lead, with 85 percent market share over Yahoo!'s 8 percent and Microsoft's 3 percent. Google's revenues topped $59 billion in 2013, and the company was ranked

the second most powerful brand in the world with a brand value of $107 billion. In addition, Google's $400 billion market capitalization in 2014 edged out companies like Walmart and Microsoft to become the second most valuable company in the world.

### Questions

1. With a portfolio as diverse as Google's, what are the company's core brand values?

2. What's next for Google? Is the company right to put so much focus on Mobile?

**Sources:** www.google.com; Catherine P. Taylor, "Google Flex," *Adweek*, March 20, 2006, cover story; Richard Karpinski, "Keywords, Analytics Help Define User Lifetime Value," *Advertising Age*, April 24, 2006, p. S2; Danny Gorog, "Survival Guide," *Herald Sun*, March 29, 2006; Julie Schlosser, "Google," *Fortune*, October 31, 2005, pp. 168–69; Jefferson Graham, "Google's Profit Sails Past Expectations," *USA Today*, October 21, 2005; Dan Frommer, "Google's Android Mobile Platform Is Getting Huge," *Advertising Age*, October 8, 2009; Rita Chang, "Google Set for Richer Advertising on Smartphones," *Advertising Age*, October 5, 2009; "comScore Releases September 2012 U.S. Search Engine Rankings," comScore.com, October 11, 2012; Claire Cain Miller, "As Google Changes, Its Revenue Keeps Rising," *The New York Times*, July 19, 2012; Roben Farzad, "Google at $400 Billion: A New No. 2 in Market Cap," *Bloomberg Businessweek*, February 12, 2104.

## In This Chapter, We Will Address the Following **Questions**

1.  How does marketing affect customer value? (p. 35)

2.  How is strategic planning carried out at the corporate and divisional levels? (p. 38)

3.  How is strategic planning carried out at the business unit level? (p. 48)

4.  What does a marketing plan include? (p. 55)

HP, led by President and CEO Meg Whitman, is revising its corporate strategy to reflect significant changes in the marketing environment.

*Source: ChinaFotoPress via Getty Images*

# 2 Developing Marketing Strategies and Plans

**Developing the right marketing strategies over time requires a blend of discipline and** flexibility. Firms must stick to a strategy but also constantly improve it. In today's fast-changing marketing world, identifying the best long-term strategies is crucial—but challenging—as HP has been finding out.[1]

 *A true technology pioneer, Hewlett-Packard (HP) has encountered much difficulty in recent years, culminating in a massive quarterly charge of more than $9.5 billion in 2012, its biggest ever. Of that total, $8 billion was a write-down in the value of its IT services unit as the result of a disastrous acquisition of EDS. Revenue for the unit dropped when customers stopped signing large, long-term outsourcing contracts that were at the core of the unit's business model. A feud with Oracle, among other factors, hurt HP's sales of large servers to business customers. In a maturing market with few good new products, PC sales slowed so much that HP announced it was exiting the business. Printer and ink sales dropped as consumers began to print less. New CEO Meg Whitman vowed to increase the company's emphasis on design, reorganizing the PC group to come up with a cleaner, minimalist sensibility. Admitting that the company did not yet have a strategy for mobile phones, Whitman acknowledged there was much work to be done.*

**This chapter begins by examining** some of the strategic marketing implications in creating customer value. We'll look at several perspectives on planning and describe how to draw up a formal marketing plan.

# Marketing and Customer Value

The task of any business is to deliver customer value at a profit. A company can win only by fine-tuning the value delivery process and choosing, providing, and communicating superior value to increasingly well-informed buyers.

## THE VALUE DELIVERY PROCESS

The traditional—but dated—view of marketing is that the firm makes something and then sells it, with marketing taking place during the selling process. Companies that take this view succeed only in economies marked by goods shortages where consumers are not fussy about quality, features, or style—for example, basic staple goods in developing markets.

In economies with many different types of people, each with individual wants, perceptions, preferences, and buying criteria, the smart competitor must design and deliver offerings for well-defined target markets. This realization inspired a new view of business processes that places marketing at the *beginning* of planning. Instead of emphasizing making and selling, companies now see themselves as part of a value delivery process.

We can divide the value creation and delivery sequence into three phases.[2] First, *choosing the value* is the "homework" marketers must do before any product exists. They must segment the market, select the appropriate target, and develop the offering's value positioning. The formula "segmentation, targeting, positioning (STP)" is the essence of strategic marketing. The second phase is *providing the value*. Marketing must identify specific product features, prices, and distribution. The task in the third phase is *communicating the value* by utilizing the Internet, advertising, sales force, and any other communication tools to announce and promote the product. The value delivery process begins before there is a product and continues through development and after launch. Each phase has cost implications.

# THE VALUE CHAIN

Harvard's Michael Porter has proposed the **value chain** as a tool for identifying ways to create more customer value.[3] According to this model, every firm is a synthesis of activities performed to design, produce, market, deliver, and support its product. Nine strategically relevant activities—five primary and four support activities—create value and cost in a specific business.

The *primary activities* are (1) inbound logistics, or bringing materials into the business; (2) operations, or converting materials into final products; (3) outbound logistics, or shipping out final products; (4) marketing, which includes sales; and (5) service. Specialized departments handle the *support activities*—(1) procurement, (2) technology development, (3) human resource management, and (4) firm infrastructure. (Infrastructure covers the costs of general management, planning, finance, accounting, legal, and government affairs.)

The firm's task is to examine its costs and performance in each value-creating activity, *benchmarking* against competitors, and look for ways to improve. Managers can identify the "best of class" practices of the world's best companies by consulting customers, suppliers, distributors, financial analysts, trade associations, and the media to see who seems to be doing the best job. Even the best companies can benchmark, against other industries if necessary, to improve their performance. GE has benchmarked against P&G as well as developing its own best practices.[4]

The firm's success depends not only on how well each department performs its work, but also on how well the company coordinates departmental activities to conduct *core business processes*.[5] These processes include:

- *The market-sensing process*—gathering and acting upon information about the market
- *The new-offering realization process*—researching, developing, and launching new high-quality offerings quickly and within budget
- *The customer acquisition process*—defining target markets and prospecting for new customers
- *The customer relationship management process*—building deeper understanding, relationships, and offerings to individual customers
- *The fulfillment management process*—receiving and approving orders, shipping goods on time, and collecting payment

Strong companies are reengineering their work flows and building cross-functional teams to be responsible for each process.[6] Ford established a cross-functional team to help reduce water usage per vehicle by 30 percent.[7] AT&T, LexisNexis, and Pratt & Whitney have reorganized their employees into cross-functional teams; cross-functional teams operate in nonprofit and government organizations as well.[8]

A firm also needs to look for competitive advantages beyond its own operations in the value chains of suppliers, distributors, and customers. Many companies today have partnered with specific suppliers and distributors to create a superior **value delivery network**, also called a **supply chain**.

# CORE COMPETENCIES

Companies today outsource less-critical resources if they can obtain better quality or lower cost. The key is to own and nurture the resources and competencies that make up the *essence* of the business. Many textile, chemical, and computer/electronic product firms use offshore manufacturers and focus on product design and development and marketing, their core competencies. A **core competency** has three characteristics: (1) It is a source of competitive advantage and makes a significant contribution to perceived customer benefits; (2) It has applications in a wide variety of markets; and (3) It is difficult for competitors to imitate.

Competitive advantage also accompanies *distinctive capabilities* or excellence in broader business processes. Wharton's George Day sees market-driven organizations as excelling in three distinctive capabilities: market sensing, customer linking, and channel bonding.[9] In terms of market sensing, Day believes tremendous opportunities and threats often begin as "weak signals" from the "periphery" of a business.[10] He suggests systematically developing peripheral vision by asking three questions related to learning from the past, evaluating the present, and envisioning the future.

Businesses may need to realign themselves to maximize core competencies. Realignment has three steps: (1) (re)defining the business concept or "big idea"; (2) (re)shaping the business scope, sometimes geographically; and (3) (re)positioning the company's brand identity. Peabody Energy implemented a new global organizational structure—creating geographic business units in the Americas, Australia, and Asia—to reflect its growing global footprint.[11] Changes in business fortunes often necessitate realignment and restructuring, as Panasonic and other Japanese technology and electronic companies found.[12]

Panasonic has encountered some marketplace challenges in recent years, forcing it to make changes in what businesses it is in and how they are run.

Source: Alberto Cristofari/A3/contrasto/Redux

**PANASONIC** As Panasonic approaches its 100th anniversary in 2018, it faces unprecedented difficulties, notably a massive loss of roughly $19 billion over 2011 and 2012. For years, its "Ideas for Life" positioning had fueled innovation, generating successful products like its rugged Toughbook notebook computers. Its television sets and other home electronics ran into trouble, however, when the economy stalled just as consumers began to treat flat-screen LCD televisions as a commodity. Further, a strong yen and high manufacturing costs in Japan made it difficult for Panasonic to compete on price. Anti-Japanese sentiment from a territorial dispute proved a stumbling block in China. Finally, the acquisition of Sanyo in 2009, designed to help the company sell more green-energy products, was disappointing. A major restructuring by new president Kazuhiro Tsuga in fall 2012 scaled back manufacturing in Japan, abandoned the mobile phone market overseas, and cut back investment in solar panels and rechargeable batteries. Tsuga emphasized that Panasonic will streamline business units and emphasize profit, not just revenue growth.

## THE CENTRAL ROLE OF STRATEGIC PLANNING

Only a select group of companies have historically stood out as master marketers (see Table 2.1). These companies focus on the customer and are organized to respond effectively to changing needs. They all have well-staffed marketing departments, and their other departments accept that the customer is king. They also often have strong marketing leadership in the form of a successful CMO (see "Marketing Memo: What Does It Take to Be a Successful CMO?").

To ensure they execute the right activities, marketers must prioritize strategic planning in three key areas: (1) managing the businesses as an investment portfolio, (2) assessing the market's growth rate and the company's position in that market, and (3) establishing a strategy. The company must develop a game plan for achieving each business's long-run objectives.

Most large companies consist of four organizational levels: (1) corporate, (2) division, (3) business unit, and (4) product. Corporate headquarters is responsible for designing a corporate strategic plan to guide the whole enterprise; it makes decisions on the amount of resources to allocate to each division as well as on which businesses to start or eliminate. Each division establishes a plan covering the allocation of funds to each business unit within the division. Each business unit develops a strategic plan to carry that business unit into a profitable future. Finally, each product level (product line, brand) develops a marketing plan for achieving its objectives.

The **marketing plan** is the central instrument for directing and coordinating the marketing effort. It operates at two levels: strategic and tactical. The **strategic marketing plan** lays out the target markets and the firm's value proposition, based on an analysis of the best market opportunities. The **tactical marketing plan** specifies the marketing tactics, including product features, promotion, merchandising, pricing, sales channels, and service. The complete planning, implementation, and control cycle of strategic planning is shown in Figure 2.1. Next, we consider planning at each of the four levels of the organization.

| TABLE 2.1 | Some Examples of Master Marketers | | |
|-----------|-----------|-----------|-----------|
| Amazon.com | Enterprise Rent-A-Car | Red Bull |
| Apple | Google | Ritz-Carlton |
| Bang & Olufsen | Harley-Davidson | Samsung |
| Best Buy | Honda | Southwest Airlines |
| BMW | IKEA | Starbucks |
| Caterpillar | LEGO | Target |
| Club Med | McDonald's | Tesco |
| Costco | Nike | Toyota |
| Disney | Nordstrom | Virgin |
| eBay | Procter & Gamble | Walmart |
| Electrolux | Progressive Insurance | Whole Foods |

| Fig. 2.1 |

The Strategic Planning, Implementation, and Control Processes

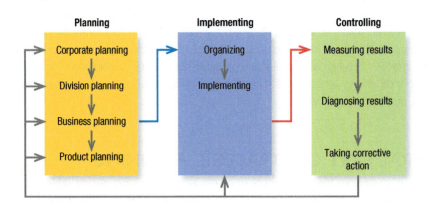

# Corporate and Division Strategic Planning

Whether they let their business units set their own goals and strategies or collaborate in doing so, all corporate headquarters undertake four planning activities:

1. Defining the corporate mission
2. Establishing strategic business units
3. Assigning resources to each strategic business unit
4. Assessing growth opportunities

We'll briefly look at each process.

## marketing memo

### What Does it Take to Be a Successful CMO?

The challenge chief marketing officers (CMOs) face is that success factors are many and varied. CMOs must have strong quantitative *and* qualitative skills; they must have an independent, entrepreneurial attitude but work closely with other departments; and they must capture the "voice" of consumers yet have a keen bottom-line understanding of how marketing creates value. Two-thirds of top CMOs think return-on-marketing-investment (ROMI) will be the primary measure of their effectiveness in 2015.

One survey asking 200 senior-level marketing executives which innate and learned qualities were most important yielded these answers:

| Innate Qualities | Learned Qualities |
| --- | --- |
| • Risk taker | • Global experience |
| • Willingness to make decisions | • Multichannel expertise |
| • Problem-solving ability | • Cross-industry experience |
| • Change agent | • Digital focus |
| • Results-oriented | • Operational knowledge |

Marketing experts George Day and Robert Malcolm believe three driving forces will change the role of the CMO in the coming years: (1) predictable marketplace trends, (2) the changing role of the C-suite, and (3) uncertainty about the economy and organizational design. They identify five priorities for any successful CMO:

1. Act as the visionary for the future of the company.
2. Build adaptive marketing capabilities.
3. Win the war for marketing talent.
4. Tighten the alignment with sales.
5. Take accountability for returns on marketing spending.

Perhaps the most important role for any CMO is to infuse a customer perspective in business decisions affecting any customer *touch point* (where a customer directly or indirectly interacts with the company). Increasingly, these customer insights must have a global focus. As one top executive search firm leader said, "Tomorrow's CMO will have to have global and international experience. You can do it without living abroad...but you have to get exposure to those markets. It opens your eyes to new ways of doing business, increases cultural sensitivity and increases flexibility."

**Sources**: Jennifer Rooney, "CMO Tenure Hits 43-Month Mark," *Forbes*, June 14, 2012; Steven Cook, "It's Time to Raise the CMO Bar," www.cmo.com, January 24, 2012; "From Stretched to Strengthened: Insights from the Global Chief Marketing Officer Study," *IBM CMO C-Suite Studies*, October 2011; Natalie Zmuda, "Global Experience Rises as Prerequisite to Getting Ahead," *Advertising Age*, June 10, 2012; George S. Day and Robert Malcolm, "The CMO and the Future of Marketing," *Marketing Management*, Spring 2012, pp. 34–43; Marc De Swann Arons and Frank Van Den Driest, *The Global Brand CEO: Building the Ultimate Marketing Machine* (New York: Airstream, 2011); Marylee Sachs, *The Changing MO of the CMO: How the Convergence of Brand and Reputation Is Affecting Marketers* (Surry, England: Gower, 2011); Marylee Sachs, *What the New Breed of CMOs Know That You Don't* (Surry, England: Gower, 2013).

## DEFINING THE CORPORATE MISSION

An organization exists to accomplish something: to make cars, lend money, provide a night's lodging. Over time, the mission may change to respond to new opportunities or market conditions. Amazon.com changed its mission from being the world's largest online bookstore to aspiring to be the world's largest online store; eBay changed from running online auctions for collectors to running online auctions of all kinds of goods; and Dunkin' Donuts switched its emphasis from doughnuts to coffee.

To define its mission, a company should address Peter Drucker's classic questions:[13] What is our business? Who is the customer? What is of value to the customer? What will our business be? What should our business be? These simple-sounding questions are among the most difficult a company will ever face. Successful companies continuously ask and answer them.

**BUSINESS DEFINITION** Companies often define themselves in terms of products: They are in the "auto business" or the "clothing business." *Market definitions* of a business, however, describe the business as a customer-satisfying process. Products are transient; basic needs and customer groups endure forever. Transportation is a need: the horse and carriage, automobile, railroad, airline, ship, and truck are products that meet that need. Consider how Steelcase takes a market definition approach to its business.[14]

Steelcase has found much success by redefining its business as more broadly than office furniture.

Source: ©Steelcase 2014

▮ STEELCASE   The world's best-selling maker of office furniture, Steelcase describes itself as "the global leader in furnishing the work experience in office environments." Defining its business broadly, former CEO James Hackett believes, "enabled a lot of the great insights that we had found out about work to be transferred beyond the office (and into furnishing home offices, schools and health care facilities)." Steelcase uses a 23-person research team to gain those insights and conducts interviews and surveys, films office activities, and uses sensors to measure how workers use rooms and furnishings. Firms are ordering fewer cubicles and filing cabinets, for instance, and more benches, tables, and café seating to free employees to brainstorm and collaborate. Hackett defines the trend as the move from an "I/Fixed" to a "We/Mobile" mentality. Increased performance is the company's key goal. If it feels it will make workers happier and more productive, Steelcase can convince a firm to modernize and upgrade its office furniture.

Viewing businesses in terms of customer needs can suggest additional growth opportunities. Table 2.2 lists companies that have moved from a product to a market definition of their business.

A *target market definition* tends to focus on selling a product or service to a current market. Pepsi could define its target market as everyone who drinks carbonated soft drinks, and competitors would therefore be other carbonated soft drink companies. A *strategic market definition,* however, also focuses on the potential market. If Pepsi considered everyone who might drink something to quench his or her thirst, its competition would include noncarbonated soft drinks, bottled water, fruit juices, tea, and coffee.

| TABLE 2.2 | Product-Oriented versus Market-Oriented Definitions of a Business | |
|---|---|---|
| **Company** | **Product Definition** | **Market Definition** |
| Union Pacific Railroad | We run a railroad. | We are a people-and-goods mover. |
| Xerox | We make copying equipment. | We help improve office productivity. |
| Hess Corporation | We sell gasoline. | We supply energy. |
| Paramount Pictures | We make movies. | We market entertainment. |
| Encyclopaedia Britannica | We sell encyclopedias online. | We distribute information. |
| Carrier | We make air conditioners and furnaces. | We provide climate control in the home. |

CRAFTING A MSSION STATEMENT  A clear, thoughtful **mission statement**, developed collaboratively with and shared with managers, employees, and often customers, provides a shared sense of purpose, direction, and opportunity. At its best it reflects a vision, an almost "impossible dream," that provides direction for the next 10 to 20 years. Sony's former president, Akio Morita, wanted everyone to have access to "personal portable sound," so his company created the Walkman and portable CD player. Fred Smith wanted to deliver mail anywhere in the United States before 10:30 AM the next day, so he created FedEx.

Good mission statements have five major characteristics.

1. *They focus on a limited number of goals.* Compare a vague mission statement such as "To build total brand value by innovating to deliver customer value and customer leadership faster, better, and more completely than our competition" to Google's ambitious but more focused mission statement, "To organize the world's information and make it universally accessible and useful."

2. *They stress the company's major policies and values.* Narrowing the range of individual discretion lets employees act consistently on important issues.

3. *They define the major competitive spheres within which the company will operate.* Table 2.3 summarizes some key competitive dimensions for mission statements.

4. *They take a long-term view.* Management should change the mission only when it ceases to be relevant.

5. *They are as short, memorable, and meaningful as possible.* Marketing consultant Guy Kawasaki advocates developing three- to four-word corporate mantras—like "Enriching Women's Lives" for Mary Kay—rather than mission statements.[15]

| TABLE 2.3 | Defining Competitive Territory and Boundaries in Mission Statements |
|---|---|

- **Industry.** *Some companies operate in only one industry; some only in a set of related industries; some only in industrial goods, consumer goods, or services; and some in any industry.*
  - Caterpillar focuses on the industrial market; John Deere operates in the industrial and consumer markets.
- **Products and applications.** *Firms define the range of products and applications they will supply.*
  - St. Jude Medical's mission is "develop medical technology and services that put more control into the hands of those who treat cardiac, neurological and chronic pain patients, worldwide. We do this because we are dedicated to advancing the practice of medicine by reducing risk wherever possible and contributing to successful outcomes for every patient."
- **Competence.** *The firm identifies the range of technological and other core competencies it will master and leverage.*
  - Japan's NEC has built its core competencies in computing, communications, and components to support production of laptop computers, television receivers, and handheld telephones.
- **Market segment.** *The type of market or customers a company will serve is the market segment.*
  - Aston Martin makes only high-performance sports cars. Gerber serves primarily the baby market.
- **Vertical.** *The vertical sphere is the number of channel levels, from raw material to final product and distribution, in which a company will participate.*
  - At one extreme are companies with a large vertical scope. American Apparel dyes, designs, sews, markets, and distributes its line of clothing apparel out of a single building in downtown Los Angeles.[16]
  - At the other extreme are "hollow corporations," which outsource the production of nearly all goods and services to suppliers. Metro newspaper is published in 56 editions in 22 countries on four continents and is read by more than 17 million people every day. It employs few reporters and owns no printing presses; instead it purchases its articles from other news sources and outsources all its printing and much of its distribution to third parties.[17]
- **Geographical.** *The range of regions, countries, or country groups in which a company will operate defines its geographical sphere.*
  - Some companies operate in a specific city or state. Others are multinationals like Deutsche Post DHL and Royal Dutch/Shell, which each operate in more than 100 countries.

Source: © Horizons WWP/Alamy

Metro outsources much of its production and operations for the different newspapers which it publishes in markets around the world.

## ESTABLISHING STRATEGIC BUSINESS UNITS

Large companies normally manage quite different businesses, each requiring its own strategy. At one time, General Electric classified its businesses into 49 **strategic business units (SBUs)**. An SBU has three characteristics:

1. It is a single business, or a collection of related businesses, that can be planned separately from the rest of the company.
2. It has its own set of competitors.
3. It has a manager responsible for strategic planning and profit performance, who controls most of the factors affecting profit.

The purpose of identifying the company's strategic business units is to develop separate strategies and assign appropriate funding. Senior management knows its portfolio of businesses usually includes a number of "yesterday's has-beens" as well as "tomorrow's winners." Liz Claiborne has put more emphasis on some of its younger businesses such as Juicy Couture, Lucky Brand Jeans, Mexx, and Kate Spade while selling businesses without the same buzz (Ellen Tracy, Sigrid Olsen, and Laundry).

## ASSIGNING RESOURCES TO EACH SBU[18]

Once it has defined SBUs, management must decide how to allocate corporate resources to each. The GE/McKinsey Matrix classified each SBU by the extent of its competitive advantage and the attractiveness of its industry. Management could decide to grow, "harvest" or draw cash from, or hold on to the business. BCG's Growth-Share Matrix used relative market share and annual rate of market growth as criteria for investment decisions, classifying SBUs as dogs, cash cows, question marks, and stars.

Portfolio-planning models like these have largely fallen out of favor as oversimplified and subjective. Newer methods rely on shareholder value analysis and on whether the market value of a company is greater with an SBU or without it. These value calculations assess the potential of a business based on growth opportunities from global expansion, repositioning or retargeting, and strategic outsourcing.

## ASSESSING GROWTH OPPORTUNITIES

Assessing growth opportunities includes planning new businesses, downsizing, and terminating older businesses. If there is a gap between future desired sales and projected sales, corporate management will need to develop or acquire new businesses to fill it.

Figure 2.2 illustrates this strategic-planning gap for a hypothetical manufacturer of blank DVD discs called Cineview. The lowest curve projects expected sales from the current business portfolio over the next

| Fig. 2.2 |

The Strategic-Planning Gap

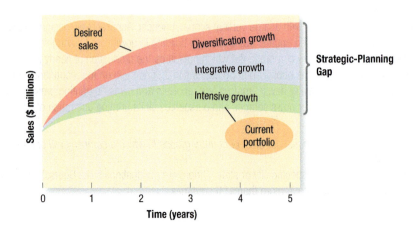

five years. The highest describes desired sales over the same period. Evidently, the company wants to grow much faster than its current businesses will permit. How can it fill the strategic-planning gap?

The first option is to identify opportunities for growth within current businesses (intensive opportunities). The second is to identify opportunities to build or acquire businesses related to current businesses (integrative opportunities). The third is to identify opportunities to add attractive unrelated businesses (diversification opportunities).

**INTENSIVE GROWTH** Corporate management should first review opportunities for improving existing businesses. One useful framework is a "product-market expansion grid," which considers the strategic growth opportunities for a firm in terms of current and new products and markets.

The company first considers whether it could gain more market share with its current products in their current markets, using a *market-penetration strategy*. Next it considers whether it can find or develop new markets for its current products, in a *market-development strategy*. Then it considers whether it can develop new products for its current markets with a *product-development strategy*. Later the firm will also review opportunities to develop new products for new markets in a *diversification strategy*. Consider how ESPN has pursued a variety of growth opportunities (see Figure 2.3).[19]

Source: © Patti McConville/Alamy

Liz Claiborne has put more emphasis on its Juicy Couture stores than its other slower-growing lines of business.

**ESPN** Through its singular focus on sports programming and news, ESPN grew from a small regional broadcaster into the biggest name in sports. In the early 1990s, the company crafted a well-thought-out plan: Wherever sports fans watched, read, and discussed sports, ESPN would be there. It pursued this strategy by expanding its brand and now encompasses 10 cable channels, a Web site, a magazine, a few restaurants (ESPN Zone), more than 600 local radio affiliates, original movies and television series, book publishing, a sports merchandise catalog and online store, music and video games, and a mobile service. ESPN International partly or wholly owns 47 television networks outside the United States and a variety of additional businesses that reach sports fans in more than 200 countries and territories across all seven continents. Now owned by The Walt Disney Company, ESPN contributes $9.4 billion a year in revenue, or roughly three-fourths of Disney's total cable network revenues. But perhaps the greatest tribute to the power of its brand came from one male focus group respondent who said, "If ESPN was a woman, I'd marry her."

So how might Cineview use these three major intensive growth strategies to increase its sales? It could try to encourage its current customers to buy more by demonstrating the benefits of using DVD discs for data storage in addition to video storage. It could try to attract competitors' customers if it noticed major weaknesses in their products or marketing programs. Finally, Cineview could try to convince nonusers to start using blank DVD discs.

How can Cineview use a market-development strategy? First, it might try to identify potential user groups in the current sales areas. If it has been selling DVD discs only to consumer markets, it might go after office and factory markets. Second, it might seek additional distribution channels by adding mass merchandising or online channels. Third, the company might sell in new locations in its home country or abroad.

Management should also consider new-product possibilities. Cineview could develop new features, such as additional data storage capabilities or greater durability. It could offer the DVD discs at two or more quality levels, or it could research an alternative technology such as flash drives.

These intensive growth strategies offer several ways to grow. Still, that growth may not be enough, and management must also look for integrative growth opportunities.

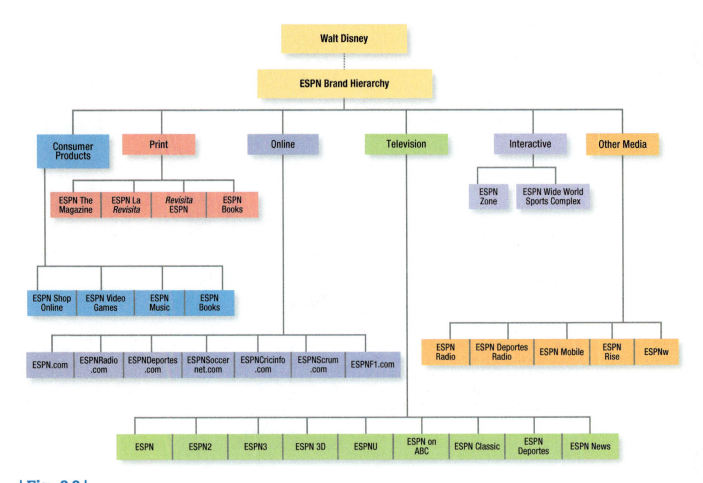

| Fig. 2.3 |

ESPN Growth
Opportunities

**INTEGRATIVE GROWTH** A business can increase sales and profits through backward, forward, or horizontal integration within its industry. Merck formed joint ventures as far back as 1989 with Johnson & Johnson to sell over-the-counter pharmaceuticals and 1991 with DuPont to expand basic research. In 1997, Merck and Rhône-Poulenc S.A. (now Sanofi-Aventis S.A.) combined their animal health and poultry genetics businesses to form Merial Limited, a fully integrated animal health company. Finally, Merck acquired Schering-Plough in 2009.[20]

Horizontal mergers and alliances don't always work out. The merger between Sears and Kmart didn't solve either retailer's problems.[21] Nextel Communications Inc. merged with Sprint in 2005 in what Bloomberg's financial analysts called one the worst mergers of the past 10 years, in part due to their incompatible networks.[22] Consider the challenges faced by United and Continental in their merger.[23]

**▌UNITED AND CONTINENTAL**   Airline mergers are notoriously tricky, laden with regulations and a host of potentially conflicting considerations about safety, cost, style, reliability, convenience, speed, and comfort. United's merger with Continental made sense strategically and financially, but logistical problems seemed endless because the two airlines ran their businesses in very different ways, from boarding procedures to the way they brought planes into the gate. Even coffee was a thorny issue; United served Starbucks while Continental used a company called Fresh Brew. After extensive research, a suitable compromise was identified—a lighter fresh blend called Journeys—but customers were unimpressed until the company discovered the two airlines had different brew baskets and United's was actually leaking water and diluting the coffee. New pillow packs were commissioned to solve the problem.

ESPN's flagship *SportsCenter* program is an anchor of its television network and related sports businesses.

Media companies, on the other hand, have long reaped the benefits of integrative growth. Consider how NBC Universal leveraged one of its properties:[24]

> Following the 2006 *Curious George* movie release via Universal Pictures, *Curious George* the TV show was released on PBS Kids as a joint production by Universal Studios Family Productions, Imagine Entertainment and WGBH Boston. Universal Studios Hollywood currently has an *Adventures of Curious George* ride where kids can "soak up the thrills of a five hundred gallon water dump and unleash thousands of flying foam balls...."

How might Cineview achieve integrative growth? The company might acquire one or more of its suppliers, such as plastic material producers, to gain more control or generate more profit through backward integration. It might acquire some wholesalers or retailers, especially if they are highly profitable, in forward integration. Finally, Cineview might acquire one or more competitors, provided the government does not bar this horizontal integration. However, these new sources may still not deliver the desired sales volume. In that case, the company must consider diversification.

United and Continental found it harder to merge their airlines than just blending their logos on their planes.

**DIVERSIFICATION GROWTH** Diversification growth makes sense when good opportunities exist outside the present businesses—the industry is highly attractive and the company has the right mix of business strengths to succeed. From its origins as an animated film producer, The Walt Disney Company has moved into licensing characters for merchandised goods, publishing general interest fiction books under the Hyperion imprint, entering the broadcast industry with its own Disney Channel as well as ABC and ESPN, developing theme parks and vacation and resort properties, and offering cruise and commercial theatre experiences.

Several types of diversification are possible for Cineview. First, the company could choose a concentric strategy and seek new products that have technological or marketing synergies with existing product lines, though appealing to a different group of customers. It might start a compact disc manufacturing operation because it knows how to manufacture DVD discs or a flash drive manufacturing operation because it knows digital storage. Second, it might use a horizontal strategy and produce plastic DVD cases, for example, though they require a different manufacturing process. Finally, the company might seek new businesses with no relationship to its current technology, products, or markets, adopting a conglomerate strategy to consider making application software or personal organizers.

**DOWNSIZING AND DIVESTING OLDER BUSINESSES** Companies must carefully prune, harvest, or divest tired old businesses to release needed resources for other uses and reduce costs. To focus on its travel and credit card operations, American Express spun off American Express Financial Advisors, which provided insurance, mutual funds, investment advice, and brokerage and asset management services (it was renamed Ameriprise Financial). American International Group (AIG) agreed to sell two of its subunits—American General Indemnity Co. and American General Property Insurance Co.—to White Mountains Insurance Group as part of a long-term growth strategy to discard redundant assets and focus on its core operations.[25]

# ORGANIZATION AND ORGANIZATIONAL CULTURE

Strategic planning happens within the context of the organization. A company's **organization** consists of its structures, policies, and corporate culture, all of which can become dysfunctional in a rapidly changing business environment. Whereas managers can change structures and policies (though with difficulty), the company's culture is very hard to change. Yet adapting the culture is often the key to successfully implementing a new strategy.

What exactly is a **corporate culture**? Some define it as "the shared experiences, stories, beliefs, and norms that characterize an organization." Walk into any company and the first thing that strikes you is the corporate culture—the way people dress, talk to one another, and greet customers.

A customer-centric culture can affect all aspects of an organization. Enterprise Rent-A-Car features its own employees in its latest "The Enterprise Way" ad campaign. Through its "Making It Right" training program,

Enterprise Rent-A-Car is known for its strong consumer-centric corporate culture.

Source: Getty Images

Enterprise empowers all employees to make their own decisions. One ad in the campaign, themed "Fix Any Problem," reinforces how any local Enterprise outlet has the authority to take actions to maximize customer satisfaction.[26]

## MARKETING INNOVATION

Innovation in marketing is critical. Imaginative ideas on strategy exist in many places within a company. Senior management should identify and encourage fresh ideas from three generally underrepresented groups: employees with youthful or diverse perspectives, employees far removed from company headquarters, and employees new to the industry. Each group can challenge company orthodoxy and stimulate new ideas.

British-based Reckitt Benckiser has been an innovator in the staid household cleaning products industry by generating 35 percent of sales from products under three years old.[27] Its multinational staff is encouraged to dig deep into consumer habits and is well rewarded for excellent performance. Slovenia-based Krka—makers of prescription pharmaceuticals, non-prescription products and animal health products—aims to generate more than 40 percent of its total sales from new products.[28] "Marketing Insight: Creating Innovative Marketing" describes how some leading companies approach innovation.

Firms develop strategy by choosing their view of the future. The Royal Dutch/Shell Group has pioneered **scenario analysis**, which develops plausible representations of a firm's possible future using assumptions about forces driving the market and different uncertainties. Managers think through each scenario with the question, "What will we do if it happens?," adopt one scenario as the most probable, and watch for signposts that might confirm or disconfirm it.[29] Consider the strategic challenges faced by the movie industry.[30]

---

## marketing insight

## Creating Innovative Marketing

When IBM surveyed top CEOs and government leaders about their priorities, business-model innovation and coming up with unique ways of doing things scored high. IBM's own drive for business-model innovation led to much collaboration, both within IBM and externally with companies, governments, and educational institutions. Then-CEO Samuel Palmisano noted how the breakthrough Cell processor, based on the company's Power architecture, would not have happened without collaboration with Sony and Nintendo, as well as competitors Toshiba and Microsoft.

Procter & Gamble (P&G) has made it a goal for 50 percent of new products to come from outside its labs—from inventors, scientists, and suppliers whose new-product ideas can be developed in-house. Mark Benioff, CEO and co-founder of Salesforce.com, believes the key to innovation is the ability to adapt. While the company spent years relying on disruptive ideas to come from within, it acquired two firms for $1 billion because it "couldn't afford to wait" and has purchased 24 firms in total. As Benioff notes, "Innovation is a continuum. You have to think about how the world is evolving and transforming. Are you part of the continuum?"

Business guru Jim Collins's research emphasizes the importance of systematic, broad-based innovation: "Always looking for the one big breakthrough, the one big idea, is contrary to what we found: To build a truly great company, it's decision upon decision, action upon action, day upon day, month upon month.... It's cumulative momentum and no one decision defines a great company." Collins cites Walt Disney in theme parks and Walmart in retailing as examples of companies that were successful by executing a big idea brilliantly over a long period of time.

To find breakthrough ideas, some companies immerse a range of employees in solving marketing problems. Samsung's Value Innovation Program (VIP) isolates product development teams of engineers, designers, and planners with a timetable and end date in the company's center just south of Seoul, Korea, while 50 specialists help guide their activities. To help make tough trade-offs, team members draw "value curves" that rank attributes such as a product's sound or picture quality on a scale from 1 to 5. To develop a new car, BMW mobilizes specialists in engineering, design, production, marketing, purchasing, and finance at its Research and Innovation Center or Project House.

Companies like Facebook and Google kickstart the creative problem-solving process by using the phrase, "How might we?" Tim Brown, CEO of IDEO, says IDEO asks "how might we" with each design challenge. "The 'How' part assumes there are solutions out there—it provides creative confidence," Brown said. "The 'Might' part says we can put ideas out there that might work or might not—either way, it's OK. And the 'We' part says we're going to do it together and build on each other's ideas."

**Sources:** Steve Hamm, "Innovation: The View from the Top," *BusinessWeek*, April 3, 2006, pp. 52–53; Jena McGregor, "The World's Most Innovative Companies," *BusinessWeek*, April 24, 2006, pp. 63–74; Rich Karlgard, "Digital Rules," *Forbes*, March 13, 2006, p. 31; Jennifer Rooney and Jim Collins, "Being Great Is *Not* Just a Matter of Big Ideas," *Point*, June 2006, p. 20; Moon Ihlwan, "Camp Samsung," *BusinessWeek*, July 3, 2006, pp. 46–47; Mohanbir Sawhney, Robert C. Wolcott, and Inigo Arroniz, "The 12 Different Ways for Companies to Innovate," *MIT Sloan Management Review* (Spring 2006), pp. 75–85; Victoria Barret, "Why Salesforce.com Ranks #1 on Forbes Most Innovative List," *Forbes*, September 2012; Warren Berger, "The Secret Phrase Top Innovators Use," *HBR Blog Network*, September 17, 2012.

Film studios are finding new ways to expand their movie franchises, as with Warner Bros. and *Batman*.

*Source: Handout/MCT/Newscom*

| **MOVIE INDUSTRY**    Netflix and the Internet started a decline in DVD sales that began in 2007 and has not stopped. The emergence of Redbox kiosks renting movies for $1 a day added yet another threat to the movie business and DVD sales. Film studios clearly need to prepare for the day when films are primarily sold not through physical distribution but through satellite and cable companies' video-on-demand services. Although studios make 70 percent on a typical $4.99 cable viewing versus 30 percent on the sale of a DVD, sales of DVDs still generate 70 percent of a film's profits. To increase electronic distribution without destroying their DVD business, studios are experimenting with new approaches. Some, such as Warner Bros., are releasing a DVD at the same time as online and cable versions of a movie. Disney cross-promotes its parent-friendly films at its theme parks, on its TV channels, and in its stores. Warner has entered the video game business (such as with *Dark Knight Batman*) in hopes of generating additional revenue on its movie characters. Warner Interactive typically spends $30 million to $40 million to make its games and generated close to $1 billion in sales in 2011. Film studios are considering all possible scenarios as they rethink their business model in a world where the DVD is no longer king.

# Business Unit Strategic Planning

The business unit strategic-planning process consists of the steps shown in Figure 2.4. We examine each step in the sections that follow.

**| Fig. 2.4 |**

The Business Unit
Strategic-Planning
Process

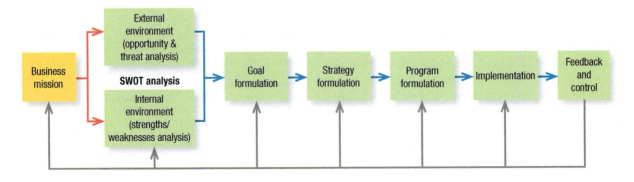

## THE BUSINESS MISSION

Each business unit needs to define its specific mission within the broader company mission. Thus, a television-studio-lighting-equipment company might define its mission as "To target major television studios and become their vendor of choice for lighting technologies that represent the most advanced and reliable studio lighting arrangements." Notice this mission does not mention winning business from smaller television studios, offering the lowest price, or venturing into non-lighting products.

## SWOT ANALYSIS

The overall evaluation of a company's strengths, weaknesses, opportunities, and threats is called SWOT analysis. It's a way of monitoring the external and internal marketing environment.

**EXTERNAL ENVIRONMENT (OPPORTUNITY AND THREAT) ANALYSIS** A business unit must monitor key *macroenvironment forces* and significant *microenvironment factors* that affect its ability to earn profits. It should set up a marketing intelligence system to track trends and important developments and any related opportunities and threats.

Good marketing is the art of finding, developing, and profiting from these opportunities.[31] A **marketing opportunity** is an area of buyer need and interest that a company has a high probability of profitably satisfying. There are three main sources of market opportunities.[32] The first is to offer something that is in short supply. This requires little marketing talent, as the need is fairly obvious. The second is to supply an existing product or service in a new or superior way. How? The *problem detection method* asks consumers for their suggestions, the *ideal method* has them imagine an ideal version of the product or service, and the *consumption chain method* asks them to chart their steps in acquiring, using, and disposing of a product. This last method can often lead to a totally new product or service, which is the third main source of market opportunities.

Marketers need to be good at spotting opportunities. Consider the following:

- *A company may benefit from converging industry trends and introduce hybrid products or services new to the market.* Cell phone manufacturers have released phones with digital photo and video capabilities, Global Positioning Systems (GPS), and so on.
- *A company may make a buying process more convenient or efficient.* Mobil introduced Speed Pass, one of the first widely deployed RFID (radio-frequency identification) payment systems, to allow consumers to quickly and easily pay for gas at the pump.
- *A company can meet the need for more information and advice.* Angie's List connects individuals with local home improvement and other services that have been reviewed by others.
- *A company can customize a product or service.* Timberland allows customers to choose colors for different parts of their boots, add initials or numbers, and select different stitching and embroidery.
- *A company can introduce a new capability.* Consumers can create and edit digital "iMovies" with the iMac and upload them to an Apple Web server or Web site such as YouTube to share with friends around the world.
- *A company may be able to deliver a product or service faster.* FedEx discovered a way to deliver mail and packages much more quickly than the U.S. Postal Service.
- *A company may be able to offer a product at a much lower price.* Pharmaceutical firms have created generic versions of brand-name drugs, and mail-order drug companies often sell for less.

To evaluate opportunities, companies can use **market opportunity analysis (MOA)** to ask questions like:

1. Can we articulate the benefits convincingly to a defined target market(s)?
2. Can we locate the target market(s) and reach them with cost-effective media and trade channels?
3. Does our company possess or have access to the critical capabilities and resources we need to deliver the customer benefits?
4. Can we deliver the benefits better than any actual or potential competitors?
5. Will the financial rate of return meet or exceed our required threshold for investment?

In the opportunity matrix in Figure 2.5(a), the best marketing opportunities facing the TV-lighting-equipment company appear in the upper-left cell (#1). The opportunities in the lower-right cell (#4) are too minor to consider. The opportunities in the upper-right cell (#2) and the lower-left cell (#3) are worth monitoring in the event that any improve in attractiveness and potential.

**| Fig. 2.5 |**

Opportunity and
Threat Matrices

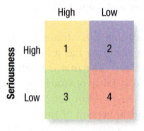

**(a) Opportunity Matrix**

**Success Probability**

1. Company develops more powerful lighting system
2. Company develops device to measure energy efficiency of any lighting system
3. Company develops device to measure illumination level
4. Company develops software program to teach lighting fundamentals to TV studio personnel

**(b) Threat Matrix**

**Probability of Occurrence**

1. Competitor develops superior lighting system
2. Major prolonged economic depression
3. Higher costs
4. Legislation to reduce number of TV studio licenses

An **environmental threat** is a challenge posed by an unfavorable trend or development that, in the absence of defensive marketing action, would lead to lower sales or profit. Figure 2.5(b) illustrates the threat matrix facing the TV-lighting-equipment company. The threats in the upper-left cell are major because they have a high probability of occurrence and can seriously hurt the company. To deal with them, the company needs contingency plans. The threats in the lower-right cell are minor and can be ignored. The firm will want to carefully monitor threats in the upper-right and lower-left cells in the event they grow more likely or serious.

**INTERNAL ENVIRONMENT (STRENGTHS AND WEAKNESSES) ANALYSIS** It's one thing to find attractive opportunities and another to be able to take advantage of them. Each business needs to evaluate its internal strengths and weaknesses. Consider Loan Bright.[33]

**LOAN BRIGHT**    At the Web site of Loan Bright, an online mortgage company, potential homebuyers can get a personalized list of lenders and available terms. At first, Loan Bright made its money by selling the homebuyer data to high-end mortgage lenders, including Wells Fargo Home Mortgage, Bank of America Mortgage, and Chase Home Mortgage. These firms turned the data into leads for their sales teams. But worrisome internal issues arose. For one thing, Loan Bright had to please every one of its big clients, yet each was becoming tougher to satisfy, eating up time and resources. The company's top managers gathered to analyze the market and Loan Bright's strengths and weaknesses. They decided that instead of serving a few choice clients, they would serve many more individual loan officers who responded to the company's Google ads and only wanted to buy a few leads. The switch required revamping the way Loan Bright salespeople brought in new business, including using a one-page contract instead of the old 12-page contract and creating a separate customer service department.

A SWOT-like analysis was instrumental in the development of the corporate strategy that drove Dell to years of success.

- Dell's *strength* was selling more effectively and efficiently directly to consumers than IBM and Compaq, its hardware competitors at the time.
- Dell's *weakness*, however, was that its brand was not as strong and it lacked a well-entrenched channel infrastructure and solid dealer relationships.

- Dell's *opportunity* was that the consumer market was becoming more sophisticated and customers increasingly knew exactly what they wanted.
- Dell's *threat* was that it would fail to generate a big enough customer base in the face of strong competitors and demanding channel partners.

With consumers desiring purchasing convenience and flexibility, however, the Internet offered a powerful direct marketing and selling option. Dell's business strategy combined direct sales, Internet marketing, mass customization, and just-in-time manufacturing to capitalize on the market opportunity it was offered.

Businesses can evaluate their own strengths and weaknesses by using a form like the one shown in "Marketing Memo: Checklist for Evaluating Strengths/Weaknesses Analysis." Clearly, the business doesn't have to correct *all* its weaknesses, nor should it gloat about all its strengths. The big question is whether it should limit itself to those opportunities for which it possesses the required strengths or consider those that might require it to find or develop new strengths.

## marketing memo
### Checklist for Evaluating Strengths/Weaknesses Analysis

| | Performance | | | | | Importance | | |
| --- | --- | --- | --- | --- | --- | --- | --- | --- |
| | Major Strength | Minor Strength | Neutral | Minor Weakness | Major Weakness | High | Med. | Low |
| **Marketing** | | | | | | | | |
| 1. Company reputation | ____ | ____ | ____ | ____ | ____ | ____ | ____ | ____ |
| 2. Market share | ____ | ____ | ____ | ____ | ____ | ____ | ____ | ____ |
| 3. Customer satisfaction | ____ | ____ | ____ | ____ | ____ | ____ | ____ | ____ |
| 4. Customer retention | ____ | ____ | ____ | ____ | ____ | ____ | ____ | ____ |
| 5. Product quality | ____ | ____ | ____ | ____ | ____ | ____ | ____ | ____ |
| 6. Service quality | ____ | ____ | ____ | ____ | ____ | ____ | ____ | ____ |
| 7. Pricing effectiveness | ____ | ____ | ____ | ____ | ____ | ____ | ____ | ____ |
| 8. Distribution effectiveness | ____ | ____ | ____ | ____ | ____ | ____ | ____ | ____ |
| 9. Promotion effectiveness | ____ | ____ | ____ | ____ | ____ | ____ | ____ | ____ |
| 10. Sales force effectiveness | ____ | ____ | ____ | ____ | ____ | ____ | ____ | ____ |
| 11. Innovation effectiveness | ____ | ____ | ____ | ____ | ____ | ____ | ____ | ____ |
| 12. Geographical coverage | ____ | ____ | ____ | ____ | ____ | ____ | ____ | ____ |
| **Finance** | | | | | | | | |
| 13. Cost or availability of capital | ____ | ____ | ____ | ____ | ____ | ____ | ____ | ____ |
| 14. Cash flow | ____ | ____ | ____ | ____ | ____ | ____ | ____ | ____ |
| 15. Financial stability | ____ | ____ | ____ | ____ | ____ | ____ | ____ | ____ |
| **Manufacturing** | | | | | | | | |
| 16. Facilities | ____ | ____ | ____ | ____ | ____ | ____ | ____ | ____ |
| 17. Economies of scale | ____ | ____ | ____ | ____ | ____ | ____ | ____ | ____ |
| 18. Capacity | ____ | ____ | ____ | ____ | ____ | ____ | ____ | ____ |
| 19. Able, dedicated workforce | ____ | ____ | ____ | ____ | ____ | ____ | ____ | ____ |
| 20. Ability to produce on time | ____ | ____ | ____ | ____ | ____ | ____ | ____ | ____ |
| 21. Technical manufacturing skill | ____ | ____ | ____ | ____ | ____ | ____ | ____ | ____ |
| **Organization** | | | | | | | | |
| 22. Visionary, capable leadership | ____ | ____ | ____ | ____ | ____ | ____ | ____ | ____ |
| 23. Dedicated employees | ____ | ____ | ____ | ____ | ____ | ____ | ____ | ____ |
| 24. Entrepreneurial orientation | ____ | ____ | ____ | ____ | ____ | ____ | ____ | ____ |
| 25. Flexible or responsive | ____ | ____ | ____ | ____ | ____ | ____ | ____ | ____ |

# GOAL FORMULATION

Once the company has performed a SWOT analysis, it can proceed to **goal formulation**, developing specific goals for the planning period. Goals are objectives that are specific with respect to magnitude and time.

Most business units pursue a mix of objectives, including profitability, sales growth, market share improvement, risk containment, innovation, and reputation. The business unit sets these objectives and then manages by objectives (MBO). For an MBO system to work, the unit's objectives must meet four criteria:

1. *They must be arranged hierarchically, from most to least important.* The business unit's key objective for the period may be to increase the rate of return on investment. Managers can increase profit by increasing revenue and reducing expenses. They can grow revenue, in turn, by increasing market share and prices.
2. *Objectives should be quantitative whenever possible.* The objective "to increase the return on investment (ROI)" is better stated as the goal "to increase ROI to 15 percent within two years."
3. *Goals should be realistic.* Goals should arise from an analysis of the business unit's opportunities and strengths, not from wishful thinking.
4. *Objectives must be consistent.* It's not possible to maximize sales and profits simultaneously.

Other important trade-offs include short-term profit versus long-term growth, deep penetration of existing markets versus development of new markets, profit goals versus nonprofit goals, and high growth versus low risk. Each choice calls for a different marketing strategy.[34]

Many believe adopting the goal of strong market share growth may mean foregoing strong short-term profits. Volkswagen has 15 times the annual revenue of Porsche—but Porsche's profit margins are seven times bigger than Volkswagen's. Other successful companies such as Google, Microsoft, and Samsung have maximized profitability *and* growth.

# STRATEGIC FORMULATION

Goals indicate what a business unit wants to achieve; **strategy** is a game plan for getting there. Every business must design a strategy for achieving its goals, consisting of a *marketing strategy* and a compatible *technology strategy* and *sourcing strategy.*

**PORTER'S GENERIC STRATEGIES** Michael Porter has proposed three generic strategies that provide a good starting point for strategic thinking: overall cost leadership, differentiation, and focus.[35]

- *Overall cost leadership.* Firms work to achieve the lowest production and distribution costs so they can underprice competitors and win market share. They need less skill in marketing. The problem is that other firms will usually compete with still-lower costs and hurt the firm that rested its whole future on cost.
- *Differentiation.* The business concentrates on achieving superior performance in an important customer benefit area valued by a large part of the market. The firm seeking quality leadership, for example, must make products with the best components, put them together expertly, inspect them carefully, and effectively communicate their quality.
- *Focus.* The business focuses on one or more narrow market segments, gets to know them intimately, and pursues either cost leadership or differentiation within the target segment.

The online air travel industry has provided a good example of these three strategies: Travelocity has pursued a differentiation strategy by offering the most comprehensive range of services to the traveler; Lowestfare has pursued a lowest-cost strategy for the leisure travel market; and Last Minute has pursued a niche strategy by focusing on travelers who have the flexibility to travel on very short notice. Some companies use a hybrid approach.

According to Porter, competing firms directing the same strategy to the same target market constitute a **strategic group**.[36] The firm that carries out the strategy best will make the most profits. Circuit City went out of business because it did not stand out in the consumer electronics industry as lowest in cost, highest in perceived value, or best in serving some market segment.

Porter draws a distinction between operational effectiveness and strategy. Competitors can quickly copy the operationally effective company using benchmarking and other tools, thus diminishing the advantage of operational effectiveness. Strategy, on the other hand, is "the creation of a unique and valuable position involving a different set of activities." A company can claim it has a strategy when it "performs different activities from rivals or performs similar activities in different ways."

**STRATEGIC ALLIANCES** Even giant companies—AT&T, Philips, and Starbucks—often cannot achieve leadership, either nationally or globally, without forming alliances with domestic or multinational companies that complement or leverage their capabilities and resources.

Just doing business in another country may require the firm to license its product, form a joint venture with a local firm, or buy from local suppliers to meet "domestic content" requirements. Many firms have developed global strategic networks, and victory is going to those who build the better one. The Star Alliance brings together 27 airlines, including Lufthansa, United Airlines, Singapore Airlines, Air New Zealand, and South Africa Airways, in a huge global partnership that allows travelers in 193 countries to make nearly seamless connections to hundreds of destinations.[37]

Many strategic partnerships take the form of marketing alliances. These fall into four major categories.

1. *Product or service alliances*—One company licenses another to produce its product, or two companies jointly market their complementary products or a new product. The credit card industry is a complicated combination of cards jointly marketed by banks such as Bank of America, credit card companies such as Visa, and affinity companies such as Alaska Airlines.

2. *Promotional alliances*—One company agrees to carry a promotion for another company's product or service. In 2011, VIBE urban music and lifestyle magazine announced a promotional alliance with Hoop It Up, the world's largest participatory 3-on-3 basketball tournament program, with competitions in 35 cities. The multi-platform partnership included VIBE digital, VIBE Cityguide App, editorial coverage and promotion in VIBE, and a highly integrated social media campaign with a strong VIBE branded presence at all Hoop It Up live events nationwide.[38]

3. *Logistics alliances*—One company offers logistical services for another company's product. Warner Music Group and Sub Pop Records created the Alternative Distribution Alliance (ADA) in 1993 as a joint venture to distribute and manufacture records owned by independent labels. ADA is the leading "indie" distribution company in the United States for both physical and digital product.

4. *Pricing collaborations*—One or more companies join in a special pricing collaboration. Hotel and rental car companies often offer mutual price discounts.

Companies need to give creative thought to finding partners that might complement their strengths and offset their weaknesses. Well-managed alliances allow companies to obtain a greater sales impact at lower cost. To keep their strategic alliances thriving, corporations have begun to develop organizational structures to support them, and many have come to view the ability to form and manage partnerships as core skills called **partner relationship management (PRM)**.

After years of growth through acquisition and buying interests in two dozen companies, the world's biggest wireless telecom operator, Vodafone, has looked outside for partners to help it leverage its existing assets.[39]

**VODAFONE**   To spur more innovation and growth, London-based Vodafone has embraced open source software and open platforms that allow it to tap into the creativity and skills of others. With its Web portal called Betavine, amateur or professional software developers can create and test their latest mobile applications on any network, not just Vodafone's. While these developers retain intellectual property rights, Vodafone gains early exposure to the latest trends and ensures that innovations are compatible with its network. Some of the new apps include real-time train arrivals and departures, movie show times, and an Amazon.com widget with personalized details. With 404 million customers in 30 countries, the £46 billion company hasn't had trouble finding help from interested corporate partners either. Dell has collaborated with Vodafone to design laptops and low-priced netbooks with built-in wireless broadband access over Vodafone's networks.

Rather than just form a partnership, a firm may choose to just acquire another firm. Kraft acquired Cadbury in 2010, in part due to Cadbury's deep roots in emerging markets like India where Kraft did not have a strong presence. The acquisition also permitted Kraft to do a restructuring and divide its businesses into two companies: one focused on grocery products, the other on snack foods.[40]

## PROGRAM FORMULATION AND IMPLEMENTATION

Even a great marketing strategy can be sabotaged by poor implementation. If the unit has decided to attain technological leadership, it must strengthen its R&D department, gather technological intelligence, develop leading-edge products, train its technical sales force, and communicate its technological leadership.

Once they have formulated marketing programs, marketers must estimate their costs. Is participating in a particular trade show worth it? Will hiring another salesperson contribute to the bottom line? Activity-based cost accounting (ABC)—described in greater detail in Chapter 5— can help determine whether each marketing program is likely to produce sufficient results to justify its cost.[41]

Source: © Andrew Hasson/Alamy

Kraft acquired Cadbury in part because of its knowledge of and presence in emerging markets.

Today's businesses recognize that unless they nurture other stakeholders—customers, employees, suppliers, distributors—they may never earn sufficient profits for the stockholders. A company might aim to delight its customers, perform well for its employees, and deliver a threshold level of satisfaction to its suppliers. It must not violate any stakeholder group's sense of fairness about the treatment it is receiving relative to the others.[42]

A dynamic relationship connects the stakeholder groups. A smart company creates a high level of employee satisfaction, which leads to higher effort, which leads to higher-quality products and services, which creates higher customer satisfaction, which leads to more repeat business, which leads to higher growth and profits, which leads to high stockholder satisfaction, which leads to more investment, and so on. This virtuous circle spells profits and growth.

According to McKinsey & Company, strategy is only one of seven elements—all of which start with the letter s—in successful business practice.[43] The first three—strategy, structure, and systems—are considered the "hardware" of success. The next four—style, skills, staff, and shared values—are the "software."

The first "soft" element, *style*, means company employees share a common way of thinking and behaving. The second, *skills*, means employees have the skills needed to carry out the company's strategy. *Staffing* means the company has hired able people, trained them well, and assigned them to the right jobs. The fourth element, *shared values*, means employees share the same guiding values. When these elements are present, companies are usually more successful at strategy implementation.[44]

## marketing insight

# Businesses Charting a New Direction

Continued prosperity or even survival may depend on how quickly and effectively a firm is able to chart a new direction. Consider these examples.

- With consumers increasingly using smart phones for directions and maps, Garmin, the biggest maker of GPS devices, found sales declining rapidly. Its solution was to concentrate on partnering with automakers to embed GPS systems in dashboard "command centers." Its selling points are that most smart phones are not optimized for use when driving and are thus dangerous to use behind the wheel. Hedging its bets, Garmin also has its own app available for smart phones.

- When Dow Chemical found its commodity chemical strategy was no longer profitable, new CEO Andrew Livirie decided to shift the company's focus to unique, innovative high-margin products like solar shingles. Dow's intent was to capitalize on four main trends:

clean energy, health and nutrition, consumerism in the emerging world, and infrastructure. R&D investments in those four areas totaled $9 billion over a five-year period.

- The runaway success of Amazon's Kindle, Apple's iPad, and other tablet products have turned the book world upside down. Bookstores, libraries, and publishers are all recognizing that the sale and delivery of a book are now just a download away. Libraries are lending e-readers in addition to "stocking" e-books for lending. When the due date arrives, the book just disappears!

- The textbook market is being transformed by new entries such as Flat World Knowledge offering customizable, discount texts. Free e-textbooks at some schools allow users to scroll page by page, highlight and annotate, and share comments with classmates and instructors. Some students buy a new or used paper version of the e-textbook anyway. As one notes, "When I'm using the e-textbook, there's the temptation to check e-mail, check my grades, or check Facebook."

**Sources:** Erik Rhey, "A GPS Maker Shifts Gears," *Fortune*, March 19, 2012; Geoff Colvin, "Dow's New Direction," *Fortune*, March 19, 2012; Ben Bradford, "Libraries Grapple with the Downside of E-books," www.npr.org, May 29, 2012; Sharon Tregaskis, "Buy the Book," *Cornell Alumni Magazine*, November–December 2012; "Great Digital Expectations," *The Economist*, September 10, 2011.

## FEEDBACK AND CONTROL

A company's strategic fit with the environment will inevitably erode because the market environment changes faster than the company's seven Ss. Thus, a company might remain efficient yet lose effectiveness. Peter Drucker pointed out that it is more important to "do the right thing"—to be effective—than "to do things right"—to be efficient. The most successful companies, however, excel at both.

Once an organization fails to respond to a changed environment, it becomes increasingly hard to recapture its lost position. Organizations, especially large ones, are subject to inertia. It's difficult to change one part without adjusting everything else. Yet organizations can be changed through strong leadership, preferably in advance of a crisis. The key to organizational health is willingness to examine the changing environment and adopt new goals and behaviors. "Marketing Insight: Businesses Charting a New Direction" describes how some different companies and industries are adjusting to the new marketing realities that have changed their fortunes.

# The Nature and Contents of a Marketing Plan

Working within the plans set by the levels above them, marketing managers come up with a marketing plan for individual products, lines, brands, channels, or customer groups. A **marketing plan** is a written document that summarizes what the marketer has learned about the marketplace and indicates how the firm plans to reach its marketing objectives.[45] It contains tactical guidelines for the marketing programs and financial allocations over the planning period.[46]

A marketing plan is one of the most important outputs of the marketing process. It provides direction and focus for a brand, product, or company. It informs and motivates key constituents inside and outside an organization about its marketing goals and how these can be achieved. Nonprofit organizations use marketing plans to guide their fund-raising and outreach efforts, and government agencies use them to build public awareness of nutrition and stimulate tourism.

More limited in scope than a business plan, the marketing plan documents how the organization will achieve its strategic objectives through specific marketing strategies and tactics, with the customer as the starting point. It is also linked to the plans of other departments. Suppose a marketing plan calls for selling 200,000 units annually. The production department must gear up to make that many units, finance must arrange funding to cover the expenses, human resources must be ready to hire and train staff, and so on. Without the appropriate level of organizational support and resources, no marketing plan can succeed.

The most frequently cited shortcomings of current marketing plans, according to marketing executives, are lack of realism, insufficient competitive analysis, and a short-run focus. (See "Marketing Memo: Marketing Plan Criteria" for questions to ask in developing marketing plans.)

---

## marketing memo          Marketing Plan Criteria

Here are some questions to ask in evaluating a marketing plan.

1. *Is the plan simple and succinct?* Is it easy to understand and act on? Does it communicate its content clearly and practically? Is it not unnecessarily long?

2. *Is the plan complete?* Does it include all the necessary elements? Does it have the right breadth and depth? Achieving the right balance between completeness and lots of detail and simplicity and clear focus is often the key to a well-constructed marketing plan.

3. *Is the plan specific?* Are its objectives concrete and measurable? Does it provide a clear course of action? Does it include specific activities, each with specific dates of completion, specific persons responsible, and specific budgets?

4. *Is the plan realistic?* Are the sales goals, expense budgets, and milestone dates realistic? Has a frank and honest self-critique been conducted to raise possible concerns and objections?

**Sources:** Adapted from Tim Berry and Doug Wilson, *On Target: The Book on Marketing Plans*, 2nd ed. (Eugene, OR: Palo Alto Software, 2000); Alexander Chernev, *The Marketing Plan Handbook* (Chicago, IL: Cerebellum Press, 2011); authors' experiences.

Most marketing plans cover one year in anywhere from 5 to 50 pages. Smaller businesses may create shorter or less formal marketing plans; corporations generally require highly structured documents. Every part of the plan must be described in considerable detail. Some companies post their marketing plan on an internal Web site so everyone can consult it and collaborate on changes. A marketing plan usually contains the following sections.

- *Executive summary and table of contents.*
- *Situation analysis.* This section presents relevant background data on sales, costs, the market, competitors, and the macroenvironment. How do we define the market, how big is it, and how fast is it growing? What are the relevant trends and critical issues? Firms will use all this information to carry out a SWOT analysis.
- *Marketing strategy.* Here the marketing manager defines the mission, marketing and financial objectives, and needs the market offering is intended to satisfy as well as its competitive positioning. All this requires inputs from other areas, such as purchasing, manufacturing, sales, finance, and human resources.
- *Marketing tactics.* Here the marketing manager outlines the marketing activities that will be undertaken to execute the marketing strategy.
  - The product or service offering section describes the key attributes and benefits that will appeal to target customers.
  - The pricing section specifies the general price range and how it might vary across different types of customers or channels, including any incentive or discount plans.
  - The channel section outlines the different forms of distribution, such as direct or indirect.
  - The communications section usually offers high-level guidance about the general message and media strategy. Firms will often develop a separate communication plan to provide the detail necessary for agencies and other media partners to effectively design the communication program.
- *Financial projections.* Financial projections include a sales forecast, an expense forecast, and a break-even analysis. On the revenue side is forecasted sales volume by month and product category, and on the expense side the expected costs of marketing, broken down into finer categories. The break-even analysis estimates how many units the firm must sell monthly (or how many years it will take) to offset its monthly fixed costs and average per-unit variable costs.

  A more complex method of estimating profit is **risk analysis**. Here we obtain three estimates (optimistic, pessimistic, and most likely) for each uncertain variable affecting profitability, under an assumed marketing environment and marketing strategy for the planning period. The computer simulates possible outcomes and computes a distribution showing the range of possible rates of returns and their probabilities.
- *Implementation controls.* The last section outlines the controls for monitoring and adjusting implementation of the plan. Typically, it spells out the goals and budget for each month or quarter so management can review each period's results and take corrective action as needed.

## THE ROLE OF RESEARCH

Marketers need up-to-date information about the environment, the competition, and the selected market segments. Often, analysis of internal data is the starting point for assessing the current marketing situation, supplemented by marketing intelligence and research investigating the overall market, the competition, key issues, threats, and opportunities. As the plan is put into effect, marketers use research to measure progress toward objectives and identify areas for improvement.

Finally, marketing research helps marketers learn more about their customers' requirements, expectations, perceptions, satisfaction, and loyalty. Thus, the marketing plan should outline what marketing research will be conducted and when, as well as how the findings will be applied.

## THE ROLE OF RELATIONSHIPS

Although the marketing plan shows how the company will establish and maintain profitable customer relationships, it also affects both internal and external relationships. First, it influences how marketing staff work with each other and with other departments to deliver value and satisfy customers. Second, it affects how the company works with suppliers, distributors, and partners to achieve the plan's objectives. Third, it influences the company's dealings with other stakeholders, including government regulators, the media, and the community at large.

## FROM MARKETING PLAN TO MARKETING ACTION

Marketers start planning well in advance of the implementation date to allow time for marketing research, analysis, management review, and coordination between departments. As each action program begins, they monitor ongoing results, investigate any deviation from plans, and take corrective steps as needed. Some prepare contingency plans; marketers must be ready to update and adapt marketing plans at any time.

The marketing plan typically outlines budgets, schedules, and marketing metrics for monitoring and evaluating results. With budgets, marketers can compare planned and actual expenditures for a given period. Schedules show when tasks were supposed to be completed and when they actually were. Marketing metrics track actual outcomes of marketing programs to see whether the company is moving forward toward its objectives, as we'll discuss in Chapter 4.

# Summary

1. The value delivery process includes choosing (or identifying), providing (or delivering), and communicating superior value. The value chain is a tool for identifying key activities that create value and costs in a specific business.

2. Strong companies develop superior capabilities in managing core business processes such as new-product realization, inventory management, and customer acquisition and retention. In today's marketing environment, managing these core processes effectively means creating a marketing network in which the company works closely with all parties in the production and distribution chain, from suppliers of raw materials to retail distributors. Companies no longer compete—marketing networks do.

3. Market-oriented strategic planning is the managerial process of developing and maintaining a viable fit between the organization's objectives, skills, and resources and its changing market opportunities. The aim of strategic planning is to shape the company's businesses and products so they yield target profits and growth.

Strategic planning takes place at four levels: corporate, division, business unit, and product.

4. The corporate strategy establishes the framework within which the divisions and business units prepare their strategic plans. Setting a corporate strategy means defining the corporate mission, establishing strategic business units (SBUs), assigning resources to each, and assessing growth opportunities.

5. Marketers should define a business or business unit as a customer-satisfying process. Taking this view can reveal additional growth opportunities.

6. Strategic planning for individual businesses includes defining the business mission, analyzing external opportunities and threats, analyzing internal strengths and weaknesses, formulating goals, formulating strategy, formulating supporting programs, implementing the programs, and gathering feedback and exercising control.

7. Each product level within a business unit must develop a marketing plan for achieving its goals. The marketing plan is one of the most important outputs of the marketing process.

MyMarketingLab

Go to **mymktlab.com** to complete the problems marked with this icon ⭐ as well as for additional Auto-graded and Assisted-graded writing questions.

# Applications

## Marketing Debate
### What Good Is a Mission Statement?

Mission statements are often the product of much deliberation and discussion. At the same time, critics claim they sometimes lack "teeth" and specificity or do not vary much from firm to firm and make the same empty promises.

**Take a position:** Mission statements are critical to a successful marketing organization *versus* Mission statements rarely provide useful marketing value.

## Marketing Discussion
### Marketing Planning

⭐ Consider Porter's value chain and the holistic marketing orientation model. What implications do they have for marketing planning? How would you structure a marketing plan to incorporate some of their concepts?

## Marketing Excellence

### >> Cisco

Cisco Systems is the worldwide leading supplier of networking equipment for the Internet. The company sells hardware (routers and switches), software, and services that make most of the Internet work. Cisco was founded in 1984 by a husband-and-wife team who worked in the computer operations department at Stanford University. They named the company cisco—with a lowercase c, short for San Francisco, and developed a logo that resembled the Golden Gate Bridge, which they frequently traveled.

Cisco went public in 1990, and the two founders left the company shortly thereafter. Over the next decade, the company grew exponentially, led by new-product launches such as patented routers, switches, platforms, and modems, which significantly contributed to the backbone of the Internet. Cisco opened its first international offices in London and France in 1991 and has expanded to more than 165 countries. During the 1990s, Cisco acquired and successfully integrated 49 companies into its core business, growing its market capitalization faster than that of any company in history—from $1 billion in 1991 to $300 billion in 1999. In March 2000, Cisco became the most valuable company in the world, with market capitalization peaking at $582 billion, or $82 per share.

By the end of the 20th century, the company was extremely successful, but brand awareness was low. Many consumers and investors knew Cisco for its stock price, but few outside the industry knew what it did. Cisco developed partnerships with Sony, Matsushita, and US West to co-brand its modems with the Cisco logo in hopes of building name recognition and brand value. In addition, it launched its first television spots as part of a campaign titled "Are You Ready?" In the ads, children and adults from around the world delivered facts about the power of the Internet and challenged viewers to ponder, "Are you ready?"

The company survived the Internet bust but reorganized in 2001 into 11 new technology groups and a marketing organization, which planned to communicate the company's product line and competitive advantages better than it had in the past. In 2003, Cisco introduced its largest marketing campaign to date, including a new slogan, "This Is the Power of the Network. Now." The international campaign targeted corporate executives and highlighted Cisco's critical role in a complicated, technological system by using a soft-sell approach. Television commercials explained how Cisco's systems change people's lives around the world, and an eight-page print ad spread didn't mention Cisco's name until the third page. Marilyn Mersereau, Cisco's vice president of corporate marketing at the time, explained, "Clever advertising involves the reader in something that's thought-provoking and provocative and doesn't slam the brand name into you from the first page."

Cisco entered the consumer segment with the acquisition of Linksys, a home and small-office network gear maker. Within a year, Cisco offered several home entertainment solutions, including wireless capabilities for music, printing, and video. The transition into the consumer segment triggered a rebranding campaign in 2006, aimed at increasing awareness among consumers and lifting the overall value of Cisco's brand.

"The Human Network" campaign tried to reposition the technology giant as more than just a supplier of switches and routers by communicating its role in connecting people through technology. The campaign evolved into "Built for the Human Network" and targeted everyone from consumers to IT professionals. As a result, Cisco developed a new marketing strategy that showcased its brand as fun and digestible, using interactive games, videos, and virtual events.

Cisco's partnership with sports and entertainment venues created the perfect opportunity to exhibit the way its technologies connected people to their passions. *Cisco Connected Sports* turned sports stadiums into digitally connected interactive venues, "the ultimate fan experience." Fans could meet the players virtually through a videoconferencing system, while digital displays throughout the stadium allowed them to pull up scores from other games, order food, and view local traffic. These flexible platforms could also work with business conferences and music concerts.

Cisco's ultimate goal is to increase overall Internet traffic, ultimately driving demand for its wide range of products. The company has recently expanded into consumer electronics, business collaboration software, and computer servers. Revenues topped $47 billion in 2014, and its market cap exceeded $118 billion. Its Web site boasts, "We help the most innovative companies in the world do things they never could before."

**Questions**

1. How is building a brand in a business-to-business context different from doing so in the consumer market?

2. Is Cisco's plan to reach out to consumers a viable one? Why or why not?

**Sources:** Marguerite Reardon, "Cisco Spends Millions on Becoming Household Name," *CNET*, October 5, 2006; Michelle Kessler, "Tech Giants Build Bridge to Consumers," *USA Today*, March 13, 2006; Marla Matzer, "Cisco Faces the Masses," *Los Angeles Times*, August 20, 1998; David R. Baker, "New Ad Campaign for Cisco," *San Francisco Chronicle*, February 18, 2003; Bobby White, "Expanding into Consumer Electronics, Cisco Aims to Jazz Up Its Stodgy Image," *Wall Street Journal*, September 6, 2006, p. B1; Burt Helm, "Best Global Brands," *BusinessWeek*, September 18, 2008; Ashlee Vance, "Cisco Buys Norwegian Firm for $3 Billion," *New York Times*, October 1, 2009; Jennifer Leggio, "10 Fortune 500 Companies Doing Social Media Right," *ZDNet*, September 28, 2009; Karen Bannan, "How Cisco Used Consumer-Based Marketing Strategies to Reach B2B Clients," *BtoB Marketing*, July 20, 2010; Cisco.com.

## Marketing Excellence

### >> Intel

Intel makes the microprocessors found in most of the world's personal computers, tablets, and smart phones. It is one of the most valuable brands in the world, with revenues exceeding $54 billion. In the early days, however, Intel microprocessors were known simply by their engineering numbers, such as "80386" or "80486." Because numbers can't be trademarked, competitors came out with their own numbered chips, and Intel had no way to distinguish itself. Nor could consumers see Intel's products, buried deep inside their PCs. Thus, Intel had a hard time convincing consumers to pay more for its high-performance products.

To correct this situation, Intel created the quintessential ingredient-branding marketing campaign. First, it chose the name Pentium for its latest microprocessor and trademarked it. Next, it launched the "Intel Inside" campaign to build brand awareness of its family of microprocessors. This campaign helped move the Intel brand name outside the PC and into the minds of consumers. To secure crucial support from the computer manufacturers who used its processors, Intel gave them significant rebates when they included its logo in their ads or placed "Intel Inside" stickers on the outside of their PCs and laptops.

Intel created several memorable marketing campaigns in the late 1990s, making it a recognizable ingredient brand name. The "Bunny People" series featured Intel technicians dressed in brightly colored contamination suits as they danced to disco music inside a processor facility. Intel also used the famous Blue Man Group in its commercials for Pentium III and Pentium IV.

As the PC industry slowed in the mid-2000s, Intel sought opportunities in new growth areas such as wireless, home entertainment, and mobile devices. The company launched a handful of new platforms: Centrino, which featured wireless capabilities, Viiv (rhymes with "five") aimed at home entertainment enthusiasts, and Centrino Duo mobile. Intel created a $2 billion global marketing campaign to help reposition itself from a brainy microprocessor company to a "warm and fuzzy company" that offered solutions for consumers as well. With a new logo, its new slogan "Leap Ahead" replaced the familiar "Intel Inside" campaign.

In 2008, reacting to the new wave of mobile Internet devices and lightweight netbooks, Intel launched the Atom, its smallest processor to date, about the size of a grain of rice. Also that year, Intel introduced its most advanced microprocessor to date, the Intel Core i7, which served the increased need for video, 3-D gaming, and advanced computer activities. Both processors were instant hits. Intel sold more than 20 million Atom processors in its first year alone and 28 million in its second year.

Intel's corresponding campaign aimed to improve the company's brand awareness among consumers and was titled "Sponsors of Tomorrow." Commercials highlighted the company's role in changing the future of technology and took a humorous tone. In one, a middle-aged man wearing his company ID tag strutted through the cafeteria as fellow employees screamed, groped, and begged for his autograph. The ad explained, "Ajay Bhatt, co-inventor of the USB. Our superheroes aren't like your superheroes."

As the post-PC era dawned, Intel, known for its relationship with the PC, found itself refocusing and taking risky steps to remain a technological leader. In 2011, it acquired two major companies, McAfee and Infineon Technologies' Wireless Solutions business, expanding its capabilities. That same year, Intel made a strategic shift in its product line and introduced the Ultrabook system, a new category of thin and secure mobile devices that combined features of tablets and netbooks.

The company launched its biggest marketing campaign in more than a decade—"A New Era of Computing"—to communicate its evolution into the category of tablets and smart phones. Kevin Sellers, vice president, Sales and Marketing Group, explained, "This is not a campaign where we're talking about the microprocessor or Intel the company. Instead, we're giving a cinematic and epic feel to how Intel-inspired Ultrabook systems are ushering in a new era of computing and making everything else seem like ancient history."

As Intel expands into mobile devices, its influence on the future of technology and its brand value will grow. The combination of effective, consistent marketing along with innovative technological launches have made its brand one of the most valuable in the world, exceeding $34 billion.

## Questions

1. Discuss how Intel changed ingredient-marketing history. What did it do so well in those initial marketing campaigns?

2. Evaluate Intel's more recent marketing efforts as the industry moves out of the PC era. What are Intel's greatest risks and strengths during this changing time?

**Sources:** Cliff Edwards, "Intel Everywhere?" *BusinessWeek,* March 8, 2004, pp. 56–62; Scott Van Camp, "ReadMe.1st," *Brandweek,* February 23, 2004, p. 17; "How to Become a Superbrand," *Marketing,* January 8, 2004, p. 15; Roger Slavens, "Pam Pollace, VP-Director, Corporate Marketing Group, Intel Corp," *BtoB,* December 8, 2003, p. 19; Kenneth Hein, "Study: New Brand Names Not Making Their Mark," *Brandweek,* December 8, 2003, p. 12; Heather Clancy, "Intel Thinking outside the Box," *Computer Reseller News,* November 24, 2003, p. 14; Cynthia L. Webb, "A Chip Off the Old Recovery?" Washingtonpost.com, October 15, 2003; "Intel Launches Second Phase of Centrino Ads," *Technology Advertising & Branding Report,* October 6, 2003; David Kirkpatrick, "At Intel, Speed Isn't Everything," *Fortune,* February 9, 2004, p. 34; Don Clark. "Intel to Overhaul Marketing in Bid to Go Beyond PCs," *Wall Street Journal,* December 30, 2005; Stephanie Clifford, "Tech Company's Campaign to Burnish Its Brand," *New York Times,* May 6, 2009, p. B7; Tim Bajarin, "Intel Makes Moves in Mobility," *PC Magazine,* October 5, 2009; "Intel Ushers in 'A New Era of Computing' with Ultrabook Campaign," *Intel press release,* April 4, 2012; *Interbrand's* Best Global Brands 2014.

# Sample Marketing Plan    Pegasus Sports International

## 1.0 Executive Summary

Pegasus Sports International is a start-up aftermarket inline skating accessory manufacturer. Inline skates have four or five wheels arranged in a single line and are often called Rollerblades by the general public after one of the early pioneers in the category. In addition to the aftermarket products, Pegasus is developing SkateTours, a service that takes clients out, in conjunction with a local skate shop, and provides them with an afternoon of skating using inline skates and some of Pegasus's other accessories such as SkateSails.

The aftermarket skate accessory market has been largely ignored. Although there are several major manufacturers of the skates themselves, the accessory market has not been addressed. This provides Pegasus with an extraordinary opportunity for market growth. Skating is a booming sport. Currently, most of the skating is recreational. There are, however, a growing number of skating competitions, including team-oriented competitions such as skate hockey as well as individual competitions such as speed skate racing. Pegasus will work to grow these markets and develop the skate transportation market, a more utilitarian use of skating.

Pegasus has outlined a go-to-market marketing program that combines highly relevant products and services with an evolving direct-to-consumer distribution strategy to tap into customer passions and loyalty.

## 2.0 Situation Analysis

Pegasus is entering its first year of operation. Its products have been well received, and marketing will be key to the development of brand and product awareness as well as the growth of the customer base. Pegasus International offers several different aftermarket skating accessories, serving the growing inline skating industry.

## 2.1 Market Summary

Pegasus possesses good information about the market and knows a great deal about the common attributes of the most prized customer. This information will be leveraged to better understand who is served, what their specific needs are, and how Pegasus can better communicate with them.

**Target Markets**

- Recreational
- Fitness
- Speed
- Hockey
- Extreme

### 2.1.1 Market Demographics

The profile for the typical Pegasus customer consists of the following geographic, demographic, and behavior factors:

**Geographics**

- Pegasus has no set geographic target area. By leveraging the expansive reach of the Internet and multiple delivery services, Pegasus can serve both domestic and international customers.
- The total targeted population is 31 million users.

**Demographics**

- There is an almost equal ratio between male and female users.
- Ages 13–46, with 48 percent clustering around ages 23–34. The recreational users tend to cover the widest age range,

| TABLE 2.4 | Target Market Forecast | | | | | | |
|---|---|---|---|---|---|---|---|
| **Target Market Forecast** | | | | | | | |
| **Potential Customers** | **Growth** | **2015** | **2016** | **2017** | **2018** | **2019** | **CAGR*** |
| Recreational | 10% | 19,142,500 | 21,056,750 | 23,162,425 | 25,478,668 | 28,026,535 | 10.00% |
| Fitness | 15% | 6,820,000 | 7,843,000 | 9,019,450 | 10,372,368 | 11,928,223 | 15.00% |
| Speed | 10% | 387,500 | 426,250 | 468,875 | 515,763 | 567,339 | 10.00% |
| Hockey | 6% | 2,480,000 | 2,628,800 | 2,786,528 | 2,953,720 | 3,130,943 | 6.00% |
| Extreme | 4% | 2,170,000 | 2,256,800 | 2,347,072 | 2,440,955 | 2,538,593 | 4.00% |
| Total | 10.48% | 31,000,000 | 34,211,600 | 37,784,350 | 41,761,474 | 46,191,633 | 10.48% |
| *Compound Annual Growth Rate | | | | | | | |

including young users through active adults. The fitness users tend to be ages 20–40. The speed users tend to be in their late 20s and early 30s. The hockey players are generally in their teens through their early 20s. The extreme segment is of similar age to the hockey players.

- Of the users who are over 20, 65 percent have an undergraduate degree or substantial undergraduate coursework.

- The adult users have a median personal income of $47,000.

**Behavior Factors**

- Users enjoy fitness activities not as a means for a healthy life but as intrinsically enjoyable activities in themselves.

- Users spend money on gear, typically sports equipment.

- Users have active lifestyles that include some sort of recreation at least two to three times a week.

## 2.1.2  Market Needs

Pegasus is providing the skating community with a wide range of accessories for all variations of skating. The company seeks to fulfill the following benefits that are important to its customers:

- *Quality craftsmanship.*  The customers work hard for their money and do not enjoy spending it on disposable products that work for only a year or two.

- *Well-thought-out designs.*  The skating market has not been addressed by well-thought-out products that serve skaters' needs. Pegasus's industry experience and personal dedication to the sport will provide it with the needed information to produce insightfully designed products.

- *Customer service.*  Exemplary service is required to build a sustainable business that has a loyal customer base.

## 2.1.3  Market Trends

Pegasus will distinguish itself by marketing products not previously available to skaters. The emphasis in the past has been to sell skates and very few replacement parts. The number of skaters is not restricted to any one single country, continent, or age group, so there is a world market. Pegasus has products for virtually every group of skaters.

The fastest-growing segment of this sport is the fitness skater (Table 2.4). Therefore, the marketing is being directed toward this group. BladeBoots will enable users to enter establishments without having to remove their skates. BladeBoots will be aimed at the recreational skater, the largest segment. SkateAids, on the other hand, are great for everyone.

The sport of skating will also grow through SkateSailing. This sport is primarily for the medium-to-advanced skater, and its growth potential is tremendous. The sails that Pegasus has manufactured have been sold in Europe, following a pattern similar to windsurfing. Windsailing originated in Santa Monica but did not take off until it had already grown big in Europe.

Another trend is group skating. More and more groups are getting together on skating excursions in cities all over the world.

For example, San Francisco has night group skating that attracts hundreds of people. The market trends are showing continued growth in all directions of skating.

## 2.1.4  Market Growth

With the price of skates going down due to competition by so many skate companies, the market has had steady growth throughout the world, although sales have slowed down in some markets. The growth statistics for 2015 were estimated to be about 31 million units. More and more people are discovering—and in many cases rediscovering—the health benefits and fun of skating.

## 2.2  SWOT Analysis

The following SWOT analysis captures the key strengths and weaknesses within the company and describes the opportunities and threats facing Pegasus.

## 2.2.1  Strengths

- In-depth industry experience and insight
- Creative yet practical product designers
- The use of a highly efficient, flexible business model utilizing direct customer sales and distribution

## 2.2.2  Weaknesses

- The reliance on outside capital necessary to grow the business
- A lack of retailers who can work face to face with the customer to generate brand and product awareness
- The difficulty of developing brand awareness as a start-up company

## 2.2.3  Opportunities

- Participation within a growing industry
- Decreased product costs through economies of scale
- The ability to leverage other industry participants' marketing efforts to help grow the general market

## 2.2.4  Threats

- Future/potential competition from an already-established market participant
- A continued slump in the economy that could have a negative effect on people's spending of discretionary income on fitness/recreational products
- The release of a study that calls into question the safety of skating or the inability to prevent major skating-induced traumas

## 2.3  Competition

Pegasus Sports International is forming its own market. Although there are a few companies that do make sails and foils that a few skaters are using, Pegasus is the only brand that is truly designed for and by skaters. The few competitors' sails on the market are not designed for skating but for windsurfing or for skateboards. In the case of foils, storage and carrying are not practical. There are different indirect competitors who are manufacturers of the actual skates. After many years in the market, these companies have yet to become direct competitors by manufacturing accessories for the skates that they make.

## 2.4 Product Offering

Pegasus Sports International now offers several products:

- The first product that has been developed is BladeBoots, a cover for the wheels and frame of inline skates, which allows skaters to enter places that normally would not allow them in with skates on. BladeBoots come with a small pouch and belt that converts to a well-designed skate carrier.

- The second product is SkateSails. These sails are specifically designed for use while skating. Feedback that Pegasus has received from skaters indicates skatesailing could become a very popular sport. Trademarking this product is currently in progress.

- The third product, SkateAid, will be in production by the end of the year. Other ideas for products are under development but will not be disclosed until Pegasus can protect them through pending patent applications.

## 2.5 Keys to Success

The keys to success are designing and producing products that meet market demand. In addition, Pegasus must ensure total customer satisfaction. If these keys to success are achieved, it will become a profitable, sustainable company.

## 2.6 Critical Issues

As a start-up business, Pegasus is still in the early stages. The critical issues are for Pegasus to:

- Establish itself as the premier skating accessory company.

- Pursue controlled growth that dictates that payroll expenses will never exceed the revenue base. This will help protect against recessions.

- Constantly monitor customer satisfaction, ensuring that the growth strategy will never compromise service and satisfaction levels.

## 3.0 Marketing Strategy

The key to the marketing strategy is focusing on the speed, health and fitness, and recreational skaters. Pegasus can cover about 80 percent of the skating market because it produces products geared toward each segment. Pegasus is able to address all of the different segments within the market because, although each segment is distinct in terms of its users and equipment, its products are useful to all of the different segments.

## 3.1 Mission

Pegasus Sports International's mission is to provide the customer with the finest skating accessories available. "We exist to attract and maintain customers. With a strict adherence to this maxim, success will be ensured. Our services and products will exceed the expectations of the customers."

## 3.2 Marketing Objectives

- Maintain positive, strong growth each quarter (notwithstanding seasonal sales patterns).

- Achieve a steady increase in market penetration.

- Decrease customer acquisition costs by 1.5 percent per quarter.

## 3.3 Financial Objectives

- Increase the profit margin by 1 percent per quarter through efficiency and economy-of-scale gains.

- Maintain a significant research and development budget (as a percentage relative to sales) to spur future product developments.

- Achieve a double- to triple-digit growth rate for the first three years.

## 3.4 Target Markets

With a projected world skating market of 31 million that is steadily growing (statistics released by the Sporting Goods Manufacturers Association), the niche has been created. Pegasus's aim is to expand this market by promoting SkateSailing, a new sport that is popular in both Santa Monica and Venice Beach in California. The breakdown of participation in skating is as follows: 1+ percent speed (growing), 8 percent hockey (declining), 7 percent extreme/aggressive (declining), 22 percent fitness (nearly 7 million—the fastest growing), and 61 percent recreational (first-timers). Pegasus's products are targeting the fitness and recreational groups because they are the fastest growing. These groups are gearing themselves toward health and fitness, and combined they can easily grow to 85 percent (or 26 million) of the market in the next five years.

## 3.5 Positioning

Pegasus will position itself as the premier aftermarket skating accessory company. This positioning will be achieved by leveraging Pegasus's competitive edge: industry experience and passion. Pegasus is a skating company formed by skaters for skaters. Its management is able to use its vast experience and personal passion for the sport to develop innovative, useful accessories for a broad range of skaters.

## 4.0 Marketing Tactics

The single objective of the marketing program is to position Pegasus as the premier skating accessory manufacturer, serving the domestic market as well as the international market. The marketing program will seek to first create customer awareness concerning the offered products and services and then develop the customer base. Specifically, Pegasus's marketing program is composed of the following approaches to product, pricing, distribution, and communications.

## 4.1 Product

Several of Pegasus's currently developed products have patents pending, and local market research indicates that there is great demand for these products. Pegasus will achieve fast, significant market penetration through a solid business model, long-range planning, and a strong management team that is able to execute this exciting opportunity. The three principals on the management team have more than 30 years of combined personal and industry experience. This extensive experience provides Pegasus with the empirical information as well as the passion to provide the skating market with much-needed after-market products.

## 4.2 Pricing

This will be based on a per-product retail price. Because of the advantages of selling directly, higher margins can be achieved with premium pricing that will still appeal to customer segments.

## 4.3 Distribution

Pegasus will sell its products initially through its Web site. In addition to allowing for higher margins, this direct-to-the-consumer approach will allow Pegasus to maintain a close relationship with customers, which is essential for producing products that have a true market demand. By the end of the year, Pegasus also will have developed relationships with different skate shops and will begin to sell some of its products through retailers.

## 4.4 Communications

The message that Pegasus will seek to communicate is that it offers the best-designed, most useful skating accessories. This message will be communicated through a variety of methods. The first will be the Pegasus Web site, which will provide a rich source of product information and offer consumers the opportunity to purchase. A lot of time and money will be invested in the site to provide the customer with the perception of total professionalism and utility for Pegasus's products and services.

The second marketing method will be advertisements placed in numerous industry magazines. The skating industry is supported by several different glossy magazines designed to promote the industry as a whole. In addition, a number of smaller periodicals serve the smaller market segments within the skating industry. The last method of communication is the use of printed sales literature. The two previously mentioned marketing methods will create demand for the sales literature, which will be sent out to customers. The cost of the sales literature will be fairly minimal because it will use the already-compiled information from the Web site.

## 4.5 Marketing Research

Pegasus is blessed with the good fortune of being located in the center of the skating world: Venice, California. It will be able to leverage this opportune location by working with many of the different skaters who live in the area. Pegasus was able to test all of its products not only with its principals, who are accomplished skaters, but also with the many other dedicated and "newbie"

| TABLE 2.5 | Break-Even Analysis |
|---|---|
| Monthly Units Break-Even | 62 |
| Monthly Sales Break-Even | $ 7,760 |
| Assumptions: | |
| Average Per-Unit Revenue | $125.62 |
| Average Per-Unit Variable Cost | $ 22.61 |
| Estimated Monthly Fixed Cost | $ 6,363 |

users located in Venice. The extensive product testing by a wide variety of users provided Pegasus with valuable product feedback and has led to several design improvements.

## 5.0 Financials

This section will offer the financial overview of Pegasus related to marketing activities. Pegasus will address break-even analysis, sales forecasts, and expense forecast and indicate how these activities link to the marketing strategy.

## 5.1 Break-Even Analysis

The break-even analysis (Table 2.5) indicates that $7,760 will be required in monthly sales revenue to reach the break-even point.

## 5.2 Sales Forecast

Pegasus feels that the sales forecast figures are conservative. It will steadily increase sales as the advertising budget allows. Although the target market forecast (Table 2.4) listed all of the potential customers divided into separate groups, the sales forecast (Table 2.6) groups customers into two categories: recreational and competitive. Reducing the number of categories allows the reader to quickly discern information, making the chart more functional.

| TABLE 2.6 | Monthly Sales Forecast | | |
|---|---|---|---|
| **Sales** | **2015** | **2016** | **2017** |
| Recreational | $455,740 | $598,877 | $687,765 |
| Competitive | $ 72,918 | $ 95,820 | $110,042 |
| Total Sales | $528,658 | $694,697 | $797,807 |
| **Direct Cost of Sales** | **2015** | **2016** | **2017** |
| Recreational | $ 82,033 | $107,798 | $123,798 |
| Competitive | $ 13,125 | $ 17,248 | $ 19,808 |
| Subtotal Cost of Sales | $ 95,158 | $125,046 | $143,606 |

## 5.3 Expense Forecast

The expense forecast will be used as a tool to keep the department on target and provide indicators when corrections/modifications are needed for the proper implementation of the marketing plan.

| TABLE 2.7 | Milestones | | | | | |
|---|---|---|---|---|---|---|
| | | | Plan | | | |
| **Milestones** | **Start Date** | **End Date** | **Budget** | **Manager** | **Department** | |
| Marketing plan completion | 1/1/15 | 2/1/15 | $ 0 | Stan | Marketing | |
| Web site completion | 1/1/15 | 3/15/15 | $20,400 | outside firm | Marketing | |
| Advertising campaign #1 | 1/1/15 | 6/30/15 | $ 3,500 | Stan | Marketing | |
| Advertising campaign #2 | 3/1/15 | 12/30/15 | $ 4,550 | Stan | Marketing | |
| Development of the retail channel | 1/1/15 | 11/30/15 | $ 0 | Stan | Marketing | |
| Totals | | | $28,450 | | | |

| TABLE 2.8 | Marketing Expense Budget | | |
|---|---|---|---|
| | **2015** | **2016** | **2017** |
| Web Site | $ 25,000 | $ 8,000 | $ 10,000 |
| Advertisements | $ 8,050 | $ 15,000 | $ 20,000 |
| Printed Material | $ 1,725 | $ 2,000 | $ 3,000 |
| Total Sales and Marketing Expenses | $ 34,775 | $ 25,000 | $ 33,000 |
| Percent of Sales | 6.58% | 3.60% | 4.14% |
| Contribution Margin | $398,725 | $544,652 | $621,202 |
| Contribution Margin/Sales | 75.42% | 78.40% | 77.86% |

# 6.0 Controls

The purpose of Pegasus's marketing plan is to serve as a guide for the organization. The following areas will be monitored to gauge performance:

- Revenue: monthly and annual
- Expenses: monthly and annual
- Customer satisfaction
- New-product development

## 6.1 Implementation

The milestones identify the key marketing programs (Table 2.7). It is important to accomplish each one on time and on budget (Table 2.8).

## 6.2 Marketing Organization

Stan Blade will be responsible for the marketing activities.

## 6.3 Contingency Planning

**Difficulties and Risks**

- Problems generating visibility, a function of being an Internet-based start-up organization
- An entry into the market by an already-established market competitor

**Worst-Case Risks**

- Determining that the business cannot support itself on an ongoing basis
- Having to liquidate equipment or intellectual capital to cover liabilities

**Source:** Adapted from a sample plan provided by and copyrighted by Palo Alto Software, Inc. Find more complete sample marketing plans at www.mplans.com. Reprinted by permission of Palo Alto Software.

# In This Chapter, We Will Address the Following Questions

1. What are the components of a modern marketing information system? (p. 67)

2. What are useful internal records for a marketing information system? (p. 69)

3. What makes up a marketing intelligence system? (p. 70)

4. What are some influential macroenvironment developments? (p. 72)

5. How can companies accurately measure and forecast demand? (p. 85)

Campbell's designed a new line of flavorful ready-to-eat soups to appeal to a discerning Millennial consumer.

*Source: CAMPBELL'S GO Soup images courtesy of Campbell Soup Company.*

MyMarketingLab™

⭐ Improve Your Grade!
Over 10 million students improved their results using the Pearson MyLabs. Visit mymktlab.com for simulations, tutorials, and end-of-chapter problems.

# 3 Collecting Information and Forecasting Demand

**Making marketing decisions in a fast-changing world is both an art and a science.** Holistic marketers recognize that the marketing environment is constantly presenting new opportunities and threats, and they understand the importance of continuously monitoring, forecasting, and adapting to that environment. Campbell is one of many companies trying to come to grips with the younger Millennial consumer.[1]

 *Campbell Soup Company's iconic red-and-white soup cans represent one of the most famous U.S. brands and were even the subject of an Andy Warhol portrait. Recently, though, the 143-year old company has suffered a double whammy: Overall consumption of canned soup has declined 13 percent, and Campbell's market share has dropped from 67% to 53% due to the popularity of fresh and premium soups. To stop the sales slide, Campbell set out to better understand the 18-to-34-year-olds who make up 25% of the U.S. population and will profoundly affect the company's future. Adopting an anthropological research approach, they sent executives to study Millennial consumers face-to-face in "hipster market hubs" such as London; Austin, TX; Portland, OR; and Washington D.C. They engaged in "live-alongs," where they shopped and ate at home with young consumers, and "eat-alongs" where they dined with them in restaurants. The key insight? Millennials loved spices and ate more exotic food than their parents—they just couldn't cook it at home! Campbell's solution was a new line, Campbell's Go! Soup ready-to-eat meals in six flavor varieties such as Moroccan Style Chicken with Chickpeas, Spicy Chorizo and Pulled Chicken with Black Beans, and Coconut Curry and Chicken with Shiitake Mushrooms. Sold in pouches rather than cans to convey freshness and at a price ($3) more than three times the basic red-and-white line, the product line was promoted entirely online, including music and humor sites, gaming platforms, and social media. Campbell also sells Pepperidge Farms baked goods, V8 vegetable juices, and Prego pasta sauce, but soups account for half its revenue, so marketing success for the new line was crucial.*

**Virtually every industry has been** touched by dramatic shifts in the economic, sociocultural, natural, technological, and political-legal environments. In this chapter, we consider how firms can identify and track relevant macroenvironment trends and develop good sales forecasts.

# Components of a Modern Marketing Information System

The major responsibility for identifying significant marketplace changes falls to the company's marketers. Marketers have two advantages for the task: (1) disciplined methods for collecting information and (2) time spent interacting with customers and observing competitors and other outside groups. Some firms have marketing information systems that provide rich detail about buyer wants, preferences, and behavior.

**DUPONT** DuPont commissioned marketing studies to uncover personal pillow behavior for its Dacron Polyester unit, which supplies filling to pillow makers and sells its own Comforel brand. One challenge is that people don't give up their old pillows: 37 percent of one sample described their relationship with their pillow as being like that of "an old married couple," and an additional 13 percent said their pillow was like "a childhood friend." Respondents fell into distinct groups in terms of pillow behavior: stackers (23 percent), plumpers (20 percent), rollers or folders (16 percent), cuddlers (16 percent), and smashers, who pound their pillows into a more comfy shape (10 percent). Women were more likely to plump, men to fold. The prevalence of stackers led the company to sell more pillows packaged as pairs and at different levels of softness or firmness.[2]

Marketers also have extensive information about how consumption patterns vary across and within countries. On a per capita annual basis, for example, the Irish consume the most chocolate (24.7 lbs.), Czechs the most beer (131.7 liters), the French the most wine (45.7 liters), and Greeks the most cigarettes (4,313).[3] Table 3.1 summarizes other comparisons across countries. Consider regional differences: Seattle's residents buy more sunglasses per person than in any other U.S. city; people in Salt Lake City (and Utah) eat the most Jell-O; Long Beach, CA, residents eat the most ice cream; and New York City dwellers buy the most country music CDs.[4]

Every firm must organize and distribute a continuous flow of information to its marketing managers. A **marketing information system (MIS)** consists of people, equipment, and procedures to gather, sort, analyze, evaluate, and distribute needed, timely, and accurate information to marketing decision makers. It relies on internal company records, marketing intelligence activities, and marketing research.

The company's marketing information system should combine what managers think they need, what they really need, and what is economically feasible. An internal MIS committee can interview a cross-section of marketing managers to discover their information needs. Table 3.2 displays some useful questions to ask them.

| TABLE 3.1 | A Global Profile of Extremes | |
|---|---|---|
| Highest fertility rate | Niger | 47.7 births per 1,000 population |
| Highest education expenditure as percent of GDP | Timor-Leste | 14.0% of GDP |
| Highest number of mobile phone subscribers | Macau | 206.4 subscribers per 100 people |
| Largest number of airports | United States | 15,079 airports |
| Highest military expenditure as percent of GDP | Saudi Arabia | 10.1% of GDP |
| Highest divorce rate | South Korea | 4.6 divorces per 1,000 population |
| Telephone lines per capita | Bermuda | 89.0 lines per 100 people |
| Highest cinema attendance | India | 4,432,700,000 cinema visits |
| Highest GDP per person | Liechtenstein | $105,190 |
| Largest aid donors as % of GDP | Norway | 1.10% of GDP |
| Most economically dependent on agriculture | Liberia | 61.3% of GDP |
| Highest population in workforce | Qatar | 74.7% |
| Highest percent of women in workforce | Mozambique | 53.5% |
| Most crowded road networks | Hong Kong | 286.7 vehicles per km of road |
| Most deaths in road accidents | Namibia | 53.4 killed per 100,000 population |
| Most tourist arrivals | France | 77,526,000 |
| Highest life expectancy | Japan | 83.7 years |
| Highest obesity rate | United States | 35.7% of adults |

**Source:** *CIA World Factbook,* www.cia.gov/library/publications/the-world-factbook, accessed July 24, 2012; *The Economist's Pocket World in Figures,* 2013 edition (London: Profile Books, 2012).

| TABLE 3.2 | Information Needs Probes |
|---|---|

1. What decisions do you regularly make?

2. What information do you need to make these decisions?

3. What information do you regularly get?

4. What special studies do you periodically request?

5. What information would you want that you are not getting now?

6. What information would you want daily? Weekly? Monthly? Yearly?

7. What online or offline newsletters, briefings, blogs, reports, or magazines would you like to see on a regular basis?

8. What topics would you like to be kept informed of?

9. What data analysis and reporting programs would you want?

10. What are the four most helpful improvements that could be made in the present marketing information system?

# Internal Records

To spot important opportunities and potential problems, marketing managers rely on internal reports of orders, sales, prices, costs, inventory levels, receivables, and payables.

## THE ORDER-TO-PAYMENT CYCLE

The heart of the internal records system is the order-to-payment cycle. Sales representatives, dealers, and customers send orders to the firm. The sales department prepares invoices, transmits copies to various departments, and back-orders out-of-stock items. Shipped items generate shipping and billing documents that go to various departments. Because customers favor firms that can promise timely delivery, companies need to perform these steps quickly and accurately.

## SALES INFORMATION SYSTEMS

Marketing managers need timely and accurate reports on current sales. Walmart operates a sales and inventory data warehouse that captures data on every item for every customer, every store, every day and refreshes it every hour.

Companies that make good use of "cookies," records of Web site usage stored on personal browsers, are smart users of targeted marketing. Many consumers are happy to cooperate: Not only do they *not* delete cookies, but they also expect customized marketing appeals and deals once they accept them.

Marketers must carefully interpret sales data, however, to avoid drawing wrong conclusions. Michael Dell illustrates: "If you have three yellow Mustangs sitting on a dealer's lot and a customer wants a red one, the salesman may be really good at figuring out how to sell the yellow Mustang. So the yellow Mustang gets sold, and a signal gets sent back to the factory that, hey, people want yellow Mustangs."[5]

## DATABASES, DATA WAREHOUSING, AND DATA MINING

The explosion of data brought by the maturation of the Internet and mobile technology gives companies unprecedented opportunities to engage their customers. It also threatens to overwhelm decision makers. "Marketing Insight: Digging into Big Data" describes opportunities and challenges in managing massive data sets.[6]

## Digging Into Big Data

Although unverified, one popular estimate says 90 percent of the data that has ever existed was created in the past two years. In one year, people stored enough data to fill 60,000 Libraries of Congress. YouTube receives 24 hours of video *every minute*. The world's 4 billion mobile phone users provide a steady source of data. Manufacturers are putting sensors and chips into appliances and products, generating even more data.

The danger, of course, is information overload. More data are not better unless they can be correctly processed, analyzed, and interpreted. In one poll of North American senior business executives, more than 90 percent reported collecting more information—86 percent more on average—than in years past. Unfortunately, roughly as many said they were missing out on new revenue growth because they could not gather the appropriate insights from those data.

And therein lies the opportunity and challenge of Big Data. Although a universally agreed-upon definition does not exist, Big Data describes data sets that cannot be effectively managed with traditional database and business intelligence tools. One industry expert, James Kobielus, sees Big Data as distinctive because of: *Volume* (from hundreds of terabytes to petabytes and beyond); *Velocity* (up to and including real-time, sub-second delivery); *Variety* (encompassing structured, unstructured, and semi-structured formats: messages, images, GPS signals, readings from sensors); and *Volatility* (with hundreds of new data sources in apps, Web services, and social networks).

Some companies are harnessing Big Data. UK supermarket giant Tesco collects 1.5 billion pieces of data every month to set prices and promotions; U.S. kitchenware retailer Williams-Sonoma uses its customer knowledge to customize versions of its catalog. Amazon reports generating 30 percent of its sales through its recommendation engine ("You may also like").

Many financial brands are putting more emphasis on Big Data. Bank of America is tracking spending and demographic data and tailoring promotions—for example, offering back-to-school deals to cardholders with children. JPMorgan Chase has improved communications to new cardholders to gain more engagement. On the production side, GE set up a team of developers in Silicon Valley to improve the efficiency of the jet engines, generators, locomotives, and CT scanners it sells. Even a 1 percent improvement in the operation of commercial aircraft would save $2 billion for GE's customers in the airline industry.

**Sources:** Schumpter, "Building with Big Data," *The Economist*, May 28, 2011; Jessica Twentyman, "Big Data Is the 'Next Frontier'" *Financial Times*, November 14, 2011; Jacques Bughin, John Livingston, and Sam Marwaha, "Seizing the Potential of Big Data," *McKinsey Quarterly* 4 (October 2011); "Mining the Big Data Goldmine," Special Advertising Section, *Fortune*, 2012; "Financial Brands Tap Big Data," www.warc.com, September 13, 2012; Thomas H. Davenport, Paul Barth, and Randy Bean, "How 'Big Data' Is Different," *MIT Sloan Management Review* 54 (Fall 2012), pp. 43–46; Andrew McAfee and Erik Brynjolfsson, "Big Data: The Management Revolution," *Harvard Business Review*, October 2012, pp. 60–68; Ashlee Vance, "GE Tries to Make Its Machines Cool and Connected," *Bloomberg Businessweek*, December 10, 2012, pp. 44–46.

# Marketing Intelligence

## THE MARKETING INTELLIGENCE SYSTEM

A **marketing intelligence system** is a set of procedures and sources that managers use to obtain everyday information about developments in the marketing environment. The internal records system supplies *results* data, but the marketing intelligence system supplies *happenings* data. Marketing managers collect marketing intelligence by reading books, newspapers, and trade publications; talking to customers, suppliers, distributors, and other company managers; and monitoring online social media.

Before the Internet, sometimes you just had to go out in the field and watch the competition. Describing how he learned about a rival's drilling activity, oil and gas entrepreneur T. Boone Pickens recalls, "We would have someone who would watch [the rival's] drilling floor from a half mile away with field glasses. Our competitor didn't like it but there wasn't anything they could do about it. Our spotters would watch the joints and drill pipe. They would count them; each [drill] joint was 30 feet long. By adding up all the joints, you would be able to tally the depth of the well." Pickens knew that the deeper the well, the more costly for his rival to get the oil or gas up to the surface, information that gave him an immediate competitive advantage.[7]

Marketing intelligence gathering must be legal and ethical. The private intelligence firm Diligence paid auditor KPMG a fine of $1.7 million after its cofounder posed as a British intelligence officer and convinced a member of the audit team to share confidential documents about a Bermuda-based investment firm for a Russian conglomerate.[8]

A company can take eight possible actions to improve the quantity and quality of its marketing intelligence. After describing the first seven, we devote special attention to the eighth: collecting marketing intelligence on the Internet.

- *Train and motivate the sales force to spot and report new developments.* The company must "sell" its sales force on their importance as intelligence gatherers. Grace Performance Chemicals, a division of W. R.

Grace, instructed its sales reps to observe the innovative ways customers used its products and suggest possible new products. Some customers used Grace waterproofing materials to soundproof their cars and patch boots and tents. Seven new-product ideas emerged, worth millions in sales.[9]

- **Motivate distributors, retailers, and other intermediaries to pass along important intelligence.** Marketing intermediaries are often closer to the customer and competition and can offer helpful insights. Combining data from its retailers Safeway, Kroger, and Walmart with its own qualitative insights, food producer ConAgra learned that many mothers switched to time-saving meals and snacks when school started. It launched its "Seasons of Mom" campaign to help grocers adjust to seasonal shifts in household needs.[10]

- **Hire external experts to collect intelligence.** Many companies hire specialists to gather marketing intelligence.[11] SavOn Convenience Stores, an enterprise of the Oneida Indian Nation, conducts 52 "mystery shopper" visits a month across its 13 stores. Stores are graded on employee responsiveness to customers, product quality, food freshness, restroom cleanliness, and stock levels. SavOn gives awards to winning stores.[12]

- **Network internally and externally.** The firm can purchase competitors' products, attend open houses and trade shows, read competitors' published reports, attend stockholders' meetings, talk to employees, collect competitors' ads, consult with suppliers, and look up news stories about competitors.

- **Set up a customer advisory panel.** Members of advisory panels might include the company's largest, most outspoken, most sophisticated, or most representative customers. GlaxoSmithKline sponsored an online community devoted to weight loss, where marketers felt they learned far more than they could have gleaned from focus groups on topics from packaging its weight-loss pill to where to place in-store marketing.[13]

- **Take advantage of government-related data resources.** The U.S. Census Bureau provides an in-depth look at the population swings, demographic groups, regional migrations, and changing family structure of the more than 311,591,917 people in the United States. Census marketer Nielsen Claritas SiteReports cross-references census figures with consumer surveys and its own grassroots research for clients such as The Weather

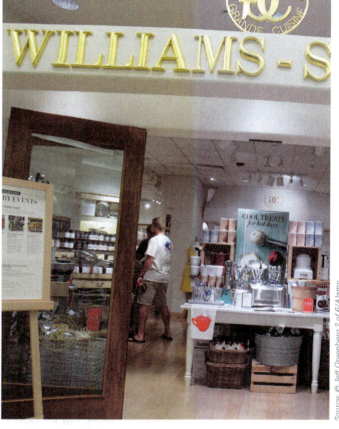

*Source: © Jeff Greenberg 2 of 6/Alamy*

Williams Sonoma uses information it has learned about its customers to customize its catalogs.

*Source: David Sacks/Getty Images*

Firms such as NPD provide detailed audits on how American consumers use their kitchens.

Channel, BMW, and Sovereign Bank. SiteReports offers more than 50 reports and maps that help companies analyze markets, select site locations, and target customers effectively.[14]

- *Purchase information from outside research firms and vendors.* Well-known data suppliers like A.C. Nielsen Company and Information Resources Inc. collect information about product sales and consumer exposure to media; they also gather consumer-panel data. Attensity offers a suite of products to monitor customer conversations from a variety of social, online, and internal sources.[15] NPD conducts its Kitchen Audit study every three years to determine what food ingredients U.S. households have on hand and what appliances, cookware, and utensils they own and to assess usage and sources of recipes.[16]

## COLLECTING MARKETING INTELLIGENCE ON THE INTERNET

Online customer review boards, discussion forums, chat rooms, and blogs can distribute one customer's experiences or evaluation to other potential buyers and, of course, to marketers seeking information. Here are five places to find competitors' product strengths and weaknesses online.

- *Independent customer goods and service review forums.* Independent forums include Web sites such as Epinions.com, RateItAll.com, ConsumerReview.com, and Bizrate.com. Bizrate.com collects millions of consumer reviews of stores and products each year from two sources: its 1.3 million volunteer members and feedback from stores that allow Bizrate.com to collect it directly from customers as they buy.
- *Distributor or sales agent feedback sites.* Feedback sites offer positive and negative product or service reviews, but the stores or distributors have built the sites themselves. Amazon.com offers an interactive feedback opportunity through which buyers, readers, editors, and others can review all products on the site, especially books. Elance.com is an online professional services provider that allows contractors to describe their experience and level of satisfaction with subcontractors.
- *Combo sites offering customer reviews and expert opinions.* Combination sites are concentrated in financial services and high-tech products that require professional knowledge. ZDNet.com offers customer and expert evaluations of technology products based on ease of use, features, and stability.
- *Customer complaint sites.* Customer complaint forums are designed mainly for dissatisfied customers. PlanetFeedback.com allows customers to voice unfavorable experiences with specific companies.
- *Public blogs.* Tens of millions of blogs and social networks offer personal opinions, reviews, ratings, and recommendations on virtually any topic—and their numbers continue to grow. Nielsen's BuzzMetrics analyzes blogs and social networks for insights into consumer sentiment and threats to the brand that may emerge online.[17]

Of course, companies can use many of these sources to monitor their own customers, products, services, and brands. Customer-service forums linked on a company's home page are a very useful tool. Customers often respond faster and provide better answers to other customers than a company could.

## COMMUNICATING AND ACTING ON MARKETING INTELLIGENCE

The competitive intelligence function works best when it is closely coordinated with the decision-making process. Given the speed of the Internet, it is important to act quickly on information gleaned online, as StubHub and Coca-Cola found:[18]

- When ticket broker StubHub detected criticism of its brand after confusion arose about refunds for a rain-delayed Yankees–Red Sox game, it quickly offered appropriate discounts and credits. The director of customer service observed, "This [episode] is a canary in a coal mine for us."
- When its monitoring software spotted a Twitter post that went to 10,000 followers from an upset consumer who couldn't redeem a prize from a MyCoke rewards program, Coke quickly posted an apology on his Twitter profile and offered to help resolve the situation. After the consumer got the prize, he changed his Twitter avatar to a photo of himself holding a Coke bottle.

# Analyzing the Macroenvironment

Successful companies recognize and respond profitably to unmet needs and trends.

Macaroni Grill revamped its menu to include more offerings to appeal to health-conscious consumers.

*Source: © Kristoffer Tripplaar/Alamy*

## NEEDS AND TRENDS

Dockers was created to meet the needs of baby boomers who could no longer fit into their jeans and wanted a physically and psychologically comfortable pair of pants. Enterprising individuals and companies create new solutions to similarly unmet needs. Let's distinguish among fads, trends, and megatrends.

- A **fad** is "unpredictable, short-lived, and without social, economic, and political significance." A company can cash in on a fad such as Crocs clogs, Elmo TMX dolls, and Pokémon gifts and toys, but getting it right requires luck and good timing.[19]
- A direction or sequence of events with momentum and durability, a **trend** is more predictable and durable than a fad; trends reveal the shape of the future and can provide strategic direction. A trend toward health and nutrition awareness has brought increased government regulation and negative publicity for firms seen as peddling unhealthy food. Macaroni Grill revamped its menu to include more low-calorie and low-fat offerings after *The Today Show* called its chicken and artichoke sandwich "the calorie equivalent of 16 Fudgesicles" and *Men's Health* declared its 1,630-calorie dessert ravioli the "worst dessert in America."[20]
- A **megatrend** is a "large social, economic, political, and technological change [that] is slow to form, and once in place, influences us for some time—between seven and ten years, or longer."[21]

Several firms offer social-cultural forecasts. The Yankelovich Monitor has tracked 35 social value and lifestyle trends since 1971, such as "anti-bigness," "mysticism," and "living for today." A new market opportunity doesn't guarantee success, of course. Even if the new product is technically feasible, market research is necessary to determine profit potential.

## IDENTIFYING THE MAJOR FORCES

The new century brought new challenges: the steep decline of the stock market, which affected savings, investment, and retirement funds; rising and long-lasting unemployment; corporate scandals; stronger indications of global warming and other signs of deterioration in the environment; and continued terrorism.

Firms must monitor six major forces in the broad environment: demographic, economic, social-cultural, natural, technological, and political-legal. We'll describe them separately, but remember their interactions will lead to new opportunities and threats. For example, explosive population growth (demographic) leads to more resource depletion and pollution (natural), which leads consumers to call for more laws (political-legal), which stimulate new technological solutions and products (technological) that, if they are affordable (economic), may actually change attitudes and behavior (social-cultural).

# THE DEMOGRAPHIC ENVIRONMENT

The main demographic factor marketers monitor is *population,* including the size and growth rate of population in cities, regions, and nations; age distribution and ethnic mix; educational levels; and household patterns.

**WORLDWIDE POPULATION GROWTH** World population growth is explosive: The world's population on July 1, 2012, was estimated at 7,027,349,193, forecasted to rise to 8.82 billion by 2040 and exceed 9 billion by 2045.[22] Table 3.3 offers an interesting perspective.[23]

Population growth is highest in countries and communities that can least afford it. Developing regions of the world house 84 percent of the world's population and are growing at 1 percent to 2 percent per year; developed countries' populations are growing at only 0.3 percent.[24] In developing countries, modern medicine is lowering the death rate, but birthrates remain fairly stable.

A growing population does not mean growing markets unless there is sufficient purchasing power. Education can raise the standard of living but is difficult to accomplish in most developing countries. Nonetheless, companies that carefully analyze these markets can find major opportunities and sometimes lessons they can apply at home. See "Marketing Memo: Finding Gold at the Bottom of the Pyramid."[25]

**POPULATION AGE MIX** Mexico has a very young population and rapid population growth. Italy, at the other extreme, has one of the world's oldest populations. Milk, diapers, school supplies, and toys will be more important products in Mexico than in Italy.

There is a global trend toward an aging population. In 1950, there were only 131 million people 65 and older; in 1995, their number had almost tripled to 371 million. By 2050, one of 10 people worldwide will be 65 or older. In the United States, baby boomers—those born between 1946 and 1964—represent a market of some 36 million, about 12 percent of the population. By 2011, the 65-and-over population was growing faster than the population as a whole in each of the 50 states.[26]

| TABLE 3.3 | The World as a Village |
|---|---|

If the world were a village of 100 people:

- Sixty-one villagers would be Asian (of those, 20 would be Chinese and 17 would be Indian), 14 would be African, 11 would be European, nine would be Latin or South American, five would be North American, and none of the villagers would be from Australia, Oceania, or Antarctica.

- At least 18 villagers would be unable to read or write, but 33 would have cellular phones and 16 would be online on the Internet.

- Twenty-seven villagers would be under 15, and seven would be over 64. There would be an equal number of males and females.

- There would be 18 cars in the village.

- Sixty-three villagers would have inadequate sanitation.

- Thirty-three villagers would be Christians, 20 would be Muslims, 13 would be Hindus, six would be Buddhists, 14 would be nonreligious, and the remaining 14 would be members of other religions.

- Thirty villagers would be unemployed or underemployed, while of those 70 who would work, 28 would work in agriculture (primary sector), 14 would work in industry (secondary sector), and the remaining 28 would work in the service sector (tertiary sector).

- Fifty-three villagers would live on less than two U.S. dollars a day. One villager would have AIDS, 26 villagers would smoke, and 14 villagers would be obese.

- By the end of a year, one villager would die and two new villagers would be born so the population would climb to 101.

**Source:** David J. Smith and Shelagh Armstrong, *If the World Were a Village: A Book about the World's People*, 2nd ed. (Tonawanda, NY: Kids Can Press, 2002).

## marketing memo
### Finding Gold at the Bottom of the Pyramid

Business writer C. K. Prahalad believes much innovation can come from developments in emerging markets such as China and India. He estimates 5 billion unserved and underserved people make up the "bottom of the pyramid." One study showed that 4 billion people live on $2 or less a day. Firms operating in those markets must learn how to do more with less.

In Bangalore, India, Narayana Hrudayalaya Hospital charges a flat fee of $1,500 for heart bypass surgery that costs 50 times as much in the United States. The hospital has low labor and operating expenses and an assembly-line view of care. The approach works—the hospital's mortality rates are half those of U.S. hospitals. Narayana also operates on hundreds of infants for free and profitably insures 2.5 million poor Indians against serious illness for 11 cents a month.

Similarly, Arvind Eye Care System, established by Govindappa Venkatswamy in 1976 in India, has performed 4 million operations using an approach likened to "McDonald's-style" high-volume assembly. Aravind also developed an intra-ocular lens, manufactured by its subsidiary, Aurolab, at a fraction of the cost of imports. SalaUno, a for-profit social enterprise based in San Francisco, replicated the Aravind model in Mexico, carrying out 133 cataract operations a month for a year—free of charge for those who could not afford the treatment.

The transfer of innovations from developing to developed markets is what Dartmouth professor Vijay Govindrajan calls *reverse innovation*. He sees opportunity in focusing on the needs and constraints of a developing market to create an inexpensive product that can succeed there and then introducing it as a cheaper alternative in developed markets. He also sees reverse innovation's public policy benefits, which can transform industries through the successful development of ultra-low-cost transportation, renewable energy, clean water, micro finance, affordable heath care, and low-cost housing.

Among successful reverse innovators, Nestlé repositioned its low-fat Maggi brand dried noodles—a popular, low-priced meal for rural Pakistan and India—as a budget-friendly health food in Australia and New Zealand. U.S.-based Harman International, known for high-end dashboard audio systems designed by German engineers, developed a radically simpler and cheaper way to create products for China, India, and emerging markets and is applying that method to its product-development centers in the West. It now can sell a range of products priced from low to high and is looking into infotainment systems for motorbikes, a popular form of transportation in emerging markets and around the world.

**Sources:** C. K. Prahalad, *The Fortune at the Bottom of the Pyramid* (Upper Saddle River, NJ: Wharton School Publishing, 2010); Bill Breen, "C. K. Prahalad: Pyramid Schemer," *Fast Company*, March 2007, p. 79; Reena Jane, "Inspiration from Emerging Economies," *BusinessWeek*, March 23, 2009, pp. 38–41; Vijay Govindarajan and Chris Trimble, *Reverse Innovation: Create Far from Home, Win Everywhere* (Boston, MA: Harvard Business School Publishing, 2012); Jeffrey R. Immelt, Vijay Govindarajan, and Chris Trimble, "How GE Is Disrupting Itself," *Harvard Business Review*, October 2009, pp. 56–65; Vijay Govindarajan, "A Reverse-Innovation Playbook," *Harvard Business Review*, April 2012, pp.120–23; Felicity Carus, "Reverse Innovation Brings Social Solutions to Developed Countries," *The Guardian*, August 29, 2012; Constantinos C. Markides, "How Disruptive Will Innovations from Emerging Markets Be?," *MIT Sloan Management Review,* 54 (Fall 2012), pp. 23–25.

Marketers generally divide the population into six age groups: preschool children, school-age children, teens, young adults age 20 to 40, middle-aged adults 40 to 65, and older adults 65 and older. Some marketers focus on **cohorts**, groups of individuals born during the same time period who travel through life together. The defining moments they experience as they come of age and become adults (roughly ages 17 through 24) can stay with them for a lifetime and influence their values, preferences, and buying behaviors.

**ETHNIC AND OTHER MARKETS** Ethnic and racial diversity varies across countries. At one extreme is Japan, where almost everyone is native Japanese; at the other extreme is the United States, 12 percent of whose people were born in another country. As of the 2010 Census, the U.S. population was: White (72 percent), Black or African American (13 percent), American Indian and Alaskan Native (0.9 percent), Asian (5 percent), Hispanic (16 percent). More than half the growth between 2000 and 2010 came from the increase in the Hispanic population, which grew by 43 percent, from 35.3 million to 50.5 million, representing a major shift in the nation's ethnic center of gravity. Geographically, the 2010 Census revealed that Hispanics were moving to states like North Carolina where they had not been concentrated before and that they increasingly live in suburbs.[27] From the food U.S. consumers eat to the clothing, music, and cars they buy, Hispanics are having a huge impact.

Companies are refining their products and marketing to reach this fastest-growing and most influential consumer group: Research by Hispanic media giant Univision suggests 70 percent of Spanish-language viewers are more likely to buy a product when it's advertised in Spanish. Fisher-Price, recognizing that many Hispanic mothers did not grow up with its brand, shifted away from appeals to their heritage. Instead, its ads emphasized the joy of mother and child playing together with Fisher-Price toys.[28] Hispanics are not the only fast-growing minority segment.[29]

**▌INDIAN-AMERICANS**   The U.S. Indian-American population has exploded over the past decade, according to the 2010 Census, surpassing Filipinos as the nation's second-largest Asian population after Chinese. Affluent, well-educated, and consumer-oriented, Indian-Americans are attractive to marketers. Nationwide Insurance developed print and TV ads for them and other South Asians in the New York tristate area and San Francisco and Silicon Valley. Cadillac has run newspaper ads and local TV spots in Chicago and New York after seeing many Indian-Americans and South Asians in its showrooms. Zee TV was the first Hindi satellite channel and is the leading network serving the South Asian audience.

Yet marketers must not overgeneralize—within each group are consumers quite different from each other.[30] Diversity also goes beyond ethnic and racial markets. More than 51 million U.S. consumers have disabilities, and they constitute a market for home delivery companies such as Internet grocer Peapod.

**EDUCATIONAL GROUPS**  The population in any society falls into five educational groups: illiterates, high school dropouts, high school diplomas, college degrees, and professional degrees. More than two-thirds of the world's 793 million illiterate adults are found in only eight countries (Bangladesh, China, Egypt, Ethiopia, India, Indonesia, Nigeria, and Pakistan); of all illiterate adults in the world, two-thirds are women; extremely low literacy rates are concentrated in three regions—the Arab states, South and West Asia, and Sub-Saharan Africa—where around one-third of the men and half of all women are illiterate (2005 est.).[31]

The United States has one of the world's highest percentages of college-educated citizens.[32] As of March 2011, just over 30 percent of U.S. adults held at least a bachelor's degree, and 10.9 percent held a graduate degree, up from 26.2 percent and 8.7 percent 10 years earlier. Half of 18- and 19-year-olds were enrolled in college in 2009, but not all college students are young. About 16 percent are 35 and older; they also make up 37 percent of part-time students. The large number of educated people in the United States drives strong demand for high-quality books, magazines, and travel and creates a supply of skills.

**HOUSEHOLD PATTERNS**  The traditional U.S. household included a husband, wife, and children under 18 (sometimes with grandparents). By 2010, only 20 percent of U.S. households met this definition, down from about 25 percent a decade before and 43 percent in 1950. Married couples have dropped below half of all U.S. households for the first time (48 percent), far below the 78 percent of 1950. The median age at first marriage has also never been higher: 26.5 for brides and 28.7 for grooms.[33]

The U.S. family has been steadily evolving toward less traditional forms. More people are divorcing, separating, choosing not to marry, or marrying later. Other types of households are single live-alones (27 percent), single-parent families (8 percent), childless married couples and empty nesters (32 percent), living with nonrelatives only (5 percent), and other family structures (8 percent).

Indian-Americans are a fast growing minority segment with much appeal to marketers.

*Source: Ashok Sinha/Taxi*

The biggest change for the decade was the jump in households headed by women without husbands—up 18 percent. Nontraditional households are growing more rapidly than traditional households. Academics and marketing experts estimate the gay and lesbian population at 4 percent to 8 percent of the total U.S. population, higher in urban areas.[34]

Each type of household has distinctive needs and buying habits. The single, separated, widowed, and divorced may need smaller apartments; inexpensive and smaller appliances, furniture, and furnishings; and smaller-size food packages. Many non-traditional households feel advertising ignores families like theirs, suggesting an opportunity for advertisers.[35]

Even traditional households have changed. Boomer dads marry later than their fathers and grandfathers did, shop more, and are much more active in raising their kids. Bugaboo makes innovative baby strollers that speaks to modern parents. Bugaboo's iconic functional strollers have unique designs and functionalities such as adjustable suspension and an extendable handle bar perfect for taller dads. And before Dyson, the high-end vacuum company, appealed to U.S. dads' inner geek by focusing on the machine's revolutionary technology, men weren't even on the radar for vacuum cleaner sales. Now they make up 40 percent of Dyson's customers.[36]

# THE ECONOMIC ENVIRONMENT

Purchasing power depends on consumers' income, savings, debt, and credit availability as well as the price level. As the recent economic downturn vividly demonstrated, fluctuating purchasing power strongly affects business, especially for products geared to high-income and price-sensitive consumers. Marketers must understand consumer psychology and levels and distribution of income, savings, debt, and credit.

**CONSUMER PSYCHOLOGY** The recession that began in 2008 initiated new consumer spending patterns. Were these temporary adjustments or permanent changes?[37] The middle class—the bread and butter of many firms—was hit hard by record declines in both wages and net worth. Some experts believed the recession had fundamentally shaken consumers' faith in the economy and their personal financial situations. "Mindless" spending would be out; willingness to comparison shop, haggle, and use discounts would become the norm.[38]

Consumers at the time certainly seemed to believe so. In one survey, almost two-thirds said the recession's economic changes would be permanent; nearly one-third said they would spend less than before the recession. Others believed tighter spending was a short-term constraint and not a fundamental behavioral change; they predicted their spending would resume when the economy improved.[39]

Identifying the more likely long-term scenario—especially for the coveted 18- to 34-year-old group—would help marketers decide how to spend their money. Executives at Sainsbury, the third-largest UK chain of supermarkets, concluded that the recession had created a more risk-averse British consumer, saving more, paying off debts instead of borrowing, and shopping in more cost-conscious ways. Even wealthy UK consumers traded down some to lower-cost items. As one retail executive said, "There's nobody who can afford not to try to save."[40]

**INCOME DISTRIBUTION** There are four types of industrial structures: *subsistence economies* like Papua New Guinea, with few opportunities for marketers; *raw-material-exporting economies* like Democratic Republic of Congo (copper) and Saudi Arabia (oil), with good markets for equipment, tools, supplies, and luxury goods for the rich; *industrializing economies* like India, Egypt, and the Philippines, where a new rich class and a growing middle class demand new types of goods; and *industrial economies* like Western Europe, with rich markets for all sorts of goods.

Marketers often distinguish countries using five income-distribution patterns: (1) very low incomes; (2) mostly low incomes; (3) very low, very high incomes; (4) low, medium, high incomes; and (5) mostly medium incomes. Consider the market for the Lamborghini, an automobile costing more than $150,000. The market would be very small in countries with type 1 or 2 income patterns. One of the largest single markets for the ultra-expensive

The unique design of Bugaboo baby strollers are especially appealing to modern parents.

*Source: Bugaboo International B.V*

High-priced Lamborghini sports cars have found success in relatively poorer countries by appealing to enough affluent buyers.

*Source: © Paul Best/Alamy*

sports car Lamborghinis is Portugal (income pattern 3), one of the poorer countries in Western Europe, but with high enough income inequality that there are also wealthy families who can afford expensive cars.[41]

**INCOME, SAVINGS, DEBT, AND CREDIT**  U.S. consumers have a high debt-to-income ratio, which slows expenditures on housing and large-ticket items. When credit became scarcer in the recession, especially for lower-income borrowers, consumer borrowing dropped for the first time in two decades. The financial meltdown that led to this contraction was due to overly liberal credit policies that allowed consumers to buy homes and other items they could not really afford. Marketers wanted every possible sale, banks wanted to earn interest on loans, and near financial ruin resulted.

An economic issue of increasing importance is the migration of manufacturers and service jobs offshore. From India, Infosys provides outsourcing services for Cisco, Nordstrom, Microsoft, and others. The 35,000 employees the fast-growing $4.2 billion company hires every year receive technical, team, and communication training in Infosys's $120 million facility outside Bangalore.[42]

## THE SOCIOCULTURAL ENVIRONMENT

From our sociocultural environment we absorb, almost unconsciously, a world view that defines our relationships to ourselves, others, organizations, society, nature, and the universe.

- *Views of ourselves.* Some "pleasure seekers" chase fun, change, and escape; others seek "self-realization." Some adopt more conservative behaviors and ambitions (see Table 3.4 for favorite consumer leisure-time activities and how they have changed, or not, in recent years).
- *Views of others.* People are concerned about the homeless, crime and victims, and other social problems. At the same time, they seek those like themselves for long-lasting relationships, suggesting a growing market for social-support products and services such as health clubs, cruises, and religious activity as well as "social surrogates" like television, video games, and social networking sites.
- *Views of organizations.* After a wave of layoffs and corporate scandals, organizational loyalty has declined. Companies need new ways to win back consumer and employee confidence. They need to ensure they are good corporate citizens and that their consumer messages are honest.
- *Views of society.* Some people defend society (preservers), some run it (makers), some take what they can from it (takers), some want to change it (changers), some are looking for something deeper (seekers), and still others want to leave it (escapers).[43] Consumption patterns often reflect these social attitudes. Makers are high achievers who eat, dress, and live well. Changers usually live more frugally, drive smaller cars, and wear simpler clothes. Escapers and seekers are a major market for movies, music, surfing, and camping.
- *Views of nature.* Business has responded to increased awareness of nature's fragility and finiteness by making more green products, seeking their own new energy sources, and reducing their environmental footprint. Companies are also literally tapping into nature more by producing wider varieties of camping, hiking, boating, and fishing gear such as boots, tents, backpacks, and accessories.
- *Views of the universe.* Most U.S. citizens are monotheistic, although religious conviction and practice have waned through the years or been redirected into an interest in evangelical movements or Eastern religions, mysticism, the occult, and the human potential movement.

Other cultural characteristics of interest to marketers are core cultural values and subcultures. Let's look at both.

| TABLE 3.4 | Favorite Leisure-Time Activities | | |
|---|---|---|---|
| | **1995 (via phone)** | | **2013 (via online)** |
| | % | | % |
| Reading | 28 | Watch TV | 42 |
| TV watching | 25 | Reading | 37 |
| Spending time with family/kids | 12 | Spending time with families and friends | 18 |
| Fishing | 10 | Watching/Going to movies | 11 |
| Gardening | 9 | Exercise/working out | 10 |
| Playing team sports | 9 | Playing video games and computer/Internet games | 10 |
| Going to movies | 8 | Walking/running/jogging | 8 |
| Walking | 8 | Gardening | 7 |
| Entertaining | 7 | Concerts/listening to/playing music | 7 |
| Golf | 6 | Hobby related activities | 5 |

**Sources:** Harris Poll, "Favorite Leisure Activities" (via online), http://www.harrisinteractive.com/NewsRoom/HarrisPolls/tabid/447/mid/1508/articleId/1345/ctl/ReadCustom%20Default/Default.aspx, Table 4, accessed July 2014; and Harris Poll, "Favorite Leisure-Time Activities" (Spontaneous, Unaided Responses, via phone), http://www.harrisinteractive.com/vault/Harris-Interactive-Poll-Research-Time-and-Leisure-2008-12.pdf, Table 1, accessed July 2014.

**CORE CULTURAL VALUES** Most people in the United States still believe in working, getting married, giving to charity, and being honest. *Core beliefs* and values are passed from parents to children and reinforced by social institutions—schools, churches, businesses, and governments. *Secondary beliefs* and values are more open to change. Believing in the institution of marriage is a core belief; believing people should marry early is a secondary belief.

Marketers have some chance of changing secondary values but little chance of changing core values. The nonprofit organization Mothers Against Drunk Drivers (MADD) does not try to stop the sale of alcohol but promotes lower legal blood-alcohol levels for driving and limited operating hours for businesses that sell alcohol.

Although core values are fairly persistent, cultural swings do take place. In the 1960s, hippies, the Beatles, Elvis Presley, and other cultural phenomena had a major impact on hairstyles, clothing, sexual norms, and life goals. Today's young people are influenced by new heroes and activities: music entertainer and mogul Jay-Z, singer Lady Gaga, and snowboarder and skateboarder Shaun White.

**SUBCULTURES** Each society contains **subcultures**, groups with shared values, beliefs, preferences, and behaviors emerging from their special life experiences or circumstances. Marketers have always loved teenagers because they are trendsetters in fashion, music, entertainment, ideas, and attitudes. Attract someone as a teen, and you will likely keep the person as a customer later in life. Frito-Lay, which draws 15 percent of its sales from teens, noted a rise in chip snacking by grown-ups. "We think it's because we brought them in as teenagers," said Frito-Lay's marketing director.[44]

# THE NATURAL ENVIRONMENT

In Western Europe, "green" parties have pressed for public action to reduce industrial pollution. In the United States, experts have documented ecological deterioration, and watchdog groups such as the Sierra Club and Friends of the Earth commit to political and social action.

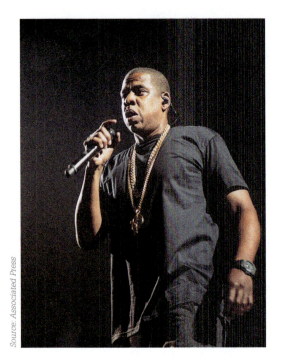

Today's youth are more likely to be influenced by contemporary music icons such as Jay-Z and Lady Gaga.

Steel companies and public utilities have invested billions of dollars in pollution-control equipment and environmentally friendly fuels, making hybrid cars, low-flow toilets and showers, organic foods, and green office buildings everyday realities. Opportunities await those who can reconcile prosperity with environmental protection. Consider these solutions to concerns about air quality:[45]

- Nearly a quarter of the carbon dioxide that makes up about 80 percent of all greenhouse gases comes from electrical power plants. Dublin-based Airtricity operates wind farms in the United States and the United Kingdom that offer cheaper and greener electricity.

- Transportation is second only to electricity generation as a contributor to global warming, accounting for roughly a fifth of carbon emissions. Vancouver-based Westport Innovations developed a conversion technology—high-pressure direct injection—that allows diesel engines to run on cleaner-burning liquid natural gas, reducing greenhouse emissions by a fourth.

- Due to millions of rural cooking fires, parts of Southern Asia suffer extremely poor air quality. A person cooking over an open wood or kerosene fire inhales the equivalent of two packs of cigarettes a day. Illinois-based Sun Ovens International makes family-sized and institutional solar ovens that use mirrors to redirect the sun's rays into an insulated box. Used in 130 countries, the oven both saves money and reduces greenhouse gas emissions.

Irish firm Airtricity is developing new wind farms as an alternative energy source.

*Corporate environmentalism* recognizes the need to integrate environmental issues into the firm's strategic plans. Trends for marketers to be aware of include the shortage of raw materials, especially water; the increased cost of energy; increased pollution levels; and the changing role of governments.[46] (See also "Marketing Insight: The Green Marketing Revolution.")

## The Green Marketing Revolution

Both consumers and companies are changing the way they view environmental issues, as the following descriptions illustrate.

### Consumer Perspective

Consumers have put their very real environmental concerns into words and actions, focusing on green products, corporate sustainability, and other environmental issues. Here are highlights of some notable studies.

- **WPP Green Brands Study.** The WPP Green Brands Study surveys 9,000 people in eight countries and evaluates 370 brands. In 2011 it found consumer interest in green products had expanded to auto, energy, and technology sectors in addition to personal care, food, and household products. Sixty percent of consumers stated they wanted to buy products from environmentally responsible companies. In developed countries such as the United States and United Kingdom, 20 percent were willing to spend more than 10 percent extra on a green product. Consumers in developing countries put even more value on green products: Ninety-five percent of Chinese consumers, for example, said they were willing to pay more for a green product.

- **Greendex.** A collaboration between National Geographic and environmental research consultants GlobeScan, Greendex is a sustainable consumption index of actual consumer behavior and material lifestyles across 17 countries. It defines environmentally friendly consumer behavior in terms of people's transportation patterns, household energy, resource use, and consumption of food and everyday goods and how well consumers minimize their environmental impact. The 2012 survey found the top-scoring consumers in developing countries: India, China, and Brazil in descending order. Developed countries scored lower, with U.S. consumers lowest, followed by Canadians, Japanese, and the French.

- **Gallup.** Gallup has consistently found U.S. consumers are most concerned about pollution of drinking water, rivers, lakes, and reservoirs and maintenance of fresh water for household needs and least concerned about global warming. Overall, the 2012 survey showed all ratings at lower levels than their 2000 peak as more U.S. adults feel environmental conditions in the United States are improving.

- **GfK Roper.** The 2012 GfK Roper Green Gauge Study showed key aspects of "green" culture—from organic purchase to recyclability—have gone mainstream. U.S. consumers increasingly turn to digital devices to learn about the environment and share their green experiences. During slow economic recovery, however, paying significantly more to be environmentally friendly was becoming a barrier for many consumers.

Interestingly, although some marketers assume younger people are more concerned about the environment, some research suggests older consumers actually take their eco-responsibilities more seriously.

### Company Perspectives

In the past, "green marketing" programs were not always entirely successful. Those that were persuaded consumers they were acting in their own and society's long-run interest at the same time by buying, for instance, organic foods that were healthier, tastier, and safer and energy-efficient appliances that cost less to run.

Some green products have emphasized their natural benefits for years, like Tom's of Maine, Burt's Bees, Stonyfield Farm, and Seventh Generation. Products offering environmental benefits are becoming more mainstream. Part of the initial success of Clorox Green Works household cleaning products, launched in January 2008, was that it found the sweet spot where a target market wanting to take smaller steps toward a greener lifestyle met a green product with a very modest price premium and sold through a grassroots marketing program.

The recession took its toll on some newly launched green products, however, and Green Works and similar products from Arm & Hammer, Windex, Palmolive, and Hefty found sales stalling. Some consumers have also become more skeptical of green claims that are hard to verify. One challenge is the difficulty consumers have in experiencing or observing the environmental benefits of products, leading to accusations of "greenwashing" where products are not nearly so green or environmentally beneficial as their marketing might suggest.

Some experts recommend avoiding "green marketing myopia" by focusing on consumer value positioning, understanding what consumers know and should know, and credible product claims. During tough economic times especially, having the right value proposition and making sure green products are seen as effective and affordable are critical.

**Sources:** Jacquelyn A. Ottman, Edwin R. Stafford, and Cathy L. Hartman, "Avoiding Green Marketing Myopia," *Environment* (June 2006), pp. 22–36; Jill Meredith Ginsberg and Paul N. Bloom, "Choosing the Right Green Marketing Strategy," *MIT Sloan Management Review* (Fall 2004), pp. 79–84; Jacquelyn Ottman, *Green Marketing: Opportunity for Innovation,* 2nd ed. (New York: BookSurge Publishing, 2004); Jacquelyn Ottman, *The New Rules of Green Marketing* (San Francisco: Berrett-Koehler, 2012); Mark Dolliver, "Deflating a Myth," *Brandweek,* May 12, 2008, pp. 30–31; Jeffrey M. Jones, "Worry about U.S. Water, Air Pollution at Historic Lows," www.gallup.com, April 13, 2012; "The 2011 Green Brands Survey," www.cohenwolfe.com, June 8, 2011; "Greendex 2012: Consumer Choice and the Environment—A Worldwide Tracking Survey," www.nationalgeographic.com, July 2012; "Green Gets Real," www.gfkamerica.com, accessed November 12, 2012; Stephanie Clifford and Andrew Martin, "As Consumers Cut Spending, 'Green' Products Lose Allure," *New York Times,* April 21, 2011; Tiffany Hsu, "Skepticism Grows over Products Touted as Eco-Friendly," *Los Angeles Times,* May 21, 2011.

Seventh Generation offers a range of household products for environmentally conscious consumers.

*Source: Andrew H. Walker/Getty Images*

- The earth's raw materials consist of the infinite, the finite renewable, and the finite nonrenewable. Firms whose products require *finite nonrenewable resources*—oil, coal, platinum, zinc, silver—face substantial cost increases as depletion approaches. Firms that can develop substitute materials have an excellent opportunity.
- One finite nonrenewable resource, oil, has created serious problems for the world economy. As oil prices soar, companies search for practical means to harness solar, nuclear, wind, and other alternative energies.
- Some industrial activity will inevitably damage the natural environment, creating a large market for pollution-control solutions such as scrubbers, recycling centers, and landfill systems as well as for alternative ways to produce and package goods.
- Many poor nations are doing little about pollution, lacking the funds or the political will. It is in the richer nations' interest to help them control their pollution, but even richer nations today lack the necessary funds.

## THE TECHNOLOGICAL ENVIRONMENT

The essence of market capitalism is a dynamism that tolerates the creative destructiveness of technology as the price of progress. Transistors hurt the vacuum-tube industry; autos hurt the railroads. Television hurt newspapers; the Internet hurt them both. When old industries fight or ignore new technologies, they decline. Tower Records, Borders, and others had ample warning they would be hurt by Internet downloads; their failure to respond led to their liquidation.

In some cases, innovation's long-run consequences are not fully foreseeable. Cell phones, video games, and the Internet allow people to stay in touch with each other and plugged in with current events but also reduce attention to traditional media as well as face-to-face social interaction as people listen to music or watch a movie on their cell phones.

Marketers should monitor the following technology trends: the accelerating pace of change, unlimited opportunities for innovation, varying R&D budgets, and increased regulation of technological change.

**ACCELERATING PACE OF CHANGE** More ideas than ever are in the works, and the time between idea and implementation is shrinking. In the first two-and-a-half years of the iPad's existence, Apple sold a staggering 97 million units worldwide.[47] In many markets, the next technological breakthrough seems right around the corner,

**UNLIMITED OPPORTUNITIES FOR INNOVATION** Consider just a few remarkable openings. Medical researchers hope to use stem cells for organ generation and hybrid positron emission tomography (PET) and magnetic resonance imaging (MRI) to dramatically improve diagnosis. Environmental researchers are exploring plasma arc waste disposal to harness lightning and turn garbage into glass or a gaseous energy source. They are developing desalination methods to safely and economically remove salt from ocean water and make it drinkable. Neuroscientists are studying how to harness brain signals via electroencephalography (EEG) as well as how to construct a "thinking" DNA neural network that can answer questions correctly.[48]

**VARYING R&D BUDGETS** The United States is the world leader in R&D, spending $436 billion in 2012. Its advantage in innovation comes from all sectors—government-funded research from the National Aeronautics and Space Administration (NASA) and National Institutes of Health (NIH); top academic institutions such as Johns Hopkins University, University of Michigan, and the University of Wisconsin; and corporations such as Merck, Pfizer, Intel, and Microsoft.

A growing portion of U.S. R&D, however, goes to the development side, not research, raising concerns about whether the United States can maintain its lead in basic science. Too many companies seem to be putting their money into copying competitors' products with minor improvements. Other countries are not standing still either. China, Israel, and Finland all are beginning to spend a larger percentage of their GDP on R&D than the United States.[49]

**INCREASED REGULATION OF TECHNOLOGICAL CHANGE** Government has expanded its agencies' powers to investigate and ban potentially unsafe products. Safety and health regulations have increased for food, automobiles, clothing, electrical appliances, and construction. Consider the Food and Drug Administration (FDA).[50]

---

**❚ THE FDA** The FDA plays a critical public health role, overseeing a wide range of products. Here is its specific charge:

> FDA is responsible for protecting the public health by assuring the safety, efficacy and security of human and veterinary drugs, biological products, medical devices, our nation's food supply, cosmetics, and products that emit radiation.
>
> FDA is also responsible for advancing the public health by helping to speed innovations that make medicines more effective, safer, and more affordable and by helping the public get the accurate, science-based information they need to use medicines and foods to maintain and improve their health. FDA also has responsibility for regulating the manufacturing, marketing and distribution of tobacco products to protect the public health and to reduce tobacco use by minors.
>
> Finally, FDA plays a significant role in the Nation's counterterrorism capability. FDA fulfills this responsibility by ensuring the security of the food supply and by fostering development of medical products to respond to deliberate and naturally emerging public health threats.

The FDA's level of enforcement has varied some through the years, in part depending on the political administration. It can also vary by product or industry. Congress recently empowered the FDA to place new restrictions on the prescribing, distribution, sale, and advertising of proposed new drugs. The FDA looks at the safety and efficacy of any proposed new drug, but also additional considerations such as the integrity of the global manufacturing chain that makes it, post-marketing studies as a condition of approval, and demonstrable superiority over existing therapies.

---

## THE POLITICAL-LEGAL ENVIRONMENT

The political and legal environment consists of laws, government agencies, and pressure groups that influence organizations and individuals. Sometimes these create new business opportunities. Mandatory recycling laws boosted the recycling industry and launched dozens of new companies making products from recycled materials. On the other hand, overseas governments can impose laws or take actions that create uncertainty and even confusion for companies. Political instability in certain Middle Eastern and African nations has created much risk for oil firms and others. Two major trends are increased business legislation and the growth of special-interest groups.[51]

**INCREASED BUSINESS LEGISLATION** Business legislation is intended to protect companies from unfair competition, protect consumers from unfair business practices, protect society from unbridled business behavior,

Political unrest in the Middle East was a major cause for concern for many large multinational firms

and charge businesses with the social costs of their products or production processes. Each new law may also have the unintended effect of sapping initiative and slowing growth.

The European Commission has established new laws covering competitive behavior, product standards, product liability, and commercial transactions for the 28 member nations of the European Union. The United States has many consumer protection laws covering competition, product safety and liability, fair trade and credit practices, and packaging and labeling, but many countries' laws are stronger.[52]

Norway bans several forms of sales promotion—trading stamps, contests, and premiums—as inappropriate or unfair. Many countries throughout the world ban or severely restrict comparative advertising. Thailand requires food processors selling national brands to also market low-price brands so low-income consumers will be served. In India, food companies need special approval to launch duplicate brands, such as another cola drink or brand of rice.

**GROWTH OF SPECIAL-INTEREST GROUPS** Political action committees (PACs) lobby government officials and pressure business executives to respect the rights of consumers, women, senior citizens, minorities, and gays and lesbians. Insurance companies directly or indirectly influence the design of smoke detectors; scientific groups affect the design of spray products. Many companies have established public affairs departments to deal with such special-interest groups.

The **consumerist movement** organized citizens and government to strengthen the rights and powers of buyers in relationship to sellers. Consumerists have won the right to know the real cost of a loan, the true cost per standard unit of competing brands (unit pricing), the basic ingredients and true benefits of a product, and the nutritional quality and freshness of food.

Privacy issues and identity theft will remain public policy hot buttons as long as consumers are willing to swap personal information for customized products—from marketers they trust.[53] Consumers worry that they will be robbed or cheated; that private information will be used against them; that they will be bombarded by solicitations; and that children will be targeted by ads. Online privacy greatly concerns consumers and regulators alike. Technology now enables firms to collect all kinds of information.[54]

> Make no mistake, your personal data isn't your own. When you update your Facebook page, "Like" something on a website, apply for a credit card, click on an ad, listen to an MP3, or comment on a YouTube video, you are feeding a huge and growing beast with an insatiable appetite for your personal data, a beast that always craves more. Virtually every piece of personal information that you provide online (and much that you provide offline) will end up being bought and sold, segmented, packaged, analyzed, repackaged, and sold again.

"Marketing Insight: Watching Out for Big Brother" describes some of the data collection practices and privacy concerns that have arisen with widespread Internet adoption and use.

## Watching Out for Big Brother

The explosion of digital data created by individuals online can nearly all be collected, bought, and sold by the *personal data economy,* including "advertisers, marketers, ad networks, data brokers, website publishers, social networks, and online tracking and targeting companies." Companies know or can find your age, race, gender, height, weight, marital status, education level, political affiliation, buying habits, hobbies, health, financial concerns, vacation dreams, and more.

The thought of such widespread transparency worries consumers. Research shows more people, especially older consumers, are refusing to reveal private information online. At the same time, consumers are accepting more privacy intrusions every day, perhaps because they don't realize what information they are giving out, don't feel they have a choice, or don't think it will really matter. Many don't realize, for example, that buried in the fine print of their agreement to buy a new smart phone may be authorization to allow third-party services to track their every move. One such firm, Carrier IQ, received permission from any purchaser of an EVO 3D HTC smart phone to see every call made and when, where text messages were sent, and which Web sites were visited. Unfortunately, once data have been collected online, they can end up in unexpected places, resulting in spam or worse.

Consumers increasingly want to know where, when, how, and why they are being watched online. Another data tracking firm is Acxion, which maintains a database on about 190 million U.S. individuals and 126 million households. Its 23,000 servers process 50 trillion data transactions a year as it attempts to assemble "360-degree views" of consumers from offline, online, and mobile sources. Its customers have included banks like Wells Fargo and HSBC, investment services like E*TRADE, automakers like Toyota and Ford, and department stores like Macy's.

Can online data profiling go too far? New parents are highly lucrative customers, but with birth records public, a slew of companies all discover them at the same time. To beat them to the punch, Target studied the buying histories of women who signed up for new-baby registries at the store and found many bought large amounts of vitamin supplements during their first trimester and unscented lotion around the start of their second trimester. Target then used these purchase markers to identify women of child-bearing age who were likely to be pregnant and sent them offers and coupons for baby products timed to the stages of pregnancy and later baby needs. When the practice became known, however, some criticized the company's tactics, which had occasionally been the means of letting family members know someone in the house was expecting. Target responded by including the offers with others unrelated to pregnancy, and sales in the promoted pregnancy-related categories soared.

This episode vividly illustrates the power of database management in an Internet era, as well as the worries it can create among consumers. Politicians and government officials are discussing a "Do Not Track" option for consumers online (like the "Do Not Call" option for unsolicited phone calls). Although it is not clear how quickly legislation can be put into place, an online privacy bill that strengthens consumer rights seems inevitable. One member of the Federal Trade Commission, Julie Brill, feels data brokers should have to tell the public what data they collect, how they collect them, with whom they share them, and how they are used.

**Sources:** Avi Goldfarb and Catherine Tucker, "Shifts in Privacy Concerns," *American Economic Review: Papers & Proceedings* 102, no. 3 (2012), pp. 349–53; Avi Goldfarb and Catherine Tucker, "Online Display Advertising: Targeting and Obtrusiveness," *Marketing Science* 30 (May–June 2011), pp. 389–404, plus commentaries and rejoinder; Alessandro Acquisti, Leslie John, and George Loewenstein, "The Impact of Relative Judgments on Concern about Privacy," *Journal of Marketing Research* 49 (April 2012), pp. 160–74; Mark Sullivan, "Data Snatchers! The Booming Market for Your Online Identity," *PC World*, June 26, 2012; Charles Duhigg, "How Companies Learn Your Secrets," *New York Times*, February 16, 2012; Joshua Topolsky, "Online Tracking Is Shady—but It Doesn't Have to Be," *Washington Post*, December 11, 2011; Natasha Singer, "You for Sale: Mapping, and Sharing, the Consumer Genome," *New York Times*, June 16, 2012; Natasha Singer, "Consumer Data, but Not for Consumers," *New York Times*, July 21, 2012; Doc Searls, "The Customer as a God," *Wall Street Journal*, July 20, 2012.

# Forecasting and Demand Measurement

Understanding the marketing environment and conducting marketing research (described in Chapter 4) can help to identify marketing opportunities. The company must then measure and forecast the size, growth, and profit potential of each new opportunity. Sales forecasts prepared by marketing are used by finance to raise cash for investment and operations; by manufacturing to establish capacity and output; by purchasing to acquire the right amount of supplies; and by human resources to hire the needed workers. If the forecast is off the mark, the company will face excess or inadequate inventory. Because it's based on estimates of demand, managers need to define what they mean by market demand. DuPont's Performance Materials group knew that even when DuPont Tyvek had 70 percent of the $100 million market for air-barrier membranes, there was greater opportunity with more products and services to tap into the entire multi-billion-dollar U.S. home construction market.[55]

Target was criticized by some for its over-zealous targeting of expecting mothers.

*Source: Bloomberg via Getty Images*

## THE MEASURES OF MARKET DEMAND

Companies can prepare as many as 90 different types of demand estimates for six different product levels, five space levels, and three time periods (see Figure 3.1). Each serves a specific purpose. A company might forecast short-run demand to order raw materials, plan production, and borrow cash. It might forecast regional demand to decide whether to set up regional distribution.

There are many productive ways to break down the market:

- The **potential market** is the set of consumers with a sufficient level of interest in a market offer. However, their interest is not enough to define a market unless they also have sufficient income and access to the product.
- The **available market** is the set of consumers who have interest, income, *and* access to a particular offer. The company or government may restrict sales to certain groups; a state might ban motorcycle sales to anyone under 21. Eligible adults constitute the *qualified available market*—the set of consumers who have interest, income, access, and qualifications for the market offer.

**| Fig. 3.1 |**

Ninety Types of Demand Measurement (6 × 5 × 3)

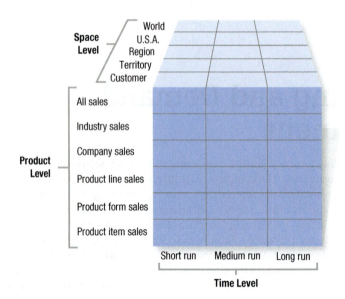

- The **target market** is the part of the qualified available market the company decides to pursue. The company might concentrate its marketing and distribution effort on the East Coast.
- The **penetrated market** is the set of consumers who are buying the company's product.

These definitions are a useful tool for market planning. If the company isn't satisfied with its current sales, it can try to attract a larger percentage of buyers from its target market. It can lower the qualifications for potential buyers. It can expand its available market by opening distribution elsewhere or lowering its price, or it can reposition itself in the minds of its customers.

# A VOCABULARY FOR DEMAND MEASUREMENT

The major concepts in demand measurement are market demand and company demand. Within each, we distinguish among a demand function, a sales forecast, and a potential.

**MARKET DEMAND**  The marketer's first step in evaluating marketing opportunities is to estimate total market demand. **Market demand** for a product is the total volume that would be bought by a defined customer group in a defined geographical area in a defined time period in a defined marketing environment under a defined marketing program.

Market demand is not a fixed number, but rather a function of the stated conditions. For this reason, we call it the *market demand function*. Its dependence on underlying conditions is illustrated in Figure 3.2(a). The horizontal axis shows different possible levels of industry marketing expenditure in a given time period. The vertical axis shows the resulting demand level. The curve represents the estimated market demand associated with varying levels of marketing expenditure.

Some base sales—called the *market minimum* and labeled $Q_1$ in the figure—would take place without any demand-stimulating expenditures. Higher marketing expenditures would yield higher levels of demand, first at an increasing rate, then at a decreasing rate. Take fruit juices. Given the indirect competition they face from other types of beverages, we would expect increased marketing expenditures to help fruit juice products stand out and increase demand and sales. Marketing expenditures beyond a certain level would not stimulate much further demand, suggesting an upper limit called the *market potential* and labeled $Q_2$ in the figure.

The distance between the market minimum and the market potential shows the overall *marketing sensitivity of demand*. We can think of two extreme types of markets, the expansible and the nonexpansible. An *expansible market*, such as the market for racquetball playing, is very much affected in size by the level of industry marketing expenditures. In terms of Figure 3.2(a), the distance between $Q_1$ and $Q_2$ is relatively large. A *nonexpansible market*—for example, the market for weekly trash or garbage removal—is *not* much affected by the level of marketing expenditures; the distance between $Q_1$ and $Q_2$ is relatively small. Organizations selling in a nonexpansible market must accept the market's size—the level of *primary demand* for the product class—and direct their efforts toward winning a larger **market share** for their product, that is, a higher level of selective demand for their product.

It pays to compare the current and potential levels of market demand. The result is the **market-penetration index**. A low index indicates substantial growth potential for all the firms. A high index suggests it will be

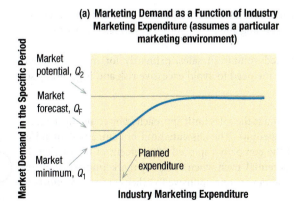

(a) Marketing Demand as a Function of Industry Marketing Expenditure (assumes a particular marketing environment)

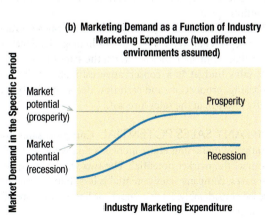

(b) Marketing Demand as a Function of Industry Marketing Expenditure (two different environments assumed)

| **Fig. 3.2** |

Market Demand Functions

expensive to attract the few remaining prospects. Generally, price competition increases and margins fall when the market-penetration index is already high.

Comparing current and potential market shares yields a firm's **share-penetration index**. If this index is low, the company can greatly expand its share. Holding it back could be low brand awareness, low availability, benefit deficiencies, or high price. A firm should calculate the share-penetration increases from removing each factor to see which investments produce the greatest improvement.[56]

Remember that the market demand function is not a picture of market demand over time. Rather, it shows alternate current forecasts of market demand associated with possible levels of industry marketing effort.

**MARKET FORECAST** Only one level of industry marketing expenditure will actually occur. The market demand corresponding to this level is called the **market forecast**.

**MARKET POTENTIAL** The market forecast shows *expected* market demand, not maximum market demand. For the latter, we need to visualize the level of market demand resulting from a very high level of industry marketing expenditure, where further increases in marketing effort would have little effect. **Market potential** is the limit approached by market demand as industry marketing expenditures approach infinity for a given marketing environment.

The phrase "for a given market environment" is crucial. Consider the market potential for automobiles. It's higher during prosperity than during a recession, as illustrated in Figure 3.2(b). Market analysts distinguish between the position of the market demand function and movement along it. Companies cannot do anything about the position of the market demand function, which is determined by the marketing environment. However, they influence their particular location on the function when they decide how much to spend on marketing.

Companies interested in market potential have a special interest in the **product-penetration percentage**, the percentage of ownership or use of a product or service in a population. The lower the product-penetration percentage, the higher the market potential, although this also assumes everyone will eventually be in the market for every product.

**COMPANY DEMAND** **Company demand** is the company's estimated share of market demand at alternative levels of company marketing effort in a given time period. It depends on how the company's products, services, prices, and communications are perceived relative to the competitors'. Other things equal, the company's market share depends on the relative scale and effectiveness of its market expenditures. As noted previously, marketing model builders have developed sales response functions to measure how a company's sales are affected by its marketing expenditure level, marketing mix, and marketing effectiveness.[57]

**COMPANY SALES FORECAST** Once marketers have estimated company demand, their next task is to choose a level of marketing effort. The **company sales forecast** is the expected level of company sales based on a chosen marketing plan and an assumed marketing environment.

We represent the company sales forecast graphically with sales on the vertical axis and marketing effort on the horizontal axis, as in Figure 3.2. We often hear that the company should develop its marketing plan on the basis of its sales forecast. This forecast-to-plan sequence is valid if *forecast* means an estimate of national economic activity or if company demand is nonexpansible. The sequence is not valid, however, where market demand is expansible or where *forecast* means an estimate of company sales. The company sales forecast does not establish a basis for deciding what to spend on marketing. On the contrary, the sales forecast is the result of an assumed marketing expenditure plan.

Two other concepts are important here. A **sales quota** is the sales goal set for a product line, company division, or sales representative. It is primarily a managerial device for defining and stimulating sales effort, often set slightly higher than estimated sales to stretch the sales force's effort.

A **sales budget** is a conservative estimate of the expected volume of sales, primarily for making current purchasing, production, and cash flow decisions. It's based on the need to avoid excessive risk and is generally set slightly lower than the sales forecast.

**COMPANY SALES POTENTIAL** **Company sales potential** is the sales limit approached by company demand as company marketing effort increases relative to that of competitors. The absolute limit of company demand is, of course, the market potential. The two would be equal if the company captured 100 percent of the market. In most cases, company sales potential is less than the market potential, even when company marketing expenditures increase considerably. Each competitor has a hard core of loyal buyers unresponsive to other companies' efforts to woo them.

# ESTIMATING CURRENT DEMAND

We are now ready to examine practical methods for estimating current market demand. Marketing executives want to estimate total market potential, area market potential, and total industry sales and market shares.

**TOTAL MARKET POTENTIAL** **Total market potential** is the maximum sales available to all firms in an industry during a given period, under a given level of industry marketing effort and environmental conditions. A common way to estimate total market potential is to multiply the potential number of buyers by the average quantity each purchases and then by the price.

If 100 million people buy books each year and the average book buyer buys three books a year at an average price of $20 each, then the total market potential for books is $6 billion (100 million × 3 × $20). The most difficult component to estimate is the number of buyers. We can always start with the total population in the nation, say, 314 million people. Next we eliminate groups that obviously would not buy the product. Assume illiterate people and children under 12 don't buy books and constitute 20 percent of the population. This means 80 percent of the population, or 251 million people, is in the potential pool. Further research might tell us that people of low income and low education rarely buy books, and they constitute more than 30 percent of the potential pool. Eliminating them, we arrive at a prospect pool of approximately 175.7 million book buyers. We use this number to calculate total market potential.

A variation on this method is the *chain-ratio method*, which multiplies a base number by several adjusting percentages. Suppose a brewery is interested in estimating the market potential for a new light beer especially designed to accompany food. It can make an estimate with the following calculation:

$$
\begin{array}{l}
\text{Demand} \\
\text{for the} \\
\text{new} \\
\text{light beer}
\end{array}
= \text{Population} \times
\begin{array}{l}
\text{Personal} \\
\text{discretionary} \\
\text{income} \\
\text{per} \\
\text{capita}
\end{array}
\times
\begin{array}{l}
\text{Average} \\
\text{percentage of} \\
\text{discretionary} \\
\text{income} \\
\text{spent} \\
\text{on food}
\end{array}
\times
\begin{array}{l}
\text{Average} \\
\text{percentage of} \\
\text{amount spent} \\
\text{on food that is} \\
\text{spent on} \\
\text{beverages}
\end{array}
\times
\begin{array}{l}
\text{Average} \\
\text{percentage of} \\
\text{amount spent} \\
\text{on beverages} \\
\text{that is spent} \\
\text{on alcoholic} \\
\text{beverages}
\end{array}
\times
\begin{array}{l}
\text{Average} \\
\text{percentage of} \\
\text{amount spent} \\
\text{on alcoholic} \\
\text{beverages that} \\
\text{is spent on beer}
\end{array}
\times
\begin{array}{l}
\text{Expected} \\
\text{percentage of} \\
\text{amount spent} \\
\text{on beer that} \\
\text{will be spent on} \\
\text{light beer}
\end{array}
$$

**AREA MARKET POTENTIAL** Because companies must allocate their marketing budget optimally among their best territories, they need to estimate the market potential of different cities, states, and nations. Two major methods are the market-buildup method, used primarily by business marketers, and the multiple-factor index method, used primarily by consumer marketers.

*Market-Buildup Method* The **market-buildup method** calls for identifying all the potential buyers in each market and estimating their potential purchases. It produces accurate results if we have a list of all potential buyers and a good estimate of what each will buy. Unfortunately, this information is not always easy to gather.

Consider a machine-tool company that wants to estimate the area market potential for its wood lathe in the Boston area. Its first step is to identify all potential buyers of wood lathes in the area, primarily manufacturing establishments that shape or ream wood as part of their operations. The company could compile a list from a directory of all manufacturing establishments in the area. Then it could estimate the number of lathes each industry might purchase, based on the number of lathes per thousand employees or per $1 million of sales in that industry.

An efficient method of estimating area market potentials makes use of the *North American Industry Classification System (NAICS)*, developed by the U.S. Bureau of the Census in conjunction with the Canadian and Mexican governments.[58] The NAICS classifies all manufacturing into 20 major industry sectors and further breaks each sector into a six-digit, hierarchical structure as follows.

| | |
|---|---|
| 51 | Industry sector (information) |
| 513 | Industry subsector (broadcasting and telecommunications) |
| 5133 | Industry group (telecommunications) |
| 51332 | Industry (wireless telecommunications carriers, except satellite) |
| 513321 | National industry (U.S. paging) |

For each six-digit NAICS number, a company can purchase business directories that provide complete company profiles of millions of establishments, subclassified by location, number of employees, annual sales, and net worth.

To use the NAICS, the lathe manufacturer must first determine the six-digit NAICS codes that represent products whose manufacturers are likely to require lathe machines. To get a full picture of these, the company can (1) identify past customers' NAICS codes; (2) go through the NAICS manual and check off all the six-digit industries that might have an interest in lathes; and (3) mail questionnaires to a wide range of companies inquiring about their interest in wood lathes.

The company's next task is to select an appropriate base for estimating the number of lathes each industry will use. Suppose customer industry sales are the most appropriate base. Once the company estimates the rate of lathe ownership relative to the customer industry's sales, it can compute the market potential.

*Multiple-Factor Index Method*  Like business marketers, consumer companies also need to estimate area market potentials, but because their customers are too numerous to list, they commonly use a straightforward index. A drug manufacturer might assume the market potential for drugs is directly related to population size. If the state of Virginia has 2.55 percent of the U.S. population, Virginia might be a market for 2.55 percent of total drugs sold.

A single factor is rarely a complete indicator of sales opportunity. Regional drug sales are also influenced by per capita income and the number of physicians per 10,000 people. Thus, it makes sense to develop a multiple-factor index and assign each factor a specific weight. Suppose Virginia has 2.00 percent of U.S. disposable personal income, 1.96 percent of U.S. retail sales, and 2.28 percent of U.S. population, and the respective weights for these factors are 0.5, 0.3, and 0.2. The buying-power index for Virginia is then 2.04 [0.5(2.00) + 0.3(1.96) + 0.2(2.28)]. Thus, 2.04 percent of the nation's drug sales (not 2.28 percent) might be expected to take place in Virginia.

The weights in the buying-power index are somewhat arbitrary, and companies can assign others if appropriate. A manufacturer might adjust the market potential for additional factors, such as competitors' presence, local promotional costs, seasonal factors, and market idiosyncrasies.

Many companies compute area indexes to allocate marketing resources. Suppose the drug company is reviewing the six cities listed in Table 3.5. The first two columns show its percentage of U.S. brand and category sales in these six cities. Column 3 shows the **brand development index (BDI)**, the index of brand sales to category sales. Seattle has a BDI of 114 because the brand is relatively more developed than the category in Seattle. Portland's BDI is 65, which means the brand is relatively underdeveloped there.

Normally, the lower the BDI, the higher the market opportunity, in that there is room to grow the brand. Other marketers would argue instead that marketing funds should go into the brand's *strongest* markets, where it might be important to reinforce loyalty or more easily capture additional brand share. Investment decisions should be based on the potential to grow brand sales.

| TABLE 3.5 | Calculating the Brand Development Index (BDI) | | |
|---|---|---|---|
| **Territory** | **(a) Percent of U.S. Brand** Sales | **(b) Percent of U.S. Category** Sales | **BDI** (a ÷ b) × 100 |
| Seattle | 3.09 | 2.71 | 114 |
| Portland | 6.74 | 10.41 | 65 |
| Boston | 3.49 | 3.85 | 91 |
| Toledo | .97 | .81 | 120 |
| Chicago | 1.13 | .81 | 140 |
| Baltimore | 3.12 | 3.00 | 104 |

Marketers can now target consumers right down to their zip code, neighborhood, or individual households.

Feeling it was underperforming in a high-potential market, Anheuser-Busch targeted the growing Hispanic population in Texas with a number of special marketing activities. Cross-promotions with Budweiser and Clamato tomato clam cocktail (to mix the popular Michiladas drink), sponsorship of the Esta Noche Toca concert series, and support of Latin music acts with three-on-three soccer tournaments helped drive higher sales. Anheuser-Busch later introduced Chelada with pre-mixed Budweiser or Bud Light and Clamato.[59]

After the company decides on the city-by-city allocation of its budget, it can refine each allocation down to census tracts or zip+4 code centers. *Census tracts* are small, locally defined statistical areas in metropolitan areas and some other counties. They generally have stable boundaries and a population of about 4,000. Zip+4 code centers (designed by the U.S. Postal Service) are a little larger than neighborhoods. Data on population size, median family income, and other characteristics are available for these geographical units. Using other sources such as loyalty card data, Mediabrands's Geomentum targets "hyper-local" sectors of zip codes, city blocks, and even individual households with ad messages delivered via interactive TV, zoned editions of newspapers, Yellow Pages, outdoor media, and local Internet searches.[60]

**INDUSTRY SALES AND MARKET SHARES** Besides estimating total potential and area potential, a company needs to know the actual industry sales taking place in its market. This means identifying competitors and estimating their sales.

The industry trade association will often collect and publish total industry sales, although it usually does not list individual company sales separately. With this information, however, each company can evaluate its own performance against the industry's. If a company's sales are increasing by 5 percent a year and industry sales are increasing by 10 percent, the company is losing its relative standing in the industry.

Another way to estimate sales is to buy reports from a marketing research firm that audits total sales and brand sales. Nielsen Media Research audits retail sales in various supermarket and drugstore product categories. A company can purchase this information and compare its performance to the total industry or any competitor to see whether it is gaining or losing share, overall or brand by brand. Because distributors typically will not supply information about how much of competitors' products they are selling, business-to-business marketers operate with less knowledge of their market share results.

## ESTIMATING FUTURE DEMAND

The few products or services that lend themselves to easy forecasting generally enjoy an absolute level or a fairly constant trend and competition that is either nonexistent (public utilities) or stable (pure oligopolies). In most markets, in contrast, good forecasting is a key factor in success.

Companies commonly prepare a macroeconomic forecast first, followed by an industry forecast, followed by a company sales forecast. The macroeconomic forecast projects inflation, unemployment, interest rates, consumer spending, business investment, government expenditures, net exports, and other variables. The end result is a forecast of gross domestic product (GDP), which the firm uses, along with other environmental indicators, to forecast industry sales. The company derives its sales forecast by assuming it will win a certain market share.

How do firms develop forecasts? They may create their own or buy forecasts from outside sources such as marketing research firms, which interview customers, distributors, and other knowledgeable parties. Specialized forecasting firms produce long-range forecasts of particular macroenvironmental components, such as population, natural resources, and technology. Examples are IHS Global Insight (a merger of Data Resources and Wharton Econometric Forecasting Associates), Forrester Research, and the Gartner Group. Futurist research firms such as the Institute for the Future, Hudson Institute, and the Futures Group produce speculative scenarios.

All forecasts are built on one of three information bases: what people say, what people do, or what people have done. Using what people say requires surveying buyers' intentions, composites of sales force opinions, and expert opinion. Building a forecast on what people do means putting the product into a test market to measure buyer response. To use the final basis—what people have done—firms analyze records of past buying behavior or use time-series analysis or statistical demand analysis.

**SURVEY OF BUYERS' INTENTIONS** Forecasting is the art of anticipating what buyers are likely to do under a given set of conditions. For major consumer durables such as appliances, research organizations conduct periodic surveys of consumer buying intentions, ask questions like *Do you intend to buy an automobile within the next six months?*, and put the answers on a **purchase probability scale:**

| 0.00 | 0.20 | 0.40 | 0.60 | 0.80 | 1.00 |
|------|------|------|------|------|------|
| No chance | Slight possibility | Fair possibility | Good possibility | High possibility | Certain |

Surveys also inquire into consumers' present and future personal finances and expectations about the economy. They combine bits of information into a consumer confidence measure (Conference Board) or a consumer sentiment measure (Survey Research Center of the University of Michigan).

For business buying, research firms can carry out buyer-intention surveys for plant, equipment, and materials, usually falling within a 10 percent margin of error. These surveys are useful in estimating demand for industrial products, consumer durables, product purchases where advanced planning is required, and new products. Their value increases to the extent that buyers are few, the cost of reaching them is low, and they have clear intentions they willingly disclose and implement.

**COMPOSITE OF SALES FORCE OPINIONS** When interviewing buyers is impractical, the company may ask its sales representatives to estimate their future sales. Few companies use these estimates without making some adjustments, however. Sales representatives might be pessimistic or optimistic, they might not know how their company's marketing plans will influence future sales in their territory, and they might deliberately underestimate demand so the company will set a low sales quota. To encourage better estimating, the company could offer incentives or assistance, such as information about marketing plans or past forecasts compared with actual sales.

Sales force forecasts do yield a number of benefits. Sales reps might have better insight into developing trends than any other group, and forecasting might give them greater confidence in their sales quotas and more incentive to achieve them. A "grassroots" forecasting procedure provides detailed estimates broken down by product, territory, customer, and sales rep.

**EXPERT OPINION** Companies can also obtain forecasts from experts, including dealers, distributors, suppliers, marketing consultants, and trade associations. Dealer estimates are subject to the same strengths and weaknesses as sales force estimates. Many companies buy economic and industry forecasts from well-known economic-forecasting firms that have more data available and more forecasting expertise.

Occasionally, companies will invite a group of experts to prepare a forecast. The experts exchange views and produce an estimate as a group (*group-discussion method*) or individually, in which case another analyst might combine the results into a single estimate (*pooling of individual estimates*). Further rounds of estimating and refining follow (the Delphi method).[61]

**PAST-SALES ANALYSIS** Firms can develop sales forecasts on the basis of past sales. *Time-series analysis* breaks past time series into four components (trend, cycle, seasonal, and erratic) and projects them into the future. *Exponential smoothing* projects the next period's sales by combining an average of past sales and the most recent sales, giving more weight to the latter. *Statistical demand analysis* measures the impact of a set of causal factors (such as income, marketing expenditures, and price) on the sales level. Finally, *econometric analysis* builds sets of equations that describe a system and statistically derives the different parameters that make up the equations statistically.

**MARKET-TEST METHOD** When buyers don't plan their purchases carefully or experts are unavailable or unreliable, a direct-market test can help forecast new-product sales or established product sales in a new distribution channel or territory. (We discuss market testing in detail in Chapter 15.)

# Summary

1. To carry out their analysis, planning, implementation, and control responsibilities, marketing managers need a marketing information system (MIS) to assess information needs, develop the needed information, and distribute it in a timely manner.

2. An MIS has three components: (a) an internal records system, which includes information about the order-to-payment cycle and sales information systems; (b) a marketing intelligence system, a set of procedures to obtain everyday information about the marketing environment; and (c) a marketing research system that allows for the systematic design, collection, analysis, and reporting of data and findings relevant to a specific marketing situation.

3. Marketers find many opportunities by identifying trends (directions or sequences of events that have some momentum and durability) and megatrends (major social, economic, political, and technological changes that have long-lasting influence).

4. Within the rapidly changing global picture, marketers must monitor six major environmental forces: demographic, economic, social-cultural, natural, technological, and political-legal.

5. In the demographic environment, marketers must be aware of worldwide population growth; changing mixes of age, ethnic composition, and educational levels; the rise of nontraditional families; and large geographic shifts in population.

6. In the economic arena, marketers need to focus on income distribution and levels of savings, debt, and credit availability.

7. In the social-cultural arena, marketers must understand people's views of themselves, others, organizations, society, nature, and the universe. Their products must correspond to society's core and secondary values and address the needs of different subcultures within a society.

8. Acknowledging the public's increased concern about the health of the natural environment, marketers are embracing sustainability and green marketing programs.

9. In the technological arena, marketers should take account of the accelerating pace of technological change, opportunities for innovation, varying R&D budgets, and the increased governmental regulation brought about by technological change.

10. In the political-legal environment, marketers must work within the many laws regulating business practices and with various special-interest groups.

11. To estimate current demand, companies attempt to determine total market potential, area market potential, industry sales, and market share. To estimate future demand, companies survey buyers' intentions, solicit their sales force's input, gather expert opinions, analyze past sales, or engage in market testing. Mathematical models, advanced statistical techniques, and computerized data collection procedures are essential to all types of demand and sales forecasting.

MyMarketingLab

Go to **mymktlab.com** to complete the problems marked with this icon ⭐ as well as for additional Auto-graded and Assisted-graded writing questions.

# Applications

## Marketing Debate

### Is Consumer Behavior More a Function of a Person's Age or Generation?

How much do consumers change over time? Some marketers who target certain age groups maintain that age differences are critical and that the needs and wants of a 25-year-old in 2015 are not that different from those of a 25-year-old in 1980. Others argue that cohort and generation effects are critical and that marketing programs must therefore suit the times.

**Take a position:** Age differences are fundamentally more important than cohort effects *versus* Cohort effects can dominate age differences.

## Marketing Discussion

### Age Targeting

⭐ What brands and products do you feel successfully speak to you and effectively target your age group? Why? Which ones do not? What could they do better?

## Marketing Excellence

### >> Microsoft

Microsoft is the world's most successful software company. Bill Gates and Paul Allen founded it in 1975 with the original mission of having "a computer on every desk and in every home, running Microsoft software." Today, Microsoft is the fifth most valuable company in the world and has a brand value of $61.2 billion.

In the early 1980s, Microsoft developed the DOS operating system for IBM computers. The company leveraged this initial success to sell software to other manufacturers, quickly becoming a major player in the industry. Initial advertising efforts communicated the company's range of products, from DOS to Excel and Windows, and unified them under the Microsoft brand.

Microsoft went public in 1986 and grew tremendously over the next decade as the Windows operating system and Microsoft Office took off. In 1990, Microsoft launched Windows 3.0, a completely revamped version of its operating system, including applications like File Manager and Program Manager that are still used today. It was an instant success; Microsoft sold more than 10 million copies of the software within two years, a phenomenal accomplishment in those days. In addition, Windows 3.0 became the first operating system to be preinstalled on certain PCs, marking another major milestone for the industry and for Microsoft.

Throughout the 1990s, Microsoft's communication efforts convinced businesses not only that its software was the best choice but also that it should be upgraded frequently. Microsoft spent millions in magazine advertising and received endorsements from the top computer magazines in the industry, making Microsoft Windows and Office the must-have software of its time. The 1998 slogan "Where Do You Want to Go Today?" promoted not individual Microsoft products like Windows 98 but rather the company itself, communicating that Microsoft could help empower companies and consumers alike.

During the mid-1990s, Microsoft entered the notorious "browser wars" as companies struggled to find their place during the Internet boom. Realizing what a good product Netscape had in its 1995 Navigator browser, Microsoft launched its own, Internet Explorer later the same year. By 1997, Explorer had grabbed 18 percent of the market.

Over the next five years, Microsoft took three major steps to overtake Netscape. First, it bundled Internet Explorer with its Office product, which included Excel, Word, and PowerPoint. This meant that consumers who wanted MS Office automatically became Internet Explorer users as well. Second, Microsoft partnered with AOL, which opened the doors to 5 million new consumers almost overnight. Third, Microsoft used its deep pockets to ensure that Internet Explorer was available free, essentially "cutting off Netscape's air supply." By 2002, Netscape's market share had fallen to a meek 4 percent.

Microsoft's fight to become the browser leader was not without controversy; some perceived that the company was monopolizing the industry. As a result, Microsoft faced antitrust charges in 1998 and numerous lawsuits based on its marketing tactics. Charges aside, the company's stock took off, peaking in 1999 at $60 per share. Microsoft continued to release new products, including Windows 2000 in 2000 and Windows XP in 2001. It also launched Xbox in 2001, marking its entrance into the multibillion-dollar gaming industry.

Over the next several years, Microsoft's stock price tumbled by more than $40 a share as consumers waited for the next operating system to be released. During this time, Apple made a strong comeback with consumer-friendly products like Mac computers, iPods, iPhones, and iTunes. Apple also launched a successful marketing campaign titled "Get a Mac" that featured a smart, creative, easygoing Mac character alongside a geeky, virus-prone, uptight PC character. Apple's campaign successfully converted many consumers and tarnished Microsoft's brand image.

In 2007, Microsoft launched the Vista operating system to great expectations; however, it was plagued by bugs and problems and the company's stock and image continued to slide, helped by the worldwide recession of 2008–2009. In response, Microsoft created a campaign titled "Windows. Life Without Walls" to help turn its image around. Its new message—that computers with Microsoft software were more cost-effective than the competition—resonated well in the recession. Microsoft also launched a series of commercials that boasted, "I'm a PC" and featured a wide variety of individuals who prided themselves on being PC owners, hoping to improve employee morale and customer loyalty.

In 2009, Microsoft launched Windows 7, an improved operating system, with the campaign "Windows 7 was my idea." Four years later, it was operating more than 30 stores like Apple's across the United States and Canada. Jonathan Adashek, general manager of Communications Strategy, explained, "We've welcomed more than 15 million customers and counting so far, and have learned a lot from them. Having this direct connection to our customers has really helped us better understand their tech needs." Travis Walter, general manager of Microsoft's International and New Store Formats, agreed, "In person, you get a very different experience and it's one we've been very delighted to provide. When you see our technology in person—when you can touch and feel it—a light goes off."

After the recession came to an end, Microsoft's image and stock started to recover, thanks to the success of its retail stores, effective marketing, and a wide range of new product launches. Microsoft went after Google's dominant position in the search marketplace, for instance, with a search engine called Bing, and it entered the growing mobile industry with its Windows Phone mobile operating system. The company's 2011 expansion into smart phones surprised many analysts, but Microsoft hoped the smart phone and Windows Phone mobile OS would forge a strong connection with its consumers around the world. It continued its innovation momentum in 2012 with the launch of Windows 8, Windows 8 Phone, and a computer called Surface Tablet. The tablet impressed consumers with a detachable keyboard that also served as its protective cover.

Today, Microsoft offers a wide range of software, mobile, and home entertainment products. Its most profitable products continue to be Microsoft Windows and Microsoft Office, which bring in approximately 80 percent of its $86 billion in annual revenue.

### Questions

1. Evaluate Microsoft's product and marketing evolution over the years. What has the company done well, and where did it falter?

2. Evaluate Microsoft's recent expansions into areas such as search engines and smart phones. Do you think these are good areas of growth for Microsoft? Why or why not?

**Sources:** Interbrand, "2014 Best Global Brands Report," *www.interbrand.com*; Stuart Elliot, "Microsoft Takes a User-Friendly Approach to Selling Its Image in a New Global Campaign," *New York Times*, November 11, 1994; "Todd Bishop, "The Rest of the Motto," *Seattle Post Intelligencer*, September 23, 2004; Devin Leonard, "Hey PC, Who Taught You to Fight Back?" *New York Times*, August 30, 2009; Suzanne Vranica and Robert A. Guth, "Microsoft Enlists Jerry Seinfeld in Its Ad Battle Against Apple," *Wall Street Journal*, August 21, 2008, p. A1; Stuart Elliott, "Echoing the Campaign of a Rival, Microsoft Aims to Redefine 'I'm a PC,'" *New York Times*, September 18, 2008, p. C4; John Furguson, "From Cola Wars to Computer Wars—Microsoft Misses Again," *BN Branding*, April 4, 2009; Microsoft press release, "Microsoft Retail Stores Maturation: Going Behind the Scenes," November 8, 2012.

## Marketing Excellence

### >> Walmart

Walmart, the giant chain of discount stores, is the third-largest company in the world, with more than $473 billion in revenue and 2.2 million associates (or employees). Its phenomenal success story began in 1962 when Sam Walton opened his first discount store in Rogers, Arkansas. Walton sold the same products as his competitors but kept prices lower by reducing his profit margin. His customers quickly caught on, and the company took off almost immediately. Walton's EDLP (Every Day Low Price) strategy remains the foundation of Walmart's success today. Through the company's economies of scale, Walmart is able to offer customers top brand-name products for the lowest possible price.

Walmart expanded throughout the United States in the 1970s and 1980s by acquiring many of its competitors and opening new stores. The first Walmart Supercenter—a discount store beefed up with food outlets and other amenities such as an optical center, photo lab, and hair salon—opened in 1988. By 1990, Walmart had become the nation's number-one retailer, with $32 billion in revenue and stores in 33 states. The company's international expansion began with a store outside Mexico City in 1991 and has grown to more than 5,600 international locations, some under a different brand name.

Walmart thrives on three basic beliefs and values: "Respect for the Individual," "Service to Our Customers," and "Striving for Excellence." Sam Walton's original 10-foot rule—"I promise that whenever I come within 10 feet of a customer, I will look him in the eye, greet him, and ask if I can help him."—still governs today, embodied by the "greeters" at the front door. In addition, Walmart embraces the communities it enters, develops strong local relationships, and works hard to foster its brand image in the area. The company donates significant amounts of money to local charities through its "Good Works" program, hires local individuals, and purchases food from local farmers.

Walmart's marketing strategy has evolved over the years. Early efforts were based on word of mouth, positive PR, and aggressive store expansion. In 1992, Walmart introduced its well-known tagline "Always Low Prices. Always," which effectively communicated the company's core brand promise and resonated with millions. In 1996, Walmart launched its price rollback campaign featuring the familiar yellow smiley face as the star of the campaign. The company's stock soared 1173 percent in the 1990s.

Walmart hit a few bumps in the road as it entered the 21st century. Critics protested its entry into small communities. Researchers at Iowa State University found that within 10 years of a new Walmart opening, as many as half the small stores in town went out of business. Walmart also faced multiple lawsuits from employees who complained about poor work conditions, exposure to health hazards, and pay below minimum wage. In some cases, employees said Walmart failed to pay for overtime, prevented them from taking rest or lunch breaks, and discriminated against women. These problems led to a very high turnover rate in the 2000s and an abundance of negative media coverage. According to one Walmart survey, 70 percent of employees left the company within the first year of employment due to lack of recognition and inadequate pay.

From 2000 to 2005, Walmart's stock price fell 27 percent, and it remained low through 2007. Negative backlash, combined with increased competition, contributed to the decline. Target, for example, reemerged on the retail scene with revamped stores, merchandise, and marketing strategy, all of which appealed to the top tier of discount shoppers. Target stores were well lit, and their wider, cleaner aisles displayed merchandise better. Even Target's television commercials featured more attractive models and trendier clothes from high-end designers. One analyst stated, "Target tends to have more upscale customers who don't feel the effects of gasoline prices and other economic factors as much as Walmart's core customers might." During the mid-2000s, Target outperformed Walmart in same-store sales growth and profit growth. In addition, Walmart lost the exclusive rights to use the smiley face in its marketing campaign.

Walmart launched a series of new initiatives to help improve sales and its image. First, it introduced a highly successful $4 generic drug campaign, a program eventually copied by Target. Walmart also launched several environmentally friendly initiatives such as constructing new buildings from recycled materials, cutting transportation costs and energy usage, and encouraging customers to buy more green products. Next, the company implemented a massive store remodeling effort called Project Impact. Stores ended up cleaner, aisles were less cluttered, and merchandise became easier to reach.

Finally, Walmart replaced its long-running slogan "Always Low Prices" with "Save Money. Live Better." Television commercials went beyond the EDLP message and highlighted other positive contributions, including Walmart's improved energy costs, 401(k) (retirement) savings, employee health care coverage, and family savings. Walmart also used the new campaign to highlight its unique product mix and low prices and to attract consumers hurt by the recession. Same-store sales rose, and the company's stock price improved during the recession. Analyst believed Walmart's product mix—45 percent consumables (food, beauty, health items)—was better fitted for a poor economy than Target's—20 percent consumables and 40 percent home and apparel products. One analyst explained, "Walmart sells what you need to have as opposed to what you want to have."

After the recession, Walmart sought new strategies to maintain its momentum and expand its consumer base. After decades of making its stores bigger, it began launching smaller-format stores—Neighborhood Markets of less than 50,000 square feet and Walmart Express shops of about 10,000 square feet—to fend off the growing dollar-store chains. Walmart also increased its presence on social media to help connect with its consumers, gain feedback, and build loyalty.

Today, Walmart has stores in 27 international markets and serves more than 250 million customers a week through Walmart Supercenters, Discount Stores, Neighborhood Markets, and Sam's Club warehouses.

## Questions

1. Evaluate the evolution of Walmart's marketing campaign and tagline over the years. What does the company continue to do well? What are the pros and cons of its most recent strategic marketing plan?

2. Walmart performs very well when the economy turns sour. How can it protect itself when the economy is on the rise? Explain.

**Sources:** Dave Goldiner, "Exxon Tops Wal-Mart on 2009 Fortune 500 List," *New York Daily News,* April 20, 2009; "Wal-Mart Seeks Smiley Face Rights," *BBC News,* August 5, 2006; David Ng, "Wal-Mart vs. Target," *Forbes,* December 13, 2004; Michael Barbaro, "A New Weapon for Wal-Mart: A War Room," *New York Times,* November 1, 2005; Kenneth E. Stone, "Impact of the Wal-Mart Phenomenon on Rural Communities," *Increasing Understanding of Public Problems and Policies* (Chicago: Farm Foundation, 1997), pp. 189–200; Suzanne Kapner, "Wal-mart Enters the Ad Age," CNNMoney.com, August 17, 2008; Jack Neff, "Why Walmart Is Getting Serious About Marketing," *Advertising Age,* June 8, 2009; Sean Gregory, "Wal-Mart's Project Impact: A Move to Crush Competition," *Time,* September 9, 2009; "Store Wars: When Wal-Mart Comes to Town," *PBS,* February 24, 2007; Sean Gregory, "Wal-Mart vs. Target: No Contest in the Recession," *Time,* March 14, 2009; Andria Cheng, "Corporate News: Wal-Mart Lays Out Strategy," *Wall Street Journal,* October 11, 2012, B.8; www.walmart.com.

## In This Chapter, We Will Address the Following **Questions**

1. What is the scope of marketing research? (p. 99)

2. What steps are involved in conducting good marketing research? (p. 102)

3. What are the best metrics for measuring marketing productivity? (p. 115)

Samsung uses marketing research to sharpen the launch of its new products.

*Source: ASSOCIATED PRESS*

# 4  Conducting Marketing Research

**To make the best possible tactical decisions in the short run and strategic decisions** in the long run, marketers need timely, accurate, and actionable information about consumers, competition, and their brands. Discovering a marketing insight and understanding its implications can often lead to a successful product launch or spur the growth of a brand. It is especially important to stay tuned in online.[1]

 *In launching its new Galaxy S III smart phone, Samsung faced a formidable opponent in Apple. To gain the upper hand, Samsung sifted through hundreds of thousands of tweets and online conversations to uncover recurring negative comments about the iPhone. One ad in its new campaign mocked Apple fanatics eagerly waiting in line for the latest iPhone model. With a tagline "The Next Big Thing Is Already Here," the ad showcased features such as screen size and NFC file-swapping technology where Samsung had an advantage. It ended with the clever twist that the Samsung phone user in the line—whose phone had all the features the Apple users were hoping for—was just saving a spot for his parents. A huge hit online, the ad attracted millions of YouTube downloads. The TV ad was a follow-up to an earlier print ad contrasting a long list of Galaxy S III features with a much smaller list for the iPhone. It also poked fun at Apple and its Genius retail employees, adding the tagline "It Doesn't Take a Genius."*

**In this chapter, we review** the scope of marketing research and the steps involved in the marketing research process. We also consider how marketers can develop effective metrics for measuring marketing productivity.

# The Scope of Marketing Research

Marketing managers often commission formal marketing studies of specific problems and opportunities, like a market survey, a product-preference test, a sales forecast by region, or an advertising evaluation. It's the job of the marketing researcher to produce insight to help the marketing manager's decision making. Formally, the American Marketing Association says:[2]

> **Marketing research** is the function that links the consumer, customer, and public to the marketer through information—information used to identify and define marketing opportunities and problems; generate, refine, and evaluate marketing actions; monitor marketing performance; and improve understanding of marketing as a process. Marketing research specifies the information required to address these issues, designs the method for collecting information, manages and implements the data collection process, analyzes the results, and communicates the findings and their implications.

## IMPORTANCE OF MARKETING INSIGHTS

Marketing research is all about generating insights. **Marketing insights** provide diagnostic information about how and why we observe certain effects in the marketplace and what that means to marketers.[3]

Good marketing insights often form the basis of successful marketing programs.

- When an extensive consumer research study of U.S. retail shoppers by Walmart revealed that the store's key competitive advantages were the functional benefit of "offers low prices" and the emotional benefit of "makes me feel like a smart shopper," its marketers used those insights to develop their "Save Money, Live Better" campaign.[4]
- When marketing research showed that consumers viewed Walgreens largely as a convenience store with a pharmacy in the back, the company took steps to reposition itself as a premium health care brand, putting more emphasis on its wellness offerings such as its walk-in clinics.[5]

Gaining marketing insights is crucial for marketing success. To improve the marketing of its $3 billion Pantene hair care brand, Procter & Gamble conducted a deep dive into women's feelings about hair, using surveys with mood scales from psychology, high-resolution EEG research to measure brainwaves, and other methods. As a result, the company reformulated Pantene products, redesigned packages, pared the line down from 14 "collections" to eight, and fine-tuned the ad campaign.[6]

If marketers lack consumer insights, they often get in trouble. When Tropicana redesigned its orange juice packaging, dropping the iconic image of an orange skewered by a straw, it failed to adequately test for consumer reactions—with disastrous results. Sales dropped by 20 percent, and Tropicana reinstated the old package design after only a few months.[7]

## WHO DOES MARKETING RESEARCH?

Spending on marketing research topped $40.2 billion globally in 2013, according to ESOMAR, the world association of opinion and market research professionals.[8] Most large companies have their own marketing research departments, which often play crucial roles within the organization. Here is how Procter & Gamble describes its marketing research department.[9]

> Consumer & Market Knowledge (CMK) Department is P&G's key internal compass guiding and championing decisions related to brand and customer business development strategy based on in-depth analysis of consumers, shoppers and the retail trade. CMK leads analysis of market trends and consumer habits/motivations, shopper behavior, customer and competitive dynamics; designs and analyzes qualitative and quantitative consumer and shopper research studies as well as syndicated market data. CMK is an integral partner, involved in all the stages of the brand life cycle starting with design of a concept to final product development and through to the in-market launch driving business growth. CMK brings to life P&G stated global strategy "Consumer is Boss."

Marketing research, however, is not limited to large companies with big budgets and marketing research departments. Often at much smaller companies, everyone carries out marketing research—including the customers. Small companies can also hire the services of a marketing research firm or conduct research in creative and affordable ways, such as:

1. ***Engaging students or professors to design and carry out projects***—AT&T, GE, Samsung, Shell Oil, and others have engaged in a "crowdcasting" exercise by sponsoring the Innovation Challenge, where top MBA students

P&G employed a wide range of research techniques to completely overhaul its Pantene product line.

Source: The Procter & Gamble Company

compete in teams to address company problems. The students gain experience and visibility; the companies get fresh sets of eyes to solve problems at a fraction of what consultants would charge.[10] The nonprofit United Way uses graduate students and interns as critical marketing research resources to collect and consolidate marketplace data and set up larger research projects.[11]

2. ***Using the Internet***—A company can collect considerable information at little cost by examining competitors' Web sites, monitoring chat rooms and blogs, and accessing published data. Social media monitoring tools from companies like Radian6, Attensity, and Lithium keep firms on top of online buzz. Home water filtration company Aquasana uses tools from NetBase to collect what people are saying about Brita and other competitors on Twitter, Facebook, news sites, blogs, message boards, and any other place there are relevant online conversations.[12]

3. ***Checking out rivals***—Many small businesses, such as restaurants, hotels, or specialty retailers, routinely visit competitors to learn about changes they have made. Tom Stemberg, who founded the office supply superstore Staples, made weekly unannounced visits to his own stores, competitors' stores, and other stores outside his category, always focused on "what the store was doing right" to get ideas for improving Staples.[13]

4. ***Tapping into marketing partner expertise***—Marketing research firms, ad agencies, distributors, and other marketing partners may be able to share relevant market knowledge they have accumulated. Partners targeting small or medium-sized businesses may be especially helpful. For example, to promote more shipping to China, UPS conducted several in-depth surveys of the Chinese market to portray its complexities but also its opportunities for even small and medium-sized businesses.[14]

5. ***Tapping into employee creativity and wisdom***—No one may come into more contact with customers and understand a company's products, services, and brands better than its employees. Software maker Intuit puts employees into four- to six-person "two pizza" teams—called that because it takes only two pizzas to feed them. They observe customers in all walks of life and try to identify problems Intuit might be able to solve. Intuit takes all the employees' proposed solutions and experiments with them, building products behind the ideas that seem to work best.[15]

Most companies use a combination of resources to study their industries, competitors, audiences, and channel strategies. They normally budget marketing research at 1 percent to 2 percent of company sales and spend a large percentage of that on the services of outside firms. Marketing research firms fall into three categories:

1. ***Syndicated-service research firms***—These firms gather consumer and trade information, which they sell for a fee. Examples include the Nielsen Company, Kantar Group, Westat, and IRI.

2. ***Custom marketing research firms***—These firms are hired to carry out specific projects. They design the study and report the findings.

3. ***Specialty-line marketing research firms***—These firms provide specialized research services. The best example is the field-service firm, which sells field interviewing services to other firms.

## OVERCOMING BARRIERS TO THE USE OF MARKETING RESEARCH

In spite of the rapid growth of marketing research, many companies still fail to use it sufficiently or correctly. They may not understand what it is capable of or provide the researcher the right problem definition and

The founder of Staples made weekly visits to stores of all kinds for insights and inspiration.

*Source: picture alliance/Frank Duenzl/Newscom*

Poorly conceived marketing research almost doomed the box office blockbuster *Star Wars*.

information from which to work. They may also have unrealistic expectations about what researchers can offer. Failure to use marketing research properly has led to numerous gaffes, including the following historic one.[16]

▌STAR WARS   In the 1970s, a successful marketing research executive left General Foods to try a daring gambit: bringing market research to Hollywood, to give film studios access to the same research that had spurred General Foods's success. A major film studio handed him a science fiction film proposal and asked him to research and predict its success or failure. His views would inform the studio's decision about whether to back the film. The research executive concluded the film would fail. For one, he argued, Watergate had made the United States less trusting of institutions and, as a result, its citizens in the 1970s prized realism and authenticity over science fiction. This particular film also had the word "*war*" in its title; the executive reasoned that viewers, suffering post-Vietnam hangover, would stay away in droves. The film was *Star Wars*, which eventually grossed more than $4.3 billion in box office receipts alone. What this researcher delivered was information, not insight. He failed to study the script itself, to see that it was a fundamentally human story—of love, conflict, loss, and redemption—that happened to play out against the backdrop of space.

# The Marketing Research Process

To take advantage of all the resources and practices available, good marketers adopt a formal marketing research process that follows the six steps shown in Figure 4.1. We illustrate these steps in the following situation.[17]

American Airlines (AA) was one of the first companies to install phone handsets on its planes. Now it's reviewing many new ideas, especially to cater to its first-class passengers on very long flights, mainly businesspeople whose high-priced tickets pay most of the freight. Among these ideas are: (1) ultra high-speed Wi-Fi service, (2) 124 channels of high-definition satellite cable TV, and (3) a 250-CD audio system that lets each passenger create a customized in-flight playlist. The marketing research manager was assigned to investigate how first-class passengers would rate these services, specifically ultra high-speed Wi-Fi, and how much extra they would be willing to pay. One source estimates revenues of $70 million from Wi-Fi access over 10 years if enough first-class passengers paid $25. AA could thus recover its costs in a reasonable time, given that making the connection available would cost $90,000 per plane.

## STEP 1: DEFINE THE PROBLEM, THE DECISION ALTERNATIVES, AND THE RESEARCH OBJECTIVES

Marketing managers must be careful not to define the problem too broadly or too narrowly for the marketing researcher. A marketing manager who says "Find out everything you can about first-class air travelers' needs" will collect a lot of unnecessary information. One who says "Find out whether enough passengers aboard a B777 flying direct between Chicago and Tokyo would pay $25 for ultra high-speed Wi-Fi service so we can break even in one year on the cost of offering this service" is taking too narrow a view of the problem.

The marketing researcher might ask, "Why does Wi-Fi have to be priced at $25 as opposed to $15, $35, or some other price? Why does American have to break even on the service, especially if it attracts new customers?" Another relevant question is, "How important is it to be first in the market, and how long can the company sustain its lead?"

The marketing manager and marketing researcher agreed to define the problem as follows: "Will offering ultra high-speed Wi-Fi service create enough incremental preference and profit to justify its cost against other service enhancements American might make?" To help design the research, management should first spell out the decisions it might face and then work backward. Suppose management outlines these decisions: (1) Should American offer ultra high-speed Wi-Fi service? (2) If so, should it offer it to first-class only or include business class and possibly economy class? (3) What price(s) should be charged? (4) On what types of planes and lengths of trips should the service be offered?

Now management and marketing researchers are ready to set specific research objectives: (1) What types of first-class passengers would respond most to ultra high-speed Wi-Fi service? (2) How many are likely to use it at different price levels? (3) How many might choose American because of this new service? (4) How much long-term goodwill will this service add to American's image? (5) How important is ultra high-speed Wi-Fi service to first-class passengers relative to other services, such as a power plug or enhanced entertainment?

Not all research can be this specific. Some is *exploratory*—its goal is to identify the problem and to suggest possible solutions. Some is *descriptive*—it seeks to quantify demand, such as how many first-class passengers would purchase ultra high-speed Wi-Fi service at $25. Some research is *causal*—its purpose is to test a cause-and-effect relationship.

## STEP 2: DEVELOP THE RESEARCH PLAN

In the second stage of marketing research we develop the most efficient plan for gathering the needed information and discover what that will cost. Suppose American made a prior estimate that launching ultra high-speed Wi-Fi service would yield a long-term profit of $50,000. If the manager believes the marketing research will lead to an improved pricing and promotional plan and a long-term profit of $90,000, he should be willing to spend up to $40,000 on this research. If the research will cost more than $40,000, it's not worth doing.

To design a research plan, we need to make decisions about the data sources, research approaches, research instruments, sampling plan, and contact methods.

**DATA SOURCES** The researcher can gather secondary data, primary data, or both. *Secondary data* are data that were collected for another purpose and already exist somewhere. *Primary data* are data freshly gathered for a specific purpose or project.

Researchers usually start their investigation by examining some of the rich variety of low-cost and readily available secondary data to see whether they can partly or wholly solve the problem without collecting costly primary data. For instance, auto advertisers looking to get a better return on their online car ads might purchase a copy of a J. D. Power and Associates survey that gives insights into who buys specific brands and where advertisers can find them online.

| Define the problem and research objectives |
| Develop the research plan |
| Collect the information |
| Analyze the information |
| Present the findings |
| Make the decision |

**| Fig. 4.1 |**

The Marketing Research Process

To help make a decision to offer ultra high-speed Wi-Fi service on its flights, an airline would want to carefully conduct consumer research.

Source: Associated Press

When the needed data don't exist or are dated or unreliable, the researcher will need to collect primary data. Most marketing research projects do include some primary-data collection.

**RESEARCH APPROACHES** Marketers collect primary data in five main ways: through observation, focus groups, surveys, behavioral data, and experiments.

*Observational Research* Researchers can gather fresh data by observing unobtrusively as customers shop or consume products. Sometimes they equip consumers with pagers and instruct them to write down or text what they're doing whenever prompted, or they hold informal interview sessions at a café or bar.[18] Photographs and videos can also provide a wealth of detailed information. Although privacy concerns have been expressed, some retailers are linking security cameras with software to record shopper behavior in stores. In its 1,000 retail stores, T-Mobile can track how people move around, how long they stand in front of displays, and which phones they pick up and for how long.[19]

**Ethnographic research** uses concepts and tools from anthropology and other social science disciplines to provide deep cultural understanding of how people live and work.[20] The goal is to immerse the researcher into consumers' lives to uncover unarticulated desires that might not surface in any other form of research.[21] Fujitsu Laboratories, Herman Miller, Steelcase, and Xerox have embraced ethnographic research to design breakthrough products. Technology companies like IBM, Microsoft, and Hewlett-Packard use anthropologists and ethnologists working alongside systems engineers and software developers.[22]

Any type of firm can benefit from the deep consumer insights of ethnographic research. To boost sagging sales for its Orville Redenbacher popcorn, ConAgra spent nine months observing families at home and studying weekly diaries of how they felt about various snacks. Researchers found a key insight: the essence of popcorn was that it was a "facilitator of interaction." Four nationwide TV ads followed with the tagline "Spending Time Together: That's the Power of Orville Redenbacher."[23]

Ethnographic research isn't limited to consumer products. UK-based Smith & Nephew, a global medical technology business, used extensive international ethnographic research with patients and clinicians to understand the physical and emotional toll of wounds, developing ALLEVYN Life, a new wound-management dressing, in the process.[24] In a business-to-business setting, a sharper focus on end users helped propel Thomson Reuters to greater financial heights.[25]

**THOMSON REUTERS**   Just before it acquired Reuters, global information services giant Thomson Corporation embarked on extensive research to better understand its ultimate customers. Thomson sold to businesses and professionals in the financial, legal, tax and accounting, scientific, and health care sectors, and it wanted to know how individual brokers and investment bankers used its data, research, and other resources to make day-to-day investment decisions for clients. Segmenting the market by its end users, rather than by its corporate purchasers, and studying the way they viewed Thomson versus competitors allowed the firm to identify market segments that offered growth opportunities. Thomson then conducted surveys and "day in the life" ethnographic research on how end users did their jobs. Using an approach called "three minutes," researchers combined observation with detailed interviews to understand what end users were doing three minutes before and after they used one of Thomson's products. Insights from the research helped the company develop new products and make acquisitions that led to significantly higher revenue and profits in the year that followed.

The American Airlines researchers might meander around first-class lounges to hear how travelers talk about different carriers and their features or sit next to passengers on planes. They can fly on competitors' planes to observe in-flight service.

*Focus Group Research* A **focus group** is a gathering of 6 to 10 people carefully selected for demographic, psychographic, or other considerations and convened to discuss various topics at length for a small payment. A professional moderator asks questions and probes based on the marketing managers' agenda; the goal is to uncover consumers' real motivations and the reasons they say and do certain things. Sessions are typically recorded, and marketing managers often observe from behind two-way mirrors. To allow more in-depth discussion, focus groups are trending smaller in size.[26]

Focus group research is a useful exploratory step, but researchers must avoid generalizing to the whole market because the sample is too small and is not drawn randomly. Some marketers feel this research setting is too contrived and prefer less artificial means. "Marketing Memo: Conducting Informative Focus Groups" has some practical tips to improve the quality of focus groups.

## marketing memo

## Conducting Informative Focus Groups

Focus groups allow marketers to hone in on issues not easily addressed by surveys. The key to using them successfully is to *thoughtfully listen* and *carefully observe,* leaving assumptions and biases behind.

Although useful insights can emerge, questions also arise about focus groups' validity. Some researchers believe consumers are so bombarded with ads, they unconsciously (or perhaps cynically) parrot back what they've heard instead of what they really think. It's always possible participants are trying to maintain their self-image and public persona, engage in "groupthink," or satisfy a need to identify with other members. They may be unwilling to acknowledge—or even recognize—their behavior patterns and motivations, and one highly opinionated person can drown out the rest of the group. Getting the right participants is crucial, but groups can be expensive too ($3,000 to $5,000 per group).

It can be difficult to generalize the results, even from multiple focus groups. For example, within the United States, findings often vary from region to region. One firm specializing in focus group research claimed Minneapolis was the best city to get a sample of fairly well-educated people who were honest and forthcoming. Many marketers interpret focus groups in New York and other northeastern cities carefully because people there tend to be highly critical and generally don't report that they like much.

Participants must feel relaxed and be strongly motivated to be truthful. Physical surroundings can be crucial. At one agency an executive noted, "We wondered why people always seemed grumpy and negative—people were resistant to any idea we showed them." Finally in one session a fight broke out between participants. The problem was the room itself: cramped, stifling, forbidding. "It was a cross between a hospital room and a police interrogation room." To fix the problem, the agency gave the room a makeover. Other firms adapt the room to fit the topic—such as designing it to look like a playroom when speaking to children. To increase interactivity among focus group members, some researchers assign pre-session homework such as diaries, photography, and videography.

Online focus groups may cost less than a quarter of an in-person focus group. They are also less intrusive, allow geographically diverse subjects to participate, and yield fast results. Proponents of traditional groups maintain that in-person sessions immerse marketers in the research process, offer a close-up look at people's emotional and physical reactions, and ensure that sensitive materials are not leaked. In-person, marketers can also adjust the flow of discussion and delve deeply into more complex topics.

Regardless of the form it takes, the focus group is still, as one marketing executive noted, "the most cost-effective, quickest, dirtiest way to get information in rapid time on an idea." Wharton's Americus Reed might have said it best: "A focus group is like a chain saw. If you know what you're doing, it's very useful and effective. If you don't, you could lose a limb."

**Sources:** Sarah Jeffrey Kasner, "Fistfights and Feng Shui," *Boston Globe,* July 21, 2001; Linda Tischler, "Every Move You Make," *Fast Company,* April 2004, pp. 73–75; Dennis Rook, "Out-of-Focus Groups," *Marketing Research* 15, no. 2 (Summer 2003), p. 11; Piet Levy, "In with the Old, In Spite of the New," *Marketing News,* May 30, 2009, p. 19; Piet Levy, "10 Minutes with … Robert J. Morais," *Marketing News*, May 30, 2011; William Boateng, "Evaluating the Efficacy of Focus Group Discussion (FGD) in Qualitative Social Research," *International Journal of Business and Social Science* 3 (April 2012), pp. 54–57; Demetrius Madrigal and Bryan McClain, "Do's and Don'ts for Focus Groups," www.uxmatters.com, July 4, 2011.

In the American Airlines research, the moderator might start with a broad question, such as "How do you feel about first-class air travel?" Questions then move to how people view the different airlines, different existing services, different proposed services, and, specifically, ultra high-speed Wi-Fi service.

Marketers can unobtrusively observe focus groups behind two-way mirrors to gain qualitative insights from consumers.

*Source: Spencer Grant/Getty Images*

Wells Fargo conducts thousands of consumer surveys to improve its banking services.

Source: Jonathan Alpeyrie/Polaris/Newscom

***Survey Research*** Companies undertake surveys to assess people's knowledge, beliefs, preferences, and satisfaction and to measure these magnitudes in the general population. A company such as American Airlines might prepare its own survey instrument, or it might add questions to an omnibus survey that carries the questions of several companies at a much lower cost. It can also pose questions to an ongoing consumer panel run by itself or another company. It may do a mall intercept study by having researchers approach people in a shopping mall and ask them questions. Or it might add a survey request at the end of calls to its customer service department.

However they conduct their surveys—online, by phone, or in person—companies must feel the information they're getting from the mounds of data makes it all worthwhile. San Francisco–based Wells Fargo bank collects more than 50,000 customer surveys each month through its bank branches. It has used customers' comments to begin more stringent new wait-time standards designed to improve customer satisfaction.

Of course, companies may risk creating "survey burnout" and seeing response rates plummet. Keeping a survey short and simple is one key to drawing participants. Offering incentives is another. Walmart, Rite Aid, Petco, and Staples include an invitation to fill out a survey on the cash register receipt with a chance to win a prize.[27]

***Behavioral Research*** Customers leave traces of their purchasing behavior in store scanning data, catalog purchases, and customer databases. Marketers can learn much by analyzing these data. Actual purchases reflect consumers' preferences and often are more reliable than statements they offer to market researchers. For example, grocery shopping data show that high-income people don't necessarily buy the more expensive brands, contrary to what they might state in interviews, and many low-income people buy some expensive brands. As Chapter 3 described, there is a wealth of online data to collect from consumers. Clearly, American Airlines can learn many useful things about its passengers by analyzing ticket purchase records and online behavior.

The most scientifically valid research is **experimental research**, designed to capture cause-and-effect relationships by eliminating competing explanations of the findings. If the experiment is well designed and executed, research and marketing managers can have confidence in the conclusions. Experiments call for selecting matched groups of subjects, subjecting them to different treatments, controlling extraneous variables, and checking whether observed response differences are statistically significant. If we can eliminate or control extraneous factors, we can relate the observed effects to the variations in the treatments or stimuli.

American Airlines might introduce ultra high-speed Wi-Fi service on one of its regular flights from Chicago to Tokyo and charge $25 one week and $15 the next week. If the plane carried approximately the same number of first-class passengers each week and the particular weeks made no difference, the airline could relate any significant difference in the number of passengers using the service to the price charged.

RESEARCH INSTRUMENTS Marketing researchers have a choice of three main research instruments in collecting primary data: questionnaires, qualitative measures, and technological devices.

***Questionnaires*** A **questionnaire** consists of a set of questions presented to respondents. Because of its flexibility, it is by far the most common instrument used to collect primary data. The form, wording, and sequence of the questions can all influence the responses, so testing and de-bugging are necessary. *Closed-end questions* specify all the possible answers, and the responses are easier to interpret and tabulate. *Open-end questions* allow respondents to answer in their own words. They are especially useful in exploratory research, where the researcher is looking for insight into how people think rather than measuring how many think a certain way. Table 4.1 provides examples of both types of questions; also see "Marketing Memo: Questionnaire Dos and Don'ts."

| TABLE 4.1 | Types of Questions |
|-----------|--------------------|

| Name | Description | Example |
|------|-------------|---------|
| **A. Closed-End Questions** | | |
| Dichotomous | A question with two possible answers | In arranging this trip, did you personally phone American? <br> Yes            No |
| Multiple choice | A question with three or more answers | With whom are you traveling on this flight? <br> ☐ No one      ☐ Children only <br> ☐ Spouse      ☐ Business associates/friends/relatives <br> ☐ Spouse and children    ☐ An organized tour group |
| Likert scale | A statement with which the respondent shows the amount of agreement/ disagreement | Small airlines generally give better service than large ones. <br> Strongly disagree    Disagree    Neither agree nor disagree    Agree    Strongly agree <br> 1_____    2_____    3_____    4_____    5_____ |
| Semantic differential | A scale connecting two bipolar words. The respondent selects the point that represents his or her opinion. | I find American Airlines ... <br> Large _____ Small <br> Experienced _____ Inexperienced <br> Modern _____ Old-fashioned |
| Importance scale | A scale that rates the importance of some attribute | Airline in-flight service to me is <br> Extremely important    Very important    Somewhat important    Not very important    Not at all important <br> 1_____    2_____    3_____    4_____    5_____ |
| Rating scale | A scale that rates some attribute from "poor" to "excellent" | American in-flight service is <br> Excellent    Very Good    Good    Fair    Poor <br> 1_____    2_____    3_____    4_____    5_____ |
| Intention-to-buy scale | A scale that describes the respondent's intention to buy | If ultra high-speed Wi-Fi service were available on a long flight, I would <br> Definitely buy    Probably buy    Not sure    Probably not buy    Definitely not buy <br> 1_____    2_____    3_____    4_____    5_____ |
| **B. Open-End Questions** | | |
| Completely unstructured | A question that respondents can answer in an almost unlimited number of ways | What is your opinion of American Airlines? |
| Word association | Words are presented, one at a time, and respondents mention the first word that comes to mind. | What is the first word that comes to your mind when you hear the following? <br> Airline_____ <br> American_____ <br> Travel_____ |
| Sentence completion | An incomplete sentence is presented and respondents complete the sentence. | When I choose an airline, the most important consideration in my decision is _____ . |
| Story completion | An incomplete story is presented, and respondents are asked to complete it. | "I flew American a few days ago. I noticed that the exterior and interior of the plane had very bright colors. This aroused in me the following thoughts and feelings . . . ." Now complete the story. |
| Picture | A picture of two characters is presented, with one making a statement. Respondents are asked to identify with the other and fill in the empty balloon. | |
| Thematic Apperception Test (TAT) | A picture is presented and respondents are asked to make up a story about what they think is happening or may happen in the picture. | |

## marketing memo

## Marketing Questionnaire Dos And Don'ts

1. **Ensure that questions are without bias.** Don't lead the respondent into an answer.

2. **Make the questions as simple as possible.** Questions that include multiple ideas or two questions in one will confuse respondents.

3. **Make the questions specific.** Sometimes it's advisable to add memory cues. For example, be specific with time periods.

4. **Avoid jargon or shorthand.** Avoid trade jargon, acronyms, and initials not in everyday use.

5. **Steer clear of sophisticated or uncommon words.** Use only words in common speech.

6. **Avoid ambiguous words.** Words such as *usually* or *frequently* have no specific meaning.

7. **Avoid questions with a negative in them.** It is better to say, "Do you ever...?" than "Do you never...?"

8. **Avoid hypothetical questions.** It's difficult to answer questions about imaginary situations. Answers aren't necessarily reliable.

9. **Do not use words that could be misheard.** This is especially important when administering the interview over the telephone. "What is your opinion of sects?" could yield interesting but not necessarily relevant answers.

10. **Desensitize questions by using response bands.** To ask people their age or ask companies about employee turnover rates, offer a range of response bands instead of precise numbers.

11. **Ensure that fixed responses do not overlap.** Categories used in fixed-response questions should be distinct and not overlap.

12. **Allow for the answer "other" in fixed-response questions.** Precoded answers should always allow for a response other than those listed.

**Source:** Adapted from Paul Hague and Peter Jackson, *Market Research: A Guide to Planning, Methodology, and Evaluation* (London: Kogan Page, 1999). See also Hans Baumgartner and Jan-Benedict E. M. Steenkamp, "Response Styles in Marketing Research: A Cross-National Investigation," *Journal of Marketing Research* (May 2001), pp. 143–56; Bert Weijters and Hans Baumgartner, "Misreponse to Reverse and Negated Items in Surveys: A Review," *Journal of Marketing Research* 49 (October 2012), pp. 737–47.

*Qualitative Measures* Some marketers prefer qualitative methods for gauging consumer opinion because they feel consumers' actions don't always match their answers to survey questions. *Qualitative research techniques* are relatively indirect and unstructured measurement approaches, limited only by the marketing researcher's creativity, that permit a range of responses. They can be an especially useful first step in exploring consumers' perceptions because respondents may be less guarded and reveal more about themselves in the process.

Qualitative research does have its drawbacks. The samples are often very small, and results may not generalize to broader populations. And different researchers examining the same qualitative results may draw very different conclusions.

Nevertheless, there is increasing interest in using qualitative methods. "Marketing Insight: Getting into the Heads of Consumers" describes the pioneering ZMET approach. Other popular methods include:[28]

1. *Word associations.* To identify the range of possible brand associations, ask subjects what words come to mind when they hear the brand's name. "What does the Timex name mean to you? Tell me what comes to mind when you think of Timex watches."

2. *Projective techniques.* Give people an incomplete or ambiguous stimulus and ask them to complete or explain it. In "bubble exercises" empty bubbles, like those in cartoons, appear in scenes of people buying or using certain products or services. Subjects fill in the bubble, indicating what they believe is happening or being said. In comparison tasks people compare brands to people, countries, animals, activities, cars, nationalities, or even other brands.

3. *Visualization.* Visualization requires people to create a collage from magazine photos or drawings to depict their perceptions.

4. *Brand personification.* Ask "If the brand were to come alive as a person, what would it be like, what would it do, where would it live, what would it wear, who would it talk to if it went to a party (and what would it talk about)?" For example, the John Deere brand might make someone think of a rugged Midwestern male who is hardworking and trustworthy.

5. *Laddering.* A series of increasingly specific "why" questions can reveal consumer motivation and deeper goals. Ask why someone wants to buy a Nokia cell phone. "They look well built" (attribute). "Why is it important that the phone be well built?" "It suggests Nokia is reliable" (a functional benefit). "Why is reliability important?" "Because my colleagues or family can be sure to reach me" (an emotional benefit). "Why must you be available to them at all times?" "I can help them if they're in trouble" (a core value). The brand makes this person feel like a Good Samaritan, ready to help others.

## marketing insight

# Getting into the Heads of Consumers

Former Harvard Business School marketing professor Gerald Zaltman, with colleagues, developed an in-depth methodology to uncover what consumers think and feel about products, services, brands, and other things. The basic assumption behind the Zaltman Metaphor Elicitation Technique (ZMET) is that most thoughts and feelings are unconscious and shaped by a set of universal **deep metaphors**, basic orientations toward the world that shape everything consumers think, hear, say, or do. According to Zaltman, there are seven main metaphors:

1. *Balance:* justice equilibrium and the interplay of elements;
2. *Transformation:* changes in substance and circumstance;
3. *Journey:* the meeting of past, present, and future;
4. *Container:* inclusion, exclusion, and other boundaries;
5. *Connection:* the need to relate to oneself and others;
6. *Resource:* acquisitions and their consequences; and
7. *Control:* sense of mastery, vulnerability, and well-being.

The ZMET technique works by first asking participants in advance to select a minimum of 12 images from their own sources (magazines, catalogs, family photo albums) to represent their thoughts and feelings about the research topic. In a one-on-one interview, the study administrator uses advanced interview techniques to explore the images with the participant and reveal hidden meanings. Finally, the participants use a computer program to create a collage with these images that communicates their subconscious thoughts and feelings about the topic. The results often significantly influence marketing actions, as the following two examples illustrate:

- In a ZMET study about pantyhose for marketers at DuPont, some respondents' pictures showed fence posts encased in plastic wrap or steel bands strangling trees, suggesting that pantyhose are tight and inconvenient. But another picture showed tall flowers in a vase, suggesting the product made a woman feel thin, tall, and sexy. The "love-hate" relationship in these and other pictures suggested a more complicated product relationship than the DuPont marketers had assumed.

- Although many older consumers told Danish hearing aid company Oticon that cost was the reason they were postponing purchase, a ZMET analysis revealed the bigger problem was fear of being seen as old or flawed. Oticon responded by creating Delta, a line of stylish new hearing aids that came in flashy colors such as sunset orange, racing green, or cabernet red.

ZMET has also been applied to help design the new Children's Hospital in Pittsburgh, PA, remake the classic soup labels for Campbell, and improve letters to prospective undergraduate applicants for the University of North Carolina at Chapel Hill.

**Sources:** Gerald Zaltman and Lindsay Zaltman, *Marketing Metaphoria: What Deep Metaphors Reveal about the Minds of Consumers* (Boston: Harvard Business School Press, 2008); Glenn L. Christensen and Jerry C. Olson, "Mapping Consumers' Mental Models with ZMET," *Psychology & Marketing* 19 (June 2002), pp. 477–502; Emily Eakin, "Penetrating the Mind by Metaphor," *New York Times*, February 23, 2002; Anne Eisenberg, "The Hearing Aid as Fashion Statement," *New York Times*, September 24, 2006; Mackenzie Carpenter, "The New Children's Hospital: Design Elements Combine to Put Patients, Parents at Ease," *Pittsburgh Post-Gazette*, April 26, 2009; Jennifer Williams, "Campbell's Soup Neuromarketing Redux: There's Chunks of Real Science in That Recipe," *Fast Company*, February 22, 2010; Jay Matthews, "Admissions Office Probes Applicants' Scary Depths," *Washington Post*, July 22, 2010.

Marketers don't have to choose between qualitative and quantitative measures. Many use both, recognizing that their pros and cons can offset each other. For example, companies can recruit someone from an online panel to participate in an in-home product use test by capturing his or her reactions and intentions with a video diary and an online survey.[29]

*Source: ©UNC-Chapel Hill*

A ZMET qualitative research study helped the University of North Carolina at Chapel Hill improve its undergraduate admission efforts.

*Technological Devices* Galvanometers can measure the interest or emotions aroused by exposure to a specific ad or picture. The tachistoscope flashes an ad to a subject with an exposure interval that may range from less than one hundredth of a second to several seconds. After each exposure, the respondent describes everything he or she recalls. Many advances in visual technology techniques studying the eyes and face have benefited marketing researchers and managers alike.[30]

---

**STUDYING THE EYES AND FACE**  A number of increasingly cost-effective methods to study the eyes and faces of consumers have been developed in recent years with diverse applications. Packaged goods companies such as P&G, Unilever, and Kimberly-Clark combine 3-D computer simulations of product and packaging designs with store layouts and use eye-tracking technology to see where consumer eyes land first, how long they linger on a given item, and so on. After doing such tests, Unilever changed the shape of its Axe body wash container, the look of the logo, and the in-store display. In the International Finance Center Mall in Seoul, Korea, two cameras and a motion detector are placed above the LCD touch screens at each of the 26 information kiosks. Facial recognition software estimates users' age and gender, and interactive ads targeting the appropriate demographic then appear. Similar applications are being developed for digital sidewalk billboards in New York, Los Angeles, and San Francisco. Facial recognition cameras and software are being tested to identify and reward participating loyal U.S. customers of retailers and restaurants via opt-in smart phone updates. In one commercial application, SceneTap uses cameras with facial detection software to post information about how full a bar is, as well as the average age and gender profile of the crowd, to help bar hoppers pick their next destination.

---

Technology now lets marketers use skin sensors, brain wave scanners, and full-body scanners to get consumer responses.[31] For example, biometric-tracking wrist sensors can measure electrodermal activity, or skin conductance, to note changes in sweat levels, body temperature and movement, and so on.[32] "Marketing Insight: Understanding Brain Science" provides a glimpse into some of the new marketing research frontiers in studying the brain.[33]

Technology has replaced the diaries that participants in media surveys used to keep. Audiometers attached to television sets in participating homes now record when the set is on and to which channel it is tuned. Electronic devices can record the number of radio programs a person is exposed to during the day or, using Global Positioning System (GPS) technology, how many billboards a person may walk or drive by during a day.

**SAMPLING PLAN**  After choosing the research approach and instruments, the marketing researcher must design a sampling plan. This calls for three decisions:

1. *Sampling unit: Whom should we survey?* In the American Airlines survey, should the sampling unit consist of only first-class business travelers, only first-class vacation travelers, or both? Should it include travelers under age 18? Both traveler and spouse? With the sampling unit chosen, marketers must next develop a sampling frame so everyone in the target population has an equal or known chance of being sampled.
2. *Sample size: How many people should we survey?* Large samples give more reliable results, but it's not necessary to sample the entire target population to achieve reliable results. Samples of less than 1 percent of a population can often provide good reliability, with a credible sampling procedure.
3. *Sampling procedure: How should we choose the respondents?* Probability sampling allows marketers to calculate confidence limits for sampling error and makes the sample more representative. Thus, after choosing the sample, marketers could conclude that "the interval five to seven trips per year has 95 chances in 100 of containing the true number of trips taken annually by first-class passengers flying between Chicago and Tokyo."

**CONTACT METHODS**  Now the marketing researcher must decide how to contact the subjects: by mail, by telephone, in person, or online.

*Mail Contacts*  The *mail questionnaire* is one way to reach people who would not give personal interviews or whose responses might

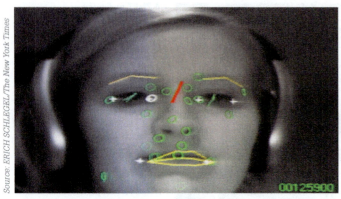

*Source: ERICH SCHLEGEL/The New York Times*

Using sophisticated equipment and methods, neuroscience researchers are studying how brain activity is affected by consumer marketing.

# marketing insight

## Understanding Brain Science

As an alternative to traditional consumer research, some researchers have begun to develop sophisticated techniques from neuroscience that monitor brain activity to better gauge consumer responses to marketing. The term **neuromarketing** describes brain research on the effect of marketing stimuli. Firms are using EEG (electroencephalograph) technology to correlate brand activity with physiological cues such as skin temperature or eye movement and thus gauge how people react to ads.

Researchers studying the brain have found different results from conventional research methods. One group of researchers at UCLA used functional magnetic resonance imaging (fMRI) to find that the Super Bowl ads for which subjects displayed the highest brain activity were different from the ads with the highest stated preferences. Other research found little effect from product placement unless the products in question played an integral role in the storyline.

Several studies have found higher correlations with brain wave research and behavior than with surveys. One study found that brain waves better predicted music purchases than stated music preferences. One major finding from neurological consumer research is that many purchase decisions appear to be characterized "as a largely unconscious habitual process, as distinct from the rational, conscious, information-processing model of economists and traditional marketing textbooks." Even basic decisions, such as the purchase of gasoline, seem to be influenced by brain activity at the subrational level.

A group of researchers in England used EEG to monitor cognitive functions related to memory recall and attentiveness for 12 different regions of the brain as subjects were exposed to advertising. Brain wave activity in different regions indicated different emotional responses. For example, heightened activity in the left prefrontal cortex is characteristic of an "approach" response to an ad and indicates an attraction to the stimulus. In contrast, a spike in brain activity in the right prefrontal cortex is indicative of a strong revulsion to the stimulus. In yet another part of the brain, the degree of memory formation activity correlates with purchase intent. Other research has shown that people activate different regions of the brain in assessing the personality traits of other people than they do when assessing brands.

Although it may offer different insights from conventional techniques, neurological research can still be fairly expensive and has not been universally accepted. Given the complexity of the human brain, many researchers caution that it should not form the sole basis for marketing decisions. The measurement devices to capture brain activity can also be highly obtrusive, using skull caps studded with electrodes or creating artificial exposure conditions.

Others question whether neurological research really offers unambiguous implications for marketing strategy. Brian Knutson, a professor of neuroscience and psychology at Stanford University, compares the use of EEG to "standing outside a baseball stadium and listening to the crowd to figure out what happened." Other critics worry that if the methods do become successful, they will only lead to more marketing manipulation by companies. Despite controversy, marketers' endless pursuit of deeper insights about consumers' response to marketing virtually guarantees continued interest in neuromarketing.

**Sources:** Carolyn Yoon, Angela H. Gutchess, Fred Feinberg, and Thad A. Polk, "A Functional Magnetic Resonance Imaging Study of Neural Dissociations between Brand and Person Judgments," *Journal of Consumer Research* 33 (June 2006), pp. 31–40; Martin Lindstrom, *Buyology: Truth and Lies about Why We Buy* (New York: Doubleday, 2008); Brian Sternberg, "How Couch Potatoes Watch TV Could Hold Clues for Advertisers," *Boston Globe*, September 6, 2009, pp. G1, G3; Kevin Randall, "Neuromarketing Hope and Hype: 5 Brands Conducting Brain Research," *Fast Company*, September 15, 2009; Todd Essig, "The Future of Focus Groups: My Brain Knows What You Like," *Forbes*, April 28, 2012; Carmen Nobel, "Neuromarketing: Tapping into the 'Pleasure Center' of Consumers," *Forbes*, February 1, 2013.

be biased or distorted by the interviewers. Mail questionnaires require simple and clearly worded questions. Unfortunately, responses are usually few or slow.

**Telephone Contacts** *Telephone interviewing* is a good method for gathering information quickly; the interviewer is also able to clarify questions if respondents do not understand them. Interviews must be brief and not too personal. Although the response rate has typically been higher than for mailed questionnaires, telephone interviewing in the United States is getting more difficult because of consumers' growing antipathy toward telemarketers.

In late 2003, Congress passed legislation allowing the Federal Trade Commission to restrict telemarketing calls through its "Do Not Call" registry. By mid-2010, consumers had registered more than 200 million phone numbers. Marketing research firms are exempt from the ruling, but the increasingly widespread resistance to telemarketing undoubtedly reduces the effectiveness of telephone surveys in the United States.

In other parts of the world, such restrictive legislation does not exist. Because mobile phone penetration in Africa had risen from just 1 in 50 people in 2000 to almost eighty percent of the population by 2014, marketers use cell phones there to convene focus groups in rural areas and to interact via text.[34]

**Personal Contacts** *Personal interviewing* is the most versatile method. The interviewer can ask more questions and record additional observations about the respondent, such as dress and body language. Personal interviewing is also the most expensive method, is subject to interviewer bias, and requires more planning and supervision. In *arranged interviews*, marketers contact respondents for an appointment and often offer a small payment or incentive. In *intercept interviews,* researchers stop people at a shopping mall or busy street corner and request an interview on the spot. Intercept interviews must be quick, and they run the risk of including nonprobability samples.

***Online Contacts***  The Internet offers many ways to do research. A company can embed a questionnaire on its Web site and offer an incentive for answering, or it can place a banner on a frequently visited site, inviting people to answer questions and possibly win a prize. Online product testing can provide information much faster than traditional new-product marketing research techniques.

Marketers can also host a real-time consumer panel or virtual focus group or sponsor a chat room, bulletin board, or blog where they introduce questions from time to time. They can ask customers to brainstorm or have the company's Twitter followers rate an idea. Insights from Kraft-sponsored online communities helped the company develop its popular line of 100-calorie snacks.[35]

Del Monte tapped its 400-member, handpicked online community called "I Love My Dog" when it was considering a new breakfast treat for dogs. The consensus request was for something with a bacon-and-egg taste and an extra dose of vitamins and minerals. Working with the online community throughout product development, the company introduced fortified "Snausages Breakfast Bites" in half the time usually required to launch a new product.[36]

Online research was a $2.4 billion dollar business in 2011. A host of new online survey providers have entered the market, such as SurveyMonkey, Survey-Gizmo, Qualtrics, and Google Consumer Surveys. Founded in 1999, SurveyMonkey has over 15 million registered users. Members can create surveys to quickly post on blogs, Websites, Facebook, or Twitter. [37] Like any survey, however, online surveys need to ask the right people the right questions on the right topic.

Other means to use the Internet as a research tool including tracking how customers *clickstream* through the company's Web site and move to other sites. Marketers can post different prices, headlines, and product features on separate Web sites or at different times to compare their relative effectiveness. Researchers like Bluefin Labs monitor all relevant Twitter tweets, Facebook posts, and broadcast television stories to provide companies with real-time trend analysis.[38]

Firms like SurveyMonkey make it easy to conduct online consumer surveys.

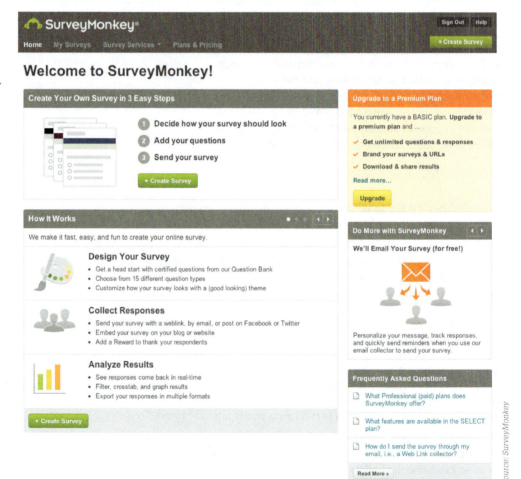

*Source: SurveyMonkey*

Yet, as popular as online research methods are, smart companies use them to augment rather than replace more traditional methods. Like any method, online research has pros and cons. Here are some advantages:

- *Online research is inexpensive.* A typical online survey can cost 20 percent to 50 percent less than a conventional survey, and return rates can be as high as 50 percent.
- *Online research is expansive.* There are essentially no geographical boundaries, allowing marketers to consider a wide range of possible respondents.
- *Online research is fast.* The survey can automatically direct respondents to applicable questions, store data, and transmit results immediately.
- *Responses tend to be honest and thoughtful.* People may be more relaxed and candid when they can answer on their own time and respond privately without feeling judged, especially on sensitive topics (such as "how often do you bathe or shower?").[39]
- *Online research is versatile.* Virtual reality software lets visitors inspect 3-D models of products such as cameras, cars, and medical equipment and manipulate product characteristics. Online community blogs allow customer participants to interact with each other.

Some disadvantages include:

- *Samples can be small and skewed.* Some 28 percent of U.S. households still lacked broadband Internet access in 2014; the percentage is higher among lower-income groups, in rural areas, and in most parts of Asia, Latin America, and Central and Eastern Europe, where socioeconomic and education levels also differ.[40] Although Internet access will increase, online market researchers must find creative ways to reach population segments on the other side of the "digital divide." Combining offline sources with online findings and providing temporary Internet access at locations such as malls and recreation centers are options. Some research firms use statistical models to fill in the gaps left by offline consumer segments.
- *Online panels and communities can suffer excessive turnover.* Members may become bored and flee or, worse, stay but participate halfheartedly. Panel and community organizers can raise recruiting standards, downplay incentives, and monitor participation and engagement levels. A constant flow of new features, events, and activities can keep members interested and engaged.
- *Online market research can suffer technological problems and inconsistencies.* Because browser software varies, the designer's final product may look very different on the research subject's screen.

Online researchers have also begun to use text messaging in various ways—to conduct a chat with a respondent, to probe more deeply with a member of an online focus group, or to direct respondents to a Web site. Text messaging is also a useful way to get teenagers to open up on topics.

## STEP 3: COLLECT THE INFORMATION

The data collection phase of marketing research is generally the most expensive and error-prone. Some respondents will be away from home, offline, or otherwise inaccessible; they must be contacted again or replaced. Others will refuse to cooperate or will give biased or dishonest answers.

Internationally, one of the biggest obstacles to collecting information is the need to achieve consistency.[41] Latin American respondents may be uncomfortable with the impersonal nature of the Internet and need interactive elements in a survey so they feel they're talking to a real person. Respondents in Asia, on the other hand, may feel more pressure to conform and may not be as forthcoming in focus groups as online. Sometimes the solution may be as simple as ensuring the right language is used.

## STEP 4: ANALYZE THE INFORMATION

The next-to-last step in the process is to extract findings by tabulating the data and developing summary measures. The researchers now compute averages and measures of dispersion for the major variables and apply some advanced statistical techniques and decision models in the hope of discovering additional findings. They may test different hypotheses and theories, applying sensitivity analysis to test assumptions and the strength of the conclusions.

## STEP 5: PRESENT THE FINDINGS

As the last step, the researcher presents the findings. Researchers are increasingly asked to play a proactive, consulting role in translating data and information into insights and recommendations for management. "Marketing Insight: Bringing Marketing Research to Life with Personas" describes an approach that some researchers are using to maximize the impact of their consumer research findings.

## marketing insight

# Bringing Marketing Research to Life with Personas

To bring all their acquired information and insights to life, some researchers are employing personas. *Personas* are detailed profiles of one, or perhaps a few, hypothetical target consumers, imagined in terms of demographic, psychographic, geographic, or other descriptive attitudinal or behavioral information. Photos, images, names, or short bios help convey how the target customer looks, acts, and feels so marketers can incorporate a well-defined target-customer point of view in all their marketing decision making. Many software companies, Microsoft in particular, have used personas to help improve user interfaces and experiences, and marketers have broadened the application. For example:

- Unilever's biggest and most successful hair-care launch, for Sunsilk, was aided by insights into the target consumer the company dubbed "Katie." The Katie persona outlined the 20-something female's hair-care needs, but also her perceptions and attitudes and the way she dealt with her everyday "dramas."

- Specialty tool and equipment maker Campbell Hausfeld relied on the many retailers it supplied, including Home Depot and Lowe's, to help it keep in touch with consumers. After developing eight consumer profiles, including a female do-it-yourselfer and an elderly consumer, the firm was able to successfully launch new products such as drills that weighed less or that included a level for picture hanging.

Although personas provide vivid information to aid marketing decision making, it's important not to overgeneralize. Any target market may have a range of consumers who vary along a number of key dimensions, so researchers sometimes employ two to six personas. Using quantitative, qualitative, and observational research, Best Buy developed five customer personas to guide the redesign and relaunch of GeekSquad.com, its national computer-support service:

- "Jill"—a suburban mom who uses her computer daily and depends on the Geek Squad as on a landscaper or plumber.

- "Charlie"—a 50-plus male who is curious about technology but needs an unintimidating guide.

- "Daryl"—a technologically savvy hands-on experimenter who occasionally needs a helping hand.

- "Luis"—a time-pressed small business owner whose primary goal is to complete tasks as expediently as possible.

- "Nick"—a prospective Geek Squad agent who views the site critically and needs to be challenged.

To satisfy Charlie, a prominent 911 button was added to the upper right-hand corner in case a crisis arose, but to satisfy Nick, Best Buy created a whole channel devoted to geek information.

**Sources:** Dale Buss, "Reflections of Reality," *Point,* June 2006, pp. 10–11; Todd Wasserman, "Unilever, Whirlpool Get Personal with Personas," *Brandweek,* September 18, 2006, p. 13; Daniel B. Honigman, "Persona-fication," *Marketing News,* April 1, 2008, p. 8; Lisa Sanders, "Major Marketers Get Wise to the Power of Assigning Personas," *Advertising Age,* April 9, 2007, p. 36; Paul Murray, "Who Are They?," www.chiefmarketer.com, June/July 2010, pp. 53–54; Lauren Sorenson, "6 Core Benefits of Well-Defined Marketing Personas," www.blog.hotspot.com, December 13, 2011.

The main survey findings for the American Airlines case showed that:

1. Passengers would use ultra high-speed Wi-Fi service primarily to stay connected and receive and send large documents and e-mails. Some would also surf the Web to download videos and songs. They would charge the cost back to their employers.

2. At $25, about 5 of 10 first-class passengers would use Wi-Fi service during a flight; at $15, about 6 would. Thus, a fee of $15 would produce less revenue ($90 = 6 × $15) than $25 ($125 = 5 × $25). Assuming the same flight takes place 365 days a year, American could collect $45,625 (= $125 × 365) annually. Given an investment of $90,000 per plane, it would take two years for each to break even.

3. Offering ultra high-speed Wi-Fi service would strengthen American Airlines' image as an innovative and progressive carrier and earn it some new passengers and customer goodwill.

## STEP 6: MAKE THE DECISION

The American Airlines managers who commissioned the research need to weigh the evidence. If their confidence in the findings is low, they may decide against introducing ultra high-speed Wi-Fi service. If they are predisposed to launching it, the findings support their inclination. They may even decide to study the issue further and do more research. The decision is theirs, but rigorously done research provides them with insight into the problem (see Table 4.2).[42]

Some organizations use marketing decision support systems to help their marketing managers make better decisions. MIT's John Little defined a **marketing decision support system (MDSS)** as a coordinated collection of data, systems, tools, and techniques, with supporting software and hardware, by which an organization gathers and interprets relevant information from business and environment and turns it into a basis for marketing action.[44] Once a year, *Marketing News* lists hundreds of current marketing and sales software programs that assist

| TABLE 4.2 | The Seven Characteristics of Good Marketing Research |
|---|---|
| **1.** Scientific method | Effective marketing research uses the principles of the scientific method: careful observation, formulation of hypotheses, prediction, and testing. |
| **2.** Research creativity | In an award-winning research study to reposition Cheetos snacks, researchers dressed up in a brand mascot Chester Cheetah suit and walked around the streets of San Francisco. The response the character encountered led to the realization that even adults loved the fun and playfulness of Cheetos. The resulting repositioning led to a double-digit sales increase despite a tough business environment.[43] |
| **3.** Multiple methods | Marketing researchers shy away from overreliance on any one method. They also recognize the value of using two or three methods to increase confidence in the results. |
| **4.** Interdependence of models and data | Marketing researchers recognize that data are interpreted from underlying models that guide the type of information sought. |
| **5.** Value and cost of information | Marketing researchers show concern for estimating the value of information against its cost. Costs are typically easy to determine, but the value of research is harder to quantify. It depends on the reliability and validity of the findings and management's willingness to accept and act on those findings. |
| **6.** Healthy skepticism | Marketing researchers show a healthy skepticism toward glib assumptions made by managers about how a market works. They are alert to the problems caused by "marketing myths." |
| **7.** Ethical marketing | Marketing research benefits both the sponsoring company and its customers. The misuse of marketing research can harm or annoy consumers, increasing resentment at what consumers regard as an invasion of their privacy or a disguised sales pitch. |

in designing marketing research studies, segmenting markets, setting prices and advertising budgets, analyzing media, and planning sales force activity.[45]

# Measuring Marketing Productivity

Although we can easily quantify marketing expenses and investments as inputs in the short run, the resulting outputs such as broader brand awareness, enhanced brand image, greater customer loyalty, and improved new product prospects may take months or years to manifest themselves. Meanwhile internal changes within the organization and external changes in the marketing environment may coincide with the marketing expenditures, making it hard to isolate its effects.[46]

Nevertheless, marketing research must assess the efficiency and effectiveness of marketing activities. Two complementary approaches to measuring marketing productivity are: (1) *marketing metrics* to assess marketing effects and (2) *marketing-mix modeling* to estimate causal relationships and measure how marketing activity affects outcomes. *Marketing dashboards* are a structured way to disseminate the insights gleaned from these two approaches.

## MARKETING METRICS

Marketers employ a wide variety of measures to assess marketing effects.[47] **Marketing metrics** is the set of measures that helps marketers quantify, compare, and interpret their performance.[48]

- The CMO of Mary Kay cosmetics would focus on four long-term brand strength metrics—market awareness, consideration, trial, and 12-month beauty consultant productivity—as well as a number of short-term program-specific metrics like ad impressions, Web site traffic, and purchase conversion.
- The VP of marketing at Virgin America would look at a broad set of online metrics—cost per acquisition, cost per click, and cost per thousand page impressions (CPM). She would also look at total dollars driven by natural and paid search and online display advertising as well as tracking results and other metrics from the offline world.

Marketers choose one or more measures based on the particular issues or problems they face. Mindbody, a web-based business management software provider for the wellness and beauty industries worldwide, tracks numerous online analytics including landing page conversions, click through rates for online ads and rankings on Google search. In addition, MINDBODY monitors the following online metrics on a weekly basis: 1) *Website analytics*, details on site navigation and online interaction; 2) *Social media presence*, different demographic and geographic responses to social media channels across different markets; and 3) *Permission marketing statistics*, measures of interactions and engagement with consumers from auto e-mails. "Marketing Memo: Measuring Social Media ROI" offers some insight into the thorny issue of measuring social media effects.

An advocate of simple, relevant marketing metrics, the University of Virginia's Paul Farris draws an analogy to the way Boeing 747 jet pilots select information from the vast array of instruments in the cockpit:[49]

> Aircraft pilots have protocols. When they are sitting on the tarmac warming their engines waiting to take off, they are looking at certain things. When they are taxiing, they look at others. When they are in flight, they look at still others. There is a sequence of knowing when to pay attention to which metrics, which lets them have their cake and eat it too, in terms of the simplicity and complexity trade-off.

London Business School's Tim Ambler believes firms can split evaluation of marketing performance into two parts: (1) short-term results and (2) changes in brand equity.[50] Short-term results often reflect profit-and-loss concerns as shown by sales turnover, shareholder value, or some combination of the two. Brand-equity measures could include customer awareness, attitudes, and behaviors; market share; relative price premium; number of complaints; distribution and availability; total number of customers; perceived quality, and loyalty and retention.[51]

Companies can also monitor an extensive set of internal metrics, such as innovation. For example, 3M tracks the proportion of sales resulting from its recent innovations. Ambler also recommends developing employee measures and metrics, arguing that "end users are the ultimate customers, but your own staff are your first; you need to measure the health of the internal market." Table 4.3 summarizes a list of popular internal and external marketing metrics from Ambler's survey in the United Kingdom.[52]

Software provider MINDBODY uses a wide variety of online statistics to monitor its brand and assess marketing effects.

Source: MINDBODY

## marketing memo

## Measuring social media ROI

Industry expenditures on social media campaigns are expected to double in the next four years, but many marketers do not know what they are getting in return for their dollars. When Audi ran the first Super Bowl ad to feature a Twitter hashtag in 2011, it had no idea how much the high engagement of its Facebook fan base translated into sales of more cars. One report showed that 50 percent of Fortune 1000 companies did not benchmark or measure the payback of their social CRM projects.

Initially, the focus of measuring social media effects was on easily observed quantities like the number of Facebook "likes" and Twitter tweets per week. These did not always correlate with marketing or business success, so researchers began digging deeper. Assessing social media value is not an easy task. Some marketing pundits compare social media to a phone: How would you assess the ROI of all the different calls you make? Josh Bernoff, Forrester Research's acclaimed digital marketing guru, sees short-term and long-term benefits of social media in four categories:

1. *Short-term financial benefits*, such as increased revenue or decreased costs. On the revenue side, when NetShops.com added ratings and reviews to its site, sales increased 26 percent within six months. On the cost side, National Instruments, makers of sophisticated technical engineering products, found members of its user community answered 46 percent of other users' questions, saving NI its typical $10 service cost per call. Similarly, AT&T's revamped online community saved the firm 16 percent in telephone customer support in one month.

2. *Short-term overall digital benefits*. When Swanson Health Products improved the visibility of its product reviews, they became more accessible to search engines, and traffic to its product pages rose 163 percent. Online videos, communities, blogs, and Twitter can similarly boost search performance.

3. *Long-term brand lift*. Social media can improve long-term brand performance measures. When P&G created a Facebook page to support ski jumper Lindsey Van, it solicited 40,000 signatures on a petition to make ski jumping an Olympic sport. Surveys of participating Facebook users found an 8 percent to 11 percent increase in brand preference and purchase intent.

4. *Long-term risk avoidance*. Dealing with a crisis can cost a firm millions of dollars over time. It is better to avoid or avert a crisis before it creates any brand damage. Firms such as McDonald's and AT&T have customer service teams who monitor Tweets about their products or services to nip any alleged problems in the bud.

Forrester social media analyst Zach Hofer-Shall believes mining actionable insights and measurable feedback from social media requires: (1) the right people to interpret the data, (2) a business purpose to drive strategy, (3) the best social listening platform for achieving goals, and (4) a formalized process for analyzing data and taking action.

The easiest way to create and measure social media's payoff is to include a contest, sweepstake, or promotion. Silicon Valley ad agency Wildfire created a promotion for Jamba Juice where the value of a "lucky coupon" was revealed only in-store. Tens of thousands of customers entered. The promotion was successful, but social media results can still be unpredictable.

V. Kumar and his colleagues suggest a seven-step process to social media success with several helpful indices that could be developed for each step:

1. Monitor the conversations.
2. Identify influential individuals.
3. Identify the factors they share.
4. Locate potential influencers who have relevant interests.
5. Recruit those influencers.
6. Incentivize them to spread positive word of mouth.
7. Reap the rewards.

Research has also shown that our use of social media differs in significant ways. People tend to be more positive in one-way communications (such as blogs and Twitter) than in two-way forums where they share and discuss brand or product experiences with others.

*Source: Getty Images*

P&G's online campaign to support ski jumper Lindsay Van produced benefits for its Secret deodorant brand too.

**Sources:** "ROI Lacking in Social CRM," www.warc.com. May 4, 2012; Josh Bernoff, "A Balanced Perspective on Social ROI," *Marketing News*, February 28, 2011; Piet Levy, "10 Minutes with…Zach Hofer-Shall," *Marketing News*, September 15, 2011; Frahad Manjoo, "Does Social Media Have a Return on Investment?," *Fast Company*, July/August 2011; David A. Schweidel, Wendy W. Moe, and Chris Boudreaux, "Social Media Intelligence: Measuring Brand Sentiment from Online Conversation," MSI Report 12-100 (Cambridge, MA: Marketing Science Institute), 2012.

| TABLE 4.3 | Sample Marketing Metrics | |
|---|---|---|
| **I. External** | | **II. Internal** |
| Awareness | | Awareness of goals |
| Market share (volume or value) | | Commitment to goals |
| Relative price (market share value/volume) | | Active innovation support |
| Number of complaints (level of dissatisfaction) | | Resource adequacy |
| Consumer satisfaction | | Staffing/skill levels |
| Distribution/availability | | Desire to learn |
| Total number of customers | | Willingness to change |
| Perceived quality/esteem | | Freedom to fail |
| Loyalty/retention | | Autonomy |
| Relative perceived quality | | Relative employee satisfaction |

**Source:** Tim Ambler, "What Does Marketing Success Look Like?," *Marketing Management* (Spring 2001), pp. 13–18.

## MARKETING-MIX MODELING

Marketing accountability also means that marketers must more precisely estimate the effects of different marketing investments. *Marketing-mix models* analyze data from a variety of sources, such as retailer scanner data, company shipment data, pricing, media, and promotion spending data, to understand more precisely the effects of specific marketing activities.[53] To deepen understanding, marketers can conduct multivariate analyses, such as regression analysis, to sort through how each marketing element influences marketing outcomes such as brand sales or market share.

Especially popular with packaged-goods marketers such as Procter & Gamble, Clorox, and Colgate, the findings from marketing-mix modeling help allocate or reallocate expenditures. Analyses explore which part of ad budgets are wasted, what optimal spending levels are, and what minimum investment levels should be.

Although marketing-mix modeling helps to isolate effects, it is less effective at assessing how different marketing elements work in combination. Wharton's Dave Reibstein also notes three other shortcomings:[54]

- Marketing-mix modeling focuses on incremental growth instead of baseline sales or long-term effects.
- The integration of important metrics such as customer satisfaction, awareness, and brand equity into marketing-mix modeling is limited.
- Marketing-mix modeling generally fails to incorporate metrics related to competitors, the trade, or the sales force (the average business spends far more on the sales force and trade promotion than on advertising or consumer promotion).

## MARKETING DASHBOARDS

Firms are also employing organizational processes and systems to make sure they maximize the value of all these different metrics. Management can assemble a summary set of relevant internal and external measures in a marketing dashboard for synthesis and interpretation. Marketing dashboards are like the instrument panel in a car or plane, visually displaying real-time indicators to ensure proper functioning. Formally, **marketing dashboards** are "a concise set of interconnected performance drivers to be viewed in common throughout the organization."[55]

Dashboards are only as good as the information on which they're based, but sophisticated visualization tools are helping bring data alive. Color-coding, symbols, and different types of charts, tables, and gauges are easy to use and effective. Some companies are also appointing marketing controllers to review budget items and expenses. Increasingly, these controllers use business intelligence software to create digital versions of marketing dashboards that aggregate data from internal and external sources.

As input to the marketing dashboard, companies should include two key market-based scorecards that reflect performance and provide possible early warning signals.

- A **customer-performance scorecard** records how well the company is doing year after year on such customer-based measures as those shown in Table 4.4. Management should set target goals for each measure and take action when results get out of bounds.
- A **stakeholder-performance scorecard** tracks the satisfaction of various constituencies who have a critical interest in and impact on the company's performance: employees, suppliers, banks, distributors, retailers, and stockholders. Again, management should take action when one or more groups register increased or above-norm levels of dissatisfaction.[56]

| TABLE 4.4 | Sample Customer-Performance Scorecard Measures |
|---|---|

- Percentage of new customers to average number of customers
- Percentage of lost customers to average number of customers
- Percentage of win-back customers to average number of customers
- Percentage of customers falling into very dissatisfied, dissatisfied, neutral, satisfied, and very satisfied categories
- Percentage of customers who say they would repurchase the product
- Percentage of customers who say they would recommend the product to others
- Percentage of target market customers who have brand awareness or recall
- Percentage of customers who say that the company's product is the most preferred in its category
- Percentage of customers who correctly identify the brand's intended positioning and differentiation
- Average perception of company's product quality relative to chief competitor
- Average perception of company's service quality relative to chief competitor

## marketing memo

### Designing Effective Marketing Dashboards

Marketing consultant Pat LaPointe sees marketing dashboards as providing all the up-to-the-minute information necessary to run the business operations for a company—such as sales versus forecast, distribution channel effectiveness, brand equity evolution, and human capital development. According to LaPointe, an effective dashboard will focus thinking, improve internal communications, and reveal where marketing investments are paying off and where they aren't.

LaPointe observes four common measurement "pathways" marketers pursue today (see Figure 4.2).

- The *customer metrics pathway* looks at how prospects become customers, from awareness to preference to trial to repeat purchase, or some less linear model. This area also examines how the customer experience contributes to the perception of value and competitive advantage.
- The *unit metrics pathway* reflects what marketers know about sales of product/service units—how much is sold by product line and/or by geography; the marketing cost per unit sold as an efficiency yardstick; and where and how margin is optimized in terms of characteristics of the product line or distribution channel.
- The *cash-flow metrics pathway* focuses on how well marketing expenditures are achieving short-term returns. Program and campaign ROI models measure the immediate impact or net present value of profits expected from a given investment.
- The *brand metrics pathway* tracks the development of the longer-term impact of marketing through brand equity measures that assess both the perceptual health of the brand from customer and prospective customer perspectives and the overall financial health of the brand.

LaPointe feels a marketing dashboard can present insights from all the pathways in a graphically related view that helps management see subtle links between them. Tabs can allow the user to toggle easily between different "families" of metrics organized by customer, product, experience, brand, channels, efficiency, organizational development, or macroenvironmental factors. Each tab presents the three or four most insightful metrics, with data filtered by business unit, geography, or customer segment based on the users' needs. (See Figure 4.3 for a sample brand metrics page.)

Ideally, over time the number of metrics on the dashboard will be reduced to a few key drivers. Meanwhile, the process of developing and refining the marketing dashboard will undoubtedly raise and resolve many key questions about the business.

**Source:** Adapted from Pat LaPointe, *Marketing by the Dashboard Light*, Association of National Advertisers, 2005, www.MarketingNPV.com.

| Fig. 4.2 |

Marketing
Measure
Pathway

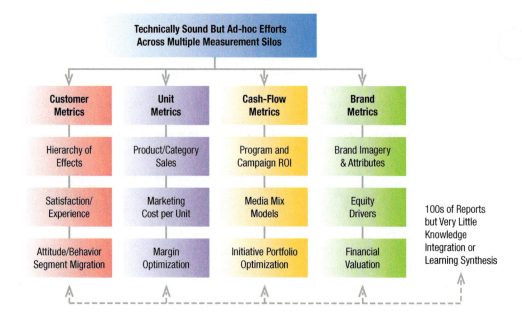

| Fig. 4.3 |

Example of
a Marketing
Dashboard

Source: Adapted from Patrick
LaPointe, *Marketing by the
Dashboard Light—How to
Get More Insight, Foresight,
and Accountability from Your
Marketing Investments.*
© 2005, Patrick LaPointe.

Some executives worry that they'll miss the big picture if they focus too much on a set of numbers on a dashboard. Some critics are concerned about privacy and the pressure the technique places on employees. But most experts feel the rewards offset the risks. "Marketing Memo: Designing Effective Marketing Dashboards" provides practical advice about the development of these marketing tools.

# Summary

1. Companies can conduct their own marketing research or hire other companies to do it for them. Some of ways companies can creatively and affordably conduct research include: engage students or professors to design and carry out projects; use the Internet; check out rivals; tap into marketing partner expertise; and tap into employee creativity and wisdom.

2. Good marketing research is characterized by the scientific method, creativity, multiple research methods, accurate model building, cost-benefit analysis, healthy skepticism, and an ethical focus.

3. The marketing research process consists of defining the problem, decision alternatives, and research objectives; developing the research plan; collecting the information; analyzing the information; presenting the findings to management; and making the decision.

4. In conducting research, firms must decide whether to collect their own data or use data that already exist. They must also choose a research approach (observational, focus group, survey, behavioral data, or experimental) and research instruments (questionnaire, qualitative measures, or technological devices). In addition, they must decide on a sampling plan and contact methods (by mail, by phone, in person, or online).

5. Two complementary approaches to measuring marketing productivity are: (1) marketing metrics to assess marketing effects and (2) marketing-mix modeling to estimate causal relationships and measure how marketing activity affects outcomes. Marketing dashboards are a structured way to disseminate the insights gleaned from these two approaches within the organization.

6. Assessing the ROI of social media is challenging but requires a range of short-term and long-term financial and brand-related measures. Although Facebook "likes" and Twitter tweets provide some sense of the engagement for a brand, a more complete set of measures is typically needed to get a more accurate picture of social media or other online activities.

---

## MyMarketingLab

Go to **mymktlab.com** to complete the problems marked with this icon ⭐ as well as for additional Auto-graded and Assisted-graded writing questions.

---

# Applications

## Marketing Debate
### What Is the Best Type of Marketing Research?

Many market researchers have their favorite research approaches or techniques, though different researchers often have different preferences. Some researchers maintain that the only way to really learn about consumers or brands is through in-depth, qualitative research. Others contend that the only legitimate and defensible form of marketing research uses quantitative measures.

**Take a position:** The best marketing research is quantitative in nature *versus* The best marketing research is qualitative in nature.

## Marketing Discussion
### Survey Quality

⭐ When was the last time you participated in a survey? How helpful do you think the information you provided was? How could the research have been done differently to make it more effective?

# Marketing Excellence

## >> IDEO

IDEO is the largest and one of the most influential design consultancy firms in the United States. The company has created many recognizable design icons of the technology age, including the first laptop computer, the first mouse for Apple, the Palm V PDA, and the TiVo digital video recorder. Beyond its high-tech wizardry, the company has designed revolutionary household items such as the Swiffer Sweeper and Crest's stand-up toothpaste tube, both for Procter & Gamble. IDEO's diverse roster of clients includes AT&T, Bank of America, Ford Motor Company, PepsiCo, Nike, Marriott, Caterpillar, Eli Lilly, Lufthansa, Prada, and the Mayo Clinic.

IDEO's success is predicated on an approach called "design thinking"—an innovative method that incorporates behavior into design. It's an unconventional way of problem solving and starts by forming teams of individuals with various backgrounds and experiences. Team members range from anthropologists and journalists to MBAs and engineers. IDEO's belief is that if you bring together a diverse group with these talents, they will build upon each other's ideas and come up a solution that one mind cannot reach alone.

Next, IDEO uses different methods of behavioral research and observation to get into the mind of the consumer. This helps IDEO uncover deep insights and understand how consumers purchase, interact with, use, and even dispose of products. For example, one method shadows consumers, takes pictures or videos of them during product purchase or use occasions, and conducts in-depth interviews with them to further evaluate their experiences. IDEO uses another method called behavioral mapping and maintains a photographic log of people within a certain area like an airline departure lounge, a hospital waiting room, or a food court to gauge how the experience can be improved. Participants keep a "camera journal" in which they record their visual impressions of a given product or category. IDEO also invites consumers to use storytelling techniques and share personal narratives, videos, skits, or even animations about their experiences with a product or service.

IDEO's human-centered approach runs counter to the prevailing wisdom of many high-tech firms that focus more on their own capabilities when designing products. David Blakely, head of IDEO's technology group, explained, "Tech companies design from the inside out, whereas we design from the outside in so that we can put customers first." Ultimately, the company designs products that consumers want and value because they offer a superior experience and solve a problem. Recent product innovations include a heart defibrillator that talks with instructions during an emergency and a renovated version of the classic wooden classroom chair.

Marriott hired IDEO to help make its Courtyard by Marriott hotels more appealing to younger guests. IDEO conducted interviews and observed guests in the hotel's lounges, lobbies, and restaurants. Its research revealed that younger guests were turned off by the lack of activity in the hotel's public places, the lack of technology offered, and poor food options. As a result, Courtyard by Marriott updated its furniture and decor to be more comfortable and inviting. The hotel added advanced technology options throughout its lobbies and lounges, such as flat-screen TVs and free Wi-Fi. Marriott converted its breakfast buffets to 24/7 coffee-shop-style cafés, where guests could quickly grab a gourmet coffee drink and healthy bite to eat anytime. Courtyard even created new outdoor hangout spots with sound speakers and fire pits. After the renovations, the chain changed its tagline to "Courtyard. It's a New Stay."

Prototyping takes place throughout IDEO's design process so individuals can physically test out the product, experience it, and improve upon it during each level of development. IDEO encourages its clients, even senior executives, to participate in the research so they get a sense of the actual consumer experience with their product or service. For example, when it created a prototype for Apple's first mouse, Steve Jobs didn't like the sound it made when it moved around on a desk and insisted that IDEO find a way to reduce the noise. The design firm overcame this huge technical obstacle and successfully rubber-coated the steel ball without interfering with its function.

IDEO's novel consumer-led approach to design has generated countless success stories and awards for the firm and its clients. Its work has also served as inspiration for the creation of Stanford University's design school—The Hasso Plattner Institute of Design—where students work on problem solving centered around design thinking.

The most important result for IDEO is that its designs solve a usability problem for clients. The company goes broad and deep to achieve this goal. Since its founding, it has been issued thousands of patents and generated hundreds of millions in revenues.

### Questions

1. Why has IDEO been so successful?

2. What is the most difficult challenge it faces in conducting its research and designing its products?

3. In the end, IDEO creates great solutions for companies that then receive all the credit. Should IDEO try to create more brand awareness for itself? Why or why not?

**Sources:** Lisa Chamberlain, "Going Off the Beaten Path for New Design Ideas," *New York Times*, March 12, 2006; Chris Taylor, "School of Bright Ideas," *Time*, March 6, 2005, p. A8; Scott Morrison, "Sharp Focus Gives Design Group the Edge," *Financial Times*, February 17, 2005, p. 8; Bruce Nussbaum, "The Power of Design," *BusinessWeek*, May 17, 2004, p. 86; Teressa Iezzi, "Innovate, but Do It for Consumers," *Advertising Age*, September 11, 2006; Barbara De Lollis, "Marriott Perks Up Courtyard with Edgier, More Social Style," *USA Today*, April 1, 2008; Tim Brown, "Change by Design," *BusinessWeek*, October 5, 2009, pp. 54–56; *60 Minutes*, January 6, 2013.

## Marketing Excellence

### >> Intuit

Intuit develops and sells financial and tax solution software for consumers and small and medium-sized businesses. The company was founded in 1983 by a former Procter & Gamble employee, Scott Cook, and a Stanford University programmer, Tom Proulx, after Cook realized there must be a better way to automate his bill-paying process. For almost 30 years, Intuit's mission has been to "revolutionize people's lives by solving their important business and financial management problems."

Intuit launched its first product, Quicken, in 1984 but almost went out of business twice during its first few years. In order to survive, Intuit changed its distribution strategy and sold its software to banks. After some favorable reviews in the trade journals and an effective print advertising campaign that featured a 1-800 number, the company got its first break. By 1988, Quicken was the best-selling finance product on the market. In 1992, Intuit launched QuickBooks, a bookkeeping and payroll software product for small businesses, and went public the following year.

Intuit grew quickly in the early 1990s, thanks to the success of Quicken, QuickBooks, and TurboTax, its tax preparation software program. Intuit's products did something for small businesses that more complicated accounting packages didn't: They solved finance and tax problems in a simple, easy-to-use manner. Intuit had recognized correctly that simplicity was the key, not in-depth accounting analysis. By 1995, the firm held a 70 percent market share, and Microsoft tried to purchase it for $2 billion. The Justice Department, however, blocked the deal as anticompetitive, and the buyout collapsed.

From 1995 to 1997, Intuit's stock tumbled 72 percent and the company was forced to refocus its strategic efforts. It turned to the growing power of the Internet, online banking capabilities, and valuable insight from extensive consumer research to develop new products. This new strategic focus and emphasis on consumer research helped improve the company's stock value and market position in the early 2000s.

In 2007, Scott Cook wanted the company to focus even more intently on innovation. As a result, he adopted an up-and-coming approach to product development called design thinking. Design thinking is an unconventional way of problem solving that incorporates extensive consumer observation and research with trial and error and ongoing product prototyping.

Today, Intuit spends a significant amount of time and money—approximately 20 percent of net revenues—on consumer research each year. This research helps Intuit understand exactly how customers use and feel about their products and keep abreast of technology, consumer needs, and competition.

Field research helps Intuit uncover insight in a variety of ways. During a *Site Visit,* Intuit researchers visit the individual's home or office to observe exactly how products are used, what works well, what frustrates users, and how products can be improved upon. A *Lab Study* invites consumers to one of Intuit's research labs to test and experiment with Intuit's new products and ideas. During a *Remote Study*, consumers are interviewed over the phone and often asked to view new design concepts over the Internet. Intuit also conducts an ongoing extensive research study with the Institute for the Future to learn more about the future trends affecting small businesses. The company uses what it learns to improve versions of its products each year and better understand the next generation of financial and tax software.

Intuit's in-depth research recently led to innovative new products and services. For example, employees watched younger consumers get frustrated using an Intuit tax software program because they couldn't take pictures of their tax forms and complete their taxes via their mobile device. This frustration and Intuit's keen empathy for the consumer led to the development of a tax app called SnapTax. Launched in 2010, it has since been downloaded more than a million times.

Demand for Intuit's products is seasonal, and its marketing efforts are typically concentrated around tax preparation time—November through April. During that time, Intuit develops promotions with original equipment manufacturers (OEMs) and major retailers via direct mail, Web marketing, print, radio, and television.

While Intuit's marketing campaigns have evolved over the years, positive word of mouth and exceptional customer service have been its most effective marketing tools since its early days. Harry Pforzheimer, chief communications officer and marketing leader, explained, "It's a little harder to measure but when you know that roughly eight out of 10 customers bought your product because of word-of-mouth that's a pretty powerful tool...So engaging with our customers directly is part of our DNA and communicating with customers on a timely basis is critical. And that timely basis now is instantaneous."

Intuit has expanded globally through new product and service offerings and through strategic acquisitions. Its purchase of Mint.com, for example, added value by giving consumers another tool to analyze their spending against a budget. Intuit also acquired Demandforce, which added the ability to provide online marketing and communications tools for small businesses. In 2009, Intuit won a rare fight against Microsoft when the software giant discontinued its Money product line after an 18-year battle with Quicken. And the company's expansion into mobile solutions has encouraged younger consumers to adopt its finance and tax software. Intuit now has more than 50 mobile applications, and more than 45 million customers have used its cloud-based services in the past five years.

As Intuit expands globally, it is developing new products for consumers worldwide. In India, for example, Intuit launched Fasal, a service that gives hundreds of thousands of farmers up-to-date marketing information to help them get the best price for their crops. Intuit earned $4.51 billion in revenue for fiscal year 2014, primarily from Quicken, QuickBooks, and TurboTax sales.

## Questions

1. Why are consumer research and design thinking so critical to Intuit's success?

2. What are the challenges Intuit faces in the near future?

3. How important are Intuit's products for mobile devices?

**Sources:** Intuit, *2012 Annual Report*; Karen E. Klein, "The Face of Entrepreneurship in 2017," *BusinessWeek*, January 31, 2007; Intuit, "Intuit Study: Next-Gen Artisans Fuel New Entrepreneurial Economy," February 13, 2008; Michael Bush, "How PR Chiefs Have Shifted Toward Center of Marketing Departments," *Advertising Age*, September 21, 2009; Jon Swartz, "More Marketers Use Social Networking to Reach Customers," *USA Today*, August 28, 2009; Mark Johnson and Joe Sinfield, "Focusing on Consumer Needs Is Not Enough," *Advertising Age*, April 28, 2008; "Intuit CEO Sees Growth in Mobile, Global Markets," *Associated Press*, September 23, 2009; Sarah Needleman, "How I Built It: For Intuit Co-Founder, the Numbers Add Up," *Wall Street Journal*, August 18, 2011, p. B4; Rachel Emma Siverman, "Companies Change Their Way of Thinking," *Wall Street Journal*, June 7, 2012; Robin Goldwyn Blumenthal, "Intuit: Lots More Than Quicken," *Wall Street Journal*, September 30, 2012.

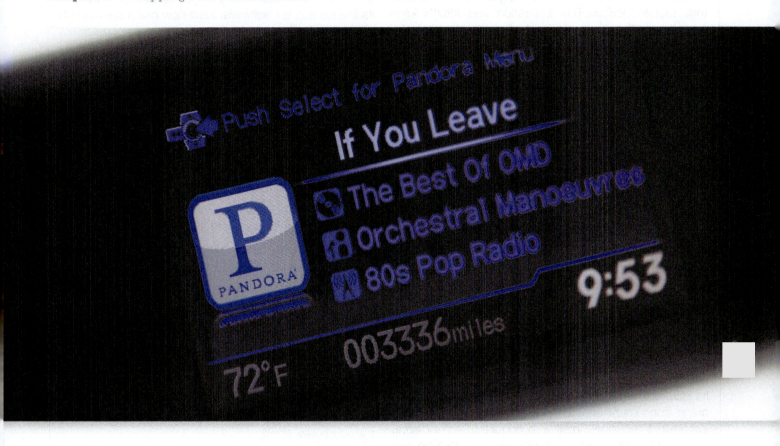

# In This Chapter, We Will Address the Following **Questions**

1. What are customer value, satisfaction, and loyalty, and how can companies deliver them? (p. 127)

2. What is the lifetime value of customers, and how can marketers maximize it? (p. 136)

3. How can companies attract and retain the right customers and cultivate strong customer relationships and communities? (p. 142)

4. How do customers' new capabilities affect the way companies conduct their marketing? (p. 146)

Pandora has created strong customer loyalty with its innovative online music discovery and recommendation services.

*Source: Bloomberg via Getty Images*

## MyMarketingLab™

⭐ **Improve Your Grade!**
Over 10 million students improved their results using the Pearson MyLabs. Visit mymktlab.com for simulations, tutorials, and end-of-chapter problems.

# **5** Creating Long-Term Loyalty Relationships

**Although their enhanced capabilities can help companies earn strong customer loyalty,** increased consumer capabilities pose challenges. Regardless, marketers must connect with customers—informing, engaging, and maybe even energizing them in the process. Customer-centered companies are adept at building customer relationships, not just products; they are skilled in market engineering, not just product engineering. Technology plays an increasing role for many companies and industries, offering new ways to satisfy customer needs and build loyalty. The music industry is a dramatic example.[1]

 *Perhaps no industry has been more thoroughly transformed than the music industry. Technological advances have changed the way consumers purchase, listen to, and share music, and music-streaming services are in a virtual arms race for their loyalty. Internet radio company Pandora has staked a claim to be the market leader with its innovative automated music discovery and recommendation service, the Music Genome Project, which has helped attract more than 200 million registered users. Based on a listener's musical selection, Pandora recommends other musical selections of a similar well-defined genre. Listener feedback to those recommendations and more than 400 different musical attributes judged by professional music lovers who pass a rigorous test are combined and analyzed to suggest future songs. Pandora launched its smart-phone app in 2008, making its service available truly "anywhere, anytime" and enriching the opportunity to provide feedback and buy music that makes it highly involving to listeners. Advertisers are able to target Pandora's audiences by key demographics and traits such as gender, birth year, zip code location, type of music, and time of day. Pandora faces steep competition, however, from Spotify, iHeartRadio, and Slacker, each of which has unique features that may drive customer preference and loyalty.*

**Successful marketers are those who** carefully cultivate customer satisfaction and loyalty. In this chapter, we spell out the different ways they can go about winning customers and beating competitors.

# Building Customer Value, Satisfaction, and Loyalty

Managers who believe the customer is the company's only true "profit center" consider the traditional organization chart in Figure 5.1(a)—a pyramid with the president at the top, management in the middle, and frontline people and customers at the bottom—obsolete.[2]

| Fig. 5.1 |

Traditional
Organization versus
Modern Customer-
Oriented Company
Organization

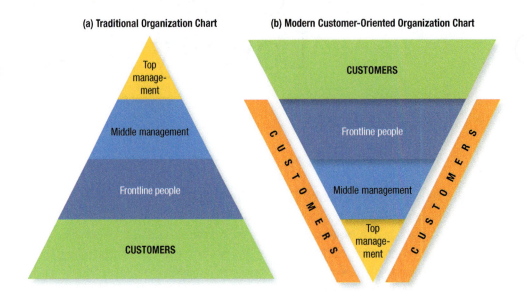

(a) Traditional Organization Chart

(b) Modern Customer-Oriented Organization Chart

Successful marketing companies invert the chart to look like Figure 5.1(b). At the top are customers; next in importance are frontline people who meet, serve, and satisfy them; under them are the middle managers, whose job is to support the frontline people so they can serve customers well; and at the base is top management, whose job is to hire and support good middle managers. We have added customers along the sides of Figure 5.1(b) to indicate that managers at every level must be personally engaged in knowing, meeting, and serving customers.

Some companies have been founded on the customer-on-top business model, and customer advocacy has been their strategy—and competitive advantage—all along. With the rise of digital technologies, increasingly informed consumers expect companies to do more than connect with them, more than satisfy them, and even more than delight them. They expect companies to *listen* and *respond* to them.

When Office Depot added customer reviews to its Web site, revenue and sales conversion increased significantly. The company also incorporated review-related terms in its paid search advertising campaign. As a result of these efforts, Web site revenue and the number of new buyers visiting the site both increased by more than 150 percent.[3]

## CUSTOMER-PERCEIVED VALUE

Consumers are better educated and better informed than ever, and they have the tools to verify companies' claims and seek out superior alternatives. Even the best-run companies have to be careful not to take customers for granted, as Dell found out.[4]

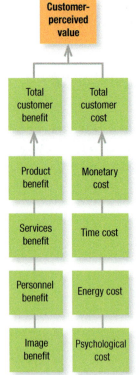

**DELL**    Dell rode to success by offering low-priced computers, logistical efficiency, and after-sales service. The firm's maniacal focus on low costs has been a key ingredient in its success. When it shifted its customer-service call centers to India and the Philippines to cut costs, however, understaffing frequently led to 30-minute waits for customers. Almost half the calls required at least one transfer. To discourage customer calls, Dell even removed its toll-free service number from its Web site. With customer satisfaction slipping, while competitors matched its product quality and prices *and* offered better service, Dell's market share and stock price both declined sharply. Dell ended up hiring more North American call center employees. "The team was managing cost instead of managing service and quality," Michael Dell confesses.

| Fig. 5.2 |

Determinants
of Customer-
Perceived Value

How do customers ultimately make choices? They tend to be value maximizers, within the bounds of search costs and limited knowledge, mobility, and income. Customers choose—for whatever reason—the offer they believe will deliver the highest value and act on it (Figure 5.2). Whether the offer lives up to

*Source: Bloomberg via Getty Images*

When Dell cut costs too much on its customer service, customer satisfaction dropped and the company's stock price sank.

expectation affects customer satisfaction and the probability that the customer will purchase the product again. In one survey asking U.S. consumers "Does [Brand X] give good value for what you pay?" the top ten–scoring brands were: Subway, Cheerios, Amazon, History Channel, Ford, Discovery Channel, Lowe's, Olive Garden, YouTube, and Google.[5]

**DEFINING VALUE** **Customer-perceived value (CPV)** is the difference between the prospective customer's evaluation of all the benefits and costs of an offering and the perceived alternatives. **Total customer benefit** is the perceived monetary value of the bundle of economic, functional, and psychological benefits customers expect from a given market offering because of the product, service, people, and image. **Total customer cost** is the perceived bundle of costs customers expect to incur in evaluating, obtaining, using, and disposing of the given market offering, including monetary, time, energy, and psychological costs.

Customer-perceived value is thus based on the difference between benefits the customer gets and costs he or she assumes for different choices. The marketer can increase the value of the offering by raising economic, functional, or emotional benefits and/or reducing one or more costs. The customer choosing between two value offerings, V1 and V2, will favor V1 if the ratio V1:V2 is larger than one, favor V2 if the ratio is smaller than one, and be indifferent if the ratio equals one.

**APPLYING VALUE CONCEPTS** Suppose the buyer for a large construction company wants to buy a tractor for residential construction from either Caterpillar or Komatsu. He wants the tractor to deliver certain levels of reliability, durability, performance, and resale value. The competing salespeople carefully describe their respective offers. The buyer decides Caterpillar has greater product benefits based on his perceptions of those attributes. He also perceives differences in the accompanying services—delivery, training, and maintenance—and decides Caterpillar provides better service as well as more knowledgeable and responsive staff. Finally, he places higher value on Caterpillar's corporate image and reputation. He adds up all the economic, functional, and psychological benefits from these four sources—product, services, people, and image—and perceives Caterpillar as delivering greater customer benefits.

Does he buy the Caterpillar tractor? Not necessarily. He also examines his total cost of transacting with Caterpillar versus Komatsu, a cost that consists of more than money. As Adam Smith observed more than two centuries ago in *The Wealth of Nations*, "The real price of anything is the toil and trouble of acquiring it." Total customer cost therefore also includes the buyer's time, energy, and psychological costs expended in product acquisition, usage, maintenance, ownership, and disposal. The buyer evaluates these elements together with the monetary cost to form a total customer cost. Then he considers whether Caterpillar's total customer cost is too high compared to total customer benefits. If it is, he might choose Komatsu. The buyer will choose whichever source delivers the highest perceived value.

Now let's use this decision-making theory to help Caterpillar succeed in selling to this buyer. Caterpillar can improve its offer in three ways. First, it can increase total customer benefit by improving economic, functional, and psychological benefits of its product, services, people, and/or image. Second, it can reduce the buyer's nonmonetary costs by reducing the time, energy, and psychological investment. Third, it can reduce its product's monetary cost to the buyer.

Suppose Caterpillar concludes the buyer sees its offer as worth $20,000. Further, suppose Caterpillar's cost of producing the tractor is $14,000. This means Caterpillar's offer generates $6,000 over its cost, so the firm needs to charge between $14,000 and $20,000. If it charges less than $14,000, it won't cover its costs; if it charges more, it will price itself out of the market.

Caterpillar's market success can be attributed in part to its focus on maximizing total customer value.

Source: James Mattil/Shutterstock

Caterpillar's price will determine how much value it delivers to the buyer and how much flows to Caterpillar. If it charges $19,000, it is creating $1,000 of customer-perceived value and keeping $5,000 for itself. The lower Caterpillar sets its price, the higher the customer's perceived value and, therefore, the higher the customer's incentive to purchase. To win the sale, the firm must offer more customer-perceived value than Komatsu does.[6] Caterpillar is well aware of the importance of taking a broad view of customer value.[7]

**CATERPILLAR**   Caterpillar has become a leading firm by maximizing total customer value in the construction equipment industry, despite challenges from a number of able competitors such as John Deere, Case, Komatsu, Volvo, and Hitachi and emerging ones such as LiuGong Machinery in China. First, Caterpillar produces high-performance equipment known for reliability and durability—key purchase considerations in heavy industrial equipment. The firm also makes it easy for customers to find the right product by providing a full line of construction equipment and a wide range of financial terms. Caterpillar maintains the largest number of independent construction-equipment dealers in the industry. These dealers all carry a complete line of Caterpillar products and are typically better trained and perform more reliably than competitors' dealers. Caterpillar has also built a worldwide parts and service system second to none in the industry. Customers recognize all the value Caterpillar creates in its offerings, allowing the firm to command a premium price 10 percent to 20 percent higher than competitors'. Caterpillar also makes strategic acquisitions to acquire new customers, such as picking up mining equipment maker Bucyrus International for $8.6 billion in 2010. Despite a recession that brought hard times to its industry and battered many of its competitors' finances, Caterpillar was one of the best-performing stocks among the 30 companies in the Dow Jones Industrial Average coming out of the recession.

Very often, managers conduct a **customer value analysis** to reveal the company's strengths and weaknesses relative to those of various competitors. The steps in this analysis are:

1. *Identify the major attributes and benefits that customers value.* Customers are asked what attributes, benefits, and performance levels they look for in choosing a product and vendors. Attributes and benefits should be defined broadly to encompass all the inputs to customers' decisions.[8]
2. *Assess the quantitative importance of the different attributes and benefits.* Customers are asked to rate the importance of different attributes and benefits. If their ratings diverge too much, the marketer should cluster them into different segments.
3. *Assess the company's and competitors' performances on the different customer values against their rated importance.* Customers describe where they see the company's and competitors' performances on each attribute and benefit.
4. *Examine how customers in a specific segment rate the company's performance against a specific major competitor on an individual attribute or benefit basis.* If the company's offer exceeds the competitor's offer on all important attributes and benefits, the company can charge a higher price (thereby earning higher profits), or it can charge the same price and gain more market share.
5. *Monitor customer values over time.* The company must periodically redo its studies of customer values and competitors' standings as the economy, technology, and product features change.

**CHOICE PROCESSES AND IMPLICATIONS** Some marketers might argue the process we have described is too rational. Suppose the customer chooses the Komatsu tractor. How can we explain this choice? Here are three possibilities.

1. *The buyer might be under orders to buy at the lowest price.* The Caterpillar salesperson's task is then to convince the buyer's manager that buying on price alone will result in lower long-term profits and customer value for the buyer's company.
2. *The buyer will retire before the company realizes the Komatsu tractor is more expensive to operate.* The buyer will look good in the short run; he is maximizing personal benefit. The Caterpillar salesperson's task is to convince other people in the customer company that Caterpillar delivers greater customer value.
3. *The buyer enjoys a long-term friendship with the Komatsu salesperson.* In this case, Caterpillar's salesperson needs to show the buyer that the Komatsu tractor will draw complaints from the tractor operators when they discover its high fuel cost and need for frequent repairs.

The point is clear: Buyers operate under various constraints and occasionally make choices that give more weight to their personal benefit than to the company's benefit.

Customer-perceived value is a useful framework that applies to many situations and yields rich insights. It suggests that the seller must assess the total customer benefit and total customer cost associated with each competitor's offer in order to know how its own offer rates in the buyer's mind. It also implies that the seller at a disadvantage has two alternatives: increase total customer benefit or decrease total customer cost. The former calls for strengthening or augmenting the economical, functional, and psychological benefits of the offering's product, services, personnel, and image. The latter calls for reducing the buyer's costs by reducing the price or cost of ownership and maintenance, simplifying the ordering and delivery process, or absorbing some buyer risk by offering a warranty.

**DELIVERING HIGH CUSTOMER VALUE** Consumers have varying degrees of loyalty to specific brands, stores, and companies. **Loyalty** has been defined as "a deeply held commitment to rebuy or repatronize a preferred product or service in the future despite situational influences and marketing efforts having the potential to cause switching behavior."[9] Table 5.1 lists brands with the highest customer loyalty, according to one 2012 survey.

The **value proposition** consists of the whole cluster of benefits the company promises to deliver; it is more than the core positioning of the offering. For example, Volvo's core positioning has been "safety," but the buyer is promised more than just a safe car; other benefits include good performance, design, and safety for the environment. The value proposition is thus a promise about the experience customers can expect from the company's market offering and their relationship with the supplier. Whether the promise is kept depends on the company's ability to manage its value delivery system. The **value delivery system** includes all the experiences the customer will have on the way to obtaining and using the offering. At the heart of a good value delivery system is a set of core business processes that help deliver distinctive consumer value.[10]

# TOTAL CUSTOMER SATISFACTION

In general, **satisfaction** is a person's feelings of pleasure or disappointment that result from comparing a product or service's perceived performance (or outcome) to expectations.[11] If the performance or experience falls short of expectations, the customer is dissatisfied. If it matches expectations, the customer is satisfied. If it exceeds expectations, the customer is highly satisfied or delighted.[12]

Customer assessments of product or service performance depend on many factors, including the type of loyalty relationship the customer has with the brand.[13] Consumers often form more favorable perceptions of a product with a brand they already feel positive about. Research has also shown an asymmetric effect of product performance and expectations on satisfaction: The negative effect on customer satisfaction of failing to meet expectations is disproportionally stronger than the positive effect of exceeding expectations.[14]

Although the customer-centered firm seeks to create high customer satisfaction, that is not its ultimate goal. Increasing customer satisfaction by lowering price or increasing services may result in lower profits. The company might be able to increase its profitability by means other than increased satisfaction (for example, by improving manufacturing processes or investing more in R&D).

The company also has many stakeholders, including employees, dealers, suppliers, and stockholders. Spending more to increase customer satisfaction might divert funds from increasing the satisfaction of other "partners." Ultimately, the company must try to deliver a high level of customer satisfaction subject to also delivering acceptable levels to other stakeholders, given its total resources.

| TABLE 5.1 | Top 30 Brands in Customer Loyalty | | |
|---|---|---|---|
| **Brand** | **Category** | **Rankings** | |
| | | **2012** | **2011** |
| Apple | Tablet | 1 | N/A |
| Amazon | Tablet | 2 | N/A |
| Apple | Smart phone | 3 | 2 |
| Amazon | Online retail | 4 | 1 |
| Apple | Computer | 5 | 5 |
| Samsung | Tablet | 6 | N/A |
| Call of Duty | Major league gaming | 7 | N/A |
| Samsung | Cellphone | 8 | 4 |
| Halo | Major league gaming | 9 | N/A |
| Twitter | Social networks | 10 | 20 |
| Kindle | E-reader | 11 | 8 |
| Mary Kay | Cosmetics | 12 | 10 |
| Grey Goose | Vodka | 13 | 15 |
| Google | Search engine | 14 | 16 |
| YouTube | Social networks | 15 | N/A |
| Facebook | Social networks | 16 | 3 |
| Dunkin' Donuts | Coffee | 17 | 12 |
| Zappos | Online retailer | 18 | 6 |
| Patron | Tequila | 19 | 9 |
| Crest Whitestrips | Tooth whitener | 20 | 10 |
| Walmart | Discount retailer | 21 | 13 |
| Maybelline | Cosmetics | 22 | 14 |
| Clinique | Cosmetics, luxury | 23 | 34 |
| Ketel One | Vodka | 24 | 17 |
| Hyundai | Automotive | 25 | 7 |
| Samsung | Smart phone | 26 | 56 |
| LG | Cellphone | 27 | 19 |
| Mary Kay | Facial moisturizer | 28 | 28 |
| Avis | Car rental | 29 | 23 |
| LinkedIn | Social networks | 30 | 24 |

**Source:** "2012 Brand Keys Customer Loyalty Leaders List," www.brandkeys.com.

CREATING LONG-TERM LOYALTY RELATIONSHIPS | CHAPTER 5    133

How do buyers form their expectations? Expectations result from past buying experience, friends' and associates' advice, public information and discourse, and marketers' and competitors' information and promises. If a company raises expectations too high, the buyer is likely to be disappointed. If it sets expectations too low, it won't attract enough buyers (although it will satisfy those who do buy).[15]

Some of today's most successful companies are raising expectations and delivering performances to match. Korean automaker Kia found success in the United States by launching low-cost, high-quality cars with enough reliability to offer 10-year, 100,000-mile warranties.

## MONITORING SATISFACTION

Many companies are systematically measuring how well they treat customers, identifying the factors shaping satisfaction, and changing operations and marketing as a result.[16]

Wise firms measure customer satisfaction regularly because it is one key to customer retention.[17] A highly satisfied customer generally stays loyal longer, buys more as the company introduces new and upgraded products, talks favorably to others about the company and its products, pays less attention to competing brands and is less sensitive to price, offers product or service ideas to the company, and costs less to serve than new customers because transactions can become routine.[18]

The link between customer satisfaction and customer loyalty is not proportional, however. Suppose customer satisfaction is rated on a scale from 1 to 5. At a very low level of satisfaction (level 1), customers are likely to abandon the company and even bad-mouth it. At levels 2 to 4, customers are fairly satisfied but still find it easy to switch when a better offer comes along. At level 5, the customer is very likely to repurchase and even spread good word of mouth about the company. High satisfaction or delight creates an emotional bond with the brand or company, not just a rational preference. Xerox's senior management found its "completely satisfied" customers were six times more likely to repurchase Xerox products over the following 18 months than even its "very satisfied" customers.[19]

The company needs to recognize, however, that customers define good performance differently. Good delivery could mean early delivery, on-time delivery, or order completeness, and two customers can report being "highly satisfied" for different reasons. One may be easily satisfied most of the time, and the other might be hard to please but was pleased on this occasion.[20] It is also important to know how satisfied customers are with competitors in order to assess "share of wallet" or how much of the customer's spending the company's brand enjoys: The more highly the consumer ranks the company's brand in terms of satisfaction and loyalty, the more the customer is likely to spend on the brand.[21]

**MEASUREMENT TECHNIQUES** *Periodic surveys* can track customers' overall satisfaction directly and ask additional questions to measure repurchase intention, likelihood or willingness to recommend the company and brand to others, and specific attribute or benefit perceptions likely to be related to customer satisfaction.

The University of Michigan's Claes Fornell has developed the American Customer Satisfaction Index (ACSI) to measure consumers' perceived satisfaction with different firms, industries, economic sectors, and national economies.[22] Research has shown a strong and consistent association between customer satisfaction, as measured by ACSI, and firm financial performance in terms of ROI, sales, long-term firm value (Tobin's Q), and other metrics.[23] Table 5.2 displays some of the 2014 ACSI leaders. "Marketing Insight: Net Promoter and Customer Satisfaction" describes why some companies believe just one well-designed question is all that is necessary to assess customer satisfaction.[24]

Companies need to monitor their competitors' performance too. They can monitor their *customer loss rate* and contact those who have stopped buying or who have switched to another supplier to find out why. Finally, as described in Chapter 3, companies can hire *mystery shoppers* to pose as potential buyers and report on strong and weak points experienced in buying the company's and competitors' products. Managers themselves can enter company and competitor sales situations where they are unknown and experience firsthand the treatment they receive, or they can phone their own company with questions and complaints to see how employees handle the calls.

**INFLUENCE OF CUSTOMER SATISFACTION** For customer-centered companies, customer satisfaction is both a goal and a marketing tool. Companies need to be especially concerned with their customer satisfaction level today because the Internet allows consumers to quickly spread both good and bad word of mouth to the rest of the world. Some customers set up their own Web sites to air grievances and galvanize protest, targeting high-profile brands such as United Airlines, Home Depot, and Mercedes-Benz.[25]

Companies that do achieve high customer satisfaction ratings make sure their target market knows it. Once they achieved number-one status in their category on J. D. Power's customer satisfaction ratings, Hyundai, American Express, Medicine Shoppe (a chain pharmacy), and Alaska Airways, among others, communicated that fact.

| TABLE 5.2 | 2014 ACSI Scores by Industry | |
|---|---|---|
| **Industry** | **Firm** | **Score** |
| Airlines | Jet Blue | 79 |
| Apparel | Levi-Strauss, V.F. | 82 |
| Automobiles & Light Vehicles | Mercedes-Benz | 84 |
| Banks | JPMorgan Chase | 76 |
| Breweries | Anheuser-Busch InBev | 81 |
| Cellular Telephones | Samsung | 81 |
| Department & Discount Stores | Nordstrom | 83 |
| Fixed Line Telephone Service | Verizon | 73 |
| Food Manufacturing | H. J. Heinz, Quaker & General Mills | 87 |
| Health Insurance | Blue Cross and Blue Shield | 74 |
| Hotels | Marriott | 81 |
| Internet Brokerage | Charles Schwab | 84 |
| Internet News & Information | FOXNews.com & USATODAY.com | 76 |
| Internet Portals & Search Engines | Google | 83 |
| Internet Retail | Amazon | 88 |
| Internet Travel | Orbitz | 77 |
| Life Insurance | New York Life | 80 |
| Personal Care & Cleaning Products | Clorox, Colgate-Palmolive & Unilever | 85 |
| Personal Computers | Apple | 84 |
| Soft Drinks | Dr Pepper Snapple | 86 |
| Supermarkets | Publix | 86 |
| Wireless Telephone Service | Verizon Wireless | 75 |

**Source:** ACSI LLC, www.theacsi.org.

## PRODUCT AND SERVICE QUALITY

Satisfaction will also depend on product and service quality. What exactly is quality? Various experts have defined it as "fitness for use," "conformance to requirements," and "freedom from variation." We will use the American Society for Quality's definition: **Quality** is the totality of features and characteristics of a product or service that bear on its ability to satisfy stated or implied needs.[26] This is clearly a customer-centered definition. We can say the seller has delivered quality whenever its product or service meets or exceeds the customers' expectations.

A company that satisfies most of its customers' needs most of the time is called a high-quality company, but we need to distinguish between *conformance* quality and *performance* quality (or grade). A Lexus provides higher performance quality than a Hyundai: The Lexus rides more smoothly, accelerates faster, and runs

# Net Promoter and Customer Satisfaction

Many companies make measuring customer satisfaction a top priority, but how should they go about doing it? Bain's Frederick Reichheld suggests only one customer question really matters: "How likely is it that you would recommend this product or service to a friend or colleague?"

Reichheld was inspired in part by the experiences of Enterprise Rent-A-Car. When the company cut its customer satisfaction survey in 1998 from 18 questions to two—one about the quality of the rental experience and the other about the likelihood customers would rent from the company again—it found those who gave the highest ratings to their rental experience were three times as likely to rent again than those who gave the second-highest rating. The firm also found that diagnostic information managers collected from dissatisfied customers helped it fine-tune its operations.

In a typical Net Promoter survey that follows Reichheld's thinking, customers are given a 1-to-10 scale on which to rate their likelihood of recommending the company. Marketers then subtract *Detractors* (those who gave a 0 to 6) from *Promoters* (those who gave a 9 or 10) to arrive at the Net Promoter Score (NPS). Customers who rate the brand with a 7 or 8 are deemed *Passively Satisfied* and are not included. A typical set of NPS scores falls in the 10 percent to 30 percent range, but world-class companies can score over 50 percent. Some firms with top NPS scores in 2014 included USAA (82 percent), Amazon (64 percent), Southwest (62 percent), Wegmans (61 percent), Apple (72 percent), and Costco (82 percent).

Reichheld has picked up many believers through the years. American Express, Dell, and Microsoft, among others, have all adopted the NPS metric. GE has tied 20 percent of its managers' bonuses to its NPS scores. When the European unit of GE Healthcare scored low, follow-up research revealed that response times to customers were a major problem. After it overhauled its call center and put more specialists in the field, GE Healthcare's Net Promoter scores jumped 10 to 15 points. Philips has focused on engaging Promoters as well as addressing the concerns of Detractors, developing a Reference Promoter program to get customers willing to recommend the brand to actually do so through taped testimonials.

Reichheld says he developed NPS in response to overly complicated—and thus ineffective—customer surveys. So it's not surprising that client firms praise its simplicity and strong relationship to financial performance. When Intuit applied Net Promoter to its TurboTax product, feedback revealed dissatisfaction with the software's rebate procedure. After Intuit dropped the proof-of-purchase requirement, sales jumped 6 percent.

Net Promoter is not without critics. A common criticism is that many different patterns of responses may lead to the same NPS. For example, NPS equals 20 percent when Promoters equal 20 percent, Passives equal 80 percent, and Detractors equal 0 percent, as well as when Promoters equal 60 percent, Passives equal 0 percent, and Detractors equal 40 percent, but the managerial implications of the two patterns of responses are very different. Another common criticism is that it is not a useful predictor of future sales or growth because it ignores important cost and revenue considerations.

Others question its actual research support. One comprehensive academic study of 21 firms and more than 15,000 consumers in Norway failed to find NPS superior to any other metrics such as the ACSI measure. Some have criticized both NPS and ACSI measures for not fully accounting for ex-customers or those who were never customers. Peoples' opinions about any of the single items or indices measuring customer satisfaction depend in part on how they value the trade-off between simplicity and complexity.

**Sources:** Fred Reichheld, *Ultimate Question: For Driving Good Profits and True Growth* (Cambridge, MA: Harvard Business School Press, 2006); Fred Reichheld, "The One Number You Need to Grow," *Harvard Business Review*, December 2003; Neil A. Morgan and Lopo Leotte Rego, "The Value of Different Customer Satisfaction and Loyalty Metrics in Predicting Business Performance," *Marketing Science* 25 (September–October 2006), pp. 426–39; Timothy L. Keiningham, Lerzan Aksoy, Bruce Cooil, and Tor W. Andreassen, "Linking Customer Loyalty to Growth," *MIT Sloan Management Review* (Summer 2008), pp. 51–57; Suhail Khan, "How Philips Uses Net Promoter Scores to Understand Customers," *HBR Blog Network*, May 10, 2011; Robert East, Jenni Romaniuk, and Wendy Lomax, "The NPS and ACSI: A Critique and an Alternative Metric," *International Journal of Market Research* 53, no. 3 (2011), pp. 327–45; Randy Hanson, "Life after NPS," *Marketing Research* (Summer 2011), pp. 8–11; Jenny van Doorn, Peter S. H. Leeflang, and Marleen Tijs, "Satisfaction as a Predictor of Future Performance: A Replication," *International Journal of Research in Marketing* 30 (September 2013), pp. 314–18; www.satmetrix.com.

problem-free longer. Yet both a Lexus and a Hyundai deliver the same conformance quality if all the units deliver their promised quality.

**IMPACT OF QUALITY** Product and service quality, customer satisfaction, and company profitability are intimately connected. Higher levels of quality result in higher levels of customer satisfaction, which support higher prices and (often) lower costs. Studies have shown a high correlation between relative product quality and company profitability.[27] The drive to produce goods that are superior in world markets has led some countries to recognize or award prizes to companies that exemplify the best quality practices, such as the Deming Prize in Japan, the Malcolm Baldrige National Quality Award in the United States, and the European Quality Award.

Companies that have lowered costs to cut corners have paid the price when the quality of the customer experience suffers. Home Depot ran into trouble when it became overly focused on cost cutting.[28]

Enterprise Rent-A-Car found its customer satisfaction surveys were more effective with just two questions.

*Source: UIG via Getty Images*

**▌HOME DEPOT** When Home Depot decided to expand into the contractor supply business, while also cutting costs and streamlining operations in 1,816 U.S. stores, it replaced many full-time workers with part-timers who soon made up about 40 percent of store staff. The chain's ACSI of customer satisfaction dropped to the bottom among major U.S. retailers, 11 points behind customer-friendly competitor Lowe's, and its share price slid 24 percent during the biggest home improvement boom in U.S. history. To turn the company around, new management simplified operations. Store managers were given three goals to achieve—cleaner warehouses, stocked shelves, and top customer service. The 200-plus e-mails sent from the corporate office on a typical Monday were replaced with one—the rest of the information was made available online. In a new practice called "power hours," on weekdays from 10 AM to 2 PM and all day Saturday and Sunday, employees were to do nothing but serve customers. To make sure the new strategy stuck, performance reviews were changed so store employees were evaluated almost entirely on customer service. These and other customer-service initiatives increased store labor hours dedicated to customer-facing activity from 40 percent to 53 percent. As the recession wore on, improved customer service, as well as new product-assortment practices and centralized distribution centers, helped Home Depot reestablish its marker leadership and distance itself from Lowe's.

Total quality is everyone's job, just as marketing is everyone's job. Nevertheless, marketing plays an especially important role in helping companies identify and deliver high-quality goods and services to target customers. How do marketers help?

- They correctly identify customers' needs and requirements.
- They communicate customer expectations properly to product designers.
- They make sure customers' orders are filled correctly and on time.
- They check that customers have received proper instructions, training, and technical assistance in the use of the product.
- They stay in touch with customers after the sale to ensure they are, and remain, satisfied.
- They gather customer ideas for product and service improvements and convey them to the appropriate departments.

When marketers do all this, they make substantial contributions to total quality management and customer satisfaction as well as to customer and company profitability.

# Maximizing Customer Lifetime Value

Ultimately, marketing is the art of attracting and keeping profitable customers. Yet every company loses money on some of its customers. The well-known 80–20 rule states that 80 percent or more of the company's profits come from the top 20 percent of its customers. Some cases may be more extreme—the most profitable 20 percent of customers (on a per capita basis) may contribute as much as 150 to 300 percent of profitability. The least profitable 10 to 20 percent, on the other hand, can actually reduce profits between 50 and 200 percent per account,

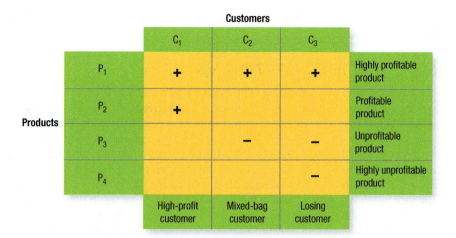

**| Fig. 5.3 |**

Customer-Product
Profitability Analysis

with the middle 60 to 70 percent breaking even.[29] The implication is that a company could improve its profits by "firing" its worst customers.

Companies need to concern themselves with Return on Customer (ROC) and how efficiently they create value from the customers and prospects available.[30] It's not always the company's largest customers who demand considerable service and deep discounts or who yield the most profit. The smallest customers pay full price and receive minimal service, but the costs of transacting with them can reduce their profitability. Midsize customers who receive good service and pay nearly full price are often the most profitable.

## CUSTOMER PROFITABILITY

A **profitable customer** is a person, household, or company that over time yields a revenue stream exceeding by an acceptable amount the company's cost stream for attracting, selling, and serving that customer. Note the emphasis is on the *lifetime* stream of revenue and cost, not the profit from a particular transaction.[31] Marketers can assess customer profitability individually, by market segment, or by channel.

Many companies measure customer satisfaction, but few measure individual customer profitability.[32] Banks claim this is a difficult task because each customer uses different banking services and the transactions are logged in different departments. However, the number of unprofitable customers in their customer database has appalled banks that have succeeded in linking customer transactions. Some report losing money on more than 45 percent of their retail customers.

**CUSTOMER PROFITABILITY ANALYSIS** A useful type of profitability analysis is shown in Figure 5.3.[33] Customers are arrayed along the columns and products along the rows. Each cell contains a symbol representing the profitability of selling that product to that customer. Customer 1 is very profitable; he buys two profit-making products (P1 and P2). Customer 2 yields mixed profitability; she buys one profitable product (P1) and one unprofitable product (P3). Customer 3 is a losing customer because he buys one profitable product (P1) and two unprofitable products (P3 and P4).

What can the company do about customers 2 and 3? (1) It can raise the price of its less profitable products or eliminate them, or (2) it can try to sell customers 2 and 3 its profit-making products. Unprofitable customers who defect should not concern the company. In fact, the company should encourage them to switch to competitors.

**Customer profitability analysis (CPA)** is best conducted with the tools of an accounting technique called **activity-based costing (ABC).** ABC accounting tries to identify the real costs associated with serving each customer—the costs of products and services based on the resources they consume. The company estimates all revenue coming from the customer, less all costs.

With ABC, the costs in a business-to-business setting should include the cost not only of making and distributing the products and services but also of taking phone calls from the customer, traveling to visit the customer, paying for entertainment and gifts—all the company's resources that go into serving that customer. ABC also allocates indirect costs like clerical costs, office expenses, supplies, and so on, to the activities that use them, rather than in some proportion to direct costs. Both variable and overhead costs are tagged back to each customer.

Companies that fail to measure their costs correctly are also not measuring their profit correctly and are likely to misallocate their marketing effort. The key to effectively employing ABC is to define and judge "activities" properly. One time-based solution calculates the cost of one minute of overhead and then decides how much of this cost each activity uses.[34]

## MEASURING CUSTOMER LIFETIME VALUE

The case for maximizing long-term customer profitability is captured in the concept of customer lifetime value.[35] **Customer lifetime value (CLV)** describes the net present value of the stream of future profits expected over the customer's lifetime purchases. The company must subtract from its expected revenues the expected costs of attracting, selling, and servicing the account of that customer, applying the appropriate discount rate (say, between 10 and 20 percent, depending on cost of capital and risk attitudes). Lifetime value calculations for a product or service can add up to tens of thousands of dollars or even run to six figures.[36]

Many methods exist to measure CLV.[37] "Marketing Memo: Calculating Customer Lifetime Value" illustrates one. CLV calculations provide a formal quantitative framework for planning customer investment and help marketers adopt a long-term perspective. One challenge, however, is to arrive at reliable cost and revenue estimates. Marketers who use CLV concepts must also take into account the short-term, brand-building marketing activities that help increase customer loyalty. One firm that has excelled in taking a short-run and long-run view of customer loyalty is Harrah's.[38]

**HARRAH'S**  Harrah's Entertainment, led by one-time academic Gary Loveman, has gone in a different direction from the big players in the Las Vegas gaming industry whose business models are based on building bigger and more opulent casinos. Back in 1997, Harrah's launched a pioneering loyalty program that pulled all customer data into a centralized warehouse and then ran sophisticated analyses to better understand the value of the investments the casino made in its customers. Harrah's has more than 40 million active members in its Total Rewards loyalty program, a system it has fine-tuned to achieve near-real-time analysis: As customers interact with slot machines, check into casinos, or buy meals, they receive reward offers—food vouchers or gambling credits, for example—based on predictive analyses from its database. Harrah's spends $100 million a year on information technology. The company has now identified hundreds of highly specific customer segments, and by targeting offers to each of them, it can almost double its share of customers' gaming budgets and generate $6.4 billion annually (80 percent of its gaming revenue). Research has shown that contrary to conventional wisdom, the most profitable customers are not the jet-setting high rollers, but older slot machine players. Harrah's also learned to dramatically cut back on its traditional ad spending, largely replacing it with direct mail and e-mail—a good customer may receive as many as 150 pieces in a year. Harrah's also rewards staff and bases compensation in part on customer service scores. To better fine-tune its Web sites and online ads, Harrah's monitors customer reviews and comments on TripAdvisor.com as well as social media sites such as Twitter and Facebook. After the company made changes to reflect customer interest in hotel amenities and the iconic views of the Las Vegas strip from its Paris Las Vegas hotel and casino, online bookings increased by double digits. Data from the Total Rewards program even influenced Harrah's decision to buy Caesars Entertainment, when company research revealed that most of Harrah's customers who visited Las Vegas without staying at a Harrah's-owned hotel were going to Caesars Palace. Harrah's latest loyalty innovation is a mobile marketing program that sends time-based and location-based offers to customers' mobile devices in real time.

## ATTRACTING AND RETAINING CUSTOMERS

Companies seeking to expand profits and sales must invest time and resources searching for new customers. To generate leads, they advertise in media that will reach new prospects, send direct mail and e-mails to possible new prospects, send their salespeople to participate in trade shows where they might find new leads, purchase names from list brokers, and so on.

Different acquisition methods yield customers with varying CLVs. One study showed that customers acquired through the offer of a 35 percent discount had about one-half the long-term value of customers acquired without any discount.[39] Many of these customers were more interested in the offer than in the product itself.

Similarly, many local restaurants, car wash services, beauty salons, and dry cleaners have launched "daily deal" campaigns from Groupon and LivingSocial to attract new customers. Unfortunately, these campaigns have sometimes turned out to be unprofitable in the long run because coupon users were not easily converted into loyal customers.[40]

Harrah's uses sophisticated customer analytics to guide its marketing activities, including filling rooms in its Paris Las Vegas hotel and casino.

Source: AFP/Getty Images

## marketing memo

# Calculating Customer Lifetime Value

Researchers and practitioners have used many different approaches for modeling and estimating CLV. Columbia's Don Lehmann and Harvard's Sunil Gupta recommend the following formula to estimate the CLV for a not-yet-acquired customer:

$$CLV = \sum_{t=0}^{T} \frac{(p_t - c_t)\, r_t}{(1 + i)^t} - AC$$

where $p_t$ = price paid by a consumer at time $t$,

   $c_t$ = direct cost of servicing the customer at time $t$,

   $i$ = discount rate or cost of capital for the firm,

   $r_t$ = probability of customer repeat buying or being "alive" at time $t$,

   $AC$ = acquisition cost, and

   $T$ = time horizon for estimating $CLV$.

   A key decision is what time horizon to use for estimating CLV. Typically, three to five years is reasonable. With this information and estimates of other variables, we can calculate CLV using spreadsheet analysis.

   Gupta and Lehmann illustrate their approach by calculating the CLV of 100 customers over a 10-year period (see Table 5.3). In this example, the firm acquires 100 customers with an acquisition cost per customer of $40. Therefore, in year 0, it spends $4,000. Some of these customers defect each year. The present value of the profits from this cohort of customers over 10 years is $13,286.52. The net CLV (after deducting acquisition costs) is $9,286.52, or $92.87 per customer.

   Using an infinite time horizon avoids having to select an arbitrary time horizon for calculating CLV. In the case of an infinite time horizon, if margins (price minus cost) and retention rates stay constant over time, the future CLV of an existing customer simplifies to the following:

$$CLV = \sum_{t=1}^{\infty} \frac{mr^t}{(1 + i)^t} = m \frac{r}{(1 + i - r)}$$

   In other words, CLV simply becomes margin ($m$) times a *margin multiple* [$r/(1 + i - r)$].

   Table 5.4 shows the margin multiple for various combinations of $r$ and $i$ and a simple way to estimate CLV of a customer. When retention rate is 80 percent and discount rate is 12 percent, the margin multiple is about two and a half. Therefore, the future CLV of an existing customer in this scenario is simply his or her annual margin multiplied by 2.5.

**Sources:** Sunil Gupta and Donald R. Lehmann, "Models of Customer Value," Berend Wierenga, ed., *Handbook of Marketing Decision Models* (Berlin, Germany: Springer Science and Business Media, 2007); Sunil Gupta and Donald R. Lehmann, "Customers as Assets," *Journal of Interactive Marketing* 17, no. 1 (Winter 2006), pp. 9–24; Sunil Gupta and Donald R. Lehmann, *Managing Customers as Investments* (Upper Saddle River, NJ: Wharton School Publishing, 2005); Peter Fader, Bruce Hardie, and Ka Lee, "RFM and CLV: Using Iso-Value Curves for Customer Base Analysis," *Journal of Marketing Research* 42, no. 4 (November 2005), pp. 415–30; Sunil Gupta, Donald R. Lehmann, and Jennifer Ames Stuart, "Valuing Customers," *Journal of Marketing Research* 41, no. 1 (February 2004), pp. 7–18.

| TABLE 5.3 | A Hypothetical Example to Illustrate CLV Calculations | | | | | | | | | | |
|---|---|---|---|---|---|---|---|---|---|---|---|
| | Year 0 | Year 1 | Year 2 | Year 3 | Year 4 | Year 5 | Year 6 | Year 7 | Year 8 | Year 9 | Year 10 |
| Number of Customers | 100 | 90 | 80 | 72 | 60 | 48 | 34 | 23 | 12 | 6 | 2 |
| Revenue per Customer | | 100 | 110 | 120 | 125 | 130 | 135 | 140 | 142 | 143 | 145 |
| Variable Cost per Customer | | 70 | 72 | 75 | 76 | 78 | 79 | 80 | 81 | 82 | 83 |
| Margin per Customer | | 30 | 38 | 45 | 49 | 52 | 56 | 60 | 61 | 61 | 62 |
| Acquisition Cost per Customer | 40 | | | | | | | | | | |
| Total Cost or Profit | −4,000 | 2,700 | 3,040 | 3,240 | 2,940 | 2,496 | 1,904 | 1,380 | 732 | 366 | 124 |
| Present Value | −4,000 | 2,454.55 | 2,512.40 | 2,434.26 | 2,008.06 | 1,549.82 | 1,074.76 | 708.16 | 341.48 | 155.22 | 47.81 |

| TABLE 5.4 | Margin Multiple | | | |
|---|---|---|---|---|
| | Discount Rate | | | |
| Retention Rate | 10% | 12% | 14% | 16% |
| 60% | 1.20 | 1.5 | 1.11 | 1.07 |
| 70% | 1.75 | 1.67 | 1.59 | 1.52 |
| 80% | 2.67 | 2.50 | 2.35 | 2.22 |
| 90% | 4.50 | 4.09 | 3.75 | 3.46 |

Promotional campaigns that reinforce the value of the brand, even if targeted to the already loyal, may be more likely to attract higher-value new customers. Two-thirds of the considerable growth spurred by UK mobile communication leader O2's loyalty strategy was attributed to recruitment of new customers; the remainder came from reduced defection.[41]

**REDUCING DEFECTION** It is not enough to attract new customers; the company must also keep them and increase their business.[42] Too many companies suffer from high **customer churn** or defection. Adding customers here is like adding water to a leaking bucket.

Cellular carriers and cable TV operators are plagued by "spinners," customers who switch carriers at least three times a year looking for the best deal. Many carriers lose 25 percent of their subscribers each year, at an estimated cost of $2 billion to $4 billion. Defecting customers cite unmet needs and expectations, poor product/service quality and high complexity, and billing errors.[43]

To reduce the defection rate, the company must:

1. *Define and measure its retention rate.* For a magazine, subscription renewal rate is a good measure of retention. For a college, it could be first- to second-year retention rate or class graduation rate.
2. *Distinguish the causes of customer attrition and identify those that can be managed better.* Not much can be done about customers who leave the region or go out of business, but poor service, shoddy products, and high prices can all be addressed.[44]
3. *Compare the lost customer's lifetime value to the costs of reducing the defection rate.* As long as the cost to discourage defection is lower than the lost profit, spend the money to try to retain the customer.

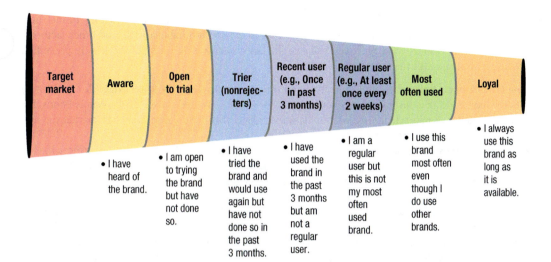

| **Fig. 5.4** |

The
Marketing
Funnel

**RETENTION DYNAMICS** Figure 5.4 shows the main steps in attracting and retaining customers, imagined in terms of a funnel, and some sample questions to measure customer progress through the funnel. The **marketing funnel** identifies the percentage of the potential target market at each stage in the decision process, from merely aware to highly loyal. Consumers must move through each stage before becoming loyal customers. Some marketers extend the funnel to include loyal customers who are brand advocates or even partners with the firm.

By calculating *conversion rates*—the percentage of customers at one stage who move to the next—the funnel allows marketers to identify any bottleneck stage or barrier to building a loyal customer franchise. If the percentage of recent users is significantly lower than triers, for instance, something might be wrong with the product or service that prevents repeat buying.

The funnel also emphasizes how important it is not just to attract new customers but to retain and cultivate existing ones. Satisfied customers are the company's *customer relationship capital.* If the company were sold, the acquiring company would pay not only for the plant and equipment and brand name but also for the delivered *customer base,* the number and value of customers who will do business with the new firm. Consider these data about customer retention:[45]

- Acquiring new customers can cost five times more than satisfying and retaining current ones. It requires a great deal of effort to induce satisfied customers to switch from their current suppliers.
- The average company loses 10 percent of its customers each year.
- A 5 percent reduction in the customer defection rate can increase profits by 25 percent to 85 percent, depending on the industry.
- Profit rate tends to increase over the life of the retained customer due to increased purchases, referrals, price premiums, and reduced operating costs to service.

Source: Courtesy of Whole Foods Market. "Whole Foods Market" is a registered trademark of Whole Foods Market IP, L.P.

Whole Foods builds customer loyalty through its skillful procurement and merchandising of natural and organic foods.

**MANAGING THE CUSTOMER BASE** Customer profitability analysis and the marketing funnel help marketers decide how to manage groups of customers that vary in loyalty, profitability, risk, and other factors.[46] A key driver of shareholder value is the aggregate value of the customer base. Winning companies improve that value by excelling at strategies like the following:

- *Reducing the rate of customer defection.* Selecting and training employees to be knowledgeable and friendly increases the likelihood that customers' shopping questions will be answered satisfactorily. Whole Foods, the world's largest retailer of natural and organic foods, woos customers with a commitment to market the best foods and a team concept for employees.
- *Increasing the longevity of the customer relationship.* The more engaged with the company, the more likely a customer is to stick around. Nearly 65 percent of new Honda purchases replace an older Honda. Drivers cited Honda's reputation for creating safe vehicles with high resale value. Seeking consumer advice can be an effective way to engage consumers with a brand and company.[47]
- *Enhancing the growth potential of each customer through "share of wallet," cross-selling, and up-selling.*[48] Sales from existing customers can be increased with new offerings and opportunities. Harley-Davidson sells more than motorcycles and accessories like gloves, leather jackets, helmets, and sunglasses. Its dealerships sell more than 3,000 items of clothing—some even have fitting rooms. Licensed goods sold by others range from predictable items (shot glasses, cue balls, and Zippo cigarette lighters) to the more surprising (cologne, dolls, and cell phones). Cross-selling isn't profitable if the targeted customer requires a lot of services for each product, generates a lot of product returns, cherry-picks promotions, or limits total spending across all products.[49]
- *Making low-profit customers more profitable or terminating them.* To avoid trying to terminate them, marketers can instead encourage unprofitable customers to buy more or in larger quantities, forgo certain features or services, or pay higher amounts or fees.[50] Banks, phone companies, and travel agencies all now charge for once-free services to ensure minimum revenue levels from these customers. Firms can also discourage those with questionable profitability prospects. Progressive Insurance screens customers and diverts the potentially unprofitable to competitors.[51] However, "free" customers who pay little or nothing and are subsidized by paying customers—as in print and online media, employment and dating services, and shopping malls—may still create useful direct and indirect network effects, an important function.[52]
- *Focusing disproportionate effort on high-profit customers.* The most profitable customers can be treated in a special way. Thoughtful gestures such as birthday greetings, small gifts, or invitations to special sports or arts events can send them a strong positive signal.

## BUILDING LOYALTY

Companies that want to form strong, tight connections to customers should heed some specific considerations (see Figure 5.5). One set of researchers sees retention-building activities as adding financial benefits, social benefits, or structural ties.[53] Next we describe three marketing activities that improve loyalty and retention.

**INTERACT CLOSELY WITH CUSTOMERS** Connecting customers, clients, patients, and others directly with company employees is highly motivating and informative. End users can offer tangible proof of the positive impact of the company's products and services, express appreciation for employee contributions, and elicit empathy. A brief visit from a student who had received a scholarship motivated university fundraisers to increase their weekly productivity by 400 percent; a patient's photograph inspired radiologists to improve the accuracy of their diagnostic findings by 46 percent.[54]

| Fig. 5.5 |

Forming
Strong
Customer
Bonds

- Create superior products, services, and experiences for the target market.
- Get cross-departmental participation in planning and managing the customer satisfaction and retention process.
- Integrate the "Voice of the Customer" to capture their stated and unstated needs or requirements in all business decisions.
- Organize and make accessible a database of information on individual customer needs, preferences, contacts, purchase frequency, and satisfaction.
- Make it easy for customers to reach appropriate company staff and express their needs, perceptions, and complaints.
- Assess the potential of frequency programs and club marketing programs.
- Run award programs recognizing outstanding employees.

Listening to customers is crucial to customer relationship management. Some companies have created an ongoing mechanism that keeps their marketers permanently plugged in to frontline customer feedback.

- Deere & Company, which makes John Deere tractors and has a superb record of customer loyalty—nearly 98 percent annual retention in some product areas—has used retired employees to interview defectors and customers.[55]
- Chicken of the Sea has 80,000 members in its Mermaid Club, a core-customer group that receives special offers, health tips and articles, new product updates, and an informative e-newsletter. In return, club members provide valuable feedback on what the company is doing and thinking of doing. Their input has helped design the brand's Web site, develop messages for TV advertising, and craft the look and text on the packaging.[56]
- Build-A-Bear Workshop uses a "Cub Advisory Board" as a feedback and decision-input body. The board is made up of twenty 5- to 16-year-olds who review new-product ideas and give a "paws up or down." Many products in the stores are customer ideas.[57]

But listening is only part of the story. It is also important to be a customer advocate and, as much as possible, take the customers' side and understand their point of view.[58]

**DEVELOP LOYALTY PROGRAMS** **Frequency programs (FPs)** are designed to reward customers who buy frequently and in substantial amounts. They can help build long-term loyalty with high CLV customers, creating cross-selling opportunities in the process. Pioneered by the airlines, hotels, and credit card companies, FPs now exist in many other industries. Most supermarket and drug store chains offer price club cards that grant discounts on certain items.

Typically, the first company to introduce an FP in an industry gains the most benefit, especially if competitors are slow to respond. After competitors react, FPs can become a financial burden to all the offering companies, but some companies are more efficient and creative in managing them. Some FPs generate rewards in a way that locks customers in and creates significant switching costs. FPs can also produce a psychological boost and a feeling of being special and elite that customers value.[59]

**Club membership programs** attract and keep those customers responsible for the largest portion of business. Clubs can be open to everyone who purchases a product or service or limited to an affinity group or those willing to pay a small fee. Although open clubs are good for building a database or snagging customers from competitors, limited membership is a more powerful long-term loyalty builder. Fees and membership conditions prevent those with only a fleeting interest in a company's products from joining.

Apple encourages owners of its computers to form local Apple user groups. There are hundreds of groups, ranging in size from fewer than 30 members to more than 1,000. The groups provide Apple owners with opportunities to learn more about their computers, share ideas, and get product discounts. They sponsor special activities and events and perform community service. A visit to Apple's Web site will help a customer find a nearby user group.[60]

**CREATE INSTITUTIONAL TIES** The company may supply business customers with special equipment or computer links that help them manage orders, payroll, and inventory. Customers are less inclined to switch to another supplier when it means high capital costs, high search costs, or the loss of loyal-customer discounts. McKesson Corporation, a leading pharmaceutical wholesaler, invested millions of dollars in EDI (Electronic Data Interchange) capabilities to help its independent-pharmacy customers manage inventory, order-entry processes, and shelf space. Another example is Milliken & Company, which provides proprietary software programs, marketing research, sales training, and sales leads to loyal customers.

# BRAND COMMUNITIES

Thanks to the Internet, companies are interested in collaborating with consumers to create value through communities built around brands. A **brand community** is a specialized community of consumers and employees whose identification and activities focus around the brand.[61] Three characteristics identify brand communities:[62]

1. A "consciousness of kind," or a sense of felt connection to the brand, company, product, or other community members;
2. Shared rituals, stories, and traditions that help convey the meaning of the community; and
3. A shared moral responsibility or duty to both the community as a whole and individual community members.

**TYPES OF BRAND COMMUNITIES** Brand communities come in many different forms.[63] Some arise organically from brand users, such as the Atlanta MGB riders club and the Porsche Rennlist online discussion

Harley-Davidson has built an active brand community through its Harley Owner's Group which boasts more than one million members.

Source: Nicholas J Reid/Getty Images

group. Others are company-sponsored and facilitated, such as Club Green Kids (official kids' fan club of the Boston Celtics) and the Harley Owners Group (H.O.G.).[64]

**HARLEY-DAVIDSON**    Founded in 1903 in Milwaukee, Wisconsin, Harley-Davidson has twice narrowly escaped bankruptcy but is today one of the most recognized motor vehicle brands in the world. In dire financial straits in the 1980s, Harley licensed its name to such ill-advised ventures as cigarettes and wine coolers. Although consumers loved the brand, sales were depressed by product-quality problems, so Harley began its return to greatness by improving manufacturing processes. It also developed a strong brand community in the form of an inclusive owners' club, called the Harley Owners Group (H.O.G.), which sponsors bike rallies, charity rides, and other motorcycle events and now numbers more than 1 million members in some 1,400 chapters. H.O.G. benefits include a magazine called *Hog Tales*, a touring handbook, emergency road service, a specially designed insurance program, theft reward service, discount hotel rates, and a Fly & Ride program enabling members to rent Harleys on vacation. The company also maintains an extensive Web site devoted to H.O.G. with information about club chapters and events and a special members-only section. Harley is active with social media too and boasts more than 3.3 million Facebook fans. One fan inspired a digital video and Twitter campaign dubbed E Pluribus Unum—"Out of Many, One"—where Harley riders from all walks of life show their diversity and their pride in their bikes.

Companies large and small can build brand communities. When New York's Signature Theatre Company built a new 70,000-square-foot facility for its shows, it made sure there was a central hub where casts, crew, playwrights, and audiences for all productions could mingle and interact.[65]

Online, marketers can tap into social media such as Facebook, Twitter, and blogs or create their own online community. Members can recommend products, share reviews, create lists of recommendations and favorites, or socialize together online.

Online forums can be especially helpful in a business-to-business setting for professional development and feedback opportunities. The Kodak Grow Your Biz blog is a place for members to learn and share insights about how Kodak products, services, and technologies can improve important company or industry business performance.[66] The Pitney Bowes User Forum is a place for members to discuss issues related to Pitney Bowes equipment and to mailing and marketing in general. Members often answer each other's business questions, though Pitney Bowes customer service representatives are available for any particularly difficult support questions.[67]

**MAXIMIZING THE BENEFITS OF BRAND COMMUNITIES** A strong brand community results in a more loyal, committed customer base. One study showed that a multichannel retailer of books, CDs, and DVDs enjoyed long-term incremental revenue of 19 percent from customers—what the authors called "social dollars"— after customers joined an online brand community. The more "connected" a member of the community was, the greater the likelihood he or she would spend more.[68]

A brand community can be a constant source of inspiration and feedback for product improvements or innovations. The activities and advocacy of members of a brand community can also substitute to some degree for activities the firm would otherwise have to engage in, creating greater marketing effectiveness and efficiency as a result.[69]

To better understand how brand communities work, one comprehensive study examined communities around brands as diverse as StriVectin cosmeceutical, BMW Mini auto, Jones soda, Tom Petty & the Heartbreakers rock and roll band, and Garmin GPS devices. Using multiple research methods such as "netnographic" research with online forums, participant and naturalistic observation of community activities, and in-depth interviews with community members, the researchers found 12 value creation practices taking place. They divided them into four categories—social networking, community engagement, impression management, and brand use—summarized in Table 5.5.

Building a positive, productive brand community requires careful thought and implementation.[70] One set of researchers offers these recommendations for making online brand communities more effective:[71]

1. *Enhance the timeliness of information exchanged.* Set appointed times for topic discussion; give rewards for timely, helpful responses; increase access points to the community.
2. *Enhance the relevance of information posted.* Keep the focus on topic; divide the forum into categories; encourage users to preselect interests.
3. *Extend the conversation.* Make it easier for users to express themselves; don't set limits on length of responses; allow user evaluation of the relevance of posts.
4. *Increase the frequency of information exchanged.* Launch contests; use familiar social networking tools; create special opportunities for visitors; acknowledge helpful members.

| TABLE 5.5 | Value Creation Practices |
|---|---|

**SOCIAL NETWORKING**

| | |
|---|---|
| **Welcoming** | Greeting new members, beckoning them into the fold, and assisting in their brand learning and community socialization. |
| **Empathizing** | Lending emotional and/or physical support to other members, including support for brand-related trials (product failure, customizing) and/or for nonbrand-related life issues (illness, death, job). |
| **Governing** | Articulating the behavioral expectations within the brand community. |

**IMPRESSION MANAGEMENT**

| | |
|---|---|
| **Evangelizing** | Sharing the brand "good news," inspiring others to use, and preaching from the mountaintop. |
| **Justifying** | Deploying rationales generally for devoting time and effort to the brand and collectively to outsiders and marginal members in the boundary. |

**COMMUNITY ENGAGEMENT**

| | |
|---|---|
| **Staking** | Recognizing variance within the brand community membership and marking intragroup distinction and similarity. |
| **Milestoning** | Noting seminal events in brand ownership and consumption. |
| **Badging** | Translating milestones into symbols and artifacts. |
| **Documenting** | Detailing the brand relationship journey in a narrative way, often anchored by and peppered with milestones. |

**BRAND USE**

| | |
|---|---|
| **Grooming** | Cleaning, caring for, and maintaining the brand or systematizing optimal use patterns. |
| **Customizing** | Modifying the brand to suit group-level or individual needs. This includes all efforts to change the factory specs of the product to enhance performance. |
| **Commoditizing** | Distancing/approaching the marketplace in positive or negative ways. May be directed at other members (you should sell/should not sell that) or may be directed at the firm through explicit link or through presumed monitoring of the site (you should fix this/do this/change this). |

**Source:** Adapted from Hope Jensen Schau, Albert M. Muniz, and Eric J. Arnould, "How Brand Community Practices Create Value," *Journal of Marketing* 73 (September 2009), pp. 30–51.

## WIN-BACKS

Regardless of how hard companies may try, some customers inevitably become inactive or drop out. The challenge is to reactivate them through win-back strategies.[72] It's often easier to reattract ex-customers (because the company knows their names and histories) than to find new ones. Exit interviews and lost-customer surveys can uncover sources of dissatisfaction and help win back only those with strong profit potential.[73]

# Cultivating Customer Relationships

Companies are using information about customers to enact precision marketing designed to build strong long-term relationships.[74] Information is easy to differentiate, customize, personalize, and dispatch over networks at incredible speed. But that capability cuts both ways. For instance, customers now comparison-shop quickly and easily through sites such as Bizrate.com, Shopping.com, and PriceGrabber.com, and Epinions.com and Yelp.com let them share information about their product and service experiences with others. Company empowerment has been matched by customer empowerment, and companies have to adjust to shifts in the nature and strength of their customer relationships.

## CUSTOMER RELATIONSHIP MANAGEMENT

**Customer relationship management (CRM)** is the process of carefully managing detailed information about individual customers and all customer "touch points" to maximize loyalty.[75] CRM is important because a major driver of company profitability is the aggregate value of the company's customer base. A related concept, **customer value management (CVM)**, describes the company's optimization of the value of its customer base. CVM focuses on the analysis of individual data on prospects and customers to develop marketing strategies to acquire and retain customers and drive customer behavior.[76]

A *customer touch point* is any occasion when a customer encounters the brand and product—from actual experience to personal or mass communications to casual observation. For a hotel, the touch points include reservations, check-in and checkout, frequent-stay programs, room service, business services, exercise facilities, laundry service, restaurants, and bars. The Four Seasons relies on personal touches, such as a staff that always addresses guests by name, high-powered employees who understand the needs of sophisticated business travelers, and at least one best-in-region facility, such as a premier restaurant or spa.[77]

CRM enables companies to provide excellent real-time customer service through the effective use of individual account information. Based on what they know about each valued customer, they can customize market offerings, services, programs, messages, and media. Companies' increased ability to track and market to individual customers is not without its controversies, as "Marketing Insight: The Behavioral Targeting Controversy" highlights.

**PERSONALIZING MARKETING**  Widespread Internet usage allows marketers to abandon the mass-market practices that built brand powerhouses in the 1950s, 1960s, and 1970s for new approaches that are a throwback to marketing practices from a century ago, when merchants literally knew their customers by name. *Personalizing marketing* is about making sure the brand and its marketing are as personally relevant as possible to as many customers as possible—a challenge, given that no two customers are identical.

Companies are using e-mail, Web sites, call centers, databases, and database software to foster continuous contact between company and customer. Although technology can help with customer relationship management, firms have to be careful not to roll out too many automated-response phone systems or social-networking tools as ways to satisfy customer service requests. Many customers still prefer to talk to a live representative to receive more personal service—an ongoing priority in marketing.[78]

Companies are recognizing the role of the personal component in CRM and its influence once customers make actual contact with the company. Employees can create strong bonds with customers by individualizing and personalizing relationships. Consider the lengths to which British Airways is going to satisfy valued customers.[79]

# The Behavioral Targeting Controversy

The emergence of *behavioral targeting* is allowing companies to track the online behavior of target customers and find the best match between ads and prospects. Tracking an individual's Internet usage behavior relies on cookies—randomly assigned numbers, codes, and data that are stored on the user's computer hard drive and reveal which sites have been visited, the amount of time spent there, which products or pages were viewed, and which search terms were entered.

The *Wall Street Journal* reviewed 1,000 top Web sites and found that 75 percent included code from social networks such as Facebook's "like" and Twitter's "tweet" buttons. The existence of the code could match people's identities with their Web-browsing activities, tracking a user's arrival on a page even if the Facebook or Twitter button was never clicked. Another *Wall Street Journal* study showed that roughly a quarter of the times a user logged into one of 70 popular Web sites, the user's real name and e-mail address or other personal details, such as username, were passed on to third-party companies.

A new customer signing up with Microsoft for a free Hotmail e-mail account, for example, is required to give the company his or her name, age, gender, and zip code. Microsoft can then combine those facts with information such as observed online behavior and characteristics of the area in which the customer lives to help advertisers better understand whether, when, and how to contact that customer. Although Microsoft maintains it carefully preserves consumer privacy—it claims it won't purchase an individual's income history—it can still provide advertising clients with behavioral targeting information.

For example, Microsoft can help a DiningIn franchisee zero in on working moms ages 30 to 40 in a given neighborhood with ads designed to reach them before 10 AM when they're most likely to be planning their evening meal. Or if a person clicks on three Web sites related to auto insurance and then visits an unrelated site for sports or entertainment, auto insurance ads may show up on that site. Microsoft claims behavioral targeting can increase the likelihood a visitor clicks an ad by as much as 76 percent.

Proponents of behavioral targeting maintain that it also brings consumers more relevant ads. Because the ads are more effective as a result, more ad revenue is available to support free online content. Supporters also maintain that many consumers would be less concerned if they knew exactly how tracking worked. They argue that practices conform with the online ad industry's self-regulation norms, ensuring anonymity by not giving firms access to "personal identifiable information" (PII).

Identity information is removed, protected, or separated from browsing history in different ways. For example, a Web site can use a formula to turn its users' e-mail addresses into jumbled strings of numbers and letters, as can an advertiser. Both can send their jumbled lists to a third company that looks for matches so the Web site can show an ad targeted to a specific person without any real e-mail addresses changing hands.

Nevertheless, as Chapter 3 pointed out, consumers have significant misgivings about advertisers tracking them online. A single Web page can contain computer code from dozens of different ad companies or tracking firms. Government regulators wonder whether industry self-regulation will be sufficient or whether legislation is needed.

**Sources:** Elisabeth Sullivan, "Behave," *Marketing News*, September 15, 2008, pp. 12–15; Stephanie Clifford, "Two-Thirds of Americans Object to Online Tracking," *New York Times*, September 30, 2009; Jessica Mintz, "Microsoft Adds Behavioral Targeting," *Associated Press*, December 28, 2006; Laurie Birkett, "The Cookie That Won't Crumble," *Forbes*, January 18, 2010, p. 32; Alden M. Hayashi, "How *Not* to Market on the Web," *MIT Sloan Management Review* (Winter 2010), pp. 14–15; Deborah L. Golemon and Laurie A. Babin, "How Marketers Are Dealing With the Controversy Surrounding Behavioral Targeting," *International Journal of Business, Marketing and Decision Sciences* 4 (Spring 2011), pp. 127–141; Jennifer Valentino-Devries and Jeremy Singer-Vine, "They Know What You're Shopping For," *Wall Street Journal*, December 7, 2012.

**BRITISH AIRWAYS**   British Airways took personalization to a higher level in the summer of 2012 with its new "Know Me" program. One goal was to centralize information about frequent fliers from every one of BA's service channels—Web site, call center, e-mail, on board planes, and inside airports—into a single database. For any one passenger booked on a flight, BA would know his or her current seating location, previous flights and meal choices, prior complaint history, and so on. BA also distributed 2,000 iPads among crew members and ground staff to allow them to access the database as well as receive personal recognition messages about passengers on any one flight. The goal was to have 4,500 daily messages, or approximately seven message updates per flight. To facilitate VIP passenger identification, British Airways also used stored photos of fliers downloaded from Google Image searches. One company representative described the program as aiming to "recreate the feeling of recognition you get in a favorite restaurant when you're welcomed there, but in our case it will be delivered by thousands of staff to millions of customers." Although some observers raised privacy concerns—even calling it "creepy"—British Airways noted that the passenger information was already available or viewed as helpful by its most valuable fliers.

As part of a broad trend towards personalization, Coca-Cola has introduced Freestyle dispensing machines that allow users to customize their soft drink choices.

Source: Scott Keeler/ZUMAPRESS/Newscom

While British Airways is personalizing its service experiences, BMW is figuring out ways to personalize its products. While 15 percent of U.S. drivers custom-ordered their cars in 2010, BMW's goal was to make that number 40 percent of its buyers by 2015. The company offers 500 side-mirror combinations, 1,300 front bumper combinations, and 9,000 center-console combinations and provides new buyers a video link to watch their car being "born" while waiting for delivery. Its detailed manufacturing and procurement system takes the slack out the production process, reduces inventory carrying costs, and avoids rebates on slow-moving sellers. Customers tend to load up with options—generating more profitability for BMW and its dealers—but are also more loyal.[80]

Even Coca-Cola is getting in on the action. The Coca-Cola Freestyle dispensing machine can dispense 125 sparkling and still brands that consumers can mix via a touchscreen, creating a beverage to suit their particular taste.[81]

To adapt to customers' increased desire for personalization, marketers have embraced concepts such as permission marketing. *Permission marketing*, the practice of marketing to consumers only after gaining their expressed permission, is based on the premise that marketers can no longer use "interruption marketing" via mass media campaigns. According to Seth Godin, a pioneer in the new technique, marketers develop stronger consumer relationships by respecting consumers' wishes and sending messages only when they express a willingness to become more engaged with the brand.[82] Godin believes permission marketing works because it is "anticipated, personal, and relevant."

Permission marketing, like other personalization approaches, presumes consumers know what they want, though they often have undefined, ambiguous, or conflicting preferences. "Participatory marketing" may be a more appropriate concept than permission marketing because marketers and consumers need to work together to find out how the firm can best satisfy consumers.

**CUSTOMER EMPOWERMENT** Marketers are helping consumers become evangelists for brands by providing them resources and opportunities to demonstrate their passion. Doritos held a contest to let consumers name its next flavor. Converse asked amateur filmmakers to submit 30-second short films that demonstrated how the iconic sneaker brand inspired them. The best of the 1,800 submissions were showcased in the Converse Gallery

Web site, and the best of the best became TV commercials. Sales of shoes via the Web site doubled in the month after the gallery's launch.[83]

As much as new technologies help customers assist or become involved in a brand's marketing, they also help them avoid marketing at the same time. For example, ad blocking is the most popular software extension for leading browsers, and the overall rate of ad blocking by users averages about 10 percent.[84]

Although much has been made of the newly empowered consumer—in charge, setting the direction of the brand, and playing a much bigger role in how it is marketed—it's still true that only *some consumers* want to get involved with *some of the brands* they use and, even then, only *some of the time*. Consumers have lives, jobs, families, hobbies, goals, and commitments, and many things matter more to them than the brands they purchase and consume. Understanding how to best market a brand given such diversity in customer interests is crucially important.[85]

When will consumers choose to engage with a brand? Many factors can come into play, but follow-up analysis of the IBM 2010 CEO Study revealed the following about customer pragmatism: "...most do not engage with companies via social media simply to feel connected.... To successfully exploit the potential of social media, companies need to design experiences that deliver tangible value in return for customers' time, attention, endorsement and data." According to these IBM analysts, that "tangible value" includes discounts, coupons, and information to facilitate purchase. They also note that many businesses overlook social media's most potent capabilities for capturing customer insights, monitoring the brand, conducting research, and soliciting new-product ideas.[86]

**CUSTOMER REVIEWS AND RECOMMENDATIONS** Although the strongest influence on consumer choice remains "recommended by relative/friend," an increasingly important decision factor is "recommendations from consumers." With increasing mistrust of some companies and their advertising, online customer ratings and reviews are playing a growing role in the customer buying process.[87]

A Forrester research study, for example, found that close to 50 percent of consumers won't book a hotel that does not have online reviews. Not surprisingly, more hotels are launching their own program to post reviews (Starwood places independent, authenticated reviews on individual hotel sites) or are using travel review sites (Wyndham streams its five most recent reviews from TripAdvisor on its site, leading to a 30 percent increase in bookings).[88] TripAdvisor has quickly grown to be a valuable online resource for travelers.[89]

**TRIPADVISOR** After being frustrated by the lack of detailed, reliable, and up-to-date information available to help him decide where to go on a Mexican holiday, Stephen Kaufer founded TripAdvisor in 2001. The pioneer in online consumer travel reviews, the company grew quickly and is now the world's largest travel Web site, with more than 170 million user reviews and opinions as of 2014. It allows users to collect and share information and make bookings for a wide variety of hotels, vacation rentals, airlines, restaurants, and other travel-related locations or businesses through its hotel and air booking partners. Users can post reviews, photos, and opinions and participate in discussions on a variety of different topics. To improve the quality and accuracy of its content, TripAdvisor uses both manual review and advanced computer algorithms, including a verification and fraud detection system that considers the IP and e-mail address of reviewers (as well as other review attributes) and monitors suspicious patterns of postings as well as inappropriate language. About 30 hotels have been blacklisted from the site for suspicious reviews. TripAdvisor has more than 280 million unique visitors monthly, and hundreds of millions of people each month view its content on 500 other sites, including Best Western International, Expedia, and Thomas Cook. In recent years, TripAdvisor has innovated to improve the personalization and social nature of its services; in fact, it was one of Facebook's initial launch partners for its "Instant Personalization" project, which allows users to personalize their TripAdvisor experience by allowing them to see TripAdvisor content posted by their Facebook friends, subject to their privacy elections. Local Picks is a Facebook app that allows users to localize TripAdvisor restaurant reviews and auto-share user reviews on Facebook Timeline. The Friends of Friends function allows TripAdvisor users to sort reviews by a user's Facebook friend status. Its acquisitions of social and mobile connectivity travel sites Wanderfly and EveryTrail have further strengthened TripAdvisor's capabilities in that area.

When online pet food retailer PETCO started using consumer product ratings and reviews in e-mails and banner ads, it found its click-through rate increased considerably as a result.[90] Brick-and-mortar retailers such as Best Buy, Staples, and Cabela's are also recognizing the power of consumer reviews and have begun to display them in their stores.[91]

Despite consumer acceptance of such reviews, however, their quality and integrity can be in question.[92] In one famous example, over a period of seven years, the cofounder and CEO of Whole Foods Market posted more than 1,100 entries on Yahoo! Finance's online bulletin board under a pseudonym, praising his company and criticizing competitors.

Some companies offer computer-recognition technology to monitor for fraud. Bazaarvoice helps companies such as Walmart and Best Buy manage and monitor online reviews using a process called device fingerprinting. The company caught one firm posting hundreds of positive reviews of one of its products and negative reviews of its competitor's.[93]

Online reviews and blogging sites such as Gawker have struggled to police comments.[94] To avoid attracting anonymous or biased reviews, Angie's List allows only paid and registered subscribers to access its Web site, which compiles about 40,000 reviews of service companies and health care professionals from its 1.5 million North American subscribers each month. Users rate providers on price, quality, responsiveness, punctuality, and professionalism using a report card–style A-to-F scale.[95]

Other sites offer summaries of professional third-party reviews. Metacritic aggregates music, game, TV, and movie reviews from leading critics—often from more than 100 publications—averaged into a single 1-to-100 score. Review sites are important in the video game industry because of the influence they wield and the product's high selling price—often $50 to $60. Some game companies tie bonuses for their developers to game scores on the more popular sites. If a major new release doesn't make the 85-plus cutoff, the publisher's stock price may even drop.[96]

Bloggers who review products or services are influential because they may have thousands of followers; blogs are often among the top links returned in online searches for certain brands or categories. A company's PR department may track popular blogs via online services such as Google Alerts and Technorati. Firms also court the favor of key bloggers via free samples and advance information. Most bloggers disclose this special treatment.

For smaller brands with limited media budgets, online word of mouth is critical. To generate prelaunch buzz for one of its new hot cereals, organic food maker Amy's Kitchen shipped out samples before its release to several of the 50 or so vegan, gluten-free, or vegetarian food bloggers the company tracks. When favorable reviews appeared on these blogs, the company was besieged by e-mails asking where to buy the cereal.[97]

As it turns out, sometimes even negative reviews can be surprisingly helpful. For one thing, although they can hurt a well-known brand, they can create awareness about an unknown or overlooked one. They can also provide valued information.

A Forrester study of 10,000 consumers of Amazon.com's electronics and home and garden products found that 50 percent found negative reviews helpful. Most purchased the products regardless of negative comments because they felt these merely reflected personal tastes and opinions different from their own. When consumers can better learn the advantages and disadvantages of products through negative reviews, fewer product returns may result, saving retailers and producers money.[98]

Online retailers often add their own recommendations to consumer selections or purchases: "If you like that black handbag, you'll love this red top." One source estimated that recommendation systems contribute 10 percent to 30 percent of an online retailer's sales. Specialized software tools help facilitate customer "discovery" or unplanned purchases.

At the same time, online companies need to make sure their attempts to create relationships with customers don't backfire, as when customers are bombarded by computer-generated recommendations that consistently miss the mark. Buy a few baby gifts on Amazon.com, and your personalized recommendations suddenly don't look so personal! E-tailers need to recognize the limitations of online personalization while searching for technology and processes that really work.

**CUSTOMER COMPLAINTS** Some companies think they're getting a sense of customer satisfaction by tallying complaints, but studies show that while customers are dissatisfied with their purchases about 25 percent of the time, only about 5 percent complain. The other 95 percent either feel complaining is not worth the effort or don't know how or to whom to complain. They just stop buying.[99]

Of the customers who register a complaint, 54 percent to 70 percent will do business with the organization again if their complaint is resolved. The figure goes up to a staggering 95 percent if the customer feels the complaint was resolved *quickly*. Customers whose complaints are satisfactorily resolved tell an average of five people about the good treatment they received.[100] The average dissatisfied customer, however, gripes to 11 people. If each of these tells still other people, the number exposed to bad word of mouth may grow exponentially.

No matter how perfectly designed and implemented a marketing program is, mistakes will happen. The best thing a company can do is make it easy for customers to complain. Suggestion forms, toll-free numbers, Web sites, and e-mail addresses allow for quick, two-way communication. The 3M Company claims that more than two-thirds of its product-improvement ideas come from listening to customer complaints.

Given that many customers may choose not to complain, companies should proactively monitor social media and other places where customer complaints and feedback may be aired. Jet Blue's 27-member customer service team is charged with monitoring the airline's Twitter account and Facebook page, among other responsibilities. When a customer's complaint about a fee for bringing a folded bike on board began to circulate online, Jet Blue quickly responded and decided it was not a service it should charge for.[101]

Given the potential downside of having an unhappy customer, it's critical that marketers deal with negative experiences properly.[102] Although challenging, the following practices can help to recover customer goodwill:[103]

1. Set up a seven-day, 24-hour toll-free hotline (by phone, fax, or e-mail) to receive and act on complaints—make it easy for the customer.
2. Contact the complaining customer as quickly as possible. The slower the company is to respond, the more dissatisfaction may grow and lead to negative word of mouth.
3. Accept responsibility for the customer's disappointment; don't blame the customer.
4. Use customer service people who are friendly and empathic.
5. Resolve the complaint swiftly and to the customer's satisfaction. Some complaining customers are not looking for compensation so much as a sign that the company cares.

Not all complaints, however, reflect actual deficiencies or problems with a company's product or service.[104] Big companies especially are targets for opportunistic customers who attempt to capitalize on even minor transgressions or generous compensation policies. Some firms fight back and even take an aggressive stance if they feel a criticism or complaint is unjustified.

When Taco Bell began to attract negative buzz online after rumors and a consumer lawsuit alleged that its taco mixture consisted of more filler than meat, it leaped into action with full-page newspaper ads headlined, "Thank you for suing us." There and in Facebook postings and a YouTube video, the company pointed out that its taco mixture was 88 percent beef, with ingredients such as water, oats, spices, and cocoa powder added only for flavor, texture, and moisture. To help spread the word, Taco Bell marketers bought the key words "taco," "bell," and "lawsuit" so that its official responses appeared as the first link on Yahoo!, Google, and Bing searches.[105]

Many senior executives worry about their firms using social media and the potential negative effects of cranky customers communicating online. Marketers, however, contend that the positives outweigh the negatives and steps can be taken to minimize the likelihood of such damage.

One strategy for companies active in corporate social responsibility is to actively shape their public image during quiet times and then leverage that goodwill in paid or other media during difficult times. Nike was once a target of Internet-savvy critics who skillfully used search engine optimization to populate unflattering portraits of the company. Now, searches for Nike yield links to sites that describe its many environmental and community initiatives (such as shoe recycling).[106]

*Source: ASSOCIATED PRESS*

Taco Bell aggressively defends the quality of its products via social media.

# Summary

1. Customers are value maximizers. They form an expectation of value and act on it. Buyers will buy from the firm that they perceive to offer the highest customer-delivered value, defined as the difference between total customer benefits and total customer cost.

2. A buyer's satisfaction is a function of the product's perceived performance and the buyer's expectations. Recognizing that high satisfaction leads to high customer loyalty, companies must ensure that they meet and exceed customer expectations.

3. Losing profitable customers can dramatically affect a firm's profits. The cost of attracting a new customer is estimated to be five times the cost of keeping a current customer happy. The key to retaining customers is relationship marketing.

4. Quality is the totality of features and characteristics of a product or service that bear on its ability to satisfy stated or implied needs. Marketers play a key role in achieving high levels of total quality so that firms remain solvent and profitable.

5. Marketing managers must calculate customer lifetime values of their customer base to understand their profit implications. They must also determine ways to increase the value of the customer base.

6. Companies are also becoming skilled in customer relationship management (CRM), which focuses on developing programs to attract and retain the right customers and meeting the individual needs of those valued customers.

MyMarketingLab

Go to **mymktlab.com** to complete the problems marked with this icon ⭐ as well as for additional Auto-graded and Assisted-graded writing questions.

# Applications

## Marketing Debate
### Online versus Offline Privacy

As more firms practice relationship marketing and develop customer databases, privacy issues are emerging as an important topic. Consumers and public interest groups are scrutinizing—and sometimes criticizing—the privacy policies of firms and raising concerns about potential theft of online credit card information or other potentially sensitive or confidential financial information. Others maintain online privacy fears are unfounded and that security issues are as much a concern offline. They argue that the opportunity to steal information exists virtually everywhere and that it's up to consumers to protect their interests.

**Take a position:** Privacy is a bigger issue online than offline *versus* Privacy is no different online than offline.

## Marketing Discussion
### Using CLV

⭐ Consider customer lifetime value (CLV). Choose a business and show how you would go about developing a quantitative formulation that captures the concept. How would that business change if it fully embraced the customer equity concept and maximized CLV?

**Excellence**

## >> Nordstrom

In 1901, John W. Nordstrom founded a small shoe store in Seattle that eventually grew into a fashion specialty chain store called Nordstrom. Nordstrom has remained in the family for four generations and now sells top-quality brand-name clothing, accessories, jewelry, cosmetics, and fragrances.

John W. Nordstrom built his company on the belief that it should always provide the highest possible level of customer service, along with top-of-the-line, high-quality merchandise to fit almost everyone's needs and budget. When he retired, his sons Everett, Elmer, and Lloyd continued to run the business with the same customer-focused attitude their father shared. As the company expanded into fashion, stores were stocked with a wide range of high-quality clothes at various price points. Nordstrom believed it was better to carry too many sizes in each style than not enough so a customer didn't get frustrated if his or her size wasn't available. The brothers also instituted a policy titled "decision by consensus," which helped move the company along even when disagreements arose.

Nordstrom grew into the billion-dollar retailer it is today under the leadership of the family's third generation: Bruce, John, and Jim Nordstrom and Jack McMillan. Their philosophy focused on empowering the managers and sales force to make decisions that favored the customer, not the company. The company rewarded energetic individuals who attained an entrepreneurial spirit, preferring to hire "nice" people who could be trained to sell rather than seasoned "salespeople" who weren't seen as nice.

During this time the company also decentralized its purchasing process, giving regional managers the freedom to purchase styles that fit the needs and tastes of their particular area. That is, managers in Minnesota could, and did, buy very differently from managers in southern California. To cater to each region, the company encouraged its sales force to continuously ask customers what products and styles they would like to see in the store. Jim Nordstrom explained, "When we go into a market, our first buy is the worst."

Today, Nordstrom is run by the fourth Nordstrom generation and continues to set the standard in customer service and loyalty. In fact, the company is so well known for its customer service that true tales of "heroics" still circulate today. Perhaps the best-known tells how in 1975 a customer came into the store after Nordstrom had purchased an Alaska-based company called Northern Commercial. The customer wanted to return a set of tires originally bought at Northern Commercial. Although Nordstrom had never carried or sold tires, it happily accepted the return and instantly provided the customer cash for his purchase. In another example, a saleswoman noticed that a customer had left her plane ticket on the store's counter. She called the airport and asked the airline to issue the customer another ticket, but the airline refused. The saleswomen immediately jumped into a cab and hand-delivered the ticket to the customer at the airport.

There are many other examples of its exceptional customer service, and Nordstrom's "no questions asked" return policy remains intact today. Its sales representatives send thank-you cards to customers who shop there, warm up their customers' cars on cold days, and have hand-delivered special orders to customers' homes. Nordstrom installed a tool called Personal Book at its registers that allows salespeople to enter and recall customers' specific preferences in order to better personalize their shopping experiences. Sales associates are also allowed to sell merchandise in any department, giving them even more opportunities to develop relationships with customers. Nordstrom also provides multiple channels for shopping, allowing customers to buy something online and pick it up at a store within an hour.

Nordstrom believes it has 15 seconds to capture the excitement of a customer with "a memorable experience" when he or she walks in the door. Aisles are neat and uncluttered, big display windows create a bright and open atmosphere, and the layout is efficient and easily navigated. Dressing rooms are large and illuminated to imitate natural light, escalators are wide to allow couples or parents with children to stand next to each other, and each fixture is chosen to create a homelike feeling. When a new store opens, Nordstrom connects with the surrounding community by hosting an opening night gala complete with live entertainment, a runway fashion show, and the ultimate shopping experience to help raise money for local charities.

Nordstrom's Fashion Rewards Program repays loyal customers on four levels based on their annual spending. Customers who spend $10,000 annually receive complimentary alterations, a 24-hour fashion emergency hotline, and access to a personal concierge service. Customers at the highest level ($20,000 annually) also receive private shopping trips complete with dressing rooms pre-stocked in their size, champagne, live piano music, tickets to Nordstrom's runway fashion shows, and access to exclusive travel and fashion packages, including red carpet events.

The company's long-term and often costly customer-focus approach has reaped great benefits. Not only has Nordstrom emerged as a luxury brand known for quality, trust, and service, but its customers remain loyal even in hard times. During the economic crisis in 2008 and 2009, many customers chose Nordstrom over its competitors due to their existing relationship and its hassle-free return policy.

Nordstrom continues to stay strategically focused on customer service and look for new ways to help deepen and develop its customer-salesperson relationship. The company currently operates in 44 countries and 31 states with 117 full-line stores, 119 Nordstrom Rack clearance stores, two Jeffrey Boutiques, and one clearance store. Sales reached $12.2 billion in 2013.

**Questions**

1. How else can Nordstrom continue to provide exceptional customer service and increase brand loyalty?

2. What are Nordstrom's greatest risks, and who are its biggest competitors?

**Sources:** "Annual Reports," Nordstrom.com; "Company History," Nordstrom.com; Chantal Todé, "Nordstrom Loyalty Program Experience," *DMNews*, May 4, 2007; Melissa Allison and Amy Martinez, "Nordstrom's Solid December Showing Suggests Some Shoppers Eager to Spend," *Seattle Times*, January 7, 2010; Robert Spector and Patrick D. McCarthy, *The Nordstrom Way: The Inside Story of America's #1 Customer Service Company* (New York: John Wiley & Sons, Inc., 1995).

## Marketing Excellence

### >> Tesco

Tesco hasn't always had a reputation as a customer-friendly retailer. Back in the early 1980s, it was a UK grocery store chain that suffered from a reputation for "piling it high and selling it cheap" and trailed behind Sainsbury's, a more upscale UK retailer. Only when the company came under the leadership of Ian MacLaurin did it began to reinvent itself as a consumer-friendly brand.

In 1983, Tesco began the long process of updating its stores and improving its product selection. Over the next decade, it took on Sainsbury's head on with brighter stores, higher-quality products, affordable prices, and more locations. Between 1990 and 1992, Tesco launched 114 separate initiatives to improve the quality of its stores, including adding baby-changing rooms, stocking specialty items such as French free-range chickens, and introducing a value-priced line of products.

The company also developed a well-received marketing campaign titled "Every Little Helps" that helped communicate these improvements and enhance its brand image in the public eye. The campaign included 20 ads, each focused on a different aspect of its new approach: "Doing right by the customer." As a result, by 1995, Tesco had attracted 1.3 million new customers and its market share surpassed Sainsbury's for the first time, making it the new market leader.

In 1996, Terry Leahy took over as CEO. During his tenure, Tesco grew from the third-largest UK supermarket chain, with $7 billion in sales, to the third-largest retailer in the world, with more than $100 billion in sales.

Under Leahy's guidance, Tesco introduced its Clubcard frequent-shopper program, an initiative that helped make the company a world-class example of how to build lasting relationships with customers. The Clubcard not only offered discounts and special offers tailored to individual shoppers but also acted as a powerful data-gathering tool, enabling Tesco to understand customers' shopping patterns and preferences better than any competitor.

Using Clubcard data, Tesco created a unique "DNA profile" for each customer based on shopping habits. It classified each product a customer purchased on as many as 40 dimensions, including price, size, brand, eco-friendliness, convenience, and healthiness. Based on these profiles, Tesco shoppers received one of 4 million variations of the quarterly Clubcard statement, containing targeted special offers and other promotions. The company also installed kiosks in its stores where Clubcard shoppers could get customized coupons.

The Clubcard data helped Tesco run its business more efficiently too. Tracking Clubcard purchases uncovered each product's price elasticity and helped set promotional schedules, which saved Tesco more than $500 million. Tesco used its customer data to pick the range of products and type of merchandising for each store and even to choose the location of new stores. Within 15 months of introduction, more than 8 million Clubcards had been issued, of which 5 million were used regularly.

Next, Tesco expanded its powerful private-label program with three distinctive brands in various price ranges; "Finest" offered the best-quality item at the highest price, "Mid-range" targeted the middle range, and the "Value" product line offered the best bargain prices available. Through this simple system, consumers came to expect a certain quality at variable prices.

By 1999, the company's market share in the United Kingdom rose to 15 percent, and it was voted Britain's most admired company. In the following years, Tesco continued to apply its winning formula of using private labels and customer data to dominate the British retail landscape.

It also moved further into "big-box" retailing of general merchandise, or nonfood products. This strategic growth plan not only provided additional convenience to consumers who preferred shopping under one roof but also improved overall profitability. In 2003, the average profit margin for nonfood products was 9 percent versus

5 percent for food products, and nearly 20 percent of Tesco's revenues came from nonfood items. That year, the company sold more CDs than Virgin Megastores, and its apparel line, Cherokee, was the fastest-growing brand in the United Kingdom. By 2005, the company had a 35 percent share of supermarket spending in the United Kingdom, almost twice that of its nearest competitor, and a 14 percent share of total retail sales.

Tesco's stores are now categorized into seven different formats, depending on where they are located and whom they target: Tesco Extra, Tesco Superstores, Tesco Metro, Tesco Express, One Stop, Tesco Homeplus, and Dobbies. Tesco Extra is the largest and offers a wide range of food and nonfood products and services like optical centers. Tesco Superstores are standard large supermarkets that offer some nonfood products. Tesco Express stores are neighborhood convenience stores that stock mostly higher-margin products and everyday essentials.

Tesco continues to diversify its product and service offerings to reach more consumers. The company partnered with existing telecoms to create Tesco Mobile and Tesco Home Phone and launched Tesco Broadband to provide Internet access to homes and businesses. In addition, it now offers insurance policies, dental plans, music downloads, and financial services. In 2008, Tesco joined forces with the Royal Bank of Scotland to create a banking division, Tesco Bank.

Its aggressive expansion into nonfood items was a departure from Tesco's core focus on groceries. That, and its determination to expand in Asia, India, and the United States, led to troubled times during the recession and a 20 percent slide in its stock price in 2010. Quality within the supermarkets slipped significantly, and customers were turned off by the abundance of nonfood items in their stores during a poor economy. Tim Green, retail analyst at Brewin Dolphin Ltd., explained, "Tesco got a little bit distracted by thinking of China, the U.S., wider Asia, Central Europe, Tesco Bank, Tesco Telephony. But that is not acceptable, because U.K. food is the main profit generator."

In 2011, Tesco came under the leadership of a new CEO, Philip Clarke, who set out to turn the company around immediately and revive its focus on supermarkets and customer service. First, he cut back on expansion programs, pulling out of Japan completely and slowing growth in the United States, India, and the rest of Europe. Next, he announced a major overhaul of the supermarket chains. Tesco hired and trained tens of thousands of employees who were dedicated to serving customers in the produce and meat departments, which had recently been deprived of sufficient staff.

The company relaunched its Tesco Value brand as Everyday Value and invested significantly to improve the quality and appearance of hundreds of Tesco products without raising the price. It renovated many of its brick-and-mortar stores to give them a homier feeling through better lighting, cleaner shelves, new fixtures and signs, warmer colors, and more spacious produce areas. Tony Hoggett, managing director of Tesco Superstores, explained how small things added up to make a big difference. "It really isn't rocket science. We've improved the look and feel of our stores to make them a much warmer, friendlier place for our customers to shop in."

In 2012, Tesco's revenues topped $108 billion and before-tax profits reached $5.7 billion. Today, Tesco is the largest British retailer measured by both sales and market share (31 percent) and the third-biggest company in the world after Walmart and Carrefour.

## Questions

1. What's most important to the Tesco brand?

2. How will Tesco grow without losing focus on its core customer?

3. How can Tesco take its customer loyalty programs to the next level?

**Sources:** Tesco Annual Report 2012; Richard Fletcher, "Leahy Shrugs Off Talk of a 'Brain Drain,'" *Sunday Times* (London), January 29, 2006; Elizabeth Rigby, "Prosperous Tesco Takes Retailing to a New Level," *Financial Times*, September 21, 2005, p. 23; Hamish Pringle and Marjorie Thompson, *Brand Spirit* (New York: John Wiley & Sons, 1999); Paul Sonne, "Tesco Loses Its Appetite for Growth," *Wall Street Journal*, November 10, 2012, B.3; Renee Schultes, "U.K. Grocers Locked in Coupon Warfare," *Wall Street Journal*, August 29, 2012; Harry Wallop, "Tesco Ditches 1bn Value Range," *BST*, April 4, 2012; Peter Evans, "Britain's Tesco Tries Out New Retail Recipe," *Wall Street Journal*, July 9, 2012, B.8; Julia Werdigier, "Tesco to Invest Heavily in a Domestic Revival," *New York Times*, April 19, 2012; Terry Leahy, "Lessons from a Retail Veteran," *Wall Street Journal*, June 27, 2012.

## In This Chapter, We Will Address the Following **Questions**

1. How do consumer characteristics influence buying behavior? (p. 157)

2. What major psychological processes influence consumer responses to the marketing program? (p. 165)

3. How do consumers make purchasing decisions? (p. 172)

4. In what ways do consumers stray from a deliberative, rational decision process? (p. 180)

Based on detailed customer insights, Domino's improved its products and how they were marketed.

*Source: Domino's Pizza, LLC*

# Analyzing Consumer Markets

**Marketers must have a thorough understanding of how consumers think, feel, and act** and offer clear value to each and every target consumer. In an award-winning marketing campaign, Domino's decided how to deal with negative consumer attitudes about its pizza.[1]

*Known more for the speed of its delivery than for the taste of its pizza, Domino's decided to address negative perceptions head on. A major communication program themed "Oh Yes We Did" featured documentary-style TV ads that opened with Domino's employees at corporate headquarters reviewing written and videotaped focus group feedback from customers. The feedback contains biting comments, such as "Domino's pizza crust to me is like cardboard" and "The sauce tastes like ketchup." Company president Patrick Doyle is shown stating that these results are unacceptable, and the ads then show Domino's chefs and executives in their test kitchens proclaiming that their pizza is new and improved with a bolder, richer sauce; a more robust cheese combination; and an herb-and-garlic-flavored crust. Many critics were stunned by the company's admission that its number-two-ranked pizza had, in effect, been inferior for years. Others countered by noting that the new product formulation and unconventional ads were addressing a widely held, difficult-to-change negative belief that was dragging the brand down and required decisive action. Doyle summed up consumer reaction: "Most really like it, some don't. And that's OK." Subsequent events proved Doyle right. Backed by additional ads and social media campaigns—and the reformulated pizza—Domino's found itself improving its image and gaining share in the following years. From the end of 2009, when Domino's announced its plans, until the end of 2011, the stock gained 233 percent, compared with 37 percent for its key rival, Papa John's. In recent years, sales have been further spurred by marketing innovations such as a mobile-optimized Web site for online ordering, new audible formats for the chain's popular Pizza Tracker, smart-phone and table apps for ordering, and the Pizza Hero game for the iPad.*

**Adopting a holistic marketing** orientation requires fully understanding customers—gaining a 360-degree view of both their daily lives and the changes that occur during their lifetimes so the right products are always marketed to the right customers in the right way. This chapter explores individual consumers' buying dynamics; the next chapter the buying dynamics of business buyers.

# What Influences Consumer Behavior?

**Consumer behavior** is the study of how individuals, groups, and organizations select, buy, use, and dispose of goods, services, ideas, or experiences to satisfy their needs and wants.[2] Marketers must fully understand both the theory and the reality of consumer behavior. Table 6.1 provides a snapshot profile of U.S. consumers.

A consumer's buying behavior is influenced by cultural, social, and personal factors. Of these, cultural factors exert the broadest and deepest influence.

## CULTURAL FACTORS

Culture, subculture, and social class are particularly important influences on consumer buying behavior. **Culture** is the fundamental determinant of a person's wants and behavior. Through family and other key institutions, a child growing up in the United States is exposed to values such as achievement and success, activity, efficiency

| TABLE 6.1 | U.S. Consumer Almanac |
|-----------|------------------------|

**Expenditures**

**Average U.S. outlays for goods and services in 2013**

|  | $ |
|---|---|
| Housing | $17,148 |
| Transportation | $9,004 |
| Food | $6,602 |
| Personal insurance and pensions | $5,528 |
| Health care | $3,631 |
| Entertainment | $2,482 |
| Apparel and services | $1,604 |
| Cash contributions | $1,834 |
| All other | $3,267 |
| Total average annual expenditures | $51,100 |

**Time use on an average workday for employed persons ages 25–54 with children in 2013**

| Working and related activities | 8.7 hours |
|---|---|
| Sleeping | 7.7 hours |
| Leisure and sports | 2.5 hours |
| Caring for others | 1.3 hours |
| Eating and drinking | 1.0 hours |
| Household activities | 1.1 hours |
| Other | 1.7 hours |

**Average time spent per person per day—Q4 2013**

|  | Hours |
|---|---|
| Watching TV in the home | 5.04 |
| Watching time-shifted TV | 0.32 |
| Video games | 0.12 |
| DVD playback | 0.09 |

**Sources:** Bureau of Labor Statistics, *Consumer Expenditure Survey*, www.bls.gov, September 9, 2014; Bureau of Labor Statistics, *American Time Use Survey*, www.bls.gov, June 18, 2014; AC Nielsen, "An Era of Growth: The Cross-Platform Report: Q4 2013," www.nielsen.com, March 5, 2014.

Cultural values differ by countries and markets.

*Source: © Blend Images/Alamy*

and practicality, progress, material comfort, individualism, freedom, external comfort, humanitarianism, and youthfulness.[3] A child growing up in another country might have a different view of self, relationship to others, and rituals.

Marketers must closely attend to cultural values in every country to understand how to best market their existing products and find opportunities for new products. Each culture consists of smaller **subcultures** that provide more specific identification and socialization for their members. Subcultures include nationalities, religions, racial groups, and geographic regions. When subcultures grow large and affluent enough, companies often design specialized marketing programs to serve them.

Virtually all human societies exhibit *social stratification,* most often in the form of **social classes**, relatively homogeneous and enduring divisions in a society, hierarchically ordered and with members who share similar values, interests, and behavior. One classic depiction of social classes in the United States defined seven ascending levels: (1) lower lowers, (2) upper lowers, (3) working class, (4) middle class, (5) upper middles, (6) lower uppers, and (7) upper uppers.[4] Social class members show distinct product and brand preferences in many areas.

## SOCIAL FACTORS

In addition to cultural factors, social factors such as reference groups, family, and social roles and statuses affect our buying behavior.

**REFERENCE GROUPS** A person's **reference groups** are all the groups that have a direct (face-to-face) or indirect influence on their attitudes or behavior. Groups having a direct influence are called **membership groups**. Some of these are **primary groups** with whom the person interacts fairly continuously and informally, such as family, friends, neighbors, and coworkers. People also belong to **secondary groups**, such as religious, professional, and trade-union groups, which tend to be more formal and require less continuous interaction.

Reference groups influence members in at least three ways. They expose an individual to new behaviors and lifestyles, they influence attitudes and self-concept, and they create pressures for conformity that may affect product and brand choices. People are also influenced by groups to which they do *not* belong. **Aspirational groups** are those a person hopes to join; **dissociative groups** are those whose values or behavior an individual rejects.

Where reference group influence is strong, marketers must determine how to reach and influence the group's opinion leaders. An **opinion leader** is the person who offers informal advice or information about a specific product or product category, such as which of several brands is best or how a particular product may be used.[5] Opinion leaders are often highly confident, socially active, and frequent users of the category. Marketers try to reach them by identifying their demographic and psychographic characteristics, identifying the media they read, and directing messages to them.[6]

**CLIQUES** Communication researchers propose a social-structure view of interpersonal communication.[7] They see society as consisting of *cliques,* small groups whose members interact frequently. Clique members are similar, and their closeness facilitates effective communication but also insulates the clique from new ideas. The challenge is to create more openness so cliques exchange information with others in society. This openness is helped along by people who function as liaisons and connect two or more cliques without belonging to either and by *bridges,* people who belong to one clique and are linked to a person in another.

Best-selling author Malcolm Gladwell claims three factors work to ignite public interest in an idea.[8] According to the first, "The Law of the Few," three types of people help to spread an idea like an epidemic. First are *Mavens,* people knowledgeable about big and small things. Second are *Connectors,* people who know and communicate with a great number of other people. Third are *Salesmen,* who possess natural persuasive power. Any idea that catches the interest of Mavens, Connectors, and Salesmen is likely to be broadcast far and wide. The second factor is "Stickiness." An idea must be expressed so that it motivates people to act. Otherwise, "The Law of the Few" will not lead to a self-sustaining epidemic. Finally, the third factor, "The Power of Context," controls whether those spreading an idea are able to organize groups and communities around it.

Not everyone agrees with Gladwell's ideas.[9] One team of viral marketing experts cautions that although influencers or "alphas" start trends, they are often too introspective and socially alienated to spread them. They advise marketers to cultivate "bees," hyperdevoted customers who are not satisfied just knowing about the next trend but live to spread the word.[10] More firms are in fact finding ways to actively engage their passionate brand evangelists. LEGO's Ambassador Program targets its most enthusiastic followers for brainstorming and feedback.[11] Some firms are exploring ways to identify the most influential and potentially lucrative customers online.[12]

**SCORING CONSUMERS ONLINE**   To better profile and market to customers, firms are exploring different ways to score consumers online. *E-scores* go beyond personal credit reports to estimate a consumer's buying power. They take into account factors such as occupation, salary, and home value as well as the amount and nature of luxury and non-luxury purchases. Independent suppliers like EBureau amass the personal information and combine it with a company's customer database to score a customer from 0 (unprofitable) to 99 (likely to return an investment). Another area of online scoring is influence measurement. A pioneer in the field, Klout measures the clout a person has online with its *Klout Scores*. Klout Scores range from 0 to 100 and are based on analysis of 400 different factors—and 12 billion pieces of data a day—like how influential your followers are and how many people retweet or respond to your messages. President Obama scored a near-perfect 99; singer Justin Bieber scored an impressive 92. Companies like Chevrolet pay Klout to identify and contact influencers for auto purchases. Those people targeted by Chevrolet are given special perks, like a three-day test drive of a Volt, in hopes that they will talk up the car on social media.

Of course, much word-of-mouth is offline person-to-person communication—face to face or over the phone. One of the most valuable sources of information is almost always "people I know and trust."[13] Some word-of-mouth tactics walk a fine line between acceptable and unethical. One controversial tactic, sometimes called *shill marketing* or *stealth marketing*, pays people to anonymously promote a product or service in public places without disclosing their financial relationship to the sponsoring firm.

To launch its T681 mobile camera phone, Sony Ericsson hired actors dressed as tourists to approach people at tourist locations and ask to have their photo taken. Handing over the mobile phone created an opportunity to discuss its merits, but many found the deception distasteful.[14] Shill marketing is also a problem online, where the legitimacy of a customer or so-called expert reviewer may be hard to verify.

**FAMILY**  The family is the most important consumer buying organization in society, and family members constitute the most influential primary reference group.[15] There are two families in the buyer's life. The **family of orientation** consists of parents and siblings. From parents a person acquires an orientation toward religion, politics, and economics and a sense of personal ambition, self-worth, and love.[16] Even if the buyer no longer interacts very much with his or her parents, parental influence on behavior can be significant. Almost 40 percent of families have auto insurance with the same company as the husband's parents.

A more direct influence on everyday buying behavior is the **family of procreation**—namely, the person's spouse and children. In the United States, in a traditional husband–wife relationship, engagement in purchases has varied widely by product category. The wife has usually acted as the family's main purchasing agent, especially for food, sundries, and staple clothing items. Now traditional purchasing roles are changing, and marketers would be wise to see both men and women as possible targets.

For expensive products and services such as cars, vacations, or housing, the vast majority of husbands and wives engage in joint decision making.[17] Men and women may respond differently to marketing messages, however. Research has shown that women value connections and relationships with family and friends and place a higher priority on people than on companies. Men, on the other hand, relate more to competition and place a high priority on action.[18] Marketers have taken direct aim at women with new products such as Quaker's Nutrition for Women cereals and Crest Rejuvenating Effects toothpaste.

Many of Disney's successful products for kids involve tie-ins with their popular TV or movie franchises.

Source: © Directphoto Collection / Alamy

Another shift in buying patterns is an increase in the amount of dollars spent by and the direct and indirect influence wielded by children and teens. Direct influence describes children's hints, requests, and demands—"I want to go to McDonald's." Indirect influence means parents know the brands, product choices, and preferences of their children without hints or outright requests—"I think Jake and Emma would want to go to Panera."

Research has shown that more than two-thirds of 13- to 21-year-olds make or influence family purchase decisions on audio/video equipment, software, and vacation destinations.[19] In total, these teens and young adults spend more than $120 billion a year. They report that to make sure they buy the right products, they watch what their friends say and do as much as what they see or hear in an ad or are told by a salesperson in a store.

Television can be especially powerful in reaching children, and marketers are using it to target them at younger ages than ever before with product tie-ins for just about everything—*Disney Princess* character pajamas, retro G.I. Joe toys and action figures, *Dora the Explorer* backpacks, and *Toy Story* playsets.

By the time children are about 2 years old, they can often recognize characters, logos, and specific brands. They can distinguish between advertising and programming by about ages 6 or 7. A year or so later, they can understand the concept of persuasive intent on the part of advertisers. By 9 or 10, they can perceive the discrepancies between message and product.[20]

**ROLES AND STATUS** We each participate in many groups—family, clubs, organizations—and these are often an important source of information and help to define norms for behavior. We can define a person's position in each group in terms of role and status. A **role** consists of the activities a person is expected to perform. Each role in turn connotes a **status**. A senior vice president of marketing may have more status than a sales manager, and a sales manager may have more status than an office clerk. People choose products that reflect and communicate their role and their actual or desired status in society. Marketers must be aware of the status-symbol potential of products and brands.

## PERSONAL FACTORS

Personal characteristics that influence a buyer's decision include age and stage in the life cycle, occupation and economic circumstances, personality and self-concept, and lifestyle and values. Because many of these have a direct impact on consumer behavior, it is important for marketers to follow them closely. See how well you do with "Marketing Memo: The Average U.S. Consumer Quiz."

**AGE AND STAGE IN THE LIFE CYCLE** Our taste in food, clothes, furniture, and recreation is often related to our age. Consumption is also shaped by the *family life cycle* and the number, age, and gender of people in the household at any point in time. U.S. households are increasingly fragmented—the traditional family of four with a husband, wife, and two kids makes up a much smaller percentage of total households than it once did. The 2010 census revealed that the average U.S. household size was 2.6 persons.[21]

In addition, *psychological* life-cycle stages may matter. Adults experience certain passages or transformations as they go through life.[22] Their behavior during these intervals, such as when becoming a parent, is not necessarily fixed but changes with the times.

Marketers should also consider *critical life events or transitions*—marriage, childbirth, illness, relocation, divorce, first job, career change, retirement, death of a spouse—as giving rise to new needs. These should alert service providers—banks, lawyers, and marriage, employment, and bereavement counselors—to ways they can help.

## The Average U.S. Consumer Quiz

Listed below is a series of statements used in attitude surveys of U.S. consumers. For each statement, estimate what percent of U.S. men and women agreed with it in 2012 and write your answer, a number between 0 percent and 100 percent, in the columns to the right. Then check your results against the correct answers in the footnote.*

| | Percent of Consumers Agreeing | |
|---|---|---|
| Statements | % Men | % Women |
| 1. Most companies today are becoming too inhuman and impersonal when it comes to connecting with their customers | _____ | _____ |
| 2. Even if others might find it offensive, it is always OK to speak what is on your mind | _____ | _____ |
| 3. I appreciate the influence that other cultures are having on the American way of life | _____ | _____ |
| 4. One of the reasons this country is losing its leadership position in the world is because parents don't push their kids hard enough to succeed | _____ | _____ |
| 5. The food and beverage industry should take more responsibility for helping solve the obesity problem in the U.S. | _____ | _____ |
| 6. I believe I will become rich in my lifetime | _____ | _____ |
| 7. I could not get by without my cell phone/smart phone (among those who have a cell phone) | _____ | _____ |
| 8. I'd really like to start my own business | _____ | _____ |
| 9. I feel that I have to take whatever I can get in this world because no one is going to give me anything | _____ | _____ |
| 10. Protecting my personal information and privacy is more of a concern now than it was a few years ago | _____ | _____ |

**Note:** Results are from a nationally representative sample of more than 4,000 respondents surveyed in 2012.

**Source:** The Futures Company Yankelovich MONITOR (with permission). Copyright 2012, Yankelovich, Inc.

*Answers

1. M = 81%, W = 81%; 2. M = 61%, W = 49%; 3. M = 63%, W = 67%; 4. M = 64%, W = 58%; 5. M = 61%, W = 60%; 6. M = 42%, W = 30%; 7. M = 45%, W = 51%; 8. M = 47%, W = 34%; 9. M = 66%, W = 52%; 10. M = 91%, W = 93%

Not surprisingly, the baby industry attracts many marketers given the enormous amount parents spend—it's estimated to be a $36 billion market annually—and its life-changing nature.[23]

**THE BABY MARKET**  Although they may not yet have reached their full earning potential, expectant and new parents seldom hold back when spending on their loved ones, making the baby industry more recession-proof than most. Spending tends to peak between the second trimester of pregnancy and the 12th week after birth. First-time mothers-to-be are especially attractive targets given the fact they will be unable to use many hand-me-downs and will need to buy the full range of new furniture, strollers, toys, and baby supplies. Recognizing the importance of reaching expectant parents early to win their trust—industry pundits call it a "first in, first win" opportunity—marketers use a variety of media including direct mail, inserts, space ads, e-mail marketing, and Web sites. Product samples are especially popular; kits are often given at childbirth education classes and other places. Many hospitals have banned the traditional bedside gift bag, though, concerned with privacy and potentially adverse effects on a vulnerable audience (for example, distributing baby formula may discourage new mothers from breast-feeding). Avenues of access still exist. Partnering with a company that sells baby bedside photos, Disney Baby hands out playful Disney Cuddly Bodysuits and solicits sign-ups for e-mail alerts from DisneyBaby.com. Not all expenditures go directly to the baby. Going through such a fundamental life change, expectant or new parents have a whole new set of needs that has them thinking differently about life insurance, financial services, real estate, home improvement, and automobiles.

**OCCUPATION AND ECONOMIC CIRCUMSTANCES** Occupation also influences consumption patterns. Marketers try to identify the occupational groups that have above-average interest in their products and services and even tailor products for certain occupational groups: Computer software companies, for example, design different products for brand managers, engineers, lawyers, and physicians.

As the recent prolonged recession clearly indicated, both product and brand choice are greatly affected by economic circumstances like spendable income (level, stability, and pattern over time), savings and assets (including the percentage that is liquid), debts, borrowing power, and attitudes toward spending and saving. Although luxury-goods makers such as Gucci, Prada, and Burberry may be vulnerable to an economic downturn, some luxury brands did surprisingly well in the latest recession.[24] If economic indicators point to a recession, marketers can take steps to redesign, reposition, and reprice their products or introduce or increase the emphasis on discount brands so they can continue to offer value to target customers.

**PERSONALITY AND SELF-CONCEPT** By **personality**, we mean a set of distinguishing human psychological traits that lead to relatively consistent and enduring responses to environmental stimuli including buying behavior. We often describe personality in terms of such traits as self-confidence, dominance, autonomy, deference, sociability, defensiveness, and adaptability.[25]

Brands also have personalities, and consumers are likely to choose brands whose personalities match their own. We define **brand personality** as the specific mix of human traits that we can attribute to a particular brand. Stanford's Jennifer Aaker researched brand personalities and identified the following traits:[26]

*Source: Paul Bradbury/Getty Images*

The baby market, targeting expectant and new parents, is highly lucrative for marketers.

1. Sincerity (down to earth, honest, wholesome, and cheerful)
2. Excitement (daring, spirited, imaginative, and up to date)
3. Competence (reliable, intelligent, and successful)
4. Sophistication (upper-class and charming)
5. Ruggedness (outdoorsy and tough)

Aaker analyzed some well-known brands and found that a number tended to be strong on one particular trait: Levi's on "ruggedness"; MTV on "excitement"; CNN on "competence"; and Campbell's on "sincerity." These brands will, in theory, attract users high on the same traits. A brand personality may have several attributes: Levi's suggests a personality that is also youthful, rebellious, authentic, and American.

A cross-cultural study exploring the generalizability of Aaker's scale outside the United States found three of the five factors applied in Japan and Spain, but a "peacefulness" dimension replaced "ruggedness" in both countries, and a "passion" dimension emerged in Spain instead of "competence."[27] Research on brand personality in Korea revealed two culture-specific factors—"passive likeableness" and "ascendancy"—reflecting the importance of Confucian values in Korea's social and economic systems.[28]

Consumers often choose and use brands with a brand personality consistent with their *actual self-concept* (how we view ourselves), though the match may instead be based on the consumer's *ideal self-concept* (how we would like to view ourselves) or even on *others' self-concept* (how we think others see us).[29] These effects may also be more pronounced for publicly consumed products than for privately consumed goods.[30] On the other hand, consumers who are high "self-monitors"—that is, sensitive to the way others see them—are more likely to choose brands whose personalities fit the consumption situation.[31]

Finally, multiple aspects of self (serious professional, caring family member, active fun-lover) may often be evoked differently in different situations or around different types of people. Some marketers carefully orchestrate brand experiences to express brand personalities. Here's how San Francisco's Joie de Vivre does this.[32]

**JOIE DE VIVRE**   Joie de Vivre Hotels operates a chain of boutique hotels and resorts in the San Francisco area as well as Arizona, Illinois, and Hawaii. Each property's unique décor, quirky amenities, and thematic style are loosely based on popular magazines. For example, The Hotel del Sol—a converted motel bearing a yellow exterior and surrounded by palm trees wrapped in festive lights—is described as "kind of *Martha Stewart Living* meets *Islands* magazine." The

Each of Joie de Vivre's hotel properties has a personality loosely based on a popular magazine, as with the *Rolling Stone*-inspired Phoenix hotel.

Source: Image provided by Commune Hotels + Resorts. Photo by Kelly Ishikawa.

Phoenix, represented by *Rolling Stone,* is, like the magazine, described as "adventurous, hip, irreverent, funky, and young at heart." Each one of Joie de Vivre's more than 30 hotels is an original concept designed to reflect its location and engage the five senses. The boutique concept enables the hotels to offer personal touches, such as vitamins in place of chocolates on pillows.

**LIFESTYLE AND VALUES** People from the same subculture, social class, and occupation may adopt quite different lifestyles. A **lifestyle** is a person's pattern of living in the world as expressed in activities, interests, and opinions. It portrays the "whole person" interacting with his or her environment. Marketers search for relationships between their products and lifestyle groups. A computer manufacturer might find that most computer buyers are achievement-oriented and then aim the brand more clearly at the achiever lifestyle.

Lifestyles are shaped partly by whether consumers are *money constrained* or *time constrained.* Companies aiming to serve the money-constrained will create lower-cost products and services. By appealing to thrifty consumers, Walmart has become the largest company in the world. Its "everyday low prices" have wrung tens of billions of dollars out of the retail supply chain, passing the larger part of savings along to shoppers in the form of rock-bottom bargain prices.

Consumers who experience time famine are prone to **multitasking**, doing two or more things at the same time. They will also pay others to perform tasks because time is more important to them than money. Companies aiming to serve them will create products and services that offer multiple time-saving benefits. For example, multitasking blemish balm (BB) skin creams offer an all-in-one approach to skin care—incorporating moisturizer, anti-aging ingredients, sunscreen, and maybe even whitening.[33]

In some categories, notably food processing, companies targeting time-constrained consumers need to be aware that these very same people want to believe they're *not* operating within time constraints. Marketers call those who seek both convenience and some involvement in the cooking process the "convenience involvement segment," as Hamburger Helper discovered.[34]

**HAMBURGER HELPER**    Launched in 1971 in response to tough economic times, the inexpensive pasta-and-powdered-mix Hamburger Helper was designed to quickly and inexpensively stretch a pound of meat into a family meal. With an estimated 44 percent of evening meals prepared in under 30 minutes and given strong competition from fast-food drive-through windows, restaurant deliveries, and precooked grocery store dishes, it might seem that Hamburger Helper's days of prosperity are numbered. Market researchers found, however, that some consumers don't want the fastest microwaveable solution possible—they also want to feel good about how they prepare a meal. In fact, on average, they prefer to use at least one pot or pan and 15 minutes of time. To remain attractive to this segment, marketers of Hamburger Helper are always introducing new flavors and varieties such as Tuna Helper, Asian Chicken Helper, and Whole Grain Helper to tap into evolving consumer taste trends. Not surprisingly, the latest economic downturn saw brand sales steadily rise.

Consumer decisions are also influenced by **core values**, the belief systems that underlie attitudes and behaviors. Core values go much deeper than behavior or attitude and at a basic level guide people's choices and desires over the long term. Marketers who target consumers on the basis of their values believe that with appeals to people's inner selves, it is possible to influence their outer selves—their purchase behavior.

# Key Psychological Processes

The starting point for understanding consumer behavior is the stimulus-response model shown in Figure 6.1. Marketing and environmental stimuli enter the consumer's consciousness, and a set of psychological processes combine with certain consumer characteristics to result in decision processes and purchase decisions. The marketer's task is to understand what happens in the consumer's consciousness between the arrival of the outside marketing stimuli and the ultimate purchase decisions. Four key psychological processes—motivation, perception, learning, and memory—fundamentally influence consumer responses.

## MOTIVATION

We all have many needs at any given time. Some needs are *biogenic*; they arise from physiological states of tension such as hunger, thirst, or discomfort. Other needs are *psychogenic*; they arise from psychological states of tension such as the need for recognition, esteem, or belonging. A need becomes a **motive** when it is aroused to a sufficient level of intensity to drive us to act. Motivation has both direction—we select one goal over another—and intensity—we pursue the goal with more or less vigor.

Three of the best-known theories of human motivation—those of Sigmund Freud, Abraham Maslow, and Frederick Herzberg—carry quite different implications for consumer analysis and marketing strategy.

**FREUD'S THEORY** Sigmund Freud assumed the psychological forces shaping people's behavior are largely unconscious and that a person cannot fully understand his or her own motivations. Someone who examines specific brands will react not only to their stated capabilities but also to other, less conscious cues such as shape, size, weight, material, color, and brand name. A technique called *laddering* lets us trace a person's motivations from the stated instrumental ones to the more terminal ones. Then the marketer can decide at what level to develop the message and appeal.[35]

Motivation researchers often collect in-depth interviews with a few dozen consumers to uncover deeper motives triggered by a product. They use various *projective techniques* such as word association, sentence completion, picture interpretation, and role playing, many pioneered by Ernest Dichter, a Viennese psychologist who settled in the United States.[36]

Dichter's research led him to believe that for women, pulling a cake out of the oven was like "giving birth." Because having women only add water to a cake mix could seem to marginalize their role, Dichter's research suggested having them also add an egg, a symbol of fertility, a practice used to this day.[37]

Another motivation researcher, cultural anthropologist Clotaire Rapaille, works on breaking the "code" behind product behavior—the unconscious meaning people give to a particular market offering. Rapaille worked with Boeing on its 787 "Dreamliner" to identify features in the airliner's interior that would have universal appeal. Based

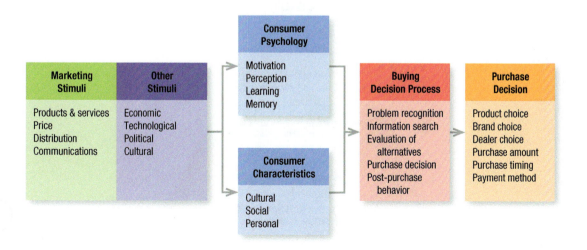

| Fig. 6.1 |

Model of Consumer Behavior

In-depth
motivational
research on
product meaning
helped Boeing
design its 787
Dreamliner.

*Source: © John Keates / Alamy*

in part on his research, the Dreamliner has a spacious foyer; larger, curved luggage bins closer to the ceiling; larger, electronically dimmed windows; and a ceiling discreetly lit by hidden LEDs.[38]

**MASLOW'S THEORY**  Abraham Maslow sought to explain why people are driven by particular needs at particular times.[39] His answer is that human needs are arranged in a hierarchy from most to least pressing—from physiological needs to safety needs, social needs, esteem needs, and self-actualization needs (see Figure 6.2). People will try to satisfy their most important need first and then move to the next. For example, a starving man (need 1) will not take an interest in the latest happenings in the art world (need 5), nor in the way he is viewed by others (need 3 or 4), nor even in whether he is breathing clean air (need 2), but when he has enough food and water, the next most important need will become salient.

**HERZBERG'S THEORY**  Frederick Herzberg developed a two-factor theory that distinguishes *dissatisfiers* (factors that cause dissatisfaction) from *satisfiers* (factors that cause satisfaction).[40] The absence of dissatisfiers is not enough to motivate a purchase; satisfiers must be present. For example, a computer that does not come with a warranty is a dissatisfier. Yet the presence of a product warranty does not act as a satisfier or motivator of a purchase because it is not a source of intrinsic satisfaction. Ease of use is a satisfier.

**| Fig. 6.2 |**

## Maslow's Hierarchy of Needs

**Source:** A. H. Maslow, *Motivation and Personality,* 3rd ed. (Upper Saddle River, NJ: Prentice Hall, 1987). Printed and electronically reproduced by permission of Pearson Education, Inc., Upper Saddle River, NJ.

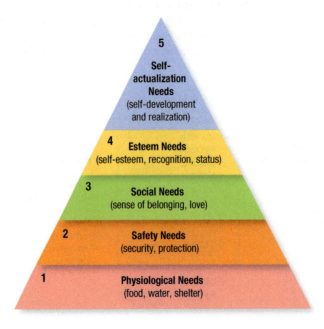

5
Self-
actualization
Needs
(self-development
and realization)

4  Esteem Needs
(self-esteem, recognition, status)

3  Social Needs
(sense of belonging, love)

2  Safety Needs
(security, protection)

1  Physiological Needs
(food, water, shelter)

Herzberg's theory has two implications. First, sellers should do their best to avoid dissatisfiers (for example, a poor training manual or a poor service policy). Although these things will not sell a product, they might easily unsell it. Second, the seller should identify the major satisfiers or motivators of purchase in the market and then supply them.

## PERCEPTION

A motivated person is ready to act—*how* is influenced by his or her perception of the situation. In marketing, perceptions are more important than reality because they affect consumers' actual behavior. **Perception** is the process by which we select, organize, and interpret information inputs to create a meaningful picture of the world.[41] Consumers perceive many different kinds of information through their senses, as reviewed in "Marketing Memo: The Power of Sensory Marketing."

---

## marketing memo — The Power of Sensory Marketing

Sensory marketing has been defined as "marketing that engages the consumers' senses and affects their perception, judgment and behavior." In other words, sensory marketing is an application of the understanding of sensation and perception to the field of marketing. All five senses may be engaged with sensory marketing: sight, sound, smell, taste, and feel. In a 2012 *Journal of Consumer Psychology* article, Aradhna Krishna offers an excellent review of the rapidly accumulating academic research on this topic.

In doing so, she notes, "Given the gamut of explicit marketing appeals made to consumers every day, subconscious 'triggers' which may appeal to the basic senses may be a more efficient way to engage consumers." In other words, consumers' own inferences about a product's attributes may be more persuasive, at least in some cases, than explicit claims from an advertiser.

Krishna argues that sensory marketing's effects can be manifested in two main ways. One, sensory marketing can be used subconsciously to shape consumer perceptions of more abstract qualities of a product or service (say, different aspects of its brand personality such as its sophistication, ruggedness, warmth, quality, and modernity). Two, sensory marketing can also be used to affect the perceptions of specific product or service attributes such as its color, taste, smell, or shape.

Marketers certainly appreciate the importance of sensory marketing. Many hotels, retailers, and other service establishments use signature scents to set a mood and distinguish themselves. Westin's White Tea scent was so popular it began to sell it for home use. Although NBC, Intel, and Yahoo! have trademarked their brand jingles (or yodels), Harley-Davidson was unsuccessful trademarking its distinctive engine roar. In packaging, companies try to find shapes that are pleasing to the touch, and in food advertising, visual and verbal depictions try to tantalize consumers' taste buds.

Based on Krishna's review of academic research in psychology and marketing, we next highlight some key considerations for each of the five senses.

### Touch (haptics)

Touch is the first sense to develop and the last sense we lose with age. People vary in their need for touch, and Peck and Childers have developed a scale to capture those differences. In one application, high need-for-touch (NFT) individuals were more confident and less frustrated about their product evaluations when they could actually touch a product than when they could only see it. For low NFT individuals, touching did not matter one way or another. Written product descriptions helped alleviate the NFT's level of frustration, though only for more concrete product attributes (such as the weight of a cell phone).

### Smell

Scent-encoded information has been shown to be more durable and last longer in memory than information encoded with other sensory cues. People can recognize scents after very long lapses of time, and using scents as reminders can cue all kinds of autobiographical memories. Pleasant scents have also been show to enhance evaluations of products and stores. Consumers also take more time shopping and engage in more variety seeking in the presence of pleasant scents.

### Sound (audition)

Marketing communications by their very nature are often auditory in nature. Even the sounds that make up a word can carry meanings. One study showed that Frosh-brand ice cream sounded creamier than Frish-brand ice cream. Language too can have its own associations. In bilingual cultures where English is the second language—such as Japan, Korea, Germany, and India—use of English in ads signals modernity, progress, sophistication, and a cosmopolitan identity. Ambient music in a store has also been shown to influence consumer mood, time spent in a location, perception of time spent in a location, and spending.

### Taste

Humans can distinguish only five pure tastes: sweet, salty, sour, bitter, and umami. Umami comes from Japanese food researchers and stands for "delicious" or "savory" as it relates to the taste of pure protein or monosodium glutonate (MSG). Taste perceptions themselves depend on all the other senses—the way a food looks, feels, smells, and sounds to eat. Thus many factors have been shown to affect taste perceptions, including physical attributes, brand name, product information (ingredients, nutritional information), product packaging, and advertising. Foreign-sounding brand names can improve ratings of yogurt, and ingredients that sound unpleasant (balsamic vinegar or soy) can affect consumers taste perceptions if disclosed before product consumption.

### Vision

Visual effects have been studied in detail in an advertising context. Many visual perception biases or illusions exist in day-to-day consumer behavior. For example, people judge tall thin containers to contain more volume than short fat ones, but after drinking from the containers, people actually feel they have consumed more from short fat containers than tall thin containers, over-adjusting their expectations. Even something as simple as the way a mug is depicted in an ad can affect product evaluations. A mug photographed with the handle on the right side was shown to elicit more mental stimulation and product purchase intent from right-handed people than if shown with the handle on the left side.

**Sources**: Aradhna Krishna, *Sensory Marketing: Research on the Sensuality of Products* (New York: Routledge, 2010); Aradhna Krishna, "An Integrative Review of Sensory Marketing: Engaging the Senses to Affect Perception, Judgment and Behavior," *Journal of Consumer Psychology* 22 (July 2012), pp. 332–51; Joann Peck and Terry L. Childers, "To Have and to Hold: The Influence of Haptic Information on Product Judgments," *Journal of Marketing* 67 (April 2003), pp. 35–48; Joann Peck and Terry L. Childers, "Individual Differences in Haptic Information Processing: On the Development, Validation, and Use of the 'Need for Touch' Scale," *Journal of Consumer Research* 30 (December 2003), pp. 430–42; Joann Peck and Terry L. Childers, "Effects of Sensory Factors on Consumer Behaviors," Frank Kardes, Curtis Haugtvedt, and Paul Herr, eds., *Handbook of Consumer Psychology* (Mahwah, NJ: Erlbaum, 2008), pp. 193–220; Aradhna Krishna, May Lwin, and Maureen Morrin, "Product Scent and Memory," *Journal of Consumer Research* 37 (June 2010), pp. 57–67; Eric Yorkston and Geeta Menon, "A Sound Idea: Phonetic Effects of Brand Names on Consumer Judgments," *Journal of Consumer Research* 31 (June 2004), pp. 43–45; Aradhna Krishna and Rohini Ahluwalia, "Language Choice in Advertising to Bilinguals: Asymmetric Effects for Multinationals versus Local Firms," *Journal of Consumer Research* 35 (December 2008), pp. 692–705; Richard F. Yalch and Eric R. Spangenberg, "The Effects of Music in a Retail Setting on Real and Perceived Shopping Times," *Journal of Business Research* 49 (August 2000), pp. 139–47; France Leclerc, Bernd H. Schmitt, and Laurette Dube, "Foreign Branding and Its Effect on Product Perceptions and Attitudes," *Journal of Marketing Research* 31 (May 1994), pp. 263–70; Priya Raghubir and Aradhna Krishna, "Vital Dimensions: Antecedents and Consequences of Biases in Volume Perceptions," *Journal of Marketing Research* 36 (August 1994), pp. 313–26; Ryan S. Elder and Aradhna Krishna, "The 'Visual Depiction Effect' in Advertising: Facilitating Embodied Mental Simulation through Product Orientation," *Journal of Consumer Research* 38 (April 2012), pp. 988–1003.

Perception depends not only on physical stimuli but also on the stimuli's relationship to the surrounding environment and on conditions within each of us. One person might perceive a fast-talking salesperson as aggressive and insincere, another as intelligent and helpful. Each will respond to the salesperson differently.

People emerge with different perceptions of the same object because of three perceptual processes: selective attention, selective distortion, and selective retention.

**SELECTIVE ATTENTION** Attention is the allocation of processing capacity to some stimulus. Voluntary attention is something purposeful; involuntary attention is grabbed by someone or something. It's estimated that the average person may be exposed to more than 1,500 ads or brand communications a day. Because we cannot possibly attend to all these, we screen most stimuli out—a process called **selective attention**. Selective attention means that marketers must work hard to attract consumers' notice. The real challenge is to explain which stimuli people will notice. Here are some findings:

1. *People are more likely to notice stimuli that relate to a current need.* A person who is motivated to buy a smart phone will notice smart phone ads and be less likely to notice non-phone-related ads.
2. *People are more likely to notice stimuli they anticipate.* You are more likely to notice laptops than portable radios in a computer store because you don't expect the store to carry portable radios.
3. *People are more likely to notice stimuli whose deviations are large in relationship to the normal size of the stimuli.* You are more likely to notice an ad offering $100 off the list price of a computer than one offering $5 off.

Though we screen out much, we are influenced by unexpected stimuli, such as sudden offers in the mail, over the Internet, or from a salesperson. Marketers may attempt to promote their offers intrusively in order to bypass selective attention filters.

**SELECTIVE DISTORTION** Even noticed stimuli don't always come across in the way the senders intended. **Selective distortion** is the tendency to interpret information in a way that fits our preconceptions. Consumers will often distort information to be consistent with prior brand and product beliefs and expectations.

For a stark demonstration of the power of consumer brand beliefs, consider that in blind taste tests, one group of consumers samples a product without knowing which brand it is while another group knows. Invariably, the groups have different opinions, despite consuming *exactly the same product*.

When consumers report different opinions of branded and unbranded versions of identical products, it must be the case that their brand and product beliefs, created by whatever means (past experiences, marketing activity for the brand, or the like), have somehow changed their product perceptions. We can find examples for virtually every

Source: © valery121283/Fotolia

The size and shape of the glass and the color and smell of the liquid are all cues which may affect consumer perceptions and evaluations when drinking a glass of orange juice.

type of product. When Coors changed its label from "Banquet Beer" to "Original Draft," consumers claimed the taste had changed even though the formulation had not.

Selective distortion can work to the advantage of marketers with strong brands when consumers distort neutral or ambiguous brand information to make it more positive. In other words, coffee may seem to taste better, a car may seem to drive more smoothly, and the wait in a bank line may seem shorter, depending on the brand.

**SELECTIVE RETENTION** Most of us don't remember much of the information to which we're exposed, but we do retain information that supports our attitudes and beliefs. Because of **selective retention**, we're likely to remember good points about a product we like and forget good points about competing products. Selective retention again works to the advantage of strong brands. It also explains why marketers need to use repetition—to make sure their message is not overlooked.

**SUBLIMINAL PERCEPTION** The selective perception mechanisms require consumers' active engagement and thought. **Subliminal perception** has long fascinated armchair marketers, who argue that marketers embed covert, subliminal messages in ads or packaging. Consumers are not consciously aware of them, yet they affect behavior. Although it's clear that mental processes include many subtle subconscious effects,[42] no evidence supports the notion that marketers can systematically control consumers at that level, especially enough to change strongly held or even moderately important beliefs.[43]

# LEARNING

When we act, we learn. **Learning** induces changes in our behavior arising from experience. Most human behavior is learned, though much learning is incidental. Learning theorists believe learning is produced through the interplay of drives, stimuli, cues, responses, and reinforcement.

A **drive** is a strong internal stimulus impelling action. **Cues** are minor stimuli that determine when, where, and how a person responds. Suppose you buy an HP laptop computer. If your experience is rewarding, your response to the laptop and HP will be positively reinforced. Later, when you want to buy a printer, you may assume that because it makes good laptops, HP also makes good printers. In other words, you *generalize* your response to similar stimuli. A countertendency to generalization is discrimination. **Discrimination** means we have learned to recognize differences in sets of similar stimuli and can adjust our responses accordingly.

Learning theory teaches marketers that they can build demand for a product by associating it with strong drives, using motivating cues, and providing positive reinforcement. A new company can enter the market by appealing to the same drives competitors use and providing similar cues because buyers are more likely to transfer loyalty to similar brands (generalization); or the company might design its brand to appeal to a different set of drives and offer strong cue inducements to switch (discrimination).

Some researchers prefer more active, cognitive approaches when learning depends on the inferences or interpretations consumers make about outcomes (Was an unfavorable consumer experience due to a bad product, or did the consumer fail to follow instructions properly?). The **hedonic bias** occurs when people have a general tendency to attribute success to themselves and failure to external causes. Consumers are thus more likely to blame a product than themselves, putting pressure on marketers to carefully explicate product functions in well-designed packaging and labels, instructive ads and Web sites, and so on.

## EMOTIONS

Consumer response is not all cognitive and rational; much may be emotional and invoke different kinds of feelings. A brand or product may make a consumer feel proud, excited, or confident. An ad may create feelings of amusement, disgust, or wonder. Brands like Hallmark, McDonald's, and Coca-Cola have made an emotional connection with loyal customers for years.

Marketers are increasingly recognizing the power of emotional appeals—especially if these are rooted in some functional or rational aspects of the brand. Given it was released 10 years after *Toy Story 2*, Disney's *Toy Story 3* used social media to tap into feelings of nostalgia in its marketing.[44]

To help teen girls and young women feel more comfortable talking about feminine hygiene and feminine care products, Kimberly-Clark used four different social media networks in its "Break the Cycle" campaign for its new U by Kotex brand. With overwhelmingly positive feedback, the campaign helped Kotex move into the top spot in terms of share of word of mouth on feminine care for that target market.[45]

An emotion-filled brand story has been shown to trigger's people desire to pass along things they hear about brands, through either word of mouth or online sharing. Firms are giving their communications a stronger human appeal to engage consumers in their brand stories.[46]

Many different kinds of emotions can be linked to brands. A classic example is Unilever's Axe brand.[47]

Source: ASSOCIATED PRESS

Axe runs edgy promotional campaigns to connect with its young male target audience, like this Showerpooling event hosted by spokesperson and actress Nikki Reed.

**AXE**    A pioneer in product development—it established the male body wash category—and in its edgy sex appeals, Unilever's Axe personal-care brand has become a favorite of young males all over the world. With scents employing different combinations of flowers, herbs, and spices, the Axe line includes deodorant body sprays, sticks, roll-ons, and shampoos. The brand was built on the promise of the "Axe Effect"—an over-the-top notion that using Axe products would get women to enthusiastically and sometimes even desperately pursue the user. For Axe, Unilever employs both traditional and nontraditional media with a heavy dose of sexual innuendo and humor. A recent social media–driven campaign gave a cheeky wink to environmentalism while advocating the practice of "showerpooling." As one ad proclaimed, "When you Showerpool, you can save water while enjoying the company of a like-minded acquaintance, or even an attractive stranger." Facebook promotions, YouTube videos, and other social media messages all helped to spread the word. By cleverly serving as the "wing man" for confidence in the "mating game" —especially for 18- to 24-year-old males—the brand has become a key player in the multibillion-dollar male grooming market. Axe has concentrated grassroots marketing efforts on college campuses with brand ambassadors who hand out products, host parties, and generate buzz. A Twitter account dispenses advice and giveaways.

Emotions can take all forms. Ray-Ban glasses and sunglasses' 75th anniversary campaign "Never Hide" showed a variety of stand-out hipsters and stylish people to suggest wearers will feel attractive and cool. Some brands have tapped into the hip-hop culture and music to market a brand in a modern multicultural way, as Apple did with its iPod.[48]

# MEMORY

Cognitive psychologists distinguish between **short-term memory (STM)**—a temporary and limited repository of information—and **long-term memory (LTM)**—a more permanent, essentially unlimited repository. All the information and experiences we encounter as we go through life can end up in our long-term memory.

Most widely accepted views of long-term memory structure assume we form some kind of associative model. For example, the **associative network memory model** views LTM as a set of nodes and links. *Nodes* are stored information connected by *links* that vary in strength. Any type of information can be stored in the memory network, including verbal, visual, abstract, and contextual.

A spreading activation process from node to node determines how much we retrieve and what information we can actually recall in any given situation. When a node becomes activated because we're encoding external information (when we read or hear a word or phrase) or retrieving internal information from LTM (when we think about some concept), other nodes are also activated if they're associated strongly enough with that node.

In this model, we can think of consumer brand knowledge as a node in memory with a variety of linked associations. The strength and organization of these associations will be important determinants of the information we can recall about the brand. **Brand associations** consist of all brand-related thoughts, feelings, perceptions, images, experiences, beliefs, attitudes, and so on, that become linked to the brand node.

In this context we can think of marketing as a way of making sure consumers have product and service experiences that create the right brand knowledge structures and maintain them in memory. Companies such as Procter & Gamble like to create mental maps of consumers that depict their knowledge of a particular brand in terms of the key associations likely to be triggered in a marketing setting and their relative strength, favorability, and uniqueness to consumers. Figure 6.3 displays a very simple mental map highlighting some brand beliefs for a hypothetical consumer for State Farm insurance.

**MEMORY PROCESSES**  Memory is a very constructive process because we don't remember information and events completely and accurately. Often we remember bits and pieces and fill in the rest based on whatever else we know.

**Memory encoding** describes how and where information gets into memory. The strength of the resulting association depends on how much we process the information at encoding (how much we think about it, for instance) and in what way.[49] In general, the more attention we pay to the meaning of information during encoding, the stronger the resulting associations in memory will be. Advertising research in a field setting suggests that high levels of repetition for an uninvolving, unpersuasive ad, for example, are unlikely to have as much sales impact as lower levels of repetition for an involving, persuasive ad.[50]

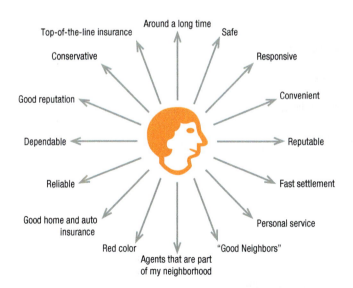

| **Fig. 6.3** |

## Hypothetical State Farm Mental Map

*Source: Courtesy of State Farm Mutual Automobile Insurance Co.*

**Memory retrieval** is the way information gets out of memory. Three facts are important about memory retrieval.

1. The presence of *other* product information in memory can produce interference effects and cause us to either overlook or confuse new data. One marketing challenge in a category crowded with many competitors—for example, airlines, financial services, and insurance companies—is that consumers may mix up brands.
2. The time between exposure to information and encoding has been shown generally to produce only gradual decay. Cognitive psychologists believe memory is extremely durable, so once information becomes stored in memory, its strength of association decays very slowly.
3. Information may be *available* in memory but not be *accessible* for recall without the proper retrieval cues or reminders. The effectiveness of retrieval cues is one reason marketing *inside* a supermarket or any retail store is so critical—the product packaging and use of in-store mini-billboard displays remind us of information already conveyed outside the store and become prime determinants of consumer decision making. Accessibility of a brand in memory is important for another reason: People talk about a brand when it is top-of-mind.[51]

# The Buying Decision Process: The Five-Stage Model

The basic psychological processes we've reviewed play an important role in consumers' actual buying decisions. Table 6.2 provides a list of some key consumer behavior questions marketers should ask in terms of who, what, when, where, how, and why.

Smart companies try to fully understand customers' buying decision process—all the experiences in learning, choosing, using, and even disposing of a product. Marketing scholars have developed a "stage model" of the

| TABLE 6.2 | Understanding Consumer Behavior |
|---|---|

Who buys our product or service?

Who makes the decision to buy the product or service?

Who influences the decision to buy the product or service?

How is the purchase decision made? Who assumes what role?

What does the customer buy? What needs must be satisfied? What wants are fulfilled?

Why do customers buy a particular brand? What benefits do they seek?

Where do they go or look to buy the product or service? Online and/or offline?

When do they buy? Any seasonality factors? Any time of day/week/month?

How is our product or service perceived by customers?

What are customers' attitudes toward our product or service?

What social factors might influence the purchase decision?

Do customers' lifestyles influence their decisions?

How do personal, demographic, or economic factors influence the purchase decision?

**Source:** Based in part on figure 1.7 from George Belch and Michael Belch, *Advertising and Promotion: An Integrated Marketing Communications Perspective*, 8th ed. (Homewood, IL: Irwin, 2009).

process (see Figure 6.4). The consumer typically passes through five stages: problem recognition, information search, evaluation of alternatives, purchase decision, and postpurchase behavior.

Clearly, the buying process starts long before the actual purchase and has consequences long afterward.[52] Some consumers passively shop and may decide to make a purchase from unsolicited information they encounter in the normal course of events.[53] Recognizing this fact, marketers must develop activities and programs that reach consumers at all decision stages. Consider how Procter & Gamble launched a new CoverGirl "Smokey Eye Look" makeup kit.[54]

.................................................................................................

■ **P&G COVERGIRL**   To create awareness at product launch, P&G sent makeup bloggers "Makeup Master" kits with packs of mascara, eyeliner, and eye shadow along with application instructions, blogging tips, product photographs, and a CoverGirl-emblazoned director's chair before the product was available in stores. At stores, CoverGirl created attention and interest with live product demonstrations, co-branded print ads with Walmart, and cardboard trays displaying product features and the product kits themselves. After they bought, purchasers were encouraged via Facebook and other online campaigns to provide feedback and write reviews to influence others. The brand's Facebook page featured testimonies from celebrities Ellen DeGeneres and Sofia Vergara. CoverGirl is one of P&G's most digitally supported brands, recognizing the high level of consumer involvement and the need to stay up to date. P&G is also supporting CoverGirl via mobile marketing through targeted ads and a microsite with experts' tips and video on proper application.

.................................................................................................

Consumers don't always pass through all five stages—they may skip or reverse some. When you buy your regular brand of toothpaste, you go directly from the need to the purchase decision, skipping information search and evaluation. The model in Figure 6.4 provides a good frame of reference, however, because it captures the full range of considerations that arise when a consumer faces a highly involving or new purchase. Later in the chapter, we will consider other ways consumers make decisions that are less calculated.

## PROBLEM RECOGNITION

The buying process starts when the buyer recognizes a problem or need triggered by internal or external stimuli. With an internal stimulus, one of the person's normal needs—hunger, thirst, sex—rises to a threshold level and becomes a drive. A need can also be aroused by an external stimulus. A person may admire a friend's new car or see a television ad for a Hawaiian vacation, which inspires thoughts about the possibility of making a purchase.

Marketers need to identify the circumstances that trigger a particular need by gathering information from a number of consumers. They can then develop marketing strategies that spark consumer interest. Particularly for discretionary purchases such as luxury goods, vacation packages, and entertainment options, marketers may need to increase consumer motivation so a potential purchase gets serious consideration.

**| Fig. 6.4 |**

**Five-Stage Model of the Consumer Buying Process**

*Source: © Vladyslav Starozhylov / Alamy*

P&G engages consumers at every stage of the buying process for its Cover Girl brand.

## INFORMATION SEARCH

Surprisingly, consumers often search for only limited information. Surveys have shown that for durables, half of all consumers look at only one store, and only 30 percent look at more than one brand of appliances. We can distinguish between two levels of engagement in the search. The milder search state is called *heightened attention*. At this level a person simply becomes more receptive to information about a product. At the next level, the person may enter an *active information search:* looking for reading material, phoning friends, going online, and visiting stores to learn about the product.

Marketers must understand what type of information consumers seek—or are at least receptive to—at different times and places.[55] Unilever, in collaboration with Kroger, the largest U.S. retail grocery chain, has learned that meal planning goes through a three-step process: discussion of meals and what might go into them; choice of exactly what will go into a particular meal, and finally purchase. Mondays turn out to be critical days for planning for the week. Conversations at breakfast time tend to focus on health, but later in the day, at lunch, discussion centers more on how meals could possibly be repurposed for leftovers.[56]

**INFORMATION SOURCES**   Major information sources to which consumers will turn fall into four groups:

- *Personal.*  Family, friends, neighbors, acquaintances
- *Commercial.*  Advertising, Web sites, e-mails, salespersons, dealers, packaging, displays
- *Public.*  Mass media, social media, consumer-rating organizations
- *Experiential.*  Handling, examining, using the product

The relative amount of information and influence of these sources vary with the product category and the buyer's characteristics. Generally speaking, although consumers receive the greatest amount of information about a product from commercial—that is, marketer-dominated—sources, the most effective information often comes from personal or experiential sources or public sources that are independent authorities.[57]

Each source performs a different function in influencing the buying decision. Commercial sources normally perform an information function, whereas personal sources perform a legitimizing or evaluation function. For example, physicians often learn of new drugs from commercial sources but turn to other doctors for evaluations. Many consumers alternate between going online and offline (in stores) to learn about products and brands.

**SEARCH DYNAMICS**   By gathering information, the consumer learns about competing brands and their features. The first box in Figure 6.5 shows the *total set* of brands available. The individual consumer will come to know a subset of these, the *awareness set*. Only some, the *consideration set*, will meet initial buying criteria. As the consumer gathers more information, just a few, the *choice set,* will remain strong contenders. The consumer makes a final choice from these.[58]

Marketers need to identify the hierarchy of attributes that guide consumer decision making in order to understand different competitive forces and how these various sets get formed. This process of identifying the hierarchy is called **market partitioning**. Years ago, most car buyers first decided on the manufacturer and then on one of its car divisions (*brand-dominant hierarchy*). A buyer might favor General Motors cars and, within this set, Chevrolet. Today, many buyers decide first on the nation or nations from which they want to buy a car (*nation-dominant hierarchy*). Buyers may first decide they want to buy a German car, then Audi, and then the A4 model of Audi.

The hierarchy of attributes also can reveal customer segments. Buyers who first decide on price are price dominant; those who first decide on the type of car (sports, passenger, hybrid) are type dominant; those who

| **Fig. 6.5** |

Successive Sets Involved in Consumer Decision Making

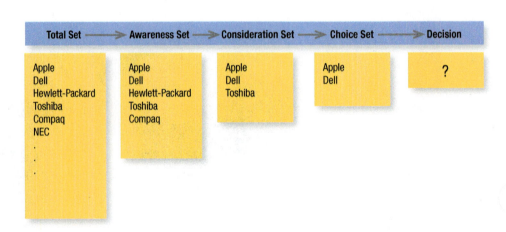

choose the brand first are brand dominant. Type/price/brand-dominant consumers make up one segment; quality/service/type buyers make up another. Each may have distinct demographics, psychographics, and mediagraphics and different awareness, consideration, and choice sets.

Figure 6.5 makes it clear that a company must strategize to get its brand into the prospect's awareness, consideration, and choice sets. If a food store owner arranges yogurt first by brand (such as Dannon and Yoplait) and then by flavor within each brand, consumers will tend to select their flavors from the same brand. However, if all the strawberry yogurts are together, then all the vanilla, and so forth, consumers will probably choose the flavors they want first and then choose the brand name they want for that particular flavor.

Search behavior can vary online, in part because of the manner in which product information is presented. For example, product alternatives may be presented in order of their predicted attractiveness for the consumer. Consumers may then choose not to search as extensively as they would otherwise.[59]

The company must also identify the other brands in the consumer's choice set so that it can plan the appropriate competitive appeals. In addition, marketers should identify the consumer's information sources and evaluate their relative importance. Asking consumers how they first heard about the brand, what information came later, and the relative importance of the different sources will help the company prepare effective communications for the target market.

# EVALUATION OF ALTERNATIVES

How does the consumer process competitive brand information and make a final value judgment? No single process is used by all consumers or by one consumer in all buying situations. There are several processes, and the most current models see the consumer forming judgments largely on a conscious and rational basis.

Some basic concepts will help us understand consumer evaluation processes. First, the consumer is trying to satisfy a need. Second, the consumer is looking for certain benefits from the product solution. Third, the consumer sees each product as a bundle of attributes with varying abilities to deliver the benefits. The attributes of interest to buyers vary by product—for example:

1. *Hotels*—Location, cleanliness, atmosphere, price
2. *Mouthwash*—Color, effectiveness, germ-killing capacity, taste/flavor, price
3. *Tires*—Safety, tread life, ride quality, price

Consumers will pay the most attention to attributes that deliver the sought-after benefits. We can often segment the market for a product according to attributes and benefits important to different consumer groups.

**BELIEFS AND ATTITUDES** Through experience and learning, people acquire beliefs and attitudes. These in turn influence buying behavior. A **belief** is a descriptive thought that a person holds about something. Just as important are **attitudes**, a person's enduring favorable or unfavorable evaluations, emotional feelings, and action tendencies toward some object or idea. People have attitudes toward almost everything: religion, politics, clothes, music, or food.

Attitudes put us into a frame of mind: liking or disliking an object, moving toward or away from it. They lead us to behave in a fairly consistent way toward similar objects. Because attitudes economize on energy and thought, they can be very difficult to change. As a general rule, a company is well advised to fit its product into existing attitudes rather than try to change attitudes. If beliefs and attitudes become too negative, however, more active steps may be necessary.

**EXPECTANCY-VALUE MODEL** The consumer arrives at attitudes toward various brands through an attribute-evaluation procedure, developing a set of beliefs about where each brand stands on each attribute.[60] The **expectancy-value model** of attitude formation posits that consumers evaluate products and services by combining their brand beliefs—the positives and negatives—according to importance.

Suppose Linda has narrowed her choice set to four laptops (A, B, C, and D). Assume she's interested in four attributes: memory capacity, graphics capability, size and weight, and price. Table 6.3 shows her beliefs about how each brand rates on the four attributes. If one computer dominated the others on all the criteria, we could predict that Linda would choose it. But, as is often the case, her choice set consists of brands that vary in their appeal. If Linda wants the best memory capacity, she should buy C; if she wants the best graphics capability, she should buy A; and so on.

If we knew the weights Linda attaches to the four attributes, we could more reliably predict her choice. Suppose she assigned 40 percent of the importance to the laptop's memory capacity, 30 percent to graphics capability, 20 percent to size and weight, and 10 percent to price. To find Linda's perceived value for each laptop according to

| TABLE 6.3 | A Consumer's Brand Beliefs about Laptop Computers | | | |
|---|---|---|---|---|
| **Laptop Computer** | **Attribute** | | | |
| | **Memory Capacity** | **Graphics Capability** | **Size and Weight** | **Price** |
| A | 8 | 9 | 6 | 9 |
| B | 7 | 7 | 7 | 7 |
| C | 10 | 4 | 3 | 2 |
| D | 5 | 3 | 8 | 5 |

**Note:** Each attribute is rated from 0 to 10, where 10 represents the highest level on that attribute. Price, however, is indexed in a reverse manner, with 10 representing the lowest price, because a consumer prefers a low price to a high price.

the expectancy-value model, we multiply her weights by her beliefs about each computer's attributes. This computation leads to the following perceived values:

$$\text{Laptop A} = 0.4(8) + 0.3(9) + 0.2(6) + 0.1(9) = 8.0$$
$$\text{Laptop B} = 0.4(7) + 0.3(7) + 0.2(7) + 0.1(7) = 7.0$$
$$\text{Laptop C} = 0.4(10) + 0.3(4) + 0.2(3) + 0.1(2) = 6.0$$
$$\text{Laptop D} = 0.4(5) + 0.3(3) + 0.2(8) + 0.1(5) = 5.0$$

An expectancy-model formulation predicts that Linda will favor laptop A, which (at 8.0) has the highest perceived value.[61]

Suppose most laptop buyers form their preferences the same way. Knowing this, the marketer of laptop B, for example, could apply the following strategies to stimulate greater interest in brand B:

- **Redesign the laptop.** This technique is called *real repositioning*.
- **Alter beliefs about the brand.** Attempting to alter beliefs about the brand is called *psychological repositioning*.
- **Alter beliefs about competitors' brands.** This strategy, called *competitive depositioning*, makes sense when buyers mistakenly believe a competitor's brand is higher quality than it actually is.
- **Alter the importance weights.** The marketer could try to persuade buyers to attach more importance to the attributes in which the brand excels.
- **Call attention to neglected attributes.** The marketer could draw buyers' attention to neglected attributes, such as styling or processing speed.
- **Shift the buyer's ideals.** The marketer could try to persuade buyers to change their ideal levels for one or more attributes.[62]

## PURCHASE DECISION

In the evaluation stage, the consumer forms preferences among the brands in the choice set and may also form an intention to buy the most preferred brand. In executing a purchase intention, the consumer may make as many as five subdecisions: brand (brand A), dealer (dealer 2), quantity (one computer), timing (weekend), and payment method (credit card).

**NONCOMPENSATORY MODELS OF CONSUMER CHOICE** The expectancy-value model is a compensatory model, in that perceived good things about a product can help to overcome perceived bad things. But consumers often take "mental shortcuts" called **heuristics** or rules of thumb in the decision process.

With **noncompensatory models** of consumer choice, positive and negative attribute considerations don't necessarily net out. Evaluating attributes in isolation makes decision making easier for a consumer, but it also increases the likelihood that she would have made a different choice if she had deliberated in greater detail. We highlight three choice heuristics here.[63]

1. Using the **conjunctive heuristic**, the consumer sets a minimum acceptable cutoff level for each attribute and chooses the first alternative that meets the minimum standard for all attributes. For example, if Linda decided all attributes had to rate at least 5, she would choose laptop B.
2. With the **lexicographic heuristic**, the consumer chooses the best brand on the basis of its perceived most important attribute. With this decision rule, Linda would choose laptop C.
3. Using the **elimination-by-aspects heuristic**, the consumer compares brands on an attribute selected probabilistically—where the probability of choosing an attribute is positively related to its importance—and eliminates brands that do not meet minimum acceptable cutoffs.

Our brand or product knowledge, the number and similarity of brand choices and time pressures present, and the social context (such as the need for justification to a peer or boss) all may affect whether and how we use choice heuristics.

Consumers don't necessarily use only one type of choice rule. For example, they might use a noncompensatory decision rule such as the conjunctive heuristic to reduce the number of brand choices to a more manageable number and then evaluate the remaining brands.

One reason for the runaway success of the Intel Inside campaign in the 1990s was that it made the brand the first cutoff for many consumers—they would buy only a personal computer that had an Intel microprocessor. Leading personal computer makers at the time, such as IBM, Dell, and Gateway, had no choice but to support Intel's marketing efforts.

A number of factors will determine the manner in which consumers form evaluations and make choices. University of Chicago professors Richard Thaler and Cass Sunstein show how marketers can influence consumer decision making through what they call the *choice architecture*—the environment in which decisions are structured and buying choices are made.

According to these researchers, in the right environment, consumers can be given a "nudge" via some small feature in the environment that attracts attention and alters behavior. They maintain Nabisco is employing a smart choice architecture by offering 100-calorie snack packs, which have solid profit margins, while nudging consumers to make healthier choices.[64]

**INTERVENING FACTORS** Even if consumers form brand evaluations, two general factors can intervene between the purchase intention and the purchase decision (see Figure 6.6). The first factor is the *attitudes of others*. The influence on us of another person's attitude depends on two things: (1) the intensity of the other person's negative attitude toward our preferred alternative and (2) our motivation to comply with the other person's wishes.[65] The more intense the other person's negativism and the closer he or she is to us, the more we will adjust our purchase intention. The converse is also true.

Related to the attitudes of others is the role played by infomediaries' evaluations: *Consumer Reports,* which provides unbiased expert reviews of all types of products and services; J. D. Power, which provides consumer-based ratings of cars, financial services, and travel products and services; professional movie, book, and music reviewers; customer reviews of books and music on such sites as Amazon.com; and the increasing number of chat rooms, bulletin boards, blogs, and other online sites like Angie's List where people discuss products, services, and companies.[66]

Consumers are undoubtedly influenced by these external evaluations, as evidenced by the runaway success of the movie *Ted.*[67]

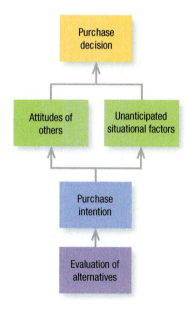

| **Fig. 6.6** |

Steps between Evaluation of Alternatives and a Purchase Decision

---

**TED**   With a modest production budget of $50 million, the R-rated comedy *Ted* became a summer blockbuster in 2012, eventually grossing more than a staggering $530 million worldwide, thanks to favorable reviews by critics and moviegoers and a carefully constructed online marketing campaign. Edgy videos and a Twitter feed with raunchy advice from Ted, the often-crude teddy bear star, created much online buzz. Fans of the movie's Facebook page approached 3 million, Twitter followers reached 400,000, and a "Talking Ted" iPhone app was downloaded 3.5 million times. Universal Pictures' marketing campaign also included several different theater trailers to attract different types of audiences. Social media targeted fans of the *Family Guy* television show, whose creator, Seth McFarlane, directed *Ted* and provided the voice of the title character. After the first trailer went online, the studio picked up much online chatter with a song, "Thunder Buddies," that the other star of the movie, Mark Wahlberg, sang to Ted while in bed. To capitalize on the buzz, the studio put out a remixed version of the song on the movie's Web site, e-cards with lyrics on Facebook, Thunder Buddy pajamas from CafePress.com, and a 30-second video clip of the song.

*Ted* became a summer blockbuster due to strong positive word-of-mouth and a well conceived and executed social media campaign.

Source: ASSOCIATED PRESS

The second factor is *unanticipated situational factors* that may erupt to change the purchase intention. Linda might lose her job before she purchases a laptop, some other purchase might become more urgent, or a store salesperson may turn her off. As Chapter 15 discusses, much marketing occurs at the point of purchase: online or in the store.

Preferences and even purchase intentions are not completely reliable predictors of purchase behavior. A consumer's decision to modify, postpone, or avoid a purchase decision is heavily influenced by one or more types of *perceived risk:*[68]

1.  *Functional risk*—The product does not perform to expectations.
2.  *Physical risk*—The product poses a threat to the physical well-being or health of the user or others.
3.  *Financial risk*—The product is not worth the price paid.
4.  *Social risk*—The product results in embarrassment in front of others.
5.  *Psychological risk*—The product affects the mental well-being of the user.
6.  *Time risk*—The failure of the product results in an opportunity cost of finding another satisfactory product.

The degree of perceived risk varies with the amount of money at stake, the amount of attribute uncertainty, and the level of consumer self-confidence. Consumers develop routines for reducing the uncertainty and negative consequences of risk, such as avoiding decisions, gathering information from friends, and developing preferences for national brand names and warranties. Marketers must understand the factors that provoke a feeling of risk in consumers and provide information and support to reduce it.

## POSTPURCHASE BEHAVIOR

After the purchase, the consumer might experience dissonance from noticing certain disquieting features or hearing favorable things about other brands and will be alert to information that supports his or her decision. Marketing communications should supply beliefs and evaluations that reinforce the consumer's choice and help him or her feel good about the brand. The marketer's job therefore doesn't end with the purchase. Marketers must monitor postpurchase satisfaction, postpurchase actions, and postpurchase product uses and disposal.

**POSTPURCHASE SATISFACTION** Satisfaction is a function of the closeness between expectations and the product's perceived performance.[69] If performance falls short of expectations, the consumer is *disappointed;* if it meets expectations, the consumer is *satisfied;* if it exceeds expectations, the consumer is *delighted.* These feelings make a difference in whether the customer buys the product again and talks favorably or unfavorably about it to others.

The larger the gap between expectations and performance, the greater the dissatisfaction. Here the consumer's coping style comes into play. Some consumers magnify the gap when the product isn't perfect and are highly dissatisfied; others minimize it and are less dissatisfied.

**POSTPURCHASE ACTIONS** A satisfied consumer is more likely to purchase the product again and will also tend to say good things about the brand to others. Dissatisfied consumers may abandon or return the product. They may seek information that confirms its high value. They may take public action by complaining to the company, going to a lawyer, or complaining directly to other groups (such as business, private, or government agencies) or to many others online. Private actions include deciding to stop buying the product (*exit option*) or warning friends (*voice option*).[70]

| **Fig. 6.7** |

# How Customers Use or Dispose of Products

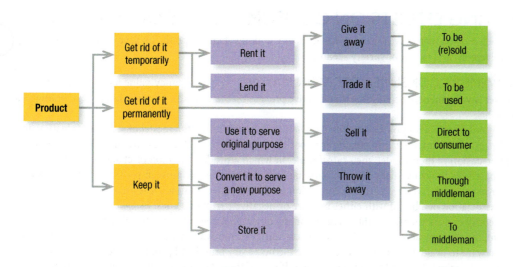

**Source:** Jacob Jacoby, et al., "What about Disposition?," *Journal of Marketing* (July 1977), p. 23. Reprinted with permission from the *Journal of Marketing*, published by the American Marketing Association.

Chapter 5 described CRM programs designed to build long-term brand loyalty. Postpurchase communications to buyers have been shown to result in fewer product returns and order cancellations. Computer companies, for example, can send a letter to new owners congratulating them on having selected a fine new tablet computer. They can place ads showing satisfied brand owners. They can solicit customer suggestions for improvements and list the location of available services. They can write intelligible instruction booklets. They can send owners e-mail updates describing new tablet applications. In addition, they can provide good channels for speedy redress of customer grievances.

**POSTPURCHASE USES AND DISPOSAL** Marketers should also monitor how buyers use and dispose of the product (Figure 6.7). A key driver of sales frequency is product consumption rate—the more quickly buyers consume a product, the sooner they may be back in the market to repurchase it.

Consumers may fail to replace some products soon enough because they overestimate product life.[71] One strategy to speed replacement is to tie the act of replacing the product to a certain holiday, event, or time of year (such as promoting changing the batteries in smoke detectors when Daylight Savings ends).

Another strategy is to provide consumers with better information about either (1) the time they first used the product or need to replace it or (2) its current level of performance. Batteries have built-in gauges that show how much power they have left; razors have color in their lubricating strips to indicate when blades may be worn; and so on. Perhaps the simplest way to increase usage is to learn when actual usage is lower than recommended and persuade customers that more regular usage has benefits, overcoming potential hurdles.

If consumers throw the product away, the marketer needs to know how they dispose of it, especially if—like batteries, beverage containers, electronic equipment, and disposable diapers—it can damage the environment. There also may be product opportunities in disposed products: Air Salvage International is the largest plane dismantler in Europe and a major player in the booming secondhand market for aircraft parts, which totaled $2.5 billion from 2009 to 2011; vintage clothing shops, such as Savers, resell 2.5 billion pounds of used clothing annually; Diamond Safety buys finely ground used tires and then makes and sells playground covers and athletic fields.[72]

Air Salvage International is a market leader in the booming business of selling used aircraft parts.

*Source: © Jim West / Alamy*

## MODERATING EFFECTS ON CONSUMER DECISION MAKING

The path by which a consumer moves through the decision-making stages depends on several factors, including the level of involvement and extent of variety seeking.

**LOW-INVOLVEMENT CONSUMER DECISION MAKING**   The expectancy-value model assumes a high level of **consumer involvement**, or engagement and active processing the consumer undertakes in responding to a marketing stimulus.

Richard Petty and John Cacioppo's *elaboration likelihood model,* an influential model of attitude formation and change, describes how consumers make evaluations in both low- and high-involvement circumstances.[73] There are two means of persuasion in their model: the *central route,* in which attitude formation or change stimulates much thought and is based on the consumer's diligent, rational consideration of the most important product information; and the *peripheral route,* in which attitude formation or change provokes much less thought and results from the consumer's association of a brand with either positive or negative peripheral cues. *Peripheral cues* for consumers include a celebrity endorsement, a credible source, or any object that generates positive feelings.

Consumers follow the central route only if they possess sufficient motivation, ability, and opportunity. In other words, they must want to evaluate a brand in detail, have the necessary brand and product or service knowledge in memory, and have sufficient time and the proper setting. If any of those factors is lacking, consumers tend to follow the peripheral route and consider less central, more extrinsic factors in their decisions.

We buy many products under conditions of low involvement and without significant brand differences. Consider salt. If consumers keep reaching for the same brand in this category, it may be out of habit, not strong brand loyalty. Evidence suggests we have low involvement with most low-cost, frequently purchased products.

Marketers use four techniques to try to convert a low-involvement product into one of higher involvement. First, they can link the product to an engaging issue, as when Crest linked its toothpaste to cavity prevention. Second, they can link the product to a personal situation—for example, fruit juice makers began to include vitamins such as calcium to fortify their drinks. Third, they might design advertising to trigger strong emotions related to personal values or ego defense, as when cereal makers began to advertise to adults the heart-healthy nature of cereals and the importance of living a long time to enjoy family life. Fourth, they might add an important feature—for example, when GE lightbulbs introduced "Soft White" versions. These strategies at best raise consumer involvement from a low to a moderate level; they do not necessarily propel the consumer into highly involved buying behavior.

If consumers will have low involvement with a purchase decision regardless of what the marketer can do, they are likely to follow the peripheral route. Marketers must give consumers one or more positive cues to justify their brand choice, such as frequent ad repetition, visible sponsorships, and vigorous PR to enhance brand familiarity. Other peripheral cues that can tip the balance in favor of the brand include a beloved celebrity endorser, attractive packaging, and an appealing promotion.

**VARIETY-SEEKING BUYING BEHAVIOR**   Some buying situations are characterized by low involvement but significant brand differences. Here consumers often do a lot of brand switching. Think about cookies. The consumer has some beliefs about cookies, chooses a brand without much evaluation, and evaluates the product during consumption. Next time, the consumer may reach for another brand out of a desire for a different taste. Brand switching occurs for the sake of variety rather than from dissatisfaction.

The market leader and the minor brands in this product category have different marketing strategies. The market leader will try to encourage habitual buying behavior by dominating the shelf space with a variety of related product versions, avoiding out-of-stock conditions, and sponsoring frequent reminder advertising. Challenger firms will encourage variety seeking by offering lower prices, deals, coupons, free samples, and advertising that tries to break the consumer's purchase and consumption cycle and presents reasons for trying something new.

# Behavioral Decision Theory and Behavioral Economics

As you might guess from low-involvement decision making and variety seeking, consumers don't always process information or make decisions in a deliberate, rational manner. One of the most active academic research areas in marketing over the past three decades has been *behavioral decision theory* (BDT). Behavioral decision theorists have identified many situations in which consumers make seemingly irrational choices. Table 6.4 summarizes some provocative findings from this research.[74]

What all these and other studies reinforce is that consumer behavior is very constructive and the context of decisions really matters. Understanding how these effects show up in the marketplace can be crucial for marketers.

| TABLE 6.4 | Selected Behavioral Decision Theory Findings |
|---|---|

- Consumers are more likely to choose an alternative (a home bread maker) after a relatively inferior option (a slightly better but significantly more expensive home bread maker) is added to the available choice set.
- Consumers are more likely to choose an alternative that appears to be a compromise in the particular choice set under consideration, even if it is not the best alternative on any one dimension.
- The choices consumers make influence their assessment of their own tastes and preferences.
- Getting people to focus their attention more on one of two considered alternatives tends to enhance the perceived attractiveness and choice probability of that alternative.
- The way consumers compare products that vary in price and perceived quality (by features or brand name) and the way those products are displayed in the store (by brand or by model type) both affect their willingness to pay more for additional features or a better-known brand.
- Consumers who think about the possibility that their purchase decisions will turn out to be wrong are more likely to choose better-known brands.
- Consumers for whom possible feelings of regret about missing an opportunity have been made more relevant are more likely to choose a product currently on sale than wait for a better sale or buy a higher-priced item.
- Consumers' choices are often influenced by subtle (and theoretically inconsequential) changes in the way alternatives are described.
- Consumers who make purchases for later consumption appear to make systematic errors in predicting their future preferences.
- Consumer's predictions of their future tastes are not accurate—they do not really know how they will feel after consuming the same flavor of yogurt or ice cream several times.
- Consumers often overestimate the duration of their overall emotional reactions to future events (moves, financial windfalls, outcomes of sporting events).
- Consumers often overestimate their future consumption, especially if there is limited availability.
- In anticipating future consumption opportunities, consumers often assume they will want or need more variety than they actually do.
- Consumers are less likely to choose alternatives with product features or promotional premiums that have little or no value, even when these features and premiums are optional (like the opportunity to purchase a collector's plate) and do not reduce the actual value of the product in any way.
- Consumers are less likely to choose products selected by others for reasons they find irrelevant, even when these other reasons do not suggest anything positive or negative about the product's values.
- Consumers' interpretations and evaluations of past experiences are greatly influenced by the ending and trend of events. A positive event at the end of a service experience can color later reflections and evaluations of the experience as a whole.
- When faced with a simple but important decision, consumers can actually make things more complicated than they should.

The work of these and other academics has also challenged predictions from economic theory and assumptions about rationality, leading to the emergence of the field of *behavioral economics*.[75] Here we review some of the issues in three broad areas: decision heuristics, framing, and other contextual effects.

# DECISION HEURISTICS

Above we reviewed some common heuristics that occur with non-compensatory decision making. Other heuristics similarly come into play in everyday decision making when consumers forecast the likelihood of future outcomes or events.[76]

1. The **availability heuristic**—Consumers base their predictions on the quickness and ease with which a particular example of an outcome comes to mind. If an example comes to mind too easily, consumers might overestimate the likelihood of its happening. For example, a recent product failure may lead consumers to inflate the likelihood of a future product failure and make them more inclined to purchase a product warranty.

2. The **representativeness heuristic**—Consumers base their predictions on how representative or similar the outcome is to other examples. One reason package appearances may be so similar for different brands in the

same product category is that marketers want their products to be seen as representative of the category as a whole.

3. The **anchoring and adjustment heuristic**—Consumers arrive at an initial judgment and then adjust it—sometimes only reluctantly—based on additional information. For services marketers, a strong first impression is critical to establishing a favorable anchor so subsequent experiences will be interpreted in a more favorable light.

Note that marketing managers also may use heuristics and be subject to biases in their own decision making.

## FRAMING

*Decision framing* is the manner in which choices are presented to and seen by a decision maker. A $200 cell phone may not seem that expensive in the context of a set of $400 phones but may seem very expensive if other phones cost $50. Framing effects are pervasive and can be powerful.[77]

We find framing effects in comparative advertising, where a brand can put its best foot forward by comparing itself to another with inferior features; in pricing where unit prices can make the product seem less expensive ("only pennies a day"); in product information where larger units can seem more desirable (a 24-month warranty versus a two-year warranty); and with new products, where consumers can better understand a new product's functions and features by seeing how it compares with existing products.[78]

Marketers can be very clever in framing decisions. To help promote its environmentally friendly cars, Volkswagen Sweden incorporated a giant working piano keyboard into the steps next to the exit escalator of a Stockholm subway station. Stair traffic rose 66 percent as a result, a fact VW cleverly captured in a YouTube video seen more than 20 million times.[79]

**MENTAL ACCOUNTING**  Researchers have found that consumers use a form of framing called "mental accounting" when they handle their money.[80] **Mental accounting** describes the way consumers code, categorize, and evaluate financial outcomes of choices. Formally, it is "the tendency to categorize *funds* or items of value even though there is no logical *basis* for the categorization, e.g., individuals often segregate their savings into separate accounts to meet different goals even though funds from any of the accounts can be applied to any of the goals."[81]

Consider the following two scenarios:

1. You spend $50 to buy a ticket for a concert.[82] As you arrive at the show, you realize you've lost your ticket. You decide to buy a replacement.
2. You decide to buy a ticket to a concert at the door. As you arrive at the show, you realize somehow you lost $50 along the way. You decide to buy the ticket anyway.

Which one are you more likely to do? Most people choose scenario 2. Although you lost the same amount in each case—$50—in the first case you may have mentally allocated $50 for going to a concert. Buying another ticket would exceed your mental concert budget. In the second case, the money you lost did not belong to any account, so you had not yet exceeded your mental concert budget.

Mental accounting has many applications to marketing.[83] According to the University of Chicago's Richard Thaler, it is based on a set of core principles:

In a clever promotion by VW to emphasize its environmental friendliness, more people used stairs when they were made into a piano keyboard coming out of a Stockholm subway station.

*Source: Li Zhong/Xinhua/Photoshot/Newscom*

1. Consumers tend to *segregate gains*. When a seller has a product with more than one positive dimension, it's desirable to have the consumer evaluate each dimension separately. Listing multiple benefits of a large industrial product, for example, can make the sum of the parts seem greater than the whole.
2. Consumers tend to *integrate losses*. Marketers have a distinct advantage in selling something if its cost can be added to another large purchase. House buyers are more inclined to view additional expenditures favorably given the already high price of buying a house.
3. Consumers tend to *integrate smaller losses with larger gains*. The "cancellation" principle might explain why withholding taxes from monthly paychecks is less painful than making large, lump-sum tax payments—the smaller withholdings are more likely to be overshadowed by the larger pay amount.
4. Consumers tend to *segregate small gains from large losses*. The "silver lining" principle might explain the popularity of rebates on big-ticket purchases such as cars.

The principles of mental accounting are derived in part from prospect theory. **Prospect theory** maintains that consumers frame their decision alternatives in terms of gains and losses according to a value function. Consumers are generally loss-averse. They tend to overweight very low probabilities and underweight very high probabilities.

# Summary

1. Consumer behavior is influenced by three factors: cultural (culture, subculture, and social class), social (reference groups, family, and social roles and statuses), and personal (age, stage in the life cycle, occupation, economic circumstances, lifestyle, personality, and self-concept). Research into these factors can provide clues to reach and serve consumers more effectively.

2. Four main psychological processes that affect consumer behavior are motivation, perception, learning, and memory.

3. To understand how consumers actually make buying decisions, marketers must identify who makes and has input into the buying decision; people can be initiators, influencers, deciders, buyers, or users. Different marketing campaigns might be targeted to each type of person.

4. The typical buying process consists of the following sequence of events: problem recognition, information search, evaluation of alternatives, purchase decision, and postpurchase behavior. The marketers' job is to understand the behavior at each stage.

5. Consumers will not necessarily go through the buying process in an orderly fashion and make skip and reverse stages and alternative between going online and offline.

6. The attitudes of others, unanticipated situational factors, and perceived risk may all affect the decision to buy, as will consumers' levels of postpurchase product satisfaction, use and disposal, and the company's actions.

7. Consumers are constructive decision makers and subject to many contextual influences. They often exhibit low involvement in their decisions, using many heuristics as a result.

## MyMarketingLab

Go to mymktlab.com to complete the problems marked with this icon ⭐ as well as for additional Auto-graded and Assisted-graded writing questions.

# Applications

## Marketing Debate
### Is Target Marketing Ever Bad?

As marketers increasingly tailor marketing programs to target market segments, some critics have denounced these efforts as exploitive. They see the preponderance of billboards advertising cigarettes and alcohol in low-income urban areas as taking advantage of a vulnerable market segment. Critics can be especially harsh in evaluating marketing programs that target African Americans and other minority groups, claiming they often employ stereotypes and inappropriate depictions. Others counter that targeting and positioning is critical to marketing and that these marketing programs are an attempt to be relevant to a certain consumer group.

**Take a position:** Targeting minorities is exploitive *versus* Targeting minorities is a sound business practice.

## Marketing Discussion
## What Are Your Mental Accounts?

⭐ What mental accounts do you have in your mind about purchasing products or services? Do you have any rules you employ in spending money? Are they different from what other people do? Do you follow Thaler's four principles in reacting to gains and losses?

## Marketing Excellence

### >> Disney

Few companies have been able to connect with their audience as well as Disney has. From its founding by brothers Walt and Roy Disney in 1923, the Disney brand has always been synonymous with trust, fun, and quality entertainment for the entire family. Walt Disney once stated, "I am interested in entertaining people, in bringing pleasure, particularly laughter, to others, rather than being concerned with 'expressing' myself with obscure creative impressions."

The Walt Disney Company has grown into the worldwide phenomenon that today includes theme parks, feature films, television networks, theatre productions, consumer products, and a growing online presence. In its first two decades, however, it was a struggling cartoon studio that introduced the world to Mickey Mouse, who went on to become its most famous character.

Few believed in Disney's vision at the time, but the smashing success of cartoons with sound and of the first full-length animated film, *Snow White and the Seven Dwarfs*, in 1937 led to other animated classics throughout the 1940s, 1950s, and 1960s, including *Pinocchio*, *Bambi*, *Cinderella,* and *Peter Pan*, live-action films such as *Mary Poppins* and *The Love Bug,* and television series like *Davy Crockett*.

When Walt Disney died in 1966, he was considered the best-known person in the world. He had expanded the Disney brand into film, television, consumer products, and Disneyland in southern California, the company's first theme park. After Walt's death, Roy Disney took over as CEO and realized his brother's dream of opening the 24,000-acre Walt Disney World theme park in Florida. Roy died in 1971, and the company stumbled for several years without the leadership of its two founding brothers. It wasn't until the late 1980s that the company reconnected with its audience and restored trust and interest in the Disney brand.

It all started with the release of *The Little Mermaid*, which turned an old fairy tale into a magical animated Broadway-style movie that won two Oscars. Between the late 1980s and 2000, Disney entered an era known as the Disney Renaissance as it released groundbreaking animated films such as *Beauty and the Beast* (1991),

*Aladdin* (1992), *The Lion King* (1994), *Toy Story* (with Pixar, 1995), and *Mulan* (1998). In addition, the company thought of creative new ways to target its core family-oriented consumers as well as expand into new areas to reach an older audience. It launched the Disney Channel, Touchstone Pictures, and Touchstone Television. Disney featured classic films during *The Disney Sunday Night Movie* and sold its classic films on video at extremely low prices, reaching a whole new generation of children. It tapped into publishing, international theme parks, and theatrical productions that helped reach a variety of audiences around the world.

Today, Disney consists of five business segments: Studio Entertainment, which creates films, recording labels, and theatrical performances; Parks and Resorts, which focuses on Disney's 11 theme parks, cruise lines, and other travel-related assets; Consumer Products, which sells all Disney-branded products; Media Networks, which includes Disney's television networks such as ESPN, ABC, and the Disney Channel; and Interactive.

Disney's greatest challenge today is keeping a 90-year-old brand relevant and current with its core audience while staying true to its heritage and core brand values. Disney's CEO Bob Iger explained, "As a brand that people seek out and trust, it opens doors to new platforms and markets, and hence to new consumers. When you deal with a company that has a great legacy, you deal with decisions and conflicts that arise from the clash of heritage versus innovation versus relevance. I'm a big believer in respect for heritage, but I'm also a big believer in the need to innovate and the need to balance that respect for heritage with a need to be relevant."

Internally, to achieve quality and recognition, Disney has focused on the *Disney Difference,* which stems from one of Walt Disney's most recognizable quotes: "Whatever you do, do it well. Do it so well that when people see you do it they will want to come back and see you do it again and they will want to bring others and show them how well you do what you do."

Disney works hard to connect with its customers on many levels and through every single detail. For example, at Disney World, "cast members" or employees are trained to be "assertively friendly" and greet visitors by waving big Mickey Mouse hands, hand out maps to adults and stickers to kids, and clean up the park so diligently that it's difficult to find a piece of garbage anywhere.

Every detail matters, right down to the behavior of custodial workers who are trained by Disney's animators to take their simple broom and bucket of water and quietly "paint" a Goofy or Mickey Mouse in water on the pavement. It's a moment of magic for guests that lasts just a minute before it evaporates in the hot sun.

Disney's broad range of businesses allows the company to connect with its audience in multiple ways, efficiently and economically. *Hannah Montana* provides an excellent example. The company took a tween-targeted television show and moved it across several divisions to become a significant franchise for the company, including millions of CD sales, video games, popular consumer products, box office movies, concerts around the world, and ongoing live performances at international Disneyland resorts in Hong Kong, India, and Russia.

Recently, Disney acquired three huge brands: Pixar, Marvel, and LucasFilms. The company has started to leverage these properties, which include the Star Wars brand and superheroes such as Spiderman, Iron Man, and the Hulk, across many of its businesses in order to create sustainable character brands and new growth opportunities for the company.

Perhaps the most anticipated new product of 2013 was the Disney Infinity gaming platform, which crossed all Disney boundaries. Disney Infinity allowed consumers to play with many of the Disney characters at the same time, interacting and working together on different adventures. For example, Andy from *Toy Story* might join forces with Captain Jack Sparrow from *Pirates of the Caribbean* and several monsters from *Monsters, Inc.* to fight villains from outer space.

With so many brands, characters, and businesses, Disney uses technology to ensure that a customer's experience is consistent across every platform. The company connects with its consumers in innovative ways through e-mail, blogs, and its Web site. It was one of the first companies to begin regular podcasts of its television shows as well as to post news about its products and interviews with Disney's employees, staff, and park officials. Disney's Web site provides insight into its movie trailers, television clips, Broadway shows, and virtual theme park experiences.

Disney's marketing campaign in recent years has focused on how it helps make unforgettable family memories. The campaign, "Let the Memories Begin," features real guests throughout Disney enjoying different rides and magical experiences. Leslie Ferraro, executive vice president of global marketing, Disney Destinations, elaborated, "The inspiration for this effort came from our guests. Each and every day people are making memories at our parks, posting them online and sharing them with friends and family."

According to internal studies, Disney estimates that consumers spend 13 billion hours "immersed" with the Disney brand each year. Consumers around the world spend 10 billion hours watching programs on the Disney Channel, 800 million hours at Disney's resorts and theme parks, and 1.2 billion hours watching a Disney movie—at home, in the theater, or on their computer. Today, Disney is the 13th most powerful brand in the world, and its revenues topped $45 billion in 2013.

## Questions

1. What does Disney do best to connect with its core consumers?

2. What are the risks and benefits of expanding the Disney brand in new ways, such as video games or superheroes?

**Sources:** "Company History," Disney.com; "Annual Reports," Disney.com; Richard Siklosc, "The Iger Difference," *Fortune*, April 11, 2008; Brooks Barnes, "After Mickey's Makeover; Less Mr. Nice Guy," *New York Times*, November 4, 2009; "World's Most Powerful Brands," *Forbes*, April 2012; Dorothy Pomerantz, "Five Lessons in Success from Disney's $40 Million CEO," *Forbes*, January 23, 2013; "Disney Launches Infinity Video Game That Costs More Than an iPad Mini," *Daily Mail*, January 16, 2013; Carmine Gallo, "Customer Service the Disney Way," *Forbes*, April 14, 2011; Hugo Martin, "Disney's 2011 Marketing Campaign Centers on Family Memories," *LA Times*, September 23, 2010; Elena Malydhina, "Disney Parks Campaign Borrows Family Memories," *Adweek*, September 23, 2010; Disney Annual Report 2013.

## Marketing Excellence

## >> IKEA

IKEA was founded in 1943 by a 17-year-old Swede named Ingvar Kamprad who sold pens, Christmas cards, and seeds out of a shed on his family's farm. The name IKEA was derived from Kamprad's initials (IK) and the first letters of the Elmtaryd farm and the village of Agunnaryd where he grew up (EA). Over the years, the company grew into a retail titan in home furnishings and a global cultural phenomenon, inspiring *BusinessWeek* to call it a "one-stop sanctuary for coolness" and "the quintessential cult brand."

IKEA inspires remarkable levels of interest and devotion from its customers. Each year more than 650 million visitors walk through its stores all over the world. Most need to drive 50 miles round-trip but happily make the effort in order to experience IKEA's unique value proposition: leading-edge design and functional home furnishings at extremely low prices.

IKEA's Scandinavian-designed products are well made and appeal to the masses. To stay relevant and fashionable, the company replaces approximately one-third of its product lines each year. Most have Swedish names, such as HEKTAR lamps, BILLY bookcases, and LACK side tables. Kamprad, who was dyslexic, believed it was easier to remember product *names* rather than codes or numbers.

Besides featuring fashionable and good-quality products, IKEA stands out in the industry because of its bargain prices. The company's vision is and always has been "to create a better everyday life for the many people." As Kamprad said, "People have very thin wallets. We should take care of their interests." A high percentage of its customers are college students and families with children.

IKEA continuously seeks out new ways to run its businesses more efficiently and pass those cost savings on to the customer. In fact, it reduces prices across its products by 1 percent to 3 percent annually. How can it do so? For starters, IKEA engages the consumer on many levels, including having the customer do all the shopping, shipping, and assembly.

IKEA's floor plan is designed in a winding, one-way format featuring different inspirational room settings, so consumers experience the entire store. Next, they can grab a shopping cart, pay for the items, visit the warehouse, and pick up their purchases in flat boxes. Consumers load the items in their car, take them home, and completely assemble the products themselves. This strategy makes storage and transportation easier and cheaper for the store.

IKEA has also implemented several company-wide strategies to keep operational costs low. The company buys in bulk, controls the supply chain, uses lighter packaging materials, and saves on electricity through solar panels, low-wattage light bulbs, and energy from its own wind farms in six different countries. Its stores are located a good distance from most city centers, which helps keep land costs down and taxes low.

When IKEA develops new products, its designers and product developers start with a low price tag first and then work with one of their 1,350 suppliers around the world to develop the product within that price range. Designs are efficient, and waste is kept to a minimum. Most stores resemble a large box with few windows and doors and are painted bright yellow and blue—Sweden's national colors.

Many of IKEA's products are sold uniformly throughout the world, but the company also caters to local and regional tastes. For example, stores in China stock specific items for each New Year. During the Chinese Year of the Rooster, IKEA stocked 250,000 plastic placemats with rooster themes, which quickly sold out. When employees realized U.S. shoppers were buying vases as drinking glasses because they considered IKEA's regular glasses too small, the company developed larger glasses for the U.S. market. After IKEA managers visited European and U.S. consumers in their homes, they learned that Europeans generally hang their clothes, whereas U.S. shoppers prefer to store them folded. As a result, IKEA designed wardrobes for the U.S. market with deeper drawers.

Showrooms in each country or region vary as well. For example, managers learned that many U.S. consumers thought IKEA sold only European-size beds. Beds are very important to U.S. consumers, so IKEA quickly changed its U.S. showrooms to feature king beds and a wide range of styles. After visiting Hispanic households in California, IKEA added more seating and dining space to its California stores, as well as brighter color palettes and more picture frames on the showroom walls. In China, IKEA set up its showrooms in small spaces to accurately reflect the small size of apartments in that country.

As the company expands globally, it is learning that attitudes towards its core DIY (do it yourself) delivery and assembly business model vary. In China, for example, consumers do not want to assemble products themselves and will pay a significant amount for home delivery and assembly. As a result, IKEA has added these services, and sales in Asia have taken off. The company plans to implement the same strategy in India, where DIY is also less common.

IKEA is known for its quirky marketing campaigns, which help generate excitement and awareness of its stores and brand. It ran a campaign inviting customers to be the "Ambassador of Kul" (Swedish for "fun"), but in order to collect the prize, the contestants had to live in an IKEA store for three full days before it opened, which they happily did.

Thousands of people will line up for a chance to win prizes and IKEA furniture. In Sweden, IKEA launched a Facebook page for the manager of a new store. Anyone who could tag his or her name to an IKEA product on the profile page won that item. The promotion generated thousands of tags.

IKEA has evolved into the largest furniture retailer in the world, with approximately 350 stores in 43 countries and revenues topping €27.9 billion, or $36 billion, in 2013. The majority of sales still come from Europe, but the company has aggressive plans to expand the $11 billion brand further into Asia, India, and the United States.

## Questions

1. What are some of the things IKEA is doing well to reach consumers in different markets? What else could it be doing?

2. IKEA has essentially changed the way people shop for furniture. Discuss the pros and cons of this strategy, especially as the company plans to continue to expand in places like Asia and India.

**Sources:** Kerry Capell, "IKEA: How the Swedish Retailer Became a Global Cult Brand," *BusinessWeek*, November 14, 2005, p. 96; "Need a Home to Go with That Sofa?," *BusinessWeek*, November 14, 2005, p. 106; Ellen Ruppel Shell, "Buy to Last," *Atlantic*, July/August 2009; Jon Henley, "Do You Speak IKEA?," *Guardian*, February 4, 2008; "Innovative Retailers: IKEA," Retailinsider.com/PCMS, March 29, 2012; Jenna Goudreau, "How IKEA Leveraged the Art of Listening to Global Dominance," *Forbes*, January 30, 2013; IKEA, www.ikea.com.

## In This Chapter, We Will Address the Following **Questions**

1. What is organizational buying? (p. 189)

2. What buying situations do business buyers face? (p. 193)

3. Who participates in the business-to-business buying process? (p. 193)

4. How do business buyers make their decisions? (p. 198)

5. In what ways can business-to-business companies develop effective marketing programs? (p. 204)

6. How can companies build strong loyalty relationships with business customers? (p. 208)

7. How do institutional buyers and government agencies do their buying? (p. 211)

CEO John Chambers has helped transform Cisco to become an exemplary customer-focused organization.

Source: ASSOCIATED PRESS

# 7 Analyzing Business Markets

**Business organizations do not only sell; they also buy vast quantities of raw materials,** manufactured components, plant and equipment, supplies, and business services. According to the Census Bureau, there were roughly 7.4 million businesses with paid employees in 2010 in the United States alone.[1] To create and capture value, sellers such as Cisco must understand these organizations' needs, resources, policies, and buying procedures.[2]

 *At the height of the dot-com boom, Cisco Systems was briefly the most valuable company in the world, with a valuation of $500 billion. Since those heady days, Cisco has faced a number of challenges and obstacles to its market leadership but has taken a series of steps to try to stay ahead. The company prides itself on staying close to its customers and sees its core competency as helping them get through big transitions by breaking down their corporate silos. Long-time CEO John Chambers cites compact and efficient blade servers as a good example of how Cisco helps companies form a common technological vision, noting that Cisco's is the only computing technology that can handle data, voice, and video. As a technology company, Cisco is constantly reinventing itself to reflect shifts in the marketplace, whether by tapping into trends to enable voice and video over the Internet or by becoming a major player in cloud computing. Acquisitions play a key role, some notable ones being the $6.9 billion purchase of set-top box maker Scientific Atlanta in 2005 and the $5 billion purchase of video software solutions provider NDS in 2012. Cisco knows that as many as a third of its acquitions will fail, as was the case when it bought Pure Digitial, maker of the Flip video camera, for $600 million in 2009. Cisco does spend $6 billion annually on research and development, and it generates 55 percent of its revenue and 70 percent of its growth from overseas.*

**Some of the world's most** valuable brands belong to business marketers: ABB, Caterpillar, DuPont, FedEx, GE, Hewlett-Packard, IBM, Intel, and Siemens, to name a few. Many principles of basic marketing also apply to business marketers. They need to embrace holistic marketing principles, such as building strong loyalty relationships with their customers, just like any marketer. But they also face some unique considerations in selling to other businesses. In this chapter, we will highlight some of the crucial similarities and differences for marketing in business markets.[3]

# What is Organizational Buying?

Frederick E. Webster Jr. and Yoram Wind define **organizational buying** as the decision-making process by which formal organizations establish the need for purchased products and services and identify, evaluate, and choose among alternative brands and suppliers.[4]

## THE BUSINESS MARKET VERSUS THE CONSUMER MARKET

The **business market** consists of all the organizations that acquire goods and services used in the production of other products or services that are sold, rented, or supplied to others. Any firm that supplies components for products is in the business-to-business marketplace. Some of the major industries making up the business market are aerospace; agriculture, forestry, and fisheries; chemical; computer; construction; defense; energy; mining; manufacturing; construction; transportation; communication; public utilities; banking, finance, and insurance; distribution; and services.

As with many products, shoes are manufactured with a wide variety of different kinds of materials and ingredients.

*Source: © edu1971/Fotolia*

More dollars and items change hands in sales to business buyers than to consumers. Consider the process of producing and selling a simple pair of shoes.[5]

A broad spectrum of materials and material combinations are used today in shoe manufacturing. Leathers, synthetics, rubber and textile materials are counted among the basic upper materials. Each material has its own specific character and they differ not only in their appearance but also in their physical properties, their service life and treatment needs. The choice of shoe material significantly influences the life of the footwear, and in many cases dictates its use.

For leather shoes, hide dealers must sell hides to tanners, who sell leather to shoe manufacturers, who sell shoes to wholesalers, who sell shoes to retailers, who finally sell them to consumers. Each party in the supply chain also buys many other goods and services to support its operations.

Given the highly competitive nature of business-to-business markets, the biggest enemy to marketers here is commoditization.[6] Commoditization eats away margins and weakens customer loyalty. It can be overcome only if target customers are convinced that meaningful differences exist in the marketplace and that the unique benefits of the firm's offerings are worth the added expense. Thus, a critical step in business-to-business marketing is to create and communicate relevant differentiation from competitors. Here is how Siemens has improved its marketing to better compete in recent years:[7]

**SIEMENS**   Although mammoth in size, with over $100 billion in revenue and approximately 336,000 employees in 190 countries, German engineering giant Siemens was still not well known in its largest market, the United States, which draws almost $20 billion in revenue. With a goal to establish "who we are, what we are about, and what we look like," the company launched the "Answers" campaign in 2007 to unify its diverse units—which design and manufacture products ranging from trains to diagnostic imaging systems to wind turbines—into one brand identity. Developed by communication agency partner Ogilvy, the campaign was thoroughly integrated across media. Over time, ads became more emotional and human in nature, focusing on how Siemens has solutions that impact customers, society, the environment and the economy. The advertising touched on Siemens' job generation, productivity and work to ensure a sustainable society. Sustainability solutions were reflected in approximately one-third of its revenue. Due to the severe economic recession, there was a strong "buy American" push. The "Siemens Answers" advertising program also helped Siemens reinforce its American credentials. With a focus on the number one Siemens market—the United States—and new emerging markets like China, Siemens began to hit its financial stride again.

Business marketers face many of the same challenges as consumer marketers, especially understanding their customers and what they value. The well-respected Institute for the Study of Business Markets (ISBM) notes that the three biggest hurdles for B-to-B marketing are: (1) building stronger interfaces between marketing and sales; (2) building stronger innovation-marketing interfaces; and (3) extracting and leveraging more granular customer and market knowledge.

Four additional imperatives cited by ISBM are: (1) demonstrating marketing's contribution to business performance; (2) engaging more deeply with customers and customers' customers; (3) finding the right mix

*Source: © Siemens AG 2014*

Business-to-business powerhouse Siemens has emphasized its American roots and sustainability accomplishments in its most important U.S. market.

of centralized versus decentralized marketing activities; and (4) finding and grooming marketing talent and competencies.[8]

Business marketers contrast sharply with consumer markets in some ways, however. They have:

- **Fewer, larger buyers.** The business marketer normally deals with far fewer and much larger buyers than the consumer marketer does, particularly in such industries as aircraft engines and defense weapons. The fortunes of Goodyear tires, Cummins engines, Delphi control systems, and other automotive part suppliers depend in large part on getting big contracts from just a handful of major automakers.

- **Close supplier–customer relationships.** Because of the smaller customer base and the importance and power of the larger customers, suppliers are frequently expected to customize their offerings to individual business customer needs. On an annual basis, Pittsburgh-based PPG Industries purchases more than $7 billion in materials and services from thousands of suppliers. The company presented seven Excellent Supplier Awards for superior performance in 2011, the criteria for which included product quality, delivery, documentation, innovation, responsiveness, continuous improvement, and participation in the Supplier Added Value Effort ($AVE) program. With its $AVE program, PPG challenges its suppliers of maintenance, repair, and operating (MRO) goods and services to deliver on annual value-added and cost-savings proposals equaling at least 5 percent of their total annual sales to PPG.[9] Business buyers also often select suppliers that also buy from them. A paper manufacturer might buy chemicals for its pulp and paper making from a chemical company that in turn buys a considerable amount of paper from the manufacturer.

- **Professional purchasing.** Business goods are often purchased by trained purchasing agents, who must follow their organizations' purchasing policies, constraints, and requirements. Many business buying instruments—for example, requests for quotations, proposals, and purchase contracts—are not typically found in consumer buying. Many professional buyers belong to the Institute for Supply Management (ISM), which seeks to improve the profession's effectiveness and status. This means business marketers must provide greater technical data about their product and its competitive advantages.

Consol Energy's revenue depends indirectly on market demand for electricity and steel-based products.

Source: ©Adam Ziaja/Shutterstock

- *Multiple buying influences.* More people typically influence business buying decisions. Buying committees that include technical experts and even senior management are common in the purchase of major goods. Business marketers need to send well-trained sales representatives and teams to deal with these equally well-trained buyers.
- *Multiple sales calls.* A study by McGraw-Hill found that it took four to four-and-a-half calls to close an average industrial sale. For capital equipment sales for large projects, it may take many attempts to fund a project, and the sales cycle—between quoting a job and delivering the product—can even take years.[10]
- *Derived demand.* The demand for business goods is ultimately derived from the demand for consumer goods. For this reason, the business marketer must closely monitor the buying patterns of end users. Pittsburgh-based Consol Energy's coal and natural gas business largely depends on orders from utilities and steel companies, which, in turn, depend on consumer demand for electricity and for steel-based products such as automobiles, machines, and appliances. Business buyers must also pay close attention to economic factors like the level of production, investment, and consumer spending and the interest rate. Business marketers can do little to stimulate total demand. They can only fight harder to increase or maintain their share of it.
- *Inelastic demand.* The total demand for many business goods and services is inelastic—that is, not much affected by price changes. Shoe manufacturers are not going to buy much more leather if the price of leather falls, nor less if the price rises unless they find satisfactory substitutes. Demand is especially inelastic in the short run because producers cannot make quick changes in production methods. Demand is also inelastic for business goods that represent a small percentage of the item's total cost, such as shoelaces.
- *Fluctuating demand.* The demand for business goods and services tends to be more volatile than the demand for consumer goods and services. A given percentage increase in consumer demand can lead to a much larger percentage increase in the demand for plant and equipment. Demand for plant and equipment is more volatile because it reflects the normal year-to-year replacement demand as well as the need to satisfy increased or decreased consumer demand. Economists refer to this as the *acceleration effect.* Sometimes a rise of only 10 percent in consumer demand can cause as much as a 200 percent rise in business demand for products in the next period; a 10 percent fall in consumer demand may cause a complete collapse in business demand as replacement needs drop considerably.
- *Geographically concentrated buyers.* For years, more than half of U.S. business buyers have been concentrated in seven states: New York, California, Pennsylvania, Illinois, Ohio, New Jersey, and Michigan. The geographical concentration of producers helps to reduce selling costs. At the same time, business marketers need to monitor regional shifts of certain industries such as the automobile industry, which is no longer concentrated around Detroit.
- *Direct purchasing.* Business buyers often buy directly from manufacturers rather than through intermediaries, especially items that are technically complex or expensive such as servers or aircraft.

## BUYING SITUATIONS

The business buyer faces many decisions in making a purchase. *How* many depends on the complexity of the problem being solved, newness of the buying requirement, number of people involved, and time required. Three types of buying situations are the straight rebuy, modified rebuy, and new task.[11]

- *Straight rebuy.* In a straight rebuy, the purchasing department reorders items like office supplies and bulk chemicals on a routine basis and chooses from suppliers on an approved list. The suppliers make an effort to maintain product and service quality and often propose automatic reordering systems to save time. "Out suppliers" attempt to offer something new or exploit dissatisfaction with a current supplier. Their goal is to get a small order and then enlarge their purchase share over time.
- *Modified rebuy.* The buyer in a modified rebuy wants to change product specifications, prices, delivery requirements, or other terms. This usually requires additional participants on both sides. The in-suppliers become nervous and want to protect the account. The out-suppliers see an opportunity to propose a better offer to gain some business.
- *New task.* A new-task purchaser buys a product or service for the first time (an office building, a new security system). The greater the cost or risk, the larger the number of participants, and the greater their information gathering—the longer the time to a decision.[12]

The business buyer makes the fewest decisions in the straight rebuy situation and the most in the new-task situation. Over time, new-buy situations become straight rebuys and routine purchase behavior.

New-task buying is the marketer's greatest opportunity and challenge. The buying process passes through several stages: awareness, interest, evaluation, trial, and adoption. Mass media can be most important during the initial awareness stage; salespeople often have their greatest impact at the interest stage; and technical sources can be most important during evaluation. Online selling efforts may be useful at all stages.

In the new-task situation, the buyer must determine product specifications, price limits, delivery terms and times, service terms, payment terms, order quantities, acceptable suppliers, and the selected supplier. Different participants influence each decision, and the order in which these decisions are made varies.

Because of the complicated selling required, many companies use a *missionary sales force* consisting of their most effective salespeople. The brand promise and the manufacturer's name recognition will be important in establishing trust and persuading the customer to consider change. The marketer also tries to reach as many key participants as possible with information and assistance.

Once a customer has been acquired, in-suppliers are continually seeking ways to add value to their market offer to facilitate rebuys. EMC has successfully acquired a series of computer software leaders to reposition the company to manage and protect—not just store—information, helping companies to "accelerate their journey to cloud computing" in the process. Where one hardware product once made up 80 percent of its sales, the company now gets about 60 percent of its revenue from software and services.[13] Oracle has also made a number of strategic acquisitions to expand its offerings.[14]

**ORACLE** Business-software giant Oracle became an industry leader by offering a range of products and services to satisfy customer needs for enterprise software. Originally known for its flagship database management systems, Oracle spent $30 billion in recent years to buy 56 companies, including $7.4 billion for Sun Microsystems, doubling its revenue to $24 billion and sending its stock soaring in the process. To become a one-stop shop for all kinds of business customers, Oracle now sells everything from server computers and data storage devices to operating systems, databases, and software for running accounting, sales, and supply-chain management. At the same time, the company has launched "Project Fusion" to unify its applications so customers can consolidate solutions to their software needs, as reinforced by their company slogan, "Hardware and Software, Engineered to Work Together." Oracle's market power has sometimes raised both criticism from customers and concerns from government regulators. At the same time, its many long-time customers speak to its track record of product innovation and customer satisfaction.

# Participants in the Business Buying Process

Who buys the trillions of dollars' worth of goods and services needed by business organizations? Purchasing agents are influential in straight-rebuy and modified-rebuy situations, whereas other employees are more influential in new-buy situations. Engineers are usually influential in selecting product components, and purchasing agents dominate in selecting suppliers.[15]

## THE BUYING CENTER

Webster and Wind call the decision-making unit of a buying organization *the buying center*. It consists of "all those individuals and groups who participate in the purchasing decision-making process, who share some common goals and the risks arising from the decisions."[16] The buying center includes all members of the organization who play any of seven roles in the purchase decision process.

1.  *Initiators*—Users or others in the organization who request that something be purchased.
2.  *Users*—Those who will use the product or service. In many cases, the users initiate the buying proposal and help define the product requirements.
3.  *Influencers*—People who influence the buying decision, often by helping define specifications and providing information for evaluating alternatives. Technical people are particularly important influencers.
4.  *Deciders*—People who decide on product requirements or on suppliers.
5.  *Approvers*—People who authorize the proposed actions of deciders or buyers.
6.  *Buyers*—People who have formal authority to select the supplier and arrange the purchase terms. Buyers may help shape product specifications, but they play their major role in selecting vendors and negotiating. In more complex purchases, buyers might include high-level managers.
7.  *Gatekeepers*—People who have the power to prevent sellers or information from reaching members of the buying center. For example, purchasing agents, receptionists, and telephone operators may prevent salespersons from contacting users or deciders.

Several people can occupy a given role such as user or influencer, and one person may play multiple roles.[17] A purchasing manager, for example, is often buyer, influencer, and gatekeeper simultaneously. She can decide which sales reps can call on other people in the organization, what budget and other constraints to place on the purchase, and which firm will actually get the business, even though others (deciders) might select two or more potential vendors that can meet the company's requirements.

A buying center typically has five or six members and sometimes dozens. Some may be outside the organization, such as government officials, consultants, technical advisors, and other members of the marketing channel.[18]

## BUYING CENTER INFLUENCES

Buying centers usually include participants with differing interests, authority, status, susceptibility to persuasion, and sometimes very different decision criteria. Engineers may want to maximize the performance of the product; production people may want ease of use and reliability of supply; financial staff focus on the economics of the purchase; purchasing may be concerned with operating and replacement costs; union officials may emphasize safety issues.

Business buyers also have personal motivations, perceptions, and preferences influenced by their age, income, education, job position, personality, attitudes toward risk, and culture. Some are "keep-it-simple" buyers, or "own-expert," "want-the-best," or "want-everything-done" buyers. Some younger, highly educated buyers are technically proficient and conduct rigorous analyses of competitive proposals before choosing a supplier. Other buyers are "toughies" from the old school who pit competing sellers against one another, and in some companies, the purchasing powers-that-be are legendary.

Webster cautions that ultimately individuals, not organizations, make purchasing decisions.[19] Individuals are motivated by their own needs and perceptions in attempting to maximize the organizational rewards they earn (pay, advancement, recognition, and feelings of achievement). But organizational needs legitimate the buying process and its outcomes.

In other words, according to Webster, businesspeople are not buying "products." They are buying solutions to two problems: the organization's economic and strategic problem and their own personal need for achievement and reward. In this sense, industrial buying decisions are both "rational" and "emotional"—they serve both the organization's and the individual's needs.[20]

Research by one industrial component manufacturer found that although top executives at its small- and medium-size customers were comfortable buying from other companies, they appeared to harbor subconscious insecurities about buying the manufacturer's product. Constant changes in technology had left them concerned about internal effects within the company. Recognizing this unease, the manufacturer retooled its selling approach to emphasize more emotional appeals and the way its product line actually enabled the customer's employees to improve their performance, relieving management of the complications and stress of using its components.[21]

## TARGETING FIRMS AND BUYING CENTERS

Successful business-to-business marketing requires that business marketers know which types of companies to focus on in their selling efforts, as well as whom to concentrate on within the buying centers in those organizations.

**TARGETING FIRMS** As we will discuss in detail in Chapter 9, business marketers may divide the marketplace in many different ways to choose the types of firms to which they will sell. Finding the sectors with the greatest growth prospects, most profitable customers, and most promising opportunities for the firm is crucial, as Timken found out.[22]

**TIMKEN** When Timken, which manufactures bearings and rotaries for companies in a variety of industries, saw its net income and shareholder returns dip compared with competitors', the firm became concerned that it was not investing in the most profitable areas. To identify businesses that operated in financially attractive sectors and would be most likely to value its offerings, it conducted an extensive market study and discovered that some customers generated a lot of business but had little profit potential, while for others the opposite was true. As a result, Timken shifted its attention away from the auto industry and into the heavy processing, aerospace, and defense industries. It also addressed customers that were financially unattractive or minimally attractive. A tractor manufacturer complained that Timken's bearings prices were too high for its medium-sized tractors. Timken suggested the firm look elsewhere but continued to sell bearings at the higher price for the manufacturer's large tractors to the satisfaction of both sides. By adjusting its products, prices, and communications to appeal to the right types of firms, Timken experienced record revenue despite a recession.

It's also true, however, that as a slowing economy has put a stranglehold on large corporations' purchasing departments, small and midsize business markets are offering new opportunities for suppliers. See "Marketing Insight: Big Sales to Small Businesses" for more on this important B-to-B market.

**TARGETING WITHIN THE BUSINESS CENTER** Once it has identified the type of businesses on which to focus marketing efforts, the firm must then decide how best to sell to them. Who are the major decision participants? What decisions do they influence, and how deeply? What evaluation criteria do they use? Consider the following example:

> A company sells nonwoven disposable surgical gowns to hospitals. The hospital staff who participate in the buying decision include the vice president of purchasing, the operating-room administrator, and the surgeons. The vice president of purchasing analyzes whether the hospital should buy disposable or reusable gowns. If disposable, the operating-room administrator compares various competitors' products on absorbency, antiseptic quality, design, and cost and normally buys the brand that meets functional requirements at the lowest cost. Surgeons influence the decision retroactively by reporting their satisfaction with the chosen brand.

The business marketer is not likely to know exactly what kind of group dynamics take place during the decision process, though whatever information he or she can obtain about personalities and interpersonal factors is useful.

Timken carefully segments business markets and adjusts the marketing programs for its bearings and rotaries to maximally satisfy target segments.

Source: PR NEWSWIRE

## marketing insight

# Big Sales to Small Businesses

In its March 2012 guidelines, the Small Business Administration (SBA) defined small businesses as those with fewer than 500 employees for most mining and manufacturing industries and $7 million in average annual receipts for most nonmanufacturing industries. Some exceptions exist in specialized industries, such as grocery and department stores and motor vehicle and electronic appliance dealers, and the guidelines are constantly being updated to reflect changes in the business environment.

The SBA counted approximately 28 million small businesses in the United States in 2013. These provide almost half of all private-sector employment and have generated almost two-thirds of net new private-sector jobs since the 1970s. Those new ventures all need capital equipment, technology, supplies, and services. Look beyond the United States and you find a huge and growing B-to-B market, one that top companies have recognized.

IBM launched Express, a line of hardware, software services, and financing, specifically for the small to midsize customers (with fewer than 1,000 employees) that supply 20 percent of its business. As one VP of marketing noted, "In today's world, we see that over 80% of the time a small or medium business makes a technology decision, it starts with a search engine.... We have to make sure we show up in their search queries, not just paid or organic search, but we want to drive stimulated search."

IBM makes heavy use of social media—including blogs, Facebook, LinkedIn, and Twitter—to drive conversations around topics of interest to small and midsize businesses, such as IT security and cloud-based computing. The company is also using events to reach small businesses, such as a series on IT security that attracted more than 10,000 attendees. It has pledged $1 billion in financing to help small and midsize businesses procure certain IBM systems and services.

Small and midsize businesses present huge opportunities and huge challenges. The market is large and fragmented by industry, size, and number of years in operation. Small business owners are notably averse to long-range planning and often have an "I'll buy it when I need

it" decision-making style. Here are some guidelines for marketing to small businesses:

- **Don't lump small and midsize businesses together.** There's a big gap between $1 million in revenue and $50 million or between a start-up with 10 employees and a more mature business with 100 or more employees. IBM distinguishes its offerings to small and medium-sized businesses on its common Web site for the two.

- **Do keep it simple.** Offer one supplier point of contact for all service problems or one bill for all services and products. AT&T serves millions of small-business customers (with fewer than 100 employees) with services that bundle Internet, local phone, long-distance phone, data management, business networking, Web hosting, and teleconferencing.

- **Do use the Internet.** Hewlett-Packard found that time-strapped small-business decision makers prefer to buy, or at least research, products and services online. So it designed a site for them that pulls visitors through extensive advertising, direct mail, e-mail campaigns, catalogs, and events.

- **Don't forget about direct contact.** Even if a small business owner's first point of contact is via the Internet, you still need to offer phone or face time.

- **Do provide support after the sale.** Small businesses want partners, not pitchmen. When the DeWitt Company, a 100-employee landscaping products business, purchased a large piece of machinery from Moeller, the company's president paid DeWitt's CEO a personal visit and stayed until the machine was up and running properly.

- **Do your homework.** The realities of small or midsize business management are different from those of a large corporation. Microsoft created a small, fictional executive research firm, Southridge, and baseball-style trading cards of its key decision makers to train its employees to tie sales strategies to small-business realities.

**Sources:** Based on Barnaby J. Feder, "When Goliath Comes Knocking on David's Door," *New York Times,* May 6, 2003; Jay Greene, "Small Biz: Microsoft's Next Big Thing?," *BusinessWeek,* April 21, 2003, pp. 72–73; Jennifer Gilbert, "Small but Mighty," *Sales & Marketing Management* (January 2004), pp. 30–35; Kate Maddox, "Driving Engagement with Small Business," *Advertising Age,* November 7, 2011; Christine Birkner, "Big Business Think Small," *Marketing News,* May 15, 2012, pp. 12–16; "IBM Luring SMBs with Expanded Finance Options," *Network World,* September 12, 2011; www.sba.gov; www.openforum.com; www-304.ibm.com/businesscenter/smb/us/en, all accessed May 20, 2014.

Small sellers concentrate on reaching the *key buying influencers*. Larger sellers go for *multilevel in-depth selling* to reach as many participants as possible. Their salespeople virtually "live with" high-volume customers. Companies must rely more heavily on their communications programs to reach hidden buying influences and keep current customers informed.[23]

Business marketers must periodically review their assumptions about buying center participants. Traditionally, SAP sold its software products to CIOs at large companies. A shift to focus on selling to individual corporate units lower down the organizational chart raised the percentage of software license sales going to new customers to 40 percent.[24]

Insights into customers and buying centers are critical. GE's ethnographic research into the plastic-fiber industry revealed that the firm wasn't in a commodity business driven by price, as it had assumed. Instead it was in an artisanal industry, with customers who wanted collaboration at the earliest stages of development. GE completely

GE learned that its plastic-fiber customers saw themselves more as artisans, completely changing how the company treated those customers.

Source: © aykuterd/Fotolia

reoriented the way it interacted with companies in the industry as a result. In developing markets, ethnographic research also can be very useful, especially in far-flung rural areas, given that marketers often do not know these consumers as well.[25]

In developing selling efforts, business marketers can also consider their customers' customers, or end users, if appropriate. Many B-to-B sales are to firms using the products they purchase as components in products they sell to the ultimate consumers. Business marketers can seek out opportunities to interact with their customers' customers and improve their offerings or even their business model. When XSENS, a Dutch supplier of three-dimensional motion-sensor technology, helped solve the problems of one of its customers' customers, it also developed a new operating procedure that improved accuracy of its products by an order of magnitude.[26]

# The Purchasing/Procurement Process

In principle, business buyers seek the highest benefit package (economic, technical, service, and social) in relationship to a market offering's costs. The strength of their incentive to purchase will be a function of the difference between perceived benefits and perceived costs.[27]

Business marketers must therefore ensure that customers fully appreciate how the firm's offerings are different and better. *Framing* occurs when customers are given a perspective or point of view that allows the seller to "put its best foot forward." It can be as simple as making sure customers recognize all the benefits or cost savings afforded by the firm's offerings or becoming more influential in the customers' thinking about the economics of purchasing, owning, using, and disposing of product offerings.

In the past, purchasing departments occupied a low position in the management hierarchy, in spite of often managing more than half the company's costs. Recent competitive pressures have led many companies to upgrade their purchasing departments and elevate administrators to vice presidential rank. These new, more strategically oriented purchasing departments have a mission to seek the best value from fewer and better suppliers.

Some multinationals have even elevated purchasing departments to "strategic supply departments" with responsibility for global sourcing and partnering. At Caterpillar, purchasing, inventory control, production scheduling, and traffic have been combined into one department. Here are two other companies that have benefited from improving their business buying practices.

- Rio Tinto is a world leader in finding, mining, and processing the earth's mineral resources, with a significant presence in North America and Australia. Coordinating with its suppliers was time-consuming, so Rio Tinto embarked on an electronic commerce strategy with one key supplier. Both parties have reaped significant benefits. In many cases, orders are being filled in the suppliers' warehouse within minutes of being transmitted, and the supplier can now use a pay-on-receipt program that has shortened Rio Tinto's payment cycle to about 10 days.[28]

- Medline Industries, the largest privately owned manufacturer and distributor of health care products in the United States, used software to integrate its view of customer activity across online and direct sales channels. The results? The firm enhanced its product margin by 3 percent, improved customer retention by 10 percent, reduced revenue lost to pricing errors by 10 percent, and enhanced the productivity of its sales representatives by 20 percent.[29]

The upgrading of purchasing means business marketers must upgrade their sales staff to match the higher caliber of today's business buyers.

Supplier diversity may not have a price tag, but it is a benefit purchasing departments and business buyers overlook at their own risk. Minority suppliers are the fastest-growing segment of today's business landscape, and CEOs of many of the largest companies see a diverse supplier base as a business imperative. In 2011, McDonald's U.S. restaurant system purchased nearly $6.7 billion in goods and services from minority- and women-owned suppliers, about two-thirds of what the system spends for food, packaging, uniforms, operating supplies, and premiums.[30]

# Stages in the Buying Process

We're ready to describe the general stages in the business buying-decision process. Patrick J. Robinson and his associates identified eight stages and called them *buyphases*.[31] The model in Table 7.1 is the *buygrid* framework.

In modified-rebuy or straight-rebuy situations, some stages are compressed or bypassed. For example, the buyer normally has a favorite supplier or a ranked list of suppliers and can skip the search and proposal solicitation stages. Here are some important considerations in each of the eight stages.

## PROBLEM RECOGNITION

The buying process begins when someone in the company recognizes a problem or need that can be met by acquiring a good or service. The recognition can be triggered by internal or external stimuli. The internal stimulus might be a decision to develop a new product that requires new equipment and materials or a machine that breaks down and requires new parts. Or purchased material turns out to be unsatisfactory and the company searches for another supplier or lower prices or better quality. Externally, the buyer may get new ideas at a trade show, see an ad, receive an e-mail, read a blog, or receive a call from a sales representative who offers a better product or a lower price. Business marketers can stimulate problem recognition by direct marketing in many different ways.

| TABLE 7.1 | Buygrid Framework: Major Stages (Buyphases) of the Industrial Buying Process in Relation to Major Buying Situations (Buyclasses) | | |
|---|---|---|---|
| | | **Buyclasses** | |
| | | **New Task** | **Modified Rebuy** | **Straight Rebuy** |
| **Buyphases** | 1. Problem recognition | Yes | Maybe | No |
| | 2. General need description | Yes | Maybe | No |
| | 3. Product specification | Yes | Yes | Yes |
| | 4. Supplier search | Yes | Maybe | No |
| | 5. Proposal solicitation | Yes | Maybe | No |
| | 6. Supplier selection | Yes | Maybe | No |
| | 7. Order-routine specification | Yes | Maybe | No |
| | 8. Performance review | Yes | Yes | Yes |

Mexican cement giant Cemex is known for its sophisticated ways to reduce costs for its customers.

*Source: © Justin Kase zsixz / Alamy*

# GENERAL NEED DESCRIPTION AND PRODUCT SPECIFICATION

Next, the buyer determines the needed item's general characteristics and required quantity. For standard items, this is simple. For complex items, the buyer will work with others—engineers, users—to define characteristics such as reliability, durability, or price. Business marketers can help by describing how their products meet or even exceed the buyer's needs.

The buying organization now develops the item's technical specifications. Often, the company will assign a product-value-analysis engineering team to the project. *Product value analysis (PVA)* is an approach to cost reduction that studies whether components can be redesigned or standardized or made by cheaper methods of production *without adversely affecting product performance.* The PVA team will identify overdesigned components, for instance, that last longer than the product itself. Tightly written specifications allow the buyer to refuse components that are too expensive or that fail to meet specified standards.

Suppliers can use product value analysis as a tool for positioning themselves to win an account. Whatever the method, it is important to eliminate excessive costs. Mexican cement giant Cemex is famed for "The Cemex Way," which uses high-tech methods to squeeze out inefficiencies.[32]

# SUPPLIER SEARCH

The buyer next tries to identify the most appropriate suppliers through trade directories, contacts with other companies, trade advertisements, trade shows, and the Internet. The move to online purchasing has far-reaching implications for suppliers and will change the shape of purchasing for years to come. Companies that purchase online are utilizing electronic marketplaces in several forms:

- *Catalog sites.* Companies can order thousands of items through electronic catalogs, such as W. W. Grainger's, distributed by e-procurement software.
- *Vertical markets.* Companies buying industrial products such as plastics, steel, or chemicals or services such as logistics or media can go to specialized Web sites called e-hubs. Plastics.com allows plastics buyers to search the best prices among thousands of plastics sellers.
- *"Pure Play" auction company.* Ritchie Bros. Auctioneers is the world's largest industrial auctioneer, with 44 auction sites worldwide. It sold $3.8 billion of used and unused equipment at more than 356 unreserved auctions in 2013, including a wide range of heavy equipment, trucks, and other assets for the construction, transportation, agricultural, material handling, oil and gas, mining, forestry, and marine industry sectors. While some people prefer to bid in person at Ritchie Bros. auctions, they can also do so online in real time at rbauction.com—the company's multilingual Web site. In 2013, 50 percent of the bidders at Ritchie Bros. auctions bid over the Internet; online bidders purchased $1.4 billion of equipment.[33]
- *Spot (or exchange) markets.* On spot electronic markets, prices change by the minute. IntercontinentalExchange (ICE) is the leading electronic energy marketplace and soft commodity exchange with billions in sales.
- *Private exchanges.* Hewlett-Packard, IBM, and Walmart operate private exchanges to link with specially invited groups of suppliers and partners over the Web.
- *Barter markets.* In barter markets, participants offer to trade goods or services.
- *Buying alliances.* Several companies buying the same goods can join together to form purchasing consortia to gain deeper discounts on volume purchases. TopSource is an alliance of firms in the retail and wholesale food-related businesses.

Richie Bros., the world's largest industrial auctioneers, conducts numerous online as well as in-person auctions for its customers.

Source: Courtesy of Ritchie Bros. Auctioneers.

Online business buying offers several advantages: It shaves transaction costs for both buyers and suppliers, reduces time between order and delivery, consolidates purchasing systems, and forges more direct relationships between partners and buyers. On the downside, it may help to erode supplier–buyer loyalty and create potential security problems.

**E-PROCUREMENT** Web sites are organized around two types of e-hubs: *vertical hubs* centered on industries (plastics, steel, chemicals, paper) and *functional hubs* (logistics, media buying, advertising, energy management). In addition to using these Web sites, companies can use e-procurement in other ways:

- *Set up direct extranet links to major suppliers.* A company can set up a direct e-procurement account at Dell or Office Depot, for instance, and its employees can make their purchases this way.
- *Form buying alliances.* A number of major retailers and manufacturers such as Acosta, Ahold, Best Buy, Carrefour, Family Dollar Stores, Lowe's, Safeway, Sears, SUPERVALU, Target, Walgreens, Walmart, and Wegmans Food Markets are part of a data-sharing alliance called 1SYNC. Several auto companies (GM, Ford, Chrysler) formed Covisint for the same reason. Covisint is the leading provider of services that can integrate crucial business information and processes between partners, customers, and suppliers. The company has now also targeted health care to provide similar services.
- *Set up company buying sites.* General Electric formed the Trading Process Network (TPN), where it posts *requests for proposals (RFPs)*, negotiates terms, and places orders.

Moving into e-procurement means more than acquiring software; it requires changing purchasing strategy and structure. However, the benefits are many. Aggregating purchasing across multiple departments yields larger, centrally negotiated volume discounts, a smaller purchasing staff, and less buying of substandard goods from outside the approved list of suppliers.

**LEAD GENERATION** The supplier's task is to ensure it is considered when customers are—or could be—in the market and searching for a supplier. Marketing must work with sales to define what makes a "sales ready" prospect and cooperate to send the right messages via sales calls, trade shows, online activities, PR, events, direct mail, and referrals.

Marketers must find the right balance between the quantity and quality of leads. Too many leads, even of high quality, and the sales force may be overwhelmed and allow promising opportunities to fall through the cracks; too few or low-quality leads and the sales force may become frustrated or demoralized.[34]

To generate high-quality leads, suppliers need to know about their customers. They can obtain background information from vendors such as Dun & Bradstreet and InfoUSA or information-sharing Web sites such as Jigsaw and LinkedIn.[35]

Suppliers that qualify may be visited by the buyer's agents, who will examine the suppliers' manufacturing facilities and meet their staff. After evaluating each company, the buyer will end up with a short list of qualified suppliers. Many professional buyers have forced suppliers to make adjustments to their marketing proposals to increase their likelihood of making the cut.

# PROPOSAL SOLICITATION

The buyer next invites qualified suppliers to submit written proposals. After evaluating them, the buyer will invite a few suppliers to make formal presentations.

Business marketers must be skilled in researching, writing, and presenting proposals as marketing documents that describe value and benefits in customer terms. Oral presentations must inspire confidence and position the company's capabilities and resources so they stand out from the competition.

Proposals and selling efforts are often team efforts that leverage the knowledge and expertise of coworkers. Pittsburgh-based Cutler-Hammer, part of Eaton Corp., developed "pods" of salespeople focused on a particular geographic region, industry, or market concentration.

# SUPPLIER SELECTION

Before selecting a supplier, the buying center will specify and rank desired supplier attributes, often using a supplier-evaluation model such as the one in Table 7.2.

To develop compelling value propositions, business marketers need to better understand how business buyers arrive at their valuations.[36] Researchers have identified eight different *customer value assessment (CVA)* methods. Companies tended to use the simpler methods, though the more sophisticated ones promise a more accurate picture of CPV (see "Marketing Memo: Developing Compelling Customer Value Propositions").

The choice of attributes and their relative importance vary with the buying situation. Delivery reliability, price, and supplier reputation are important for routine-order products. For procedural-problem products, such as a copying machine, the three most important attributes are technical service, supplier flexibility, and product reliability. For political-problem products that stir rivalries in the organization (such as the choice of a computer system or software platform), the most important attributes are price, supplier reputation, product reliability, service reliability, and supplier flexibility.

**OVERCOMING PRICE PRESSURES** Despite moves toward strategic sourcing, partnering, and participation in cross-functional teams, buyers still spend a large chunk of their time haggling with suppliers on price. The number of price-oriented buyers can vary by country, depending on customer preferences for different service configurations and characteristics of the customer's organization.[37]

Marketers can counter requests for a lower price in a number of ways, including framing as noted above. They may also be able to show that the total cost of ownership, that is, the life-cycle cost of using their product, is lower

| TABLE 7.2 | An Example of Vendor Analysis | | | | |
|---|---|---|---|---|---|
| **Attributes** | | **Rating Scale** | | | |
| | Importance Weights | Poor (1) | Fair (2) | Good (3) | Excellent (4) |
| Price | .30 | | | | X |
| Supplier reputation | .20 | | | X | |
| Product reliability | .30 | | | | X |
| Service reliability | .10 | | X | | |
| Supplier flexibility | .10 | | | X | |
| Total Score: .30(4) + .20(3) + .30(4) + .10(2) + .10(3) = 3.5 | | | | | |

## marketing memo — Developing Compelling Customer Value Propositions

To command price premiums in competitive B-to-B markets, firms must create compelling customer value propositions. The first step is to research the customer. Here are a number of productive research methods:

1. *Internal engineering assessment*—Have company engineers use laboratory tests to estimate the product's performance characteristics. Weakness: Ignores the fact that the product will have different economic values in different applications.

2. *Field value-in-use assessment*—Interview customers about how costs of using a new product compare with those of using an incumbent. The task is to assess how much each cost element is worth to the buyer.

3. *Focus-group value assessment*—Ask customers in a focus group what value they would put on potential market offerings.

4. *Direct survey questions*—Ask customers to place a direct dollar value on one or more changes in the market offering.

5. *Conjoint analysis*—Ask customers to rank their preferences for alternative market offerings or concepts. Use statistical analysis to estimate the implicit value placed on each attribute.

6. *Benchmarks*—Show customers a benchmark offering and then a new-market offering. Ask how much more they would pay for the new offering or how much less they would pay if certain features were removed from the benchmark offering.

7. *Compositional approach*—Ask customers to attach a monetary value to each of three alternative levels of a given attribute. Repeat for other attributes, then add the values together for any offer configuration.

8. *Importance ratings*—Ask customers to rate the importance of different attributes and their suppliers' performance on each.

Having done this research, firms can specify the customer value proposition, following a number of important principles. First, *clearly substantiate value claims by concretely specifying the differences between your offerings and those of competitors on the dimensions that matter most to the customer.* Rockwell Automation identified the cost savings customers would realize from purchasing its pump instead of a competitor's by using industry-standard metrics of functionality and performance: kilowatt-hours spent, number of operating hours per year, and dollars per kilowatt-hour. Also, make the financial implications obvious.

Second, *document the value delivered by creating written accounts of costs savings or added value that existing customers have actually captured by using your offerings.* Chemical producer Akzo Nobel conducted a two-week pilot on a production reactor at a prospective customer's facility to document the advantages of its high-purity metal organics product.

Finally, *make sure the method of creating a customer value proposition is well implemented within the company, and train and reward employees for developing a compelling one.* Quaker Chemical conducts training programs for its managers that include a competition to develop the best proposals.

**Sources:** James C. Anderson and Finn Wynstra, "Purchasing Higher-Value, Higher-Price Offerings in Business Markets," *Journal of Business-to-Business Marketing* 17 (2010), pp. 29–61; James C. Anderson, Marc Wouters, and Wouter van Rossum, "Why the Highest Price Isn't the Best Price," *MIT Sloan Management Review,* Winter 2010, pp. 69–76; James C. Anderson, Nirmalya Kumar, and James A. Narus, *Value Merchants: Demonstrating and Documenting Superior Value in Business Markets* (Boston: Harvard Business School Press, 2007); James C. Anderson, James A. Narus, and Wouter van Rossum, "Customer Value Propositions in Business Markets," *Harvard Business Review,* March 2006, pp. 2–10; James C. Anderson and James A. Narus, "Business Marketing: Understanding What Customers Value," *Harvard Business Review,* November 1998, pp. 53–65.

than for competitors' products. They can cite the value of the services the buyer now receives, especially if it is superior to that offered by competitors.[38] Research shows that service support and personal interactions, as well as a supplier's know-how and ability to improve customers' time to market, can be useful differentiators in achieving key-supplier status.[39]

Improving productivity helps alleviate price pressures. Burlington Northern Santa Fe Railway has tied 30 percent of employee bonuses to improvements in the number of railcars shipped per mile.[40] Some firms are using technology to devise novel customer solutions. With Web technology and tools, Vistaprint printers can offer professional printing to small businesses that previously could not afford it.[41]

Some companies handle price-oriented buyers by setting a lower price but establishing restrictive conditions: (1) limited quantities, (2) no refunds, (3) no adjustments, and (4) no services.[42]

- **Cardinal Health** set up a bonus-dollars plan and gave points according to how much the customer purchased. The points could be turned in for extra goods or free consulting.
- **GE** is installing diagnostic sensors in its airline engines and railroad engines. It is now compensated for hours of flight or railroad travel.
- **IBM** is now more of a "service company aided by products" than a "product company aided by services." It can sell computer power on demand (like video on demand) as an alternative to selling computers.

Source: © B. Leighty / Photri Images / Alamy

Burlington Northern Santa Fe (BNSF) Railway rewards employees for improvements in the number of railcars shipped per mile.

*Solution selling* can also alleviate price pressure and comes in different forms. Here are three examples.[43]

- **Solutions to enhance customer revenues.** Hendrix UTD has used its sales consultants to help farmers deliver an incremental animal weight gain of 5 percent to 10 percent over competitors.
- **Solutions to decrease customer risks.** ICI Explosives formulated a safer way to ship explosives for quarries.
- **Solutions to reduce customer costs.** W. W. Grainger employees work at large customer facilities to reduce materials-management costs.

More firms are seeking solutions that increase benefits and reduce costs enough to overcome any low-price concerns. Consider the following example.[44]

**LINCOLN ELECTRIC** Lincoln Electric has a decades-long tradition of working with its customers to reduce costs through its Guaranteed Cost Reduction (GCR) Program. When a customer insists that a Lincoln distributor lower prices to match competitors, the company and the distributor may guarantee that, during the coming year, they will find cost reductions in the customer's plant that meet or exceed the price difference between Lincoln's products and the competition's. The Holland Binkley Company, a major manufacturer of components for tractor trailers, had been purchasing Lincoln Electric welding wire for years. When Binkley began to shop around for a better price on wire, Lincoln Electric developed a package for reducing costs and working together that called for a $10,000 savings but eventually led to a six-figure savings, a growth in business, and a strong long-term partnership between customer and supplier.

*Risk and gain sharing* can offset price reductions customers request. Suppose Medline, a hospital supplier, signs an agreement with Highland Park Hospital promising $350,000 in savings over the first 18 months in exchange for getting a tenfold increase in the hospital's share of supplies. If Medline achieves less than this promised savings, it will make up the difference. If it achieves substantially more, it participates in the extra savings. To make such arrangements work, the supplier must be willing to help the customer build a historical database, reach an agreement for measuring benefits and costs, and devise a dispute resolution mechanism.

**NUMBER OF SUPPLIERS** Companies are increasingly reducing the number of their suppliers. Ford, Motorola, and Honeywell have cut their number of suppliers 20 percent to 80 percent. These companies want their chosen suppliers to be responsible for a larger component system, achieve continuous quality and performance improvement, and at the same time lower prices each year by a given percentage. They expect their suppliers to work closely with them during product development, and they value their suggestions.

There is even a trend toward single sourcing, though companies that use multiple sources often cite the threat of a labor strike, natural disaster, or any other unforseen event as the biggest deterrent to single sourcing. Companies may also fear single suppliers will become too comfortable in the relationship and lose their competitive edge.

## ORDER-ROUTINE SPECIFICATION

After selecting suppliers, the buyer negotiates the final order, listing the technical specifications, the quantity needed, the expected time of delivery, return policies, warranties, and so on. Many industrial buyers lease heavy equipment such as machinery and trucks. The lessee gains a number of advantages: the latest products, better service, the conservation of capital, and some tax advantages. The lessor often ends up with a larger net income and the chance to sell to customers that could not afford outright purchase.

For maintenance, repair, and operating items, buyers are moving toward blanket contracts rather than periodic purchase orders. A blanket contract establishes a long-term relationship in which the supplier promises to resupply the buyer as needed, at agreed-upon prices, over a specified period of time. Because the seller holds the stock, blanket contracts are sometimes called *stockless purchase plans*. They lock suppliers in tighter with the buyer and make it difficult for out-suppliers to break in unless the buyer becomes dissatisfied.

Companies that fear a shortage of key materials are willing to buy and hold large inventories. They will sign long-term contracts with suppliers to ensure a steady flow of materials. DuPont, Ford, and several other major companies regard long-term supply planning as a major responsibility of their purchasing managers. For example, General Motors wants to buy from fewer suppliers, which must be willing to locate close to its plants and produce high-quality components. Business marketers are also setting up extranets with important customers to facilitate and lower the cost of transactions. Customers enter orders that are automatically transmitted to the supplier.

Some companies go further and shift the ordering responsibility to their suppliers, using systems called *vendor-managed inventory (VMI)*. These suppliers are privy to the customer's inventory levels and take responsibility for *continuous replenishment programs*. Plexco International AG supplies audio, lighting, and vision systems to the world's leading automakers. Its VMI program with its 40 suppliers resulted in significant time and cost savings and allowed the company to use former warehouse space for productive manufacturing activities.[45]

## PERFORMANCE REVIEW

The buyer periodically reviews the performance of the chosen supplier(s) using one of three methods. The buyer may contact end users and ask for their evaluations, rate the supplier on several criteria using a weighted-score method, or aggregate the cost of poor performance to come up with adjusted costs of purchase, including price. The performance review may lead the buyer to continue, modify, or end a supplier relationship.

Many companies have set up incentive systems to reward purchasing managers for good buying performance, leading them to increase pressure on sellers for the best terms.

# Developing Effective Business-to-Business Marketing Programs

Business-to-business marketers are using every marketing tool at their disposal to attract and retain customers. They are embracing systems selling and adding valuable services to their product offerings and employing customer reference programs and a wide variety of online and offline communication and branding activities.

## COMMUNICATION AND BRANDING ACTIVITIES

Business marketers are increasingly recognizing the importance of their brand. Swiss-based ABB is a global leader in power and automation technologies with 145,000 employees in about 100 countries. The company spends $1 billion in R&D annually to fuel a long tradition of groundbreaking and nation-building projects. An extensive and carefully planned rebranding project in 2011 evaluated five alternative positioning platforms, concluding that ABB should stand for "Power and Productivity for a Better World." Magazines, posters, brochures, and digital communication were all revamped to give the brand a new look.[46] NetApp is another good example of the increased importance placed on branding in business-to-business marketing.[47]

**NETAPP**    NetApp is a *Fortune* 1000 company providing data management and storage solutions to medium- and large-sized clients. Despite some marketplace success, the company found its branding efforts in disarray by 2007. Several variations of its name were in use, leading to a formal name change to NetApp in 2008. Branding consultants Landor also created a new identity, architecture, nomenclature, tone of voice, and tagline ("Go further, faster."). Messages emphasized NetApp's superior technology, innovation, and customer-centric "get things done" culture. Some marketing efforts still left a few things to be desired, however. Called "Frankensites" because they had been modified by so many developers over a 12-year period, the company's Web sites were streamlined to organize the company's presentation and make updates easier. The new Web sites were estimated to increase sales leads from inquiries fourfold. Investing heavily in marketing communications despite the recession, NetApp also ran print and online ads and tapped into a number of social media outlets—communities and forums, bloggers, Facebook, Twitter, and YouTube. Social media initiatives helped it in Asia where it did not have an advertising presence.

In business-to-business marketing, the corporate brand is often critical because it is associated with so many of the company's products. At one time, Emerson Electric, a global provider of power tools, compressors, electrical equipment, and engineering solutions, was a conglomerate of 60 autonomous—and sometimes anonymous—companies. A new CMO, Kathy Button Bell, aligned the brands under a new global brand architecture and identity, allowing Emerson to achieve a broader presence so it could sell locally while leveraging its global brand name. She also took on the challenge of strengthening the corporate brand online. A global consolidation cut the number of company Web sites in half; Web sites and marketing campaigns were translated into local languages around the globe; and social media platforms were built out. Record sales and stock price highs have followed.[48] SAS is another firm that recognized the importance of its corporate brand.[49]

**SAS** With sales of more than $2.3 billion and a huge "fan club" of IT customers, SAS, the business analytics software and services firm, seemed to be in an enviable position in 1999. Yet its image was what one industry observer called "a geek brand." To extend the company's reach beyond IT managers with PhDs in math or statistical analysis, the company needed to connect with C-level executives in the largest companies—people who either didn't have a clue what SAS's software was or didn't think business analytics was a strategic issue. Working with its first outside ad agency ever, SAS emerged with a new logo, a new slogan, "The Power to Know[®]," and a series of TV spots and print ads in business publications such as *BusinessWeek, Forbes,* and the *Wall Street Journal.* One TV spot that exemplifies SAS's rebranding effort ran like this:

> The problem is not harvesting the new crop of e-business information. It's making sense of it. With e-intelligence from SAS, you can harness the information. And put the knowledge you need within reach. SAS. The Power to Know.

Later research showed that SAS had made the transition to a mainstream business decision-making support brand and was seen as both user-friendly and necessary. Highly profitable and now one of the world's largest privately owned software companies, more than doubling its revenue stream since the brand change, SAS has met with just as much success inside the company. For more than 15 years, *Fortune* magazine has ranked it one of the best U.S. companies to work for.

Here are some examples of the way top firms are redesigning Web sites, improving search results, engaging in social media, and launching Webinars and podcasts to improve their business performance through their B-to-B marketing.

- Chapman Kelly provides audit and other cost-containment products to help firms reduce their health care and insurance costs. The company originally tried to acquire new customers through traditional cold calling and outbound selling techniques. After it redesigned its Web site and optimized the site's search engine so the company's name moved close to the top of relevant online searches, revenue nearly doubled.[50]
- Emerson Process Management makes automation systems for chemical plants, oil refineries, and other types of factories. Readers like to hear and swap factory war stories on the company's blog about factory automation, which attracts 35,000 to 40,000 regular visitors each month and generates five to seven leads a week. Given that its systems sell for millions of dollars, ROI on the blog investment is immense.[51]
- Machinery manufacturer Makino builds relationships with end-user customers by hosting an ongoing series of industry-specific Webinars, averaging three a month. The company uses highly specialized content, such as how to get the most out of machine tools and how metal-cutting processes work, to appeal to different industries and different styles of manufacturing. Its database of Webinar participants has allowed the firm to cut marketing costs and improve its effectiveness and efficiency.[52]
- Canadian supply-chain management company Kinaxis uses a fully integrated approach to communications including blogs, white papers, and a video channel that hinges on specific keywords to drive traffic to its Web

Machinery maker Makimo employs an extensive series of webinars to build stronger ties with its customers.

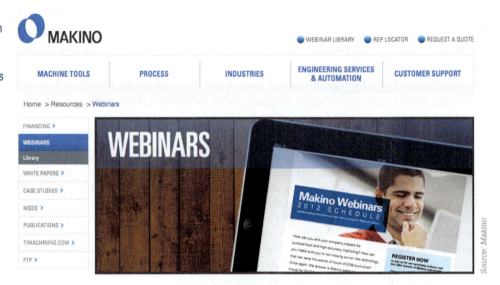

site and generate qualified leads. With research suggesting that 93 percent of all B-to-B purchases start with search, Kinaxis puts much emphasis on search engine optimization (SEO), reusing and repurposing content as much as possible to make it relevant and "Google-friendly."[53]

Some business-to-business marketers are adopting marketing practices from business-to-consumer markets to build their brand. Xerox ran a fully integrated communication campaign to cleverly reinforce the fact that 50 percent of its revenue comes from business services and not copiers. Here is how its Marriott ad unfolded:[54]

Two Marriott bellmen are sitting in an office. "Did you finish last month's invoices?" one asks the other. "No, but I did pick up your dry cleaning and have your shoes shined," the second replies. "Well, I made you a reservation at the sushi place around the corner!" the first bellman says. This voiceover follows: "Marriott knows it's better for Xerox to automate their global invoice processes so they can focus on serving their customers."

Sometimes a more personal touch can make all the difference. Customers considering dropping six or seven figures on one transaction for big-ticket goods and services want all the information they can get, especially from a trusted, independent source. "Marketing Memo: Spreading the Word with Customer Reference Programs" describes the role of that increasingly important marketing tool.

## SYSTEMS BUYING AND SELLING

Many business buyers prefer to buy a total problem solution from one seller. Called *systems buying,* this practice originated with government purchases of major weapons and communications systems. The government solicited bids from *prime contractors* that, if awarded the contract, became responsible for bidding out and assembling the system's subcomponents from *second-tier contractors*. The prime contractor thus provided a turnkey solution, so-called because the buyer simply had to turn one key to get the job done.

Sellers have increasingly recognized that buyers like to purchase in this way, and many have adopted systems selling as a marketing tool. Cisco Systems began to take share from telcommunications rival Avaya by offering customers a one-stop solution for communications technology.[55] Technology giants such as Hewlett-Packard, IBM, Oracle, Dell, and EMC are all transitioning from specialists to competing one-stop shops that can provide the core technology necessary as businesses shift to the cloud.[56]

One variant of systems selling is *systems contracting,* in which a single supplier provides the buyer with its entire requirement of MRO supplies. During the contract period, the supplier also manages the customer's inventory. Shell Oil manages the oil inventories of many of its business customers and knows when they require replenishment. The customer benefits from reduced procurement and management costs and from price protection over the term of the contract. The seller achieves lower operating costs thanks to steady demand and reduced paperwork.

Systems selling is a key industrial marketing strategy in bidding to build large-scale industrial projects such as dams, steel factories, irrigation systems, sanitation systems, pipelines, utilities, and even new towns. Project

## marketing memo
## Spreading the Word With Customer Reference Programs

In a networked economy, buyers increasingly rely on the input of others to help them make purchase decisions. One way to entice or reassure potential new buyers is to create a customer reference program in which satisfied existing customers act in concert with the company's sales and marketing department by agreeing to serve as references. Technology companies such as HP, Lucent, and Unisys have all employed such programs.

Buyers can interact with a company and its customers in a variety of ways—via social media; conferences, events, and trade shows; and their own personal and professional networks. Companies need to recognize the importance of peer-to-peer interaction and know how they can assist a potential buyer. One expert offers the following advice:

1. Establish a formal, organized customer reference program to build an army of advocates.
2. Put references at the center of your growth strategy.
3. Give your customer reference program a seat at the table by using an experienced executive as its leader.
4. Don't strive for "100 percent referenceability"—put focus on a smaller group of truly committed, impactful company advocates.
5. Revolutionize your customer value proposition; find customers who want to be advocates because of their passion for the company and not as the result of any financial inducement.

Research has shown that another potential benefit of a customer reference program is that it can increase the loyalty even of the customer advocates themselves.

**Sources:** V. Kumar, J. Andrew Petersen, and Robert P. Leone, "Defining, Measuring, and Managing Business Reference Value," *Journal of Marketing* 77 (January 2013), pp. 68–86; David Godes, "The Strategic Impact of References in Business Markets," *Marketing Science* 31 (March–April 2012), pp. 257–76; Bill Lee, "Customer Reference Programs at the Tipping Point," *HBR Blog Network*, June 7, 2012.

engineering firms must compete on price, quality, reliability, and other attributes to win contracts. Suppliers, however, are not just at the mercy of customer demands. Ideally, they're active early in the process to influence the actual development of the specifications. Or they can go beyond the specifications to offer additional value in various ways, as the following example shows.

## SELLING TO THE INDONESIAN GOVERNMENT
The Indonesian government requested bids to build a cement factory near Jakarta. A U.S. firm made a proposal that included choosing the site, designing the factory, hiring the construction crews, assembling the materials and equipment, and turning over the finished factory to the Indonesian government. A Japanese firm, in its proposal, included all these services, plus hiring and training the workers to run the factory, exporting the cement through its trading companies, and using the cement to build roads and new office buildings in Jakarta. Although the Japanese plan would cost more money, it won the contract. Clearly, the Japanese viewed the problem not just as building a cement factory (the narrow view of systems selling) but as contributing to Indonesia's economic development. They took the broadest view of the customer's needs, which is true systems selling.

## ROLE OF SERVICES

Services play an increasing strategic and financial role for many business-to-business firms selling primarily products. Adding high-quality services to their product offerings allows them to provide greater value and establish closer ties with customers.

A classic example is Rolls-Royce, which has invested heavily in developing giant jet engine models for the new jumbo planes being introduced by Boeing and Airbus. An important source of profits for Rolls-Royce, beyond selling engines and replacement parts, is the add-on "power by the hour" long-term repair and maintenance contracts it sells. Margins are higher because customers are willing to pay a premium for the peace of mind and predictability the contracts offer.[57]

Mondo combines state-of-the-art running tracks with value-added services to successfully sell to stadiums all over the world.

Source: Mondo S.p.A.

Technology firms are also bundling services to improve customer satisfaction and increase profits. Like many software firms, Adobe Systems is making the transition to a digital-marketing business with cloud-based monthly subscriptions. Revenue is increasing because the company is able to sell support services, Web site hosting, and server management to its cloud customers.[58]

All kinds of firms are finding ways to bundle value-added services to their products. Italian firm Mondo makes state-of-the-art running tracks for stadiums all over the world. Despite competition, it has continued to win new clients, such as the London Olympics, in part because of the installation and maintenance services it offers.[59]

# Managing Business-to-Business Customer Relationships

Business suppliers and customers are exploring different ways to manage their relationships.[60] Loyalty is driven in part by supply chain management, early supplier involvement, and purchasing alliances.[61]

Business-to-business marketers are avoiding "spray and pray" approaches to attracting and retaining customers in favor of honing in on their targets and developing one-to-one marketing approaches.[62] Nearly 80 percent of the *Fortune* 500 use SAP software, but the software giant begin to lose market share and revenue when, as one cofounder observed, "We had lost the trust in relationships with our customers, and employees did not believe in management." Embracing innovation with new cloud-based services was a big part of the company's turnaround strategy; the other was focusing on improving customer relationships. A controversial price hike introduced during the financial crisis was reversed, and new co-CEOs vowed to listen more closely to customer concerns.[63]

## THE BENEFITS OF VERTICAL COORDINATION

Much research has advocated greater vertical coordination between buying partners and sellers so they can transcend merely transacting and instead create more value for both parties.[64] Building trust is one prerequisite to enjoying healthy long-term relationships. "Marketing Insight: Establishing Corporate Trust, Credibility, and Reputation" identifies some key dimensions of such trust. Knowledge that is specific and relevant to a relationship partner is also an important factor in the strength of interfirm ties.[65]

A number of forces influence the development of a relationship between business partners. Four relevant ones are availability of alternatives, importance of supply, complexity of supply, and supply market dynamism. Based on these we can classify buyer–supplier relationships into eight categories:[66]

1. **Basic buying and selling**—These are simple, routine exchanges with moderate levels of cooperation and information exchange.
2. **Bare bones**—These relationships require more adaptation by the seller and less cooperation and information exchange.
3. **Contractual transaction**—These exchanges are defined by formal contract and generally have low levels of trust, cooperation, and interaction.

## marketing insight

# Establishing Corporate Trust, Credibility, and Reputation

*Corporate credibility* is the extent to which customers believe a firm can design and deliver products and services that satisfy their needs and wants. It reflects the supplier's reputation in the marketplace and is the foundation of a strong relationship.

Corporate credibility depends on three factors:

- *Corporate expertise,* the extent to which a company is seen as able to make and sell products or conduct services.

- *Corporate trustworthiness,* the extent to which a company is seen as motivated to be honest, dependable, and sensitive to customer needs.

- *Corporate likability*, the extent to which a company is seen as likable, attractive, prestigious, and dynamic.

In other words, a credible firm is good at what it does; it keeps its customers' best interests in mind and is enjoyable to work with.

*Trust* is a firm's willingness to rely on a business partner. It depends on a number of interpersonal and interorganizational factors, such as the firm's perceived competence, integrity, honesty, and benevolence. Personal interactions with employees of the firm,

opinions about the company as a whole, and perceptions of trust will evolve with experience. A firm is more likely to be seen as trustworthy when it:

- Provides full, honest information
- Provides employee incentives aligned to meet customer needs
- Partners with customers to help them learn and help themselves
- Offers valid comparisons with competitive products

Building trust can be especially tricky in online settings, and firms often impose more stringent requirements on their online business partners than on others. Business buyers worry that they won't get products of the right quality delivered to the right place at the right time. Sellers worry about getting paid on time—or at all—and debate how much credit they should extend. Some firms, such as transportation and supply chain management company Ryder System, use automated credit-checking applications and online trust services to assess the creditworthiness of trading partners.

**Sources:** Kevin Lane Keller and David A. Aaker, "Corporate-Level Marketing: The Impact of Credibility on a Company's Brand Extensions," *Corporate Reputation Review* 1 (August 1998), pp. 356–78; Robert M. Morgan and Shelby D. Hunt, "The Commitment–Trust Theory of Relationship Marketing," *Journal of Marketing* 58, no. 3 (July 1994), pp. 20–38; Christine Moorman, Rohit Deshpande, and Gerald Zaltman, "Factors Affecting Trust in Market Research Relationships," *Journal of Marketing* 57 (January 1993), pp. 81–101; Glen Urban, "Where Are You Positioned on the Trust Dimensions?," *Don't Just Relate-Advocate: A Blueprint for Profit in the Era of Customer Power* (Upper Saddle River, NJ: Pearson Education/Wharton School Publishers, 2005).

4. *Customer supply*—In this traditional supply situation, competition rather than cooperation is the dominant form of governance.
5. *Cooperative systems*—The partners in cooperative systems are united in operational ways, but neither demonstrates structural commitment through legal means or adaptation.
6. *Collaborative*—In collaborative exchanges, much trust and commitment lead to true partnership.
7. *Mutually adaptive*—Buyers and sellers make many relationship-specific adaptations, but without necessarily achieving strong trust or cooperation.
8. *Customer is king*—In this close, cooperative relationship, the seller adapts to meet the customer's needs without expecting much adaptation or change in exchange.

Over time, however, relationship roles may shift or be activated under different circumstances.[67] Some needs can be satisfied with fairly basic supplier performance. Buyers then neither want nor require a close relationship with a supplier. Likewise, some suppliers may not find it worth their while to invest in customers with limited growth potential.

One study found the closest relationships between customers and suppliers arose when supply was important to the customer and there were procurement obstacles, such as complex purchase requirements and few alternate suppliers.[68] Another study suggested that greater vertical coordination between buyer and seller through information exchange and planning is usually necessary only when high environmental uncertainty exists and specific investments (described next) are modest.[69]

## RISKS AND OPPORTUNISM IN BUSINESS RELATIONSHIPS

Researchers have noted that establishing a customer–supplier relationship creates tension between safeguarding (ensuring predictable solutions) and adapting (allowing for flexibility for unanticipated events). Vertical coordination can facilitate stronger customer–seller ties but may also increase the risk to the customer's and supplier's specific investments.[70]

*Specific investments* are those expenditures tailored to a particular company and value chain partner (investments in company-specific training, equipment, and operating procedures or systems).[71] They help firms grow profits and achieve their positioning.[72] Xerox worked closely with its suppliers to develop customized processes and components that reduced its copier manufacturing costs by 30 percent to 40 percent. In return, suppliers received sales and volume guarantees, an enhanced understanding of their customer's needs, and a strong position with Xerox for future sales.[73]

Specific investments, however, also entail considerable risk to both customer and supplier. Transaction theory from economics maintains that because these investments are partially sunk, they lock firms into a particular relationship. Sensitive cost and process information may need to be exchanged. A buyer may be vulnerable to holdup because of switching costs; a supplier may be more vulnerable because it has dedicated assets and/or technology/knowledge at stake. In terms of the latter risk, consider the following example.[74]

> An automobile component manufacturer wins a contract to supply an under-hood component to an original equipment manufacturer (OEM). A one-year, sole-source contract safeguards the supplier's OEM-specific investments in a dedicated production line. However, the supplier may also be obliged to work (noncontractually) as a partner with the OEM's internal engineering staff, using linked computing facilities to exchange detailed engineering information and coordinate frequent design and manufacturing changes over the term of the contract. These interactions could reduce costs and/or increase quality by improving the firm's responsiveness to marketplace changes. But they could also magnify the threat to the supplier's intellectual property.

When buyers cannot easily monitor supplier performance, the supplier might shirk or cheat and not deliver the expected value. *Opportunism* is "some form of cheating or undersupply relative to an implicit or explicit contract."[75] When it was discovered in 2007 that a supplier to a supplier to a supplier to a supplier of Mattel chose to use lead-based ingredients outside Mattel's specification, the toy-makers reputation took a significant PR hit.

A more passive form of opportunism might be a refusal or unwillingness to adapt to changing circumstances or just negligence in satisfying contractual obligations. When a peanut-processing company, Peanut Corporation of America, with only $25 million in sales was found to have a contaminated product, a $1 billion recall resulted because the ingredient was found in 2,000 other products.[76]

Opportunism is a concern because firms must devote resources to control and monitoring that they could otherwise allocate to more productive purposes. Contracts may become inadequate to govern supplier transactions when supplier opportunism becomes difficult to detect, when firms make specific investments in assets they cannot use elsewhere, and when contingencies are harder to anticipate. Customers and suppliers are more likely to form a joint venture (instead of signing a simple contract) when the supplier's degree of asset specificity is high, monitoring the supplier's behavior is difficult, and the supplier has a poor reputation.[77] When a supplier has a good reputation, it is more likely to avoid opportunism to protect this valuable intangible asset.

The presence of a significant future time horizon and/or strong solidarity norms typically causes customers and suppliers to strive for joint benefits. Their specific investments shift from expropriation (increased opportunism on the receiver's part) to bonding (reduced opportunism).[78]

A firm like Mattel must carefully monitor its suppliers' behaviors to ensure they conform to company standards and values.

*Source: ASSOCIATED PRESS*

# Institutional and Government Markets

Our discussion has concentrated largely on the buying behavior of profit-seeking companies. Much of what we have said also applies to the buying practices of institutional and government organizations. However, we want to highlight certain special features of these markets.

The **institutional market** consists of schools, hospitals, nursing homes, prisons, and other institutions that must provide goods and services to people in their care. Many of these organizations are characterized by low budgets and captive clienteles. For example, hospitals must decide what quality of food to buy for patients. The buying objective here is not profit because the food is provided as part of the total service package; nor is cost minimization the sole objective because poor food will cause patients to complain and hurt the hospital's reputation. The hospital purchasing agent must search for institutional-food vendors whose quality meets or exceeds a certain minimum standard and whose prices are low. In fact, many food vendors set up a separate sales division to cater to institutional buyers' special needs and characteristics. Heinz produces, packages, and prices its ketchup differently to meet the requirements of hospitals, colleges, and prisons. ARAMARK, which provides food services for stadiums, arenas, campuses, businesses, and schools, also has a competitive advantage in providing food for the nation's prisons, a direct result of refining its purchasing practices and supply chain management.[79]

**ARAMARK** Where ARAMARK once merely selected products from lists provided by potential suppliers, it now collaborates with suppliers to develop products customized to meet the needs of individual segments. In the corrections segment, quality has historically been sacrificed to meet food cost limits that operators outside the market would find impossible to work with. "When you go after business in the corrections field, you are making bids that are measured in hundredths of a cent," says John Zillmer, president of ARAMARK's Food & Support Services, "so any edge we can gain on the purchasing side is extremely valuable." ARAMARK sourced a series of protein products with unique partners at price points it never could have imagined before. These partners were unique because they understood the chemistry of proteins and knew how to lower the price while still creating a product acceptable to ARAMARK's customers, allowing the company to drive down costs. Then ARAMARK replicated this process with 163 different items formulated exclusively for corrections. Rather than reducing food costs by 1 cent or so a meal as usual, ARAMARK took 5 to 9 cents off—while maintaining or even improving quality.

In most countries, government organizations are a major buyer of goods and services. They typically require suppliers to submit bids and often award the contract to the lowest bidder, sometimes making allowance for superior quality or a reputation for completing contracts on time. Governments will also buy on a negotiated-contract basis, primarily in complex projects with major R&D costs and risks and those where there is little competition.

A major complaint of multinationals operating in Europe is that each country shows favoritism toward its nationals despite superior offers from foreign firms. Although such practices are fairly entrenched, the European Union is attempting to remove this bias. Another challenge is the volatility of spending due to economic swings and cycles. When state governments suddenly cut back their spending, a firm like Cisco, which makes 22 percent of its sales to the public sector, is likely to feel the effects.[80] When the U.S. government announced a long-term cutback of hundreds of billions of dollars in defense spending in 2011—with more cuts anticipated—many defense contractors prepared to take signficant hits.[81]

Because their spending decisions are subject to public review, government organizations require considerable paperwork from suppliers, who often complain about bureaucracy, regulations, decision-making delays, and frequent shifts in procurement staff. But the fact remains that the U.S. government now spends more than $500 billion a year—or roughly 14 percent of the federal budget—on private-sector contractors, making it the largest and potentially the most attractive customer in the world.[82] Motorola Solutions, created when Motorola was split into two companies, sells wireless communications equipment to public-safety agencies around the world that need state-of-the-art communications networks for police cars in a multibillion-dollar government market.[83]

Not only the dollar figure is large; so is the number of individual buys. According to the General Services Administration Procurement Data Center, more than 20 million individual contract actions are processed every year. Although most items purchased cost between $2,500 and $25,000, the government also makes purchases in the billions, many in technology.

Government decision makers often think vendors have not done their homework. Different types of agencies—defense, civilian, intelligence—have different needs, priorities, purchasing styles, and time frames. In addition, vendors often do not pay enough attention to cost justification, a major activity for government procurement professionals. Companies hoping to be government contractors need to help government agencies see the bottom-line impact of products. Demonstrating useful experience and successful past performance through case studies, especially with other government organizations, can be influential.[84]

Just as companies provide government agencies with guidelines about how best to purchase and use their products, governments provide would-be suppliers with detailed guidelines describing how to sell to the government. Failure to follow the guidelines or to fill out forms and contracts correctly can create a legal nightmare.[85]

Fortunately for businesses of all sizes, the federal government has been trying to simplify the contracting procedure and make bidding more attractive. Reforms place more emphasis on buying off-the-shelf items instead of customizing, communicating with vendors online to eliminate paperwork, and debriefing losing vendors to improve their chances of winning the next time around.[86] More purchasing is being done online via Web-based forms, digital signatures, and electronic procurement cards (P-cards).

Several federal agencies that act as purchasing agents for the rest of the government have launched Web-based catalogs that allow authorized defense and civilian agencies to buy everything from medical and office supplies to clothing online. The General Services Administration, for example, not only sells stocked merchandise through its Web site but also creates direct links between buyers and contract suppliers. A good starting point for any work with the U.S. government is to make sure the company is in the Central Contractor Registration (CCR) database (www.ccr.gov), which collects, validates, stores, and disseminates data in support of agency acquisitions.[87]

Still, many companies that sell to the government have not used a marketing orientation, though some have established separate government marketing departments. Gateway, Rockwell, Kodak, and Goodyear anticipate government needs and projects, participate in the product specification phase, gather competitive intelligence, prepare bids carefully, and produce strong communications to describe and enhance their companies' reputations.

# Summary

1. Organizational buying is the decision-making process by which formal organizations establish the need for purchased products and services, then identify, evaluate, and choose among alternative brands and suppliers. The business market consists of all the organizations that acquire goods and services used in the production of other products or services that are sold, rented, or supplied to others.

2. Compared with consumer markets, business markets generally have fewer and larger buyers, a closer customer supplier relationship, and more geographically concentrated buyers. Demand in the business market is derived from demand in the consumer market and fluctuates with the business cycle. Nonetheless, the total demand for many business goods and services is quite price inelastic. Business marketers need to be aware of the role of professional purchasers and their influencers, the need for multiple sales calls, and the importance of direct purchasing, reciprocity, and leasing.

3. The buying center is the decision-making unit of a buying organization. It consists of initiators, users, influencers, deciders, approvers, buyers, and gatekeepers. To influence these parties, marketers must consider environmental, organizational, interpersonal, and individual factors.

4. The buying process consists of eight stages called buyphases: (1) problem recognition, (2) general need description, (3) product specification, (4) supplier search, (5) proposal solicitation, (6) supplier selection, (7) order-routine specification, and (8) performance review.

5. Business marketers are strengthening their brands and using technology and other communication tools to develop effective marketing programs. They are also using systems selling and adding services to provide customers added value.

6. Business marketers must form strong bonds and relationships with their customers. Some customers, however, may prefer a transactional relationship.

7. The institutional market consists of schools, hospitals, nursing homes, prisons, and other institutions that provide goods and services to people in their care. Buyers for government organizations tend to require a great deal of paperwork from their vendors and to favor open bidding and domestic companies. Suppliers must be prepared to adapt their offers to the special needs and procedures found in institutional and government markets.

MyMarketingLab

Go to mymktlab.com to complete the problems marked with this icon ⭐ as well as for additional Auto-graded and Assisted-graded writing questions.

# Applications

## Marketing Debate
### How Different Is Business-to-Business Marketing?

Some business-to-business marketing executives lament the challenges of business-to-business marketing, maintaining that many traditional marketing concepts and principles do not apply and that selling products and services to a company is fundamentally different from selling to individuals. Others disagree, claiming marketing theory is still valid and only requires some adaptation in marketing tactics.

**Take a position:** Business-to-business marketing requires a special, unique set of marketing concepts and principles *versus* Business-to-business marketing is really not that different, and the basic marketing concepts and principles apply.

## Marketing Discussion
### Applying B-to-C Concepts to B-to-B

⭐ Consider some of the consumer behavior topics for business-to-consumer (B-to-C) marketing from Chapter 6. How might you apply them to business-to-business (B-to-B) settings? For example, how might noncompensatory models of choice work? Mental accounting?

## Marketing Excellence

### >> Accenture

Accenture was launched as the Administrative Accounting Group in 1942 and was the consulting arm of accounting firm Arthur Andersen. In 1989, it became a separate business unit focused on IT consulting and bearing the name Andersen Consulting. At that time, though it was earning $1 billion annually, Andersen Consulting had low brand awareness among information technology consultancies and was commonly mistaken for its corporate parent. To build a strong brand and separate itself from the accounting firm, Andersen Consulting launched the first large-scale advertising campaign in the professional services area. By the end of the decade, it was the world's largest management and technology consulting organization.

In 2000, following arbitration against its former parent, Andersen Consulting was granted full independence from Arthur Andersen but had to relinquish the Andersen name. Andersen Consulting was given three months to find a name that could be trademarked in 47 countries, was effective and inoffensive in more than 200 languages, was acceptable to employees and clients, *and* corresponded with an available URL. The effort that followed was one of the largest and most successful rebranding campaigns in corporate history.

The company's new name came from one of the company's own consultants at its Oslo office. As part of an internal name-generation initiative dubbed "Brandstorming," he submitted the Accenture name because it rhymed with "adventure" and suggested an "accent on the future." The name also retained the "Ac" of the original Andersen Consulting name (echoing the Ac.com Web site), which would help the firm retain some of its former brand equity. At midnight on December 31, 2000, Andersen Consulting officially adopted the Accenture name and launched a global advertising, marketing, and communications campaign targeting senior executives at its clients and prospects, all partners and employees, the media, leading industry analysts, potential recruits, and academia.

The results were quick and impressive. Accenture's brand equity increased 11 percent the first year, and the number of firms that inquired about its services increased 350 percent. Awareness of the company's breadth and depth of services reached 96 percent of its previous level, and awareness of Accenture as a provider of management and technology consulting services already topped 76 percent of its previous level. These results enabled Accenture to successfully complete a $1.7 billion IPO in July 2001.

Accenture believed its differentiator was the ability both to provide innovative ideas—ideas grounded in business processes as well as IT—and to execute them. Competitors such as McKinsey were seen as highly specialized at developing strategy, whereas other competitors such as IBM were seen as highly skilled in technological implementation. Accenture wanted to be seen as excelling at both. As Ian Watmore, its UK chief, explained: "Unless you can provide both transformational consulting and outsourcing capability, you're not going to win. Clients expect both."

In 2002, Accenture unveiled a new positioning statement, which reflected its role as a partner that helped create strategies and execute them. The tagline "Innovation Delivered" was supported by the statement "From innovation to execution, Accenture helps accelerate your vision."

As part of its new commitment to helping clients achieve their business objectives, Accenture also introduced a policy whereby many of its contracts contained incentives that it realized only if specific business targets were met. For instance, a contract with British travel agent Thomas Cook was structured such that Accenture's bonus depended on five metrics, including a cost-cutting one.

In late 2003, Accenture built upon the "Innovation Delivered" theme and announced its new tagline, "High Performance. Delivered," along with a campaign that featured golf superstar Tiger Woods as spokesperson. When Accenture sought Woods as its spokesperson, the athlete was at the top of his game—the world's best golfer with an impeccable image and an ideal symbol of high performance. Accenture's message communicated that it could help client companies become "high-performing business leaders," and the Woods endorsement drove home the importance of high performance.

Over the next six years, Accenture spent nearly $300 million in ads that mostly featured Tiger Woods, alongside slogans such as "We know what it takes to be a Tiger" and "Go on. Be a Tiger." The campaign capitalized on Woods's international appeal, ran all over the world, and became the central focus of Accenture-sponsored events such as the World Golf Championships and the Chicago Marathon.

That all changed when the scandal surrounding Tiger Woods, his extramarital affairs, and his indefinite absence from golf hit the press in late 2009. Accenture dropped Woods as a spokesperson, saying he was no longer a good fit for its brand. Indeed, focus groups showed that consumers were too distracted by the scandal to focus on Accenture's strategic message. Accenture found itself in familiar territory and worked on developing and executing a groundbreaking campaign that not only resonated across the world and translated appropriately into different cultures but also elevated Accenture's brand to the next level.

In 2011, Accenture launched the "Greater Than" campaign to an international audience across 35 countries. The campaign highlighted successful case studies from clients like Unilever, Starwood Hotels, and Caterpillar and focused on Accenture's capabilities in areas such as emerging technologies and globalization. The company conducted extensive research to ensure that its brand positioning—"High performance. Delivered."—was not only effective but also still relevant to business leaders. Lastly, Accenture created a new marketing twist to the campaign. The "greater than" symbol, >, which had always appeared in the Accenture logo, was pulled out and used as a major element of the campaign. It appeared on cabs and billboards in major cities and became a critical unifying element across all Accenture's print, digital, and social media as well as among employees.

Today, Accenture continues to excel as a global management consulting, technology services, and outsourcing company. Its clients include 99 of the *Fortune* Global 100 and more than three-quarters of the *Fortune* Global 500. The company ended fiscal 2013 with revenues of $28.6 billion and has a brand value close to $9 billion.

### Questions

1. How does Accenture target its B-to-B audience so effectively?

2. Evaluate Accenture's history of branding campaigns. What remains consistent throughout?

**Sources:** Accenture.com, "Annual Reports," Accenture.com; "Lessons Learned from Top Firms' Marketing Blunders," *Management Consultant International*, December 2003, p. 1; Sean Callahan, "Tiger Tees Off in New Accenture Campaign," *BtoB Magazine*, October 13, 2003, p. 3; "Inside Accenture's Biggest UK Client," *Management Consultant International*, October 2003, pp. 1–3; "Accenture's Results Highlight Weakness of Consulting Market," *Management Consultant International*, October 2003, pp. 8–10; "Accenture Re-Branding Wins UK Plaudits," *Management Consultant International*, October 2002, p. 5; Mary Ellen Podmolik, "Accenture Turns to Tiger for Global Marketing Effort," *BtoB Magazine*, October 25, 2004; Sean Callahan, "Tiger Tees Off in New Accenture Campaign," *BtoB Magazine*, October 13, 2003; Emily Steel, "After Ditching Tiger, Accenture Tries New Game," *Wall Street Journal*, January 14, 2010; "Best Global Brands 2012," *Interbrand*.

## Marketing Excellence

### >> GE

Thomas Edison founded the Edison Electric Light Company in 1878. The company, which soon changed its name to General Electric (GE), became an early pioneer in lightbulbs and electrical appliances and served the electrical needs of various industries, such as transportation, utilities, manufacturing, and broadcasting. GE became the acknowledged pioneer in business-to-business marketing in the 1950s and 1960s under the tagline "Progress Is Our Most Important Product."

As the company diversified its business-to-business product lines in the 1970s and 1980s, it created new corporate campaigns, including "Progress for People" and "We Bring Good Things to Life." In 1981, Jack Welch succeeded Reginald Jones as GE's eighth CEO. During Welch's two decades of leadership, he helped grow GE from an "American manufacturer into a global services giant" and increased the company's market value from $12 billion in 1981 to $280 billion in 2001, making it the world's most valuable corporation at the time.

Over the years, GE has exhibited a keen understanding of the business market and the business buying process by putting itself in the shoes of its business customers. For example, the company understands that buying an aircraft engine is a multimillion-dollar expenditure that doesn't end with the purchase. Customers (the airlines) face substantial maintenance costs to meet FAA guidelines and ensure reliability of the engines. In 1999, GE pioneered a new pricing option called "Power by the Hour," giving customers an opportunity to pay a fixed fee each time they run the engine. In return, GE performs all the maintenance and guarantees the engine's reliability. When demand for air travel is uncertain, "Power by the Hour" provides GE's customers with a lower cost of ownership.

In 2003, GE and its new CEO, Jeffrey Immelt, faced a fresh challenge: how to promote its diversified brand with a unified global message. A source at GE explained, "(Immelt) wants advertising that's more high-tech, more innovative and contemporary. Something that will make GE look more advanced, out in front." So, after 24 years and $1 billion in financial support, GE dropped its signature slogan "We Bring Good Things to Life" for the new tagline "Imagination at Work," highlighting its renewed focus on innovation and new technology.

The award-winning new campaign promoted units such as GE Aircraft Engines, Medical Systems, and Plastics, focusing on the breadth of the company's product offerings, and it got results. "Research indicates GE is now being associated with attributes such as being high tech, leading edge, innovative, contemporary, and creative," stated Judy Hu, GE's general manager for global advertising and branding. In addition, survey respondents continued to associate GE with some of its traditional attributes, including trust and reliability.

In 2005, GE evolved the campaign into a company-wide initiative that continues today, "Ecomagination." Ecomagination highlighted the company's efforts to develop environmentally friendly "green" technologies such as solar energy, lower-emission engines, and water purification technologies. GE initially set several aggressive goals for the new initiative, including doubling the revenue from "Ecomagination" products to $20 billion in five years and promising to reduce greenhouse gas emissions by 1 percent within seven years. The company believed then and still believes that embracing innovation around Ecomagination is critical to its growth.

Immelt made some strategic restructuring decisions that helped the company survive the worldwide recession of 2008 and 2009 and also helped shift it even more in the B-to-B direction. GE moved from 11 divisions to five and sold off some of its consumer-focused businesses, including 51 percent of NBC Universal (sold to Comcast). This shift allowed the company to spend more resources on innovation, green initiatives, and its growing businesses such as power generation, aviation, medical imaging, and fuel cell technologies.

GE understood that it needed another huge initiative to help pull the conglomerate out of its current poor financial situation. Management believed there was huge growth potential in affordable health care around the world. As a result, the company embraced a $6 billion company-wide initiative called Healthymagination. The business strategy aimed at growing GE's health care business by providing innovative solutions to more people around the world, and the company launched an integrated marketing plan for it.

GE's B-to-B marketing savvy has helped it lock in the top position in the *Financial Times*'s "World's Most Respected Companies" ranking for years. The company's in-depth understanding of each of its business markets has kept its B-to-B marketing strategies progressive, relevant, and effective. In addition, its global marketing campaign helps keep brand equity strong. GE was ranked sixth in Interbrand/*BusinessWeek*'s "Top 100 Global Brands" report, with a brand value of $45 billion. "The GE brand is what connects us all and makes us so much better than the parts," Chief Marketing Officer Beth Comstock said.

Today, General Electric operates in a wide range of industries, including power and water, oil and gas, energy management, aviation, health care, transportation, home and business solutions, and capital. As a result, the firm sells a diverse array of products and services from home appliances to jet engines, security systems, wind turbines, and financial services. Its revenues topped $146 billion in 2013, making it so large that its largest business units could rank separately in the *Fortune* 200. If GE were a country, it would be the 50th largest in the world, ahead of Kuwait, New Zealand, and Iraq.

## Questions

1. Discuss GE's B-to-B marketing strategy. Why has the company been so successful over the years at targeting such a large business audience?

2. Have "Ecomagination" and "Healthymagination" successfully communicated GE's focus on its newer endeavors? Why or why not?

**Sources:** "A New Life. General Elective to Change Corporate Image," *Delaney Report*, June 10, 2002; Geoffrey Colvin, "What Makes GE Great?," *Fortune*, March 6, 2006, pp. 90–104; Thomas A. Stewart, "Growth as a Process," *Harvard Business Review*, June 2006, pp. 60–70; Kathryn Kranhold, "The Immelt Era, Five Years Old, Transforms GE," *Wall Street Journal*, September 11, 2006; Daniel Fisher, "GE Turns Green," *Forbes*, August 15, 2005, pp. 80– 85; John A. Byrne, "Jeff Immelt," *Fast Company*, July 2005, pp. 60–65; Rachel Layne, "GE's NBC Sale Brings Immelt Cash, Scrutiny," *BusinessWeek*, December 3, 2009; GE Annual Report, 2013.

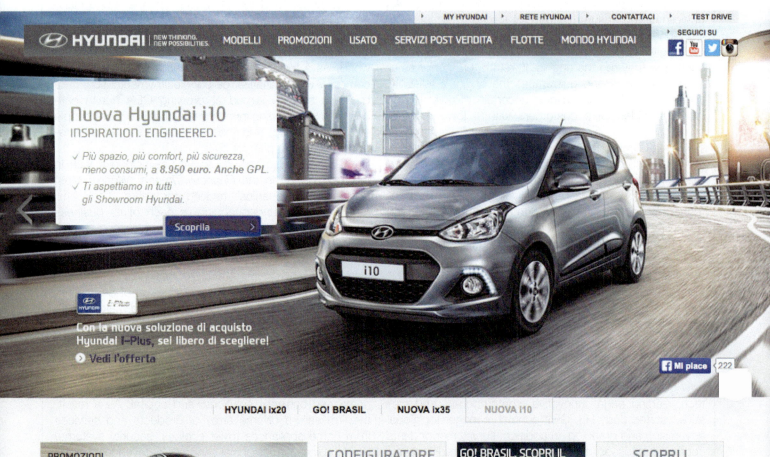

## In This Chapter, We Will Address the Following **Questions**

1. What factors should a company review before deciding to go abroad? (p. 217)

2. How can companies evaluate and select specific international markets to enter? (p. 219)

3. What are the differences between marketing in a developing and a developed market? (p. 220)

4. What are the major ways of entering a foreign market? (p. 226)

5. To what extent must the company adapt its products and marketing program to each foreign country? (p. 229)

6. How do marketers influence country-of-origin effects? (p. 238)

By skillfully combining quality, reliability, and style, Korean automaker Hyundai is finding success in markets all over the world.

Source: HYUNDAI MOTOR COMPANY. Andy Glass Wyatt-Clarke & Jones.

# 8 Tapping into Global Markets

**The world has dramatically shrunk in recent years. Countries are increasingly multicultural,** and products and services developed in one country are finding enthusiastic acceptance in others. A German businessman may wear an Italian suit to meet an English friend at a Japanese restaurant, who later returns home to drink Russian vodka and watch a U.S. movie on a Korean TV. Emerging markets that embrace capitalism and consumerism are especially attractive targets. Some marketers are finding success both in developing and developed markets. Consider the rapid ascent of Hyundai.[1]

*Once synonymous with cheap and unreliable cars, Hyundai Motor Company has experienced a massive global transformation. In 1999, its new chairman, Mong-Koo Chung, declared that Hyundai would focus not on volume and market share but on quality instead. The company began to benchmark industry leader Toyota, adopted Six Sigma processes, organized product development cross-functionally, partnered more closely with suppliers, and increased quality oversight meetings. From a place near the bottom of J. D. Power's study of U.S. new vehicle quality in 2001—32nd of 37 brands—Hyundai zoomed to number 4 by 2009, surpassed only by luxury brands Lexus, Porsche, and Cadillac. Hyundai also transformed its marketing. Its groundbreaking 10-year warranty sent a strong signal of reliability and quality, and more consumers began to appreciate the value its stylish cars had to offer. The U.S. market was not the only one receiving attention from Hyundai and its younger, more affordable brand sibling, Kia. Hyundai is the second-largest carmaker in India. In Europe, it invested in a $1.4 billion factory in the Czech Republic and a new $7.5 research center near a famed German racetrack, and its market share has surpassed Toyota's. A joint venture with Beijing Automotive is targeting China.*

**Although opportunities to compete** in international markets are significant, the risks can be high. Companies selling in global industries have no choice, however, but to internationalize their operations. In this chapter, we review the major decisions in expanding into global markets.

# Competing on a Global Basis

Some companies have long been successful global marketers—firms like Shell, Bayer, and Toshiba have sold around the world for years. In luxury goods such as jewelry, watches, and handbags, where the addressable market is relatively small, a global profile is essential for firms like Prada, Gucci, and Louis Vuitton to profitably grow. But global competition is intensifying in more product categories as new firms make their mark on the international stage.

In China's fast-moving mobile-phone market, Motorola found its once-promising share drop to the point where it was only the eighth-ranked competitor behind a slew of new entrants.[2] To better understand the Chinese market, Starwood's CEO and top management team even temporarily relocated to Shanghai for five weeks in 2011. Sixty percent of guests in their hotels in China were native Chinese, and the firm anticipated a wave of Chinese travelers going abroad.[3]

Competition from developing-market firms is also heating up. Founded in Guatemala, Pollo Campero (Spanish for "country chicken") has launched more than 50 stores in different parts of the United States—including three as far north as Massachusetts—blending old favorites such as fried plantains and milky *horchata* drinks with traditional U.S. fare such as grilled chicken and mashed potatoes.[4] Tata has created a marketing powerhouse in India and set its sights on other parts of the world.[5]

**TATA NANO** Tata Group, India's biggest conglomerate, is also its largest commercial vehicle maker. The company created a stir with the 2009 launch of its $2,500 Tata Nano, dubbed the "People's Car." Although impossibly low by Western standards, the Nano's price of 1 Indian lakh is three times India's annual per capita income. Looking somewhat like an egg on wheels, the Nano comfortably seats five while running a 33-horsepower engine that gets nearly 50 miles per gallon. Aiming to sell 250,000 units annually, Tata targeted the 7 million Indians who buy scooters and motorcycles every year, in part because they cannot afford a car. Huge market potential exists in the country, which has just seven automobiles per 1,000 people. Tata is also targeting other "bottom of the pyramid" markets such as Africa and Southeast Asia, and perhaps even parts of Eastern Europe and Latin America, as well as the U.S. market. Despite its positive features, the Nano got off to a rocky start in India due in part to the stigma attached to buying a "cheap" car. In a country where incomes have risen dramatically in recent years, some saw it as a glorified version of a tuk-tuk, the three-wheeled motorized rickshaw often seen on the streets of developing nations. Many low-income consumers decided to try to stretch their budgets to buy the Maruti-Suzuki Alto instead, with its bigger 800cc engine. On the other hand, some target customers who had never owned a car before were intimidated by Tata's glittering showrooms. After sales reached a low point in November 2012—only 3,500 cars sold against a target of 10,000—another makeover was announced—the third since launch in 2009, including a possible 800cc engine and a diesel option.

Although some U.S. businesses may want to eliminate foreign competition through protective legislation, the better way to compete is to continuously improve products at home and expand into foreign markets. In a **global industry,** competitors' strategic positions in major geographic or national markets are affected by their overall global positions.[6] A **global firm** operates in more than one country and captures R&D, production, logistical, marketing, and financial advantages not available to purely domestic competitors.

Global firms plan, operate, and coordinate their activities on a worldwide basis. Otis Elevator uses door systems from France, small geared parts from Spain, electronics from Germany, and motor drives from Japan; systems integration happens in the United States. Although some countries have erected entry barriers or regulations, the World Trade Organization, consisting of 160 countries, continues to press for more free trade in international services and other areas.[7] An interconnected world and global supply chains can have drawbacks, though, as the 2011 tsunami and earthquake in Japan vividly demonstrated.[8]

To sell overseas, many successful global U.S. brands have tapped into universal consumer values and needs—such as Nike with athletic performance, MTV with youth culture, and Coca-Cola with youthful optimism. These firms hire thousands of employees abroad and make sure their products and marketing activities are consistent with local sensibilities. Global marketing extends beyond products. Services represent the fastest-growing sector of the global economy and account for two-thirds of global output, one-third of global employment, and nearly 20 percent of global trade.

Tata is attacking automobile markets all over the world with its extraordinarily inexpensive Nano or "People's Car."

Source: © Neil McAllister/Alamy

For a company of any size or any type to go global, it must make a series of decisions (see Figure 8.1). We'll examine each of these decisions here.[9]

# Deciding Whether to Go Abroad

Most companies would prefer to remain domestic if their domestic market were large enough. Managers would not need to learn other languages and laws, deal with volatile currencies, face political and legal uncertainties, or redesign their products to suit different customer needs and expectations. Business would be easier and safer. Yet several factors can draw companies into the international arena:

- Some international markets present better profit opportunities than the domestic market.
- The company needs a larger customer base to achieve economies of scale.
- The company wants to reduce its dependence on any one market.
- The company decides to counterattack global competitors in their home markets.
- Customers are going abroad and require international service.

As cultures blend across countries, another benefit of global expansion is the ability to transfer ideas and products or services from one market into another market. Cinnabon discovered that products it developed for Central and South America were finding success in the United States, too, given its large Hispanic population.[10]

Reflecting the power of these forces, exports accounted for roughly 14 percent of U.S. GDP in 2013, more than double the figure 40 years ago.[11] Before making a decision to go abroad, the company must also weigh several risks:

- The company might not understand foreign preferences and could fail to offer a competitively attractive product.
- The company might not understand the foreign country's business culture.
- The company might underestimate foreign regulations and incur unexpected costs.
- The company might lack managers with international experience.
- The foreign country might change its commercial laws, devalue its currency, or undergo a political revolution and expropriate foreign property.

Some companies don't act until events thrust them into the international arena. The *internationalization process* typically has four stages:[12]

Stage 1: No regular export activities
Stage 2: Export via independent representatives (agents)
Stage 3: Establishment of one or more sales subsidiaries
Stage 4: Establishment of production facilities abroad

The first task is to move from stage 1 to stage 2. Most firms work with an independent agent and enter a nearby or similar country. Later, the firm establishes an export department to manage its agent relationships. Still later, it

**Deciding whether to go abroad**

⬇

**Deciding which markets to enter**

⬇

**Deciding how to enter the market**

⬇

**Deciding on the marketing program**

⬇

**Deciding on the marketing organization**

**|Fig. 8.1|**

Major Decisions in International Marketing

Source: Associated Press

Cinnabon found that some products developed for Central and South America found acceptance in the U.S. too.

replaces agents with its own sales subsidiaries in its larger export markets. This increases investment and risk but also earning potential. Next, to manage subsidiaries, the company replaces the export department with an international department or division. If markets are large and stable or the host country requires local production, the company will locate production facilities there.

By this time, the firm is operating as a multinational and optimizing its sourcing, financing, manufacturing, and marketing as a global organization. According to some researchers, top management begins to focus on global opportunities when more than 15 percent of revenue comes from international markets.[13]

# Deciding Which Markets to Enter

In deciding to go abroad, the company needs to define its marketing objectives and policies. What proportion of international to total sales will it seek? Most companies start small when they venture abroad. Some plan to stay small; others have bigger plans.

## HOW MANY MARKETS TO ENTER

The company must decide how many countries to enter and how fast to expand. Typical entry strategies are the *waterfall* approach, gradually entering countries in sequence, and the *sprinkler* approach, entering many countries simultaneously. Increasingly, firms—especially technology-intensive firms or online ventures—are *born global* and market to the entire world from the outset.[14]

Matsushita, BMW, General Electric, Benetton, and The Body Shop followed the waterfall approach. It allows firms to carefully plan expansion and is less likely to strain human and financial resources. When first-mover advantage is crucial and a high degree of competitive intensity prevails, the sprinkler approach is better. Microsoft sold more than 60 million licenses and upgrades of Windows 8 in the first 10 weeks after its October 26, 2012, global launch. Marketing spanned 42 countries with TV, print, and banner ads, outdoor posters, and branded entertainment. The main risk in the sprinkler approach is the substantial resources needed and the difficulty of planning entry strategies for many diverse markets.[15]

The company must also choose the countries to enter based on the product and on factors such as geography, income, population, and political climate. Competitive considerations come into play too. It may make sense to go into markets where competitors have already entered to force them to defend their market share as well as to learn from them how they are marketing in that environment.

A critical consideration without question is market growth. Getting a toehold in a fast-growing market can be a very attractive option even if that market is likely to soon be crowded with more competitors.[16] KFC has entered scores of countries as a pioneer by franchising its retail concept and making its marketing culturally relevant.[17]

**KFC**   KFC is the world's largest fast-food chicken chain, serving more than 12 million customers at more than 4,600 restaurants in the United States and more than 18,000 restaurants in 120 countries and territories around the world. The company is world famous for its Original Recipe fried chicken—made with the same secret blend of 11 herbs and spices Colonel Harland Sanders perfected more than a half-century ago. In China, KFC is the largest, oldest, most popular, and fastest-growing quick-service restaurant chain, with more than 4,260 locations in 850 towns or cities, often enjoying healthy margins of 20 percent per store. The company has tailored its menu in China to local tastes with items such as the Dragon Twister, a wrap stuffed with chicken strips, Peking duck sauce, cucumbers, and scallions. KFC even has a Chinese mascot—a kid-friendly character named Chicky, which the company boasts has become "the Ronald McDonald of China." Like any emerging market, China does pose challenges to KFC. Sales there took a stumble early in 2013 when state-owned Chinese media accused the company of using local suppliers that gave their chickens excessive antibiotics to stimulate faster growth. A social media firestorm followed, eventually causing KFC to apologize for not having tighter controls. Supply chain problems have posed a different challenge in Africa, KFC's next growth target. Without enough domestic supply of chickens, the company has to import them, but that is illegal in Nigeria and Kenya. To overcome the supply problem in Nigeria, it added fish to the menu. By 2013, KFC had more than 1,000 restaurants in 17 countries in Africa. As it moved into more and more African markets, the company made sure to localize its menu—selling Ugali, a type of porridge, in Kenya and jollof rice in Nigeria—and to showcase local culture on the walls and in the advertising.

KFC has become one of the world's biggest global brands by adapting its products appropriately and overcoming any local market obstacles.

Source: © Jeff Greenberg 5 of 6/Alamy

# EVALUATING POTENTIAL MARKETS

However much nations and regions integrate their trading policies and standards, each market still has unique features. Readiness for different products and services and attractiveness as a market depend on the market's demographic, economic, sociocultural, natural, technological, and political-legal environments.

How does a company choose among potential markets to enter? Many companies prefer to sell to neighboring countries because they understand them better and can control their entry costs more effectively. It's not surprising that the two largest U.S. export markets are Canada and Mexico or that Swedish companies first sold to their Scandinavian neighbors.

At other times, *psychic proximity* determines choices. Given more familiar language, laws, and culture, many U.S. firms prefer to sell in Canada, England, and Australia rather than in larger markets such as Germany and France. Companies should be careful, however, in choosing markets according to cultural distance. Besides overlooking potentially better markets, they may only superficially analyze real differences that put them at a disadvantage.[18]

It often makes sense to operate in fewer countries, with a deeper commitment and penetration in each. In general, a company prefers to enter countries that have high market attractiveness and low market risk and in which it possesses a competitive advantage. Digicel has a very unusual market expansion strategy, an interesting twist on those market-entry criteria.[19]

**DIGICEL** In its 11-year existence, Jamaica-based Digicel has conquered politically unstable developing countries such as Papua New Guinea, Haiti, and Tonga with mobile telecommunication products and services appealing to poor and typically overlooked consumers. The company strives for 100 percent population coverage with its networks, bringing affordable mobile service to local and rural residents who have never had the opportunity for coverage before and whose fierce loyalty helps protect Digicel from aggressive government interventions. It operates in 32 markets in the Caribbean, South Pacific, and Central and South America, serving 13 million customers. To be locally relevant, Digicel sponsors local cricket, rugby and other high-profile sports teams in each of these areas. Well-known champion Olympic sprinter Usain Bolt is the chief Digicel Brand Ambassador for various advertising and promotions across the region. The company also runs a host of community-based initiatives in each market through the educational, cultural, and social development programs of its Digicel Foundation. The company's marketing efforts in Fiji are instructive. Pitched in a fierce battle with incumbent Vodafone only two years after entry, Digicel Fiji even added a shade of light blue from the bottom of the Fiji national flag to its own red logo to reflect the company's pride in its contributions to Fijian life and sport, as reflected in its campaign, "Fiji Matters to Us."

# SUCCEEDING IN DEVELOPING MARKETS

One of the sharpest distinctions in global marketing is between developed and developing or emerging markets such as Brazil, Russia, India, China, and South Africa. These five countries have formed an

Digicel offers affordable mobile phone service and locally relevant marketing programs to overlooked consumers in developing markets.

association dubbed "BRICS" (for Brazil, Russia, India, China, and South Africa).[20] Another developing market with much economic and marketing significance is Indonesia. Some have begun grouping that country and South Africa with Columbia, Vietnam, Egypt, and Turkey, dubbing them CIVETS to raise their profile.[21] These markets offer many opportunities but also many challenges.

The unmet needs of the developing world represent huge potential markets for food, clothing, shelter, consumer electronics, appliances, and many other goods. Many market leaders are relying on developing markets to fuel their growth. Nestlé estimates about 1 billion consumers in emerging markets have increased their incomes enough to afford its products within the next decade. The world's largest food company now gets about 40 percent of its revenue from emerging markets. Developing markets make up more than 50 percent of Unilever's sales and 30 percent of Kraft's total business, as well as more than 40 percent of its newly spun-off snack business, Mondelēz.[22]

Developing markets account for about 82 percent of the world's population, and 90 percent of future population growth is projected to occur there.[23] Can marketers serve this huge population, which has much less purchasing power and lives in conditions ranging from mild deprivation to severe deficiency? Next we highlight some important developments in each of the BRICS countries and Indonesia.

**BRAZIL**[24]  Resource-rich Brazil is the biggest economy in Latin America and the sixth largest in the world. According to a study by Goldman Sachs, it will likely move into fourth place by 2050, meaning it would economically be larger than countries like Germany, Japan, and the United Kingdom. The 2014 World Cup in soccer and the 2016 Summer Olympics in Rio de Janeiro will put the world's spotlight on recent progress made by Brazil, though also highlighting some of the country's unease in huge investments in athletic events as opposed to addressing pressing domestic concerns such as education and infrastructure.

Brazil is also the fifth-largest country globally in terms of digital users, with about 91 million people online, making digital strategies attractive. Social media are especially popular. Firms are increasingly using mobile marketing, with a strong local flavor in their marketing communications.

Marketers are finding innovative ways to sell products and services to Brazil's poor and low-income residents. Nestlé Brazil boosted sales of Bono cookies 40 percent after shrinking the package from 200 to 140 grams and lowering the price. One Unilever Brasil marketing vice president noted:

> There are common themes that resonate well with Brazilians—family life, happiness, optimism, and pride at being from Brazil. Brazilians are natural optimists, and notoriously upbeat, and the way brands engage with them must reflect this.

Brazil experienced some "go-go" growth years in the 1960s and 1970s, when it was the world's second-fastest-growing large economy. As a result, it now boasts large and well-developed agricultural, mining, manufacturing, and service sectors.

Brazilian firms that have succeeded internationally include aircraft manufacturer Embraer, sandal maker Havaianas, and brewer and beverage producer AmBev, which merged with Interbrew to form InBev. Brazil also differs from other emerging markets in being a full-blown democracy, unlike Russia and China, and it has no serious disputes with neighbors, unlike India.

A number of obstacles exist, however, that are popularly called *custo Brasil* ("the cost of Brazil"). The cost of transporting products eats up nearly 13 percent of Brazil's GDP, five percentage points more than in the United States. Unloading a container is twice as expensive as in India and takes three times longer than in China. Strict and costly labor laws have inspired a massive underground economy that McKinsey estimated accounted for as much as 40 percent of Brazil's gross domestic product, taking about half of all urban jobs. Crime and corruption are still problems.

**RUSSIA**[25]  The 1991 splintering of the Soviet Union transformed Russia's isolated, centrally planned economy into a globally integrated, market-based economy. Russia is the largest exporter of natural gas, the second-largest exporter of oil, and the third-largest exporter of steel and primary aluminum. Reliance on commodities has its downside, however. The country's economy was hammered in the recent recession by plunging commodity prices and the credit crunch.

Russians make heavy use of social media, spending an average of 9.8 hours per visitor on a monthly basis, twice the world average, though Facebook has lagged behind local competitors. The company is engaging Russian developers of apps, games, and similar tools to provide more local content.

Russia has a dwindling workforce and poor infrastructure. The Organization for Economic Cooperation & Development (OECD) cautions that economic reforms have stagnated and ranks Russia as one of the most corrupt countries in the world. Many feel the government of Vladimir Putin has been unpredictable and difficult to work with.

For these and other reasons, market entry can be daunting. To distribute in Russia, Cyclo Industries, a U.S. manufacturer of chemicals for the automotive industry, had to translate its labeling, determine how to competitively price its products, and develop specialized marketing plans. Logistical problems caused one of the company's marketers to note, "The roads are just terrible and there's no way to get from one part of Russia to another." Although it took the company more than a year to even establish a presence there, within six months the Russian market was contributing 10 percent of Cyclo's revenue.

**INDIA**[26] India's transformation over a generation has been staggering. Reforms in the early 1990s lowered trade barriers and liberalized capital markets, bringing booming investment and consumption. India boasts a lively democracy and a youthful population. The world's second most populous nation with 1.21 billion people, it is also one of the youngest large economies, with a median age of 25. In fact, one-quarter of the entire world's under-25 population lives in India.

A strong economy has been matched by progress in literacy and access to financial services and modern technology. India has fully embraced mobile technology; mobile phone density is approximately 75 percent of the population, of whom around 15 percent use their mobile devices to go online. Enjoying some of the lowest prices anywhere, one-third of Indian mobile subscribers live in rural areas.

India's ascent opens a larger market for U.S. and Western goods. About 16 million, or 3 percent, of Indian consumers are high-earning targets of youth lifestyle brands connoting status and affluence, like luxury cars and shiny motorbikes, followed by clothing, food, entertainment, consumer durables, and travel. Opportunities abound for firms of all types. Indians drank an average of only 14 eight-ounce bottles of Coke in 2012, compared with an average of 241 bottles in Brazil and 745 bottles in Mexico, leading Coca-Cola to announce a $5 billion investment over 2012–2020.

As the seventh-largest country in size, however, India has important regional differences. Its 28 separate states each have their own policies and tax rules, 23 official languages, 1,500 dialects, and a multitude of faiths. Areas around Mumbai and Bangalore are richer and more highly literate, while poorer, less educated states lie in the east. Even the weather is significant to marketers. Cool winters in the north create dry skin conditions, in stark contrast to the humid climates of Mumbai and Chennai.

Some Indian firms—such as Mittal, Reliance Group, Tata, Wipro, Infosys, and Mahindra—have achieved international success. Reliance touches the life of one in 10 Indians every day, and its worldwide customer base numbers 100 million.

For all its opportunities, India struggles with poor infrastructure and public services—education, health, and water supply—and restrictive labor laws. The national government in New Delhi vows to spend $1 trillion on infrastructure over five years, although, as in many emerging markets, corruption remains a huge problem at virtually all levels of government. A complicated retail network has been slow to modernize, leading to distribution problems.

**CHINA**[27] China's 1.34 billion people have marketers scrambling to gain a foothold, and competition has heated up between domestic and international firms. Its 2001 entry into the World Trade Organization (WTO) eased China's manufacturing and investment rules and modernized retail and logistics industries. Greater competition in pricing, products, and channels resulted, though some industries remained fiercely protected or off-limits to foreigners altogether.

Foreign businesses complain about subsidized competition, restricted access, conflicting regulations, opaque and seemingly arbitrary bureaucracy, and lack of protection for intellectual property; 90 percent of PC software is reportedly pirated in China. The Chinese government encourages partnerships with foreign companies, in part so that its firms can learn enough to become global powerhouses themselves.

Nevertheless, opportunities exist. Although China is Nestlé's ninth-biggest market, the company sells half what it does in Brazil, despite China's having seven times the population. While it's the largest auto market in the world, at 60 vehicles per 1,000 people, China lags in car ownership at half the world average. PepsiCo has big plans for its food and beverage brands knowing that consumption of potato chips in China is around one small bag every two to four weeks, compared with 15 bags in the United States, and that the average Chinese buys a beverage 230 times per year while the average U.S. consumer buys 1,500.

Selling in China means going beyond the big cities to the second- and third-tier cities, as well as to the 700 million potential consumers in small communities in the rural interior. Chengdu and Chongqing are two second-tier economic powerhouses in western China and experiencing much growth. Rural consumers can be challenging; they have lower incomes (the income ratio between China's coastal cities and rural interior is six to one), are less sophisticated, and often cling to local habits. China is also ethnically diverse—the banknote features eight languages, including Arabic, Mongolian, and Tibetan.

China's emerging urban middle class is active and discerning, demanding higher-quality products and variety. Although they number four times the U.S. population, Chinese consumers spend a fraction of what U.S. consumers do. China is now the world's top consumer of luxury consumer goods, with many Chinese consumers viewing these as trophies of success. Luxury cars are the fastest-growing auto segment thanks to the swelling ranks of Chinese millionaires. Burberry's sales in China now almost match those in Europe as a whole.

Competition among foreign firms is fierce as they attempt to get the upper hand in the fast-growing market. Walmart contends with Carrefour, General Motors fights Volkswagen, and Nike battles Adidas. In competing with local firms, many Western companies benefit from their reputation of quality, safety, and dependability with Chinese consumers, who have seen numerous scandals from their domestic companies. At the same time, Western companies need to be locally relevant. Starbucks has a localized menu of beverages particularly tailored for Chinese consumers—including a unique "East meets West" blend—from which local stores can choose.

**SOUTH AFRICA**[28]   Although South Africa is a developed market, we include it here not only as an important market in its own right but also for its role as an access point to the African region; many international companies are using it as a launch pad for African expansion. The 2010 World Cup in soccer offered a chance to reexamine economic progress in South Africa and other African countries.

Africa has experienced much change in recent years. Although political turmoil in Egypt, Tunisia, and Libya during the "Arab Spring" is a reminder of the instability that has plagued the continent and logistical and infrastructure problems prevail, improvements in many other areas such as health, education, and social services paint a rosier picture of the continent's future, as do economic forecasts. McKinsey Global Institute estimates the number of African households with discretionary income—money available to spend on items other than food—is expected to increase by a robust 50 percent to 128 million people by 2020.

Additional McKinsey research shows that many African consumers seek high-quality products and are brand conscious, "belying the view that the continent is a backwater where companies can sell second-rate merchandise." Unilever is finding success by tailoring products for African customers: affordable food, water-conserving washing powders, and grooming products to fit local tastes. Its best-selling Motions range of shampoos and conditioners were made especially for African hair and black skin.

Some firms have worked for years to develop their African business. General Motors now sells in more than 50 African countries and has manufacturing facilities in South Africa, Egypt, and Kenya. Like any other continent, Africa is highly heterogeneous, and some experts emphasize that it should be seen as 53 separate and often very different countries. The Boston Consulting Group has dubbed eight of Africa's strongest economies the "African Lions": Algeria, Botswana, Egypt, Libya, Mauritius, Morocco, South Africa, and Tunisia. Nestlé is especially bullish on Kenya, Ethiopia, Mozambique, Angola, and the Democratic Republic of the Congo.

Although agriculture is the largest economic sector, telecommunications, energy, consumer products, and health care are experiencing the fastest growth. More than 650 million Africans had mobile phones by the end of 2011; more than 300 million of them are new subscribers since 2000. Mobile phones are used not just for talking but also as a platform to support daily living, playing a crucial role in health care and banking, for example, where extensive infrastructure does not exist. Two-thirds of adults used a mobile money service, with Vodafone and MTN leading the way. The Internet is playing an increasingly important marketing role in Africa, often accessed by mobile phones.

**INDONESIA**[29]   Indonesia's reputation as a country historically struggling with natural disasters, terrorism, and economic uncertainty is quickly being replaced by a profile of political stability and economic growth. The fourth-largest country in the world and the largest Muslim country, given all its progress, Indonesia strikes many as ready to join the BRICS countries.

It has become the third-fastest-growing economy in the region—behind India and China—largely on the basis of its 240 million consumers. By 2030, forecasts expect the number of middle-class Indonesians—those making between $2 and $20 per day—to increase from 131 million to 244 million and those in the "consumer class"—who make more than $3,600 per year—to increase from 45 million to 135 million. Marketers have found Indonesian consumers to be very brand conscious, an important preference given their rising incomes.

An archipelago with more than 14,000 islands in a hot and humid climate, Indonesia does present challenges. Effective, efficient distribution is critical. Large importers have established distribution networks that allow them to reach beyond the one-third of the population living in the six or seven largest cities, but as in many developing countries, infrastructure can be lacking.

Recent progress is noteworthy, however. Indonesia is L'Oréal's fastest-growing market in Asia-Pacific, leading the firm to build a plant there. IKEA has made a recent entry. With more than 20 percent of its Internet users having a Twitter account, Indonesia is the fifth-most active country on the microblogging site.

**MARKETING STRATEGIES FOR DEVELOPING MARKETS** Successfully entering developing markets requires a special set of skills and plans and an ability to do a number of things differently and well.[30] Consider how these companies pioneered ways to serve "invisible" consumers in these markets:[31]

- Grameenphone marketed cell phones to 35,000 villages in Bangladesh by hiring village women as agents who leased phone time to other villagers, one call at a time.
- Colgate-Palmolive rolled into Indian villages with video vans that showed the benefits of toothbrushing.
- Corporación GEO builds low-income housing in Mexico, featuring two-bedroom homes that are modular and expandable.

These marketers capitalized on the potential of developing markets by changing their conventional marketing practices. Selling in developing areas can't be "business as usual." Economic and cultural differences abound, a marketing infrastructure may barely exist, and local competition can be surprisingly stiff.[32]

Many companies are tapping into the growing middle class in developing markets. Boston Consulting Group estimates there will be nearly a billion middle-class Chinese and Indians by 2020.[33] Many will have aspirations that include the purchase of premium products and global brands.[34]

For example, when Unilever introduced TRESemmé in Brazil, it secured the support of 40 big retailers, courted fashion bloggers, distributed 10 million free samples, and launched the company's biggest-ever single-day online ad blitz, which eventually lured 1 million fans to the brand's Brazilian Facebook page. In under a year, sales of TRESemmé surpassed those of P&G shampoo stalwart Pantene in hypermarkets and drugstores, giving Unilever confidence to set its sights on India and Indonesia next.[35]

Because the needed marketing practices are more similar to those employed in developing markets, it is typically much easier to tap into the middle class in developing markets than to reach the 4 billion people at the "bottom of the pyramid." Although they may collectively be worth $3 trillion, each individual low-income consumer may have very little to spend.

Satisfying the bottom of the pyramid also requires careful planning and execution. Conventional wisdom says a "low price, low margin, high volume" business model is the key to successfully appealing to lower-income markets in developing markets. Although there are some good examples of such a strategy—Hindustan Unilever with Wheel detergent in India, for one—others have struggled. Procter & Gamble launched its Pur water-purification product in India, and although priced at only 10 cents a sachet, the product yielded a 50 percent margin. But after disappointing overall results, the company transitioned the brand to a philanthropic venture.[36]

Marketers are learning the nuances in marketing to a broader population in emerging markets, especially when cost reductions are difficult to realize because of the firm's established supply chain and when production methods and distribution strategy and price premiums are hard to command because of consumer price sensitivity.

Getting the marketing equation right in developing markets can pay big dividends:

- Smaller packaging and lower prices are often critical when income and space are limited. Unilever's four-cent sachets of detergent and shampoo were a big hit in rural India, where 70 percent of the population still lives.[37]
- The vast majority of consumers in emerging markets buy their products from tiny bodegas, stalls, kiosks, and mom-and-pop stores not much bigger than a closet, which Procter & Gamble calls "high-frequency stores." In India, food is largely purchased from the 12 million neighborhood mom-and-pop outfits called kirana stores. These thrive by offering convenience, credit, and even home delivery, though modern retailing is beginning to make inroads.[38]
- Nokia sent marketing, sales, and engineering staff from its entry-level phone group to spend a week in people's homes in rural China, Thailand, and Kenya to observe how they used phones. By developing rock-bottom-priced phones with just the right functionality, Nokia has retained market-share leadership in some parts of Africa and Asia despite being surpassed by other brands in parts of the developed world.[39]

Digital strategies will be crucial in developing markets given the rapid penetration of smart phones as more than a means of communication. One research study showed that social media is six times more important for brands in developing markets such as Indonesia and Thailand than it is in Japan or the United Kingdom. [40]

In India, millions of consumers buy their food from the ubiquitous kirana or "mom & pop" shops.

Source: © imageBROKER/Alamy

**DEVELOPING AND DEVELOPED MARKETS** Competition is also growing from companies based in developing markets. Wipro of India, Cemex of Mexico, HTC from Taiwan, and Petronas of Malaysia have emerged from developing markets to become strong multinationals selling in many countries. Often the key is to both develop a global business model and build a global brand that will effectively work in all the targeted markets.[41]

One strategy successfully employed by some companies from emerging markets is to identify neglected niches in larger markets.[42] Mahindra has been selling U.S. farmers small tractors from its three U.S. assembly plants for more than 20 years. It has used its expertise in manufacturing small tractors to also expand into niche markets for lawn care and golf course maintenance.

Another strategy for going global is to acquire one or more firms in developed markets. India's Apollo Tyres acquired businesses in the Netherlands and South Africa. After Lenovo bought IBM's PC business for $1.25 billion in 2005, many other Chinese firms began to look overseas for possible acquisitions, leading one pundit to declare that the well-known phrase "Made in China" would soon be replaced by "Owned by China."[43]

On the other hand, many firms from developed markets are using lessons gleaned from developing markets to better compete in their home or existing markets (recall the "bottom of the pyramid" discussion from Chapter 3). Product innovation has become a two-way street between developing and developed markets. The challenge is to think creatively about how marketing can fulfill the dreams of most of the world's population for a better standard of living.[44]

Many companies are betting they can do that. To feed a projected world population of 9 billion by 2050, analysts estimate that food production globally must increase by 60 percent, a challenge John Deere is addressing.[45]

---

**JOHN DEERE** John Deere's new 8R line was the first tractor line designed to accommodate the needs of different farmers in 130 countries worldwide. The 8R is powerful but agile and fuel-efficient, best suited for larger farms. But it is highly customizable to suit the needs of growers in developing markets like Brazil and Russia as much as the developed markets of the United States or Germany. From March 2011 to March 2012, customers ordered more than 7,800 different configurations of the 8R tractor. Deere has nine factories outside the United States in both developed and developing markets, including Germany, India, China, Mexico, and Brazil.

---

Regional economic integration—the creation of trading agreements between blocs of countries—has intensified in recent years. This means companies are more likely to enter entire regions at the same time. Certain countries have formed free trade zones or economic communities—groups of nations organized to work toward common goals in the regulation of international trade.

**Commitment, Risk, Control, and Profit Potential**

Direct investment

↑

Joint ventures

↑

Licensing

↑

Direct exporting

↑

Indirect exporting

| **Fig. 8.2** |

Five Modes of Entry into Foreign Markets

# Deciding How to Enter the Market

Once a company decides to target a particular country, it must choose the best mode of entry with its brands. Its broad choices are *indirect exporting*, *direct exporting*, *licensing*, *joint ventures*, and *direct investment*, shown in Figure 8.2. Each succeeding strategy entails more commitment, risk, control, and profit potential.

# INDIRECT AND DIRECT EXPORT

Companies typically start with export, specifically *indirect exporting*—that is, they work through independent intermediaries. *Domestic-based export merchants* buy the manufacturer's products and then sell them abroad. *Domestic-based export agents,* including trading companies, seek and negotiate foreign purchases for a commission. *Cooperative organizations* conduct exporting activities for several producers—often of primary products such as fruits or nuts—and are partly under their administrative control. *Export-management companies* agree to manage a company's export activities for a fee.

Indirect export has two advantages. First, there is less investment: The firm doesn't have to develop an export department, an overseas sales force, or a set of international contacts. Second, there's less risk: Because international marketing intermediaries bring know-how and services to the relationship, the seller will make fewer mistakes.

Companies may eventually decide to handle their own exports. The investment and risk are somewhat greater, but so is the potential return. Direct exporting happens in several ways:

- **Domestic-based export department or division.** A purely service function may evolve into a self-contained export department operating as its own profit center.
- **Overseas sales branch or subsidiary.** The sales branch handles sales and distribution and perhaps warehousing and promotion as well. It often serves as a display and customer service center.
- **Traveling export sales representatives.** Home-based sales representatives travel abroad to find business.
- **Foreign-based distributors or agents.** These third parties can hold limited or exclusive rights to represent the company in that country.

Many companies use direct or indirect exporting to "test the waters" before building a plant and manufacturing their product overseas. A company does not necessarily have to attend international trade shows if it can effectively use the Internet to attract new customers overseas, support existing customers who live abroad, source from international suppliers, and build global brand awareness.

Successful companies adapt their Web sites to provide country-specific content and services to their highest-potential international markets, ideally in the local language. Finding free information about trade and exporting has never been easier. Here are some places to start a search:

| | |
|---|---|
| www.trade.gov | U.S. Department of Commerce's International Trade Administration |
| www.exim.gov | Export-Import Bank of the United States |
| www.sba.gov | U.S. Small Business Administration |
| www.bis.doc.gov | Bureau of Industry and Security, a branch of the Commerce Department |

Many states' export-promotion offices also have online resources and allow businesses to link to their sites.

# LICENSING

Licensing is a simple way to engage in international marketing. The licensor issues a license to a foreign company to use a manufacturing process, trademark, patent, trade secret, or other item of value for a fee or royalty. The licensor gains entry at little risk; the licensee gains production expertise or a well-known product or brand name.

The licensor, however, has less control over the licensee than over its own production and sales facilities. If the licensee is very successful, the firm has given up profits, and if and when the contract ends, it might find it has created a competitor. To prevent this, the licensor usually supplies some proprietary product ingredients or components (as Coca-Cola does). But the best strategy is to lead in innovation so the licensee will continue to depend on the licensor.

Licensing arrangements vary. Companies such as Hyatt and Marriott sell *management contracts* to owners of foreign hotels to manage these businesses for a fee. The management firm may have the option to purchase some share in the managed company within a stated period.

In *contract manufacturing,* the firm hires local manufacturers to produce the product. Volkswagen has a contract agreement with the GAZ Group through 2019, whereby GAZ will build the Volkswagen Jetta, Skoda Octavia, and Skoda Yeti models in Nizhny Novgorod for the Russian market, with planned production volume of 110,000 vehicles per year.[46] Toshiba, Hitachi, and other Japanese television manufacturers use contract manufacturing to service the Eastern European market.[47]

Source: © Tupungato /Shutterstock

Companies such as Best Western have used franchise arrangements to cost-effectively enter markets all over the world.

Contract manufacturing reduces the company's control over the process and risks loss of potential profits. However, it offers a chance to start faster, with the opportunity to partner with or buy out the local manufacturer later.

Finally, a company can enter a foreign market through *franchising,* a more complete form of licensing. The franchisor offers a complete brand concept and operating system. In return, the franchisee invests in and pays certain fees to the franchisor. Quick-service operators like McDonald's, Subway, and Burger King have franchised all over the world, as have service and retail companies such as 7-Eleven, Hertz, and Best Western Hotels.[48]

## JOINT VENTURES

Historically, foreign investors have often joined local investors in a **joint venture** company in which they share ownership and control. To reach more geographic and technological markets and to diversify its investments and risk, GE Capital—GE's retail lending arm—views joint ventures as one of its "most powerful strategic tools." It has formed joint ventures with financial institutions in South Korea, Spain, Turkey, and elsewhere.[49] Emerging markets, especially large, complex countries such as China and India, see much joint venture action.

A joint venture may be necessary or desirable for economic or political reasons. The foreign firm might lack the financial, physical, or managerial resources to undertake the venture alone, or the foreign government might require joint ownership as a condition for entry. Joint ownership has drawbacks. The partners might disagree over investment, marketing, or other policies. One might want to reinvest earnings for growth, the other to declare more dividends. Joint ownership can also prevent a multinational company from carrying out specific manufacturing and marketing policies on a worldwide basis.

The value of a partnership can extend far beyond increased sales or access to distribution. Good partners share "brand values" that help maintain brand consistency across markets. For example, McDonald's fierce commitment to product and service standardization is one reason its retail outlets are so similar around the world. McDonald's handpicks its global partners one by one to find "compulsive achievers" who will put forth the desired effort.

## DIRECT INVESTMENT

The ultimate form of foreign involvement is direct ownership: The foreign company can buy part or full interest in a local company or build its own manufacturing or service facilities. Cisco had no presence in India before 2005, but it has already opened a second headquarters in Bangalore to take advantage of opportunities in India and other locations such as Dubai.[50]

If the market is large enough, direct investment offers distinct advantages. First, the firm secures cost economies through cheaper labor or raw materials, government incentives, and freight savings. Second, the firm strengthens its image in the host country because it creates jobs. Third, the firm deepens its relationship with the government, customers, local suppliers, and distributors, enabling it to better adapt its products to the local environment. Fourth, the firm retains full control over its investment and can develop manufacturing and marketing policies that serve its long-term international objectives. Fifth, the firm ensures its access to the market in case the host country insists that locally purchased goods must have domestic content.

The main disadvantage of direct investment is that the firm exposes a large investment to risks like blocked or devalued currencies, worsening markets, or expropriation. If the host country requires high severance pay for local employees, reducing or closing operations can be expensive.

## ACQUISITION

Rather than bringing their brands into certain countries, many companies choose to acquire local brands for their brand portfolio. Strong local brands can tap into consumer sentiment in a way international brands may find difficult. A good example of a company assembling a collection of "local jewels" is SABMiller.[51]

**SABMILLER** From its isolated origins as the dominant brewery in South Africa, SABMiller now has a presence in 75 different countries all over the world, thanks to a series of acquisitions including its 2002 purchase of Miller Brewing in the United States for $5.6 billion. The company is the world's second-largest beer maker, producing such well-known brands as Grolsch, Miller Lite, Peroni, Pilsner Urquell, South Africa's Castle Lager, and Australia's Victoria Bitter. Its global strategy, however, is in stark contrast to that of its main competitor. Anheuser-Busch InBev's strategy with Budweiser is to sell the brand all over the world, positioned as "The American Dream in a Bottle." SABMiller calls itself "the most local of global brewers" and believes the key to global success is pushing local brands that appeal to a home country's customs, attitudes, and traditions. The company relies on sociologists, anthropologists, and historians to find the right way to create "local intimacy" and also employs 10 analysts whose sole responsibility is segmentation research in different markets. Peru's Cusquena brand "pays tribute to the elite standard of Inca craftsmanship." Romania's Timisoreana brand taps into its own 18th-century roots. In Ghana and other parts of Africa, cloudy Chibuku beer is priced at only 58¢ a liter to compete with home brews. When research revealed that many beer drinkers in Poland felt "no one takes us seriously," SABMiller launched a campaign for its Tyskie brand featuring foreigners lauding the brew and the Polish people.

# Deciding on the Marketing Program

International companies must decide how much to adapt their marketing strategy to local conditions.[52] At one extreme is a *standardized marketing program* worldwide, which promises the lowest costs; Table 8.1 summarizes some pros and cons. At the other extreme is an *adapted marketing program* in which the company, consistent with the marketing concept, believes consumer needs vary and tailors marketing to each target group. A good example of the latter strategy is Oreo cookies.[53]

| TABLE 8.1 | Globally Standardized Marketing Pros and Cons |
|---|---|
| **Advantages** | |
| Economies of scale in production and distribution | |
| Lower marketing costs | |
| Power and scope | |
| Consistency in brand image | |
| Ability to leverage good ideas quickly and efficiently | |
| Uniformity of marketing practices | |
| **Disadvantages** | |
| Ignores differences in consumer needs, wants, and usage patterns for products | |
| Ignores differences in consumer response to marketing programs and activities | |
| Ignores differences in brand and product development and the competitive environment | |
| Ignores differences in the legal environment | |
| Ignores differences in marketing institutions | |
| Ignores differences in administrative procedures | |

SABMiller has assembled a diverse portfolio of iconic local beer brands from all over the world.

Source: Associated Press

**OREO**  In launching its Oreo brand of cookies worldwide, Kraft chose to adopt a consistent global positioning, "Milk's Favorite Cookie." Although not necessarily highly relevant in all countries, it did reinforce generally desirable associations like nurturing, caring, and health. To help ensure global understanding, Kraft created a brand book with a CD in an Oreo-shaped box that summarized brand management fundamentals—what needed to be common across countries, what could be changed, and what could not. At first, Kraft tried to sell the U.S. Oreo everywhere. When research showed cultural differences in taste preferences—Chinese found the cookies too sweet whereas Indians found them too bitter—new formulas were introduced across markets. In China, the cookie was made less sweet and with different fillings, such as green tea ice cream, grape–peach, mango–orange, and raspberry–strawberry. Indonesia has a chocolate-and-peanut variety; Argentina has banana and dulce de leche varieties. In an example of reverse innovation, Kraft successfully introduced some of these new flavors into other countries. The company also tailors its marketing efforts to better connect with local consumers. One Chinese commercial has a child showing China's first NBA star Yao Ming how to dunk an Oreo cookie.

## GLOBAL SIMILARITIES AND DIFFERENCES

The vast penetration of the Internet, the spread of cable and satellite TV, and the global linking of telecommunications networks have led to a convergence of lifestyles. Increasingly shared needs and wants have created global markets for more standardized products, particularly among the young middle class. Once the butt of jokes like "Why do you need a rear-window defroster on a Skoda? To keep your hands warm when pushing it," the Czech carmaker Skoda was acquired by VW, which invested to upgrade quality and image and offer an affordable option to lower-income consumers worldwide.[54]

At the same time, consumers can still vary in significant ways.[55]

- The median age is only about 26 or 27 in India and Mexico and 35 in China but about 43 to 45 in Japan, Germany, and Italy.[56]
- Doughnuts don't appeal to British consumers for breakfast, while Kenyans need to be convinced that cereal is a good option.[57]
- When asked whether they are more concerned with getting a specific brand rather than the best price, roughly two-thirds of U.S. consumers agreed, compared with about 80 percent in Russia and India.[58]
- The percentage of the population online varies wildly across countries: United Kingdom (85 percent), Japan (80 percent), United States (79 percent), Brazil (40 percent), China (34 percent), and India (7.5 percent). U.S. Internet users spend an average of 32 hours per month, compared with 16 hours globally.[59]

Consumer behavior may reflect cultural differences that can be pronounced across countries.[60] Hofstede identifies four cultural dimensions that differentiate countries:[61]

1. **Individualism versus collectivism**—In collectivist societies, the self-worth of an individual is rooted more in the social system than in individual achievement (high collectivism: Japan; low: United States).
2. **High versus low power distance**—High power distance cultures tend to be less egalitarian (high: Russia; low: Nordic countries).

3. *Masculine versus feminine*—This dimension measures how much the culture reflects assertive characteristics more often attributed to males versus nurturing characteristics more often attributed to females (highly masculine: Japan; low: Nordic countries).

4. *Weak versus strong uncertainty avoidance*—Uncertainty avoidance indicates how risk-aversive people are (high avoidance: Greece; low: Jamaica).

Consumer behavior differences as well as historical market factors have led marketers to position brands differently in different markets.

- Heineken beer is a high-end super-premium offering in the United States but more middle-of-the-road in its Dutch home market.
- Honda automobiles denote speed, youth, and energy in Japan and quality and reliability in the United States.
- The Toyota Camry is the quintessential middle-class car in the United States but is at the high end in China, though in the two markets the cars differ only in cosmetic ways.

## MARKETING ADAPTATION

Because of all these differences, most products require at least some adaptation.[62] Even Coca-Cola is sweeter or less carbonated in certain countries. Rather than assuming it can introduce its domestic product "as is" in another country, a company should review the following elements and determine which add more revenue than cost if adapted:

- Product features
- Labeling
- Colors
- Materials
- Sales promotion
- Prices
- Advertising media
- Brand name
- Packaging
- Advertising execution
- Advertising themes

The best global brands are consistent in theme but reflect significant differences in consumer behavior, brand development, competitive forces, and the legal or political environment.[63] Oft-heard—and sometime modified—advice to marketers of global brands is to "Think Global, Act Local." In that spirit, HSBC was explicitly positioned for years as "The World's Local Bank."

Take McDonald's, for example.[64] It allows countries and regions to customize its basic layout and menu staples (see Table 8.2). In cities plagued by traffic tie-ups like Manila, Taipei, Jakarta, and Cairo, McDonald's delivers via fleets of motor scooters.

| TABLE 8.2 | McDonald's Global Menu Variations |
|---|---|
| **Country** | **Noteworthy Menu Items** |
| United States | Big Mac, Chicken McNuggets, Filet-o-Fish, Egg McMuffin, Fries |
| India | McVeggie, Chicken Maharaja-Mac, McSpicy Paneer |
| France | Le McBaguette, Le Croque McDo, Le Royal Cheese |
| Egypt | Beef N Pepper, McArabia (grilled kofta), McFalafel |
| Israel | McKebab, McFalafel, Big New York and Big Texas (hamburgers) |
| Japan | Ebi Filet-O, Mega Teriyaki Burger, Bacon Egg and Lettuce Wrap, Shaka Shaka Chicken |
| China | Prosperity Burger, Taro Pie, McWings, McNuggets with Chili Garlic sauce |
| Brazil | Banana Pie, McNífico Bacon, Cheddar McMelt, Big Tasty |
| Mexico | Big Mac, McChicken, Fries, etc. |

Sources: "Discover McDonald's Around the World," www.aboutmcdonalds.com/mcd/country/map.html, accessed May 20, 2014; David Griner, "McDonald's 60-Second Meals in Japan Aren't Going So Well," *Adweek*, January 7, 2013; Richard Vines and Caroline Connan, "McDonald's Wins Over French Chef with McBaguette Sandwich," www.bloomberg.com, January 15, 2013; Ségolène Poirier, "McDonald's Brazil Has Big Plans," *The Rio Times*, April 8, 2012; Susan Postlewaite, "McDonald's McFalafel a Hit with Egyptians, *Advertising Age*, June 19, 2001.

Companies must make sure their brands are relevant to consumers in every market they enter. After highlighting how Amazon and Netflix are entering global markets, we next consider some specific issues in developing global product, communications, pricing, and distribution strategies.[65]

**AMAZON AND NETFLIX** Two of the most successful marketing companies in recent years, Amazon and Netflix are going overseas to fuel their rapid growth, but they are also finding themselves butting heads as they both seek to become the market leader for digital movie downloads. The older of the two, Amazon has been overseas longer, finding much success in the United Kingdom, Germany, and other parts of Europe. Amazon has also moved into Asia-Pacific but has found progress in emerging markets like China to be slow. Amazon acquired LoveFilm, a European DVD rental and movie-streaming business, to compete with Netflix. It also opened up a massive media R&D center in London and expanded its Android-based Appstore distribution business to cover 200 countries. Netflix has expanded aggressively overseas, starting with Canada in 2010 and Latin America in 2011 and then the United Kingdom, Ireland, and Nordic countries in 2012. Although its international base of more than 6 million consumers is formidable, the company faces heavy local and regional competition and has to negotiate with local broadcasters and distributors for its streaming TV licenses. To attract new users, Netflix is emphasizing breadth of content and original programming such as the Emmy- and Golden Globe–winning political thriller "House of Cards."

## GLOBAL PRODUCT STRATEGIES

Developing global product strategies requires knowing what types of products or services are easily standardized and what are appropriate adaptation strategies.

**PRODUCT STANDARDIZATION** Some products cross borders without adaptation better than others, and consumer knowledge about new products is generally the same everywhere because perceptions have yet to be formed. Many leading Internet brands—such as Google, eBay, Twitter, and Facebook—made quick progress in overseas markets.

High-end products also benefit from standardization because quality and prestige often can be marketed similarly across countries. Culture and wealth factors influence how quickly a new product takes off in a country, though adoption and diffusion rates are becoming more alike across countries over time. Food and beverage marketers find it more challenging to standardize, of course, given widely varying tastes and cultural habits.[66]

A company may emphasize its products differently across markets. In its medical-equipment business, Philips traditionally reserved higher-end, premium products for developed markets and emphasized products with basic functionality and affordability in developing markets. Increasingly, however, the company is designing, engineering, and manufacturing locally in emerging markets like China and India.[67]

Amazon has found great success moving into global markets, especially in Europe.

Milkuat is a popular milk beverage in Indonesia due to its six month shelf life and affordability.

Source: Groupe Danone. Used with permission.

With a growing middle class in many emerging markets, many firms are assembling product portfolios to tap into different income segments. French food company Danone has many high-end healthy products, such as Dannon yogurt, Evian water, and Bledina baby food, but it also sells much lower priced products targeting consumers with "dollar-a-day" food budgets. In Indonesia, where average per-capita income is about US$10 a day, the company sells Milkuat, a 6 month shelf life neutral ph milk beverage. Danone now generates over 60% of its sales from growth markets (i.e. all except Western Europe), up from just 23% in 1996 (source: www.danone.com).[68]

**PRODUCT ADAPTATION STRATEGIES** Warren Keegan has distinguished five product and communications adaptation strategies (see Figure 8.3).[69] We review the product strategies here and the communication strategies in the next section.

**Straight extension** introduces the product in the foreign market without any change. Tempting because it requires no additional R&D expense, manufacturing retooling, or promotional modification, the strategy has been successful for cameras, consumer electronics, and many machine tools. In other cases, it has been a disaster. Campbell Soup Company lost an estimated $30 million introducing condensed soups in England; consumers saw expensive small-sized cans and didn't realize water needed to be added.

**Product adaptation** alters the product to meet local conditions or preferences. Flexible manufacturing makes it easier to do so on several levels.

- A company can produce a *regional version* of its product. Dunkin' Donuts has been introducing more regionalized products, such as Coco Leche donuts in Miami and sausage kolaches in Dallas.[70]
- A company can produce a *country version*. Kraft blends different coffees for the British (who drink coffee with milk), the French (who drink it black), and Latin Americans (who want a chicory taste).
- A company can produce a *city version*—for instance, a beer to meet Munich's or Tokyo's tastes.
- A company can produce different *retailer versions*, such as one coffee brew for the Migros chain store and another for the Cooperative chain store, both in Switzerland.

Some companies have learned adaptation the hard way. The Euro Disney theme park, launched outside Paris in 1992, was harshly criticized as an example of U.S. cultural imperialism that ignored French customs and values, such as the serving of wine with meals. As one

|  | Product | | |
|---|---|---|---|
|  | Do Not Change Product | Adapt Product | Develop New Product |
| **Do Not Change Communications** | Straight extension | Product adaptation | Product invention |
| **Adapt Communications** | Communication adaptation | Dual adaptation | Product invention |

(Communications)

**| Fig. 8.3 |**

Five International Product and Communication Strategies

Euro Disney executive noted, "When we first launched, there was the belief that it was enough to be Disney. Now we realize our guests need to be welcomed on the basis of their own culture and travel habits." Renamed Disneyland Paris, the theme park eventually became one of Europe's biggest tourist attraction—even more popular than the Eiffel Tower—by implementing a number of local touches.[71]

On the other hand, South Korea's LG Electronics has found success in India by investing in local design and manufacturing facilities that helped it develop TVs with higher-quality speakers, refrigerators with brighter colors and smaller freezers, and microwaves with one-touch "Indian menu" functions, all reflecting Indian preferences.[72]

**Product invention** creates something new. It can take two forms:

- **Backward invention** reintroduces earlier product forms well adapted to a foreign country's needs. A big hit in developing markets in Latin America, Mexico, and the Middle East, the powdered drink Tang has added local flavors like lemon pepper and soursop. Although its U.S. sales have fallen precipitously, its worldwide sales doubled from 2006 to 2011.[73]
- **Forward invention** creates a new product to meet a need in another country. Less-developed countries need low-cost, high-protein foods. Companies such as Quaker Oats, Swift, and Monsanto have researched their nutrition requirements, formulated new foods, and developed advertising to gain product trial and acceptance.

**BRAND ELEMENT ADAPTATION** When they launch products and services globally, marketers may need to change certain brand elements.[74] Even a brand name may require a choice between phonetic and semantic translations.[75] When Clairol introduced the "Mist Stick," a curling iron, in Germany, it found that *mist* is slang for *manure*. In China, Coca-Cola and Nike have both found sets of Chinese characters that sounds broadly like their names but also offer some relevant meaning at the same time ("Can Be Tasty, Can Be Happy" and "Endurance Conquer," respectively).[76]

Numbers and colors can take on special meaning in certain countries. The number four is considered unlucky throughout much of Asia because the Japanese word sounds like "death." Some East Asian buildings skip not only the fourth floor but often every floor that has a four in it (14, 24, 40–49). Nokia doesn't release phone models with the number four in them in Asia.[77]

Purple is associated with death in Burma and some Latin American nations, white is a mourning color in India, and in Malaysia green connotes disease. Red generally signifies luck and prosperity in China.[78]

Brand slogans or ad taglines sometimes need to be changed too:[79]

- When Coors put its brand slogan "Turn it loose" into Spanish, some read it as "suffer from diarrhea."
- A laundry soap ad claiming to wash "really dirty parts" was translated in French-speaking Quebec to read "a soap for washing private parts."
- Perdue's slogan—"It takes a tough man to make a tender chicken"—was rendered into Spanish as "It takes a sexually excited man to make a chicken affectionate."

Table 8.3 lists some other famous marketing mistakes in this area.

| TABLE 8.3 | Classic Blunders in Global Marketing |
|---|---|

- Hallmark cards failed in France, where consumers dislike syrupy sentiment and prefer writing their own cards.
- Philips became profitable in Japan only after reducing the size of its coffeemakers to fit smaller kitchens and its shavers to fit smaller hands.
- Coca-Cola withdrew its big two-liter bottle in Spain after discovering that few Spaniards owned refrigerators that could accommodate it.
- General Foods' Tang initially failed in France when positioned as a substitute for orange juice at breakfast. The French drink little orange juice and almost never at breakfast.
- Kellogg's Pop-Tarts failed in Britain because fewer homes have toasters than in the United States and the product was too sweet for British tastes.
- The U.S. campaign for Procter & Gamble's Crest toothpaste initially failed in Mexico. Mexicans did not care as much about the decay-prevention benefit nor the scientifically oriented advertising appeal.
- General Foods squandered millions trying to introduce packaged cake mixes to Japan, where only 3 percent of homes at the time were equipped with ovens.
- S. C. Johnson's wax floor polish initially failed in Japan. It made floors too slippery for a culture where people do not wear shoes at home.

# GLOBAL COMMUNICATION STRATEGIES

Changing marketing communications for each local market is a process called **communication adaptation.** If it adapts both the product and the communications, the company engages in **dual adaptation.**

Consider the message. The company can use one message everywhere, varying only the language and name.[80] General Mills positions its Häagen-Dazs brand in terms of "indulgence," "affordable luxury," and "intense sensuality." To communicate that message, it ran a 30-second TV spot called "Sensation," with the tagline "Anticipated Like No Other" in markets all over the world, substituting only the voice-over in the language of each country.[81]

The second possibility is to use the same message and creative theme globally but adapt the execution. GE's global "Ecomagination" ad campaign substitutes creative content in Asia and the Middle East to reflect cultural interests there. Even in the high-tech space, local adaptations may be necessary.[82]

The third approach, which Coca-Cola and Goodyear have used, consists of developing a global pool of ads from which each country selects the most appropriate. Finally, some companies allow their country managers to create country-specific ads—within guidelines, of course. The challenge is to make the message as compelling and effective as in the home market.

**GLOBAL ADAPTATIONS** Companies that adapt their communications wrestle with a number of challenges. They first must ensure their communications are legally and culturally acceptable. U.S. toy makers were surprised to learn that in many countries (Norway and Sweden, for example), no TV ads may be directed at children under 12. To foster a culture of gender neutrality, Sweden also now prohibits "sexist" advertising—a commercial that spoke of "cars for boys, princesses for girls" was criticized by government advertising regulators.[83]

A number of countries are taking steps to eliminate "super skinny" and airbrushed models in ads. Israel has banned "underweight" models from print and TV ads and runway shows. Models must have a body-mass index—a calculation based on height and weight—of greater than 18.5. According to that BMI standard, a female model who is 5 feet, 8 inches tall can weigh no less than 119 pounds.[84]

Firms next must check their creative strategies and communication approaches for appropriateness. Comparative ads, though acceptable and even common in the United States and Canada, are less frequent in the United Kingdom, unacceptable in Japan, and illegal in India and Brazil. The EU seems to have a very low tolerance for comparative advertising and prohibits bashing rivals in ads.

Companies also must be prepared to vary their messages' appeal.[85] In advertising its hair care products, Helene Curtis observed that middle-class British women wash their hair frequently, Spanish women less so. Japanese women avoid overwashing for fear of removing protective oils. Language can vary too, whether the local language, another such as English, or some combination.[86]

When the brand is at an earlier stage of development in its new market, consumer education may need to accompany brand development efforts. In launching Chik shampoo in rural areas of South India, where hair is washed with soap, CavinKare showed people how to use the product through live "touch and feel" demonstrations and free sachets at fairs.[87]

Personal selling tactics may need to change too. The direct, no-nonsense approach favored in the United States ("let's get down to business" and "what's in it for me") may not work as well in Europe or Asia as an indirect, subtle approach.[88]

# GLOBAL PRICING STRATEGIES

Multinationals selling abroad must contend with price escalation and transfer prices (and dumping charges). As part of those issues, two particularly thorny pricing problems are gray markets and counterfeits.

**PRICE ESCALATION** A Gucci handbag may sell for $120 in Italy and $240 in the United States. Why? Gucci must add the cost of transportation, tariffs, importer margin, wholesaler margin, and retailer margin to its factory price. **Price escalation** from these added costs and currency-fluctuation risk might require the price to be two to five times as high for the manufacturer to earn the same profit.

Marketers in Israel must observe the body-mass restrictions prohibiting overly-skinny models.

Companies have three choices for setting prices in different countries:

1. ***Set a uniform price everywhere.*** PepsiCo might want to charge $1 for Pepsi everywhere in the world, but then it would earn quite different profit rates in different countries. Also, this strategy would make the price too high in poor countries and not high enough in rich countries.
2. ***Set a market-based price in each country.*** PepsiCo would charge what each country could afford, but this strategy ignores differences in the actual cost from country to country. It could also motivate intermediaries in low-price countries to reship their Pepsi to high-price countries.[89]
3. ***Set a cost-based price in each country.*** Here PepsiCo would use a standard markup of its costs everywhere, but this strategy might price it out of markets where its costs are high.

When companies sell their wares over the Internet, price becomes transparent and price differentiation between countries declines. Consider an online training course. Whereas the cost of a classroom-delivered day of training can vary significantly from the United States to France to Thailand, the price of an online-delivered day would be similar everywhere.

In another new global pricing challenge, countries with overcapacity, cheap currencies, and the need to export aggressively have pushed their prices down and devalued their currencies. Sluggish demand and reluctance to pay higher prices make selling in these markets difficult. Here is what IKEA did to compete in China's challenging pricing market.[90]

**IKEA**   When the Swedish home furnishings giant IKEA opened its first store in Beijing in 2002, local stores were selling copies of its designs at a fraction of IKEA's prices. The only way to lure China's frugal customers was to drastically slash prices. Western brands in China usually price products such as makeup and running shoes 20 percent to 30 percent higher than in their other markets, both to make up for China's high import taxes and to give their products added cachet. By stocking its Chinese stores with Chinese-made products, IKEA has been able to slash prices as low as 70 percent below their level outside China. Western-style showrooms provide model bedrooms, dining rooms, and family rooms and suggest how to furnish them, an important consideration given home ownership in China has gone from practically zero in 1995 to about 70 percent today. Young couples are especially drawn to IKEA's stylish, functional modern styles. Although it still contends with persistent knockoffs, IKEA maintains sizable stores in eight locations and aims to have 15 by 2015.

IKEA has gone to great lengths to draw customers into its showrooms and establish a market presence in China.

**TRANSFER PRICES**   A different problem arises when one unit charges another unit in the same company a **transfer price** for goods it ships to its foreign subsidiaries. If the company charges a subsidiary too *high* a price, it may end up paying higher tariff duties, though it may pay lower income taxes in the foreign country. If the company charges its subsidiary too *low* a price, it can be accused of **dumping,** charging either less than its costs or less than it charges at home in order to enter or win a market. Various governments are watching for abuses and often force companies to charge the **arm's-length price**—the price charged by other competitors for the same or a similar product.

When the U.S. Department of Commerce finds evidence of dumping, it can levy a dumping tariff on the guilty company. After much debate over government support for clean-energy products, the United States chose to set anti-dumping duties of 44.99 percent to 47.59 percent on wind towers produced in China and Vietnam and sent to the United States.[91]

**GRAY MARKETS**   Many multinationals are plagued by the **gray market,** which diverts branded products from authorized distribution channels either in-country or across international borders. Often a company finds some enterprising distributors buying more than they can sell in their own country and reshipping the goods to another country to take advantage of price differences.

Gray markets create a free-rider problem, making legitimate distributors' investments in supporting a manufacturer's product less productive and selective distribution systems more intensive to reduce the number of gray market possibilities. They harm distributor relationships, tarnish the manufacturer's brand equity, and undermine the integrity of the distribution channel. They can even pose risks to consumers if the product is damaged, relabeled, obsolete, without warranty or support, or just counterfeit. Because of their high prices, prescription drugs are often a gray market target, though U.S. government regulators are looking at the industry more closely after fake vials of Riche Holding AG's cancer drug Avastin were shipped to U.S. doctors.[92]

Multinationals try to prevent gray markets by policing distributors, raising their prices to lower-cost distributors, or altering product characteristics or service warranties for different countries.[93] 3Com successfully sued several companies in Canada (for a total of $10 million) for using written and oral misrepresentations to get deep discounts on 3Com networking equipment. The equipment, worth millions of dollars, was to be sold to a U.S. educational software company and sent to China and Australia but instead ended up back in the United States.

One research study found that gray market activity was most effectively deterred when penalties were severe, manufacturers were able to detect violations or mete out punishments in a timely fashion, or both.[94]

**COUNTERFEIT PRODUCTS** As companies develop global supply chain networks and move production farther from home, the chance for corruption, fraud, and quality-control problems rises.[95] Sophisticated overseas factories seem able to reproduce almost anything. Name a popular brand, and chances are a counterfeit version of it exists somewhere in the world.[96]

Counterfeiting is estimated to cost more than a trillion dollars a year. U.S. Customs and Border Protection seized $1.26 billion worth of goods in 2012; the chief culprits were China (81 percent) and Hong Kong (12 percent), and the chief products were apparel and accessories, followed by electronics, optical media, handbags and wallets, and watches and jewelry.[97]

At the Summer Olympics in London in 2012, the Egyptian Olympic team even admitted to buying fake Nike gear from a Chinese distributor because of the country's dire economic situation. Once Nike found out what had happened, the company donated all the necessary training and village wear to the team.[98]

Fakes take a big bite of the profits of luxury brands such as Hermès, LVMH Moët Hennessy Louis Vuitton, and Tiffany, but faulty counterfeits can literally kill people. Cell phones with counterfeit batteries, fake brake pads made of compressed grass trimmings, and counterfeit airline parts pose safety risks to consumers. Pharmaceuticals are especially worrisome. Toxic cough syrup in Panama, tainted baby formula in China, and fake teething powder in Nigeria have all led to the deaths of children in recent years.[99]

Virtually every product is vulnerable. Microsoft estimates that four-fifths of Windows OS software in China is pirated.[100] As one anti-counterfeit consultant observed, "If you can make it, they can fake it." Defending against counterfeiters is a never-ending struggle; some observers estimate that a new security system can be just months old before counterfeiters start nibbling at sales again.[101]

The Internet has been especially problematic. After surveying thousands of items, LVMH estimated 90 percent of Louis Vuitton and Christian Dior pieces listed on eBay were fakes, prompting the firm to sue. Manufacturers are fighting back online with Web-crawling software that detects fraud and automatically warns apparent violators without the need for any human intervention. Acushnet, maker of Titleist golf clubs and balls, shut down 75 auctions of knockoff gear in one day with a single mouse click.[102]

Web-crawling technology searches for counterfeit storefronts and sales by detecting domain names similar to legitimate brands and unauthorized Internet sites that plaster brand trademarks and logos on their homepages. It also checks for keywords such as *cheap, discount, authentic,* and *factory variants,* as well as colors that products were never made in and prices that are far too low.

# GLOBAL DISTRIBUTION STRATEGIES

Too many U.S. manufacturers think their job is done once the product leaves the factory. They should instead note how the product moves within the foreign country and take a whole-channel view of distributing products to final users.

**CHANNEL ENTRY** Figure 8.4 shows three links between the seller and the final buyer. In the first, *seller's international marketing headquarters,* the export department or international division makes decisions about channels and other marketing activities. The second

*Source: Associated Press*

Nike came to the rescue of the Egyptian Olympic team after they admitted buying fake Nike gear because of the country's budgetary problems.

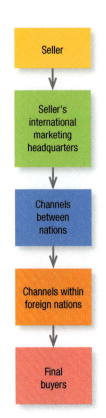

**| Fig. 8.4 |**

Whole-Channel Concept for International Marketing

link, *channels between nations,* gets the products to the borders of the foreign nation. Decisions made in this link include the types of intermediaries (agents, trading companies), type of transportation (air, sea), and financing and risk management. The third link, *channels within foreign nations,* gets products from their entry point to final buyers and users.

When multinationals first enter a country, they prefer to work with local distributors with good local knowledge, but friction often arises later.[103] The multinational complains that the local distributor doesn't invest in business growth, doesn't follow company policy, and doesn't share enough information. The local distributor complains of insufficient corporate support, impossible goals, and confusing policies. The multinational must choose the right distributors, invest in them, and set up performance goals to which they can both agree.[104]

**CHANNEL DIFFERENCES** Distribution channels across countries vary considerably. To sell consumer products in Japan, companies must work through one of the most complicated distribution systems in the world. They sell to a general wholesaler, who sells to a product wholesaler, who sells to a product-specialty wholesaler, who sells to a regional wholesaler, who sells to a local wholesaler, who finally sells to retailers. All these distribution levels can make the consumer's price double or triple the importer's price. Taking these same consumer products to tropical Africa, the company might sell to an import wholesaler, who sells to several jobbers, who sell to petty traders (mostly women) working in local markets.

Another difference is the size and character of retail units abroad. Large-scale retail chains dominate the U.S. scene, but much foreign retailing is in the hands of small, independent retailers. Millions of Indian retailers operate tiny shops or sell in open markets. Markups are high, but the real price comes down through haggling. Incomes are low, most homes lack storage and refrigeration, and people shop daily for whatever they can carry home on foot or bicycle. In India, people often buy one cigarette at a time. Breaking bulk remains an important function of intermediaries and helps perpetuate long channels of distribution, a major obstacle to the expansion of large-scale retailing in developing countries.

Nevertheless, retailers are increasingly moving into new global markets, offering firms the opportunity to sell across more countries and creating a challenge to local distributors and retailers.[105] France's Carrefour, Germany's Aldi and Metro, and United Kingdom's Tesco have all established global positions. But even some of the world's most successful retailers have had mixed success abroad. Despite concerted efforts and earlier success in Latin America and China, Walmart had to withdraw from both the German and South Korean markets after heavy losses. Walmart now earns a quarter of its revenue overseas by being more sensitive to local market needs in different countries.[106]

# Country-of-Origin Effects

*Country-of-origin perceptions* are the mental associations and beliefs triggered by a country. Government officials want to strengthen their country's image to help domestic marketers that export and to attract foreign firms and investors. Marketers want to use positive country-of-origin perceptions to sell their products and services.

## BUILDING COUNTRY IMAGES

Governments now recognize that the images of their cities and countries affect more than tourism and have important value in commerce. Foreign business can boost the local economy, provide jobs, and improve infrastructure. Image can also help sell products. For its first global ad campaign for Infiniti luxury cars, Nissan chose to tap into its Japanese roots and association with Japanese-driven art and engineering.[107]

Countries are being marketed like any other brand. New Zealand has developed concerted marketing programs both to sell its products outside the country, via its New Zealand Way program, and to attract tourists, by showing the dramatic landscapes featured in *The Lord of the Rings* film trilogy. Both efforts reinforce the image of New Zealand as fresh and pure. The launch of the new *Hobbit* trilogy in November 2012—with the fictional Middle Earth again being depicted by New Zealand—has attracted a new wave of visitors.[108]

Another film affected the image of a country in an entirely different way. Kazakhstan has a positive story to tell given its huge size, rich natural resources, and rapid modernization. British comedian Sacha Baron Cohen's mock documentary *Borat,* however, portrayed the country in a sometimes crude and vulgar light, and the character Borat was sexist, homophobic, and anti-Semitic. Despite that fact, Yerzhan Kazykhanov, Kazakhstan's foreign minister, observed: "After this film, the number of visas issued to Kazakhstan grew by ten times. This is a big victory for us, and I thank Borat for attracting tourists to Kazakhstan." Evidently, enough publicity about the country surrounded the film to boost its awareness.[109]

A strong company that emerges as a global player can do wonders for a country's image. Before World War II, Japan had a poor image, which the success of Sony with its Trinitron TV sets and of Japanese automakers Honda, Nissan, and Toyota helped change. Relying partly on the global success of Nokia, Finland campaigned to enhance

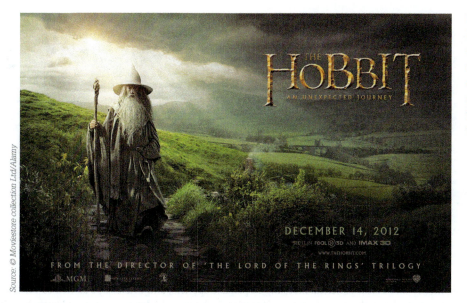

Source: © Moviestore collection Ltd/Alamy

The government of New Zealand markets the country as fresh and pure, a message reinforced by the use of stunning New Zealand scenery in many popular films such as the *Hobbit* trilogy.

its image as a center of high-tech innovation. Current events can also shape the image of a country. When public unrest and violent protests surrounded the government's austerity program to address Greece's debt crisis, tourist bookings there dropped as much as 30 percent.[110]

## CONSUMER PERCEPTIONS OF COUNTRY OF ORIGIN

Global marketers know that buyers hold distinct attitudes and beliefs about brands or products from different countries.[111] These perceptions can be attributes in decision making or influence other attributes in the process ("If it's French, it must be stylish"). Coca-Cola's success against local cola brand Jianlibao in China was partly due to its symbolic values of U.S. modernity and affluence.[112]

The mere fact that a brand is perceived as successful on a global stage—whether it sends a quality signal, taps into cultural myths, or reinforces a sense of social responsibility—may lend credibility and respect.[113] Research studies have found the following:[114]

- People are often ethnocentric and favorably predisposed to their own country's products, unless they come from a less developed country.
- The more favorable a country's image, the more prominently the "Made in…" label should be displayed.
- The impact of country of origin varies with the type of product. Consumers want to know where a car was made, but not the lubricating oil.
- Certain countries enjoy a reputation for certain goods: Japan for automobiles and consumer electronics; the United States for high-tech innovations, soft drinks, toys, cigarettes, and jeans; France for wine, perfume, and luxury goods.
- Sometimes country-of-origin perception can encompass an entire country's products. In one study, Chinese consumers in Hong Kong perceived U.S. products as prestigious, Japanese products as innovative, and Chinese products as cheap.

Marketers must look at country-of-origin perceptions from both a domestic and a foreign perspective. In the domestic market, these perceptions may stir consumers' patriotic notions or remind them of their past. As international trade grows, consumers may view certain brands as symbolically important in their own cultural identity or as playing an important role in keeping jobs in their own country. More than three-quarters of U.S. consumers said that, given a choice between a product made at home and an identical one made abroad, they would choose the U.S. product.[115]

Patriotic appeals underlie marketing strategies all over the world, but they can lack uniqueness and even be overused, especially in economic or political crises. Many small businesses tap into community pride to emphasize their local roots. To be successful, these need to be clearly local and offer appealing product and service offerings.[116]

Sometimes consumers don't know where brands come from. In surveys, they routinely guess that Heineken is German and Nokia is Japanese (they are Dutch and Finnish, respectively). Few consumers know Häagen-Dazs and Estée Lauder originated in the United States.

With outsourcing and foreign manufacturing, it's hard to know what the country of origin really is anyway. Only 65 percent of the content of a Ford Mustang comes from the United States or Canada, whereas the Toyota Avalon is assembled in Georgetown, Kentucky, with one of the highest percentages of local components, 85 percent. Foreign automakers

China's large appliance maker Haier has made being seen as a localized U.S. brand one of their top business priorities.

Source: Wang Jun qd · Imaginechina

are pouring money into North America, investing in plants, suppliers, and dealerships as well as design, testing, and research centers. But what makes a product more "American"—having a higher percentage of North American components or creating more jobs in North America? The two measures may not lead to the same conclusion.[117]

Many brands have gone to great lengths to weave themselves into the cultural fabric of their foreign markets. One Coca-Cola executive tells of a young child visiting the United States from Japan who commented to her parents on seeing a Coca-Cola vending machine—"Look, they have Coca-Cola too!" As far as she was concerned, Coca-Cola was a Japanese brand. Haier is another global brand working hard to establish local roots in other countries.[118]

**HAIER** As China's leading maker of refrigerators, washing machines, and air conditioners, Haier was well known and respected in its home market for its well-designed products. For rural customers, Haier sold extra-durable washing machines that could wash vegetables as well as clothes; for urban customers, it made smaller washing machines to fit in tiny apartments. In 1999, the company set its sights on a much bigger goal: building a truly global brand. Unlike most other Asian companies that chose to enter Asian markets before considering Western markets, Haier decided to first target the United States and Western Europe. The company felt success there would enable greater success elsewhere in the world. In the United States, Haier established a beachhead by tapping a neglected market—mini-fridges for homes, offices, dorms, and hotels—and securing distribution at Walmart, Target, Home Depot, and other top retailers. After some initial success, the company began to sell higher-end refrigerators and other appliances such as air conditioners, washing machines, and dishwashers. Its goal is to be seen as a "localized U.S. brand," not an "imported Chinese brand." Thus, Haier invested $40 million in a manufacturing plant in South Carolina and became a marketing partner with the National Basketball Association. The firm's global marketing efforts have paid off. By 2012, 30 percent of U.S. households owned a Haier product, and Haier is now the world's top-selling home appliance brand.

Interestingly, even when the United States has not been that popular, its brands typically have been. As one marketer noted, "Regardless of all the problems we have as a country, we are still looked to as the consumer capital of the world."[119]

# Summary

1. Despite shifting borders, unstable governments, foreign-exchange problems, corruption, and technological pirating, companies selling in global industries need to internationalize their operations.

2. Upon deciding to go abroad, a company needs to define its international marketing objectives and poli-

cies. It must determine whether to market in a few or many countries and rate candidate countries on three criteria: market attractiveness, risk, and competitive advantage.

3. Developing countries offer a unique set of opportunities and risks. The "BRICS" countries—Brazil, Russia, India,

China, and South Africa—plus other significant markets such as Indonesia are a top priority for many firms.

4. Modes of entry are indirect exporting, direct exporting, licensing, joint ventures, and direct investment. Each succeeding strategy entails more commitment, risk, control, and profit potential.

5. In deciding how much to adapt their marketing programs at the product level, firms can pursue a strategy of straight extension, product adaptation, or product invention. At the communication level, they may choose communica-

tion adaptation or dual adaptation. At the price level, firms may encounter price escalation, dumping, gray markets, and discounted counterfeit products. At the distribution level, firms need to take a whole-channel view of distributing products to the final users. Firms must always consider the cultural, social, political, technological, environmental, and legal limitations they face in other countries.

6. Country-of-origin perceptions can affect consumers and businesses alike. Managing those perceptions to best advantage is a marketing priority.

# Applications

## Marketing Debate
### Is the World Coming Closer Together?

Many social commentators maintain that youth and teens are becoming more alike across countries over time. Others, though not disputing the fact, point out that differences between cultures at even younger ages by far exceed the similarities.

**Take a position:** People are becoming more and more similar *versus* The differences between people of different cultures far outweigh their similarities.

## Marketing Discussion
### Country of Origin

⭐ Think of some of your favorite brands. Do you know where they come from? Where and how are they made or provided? Do you think knowing these answers would affect your perceptions of quality or satisfaction?

## Marketing Excellence

### >> Twitter

Few companies have had such a vast global impact in so short a time as Twitter. The online social networking company was the brainchild of Jack Dorsey, Evan Williams, Biz Snow, and Noah Glass back in 2005. Dorsey thought it would be revolutionary if people could send a text to one number and have it broadcast to all their friends: "I want to make something so simple, you don't even think about it, you just write." The code name for the concept was "twttr," which eventually morphed into Twitter. Dorsey sent the first Twitter message on March 21, 2006.

At the heart of Twitter are tweets, text messages limited to 140 characters. Dorsey once tweeted, "One could change the world with 140 characters." Registered users can send and receive tweets, while unregistered users can

only read them. In response to users' comments and ideas, the company added more features to help organize the ongoing communication on Twitter, including the @ sign in front of usernames, direct messages, and the retweet. Web developer Chris Messina suggested adding a hashtag (#) symbol to help organize categories of conversation or search for tweets on a common topic. For example, #Grammys will bring a user to conversations about the Grammys.

Twitter grew slowly during its first year, but things started to heat up in 2007 when the company set up 51-inch plasma screens around the grounds of the South by Southwest interactive festival and broadcast tweets sent by attendees. Overnight, activity increased from 20,000 to 60,000 tweets a day.

Another milestone came on January 15, 2009, when US Airways flight 1549 landed safely on the Hudson River in New York City during an emergency. An eyewitness on a commuter ferry broke the news worldwide when he snapped a photo of the plane on the river, wrote a tweet, and sent it to his 170 followers. The tweet and #Flight1549 went viral within minutes and proved that Twitter had transformed the way we get news.

Seth Mnookin, MIT's Associate Director of Science Writing, explained why Twitter has been so revolutionary in media: "What the advent of television or radio did was give a small group of people a new way to reach the masses. And this essentially is doing the same thing, for the masses." Twitter captures and records history in real time with eyewitness accounts, pictures, and thoughts.

Celebrities and sports figures started to embrace Twitter in 2009. Perhaps the most influential early adopter was Ashton Kutcher, the first celebrity to reach 1 million followers. Katy Perry, Barack Obama, Lady Gaga, and Justin Bieber are now among the most followed Tweeters, with tens of millions followers each.

By 2011, Twitter had expanded across seven different countries and languages. The medium had a huge impact on the Arab Spring, when millions demanded the overthrow of oppressive Middle East regimes. Bahraini protester Maryam Al-Khawaja explained that in many countries Twitter is about entertainment, but in the Middle East and North Africa, it can make the difference between life and death. Twitter gave activists a means to share accurate and uncensored information, connect with like-minded individuals, and organize street operations at unheard-of speed. Hussein Amin, professor of mass communication at the American University in Cairo, explained, "[Social networks] for the first time provided activists with an opportunity to quickly disseminate information while bypassing government restrictions."

During the 2012 U.S. presidential election, Twitter had enormous impact on campaigns and communications with voters. In fact, the most popular tweet of 2012 was "Four more years," posted by Barack Obama after he won the reelection. It was retweeted almost 1 million times.

Twitter went public in November 2013 and raised $2.1 billion in the second-biggest Internet IPO in history (Facebook raised $16 billion in 2012). Its global impact has grown so great that it operates in 35 languages and 70 percent of users live outside the United States. In 2014, 500 million users were registered on Twitter, 250 million were active, and more than 400 million tweets were posted each day around the globe.

Today, people use Twitter for many reasons, including promoting a brand or company, raising money for charities, breaking news, following favorite celebrities, or, as Dorsey said, changing the world. Twitter describes itself as a global platform for public self-expression and conversation in real time. Mark Burnett, the producer of shows like *The Voice, Survivor,* and *The Apprentice,* stated, "Twitter actually is the real time, water cooler conversation of young America." The company's ultimate goal is to reach everyone in the world.

### Questions

1. Discuss Twitter's global impact since its inception.

2. Who are Twitter's biggest competitors? How does Twitter differ from other social media companies?

3. What marketing challenges does Twitter face as it continues to expand its brand globally?

**Sources:** Dom Sagolla, 140Characters.com, January 30, 2009; Nicholas Carlson, "The Real History of Twitter," BusinessInsider.com, April 13, 2011; Victor Luckerson, "The 7 Most Important Moments in Twitter History," *Time,* November 7, 2013; Drew Olanoff, "Twitter's Social Impact Can't Be Measured, but It's the Pulse of the Planet," Techcrunch.com, January 15, 2013; Heesun Wee, "Twitter May Be Going Public but Can It Make Money?" *CNBC,* November 5, 2013; Elizabeth Kricfalusi, "The Twitter Hashtag: What Is It and How Do You Use It?" *Tech for Luddites,* November 12, 2013; Julianne Pepitone, "#WOW! Twitter Soars 73% in IPO," CNNMoney.com, November 7, 2013; "#Twitter Revolution," CNBC.com, August 7, 2013; David Wolman, "Facebook, Twitter Help the Arab Spring Blossom," *Wired,* April 16, 2013; David Jolly, Mark Scott, and Eric Pfanner, "Twitters IPO Plan Has an International Focus," *New York Times,* October 5, 2013; Saleem Kassim, "Twitter Revolution: How the Arab Spring Was Helped by Social Media," PolicyMic.com, July 3, 2012; www.twitter.com.

## Marketing Excellence

### >> L'Oréal

When it comes to globalizing beauty, no one does it better than L'Oréal. The company was founded in Paris more than 100 years ago by a young chemist, Eugene Schueller, who sold his patented hair dyes to local hairdressers and salons. By the 1930s, Schueller had invented beauty products like suntan oil and the first mass-marketed shampoo. Today, the company has evolved into the world's largest beauty and cosmetics company, with distribution in 130 countries, 27 global brands, and more than $30.8 billion in sales.

Much of the company's early international expansion is credited to Sir Lindsay Owen-Jones, who transformed L'Oréal from a small French business into an international cosmetics phenomenon with strategic vision and precise brand management. During his almost 20 years as CEO and chairman, Owen-Jones divested weak brands, invested heavily in product innovation, acquired ethnically diverse brands, and expanded into markets no one had dreamed of, including China, South America, and the former Soviet Union. His quest was to achieve diversity and "meet the needs of men and women around the globe, and make beauty products available to as many people as possible."

Today, L'Oréal focuses on five areas of beauty expertise: skin care, hair care, makeup, hair coloring, and perfume. Its brands fall into four different groups: (1) *Consumer Products* (52 percent of sales, includes mass-marketed brands like Maybelline and high-technology products sold at competitive prices through mass-market retailing chains), (2) *L'Oreal Luxe* (27 percent of sales, includes prestigious brands like Ralph Lauren perfume that are available only in premium stores, department stores, or specialty stores), (3) *Professional Products* (14 percent of sales, includes brands such as Redken designed specifically for professional hair salons), and (4) *Active Cosmetics* (7 percent of sales, includes dermo-cosmetic products sold at pharmacies, drugstores, and medi-spas).

L'Oréal believes precise target marketing—hitting the right audience with the right product and message at the right place—is crucial to its global success. Owen-Jones explained, "Each brand is positioned on a very precise [market] segment, which overlaps as little as possible with the others."

The company has built its portfolio primarily by purchasing local beauty companies all over the world, revamping them with strategic direction, and expanding the brand into new areas through its powerful marketing arm. For example, L'Oréal instantly became a player (with 20 percent market share) in the growing ethnic hair care industry when it purchased and merged the U.S. companies Soft Sheen Products in 1998 and Carson Products in 2000. L'Oréal believed the competition had overlooked this category because it was fragmented and misunderstood. Backed by a deep portfolio of brands and products, SoftSheen-Carson is now the market leader in the ethnic hair care industry.

L'Oréal also invests significant money and time in its 22 local research centers around the world. The company spends 3.5 percent of annual sales on R&D, more than one percentage point above the industry average, researching and innovating products that meet the local needs of each region.

Understanding the unique beauty routines and needs of different cultures, climates, traditions, and physiologies is critical to L'Oréal's global success. Hair and skin greatly differ from one part of the world to another, so L'Oreal listens to and observes consumers across the globe to gather a deep understanding of their beauty needs. L'Oréal scientists study consumers in laboratory bathrooms and in their own homes, sometimes achieving scientific beauty milestones.

In Japan, for example, L'Oréal developed Wondercurl mascara specially formulated to curl Asian women's eyelashes, which are usually short and straight. Within three months, Wondercurl mascara had become Japan's number-one selling mascara, and young women lined up outside stores to buy it. L'Oréal continued to research the market and developed nail polish, blush, and other cosmetics aimed at this new Asian generation.

L'Oréal believes its future lies in emerging areas such as Asia, Africa, and Latin America, where it expects to find millions of new customers over the next few years. Marc Menesguen, L'Oréal's managing director-strategic marketing, explained, "Our projection for 2020 is that 50% to 60% of sales will be coming from [emerging] markets." As a result, new research centers have popped up in these countries, and the company is working aggressively on understanding these consumers' needs and developing beauty products to satisfy them.

Well known for its 1973 advertising tagline—"Because I'm Worth It"—L'Oréal is the leader in beauty products around the world. The company spends approximately $5 billion in advertising each year, making it the third-largest advertiser. As Gilles Weil, its head of luxury products, explained, "You have to be local and as strong as the best locals, but backed by an international image and strategy."

## Questions

1. Review L'Oréal's brand portfolio. What role have local and global marketing, smart acquisitions, and R&D played in growing those brands?

2. What are the keys to successful local product launches like Maybelline's Wondercurl in Japan?

3. What's next for L'Oréal on a global level? Who are its biggest competitors? If you were CEO, how would you sustain the company's global leadership?

**Sources:** Andrew Roberts, "L'Oréal Quarterly Sales Rise Most since 2007 on Luxury Perfume," *Bloomberg BusinessWeek*, April 22, 2010; Richard Tomlinson, "L'Oréal's Global Makeover," *Fortune*, September 30, 2002; Doreen Carvajal, "International Business; Priming for the Cameras in the Name of Research," *New York Times*, February 7, 2006; Richard C. Morais, "The Color of Beauty," *Forbes*, November 27, 2000; Jack Neff, "How L'Oreal Zen Master Menesguen Shares Best Practices around the Globe," *Advertising Age*, June 11, 2012; L'Oréal, www.loreal.com.

## In This Chapter, We Will Address the Following **Questions**

1.  In what ways can a company divide the consumer market into segments? (p. 246)

2.  How should business markets be segmented? (p. 261)

3.  How should a company choose the most attractive target markets? (p. 262)

4.  What are the requirements for effective segmentation? (p. 263)

5.  What are the different levels of market segmentation? (p. 263)

LinkedIn offers a variety of relevant value-added online services to its target market of career-minded professionals.

*Source: © PSL Images/Alamy*

MyMarketingLab™
⭐ Improve Your Grade!
Over 10 million students improved their results using the Pearson MyLabs. Visit mymktlab.com for simulations, tutorials, and end-of-chapter problems.

# 9    Identifying Market Segments and Targets

**Companies cannot connect with all customers in large, broad, or diverse markets.**
They need to identify the market segments they can serve effectively. This decision requires a keen understanding of consumer behavior and careful strategic thinking about what makes each segment unique and different. Identifying and uniquely satisfying the right market segments are often the key to marketing success. LinkedIn has built an online powerhouse by fulfilling the needs of career-minded professionals.[1]

 *LinkedIn was the first major social network to issue an IPO, after being one of the first entries into social networking back in 2003. The company targeted a different audience than most other social networks, establishing itself as the premier professional networking site with a vision "…to create economic opportunity for every professional in the world." Also separating LinkedIn from other social networks is the fact that it has diverse revenue streams, driven by three distinct customer segments: job seekers who buy premium subscriptions with various special services; advertisers large and small who rely on its marketing solutions unit; and, supporting its largest and fastest-growing business, corporate recruiters who buy special search tools from its talent solutions unit. At the time of its IPO on May 19, 2011, LinkedIn had amassed 100 million registered users, adding a new one literally every second and a million every 10 days, half of them outside the United States. These users were attracted by the ability to manage their careers by networking with other professionals, seeking and sharing insights, and searching for jobs if the need arose.*

*Like most online services, LinkedIn strives to engage users on its site for as long as possible through continually improved content and new features. Toward that goal, the company acquired SlideShare, a presentation-hosting site, and Pulse, a news-reading application, and also launched Talent Pipeline to help recruiters manage their leads. LinkedIn sees much growth from its mobile users, who in 2013 accounted for more than 30 percent of unique visits to the site, leading to a complete makeover of its apps for easier navigation and greater personalization. Although LinkedIn's well-targeted and positioned brand has led to much initial success, competition looms from other online giants, such as Facebook, and from established professional network services overseas, such as Viadeo SA in Europe and elsewhere.*

**To compete more effectively, many** companies are now embracing target marketing. Instead of scattering their marketing efforts, they're focusing on those consumers they have the greatest chance of satisfying.

Effective target marketing requires that marketers:

1. Identify and profile distinct groups of buyers who differ in their needs and wants (market segmentation).
2. Select one or more market segments to enter (market targeting).
3. For each target segment, establish, communicate, and deliver the right benefit(s) for the company's market offering (market positioning).

Market segmentation, targeting, and positioning are known as the "STP" of marketing. This chapter will focus on the first two steps; Chapter 10 discusses the third step. Chapters 11 and 12 describe how effective market segmentation, targeting, and positioning can build strong brands that grow over time and withstand competitive attacks.

# Bases for Segmenting Consumer Markets

Market segmentation divides a market into well-defined slices. A *market segment* consists of a group of customers who share a similar set of needs and wants. The marketer's task is to identify the appropriate number and nature of market segments and decide which one(s) to target.

We use two broad groups of variables to segment consumer markets. Some researchers define segments by looking at descriptive characteristics—geographic, demographic, and psychographic—and asking whether these segments exhibit different needs or product responses. For example, they might examine the differing attitudes of "professionals," "blue collars," and other groups toward, say, "safety" as a product benefit.

Other researchers define segments by looking at behavioral considerations, such as consumer responses to benefits, usage occasions, or brands, then seeing whether different characteristics are associated with each consumer-response segment. For example, do people who want "quality" rather than "low price" in an automobile differ in their geographic, demographic, and/or psychographic makeup?

Regardless of which type of segmentation scheme we use, the key is adjusting the marketing program to recognize customer differences. The major segmentation variables—geographic, demographic, psychographic, and behavioral segmentation—are summarized in Table 9.1.

## GEOGRAPHIC SEGMENTATION

Geographic segmentation divides the market into geographical units such as nations, states, regions, counties, cities, or neighborhoods. The company can operate in one or a few areas, or it can operate in all but pay attention to local variations. In that way it can tailor marketing programs to the needs and wants of local customer groups in trading areas, neighborhoods, even individual stores. In a growing trend called *grassroots marketing*, marketers concentrate on making such activities as personally relevant to individual customers as possible.

*Source: Denver Post via Getty Images*

Outdoor goods retailer REI emphasizes local marketing initiatives in engaging its customers.

Much of Nike's initial success came from engaging target consumers through grassroots marketing efforts such as sponsorship of local school teams, expert-conducted clinics, and provision of shoes, clothing, and equipment to young athletes. Citibank provides different mixes of banking services in its branches depending on neighborhood demographics. Retail firms such as Starbucks, Costco, Trader Joe's, and REI have all found great success emphasizing local marketing initiatives, and other types of firms have also jumped into the action.[2]

More and more, regional marketing means marketing right down to a specific zip code. Many companies use mapping software to pinpoint the geographic locations of their customers, learning, say, that most customers are within a 10-mile radius of the store and are further concentrated within certain zip+4 areas. By mapping the densest areas, the retailer can rely on *customer cloning*, assuming the best prospects live where most of the customers already come from.

Some approaches combine geographic data with demographic data to yield even richer descriptions of consumers and neighborhoods. Nielsen Claritas has developed a geoclustering approach called PRIZM (Potential Rating Index by Zip Markets) NE that classifies more than half a million U.S. residential neighborhoods into 14 distinct groups and 66 distinct lifestyle segments called PRIZM Clusters.[3] The groupings take into consideration 39 factors in five broad categories: (1) education and affluence, (2) family life cycle, (3) urbanization, (4) race and ethnicity, and (5) mobility. The neighborhoods are broken down by zip code, zip+4, or census tract and block group. The clusters have descriptive titles such as *Blue Blood Estates, Winner's Circle, Hometown Retired, Shotguns and Pickups,* and *Back Country Folks.* The inhabitants in a cluster tend to lead similar lives, drive similar cars, have similar jobs, and read similar magazines. Table 9.2 has examples of three PRIZM clusters.

Geoclustering captures the increasing diversity of the U.S. population. PRIZM has been used to answer questions such as: Which neighborhoods or zip codes contain our most valuable customers? How deeply have we already penetrated these segments? Which distribution channels and promotional media work best in reaching our target clusters in each area? Barnes & Nobles placed its stores

| TABLE 9.1 | Major Segmentation Variables for Consumer Markets |
|---|---|
| Geographic region | Pacific Mountain, West North Central, West South Central, East North Central, East South Central, South Atlantic, Middle Atlantic, New England |
| City or metro size | Under 5,000; 5,000–20,000; 20,000–50,000; 50,000–100,000; 100,000–250,000; 250,000–500,000; 500,000–1,000,000; 1,000,000–4,000,000; 4,000,000+ |
| Density | Urban, suburban, rural |
| Climate | Northern, southern |
| Demographic age | Under 6, 6–11, 12–17, 18–34, 35–49, 50–64, 64+ |
| Family size | 1–2, 3–4, 5+ |
| Family life cycle | Young, single; young, married, no children; young, married, youngest child under 6; young; married, youngest child 6 or older; older, married, with children; older, married, no children under 18; older, single; other |
| Gender | Male, female |
| Income | Under $10,000; $10,000–$15,000; $15,000–$20,000; $20,000–$30,000; $30,000–$50,000; $50,000–$100,000; $100,000+ |
| Occupation | Professional and technical; managers, officials, and proprietors; clerical sales; craftspeople; forepersons; operatives; farmers; retired; students; homemakers; unemployed |
| Education | Grade school or less; some high school; high school graduate; some college; college graduate; post college |
| Religion | Catholic, Protestant, Jewish, Muslim, Hindu, other |
| Race | White, Black, Asian, Hispanic, Other |
| Generation | Silent Generation, Baby Boomers, Gen X, Millennials (Gen Y) |
| Nationality | North American, Latin American, British, French, German, Italian, Chinese, Indian, Japanese |
| Social class | Lower lowers, upper lowers, working class, middle class, upper middles, lower uppers, upper uppers |
| Psychographic lifestyle | Culture-oriented, sports-oriented, outdoor-oriented |
| Personality | Compulsive, gregarious, authoritarian, ambitious |
| Behavioral occasions | Regular occasion, special occasion |
| Benefits | Quality, service, economy, speed |
| User status | Nonuser, ex-user, potential user, first-time user, regular user |
| Usage rate | Light user, medium user, heavy user |
| Loyalty status | None, medium, strong, absolute |
| Readiness stage | Unaware, aware, informed interested, desirous, intending to buy |
| Attitude toward product | Enthusiastic, positive, indifferent, negative, hostile |

| TABLE 9.2 | Examples of PRIZM Clusters |
| --- | --- |

- **Young Digerati.** Young Digerati are the nation's tech-savvy singles and couples living in fashionable neighborhoods on the urban fringe. Affluent, highly educated, and ethnically mixed, they live in areas typically filled with trendy apartments and condos, fitness clubs and clothing boutiques, casual restaurants, and all types of bars—from juice to coffee to microbrew.

- **Beltway Boomers.** One segment of the huge baby boomer cohort—college-educated, upper-middle-class, and home-owning—is Beltway Boomers. Like many of their peers who married late, these boomers are still raising children in comfortable suburban subdivisions and pursuing kid-centered lifestyles.

- **The Cosmopolitans.** Educated, midscale, and multiethnic, the Cosmopolitans are urbane couples in America's fast-growing cities. Concentrated in a handful of metros—such as Las Vegas, Miami, and Albuquerque—these households feature older homeowners, empty nesters, and college graduates. A vibrant social scene surrounds their older homes and apartments, and residents love the nightlife and enjoy leisure-intensive lifestyles.

**Source:** *Nielsen*, www.claritas.com.

where the "Money & Brains" segment hangs out. Hyundai successfully targeted a promotional campaign to neighborhoods where the "Kids & Cul-de-Sacs," "Bohemian Mix," and "Pool & Patios" could be found.[4]

Marketing to microsegments has become possible even for small organizations as database costs decline, software becomes easier to use, and data integration increases. Going online to reach customers directly can open a host of local opportunities, as Yelp has found out.[5]

**YELP** Founded in 2004, Yelp.com wants to "connect people with great local businesses" by targeting consumers who seek or want to share reviews of local businesses in 96 markets around the world. Almost two-thirds of the Web site's millions of vetted online reviews are for restaurants and retailers. Yelp was launched in San Francisco, where monthly parties with preferred users evolved into a formal program, Yelp Elite, now used to launch the service into new cities. The company's recently introduced mobile app allows it to bypass the Internet and connect with consumers directly; almost 50 percent of searches on the site now come from its mobile platform. Yelp generates revenue by selling designated Yelp Ads to local merchants via hundreds of salespeople. The local advertising business is massive—estimated to be worth between $90 billion and $130 billion—but relatively untapped given that many local businesses are not that tech-savvy. Sheryl Sandberg, COO of Facebook (a Yelp competitor), calls local advertising the Internet's "Holy Grail." Local businesses also benefit from Yelp—several research studies have demonstrated the potential revenue payback from having reviews of their businesses on the site.

Yelp has attracted scores of consumers and advertisers with its carefully vetted online reviews of local businesses.

*Source: © Don Snetzer/Alamy*

Those who favor such localized marketing see national advertising as wasteful because it is too "arm's length" and fails to address local needs. Those against local marketing argue that it drives up manufacturing and marketing costs by reducing economies of scale and magnifying logistical problems. A brand's overall image might be diluted if the product and message are too different in different localities.

## DEMOGRAPHIC SEGMENTATION

One reason demographic variables such as age, family size, family life cycle, gender, income, occupation, education, religion, race, generation, nationality, and social class are so popular with marketers is that they're often associated with consumer needs and wants. Another is that they're easy to measure. Even when we describe the target market in nondemographic terms (say, by personality type), we may need the link back to demographic characteristics in order to estimate the size of the market and the media we should use to reach it efficiently.

Here's how marketers have used certain demographic variables to segment markets.

**AGE AND LIFE-CYCLE STAGE** Consumer wants and abilities change with age. Toothpaste brands such as Crest and Colgate offer three main lines of products to target kids, adults, and older consumers. Age segmentation can be even more refined. Pampers divides its market into prenatal, new baby (0–5 months), baby (6–12 months), toddler (13–23 months), and preschooler (24 months+). Indirect age effects also operate for some products. One study of kids ages 8–12 found that 91 percent decided or influenced clothing or apparel buys, 79 percent grocery purchases, and 54 percent vacation choices, while 14 percent even made or swayed vehicle purchase decisions.[6]

Nevertheless, age and life cycle can be tricky variables. The target market for some products may be the *psychologically* young. To target 21-year-olds with its boxy Element, which company officials described as a "dorm room on wheels," Honda ran ads depicting sexy college kids partying near the car at a beach. So many baby boomers were attracted to the ads, however, that the average age of Element buyers turned out to be 42! With baby boomers seeking to stay young, Honda decided the lines between age groups were getting blurred. When sales fizzled, Honda decided to discontinue sales of the Element. When it was ready to launch a new subcompact called the Fit, the firm deliberately targeted Gen Y buyers as well as their empty-nest parents.[7]

**LIFE STAGE** People in the same part of the life cycle may still differ in their life stage. **Life stage** defines a person's major concern, such as going through a divorce, going into a second marriage, taking care of an older parent, deciding to cohabit with another person, buying a new home, and so on. As Chapter 6 noted, these life stages present opportunities for marketers who can help people cope with the accompanying decisions.

For example, the wedding industry attracts marketers of a vast range of products and services. No surprise—the average U.S. couple spends almost $27,000 on their wedding (see Table 9.3 for some major wedding expenditures).[8] But that's just the start. Newlyweds in the United States spend a total of about $70 billion on their households in the first year after marriage—and they buy more in the first six months than an established household does in five years!

The Honda Fit targets young Gen Y buyers as well as psychologically young empty nest parents.

Source: Courtesy American Honda Motor Co., Inc

| TABLE 9.3 | Major Wedding Expenditures |
|---|---|
| Reception: $11,599 | |
| Engagement ring: $5,229 | |
| Wedding rings: $1,594 | |
| Photography: $2,186 | |
| Wedding gown: $1,355 | |
| Flowers: $1,334 | |
| Wedding cake: $486 | |

**Source:** May 2012 survey from *Brides* magazine.

Marketers know marriage often means two sets of shopping habits and brand preferences must be blended into one. Procter & Gamble, Clorox, and Colgate-Palmolive include their products in "Newlywed Kits," distributed when couples apply for a marriage license. JCPenney has identified "Starting Outs" as one of its two major customer groups. Marketers pay a premium for name lists to assist their direct marketing because, as one noted, newlywed names "are like gold."[9]

But not everyone goes through that life stage at a certain time—or at all, for that matter. More than a quarter of all U.S. households now consist of only one person—a record high. It's no surprise this $1.9 trillion market is attracting interest from marketers: Lowe's has run an ad featuring a single woman renovating her bathroom; DeBeers sells a "right-hand ring" for unmarried women; and at the recently opened, ultra-hip Middle of Manhattan 63-floor tower, two-thirds of the occupants live alone in one-bedroom and studio rental apartments.[10]

**GENDER**   Men and women have different attitudes and behave differently, based partly on genetic makeup and partly on socialization.[11] Research shows that women have traditionally tended to be more communal-minded and men more self-expressive and goal-directed; women have tended to take in more of the data in their immediate environment and men to focus on the part of the environment that helps them achieve a goal.

A research study of shopping found that men often need to be invited to touch a product, whereas women are likely to pick it up without prompting. Men often like to read product information; women may relate to a product on a more personal level.

Marketers can now reach women more easily via media like Lifetime, Oxygen, and WE television networks and scores of women's magazines and Web sites; men are more easily found at ESPN, Comedy Central, and Spike TV channels and through magazines such as *Maxim* and *Men's Health*.[12] After Pinterest proved its

Given their elevated household spending rates, newlyweds are a lucrative target segment for marketers.

*Source: © MNStudio/Fotolia*

popularity among women, five different Web sites with similar functionality but targeted at men sprang up, including MANinteresting, Dudepins, and Gentlemint.[13]

Gender differences are shrinking in some other areas as men and women expand their roles. One Yahoo survey found that more than half of men identified themselves as the primary grocery shoppers in their households. Procter & Gamble now designs some ads with men in mind, such as for its Gain and Tide laundry detergents, Febreze air freshener, and Swiffer sweepers. On the flip side, according to some studies, women in the United States and the United Kingdom make 75 percent of decisions about buying new homes and purchase 60 percent of new cars.[14]

Nevertheless, gender differentiation has long been applied in clothing, hairstyling, and cosmetics. Avon, for one, has built a $6 billion-plus business by selling beauty products to women. Gillette has found similar success with its Venus razor.[15]

## VENUS RAZOR

Gillette's Venus razor has become the most successful women's shaving line ever—holding more than 50 percent of the global women's shaving market—as a result of insightful consumer research and extensive market tests revealing product design, packaging, and advertising cues. The razor was a marked departure from earlier designs, which had essentially been colored or repackaged versions of men's razors. Venus was designed to uniquely meet women's needs, instead of men's. Extensive research identified unique shaving needs for women, including shaving a surface area 9X greater than the male face; in a wet environment and across the unique curves of the body. The resulting female design included an oval shaped cartridge to better fit in to tight areas like underarms and bikini and additional lubrication for better glide. Furthermore, after discovering that women change their grip on a razor about 30 times during each shaving session, Gillette designed Venus razor with a wide, sculpted rubberized handle offering superior grip and control. Design work did not stop with the differences between men and women's shaving needs, when Gillette later found four distinct segments of female shavers—perfect shave seekers (no missed hairs), skin pamperers, pragmatic functionalists, and EZ seekers—the company designed Venus products for each of them. It also commissioned Harris Interactive to conduct an online study among more than 6,500 women in 13 countries that found seven of 10 wanted so-called goddess skin, defined as smooth (68 percent), healthy (66 percent), and soft (61 percent), leading to the introduction of the new Gillette Venus & Olay razor.

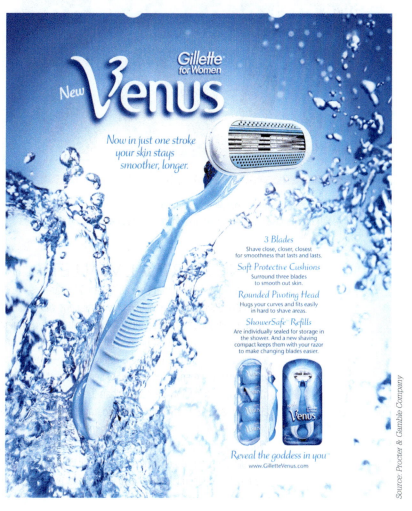

Years of in-depth consumer research with women has been critical to the long-term success of Gillette's Venus razor.

Source: Procter & Gamble Company

**INCOME** Income segmentation is a long-standing practice in such categories as automobiles, clothing, cosmetics, financial services, and travel. However, income does not always predict the best customers for a given product. Blue-collar workers were among the first purchasers of color television sets; it was cheaper for them to buy a television than to go to movies and restaurants.

Many marketers are deliberately going after lower-income groups, in some cases discovering fewer competitive pressures or greater consumer loyalty. Procter & Gamble launched two discount-priced brand extensions in 2005—Bounty Basic and Charmin Basic—which have met with some success. Other marketers are finding success with premium-priced products. When Whirlpool launched a pricey Duet washer line, sales doubled their forecasts in a weak economy, due primarily to middle-class shoppers who traded up.

Increasingly, companies are finding their markets are hourglass-shaped, as middle-market U.S. consumers

Source: PR NEWSWIRE

The Signature by Levi Strauss & Co. line of jeans allows the company to effectively and efficiently reach more mass-market consumers than with its other existing jeans lines.

migrate toward both discount *and* premium products. Companies that miss out on this new market risk being "trapped in the middle" and seeing their market share steadily decline. Recognizing that its channel strategy emphasized retailers like Sears selling primarily to the middle class, Levi-Strauss has since introduced premium lines such as Levi's Made & Crafted to upscale retailers Bloomingdales and Saks Fifth Avenue and the less-expensive Signature by Levi Strauss & Co. line to mass-market retailers Walmart and Kmart.

**GENERATION** Each generation or *cohort* is profoundly influenced by the times in which it grows up—the music, movies, politics, and defining events of that period. Members share the same major cultural, political, and economic experiences and often have similar outlooks and values. Marketers may choose to advertise to a cohort by using the icons and images prominent in its experiences. They can also try to develop products and services that uniquely meet the particular interests or needs of a generational target.

Although the beginning and ending birth dates of any generation are always subjective—and generalizations can mask important differences within the group—here are some general observations about the four main generation cohorts of U.S. consumers, from youngest to oldest.[16]

*Millennials (or Gen Y)* Although different age splits are used to define Millennials, or Gen Y, the term usually means people born between 1977 and 1994. That's about 78 million people in the United States, with annual spending power approaching $200 billion. If you factor in career growth and household and family formation and multiply by another 53 years of life expectancy, trillions of dollars in consumer spending are at stake over their life spans. It's not surprising that marketers are racing to get a bead on Millennials' buying behavior. Here is how one bank has targeted these consumers.[17]

**PNC'S VIRTUAL WALLET**   In early 2007, PNC Bank hired design consultants IDEO to study Gen Y—defined by PNC at that time as 18- to 34-year-olds—to help develop a marketing plan to appeal to them. IDEO's research found this cohort (1) didn't know how to manage money and (2) found bank Web sites clunky and awkward to use. PNC thus chose to introduce a new offering, Virtual Wallet, that combined three accounts—"Spend" (regular checking and bill payments), "Reserve" (backup interest-bearing checking for overdraft protection and emergencies), and "Grow" (long-term savings)—with a slick personal finance tool—the "Money Bar"—by which customers can drag money from account to account online by adjusting an on-screen slider. Instead of seeing a traditional ledger, customers can view balances on a calendar that displays estimated future cash flow based on when they get paid, when they pay their bills, and what their spending habits are. Customers also can set a "Savings Engine" tool to transfer money to savings when they receive a paycheck as well as get their account balances via text. PNC has added even more features to Virtual Wallet, such as transaction information for credit cards and a joint calendar view for joint account holders, which has expanded the service's appeal beyond its 1 million Gen Y customers. PNC also engages 80,000-plus of its Virtual Wallet customers in an "Inside the Wallet" blog, which the bank feels provides more detailed feedback than it can get with its Twitter and Facebook accounts.

Also known as the Echo Boomers, "digital native" Millennials have been wired almost from birth—playing computer games, navigating the Internet, downloading music, and connecting with friends via texting and social media. They are much more likely than other age groups to own multiple devices and multitask while online, moving across mobile, social, and PC platforms. They are also more likely to go online to broadcast their thoughts and experiences and to contribute user-generated content. They tend to trust friends more than corporate sources of information.[18]

Although they may have a sense of entitlement and abundance from growing up during the economic boom and being pampered by their boomer parents, Millennials are also often highly socially conscious, concerned about environmental issues, and receptive to cause marketing efforts. The recession hit them hard, and many have accumulated sizable debt. One implication is they are less likely to have bought their first homes and more likely to still live with their parents, influencing their purchases in what demographers are calling a "boom-boom" or boomerang effect. That is, the same products that appeal to 20-somethings also appeal to many of their youth-obsessed parents.

Because Gen Y members are often turned off by overt branding practices and "hard sell," marketers have tried many different approaches to reach and persuade them.[19] Consider these widely used experiential tactics.

1. *Student ambassadors*—Red Bull enlisted college students as Red Bull Student Brand Managers to distribute samples, research drinking trends, design on-campus marketing initiatives, and write stories for student newspapers. American Eagle, among other brands, has also developed an extensive campus ambassador program.
2. *Street teams*—Long a mainstay in the music business, street teams help to promote bands both big and small. Rock band Foo Fighters created a digital street team that sends targeted e-mail blasts to members who "get the latest news, exclusive audio/video sneak previews, tons of chances to win great Foo Fighters prizes, and become part of the Foo Fighters Family."
3. *Cool events*—Hurley, which defined itself as an authentic "Microphone for Youth" brand rooted in surf, skate, art, music, and beach cultures, has been a long-time sponsor of the U.S. Open of Surfing. The actual title sponsor for the 2013 event was Vans, whose shoes and clothing also have strong Millennial appeal. Vans has also been the title sponsor for almost 20 years of the Warped tour, which blends music with action (or extreme) sports.

**Gen X** Often lost in the demographic shuffle, the 50 million or so Gen X consumers, named for a 1991 novel by Douglas Coupland, were born between 1964 and 1978. The popularity of Kurt Cobain, rock band Nirvana, and the lifestyle portrayed in the critically lauded film *Slacker* led to the use of terms like *grunge* and *slacker* to characterize Gen X when they were teens and young adults. They bore an unflattering image of disaffection, short attention spans, and weak work ethic.

These stereotypes have slowly disappeared. Gen Xers were certainly raised in more challenging times, when working parents relied on day care or left "latchkey kids" on their own after school and corporate downsizing led to the threat of layoffs and economic uncertainty. At the same time, social and racial diversity were more widely accepted, and technology changed the way people lived and worked. Although Gen Xers raised standards in educational achievement, they were also the first generation to find surpassing their parents' standard of living a serious challenge.

These realities had a profound impact. Gen Xers prize self-sufficiency and the ability to handle any circumstance. Technology is an enabler for them, not a barrier. Unlike the more optimistic, team-oriented Gen Yers, Gen Xers are more pragmatic and individualistic. As consumers, they are wary of hype and pitches that seem inauthentic

The Foo Fighters have used digital street teams to build stronger ties and a sense of community with their devoted fan base.

or patronizing. Direct appeals where value is clear often work best, especially as Gen Xers have become parents raising families.[20]

***Baby Boomers*** Baby boomers are the approximately 76 million U.S. consumers born between 1946 and 1964. Though they represent a wealthy target, possessing $1.2 trillion in annual spending power and controlling three-quarters of the country's wealth, marketers often overlook them. In network television circles, because advertisers are primarily interested in 18- to 49-year-olds, viewers over 50 are referred to as "undesirables," though ironically the average age of the prime-time TV viewer is 51.

With many baby boomers approaching their 70s and even the last and youngest wave cresting 50, demand has exploded for products to turn back the hands of time. According to one survey, nearly one in five boomers was actively resisting the aging process, driven by the mantra "Fifty is the new thirty." As they search for the fountain of youth, sales of hair replacement and hair coloring aids, health club memberships, home gym equipment, skin-tightening creams, nutritional supplements, and organic foods have all soared.

Contrary to conventional marketing wisdom that brand preferences of consumers over 50 are fixed, one study of boomers ages 55 to 64 found a significant number are willing to change brands, spend on technology, use social networking sites, and purchase online.[21] Although they love to buy things, they hate being sold to, and as one marketer noted, "You have to earn your stripes every day." But abundant opportunity exists. Boomers are also less likely to associate retirement with "the beginning of the end" and see it instead as a new chapter in their lives with new activities, interests, careers, and even relationships.[22]

***Silent Generation*** Those born between 1925 and 1945—the "Silent Generation"—are redefining what *old age* means. To start with, many people whose chronological age puts them in this category don't see themselves as old.[23] One survey found that 60 percent of respondents over 65 said they felt younger than their actual age. A third of those 65 to 74 said they felt 10 to 19 years younger, and one in six felt at least 20 years younger than their actual age.[24]

Consistent with what they say, many older consumers lead very active lives. As one expert noted, it is if they were having a second middle age before becoming elderly. Advertisers have learned that older consumers don't mind seeing other older consumers in ads targeting them, as long as they appear to be leading vibrant lives. But marketers have learned to avoid clichés like happy older couples riding bikes or strolling hand in hand on a beach at sunset.

Strategies emphasizing seniors' roles as grandparents are well received. Many older consumers not only happily spend time with their grandkids, they often provide for their basic needs and at least occasional gifts. The founders of eBeanstalk.com, which sells children's learning toys, thought their online business would be driven largely by young consumers starting families. They were surprised to find that as much as 40 percent of their customers were older, mainly grandparents. These customers are very demanding but also more willing to pay full price than their younger counterparts.[25]

But they also need their own products. To design better appliances for the elderly, GE holds empathy sessions to help designers understand the challenges of aging. They tape their knuckles to represent arthritic hands, put kernels of popcorn in their shoes to create imbalance, and weigh down pans to simulate the challenge of putting food into ovens. Researchers at the MIT AgeLab use a suit called AGNES (<u>A</u>ge <u>G</u>ain <u>N</u>ow <u>E</u>mpathy <u>S</u>ystem) to research

Researchers at the MIT AgeLab use special suits in their shopping experiments to mimic the physical limitations of being elderly.

*Source: Nathan-Fried-Lipiski/MIT AgeLab*

the changing needs of the elderly. The suit has a pelvic harness that connects to a headpiece, mimicking an aging spine and restricted mobility, range of motion, joint function, balance, and vision.[26]

***Race and Culture*** *Multicultural marketing* is an approach recognizing that different ethnic and cultural segments have sufficiently different needs and wants to require targeted marketing activities and that a mass market approach is not refined enough for the diversity of the marketplace. Consider that McDonald's now does 40 percent of its U.S. business with ethnic minorities. Its highly successful "I'm Lovin' It" campaign was rooted in hip-hop culture but has had an appeal that transcended race and ethnicity.[27]

The Hispanic American, African American, and Asian American markets are all growing at two to three times the rate of nonmulticultural populations, with numerous submarkets, and their buying power is expanding. Multicultural consumers also vary in whether they are first, second, or a later generation and whether they are immigrants or born and raised in the United States.

Marketers need to factor the norms, language nuances, buying habits, and business practices of multicultural markets into the initial formulation of their marketing strategy, rather than adding these as an afterthought. All this diversity also has implications for marketing research; it takes careful sampling to adequately profile target markets.

Multicultural marketing can require different marketing messages, media, channels, and so on. Specialized media exist to reach virtually any cultural segment or minority group, though some companies have struggled to provide financial and management support for fully realized programs.

Fortunately, as countries become more culturally diverse, many marketing campaigns targeting a specific cultural group can spill over and positively influence others. Ford developed a TV ad featuring comedian Kevin Hart to launch its new Explorer model that initially targeted the African American market, but it became one of the key ads for the general market launch too.[28]

Next, we consider issues in the three largest multicultural markets—Hispanic Americans, African Americans, and Asian Americans. Table 9.4 lists some important facts and figures about them.[29]

***Hispanic Americans*** Accounting for more than half the growth in the U.S. population from 2000 to 2010, Hispanic Americans have become the largest minority in the country. It's projected that by 2020, 17 percent of U.S. residents will be of Hispanic origin. With annual purchasing power of more than $1 trillion in 2010—and expected to rise to $1.5 trillion by 2015—Hispanic Americans would be the world's *ninth-largest* market if they were a separate nation.[30]

This segment is youthful. The median age of U.S. Hispanics is 27—right in the middle of the highly coveted 18-to-34 Millennial age range—compared with a median age of 42 for non-Hispanic whites. In fact, every 30 seconds, two non-Hispanics retire while a Hispanic turns 18.[31] Hispanic Millennials have been called "fusionistas" because

| TABLE 9.4 | Multicultural Market Profile | | |
|---|---|---|---|
| | **Hispanic Americans** | **Asian Americans** | **African Americans** |
| Estimated population—2012 | 52.4 million | 15.7 million | 41.1 million |
| Forecasted population—2060 | 128.8 million | 34.4 million | 61.8 million |
| Number of minority-owned businesses in 2007 | 2.3 million | 1.5 million | 1.9 million |
| Revenue generated by minority-owned businesses in 2007 | $345.2 billion | $507.6 billion | $137.5 billion |
| Median household income in 2011 | $38,624 | $65,129 | $32,229 |
| Poverty rate 2011 | 25.3% | 12.3% | 27.6% |
| Percentage of those ages >25 with at least a high school education in 2012 | 65% | 88.8% | 84.9% |
| Number of veterans of U.S. armed forces in 2011 | 1.2 million | 264,695 | 2.3 million |
| Median age in 2011 | 27.0 | 36.0 | 31.7 |
| Percent of population under 18 years old in 2011 | 35% | 23% | 28% |

**Sources:** www.selig.uga.edu and www.census.gov.

they see themselves as both fully American and Latino.[32] As one marketing executive noted, "they eat tamales and burgers and watch football and *fútbol*."[33]

More than half the U.S. Hispanic population lives in just three states—California, Texas, and Florida—and more than 4 million Hispanics live in New York and Los Angeles. The Hispanic American market holds a wide variety of subsegments. Hispanics of Mexican origin are the dominant segment, followed by those of Puerto Rican and Cuban descent, though numbers of Salvadorans, Dominicans, Guatemalans, and Columbians are growing faster.[34]

To meet these divergent needs, Goya, the largest U.S. Hispanic food company with $1.3 billion in annual revenue, sells 1,600 products ranging from bags of rice to ready-to-eat, frozen empanadas and 38 varieties of beans alone. The company also has found much success selling key products directly to non-Hispanics. Its new philosophy: "We don't market to Latinos, we market as Latinos."[35]

Hispanic Americans often share strong family values—several generations may reside in one household—and strong ties to their country of origin. Even young Hispanics born in the United States tend to identify with the country their families are from. Hispanic Americans desire respect, are brand loyal, and take a keen interest in product quality. Procter & Gamble's research revealed that Hispanic consumers believe "*lo barato sale caro*" ("cheap can be expensive," or in the English equivalent, "you get what you pay for"). P&G found Hispanic consumers were so value-oriented they would even do their own product tests at home. One woman was using different brands of tissues and toilet paper in different rooms to see which her family liked best.[36]

U.S.-born Hispanic Americans also have different needs and tastes than their foreign-born counterparts and, though bilingual, often prefer to communicate in English. Though two-thirds of U.S. Hispanics are considered "bicultural" and comfortable with both Spanish- and English-speaking cultures, most firms choose to run Spanish-only ads on traditional Hispanic networks Univision and Telemundo. Univision is the long-time market-leader, which has found great success with its DVR-proof telenovelas (like daily soap operas), though new competition is emerging from Fox and other media companies.[37]

Clorox developed its Fraganzia line of cleaning products to appeal to those Hispanics who had strong preferences for hygiene and scent.

Marketers are reaching out to Hispanic Americans with targeted promotions, ads, and Web sites, but they need to capture the nuances of cultural and market trends.[38] Consider two companies that did so.

- Although Kleenex was the market-share leader in facial tissues among Hispanics, brand owner Kimberly-Clark felt there was much room to grow. Relying on research showing that more than twice as many Hispanics base their purchase decisions on package and design as in the general population, it launched the "Con Kleenex, Expresa Tu Hispanidad" campaign. Amateur artists were solicited to submit designs for customized packages sold during National Hispanic Heritage Month. Public voting chose three winners, and the campaign increased Kleenex sales at participating retailers by an impressive 476 percent.[39]
- The Clorox Company found its Hispanic American customers were relatively more likely to agree or over-index on "cleaning more to prevent family and friends from getting sick," especially in spring and summer months and when visitors came. Additional research also revealed the importance of packaging and a preference for scent as the final step in the cleaning process. Product development led to the launch of the FRANGAZIA line of cleaning products with lavender and other scents that had tested well. As support, Spanish-only ads were run on Hispanic media.[40]

General Motors, Southwestern Airlines, and Toyota have used a "Spanglish" approach in their ads, conversationally mixing some Spanish with English in dialogue among Hispanic families.[41] Continental Airlines, General Mills, and Sears have used mobile marketing to reach Hispanics.[42] With a mostly younger population that may have less access to Internet or landline service, Hispanics are much more active with mobile technology and social media than the general population. Staying connected to friends and family is important for them.[43]

***Asian Americans*** According to the U.S. Census Bureau, "Asian" refers to people having origins in any of the original peoples of the Far East, Southeast Asia, or the Indian subcontinent. Six countries represent 79 percent of the Asian American population: China (21 percent), the Philippines (18 percent), India (11 percent), Vietnam (10 percent), Korea (10 percent), and Japan (9 percent).

The diversity of these national identities limits the effectiveness of pan-Asian marketing appeals. For example, in terms of general food trends, research has uncovered that Japanese eat much more raw food than Chinese; Koreans are more inclined to enjoy spicy foods and drink more alcohol than other Asians; and Filipinos tend to be the most Americanized and Vietnamese the least Americanized in terms of food choices.[44]

The Asian American market has been called the "invisible market" because, compared with the Hispanic Americans and African American markets, it has traditionally received a disproportionally small fraction of U.S. companies' total multicultural marketing expenditure.[45] Yet it is getting easier to reach this market, given Asian-language newspapers, magazines, cable TV channels, and radio stations targeting specific groups.[46]

Telecommunications and financial services are a few of the industries more actively targeting Asian Americans. Wells Fargo Bank has a long tradition of marketing to Asian Americans, aided by its deep historical roots in California where a heavy concentration exists. The bank has engaged its Asian American agency partner, Dae Partners, for years. Wells Fargo itself is diverse with an internal team of multicultural experts and a significant group of Asian American executives. It has developed products and programs specifically for the Asian American market and is highly engaged in volunteerism and community efforts.[47]

Asian Americans tend to be more brand-conscious than other minority groups yet are the least loyal to particular brands. They also tend to care more about what others think (for instance, whether their neighbors will approve of them) and share core values of safety and education. Comparatively affluent and well educated, they are an attractive target for luxury brands. The most computer-literate group, Asian Americans are more likely to use the Internet on a daily basis.[48]

***African Americans*** African Americans are projected to have a combined spending power of $1.1 trillion by 2015. They have had a significant economic, social, and cultural impact on U.S. life, contributing inventions, art, music, sports achievements, fashion, and literature. Like many cultural segments, they are deeply rooted in the U.S. landscape while also proud of their heritage and respectful of family ties.[49]

Based on survey findings, African Americans are the most fashion-conscious of all racial and ethnic groups but are strongly motivated by quality and selection. They're also more likely to be influenced by their children when selecting a product and less likely to buy unfamiliar brands. African Americans watch television and listen to the radio more than other groups and are heavy users of mobile data. Nearly three-fourths have a profile on more than one social network, with Twitter being extremely popular.[50]

Media outlets directed at black audiences received only 2 percent of the $120 billion firms spent on advertising in 2011, however.[51] A Nielsen research study found that roughly half of African Americans say they are more likely to buy a product if its advertising portrays the black community in a positive manner. More than 90 percent said black media are more relevant to them than generic media outlets.[52] To encourage more marketing investment, the Cabletelevision Advertising Bureau trade organization even created an information-laden Web site, www.reachingblackconsumers.com.

Ad messages targeting African Americans must be seen as relevant. In a campaign for Lawry's Seasoned Salt targeting African Americans, images of soul food appeared; a campaign for Kentucky Fried Chicken showed an African American family gathered at a reunion—demonstrating an understanding of both the market's values and its lifestyle.[53] P&G's "My Black Is Beautiful" campaign was started by women inside the company who saw a lack of positive images of African American women in mainstream media. The campaign has a dedicated Web site, a national television show on BET network, and various promotional efforts featuring P&G's beauty, health, and personal care brands.[54]

Many companies have successfully tailored products to meet the needs of African Americans. Sara Lee Corporation's L'eggs discontinued its separate line of pantyhose for black women; now shades and styles popular among black women make up half the company's general-focus sub-brands. In some cases, campaigns have expanded beyond their African American target. State Farm's "50 Million Pound Challenge" weight-loss campaign began in the African American community but expanded to the general market.

Cigarette, liquor, and fast-food firms have been criticized for targeting urban African Americans. As one writer noted, with obesity a problem, it is disturbing that it is easier to find a fast-food restaurant than a grocery store in many black neighborhoods.[55]

***Lesbian, Gay, Bisexual, and Transgender (LGBT)*** The lesbian, gay, bisexual, and transgender (LGBT) market is estimated to make up 5 percent to 10 percent of the population and have approximately $700 billion in buying power.[56] Many firms have recently created initiatives to target this market.[57]

American Airlines created a Rainbow Team with a dedicated LGBT staff and Web site that has emphasized community-relevant services such as a calendar of gay-themed national events. JCPenney hired openly gay Ellen DeGeneres as its spokesperson, featured both male and female same-sex couples in its catalogs, and sponsored a float in New York's Gay Pride parade. Wells Fargo, General Mills, and Kraft are also often identified as among the most gay-friendly businesses.[58]

Logo, MTV's television channel for a gay and lesbian audience, has 150 advertisers in a wide variety of product categories and is available in more than 52 million homes. Increasingly, advertisers are using digital efforts to reach the market. Hyatt's online appeals to the LGBT community target social sites and blogs where customers share their travel experiences.

Some firms worry about backlash from organizations that will criticize or even boycott firms supporting gay and lesbian causes. Although Pepsi, Campbell's, and Wells Fargo all experienced such boycotts in the past, they continue to advertise to the gay community.

## PSYCHOGRAPHIC SEGMENTATION

**Psychographics** is the science of using psychology and demographics to better understand consumers. In *psychographic segmentation,* buyers are divided into groups on the basis of psychological/personality traits, lifestyle, or values. People within the same demographic group can exhibit very different psychographic profiles.

One of the most popular commercially available classification systems based on psychographic measurements is Strategic Business Insight's (SBI) VALS™ framework. VALS is based on psychological traits for people and classifies U.S. adults into eight primary groups based on responses to a questionnaire featuring four demographic and 35 attitudinal questions. The VALS system is continually updated with new data from more than 80,000 surveys per year (see Figure 9.1). You can find out which VALS type you are by going to the SBI Web site.[59]

The main dimensions of the VALS segmentation framework are consumer motivation (the horizontal dimension) and consumer resources (the vertical dimension). Consumers are inspired by one of three primary motivations: ideals, achievement, and self-expression. Those primarily motivated by ideals are guided by knowledge and principles. Those motivated by achievement look for products and services that demonstrate success to their peers. Consumers whose motivation is self-expression desire social or physical activity, variety, and risk. Personality traits such as energy, self-confidence, intellectualism, novelty seeking, innovativeness, impulsiveness, leadership, and

| Fig. 9.1 |

The VALS Segmentation System: An Eight-Part Typology

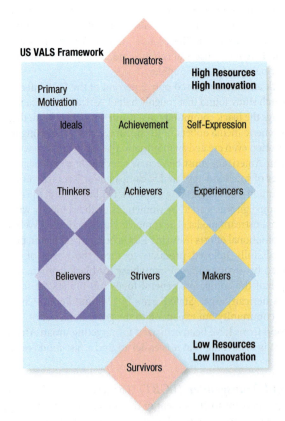

vanity—in conjunction with key demographics—determine an individual's resources. Different levels of resources enhance or constrain a person's expression of his or her primary motivation.

# BEHAVIORAL SEGMENTATION

Although psychographic segmentation can provide a richer understanding of consumers, some marketers fault it for being somewhat removed from actual consumer behavior.[60] In *behavioral segmentation,* marketers divide buyers into groups on the basis of their knowledge of, attitude toward, use of, or response to a product.

**NEEDS AND BENEFITS** Not everyone who buys a product has the same needs or wants the same benefits from it. Needs-based or benefit-based segmentation identifies distinct market segments with clear marketing implications. For example, Constellation Brands identified six different benefit segments in the U.S. premium wine market ($5.50 a bottle and up).[61]

- *Enthusiast (12 percent of the market).* Skewing female, their average income is about $76,000 a year. About 3 percent are "luxury enthusiasts" who skew more male with a higher income.
- *Image Seekers (20 percent).* The only segment that skews male, with an average age of 35. They use wine basically as a badge to say who they are, and they're willing to pay more to make sure they're getting the right bottle.
- *Savvy Shoppers (15 percent).* They love to shop and believe they don't have to spend a lot to get a good bottle of wine. Happy to use the bargain bin.
- *Traditionalist (16 percent).* With very traditional values, they like to buy brands they've heard of and from wineries that have been around a long time. Their average age is 50, and they are 68 percent female.
- *Satisfied Sippers(14 percent).* Not knowing much about wine, they tend to buy the same brands. About half of what they drink is white zinfandel.
- *Overwhelmed (23 percent).* A potentially attractive target market, they find purchasing wine confusing.

**DECISION ROLES** It's easy to identify the buyer for many products. In the United States, men normally choose their shaving equipment and women choose their pantyhose, but even here marketers must be careful in making targeting decisions because buying roles change. When ICI, the giant British chemical company now called AkzoNobel, discovered that women made 60 percent of decisions on the brand of household paint, it decided to advertise its Dulux brand to women.

People play five roles in a buying decision: *Initiator, Influencer, Decider, Buyer,* and *User.* For example, assume a wife initiates a purchase by requesting a new treadmill for her birthday. The husband may then seek information from many sources, including his best friend who has a treadmill and is a key influencer in what models to consider. After presenting the alternative choices to his wife, he purchases her preferred model, which ends up being used by the entire family. Different people are playing different roles, but all are crucial in the decision process and ultimate consumer satisfaction.

**USER AND USAGE-RELATED VARIABLES** Many marketers believe variables related to users or their usage—occasions, user status, usage rate, buyer-readiness stage, and loyalty status—are good starting points for constructing market segments.

*Occasions* Occasions mark a time of day, week, month, year, or other well-defined temporal aspects of a consumer's life. We can distinguish buyers according to the occasions when they develop a need, purchase a product, or use a product. For example, air travel is triggered by occasions related to business, vacation, or family. Occasion segmentation can help expand product usage.

*User Status* Every product has its nonusers, ex-users, potential users, first-time users, and regular users. Blood banks cannot rely only on regular donors to supply blood; they must also recruit new first-time donors and contact ex-donors, each with a different marketing strategy. The key to attracting potential users, or even possibly nonusers, is understanding the reasons they are not using. Do they have deeply held attitudes, beliefs, or behaviors or just lack knowledge of the product or brand benefits?

Included in the potential-user group are consumers who will become users in connection with some life stage or event. Mothers-to-be are potential users who will turn into heavy users. Producers of infant products and services learn their names and shower them with products and ads to capture a share of their future purchases. Market-share leaders tend to focus on attracting potential users because they have the most to gain from them. Smaller firms focus on trying to attract current users away from the market leader.

*Usage Rate* We can segment markets into light, medium, and heavy product users. Heavy users are often a small slice but account for a high percentage of total consumption. Heavy beer drinkers account for

87 percent of beer consumption—almost seven times as much as light drinkers. Marketers would rather attract one heavy user than several light users. A potential problem, however, is that heavy users are often either extremely loyal to one brand or never loyal to any brand and always looking for the lowest price. They also may have less room to expand their purchase and consumption. Light users may be more responsive to new marketing appeals.[62]

***Buyer-Readiness Stage*** Some people are unaware of the product, some are aware, some are informed, some are interested, some desire the product, and some intend to buy. To help characterize how many people are at different stages and how well they have converted people from one stage to another, recall from Chapter 5 that marketers can employ a *marketing funnel* to break the market into buyer-readiness stages.

The proportions of consumers at different stages make a big difference in designing the marketing program. Suppose a health agency wants to encourage women to have an annual Pap test to detect cervical cancer. At the beginning, most women may be unaware of the Pap test. The marketing effort should go into awareness-building advertising using a simple message. Later, the advertising should dramatize the benefits of the Pap test and the risks of not getting it. A special offer of a free health examination might motivate women to actually sign up for the test.

Figure 9.2 displays a funnel for two hypothetical brands. Compared with Brand B, Brand A performs poorly at converting one-time users to more recent users (only 46 percent convert for Brand A compared with 61 percent for Brand B). Depending on the reasons consumers didn't use again, a marketing campaign could introduce more relevant products, find more accessible retail outlets, or dispel rumors or incorrect beliefs consumers hold.

***Loyalty Status*** Marketers usually envision four groups based on brand loyalty status:

1. ***Hard-core loyals***—Consumers who buy only one brand all the time
2. ***Split loyals***—Consumers who are loyal to two or three brands
3. ***Shifting loyals***—Consumers who shift loyalty from one brand to another
4. ***Switchers***—Consumers who show no loyalty to any brand[63]

A company can learn a great deal by analyzing degrees of brand loyalty: Hard-core loyals can help identify the products' strengths; split loyals can show the firm which brands are most competitive with its own; and by looking at customers dropping its brand, the company can learn about its marketing weaknesses and attempt to correct them. One caution: What appear to be brand-loyal purchase patterns may reflect habit, indifference, a low price, a high switching cost, or the unavailability of other brands.

***Attitude*** Five consumer attitudes about products are enthusiastic, positive, indifferent, negative, and hostile. Workers in a political campaign use attitude to determine how much time and effort to spend with each voter. They thank enthusiastic voters and remind them to vote, reinforce those who are positively disposed, try to win the votes of indifferent voters, and spend no time trying to change the attitudes of negative and hostile voters.

***Multiple Bases*** Combining different behavioral bases can provide a more comprehensive and cohesive view of a market and its segments. Figure 9.3 depicts one possible way to break down a target market by various behavioral segmentation bases.

| Fig. 9.2 |

Example of Marketing Funnel

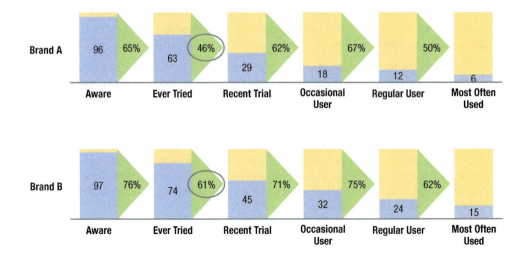

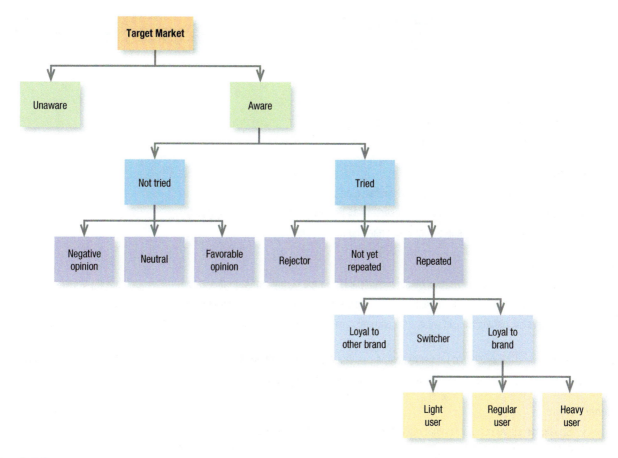

**| Fig. 9.3 |**

Behavioral Segmentation Breakdown

# How Should Business Markets Be Segmented?

We can segment business markets with some of the same variables we use in consumer markets, such as geography, benefits sought, and usage rate, but business marketers also use other variables. Table 9.5 shows one set of these. The demographic variables are the most important, followed by the operating variables—down to the personal characteristics of the buyer.

The table lists major questions that business marketers should ask in determining which segments and customers to serve. A rubber-tire company can sell tires to manufacturers of automobiles, trucks, farm tractors, forklift trucks, or aircraft. Within a chosen target industry, it can further segment by company size and set up separate operations for selling to large and small customers.

A company can segment further by purchase criteria. Government laboratories need low prices and service contracts for scientific equipment, university laboratories need equipment that requires little service, and industrial labs need equipment that is highly reliable and accurate.

Business marketers generally identify segments through a sequential process. Consider an aluminum company: The company first undertook macrosegmentation. It looked at which end-use market to serve: automobile, residential, or beverage containers. It chose the residential market, and it needed to determine the most attractive product application: semifinished material, building components, or aluminum mobile homes. Deciding to focus on building components, it considered the best customer size and chose large. The second stage consisted of microsegmentation. The company distinguished among customers buying on price, service, and quality. Because it had a high-service profile, the firm decided to concentrate on the service-motivated segment of the market.

| TABLE 9.5 | Major Segmentation Variables for Business Markets |
|---|---|

**Demographic**

1. *Industry:* Which industries should we serve?
2. *Company size:* What size companies should we serve?
3. *Location:* What geographical areas should we serve?

**Operating Variables**

4. *Technology:* What customer technologies should we focus on?
5. *User or nonuser status:* Should we serve heavy users, medium users, light users, or nonusers?
6. *Customer capabilities:* Should we serve customers needing many or few services?

**Purchasing Approaches**

7. *Purchasing-function organization:* Should we serve companies with a highly centralized or decentralized purchasing organization?
8. *Power structure:* Should we serve companies that are engineering dominated, financially dominated, and so on?
9. *Nature of existing relationship:* Should we serve companies with which we have strong relationships or simply go after the most desirable companies?
10. *General purchasing policies:* Should we serve companies that prefer leasing? Service contract? Systems purchases? Sealed bidding?
11. *Purchasing criteria:* Should we serve companies that are seeking quality? Service? Price?

**Situational Factors**

12. *Urgency:* Should we serve companies that need quick and sudden delivery or service?
13. *Specific application:* Should we focus on a certain application of our product rather than all applications?
14. *Size or order:* Should we focus on large or small orders?

**Personal Characteristics**

15. *Buyer-seller similarity:* Should we serve companies whose people and values are similar to ours?
16. *Attitude toward risk:* Should we serve risk-taking or risk-avoiding customers?
17. *Loyalty:* Should we serve companies that show high loyalty to their suppliers?

**Source:** Adapted from Thomas V. Bonoma and Benson P. Shapiro, *Segmenting the Industrial Market* (Lexington, MA: Lexington Books, 1983).

Business-to-business marketing experts James C. Anderson and James A. Narus have urged marketers to present flexible market offerings to all members of a segment.[64] A **flexible market offering** consists of two parts: a *naked solution* containing the product and service elements that all segment members value and *discretionary options* that some segment members value. Each option might carry an additional charge. Siemens Electrical Apparatus Division sells metal-clad boxes to small manufacturers at prices that include free delivery and a warranty, but it also offers installation, tests, and communication peripherals as extra-cost options.

# Market Targeting

There are many statistical techniques for developing market segments.[65] Once the firm has identified its market-segment opportunities, it must decide how many and which ones to target. Marketers are increasingly combining several variables in an effort to identify smaller, better-defined target groups. Thus, a bank may not only identify a group of wealthy retired adults but within that group distinguish several segments depending on current income, assets, savings, and risk preferences. This has led some market researchers to advocate a *needs-based market segmentation approach*. Roger Best proposed the seven-step approach shown in Table 9.6.

| TABLE 9.6 | Steps in the Segmentation Process |
|---|---|

| | **Description** |
|---|---|
| 1. Needs-Based Segmentation | Group customers into segments based on similar needs and benefits sought by customers in solving a particular consumption problem. |
| 2. Segment Identification | For each needs-based segment, determine which demographics, lifestyles, and usage behaviors make the segment distinct and identifiable (actionable). |
| 3. Segment Attractiveness | Using predetermined segment attractiveness criteria (such as market growth, competitive intensity, and market access), determine the overall attractiveness of each segment. |
| 4. Segment Profitability | Determine segment profitability. |
| 5. Segment Positioning | For each segment, create a "value proposition" and product-price positioning strategy based on that segment's unique customer needs and characteristics. |
| 6. Segment "Acid Test" | Create "segment storyboard" to test the attractiveness of each segment's positioning strategy. |
| 7. Marketing-Mix Strategy | Expand segment positioning strategy to include all aspects of the marketing mix: product, price, promotion, and place. |

**Source:** Adapted from Roger J. Best, *Market-Based Management,* 6th ed. (Upper Saddle River NJ: Prentice Hall, 2013). © 2013. Printed and electronically reproduced by permission of Pearson Education, Inc. Upper Saddle River, New Jersey.

# Effective Segmentation Criteria

Not all segmentation schemes are useful. We could divide buyers of table salt into blond and brunette customers, but hair color is undoubtedly irrelevant to the purchase of salt. Furthermore, if all salt buyers buy the same amount of salt each month, believe all salt is the same, and would pay only one price for salt, this market is minimally segmentable from a marketing point of view.

To be useful, market segments must rate favorably on five key criteria:

- *Measurable.* The size, purchasing power, and characteristics of the segments can be measured.
- *Substantial.* The segments are large and profitable enough to serve. A segment should be the largest possible homogeneous group worth going after with a tailored marketing program. It would not pay, for example, for an automobile manufacturer to develop cars for people who are under four feet tall.
- *Accessible.* The segments can be effectively reached and served.
- *Differentiable.* The segments are conceptually distinguishable and respond differently to different marketing-mix elements and programs. If married and single women respond similarly to a sale on perfume, they do not constitute separate segments.
- *Actionable.* Effective programs can be formulated for attracting and serving the segments.

Michael Porter has identified five forces that determine the intrinsic long-run attractiveness of a market or market segment: industry competitors, potential entrants, substitutes, buyers, and suppliers. The threats these forces pose are as follows.[66]

1. *Threat of intense segment rivalry*—A segment is unattractive if it already contains numerous, strong, or aggressive competitors. It's even more unattractive if it's stable or declining, if plant capacity must be added in large increments, if fixed costs or exit barriers are high, or if competitors have high stakes in staying in the segment. These conditions will lead to frequent price wars, advertising battles, and new-product introductions and will make it expensive to compete. The mobile phone market has seen fierce competition due to segment rivalry.

2. *Threat of new entrants*—The most attractive segment is one in which entry barriers are high and exit barriers are low. Few new firms can enter the industry, and poorly performing firms can easily exit. When both entry and exit barriers are high, profit potential is high, but firms face more risk because poorer-performing firms stay in and fight it out. When both entry and exit barriers are low, firms easily enter and leave the industry, and returns are stable but low. The worst case occurs when entry barriers are low and exit barriers are high: Here firms enter during good times but find it hard to leave during bad times. The result is chronic

overcapacity and depressed earnings for all. The airline industry has low entry barriers but high exit barriers, leaving all carriers struggling during economic downturns.

3. *Threat of substitute products*—A segment is unattractive when there are actual or potential substitutes for the product. Substitutes place a limit on prices and on profits. If technology advances or competition increases in these substitute industries, prices and profits are likely to fall. Air travel has severely challenged profitability for Greyhound and Amtrak.

4. *Threat of buyers' growing bargaining power*—A segment is unattractive if buyers possess strong or growing bargaining power. The rise of retail giants such as Walmart has led some analysts to conclude that the potential profitability of packaged-goods companies will become curtailed. Buyers' bargaining power grows when they become more concentrated or organized, when the product represents a significant fraction of their costs, when the product is undifferentiated, when buyers' switching costs are low, or when they can integrate upstream. To protect themselves, sellers might select buyers who have the least power to negotiate or switch suppliers. A better defense is developing superior offers that strong buyers cannot refuse.

5. *Threat of suppliers' growing bargaining power*—A segment is unattractive if the company's suppliers are able to raise prices or reduce quantity supplied. Suppliers tend to be powerful when they are concentrated or organized, when they can integrate downstream, when there are few substitutes, when the supplied product is an important input, and when the costs of switching suppliers are high. The best defenses are to build win-win relationships with suppliers or use multiple supply sources.

## EVALUATING AND SELECTING THE MARKET SEGMENTS

In evaluating market segments, the firm must look at two factors: the segment's overall attractiveness and the company's objectives and resources. How well does a potential segment score on the five criteria? Does it have characteristics that make it generally attractive, such as size, growth, profitability, scale economies, and low risk? Does investing in it make sense given the firm's objectives, competencies, and resources? Some attractive segments may not mesh with the company's long-run objectives, or the company may lack one or more competencies necessary to offer superior value.

Marketers have a range or continuum of possible levels of segmentation that can guide their target market decisions. As Figure 9.4 shows, at one end is a mass market of essentially one segment; at the other are individuals or segments of one person each. Between lie multiple segments and single segments. We describe approaches to each of the four levels next.

**FULL MARKET COVERAGE** With full market coverage, a firm attempts to serve all customer groups with all the products they might need. Only very large firms such as Microsoft (software market), General Motors (vehicle market), and Coca-Cola (nonalcoholic beverage market) can undertake a full market coverage strategy. Large firms can cover a whole market in two broad ways: through differentiated or undifferentiated marketing.

In *undifferentiated* or *mass marketing*, the firm ignores segment differences and goes after the whole market with one offer. It designs a marketing program for a product with a superior image that can be sold to the broadest number of buyers via mass distribution and mass communications. Undifferentiated marketing is appropriate when all consumers have roughly the same preferences and the market shows no natural segments. Henry Ford epitomized this strategy when he offered the Model-T Ford in one color, black.

The argument for mass marketing is that it creates the largest potential market, which leads to the lowest costs, which in turn can lead to lower prices or higher margins. The narrow product line keeps down the costs of research and development, production, inventory, transportation, marketing research, advertising, and product management. The undifferentiated communication program also reduces costs. However, many critics point to the increasing splintering of the market and the proliferation of marketing channels and communication, which make it difficult and increasingly expensive to reach a mass audience.

| **Fig. 9.4** |

Possible
Levels of
Segmentation

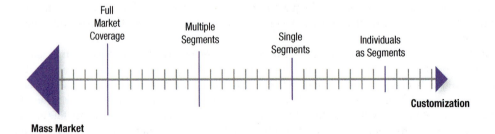

When different groups of consumers have different needs and wants, marketers can define multiple segments. The company can often better design, price, disclose, and deliver the product or service and also fine-tune the marketing program and activities to better reflect competitors' marketing. In *differentiated marketing*, the firm sells different products to all the different segments of the market. Cosmetics firm Estée Lauder markets brands that appeal to women (and men) of different tastes: The flagship brand, the original Estée Lauder, appeals to older consumers; Clinique caters to middle-aged women; M.A.C. to youthful hipsters; Aveda to aromatherapy enthusiasts; and Origins to ecoconscious consumers who want cosmetics made from natural ingredients.[67] Perhaps no firm practices differentiated marketing like Hallmark Cards, which celebrated its 100th birthday in 2010.[68]

**HALLMARK**  Hallmark's personal expression products are sold in more than 40,000 retail outlets nationwide and in 100 countries worldwide. Each year the company produces 10,000 new and redesigned greeting cards, as well as related products including party goods, gift wrap, and ornaments. Its success is due in part to its vigorous segmentation of the greeting card business. In addition to popular sub-branded card lines such as the humorous Shoebox Greetings, Hallmark has introduced lines targeting specific market segments. Fresh Ink targets 18- to 39-year-old women. The Simple Motherhood line targets moms with designs featuring fresh photography and simple, relatable sentiments. Hallmark's three ethnic lines—Mahogany, Sinceramente Hallmark, and Tree of Life—target African American, Hispanic, and Jewish consumers, respectively. Specific greeting cards also benefit charities such as (PRODUCT) RED™, UNICEF, and the Susan G. Komen Race for the Cure. Hallmark has also embraced technology. Musical greeting cards incorporate sound clips from popular movies, TV shows, and songs. Hallmark recently introduced its Magic Prints line of interactive products, with "magic mitt" technology that lets kids leave an imprint of their hand on an insert in a card or other keepsake for parents or grandparents. Online, Hallmark offers e-cards as well as personalized printed greeting cards that it mails for consumers. For business needs, Hallmark Business Expressions offers personalized corporate holiday cards and greeting cards for all occasions and events.

Differentiated marketing typically creates more total sales than undifferentiated marketing. However, it also increases the costs of doing business. Because differentiated marketing leads to both higher sales and higher costs, no generalizations about its profitability are valid.

**MULTIPLE SEGMENT SPECIALIZATION** With *selective specialization*, a firm selects a subset of all the possible segments, each objectively attractive and appropriate. There may be little or no synergy among the segments, but each promises to be a moneymaker. When Procter & Gamble launched Crest Whitestrips, initial target segments included newly engaged women and brides-to-be as well as gay males. The multisegment strategy also has the advantage of diversifying the firm's risk.

Keeping synergies in mind, companies can try to operate in supersegments rather than in isolated segments. A **supersegment** is a set of segments sharing some exploitable similarity. For example, many symphony orchestras target people who have broad cultural interests, rather than only those who regularly attend concerts. A firm can also attempt to achieve some synergy with product or market specialization.

Hallmark has thoroughly segmented the greeting card market according to occasion, personality, race, and other factors.

*Source: Greenberg 1 of 6/Alamy*

- With *product specialization*, the firm sells a certain product to several different market segments. A microscope manufacturer, for instance, sells to university, government, and commercial laboratories, making different instruments for each and building a strong reputation in the specific product area. The downside risk is that the product may be supplanted by an entirely new technology.
- With *market specialization*, the firm concentrates on serving many needs of a particular customer group, such as by selling an assortment of products only to university laboratories. The firm gains a strong reputation among this customer group and becomes a channel for additional products its members can use. The downside risk is that the customer group may suffer budget cuts or shrink in size.

**SINGLE-SEGMENT CONCENTRATION**  With single-segment concentration, the firm markets to only one particular segment. Porsche concentrates on the sports car enthusiast and Volkswagen on the small-car market—its foray into the large-car market with the Phaeton was a failure in the United States. Through concentrated marketing, the firm gains deep knowledge of the segment's needs and achieves a strong market presence. It also enjoys operating economies by specializing its production, distribution, and promotion. If it captures segment leadership, the firm can earn a high return on its investment.

A *niche* is a more narrowly defined customer group seeking a distinctive mix of benefits within a segment. Marketers usually identify niches by dividing a segment into subsegments. Whereas Hertz, Avis, Alamo, and others specialize in airport rental cars for business and leisure travelers, Enterprise has attacked the low-budget, insurance-replacement market by primarily renting to customers whose cars have been wrecked or stolen. By creating unique associations to low cost and convenience in an overlooked niche market, Enterprise has been highly profitable. Another up-and-coming niche marketer is Allegiant Air.[69]

**ALLEGIANT AIR**  The recent prolonged recession wreaked havoc on the financial performance of all the major U.S. domestic airlines. Up-and-comer Allegiant Air, however, managed to turn a profit quarter after quarter. Founded in Eugene, OR, in 2007, Allegiant has developed a highly successful niche strategy by providing leisure travelers affordable nonstop flights from smaller markets such as Great Falls, MT; Grand Forks, ND; Knoxville, TN; and Plattsburgh, NY; to popular vacation spots in Florida, California, and Hawaii and to Las Vegas, Phoenix, and Myrtle Beach. By staying off the beaten track, it avoids competition on all but a handful of its 100-plus routes. Much of its passenger traffic is additive and incremental, attracting tourist travel that might not have otherwise even happened. If a market doesn't seem to be taking hold, Allegiant quickly drops it. The carrier carefully balances revenues and costs. It charges for services—like in-flight beverages and overhead storage space—that are free on other airlines. It also generates additional revenue by cross-selling vacation products and packages. Allegiant owns its 64 used MD-80 planes and also cuts costs by flying only a few times a week instead of a few times a day like most airlines. It even fixes its seats at a pitch halfway between fully upright and fully reclined—adjustable seats add weight, burn fuel, and are a "maintenance nightmare." The formula seems to be working. Passengers in its local markets love the convenience, keeping Allegiant's planes full and the company profitable.

Allegiant Air has found a niche flying leisure travelers from smaller markets.

Source: © Michael Matthews/Alamy

What does an attractive niche look like? Niche customers have a distinct set of needs; they will pay a premium to the firm that best satisfies them; the niche is fairly small but has size, profit, and growth potential and is unlikely to attract many competitors; and it gains certain economies through specialization. As marketing efficiency increases, niches that seemed too small may become more profitable. See "Marketing Insight: Chasing the Long Tail."

**INDIVIDUAL MARKETING** The ultimate level of segmentation leads to "segments of one," "customized marketing," or "one-to-one marketing."[70] As companies have grown proficient at gathering information about individual customers and business partners (suppliers, distributors, retailers), and as their factories are being designed more flexibly, they have increased their ability to individualize market offerings, messages, and media. **Mass customization** is the ability of a company to meet each customer's requirements—to prepare on a mass basis individually designed products, services, programs, and communications.[71]

---

## marketing insight

## Chasing the Long Tail

The advent of online commerce, made possible by technology and epitomized by Amazon.com, eBay, iTunes, and Netflix, has led to a shift in consumer buying patterns, according to Chris Anderson, editor-in-chief of *Wired* magazine and author of *The Long Tail*.

In most markets, the distribution of product sales conforms to a curve weighted heavily to one side—the "head"—where the bulk of sales are generated by a few products. The curve falls rapidly toward zero and hovers just above it far along the X-axis—the "long tail"—where the vast majority of products generate very little sales. The mass market traditionally focused on generating "hit" products that occupy the head, disdaining the low-revenue market niches comprising the tail. The Pareto principle–based "80–20" rule—that 80 percent of a firm's revenue is generated by 20 percent of a firm's products—epitomizes this thinking.

Anderson asserts that as a result of consumers' enthusiastic adoption of the Internet as a shopping medium, the long tail holds significantly more value than before. In fact, he argues, the Internet has directly contributed to the shifting of demand "down the tail, from hits to niches" in a number of product categories including music, books, clothing, and movies. According to this view, the rule that now prevails is more like "50–50," with lower-selling products adding up to half a firm's revenue.

Anderson's long-tail theory is based on three premises: (1) Lower costs of distribution make it economically easier to sell products without precise predictions of demand; (2) The more products available for sale, the greater the likelihood of tapping into latent demand for niche tastes unreachable through traditional retail channels; and (3) If enough niche tastes are aggregated, a big new market can result.

Anderson identifies two aspects of Internet shopping that support these premises. First, the increased inventory and variety afforded online permit greater choice. Second, the search costs for relevant new products are lowered due to the wealth of information online, the filtering of product recommendations based on user preferences that vendors can provide, and the word-of-mouth network of Internet users.

Some critics challenge the notion that old business paradigms have changed as much as Anderson suggests. Especially in entertainment, they say, the "head" where hits are concentrated is valuable also to consumers, not only to the content creators. One critique argued that "most hits are popular because they are of high quality," and another noted that the majority of products and services making up the long tail originate from a small concentration of online "long-tail aggregators."

Although some academic research supports the long-tail theory, other research is more challenging, finding that poor recommendation systems render many very low share products in the tail so obscure and hard to find they disappear before they can be purchased frequently enough to justify their existence. For companies selling physical products, inventory, stocking, and handling costs can outweigh any financial benefits of such products.

Harvard's Anita Elberse provides an especially detailed analysis of various media and entertainment options via sources such as sales data from Nielsen Soundscan and online music service Rhapsody, with some provocative findings. Blockbusters are capturing even more of the market than they used to, which Elberse attributes to humans' social nature and desire to share experiences. Consumers in the tail tend to be heavier users in the category but actually don't like niche products as much as they like the hit products.

Elberse concluded that consumer behavior online and offline in the media and entertainment industries was highly similar and favored hit products in both cases. She notes that niche products at the tail end of a distribution can have value, but keeping costs low is critical. The debate over the importance of the long tail is likely to continue; perhaps the answer is that it is not so much either/or, but how hit and niche products can best be created and marketed.

**Sources:** Chris Anderson, *The Long Tail* (New York: Hyperion, 2006); "Reading the Tail," interview with Chris Anderson, *Wired*, July 8, 2006, p. 30; "Wag the Dog: What the Long Tail Will Do," *The Economist*, July 8, 2006, p. 77; John Cassidy, "Going Long," *New Yorker*, July 10, 2006; Erik Brynjolfsson, Yu "Jeffrey" Hu, and Michael D. Smith, "From Niches to Riches: Anatomy of a Long Tail," *MIT Sloan Management Review* (Summer 2006), p. 67; Anita Elberse, "Should You Invest in the Long Tail," *Harvard Business Review*, July–August 2008, pp. 88–96 (with online commentary); Lee Gomes, "Study Refutes Niche Theory Spawned by Web," Wall Street Journal, July 2, 2008; Erick Schonfeld, "Poking Holes in the Long Tail Theory," www.techcrunch.com, July 2, 2008; "Rethinking the Long Tail Theory: How to Define 'Hits' and 'Niches,'" *Knowledge@Wharton*, September 16, 2009.

Consumers increasingly value self-expression and the ability to capitalize on user-generated products (UGP) as much as user-generated content (UGC).[72] MINI Cooper's online "configurator" allows prospective buyers to virtually select and try out many options for a new MINI. Coke's Freestyle vending machine allows users to choose from more than 100 Coke brands or custom flavors or to create their own.[73]

Consumers can buy customized jeans, cowboy boots, and bicycles that cost thousands of dollars.[74] Peter Wagner started Wagner Custom Skis in Telluride, Colorado, in 2006. His company now makes about 1,000 snowboards and pairs of skis a year, with prices that start at $1,750. Each ski or snowboard is unique and precisely fitted to the preferences and riding style of its owner. Strategies like using NASA-like materials and making adjustments of thousands of an inch send a strong performance message, matched by the attractive aesthetic of the skis.[75]

Services are also a natural setting to apply customized marketing; airlines, hotels, and rental car agencies are attempting to offer more individualized experiences. Even political candidates are embracing customized marketing. On Facebook, politicians can find an individual's preferences by observing the groups or causes he or she joins, and then, using Facebook's ad platform, the campaign team can test hundreds of ad messages designed to reflect the theme of these other interests. Hikers may get an environmentally themed message; members of particular religious groups may get a Christian-themed message.[76]

Early pioneers in individual marketing Don Peppers and Martha Rogers outlined a four-step framework for what they called *one-to-one marketing* as follows:[77]

1. *Identify your prospects and customers.* Don't go after everyone. Build, maintain, and mine a rich customer database with information from all the channels and customer touch points.
2. *Differentiate customers in terms of (1) their needs and (2) their value to your company.* Spend proportionately more effort on the most valuable customers (MVCs). Apply activity-based costing and calculate customer lifetime value. Estimate net present value of all future profits from purchases, margin levels, and referrals, less customer-specific servicing costs.
3. *Interact with individual customers to improve your knowledge about their individual needs and to build stronger relationships.* Formulate customized offerings you can communicate in a personalized way.
4. *Customize products, services, and messages to each customer.* Facilitate customer interaction through the company contact center and Web site.

One-to-one marketing is not for every company. It works best for firms that normally collect a great deal of individual customer information and carry a lot of products that can be cross-sold, need periodic replacement or upgrading, and offer high value. For others, the required investment in information collection, hardware, and software may exceed the payout. The cost of goods is raised beyond what the customer is willing to pay.

Customers must know how to express their personal product preferences, however, or be given assistance to best customize a product.[78] Some customers don't know what they want until they see actual products, but they also cannot cancel the order after the company has started to work on it. The product may be hard to repair and have little resale value. In spite of this, customization has worked well for some products.

**LEGAL AND ETHICAL ISSUES WITH MARKET TARGETS** Marketers must target carefully to avoid consumer backlash. Some consumers resist being labeled.[79] Singles may reject single-serve food packaging if they don't want to be reminded they are eating alone. Elderly consumers who don't feel their age may not appreciate products that label them "old."

Market targeting also can generate public controversy when marketers take unfair advantage of vulnerable groups (such as children) or disadvantaged groups (such as inner-city residents) or promote potentially harmful products. The cereal industry has been criticized through the years for marketing efforts directed toward children. Critics worry that high-powered appeals presented by lovable animated characters will overwhelm children's defenses and lead them to want sugared cereals or poorly balanced breakfasts. Toy marketers have been similarly criticized. A key area of concern for many consumer protection advocates is the millions of kids who are online, as discussed in "Marketing Memo: Protecting Kids Online."

Not all attempts to target children, minorities, or other special segments draw criticism. Colgate-Palmolive's Colgate Junior toothpaste has special features designed to get children to brush longer and more often. Thus, the issue is not who is targeted, but how and for what purpose. Socially responsible marketing calls for targeting that serves not only the company's interests but also the interests of those targeted.

This is the case many companies make in marketing to the nation's preschoolers. With nearly one in four youngsters under the age of five attending some kind of organized child care, they feel the potential market—including kids and parents—is too great to pass up.[80] So in addition to standards such as art easels, gerbil cages,

## marketing memo

## Protecting Kids Online

With the explosion of cell phones, tablets, software apps, and social networking sites, an important concern is protecting unknowing or unsuspecting children in an increasingly complex technological world. The 8-to-12 tween market today is highly mobile and happy to share locations via an app and communicate with others by phone, leading one trendspotting expert to characterize them as "SoLoMo" (Social Local Mobile). Only one in five parents, however, uses basic content control features on smart phones, tablets, and game consoles. Thus, establishing ethical and legal boundaries in marketing to children online—and offline—continues to be a hot topic.

The Children's Online Privacy Protection Act (COPPA) was designed to better control the online collection of personal information from children under 13. It became law in July 2000 and helped ensure that Web sites targeted to children could not inappropriately collect names, e-mail addresses, and other sensitive information. Updates to the law in 2010 reflect the rapid technological developments that allowed marketers to collect so much more information from kids.

COPPA spells out "what a Web site operator must include in a privacy policy, when and how to seek verifiable consent from a parent and what responsibilities an operator has to protect children's privacy and safety online." The act forbids the collection of certain information about children unless a parent first gives permission. That information includes photos, videos, and audio files containing a human image or voice, as well as location data generated by a cell phone. "Personal identifiers" that allow a person to be tracked over time and across Web sites were deemed personal information and covered by the law. The updated law also outlined how parental consent could be verified through electronically scanned consent forms, video conferencing, and e-mail.

Some software developers were opposed to the amended COPPA, complaining that the cost of compliance and the risk of violations were too great. Penalties can be stiff. In 2008, Sony BMG Music Entertainment agreed to pay $1 million as part of a settlement with the FTC after being charged with improperly collecting information from 30,000 children under 13 on its Web sites. Mrs. Fields Cookies and Hershey Foods were fined early on.

Despite the restrictions of COPPA and other regulations, businesses continue to eye the potentially rewarding youth market. eBay has explored allowing consumers under 18 to set up accounts with parental authorization and shop, with some safeguards to prevent access to adult content and products. Facebook's stated interest in allowing children 12 and under to join its site has met with criticism from consumer, privacy, and child advocacy groups.

**Sources:** Anton Troianovski, "New Rules on Kids' Web Ads," *Wall Street Journal*, August 1, 2012; www.ftc.gov/ogc/coppa1.htm; "How to Comply with the Children's Online Privacy Protection Rule, www.business.ftc.gov/documents/; Richard Lardner, "Government Issues New Online Child Privacy Rules," www.news.terra.com, December 19, 2012; Greg Bensinger, "EBay to Target Under-18 Set," *Wall Street Journal*, July 26, 2012; Tim Peterson, "Tweenage Wasteland," *Adweek*, June 25, 2012, p.11; Sharon M. Goldman, "The Social Tween," *Adweek*, June 25, 2012, p. T1; Heather Chaet, "The Tween Machine," *Adweek*, June 25, 2012; Bruce Levinson, "Does Technology Change the Ethics of Marketing to Children," *Fast Company*, April 11, 2013.

and blocks, the nation's preschools are likely to have Care Bear worksheets, Pizza Hut reading programs, and Nickelodeon magazines.

Teachers and parents are divided about the ethics of this increasingly heavy preschool marketing push. Some side with groups such as Campaign for a Commercial-Free Childhood, whose members feel preschoolers are incredibly susceptible to advertising and that schools' endorsements of products make children believe the product is good for them—no matter what it is. Yet many preschools and day care centers operating on tight budgets welcome the free resources marketers offer.[81]

# Summary

1. Target marketing includes three activities: market segmentation, market targeting, and market positioning. Market segments are large, identifiable, distinct groups within a market.

2. The major segmentation variables for consumer markets are geographic, demographic, psychographic, and behavioral. Marketers use them singly or in combination.

3. Business marketers use all these variables along with operating variables, purchasing approaches, and situational factors.

4. To be useful, market segments must be measurable, substantial, accessible, differentiable, and actionable.

5. We can target markets at four main levels: mass, multiple segments, single (or niche) segment, and individuals.

6. A mass market targeting approach is adopted only by the biggest companies. Many companies target multiple segments defined in various ways such as various demographic groups who seek the same product benefit.

7. A niche is a more narrowly defined group. Globalization and the Internet have made niche marketing more feasible for many.

8. More companies now practice individual and mass customization. The future is likely to see more individual consumers take the initiative in designing products and brands.

9. Marketers must choose target markets in a socially responsible manner at all times.

---

## MyMarketingLab

Go to mymktlab.com to complete the problems marked with this icon ⭐ as well as for additional Auto-graded and Assisted-graded writing questions.

---

# Applications

---

## Marketing Debate
### Is Mass Marketing Dead?

With marketers increasingly adopting more and more refined market segmentation schemes—fueled by the Internet and other customization efforts—some claim mass marketing is dead. Others counter there will always be room for large brands employing marketing programs to target the mass market.

**Take a position:** Mass marketing is dead versus Mass marketing is still a viable way to build a profitable brand.

## Marketing Discussion
### Marketing Segmentation Schemes

⭐ Think of various product categories. In each segmentation scheme, to which segment do you feel you belong? How would marketing be more or less effective for you depending on the segment? How would you contrast demographic and behavioral segment schemes? Which one(s) do you think would be most effective for marketers trying to sell to you?

---

## Marketing Excellence

### >> HSBC

HSBC, originally known as the Hong Kong and Shanghai Banking Corporation Limited, was established in 1865 to finance the growing trade between China and the United Kingdom. Over the years, the bank has pioneered many modern banking practices in different countries. For example, it was the first bank in Thailand and printed the country's first banknotes. During the early 20th century, HSBC issued significant loans to several national governments, including China, which helped finance projects such as its railway development. The bank was also a key player in reestablishing Hong Kong's economy after World War II. By the end of the 20th century, it had acquired numerous companies in hopes of implementing a "three-legged stool" strategy; the three legs represented a foothold in the United Kingdom, the United States, and Asia. HSBC continued to grow around the world for many years, and by the early 21st century, it was the second-largest bank in the world.

HSBC has successfully grown its business under a single global brand and for years kept the tagline "The World's Local Bank." The aim was to link its huge international size with the close relationships it nurtures in each of the countries in which it operates. Sir John Bond, HSBC's former chairman, said, "Our position as the world's local bank enables us to approach each country uniquely, blending local knowledge with a worldwide operating platform."

HSBC launched one global campaign titled "Different Values," which embraced this exact notion of understanding multiple viewpoints and different interpretations. Print ads showed the same picture three times with a different interpretation in each. For example, an old classic car appeared with the words *freedom*, *status symbol*, and *polluter*. Next to the picture the copy read, "The more you look at the world, the more you realize that what one person values may be different from the next." In another set of print ads, the word *accomplishment* is first shown on a picture of a woman winning a beauty pageant, then an astronaut walking on the moon, and a young child tying his sneaker. The copy read, "The more you look at the world, the more you realize what really matters to people." Tracy Britton, head of marketing for HSBC Bank, USA, explained the strategy behind the campaign: "It encapsulates our global outlook that acknowledges and respects that people value things in very different ways. HSBC's global footprint gives us the insight and the opportunity not only to be comfortable, but confident in helping people with different values achieve what's really important to them."

HSBC revised its business strategy in 2011, consolidating in underperforming markets and investing in growth markets and businesses. As a result, it made a strategic shift in its branding efforts, moving away from the familiar "World's Local Bank" message and introducing "HSBC helps you unlock the world's potential." HSBC hoped to communicate how it connects local businesses to the world economy and, ultimately, how it focuses on the business elements that affect the world of the future. Chris Clark, HSBC's marketing director, explained that the new ads and campaign "are symptomatic of a shift from pure brand-led advertising to a more product-driven approach."

In one television ad, a young girl and her father set up a lemonade stand advertising lemonade for 50 cents. As customers passing by scramble to find a few quarters, the girl explains (in a different language) that she accepts other global currencies, including Hong Kong dollars and Brazilian reals. The voiceover says, "At HSBC we believe that in the future even the smallest business will be multinational." The ads were meant to make consumers feel reassured about banking with HSBC. In a corresponding print ad, a lemonade stand sign displayed the cost of a glass as 50¢, €0.4, and ¥3. The copy read, "Whether you

trade in dollars, euros or renminbi, global markets are opening up to everyone. At HSBC we can connect your business to new opportunities on six continents—in more than 90 currencies."

HSBC has traditionally focused much of its advertising in airports but also sponsors more than 250 cultural and sporting events, with a special concentration on helping youth, growing education, and embracing communities. These sponsorships allow the company to learn from different people and cultures around the world.

The bank has gained insight into how to target consumer niches with unique products and services. For example, it found a little-known product area growing at 125 percent a year: pet insurance. HSBC now distributes nationwide pet insurance to its depositors through its HSBC Insurance agency. In Malaysia, it offered a "smart card" and no-frills credit cards to the underserved student segment and targeted high-value customers with special "Premium Center" bank branches.

Today, HSBC remains one of the largest banks in the world, with four global businesses: retail banking and wealth management, commercial banking, global banking and markets, and global private banking. It serves 60 million customers through 6,600 branches in 80 countries and earned $22.6 billion in profit in 2013, with a brand value of $11.4 billion, according to Interbrand/*BusinessWeek* global brand rankings.

## Questions

1. What were the risks and benefits of HSBC's positioning itself as the "World's Local Bank"?

2. Evaluate HSBC's recent business and marketing shift. How do you think its current ad campaign and tagline, "HSBC helps you unlock the world's potential," resonate with its key consumers?

**Sources:** Carrick Mollenkamp, "HSBC Stumbles in Bid to Become Global Deal Maker," *Wall Street Journal*, October 5, 2006; Kate Nicholson, "HSBC Aims to Appear Global yet Approachable," *Campaign*, December 2, 2005, p. 15; Deborah Orr, "New Ledger," *Forbes*, March 1, 2004, pp. 72–73; "HSBC's Global Marketing Head Explains Review Decision," *Adweek*, January 19, 2004; "Now Your Customers Can Afford to Take Fido to the Vet," *Bank Marketing*, December 2003; Kenneth Hein, "HSBC Bank Rides the Coattails of Chatty Cabbies," *Brandweek*, December 1, 2003, p. 30; Sir John Bond and Stephen Green, "HSBC Strategic Overview," presentation to investors, November 27, 2003; "Lafferty Retail Banking Awards 2003," *Retail Banker International*, November 27, 2003, pp. 4–5; "Ideas That Work," *Bank Marketing*, November 2003; "HSBC Enters the Global Branding Big League," *Bank Marketing International*, August 2003; Normandy Madden, "HSBC Rolls Out Post-SARS Effort," *Advertising Age*, June 16, 2003, p. 12; Douglas Quenqua, "HSBC Dominates Ad Pages in New York Magazine Issue," *New York Times*, October 20, 2008, pg. B.6; Kimia M. Ansari, "A Different Point of View: HSBC." *Unbound Edition*, July 10, 2009; "The Evolution of "Your Point of View," press release, October 20, 2008; *Fortune*, Global 500; Alex Brownsell, "HSBC's Chris Clark on a New Era for the Bank's Marketing," *Marketingmagazine.co.uk*, May 31, 2012; "Best Global Brands 2012," *Interbrand*; HSBC.com; 2013 HSBC Annual Report.

## >> BMW

BMW is the ultimate driving machine. Manufactured by the German company Bayerische Motoren Werke AG, BMW stands for both performance and luxury. The company was founded in 1916 as an aircraft-engine manufacturer and produced engines during World Wars I and II. It evolved into a motorcycle and automobile maker by the mid-20th century, and today it is an internationally respected company and brand with $106 billion in sales in 2012.*

BMW's logo is one of the most distinctive and globally recognized symbols ever created. The signature BMW roundel looks like a spinning propeller blade set against a blue sky background—originally thought to be a tribute to the company's founding days as an aircraft-engine manufacturer. Recently, however, a *New York Times* reporter revealed that the logo, which features the letters *BMW* at the top of the outer ring and a blue-and-white checkered design in the inner ring, was trademarked in 1917 and meant to show the colors of the Free State of Bavaria, where the company is headquartered.

BMW's growth exploded in the 1980s and 1990s, when it successfully targeted the growing market of baby boomers and professional yuppies who put work first and wanted a car that spoke of their success. BMW gave them sporty sedans with exceptional performance and a brand that stood for prestige and achievement. The cars, which came in a 3, 5, or 7 Series, were basically the same design in three sizes. It was at this time that yuppies made Beemer and Bimmer the slang terms for BMW's cars and motorcycles, popular names still used today.

At the turn of the century, consumers' attitudes toward cars changed. Research showed that they cared less about the bragging rights of the BMW brand and instead desired a variety of design, size, price, and style choices. As a result, the company took several steps to grow its product line by targeting specific market segments. This resulted in unique premium-priced cars such as SUVs, convertibles, and roadsters, as well as less expensive compact cars like the 1 Series. In addition, BMW redesigned its 3, 5, and 7 Series cars, making them unique in appearance yet maintaining their exceptional performance. BMW's full range of cars now includes the 1 Series, 3 Series, 5 Series, 6 Series, 7 Series, X Series, Z4 Roadster, M Series, Hybrids, and BMWi.

BMW created the lower-priced 1 Series and X1 SUV to target the "modern mainstream," a group who are also family-focused and active but had previously avoided BMWs because of their premium cost. The 1 Series reached this group with its lower price point, sporty design, and luxury brand. The X1 and X3 also hit home with a smaller, less expensive SUV design.

The redesign of the 7 Series, BMW's most luxurious car, targeted a group called "upper conservatives." These wealthy, traditional consumers don't usually like sportier cars, so BMW added electronic components such as multiple options to control the windows, seats, airflow, and lights, a push-button ignition, and night vision, all controlled by a point-and-click system called iDrive. These enhancements added comfort and luxury, attracting drivers away from competitors like Jaguar and Mercedes.

BMW successfully launched the X Series by targeting "upper liberals" who had achieved success in the 1990s and gone on to have children and take up extracurricular activities such as biking, golf, and skiing. These consumers needed a bigger car for their active lifestyles and growing families, so BMW created a high-performance luxury SUV. BMW refers to its SUVs as sport *activity* vehicles in order to appeal even more to these active consumers.

BMW introduced convertibles and roadsters to target "post-moderns," a high-income group that continues to attract attention with more showy, flamboyant cars.

---

*BMW Group includes BMW, MINI, and Rolls-Royce brands.

BMW's 6 Series, a flashier version of the high-end 7 Series, also targeted this group.

BMW uses a wide range of advertising tactics to reach each of its target markets. However, the company's U.S. tagline, "The Ultimate Driving Machine," has remained consistent since it first launched there in 1974. During that time, sales have grown to more than 300,000 units in the United States in 2013. In recent years, BMW has returned to emphasizing performance over status, stating, "We only make one thing, the ultimate driving machine."

BMW owners are very loyal to the brand, and enthusiasts host an annual Bimmerfest each year to celebrate their cars. The company nurtures these loyal consumers and continues to research, innovate, and reach out to specific segment groups year after year.

## Questions

1. How does BMW segment its consumers? Why does this work for BMW?

2. What does BMW do well to market to each segment group? Where could it improve its marketing strategy?

3. Should BMW ever change its tagline, "The Ultimate Driving Machine"? Why or why not?

**Sources:** Mark Clothier, "Mercedes Outlasts BMW's Late Surge to Capture U.S. Luxury Crown," www.bloomberg.com, January 4, 2014; Stephen Williams, "BMW Roundel: Not Born from Planes," *New York Times,* January 7, 2010; Gail Edmondson, "BMW: Crashing the Compact Market," *BusinessWeek,* June 28, 2004; Neil Boudette, "BMW's Push to Broaden Line Hits Some Bumps in the Road," *Wall Street Journal,* January 10, 2005; Boston Chapter BMW Club Car of America, http://boston-bmwcca.org; Rupal Parekh, "BMW Changes Gears with New Campaign from KBS&P," *Advertising Age,* January 6, 2012; BMW.com; BMWgroup.com; BMW 2013 Annual Report, Company History.

Goodbye wires.

With DIRECTV, say goodbye to messy cable wires and boxes in every room.
1.800.DIRECTV | directv.com

DIRECTV

## In This Chapter, We Will Address the Following **Questions**

1. How can a firm develop and establish an effective positioning in the market? (p. 275)

2. How do marketers identify and analyze competition? (p. 276)

3. How are brands successfully differentiated? (p. 278)

4. How do firms communicate their positioning? (p. 286)

5. What are some alternative approaches to positioning? (p. 291)

6. What are the differences in positioning and branding for a small business? (p. 292)

DirecTV has established a unique position in the marketplace as the world's leading provider of digital television entertainment services.

*Source: Courtesy of DIRECTV*

# **10** Crafting the Brand Positioning

**No company can win if its products and services resemble every other product and** offering. As part of the strategic brand management process, each offering must represent the right kinds of things in the minds of the target market. Consider how DirecTV has positioned itself.[1]

 *Launched a little more than two decades ago, DirecTV now has more than 32 million subscribers in the United States and Latin America. The direct-broadcast satellite service provider faces competition on a number of fronts: from classic cable companies (Comcast and TimeWarner Cable), from other direct broadcast satellite service providers (Dish), and from alternate ways to watch television digitally through downloads and streaming (Hulu, Netflix, and Amazon). The world's leading provider of digital television entertainment services, DirecTV carries the slogan "Don't Just Watch TV, DirecTV," reflecting the unique positioning it has crafted thanks to a combination of features not easily matched by any competitor. Three pillars of that positioning are captured by its claims to "state-of-the-art technology, unmatched programming, and industry leading customer service." The company puts much emphasis on its comprehensive set of sports packages, its wide array of HD channels, and its broad broadcast platform that lets customers watch programming on their TVs at home and on their laptops, tablets, and cell phones. With its Genie service, users can record as many as five shows at once. In exaggerated fashion, its "Get Rid of Cable" TV ad campaign shows how customers who get mad at cable have their lives turn for the worse through a series of unfortunate events. DirecTV has made a strategic targeting shift to focus on "high quality" subscribers: loyal customers who purchase premium services, pay their bills on time, and call less often to complain.*

**As the success of DirecTV** demonstrates, a company can reap the benefits of carving out a unique position in the marketplace. Creating a compelling, well-differentiated brand position requires a keen understanding of consumer needs and wants, company capabilities, and competitive actions. It also requires disciplined but creative thinking. In this chapter, we outline a process by which marketers can uncover the most powerful brand positioning.

# Developing a Brand Positioning

All marketing strategy is built on segmentation, targeting, and positioning (STP). A company discovers different needs and groups of consumers in the marketplace, targets those it can satisfy in a superior way, and then positions its offerings so the target market recognizes its distinctive offerings and images. By building customer advantages, companies can deliver high customer value and satisfaction, which lead to high repeat purchases and ultimately to high company profitability.

## UNDERSTANDING POSITIONING AND VALUE PROPOSITIONS

**Positioning** is the act of designing a company's offering and image to occupy a distinctive place in the minds of the target market.[2] The goal is to locate the brand in the minds of consumers to maximize the potential benefit to the firm. A good brand positioning helps guide marketing strategy by clarifying the brand's essence, identifying the goals it helps the consumer achieve, and showing how it does so in a unique way. Everyone in the organization should understand the brand positioning and use it as context for making decisions.

| TABLE 10.1 | Examples of Value Propositions | |
|---|---|---|
| **Company and Product** | **Target Customers** | **Value Proposition** |
| Hertz (car rental) | Busy professionals | Fast, convenient way to rent the right type of a car at an airport |
| Volvo (station wagon) | Safety-conscious upscale families | The safest, most durable wagon in which your family can ride |
| Domino's (pizza) | Convenience-minded pizza lovers | A delicious hot pizza, delivered promptly to your door |

A useful measure of the effectiveness of the organization's positioning is the *brand substitution test*. If, in some marketing activity—an ad campaign, a viral video, a new product introduction—the brand were replaced by a competitive brand, then that marketing activity should not work as well in the marketplace. A well-positioned brand should be distinctive in its meaning and execution. If a sport or music sponsorship, for example, would work as well if it were for a leading competitor, then either the positioning is not sharply defined well enough or the sponsorship as executed does not tie closely enough to the brand positioning.

A good positioning has one foot in the present and one in the future. It needs to be somewhat aspirational so the brand has room to grow and improve. Positioning on the basis of the current state of the market is not forward-looking enough, but at the same time, the positioning cannot be so removed from reality that it is essentially unobtainable. The real trick is to strike just the right balance between what the brand is and what it could be.

One result of positioning is the successful creation of a customer-focused *value proposition,* a cogent reason why the target market should buy a product or service. As introduced in Chapter 1, a value proposition captures the way a product or service's key benefits provide value to customers by satisfying their needs. Table 10.1 shows how three companies—Hertz, Volvo, and Domino's—have defined their value proposition through the years with their target customers.[3]

Positioning requires that marketers define and communicate similarities and differences between their brand and its competitors. Specifically, deciding on a positioning requires: (1) choosing a frame of reference by identifying the target market and relevant competition, (2) identifying the optimal points-of-parity and points-of-difference brand associations given that frame of reference, and (3) creating a brand mantra summarizing the positioning and essence of the brand.

# Choosing a Competitive Frame of Reference

The **competitive frame of reference** defines which other brands a brand competes with and which should thus be the focus of competitive analysis. Decisions about the competitive frame of reference are closely linked to target market decisions. Deciding to target a certain type of consumer can define the nature of competition because certain firms have decided to target that segment in the past (or plan to do so in the future) or because consumers in that segment may already look to certain products or brands in their purchase decisions.

**IDENTIFYING COMPETITORS** A good starting point in defining a competitive frame of reference for brand positioning is **category membership**—the products or sets of products with which a brand competes and that function as close substitutes. It would seem a simple task for a company to identify its competitors. PepsiCo knows Coca-Cola's Dasani is a major bottled-water competitor for its Aquafina brand; Wells Fargo knows Bank of America is a major banking competitor; and Petsmart.com knows a major online retail competitor for pet food and supplies is Petco.com.

The range of a company's actual and potential competitors, however, can be much broader than the obvious. To enter new markets, a brand with growth intentions may need a broader or maybe even a more aspirational competitive frame. And it may be more likely to be hurt by emerging competitors or new technologies than by current competitors.

The energy-bar market created by PowerBar ultimately fragmented into a variety of subcategories, including those directed at specific segments (such as Luna bars for women) and some possessing specific attributes (such as the protein-laden Balance and the calorie-control bar Pria). Each represented a subcategory for which the original PowerBar may not be as relevant.[4]

Firms should broaden their competitive frame to invoke more advantageous comparisons. Consider these examples:

Source: © RGB Ventures LLC dba SuperStock/Alamy

- In the United Kingdom, the Automobile Association positioned itself as the fourth "emergency service"—along with police, fire, and ambulance—to convey greater credibility and urgency.
- The International Federation of Poker is attempting to downplay some of the gambling image of poker to emphasize the similarity of the card game to other "mind sports" such as chess and bridge.[5]
- The U.S. Armed Forces changed the focus of its recruitment advertising from the military as patriotic duty to the military as a place to learn leadership skills—a much more rational than emotional pitch that better competes with private industry.[6]

We can examine competition from both an industry and a market point of view.[7] An **industry** is a group of firms offering a product or class of products that are close substitutes for one another. Marketers classify industries according to several different factors, such as the number of sellers; degree of product differentiation; presence or absence of entry, mobility, and exit barriers; cost structure; degree of vertical integration; and degree of globalization.

Using the market approach, we define *competitors* as companies that satisfy the same customer need. For example, a customer who buys a word-processing software package really wants "writing ability"—a need that can also be satisfied by pencils, pens, or, in the past, typewriters. Marketers must overcome "marketing myopia" and stop defining competition in traditional category and industry terms.[8] Coca-Cola, focused on its soft drink business, missed seeing the market for coffee bars and fresh-fruit-juice bars that eventually impinged on its soft-drink business.

The U.S. Armed Forces is putting more emphasis on its opportunities for leadership and career development vs. patriotic appeals for serving.

The market concept of competition reveals a broader set of actual and potential competitors than competition defined in just product category terms. Jeffrey Rayport and Bernard Jaworski suggest profiling a company's direct and indirect competitors by mapping the buyer's steps in obtaining and using the product. This type of analysis highlights both the opportunities and the challenges a company faces.[9]

**ANALYZING COMPETITORS** Chapter 2 described how to conduct a SWOT analysis that includes a competitive analysis. A company needs to gather information about each competitor's real and perceived strengths and weaknesses.

Table 10.2 shows the results of a company survey that asked customers to rate its three competitors, A, B, and C, on five attributes. Competitor A turns out to be well known and respected for producing high-quality products sold by a good sales force, but poor at providing product availability and technical assistance. Competitor B is good across the board and excellent in product availability and sales force. Competitor C rates poor to fair on most attributes. This result suggests that in its positioning, the company could attack Competitor A on product availability and technical assistance and Competitor C on almost anything, but it should not attack B, which has no glaring weaknesses. As part of this competitive analysis for positioning, the firm should also ascertain the strategies and objectives of its primary competitors.

Source: © Blend Images/Alamy

The International Federation of Poker is putting more emphasis on the intellectual rewards from playing poker vs. the thrill from gambling.

| TABLE 10.2 | Customers' Ratings of Competitors on Key Success Factors | | | | |
|---|---|---|---|---|---|
| | Customer Awareness | Product Quality | Product Availability | Technical Assistance | Selling Staff |
| Competitor A | E | E | P | P | G |
| Competitor B | G | G | E | G | E |
| Competitor C | F | P | G | F | F |

*Note:* E = excellent, G = good, F = fair, P = poor.

Once a company has identified its main competitors and their strategies, it must ask: What is each competitor seeking in the marketplace? What drives each competitor's behavior? Many factors shape a competitor's objectives, including size, history, current management, and financial situation. If the competitor is a division of a larger company, it's important to know whether the parent company is running it for growth or for profits, or milking it.[10]

Finally, based on all this analysis, marketers must formally define the competitive frame of reference to guide positioning. In stable markets where little short-term change is likely, it may be fairly easy to define one, two, or perhaps three key competitors. In dynamic categories where competition may exist or arise in a variety of different forms, multiple frames of reference may be present, as we discuss below.

## IDENTIFYING POTENTIAL POINTS-OF-DIFFERENCE AND POINTS-OF-PARITY

Once marketers have fixed the competitive frame of reference for positioning by defining the customer target market and the nature of the competition, they can define the appropriate points-of-difference and points-of-parity associations.[11]

**POINTS-OF-DIFFERENCE** **Points-of-difference (PODs)** are attributes or benefits that consumers strongly associate with a brand, positively evaluate, and believe they could not find to the same extent with a competitive brand.

Associations that make up points-of-difference can be based on virtually any type of attribute or benefit.[12] Louis Vuitton may seek a point-of-difference as having the most stylish handbags, Energizer as having the longest-lasting battery, and Fidelity Investments as offering the best financial advice and planning.

Strong brands often have multiple points-of-difference. Some examples are Apple (*design, ease-of-use,* and *irreverent attitude*), Nike (*performance, innovative technology,* and *winning*), and Southwest Airlines (*value, reliability,* and *fun personality*).

Creating strong, favorable, and unique associations is a real challenge, but an essential one for competitive brand positioning. Although successfully positioning a new product in a well-established market may seem particularly difficult, Method Products shows that it is not impossible.[13]

**METHOD PRODUCTS**   The brainchild of former high school buddies Eric Ryan and Adam Lowry, Method Products was started with the realization that although cleaning and household products are sizable categories by sales, taking up an entire supermarket aisle or more, they are also incredibly boring ones. Method launched a sleek, uncluttered dish soap container that also had a functional advantage—the bottle, shaped like a chess piece, was built to let soap flow out the bottom so users would never have to turn it upside down. This signature product, with its pleasant fragrance, was designed by award-winning industrial designer Karim Rashid. Sustainability also became part of the core of the brand, from sourcing and labor practices to material reduction and the use of nontoxic materials. By creating a line of unique eco-friendly, biodegradable household cleaning products with bright colors and sleek designs, Method grew to a $100 million company in revenues. A big break came with the placement of its product in Target, known for partnering with well-known designers to produce standout products at affordable prices. Because of its limited advertising budget, the company believes its attractive packaging and innovative products must work harder to express the brand positioning. Social media campaigns have been able to put some teeth into the company's "People Against Dirty" slogan and its desire to make full disclosure of ingredients an industry requirement. Method was acquired by Belgium-based Ecover in 2012; its strong European distribution network will help launch the brand overseas.

Three criteria determine whether a brand association can truly function as a point-of-difference: desirability, deliverability, and differentiability. Some key considerations follow.

- *Desirable to consumer.* Consumers must see the brand association as personally relevant to them. Select Comfort made a splash in the mattress industry with its Sleep Number beds, which allow consumers to adjust the support and fit of the mattress for optimal comfort with a simple numbering index. Consumers must also be given a compelling reason to believe and an understandable rationale for why the brand can deliver the desired benefit. Mountain Dew may argue that it is more energizing than other soft drinks and support this claim by noting that it has a higher level of caffeine. Chanel No. 5 perfume may claim to be the quintessentially elegant French perfume and support this claim by noting the long association between Chanel and haute couture. Substantiators can also come in the form of patented, branded ingredients, such as NIVEA Wrinkle Control Crème with Q10 co-enzyme.
- *Deliverable by the company.* The company must have the internal resources and commitment to feasibly and profitably create and maintain the brand association in the minds of consumers. The product design and marketing offering must support the desired association. Does communicating the desired association require real changes to the product itself or just perceptual shifts in the way the consumer thinks of the product or brand? Creating the latter is typically easier. General Motors has had to work to overcome public perceptions that Cadillac is not a youthful, modern brand and has done so through bold designs, solid craftsmanship, and active, contemporary images.[14] The ideal brand association is preemptive, defensible, and difficult to attack. It is generally easier for market leaders such as ADM, Visa, and SAP to sustain their positioning, based as it is on demonstrable product or service performance, than it is for market leaders such as Fendi, Prada, and Hermès, whose positioning is based on fashion and is thus subject to the whims of a more fickle market.
- *Differentiating from competitors.* Finally, consumers must see the brand association as distinctive and superior to relevant competitors. Splenda sugar substitute overtook Equal and Sweet'N Low to become the leader in its category in 2003 by differentiating itself as a product derived from sugar without the associated

Method cleaning products has met with great success from being uniquely positioned on the basis of sustainability and attractive and functional product designs.

*Source: Method Products, PBC*

drawbacks.[15] In the crowded energy drink category, Monster has become a nearly $2 billion brand and a threat to category pioneer Red Bull by differentiating itself on its innovative 16-ounce can and an extensive line of products targeting nearly every need state related to energy consumption.[16]

**POINTS-OF-PARITY** **Points-of-parity (POPs)**, on the other hand, are attribute or benefit associations that are not necessarily unique to the brand but may in fact be shared with other brands.[17] These types of associations come in three basic forms: category, correlational, and competitive.

*Category points-of-parity* are attributes or benefits that consumers view as essential to a legitimate and credible offering within a certain product or service category. In other words, they represent necessary—but not sufficient—conditions for brand choice. Consumers might not consider a travel agency truly a travel agency unless it is able to make air and hotel reservations, provide advice about leisure packages, and offer various ticket payment and delivery options. Category points-of-parity may change over time due to technological advances, legal developments, or consumer trends, but to use a golfing analogy, they are the "greens fees" necessary to play the marketing game.

*Correlational points-of-parity* are potentially negative associations that arise from the existence of positive associations for the brand. One challenge for marketers is that many attributes or benefits that make up their POPs or PODs are inversely related. In other words, if your brand is good at one thing, such as being inexpensive, consumers can't see it as also good at something else, like being "of the highest quality." Consumer research into the trade-offs consumers make in their purchasing decisions can be informative here. Below, we consider strategies to address these trade-offs.

*Competitive points-of-parity* are associations designed to overcome perceived weaknesses of the brand in light of competitors' points-of-difference. One good way to uncover key competitive points-of-parity is to role-play competitors' positioning and infer their intended points-of-difference. Competitor's PODs will, in turn, suggest the brand's POPs.

Regardless of the source of perceived weaknesses, if, in the eyes of consumers, a brand can "break even" in those areas where it appears to be at a disadvantage *and* achieve advantages in other areas, it should be in a strong—and perhaps unbeatable—competitive position. Consider the introduction of Miller Lite beer—the first major light beer in North America.[18]

**MILLER LITE**    The initial advertising strategy for Miller Lite beer had two goals: ensuring parity with key competitors in the regular, full-strength beer category by stating that Miller Lite "tastes great," while at the same time creating a point-of-difference around the fact that it contained one-third fewer calories and was thus "less filling." As often happens, the point-of-parity and point-of-difference were somewhat conflicting because consumers tend to equate taste with calories. To overcome potential resistance, Miller employed credible spokespeople, primarily popular former professional athletes, who would presumably not drink a beer unless it tasted good. These ex-jocks humorously debated which of the two product benefits—"tastes great" or "less filling"—was more descriptive of the beer. The ads ended with the clever tagline "Everything You've Always Wanted in a Beer…and Less." As time went on, the brand positioning evolved to encompass "Miller Time" in its advertising, an emotional appeal about the brand's "sociability" and ability to serve as a catalyst for good times with friends.

**POINTS-OF-PARITY VERSUS POINTS-OF-DIFFERENCE**    For an offering to achieve a point-of-parity on a particular attribute or benefit, a sufficient number of consumers must believe the brand is "good enough" on that dimension. There is a zone or range of tolerance or acceptance with points-of-parity. The brand does not literally need to be seen as equal to competitors, but consumers must feel it does well enough on that particular

Miller Lite pioneered the light beer category by successfully establishing a point-of-difference on low calories <u>and</u> a point-of-parity on taste vs. full-strength beers.

Source: MillerCoors LLC

attribute or benefit. If they do, they may be willing to base their evaluations and decisions on other factors more favorable to the brand. A light beer presumably would never taste as good as a full-strength beer, but it would need to taste close enough to be able to effectively compete.

Often, the key to positioning is not so much achieving a point-of-difference as achieving points-of-parity!

**VISA VERSUS AMERICAN EXPRESS** Visa's point-of-difference in the credit card category is that it is the most widely available card, which underscores the category's main benefit of convenience. American Express, on the other hand, has built the equity of its brand by highlighting the prestige associated with the use of its card. Visa and American Express now compete to create points-of-parity by attempting to blunt each other's advantage. Visa offers gold and platinum cards to enhance the prestige of its brand, and for years it advertised, "It's Everywhere You Want to Be," showing desirable travel and leisure locations that accept only the Visa card to reinforce both its own exclusivity and its acceptability. American Express has substantially increased the number of merchants that accept its cards and created other value enhancements while also reinforcing its cachet through advertising that showcases celebrities such as Robert De Niro, Tina Fey, Ellen DeGeneres, and Beyoncé as well as promotions for exclusive access to special events.

**MULTIPLE FRAMES OF REFERENCE** It is not uncommon for a brand to identify more than one actual or potential competitive frame of reference, if competition widens or the firm plans to expand into new categories. For example, Starbucks could define very distinct sets of competitors, suggesting different possible POPs and PODs as a result:[19]

1. *Quick-serve restaurants and convenience shops (McDonald's and Dunkin' Donuts)*—Intended PODs might be quality, image, experience, and variety; intended POPs might be convenience and value.
2. *Home and office consumption (Folgers, NESCAFÉ instant, and Green Mountain Coffee K-Cups)*—Intended PODs might be quality, image, experience, variety, and freshness; intended POPs might be convenience and value.
3. *Local cafés*—Intended PODs might be convenience and service quality; intended POPs might be product quality, variety, price, and community.

Note that some potential POPs and PODs for Starbucks are shared across competitors; others are unique to a particular competitor.

Under such circumstances, marketers have to decide what to do. There are two main options with multiple frames of reference. One is to first develop the best possible positioning for each type or class of competitors and then see whether there is a way to create one combined positioning robust enough to effectively address them all. If competition is too diverse, however, it may be necessary to prioritize competitors and then choose the most important set of competitors to serve as the competitive frame. One crucial consideration is not to try to be all things to all people—that leads to lowest-common-denominator positioning, which is typically ineffective.

Finally, if there are many competitors in different categories or subcategories, it may be useful to either develop the positioning at the categorical level for all relevant categories ("quick-serve restaurants" or "supermarket take-home coffee" for Starbucks) or with an exemplar from each category (McDonald's or NESCAFÉ for Starbucks).

**STRADDLE POSITIONING** Occasionally, a company will be able to straddle two frames of reference with one set of points-of-difference and points-of-parity. In these cases, the points-of-difference for one category become points-of-parity for the other and vice versa. Subway restaurants are positioned as offering healthy, good-tasting sandwiches. This positioning allows the brand to create a POP on taste and a POD on health with respect to quick-serve restaurants such as McDonald's and Burger King and, at the same time, a POP on health and a POD on taste with respect to health food restaurants and cafés.

Straddle positions allow brands to expand their market coverage and potential customer base. Another example is BMW.[20]

**BMW** When BMW first made a strong competitive push into the U.S. market in the late 1970s, it positioned the brand as the only automobile that offered both luxury *and* performance. At that time, consumers saw U.S. luxury cars

By combining the seemingly incompatible benefits of luxury and performance, BMW has found great success in the American automotive market.

*Source: BMW of North America*

as lacking performance and U.S. performance cars as lacking luxury. By relying on the design of its cars, its German heritage, and other aspects of a well-conceived marketing program, BMW was able to simultaneously achieve: (1) a point-of-difference on luxury and a point-of-parity on performance with respect to U.S. performance cars like the Chevy Corvette and (2) a point-of-difference on performance and a point-of-parity on luxury with respect to U.S. luxury cars like Cadillac. The clever slogan "The Ultimate Driving Machine" effectively captured the newly created umbrella category: luxury performance cars.

Although a straddle positioning is often attractive as a means of reconciling potentially conflicting consumer goals and creating a "best of both worlds" solution, it also carries an extra burden. If the points-of-parity and points-of-difference are not credible, the brand may not be viewed as a legitimate player in either category. Many early personal digital assistants (PDAs), or palm-sized computers, that unsuccessfully tried to straddle categories ranging from pagers to laptop computers provide a vivid illustration of this risk.

## CHOOSING SPECIFIC POPs AND PODs

To build a strong brand and avoid the commodity trap, marketers must start with the belief that you can differentiate anything. Michael Porter urged companies to build a sustainable competitive advantage.[21] **Competitive advantage** is a company's ability to perform in one or more ways that competitors cannot or will not match.

Some companies are finding success. Pharmaceutical companies are developing biologics, medicines produced using the body's own cells rather than through chemical reactions in a lab, because they are difficult for copycat pharmaceutical companies to make a generic version of when they go off patent. Roche Holding will enjoy an advantage of at least three years with its $7 billion-a-year in sales biologic rheumatoid arthritis treatment Rituxan before a biosimilar copycat version is introduced.[22]

But few competitive advantages are inherently sustainable. At best, they may be leverageable. A *leverageable advantage* is one that a company can use as a springboard to new advantages, much as Microsoft has leveraged its operating system to Microsoft Office and then to networking applications. In general, a company that hopes to endure must be in the business of continuously inventing new advantages that can serve as the basis of points-of-difference.[23]

Marketers typically focus on brand benefits in choosing the points-of-parity and points-of-difference that make up their brand positioning. Brand attributes generally play more of a supporting role by providing "reasons to believe" or "proof points" as to why a brand can credibly claim it offers certain benefits. Marketers of Dove soap, for example, will talk about how its attribute of one-quarter cleansing cream uniquely creates the benefit of softer skin. Singapore Airlines can boast about its superior customer service because of its better-trained flight attendants and strong service culture. Consumers are usually more interested in benefits and what exactly they will get from a product. Multiple attributes may support a certain benefit, and they may change over time.

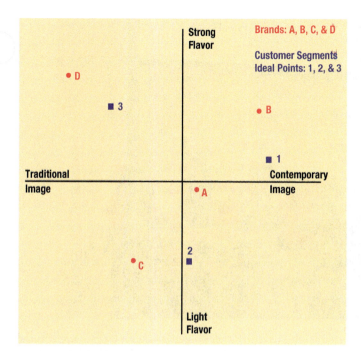

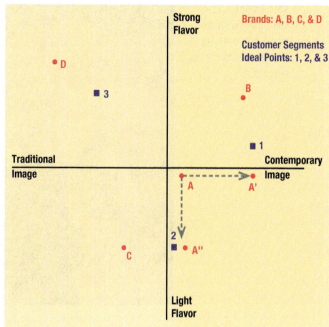

| Fig. 10.1a |

(a) Hypothetical Beverage Perceptual Map: Current Perceptions

| Fig. 10.1b |

(b) Hypothetical Beverage Perceptual Map: Possible Repositioning for Brand A

**MEANS OF DIFFERENTIATION** Any product or service benefit that is sufficiently desirable, deliverable, and differentiating can serve as a point-of-difference for a brand. The obvious, and often the most compelling, means of differentiation for consumers are benefits related to performance (Chapters 13 and 14). Swatch offers colorful, fashionable watches; GEICO offers reliable insurance at discount prices.

Sometimes changes in the marketing environment can open up new opportunities to create a means of differentiation. Eight years after it launched Sierra Mist and with sales stagnating, Pepsico tapped into rising consumer interest in natural and organic products to reposition the lemon-lime soft drink as all-natural with only five ingredients: carbonated water, sugar, citric acid, natural flavor, and potassium citrate.[24]

Often a brand's positioning transcends its performance considerations. Companies can fashion compelling images that appeal to consumers' social and psychological needs. The primary explanation for Marlboro's extraordinary worldwide market share (about 30 percent) is that its "macho cowboy" image has struck a responsive chord with much of the cigarette-smoking public. Wine and liquor companies also work hard to develop distinctive images for their brands. Even a seller's physical space can be a powerful image generator. Hyatt Regency Hotels developed a distinctive image with its atrium lobbies.

To identify possible means of differentiation, marketers have to match consumers' desire for a benefit with their company's ability to deliver it. For example, they can design their distribution channels to make buying the product easier and more rewarding. Back in 1946, pet food was cheap, not too nutritious, and available exclusively in supermarkets and the occasional feed store. Dayton, Ohio–based Iams found success selling premium pet food through regional veterinarians, breeders, and pet stores.

**PERCEPTUAL MAPS** For choosing specific benefits as POPs and PODs to position a brand, perceptual maps may be useful. *Perceptual maps* are visual representations of consumer perceptions and preferences. They provide quantitative pictures of market situations and the way consumers view different products, services, and brands along various dimensions. By overlaying consumer preferences with brand perceptions, marketers can reveal "holes" or "openings" that suggest unmet consumer needs and marketing opportunities.[25]

For example, Figure 10.1(a) shows a hypothetical perceptual map for a beverage category. The four brands—A, B, C, and D—vary in terms of how consumers view their taste profile (light versus strong) and personality and imagery (contemporary versus modern). Also displayed on the map are ideal point "configurations" for three

Kate Spade found a consumer sweet spot by skillfully blending form and function in its products.

Source: © Lou Linwei/Alamy

market segments (1, 2, and 3). The ideal points represent each segment's most preferred ("ideal") combination of taste and imagery.

Consumers in Segment 3 prefer beverages with a strong taste and traditional imagery. Brand D is well positioned for this segment because the market strongly associates it with both these benefits. Given that none of the competitors is seen as anywhere close, we would expect Brand D to attract many of the Segment 3 customers.

Brand A, on the other hand, is seen as more balanced in terms of both taste and imagery. Unfortunately, no market segment seems to really desire this balance. Brands B and C are better positioned with respect to Segments 2 and 3, respectively.

- By making its image more contemporary, Brand A could move to A' to target consumers in Segment 1 and achieve a point-of-parity on imagery and maintain its point-of-difference on taste profile with respect to Brand B.
- By changing its taste profile to make it lighter, Brand A could move to A" to target consumers in Segment 2 and achieve a point-of-parity on taste profile and maintain its point-of-difference on imagery with respect to Brand C.

Deciding which repositioning is most promising, A' or A", would require detailed consumer and competitive analysis on a host of factors—including the resources, capabilities, and likely intentions of competing firms—to identify the markets where consumers can profitably be served.

**EMOTIONAL BRANDING**  Many marketing experts believe a brand positioning should have both rational and emotional components. In other words, it should contain points-of-difference and points-of-parity that appeal to both the head and the heart.[26]

Strong brands often seek to build on their performance advantages to strike an emotional chord with customers. When research on scar-treatment product Mederma found that women were buying it not just for the physical treatment but also to increase their self-esteem, the marketers of the brand added emotional messaging to what had traditionally been a practical message that stressed physician recommendations: "What we have done is supplement the rational with the emotional."[27] Kate Spade is another brand that blends functional and emotional in its positioning.[28]

**❙ KATE SPADE**  Although only a little more than 20 years old, Kate Spade has evolved from a bags-only brand to a much more diversified fashion brand. Launched by husband-and-wife team Kate and Andy Spade—who have since sold their stake—the brand was initially known for a tiny, minimalist-looking black bag. In 2007, a new creative director, Deborah Lloyd, brought a stronger style sensibility to help hit the Kate Spade customer sweet spot of being "the most interesting person in the room." With greater emphasis on marrying form and function, the brand expanded into apparel and jewelry and has become the centerpiece of a revamped Liz Claiborne (now known as Fifth & Pacific). Accessories are updated constantly, and there are frequent new merchandise introductions. A men's brand (Jack Spade) and a more casual, affordable fashion brand targeting younger millennium consumers (Kate Spade Saturday) have also been launched. Kate Spade has made a strong e-commerce push to complement its 200-plus stores; 20 percent of sales come from online channels. The company has also made a well-integrated social media foray, using Facebook, Twitter, Instagram, Tumblr, Pinterest, YouTube, FourSquare, and Spotify to reinforce its core brand values of "patterns, colors, fun food and classic New York moments." It has made a move into Europe and Asia and has especially set its sights on China.

A person's emotional response to a brand and its marketing will depend on many factors. An increasingly important one is the brand's authenticity.[29] Brands such as Hershey's, Kraft, Crayola, Kellogg's, and Johnson & Johnson that are seen as authentic and genuine can evoke trust, affection, and strong loyalty.[30]

Authenticity also has functional value. Family farmer–owned Welch's—1,150 Concord and Niagara grape farmers make up the National Grape Cooperative—is seen by consumers as "wholesome, authentic and real." The brand reinforces those credentials by focusing on its local sourcing of ingredients, increasingly important for consumers who want to know where their foods come from and how they were made.[31]

By successfully differentiating themselves, emotional brands can also provide financial payoffs. As part of its IPO, the UK mobile phone operator O2 was rebranded from British Telecom's struggling BT Cellnet, based on a powerful emotional campaign about freedom and enablement. When customer acquisition, loyalty, and average revenue soared, the business was quickly acquired by Spanish multinational Telefonica for more than three times its IPO price.[32]

# BRAND MANTRAS

To further focus brand positioning and guide the way their marketers help consumers think about the brand, firms can define a brand mantra.[33] A *brand mantra* is a three- to five-word articulation of the heart and soul of the brand and is closely related to other branding concepts like "brand essence" and "core brand promise." Its purpose is to ensure that all employees within the organization and all external marketing partners understand what the brand is most fundamentally to represent with consumers so they can adjust their actions accordingly.

**ROLE OF BRAND MANTRAS** Brand mantras are powerful devices. By highlighting points-of-difference, they provide guidance about what products to introduce under the brand, what ad campaigns to run, and where and how to sell the brand. Their influence can even extend beyond these tactical concerns. Brand mantras can guide the most seemingly unrelated or mundane decisions, such as the look of a reception area and the way phones are answered. In effect, they create a mental filter to screen out brand-inappropriate marketing activities or actions of any type that may have a negative bearing on customers' impressions.

Brand mantras must economically communicate what the brand is and what it is *not*. What makes a good brand mantra? McDonald's "Food, Folks, and Fun" captures its brand essence and core brand promise. Two other high-profile and successful examples—Nike and Disney—show the power and utility of a well-designed brand mantra.

Nike's brand mantra of "authentic athletic performance" is visibly reinforced by its endorsements of top athletes like champion tennis player Rafael Nadal.

Source: © Presselect/Alamy

▎ **NIKE**    Nike has a rich set of associations with consumers, based on its innovative product designs, its sponsorships of top athletes, its award-winning communications, its competitive drive, and its irreverent attitude. Internally,

Disney's "fun family entertainment" brand mantra has been an invaluable guide for its product and marketing decisions.

Source: © Jim Nicholson/Alamy

Nike marketers adopted the three-word brand mantra, "authentic athletic performance," to guide their marketing efforts. Thus, in Nike's eyes, its entire marketing program—its products and the way they are sold—must reflect that key brand value. Over the years, Nike has expanded its brand meaning from "running shoes" to "athletic shoes" to "athletic shoes and apparel" to "all things associated with athletics (including equipment)." Each step of the way, however, it has been guided by its "authentic athletic performance" brand mantra. For example, as Nike rolled out its successful apparel line, one important hurdle was that the products must be made innovative enough through material, cut, or design to truly benefit top athletes. At the same time, the company has been careful to avoid using the Nike name to brand products that do not fit with the brand mantra (like casual "brown" shoes).

**DISNEY**  Disney developed its brand mantra in response to its incredible growth through licensing and product development during the mid-1980s. In the late 1980s, Disney became concerned that some of its characters, such as Mickey Mouse and Donald Duck, were being used inappropriately and becoming overexposed. The characters were on so many products and marketed in so many ways that in some cases it was difficult to discern what could have been the rationale behind the deal to start with. Moreover, because of the broad exposure of the characters in the marketplace, many consumers had begun to feel Disney was exploiting its name. Disney moved quickly to ensure that a consistent image—reinforcing its key brand associations—was conveyed by all third-party products and services. To that end, Disney adopted an internal brand mantra of "fun family entertainment" to filter proposed ventures. Opportunities that were not consistent with the brand mantra—no matter how appealing—were rejected. As useful as that mantra was to Disney, adding the word "magical" might have made it even more so.

**DESIGNING A BRAND MANTRA**  Unlike brand slogans meant to engage, brand mantras are designed with internal purposes in mind. Although Nike's internal mantra was "authentic athletic performance," its external slogan was "Just Do It." Here are the three key criteria for a brand mantra.

- *Communicate.* A good brand mantra should clarify what is unique about the brand. It may also need to define the category (or categories) of business for the brand and set brand boundaries.
- *Simplify.* An effective brand mantra should be memorable. For that, it should be short, crisp, and vivid in meaning.
- *Inspire.* Ideally, the brand mantra should also stake out ground that is personally meaningful and relevant to as many employees as possible.

For brands anticipating rapid growth, it is helpful to define the product or benefit space in which the brand would like to compete, as Nike did with "athletic performance" and Disney with "family entertainment." Words that describe the nature of the product or service, or the type of experiences or benefits the brand provides, can be critical to identifying appropriate categories into which to extend. For brands in more stable categories where extensions into more distinct categories are less likely to occur, the brand mantra may focus more exclusively on points-of-difference.

Other brands may be strong on one, or perhaps even a few, of the brand associations making up the brand mantra. But for it to be effective, no other brand should singularly excel on all dimensions. Part of the key to both Nike's and Disney's success is that for years no competitor could really deliver on the combined promise suggested by their brand mantras.

# Establishing a Brand Positioning

Once they have fashioned the brand positioning strategy, marketers should communicate it to everyone in the organization so it guides their words and actions. One helpful schematic with which to do so is a brand-positioning bull's-eye. "Marketing Memo: Constructing a Brand Positioning Bull's-eye" outlines one way marketers can formally express brand positioning without skipping any steps.

Often a good positioning will have several PODs and POPs. Of those, often two or three really define the competitive battlefield and should be analyzed and developed carefully. A good positioning should also follow the "90–10" rule and be highly applicable to 90 percent (or at least 80 percent) of the products in the brand. Attempting to position to all 100 percent of a brand's product often yields an unsatisfactory "lowest common denominator" result. The remaining 10 percent or 20 percent of products should be reviewed to ensure they have the proper branding strategy and to see how they could be changed to better reflect the brand positioning.

COMMUNICATING CATEGORY MEMBERSHIP Category membership may be obvious. Target customers are aware that Maybelline is a leading brand of cosmetics, Cheerios is a leading brand of cereal, Accenture is a leading consulting firm, and so on. When a product is new, marketers must inform consumers of the brand's category membership.

Sometimes consumers may know the category membership but not be convinced the brand is a valid member of the category. They may be aware that HP produces digital cameras, but they may not be certain whether HP cameras are in the same class as those made by Canon, Nikon, and Sony. In this instance, HP might find it useful to reinforce category membership.

Brands are sometimes affiliated with categories in which they do *not* hold membership. This approach is one way to highlight a brand's point-of-difference, providing consumers know its actual membership. Instead of putting it in the frozen pizza category, the marketers of DiGiorno's frozen pizza have positioned it in the delivered pizza category with ads that claim "It's Not Delivery, It's DiGiorno!" Similarly, pay channel HBO has developed original, edgy programming to justify its premium fee, adopting the slogan "It's Not TV, It's HBO."

---

## marketing memo

### Constructing a Brand Positioning Bull's-eye

A brand bull's-eye provides content and context to improve everyone's understanding of the positioning of a brand in the organization. Here we look at a hypothetical Starbucks example.

In the inner two circles is the heart of the bull's-eye—key points-of-parity and points-of-difference as well as the brand mantra. Points-of-parity and points-of-difference should be made as specific as possible without being too narrow. A POD of "gives confidence" for P&G's Bounty paper towels—known as the "Quicker Picker-Upper"—is very broad compared to the much more brand-relevant POD of "helps to relieve tense situations."

Points-of-parity and points-of-difference should be constructed in terms of the benefits a customer would actually derive from the product or service. "Leading Brand in the Category" as a point-of-difference fails to answer the question: What's in it for the customer? Does being the leading brand give the customer greater peace of mind, greater convenience, access to more innovative products, and/or social approval or self-respect from being associated with a "winner"?

Points-of-difference should also be stated in positive, aspirational terms, like "Irresistible Taste," "Superior Value," Tireless Customer Service," and "Unimpeachable Trust." Points-of-parity are often stated in more muted terms to recognize the potential deficiencies they represent, such as "Sufficiently Accessible," "Appropriately Relevant," and "Fairly Priced."

In the next circle out are the substantiators or reasons-to-believe (RTB)—attributes or benefits that provide factual or demonstrable support for the points-of-parity and points-of-difference. Finally, the outer circle contains two other useful branding concepts: (1) the brand values, personality, or character—intangible associations that help to establish the tone for the words and actions for the brand; and (2) executional properties and visual identity—more tangible components of the brand that affect the way customers see it.

Three boxes outside the bull's-eye provide useful context and interpretation. To the left, two boxes highlight some of the input to the positioning analysis. One includes the consumer target and a key insight about consumer attitudes or behavior that significantly influenced the actual positioning; the other provides competitive information about the key consumer need the brand is attempting to satisfy and some competitive products or brands that need suggests. To the right of the bull's-eye, one box offers a "big picture" view of the output—the ideal consumer takeaway if the brand positioning efforts are successful.

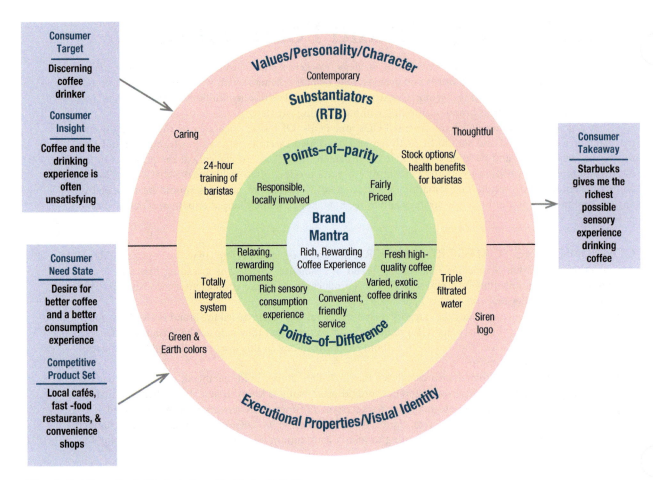

A Hypothetical Example of a Starbucks Brand Positioning Bull's Eye

The typical approach to positioning is to inform consumers of a brand's membership before stating its point-of-difference. Presumably, consumers need to know what a product is and what function it serves before deciding whether it is superior to the brands against which it competes. For new products, initial advertising often concentrates on creating brand awareness, and subsequent advertising attempts to create the brand image. Ally Bank tapped into a distrust of financial institutions to stake out a unique positioning. [34]

**ALLY FINANCIAL**  In rebranding GMAC Financial as Ally Financial and launching its Ally Bank subsidiary, the firm initially ran a campaign featuring a smarmy man in a suit—who symbolically represented the typical bank—being mean to unsuspecting children—who symbolically represented typical bank customers. The idea was to show Ally Bank as simple and direct. One ad had the slick spokesperson sitting with two young girls at a small table asking one of them whether she wanted a pony. When the girl said yes, he gave her a small toy pony. When the other girl said yes, he gave her a real pony. The clearly unhappy first girl asked why she didn't get a real pony, and the man answered, in effect, "You didn't ask." Having established initial awareness, the campaign developed its "straightforward" positioning with several follow-up ads relaying a "Your Money Needs an Ally" theme and touting customers' ability to reach humans at Ally Bank instead of machines. In the "Dry Cleaner" ad, seemingly real customers of a dry cleaner are captured via hidden camera as they attempt to cope with a blender that a sign indicates they should use for help. The ad ends with the words "Ally Bank. Helpful People. Not Machines."

Ally has positioned itself as a consumer-friendly banking alternative.

*Source: Used with permission from Ally Financial Inc.*

There are three main ways to convey a brand's category membership:

1. *Announcing category benefits*—To reassure consumers that a brand will deliver on the fundamental reason for using a category, marketers frequently use benefits to announce category membership. Thus, industrial tools might claim to have durability, and antacids might announce their efficacy. A brownie mix might attain membership in the baked desserts category by claiming the benefit of great taste and support this claim by including high-quality ingredients (performance) or by showing users delighting in its consumption (imagery).

2. *Comparing to exemplars*—Well-known, noteworthy brands in a category can also help a brand specify its category membership. When Tommy Hilfiger was an unknown, advertising announced his status as a great U.S. designer by associating him with Geoffrey Beene, Stanley Blacker, Calvin Klein, and Perry Ellis, recognized members of that category.

3. ***Relying on the product descriptor***—The product descriptor that follows the brand name is often a concise means of conveying category origin. Ford Motor Co. invested more than $1 billion in a radical new 2004 model called the X-Trainer, which combined the attributes of an SUV, a minivan, and a station wagon. To communicate its unique position—and to avoid association with its Explorer and Country Squire models—the vehicle, eventually called Freestyle, was designated a "sports wagon."[35]

**COMMUNICATING POPs AND PODs** We saw above that one common challenge in positioning is that many of the benefits that make up points-of-parity and points-of-difference are negatively correlated. ConAgra must convince consumers that Healthy Choice frozen foods both taste good *and* are good for you. Consider these examples of negatively correlated attributes and benefits:

| | |
|---|---|
| Low price vs. High quality | Powerful vs. Safe |
| Taste vs. Low calories | Strong vs. Refined |
| Nutritious vs. Good tasting | Ubiquitous vs. Exclusive |
| Efficacious vs. Mild | Varied vs. Simple |

Moreover, individual attributes and benefits often have positive *and* negative aspects. For example, consider a long-lived brand such as La-Z-Boy recliners, Burberry outerwear, or the *New York Times*. The brand's heritage could suggest experience, wisdom, and expertise as well as authenticity. On the other hand, it could also imply being old-fashioned and not contemporary and up to date.

Unfortunately, consumers typically want to maximize *both* the negatively correlated attributes or benefits. Much of the art and science of marketing consists of dealing with trade-offs, and positioning is no different. The best approach clearly is to develop a product or service that performs well on both dimensions. GORE-TEX was able to overcome the conflicting product images of "breathable" and "waterproof" through technological advances. When in-depth and quantitative interviews and focus groups suggested that consumers wanted the benefits of technology without the hassles, Royal Philips launched its "Sense and Simplicity" campaign for its Philips brand of electronics, using print, online, and television advertising.[36]

Other approaches include launching two different marketing campaigns, each devoted to a different brand attribute or benefit; linking the brand to a person, place, or thing that possesses the right kind of equity to establish an attribute or benefit as a POP or POD; and convincing consumers that the negative relationship between attributes and benefits, if they consider it differently, is in fact positive.

Heritage brands like the *New York Times* may be seen as experienced and expert, but also may be seen as old-fashioned and not up-to-date if they are not sufficiently innovative and relevant.

**MONITORING COMPETITION** Positioning requires an organizational commitment. It is not something that is constantly overhauled or changed. At the same time, it is important to regularly research the desirability, deliverability, and differentiability of the brand's POPs and PODs in the marketplace to understand how the brand positioning might need to evolve or, in relatively rare cases, be completely replaced.

In assessing potential threats from competitors, three high-level variables are useful:

1. ***Share of market***—The competitor's share of the target market.
2. ***Share of mind***—The percentage of customers who named the competitor in responding to the statement "Name the first company that comes to mind in this industry."
3. ***Share of heart***—The percentage of customers who named the competitor in responding to the statement "Name the company from which you would prefer to buy the product."

There's an interesting relationship among these three measures. Table 10.3 shows them as recorded for three hypothetical competitors. Competitor A enjoys the highest market share but is slipping. Its mind share and heart share are also slipping, probably because it's not providing good product availability and technical assistance. Competitor B is steadily gaining market share, probably due to strategies that are increasing its mind share and heart share. Competitor C seems to be stuck at a low level of market, mind, and heart share, probably because of its poor product and marketing attributes.

| TABLE 10.3 | Market Share, Mind Share, and Heart Share | | | | | | | | |
|---|---|---|---|---|---|---|---|---|---|
| | **Market Share** | | | **Mind Share** | | | **Heart Share** | | |
| | **2015** | **2016** | **2017** | **2015** | **2016** | **2017** | **2015** | **2016** | **2017** |
| Competitor A | 50% | 47% | 44% | 60% | 58% | 54% | 45% | 42% | 39% |
| Competitor B | 30 | 34 | 37 | 30 | 31 | 35 | 44 | 47 | 53 |
| Competitor C | 20 | 19 | 19 | 10 | 11 | 11 | 11 | 11 | 8 |

We could generalize as follows: *Companies that make steady gains in mind share and heart share will inevitably make gains in market share and profitability.* Firms such as CarMax, Timberland, Jordan's Furniture, Wegmans, and Toyota are all reaping the benefits of providing emotional, experiential, social, and financial value to satisfy customers and all their constituents.[37]

# Alternative Approaches to Positioning

The competitive brand positioning model we've reviewed in this chapter is a structured way to approach positioning based on in-depth consumer, company, and competitive analysis. Some marketers have proposed other, less-structured approaches in recent years that offer provocative ideas on how to position a brand. We highlight a few of those here.

## BRAND NARRATIVES AND STORYTELLING

Rather than outlining specific attributes or benefits, some marketing experts describe positioning a brand as telling a narrative or story. Companies like the richness and imagination they can derive from thinking of the story behind a product or service. To help sharpen its marketing and positioning, Jim Beam, with its namesake Jim Beam and Maker's Mark brands, hired The Moth, a group of professional storytellers best known for a weekly public radio broadcast, to kick off a three-day biannual gathering of its marketing teams.[38]

Randall Ringer and Michael Thibodeau see *narrative branding* as based on deep metaphors that connect to people's memories, associations, and stories.[39] They identify five elements of narrative branding: (1) the brand story in terms of words and metaphors, (2) the consumer journey or the way consumers engage with the brand over time and touch points where they come into contact with it, (3) the visual language or expression for the brand, (4) the manner in which the narrative is expressed experientially or the brand engages the senses, and (5) the role the brand plays in the lives of consumers. Based on literary convention and brand experience, they also offer the following framework for a brand story:

- *Setting.* The time, place, and context
- *Cast.* The brand as a character, including its role in the life of the audience, its relationships and responsibilities, and its history or creation myth
- *Narrative arc.* The way the narrative logic unfolds over time, including actions, desired experiences, defining events, and the moment of epiphany
- *Language.* The authenticating voice, metaphors, symbols, themes, and leitmotifs

Patrick Hanlon developed the related concept of "primal branding" that views brands as complex belief systems. According to Hanlon, diverse brands such as Google, MINI Cooper, the U.S. Marine Corps, Starbucks, Apple, UPS, and Aveda all have a "primal code" or DNA that resonates with their customers and generates their passion and fervor. He outlines seven assets that make up this belief system or primal code: a creation story, creed, icon, rituals, sacred words, a way of dealing with nonbelievers, and a good leader.[40]

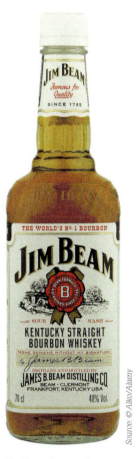

Jim Beam has used professional story-tellers to sharpen its marketing and positioning.

## CULTURAL BRANDING

Douglas Holt believes that for companies to build iconic, leadership brands, they must assemble cultural knowledge, strategize according to cultural branding principles, and hire and train cultural experts.[41] The University of Wisconsin's Craig Thompson views brands as sociocultural templates, citing research investigating brands as cultural resources. ESPN Zone restaurants tap into competitive masculinity, for instance, and American Girl dolls tap into mother–daughter relationships and the cross-generational transfer of femininity.[42] Experts who see consumers actively cocreating brand meaning and positioning even refer to this as "Brand Wikification," given that wikis are written by contributors from all walks of life and points of view.[43]

# Positioning and Branding for A Small Business

Building brands is a challenge for a small business with limited resources and budgets. Nevertheless, numerous success stories exist of entrepreneurs who have built their brands up essentially from scratch to become powerhouse brands. Consider the global success of UNIQLO.[44]

.........................................................................................................................................

**UNIQLO**     Founded by Tadashi Yanai, now the wealthiest person in Japan, UNIQLO (short for Unique Clothing Warehouse) has followed its mission statement and credo of "Made for All" (see Table 10.4) to become a brand with a goal of reaching $50 billion in sales in 2020 and becoming the number-one retailer in the world. UNIQLO stands out … by not standing out! Heavily inspired in its early days by the Gap and its one-time president Mickey Drexler, the company expressly states that it does not want to be in the fashion game of chasing ever-changing trends. With a strong technology emphasis, the company focuses on continual process improvement and the creation of new, innovative products. Its signature mix of fleece, synthetic thermal underwear, down jackets, jeans, and other basics is designed to capture the essence of each type of product. UNIQLO feels it provides the perfect components for its customer's everyday lives, products they can combine in different ways to create their own unique expressions. The company's marketing strategy combines active social media campaigns with aggressive in-store activities to connect with customers and pull them into the stores.

.........................................................................................................................................

By being inclusive and focusing on how its products can fit into consumers' everyday lives, UNIQLO has experienced remarkable growth.

Source: Lou-Foto/Alamy

| TABLE 10.4 | UNIQLO Made for All Credo |
|---|---|

# UNIQLO. MADE FOR ALL

It doesn't matter who you are or where you live, UNIQLO makes clothes that transcend all categories and social groups. Our clothes are made for all, going beyond age, gender, occupation, ethnicity and all the other ways that define people. Our clothes are simple and essential yet universal, so people can freely combine them with their own unique styles, in any way they choose, every day of the year. Everything we do is rooted deeply in our Japanese origin, always aspiring to excellence in quality, design and technology. However, we will always ensure that our clothes are affordable and accessible to everyone. UNIQLO is a way of thinking that's about constant change, diversity, and challenging conventional wisdom. At UNIQLO, we believe that everyone can benefit from simple, well-designed clothes. Because if all people can look and feel better every day, then maybe the world can be a little better too.

MADE FOR ALL  UNI QLO

When resources are limited, focus and consistency in marketing programs become critically important. Creativity is also paramount—finding new ways to market new ideas about products to consumers. Here are some specific branding guidelines for small businesses.

- *Find a compelling product or service performance advantage.* As for any brand, demonstrable, meaningful differences in product or service performance can be the key to success. Upstart Dropbox.com has carved out a strong position in the face of a slew of competitors large (Microsoft) and small (Box) that also offer consumers a means to conveniently store massive amounts of documents, photos, videos, and other files, in part by virtue of its convenient single-folder approach to accommodate multiple devices for a user.[45]
- *Focus on building one or two strong brands based on one or two key associations.* Small businesses often must rely on only one or two brands and key associations as points-of-difference for them. These associations must be consistently reinforced across the marketing program and over time. Rooted in the snowboarding and surfing cultures, Volcom has adopted a "Youth Against Establishment" credo that has resulted in steady sales of its music, athletic apparel, and jewelry.
- *Encourage product or service trial in any way possible.* A successful small business has to distinguish itself in ways consumers can learn about and experience. One way is to encourage trial through sampling, demonstrations, or any means to engage consumers with the brand. See's Candies allows walk-in customers to sample any piece of candy in the shop they choose. As one senior executive noted, "That's the best marketing we have, if people try it, they love it." See's uses all fresh ingredients and no added preservatives to create its enticing flavors.[46]
- *Develop cohesive digital strategy to make the brand "bigger and better."* One advantage of the Internet is it allows small firms to have a larger profile than they might otherwise. Urbane Apartments, a property investment and management company from Royal Oak, Michigan, has a virtual prominence that far exceeds its real-world scope. The company boasts a resident-penned blog touting favorite Royal Oak destinations, its own Urbane Lobby social networking site for tenants, and active YouTube, Facebook, and Twitter profiles.[47] Sales for Rider Shack surf shop in Los Angeles increased when the firm began to emphasize Facebook and its

Promoted Post service feature as a way to keep the brand in front of people.[48] Mobile marketing can be especially important given the local nature of many small businesses.[49]

- *Create buzz and a loyal brand community.*  Small businesses often must rely on word of mouth to establish their positioning, but they can find public relations, social networking, and low-cost promotions and sponsorship to be inexpensive alternatives. As discussed in Chapter 5, creating a vibrant brand community among current and prospective customers can also be a cost-effective way to reinforce loyalty and help spread the word to new prospects. Evernote has several dozen "power users" who serve as passionate ambassadors to spread the word about the personal-organization application brand touted by the online company as the everything-in-one-place "external brain" for its customers.[50]

- *Employ a well-integrated set of brand elements.*  Tactically, it is important for small businesses to maximize the contribution of all types of brand equity drivers. In particular, they should develop a distinctive, well-integrated set of brand elements—brand names, logos, packaging—that enhances both brand awareness and brand image. Brand elements should be memorable and meaningful, with as much creative potential as possible. Innovative packaging can substitute for ad campaigns by capturing attention at the point of purchase. SMARTFOOD introduced its first product without any advertising by means of both a unique package that served as a strong visual symbol on the shelf and an extensive sampling program that encouraged trial. Proper names or family names, which often characterize small businesses, may provide some distinctiveness but can suffer in terms of pronounceability, meaningfulness, memorability, or other branding considerations. If these deficiencies are too great, alternative brand elements should be explored.

- *Leverage as many secondary associations as possible.*  Secondary associations—any persons, places, or things with potentially relevant associations—are often a cost-effective, shortcut means to build brand equity, especially those that help to signal quality or credibility. In 1996, J. Darius Bickoff launched an electrolyte-enhanced line of bottled water called Smartwater, followed in two years by the introduction of Vitaminwater, a vitamin-enhanced and flavored alternative to plain bottled water, and by Fruitwater two years after that. Clever marketing including endorsement deals with rapper 50 Cent, singer Kelly Clarkson, actress Jennifer Aniston, and football star Tom Brady helped drive success. Less than 10 years after its launch, Bickoff's Energy Brands company, also known as Glacéau, was sold to the Coca-Cola company for $4.2 billion in cash.[51]

- *Creatively conduct low-cost marketing research.*  A variety of low-cost marketing research methods help small businesses connect with customers and study competitors (Chapter 4). One way is to set up course projects at local colleges and universities to access the expertise of both students and professors. Many online options exist too.

Unlike major brands that often have more resources at their disposal, small businesses usually do not have the luxury of making mistakes and must design and implement marketing programs much more carefully.

Vitaminwater built its brand, in part, through endorsements from popular entertainers and athletes.

*Source: © Richard Levine/Alamy*

# Summary

1. To develop an effective positioning, a company must study competitors as well as actual and potential customers. Marketers need to identify competitors' strategies, objectives, strengths, and weaknesses.

2. Developing a positioning requires identifying a frame of reference—by locating the target market and the nature of the competition—and the optimal points-of-parity and points-of-difference brand associations.

3. A company's closest competitors are those seeking to satisfy the same customers and needs and making similar offers. A company should also pay attention to latent competitors, who may offer new or different ways to satisfy the same needs. Industry- and market-based analyses both help uncover competitors.

4. Points-of-difference are those associations unique to the brand that are also strongly held and favorably evaluated by consumers. These differences may be based directly on the product or service itself or on other considerations related to employees, channels, image, or services. Points-of-difference must be desirable (from a consumer standpoint), deliverable (from a company standpoint), and differentiated (from a competitor standpoint).

5. Points-of-parity are those associations not necessarily unique to the brand but perhaps shared with other brands. They help to negate any potential weaknesses for the brand. Category point-of-parity are associations consumers view as being necessary to a legitimate and credible product offering within a certain category. Correlational points-of-parity are associations designed to overcome perceived weaknesses or vulnerabilities of the brand. Competitive point-of-parity are associations designed to negate competitors' points-of-difference.

6. Emotional branding is becoming an important way to connect with customers and create differentiation from competitors. Emotional differences are often most powerful when they are connected to underlying functional differences.

7. Several different alternative approaches exist to position a product or service. These less structured, more qualitative approaches are based on concepts such as brand narratives, storytelling, and cultural branding.

8. Although small businesses should adhere to many of the branding and positioning principles larger companies use, they must place extra emphasis on their brand elements and secondary associations, be more focused, and create buzz for their brand.

---

## MyMarketingLab

Go to **mymktlab.com** to complete the problems marked with this icon ⭐ as well as for additional Auto-graded and Assisted-graded writing questions.

---

# Applications

## Marketing Debate
### What Is the Best Way to Position?

Marketers have different views about how to position a brand. Some value structured approaches such as the competitive positioning model described in the chapter, which focuses on specific points-of-parity and points-of-difference. Others prefer unstructured approaches that rely more on stories, narratives, and other flowing depictions.

**Take a position:** The best way to position a brand is through a structured approach *versus* The best way to position a brand is through an unstructured approach.

## Marketing Discussion
### Attributes and Benefits

⭐ Identify negatively correlated attributes and benefits *not* described in this chapter. What strategies do firms use to try to position themselves on the basis of pairs of attributes and benefits?

# Marketing Excellence

## >> Louis Vuitton

Louis Vuitton (LV) is one of the world's legendary brands and synonymous with luxury, wealth, and fashion. Currently the highest-ranking luxury brand in the world, the company is best known for its iconic handbags, leather goods, shoes, watches, jewelry, accessories, and sunglasses.

Louis Vuitton opened his first store in Paris in 1854, selling handmade, high-quality trunks and luggage. Word of his skill and craftsmanship traveled quickly, but it wasn't until Napoleon's wife challenged him to "pack the most beautiful clothes in an exquisite way" that he truly made a name for himself in the industry. In 1872, Vuitton introduced a simple, luxurious design that attracted Paris's most elite customers. He also created the signature Damier and Monogram Canvas materials, featuring the famous design still used in most of the company's products today.

Throughout the 20th century, the company that carries his name continued to grow internationally, expanding into the fashion world by the 1950s and reaching $10 million in sales by 1977. In 1987, Louis Vuitton merged with Moët et Chandon and Hennessy, leading manufacturers of champagne and cognac respectively, and created LVMH, a luxury goods conglomerate.

Louis Vuitton's products stand out in both quality and design. Everything is made with state-of-the-art materials, combining art, precision, and craftsmanship, and tested rigorously. For example, the company spends as long as 60 hours making one piece of luggage by hand—the same way it did 150 years ago—and tests zippers 5,000 times before putting them in its luxurious handbags. The legendary LV monogram appears on all its products and continues to stand for the highest quality, premium status, and luxury travel.

Until the 1980s, Louis Vuitton products were available in a wide variety of department stores. However, this led to a high rate of counterfeiting—one of the brand's most difficult challenges—so the company now maintains tighter control over its distribution channels. It sells only through its 3,200 authentic Louis Vuitton boutiques, located in upscale shopping areas and high-end department stores and run by its own employees and managers. The company limits store openings each year to help maintain a sense of exclusivity. Only recently did it start selling products through louisvuitton.com in hopes of reaching new consumers and regions.

Louis Vuitton prices are never reduced. In fact, the company recently increased prices as much as 13 percent and has been primarily marketing its more expensive line of bags in order to push the concept that owning an LV product is a rare luxury. Strategies like this have built barriers to entry and have helped create a status brand that is resilient even during tough economic times.

Louis Vuitton is careful not to dilute its brand through overexposure or over-marketing. This presents the company with the challenge of trying to sell as much as possible while maintaining an aura of exclusivity, luxury, and prestige. Over the years, it has used high-profile celebrities and supermodels to showcase its products, including Madonna, Angelina Jolie, Jennifer Lopez, and images of the late Audrey Hepburn. Marketing campaigns often include a combination of high-fashion celebrities, billboards, print ads, and Vuitton's own international regatta—the Louis Vuitton Cup.

In hopes of keeping the brand fresh, the company recently broke tradition and featured celebrities such as Michael Phelps, Steffi Graf, Mikhail Gorbachev, Buzz Aldrin, Bono, and Keith Richards in a noteworthy campaign titled "Core Values." It also launched its first television commercial focused on luxury travel rather than on fashion and formed new partnerships with international artists, museums, and cultural organizations.

Today, Louis Vuitton holds a brand value of $22.5 billion according to *Forbes* and is ranked the 19th most powerful global brand according to *Interbrand*. The company is focused on expanding its luxury brand into growing markets such as China and India as well as continuing to grow in already strong markets like Japan and Europe.

### Questions

1. How does an exclusive brand such as Louis Vuitton grow and sell more while remaining fresh and retaining its cachet?

2. Is the counterfeiting of Louis Vuitton always a negative? Are there any circumstances in which it could be seen as having some positive aspects?

**Sources:** Reena Jana, "Louis Vuitton's Life of Luxury," *Business Week*, August 6, 2007; Eric Pfanner, "Luxury Firms Move to Make Web Work for Them," *New York Times*, November 17, 2009; Louis Vuitton, *bio.com*; William Alden, "LVMH Is Buying the Luxury Clothier Loro," *The New York Times*, July 8, 2013; Christina Passariello, "Louis Vuitton Sports a Richer Price Tag," *Wall Street Journal*, April 16, 2013; 2012 LVMH Annual Report; www.louisvuitton.com.

# Marketing Excellence

## >> American Express

American Express is one of the world's most respected brands, known globally for its charge cards, travel services, and financial services. It began as a 19th-century express shipping company, grew into a travel services company, and eventually evolved into a global payments company with a strong brand image via perceptions such as prestige, trust, security, customer service, international acceptability, and integrity.

American Express created the first internationally accepted "Travelers Cheque" in 1891, which used the same signature security system and exchange rate guarantees employed today. In 1958, the company issued its first charge card—a card that requires customers to pay outstanding balances each month, unlike credit cards that allow for revolving debt. American Express charged a higher annual fee than its competitors in order to create the feeling of prestige and sense of membership.

In the 1960s and 1970s, American Express stepped up its marketing efforts in response to strong competitive pressure from Master Charge (now MasterCard) and BankAmericard (later to become Visa). Ad agency Ogilvy & Mather created the now-famous "Don't Leave Home Without It" cue in the early 1970s as a "synergy" tagline. In 1974, the now-familiar blue-box logo first appeared, with the words *American Express* printed in white.

Many perceived American Express cards as a status symbol signifying success and achievement. The company called its cardholders "card members" and printed the year they became members on their cards, suggesting they held membership in a prestigious club. It maintained this exclusive image through its advertising, impeccable customer service, and elite promotions and events.

During the 1980s, the firm increased the number of merchants that accepted its cards, adding Walmart, and developed new card offerings, including co-branded cards. To communicate the transformation of the 1990s, it launched a corporate ad campaign called "Do More."

These efforts helped American Express compete alongside Visa and MasterCard. In addition, the company rebranded its Small Business Services division as "OPEN: The Small Business Network" and added benefits such as flexible payments as well as special offers, partnerships, and resources for small businesses.

At the turn of the century, American Express introduced two revolutionary new credit cards, Blue and Centurion Black. Blue contained a chip that enhanced Internet security and targeted younger, tech-savvy consumers with a hip image and no annual fee. The Black Card, on the other hand, targeted the most elite clients, who spent more than $150,000 annually and desired amenities such as a 24-hour personal concierge service and invitations to exclusive events.

The company also expanded its Membership Rewards program, which at the time was the world's largest card-based rewards program. Cardholders could redeem points for travel, entertainment, gift certificates, and other predetermined offerings.

In response, Visa and MasterCard turned on the competitive pressure. Visa took ownership of check cards, which were debit cards that subtracted money for purchases directly from a cardholders' bank account. MasterCard surged in popularity as well when it created the "Priceless" ad campaign, which became a ubiquitous pop-culture reference point. However, American Express scored a huge legal victory against Visa and MasterCard

in 2004 when the Supreme Court ruled that it could pursue relationships with any and all banks, which technicalities had prevented it from doing before.

Over the next three years, American Express partnered with banks such as MBNA, Citigroup, UBS, and USAA. The company also launched a handful of strong marketing campaigns and taglines throughout the 2000s to help increase membership. The "My Life. My Card" campaign featured celebrities like Robert De Niro, Ellen DeGeneres, and Tiger Woods, and the "Are You a Cardmember?" campaign served as a call to action to join American Express. The result: Card accounts surged from 60 million in 2003 to 86 million in 2007.

Things turned for the worse when the global economy collapsed in 2008 and 2009, but American Express bounced back more quickly than most credit card and financial services companies. The company returned to focusing on an affluent customer base and closed many of its bad accounts. It pushed more cards that carried an annual fee, broadened its marketing focus to bring in affluent new customers, and wooed small businesses with better rewards and technological innovations. In addition, American Express made big strides in social and digital media, including a partnership with Twitter that enabled cardholders to make a purchase or receive rewards with a hashtag.

American Express has successfully developed and nurtured its strong brand and reputation over the years. *Business Week* and Interbrand rank it among the top 25 "Most Valuable Brands in the World" year after year, *Fortune* includes it as one of the top "Most Admired Companies," and J. D. Powers has ranked it the top U.S. payment card company since 2007. These results are testament not only to the company's ongoing innovation in product development and marketing, but also to its commitment to customers, providing them all with outstanding service at any location in the world.

### Questions

1. Evaluate American Express in terms of its competitors. How has its positioning changed over time? Where does American Express face the most competition?

2. Evaluate American Express's integration of its various businesses. What recommendations would you make to maximize the contribution to equity of all its business units? Is the corporate brand sufficiently coherent?

**Sources:** Hilary Cassidy, "Amex Has Big Plans for Small Business Unit," *Brandweek*, January 21, 2002; American Express, "Ellen DeGeneres, Laird Hamilton, Tiger Woods & Robert De Niro Featured in New American Express Global Ad Campaign," November 8, 2004; "The VISA Black Card: A Smart Strategy in Trying Times," *BusinessPundit.com*, December 8, 2008; "Credit Cards: Loyalty and Retention—US—November 2007," Mintel Reports, November 2007; Scott Cendrowski, "Is It Time to Buy American Express?" *CNN Money*, April 17, 2009; American Express, "Membership Rewards Program from American Express Adds Practical Rewards for Tough Economic Times," February 19, 2009; "World's Most Admired Companies 2013," *Fortune*; "Best Global Brands 2013," *Interbrand*.

## In This Chapter, We Will Address the Following **Questions**

1. What is a brand, and how does branding work? (p. 299)

2. What is brand equity? (p. 302)

3. How is brand equity built? (p. 309)

4. How is brand equity measured? (p. 315)

5. How is brand equity managed? (p. 318)

6. What is brand architecture? (p. 321)

7. What is customer equity? (p. 328)

Market leader Gatorade has refocused on its core target market of athletes with a broad assortment of new products and a revamped ad campaign.

*Source: The Gatorade Company*

# 11 Creating Brand Equity

**One of the most valuable intangible assets of a firm is its brands, and it is incumbent** on marketing to properly manage their value. Building a strong brand is both an art and a science. It requires careful planning, a deep long-term commitment, and creatively designed and executed marketing. A strong brand commands intense consumer loyalty—and at its heart is a great product or service. Building a strong brand is a never-ending process, as the marketers of Gatorade have found out.[1]

 *Gatorade's roots go back nearly five decades. The product was first developed by researchers at the University of Florida to help the school's athletes cope with the debilitating effects of the hot and humid climate. Its subsequent success as the pioneering leader of the sports drink category led PepsiCo to acquire its parent company, Quaker Oats, in 2001 for $13.4 billion in stock. The brand took off even more in the following years as a result of PepsiCo's massive distribution system and a slew of new product and packaging introductions. But when market share dropped from 80 percent to 75 percent and the brand seemed tired. Pepsico decided a change was needed, so Gatorade marketers returned the brand to its roots, walking away from the mass market to focus more on athletes. Their goal was to transcend the $7 billion a year sports drink market and become a major player in the $20 billion a year sports nutrition market. Three new lines, labeled 01 Prime, 02 Perform, and 03 Recover, were introduced for pre-, during-, and post-workout, respectively. Three different markets were targeted as well. The G Series line aimed at "performance" athletes who engaged in scholastic, collegiate, or high-intensity recreational sports; the G Series Fit line targeted less competitive 18- to 34-year-olds who exercised three to four times a week; and the G Series Pro line targeted professional athletes. A new advertising tagline, "Win From Within," reflected the new Gatorade brand strategy. Gatorade wanted to be all about what is inside an athlete's body, as much as Nike was seen as being all about what is outside the body. Other changes included a shift in the brand's communication budget from 90 percent advertising to include a 30 percent digital component.*

**Marketers of successful 21st-century brands** must excel at the *strategic brand management* process. Strategic brand management combines the design and implementation of marketing activities and programs to build, measure, and manage brands to maximize their value. It has four main steps:[2]

- Identifying and establishing brand positioning
- Planning and implementing brand marketing
- Measuring and interpreting brand performance
- Growing and sustaining brand value

Chapter 10 reviewed positioning; the latter three topics are discussed in this chapter. Chapter 12 reviews important concepts dealing with competitive dynamics.

# How Does Branding Work?

Perhaps the most distinctive skill of professional marketers is their ability to create, maintain, enhance, and protect brands, whether established brands such as Mercedes, Sony, and Nike or new ones like Pure Leaf Teas, Taste Nirvana Coconut Waters, and Alexia All Natural Foods. Some of the hottest brands in recent years have emerged online. Consider the runaway success of Tumblr and Instagram.[3]

**TUMBLR**    Founded by technical wizard and high-school dropout David Karp, Tumblr is a multimedia platform that allows users to post images, videos, and music in the form of a personal blog and, as the company's motto says, "to follow the world's creators." A combination of publishing platform and social network, Tumblr allows users to express themselves publicly and then follow the feedback on their posts and other people's on a convenient dashboard. Boasting more than 200 million blogs as of October 2014, the site is seen as a must-have for creative types, with most users between 18 and 24. Formally launched in February 2007, Tumblr was purchased by Yahoo! for approximately $1.1 billion in cash in June 2013 with the hope of making it commercially more successful. Advertisers can create their own blogs for free but have to pay to participate in two popular Tumblr modules: Spotlight (an accounts-to-follow suggestion) and the Radar (editor's picks).

**INSTAGRAM**    Launched in October 2010 by Stanford grads Kevin Systrom and Mike Krieger, Instagram is known for its photo-sharing app that uses filters to make photos from smart-phone cameras look more professional and allows them to be easily uploaded and shared across multiple platforms simultaneously. These highly valued benefits led the brand to quickly attract more than 100 million users, including some top brands such as Nike, MTV, Starbucks, Burberry, and Gucci. Instagram's name was chosen because it combines the concept of "instant" with the notion of connecting with people via a "telegram." Its success led Facebook to acquire it in April 2012 for approximately $1 billion in stock and cash. A controversial change in its terms of service in December 2012 led users to think Instagram could sell their photos for use in advertising. In the face of an uproar about a violation of privacy, the founders quickly reverted to the original terms.

The American Marketing Association defines a **brand** as "a name, term, sign, symbol, or design, or a combination of them, intended to identify the goods or services of one seller or group of sellers and to differentiate them from those of competitors." A brand is thus a product or service whose dimensions differentiate it in some way from other products or services designed to satisfy the same need. These differences may be functional, rational, or tangible—related to product performance of the brand. They may also be more symbolic, emotional, or intangible—related to what the brand represents or means in a more abstract sense.

Branding has been around for centuries as a means to distinguish the goods of one producer from those of another.[4] Medieval guilds in Europe required that craftspeople put trademarks on their products to protect themselves and their customers against inferior quality. In the fine arts, branding began with artists signing their works. Brands today play a number of important roles that improve consumers' lives and enhance the financial value of firms.

## THE ROLE OF BRANDS

Brands identify the maker of a product and allow consumers to assign responsibility for its performance to that maker or distributor. Brands perform a number of functions for both consumers and firms.

**BRANDS' ROLE FOR CONSUMERS**    A brand is a promise between the firm and the consumer. It is a means to set consumers' expectations and reduce their risk. In return for customer loyalty, the firm promises to reliably deliver a predictably positive experience and set of desirable benefits with its products and services. A brand may even be "predictably unpredictable" if that is what consumers expect, but the key is that it fulfills or exceeds customer expectations in satisfying their needs and wants.

Consumers may evaluate the identical product differently depending on how it is branded.[5] They learn about brands through past experiences with the product and its marketing program, finding out which brands satisfy their needs and which do not. As consumers' lives become more rushed and complicated, a brand's ability to simplify decision making and reduce risk becomes invaluable.[6]

Brands can also take on personal meaning to consumers and become an important part of their identity.[7] They can express who consumers are or who they would like to be. For some consumers, brands can even take on human-like characteristics.[8] Brand relationships, like any relationship, are not cast in stone, and marketers must be sensitive to all the words and actions that might strengthen or weaken consumer ties.[9]

**BRANDS' ROLE FOR FIRMS**    Brands also perform valuable functions for firms.[10] First, they simplify product handling by helping organize inventory and accounting records. A brand also offers the firm legal protection for unique features or aspects of the product.[11] The brand name can be protected through registered trademarks, manufacturing processes can be protected through patents, and packaging can be protected through copyrights and proprietary designs. These intellectual property rights ensure that the firm can safely invest in the brand and reap the benefits of a valuable asset.

A credible brand signals a certain level of quality so satisfied buyers can easily choose the product again.[12] Brand loyalty provides predictability and security of demand for the firm, and it creates barriers to entry that make it difficult for other firms to enter the market. Loyalty also can translate into customer willingness to pay a higher price—often even 20 percent to 25 percent more than competing brands.[13]

Although competitors may duplicate manufacturing processes and product designs, they cannot easily match lasting impressions left in the minds of individuals and organizations by years of favorable product experiences and marketing activity. In this sense, branding can be a powerful means to secure a competitive advantage.[14] Sometimes marketers don't see the real importance of brand loyalty until they change a crucial element of the brand, as the classic tale of New Coke illustrates.[15]

**COCA-COLA** Battered by a nationwide series of taste-test challenges from sweeter-tasting Pepsi-Cola, Coca-Cola decided in 1985 to replace its old formula with a sweeter variation, dubbed New Coke. The company spent $4 million on market research, and blind taste tests showed Coke drinkers preferred the new, sweeter formula. But the launch of New Coke provoked a national uproar. Market researchers had measured the taste but failed to adequately measure the emotional attachment consumers had to Coca-Cola. There were angry letters, formal protests, and even lawsuit threats to force the retention of "The Real Thing." Ten weeks later, the company reintroduced its century-old formula as "Classic Coke." Efforts to resuscitate New Coke eventually failed, and the brand disappeared around 1992. Ironically, the failed introduction of New Coke actually ended up giving the old formula measurably stronger status in the marketplace, with more favorable attitudes and greater sales as a result.

For better or worse, branding effects are pervasive.[16] One research study that provoked much debate about the effects of marketing on children showed that preschoolers felt identical food items—even carrots, milk, and apple juice—tasted better when wrapped in McDonald's familiar packaging than when in unmarked wrappers.[17]

To firms, brands represent enormously valuable pieces of legal property that can influence consumer behavior, be bought and sold, and provide their owner the security of sustained future revenues.[18] Companies have paid dearly for brands in mergers or acquisitions, often justifying the price premium on the basis of the extra profits expected and the difficulty and expense of creating similar brands from scratch.[19] Wall Street believes strong brands result in better earnings and profit performance for firms, which, in turn, create greater value for shareholders.[20]

## THE SCOPE OF BRANDING

How do you "brand" a product? Although firms provide the impetus to brand creation through marketing programs and other activities, ultimately a brand resides in the minds and hearts of consumers. It is a perceptual entity rooted in reality but reflecting the perceptions and idiosyncrasies of consumers.

**Branding** is the process of endowing products and services with the power of a brand. It's all about creating differences between products. Marketers need to teach consumers "who" the product is—by giving it a name and other brand elements to identify it—as well as what the product does and why consumers should care. Branding creates mental structures that help consumers organize their knowledge about products and services in a way that clarifies their decision making and, in the process, provides value to the firm.

For branding strategies to be successful and brand value to be created, consumers must be convinced there are meaningful differences among brands in the product or service category. Brand differences often relate to attributes or benefits of the product itself. Gillette, Merck, and 3M have led their product categories for decades, due in part to continual innovation. Other brands create competitive advantages through nonproduct-related means. Gucci, Chanel, and Louis Vuitton have become category leaders by understanding consumer motivations and desires and creating relevant and appealing images around their stylish products.

Successful brands are seen as genuine, real, and authentic in what they sell as well as who they are. A successful brand makes itself an indispensable part of its customers' lives. Once a faded preppy afterthought, J.Crew tripled its revenue to $2.2 billion from 2002 to 2012 by becoming a highly creative force in fashion. By constantly introducing new styles—but retaining a cohesive look—the brand enjoys intense loyalty, numerous fan blogs, and high-profile celebrity supporters like Michelle Obama and Anna Wintour.[21]

Home to some of the top soccer players in the world, like Cristiano Ronaldo, Real Madrid is an iconic sports brand with multiple lines of revenue.

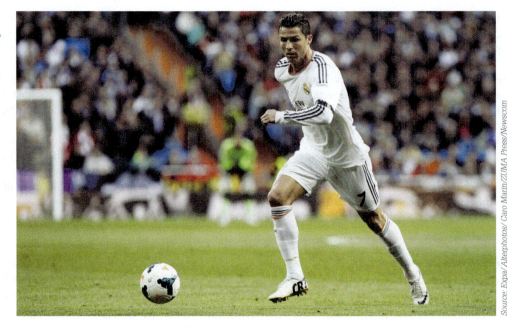

Source: Expa/Alterphotos/ Caro Marin/ZUMA Press/Newscom

Marketers can apply branding virtually anywhere a consumer has a choice. It's possible to brand a physical good (Ford Focus automobile or Lipitor cholesterol medication), a service (Singapore Airlines or Blue Cross and Blue Shield medical insurance), a store (Nordstrom or Dick's Sporting Goods), a person (actress Angelina Jolie or tennis player Roger Federer), a place (the city of Sydney or the country of Ireland), an organization (U2 or the American Automobile Association), or an idea (abortion rights or free trade).[22]

Branding has become of great importance in sports, arts, and entertainment. One of the world's top sports brands comes from Madrid, Spain.[23]

**REAL MADRID**    For the first time since *Forbes* magazine began its ranking in 2004, Real Madrid surpassed Manchester United in 2013 to become the world's most valuable team in soccer—or football as it is known as outside the United States—with an estimated value of $3.3 billion. Also known by fans as "Los Merengues," the iconic but floundering club began to thrive when the billionaire construction tycoon Florentine Perez took over in 2000. Perez's strategy was to attract some of the very top players in the game, brand names in their own right, such as David Beckham, Zinedine Zidane, and, later on, Cristiano Ronaldo and Kaka. Success on the pitch allowed Perez to develop three distinct and lucrative lines of business: broadcast rights (worth $250 million annually), sponsorship and endorsement revenue (worth $240 million annually), and match-day revenue (worth $160 million annually). Real Madrid is truly a global brand and derives 65 percent of its revenue abroad. Sponsorship includes high-profile deals with Adidas, Emirates Airlines, and Spanish banking group BBVA.

# Defining Brand Equity

**Brand equity** is the added value endowed to products and services with consumers. It may be reflected in the way consumers think, feel, and act with respect to the brand, as well as in the prices, market share, and profitability it commands.

Marketers and researchers use various perspectives to study brand equity.[24] Customer-based approaches view it from the perspective of the consumer—either an individual or an organization—and recognize that the power of a brand lies in what customers have seen, read, heard, learned, thought, and felt about the brand over time.[25]

**Customer-based brand equity** is thus the differential effect brand knowledge has on consumer response to the marketing of that brand.[26] A brand has *positive* customer-based brand equity when consumers react more favorably to a product and the way it is marketed when the brand is *identified* than when it is not identified. A brand has negative customer-based brand equity if consumers react less favorably to marketing activity for the brand under the same circumstances. There are three key ingredients of customer-based brand equity.

| TABLE 11.1 | Marketing Advantages of Strong Brands |  |
|---|---|---|
| Improved perceptions of product performance | | Greater trade cooperation and support |
| Greater loyalty | | Increased marketing communications effectiveness |
| Less vulnerability to competitive marketing actions | | Possible licensing opportunities |
| Less vulnerability to marketing crises | | Additional brand extension opportunities |
| Larger margins | | Improved employee recruiting and retention |
| More inelastic consumer response to price increases | | Greater financial market returns |
| More elastic consumer response to price decreases | | |

1. Brand equity arises from differences in consumer response. If no differences occur, the brand-name product is essentially a commodity, and competition will probably be based on price.
2. Differences in response are a result of consumers' **brand knowledge**, all the thoughts, feelings, images, experiences, and beliefs associated with the brand. Brands must create strong, favorable, and unique brand associations with customers, as have Toyota *(reliability)*, Hallmark *(caring)*, and Amazon.com *(convenience and wide selection)*.
3. Brand equity is reflected in perceptions, preferences, and behavior related to all aspects of the marketing of a brand. Stronger brands earn greater revenue.[27] Table 11.1 summarizes some key benefits of brand equity.

The challenge for marketers is therefore ensuring customers have the right type of experiences with products, services, and marketing programs to create the desired thoughts, feelings and brand knowledge. In an abstract sense, we can think of brand equity as providing marketers with a vital strategic bridge from their past to their future.[28]

Marketers should also think of the marketing dollars spent on products and services each year as investments in consumer brand knowledge. The *quality* of that investment is the critical factor, not necessarily the *quantity* (beyond some threshold amount). It's actually possible to overspend on brand building if money is not spent wisely.

Customers' brand knowledge dictates appropriate future directions for the brand. Consumers will decide, based on what they think and feel about the brand, where (and how) they believe the brand should go and grant permission (or not) to any marketing action or program. New-product ventures such as BENGAY aspirin, Cracker Jack cereal, Frito-Lay lemonade, Fruit of the Loom laundry detergent, and Smucker's premium ketchup all failed because consumers found them inappropriate extensions of the brand.

A **brand promise** is the marketer's vision of what the brand must be and do for consumers. Virgin's brand promise is to enter categories where customers' needs are not well met, do different things, and do things differently, all in a way that better meets those needs. With Virgin America, the company appears to have come up with another brand winner.[29]

**VIRGIN AMERICA** After flying for only a few years, Virgin America became an award-winning airline that passengers adore *and* that can make money. It is not unusual for the company to receive e-mails from customers saying they actually wished their flights lasted longer! Virgin America set out to reinvent the entire travel experience, starting with an easy-to-use and friendly Web site and check-in. In flight, passengers revel in Wi-Fi, spacious leather seats, mood lighting, and in-seat food and beverage ordering through touch-screen panels. Some passengers remark that Virgin America is like "flying in an iPod or nightclub." The brand is seeking to be positioned as "an established player featuring discount pricing and a hip, stylish customer experience for travelers." Without a national TV ad campaign, Virgin America has relied on PR, word of mouth, social media, and exemplary customer service to create that customer experience and build the brand. To get customers more involved with the brand, Virgin America launched a digital marketing campaign offering the opportunity to upload a photo to Instagram from the flight. By tweeting the company's Twitter account, travelers can also upload their photo onto Virgin America's Times Square billboard or share it via their own social media accounts.

Virgin America airline exemplifies Virgin's corporate mission to better satisfy customers by doing different things and doing things differently.

*Source: PR NEWSWIRE*

Violating a brand promise can have severe consequences. Founded in 1984, TED talks ("Technology, Entertainment, and Design") became widely admired for their thought-provoking, leading-edge content. After deciding to let anyone apply to manage and stage local events called TEDx with relatively minor oversight, the organizers of TED saw thousands of events of varying quality spring up all over the world, leading some critics to question whether the organization was losing control of its brand.[30]

## BRAND EQUITY MODELS

Although marketers agree about basic branding principles, a number of models of brand equity offer some differing perspectives. Here we highlight three more established ones.

**BRANDASSET® VALUATOR** Advertising agency Young and Rubicam (Y&R) developed a model of brand equity called the BrandAsset® Valuator (BAV). Based on research with more than 800,000 consumers in 51 countries, BAV compares the brand equity of thousands of brands across hundreds of different categories. There are four key components—or pillars—of brand equity, according to BAV (see Figure 11.1):

**| Fig. 11.1 |**

### BrandAsset® Valuator Model

Source: Courtesy of BrandAsset® Consulting, a division of Young & Rubicam.

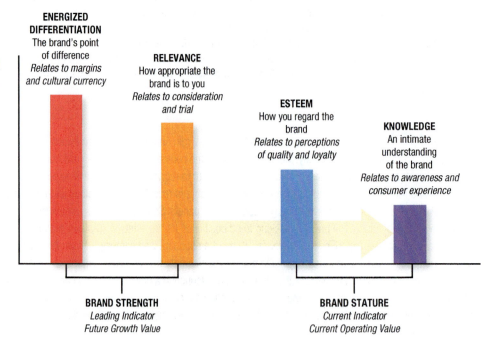

- *Energized differentiation* measures the degree to which a brand is seen as different from others as well as its pricing power.
- *Relevance* measures the appropriateness and breadth of a brand's appeal.
- *Esteem* measures perceptions of quality and loyalty, or how well the brand is regarded and respected.
- *Knowledge* measures how aware and familiar consumers are with the brand and the depth of their experience.

Energized differentiation and relevance combine to determine *brand strength*—a leading indicator that predicts future growth value. Esteem and knowledge together create *brand stature,* a "report card" of past performance and a lagging indicator of current operating value.

The relationships among these dimensions—a brand's "pillar pattern"—reveal much about a brand's current and future status. Brand strength and brand stature combine to form the *power grid,* depicting stages in the cycle of brand development in successive quadrants (see Figure 11.2). Strong new brands show higher levels of energized differentiation and energy than relevance, whereas both esteem and knowledge are lower still. Leadership brands

By plotting a representative group of brands' scores for both strength and stature, this matrix derived from the BrandAsset Valuator shows an accurate picture of a brand's status and overall performance.

| Fig. 11.2 |

## The Universe of Brand Performance

Source: Young & Rubicam BrandAsset Valuator.

These brands have low brand strength but high potential. They have built some energy and relevance, but are known to only a relatively small audience. Consumers are expressing curiosity and interest.

These brands have become irresistible, combining high brand strength with high brand stature. They have high earnings, high margin power, and the greatest potential to create future value.

These brands, with both low brand stature and low brand strength, are not well known among the general population. Many are new entrants; others are middling brands that have lost their way.

These brands show why high brand stature by itself is insufficient for maintaining a leading position. They struggle to overcome what consumers already know about and expect from them.

show high levels on all pillars, with strength greater than stature. As strength slips, they become mass market brands. Finally, declining brands show high knowledge—evidence of past performance—a lower level of esteem, and even lower relevance and energized differentiation.

According to BAV analysis, consumers are concentrating their devotion and purchasing power on an increasingly smaller portfolio of special brands—brands with energized differentiation that keep evolving. These brands connect better with consumers—commanding greater usage loyalty and pricing power and creating greater shareholder value. Some recent insights from the BAV data are summarized in "Marketing Insight: Brand Bubble Trouble."

## marketing insight

# Brand Bubble Trouble

In *The Brand Bubble*, brand consultants Ed Lebar and John Gerzema use Y&R's historical BAV database to conduct a comprehensive examination of the state of brands. Beginning with data from mid-2004, they discovered several odd trends. For thousands of consumer goods and services brands, key brand value measures such as consumer "top-of-mind" awareness, trust, regard, and admiration experienced significant drops.

At the same time, however, share prices for a number of years were being driven higher by the intangible value the markets were attributing to consumer brands. Digging deeper, Lebar and Gerzema found the increase was actually due to a very few extremely strong brands such as Google, Apple, and Nike. The value created by the vast majority of brands was stagnating or falling.

The authors viewed this mismatch between the value consumers see in brands and the value the markets were ascribing to them as a recipe for disaster in two ways. At the macroeconomic level, it implied that stock prices of most consumer companies were overstated. At the microeconomic, company level, it pointed to a serious and continuing problem in brand management.

Why have consumer attitudes toward brands declined? The research identified three fundamental causes. First, there has been a proliferation of brands. New product introductions have accelerated, but many fail to register with consumers. Two, consumers expect creative "big ideas" from brands and feel they are just not getting them. Finally, due to corporate scandals, product crises, and executive misbehavior, trust in brands has declined.

Yet vital brands are still being successfully built. Although all four pillars of the BAV model play a role, the strongest brands resonated with consumers in a special way. Amazon.com, Axe, Facebook, Innocent, IKEA, Land Rover, LG, LEGO, Tata, Nano, Twitter, Whole Foods, and Zappos exhibited notable energized differentiation by communicating dynamism and creativity in ways most other brands did not.

Formally, the BAV analysis identified three factors that help define energy and the marketplace momentum it creates:

1. *Vision*—A clear direction and point of view on the world and how it can and should be changed.

2. *Invention*—An intention for the product or service to change the way people think, feel, and behave.

3. *Dynamism*—Excitement and affinity in the way the brand is presented.

John Gerzema's follow-up research with Michael D'Antonio, published in *Spend Shift*, examined developments later in the decade and the way consumers were changing—or not—as a result of the traumatic economic recession. The authors describe "Spend Shift" as "a consumer-led movement to express their values through the power of their spending. We're moving from mindless to mindful consumption. People are returning to old-fashioned virtues, such as self-reliance, thrift, faith, creativity, hard work and community—and powering them with social behaviors and technology."

The authors make several telling observations: Trust is declining across industries, and brand attribute characteristics such as "kind," "empathetic," "socially responsible," and "leader" are rising in importance with consumers. The authors offer 10 "post-consumer learnings":

| | |
|---|---|
| 1. We are moving from a credit to a debit society. | 2. There are no longer consumers, only customers. |
| 3. Industries are revealed as collections of individuals. | 4. Generational divides are disappearing. |
| 5. Human regulation is remaking the marketplace. | 6. Generosity is now a business model. |
| 7. Society is shifting from consumption to production. | 8. We must think small to solve big. |
| 9. We are seeking better vs. more. | 10. America is an emerging market for value-led innovation. |

**Sources:** John Gerzema and Ed Lebar, *The Brand Bubble: The Looming Crisis in Brand Value and How to Avoid It* (San Francisco, CA: Jossey-Bass, 2008); John Gerzema and Ed Lebar, "The Trouble with Brands," *Strategy+Business* 55 (Summer 2009); John Gerzema and Michael D'Antonio, *Spend Shift: How the Post-Crisis Values Revolution Is Changing the Way We Buy, Sell and Live* (San Francisco, CA: Jossey-Boss, 2011).

Source: Fruit Towers

Innocent is a brand which consumers rate as being highly dynamic and creative.

**BRANDZ** Marketing research consultants Millward Brown and WPP have developed the Brandz model of brand strength, at the heart of which is the BrandDynamics™ model, a system of brand equity measurements, based on Millward Brown's Meaningfully Different Framework, that reveals a brand's current equity and opportunities for growth (Figure 11.3).* BrandDynamics employs a set of simple scores that summarize a brand's equity and are relatable directly to real world financial and business outcomes.

BrandDynamics maintain that three different types of brand associations are crucial for building customer predisposition to buy a brand—meaningful, different, and salient brand associations. The success of a brand along those three dimensions, in turn, is reflected in three important outcome measures:

- **Power:** a prediction of the brand's volume share
- **Premium:** a brand's ability to command a price premium relative to the category average
- **Potential:** the probability that a brand will grow value share

According to the model, how well a brand is activated in the marketplace and the competition that exists there will determine how strongly brand predisposition ultimately translates into sales.

**BRAND RESONANCE MODEL** The brand resonance model also views brand building as an ascending series of steps, from bottom to top: (1) ensuring customers identify the brand and associate it with a specific

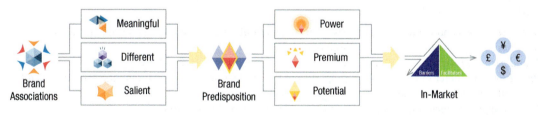

**| Fig. 11.3 |**

**BrandDynamics™ Model**

Source: BrandDynamics™ Model. Reprinted with permission of Millward Brown.

---

*Nigel Hollis, "Making Marketing Meaningful Again," talk given at MSI conference, *Brands in the Balance: Managing Continuity and Change*," Charleston, SC, February 11-12, 2014.

**| Fig. 11.4 |**

Brand
Resonance
Pyramid

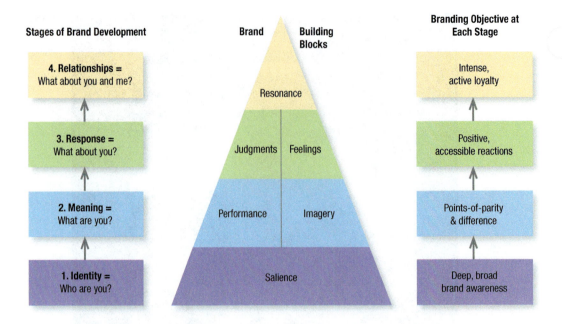

product class or need; (2) firmly establishing the brand meaning in customers' minds by strategically linking a host of tangible and intangible brand associations; (3) eliciting the proper customer responses in terms of brand-related judgment and feelings; and (4) converting customers' brand responses to intense, active loyalty.

According to this model, enacting the four steps means establishing a pyramid of six "brand building blocks" as illustrated in Figure 11.4. The model emphasizes the duality of brands—the rational route to brand building is on the left side of the pyramid, and the emotional route is on the right side.[31] One brand that has found much success going up both sides of the pyramid is MasterCard.[32]

**▌ MASTERCARD**   In the mid-1990s, Visa and American Express were battling fiercely for market leadership. To get back into the picture, MasterCard, with its ad agency McCann Erickson, launched the now iconic "Priceless" ad campaign in 1997 to strengthen its brand image. Each ad focused on a consumer activity (such as a father and son going to a baseball game) and identified three tangible products or services purchased as part of that activity and their prices ("One autographed baseball. $50") before ending with the true but intangible payoff ("Real conversation with 11-year-old son. Priceless."). The ads always ended with the campaign tagline, "There are some things money can't buy; for everything else, there's MasterCard." The campaign stressed the duality of the MasterCard brand, communicating both its rational advantages—acceptance at establishments worldwide—and the emotional payoffs those advantages permitted. The campaign has been a global success for more than 17 years, running similarly structured ads in 102 markets and 50 languages. Lately, it has emphasized *enabling* "priceless" moments with the "Priceless Cities" initiative, launched in 2011 to create special events for MasterCard cardholders in major cities around the world.

Creating significant brand equity requires reaching the top of the brand pyramid, which occurs only if the right building blocks are put into place.

- **Brand salience** is how often and how easily customers think of the brand under various purchase or consumption situations—the depth and breadth of brand awareness.
- **Brand performance** is how well the product or service meets customers' functional needs.
- **Brand imagery** describes the extrinsic properties of the product or service, including the ways in which the brand attempts to meet customers' psychological or social needs.
- **Brand judgments** focus on customers' own personal opinions and evaluations.
- **Brand feelings** are customers' emotional responses and reactions with respect to the brand.
- **Brand resonance** describes the relationship customers have with the brand and the extent to which they feel they're "in sync" with it.

Resonance is the intensity of customers' psychological bond with the brand and the level of activity it engenders.[33] Brands with high resonance include Harley-Davidson, Apple, and eBay. Fox News has found that the higher levels of resonance and engagement its programs engender often lead to greater recall of the ads it runs.[34]

# Building Brand Equity

Marketers build brand equity by creating the right brand knowledge structures with the right consumers. The success of this process depends on *all* brand-related contacts—whether marketer-initiated or not.[35] From a marketing management perspective, however, there are three main sets of **brand equity drivers**:

1. ***The initial choices for the brand elements or identities making up the brand (brand names, URLs, logos, symbols, characters, spokespeople, slogans, jingles, packages, and signage)***—Microsoft chose the name Bing for its new search engine because it felt it unambiguously conveyed search and the "aha" moment of finding what you are looking for. It is also short, appealing, memorable, active, and effective multiculturally.[36]
2. ***The product and service and all accompanying marketing activities and supporting marketing programs***—General Mills and its long-time CMO Mark Addicks are employing a number of new marketing activities to sell cereals, cake mixes, and yogurt. The company is exploring how to best use smart phones with consumers via QR codes, apps, and augmented reality, developing new packaging strategies in the process.[37]
3. ***Other associations indirectly transferred to the brand by linking it to some other entity (a person, place, or thing)***—The brand name of New Zealand vodka 42BELOW refers to both a latitude that runs through New Zealand and the percentage of the drink's alcohol content. The packaging and other visual cues are designed to leverage the perceived purity of the country to communicate the positioning for the brand.[38]

**CHOOSING BRAND ELEMENTS** **Brand elements** are devices, which can be trademarked, that identify and differentiate the brand. Most strong brands employ multiple brand elements. Nike has the distinctive "swoosh" logo, the empowering "Just Do It" slogan, and the "Nike" name from the Greek winged goddess of victory.

Marketers should choose brand elements to build as much brand equity as possible. The test is what consumers would think or feel about the product *if* the brand element were all they knew. Based on its name alone, for instance, a consumer might expect SnackWell's products to be healthful snack foods and Panasonic Toughbook laptop computers to be durable and reliable.

**BRAND ELEMENT CHOICE CRITERIA** There are six criteria for choosing brand elements. The first three—memorable, meaningful, and likable—are brand building. The latter three—transferable, adaptable, and protectable—are defensive and help leverage and preserve brand equity against challenges.

1. *Memorable*—How easily do consumers recall and recognize the brand element, and when—at both purchase and consumption? Short names such as Tide, Crest, and Puffs are memorable brand elements.
2. *Meaningful*—Is the brand element credible? Does it suggest the corresponding category and a product ingredient or the type of person who might use the brand? Consider the inherent meaning in names such as DieHard auto batteries, Mop & Glo floor wax, and Lean Cuisine low-calorie frozen entrées.
3. *Likable*—How aesthetically appealing is the brand element? A recent trend is for playful names that also offer a readily available URL, especially for online brands like Flickr, Instagram, Pinterest, Tumblr, Dropbox, and others.
4. *Transferable*—Can the brand element introduce new products in the same or different categories? Does it add to brand equity across geographic boundaries and market segments? Although initially an online bookseller, Amazon.com was smart enough not to call itself "Books 'R' Us." The Amazon is famous as the world's biggest river, and the name suggests the staggeringly diverse range of products the company now sells.
5. *Adaptable*—How adaptable and updatable is the brand element? Logos can easily be updated. The past 100 years have seen the Shell logo updated 10 times.
6. *Protectable*—How legally protectable is the brand element? How competitively protectable? When names are in danger of becoming synonymous with product categories—as happened to Kleenex, Kitty Litter, Jell-O, Scotch Tape, Xerox, and Fiberglass—their makers should retain their trademark rights and not allow the brand to become generic.

**DEVELOPING BRAND ELEMENTS** Brand elements can play a number of brand-building roles.[39] If consumers don't examine much information in making product decisions, brand elements should be easy to recall and inherently descriptive and persuasive. But choosing a name with inherent meaning may make it harder to later add a different meaning or update the positioning.[40]

The likability of brand elements can increase awareness and associations.[41] "Marketing Memo: The Marketing Magic of Characters" describes some of the marketing advantages of using brand characters.

## marketing memo

### The Marketing Magic of Characters

Brand characters have a long and important history in marketing. The Keebler elves reinforce home-style baking quality and a sense of magic and fun for their line of cookies. In the insurance industry, the AFLAC duck competes for consumer attention with GEICO's gecko, and Progressive's chatty Flo competes with Met Life's adorable Peanuts characters. Michelin's friendly tire-shaped Bibendum—the "Michelin Man"—helps to convey safety for the family and is credited with helping the brand achieve 80 percent awareness around the world. Each year Michelin distributes a "Passport" for Bibendum that sets boundaries on the character's use by marketers in advertising. Bibendum is never aggressive, for example, and never delivers a sales pitch.

Brand characters represent a special type of brand symbol—one with human characteristics that in turn enhance likeability and tag the brand as interesting and fun. Consumers can more easily form relationships with a brand when it has a human or other character's presence. Brand characters typically are introduced through advertising and can play a central role in ad campaigns and package designs. M&M's "spokescandies" are an integral part of all the brand's advertising, promotion, and digital communications. Some brand characters are animated, like the Pillsbury Doughboy, Peter Pan (from the peanut butter), and numerous cereal characters like Tony the Tiger and Snap, Crackle, & Pop. Others are live-action figures like Juan Valdez (Colombian coffee) and Ronald McDonald.

Because they are often colorful and rich in imagery, brand characters can help brands break through marketplace clutter and communicate a key product benefit in a soft-sell manner. Maytag's Lonely Repairman reinforced the company's key "reliability" product association for years. Characters also avoid many of the problems that plague human spokespeople—they don't demand pay raises, cheat on their spouses, or grow old. Betty Crocker may be over 90, but after seven makeovers, she doesn't look a day over 39!

With the opportunity to shape the brand's personality and facilitate consumer interactions, brand characters play an increasingly important role in a digital world. The success of Mr. Peanut in viral videos led to the introduction of a new peanut butter line. For the namesake character of Captain Morgan rum, Diageo has a team of eight people who work with its New York ad firm Anomaly to create daily online content. Even old-timers are making their way onto the Web. First introduced in 1957, Mr. Clean has amassed almost 900,000 Facebook fans.

The online popularity and effectiveness of brand characters was demonstrated by a research study revealing that the Pillsbury Doughboy garners 10 times the social media buzz for the Pillsbury brand as NBA star LeBron James does for his Nike sponsor!

**Sources:** Bruce Horovitz, "Mascots Top Celebrities in Social Media Buzz," *USA Today*, June 10, 2013; Rupal Parekh, "Meet the Woman behind the Michelin Man," *Advertising Age*, June 11, 2012; Suzanne Vranica, "Knights, Pirates and Trees Flock to Facebook," *Wall Street Journal*, March 26, 2012; David Welch, "Mr. Peanut Gets Smashed," *Bloomberg Businessweek*, March 12, 2012; "Betty Crocker Celebrates 90th Birthday," www.marketwatch.com, November 18, 2011; Dorothy Pomerantz and Lacey Rose, "America's Most Loved Spokescreatures," *Forbes*, March 18, 2010; Judith A. Garretson and Scot Burton, "The Role of Spokescharacters as Advertisement and Package Cues in Integrated Marketing Communications," *Journal of Marketing* 69 (October 2005), pp. 118–32; Judith Anne Garretson Folse, Richard G. Netemeyer, and Scot Burton, "Spokescharacters: How the Personality Traits of Sincerity, Excitement, and Competence Help to Build Equity," *Journal of Advertising* 41 (Spring 2012), pp. 17–32.

Often, the less concrete brand benefits are, the more important that brand elements capture intangible characteristics. Many insurance firms use symbols of strength for their brands (the Rock of Gibraltar for Prudential and the stag for Hartford) or security (the "good hands" of Allstate, the Traveler's umbrella, and the hard hat of Fireman's Fund).

Like brand names, slogans are an extremely efficient means to build brand equity.[42] They can function as useful "hooks" to help consumers grasp what the brand is and what makes it special, as in "Like a Good Neighbor, State Farm Is There," "Nothing Runs Like a Deere," and "Every Kiss Begins with Kay" for the jeweler.

Firms should be careful in replacing a good slogan. Citi walked away from its famous "Citi Never Sleeps" slogan, replacing it with "Let's Get It Done," only to return when the new slogan failed to catch on.[43] After 50 years, Avis Car Rental dropped "We Try Harder" for "It's Your Space." It's not clear whether this new slogan will have the staying power of the one it replaced.[44]

## DESIGNING HOLISTIC MARKETING ACTIVITIES

Brands are not built by advertising alone. Customers come to know a brand through a range of contacts and touch points: personal observation and use, word of mouth, interactions with company personnel, online or telephone experiences, and payment transactions. A **brand contact** is any information-bearing experience, whether positive or negative, a customer or prospect has with the brand, its product category, or its market.[45] The company must put as much effort into managing these experiences as into producing its ads. Any brand contact can affect consumers' brand knowledge and the way they think, feel, or act toward the brand.

As we describe throughout this text, marketing strategy and tactics have changed dramatically.[46] Marketers are creating brand contacts and building brand equity through new avenues such as online clubs and consumer communities, trade shows, event marketing, sponsorship, factory visits, public relations and press releases, and social cause marketing. Consider how BMW has built the MINI Cooper brand in the United States.[47]

Source: MINI USA

MINI Cooper has been supported since its American launch by a creative and full-integrated marketing program.

**MINI COOPER** When BMW launched the modernized MINI Cooper in the United States in 2002, it employed a broad mix of media: billboards, posters, Internet, print, PR, product placement, and grassroots activities. Many were linked to a cleverly designed Web site with product and dealer information. The car was placed atop Ford Excursion SUVs at 21 auto shows across the United States; it was used as seats in a sports stadium; and it appeared in *Playboy* magazine as a centerfold. The imaginative integrated campaign built a six-month waiting list for the MINI Cooper. Despite its relatively limited communications budget, the brand has continued to develop innovative, award-winning campaigns ever since. MINI has especially used outdoor advertising creatively: Two curved palm trees planted next to a speeding MINI on a billboard

Source: uggaustralia.com

Source: FGA WENN Photos/Newscom

Supported by an ad campaign featuring star NFL quarterback Tom Brady, UGG has been targeting men as one of its new avenues for growth.

The Volvo Ocean race is a way to help the Volvo brand be seen as modern, active and energetic.

Source: ASSOCIATED PRESS

created an illusion of speed and power; a digital billboard personally greeted passing MINI drivers by using a signal from a radio chip embedded in their key fobs; and a real MINI on the side of a building was able to move up and down like a yo-yo. A new worldwide campaign, "Not Normal," spotlights MINI's strong, independent character through classic and digital media. Now sold in 100 countries around the world, MINI has expanded into a six-model lineup, including a convertible, a coupe, the Clubman four-door, and the Countryman wagon. These product introductions reinforce that MINI is agile, versatile, and fun to drive, and the marketing campaign as a whole builds strong emotional connections with drivers.

**Integrated marketing** is about mixing and matching marketing activities to maximize their individual and collective effects.[48] Marketers need a variety of different marketing activities that consistently reinforce the brand promise. Consider what Deckers is doing to make sure UGG does not become yesterday's news.[49]

**UGG**    UGG sheepskin boots were originally made for men; surfers in Australia wore them on the beach to warm their feet after surfing. Acquired by Deckers in 1995, UGGs took off among women in 2000 after Oprah Winfrey showcased them on her famous "Favorite Things" show. By 2011, sales had cracked $1 billion. The following year, women's tastes in boots shifted to leather, and sales of UGGs slipped. To bolster the brand, Deckers is using the credibility and influence of bloggers who make up the "UGG Creative Council" to expand the brand's social media footprint and build awareness of the full range of its product line. To appeal to men, rugged New England Patriots quarterback Tom Brady was hired as an endorser in a campaign featuring the comfort, craftsmanship, and quality of the brand. To broaden the brand's appeal beyond its quintessential winter boot, spring and summer lines including sandals and beach cover-ups were launched to position UGG as an active, outdoor lifestyle brand.

We can evaluate integrated marketing activities in terms of the effectiveness and efficiency with which they affect brand awareness and create, maintain, or strengthen brand associations and image. Although Volvo may invest in R&D and engage in advertising, promotions, and other communications to reinforce its "safety" brand association, it also sponsors events to make sure it is seen as active, contemporary, and up to date. Notable Volvo sponsorships include golf tournaments and the European professional golf tour, the Volvo Ocean race, the famed Gothenburg horse show, and cultural events.

Marketing programs should be put together so the whole is greater than the sum of the parts. In other words, marketing activities should work singularly and in combination.

## LEVERAGING SECONDARY ASSOCIATIONS

The third and final way to build brand equity is, in effect, to "borrow" it. That is, create brand equity by linking the brand to other information in memory that conveys meaning to consumers (see Figure 11.5).

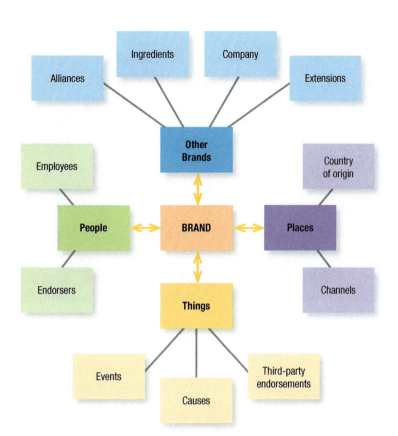

| **Fig. 11.5** |
Secondary Sources of
Brand Knowledge

These "secondary" brand associations can link the brand to sources such as the company itself (through branding strategies), to countries or other geographical regions (through identification of product origin), and to channels of distribution (through channel strategy), as well as to other brands (through ingredient or co-branding), characters (through licensing), spokespeople (through endorsements), sporting or cultural events (through sponsorship), or some other third-party sources (through awards or reviews).

Suppose Burton—the maker of snowboards, snowboard boots, bindings, clothing, and outerwear—decided to introduce a new surfboard called the "Dominator." Burton has gained more than a third of the snowboard market by closely aligning itself with top professional riders and creating a strong amateur snowboarder community around the country.[50] To support the new surfboard, Burton could leverage secondary brand knowledge in a number of ways:

- It could "sub-brand" the product, calling it "Dominator by Burton." Consumers' evaluations of the new product would be influenced by how they felt about Burton and whether they felt that such knowledge predicted the quality of a Burton surfboard.
- Burton could rely on its rural New England origins, but such a geographical location would seem to have little relevance to surfing.
- Burton could sell through popular surf shops in the hope that their credibility would rub off on the Dominator brand.
- Burton could co-brand by identifying a strong ingredient brand for its foam or fiberglass materials (as Wilson did by incorporating Goodyear tire rubber on the soles of its Pro Staff Classic tennis shoes).
- Burton could find one or more top professional surfers to endorse the surfboard, or it could sponsor a surfing competition or even the entire Association of Surfing Professionals (ASP) World Tour.
- Burton could secure and publicize favorable ratings from third-party sources such as *Surfer* or *Surfing* magazine.

Thus, independent of the associations created by the surfboard itself, its brand name, or any other aspects of the marketing program, Burton could build equity by linking the brand to these other entities.

Leveraging secondary associations can be an efficient and effective way to strengthen a brand. But linking a brand to someone or something else can be risky because anything bad that happens to that other entity can also be linked to the brand. When popular endorsers Tiger Woods and Lance Armstrong got into trouble, many of the firms using them to promote their brands chose to cut ties.

If Burton were to introduce a surfboard, there are many ways it could leverage secondary brand knowledge and associations.

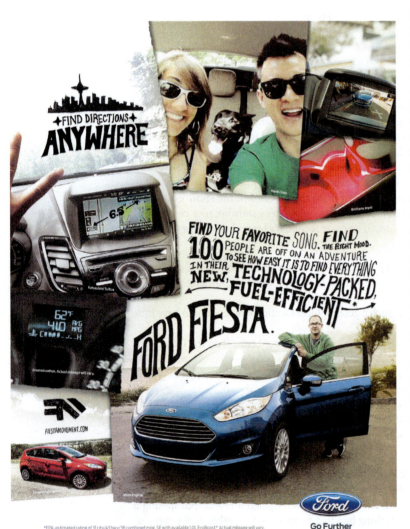

Ford's external marketing efforts are matched by a strong internal branding program within the company.

## INTERNAL BRANDING

Marketers must now "walk the walk" to deliver the brand promise. They must adopt an *internal* perspective to be sure employees and marketing partners appreciate and understand basic branding notions and how they can help—or hurt—brand equity.[51] **Internal branding** consists of activities and processes that help inform and inspire employees about brands.[52] Holistic marketers must go even further and train and encourage distributors and dealers to serve their customers well. Poorly trained dealers or other intermediaries can ruin the best efforts to build a strong brand image.

*Brand bonding* occurs when customers experience the company as delivering on its brand promise. All the customers' contacts with company employees and communications must be positive.[53] *The brand promise will not be delivered unless everyone in the company lives the brand.* Disney is so successful at internal branding that it holds seminars on the "Disney Style" for employees from other companies. Chevrolet chose to send almost 3,000 of its dealers to the Disney Institute in Walt Disney World to help them learn how to apply Disney principles to improve the car-buying experience for their customers.[54]

When employees care about and believe in the brand, they're motivated to work harder and feel greater loyalty to the firm. Some important principles for internal branding are:[55]

1. *Choose the right moment.* Turning points are ideal opportunities to capture employees' attention and imagination. After it ran an internal branding campaign to accompany its external repositioning, the "Beyond Petroleum" ad campaign, BP found most employees were positive about the new brand and thought the company was going in the right direction.

2. *Link internal and external marketing.* Internal and external messages must match. Ford's new

branding push to "Go Further" targets car buyers as well as Ford employees. The company believes that making Ford's internal branding efforts consistent with its external branding can "create profound synergies that will benefit the company in significant ways." Internally, Ford CMO Jim Farley is emphasizing three areas to help Ford employees "go further": "people serving people," "ingenuity," and "attainable."[56]

3. ***Bring the brand alive for employees.*** Internal communications should be informative and energizing. Starbucks created a major facility and exhibit to physically immerse managers and employees in the brand experience. To help its staff better understand how the brand positioning and promise affected their daily work, a major services company invested more than 100,000 hours in deep manager and employee training, with role-playing scenarios, exercises, and interactive tools.[57]

4. ***Keep it simple.*** Don't overwhelm employees with too many details. Focus on the key brand pillars, ideally in the form of a brand mantra. Walmart uses three very simple brand pillars: "Quality Products; Unbeatable Prices; Easy Shopping." [58]

# Measuring Brand Equity

How do we measure brand equity? An *indirect* approach assesses potential sources of brand equity by identifying and tracking consumer brand knowledge structures.[59] A *direct* approach assesses the actual impact of brand knowledge on consumer response to different aspects of the marketing. "Marketing Insight: The Brand Value Chain" shows how to link the two approaches.

---

## The Brand Value Chain

The **brand value chain** is a structured approach to assessing the sources and outcomes of brand equity and the way marketing activities create brand value (Figure 11.6). It is based on several premises.

First, brand value creation begins when the firm targets actual or potential customers by investing in a marketing program to develop the brand, including marketing communications, trade or intermediary support, and product research, development, and design. This marketing activity will change customers' mind-sets—what customers think and feel and everything that becomes linked to the brand. Next, these customers' mind-sets will affect buying behavior and the way consumers respond to all subsequent marketing activity—pricing, channels, communications, and the product itself—and the resulting market share and profitability of the brand. Finally, the investment community will consider this market performance of the brand to assess shareholder value in general and the value of a brand in particular.

The model also assumes that three multipliers increase or decrease the value that can flow from one stage to another.

- The *program multiplier* determines the marketing program's ability to affect the customer mind-set and is a function of the quality of the program investment.

- The *customer multiplier* determines the extent to which value created in the minds and hearts of customers affects market performance. This result depends on competitive superiority (how effective the quantity and quality of the marketing investment of other competing brands are), channel and other intermediary support (how much brand reinforcement and selling effort various marketing partners are putting forth), and customer size and profile (how many and what types of customers, profitable or not, are attracted to the brand).

- The *market multiplier* determines the extent to which the value shown by the market performance of a brand is manifested in shareholder value. It depends, in part, on the actions of financial analysts and investors.

Researchers at Millward Brown adopt a very similar perspective. They maintain that a brand's financial success depends on its ability to be meaningful, different, and salient. These three brand qualities (MD&S) predispose someone to positive purchase behavior (choose the brand over others, pay more for it, stick with or try it in the future), which in turn generates financial benefits to the company (increased volume share, higher price premium, increased likelihood to grow value share in the future).

Millward Brown asserts that this brand predisposition is measured by three brand equity metrics: power, premium and potential.

- People are predisposed to choose the brand over others. This will drive brand volume, so *power* predicts volume share based entirely on perceptions, absent of activation factors.

- People are predisposed to pay more for the brand. This will allow the brand to charge more, so *premium* predicts the price index your brand can command.

- *Potential* indicates the likelihood of value share growth for the brand in the next 12 months, based on people's predisposition to stick to the brand or try it in the future.

**Sources:** Kevin Lane Keller and Don Lehmann, "How Do Brands Create Value," *Marketing Management* (May–June 2003), pp. 27–31. See also Marc J. Epstein and Robert A. Westbrook, "Linking Actions to Profits in Strategic Decision Making," *MIT Sloan Management Review* (Spring 2001), pp. 39–49; Rajendra K. Srivastava, Tasadduq A. Shervani, and Liam Fahey, "Market-Based Assets and Shareholder Value," *Journal of Marketing* 62 (January 1998), pp. 2–18; Shuba Srinivasan, Marc Vanheule, and Koen Pauwels, "Mindset Metrics in Market Response Models: An Integrative Approach," *Journal of Marketing Research* 47 (August 2010), pp. 672–84; Josh Samuel, "The Power of Being Meaningful, Different and Salient," *Point of View*, www.millwardbrown.com; Jorge Alagon and Josh Samuel, "The Meaningfully Different Framework," white paper, www.millwardbrown.com, April 2013.

| **Fig. 11.6** |

# Brand Value Chain

Source: Kevin Lane Keller, *Strategic Brand Management*, 4th ed. (Upper Saddle River, NJ: Prentice Hall, 2013). Printed and electronically reproduced by permission of Pearson Education, Inc. Upper Saddle River, New Jersey.

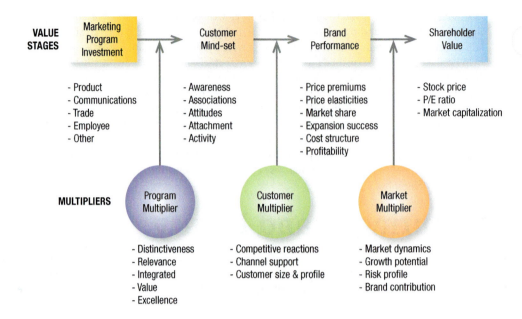

The two general approaches are complementary, and marketers can employ both. In other words, for brand equity to perform a useful strategic function and guide marketing decisions, marketers need to fully understand (1) the sources of brand equity and how they affect outcomes of interest and (2) how these sources and outcomes change, if at all, over time. Brand audits are important for the former; brand tracking for the latter.

- A **brand audit** is a focused series of procedures to assess the health of the brand, uncover its sources of brand equity, and suggest ways to improve and leverage its equity. Marketers should conduct a brand audit when setting up marketing plans and when considering shifts in strategic direction. Conducting brand audits on a regular basis, such as annually, allows marketers to keep their fingers on the pulse of their brands so they can manage them more proactively and responsively. A good brand audit provides keen insights into consumers, brands, and the relationship between the two.
- **Brand-tracking studies** use the brand audit as input to collect quantitative data from consumers over time, providing consistent, baseline information about how brands and marketing programs are performing. Tracking studies help us understand where, how much, and in what ways brand value is being created to facilitate day-to-day decision making.

One firm that recently conducted an influential major brand audit is Kellogg's.[60]

**KELLOGG'S**   The ready-to-eat cereal category has been under siege in recent years as busy consumers choose to eat on the run while nutrition-minded consumers worry about genetically modified ingredients. With a history spanning more than a century, Kellogg decided it needed to refresh the brand and address the issues head-on. An extensive brand audit, dubbed "Project Signature," was launched to provide strategic direction and creative inspiration. After a year of work with brand consulting partner Interbrand, the result was a new tagline, "Let's Make Today Great"; an updated, more contemporary logo and design look; clear identification of the brand's core purpose as highlighting the "power of breakfast"; explicit incorporation of the Kellogg's master brand into all its marketing campaigns; and consolidation of 42 company Web sites around the world into one. The brand audit influenced a number of Kellogg's specific marketing programs and activities, from the cause-related "Share Your Breakfast" campaign (to help the one in five U.S. children who might not have access to breakfast) to the "Love Your Cereal" social media program debunking myths about cereal. An Olympic sponsor, Kellogg also devotes 20 percent of its communication budget to online engagement.

Marketers should distinguish brand equity from **brand valuation,** which is the job of estimating the total financial value of the brand. Table 11.2 displays the world's most valuable brands in 2012 according to the Interbrand rankings, as described below in "Marketing Insight: What Is a Brand Worth?"[61] In these well-known companies, brand value is typically more than half the total company market capitalization. John Stuart, cofounder of Quaker Oats, said: "If this business were split up, I would give you the land and bricks and mortar, and I would take the

| Rank | Brand | 2014 Brand Value (Billions) |
|------|-------|------------------------------|
| TABLE 11.2 | The World's 10 Most Valuable Brands in 2014 | |
| 1 | Apple | $118.9 |
| 2 | Google | $107.4 |
| 3 | Coca-Cola | $81.6 |
| 4 | IBM | $72.2 |
| 5 | Microsoft | $61.2 |
| 6 | GE | $45.5 |
| 7 | Samsung | $45.5 |
| 8 | Toyota | $42.4 |
| 9 | McDonald's | $42.3 |
| 10 | Mercedes-Benz | $34.3 |

*Source:* Interbrand. Used with permission.

brands and trademarks, and I would fare better than you." U.S. companies do not list brand equity on their balance sheets, in part because of differences in opinion about what constitutes a good estimate. However, companies do give it a value in countries such as the United Kingdom, Hong Kong, and Australia.

# What Is a Brand Worth?

Top brand-management firm Interbrand has developed a model to formally estimate the dollar value of a brand. It defines brand value as the net present value of the future earnings that can be attributed to the brand alone. The firm believes marketing and financial analyses are equally important in determining the value of a brand. Its process follows five steps (see Figure 11.7 for a schematic overview):

1. **Market Segmentation**—The first step is to divide the market(s) in which the brand is sold into mutually exclusive segments that help determine variations among the brand's different customer groups.

2. **Financial Analysis**—Interbrand assesses purchase price, volume, and frequency to help calculate accurate forecasts of future brand sales and revenues. Once it has established Brand Revenues, it deducts all associated operating costs to derive earnings before interest and tax (EBIT). It also deducts the appropriate

taxes and a charge for the capital employed to operate the underlying business, leaving Economic Earnings, that is, the earnings attributed to the branded business.

3. **Role of Branding**—Interbrand next attributes a proportion of Economic Earnings to the brand in each market segment by first identifying the various drivers of demand and then determining the degree to which the brand directly influences each. The Role of Branding assessment is based on market research, client workshops, and interviews and represents the percentage of Economic Earnings the brand generates. Multiplying the Role of Branding by Economic Earnings yields Brand Earnings.

4. **Brand Strength**—Interbrand then assesses the brand's strength profile to determine the likelihood that the brand will realize forecasted Brand Earnings. This step relies on competitive benchmarking and a structured evaluation of the brand's clarity, commitment, protection, responsiveness, authenticity, relevance, differentiation, consistency, presence, and understanding. For each segment, Interbrand applies industry and brand equity metrics to determine a risk premium for the brand. The company's analysts derive the overall Brand Discount Rate by adding a brand-risk premium to

| Fig. 11.7 |

Interbrand Brand
Valuation Method

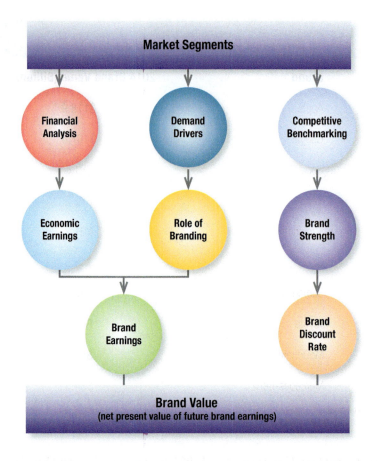

the risk-free rate, represented by the yield on government bonds. The Brand Discount Rate, applied to the forecasted Brand Earnings forecast, yields the net present value of the Brand Earnings. The stronger the brand, the lower the discount rate, and vice versa.

5.  **Brand Value Calculation**—Brand Value is the net present value (NPV) of the forecasted Brand Earnings, discounted by the Brand Discount Rate. The NPV calculation is composed of both the forecast period and the period beyond, reflecting the ability of brands to continue generating future earnings.

Increasingly, Interbrand uses brand value assessments as a dynamic, strategic tool to identify and maximize return on brand investment across a whole host of areas.

**Sources:** Interbrand, the Interbrand Brand Glossary, and Interbrand's Nik Stucky and Rita Clifton, January 2009. For an alternative brand valuation method, see Millward Brown's BrandZ brand valuation methodology: http://www.millwardbrown.com/BrandZ/Top_100_Global_Brands/Methodology.aspx.

# Managing Brand Equity

Because consumer responses to marketing activity depend on what they know and remember about a brand, as the brand value chain suggests, short-term marketing actions, by changing brand knowledge, necessarily increase or decrease the long-term success of future marketing actions.

## BRAND REINFORCEMENT

As a company's major enduring asset, a brand needs to be carefully managed so its value does not depreciate.[62] Brand leaders of 70 years ago that remain leaders today—companies such as Wrigley's, Coca-Cola, Heinz, and Campbell Soup—only do so by constantly striving to improve their products, services, and marketing.

Marketers can reinforce brand equity by consistently conveying the brand's meaning in terms of (1) what products it represents, what core benefits it supplies, and what needs it satisfies; and (2) how the brand makes products superior and which strong, favorable, and unique brand associations should exist in consumers' minds.[63] NIVEA, one of Europe's strongest brands, expanded from a skin cream brand to a skin care and personal care brand through carefully designed and implemented brand extensions that reinforced the brand promise of "mild," "gentle," "caring," and "protective."

Reinforcing brand equity requires that the brand always be moving forward—in the right direction and with new and compelling offerings and ways to market them. In virtually every product category, once-prominent and admired brands—such as Circuit City, Fila, Polaroid, and Slim-Fast—have fallen on hard times or gone out of business.[64] Consider the plight of one-time highflier Nokia.[65]

By failing to sufficiently innovate and stay relevant, Nokia quickly lost market leadership.

**| NOKIA**   For 14 years, Nokia dominated cell phone sales as the world's industry leader before being surpassed by Samsung in 2012, marking the end of an era. Once the pride of Finland, the company has found itself outsold by Samsung even on its home soil. How could such a high-flying brand come crashing to earth? In a nutshell, it failed to innovate and stay relevant. Nokia did not respond to the wildly successful iPhone and the shifting consumer demand that accompanied it. The company thought the iPhone was too expensive to manufacture and was not up to its own product standards. The iPhone reportedly failed Nokia's "drop test," in which a phone is dropped on concrete from a height of five feet at different angles. Nokia had actually spent $40 billion on R&D over the preceding decade and was a smart phone pioneer, but it chose not to invest in devices that anticipated what the iPhone eventually became. Without the right new products, Nokia began to be associated by consumers with a different era of technology, a fatal blow in the fast-moving, technologically intensive smart phone market.

An important part of reinforcing brands is providing consistent marketing support. Consistency doesn't mean uniformity with no changes: While there is little need to deviate from a successful position, many tactical changes may be necessary to maintain the strategic thrust and direction of the brand. When change *is* necessary, marketers should vigorously preserve and defend sources of brand equity.

Marketers must recognize the trade-offs between activities that fortify the brand and reinforce its meaning, such as a well-received product improvement or a creatively designed ad campaign, and those that leverage or borrow from existing brand equity to reap some financial benefit, such as a short-term promotional discount.[66] At some point, failure to reinforce the brand will diminish brand awareness and weaken brand image. Consider what happened to Sears.[67]

**| SEARS**   A classic U.S. company, Sears was one of the strongest department store brands for more than 100 years, associated with high-quality merchandise and responsive customer service. Facing financial difficulties in the early 2000s, the company started aggressively selling assets and cutting costs to maintain its revenue targets. As a result of spending only $2 to $3 per square foot on annual maintenance and repair of its stores, far less than the $6 to $8 per square foot spent by competitors Target and Walmart, Sears began hearing customer complaints about inattentive sales associates, disorganized sales racks, and stores in disrepair. As one analyst noted, "[T]hey weren't keeping [their] promise. Consumers are pretty sophisticated, and they walked into these stores and it was the same old place ... without the freshness, the excitement or the interactivity of the experience." According to the ACS index of customer satisfaction, in 2012 Sears was ranked 10th among 11 department and discount stores, and same-store sales had been in a prolonged six-year decline.

## BRAND REVITALIZATION

Any new development in the marketing environment can affect a brand's fortunes. Nevertheless, a number of brands have managed to make impressive comebacks in recent years.[68] After some hard times in the automotive market, Cadillac, Fiat, and Volkswagen have all turned their brand fortunes around to varying degrees. General Motors's rescue of its fading Cadillac brand was fueled by a complete overhaul of its product lineup with new designs that redefined its look and styling, such as the SRX crossover, the XTS and CTS sedans, the Escalade

SUV, and the new ATS sports sedan. A healthy dose of breakthrough marketing, including the first use of Led Zeppelin's music in advertising, also helped.[69]

Often, the first thing to do in revitalizing a brand is understand what the sources of brand equity were to begin with. Are positive associations losing their strength or uniqueness? Have negative associations become linked to the brand? Then decide whether to retain the same positioning or create a new one and, if so, which new one.[70]

Sometimes the actual marketing program is the source of the problem because it fails to deliver on the brand promise. Then a "back to basics" strategy may make sense. We've mentioned that Harley-Davidson regained its market leadership by doing a better job of living up to customer expectations for product performance. Pabst Brewing Company did it by returning to its roots and leveraging iconic packaging and imagery and a perception of authenticity.

In other cases, however, the old positioning is just no longer viable and a reinvention strategy is necessary. Mountain Dew completely overhauled its brand image to become a soft-drink powerhouse. As its history reveals, it is often easier to revive a brand that is alive but has been more or less forgotten. Old Spice is another example of a brand that transcended its roots as the classic aftershave and cologne gift set that baby boomers gave their dads on Father's Day to become positively identified with contemporary male grooming products for a younger Millennial audience. To revitalize Old Spice, P&G used product innovation and tongue-in-cheek communications that stressed the brand's "experience."[71]

There is obviously a continuum of revitalization strategies, with pure "back to basics" at one end, pure "reinvention" at the other, and many combinations in between. The challenge is often to change enough to attract some new customers, but not enough to alienate old customers. Regardless of the strategy, brand revitalization of almost any kind starts with the product.[72] Consider how Burberry made its comeback.[73]

**❚ BURBERRY**   Burberry has an incredible 150-year history. The company's classic English trenchcoats were worn by British soldiers in World War I; Sir Ernest Shackleton wore a Burberry during his Antarctic expedition; and Burberry has even been designated an official supplier to the royal family. By 2006, though, the brand's distinctive plaid pattern was no longer cool; it had been splashed over too many products and knocked off by too many counterfeiters. A new CEO, Angela Ahrendts, who had grown up in the U.S. Midwest, was shocked to find that despite the trenchcoat's iconic status, outerwear made up only 20 percent of Burberry's global business. Despite some misgivings from others, she decided to "reinforce our heritage, our Britishness, by emphasizing and growing our core luxury products, innovating them and keeping them at the heart of everything we did." Targeting the luxury customer of the future,

Burberry revitalized its brand by focusing on core products and refocusing on its heritage and style.

*Source: © Camera Press Ltd/Alamy*

Ahrendt removed the overworked plaid pattern from 90 percent of products. A new global design czar, Christopher Bailey, gave the brand a more unified and contemporary sensibility, resulting in the creation of more than 300 different coats, from capes and cropped jackets to classic trenches in a variety of colors and styles. New stores were opened in desirable locations, and training for sales associates was increased. The Web site was redesigned to be more appealing to Millennials, featuring emotive brand content like music, movies, heritage, and storytelling, including simulcasts of Burberry's runway shows.

# Devising a Branding Strategy

A firm's **branding strategy**—often called its **brand architecture**—reflects the number and nature of both common and distinctive brand elements. Deciding how to brand new products is especially critical. A firm has three main choices:

1. It can develop new brand elements for the new product.
2. It can apply some of its existing brand elements.
3. It can use a combination of new and existing brand elements.

When a firm uses an established brand to introduce a new product, the product is called a **brand extension.** When marketers combine a new brand with an existing brand, the brand extension can also be called a **sub-brand,** such as Hershey Kisses candy, Adobe Acrobat software, Toyota Camry automobiles, and American Express Blue cards. The existing brand that gives birth to a brand extension or sub-brand is the **parent brand.** If the parent brand is already associated with multiple products through brand extensions, it can also be called a **master brand** or **family brand.**

Brand extensions fall into two general categories. In a **line extension,** the parent brand covers a new product within a product category it currently serves, such as with new flavors, forms, colors, ingredients, and package sizes. Dannon has introduced several types of Dannon yogurt line extensions through the years—Fruit on the Bottom, All Natural Flavors, Dan-o-nino, and Light & Fit. In a **category extension,** marketers use the parent brand to enter a different product category, such as Swiss Army watches. Honda has used its company name to cover such different products as automobiles, motorcycles, snowblowers, lawn mowers, marine engines, and snowmobiles. This allows the firm to advertise that it can fit "six Hondas in a two-car garage."

A **brand line** consists of all products—original as well as line and category extensions—sold under a particular brand. A **brand mix** (or brand assortment) is the set of all brand lines that a particular seller makes. Many companies are introducing **branded variants,** which are specific brand lines supplied to specific retailers or distribution channels. They result from the pressure retailers put on manufacturers to provide distinctive offerings. A camera company may supply its low-end cameras to mass merchandisers while limiting its higher-priced items to specialty camera shops. Valentino may design and supply different lines of suits and jackets to different department stores.[74]

A **licensed product** is one whose brand name has been licensed to other manufacturers that actually make the product. Corporations have seized on licensing to push their company names and images across a wide range of products—from bedding to shoes—making licensing a multibillion-dollar business. It is perhaps not surprising that in a high-involvement category such as automobiles, licensing is big business.[75]

**AUTOMOTIVE LICENSING** Several automotive brands have created lucrative licensing businesses. Jeep's licensing program, with 600 products and 150 licensees, includes everything from strollers built for a father's longer arms to apparel with Teflon in the denim—as long as the product fits the brand's positioning of "Life without Limits." Thanks to 600-plus dedicated shop-in-shops and 80 freestanding stores around the world, Jeep's licensing revenue now exceeds $550 million in retail sales. New areas of emphasis include outdoor and travel gear, juvenile products, and sporting goods. As of 2014, Ford was generating $2 billion in licensing revenue from 18,000 different items sold through 400 licensees. Products range from apparel branded with the Ford Blue Oval logo and the popular Mustang nameplate logo to radio-controlled cars sold in major retailers like Walmart and Toys R Us. An area of growth is products designed to equip male fans and their "man caves."

Jeep generates over $550 million in revenues by licensing its brand to other companies for other products.

*Source: © MARKA/Alamy*

# BRANDING DECISIONS

**ALTERNATIVE BRANDING STRATEGIES** Today, branding is such a strong force that hardly anything goes unbranded. Assuming a firm decides to brand its products or services, it must choose which brand names to use. Three general strategies are popular:

- *Individual or separate family brand names.* Consumer packaged-goods companies have a long tradition of branding different products by different names. General Mills largely uses individual brand names, such as Bisquick, Gold Medal flour, Nature Valley granola bars, Old El Paso Mexican foods, Progresso soup, Wheaties cereal, and Yoplait yogurt. If a company produces quite different products, one blanket name is often not desirable. Swift & Company developed separate family names for its hams (Premium) and fertilizers (Vigoro). Companies often use different brand names for different quality lines within the same product class. A major advantage of separate family brand names is that if a product fails or appears to be of low quality, the company has not tied its reputation to it.[76]
- *Corporate umbrella or company brand name.* Many firms, such as Heinz and GE, use their corporate brand as an umbrella brand across their entire range of products.[77] Development costs are lower with umbrella names because there's no need to research a name or spend heavily on advertising to create recognition. Campbell Soup introduces new soups under its brand name with extreme simplicity and achieves instant recognition. Sales of the new product are likely to be strong if the manufacturer's name is good. Corporate-image associations of innovativeness, expertise, and trustworthiness have been shown to directly influence consumer evaluations.[78] Finally, a corporate branding strategy can lead to greater intangible value for the firm.[79]
- *Sub-brand name.* Sub-brands combine two or more of the corporate brand, family brand, or individual product brand names. Kellogg employs a sub-brand or hybrid branding strategy by combining the corporate brand with individual product brands as with Kellogg's Rice Krispies, Kellogg's Raisin Bran, and Kellogg's Corn Flakes. Many durable-goods makers such as Honda, Sony, and Hewlett-Packard use sub-brands for their products. The corporate or company name legitimizes, and the individual name individualizes, the new product.

**HOUSE OF BRANDS VERSUS A BRANDED HOUSE** The use of individual or separate family brand names has been referred to as a "house of brands" strategy, whereas the use of an umbrella corporate or company brand name is a "branded house" strategy. These two strategies represent two ends of a continuum. A sub-brand strategy falls somewhere between, depending on which component of the sub-brand receives more emphasis. A good example of a house of brands strategy is United Technologies.[80]

**▌ UNITED TECHNOLOGIES** United Technology Corporation (UTC) provides a broad range of high-technology products and services for the aerospace and commercial building industries, generating nearly $63 billion in revenues. Its aerospace businesses include Sikorsky helicopters, Pratt & Whitney aircraft engines, and UTC Aerospace

Systems (which includes Goodrich Corporation and Hamilton Sundstrand aerospace systems). UTC Building & Industrial Systems, the world's largest provider of building technologies, includes Otis elevators and escalators; Carrier heating, air-conditioning, and refrigeration systems; and fire and security solutions from brands such as Kidde and Chubb. Most of its in-market brands are the names of the individuals who invented the product or created the company decades ago; they have more power and are more recognizable in the business buying marketplace than the name of the parent brand, and employees are loyal to the individual companies. The UTC name is advertised only to small but influential audiences—the financial community and opinion leaders in New York and Washington, DC. "My philosophy has always been to use the power of the trademarks of the subsidiaries to improve the recognition and brand acceptance, awareness, and respect for the parent company itself," said UTC's one-time CEO George David.

With a branded house strategy, it is often useful to have a well-defined flagship product. A **flagship product** is one that best represents or embodies the brand as a whole to consumers. It often is the first product by which the brand gained fame, a widely accepted best-seller, or a highly admired or award-winning product.[81]

Flagship products play a key role in the brand portfolio in that marketing them can have short-term benefits (increased sales) as well as long-term benefits (improved brand equity for a range of products). Certain models play important flagship roles for many car manufacturers. Besides generating the most sales, family sedans Toyota Camry and Honda Accord represent brand values that all cars from those manufacturers share.[82] In justifying the large investments incurred in launching its new 2014 Mercedes S-class automobiles, Daimler's chief executive Dieter Zetsche explained, "This car is for Mercedes-Benz what the harbor is for Hamburg, the Mona Lisa for Leonardo da Vinci and 'Satisfaction' for the Rolling Stones: the most important symbol of the reputation of the whole."[83]

Two key components of virtually any branding strategy are brand portfolios and brand extensions. (Chapter 13 discusses co-branding and ingredient branding, as well as line-stretching through vertical extensions.)

# BRAND PORTFOLIOS

A brand can be stretched only so far, and all the segments the firm would like to target may not view the same brand equally favorably. Marketers often need multiple brands in order to pursue these multiple segments. Some other reasons for introducing multiple brands in a category include:[84]

1. Increasing shelf presence and retailer dependence in the store
2. Attracting consumers seeking variety who may otherwise have switched to another brand
3. Increasing internal competition within the firm
4. Yielding economies of scale in advertising, sales, merchandising, and physical distribution

The **brand portfolio** is the set of all brands and brand lines a particular firm offers for sale in a particular category or market segment. Building a good brand portfolio requires careful thinking and creative execution. In the hotel industry, brand portfolios are critical. Consider Starwood.[85]

Source: © Stocktrek Images, Inc./Alamy

United Technology has adopted a "house of brands" strategy with a diverse brand portfolio, including Pratt & Whitney aircraft engines.

**STARWOOD HOTELS & RESORTS**   One of the leading hotel and leisure companies in the world, Starwood Hotels & Resorts Worldwide has more than 1,200 properties in 100 countries and 181,400 employees at its owned and managed properties. In its rebranding attempt to go "beyond beds," Starwood has differentiated its hotels along emotional, experiential lines. Its hotel and call center operators convey different experiences at the firm's different chains, as does the firm's advertising. Starwood has nine distinct lifestyle brands in its portfolio. Here is how some of them are positioned:

- *Sheraton.* The largest brand, Sheraton is about warm, comforting, and casual. Its core value centers on "connections"—Sheraton enables you to connect to your location and to those back home.
- *Four Points by Sheraton.* For the self-sufficient traveler, Four Points is a select-service hotel that strives to be honest and uncomplicated. The brand is all about providing the comforts of home with little indulgences like local craft beers and free high-speed Internet access and bottled water.
- *W.* With a brand personality defined as flirty, for the insider, and an escape, W offers guests unique locally inspired experiences with a "What's New/What's Next" attitude. W's "Whatever/Whenever" service complements the sylish designs in its lobby gathering places and signature bars and restaurants.
- *Westin.* Westin's emphasis on "personal, instinctive, and renewal" has led to a new sensory welcome featuring a white tea scent, signature music and lighting, and refreshing towels. Each room features Westin's own "Heavenly" bed and bath products.

The hallmark of an optimal brand portfolio is the ability of each brand in it to maximize equity in combination with all the other brands in it. Marketers generally need to trade off market coverage with costs and profitability. If they can increase profits by dropping brands, a portfolio is too big; if they can increase profits by adding brands, it's not big enough.

The basic principle in designing a brand portfolio is to maximize market coverage so no potential customers are being ignored, but minimize brand overlap so brands are not competing for customer approval. Each brand should be clearly differentiated and appealing to a sizable enough marketing segment to justify its marketing and production costs. Consider these two B-to-B and B-to-C examples.

- Dow Corning has adopted a dual-brand approach to sell its silicon, which is used as an ingredient by many companies. Silicon under the Dow Corning name uses a "high touch" approach where customers receive much attention and support; silicon sold under the Xiameter name uses a "no frills" approach emphasizing low prices.[86]
- Unilever, partnering with PepsiCo, sells four distinct brands of ready-to-drink iced tea. Brisk Iced Tea is an "on ramp" brand that is an entry point and a "flavor-forward" value brand; Lipton Iced Tea is a mainstream brand with an appealing blend of flavor and tea; Lipton Pure Leaf Iced Tea is premium and "tea-forward" for tea purists; and Tazo is a super-premium, niche brand.[87]

Marketers carefully monitor brand portfolios over time to identify weak brands and kill unprofitable ones.[88] Brand lines with poorly differentiated brands are likely to be characterized by much cannibalization and require pruning. There are scores of cereals, beverages, and snacks and thousands of mutual funds. Students can choose among hundreds of business schools. For the seller, this spells hypercompetition. For the buyer, as Chapter 13 points out, it may mean too much choice.

Brands can also play a number of specific roles as part of a portfolio.

**FLANKERS**   Flanker or fighter brands are positioned with respect to competitors' brands so that more important (and more profitable) *flagship brands* can retain their desired positioning. Busch Bavarian is priced and marketed to protect Anheuser-Busch's premium Budweiser.[89] Marketers walk a fine line in designing fighter brands, which must be neither so attractive that they take sales away from their higher-priced comparison brands nor designed so cheaply that they reflect poorly on them.

**CASH COWS**   Some brands may be kept around despite dwindling sales because they manage to maintain their profitability with virtually no marketing support. Companies can effectively milk these "cash cow" brands by capitalizing on their reservoir of brand equity. Gillette still sells the older Atra, Sensor, and Mach III razors because withdrawing them may not necessarily move customers to another Gillette razor brand.

**LOW-END ENTRY LEVEL**   The role of a relatively low-priced brand in the portfolio often may be to attract customers to the brand franchise. Retailers like to feature these "traffic builders" because they are able to trade up customers to a higher-priced brand. Toyota's Scion, with its quirky design and low prices, has a very specific

Toyota Scion plays an important role as an entry level offering for the entire Toyota product line.

target: people in their early 30s or under. Its specific marketing mission is to capture buyers who have not purchased anything from Toyota to move them into the franchise. The youngest average customers in the industry for eight years running, Scion drivers are in fact three-quarters first-time Toyota buyers[90].

**HIGH-END PRESTIGE** The role of a relatively high-priced brand often is to add prestige and credibility to the entire portfolio. One analyst argued that the real value to Chevrolet of its high-performance Corvette sports car was "its ability to lure curious customers into showrooms and at the same time help improve the image of other Chevrolet cars. It does not mean a hell of a lot for GM profitability, but there is no question that it is a traffic builder."[91] Corvette's technological image and prestige cast a halo over the entire Chevrolet line.

# BRAND EXTENSIONS

Many firms have decided to leverage their most valuable asset by introducing a host of new products under their strongest brand names. Most new products are in fact brand extensions—typically 80 percent to 90 percent in any one year. Moreover, many of the most successful new products, as rated by various sources, are brand extensions. Among the most successful in supermarkets in 2012 were Dunkin' Donuts coffee, Progresso Light soups, and Hormel Compleats microwave meals. Nevertheless, many new products are introduced each year as new brands. The year 2012 also saw the launch of Zyrtec allergy relief medicine and Ped Egg foot files.

**ADVANTAGES OF BRAND EXTENSIONS** Two main advantages of brand extensions are that they can facilitate new-product acceptance and provide positive feedback to the parent brand and company.

*Improved Odds of New-Product Success* Consumers form expectations about a new product based on what they know about the parent brand and the extent to which they feel this information is relevant. When Sony introduced a new personal computer tailored for multimedia applications, the Vaio, consumers may have felt comfortable with its anticipated performance because of their experience with and knowledge of other Sony products.

By setting up positive expectations, extensions reduce risk. It also may be easier to convince retailers to stock and promote a brand extension because of anticipated increased customer demand. An introductory campaign for an extension doesn't need to create awareness of both the brand *and* the new product; it can concentrate on the new product itself.[92]

Extensions can thus reduce launch costs, important given that establishing a major new brand name for a consumer packaged good in the U.S. marketplace can cost more than $100 million! Extensions also can avoid the difficulty—and expense—of coming up with a new name and allow for packaging and labeling efficiencies. Similar or identical packages and labels can lower production costs for extensions and, if coordinated properly, provide more prominence in the retail store via a "billboard" effect.[93] Stouffer's offers a variety of frozen entrees with identical orange packaging that increases their visibility when they're stocked together in the freezer. With a portfolio of brand variants within a product category, consumers who want a change can switch to a different product type without having to leave the brand family.

*Positive Feedback Effects* Besides facilitating acceptance of new products, brand extensions can provide feedback benefits.[94] They can help to clarify the meaning of a brand and its core values or improve consumer loyalty to the company behind the extension.[95] Through their brand extensions, Crayola means "colorful arts and crafts for kids," Aunt Jemima means "breakfast foods," and Weight Watchers means "weight loss and maintenance."

Brand extensions can renew interest and liking for the brand and benefit the parent brand by expanding market coverage. AB InBev introduced its Budweiser Black Crown line extension—a beer with more alcohol and a stronger hops taste than regular Budweiser—with several purposes. The company hoped to both attract a younger audience being wooed by the explosion of craft brews and reinvigorate the core brand with its established base.[96]

A successful category extension may not only reinforce the parent brand and open up a new market but also facilitate even more new category extensions.[97] The success of Apple's iPod and iTunes products was that they: (1) opened up a new market, (2) helped sales of core Mac products, and (3) paved the way for the launch of the iPhone and iPad products.

**DISADVANTAGES OF BRAND EXTENSIONS** On the downside, line extensions may cause the brand name to be less strongly identified with any one product. Al Ries and Jack Trout call this the "line-extension trap."[98] By linking its brand to mainstream food products such as mashed potatoes, powdered milk, soups, and beverages, Cadbury ran the risk of losing its more specific meaning as a chocolate and candy brand.[99]

**Brand dilution** occurs when consumers no longer associate a brand with a specific or highly similar set of products and start thinking less of the brand. Porsche found sales success with its Cayenne sport-utility vehicle and Panamera four-door sedan, which accounted for three-quarters of its vehicle sales in 2012, but some critics felt the company was watering down its sports car image in the process. Perhaps in response, Porsche has dialed up its on- and off-road test tracks, driving courses, and roadshow events in recent years to help customers get the adrenaline rush of driving a legendary Porsche 911 or Boxster roadster.[100]

If a firm launches extensions consumers deem inappropriate, they may question the integrity of the brand or become confused or even frustrated: Which version of the product is the "right one" for them? Do they know the brand as well as they thought they did? Retailers reject many new products and brands because they don't have the shelf or display space for them. And the firm itself may become overwhelmed.

The worst possible scenario is for an extension not only to fail, but to harm the parent brand in the process. Fortunately, such events are rare. "Marketing failures," in which too few consumers are attracted to a brand, are typically much less damaging than "product failures," in which the brand fundamentally fails to live up to its promise. Even then, product failures dilute brand equity only when the extension is seen as very similar to the parent brand. The Audi 5000 car suffered from a tidal wave of negative publicity and word of mouth in the mid-1980s when it was alleged to have a "sudden acceleration" problem. The adverse publicity spilled over to the 4000 model. But the Quattro was relatively insulated because it was distanced from the 5000 by its more distinct branding and advertising strategy.[101]

Even if sales of a brand extension are high and meet targets, the revenue may be coming from consumers switching to the extension from existing parent-brand offerings—in effect cannibalizing the parent brand. Intrabrand shifts in sales may not necessarily be undesirable if they're a form of *preemptive cannibalization*. In other words, consumers who switched to a line extension might otherwise have switched to a competing brand instead. Tide laundry detergent maintains the same market share it had 50 years ago because of the sales contributions of its various line extensions—scented and unscented powder, tablet, liquid, and other forms.

One easily overlooked disadvantage of brand extensions is that the firm forgoes the chance to create a new brand with its own unique image and equity. Consider the long-term financial advantages to Disney of having introduced more grown-up Touchstone films, to Levi's of creating casual Dockers pants, and to Black & Decker of introducing high-end DeWALT power tools.

**SUCCESS CHARACTERISTICS** Marketers must judge each potential brand extension by how effectively it leverages existing brand equity from the parent brand as well as how effectively, in turn, it contributes to the parent brand's equity. Crest Whitestrips leveraged the strong reputation of Crest and dental care to provide reassurance in the teeth-whitening arena while also reinforcing its dental authority image.

Marketers should ask a number of questions in judging the potential success of an extension.[102]

- Does the parent brand have strong equity?
- Is there a strong basis of fit?
- Will the extension have the optimal points-of-parity and points-of-difference?
- How can marketing programs enhance extension equity?
- What implications will the extension have for parent brand equity and profitability?
- How should feedback effects best be managed?

| TABLE 11.3 | Brand Extendibility Scorecard |
|---|---|

Allocate points according to how well the new product concept rates on the specific dimensions in the following areas:

**Consumer Perspectives: Desirability**

10 pts. _____ Product category appeal (size, growth potential)

10 pts. _____ Equity transfer (perceived brand fit)

5 pts. _____ Perceived consumer target fit

**Company Perspectives: Deliverability**

10 pts. _____ Asset leverage (product technology, organizational skills, marketing effectiveness via channels and communications)

10 pts. _____ Profit potential

5 pts. _____ Launch feasibility

**Competitive Perspectives: Differentiability**

10 pts. _____ Comparative appeal (many advantages; few disadvantages)

10 pts. _____ Competitive response (likelihood; immunity or invulnerability from)

5 pts. _____ Legal/regulatory/institutional barriers

**Brand Perspectives: Equity Feedback**

10 pts. _____ Strengthens parent brand equity

10 pts. _____ Facilitates additional brand extension opportunities

5 pts. _____ Improves asset base

**TOTAL** _____ pts.

To help answer these questions, Table 11.3 offers a sample scorecard with specific weights and dimensions that users can adjust for each application.

Table 11.4 lists a number of academic research findings on brand extensions.[103] One major mistake in evaluating extension opportunities is failing to take *all* consumers' brand knowledge structures into account and focusing instead on one or a few brand associations as a potential basis of fit.[104] Bic is a classic example of that mistake.[105]

| TABLE 11.4 | Research Insights on Brand Extensions |
|---|---|

- Successful brand extensions occur when the parent brand is seen as having favorable associations and there is a perception of fit between the parent brand and the extension product.

- There are many bases of fit: product-related attributes and benefits, as well as nonproduct-related attributes and benefits related to common usage situations or user types.

- Depending on consumer knowledge of the categories, perceptions of fit may be based on technical or manufacturing commonalties or more surface considerations such as necessary or situational complementarity.

- High-quality brands stretch farther than average-quality brands, although both types of brands have boundaries.

- A brand that is seen as prototypical of a product category can be difficult to extend outside the category.

- Concrete attribute associations tend to be more difficult to extend than abstract benefit associations.

*(continued)*

| TABLE 11.4 | Continued |
| --- | --- |

- Consumers may transfer associations that are positive in the original product class but become negative in the extension context.
- Consumers may infer negative associations about an extension, perhaps even based on other inferred positive associations.
- It can be difficult to extend into a product class that is seen as easy to make.
- A successful extension cannot only contribute to the parent brand image but also enable a brand to be extended even farther.
- An unsuccessful extension hurts the parent brand only when there is a strong basis of fit between the two.
- An unsuccessful extension does not prevent a firm from "backtracking" and introducing a more similar extension.
- Vertical extensions can be difficult and often require sub-branding strategies.
- The most effective advertising strategy for an extension emphasizes information about the extension (rather than reminders about the parent brand).

**Source:** Kevin Lane Keller, *Strategic Brand Management*, 4th ed. (Upper Saddle River, NJ: Pearson, 2013). Printed and electronically reproduced by permission of Pearson Education, Inc., Upper Saddle River, NJ.

**BIC**   The French company Société Bic, by emphasizing inexpensive, disposable products, was able to create markets for nonrefillable ballpoint pens in the late 1950s, disposable cigarette lighters in the early 1970s, and disposable razors in the early 1980s. It unsuccessfully tried the same strategy in marketing BIC perfumes in the United States and Europe in 1989. The perfumes—two for women ("Nuit" and "Jour") and two for men ("BIC for Men" and "BIC Sport for Men")—were packaged in quarter-ounce glass spray bottles that looked like fat cigarette lighters and sold for $5 each. The products were displayed on racks at checkout counters throughout Bic's extensive distribution channels. At the time, a Bic spokeswoman described the new products as extensions of the Bic heritage—"high quality at affordable prices, convenient to purchase, and convenient to use." The brand extension was launched with a $20 million advertising and promotion campaign containing images of stylish people enjoying themselves with the perfume and using the tagline "Paris in Your Pocket." Nevertheless, Bic was unable to overcome its lack of cachet and negative image associations, and the extension was a failure.

# Customer Equity

Achieving brand equity should be a top priority for any organization. "Marketing Memo: Twenty-First-Century Branding" offers some wise advice on continued brand success.

Finally, we can relate brand equity to one other important marketing concept: **customer equity.** The aim of customer relationship management (CRM) is to produce high customer equity.[106] Although we can calculate it in different ways, one definition is "the sum of lifetime values of all customers."[107] As Chapter 5 reviewed, customer lifetime value is affected by revenue and by the costs of customer acquisition, retention, and cross-selling.[108]

- *Acquisition* depends on the number of prospects, the acquisition probability of a prospect, and acquisition spending per prospect.
- *Retention* is influenced by the retention rate and retention spending level.
- *Add-on spending* is a function of the efficiency of add-on selling, the number of add-on selling offers given to existing customers, and the response rate to new offers.

The brand equity and customer equity perspectives certainly share many common themes.[109] Both emphasize the importance of customer loyalty and the notion that we create value by having as many customers as possible pay as high a price as possible.

<table>
<tr><td>**marketing memo**</td><td>**Twenty-First-Century Branding**</td></tr>
</table>

An early pioneer in the study of branding and still active as a brand strategist, David Aaker has much experience with what makes brands successful. Here are his top ten "to do tasks" for marketers—what you need to know to excel at brand building.

1. Treat brands as assets. Brand strategy needs to be developed in tandem with business strategy.

2. Show the strategic payoff of brand building. Show how the success of a business strategy depended on brand assets.

3. Recognize the richness of brands—go beyond the three-word phrase. Although two to four associations are often the most import, understand the full range of associations that are cued by the brand.

4. Get beyond functional benefits. Emotional and self-expressive benefits and brand personality can provide a basis for sustainable differentiation and a deep customer relationship.

5. Consider organizational associations—people, programs, values, strategies, and heritage that are unique to the company and meaningful to customers.

6. Look to role models. What other companies have been successful with similar branding efforts? Are there any people or programs internal to the firm that exemplify desired characteristics for the brand?

7. Understand the brand relationship spectrum and the right degree of separation for new offerings.

8. Look for branded differentiators. Even functional benefits, if copied, can remain distinctive if given a strong brand identify initially.

9. Use branded energizers—a branded person or program you can associate with your brand.

10. Win the brand relevance battle—make your competitors seem irrelevant.

**Source:** "David Aaker's Top 10 Brand Precepts," white paper, www.prophet.com. For more insights into branding best practices, see Allen Adamson, *The Edge: 50 Tips from Brands That Lead* (New York: Palgrave Macmillan, 2013).

In practice, however, the two perspectives emphasize different things. The customer equity perspective focuses on bottom-line financial value. Its clear benefit is its quantifiable measures of financial performance. But it offers limited guidance for go-to-market strategies. It largely ignores some of the important advantages of creating a strong brand, such as the ability to attract higher-quality employees, elicit stronger support from channel and supply chain partners, and create growth opportunities through line and category extensions and licensing. The customer equity approach can overlook the "option value" of brands and their potential to affect future revenues and costs. It does not always fully account for competitive moves and countermoves or for social network effects, word of mouth, and customer-to-customer recommendations.

Brand equity, on the other hand, tends to emphasize strategic issues in managing brands and creating and leveraging brand awareness and image with customers. It provides much practical guidance for specific marketing activities. With a focus on brands, however, managers don't always develop detailed customer analyses in terms of the brand equity they achieve or the resulting long-term profitability they create.[110] Brand equity approaches could benefit from sharper segmentation schemes afforded by customer-level analyses and more consideration of how to develop personalized, customized marketing programs—whether for individuals or for organizations such as retailers. There are generally fewer financial considerations put into play with brand equity than with customer equity.

Nevertheless, both brand equity and customer equity matter. There are no brands without customers and no customers without brands. Brands serve as the "bait" that retailers and other channel intermediaries use to attract customers from whom they extract value. Customers are the tangible profit engine for brands to monetize their brand value.

# Summary

1. A brand is a name, term, sign, symbol, design, or some combination of these elements, intended to identify the goods and services of one seller or group of sellers and to differentiate them from those of competitors. The different components of a brand—brand names, logos, symbols, package designs, and so on—are called brand elements.

2. Brands are valuable intangible assets that offer a number of benefits to customers and firms and need to be managed carefully. The key to branding is that consumers perceive differences among brands in a product category.

3. Brand equity should be defined in terms of marketing effects uniquely attributable to a brand. That is, different outcomes result when a product or service is marketed under its brand than when it is not.

4. Building brand equity depends on three main factors: (1) The initial choices for the brand elements or identities making up the brand; (2) the way the brand is integrated into the supporting marketing program; and (3) the associations indirectly transferred to the brand by links to some other entity (the company, country of origin, channel of distribution, or another brand).

5. Brand audits measure "where the brand has been," and tracking studies measure "where the brand is now" and whether marketing programs are having the intended effects.

6. A branding strategy identifies which brand elements a firm chooses to apply across the various products it sells. In a brand extension, a firm uses an established brand name to introduce a new product. Potential extensions must be judged by how effectively they leverage existing brand equity to a new product, as well as how effectively they contribute to the equity of the parent brand in turn.

7. Brands may expand coverage, provide protection, extend an image, or fulfill a variety of other roles for the firm. Each brand-name product must have a well-defined positioning to maximize coverage, minimize overlap, and thus optimize the portfolio.

8. Customer equity is a concept that is complementary to brand equity and reflects the sum of lifetime values of all customers for a brand.

---

## MyMarketingLab

Go to **mymktlab.com** to complete the problems marked with this icon ⭐ as well as for additional Auto-graded and Assisted-graded writing questions.

---

# Applications

---

## Marketing Debate
### Are Brand Extensions Good or Bad?

Some critics vigorously denounce the practice of brand extensions because they feel that too often companies lose focus and consumers become confused. Other experts maintain that brand extensions are a critical growth strategy and source of revenue for the firm.

**Take a position:** Brand extensions can endanger brands *versus* Brand extensions are an important brand-growth strategy.

## Marketing Discussion
### Brand Equity Models

⭐ How can you relate the different models of brand equity in this chapter to one another? How are they similar? How are they different? Can you construct a brand-equity model that incorporates the best aspects of each model?

## Marketing Excellence

### >> McDonald's

McDonald's is the world's leading hamburger fast-food chain with more than 34,000 restaurants in 119 countries. More than 80 percent of McDonald's restaurants are owned and operated by franchisees, which decreases the risk associated with expansion and ensures long-term tenants for the company. McDonald's serves 70 million people each day and promises an easy and enjoyable food experience for its customers.

McDonald's Corporation dates back to 1955 when Ray Kroc, a multi-mixer salesman, franchised a hamburger restaurant from the McDonald brothers. Kroc named it McDonald's and offered simple foods such as the famous 15-cent hamburger. He helped design the building, which featured red and white sides and a single golden arch that attracted local attention. Just 10 years later, McDonald's had expanded to more than 700 U.S. restaurants, and the brand was on its way to becoming a household name.

During the 1960s and 1970s, Kroc led McDonald's growth domestically and internationally but always reinforced the importance of quality, service, cleanliness, and value. The menu expanded to include iconic items such the Big Mac, the Quarter Pounder, the Happy Meal, Filet-O-Fish, and breakfast items like the Egg McMuffin. The company ramped up its advertising as well. To target its core audience—children and families—it introduced Ronald McDonald during a 60-second commercial in 1965. Soon, characters like Grimace, the Hamburgler, and Mayor McCheese made their debut in McDonald's advertising and helped lure children into its restaurants for familiar food and a fun experience.

In 1974, McDonald's opened the Ronald McDonald House, a charitable cause to help children with leukemia. Since then, it has expanded into a global effort called Ronald McDonald House Charities that consists of three major programs: Ronald McDonald House, Ronald McDonald Family Room, and Ronald McDonald Care Mobile.

McDonald's aggressively expanded overseas during the 1980s by adding locations throughout Europe, Asia, the Philippines, and Malaysia. However, this rapid growth led to many struggles during the 1990s and early 2000s. The company lost focus and direction as it added as many as 2,000 new restaurants a year. New employees weren't trained fast enough or well enough, which led to poor customer service and dirtier restaurants. In addition, new healthier-option competitors popped up such as Subway and Panera Bread.

Consumers' tastes and eating trends also started to change in the early 2000s, and McDonald's new food offerings failed on many fronts. Product launches like pizza, the Arch Deluxe, fajitas, and deli sandwiches did not connect with consumers, nor did tweaks to the current menu like multiple changes to the Big Mac special sauce. Jim Skinner, McDonald's former chief executive, explained, "We got distracted from the most important thing: hot, high-quality food at a great value at the speed and convenience of McDonald's."

In 2003, McDonald's implemented a strategic effort called the Plan to Win. Still in effect, the plan helped McDonald's restaurants refocus on offering a better, higher-quality consumer experience rather than a quick and cheap fast-food option. Its "playbook" provided strategic insight on how to improve on the company's 5 Ps—people, products, promotions, price, and place—yet allow local restaurants to adapt to different environments and cultures. For example, McDonald's introduced a Bacon Roll breakfast sandwich in the United Kingdom, a premium M burger in France, and an egg, tomato, and pepper McPuff in China. Prices also varied slightly across the United States to better reflect different regional tastes.

Some changes that initially helped turn the company around included offering more chicken options as beef consumption started to decline, selling milk in a bottle instead of a carton, and removing "Super Size" options after the documentary "Super Size Me" targeted McDonald's and its link to obesity. The company responded to customers' desire for healthy foods with premium salads and apple slices instead of French fries in its Happy Meals. It also dismissed claims of "mystery meat" by introducing all-white-meat McNuggets.

Many of these healthier options targeted moms and charged a premium price. Meanwhile, McDonald's targeted teenagers and its lower-income consumers with the introduction of the $1 menu. The company improved its drive-thru service, added more snack options, and refurbished restaurants with leather seats, warm paint colors, Wi-Fi, and flat-screen TVs. In many locations it created three different "zones" that fit the needs of each target audience: a linger zone with comfortable sofas where teenagers could hang out and socialize, a family zone with tables and chairs that could easily be reconfigured, and an efficient zone for consumers who needed to grab a quick bite and go.

Initial results were staggering; from 2003 to 2006, revenues increased 33 percent and share price soared 170 percent. In 2008, McDonald's was one of only two companies in the Dow Jones industrial average whose share price rose during the worldwide recession. Sales continued to increase, and in 2012, McDonald's experienced record revenues of $27 billion.

Today, McDonald's increases its consumer base through global growth and product expansion. For example, the successful introduction of McCafé directly targeted consumers in the booming coffee industry and stole share from companies like Starbucks, Dunkin' Donuts, and Caribou Coffee. It is a good example of how McDonald's works to appeal to new consumers and aims to stay relevant through the years. Its current campaign, "I'm Lovin' It," seems to connect with McDonald's large consumer base and keep them coming back again and again.

## Questions

1. What are McDonald's core brand values? Have these changed over the years?

2. How has McDonald's grown its brand equity over the years? Has McDonald's changed in different economic times or in different parts of the world? Explain.

3. What risks do you think McDonald's will face in the future?

Sources: Andrew Martin, "At McDonald's, the Happiest Meal Is Hot Profits," *The New York Times*, January 10, 2009; Janet Adamy, "McDonald's Seeks Way to Keep Sizzling," *Wall Street Journal*, March 10, 2009; Matt Vella, "McDonald's Thinks about the Box," *Businessweek*, December 8, 2008; Jessica Wohl, "McDonald's CEO: Tough Economy, but Some 'Thawing,'" *Reuters*, April 17, 2009; "Interbrand's Best Global Brands 2012," *Interbrand.com*; Rance Crain, "Has Time Run Out for McDonald's Brand Chronicle after 10 years?" *Ad Age*, December 2, 2013; McDonald's 2012 Annual Report.

---

## Marketing Excellence

## >> Procter & Gamble

Procter & Gamble (P&G) began in 1837 when brothers-in-law William Procter and James Gamble formed a small candle and soap company. Over the next 150 years, P&G innovated and launched scores of revolutionary products with superior quality and value, including Ivory soap in 1882, Tide laundry detergent in 1946, Crest toothpaste with fluoride in 1955, and Pampers disposable diapers in 1961. The company also opened the door to new product categories by acquiring a number of companies, including Richardson-Vicks (makers of personal care products like Pantene, Olay, and Vicks), Norwich Eaton Pharmaceuticals (makers of Pepto-Bismol), Gillette, Noxell (makers of Noxzema), Shulton's Old Spice, Max Factor, and the Iams pet food company.

Today, Procter & Gamble is one of the most skillful marketers of consumer-packaged goods in the world and holds one of the most powerful portfolios of trusted brands. The company employs 121,000 people in about 80 countries worldwide, has 25 billion-dollar global brands, spends more than $2 billion annually on R&D, and has total worldwide sales in excess of $84 billion a year. Its sustained market leadership rests on a number of different capabilities and philosophies. These include:

**Customer knowledge:** P&G studies its customers—both the end consumers and its trade partners—through continuous marketing research and intelligence gathering. It spends more than $100 million annually on more than 10,000 formal consumer research projects and generates more than 3 million consumer contacts via its e-mail and phone center. The company also encourages its marketers and researchers to be out in the field, interacting with consumers and retailers in their home environment.

**Long-term outlook:** P&G takes the time to analyze each opportunity carefully before acting. Once committed, the company develops the best product possible and executes it with the determination to make it a success. For example, it struggled with Pringles potato chips for almost a decade before achieving market success. Recently, P&G has increased its presence in developing markets by focusing on affordability, brand awareness, and distribution through e-commerce and high-frequency stores.

**Product innovation:** P&G is an active product innovator. The company employs 1,000 science PhDs, more than Harvard, Berkeley, and MIT combined, and applies for roughly 3,800 patents each year. Part of its innovation process is to develop brands that offer new consumer benefits. Recent innovations that created entirely new categories include Febreze, an odor-eliminating fabric spray; Dryel, a product that helps "dry-clean" clothes at home in the dryer; and Swiffer, a cleaning system that effectively removes dust, dirt, and hair from floors. Larry Huston, former innovation officer at P&G, stated, "P&G is largely a branded science company."

**Quality strategy:** P&G designs products of above-average quality and continuously improves and reformulates them. When the company says "new and improved," it means it. Recent examples include Tide Pods, a compact laundry detergent tablet; Pampers Rash Guard, a diaper that treats and prevents diaper rash; and improved two-in-one shampoo and conditioner products Pantene, Vidal Sassoon, and Pert Plus.

**Brand extension strategy:** P&G produces its brands in several sizes and forms. This strategy gains more shelf space and prevents competitors from moving in to satisfy unmet market needs. P&G also uses its strong brand names to launch new products with instant recognition and much less advertising outlay. The Mr. Clean brand has been extended from household cleaner to bathroom cleaner and even to a carwash system. Old Spice extended its brand from men's fragrances to deodorant. Often, P&G will leverage the technologies already in place to create a brand extension. For example, when Crest successfully extended its brand into a new tooth-whitening system called Crest Whitestrips, the company used bleaching methods from P&G's laundry division, film technology from the food wrap division, and glue techniques from the paper division.

***Multibrand strategy:*** P&G markets several brands in the same product category, such as Luvs and Pampers diapers and Oral-B and Crest toothbrushes. Each brand meets a different consumer want and competes against specific competitors' brands. At the same time, the company is careful not to sell too many brands and recently reduced its vast array of products, sizes, flavors, and varieties to assemble a stronger brand portfolio.

***Strong sales force:*** P&G's sales force has been named one of the top 25 sales forces by *Sales & Marketing Management* magazine. A key to its success is the close tie its sales force forms with retailers, notably Walmart. The 150-person team that serves the retail giant works closely with Walmart to improve both the products that go to the stores and the process by which they get there.

***Manufacturing efficiency and cost cutting:*** P&G's reputation as a great marketing company is matched by its excellence as a manufacturing company. The company has successfully developed and continually improves its production operations, which keep costs among the lowest in the industry. As a result, it is able to offer reduced prices for its premium products.

***Brand-management system:*** P&G originated the brand-management system, in which one executive is responsible for each brand. The system has been copied by many competitors but not often with P&G's success. Recently, P&G modified its general management structure so that a category manager runs each brand category and has volume and profit responsibility. Although this new organization does not replace the brand-management system, it helps to sharpen strategic focus on key consumer needs and competition in the category.

P&G's accomplishments over the past 177 years have come from successfully managing the numerous factors that contribute to market leadership. Today, the company's wide range of products are used by 4.8 billion people around the world in 180 different countries.

### Questions

1. P&G's impressive portfolio includes some of the strongest brand names in the world. What are some of the challenges associated with being the market leader in so many different categories?

2. With social media becoming increasingly important and fewer people watching traditional commercials on television, what does P&G need to do to maintain its strong brand images?

3. What risks will P&G face in the future?

**Sources:** Robert Berner, "Detergent Can Be So Much More," *Business Week*, May 1, 2006, pp. 66–68; "A Post-Modern Proctoid," *The Economist*, April 15, 2006, p. 68; *P&G Fact Sheet* (December 2006); John Galvin, "The World on a String," *Point*, February 2005, pp. 13–24; Jack Neff, "P&G Kisses Up to the Boss: Consumers," *Advertising Age*, May 2, 2005, p. 18; "The Nielsen Company Issues Top Ten U.S. Lists for 2008," press release, *The Nielsen Company*, December 12, 2008; Lauren Coleman-Lochner and Carol Hymowitz, "At Procter and Gamble, the Innovation Well Runs Dry," *Business week*, September 6, 2012; www.pg.com; Procter and Gamble 2013 Annual Report.

## In This Chapter, We Will Address the Following **Questions**

1. Why is it important for companies to grow the core of their business? (p. 335)

2. How can market leaders expand the total market and defend market share? (p. 337)

3. How should market challengers attack market leaders? (p. 342)

4. How can market followers or nichers compete effectively? (p. 344)

5. What marketing strategies are appropriate at each stage of the product life cycle? (p. 348)

6. How should marketers adjust their strategies and tactics during slow economic growth? (p. 359)

FedEx now offers ground shipping and UPS now offers air shipping so each company can better compete with the other.

*Source: Andrew Kelly/Insider Images/Polaris/Newscom*

MyMarketingLab™

⭐ **Improve Your Grade!**
Over 10 million students improved their results using the Pearson MyLabs. Visit mymktlab.com for simulations, tutorials, and end-of-chapter problems.

# **12** Addressing Competition and Driving Growth

**Growth is essential for the success of any firm. Thus, to be a long-term market leader** is the goal of any marketer. Today's challenging marketing circumstances often dictate that companies reformulate their marketing strategies and offerings several times. Economic conditions change, competitors launch new assaults, and buyer interest and requirements evolve. Though the years an interesting competitive battle has been fought between FedEx and UPS in which each has been a challenger on the other's home turf.[1]

 *After FedEx watched UPS successfully invade its airborne delivery system, it invested heavily in ground delivery through a series of acquisitions to challenge UPS on its home turf. The two firms are now in a heated battle to gain the upper hand in the marketplace. Both are moving into the fast-growing, multi-billion-dollar Chinese domestic delivery market, where FedEx has a head start and a bigger operation.*

*Overseas markets are attractive for both firms, given that a little more than half of FedEx revenue and almost two-thirds of UPS revenue comes from the domestic U.S. market. Combined, the two companies account for an impressive 10 percent of U.S. gross domestic product (GDP). To expand their reach and the range of services they can provide, both are making strategic acquisitions of delivery companies all over the world, none bigger than UPS's attempted purchase of TNT, blocked at least initially by European regulators. Back in their home U.S. markets, both firms are trying to lock in customers with customized door-to-door deliveries. Fueled by the rapid rise of online shopping, residential deliveries are growing fast, and FedEx has the advantage of being able to make Saturday deliveries. Advertising "UPS Loves Logistics," UPS has made a strong play with businesses, positioning itself as the "logistics expert" capable of providing a broader range of supply-chain services than just deliveries.*

**This chapter examines growth,** the role competition plays, and how marketers can best manage their brands given their market position and stage of the product life cycle. Competition grows more intense every year—from global competitors eager to enter new markets, from online competitors seeking cost-efficient ways to expand distribution, from private-label and store brands providing low-price alternatives, and from brand extensions by mega-brands moving into new categories. For these reasons and more, product and brand fortunes change over time, and marketers must respond accordingly.

# Growth

An important function of marketing is to drive growth in sales and revenue for a company. Marketing is especially adept at doing so for a new product with many competitive advantages and much potential. Good marketing can help to induce trial and promote word of mouth and diffusion. Marketing in more mature markets can be more challenging. In some cases, fighting over market share is less productive than expanding the size of the market as a whole.

## GROWTH STRATEGIES

Chapter 2 introduced how companies can grow through expansion with new products and new markets, the detailed focus of Chapters 8 and 15. Along those lines, Phil and Milton Kotler stress the following strategies:[2]

- Grow by building your market share
- Grow by developing committed customers and stakeholders

- Grow by building a powerful brand
- Grow by innovating new products, services, and experiences
- Grow by international expansion
- Grow by acquisitions, mergers, and alliances
- Grow by building an outstanding reputation for social responsibility
- Grow by partnering with government and NGOs

Consider how Under Armour has grown in recent years.[3]

**UNDER ARMOUR**   In his days as a University of Maryland football player, Kevin Plank had been dissatisfied with cotton T-shirts that retained water and became heavy during practice. Under Armour was born when, with $500 and several yards of coat lining, Plank worked with a local tailor to create seven prototypes of snug-fitting T-shirts that absorbed perspiration and kept athletes dry. With a focus on performance and authenticity and backed by intense, in-your-face advertising, the brand quickly became a favorite at high schools, colleges, and universities, later introducing a wide range of athletic apparel as well as football cleats, basketball shoes, and running shoes. By 2009, it was squarely in competition with formidable opponents Nike and Adidas. A traditionally male-oriented brand, Under Armour soon recognized the value of a new target demographic—women. Not wanting to fall back on a "shrink it and pink it" approach, the company united its marketing, product design, and consumer insights departments to develop focused solutions for women. The fully integrated "What's Beautiful" media campaign—with its tagline urging women to "No Matter What, Sweat Every Day"—and the success of its footwear lines have helped the women's division become the fastest-growing Under Armour business. The company is also looking to expand internationally, focusing initially on Europe and Latin America. While Nike and Adidas both generate about 60 percent of their revenue outside their home regions, Under Armour generates only 6 percent outside North America, with very little of that in fast-growing emerging markets like India, China, and Brazil.

## GROWING THE CORE

Although many different growth strategies are available to firms, some of the best opportunities come from growing the core—focusing on their most successful existing products and markets. Marketers must avoid the trap of thinking the "grass is always greener" and overestimating the upside of new ventures that stretch the company into uncharted territory.

Often a firm's unique capabilities don't effectively translate to a new industry. Mattel's disastrous acquisition of the Learning Company in 1999 failed in part because the toy company's expertise was not as valuable in the interactive-learning market. Further, an industry that is red-hot today may be ice-cold tomorrow.[4]

Growing the core can be a less risky alternative than expansion into new product categories. It strengthens a brand's credentials as a source of authority and credibility and can yield economies of scale. Through improved revenues and lower costs, growing the core can also lead to greater profits. UK marketing guru David Taylor advocates three main strategies, citing these examples:[5]

1. *Make the core of the brand as distinctive as possible.* Galaxy chocolate has successfully competed with Cadbury by positioning itself as "your partner in chocolate indulgence" and featuring smoother product shapes, more refined taste, and sleeker packaging,
2. *Drive distribution through both existing and new channels.* Costa Coffee, the number-one coffee shop in the United Kingdom, has found new distribution routes using drive-through outlets, vending machines at service stations, and in-school coffee shops.
3. *Offer the core product in new formats or versions.* WD40 offers a Smart Straw version of its popular multi-purpose lubricant with a built-in straw that pops up for use.

Many firms are seeking success by focusing on their core businesses. London-based Aegis Group sold market research firm Synovate in order to focus on becoming media and digital communication specialists.[6] Levi Strauss phased out its Denizen brand in Asia to focus on its core Levi's brand.[7]

Growth strategies are not necessarily "either/or" propositions. A focus on core businesses does not mean foregoing new market opportunities. Vancouver, Canada's Fortuna Silver Mines has focused on its two fully owned, fully integrated silver mines in Peru and Mexico to spur organic growth while looking for a third mine to drive further growth.[8] And sometimes the core business is just not expandable. With personal computer sales steadily declining, leading PC maker Lenovo began to look at smart phones as a new source of business for its brand.[9]

# Competitive Strategies for Market Leaders

Suppose a market is occupied by the firms shown in Figure 12.1. Forty percent is in the hands of a *market leader,* another 30 percent belongs to a *market challenger,* and 20 percent is claimed by a *market follower* willing to maintain its share and not rock the boat. *Market nichers,* serving small segments larger firms don't reach, hold the remaining 10 percent. Sometimes growth depends on adopting the right competitive strategies.

A market leader has the largest market share and usually leads in price changes, new-product introductions, distribution coverage, and promotional intensity. Some historical market leaders are Microsoft (computer software), Gatorade (sports drinks), Best Buy (retail electronics), McDonald's (fast food), BlueCross BlueShield (health insurance), and Visa (credit cards).

Although marketers assume well-known brands are distinctive in consumers' minds, unless a dominant firm enjoys a legal monopoly, it must maintain constant vigilance. A powerful product innovation may come along, a competitor might find a fresh marketing angle or commit to a major marketing investment, or the leader's cost structure might spiral upward. One well-known brand and market leader that has worked hard to stay on top is Xerox.[10]

Source: PR NEWSWIRE

Under Armour's fastest growing business has been with women.

---

**XEROX**  Xerox has had to become much more than just a copier company. Now a blue-chip icon with the name that became a verb, the company sports the broadest array of imaging products in the world and dominates the market for high-end printing systems while also offering a new range of printing and business-related services. It has made a product line transition from the old light lens technology to digital systems and is finding ways to make color copying less expensive and even to print in 3-D. Xerox provides broader document and print-manager services to help companies lower costs by eliminating desktop printers, reducing paper use, and installing multifunction multi-user devices that are more efficient, break down less, and use cheaper supplies. Under CEO Ursula Burns, the firm is becoming more of a services company, providing bill processing, business processing, and IT outsourcing. A $6.4 billion acquisition of Affiliated Computer Services (ACS) allowed Xerox to plunge its technology into back-office operations. A call to Virgin America customer care, a paper or online submission of a health insurance claim, and a query to solve a smart phone problem all might be handled by a Xerox employee. A new Xerox device—a compact computer with scanning, printing, and Internet capabilities—allows ACS insurance agents in the field to scan claims on-site to be sorted, routed, and put immediately into a workflow system. Xerox is embracing technology in its marketing too. The company's "Information Overload" campaign employed a personalized video, e-mail campaign, and direct mail piece. Each customer received a personalized URL (PURL) based on his or her behavior and interests, leading to click-through rates of 35 percent to 40 percent as opposed to the typical 1 percent to 2 percent industry rates. A new print and TV ad campaign, "Simplicity by the Numbers," acknowledges the brand's heritage while highlighting its new capabilities. One TV ad opened with a women standing in front of a copier saying, "When I say Xerox, I know what you're thinking," After printing the image of a transit map, she states, "Transit fares, as in the 37 billion transit ares we help collect each year."

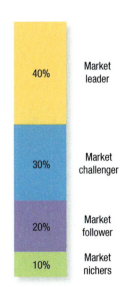

| 40% | Market leader |
| 30% | Market challenger |
| 20% | Market follower |
| 10% | Market nichers |

**| Fig. 12.1 |**

Hypothetical Market Structure

To stay number one, the firm must first find ways to expand total market demand. Second, it must protect its current share through good defensive and offensive actions. Third, it should increase market share, even if market size remains constant. Let's look at each strategy.

# EXPANDING TOTAL MARKET DEMAND

When the total market expands, the dominant firm usually gains the most. If Heinz can convince more people to use ketchup, or to use ketchup with more meals, or to use more ketchup on each occasion, the firm will benefit considerably because it already sells almost two-thirds of the country's ketchup. In general, the market leader should look for new customers or more usage from existing customers.

NEW CUSTOMERS As Chapter 2 suggested, a company can search for new users among three groups: those who might use it but do not *(market-penetration strategy)*, those who have never used it *(new-market segment strategy)*, or those who live elsewhere *(geographical-expansion strategy)*. Here is how Starbucks has described its multipronged approach to growth on its corporate Web site.[11]

> Starbucks purchases and roasts high-quality whole bean coffees and sells them along with fresh, rich-brewed, Italian style espresso beverages, a variety of pastries and confections, and coffee-related accessories and equipment—primarily through its company-operated retail stores. In addition to sales through our company-operated retail stores, Starbucks sells whole bean coffees through a specialty sales group and supermarkets. Additionally, Starbucks produces and sells bottled Frappuccino® coffee drinks and a line of premium ice creams through its joint venture partnerships and offers a line of innovative premium teas produced by its wholly owned subsidiary, Tazo Tea Company. The Company's objective is to establish Starbucks as the most recognized and respected brand in the world.

In targeting new customers, the firm should not lose sight of existing ones. Daimler, maker of Mercedes-Benz, has developed a balanced approach to capitalize on both the established demand from mature markets in the European Union, United States, and Japan and the enormous potential offered by fast-growing emerging markets. As the company's chairman Dieter Zetsche proclaimed, "You cannot do either/or. You have to maintain your strength in traditional markets and even expand it."[12]

MORE USAGE Marketers can try to increase the amount, level, or frequency of consumption. They can sometimes boost the *amount* through packaging or product redesign. Larger package sizes increase the amount of product consumers use at one time.[13] Consumers use more of impulse products such as soft drinks and snacks when the product is made more available.

Ironically, some food firms such as Hershey's have developed smaller packaging sizes that have actually increased sales volume through more frequent usage.[14] In general, increasing *frequency* of consumption requires either (1) identifying additional opportunities to use the brand in the same basic way or (2) identifying completely new and different ways to use the brand.

*Additional Opportunities to Use the Brand* A marketing program can communicate the appropriateness and advantages of using the brand. Pepto-Bismol stomach remedies are in 40 percent of U.S. households, but only 7 percent of people claim to have used them in the previous 12 months. To expand usage and make the brand more top of mind, a holiday campaign linked it to party festivities and celebrations with the tag line "Eat, Drink, and Be Covered." In a somewhat similar vein, on the inside of the front flap of its package, Orbit chewing gum puts the message, "Eat. Drink. Chew. A Good Clean Feeling." to reinforce that the brand can be a substitute for brushing teeth.[15]

Another opportunity arises when consumers' perceptions of their usage differs from reality. Consumers may fail to replace a short-lived product when they should because they overestimate how long it stays fresh or operates effectively.[16] One strategy is to tie the act of replacing the product to a holiday, event, or time of year. Marketers of household products such as batteries for alarms and filters for vacuum cleaners, furnaces, and air conditioners use the beginning and end of Daylight Savings Time twice a year as a means to remind consumers.

Another approach might be to provide consumers with (1) better information about when they first used the product or need to replace it or (2) a gauge of the current level of product performance. Gillette razor cartridges feature colored stripes that slowly fade with repeated use, signaling the user to move on to the next cartridge. Marketers for Monroe® shock absorbers and struts launched the clever, fully integrated "Everything Gets Old. Even Your Shocks." campaign, which drew comparisons between worn shocks and struts and familiar consumer items that eventually wear out and need to be replaced such as shoes, socks, tires, and even bananas![17]

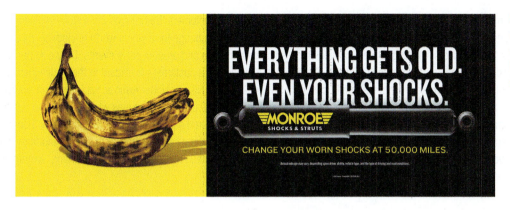

Monroe advertises to remind consumers to make sure they do not forget to change their shocks.

*New Ways to Use the Brand* The second approach to increasing frequency of consumption is to identify completely new and different applications. Food product companies have long advertised recipes that use their branded products in different ways. After discovering that some consumers used Arm & Hammer baking soda as a refrigerator deodorant, the company launched a heavy promotion campaign focusing on this use and succeeded in getting half the homes in the United States to adopt it. Next, the company expanded the brand into a variety of new product categories such as toothpaste, antiperspirant, and laundry detergent.

## PROTECTING MARKET SHARE

While trying to expand total market size, the dominant firm must actively defend its current business: Boeing against Airbus, Staples against Office Depot, and Google against Yahoo! and Microsoft.[18] How can the leader do so? The most constructive response is *continuous innovation*. The front-runner should lead the industry in developing new products and customer services, distribution effectiveness, and cost cutting. Comprehensive solutions increase competitive strength and value to customers so they feel appreciative or even privileged to be a customer as opposed to feeling trapped or taken advantage of.[19]

**PROACTIVE MARKETING** In satisfying customer needs, we can draw a distinction between responsive marketing, anticipative marketing, and creative marketing. A *responsive* marketer finds a stated need and fills it. An *anticipative* marketer looks ahead to needs customers may have in the near future. A *creative* marketer discovers solutions customers did not ask for but to which they enthusiastically respond. Creative marketers are proactive *market-driving* firms, not just market-driven ones.[20]

Many companies assume their job is simply to adapt to customer needs. They are reactive mostly because they are overly faithful to the customer-orientation paradigm and fall victim to the "tyranny of the served market." Successful companies instead proactively shape the market to their own interests. Instead of trying to be the best player, they change the rules of the game.[21]

A company needs two proactive skills: (1) *responsive anticipation* to see the writing on the wall, as when IBM changed from a hardware producer to a service business, and (2) *creative anticipation* to devise innovative solutions. Note that *responsive anticipation* is performed before a given change, while *reactive response* happens after the change takes place. Accenture maintains that 10 consumer trends covering areas like e-commerce, social media, and a desire to express individuality will yield market opportunities worth more than $2 trillion between 2013 and 2016.[22] Proactive companies will reap the most benefit from those shifts.

Proactive companies create new offers to serve unmet—and maybe even unknown—consumer needs. In the late 1970s, Akio Morita, the Sony founder, was working on a pet project that would revolutionize the way people listened to music: a portable cassette player he called the Walkman. Engineers at the company insisted there was little demand for such a product, but Morita refused to part with his vision. By the 20th anniversary of the Walkman, Sony had sold more than 250 million in nearly 100 different models.[23]

Proactive companies may redesign relationships within an industry, like Toyota did with its relationship to its suppliers. Or they may educate and engage customers, as lululemon does with yoga and workouts.[24]

**LULULEMON**    While attending yoga classes, Canadian entrepreneur Chip Wilson decided the cotton-polyester blends most fellow students wore were too uncomfortable. After designing a well-fitting, sweat-resistant black garment to sell, he also decided to open a yoga studio, and lululemon was born. The company has taken a grassroots approach to growth that creates a strong emotional connection with its customers. Before it opens a store in a new city, it first identifies influential yoga instructors or other fitness teachers. In exchange for a year's worth of clothing, these yogi serve as "ambassadors," hosting students at lululemon-sponsored classes and product sales events. They also provide product design advice to the company. The cult-like devotion of lululemon's customers is evident in their willingness to pay $92 for a pair of workout pants that might cost only $60 to $70 from Nike or Under Armour. lululemon can sell as much as $1,800 worth of product per square feet in its approximately 100 stores, three times what established retailers Abercrombie & Fitch and J.Crew sell. Although the company has encountered some challenges with inventory management issues, production snafus, and negative publicity surrounding statements by its founder, it is still looking to expand beyond yoga-inspired athletic apparel and accessories into similar products in other sports such as running, swimming, and biking.

Companies need to practice "uncertainty management." Proactive firms:

- are ready to take risks and make mistakes,
- have a vision of the future and of investing in it,
- have the capabilities to innovate,
- are flexible and non-bureaucratic, and
- have many managers who think proactively.

Companies that are *too* risk-averse won't be winners.

**DEFENSIVE MARKETING** Even when it does not launch offensives, the market leader must not leave any major flanks exposed. The aim of defensive strategy is to reduce the probability of attack, divert attacks to less-threatened areas, and lessen their intensity. A leader would like to do anything it legally and ethically can to reduce competitors' ability to launch a new product, secure distribution, and gain consumer awareness, trial, and repeat.[25] In any strategy, speed of response can make an important difference to profit.

A dominant firm can use the six defense strategies summarized in Figure 12.2.[26] Decisions about which strategy to adopt will depend in part on the company's resources and goals and its expectations about how competitors will react.[27]

- *Position defense.* Position defense means occupying the most desirable position in consumers' minds, making the brand almost impregnable. Procter & Gamble "owns" the key functional benefit in many product categories, with Tide detergent for cleaning, Crest toothpaste for cavity prevention, and Pampers diapers for dryness.
- *Flank defense.* The market leader should erect outposts to protect a weak front or support a possible counterattack. Procter & Gamble brands such as Gain and Cheer laundry detergent and Luvs diapers have played strategic offensive and defensive roles in support of the Tide and Pampers brands, respectively.
- *Preemptive defense.* A more aggressive maneuver is to attack first, perhaps with guerrilla action across the market—hitting one competitor here, another there—and keeping everyone off balance. Another is to achieve broad market envelopment that signals competitors not to attack.[28] Bank of America's 16,220 ATMs and 5,858 retail branches nationwide provide steep competition to local and regional banks.[29] Yet another preemptive defense is to introduce a stream of new products and announce them in advance, signaling competitors that they will need to fight to gain market share. If Microsoft announces plans for a new-product development,

| **Fig. 12.2** |

Six Types of Defense Strategies

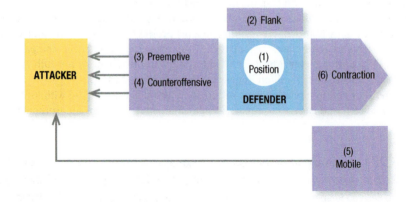

smaller firms may concentrate their development efforts in other directions to avoid head-to-head competition. Some high-tech firms have been accused of selling "vaporware"—announcing products that miss delivery dates or are never introduced.[30]

- *Counteroffensive defense.* In a counteroffensive, the market leader can meet the attacker frontally and hit its flank or launch a pincer movement so the attacker will have to pull back to defend itself. Another form of counteroffensive is the exercise of economic or political clout. The leader may try to crush a competitor by subsidizing lower prices for a vulnerable product with revenue from its more profitable products, or it may prematurely announce a product upgrade to prevent customers from buying the competitor's product. Or the leader may lobby legislators to take political action to inhibit the competition or initiate appropriate legal actions. Tech leaders like Apple, Intel, and Microsoft have aggressively defended their brands in court.

- *Mobile defense.* In mobile defense, the leader stretches its domain over new territories through market broadening and market diversification. *Market broadening* shifts the company's focus from the current product to the underlying generic need. Thus, "petroleum" companies such as BP sought to recast themselves as "energy" companies. This change required them to research the oil, coal, nuclear, hydroelectric, and chemical industries. *Market diversification* shifts the company's focus into unrelated industries. When U.S. tobacco companies such as Reynolds and Philip Morris acknowledged the growing curbs on cigarette smoking, instead of defending their market position or looking for cigarette substitutes, they moved quickly into new industries such as beer, liquor, soft drinks, and frozen foods.

- *Contraction defense.* Sometimes large companies can no longer defend all their territory. In *planned contraction* (also called *strategic withdrawal*), they give up weaker markets and reassign resources to stronger ones. Beginning in 2006, Sara Lee sold off products that accounted for a large percentage of its revenues—including its strong Hanes hosiery brand and global body care and European detergents businesses. In 2012, it split its remaining products into two businesses. Hillshire Brands became the new name of the company, which focused on its core Hillshire Farms packaged meats business in North America, and D.E. Master Blenders 1753 was a spin-off company for its successful European coffee-and-tea business.[31]

P&G sold Pringles to Kellogg for almost $2.7 billion in an all-cash transaction when it decided it wanted to get out of the foods business to focus on its core household and consumer products.[32] Another company that restructured its business to improve competitiveness was Kraft.[33]

**KRAFT**  After years of acquisitions, CEO Irene Rosenfeld announced in 2011 that Kraft would split into two businesses by the end of 2012: A fast-growing global snacks and candy business to include Oreo cookies and Cadbury candy and a slower-growing North American grocery business with long-terms stalwarts Maxwell House coffee, Planters peanuts, Kraft cheese, and Jell-O. The rationale was to improve performance and give investors distinctly different choices. The snacks and candy business was branded as Mondelēz International and was positioned as a high-growth company with many opportunities in emerging markets such as China and India. Coined by two employees, Mondelēz is a mash-up of the words for "world" and "delicious" in Latin and several other Romance languages. The grocery business retained the Kraft Foods name, and because it consisted of many category-dominant meat and cheese brands, it was seen as more of a cash cow for investors interested in consistent dividends. Mondelēz has ramped up for rapid expansion, while Kraft Foods has focused on cost-cutting and selective investment behind its power brands.

## INCREASING MARKET SHARE

No wonder competition has turned fierce in so many markets: One share point can be worth tens of millions of dollars. Gaining increased share does not automatically produce higher profits, however—especially for labor-intensive service companies that may not experience many economies of scale. Much depends on the company's strategy.[34]

Because the cost of buying higher market share through acquisition may far exceed its revenue value, a company should consider four factors first:

- *The possibility of provoking antitrust action.* Frustrated competitors are likely to cry "monopoly" and seek legal action if a dominant firm makes further inroads. Microsoft and Intel have had to fend off numerous lawsuits and legal challenges around the world as a result of what some feel are inappropriate or illegal business practices and abuse of market power.

Kraft split its company into two to better focus on fast-growing categories and markets, as well as to adequately support its solid core of heritage brands.

Source: Bloomberg via Getty Images

- *Economic cost.* Figure 12.3 shows that profitability might *fall* with market share gains after some level. In the illustration, the firm's *optimal market share* is 50 percent. The cost of gaining further market share might exceed the value if holdout customers dislike the company, are loyal to competitors, have unique needs, or prefer dealing with smaller firms. And the costs of legal work, public relations, and lobbying rise with market share. Pushing for higher share is less justifiable when there are unattractive market segments, buyers who want multiple sources of supply, high exit barriers, and few scale or experience economies. Some market leaders have even increased profitability by selectively *decreasing* market share in weaker areas.[35]
- *The danger of pursuing the wrong marketing activities.* Companies successfully gaining share typically outperform competitors in three areas: new-product activity, relative product quality, and marketing expenditures.[36] Companies that attempt to increase market share by cutting prices more deeply than competitors typically don't achieve significant gains because rivals meet the price cuts or offer other values so buyers don't switch.
- *The effect of increased market share on actual and perceived quality.* Too many customers can put a strain on the firm's resources, hurting product value and service delivery. Charlotte-based FairPoint Communications struggled to integrate the 1.3 million customers it gained in buying Verizon Communications's New England franchise. A slow conversion and significant service problems led to customer dissatisfaction, regulator's anger, and eventually short-term bankruptcy.[37]

| Fig. 12.3 |

The Concept of Optimal Market Share

# Other Competitive Strategies

Firms that occupy second, third, and lower ranks in an industry are often called runner-up or trailing firms. Some, such as PepsiCo, Ford, and Avis, are quite large in their own right. These firms can adopt one of two postures. They can attack the leader and other competitors in an aggressive bid for further market share as *market challengers,* or they can choose to not "rock the boat" as *market followers.*

## MARKET-CHALLENGER STRATEGIES

Many market challengers have gained ground or even overtaken the leader. Toyota today produces more cars than General Motors, Lowe's is putting pressure on Home Depot, and AMD has found some success chipping away at Intel's market share. Challengers set high aspirations, while market leaders can fall prey to running business as usual. Challengers can also tap into public perceptions that they are the underdog.[38] Now let's examine the competitive attack strategies available to them.[39]

**DEFINING THE STRATEGIC OBJECTIVE AND OPPONENT(S)** A market challenger must first define its strategic objective, which is usually to increase market share. It then must decide whom to attack:

- *It can attack the market leader.* This is a high-risk but potentially high-payoff strategy and makes good sense if the leader is not serving the market well. Xerox wrested the copy market from 3M by developing a better copying process. Later, Canon grabbed a large chunk of Xerox's market by introducing desk copiers. This strategy often has the added benefit of distancing the firm from other challengers.
- *It can attack firms its own size that are not doing the job and are underfinanced.* These firms have aging products, are charging excessive prices, or are not satisfying customers in other ways.
- *It can attack small local and regional firms.* Several major banks grew to their present size by gobbling up smaller regional banks, or "guppies."
- *It can attack the status quo.* A challenger might not attack a specific firm as much as an industry as a whole or a pervasive way of thinking that doesn't adequately address customer needs. Firms like Jet Blue, Ally Bank, and Netflix have succeeded by contrasting their services with those of competitors.[40]

**CHOOSING A GENERAL ATTACK STRATEGY** Given clear opponents and objectives, what attack options are available? As Figure 12.4 shows, we can distinguish five: frontal, flank, encirclement, bypass, and guerilla attacks.

- *Frontal attack.* In a pure *frontal attack,* the attacker matches its opponent's product, advertising, price, and distribution. The principle of force says the side with the greater resources will win. A modified frontal attack, such as cutting price, can work if the market leader doesn't retaliate and if the competitor convinces the market its product is equal to the leader's. Helene Curtis is a master at convincing the market that its hair-care brands—such as Suave and Finesse—are equal in quality but a better value than higher-priced brands.
- *Flank attack.* A *flanking* strategy is another name for identifying shifts that cause gaps to develop in the market, then rushing to fill the gaps. Flanking is particularly attractive to a challenger with fewer resources and can be more likely to succeed than frontal attacks. Top communications companies such as Verizon, AT&T, and T-Mobile found themselves losing sales in the specialized but fast-growing prepaid smart-phone market when smaller carriers such as Boost Mobile, Virgin Mobile, and MetroPCS offered lower prices and greater selection.[41] Another flanking strategy is to serve uncovered market needs. Ariat's cowboy boots have challenged long-time market leaders Justin Boots and Tony Lama by making boots that are every bit as ranch-ready but ergonomically designed to feel as comfortable as a running shoe—a totally new benefit in the category.[42] With a geographic attack, the challenger spots areas where the opponent is underperforming.
- *Encirclement attack.* *Encirclement* attempts to capture a wide slice of territory by launching a grand offensive on several fronts. It makes sense when the challenger commands superior resources. Back when it was pitched in a heated battle with much bigger rival Microsoft, Sun Microsystems licensed its Java software to hundreds of companies and thousands of software developers for all sorts of consumer devices. As consumer electronics began to go digital, Java started appearing in a wide range of gadgets.
- *Bypass attack.* *Bypassing* the enemy altogether to attack easier markets instead offers three lines of approach: diversifying into unrelated products, diversifying into new geographical markets, and leapfrogging into new technologies. In the "cola wars," Pepsi used a bypass strategy against Coke by (1) rolling out Aquafina bottled water nationally in 1997 before Coke launched its Dasani brand; (2) purchasing orange juice giant Tropicana in 1998, when it owned almost twice the market share of Coca-Cola's Minute Maid;

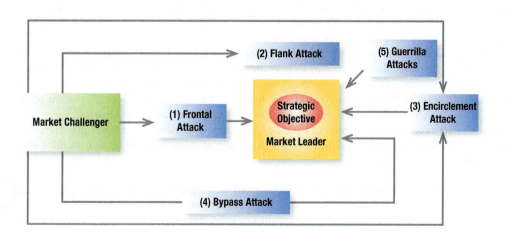

**| Fig. 12.4 |**

General Attack Strategies

and (3) purchasing the Quaker Oats Company, owner of market leader Gatorade sports drink, for $14 billion in 2000.[43] Coca-Cola has responded in turn with its own acquisitions. In *technological leapfrogging*, the challenger patiently researches and develops the next technology, shifting the battleground to its own territory where it has an advantage. Google used technological leapfrogging to overtake Yahoo! and become the market leader in search.

- *Guerrilla attack. Guerrilla attacks* consist of small, intermittent attacks, conventional and unconventional, including selective price cuts, intense promotional blitzes, and occasional legal action, to harass the opponent and eventually secure permanent footholds. A guerrilla campaign can be expensive, though less so than a frontal, encirclement, or flank attack, but it typically must be backed by a stronger attack to beat the opponent.

**CHOOSING A SPECIFIC ATTACK STRATEGY** Any aspect of the marketing program can serve as the basis for attack, such as lower-priced or discounted products, new or improved products and services, a wider variety of offerings, and innovative distribution strategies. A challenger's success depends on combining several, more specific strategies to improve its position over time. Once successful, a challenger brand must retain a challenger mentality even if it becomes a market leader, highlighting the way it does things differently.

## MARKET-FOLLOWER STRATEGIES

Theodore Levitt argues that a strategy of *product imitation* might be as profitable as a strategy of *product innovation*.[44] In "innovative imitation," as he calls it, the innovator bears the expense of developing the new product, getting it into distribution, and informing and educating the market. The reward for all this work and risk is normally market leadership. However, another firm can come along and copy or improve on the new product. Although it may not overtake the leader, the follower can achieve high profits because it did not bear any of the innovation expense.

Many companies prefer to follow rather than challenge the market leader. Patterns of "conscious parallelism" are common in capital-intensive, homogeneous-product industries such as steel, fertilizers, and chemicals. The opportunities for product differentiation and image differentiation are low, service quality is comparable, and price sensitivity runs high. The mood in these industries is against short-run grabs for market share because that only provokes retaliation. Instead, most firms present similar offers to buyers, usually by copying the leader. Market shares show high stability.

That's not to say market followers lack strategies. They must know how to hold current customers and win a fair share of new ones. Each follower tries to bring distinctive advantages to its target market—location, services, financing—while defensively keeping its manufacturing costs low and its product quality and services high. It must also enter new markets as they open up. "Marketing Insight: The Costs and Benefits of Fast Fashion" describes how a set of firms is changing the fashion industry, both for better and for worse.

Followers must define a growth path, but one that doesn't invite competitive retaliation. We distinguish three broad strategies:

1. *Cloner*—The cloner emulates the leader's products, name, and packaging with slight variations. Technology firms are often accused of being cloners: Similar-sounding knockoffs copy mobile-messaging app maker WhatsApp's products, and Berlin-based Rocket Internet has copied competitors' business models and attempted to out-execute them.[45] Ralston Foods, now owned by ConAgra, sells imitations of name-brand cereals in look-alike boxes as part of its "Value+Brands" platform. Its Apple Cinnamon Tasteeos (versus Cheerios), Cocoa Crunchies (versus Cocoa Puffs), and Corn Biscuits (versus Corn Chex) take aim at successful General Mills brands, but with much lower price points.[46]
2. *Imitator*—The imitator copies some things from the leader but differentiates on packaging, advertising, pricing, or location. The leader doesn't mind as long as the imitator doesn't attack aggressively. Fernandez Pujals grew up in Fort Lauderdale, Florida, and took Domino's pizza home delivery idea to Spain, where he borrowed $80,000 to open his first store in Madrid. His Telepizza chain now holds about 70 percent of the Spanish pizza delivery market and operates more than 1,200 stores in Europe and Latin America.[47]
3. *Adapter*—The adapter takes the leader's products and adapts or improves them. The adapter may choose to sell to different markets, but often it grows into a future challenger, as many Japanese firms have done after improving products developed elsewhere.

Note that we can contrast these three follower strategies from an illegal and unethical follower strategy. Counterfeiters duplicate the leader's product and packages and sell them on the black market or through disreputable dealers. High-tech firms like Apple and luxury brands like Rolex have been plagued by the counterfeiter

## The Costs and Benefits of Fast Fashion

In the fashion industry, styles and tastes can change quickly, and some savvy businesses and retailers are developing business models to allow them to quickly capitalize. Notable among them are Sweden's Hennes & Mauritz, or H&M, and Spain's Inditext with its Zara brand. These firms can take a new garment or accessory from design to store in a mere two weeks. Their success is forcing established luxury brands like Burberry, Chanel, and Saint Tropez to speed up and increase the frequency of their new product introductions beyond the traditional fashion-week-driven fall and spring collections.

By sourcing more than half its products from Spain, Portugal, and Morocco, Indetix pays more in production, but thanks to its tightly integrated supply chain, the company can quickly stock and supply what is selling and avoid having to discount what is not. Because there is almost always something new at appealing price points, shoppers always have a reason to stop by and check out what has just arrived. H&M has adopted a similar fast-fashion model that allows it to closely follow and respond to what is selling in the marketplace.

Both firms generate most of their sales in Europe—four-fifths for H&M and two-thirds for Zara—so they are furiously moving into China, Russia, and elsewhere and opening up hundreds of new stores. But this rapid growth and continual replenishment has both an environmental and social cost that fast-fashion companies are trying to address.

The social cost came to light when a tragic 2012 fire in a subcontracted Bangladesh garment factory killed 111 workers. Competition in the $18 billion fashion industry is fierce, and with a focus on lean production costs, safety concerns took a backseat. Prodded by labor rights activists, Western firms finally signed a building and fire safety agreement that provided greater regulation to improve worker safety.

Another negative by-product of the fast-fashion business model is the environmental cost of making and disposing of clothing with a limited shelf life. To deflect some of the criticism, H&M adopted a series of "Recycle, Resell, or Reuse" programs and activities. Products were made using fewer, recycled materials, and customer were able to trade in old clothes for vouchers for new ones. The company also required all contract suppliers to sign a code of conduct to ensure good working conditions.

**Sources:** William Mauldin and Suzanne Kapner, "Wal-Mart and Other U.S. Retailers Commit to Factory Safety in Bangladesh," *Wall Street Journal*, July 10, 2013; Katarina Gustafsson, "H&M's New Love for Old Clothes," *Bloomberg Businessweek*, July 1, 2013; Kyle Stock, "H&M Has Been Slower than Its Fast-Fashion Rival in Escaping Europe," *Bloomberg Businessweek,* June 13, 2013; Calum Macleod, "H&M, Zara to Sign Bangladesh Factory Safety Accord," *USA Today,* May 13, 2013; Oliver Balch, "H&M: Can Fast Fashion and Sustainability Ever Really Mix?," *The Guardian*. May 3, 2013; Renee Dudley, Arun Devanth, and Matt Townsend, "The Hidden Cost of Fast Fashion: Worker Safety," *Bloomberg Businessweek*, February 7, 2013; Lucy Siegle, "Is H&M the New Home of Ethical Fashion?," *The Guardian*, April 7, 2012; "Fashion Forward," *The Economist*, March 24, 2012; Gerard Cachon and Robert Swinney, "The Value of Fast Fashion: Quick Response, Enhanced Design, and Strategic Consumer Behavior," *Management Science* 57 (April 2011); Andrew Roberts, "H&M, Zara Fast Fashion Pressures Luxury to Speed Up," www.bloomberg.com, September 30, 2010.

*Source: ASSOCIATED PRESS*

Companies who have adopted fast fashion practices emphasize low cost manufacturing with quick replenishment but must ensure that working conditions and safety are not sacrificed in the process.

problem for years, especially in Asia. Pharmaceutical counterfeits have become an enormous and potentially lethal $75 billion business. Unregulated, drug fakes have been found to contain traces of chalk, brick dust, paint, and even pesticides.[48]

What does a follower earn? Normally, less than the leader. A study of food-processing companies showed the largest averaging a 16 percent return on investment, the number-two firm, 6 percent, the number-three

Popchips adopted an introductory marketing program similar to vitaminwater using celebrities like Katy Perry and much product sampling with consumers.

Sriracha hot chili sauce has grown its sales organically with little marketing support.

firm, –1 percent, and the number-four firm, –6 percent. No wonder Jack Welch, former CEO of GE, told his business units that each must reach the number-one or -two position in its market or else!

Followership is often not a rewarding path. Some follower firms have found success, but in another industry. Les Wexner, who runs Limited Brands and its Victoria's Secret lingerie retailer, fully embraces imitation. One month a year, he travels the world looking for ideas he can borrow from other companies ranging from airlines to consumer goods makers.[49]

Popchips has developed a $100 million business in part by expressly copying the successful marketing formula for vitaminwater (described in Chapter 10). As vitaminwater did, Popchips started with a novel and appealing product, converting a Los Angeles rice-cake plant to produce a new potato chip. Also like vitaminwater, Popchips then used an aggressive sampling strategy to create consumer interest and secure distribution in top retailers such as Safeway and Whole Foods. To generate buzz and broaden appeal, Popchips brought in celebrities Ashton Kutcher and Katy Perry as minority investors and marketing spokespeople.[50]

## MARKET-NICHER STRATEGIES

An alternative to being a follower in a large market is to be a leader in a small market, or niche, as we introduced in Chapter 8. Smaller firms normally avoid competing with larger firms by targeting small markets of little or no interest to the larger firms. Over time, those markets can sometimes end up being sizable in their own right, as Huy Fong Foods has found.[51]

**▌SRIRACHA HOT CHILI SAUCE**    David Tran started Huy Fong Foods in Los Angeles's Chinatown in 1980, naming the company after the Taiwanese freighter that brought him to the United States as a refugee from Vietnam. Based in part on a condiment made in Si Racha, Thailand, Tan's Sriracha hot chili sauce is known as the "rooster sauce" for the distinctive rooster (Tan's astrological sign) on its green-capped squeeze bottle. A unique combination of locally sourced jalapeño peppers, vinegar, sugar, salt, and garlic created a taste that his packaging suppliers thought would be too spicy. Tran refused to change the recipe, saying, "Hot sauce must be hot. If you don't like it hot, use less. We don't make mayonnaise here." Fortunately, many consumers agreed. Huy Fong's Sriracha sauce can be bought at Walmart and enjoyed in dishes at Applebee's restaurants and in street foods in major cities. The product tastes so good that NASA has supplied it to its astronauts in space to help stave off dulled taste buds. It has never been advertised, has no Facebook page and no Twitter account, and at one point had not updated its Web site in years. Because of Sriracha's popularity, however, Huy Fong has become one of the fastest-growing U.S. food companies. Success has attracted imitators, but the firm's revenues continue to grow by at least 20 percent a year.

Firms with low shares of the total market can become highly profitable through smart niching. They know their target customers so well they can meet their needs better than other firms by offering high value, but they can also charge a premium price, achieve lower manufacturing costs, and shape a strong corporate culture and vision.[52] The nicher achieves *high margin,* whereas the mass marketer achieves *high volume.*

Paul Reed Smith founded PRS Guitars to compete with big rivals Fender and Gibson and supply "the Stradivarius of guitars." PRS instruments are carefully constructed of selected mahogany and figured maple, kiln-dried and sanded five times, followed by eight very thin coats of finish. They cost from $3,000 to $60,000, but endorsements from top musicians like Carlos Santana and distribution through well-respected retailers like Rudy's Music Shop in Manhattan have helped the brand establish a foothold.[53]

PRS Guitars has found a niche with its carefully-crafted, high-end guitars coveted by top musicians.

Nichers have three tasks: creating niches, expanding niches, and protecting niches. The risk is that the niche might dry up or be attacked. The company is then stuck with highly specialized resources that may not have high-value alternative uses. Zippo has successfully addressed the problem of a fast-shrinking niche market.[54]

**ZIPPO** With smoking on a steady decline, Pennsylvania-based Zippo Manufacturing found the market for its iconic brass and chrome "windproof" cigarette lighters shrinking from 18 million units sold in 1998 to 12 million in 2011. With the writing on the wall, the company decided to broaden its focus to selling "flame," warmth, and much more, reducing its reliance on tobacco-related products to 50 percent of revenue by 2010. Although an earlier attempt to diversify into tape measures, key holders, and belt buckles in the 1960s and 1970s had diminished in the 1990s and finally discontinued in 2007, Zippo came close to meeting its new goal. It introduced a long, slender multipurpose lighter for candles, grills, and fireplaces; launched an Outdoors Line including hand warmers and fire starters sold through Dick's Sporting Goods, REI, and True Value; and acquired W.R. Case & Sons Cutlery, a knife maker. Zippo has even launched a clothing line and men's and women's fragrances as a way to become more of a lifestyle brand. The company still sells its fair share of lighters by promoting new designs as well as perennial favorites like lighters with Elvis Presley's image and the Playboy logo. It now gets 60 percent of its sales outside the United States, with China the biggest foreign market at 10 percent of sales.

Because niches can weaken, the firm must continually create new ones. "Marketing Memo: Niche Specialist Roles" outlines some options. The firm should "stick to its niching," but not necessarily to its niche. That is why *multiple niching* can be preferable to *single niching*. With strength in two or more niches, the company increases its chances for survival.

Firms entering a market should initially aim at a niche rather than the whole market. The cell phone industry has experienced phenomenal growth but is now facing fierce competition as the number of new potential users dwindles.

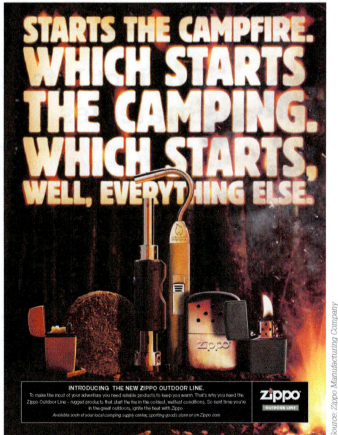

Zippo has expanded its product offerings beyond lighters to sell "flame" and more.

## Niche Specialist Roles

The key idea in successful nichemanship is specialization. Here are some possible niche roles:

- **End-user specialist.** The firm specializes in one type of end-use customer. For example, a *value-added reseller (VAR)* customizes computer hardware and software for specific customer segments and earns a price premium in the process.

- **Vertical-level specialist.** The firm specializes at some vertical level of the production-distribution value chain. A copper firm may concentrate on producing raw copper, copper components, or finished copper products.

- **Customer-size specialist.** The firm concentrates on either small, medium-sized, or large customers. Many nichers serve small customers neglected by the majors.

- **Specific-customer specialist.** The firm limits its selling to one or a few customers. Many firms sell their entire output to a single company, such as Walmart or General Motors.

- **Geographic specialist.** The firm sells only in a certain locality, region, or area of the world.

- **Product or product line specialist.** The firm carries or produces only one product line or product. A manufacturer may produce only lenses for micro-scopes. A retailer may carry only ties.

- **Product-feature specialist.** The firm specializes in producing a certain type of product or product feature.

- **Job-shop specialist.** The firm customizes its products for individual customers.

- **Quality-price specialist.** The firm operates at the low- or high-quality ends of the market. McIntosh Laboratory only makes high-performance luxury audio systems—its hand-built audio products appeal to audiophiles everywhere.

- **Service specialist.** The firm offers one or more services not available from other firms. A bank might take loan requests over the phone and hand-deliver the money to the customer.

- **Channel specialist.** The firm specializes in serving only one channel of distribution. For example, a soft drink company makes a very large-sized serving available only at gas stations.

# Product Life-Cycle Marketing Strategies

A company's positioning and differentiation strategy must change as its product, market, and competitors change over the *product life cycle* (PLC). To say a product has a life cycle is to assert four things:

1. Products have a limited life.
2. Product sales pass through distinct stages, each posing different challenges, opportunities, and problems to the seller.
3. Profits rise and fall at different stages of the product life cycle.
4. Products require different marketing, financial, manufacturing, purchasing, and human resource strategies in each life-cycle stage.

## PRODUCT LIFE CYCLES

Most product life cycles are portrayed as bell-shaped curves, typically divided into four stages: introduction, growth, maturity, and decline[55] (see Figure 12.5).

1. *Introduction*—A period of slow sales growth as the product is introduced in the market. Profits are nonexistent because of the heavy expenses of product introduction.
2. *Growth*—A period of rapid market acceptance and substantial profit improvement.
3. *Maturity*—A slowdown in sales growth because the product has achieved acceptance by most potential buyers. Profits stabilize or decline because of increased competition.
4. *Decline*—Sales show a downward drift and profits erode.

We can use the PLC concept to analyze a product category (liquor), a product form (white liquor), a product (vodka), or a brand (Absolut). Not all products exhibit a bell-shaped PLC.[56] Three common alternate patterns are shown in Figure 12.6.

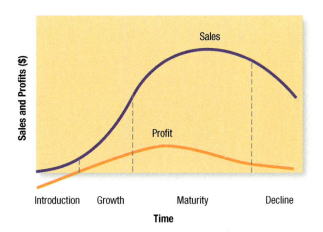

| Fig. 12.5 |

Sales and Profit
Life Cycles

Figure 12.6(a) shows a *growth-slump-maturity pattern*, characteristic of small kitchen appliances like bread makers and toaster ovens. Sales grow rapidly when the product is first introduced and then fall to a "petrified" level sustained by late adopters buying the product for the first time and early adopters replacing it.

The *cycle-recycle pattern* in Figure 12.6 (b) often describes the sales of new drugs. The pharmaceutical company aggressively promotes its new drug, producing the first cycle. Later, sales start declining, and another promotion push produces a second cycle (usually of smaller magnitude and duration).[57]

Another common pattern is the *scalloped PLC* in Figure 12.6 (c). Here, sales pass through a succession of life cycles based on the discovery of new product characteristics, uses, or users. Sales of nylon showed a classic scalloped pattern because of the many new uses—parachutes, hosiery, shirts, carpeting, boat sails, automobile tires—discovered over time.[58]

## STYLE, FASHION, AND FAD LIFE CYCLES

We need to distinguish three special categories of product life cycles: styles, fashions, and fads (Figure 12.7). A *style* is a basic and distinctive mode of expression appearing in a field of human endeavor. Homes can be colonial, ranch, or Cape Cod; clothing is formal, business casual, or sporty; art is realistic, surrealistic, or abstract. A style can last for generations and go in and out of vogue. A *fashion* is a currently accepted or popular style in a given field. Fashions pass through four stages: distinctiveness, emulation, mass fashion, and decline.[59]

The length of a fashion cycle is hard to predict. One view is that fashions end because they represent a compromise, and consumers start looking for the missing attributes.[60] For example, as automobiles become smaller, they become less comfortable, and then a growing number of buyers start wanting larger cars. Another explanation is that too many consumers adopt the fashion, discouraging others. Still another is that the length of a fashion cycle depends on whether the fashion meets a genuine need, is consistent with other trends, satisfies societal norms and values, and keeps within technological limits as it develops.[61]

*Fads* are fashions that come quickly into public view, are adopted with great zeal, peak early, and decline very fast. Their acceptance cycle is short, and they tend to attract only a limited following searching for excitement or wanting

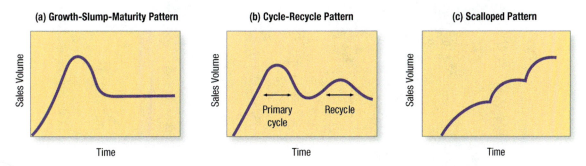

**Fig. 12.6 |**

Common Product Life-Cycle Patterns

| Fig. 12.7 |

Style, Fashion, and Fad Life Cycles

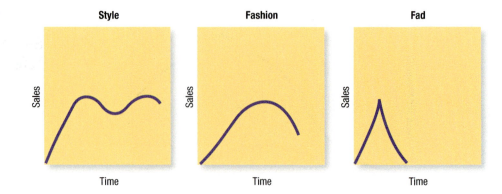

to distinguish themselves from others. Heelys wheeled shoes were the rage with kids—for a while. Dwindling sales resulted in a sale to a private equity company for a fraction of what the company was worth at its IPO.[62]

Fads decline because they don't normally satisfy a strong need. The marketing winners are those who recognize fads early and leverage them into products with staying power, as Crocs has tried to do.[63]

**CROCS**  Crocs' signature plastic clogs or "boat shoes"—colorful, comfortable, perfect for summer—succeeded soon after their introduction in Boulder, CO, in 2002. The company's 2006 IPO was the largest ever in U.S. footwear, raising $208 million. Its stock peaked a year later when Crocs' sales reached $847 million. But the recession and consumer fatigue with the brand were a double whammy that led to a steep drop in sales and drove the stock price down to a mere $1 in what the CFO now calls a "near-death experience." By 2011, however, Crocs had rebounded with more than $1 billion in revenues and growth goals of 15 percent to 20 percent. What happened? The company had diversified into more than 300 styles of stylish, comfortable boots, loafers, sneakers, and other shoes that helped to reduce its reliance on clogs to less than 50 percent of sales. It also adopted a multichannel distribution approach to sell wholesale through retailers like Kohl's and Dick's Sporting Goods (60 percent of business), as well as directly online (10 percent) and through more than 500 of its own retail stores (30 percent). International sales now make up more than half its sales, including in emerging marketing and the growing middle-class markets in Asia and Latin America.

With sales fading fast, Crocs turned around its fortunes by expanding its product line, adopting a multichannel distribution approach, and tapping into global markets.

Source: © Per Andersen/Alamy

# MARKETING STRATEGIES: INTRODUCTION STAGE AND THE PIONEER ADVANTAGE

Because it takes time to roll out a new product, work out technical problems, fill dealer pipelines, and gain consumer acceptance, sales growth tends to be slow in the introduction stage. Profits are negative or low, and promotional expenditures are at their highest ratio to sales because of the need to (1) inform potential consumers, (2) induce product trial, and (3) secure distribution in retail outlets.[64] Prices tend to be higher because costs are high, and firms focus on buyers who are the most ready to buy. Consider the challenges Zipcar faced in trying to establish itself in the hourly car rental market.[65]

**ZIPCAR** Car sharing started in Europe as a means to serve those who frequently used public transportation but still needed a car a few times a month. In the United States, the appeal of Zipcar, the market leader and pioneer in car sharing, has been both environmental and economic. With a $50 membership fee and rates that total less than $100 a day—including gas, insurance, and parking—a typical family could save $3,000 to $4,000 a year by substituting Zipcar use for car ownership. The firm estimated that every car it added kept up to 20 private cars off the road. Targeting major cities and college campuses, offering a wide variety of vehicles, and facing little competition, it grew about 30 percent annually for a number of years. Rental leader Hertz decided to enter the hourly car rental business in 2012, however, equipping its entire 375,000-vehicle U.S. fleet with devices that let customers use a computer or smart phone to reserve and unlock a rental car. Unlike Zipcar, Hertz offers one-way rentals and charges no membership or annual fees. With Enterprise also entering the market at home, Zipcar set its sights overseas, concentrating initially on the United Kingdom and Spain. Needing resources to capitalize on global opportunities, in January 2013 it agreed to be acquired by Avis Budget, the number-two rental car company.

Companies that plan to introduce a new product must decide when to do so. To be first can be rewarding, but risky and expensive. To come in later makes sense if the firm can bring superior technology, quality, or brand strength to create a market advantage. We next consider some of the pros and cons of being a pioneer in a new market.

**PIONEERING ADVANTAGES** Studies show that a market pioneer can gain a great advantage.[66] Campbell, Coca-Cola, Hallmark, and Amazon.com developed sustained market dominance. Nineteen of 25 market leaders in 1923 were still the market leaders 60 years later.[67] In a sample of industrial-goods businesses, 66 percent of pioneers survived at least 10 years versus 48 percent of early followers.[68]

Zipcar pioneered the hourly car rental market in the U.S. but encountered stiff competition from established car rental companies.

## Understanding Double Jeopardy

Double jeopardy is an empirical generalization that has roots in many areas but was popularized in marketing by the British academic Andrew Ehrenberg. It boils down to the fact that a small-share brand is penalized twice—it has fewer buyers than a large-share brand, and they buy less frequently. As a consequence, most of a brand's market share is explained by its market penetration and the size of its customer base, rather than by customers' repeat purchases.

Implicit in the principle of double jeopardy is the assumption that brands are substitutable and have target segments in common. It is, in fact, most often observed with weakly differentiated brands targeting the same group of people. Exceptions are highly differentiated niche brands that thrive on small shares and high loyalty and seasonal brands that offer unique value and tally cluster purchases in short periods of time.

One implication drawn by double jeopardy proponents is that marketers seeking growth should focus on increasing the size of the customer base rather than on deepening the loyalty of existing customers. They see PR efforts, distribution plans, and any means to increase brand exposure, familiarity, and availability as more important than persuasive advertising to target switchers or CRM efforts to reward loyal customers.

Critics of double jeopardy question how inevitable it is and see other implications for marketers. For example, they view new or established brands with a new positioning or message as differentiated enough to avoid double jeopardy's predicted results.

**Sources:** John Scriven and Gerald Goodhardt, "The Ehrenberg Legacy," *Journal of Advertising Research*, June 2012, pp. 198–202; Byron Sharp, *How Brands Grow: What Marketers Don't Know* (Melbourne, Australia: Oxford University Press, 2010); Nigel Hollis, "The Jeopardy in Double Jeopardy," www.millwardbrown.com, September 2, 2009; Andrew Ehrenberg and Gerald Goodhardt, "Double Jeopardy Revisited, Again," *Marketing Research*, 2002. See also *Andrew Ehrenberg: A Tribute (1926–2010),* Special Section, *Journal of Advertising Research* 52 (June 2012).

What are the sources of the pioneer's advantage? "Marketing Insight: Understanding Double Jeopardy" describes one way market leaders can benefit from loyalty due to their size. Early users will recall the pioneer's brand name if the product satisfies them. The pioneer's brand also establishes the attributes the product class should possess.[69] It normally aims at the middle of the market and so captures more users. Customer inertia also plays a role, and there are producer advantages: economies of scale, technological leadership, patents, ownership of scarce assets, and the ability to erect other barriers to entry. Pioneers can spend marketing dollars more effectively and enjoy higher rates of repeat purchases. An alert pioneer can lead indefinitely.

**PIONEERING DRAWBACKS** But the pioneering advantage is not inevitable.[70] Bowmar (hand calculators), Apple's Newton (personal digital assistant), Netscape (Web browser), Reynolds (ballpoint pens), and Osborne (portable computers) were market pioneers overtaken by later entrants. First movers also have to watch out for the "second-mover advantage."

Steven Schnaars studied 28 industries in which imitators surpassed the innovators.[71] He found several weaknesses among the failing pioneers, including new products that were too crude, were improperly positioned, or appeared before there was strong demand; product-development costs that exhausted the innovator's resources; a lack of resources to compete against entering larger firms; and managerial incompetence or unhealthy complacency. Successful imitators thrived by offering lower prices, continuously improving the product, or using brute market power to overtake the pioneer.

Peter Golder and Gerald Tellis raise further doubts about the pioneer advantage.[72] They distinguish between an *inventor,* first to develop patents in a new-product category, a *product pioneer,* first to develop a working model, and a *market pioneer,* first to sell in the new-product category. Including nonsurviving pioneers in their sample, they conclude that although pioneers may still have an advantage, more market pioneers fail than has been reported, and more early market leaders (though not pioneers) succeed. Later entrants overtaking market pioneers through the years included Matsushita over Sony in VCRs, GE over EMI in CAT scan equipment, and Google over Yahoo! in search.

Follow-up research by Golder and his colleagues of 625 brand leaders in 125 categories from 1921 to 2010 provides further insight:[73]

- Leading brands are more likely to persist during economic slowdowns and when inflation is high and less likely to persist during economic expansion and when inflation is low.
- Half the leading brands in the sample lost their leadership after being a leader over periods ranging from 12 to 39 years.

- The rate of brand leadership persistence has been substantially lower in recent eras than in earlier eras (e.g., more than 30 years ago).
- Once brand leadership has been lost, it is rarely regained.
- Categories with above-average brand leadership persistence are food and household supplies; those with below-average rates are durables and clothing.

**GAINING A PIONEERING ADVANTAGE** Tellis and Golder also identified five factors underpinning long-term market leadership: vision of a mass market, persistence, relentless innovation, financial commitment, and asset leverage.[74] Other research has highlighted the role of genuine product innovation.[75] When a pioneer starts a market with a really new product, like the Segway Human Transporter, surviving can be very challenging. For incremental innovators, like MP3 players with video capabilities, survival rates are much higher.

Speeding up innovation is essential in an age of shortening product life cycles. Being early has been shown to pay. One study found that products debuting six months late but on budget earned an average of 33 percent less profit in their first five years; products that came out on time but 50 percent over budget sacrificed only 4 percent of potential profits.[76]

Companies should not try to move too fast; they must carefully design and execute their product-launch marketing. General Motors rushed out its newly designed Malibu to get a leg up over its Honda, Nissan, and Ford midsize competitors. When all the different versions were not ready for production at launch, the brand's momentum stalled.[77] One study found Internet companies that realized benefits from moving fast (1) were first movers in large markets, (2) erected barriers of entry against competitors, and (3) directly controlled critical elements necessary for starting a company.[78]

The pioneer should visualize the product markets it could enter, knowing it cannot enter all of them at once. Suppose market-segmentation analysis reveals the segments shown in Figure 12.8. The pioneer should analyze the profit potential of each singly and of all together and decide on a market expansion path. Thus, the pioneer in Figure 12.8 plans first to enter product market $P_1M_1$, then move into a second market ($P_1M_2$), then surprise the competition by developing a second product for the second market ($P_2M_2$), then take the second product back into the first market ($P_2M_1$), then launch a third product for the first market ($P_3M_1$). If this game plan works, the pioneer firm will own a good part of the first two segments, serving each with two or three products.

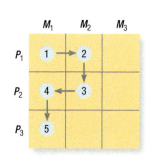

| **Fig. 12.8** |

Long-Range Product Market Expansion Strategy ($P_i$ = product i; $M_j$ = market j)

# MARKETING STRATEGIES: GROWTH STAGE

The growth stage is marked by a rapid climb in sales. Early adopters like the product, and additional consumers start buying it. New competitors enter, attracted by the opportunities. They introduce new product features and expand distribution. Prices stabilize or fall slightly, depending on how fast demand increases.

Companies maintain marketing expenditures or raise them slightly to meet competition and continue to educate the market. Sales rise much faster than marketing expenditures, causing a welcome decline in the marketing-to-sales ratio. Profits increase as marketing costs are spread over a larger volume, and unit manufacturing costs fall faster than price declines, owing to the producer-learning effect. Firms must watch for a change to a decelerating rate of growth in order to prepare new strategies.

To sustain rapid market share growth now, the firm:

- improves product quality and adds new features and improved styling.
- adds new models and flanker products (of different sizes, flavors, and so forth) to protect the main product.
- enters new market segments.
- increases its distribution coverage and enters new distribution channels.
- shifts from awareness and trial communications to preference and loyalty communications.
- lowers prices to attract the next layer of price-sensitive buyers.

By spending money on product improvement, promotion, and distribution, the firm can capture a dominant position. It trades off maximum current profit for high market share and the hope of even greater profits in the next stage.

Sustaining a competitive advantage in the face of many possible marketplace changes can be challenging but not impossible, as evidenced by some of the long-time market leaders noted above. Finding new ways to consistently improve customer satisfaction can go a long way. Brambles, a leading Australian logistics supplier, designed plastic bins for its grocery customers that could be filled in farmers' fields and placed directly on store shelves, saving the grocers significant labor costs in the process.[79]

## MARKETING STRATEGIES: MATURITY STAGE

At some point, the rate of sales growth will slow, and the product will enter a stage of relative maturity. Most products are in this stage of the life cycle, which normally lasts longer than the preceding ones.

The maturity stage divides into three phases: growth, stable, and decaying maturity. In the first, sales growth starts to slow. There are no new distribution channels to fill. New competitive forces emerge. In the second phase, sales per capita flatten because of market saturation. Most potential consumers have tried the product, and future sales depend on population growth and replacement demand. In the third phase, decaying maturity, the absolute level of sales starts to decline, and customers begin switching to other products.

This third phase poses the most challenges. The sales slowdown creates overcapacity in the industry, which intensifies competition. Weaker competitors withdraw. A few giants dominate—perhaps a quality leader, a service leader, and a cost leader—and they profit mainly through high volume and lower costs. Surrounding them is a multitude of market nichers, including market specialists, product specialists, and customizing firms.

The question is whether to struggle to become one of the big three and achieve profits through high volume and low cost or to pursue a niching strategy and profit through low volume and high margins. Sometimes the market will divide into low- and high-end segments, and market shares of firms in the middle will steadily erode. Here's how Swedish appliance manufacturer Electrolux has coped with this situation.[80]

**❚ ELECTROLUX AB**  In 2002, Swedish manufacturer Electrolux faced a rapidly polarizing appliance market. Low-cost Asian companies such as Haier, LG, and Samsung were applying downward price pressure, while premium competitors like Bosch, Sub-Zero, and Viking were growing at the expense of the middle-of-the-road brands. Electrolux's CEO at the time, Hans Stråberg, decided to escape the middle by rethinking customers' wants and needs. He segmented the market according to the lifestyle and purchasing patterns of about 20 different types of consumers to help target and position the company's broad portfolio of brands, which includes Electrolux as well as Frigidaire refrigerators, AEG ovens, and Zanussi coffee machines. Electrolux now successfully markets its steam ovens to health-oriented consumers, for example, and its compact dishwashers, originally for smaller kitchens, to a broader consumer segment that washes dishes more often. To companies stuck in the middle of a mature market, Stråberg offered this advice: "Start with consumers and understand what their latent needs are and what problems they experience…then put the puzzle together yourself to discover what people really want to have. Henry Ford is supposed to have said, 'If I had asked people what they really wanted, I would have made faster horses' or something like that. You need to figure out what people really want, although they can't express it." Under new CEO Keith McLoughlin, Electrolux is concentrating on the top end of the appliance market, selling professional-grade ranges to the ultra-luxury consumer segment. With distribution and local market presence in more than 150 countries, the company is well positioned for global growth, especially in emerging markets.

Some companies abandon weaker products to concentrate on new and more profitable ones. Yet they may be ignoring the high potential many mature markets and old products still have. Industries widely thought to be mature—autos, motorcycles, television, watches, cameras—were proved otherwise by Japanese firms, who found ways to offer customers new value. Three ways to change the course for a brand are market, product, and marketing program modifications.

**MARKET MODIFICATION**  A company might try to expand the market for its mature brand by working with the two factors that make up sales volume, number of brand users and usage rate per customer, as in Table 12.1, but competitors may match this strategy.

**PRODUCT MODIFICATION**  Managers also try to stimulate sales by improving quality, features, or style. *Quality improvement* increases functional performance by launching a "new and improved" product. *Feature*

| TABLE 12.1 | Alternate Ways to Increase Sales Volume |
|---|---|
| **Expand the Number of Users** | **Increase the Usage Rates among Users** |
| • *Convert nonusers.* The key to the growth of air freight service was the constant search for new users to whom air carriers could demonstrate the benefits of using air freight rather than ground transportation. | • *Have consumers use the product on more occasions.* Serve Campbell's soup for a snack. Use Heinz vinegar to clean windows. |
| • *Enter new market segments.* When Goodyear decided to sell its tires in Walmart, Sears, and Discount Tire, it immediately boosted its market share. | • *Have consumers use more of the product on each occasion.* Drink a larger glass of orange juice. |
| • *Attract competitors' customers.* Marketers of Puffs facial tissues are always wooing Kleenex customers. | • *Have consumers use the product in new ways.* Use Tums antacid as a calcium supplement. |

*improvement* adds size, weight, materials, supplements, and accessories that expand the product's performance, versatility, safety, or convenience. *Style improvement* increases the product's esthetic appeal.

Any of these improvements can attract consumer attention. In the highly competitive digital photography space, Shutterfly has grown revenue to $600 million in annual sales by converting customers' digital images to tangible items: photo books, calendars, greeting cards, wedding invitations, wall decals, and more.[81]

The paper industry is also coping with the challenges of the digital era. As long as some consumers prefer to read, store, or share hard-copy documents, the industry recognizes it must also provide as environmentally sound a solution as possible. Suppliers have worked to develop a more environmentally friendly supply chain from seedlings and reforestation, adopt greener pulp and paper production, recycle, and reduce their carbon footprint.[82] Such efforts are crucial for success and even survival. Due to the rise of e-mail, online bill payments, and other digital developments, leading envelope maker National Envelope declared Chapter 11 bankruptcy twice from 2011 to 2013 as a result of dwindling sales, while leading postage meter supplier Pitney Bowes expanded its digital operations.[83]

**MARKETING PROGRAM MODIFICATION** Finally, brand managers might also try to stimulate sales by modifying non-product elements—price, distribution, and communications in particular—as we will review in later chapters. They should assess the likely success of any changes in terms of their effects on new and existing customers.

## MARKETING STRATEGIES: DECLINE STAGE

Sales decline for a number of reasons, including technological advances, shifts in consumer tastes, and increased domestic and foreign competition. All can lead to overcapacity, increased price cutting, and profit erosion. The decline might be slow, as for sewing machines and newspapers, or rapid, as it was for 5.25 floppy disks and eight-track cartridges. Sales may plunge to zero or petrify at a low level. These structural changes are different from a short-term decline resulting from a marketing crisis of some sort. "Marketing Memo: Managing a Marketing Crisis" describes strategies for a brand in temporary trouble.

As sales and profits decline, some firms withdraw. Those remaining may reduce the number of products they offer, exiting smaller segments and weaker trade channels, cutting marketing budgets, and reducing prices further. Unless strong reasons for retention exist, carrying a weak product is often very costly. Encyclopædia Britannica ceased production of its iconic bound sets of encyclopedias once consumers felt they could get adequate content elsewhere for much less or free. The company rebounded by focusing on the online educational market. Valuing

# marketing memo
## Managing a Marketing Crisis

Marketing managers must assume a brand crisis will someday arise. Chick-fil-A, BP, Domino's, and Toyota have all experienced damaging and even potentially crippling brand crises. Bank of America, JPMorgan, AIG, and other financial services firms have been rocked by scandals that significantly eroded investor trust. Repercussions include (1) lost sales, (2) reduced effectiveness of marketing activities, (3) increased sensitivity to rivals' marketing activities, and (4) reduced impact of the firm's marketing activities on competing brands.

In general, the stronger the brand equity and corporate image—especially credibility and trustworthiness—the more likely the firm can weather the storm. Careful preparation and a well-managed crisis management program are also critical, however. As Johnson & Johnson's legendary and nearly flawless handling of the Tylenol product-tampering incident taught marketers everywhere, consumers must see the firm's response as both *swift* and *sincere*. They must feel an immediate sense that the company truly cares. Listening is not enough.

The longer the firm takes to respond, the more likely consumers can form negative impressions from unfavorable media coverage or word of mouth. Perhaps worse, they may find they don't like the brand after all and permanently switch. Getting in front of a problem with PR, and perhaps even ads, can help avoid those problems.

A classic example is Perrier—the one-time brand leader in the bottled water category. In 1994, Perrier was forced to halt production worldwide and recall all existing product when traces of benzene, a known carcinogen, were found in excessive quantities in its bottled water. Over the next weeks it offered several explanations, creating confusion and skepticism. Perhaps more damaging, the product was off shelves for more than three months. Despite an expensive relaunch featuring ads and promotions, the brand struggled to regain lost market share, and a full year later sales were less than half what they had been. With its key "purity" association tarnished, Perrier had no other compelling points-of-difference. Consumers and retailers had found satisfactory substitutes, and the brand never recovered. Eventually it was taken over by Nestlé SA.

The more sincere the firm's response—ideally a public acknowledgment of the impact on consumers and willingness to take necessary steps—the less likely consumers will form negative attributions. When shards of glass were found in some jars of its baby food, Gerber tried to reassure the public there were no problems in its manufacturing plants but adamantly refused to withdraw products from stores. After market share slumped from 66 percent to 52 percent within a couple of months, one company official admitted, "Not pulling our baby food off the shelf gave the appearance that we aren't a caring company."

If a problem exists, consumers need to know without a shadow of a doubt that the company has found the proper solution. One of the keys to Tylenol's recovery was J&J's introduction of triple tamper-proof packaging, successfully eliminating consumer worry that the product could ever be tampered with again.

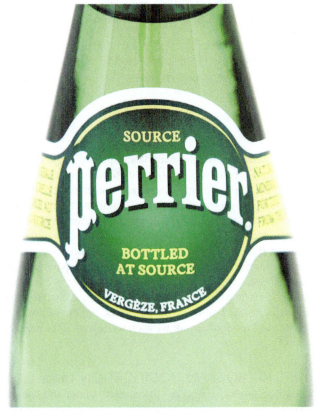

Source: © SQUIB/Alamy

By mishandling a brand crisis, Perrier lost market share which it never recovered.

**Sources:** Norman Klein and Stephen A. Greyser, "The Perrier Recall: A Source of Trouble," Harvard Business School Case #9-590-104 and "The Perrier Relaunch," Harvard Business School Case #9-590-130; Harald Van Heerde, Kristiaan Helsen, and Marnik G. Dekimpe, "The Impact of a Product-Harm Crisis on Marketing Effectiveness," *Marketing Science* 26 (March–April 2007), pp. 230–45; Michelle L. Roehm and Alice M. Tybout, "When Will a Brand Scandal Spill Over and How Should Competitors Respond?" *Journal of Marketing Research* 43 (August 2006), pp. 366–73; Michelle L. Roehm and Michael K. Brady, "Consumer Responses to Performance Failures by High Equity Brands," *Journal of Consumer Research* 34 (December 2007), pp. 537–45; Alice M. Tybout and Michelle Roehm, "Let the Response Fit the Scandal," *Harvard Business Review*, December 2009, pp. 82–88; Andrew Pierce, "Managing Reputation to Rebuild Battered Brands, *Marketing News*, March 15, 2009, p. 19; Kevin O'Donnell, "In a Crisis Actions Matter," *Marketing News*, April 15, 2009, p. 22; Anne Marie Kelly, "Has Toyota's Image Recovered from the Brand's Recall Crisis?," *Forbes*, March 5, 2012; Mark Guarino, "Chick-fil-A: Will the Controversy Hurt Chain's Expansion Plans?," *Christian Science Monitor*, August 3, 2012; Mark McNeilly, "5 Steps to Handling Your Next Brand Crisis," *Fast Company*, August 15, 2012; Kathleen Cleeren, Harald J. van Heerde, and Marnik G. Dekimpe, "Rising from the Ashes: How Brands and Categories Can Overcome Product-Harm Crises," *Journal of Marketing* 77 (March 2013), pp. 58–77.

the company's long-standing mission to bring expert knowledge to the general public, more than half of U.S. students and teachers have access to some Britannica content.[84]

**ELIMINATING WEAK PRODUCTS** Besides being unprofitable, weak products consume a disproportionate amount of management's time, require frequent price and inventory adjustments, incur expensive setup for what are usually short production runs, draw advertising and sales force attention better used to make healthy products more profitable, and cast a negative shadow on company image. Maintaining them also delays the aggressive search for replacement products, creating a lopsided product mix long on yesterday's breadwinners and short on tomorrow's.

Recognizing these drawbacks, General Motors decided to drop the floundering Oldsmobile and Pontiac lines.[85] Unfortunately, most companies have not developed a policy for handling aging products. The first task is to establish a system for identifying them. Many companies appoint a product-review committee with representatives from marketing, R&D, manufacturing, and finance who, based on all available information, make a recommendation for each product—leave it alone, modify its marketing strategy, or drop it.[86]

Some firms abandon declining markets earlier than others. Much depends on the height of exit barriers in the industry. The lower the barriers, the easier for firms to leave the industry, and the more tempting for the remaining firms to stay and attract the withdrawing firms' customers. Procter & Gamble stayed in the declining liquid-soap business and improved its profits as others withdrew.

The appropriate strategy also depends on the industry's relative attractiveness and the company's competitive strength in it. A company in an unattractive industry that possesses competitive strength should consider shrinking selectively. A company in an attractive industry that has competitive strength should consider strengthening its investment. Companies that successfully restage or rejuvenate a mature product often do so by adding value to it.

**HARVESTING AND DIVESTING** Strategies for harvesting and for divesting are quite different. *Harvesting* calls for gradually reducing a product or business's costs while trying to maintain sales. The first step is to cut R&D costs and plant and equipment investment. The company might also reduce product quality, sales force size, marginal services, and advertising expenditures, ideally without letting customers, competitors, and employees know what is happening. Harvesting is difficult to execute, yet many mature products warrant this strategy. And it can substantially increase current cash flow.[87]

When a company decides to *divest* a product with strong distribution and residual goodwill, it can probably sell it to another firm. Some firms specialize in acquiring and revitalizing "orphan" or "ghost" brands that larger firms want to divest or that have encountered bankruptcy, such as Linens n' Things, Folgers and Brim coffee, Nuprin

Source: © John Gaffen 2/Alamy

Despite its history with one-time popular models like the GTO, General Motors chose to cease production of the floundering Pontiac product line.

pain reliever, and Salon Selective shampoos.[88] These firms attempt to capitalize on the residue of awareness in the market to develop a brand revitalization strategy. Reserve Brands bought Eagle Snacks in part because research showed 6 of 10 adults remembered the brand, leading Reserve's CEO to observe, "It would take $300 million to $500 million to recreate that brand awareness today."[89]

If the company can't find any buyers, it must decide whether to liquidate the brand quickly or slowly. It must also decide how much inventory and service to maintain for past customers.

## EVIDENCE FOR THE PRODUCT LIFE-CYCLE CONCEPT

Table 12.2 summarizes the characteristics, marketing objectives, and marketing strategies of the four stages of the product life cycle. The PLC concept helps marketers interpret product and market dynamics, conduct planning and control, and do forecasting. Another study by Golder and Tellis of 30 product categories unearthed a number of interesting findings about the PLC:[90]

- New consumer durables show a distinct takeoff, after which sales increase by roughly 45 percent a year, but they also show a distinct slowdown, when sales decline by roughly 15 percent a year.
- Slowdown occurs at 34 percent penetration on average, well before most households own a new product.

| TABLE 12.2 | Summary of Product Life-Cycle Characteristics, Objectives, and Strategies | | | |
|---|---|---|---|---|
| | **Introduction** | **Growth** | **Maturity** | **Decline** |
| ***Characteristics*** | | | | |
| Sales | Low sales | Rapidly rising sales | Peak sales | Declining sales |
| Costs | High cost per customer | Average cost per customer | Low cost per customer | Low cost per customer |
| Profits | Negative | Rising profits | High profits | Declining profits |
| Customers | Innovators | Early adopters | Middle majority | Laggards |
| Competitors | Few | Growing number | Stable number beginning to decline | Declining number |
| ***Marketing Objectives*** | | | | |
| | Create product awareness and trial | Maximize market share | Maximize profit while defending market share | Reduce expenditure and milk the brand |
| ***Strategies*** | | | | |
| Product | Offer a basic product | Offer product extensions, service, warranty | Diversify brands and items models | Phase out weak products |
| Price | Charge cost-plus | Price to penetrate market | Price to match or best competitors' | Cut price |
| Distribution | Build selective distribution | Build intensive distribution | Build more intensive distribution | Go selective: phase out unprofitable outlets |
| Communications | Build product awareness and trial among early adopters and dealers | Build awareness and interest in the mass market | Stress brand differences and benefits and encourage brand switching | Reduce to minimal level needed to retain hard-core loyals |

**Sources:** Chester R. Wasson, *Dynamic Competitive Strategy and Product Life Cycles* (Austin, TX: Austin Press, 1978); John A. Weber, "Planning Corporate Growth with Inverted Product Life Cycles," *Long Range Planning* (October 1976), pp. 12–29; Peter Doyle, "The Realities of the Product Life Cycle," *Quarterly Review of Marketing* (Summer 1976).

- The growth stage lasts a little more than eight years and does not seem to shorten over time.
- Informational cascades exist, meaning people are more likely to adopt over time if others already have, instead of making careful product evaluations. One implication is that product categories with large sales increases at takeoff tend to have larger sales declines at slowdown.

## CRITIQUE OF THE PRODUCT LIFE-CYCLE CONCEPT

PLC theory has its share of critics, who claim life-cycle patterns are too variable in shape and duration to be generalized and that marketers can seldom tell what stage their product is in. A product may appear mature when it has actually reached a plateau prior to another upsurge. Critics also charge that, rather than an inevitable course, the PLC pattern is the self-fulfilling result of marketing strategies and that skillful marketing can in fact lead to continued growth.[91]

## MARKET EVOLUTION

Because the PLC focuses on what's happening to a particular product or brand rather than the overall market, it yields a product-oriented rather than a market-oriented picture. Firms also need to visualize a *market's* evolutionary path as it is affected by new needs, competitors, technology, channels, and other developments and change product and brand positioning to keep pace.[92] Like products, markets evolve through four stages: emergence, growth, maturity, and decline. Consider the evolution of the paper towel market.

**PAPER TOWELS**   Homemakers originally used cotton and linen dishcloths and towels in their kitchens. Then a paper company looking for new markets developed paper towels, crystallizing a latent market that other manufacturers entered. The number of brands grew and created market fragmentation. Industry overcapacity led manufacturers to search for new features. One manufacturer, hearing consumers complain that paper towels were not absorbent, introduced "absorbent" towels and increased its market share. Competitors produced their own versions of absorbent paper towels, and the market fragmented again. One manufacturer introduced a "superstrength" towel that was soon copied. Another introduced a "lint-free" towel, subsequently copied. A later innovation was wipes containing a cleaning agent (like Clorox Disinfecting Wipes) that are often surface-specific (for wood, metal, or stone). Thus, driven by innovation and competition, paper towels evolved from a single product to one with various absorbencies, strengths, and applications.

# Marketing in a Slow-Growth Economy

Given economic cycles, there will always be tough times, such as the recession of 2008–2009 and the slow recovery that has followed. Despite reduced funding for marketing programs and intense pressure to justify them as cost effective, some marketers have survived—or even thrived—in tough economic times. Here are five guidelines for improving the odds for marketing success in a slow-growth economy.[93]

## EXPLORE THE UPSIDE OF INCREASING INVESTMENT

Forty years of evidence suggests those willing to invest during a recession have, on average, improved their fortunes more than those that cut back.[94] Marketers should consider the potential upside of increasing investment to exploit a marketplace advantage like an appealing new product, a weakened rival, or a neglected target market to develop. Here are two companies that did.

- General Mills increased marketing expenditures for the 2009 fiscal year by 16 percent, increased revenues by 8 percent to $14.7 billion, and increased operating profit by 4 percent. As CEO Ken Powell explained, "In an environment where you have consumers going to the grocery store more often and thinking more about meals at home, we think that is a great environment for brand building, to remind consumers about our products."[95]

- UK supermarket giant Sainsbury launched an advertising and point-of-sale campaign called "Feed Your Family for a Fiver" that played off its corporate slogan, "Try Something New Today," to encourage shoppers to try new recipes that would feed families for only £5 (or $9).

## GET CLOSER TO CUSTOMERS

Consumers with leveling incomes may change what they want and where and how they shop. A downturn or slow-growth period is an opportunity to learn even more about what consumers are thinking, feeling, and doing, especially the loyal base that yields so much profitability.[96]

Firms should characterize any changes as temporary rather than permanent shifts.[97] In explaining the need to look forward, Eaton CEO Alex Cutler noted, "It is a time when businesses shouldn't be assuming that the future will be like the past. And I mean that in virtually every dimension whether it is economic growth, value propositions, or the level of government regulation and involvement."[98]

A recent Booz & Company survey of 1,000 U.S. households found 43 percent were eating at home more and 25 percent were cutting spending on hobbies and sports activities; respondents said they would likely continue to do so.[99] Spending has shifted in many ways, and the potential value and profitability of some customers may change. As one retail analyst commented, "Moms who used to buy every member of the family their own brand of shampoo are buying one big cheap one."[100]

## REVIEW BUDGET ALLOCATIONS

Slowed growth provides an opportunity for marketers to review their spending, opening promising new options and eliminating sacred cows if they don't yield results. It can be a good time to experiment. In London, T-Mobile created spontaneous "happenings" to convey its brand positioning that "Life's for Sharing" and generate massive publicity. Its "Dance" video, featuring 400 dancers getting subway riders to dance, was viewed millions of times on YouTube.[101]

Firms as diverse as Century 21 realtors and Red Robin gourmet burgers have increased online marketing activities.[102] Dentists are turning to marketing, communicating with patients via e-mail newsletters, calling to set up appointments, and sending Twitter messages about new products or services.[103]

## PUT FORTH THE MOST COMPELLING VALUE PROPOSITION

Focusing heavily on price reductions and discounts can harm long-term brand equity and price integrity. Marketers should increase—and clearly communicate—their brands' value, conveying all the financial, logistical, and psychological benefits.[104] GE changed its ad messages for the $3,500 Profile washer-and-dryer set during the

In a slow growth economy, many dentists have embraced marketing to better connect with their patients.

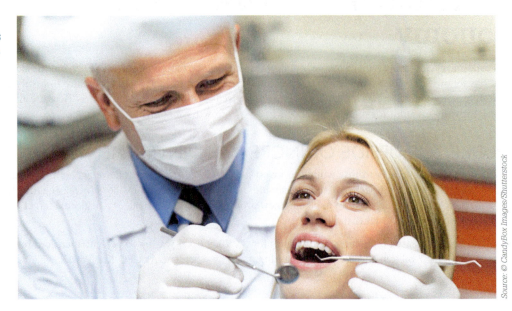

Source: © CandyBox Images/Shutterstock

downturn to emphasize its practicality—it optimizes the use of soap and water per load and is gentle on clothes, extending their life.[105]

Marketers should ensure pricing has not crept up unduly over time.[106] Procter & Gamble adopted a "surgical" approach during the recession, reducing prices in some categories while communicating about innovation and value to support premium prices in others. Ads for Bounty claimed it was more absorbent than a "bargain brand"; ads for Olay Professional Pro-X's Intensive Wrinkle Protocol called it as effective as prescription "at half the price."[107]

Discounting successful brands is not a good option because it tells the market two things: your prices were too high before, and your products won't be worth the price once the discounts are gone. Appealing to frugal customers with a new brand at lower prices avoids alienating those still willing to pay for higher-priced brands.

## FINE-TUNE BRAND AND PRODUCT OFFERINGS

Marketers can review product portfolios and brand architecture to confirm that brands and sub-brands are clearly differentiated, targeted, and supported based on their prospects. Luxury brands can benefit from lower-priced brands or sub-brands in their portfolios. Armani is an example.[108]

**ARMANI** Armani differentiates its product line into three tiers distinct in style, luxury, customization, and price. In the most expensive, Tier I, are Giorgio Armani and Giorgio Armani Privé, custom-made couture products selling for thousands of dollars. In Tier II are Emporio Armani—young, modern, more affordable styles—and Armani jeans. In lower-priced Tier III are youthful and street-savvy versions, A|X Armani Exchange, sold exclusively at 268 retail locations. Each extension lives up to the Armani brand's core promise without diluting the parent's image. But clear differentiation minimizes consumer confusion and brand cannibalization. During slow growth, the lower end picks up the slack and helps maintain profitability. In 2011, the Giorgio Armani line accounted for 32 percent of total sales, Emporio Armani for 27 percent, and Armani Exchange for 14 percent.

Brands and sub-brands targeting the lower end of the socioeconomic spectrum may be particularly important during slow growth. Value-driven companies like McDonald's, Walmart, Costco, Aldi, Dell, E*TRADE, Southwest Airlines, and IKEA may benefit most. Spam, the oft-maligned can of spiced ham and pork, found sales soaring during the recession.[109]

Slow times also are an opportunity to prune products with diminished prospects. In the post-9/11 recession, Procter & Gamble divested stagnant brands including Comet cleanser, Folgers coffee, Jif peanut butter, and Crisco oil and shortening to concentrate on higher-growth opportunities.

Armani's three price tiers within its product lines helps the company survive and prosper in good and bad times.

Source: © Michael Kemp/Alamy

# Summary

1. Growing the core or seeking organic growth—focusing on opportunities with existing products and markets—is often a prudent way to increase sales and profits.

2. A market leader has the largest market share in the relevant product market. To remain dominant, it looks to expand total demand and protect and perhaps increase its current share.

3. A market challenger attacks the market leader and other competitors in an aggressive bid for more market share. There are five types of general attack and specific attack strategies.

4. A market follower is a runner-up firm willing to maintain its market share and not rock the boat. It can be a cloner, imitator, or adapter.

5. A market nicher serves small market segments ignored by larger firms. The key is specialization, which can command a premium price in the process.

6. Companies should maintain a good balance of consumer and competitor monitoring and not overly focus on competitors.

7. Technologies, product forms, and brands exhibit life cycles with distinct stages, usually introduction, growth, maturity, and decline. Most products today are in the maturity stage.

8. The introduction stage is marked by slow growth and minimal profits. If successful, the product enters a growth stage marked by rapid sales growth and increasing profits. In the maturity stage, sales growth slows and profits stabilize. Finally, the product enters a decline stage. The company's task is to identify truly weak products and phase them out with minimal impact on company profits, employees, and customers.

9. Like products, markets evolve through stages: emergence, growth, maturity, and decline.

10. In a slow-growth economy, marketers must explore the upside of increasing investments, get closer to customers, review budget allocations, put forth the most compelling value proposition, and fine-tune brand and product offerings.

---

## MyMarketingLab

Go to mymktlab.com to complete the problems marked with this icon ✪ as well as for additional Auto-graded and Assisted-graded writing questions.

---

# Applications

## Marketing Debate
### Do Brands Have Finite Lives?

Often, after a brand begins to slip in the marketplace or disappears altogether, commentators observe, "All brands have their day," implying brands have a finite life and cannot be expected to be leaders forever. Other experts contend brands *can* live forever and that their long-term success depends on marketers' skill and insight.

**Take a position:** Brands cannot be expected to last forever *versus* There is no reason for a brand to ever become obsolete.

## Marketing Discussion:
### Industry Roles

✪ Pick an industry. Classify firms according to the four different roles they might play: leader, challenger, follower, and nicher. How would you characterize the nature of competition? Do the firms follow the principles described in this chapter?

## >> Samsung

Korean consumer electronics giant Samsung has made a remarkable transformation since its founding in 1938. Originally created as an exporter of dried Korean fish, vegetables, and fruit, the company evolved into a provider of value-priced commodity products during the 1970s and 1980s that original equipment manufacturers (OEMs) sold under their own brands. When Samsung's founder passed away in 1987, his son Kun-Hee Lee succeeded him and restructured the company with the goal of becoming one of the world's top electronic companies.

Samsung initially focused on volume and market domination rather than profitability. During the Asian financial crisis of the late 1990s, other Korean *chaebols* or conglomerates collapsed beneath a mountain of debt, but Samsung took a different approach. The company cut costs and refocused its vision on product quality, complete customer satisfaction, and manufacturing flexibility. This revolutionary strategy allowed its consumer electronic products to go from project phase to store shelves within six months. Samsung invested heavily in innovation, and many of its products—from semiconductors to LCD screens—gained significant market share and became industry leaders in their respective categories. The company also focused intently on its memory-chip business, which established an important cash cow and made it the largest chipmaker in the world.

Samsung continued to pour money into R&D during the 2000s, budgeting $40 billion for 2005–2010 alone. The company made innovation one of its highest priorities and emphasized its importance through extensive training and recruiting. As a result, it introduced a wide range of electronic products under its strong brand umbrella. Samsung also partnered with longtime market leader Sony to create a $2 billion state-of-the-art LCD factory in South Korea and signed a milestone agreement to share 24,000 basic patents for components and production processes.

Today, Samsung is a global marketer of premium-priced, Samsung-branded consumer electronics such as smart phones, flat-screen TVs, digital cameras, batteries, digital appliances, and semiconductors. The company's high-end smart phones and cell phones are now its growth engines, leading to a steady stream of innovations including the first cell phone with an MP3 player, the first Blu-ray disc player, and the first Smartwatch.

Samsung's success has been driven not only by successful product innovation, but also by aggressive brand building. The company has spent billions of dollars in marketing over the past decade, including sponsoring the Olympics since 1998 and running several global ad campaigns themed "Imagine," "Quietly Brilliant," and "Men Are Idiots," all of which included brand messages such as "technology," "design," and "human sensation." In 2005, Samsung surpassed Sony in the Interbrand ranking for the first time, and it continues to outperform Sony today.

Samsung faces competitors in several different industries, including Google and Apple. However, the company is unique because, unlike rival firms, it has become a global leader in making both the components for electronics products and the actual devices sold to consumers. It controls virtually everything in the smart phone supply chain, from the chips to the screen, while Apple has to outsource these products. As a result, Samsung can keep costs low, create many products for many needs, make design changes quickly, and introduce new products at an unusually fast pace. The company recently passed Apple as the number-one player in smart phones.

With record sales of $327 billion in 2013 and more than 275,000 employees worldwide, Samsung continues to work toward its goal of earning $400 billion in revenue by the year 2020.

### Questions

1. What are some of Samsung's greatest competitive strengths?

2. Samsung's goal of earning $400 billion in sales by 2020 would bring it to the same level as Walmart. Is this a feasible goal? Why or why not?

**Sources:** Moon Ihlwan, "Samsung Is Having a Sony Moment," *BusinessWeek*, July 30, 2007, p. 38; Martin Fackler, "Raising the Bar at Samsung," *New York Times*, April 25, 2006; "Brand New," *Economist*, January 15, 2005, pp. 10–11; Patricia O'Connell, "Samsung's Goal: Be Like BMW," *BusinessWeek*, August 1, 2005; Heidi Brown and Justin Doeble, "Samsung's Next Act," *Forbes*, July 26, 2004; John Quelch and Anna Harrington, "Samsung Electronics Company: Global Marketing Operations," *Harvard Business School*, January 16, 2008; Evan Ramstad, "Samsung's Swelling Size Brings New Challenges," *Wall Street Journal*, November 11, 2009; "Looking Good? LG v. Samsung," *Economist*, January 24, 2009; Haydn Shaughnessy, "What Makes Samsung Such an Innovative Company," *Forbes*, March 7, 2013; Zach Epstein, "Samsung Smashes Apple as Smartphone Explosion Continues in Q2," BGR.org, July 26, 2013; Darrell Etherington, "Samsung Goes First, Google Experiments and Apple Refines," Techcrunch.com, October 9, 2013; Chuck Jones, "Apple vs. Samsung: Who Could Win the Smartphone War?," *Forbes*, August 20, 2013; Ashraf Eassa, "Apple Has a Problem," *The Motley Fool*, September 27, 2013; Tim Worstall, "Why Samsung Beats Apple or Perhaps Vice Versa," *Forbes*, September 9, 2013; Samsung.com.

## Marketing Excellence

### >> IBM

International Business Machines Corporation (IBM) manufactures and sells computer hardware and software, offers infrastructure services, and provides global consulting services. The company's roots date back to the 1880s, but it officially became known as IBM in 1924, under the leadership of then-president Thomas J. Watson Sr.

IBM flourished during the 1930s and 1940s, growing primarily through sales of technologies developed for the military during World War I and World War II and of tabulating machines, which helped underpin the Social Security system in the 1930s. Watson Sr. led the company for four decades and helped establish some of its most successful business tactics, including exceptional customer service, a professional and knowledgeable sales force, and a focus on large-scale, custom-built solutions for businesses. Watson Sr. also created the company's first slogan, "THINK," which quickly became a corporate mantra.

Thomas J. Watson Jr. took over as CEO in 1952, and under his management IBM paved the way for innovations in computation. The company worked with the government during the Cold War and built the air-defense SAGE computer system for $30 million. In 1964, it launched a revolutionary family of computers called the System/360, which used interchangeable software and peripheral equipment. For the system to succeed, however, IBM had to cannibalize its own computer product lines and move its current systems to the new technology. Fortunately, the risk paid off, and IBM architecture became the industry standard. By the 1960s, the company was producing approximately 70 percent of all computers, beating out early competitors like General Electric, RCA, and Honeywell.

The 1980s were a pivotal time in IBM's history. In 1981, the firm launched the first personal computer, which offered 18KB of memory, floppy disk drives, and an optional color monitor. It also opened new channels of distribution through companies like Sears and ComputerLand. However, IBM's decision to outsource components of the PC to companies like Microsoft and Intel marked the end of the company's monopoly in computing. During the 1980s, its market share and profits eroded as the PC revolution changed the way consumers viewed and bought technology. IBM's sales dropped from $5 billion in the early 1980s to $3 billion by 1989. The dip continued into the early 1990s when the company felt pressure from Compaq and Dell and tried to split into smaller business units to compete. The results were disastrous, and IBM posted net losses of $16 billion between 1991 and 1993.

Things turned around when a new CEO, Louis Gerstner, refocused IBM in a new strategic direction. He reconnected the company's business units, shed its commodity products, and focused on high-margin businesses like consulting and middleware software. The company then introduced the iconic ThinkPad, which helped regain lost share. To rebuild its brand image, it consolidated marketing efforts from 70 advertising agencies to one and created a consistent, universal message. In 1997, IBM's chess-playing computer system, Deep Blue, also helped lift the company's brand image by defeating the world's reigning chess champion in a historic event that captured the attention of millions.

At the turn of the 21st century, IBM achieved new levels of success in the wake of the dot-com bust. The company moved further away from hardware by selling its ThinkPad division to Lenovo and exiting disk drives. In addition, it embraced global consulting and data analytics by acquiring close to 100 firms, including PricewaterhouseCoopers.

IBM's strategic focus on smart technologies is reflected in its ongoing campaign titled "Smarter Planet." The campaign highlights a few of the company's accomplishments to date and explores its ideas for the future. IBM is now focused on solving the world's most challenging high-tech problems, such as water management, traffic congestion, and collaborative health care. The company continuously changes its business mix in order to embrace profitable technologies and market opportunities. For example, 27 percent of its year 2000 income came from software, and in 2012, 45 percent. IBM believes that by 2015, 50 percent of its income will come from software.

Today, IBM is the largest and most profitable information technology company in the world, with almost $100 billion in sales and 431,000 employees worldwide. It employs scientists, engineers, consultants, and sales professionals in more than 170 countries and holds more patents than any other U.S.-based technology company.

From 2000 to 2012, IBM spent more than $75 billion on R&D, and approximately 30 percent of its annual R&D budget has funded long-term research to prepare for major changes in technologies, global economies, and businesses.

## Questions

1  Few companies have had such a long history of ups and downs as IBM. What were some of the keys to its successes? Can IBM's plans to solve some of the world's most challenging problems succeed? Why or why not?

2  Who are IBM's biggest competitors today, and what risks does IBM face with its current strategy?

**Sources:** Steve Lohr, "IBM Showing That Giants Can Be Nimble," *New York Times,* July 18, 2007; Jeffrey M. O'Brien, "IBM's Grand Plan to Save the Planet," *Fortune,* April 21, 2009; "IBM Archives," *IBM,* www.ibm.com; Louis V. Gerstner Jr., *Who Says Elephants Can't Dance? Inside IBM's Historic Turnaround* (New York: Harper Business, 2002); IBM 2012 Annual Report; www.ibm.com.

## Part 5  Creating Value

## In This Chapter, We Will Address the Following **Questions**

1. What are the characteristics of products, and how do marketers classify products? (p. 367)

2. How can companies differentiate products? (p. 370)

3. Why is product design important, and what are the different approaches taken? (p. 374)

4. How can marketers best manage luxury brands? (p. 376)

5. What environmental issues must marketers consider in their product strategies? (p. 378)

6. How can a company build and manage its product mix and product lines? (p. 379)

7. How can companies combine products to create strong co-brands or ingredient brands? (p. 387)

8. How can companies use packaging, labeling, warranties, and guarantees as marketing tools? (p. 390)

With its relentless focus on quality and strong dealer network, Lexus has become one of the top luxury automotive brands in the world.

*Source: Robert Duyos/MCT/Newscom*

MyMarketingLab™

⭐ Improve Your Grade!
Over 10 million students improved their results using the Pearson MyLabs. Visit mymktlab.com for simulations, tutorials, and end-of-chapter problems.

# **13** Setting Product Strategy

**At the heart of a great brand is a great product. To achieve market leadership, firms** must offer products and services of superior quality that provide unsurpassed customer value. Lexus has conquered the luxury car market in the United States and elsewhere, in part due to a relentless focus on product and service quality.[1]

 *Since its inception in 1989, Lexus has emphasized top-notch product quality and customer care, as reflected by its long-time slogan, "The Relentless Pursuit of Perfection." At one point, in response to customer complaints over minor problems with its LS 400, the company sent technicians to each owner's home to fix the vehicles for free. As part of its "Lexus Covenant," it has vowed to "have the finest dealer network in the industry, and treat each customer as we would a guest in our own home." To this end, Lexus built its dealership framework from the ground up, hand-picking dealers committed to its promise to provide an exceptional experience to customers, a system competitors acknowledge is the industry ideal. The company offers a full product line anchored by its flagship LS sedan, as well as its GS sports coupe, RX SUVs, and ES midsize car. It is consistently highly rated in the Luxury Institute's annual Luxury Consumer Experience surveys, bolstered by strong dealership experience. In addition, J. D. Power and Associates has ranked Lexus the "most dependable" automotive brand 16 times since 1995, and the company consistently ranks above the industry average in customer retention. With its average buyer in his or her mid-50s, Lexus has set its sights on attracting younger buyers by emphasizing more aggressive styling, handling dynamics, and driver engagement. A new marketing initiative uses television advertising to link the brand and the LS sedan to a lavish, cool lifestyle. Social media and other promotions and events also create novel customer experiences around food, fashion, entertainment, and travel.*

**Marketing planning begins with formulating** an offering to meet target customers' needs or wants. The customer will judge the offering on three basic elements: product features and quality, service mix and quality, and price (see Figure 13.1). In this chapter we examine product, in Chapter 14, services, in Chapter 15, new products and services, and in Chapter 16, price. All three elements—products, services, and pricing—must be meshed into a competitively attractive market offering.

# **Product Characteristics and Classifications**

Many people think a product is tangible, but technically a **product** is anything that can be offered to a market to satisfy a want or need, including physical goods, services, experiences, events, persons, places, properties, organizations, information, and ideas.

## PRODUCT LEVELS: THE CUSTOMER-VALUE HIERARCHY

In planning its market offering, the marketer needs to address five product levels (see Figure 13.2).[2] Each level adds more customer value, and together the five constitute a **customer-value hierarchy**.

Value-based prices

**Attractiveness of the market offering**

Product features and quality

Services mix and quality

| **Fig. 13.1** |

Components of the Market Offering

- The fundamental level is the **core benefit:** the service or benefit the customer is really buying. A hotel guest is buying rest and sleep. The purchaser of a drill is buying holes. Marketers must see themselves as benefit providers.
- At the second level, the marketer must turn the core benefit into a **basic product.** Thus a hotel room includes a bed, bathroom, towels, desk, dresser, and closet.
- At the third level, the marketer prepares an **expected product,** a set of attributes and conditions buyers normally expect when they purchase this product. Hotel guests minimally expect a clean bed, fresh towels, working lamps, and a relative degree of quiet.
- At the fourth level, the marketer prepares an **augmented product** that exceeds customer expectations. In developed countries, brand positioning and competition take place at this level. In developing and emerging markets such as India and Brazil, however, competition takes place mostly at the expected product level.
- At the fifth level stands the **potential product,** which encompasses all the possible augmentations and transformations the product or offering might undergo in the future. Here companies search for new ways to satisfy customers and distinguish their offering.

Differentiation arises and competition increasingly occurs on the basis of product augmentation. Each augmentation adds cost, however, and augmented benefits soon become expected benefits and necessary points-of-parity in the category. If today's hotel guests expect large-screen HD TVs, wireless Internet access, and a fully equipped fitness center, competitors must search for still other features and benefits to differentiate themselves.

As some companies raise the price of their augmented product, others offer a stripped-down version for less. Thus, alongside the growth of expensive luxury hotels such as Four Seasons and Ritz-Carlton, we see lower-cost discount hotels and motels emerge such as Motel 6 and Comfort Inn, catering to clients who want simply the basic product. Marketers must be sure, however, that consumers not see lower quality or limited capability versions as unfair.[3]

Great companies make great products and services, as evident by Lego.[4]

**LEGO** LEGO may have been one of the first mass-customized brands. Every child who has ever had a set of the Danish company's most basic blocks has built his or her own unique creations with it, brick by plastic brick. Although LEGO defines itself as being in the "business of play," parents like the idea of buying LEGO's products as a means of also enhancing their children's motor skills, creativity, and other cognitive capabilities. Some bricks and systems are exactly the same as 50 years ago, but the company is always developing new product offerings. Popular play sets tied in with the *Pirates of the Caribbean* and *Star Wars* film franchises also include video games. LEGO Design byME lets customers design, share, and build their own custom products by downloading free Digital Designer 3.0 software. The creations that result can exist—and be shared with other enthusiasts—solely online, or, if customers want to build them, the software tabulates the pieces required and sends an order to LEGO's Enfield, Connecticut, warehouse. Customers can request step-by-step building guide instructions and even design their own box to store the pieces. The success of *The LEGO Movie* in 2014 further underscored the widespread popularity of the brand.

Timeless toy manufacturer Lego constantly innovates so that its brand stays relevant with kids of all ages.

Source © Richard McDowell/Alamy

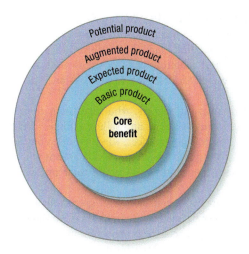

| Fig. 13.2 |

Five Product Levels

## PRODUCT CLASSIFICATIONS

Marketers classify products on the basis of durability, tangibility, and use (consumer or industrial). Each type has an appropriate marketing-mix strategy.[5]

**DURABILITY AND TANGIBILITY** Products fall into three groups according to durability and tangibility:

1. **Nondurable goods** are tangible goods normally consumed in one or a few uses, such as beer and shampoo. Because these goods are purchased frequently, the appropriate strategy is to make them available in many locations, charge only a small markup, and advertise heavily to induce trial and build preference.
2. **Durable goods** are tangible goods that normally survive many uses: refrigerators, machine tools, and clothing. They normally require more personal selling and service, command a higher margin, and require more seller guarantees.
3. **Services** are intangible, inseparable, variable, and perishable products that normally require more quality control, supplier credibility, and adaptability. Examples include haircuts, legal advice, and appliance repairs.

**CONSUMER-GOODS CLASSIFICATION** When we classify the vast array of consumer goods on the basis of shopping habits, we distinguish among convenience, shopping, specialty, and unsought goods.

The consumer usually purchases **convenience goods** frequently, immediately, and with minimal effort. Examples include soft drinks, soaps, and newspapers. *Staples* are convenience goods consumers purchase on a regular basis. A buyer might routinely purchase Heinz ketchup, Crest toothpaste, and Ritz crackers. *Impulse goods* are purchased without any planning or search effort, like candy bars and magazines. *Emergency goods* are purchased when a need is urgent—umbrellas during a rainstorm, boots and shovels during the first winter snow. Manufacturers of impulse and emergency goods will place them where consumers are likely to experience an urge or compelling need to purchase.

**Shopping goods** are those the consumer characteristically compares on such bases as suitability, quality, price, and style. Examples include furniture, clothing, and major appliances. *Homogeneous shopping goods* are similar in quality but different enough in price to justify shopping comparisons. *Heterogeneous shopping goods* differ in product features and services that may be more important than price. The seller of heterogeneous shopping goods carries a wide assortment to satisfy individual tastes and trains salespeople to inform and advise customers.

**Specialty goods** have unique characteristics or brand identification for which enough buyers are willing to make a special purchasing effort. Examples include cars, audio-video components, and men's suits. A Mercedes is a specialty good because interested buyers will travel far to buy one. Specialty goods don't require comparisons; buyers invest time only to reach dealers carrying the wanted products. Dealers don't need convenient locations, though they must let prospective buyers know where to find them.

**Unsought goods** are those the consumer does not know about or normally think of buying, such as smoke detectors. Other classic examples are life insurance, cemetery plots, and gravestones. Unsought goods require advertising and personal-selling support.

**INDUSTRIAL-GOODS CLASSIFICATION** We classify industrial goods in terms of their relative cost and the way they enter the production process: materials and parts, capital items, and supplies and business services. **Materials and parts** are goods that enter the manufacturer's product completely. They fall into two classes: raw materials and manufactured materials and parts. *Raw materials* in turn fall into two major groups: *farm products* (wheat, cotton, livestock, fruits, and vegetables) and *natural products* (fish, lumber, crude petroleum, iron ore).

Farm products are supplied by many producers, who turn them over to marketing intermediaries, who provide assembly, grading, storage, transportation, and selling services. The perishable and seasonal nature of farm products gives rise to special marketing practices, whereas their commodity character results in relatively little advertising and promotional activity. At times, commodity groups will launch campaigns to promote their product—potatoes, cheese, and beef. Some producers brand their products—Dole salads, Mott's apples, and Chiquita bananas.

Natural products are limited in supply. They usually have great bulk and low unit value and must be moved from producer to user. Fewer and larger producers often market them directly to industrial users. Because users depend on these materials, long-term supply contracts are common. The homogeneity of natural materials limits the amount of demand-creation activity. Price and reliable delivery are the major factors influencing the selection of suppliers.

*Manufactured materials and parts* fall into two categories: component materials (iron, yarn, cement, wires) and component parts (small motors, tires, castings). *Component materials* are usually fabricated further—pig iron is made into steel, and yarn is woven into cloth. The standardized nature of component materials usually makes price and supplier reliability key purchase factors. *Component parts* enter the finished product with no further change in form, as when small motors are put into vacuum cleaners and tires are put on automobiles. Most manufactured materials and parts are sold directly to industrial users. Price and service are major marketing considerations, with branding and advertising less important.

**Capital items** are long-lasting goods that facilitate developing or managing the finished product. They fall into two groups: installations and equipment. *Installations* consist of buildings (factories, offices) and heavy equipment (generators, drill presses, mainframe computers, elevators). Installations are major purchases. They are usually bought directly from the producer, whose sales force includes technical staff, and a long negotiation precedes the typical sale. Producers must be willing to design to specification and to supply postsale services. Advertising is much less important than personal selling.

*Equipment* includes portable factory equipment and tools (hand tools, lift trucks) and office equipment (desktop computers, desks). These types of equipment don't become part of a finished product. They have a shorter life than installations but a longer life than operating supplies. Although some equipment manufacturers sell direct, more often they use intermediaries because the market is geographically dispersed, buyers are numerous, and orders are small. Quality, features, price, and service are major considerations. The sales force tends to be more important than advertising, though advertising can be used effectively.

**Supplies and business services** are short-term goods and services that facilitate developing or managing the finished product. Supplies are of two kinds: *maintenance and repair items* (paint, nails, brooms) and *operating supplies* (lubricants, coal, writing paper, pencils). Together, they go under the name of MRO goods. Supplies are the equivalent of convenience goods; they are usually purchased with minimum effort on a straight-rebuy basis. They are normally marketed through intermediaries because of their low unit value and the great number and geographic dispersion of customers. Price and service are important considerations because suppliers are standardized and brand preference is often not high.

Business services include *maintenance and repair services* (window cleaning, copier repair) and *business advisory services* (legal, management consulting, advertising). Maintenance and repair services are usually supplied under contract by small producers or from the manufacturers of the original equipment. Business advisory services are usually purchased on the basis of the supplier's reputation and staff.

# Differentiation

To be branded, products must be differentiated. At one extreme are products that allow little variation: chicken, aspirin, and steel. Yet even here some differentiation is possible: Perdue chickens, Bayer aspirin, and India's Tata Steel have carved out distinct identities in their categories. Procter & Gamble makes Tide, Cheer, and Gain laundry detergents, each with a separate brand identity. At the other extreme are products capable of high differentiation, such as automobiles, commercial buildings, and furniture. Here the seller faces an abundance of differentiation possibilities.

As Chapter 10 described, well-differentiated products can create significant competitive advantages. Intuitive Surgical sells million-dollar robotic systems for operating rooms. Watching a high-definition video feed from a camera inside the patient, surgeons use a joystick, pedals, and a robotic arm with tiny scalpels and needles to perform minimally invasive cardiac and urological procedures. One analyst said of Intuitive Surgical in 2010, "In our view, they've got a decade's worth of technological lead."[6]

Means for differentiation include form, features, performance quality, conformance quality, durability, reliability, repairability, and style.[7] Design has become an increasingly important differentiator, and we discuss it separately later in the chapter.

# PRODUCT DIFFERENTIATION

FORM Many products can be differentiated in **form**—the size, shape, or physical structure of a product. Consider the many possible forms of aspirin. Although essentially a commodity, it can be differentiated by dosage, size, shape, color, coating, or action time.

FEATURES Most products can be offered with varying **features** that supplement their basic function. A company can identify and select appropriate new features by surveying recent buyers and then calculating *customer value* versus *company cost* for each potential feature. Marketers should consider how many people want each feature, how long it would take to introduce it, and whether competitors could easily copy it.[8]

To avoid "feature fatigue," the company must prioritize features and tell consumers how to use and benefit from them.[9] Marketers must also think in terms of feature bundles or packages. Auto companies often manufacture cars at several "trim levels." This lowers manufacturing and inventory costs. Each company must decide whether to offer feature customization at a higher cost or a few standard packages at a lower cost.

PERFORMANCE QUALITY Most products occupy one of four performance levels: low, average, high, or superior. **Performance quality** is the level at which the product's primary characteristics operate. Quality is growing increasingly important for differentiation as companies adopt a value model and provide higher quality for less money. Firms should design a performance level appropriate to the target market and competition, however, not necessarily the highest level possible. They must also manage performance quality through time. Continuously improving the product can produce high returns and market share; failing to do so can have negative consequences.

**MERCEDES-BENZ** From 2003 to 2006, Mercedes-Benz endured one of the most painful stretches in its 127-year history. The company saw its reputation for stellar quality take a beating in J. D. Power and other surveys, and BMW surpassed it in global sales. To recoup, a new management team reorganized around functional elements—motors, chassis, and electronic systems—instead of model lines. Engineers now begin testing electronic systems a year earlier and put each new model through 10,000 diagnostics that run 24 hours a day for three weeks. Mercedes-Benz also tripled its number of prototypes for new designs, allowing engineers to drive them 3 million miles before production. With these and other changes, the number of flaws in the company's cars dropped 72 percent from their 2002 peak, and warranty costs decreased 25 percent. As an interesting side effect, Mercedes-Benz dealers have had to contend with a sizable drop in their repair and service businesses! The challenge now is to match the impressive levels of quality and reliability set by Japanese luxury foes.[10]

CONFORMANCE QUALITY Buyers expect a high **conformance quality,** the degree to which all produced units are identical and meet promised specifications. Suppose a Porsche 911 is designed to accelerate to 60 miles per hour within 10 seconds. If every Porsche 911 coming off the assembly line does this, the model is said to have high conformance quality. A product with low conformance quality will disappoint some buyers. Firms thoroughly test finished products to ensure conformance. Although men account for almost three-quarters of the world's beer sales, SABMiller found that women were actually more sensitive to levels of flavor in beer and thus were better product testers.[11]

DURABILITY **Durability,** a measure of the product's expected operating life under natural or stressful conditions, is a valued attribute for vehicles, kitchen appliances, and other durable goods. The extra price for

After experiencing some declines in product quality, Mercedes-Benz changed how it made and tested its cars, with positive results.

*Source: TRIPPLAAR KRISTOFFER/SIPA/Newscom*

durability must not be excessive, however, and the product must not be subject to rapid technological obsolescence, as personal computers, televisions, and cell phones have sometimes been.

**RELIABILITY** Buyers normally will pay a premium for more reliable products. **Reliability** is a measure of the probability that a product will not malfunction or fail within a specified time period. Maytag has an outstanding reputation for creating reliable home appliances. Its long-running "Lonely Repairman" ad campaign was designed to highlight that attribute.

**REPAIRABILITY** **Repairability** measures the ease of fixing a product when it malfunctions or fails. Ideal repairability would exist if users could fix the product themselves with little cost in money or time. Some products include a diagnostic feature that allows service people to correct a problem over the telephone or advise the user how to correct it. Many computer hardware and software companies offer technical support over the phone, by fax or e-mail, or via real-time chat online.

**STYLE** **Style** describes the product's look and feel to the buyer and creates distinctiveness that is hard to copy. Car buyers pay a premium for Jaguars because of their extraordinary looks. Aesthetics play a key role for such brands as Apple computers, Godiva chocolate, and Harley-Davidson motorcycles.[12] Strong style does not always mean high performance, however. A car may look sensational but spend a lot of time in the repair shop.

**CUSTOMIZATION** As Chapter 9 described, customized products and marketing allow firms to be highly relevant and differentiating by finding out exactly what a person wants—and doesn't want—and delivering on that. Online retailers such as Zazzle and CafePress allow users to upload images and create their own clothing and posters or buy merchandise created by other users. NikeiD, which allows customers to personalize and design their own shoes and clothing either online or in store at NikeiD Studios, now generates hundreds of millions of dollars in revenue.[13]

The demand for customization is certainly there. One Forrester study found that more than one-third of U.S. online consumers were interested in customizing product features or in purchasing build-to-order products that use their specifications. And companies have responded: M&M's allows you to print specialized messages on your candies; Pottery Barn Kids allows you to personalize a children's book; and for $2,000 or so, Burberry allows you to select the fabric, color, style, and five other features for your own personalized trench coat.[14]

## SERVICES DIFFERENTIATION

When the physical product cannot easily be differentiated, the key to competitive success may lie in adding valued services and improving their quality. Rolls-Royce PLC has ensured its aircraft engines are in high demand by continuously monitoring their health for 1,300 airplane engines around the world through live satellite feeds Under its TotalCare and CorporateCare programs, airlines pay Rolls a fee for every hour an engine is in flight and Rolls assumes the risks and costs of downtime and repairs.[15]

The main service differentiators are ordering ease, delivery, installation, customer training, customer consulting, maintenance and repair, and returns.

**ORDERING EASE** **Ordering ease** describes how easy it is for the customer to place an order with the company. Baxter Healthcare supplies hospitals with computer terminals through which they send orders directly to the firm. Many financial service institutions offer secure online sites to help customers get information and complete transactions more efficiently.

**DELIVERY** **Delivery** refers to how well the product or service is brought to the customer, including speed, accuracy, and care throughout the process. Today's customers have grown to expect speed: pizza delivered in half an hour, eyeglasses made in 60 minutes, cars lubricated in 15 minutes. Many firms have computerized *quick response systems* (QRS) that link the information systems of their suppliers, manufacturing plants, distribution centers, and retailing outlets to improve delivery.

Cemex, a giant cement company based in Mexico, has transformed its business by promising to deliver concrete faster than pizza, equipping every truck with a global positioning system (GPS) so dispatchers know its real-time location. Its 24/7 LOAD service program guarantees delivery within a 20-minute window, providing important flexibility in an industry where delays are costly but common.[16]

**INSTALLATION** **Installation** refers to the work done to make a product operational in its planned location. Ease of installation is a true selling point for technology novices and for buyers of complex products like heavy equipment.

**CUSTOMER TRAINING** **Customer training** helps the customer's employees use the vendor's equipment properly and efficiently. General Electric not only sells and installs expensive X-ray equipment in hospitals, it also gives users extensive training. McDonald's requires its new franchisees to attend Hamburger University in Oak Brook, Illinois, for two weeks to learn how to manage the franchise properly.

**CUSTOMER CONSULTING** **Customer consulting** includes data, information systems, and advice services the seller offers to buyers. Technology firms such as IBM, Oracle, and others have learned that such consulting is an increasingly essential—and profitable—part of their business.

**MAINTENANCE AND REPAIR** **Maintenance and repair** programs help customers keep purchased products in good working order. These services are critical in business-to-business settings. Goodyear's TVTrack program helps its fleet customers monitor and manage tires more effectively.[17] Many firms offer online technical support, or "e-support," for customers, who can search an online database for fixes or seek online help from a technician. Appliance makers such as LG, Kenmore, and Miele have introduced products that can transmit self-diagnostic data over the phone to a customer service number that electronically describes the nature of any technical problems.[18]

Makers of luxury products especially recognize the importance of a smooth repair process. Although Movado watches are high-end, its repair process had been anything but, requiring time-consuming manual labor and customer inconvenience. Recognizing the need to offer more digital services in general, Movado created a Web site where customers can buy products directly from the company as well as execute many of the initial steps in the repair process online, such as registering any problems and identifying possible repair options before contacting customer service directly. The database created by users of the site has also allowed the company to recruit potential focus group participants and identify repair trends that may suggest recurring production problems.[19]

**RETURNS** A nuisance to customers, manufacturers, retailers, and distributors alike, product returns are also an unavoidable reality of doing business, especially in online purchases. Free shipping, growing more popular, makes it easier for customers to try out an item, but it also increases the likelihood of returns.

Returns can add up. One estimate is that 10 percent to 15 percent of overall holiday sales come back as returns or exchanges, and the total annual cost may be $100 billion.[20] To the consumer, returns can be inconvenient, embarrassing, or difficult to complete. Returns have a downside for merchants too, when the returned merchandise is not in re-sellable condition, lacks proper proof of purchase, or is returned to the wrong store. It may even be used or stolen. Yet if the merchant is reluctant to accept returns, customers can become annoyed.[21]

Of course, product returns do have an upside. Physically returning a product can get the consumer into the store, maybe for the first time. One research study found that a lenient return policy left customers more willing to make other purchases and refer the company to others.[22]

We can think of product returns in two ways:[23]

- *Controllable returns* result from problems or errors made by the seller or customer and can mostly be eliminated with improved handling or storage, better packaging, and improved transportation and forward logistics by the seller or its supply chain partners.
- *Uncontrollable returns* result from the need for customers to actually see, try, or experience products in person to determine suitability and can't be eliminated by the company in the short run.

One basic strategy is to eliminate the root causes of controllable returns while developing processes for handling uncontrollable returns. The goal is to have fewer products returned and put a higher percentage back into the distribution pipeline to be sold again. San Diego-based Road Runner Sports, which sells running shoes, clothing, and equipment through multiple stores, catalogs, and a Web site, trains its salespeople to be as knowledgeable as possible in order to recommend the right products. As a result, its return rate on running shoes has been 12 percent, noticeably below the industry average of 15 percent to 20 percent. [24]

# Design

As competition intensifies, design offers a potent way to differentiate and position a company's products and services. **Design** is the totality of features that affect the way a product looks, feels, and functions to a consumer. It offers functional and aesthetic benefits and appeals to both our rational and emotional sides.[25]

Herman Miller has brought form and function to office furniture with their stylish, well-designed products.

## DESIGN LEADERS

As holistic marketers recognize the emotional power of design and the importance to consumers of look and feel as well as function, design is exerting a stronger influence in categories where it once played a small role. Herman Miller office furniture, Viking ranges and kitchen appliances, and Kohler kitchen and bathroom fixtures and faucets are among the brands that now stand out in their categories thanks to attractive looks added to efficient and effective performance.[26]

Some countries have developed strong reputations for their design skills and accomplishments, such as Italy in apparel and furniture and Scandinavia in products designed for functionality, aesthetics, and environmental consciousness. Finland's Nokia was the first to introduce user-changeable covers for cell phones, the first to have elliptical-shaped, soft, and friendly forms, and the first with big screens, all contributing to its remarkable ascent. When it later failed to innovate its smart-phone designs, its fortunes dramatically declined. Braun, a German division of Gillette, has elevated design to a high art in its electric shavers, coffeemakers, hair dryers, and food processors.

The International Design and Excellence Awards (IDEA) are given each year based on benefit to the user, benefit to the client/business, benefit to society, ecological responsibility, appropriate aesthetics and appeal, and usability testing. IDEO has been one of the more successful design companies through the years. Then in 2013 Samsung Electronics won 10 awards, 3M four, and Coway, Lenovo, LG Electronics, Nokia, and PearsonLloyd three each.[27] Samsung's design accomplishments have been a result of a concerted effort.[28]

**SAMSUNG** Much of Samsung's remarkable marketing success comes from innovative new products that have captured the imagination of consumers all over the world. The company has invested heavily in R&D and in design capabilities, with big payoffs. It has a clear design philosophy it calls "Design 3.0," and an internal design slogan, "Make it Meaningful," that reflects its relentless focus on making beautiful and intuitive products that will be integrated into customers' lifestyles. Samsung applies three design criteria: (1) simple and intuitive, (2) efficient and long-lasting, and (3) adaptive and engaging. Like its chief rival Apple, the company organizes its design efforts through a cross-divisional Corporate Design Center that reports directly to the CEO. The Corporate Design Center aligns the design efforts of various divisions and analyzes cultural trends to help forecast the future of design. It also coordinates the work done at Samsung's five Global Design Centers, located in London, San Francisco, Shanghai, Tokyo, and Delhi. Among the many awards the company has received for design were two IF Gold Awards in 2013—from one of the world's top three design contests— for its "split concept" color printer and its twin-tub washing machine especially designed for Southeast Asia users.

## POWER OF DESIGN

In a visually oriented culture, transmitting brand meaning and positioning through design is critical. "In a crowded marketplace," writes Virginia Postrel in *The Substance of Style,* "aesthetics is often the only way to make a product stand out."[29]

Design is especially important with long-lasting durable goods such as automobiles. As GM's VP of Design Ed Welburn notes, "…every car has its own mood, whether it's a van for India or a Cadillac for China, and needs to connect with customers at an emotional level." The GM design team for the 2011 plug-in electric Chevy Volt wanted to make sure the car looked better than other electric cars. As the Volt design director said, "Most electric cars are like automotive Brussels sprouts. They're good for you, but you don't want to eat them."[30]

Design can shift consumer perceptions to make brand experiences more rewarding. Consider the lengths Boeing went to in making its 777 airplane seem roomier and more comfortable. Raised center bins, side luggage bins, divider panels, gently arched ceilings, and raised seats make the aircraft interior seem bigger. One design engineer noted, "If we do our jobs, people don't realize what we have done. They just say they feel more comfortable."

## APPROACHES TO DESIGN

"Design is more than just creativity, or a phase in creating a product, service, or application. It's a way of thinking that can transform an entire enterprise."[31] Design should penetrate all aspects of the marketing program so all design aspects work together. To the company, a well-designed product is easy to manufacture and distribute. To the customer, it is pleasant to look at and easy to open, install, use, repair, and dispose of. The designer must take all these goals into account.[32]

Given the creative nature of design, it's no surprise there isn't one widely adopted approach. Some firms employ formal, structured processes. *Design thinking* is a very data-driven approach with three phases: observation, ideation, and implementation. Design thinking requires intensive ethnographic studies of consumers, creative brainstorming sessions, and collaborative teamwork to decide how to bring the design idea to reality. Whirlpool used design thinking to develop the KitchenAid Architect Series II kitchen appliances with a more harmonized look than had existed in the category.[33] Not everyone employs design thinking, however.[34]

**BANG & OLUFSEN** The Danish firm Bang & Olufsen (B&O)—which has received many kudos for the design of its stereos, TV equipment, and telephones—trusts the instincts of a handful of designers who rarely consult with consumers. The company does not introduce many new products in any given year, so each one is expected to be sold for a long time. Its BeoLab 8000 speakers sold for $3,000 a pair when introduced in 1992 and retailed for more than $5,000 almost 20 years later. When the company was the subject of a special exhibition at the Museum of Modern Art in New York City, the museum noted, "Bang & Olufsen design their sound equipment as beautiful objects in their own right that do not inordinately call attention to themselves." Today, 15 B&O products are part of MOMA's permanent design collection.

# Luxury Products

Design is often an important aspect of luxury products, though these products also face some unique issues. They are perhaps one of the purest examples of the role of branding because the brand and its image are often key competitive advantages that create enormous value and wealth. Marketers for luxury brands such as Prada, Gucci, Cartier, and Louis Vuitton manage lucrative franchises that have endured for decades in what some believe is now a $270 billion industry.[35]

## CHARACTERIZING LUXURY BRANDS

Significantly higher priced than typical items in their categories, luxury brands for years were about social status and who a customer was—or perhaps wanted to be. Times have changed, and especially in the aftermath of a crippling recession, luxury for many has become more about style and substance, combining personal pleasure and self-expression.[36]

A luxury shopper must feel he or she is getting something truly special. Thus the common denominators of luxury brands are quality and uniqueness. A winning formula for many is craftsmanship, heritage, authenticity, and history, often critical to justifying a sometimes extravagant price. Hermès, the French luxury leather-goods maker, sells its classic designs for hundreds or even thousands of dollars, "not because they are in fashion," as one writer put it, "but [because] they never go out of fashion."[37] Here is how several luxury brands have become enduring market successes:

- *Sub-Zero refrigerators.* Sub-Zero sells refrigerators that range from $1,600 for small, under-counter models to $12,000 for a specialty Pro 48 with a stainless steel interior. The target is customers with high standards of performance and design who cherish their home and what they buy to furnish it. Sub-Zero extensively surveys this group as well as the kitchen designers, architects, and retailers who recommend and sell its products.[38]
- *Patrón tequila.* Cofounded by Paul Mitchell hair care founder John Paul DeJoria, Patrón came about after a 1989 trip to a distillery in the small Mexican state of Jalisco. Named Patrón to convey "the boss, the cool guy," the smooth agave tequila comes in an elegant hand-blown decanter and is sold in individually numbered bottles for $45 or more. Essentially creating the high-end tequila market, with more than $1.1 billion in retail sales, Patrón has surpassed Jose Cuervo to become the world's largest tequila brand.[39]
- *Montblanc luxury goods.* The goal of Montblanc, whose products now range from pens to watches to leather goods and fragrances, is to be a strong luxury brand to as many classes of luxury customers as possible, while still retaining a prominent public image. The brand promise is that "the product you buy is of highest esteem, based on its timeliness, elegant design and the high quality, which is derived from the excellence of our craftsmen." The company branched out from its origins in writing instruments into categories such as leather goods and timepieces, where it could "rely on the trust of our customers, who believed in Montblanc as a brand that provides excellence in its core category writing instruments based on its philosophy of manufacturing competence, highest quality, sustainable value and creativity."[40]

With its unique product formulation and bottle, Patron pioneered the high end tequila market.

Source: ©David Pruter/Shutterstock

## GROWING LUXURY BRANDS

The recent recession challenged many luxury brands as they tried to justify their value proposition and avoid discounting their products.[41] Those that had already successfully extended their brands vertically across a range of price points were usually the most immune to economic downturns.

The Armani brand has extended from high-end Giorgio Armani and Giorgio Armani Privé to mid-range luxury with Emporio Armani to affordable luxury with Armani Jeans and Armani Exchange. Clear differentiation exists between these brands, minimizing the potential for consumer confusion and brand cannibalization. Each also lives up to the core promise of the parent brand, reducing chances of hurting the parent's image.

Horizontal extensions into new categories can also be tricky for luxury brands. Even the most loyal consumer might question a $7,300 Ferragamo watch or an $85 bottle of Roberto Cavalli vodka. Jewelry maker Bulgari has moved into hotels, fragrances, chocolate, and skin care, prompting some branding experts to deem the brand overstretched.[42] In the past, iconic fashion designers Pierre Cardin and Halston licensed their names to so many ordinary products that the brands were badly tarnished.

Ralph Lauren, however, has successfully marketed an aspirational luxury brand with wholesome all-American lifestyle imagery across a wide range of products. Besides clothing and fragrances, Lauren boutiques sell linens, candles, beds, couches, dishware, photo albums, and jewelry. Calvin Klein has adopted a similarly successful expansive strategy, though with different lifestyle imagery.

Much of the growth in luxury brands in recent years has been geographical. China has overtaken the United States as the world's largest luxury market; it's forecast that one-third of all high-end goods will be sold there in the coming years. Although initially very "logo-driven" and interested in conspicuous brand signals, Chinese luxury consumers have also become more quality and design conscious, like luxury consumers in other parts of the world.[43]

## MARKETING LUXURY BRANDS

Luxury marketers have learned that luxury is not viewed the same way around the world. In post-communist Russia for a time, as in China, the bigger and gaudier the logo, the better. But in the end, luxury brand marketers have to remember they are often selling a dream, anchored in product quality, status, and prestige.

Just like marketers in less expensive categories, those guiding the fortunes of luxury brands operate in a constantly evolving marketing environment. Globalization, new technologies, financial crises, shifting consumer cultures, and other forces require them to be skillful and adept at their brand stewardship to succeed. Table 13.1 summarizes some key guidelines in marketing luxury brands.

One trend for luxury brands is to wrap personal experiences around the products. Top-end fashion retailers are offering such experiences alongside their wares, expecting that customers who have visited a workshop or met the designer will feel closer to the brand. Gucci is inviting its biggest spenders to fashion shows, equestrian events, and the Cannes Film Festival.[44]

Porsche Sport Driving Schools and Experience Centers in Germany, the United States, and other parts of the world allow Porsche drivers to "train their driving skills and enjoy the all-out pleasure of driving, on-road, off-road, or on snow and ice." The recently opened state-of-the-art facility in Southern California features 45-degree off-road inclines and a simulated ice hill.[45]

| TABLE 13.1 | Guidelines for Marketing Luxury Brands |
| --- | --- |

1. Maintaining a premium image for luxury brands is crucial; controlling that image is thus a priority.
2. Luxury branding typically includes the creation of many intangible brand associations and an aspirational image.
3. All aspects of the marketing program for luxury brands must be aligned to ensure high-quality products and services and pleasurable purchase and consumption experiences.
4. Besides brand names, other brand elements—logos, symbols, packaging, signage—can be important drivers of brand equity for luxury products.
5. Secondary associations from linked personalities, events, countries, and other entities can boost luxury-brand equity as well.
6. Luxury brands must carefully control distribution via a selective channel strategy.
7. Luxury brands must employ a premium pricing strategy, with strong quality cues and few discounts and markdowns.
8. Brand architecture for luxury brands must be managed carefully.
9. Competition for luxury brands must be defined broadly because it often comes from other categories.
10. Luxury brands must legally protect all trademarks and aggressively combat counterfeits.

**Source:** Based on Kevin Lane Keller, "Managing the Growth Tradeoff: Challenges and Opportunities in Luxury Branding," *Journal of Brand Management* 16 (March–May 2009), pp. 290–301.

Porsche has created driving tracks and schools so its owners can learn and experience more about their vehicles.

Source: © Caro/Alamy

In an increasingly wired world, some luxury marketers have struggled to find the appropriate online selling and communication strategies for their brand.[46] Some fashion brands have begun to go beyond glossy magazine spreads to listening to and communicating with consumers through Facebook, Twitter, Foursquare, and other digital and social media channels. Coach and Tiffany are two luxury brands praised for their Web site and digital operations. E-commerce has also begun to take hold for some luxury brands. Sites such as Gilt Groupe and Ideel now offer new ways for fashion brands to move high-end goods.[47]

Ultimately, luxury marketers are learning that, as for all marketers, success depends on getting the right balance of classic and contemporary imagery and continuity and change in marketing programs and activities.

# Environmental Issues

Environmental issues are also playing an increasingly important role in product design and manufacturing. Many firms are considering ways to reduce the negative environmental consequences of conducting business, and some are changing the manufacture of their products or the ingredients that go into them. "Marketing Memo: A Sip or a Gulp: Environmental Concerns in the Water Industry" considers some of the environmental issues raised by the sale of bottled water.

In a fascinating twist, Levi-Strauss found a highly creative way to address the problem of proliferating plastic bottles.[48]

▌LEVI'S WASTE<LESS    If someone said your jeans were "made of garbage," you might be insulted, but not if they were made by Levi-Strauss. Levi's new "Waste<Less" jeans and jackets carry a clothing tag that says exactly that—because they are! Twenty percent of the material in the denim comes from plastic bottles and black food trays recycled from municipal sites, including about eight 12- to 20-ounce bottles per pair. Much research and development went into creating the Waste<Less line, for which the plastic is cleaned, sorted, shredded into flakes, and made into a polyester fiber that's then blended with cotton. The resulting fabric looks and feels like traditional denim except for the color of the underside, which varies according to the hue of the plastic. The jeans retail for $69 to $128. Levi's is not a newcomer to the market for environmentally friendly products; sustainability is a company-wide priority. "Water<Less" jeans helped farmers grow cotton with less water, let Levi's manufacture with less water, and educated consumers about cleaning and disposing of the garments with less water. Both lines have made a tangible difference: The Water<Less line saved more than 360 million liters of water in its first full year, while the Waste<Less line recycled 3.5 million bottles and trays in its first full year.

## A Sip or A Gulp: Environmental Concerns in the Water Industry

The huge popularity of bottled water has been a boon to many companies, but at a high cost to the environment. One estimate put the amount of plastic used in disposable bottles at 2.7 million tons a year, which requires about 47 million gallons of oil to manufacture. Unfortunately, fewer than 20 percent of these bottles are believed to be recycled in the United States. These high environmental costs have a number of implications for marketers.

Colleges all over the country—from Western Washington University to Brown University, the University of Vermont, and the University of California at Berkeley—have banned the sale of plain bottled water, typically as part of a student-led movement toward greater sustainability on campus. The College of Saint Benedict in Minnesota equipped 31 fountains with an extra spigot to make them "hydration stations," a practice adopted by many other schools that banned bottled water. Nor are schools alone. Many public institutions from zoos to national parks are similarly installing water filling stations and banning the sale of bottled water.

As more consumers seek to reduce their personal environmental foot-print, sales of reusable water bottles have exploded. Sigg Switzerland sells cleverly designed lightweight aluminum water bottles for $25 to $30, choosing 100 new products from among 3,000 different designs each year. Features popular in other brands include caps with built-in micro-filtration systems.

Glass bottles promote their environmental advantages over plastic and re-assure consumers who fear chemicals can leak into foods and beverages from plastic. They now account for an increasingly large percentage of water bottle sales. Glass is also being developed for greater safety if broken; for instance, PURE glass bottles uses clear protective Safe-Shell coating.

Soft drink makers face similar pressures from environmentally aware con-sumers. Soda Stream sells equipment that allows people to carbonate and fla-vor plain tap water using reusable glass bottles. The company promotes three key benefits: Using tap water is cheaper, it can be slightly healthier, and there is no waste. Coca-Cola reports reclaiming more than one-third of its bottles and cans in North America, diverting 250 million pounds of waste from landfills each year. When PepsiCo launched Eco-Fina packaging for its Aquafina water brand, which uses 50 percent less plastic, it estimated it would save more than 75 million pounds of plastic annually.

Perhaps the most important lesson here is that environmental concerns matter to consumers, and they expect companies to make changes to address their concerns. Second, competition will emerge in all forms as companies try to find ways to better suit consumers' unmet needs, even for a sip of water.

*Source: SIGG Switzerland AG. Creators of "The Original Bottle" made in Switzerland.*

Emphasizing product design and variety, Swiss made Sigg has caught on as sales of reusable water bottles exploded.

**Sources:** Caleb Melby, "SodaStream's Moneymaking Battle Cry: Get Rid of Plastic Bottles," *Forbes*, July 19, 2012; Stephanie Strom, "Wary of Plastic, and Waste, Some Consumers Turn to Glass," *New York Times*, June 20, 2012; Kirsti Marohn, "Colleges Moving Away from Plastic Water Bottles," *USA Today*, September 15, 2011; Lindsay Armstrong, "The Best Reusable Water Bottles," *Huffington Post*, May 25, 2011; Helen Coster, "The $25 Water Bottle," *Fortune*, March 19, 2009; "PepsiCo's Aquafina Launches the Eco-Fina Bottle, the Lightest Weight Bottle in the Market," www.pepsico.com, March 25, 2009.

# Product and Brand Relationships

Each product can be related to other products to ensure that a firm is offering and marketing the optimal set of products.

# THE PRODUCT HIERARCHY

The product hierarchy stretches from basic needs to particular items that satisfy those needs. We can identify six levels of the product hierarchy, using life insurance as an example:

1. *Need family*—The core need that underlies the existence of a product family. Example: security.
2. *Product family*—All the product classes that can satisfy a core need with reasonable effectiveness. Example: savings and income.
3. *Product class*—A group of products within the product family recognized as having a certain functional coherence, also known as a product category. Example: financial instruments.
4. *Product line*—A group of products within a product class that are closely related because they perform a similar function, are sold to the same customer groups, are marketed through the same outlets or channels, or fall within given price ranges. A product line may consist of different brands, a single family brand, or an individual brand that has been line extended. Example: life insurance.
5. *Product type*—A group of items within a product line that share one of several possible forms of the product. Example: term life insurance.
6. *Item* (also called *stock-keeping unit* or *product variant*)—A distinct unit within a brand or product line distinguishable by size, price, appearance, or some other attribute. Example: Prudential renewable term life insurance.

# PRODUCT SYSTEMS AND MIXES

A **product system** is a group of diverse but related items that function in a compatible manner.[49] For example, the extensive iPod product system includes headphones and headsets, cables and docks, armbands, cases, power and car accessories, and speakers. A **product mix** (also called a **product assortment**) is the set of all products and items a particular seller offers for sale.

A product mix consists of various product lines. NEC's (Japan) product mix consists of communication products and computer products. Michelin has three product lines: tires, maps, and restaurant-rating services. At Northwestern University, separate academic deans oversee the schools of medicine, law, business, engineering, music, speech, journalism, and liberal arts, among others.

A company's product mix has a certain width, length, depth, and consistency. These concepts are illustrated in Table 13.2 for selected Procter & Gamble consumer products.

- The *width* of a product mix refers to how many different product lines the company carries. Table 13.2 shows a product mix width of five lines. (In fact, P&G produces many additional lines.)

| TABLE 13.2 | Product Mix Width and Product Line Length for Procter & Gamble Products (including year of introduction) | | | | |
|---|---|---|---|---|---|
| | **Product Mix Width** | | | | |
| | **Detergents** | **Toothpaste** | **Bar Soap** | **Disposable Diapers** | **Paper Products** |
| | Ivory Snow (1930) | Gleem (1952) | Ivory (1879) | Pampers (1961) | Charmin (1928) |
| | Dreft (1933) | Crest (1955) | Camay (1926) | Luvs (1976) | Puffs (1960) |
| **Product Line Length** | Tide (1946) | | Zest (1952) | | Bounty (1965) |
| | Cheer (1950) | | Safeguard (1963) | | |
| | Dash (1954) | | Oil of Olay (1993) | | |
| | Bold (1965) | | | | |
| | Gain (1966) | | | | |
| | Era (1972) | | | | |

Tide comes in many forms and varieties to suit different consumer needs.

- The *length* of a product mix refers to the total number of items in the mix. In Table 13.2, it is 20. We can also talk about the average length of a line. We obtain this by dividing the total length (here 20) by the number of lines (here 5), for an average product line length of 4.
- The *depth* of a product mix refers to how many variants are offered of each product in the line. If Tide came in two scents (Clean Breeze and Regular), two formulations (liquid and powder), and with two additives (with or without bleach), it would have a depth of eight because there are eight distinct variants.[50] We can calculate the average depth of P&G's product mix by averaging the number of variants within the brand groups.
- The *consistency* of the product mix describes how closely related the various product lines are in end use, production requirements, distribution channels, or some other way. P&G's product lines are consistent in that they are consumer goods that go through the same distribution channels. The lines are less consistent in the functions they perform for buyers.

These four product mix dimensions permit the company to expand its business in four ways. It can add new product lines, thus widening its product mix. It can lengthen each product line. It can add more product variants to each product and deepen its product mix. Finally, a company can pursue more product line consistency. To make these product and brand decisions, marketers can conduct product line analysis.

## PRODUCT LINE ANALYSIS

In offering a product line, companies normally develop a basic platform and modules that can be added to meet different customer requirements and lower production costs. Car manufacturers build cars around a basic platform. Homebuilders show a model home to which buyers can add additional features. Product line managers need to know the sales and profits of each item in their line to determine which items to build, maintain, harvest, or divest.[51] They also need to understand each product line's market profile and image.[52]

**SALES AND PROFITS** Figure 13.3 shows a sales and profit report for a five-item product line. The first item accounts for 50 percent of total sales and 30 percent of total profits. The first two items account for 80 percent of total sales and 60 percent of total profits. If these two items were suddenly hurt by a competitor, the line's sales and profitability could collapse. These items must be carefully monitored and protected. At the other end, the last item delivers only 5 percent of the product line's sales and profits. The product line manager may consider dropping this item unless it has strong growth potential.

Every company's product portfolio contains products with different margins. Supermarkets make almost no margin on bread and milk, reasonable margins on canned and frozen foods, and better margins on flowers, ethnic food lines, and freshly baked goods. Companies should recognize that different items will allow for different margins and respond differently to changes in level of advertising.[53]

**MARKET PROFILE AND IMAGE** The product line manager must review how the line is positioned against competitors' lines. Consider paper company X with a paperboard product line.[54] Two paperboard attributes are weight and finish quality. Paper is usually offered at standard levels of 90, 120, 150, and 180 weights. Finish quality is offered at low, medium, and high levels.

| Fig. 13.3 |

Product-Item
Contributions to a
Product Line's Total
Sales and Profits

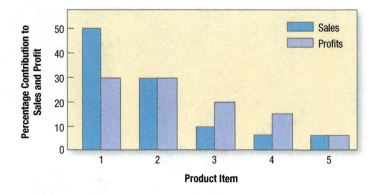

The **product map** in Figure 13.4 shows the location of the various product line items of company X and four competitors, A, B, C, and D. Competitor A sells two product items in the extra-high weight class ranging from medium to low finish quality. Competitor B sells four items that vary in weight and finish quality. Competitor C sells three items in which the greater the weight, the greater the finish quality. Competitor D sells three items, all lightweight but varying in finish quality. Company X offers three items that vary in weight and finish quality.

The product map also shows which competitors' items are competing against company X's items. For example, company X's low-weight, medium-quality paper competes against competitor D's and B's papers, but its high-weight, medium-quality paper has no direct competitor. The map also reveals possible locations for new items. No manufacturer offers a high-weight, low-quality paper. If company X estimates a strong unmet demand and can produce this paper at low cost and price it accordingly, it could consider adding it to its line.

Another benefit of product mapping is that it identifies market segments. Figure 13.4 shows the types of paper, by weight and quality, preferred by the general printing industry, the point-of-purchase display industry, and the office supply industry. The map shows that company X is well positioned to serve the needs of the general printing industry but less effective in serving the other two markets.

Product line analysis provides information for two key decision areas: product line length and product mix pricing.

## PRODUCT LINE LENGTH

Company objectives influence product line length. One objective is to create a product line to induce up-selling. Mercedes C-Class plays a critical function as an entry point to the brand. As one industry analyst notes: "The C-Class is critical for the luxury race because it creates the most amount of volume for Benz. It also opens the Benz brand to potential future buyers by catching them while they're young with the hopes that they upgrade as they get more affluent and older."[55]

A different objective is to create a product line that facilitates cross-selling: Hewlett-Packard sells printers as well as computers. Still another is to protect against economic ups and downs: Electrolux offers white goods such as refrigerators, dishwashers, and vacuum cleaners under different brand names in the discount, middle-market, and premium segments, in part as a hedge when the economy moves up or down. Companies seeking high market

| Fig. 13.4 |

Product Map for a
Paper-Product Line

Source: Benson P. Shapiro, *Industrial Product Policy: Managing the Existing Product Line* (Cambridge, MA: Marketing Science Institute Report No. 77–110). Copyright © 2003. Reprinted by permission of Marketing Science Institute and Benson P. Shapiro.

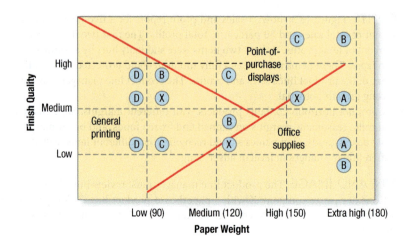

share and market growth will generally carry longer product lines. Those emphasizing high profitability will carry shorter lines consisting of carefully chosen items.

Product lines tend to lengthen over time. Excess manufacturing capacity puts pressure on the product line manager to develop new items. The sales force and distributors also lobby for a more complete product line to satisfy customers. But as items are added, costs rise for design and engineering, inventory carrying, manufacturing changeover, order processing, transportation, and new-item promotions. Eventually, top management may stop development because of insufficient funds or manufacturing capacity. A pattern of product line growth followed by massive pruning may repeat itself many times. Increasingly, consumers are growing weary of dense product lines, overextended brands, and feature-laden products (see "Marketing Insight: When Less Is More").[56]

A company lengthens its product line in two ways: line stretching and line filling.

**LINE STRETCHING** Every company's product line covers a certain part of the total possible range. For example, Mercedes automobiles are located in the upper price range of the automobile market. **Line stretching** occurs when a company lengthens its product line beyond its current range, whether down-market, up-market, or both ways.

*Down-Market Stretch* A company positioned in the middle market may want to introduce a lower-priced line for any of three reasons:

1. The company may notice strong growth opportunities. Mass retailers such as Walmart, Target, and others attract a growing number of shoppers who want value-priced goods.
2. The company may wish to tie up lower-end competitors who might otherwise try to move up-market. If the company has been attacked by a low-end competitor, it often decides to counterattack by entering the low end of the market.
3. The company may find the middle market stagnating or declining.

Marketers face a number of naming choices in deciding to move a brand down-market:

1. Use the parent brand name on all its offerings. Sony has used its name on products in a variety of price tiers.
2. Introduce lower-priced offerings using a sub-brand name, such as P&G's Charmin Basic and Bounty Basic.
3. Introduce the lower-priced offerings under a different name, such as the Gap's Old Navy brand. This strategy is expensive to implement and means brand equity will have to be built from scratch, but the equity of the parent brand name is protected.

# When Less Is More

With thousands of new products introduced each year, consumers find it ever harder to navigate store aisles. One study found the average shopper spent 40 seconds or more in the supermarket soda aisle, compared with 25 seconds six or seven years ago.

Although consumers may think greater product variety increases their likelihood of finding the right product for them, the reality is often different. One study showed that although consumers expressed greater interest in shopping a larger assortment of 24 flavored jams than a smaller assortment of 6, they were 10 times more likely to actually make a selection when given the smaller assortment. Presented with too many options, people "choose not to choose," even if it may not be in their best interests.

Similarly, if product quality in an assortment is high, consumers actually prefer fewer choices. Those with well-defined preferences may benefit from more-differentiated products that offer specific benefits, but others may experience frustration, confusion, and regret. Product proliferation has another downside. Constant product changes and introductions may nudge customers into reconsidering their choices and perhaps switching to a competitor's product.

Some companies are getting the message. When Procter & Gamble went from 20 different kinds of Head & Shoulders to 15, sales for the brand increased by 10 percent. Smart marketers realize it's not just product lines making consumer heads spin—many products themselves are too complicated. Technology marketers need to be especially sensitive to the problems of information overload. The launch of the HTC One smartphone succeeded in part because the company adopted a "less is more" approach instead of just adding features.

**Sources:** John Davidson, "One Classic Example of When Less Is More," *Financial Review*, April 9, 2013; Carolyn Cutrone, "Cutting Down on Choice Is the Best Way to Make Better Decisions," *Business Insider*, January 10, 2013; Dimitri Kuksov and J. Miguel Villas-Boas, "When More Alternatives Lead to Less Choice," *Marketing Science*, 29 (May/June 2010), pp. 507–24; Kristin Diehl and Cait Poynor, "Great Expectations?! Assortment Size, Expectations, and Satisfaction," *Journal of Marketing Research* 46 (April 2009), pp. 312–22; Joseph P. Redden and Stephen J. Hoch, "The Presence of Variety Reduces Perceived Quantity," *Journal of Consumer Research* 36 (October 2009), pp. 406–17; Alexander Chernev and Ryan Hamilton, "Assortment Size and Option Attractiveness in Consumer Choice Among Retailers," *Journal of Marketing Research* 46 (June 2009), pp. 410–20; Richard A. Briesch, Pradeep K. Chintagunta, and Edward J. Fox, "How Does Assortment Affect Grocery Store Choice," *Journal of Marketing Research* 46 (April 2009), pp. 176–89; Susan M. Broniarczyk, "Product Assortment," Curt P. Haugtvedt, Paul M. Herr, and Frank R. Kardes, eds., *Handbook of Consumer Psychology* (New York: Taylor & Francis, 2008), pp. 755–79.

Moving down-market carries risks. In one classic example, when Kodak introduced Kodak Funtime Film to counter lower-priced brands, it did not price it low enough to match competitors. It also found some of its regular customers buying Funtime, so it was cannibalizing its core brand. Kodak withdrew the product and may have also lost some of its quality image in the process. P&G also introduced Tide Basic in test markets—priced lower but also lacking some of the latest detergent technology of its famous parent brand—and decided against rolling it out.[57]

On the other hand, Mercedes successfully introduced its C-Class cars at $30,000 without injuring its ability to sell other Mercedes cars for $100,000. John Deere introduced a lower-priced line of lawn tractors called Sabre from John Deere, while still selling its more expensive tractors under the John Deere name. In these cases, consumers may have been better able to compartmentalize the different offerings and understand the functional differences between them.[58]

*Up-Market Stretch* Companies may wish to enter the high end of the market to achieve more growth, realize higher margins, or simply position themselves as full-line manufacturers. Many markets have spawned surprising upscale segments: Starbucks in coffee, Häagen-Dazs in ice cream, and Evian in bottled water. The leading Japanese auto companies each introduced a highly successful upscale automobile nameplate: Toyota's Lexus, Nissan's Infiniti, and Honda's Acura. They invented entirely new names because consumers might not have given the brand "permission" to stretch upward when those lines were first introduced.

Other companies have included their own names in moving up-market. Gallo sells Gallo Family Vineyards (priced at $10 to $30 a bottle) with a hip, younger image to compete in the premium wine segment. General Electric introduced the GE Profile brand for its large-appliance offerings in the upscale market. Some brands have used modifiers to signal a quality improvement, such as Ultra Dry Pampers, Extra Strength Tylenol, and Power Pro Dustbuster Plus.

*Two-Way Stretch* Companies serving the middle market might stretch their line in both directions. Robert Mondavi Winery, now owned by Constellation Brands, sells $35 bottles of wines as the first premium "New World" wine, but it also sells $125 bottles of Mondavi Reserve at high-end wineries, restaurants, and vineyards and through direct order, as well as $11 bottles of Woodbridge created during the grape oversupply of the mid-1990s. Purina Dog Food has stretched up and down to create a product line differentiated by benefits to dogs, breadth of varieties, ingredients, and price:

- Pro Plan ($38.99/18 lb. bag)—helps dogs live long and healthy lives with high-quality ingredients (real meat, fish, and poultry)
- Purina ONE ($22.99/16.5 lb. bag)—meets dogs' changing and unique nutritional needs and provides super-premium nutrition for good health
- Purina Dog Chow ($12.24/18.5 lb. bag)—provides dogs with complete nutrition to build, replenish, and repair at each life stage
- Alpo by Purina ($8.69/17.6 lb. bag)—offers beef, liver, and cheese flavor combinations and three meaty varieties

**LINE FILLING** A firm can also lengthen its product line by adding more items within the present range. Motives for *line filling* include reaching for incremental profits, satisfying dealers who complain about lost sales because of items missing from the line, utilizing excess capacity, trying to become the leading full-line company, and plugging holes to keep out competitors. Consider BMW.[59]

**BMW AG** In four years, BMW has morphed from a one-brand, five-model carmaker into a powerhouse with three brands, 14 "Series," and roughly 30 distinct models. Not only has the carmaker expanded its product range downward with MINI Coopers and its compact 1-series models, but it has also built it upward with Rolls-Royce and filled the gaps in between with its X1, X3, X5, and X6 sports activity vehicles, Z4 roadsters, and a 6-series coupe. The company has used line filling successfully to boost its appeal to the rich, the super-rich, and the hope-to-be-rich, all without departing from its pure premium positioning. BMW has also built a clear brand migration strategy within its product line. It would like to move customers up from a 1-series or 3-series vehicle to a 5-series and eventually even a 7-series.

Line filling is overdone if it results in cannibalization and customer confusion. The company needs to differentiate each item in the consumer's mind with a *just-noticeable difference*. According to Weber's law, customers are

BMW has filled its product line to offer more vehicle choices to its customers.

more attuned to relative than to absolute difference.[60] They will perceive the difference between boards 2 and 3 feet long and boards 20 and 30 feet long, but not between boards 29 and 30 feet long. The proposed item should also meet a market need and not be added simply to satisfy an internal need. The infamous Edsel automobile, on which Ford lost $350 million in the late 1950s, met Ford's internal positioning need for a car between its Ford and Lincoln lines, but not the market's needs.

**LINE MODERNIZATION, FEATURING, AND PRUNING** Product lines regularly need to be modernized. The question is whether to overhaul the line piecemeal or all at once. A piecemeal approach allows the company to see how customers and dealers take to the new style. It is also less draining on the company's cash flow, but it lets competitors see changes and start redesigning their own lines.

In rapidly changing markets, modernization is continuous. Companies plan improvements to encourage customer migration to higher-value, higher-price items. Microprocessor companies such as Intel and AMD and software companies such as Microsoft and Oracle continually introduce more advanced versions of their products. Marketers want to time improvements so they do not appear too early (damaging sales of the current line) or too late (giving the competition time to establish a strong reputation).[61]

The product line manager typically selects one or a few items in the line to feature. Best Buy will announce a special low-priced big-screen TV to attract customers. At other times, managers will feature a high-end item to lend prestige to the product line. Sometimes a company finds one end of its line selling well and the other end selling poorly.

It may try to boost demand for slower sellers, especially if a factory is idled by lack of demand, but it could be counterargued that the firm should promote strong sellers rather than prop up weak ones. Nike's Air Force 1 basketball shoe, introduced in the 1980s, is a billion-dollar brand that is still a consumer and retailer favorite and a moneymaker for the company thanks to collectable styles and tight supplies. Since their introduction, the shoes have been designed or inspired by many celebrities and athletes.[62]

Using sales and cost analysis, product line managers must periodically review the line for deadwood that depresses profits.[63] One study found that for a big Dutch retailer, a major assortment reduction led to a short-term drop in category sales, caused mainly by fewer category purchases by former buyers, but it also attracted new category buyers who partially offset the losses.[64]

Multi-brand companies all over the world try to optimize their brand portfolios. This often means focusing on core brand growth and concentrating resources on the biggest and most established brands. Hasbro has designated a set of core toy brands to emphasize in its marketing, including GI Joe, Transformers, and My Little Pony. Procter & Gamble's "back to basics" strategy concentrated on brands with more than $1 billion in revenue, such as Tide, Crest, Pampers, and Pringles. Every product in a product line must play a role, as must any brand in the brand portfolio.[65]

**VOLKSWAGEN** Volkswagen has four different core brands of particular importance in its European portfolio. Initially, Audi and Seat had a sporty image and VW and Skoda had a family-car image. Audi and VW were in a higher price-quality tier than Skoda and Seat, which had spartan interiors and utilitarian engine performance. To reduce costs, streamline part/systems designs, and eliminate redundancies, Volkswagen upgraded the Seat and Skoda brands, which captured market share with splashy interiors, a full array of safety systems, and reliable power trains. The danger, of course, is that by borrowing from its upper-echelon Audi and Volkswagen products, Volkswagen could dilute their cachet. Frugal European consumers may convince themselves that a Seat or Skoda is almost identical to its VW sister, at several thousand euros less.

## PRODUCT MIX PRICING

Marketers must modify their price-setting logic when the product is part of a product mix. In **product mix pricing,** the firm searches for a set of prices that maximizes profits on the total mix. The process is challenging because the various products have demand and cost interrelationships and are subject to different degrees of competition. We can distinguish six situations calling for product-mix pricing: product line pricing, optional-feature pricing, captive-product pricing, two-part pricing, by-product pricing, and product-bundling pricing.

**PRODUCT LINE PRICING** Companies normally develop product lines rather than single products, so they introduce price steps. A men's clothing store might carry men's suits at three price levels: $300, $600, and $900, which customers associate with low, average, and high quality. The seller's task is to establish perceived quality differences that justify the price differences.[66]

**OPTIONAL-FEATURE PRICING** Many companies offer optional products, features, and services with their main product. The 2013 Subaru Outback 2.5i was available in five trim levels. Premium trim additional features included an eight-way power driver's seat, windshield wiper de-icer, leather-wrapped steering wheel, and 17-inch aluminum wheels; the more luxurious Limited trim added even more features, including perforated leather, dual-zone automatic climate control, heated front seats, heated side mirrors, and a Harman/Kardon audio system with satellite radio.[67]

Pricing options is a sticky problem because companies must decide which to include in the standard price and which to offer separately. Many restaurants price their beverages high and their food low. The food revenue covers costs, and the beverages—especially liquor—produce the profit. This explains why servers often press hard to get customers to order drinks. Other restaurants price their liquor low and food high to draw in a drinking crowd.

**CAPTIVE-PRODUCT PRICING** Some products require the use of ancillary or **captive products.** Manufacturers of razors often price them low and set high markups on razor blades. Movie theaters and concert venues often make more from concessions and merchandise sales than from ticket receipts.[68] AT&T may give a cell phone for free if the person commits to buying two years of phone service.

If the captive product is priced too high in the aftermarket, however, counterfeiting and substitutions can erode sales. Consumers now can buy cartridge refills for their printers from discount suppliers and save 20 percent to 30 percent off the manufacturer's price. Hewlett-Packard has attempted to strike the right balance in its printer pricing, though changes in the marketing environment are upending its well-honed profit machine.[69]

**HEWLETT-PACKARD** In 1996, Hewlett-Packard (HP) began drastically cutting prices on its printers, by as much as 60 percent in some cases. The company could afford to make these cuts because over the life of the product customers typically spend twice as much on replacement ink cartridges, toner, and specialty paper as on the printer, and inkjet supplies typically carry 45 percent to 60 percent profit margins. As the price dropped, printer sales rose, and so did aftermarket sales. Over the next decade, with a market share above 40 percent, the printer division was a highly profitable cash cow for the company. But with more consumers using tablets and smart phones and sharing images and information via cloud computing, HP's bigger challenge now is countering the continuing decline in sales of PCs. Lower PC sales have meant lower printer sales and a steady drop in profit margin and revenue in recent years.

Source: Handout/MCT/Newscom

HP prices its printers recognizing that its real profits comes from the supplies it sells customers afterwards.

**TWO-PART PRICING** Service firms engage in **two-part pricing,** consisting of a fixed fee plus a variable usage fee. Cell phone users may have to pay a minimum monthly fee plus charges for calls that exceed their allotted minutes. Amusement parks charge an admission fee plus fees for rides over a certain minimum. The service firm faces a problem similar to captive-product pricing—namely, how much to charge for the basic service and how much for the variable usage. The fixed fee should be low enough to induce purchase; profit can then come from the usage fees.

**BY-PRODUCT PRICING** The production of certain goods—meats, petroleum products, and other chemicals—often yields by-products that should be priced on their value. Any income earned on the by-products will make it easier for the company to charge a lower price on its main product if competition forces it to do so. Formed in 1855, Australia's CSR was originally named Colonial Sugar Refinery and forged its early reputation as a sugar company. The company began to sell by-products of its sugar cane; waste sugar cane fiber was used to manufacture wallboard. Today, through product development and acquisition, the renamed CSR has become one of the top 10 companies in Australia selling building and construction materials.

**PRODUCT-BUNDLING PRICING** Sellers often bundle products and features.[70] **Pure bundling** occurs when a firm offers its products only as a bundle. Providers of aftermarket products for automobiles increasingly are bundling their offerings in customizable three-in-one and four-in-one programs, especially second-tier products such as tire-and-wheel protection and paintless dent repair.[71] A talent agency might insist that a "hot" actor can be signed to a film only if the film company also accepts other talent the agency represents such as directors or writers. This is a form of *tied-in sales.*

In **mixed bundling,** the seller offers goods both individually and in bundles, normally charging less for the bundle than if the items were purchased separately. A theater will price a season subscription lower than the cost of buying all the performances separately. Customers may not have planned to buy all the components, so savings on the price bundle must be enough to induce them to buy it.[72]

Some customers want less than the whole bundle in exchange for a lower price.[73] These customers ask the seller to "unbundle" or "rebundle" its offer. If a supplier saves $100 by not supplying unwanted delivery and reduces the customer's price by $80, it has kept the customer happy while increasing its profit by $20. "Marketing Memo: Product-Bundle Pricing Considerations" offers a few tips.

## CO-BRANDING AND INGREDIENT BRANDING

**CO-BRANDING** Marketers often combine their products with products from other companies in various ways. In **co-branding**—also called dual branding or brand bundling—two or more well-known brands are combined into a joint product or marketed together in some fashion.

## marketing memo

### Product-Bundle Pricing Considerations

As promotional activity increases on individual items in the bundle, buyers perceive less savings from the bundle and are less apt to pay for it. Research suggests the following guidelines for implementing a bundling strategy:

- Don't promote individual products in a package as frequently or for as little as the bundle. The bundle price should be much lower than the sum of individual products or the consumer will not perceive its attractiveness.

- If you still want to promote individual products, choose a single item in the mix. Another option is to alternate promotions to avoid running conflicting ones.

- If you offer large rebates on individual products, do so with discretion and make them the absolute exception. Otherwise, the consumer uses the price of individual products as an external reference for the bundle, which then loses value.

- Consider how experienced and knowledgeable your customer is. More knowledgeable customers may be less likely to need or want bundled offerings and prefer the freedom to choose components individually.

- Make sure the value of the bundle is easily understood. Bundles can streamline choices and make it easier for a consumer to appreciate different sets of benefits.

- Remember costs play a role. If marginal costs for the products are low—such as for proprietary software components that can be easily copied and distributed—a bundling strategy can be preferable to a pure component strategy where each component is purchased separately.

- Firms with single products that bundle their products together to compete against a multiproduct firm may not be successful if a price war ensues.

**Sources:** Dina Gerdeman, "Product Bundling Is a Smart Strategy—But There's a Catch," *Forbes*, January 18, 2013; Timothy P. Derdenger and Vineet Kumar, "The Dynamic Effects of Bundling as a Product Strategy," *Marketing Science* 32 (November–December 2013), pp. 827–59; Aaron Brough and Alexander Chernev, "When Opposites Detract: Categorical Reasoning and Subtractive Valuations of Product Combinations" *Journal of Consumer Research* 39 (August 2012), pp. 399–414; Amiya Basu and Padmal Vitharana, "Impact of Customer Knowledge Heterogeneity on Bundling Strategy," *Marketing Science* 28 (July–August 2009), pp. 792–801; Bikram Ghosh and Subramanian Balachnadar, "Competitive Bundling and Counterbundling with Generalist and Specialist Firms," *Management Science* 53 (January 2007), pp. 159–68.

One form of co-branding is *same-company co-branding,* as when General Mills advertises Trix cereal and Yoplait yogurt. Another form is *joint-venture co-branding,* such as General Electric and Hitachi lightbulbs in Japan or the Citi Platinum Select AAdvantage Visa Signature credit card in which three different parties are involved. There is *multiple-sponsor co-branding,* such as Taligent, a one-time technological alliance of Apple, IBM, and Motorola. Finally, there is *retail co-branding* in which two retail establishments use the same location to optimize space and profits, such as jointly owned Pizza Hut, KFC, and Taco Bell restaurants.

The main advantage of co-branding is that a product can be convincingly positioned by virtue of the multiple brands. Co-branding can generate greater sales from the existing market and open opportunities for new consumers and channels. It can also reduce the cost of product introduction because it combines two well-known images and speeds adoption. And co-branding may be a valuable means to learn about consumers and how other companies approach them. Companies in the automotive industry have reaped all these benefits.

The potential disadvantages of co-branding are the risks and lack of control in becoming aligned with another brand in consumers' minds. Consumer expectations of co-brands are likely to be high, so unsatisfactory performance could have negative repercussions for both brands. If the other brand enters a number of co-branding arrangements, overexposure may dilute the transfer of any association. It may also result in a lack of focus on existing brands. Consumers may feel less sure of what they know about the brand.[74]

For co-branding to succeed, the two brands must separately have brand equity—adequate brand awareness and a sufficiently positive brand image. The most important requirement is a logical fit between the two brands, to maximize the advantages of each while minimizing disadvantages. Consumers are more apt to perceive co-brands favorably if they are complementary and offer unique quality, rather than being overly similar and redundant.

Managers must enter co-branding ventures carefully, looking for the right fit in values, capabilities, and goals and an appropriate balance of brand equity. There must be detailed plans to legalize contracts, make financial arrangements, and coordinate marketing programs. As one executive at Nabisco put it, "Giving away your brand is a lot like giving away your child—you want to make sure everything is perfect." Financial arrangements between brands vary; one common approach is for the brand more deeply invested in the production process to pay the other a licensing fee and royalty.

Brand alliances require a number of decisions.[75] What capabilities do you *not* have? What resource constraints do you face (people, time, money)? What are your growth goals or revenue needs? Ask whether the opportunity is a profitable business venture. How does it help maintain or strengthen brand equity? Is there any risk of diluting brand equity? Does the opportunity offer extrinsic advantages such as learning opportunities?

INGREDIENT BRANDING **Ingredient branding** is a special case of co-branding.[76] It creates brand equity for materials, components, or parts that are necessarily contained within other branded products. For host products whose brands are not that strong, ingredient brands can provide differentiation and important signals of quality.[77]

Successful ingredient brands include Dolby noise reduction technology, GORE-TEX water-resistant fibers, and Scotchgard fabrics. Vibram is the world leader in high-performance rubber soles for outdoor, work, military, recreation, fashion, and orthopedic shoes. Look under your shoe and you may find Vibram soles—they are used by a wide range of footwear manufacturers, including The North Face, Saucony, Timberland, Lacoste, L.L. Bean, Wolverine, Rockport, Columbia, Nike, and Frye.[78]

An interesting take on ingredient branding is *self-branded ingredients* that companies advertise and even trademark.[79] Westin Hotels advertises its own "Heavenly Bed"—a critically important ingredient to a guest's good night's sleep. The brand has been so successful that Westin now sells the bed, pillows, sheets, and blankets via an online catalog, along with other "Heavenly" gifts, bath products, and even pet items. The success of the bed has also created a halo for the Westin brand as a whole. Heavenly Bed enthusiasts are more likely to rate other aspects of their room or stay as more positive.[80] If it can be done well, using self-branded ingredients makes sense because firms have more control over them and can develop them to suit their purposes.

Ingredient brands try to create enough awareness and preference for their product so consumers will not buy a host product that doesn't contain it. DuPont has introduced a number of innovative products, such as Corian® solid-surface material, for use in markets ranging from apparel to aerospace. Many of its products, such as Tyvek® house wrap, Teflon® non-stick coating, and Kevlar® fiber, became household names as ingredient brands in consumer products manufactured by other companies. Since 2004, DuPont has introduced more than 5,000 new products and received more than 2,400 new patents.[81]

Many manufacturers make components or materials that enter final branded products but lose their individual identity. One of the few companies that avoided this fate is Intel. Intel's consumer-directed brand campaign convinced many personal computer buyers to buy only brands with "Intel Inside." As a result, major PC manufacturers—Dell, HP, Lenovo—typically purchase their chips from Intel at a premium price rather than buy equivalent chips from an unknown supplier.

Source: © David L. Moore - CA/Alamy

Westin has successfully built an ingredient brand around their "Heavenly Bed" innovation.

What are the requirements for successful ingredient branding?[82]

1. Consumers must believe the ingredient matters to the performance and success of the end product. Ideally, this intrinsic value is easily seen or experienced.
2. Consumers must be convinced that not all ingredient brands are the same and that the ingredient is superior.
3. A distinctive symbol or logo must clearly signal that the host product contains the ingredient. Ideally, this symbol or logo functions like a "seal" and is simple and versatile, credibly communicating quality and confidence.
4. A coordinated "pull" and "push" program must help consumers understand the advantages of the branded ingredient. Channel members must offer full support such as consumer advertising and promotions and—sometimes in collaboration with manufacturers—retail merchandising and promotion programs.

# Packaging, Labeling, Warranties, and Guarantees

Some product packages—such as the Coke bottle and Red Bull can—are world famous. Many marketers have called packaging a fifth P, along with price, product, place, and promotion. Most, however, treat packaging and labeling as an element of product strategy. Warranties and guarantees can also be an important part of the product strategy and often appear on the package.

## PACKAGING

**Packaging** includes all the activities of designing and producing the container for a product. Packages might have up to three layers. Cool Water by Davidoff For Men cologne comes in a bottle (*primary package*) inside a cardboard box (*secondary package*), shipped in a corrugated box (*shipping package*) containing six dozen bottles in cardboard boxes.

Packaging is important because it is the buyer's first encounter with the product. A good package draws the consumer in and encourages product choice. In effect, it can act as a "five-second commercial" for the product. It also affects consumers' later product experiences when they open it and use what's inside. Some packages can even be attractively displayed at home. Distinctive packaging like that for Kiwi shoe polish, Altoids mints, and Absolut vodka is an important part of a brand's equity.

Several factors contribute to the growing use of packaging as a marketing tool.

- *Self-service.* In an average supermarket, which may stock 15,000 items, the typical shopper passes some 300 products per minute. Given that 50 percent to 70 percent of all purchases are made in the store, the effective package must perform many sales tasks: attract attention, describe the product's features, create consumer confidence, and make a favorable overall impression.
- *Consumer affluence.* Rising affluence means consumers are willing to pay a little more for the convenience, appearance, dependability, and prestige of better packages.
- *Company and brand image.* Packages contribute to instant recognition of the company or brand. In the store, they can create a billboard effect, as Garnier Fructis does with its bright green packaging in the hair care aisle.
- *Innovation opportunity.* Unique or innovative packaging can bring big benefits to consumers and profits to producers. Companies are always looking for a way to make their products more convenient and easier to use—often charging a premium when they do so. The SC Johnson Smart Twist Cleaning System has a hand-held sprayer and carousel that rotates between concentrated versions of three different cleaning products; Kleenex hand towels use a dispenser that fits upside down in a bathroom towel rack; and Kiwi Express Shine shoe polish has a dispenser and applicator to shine shoes without the need to spread newspaper, wear a glove, or use a brush.[83]

Formally, packaging must achieve a number of objectives:

1. Identify the brand.
2. Convey descriptive and persuasive information.
3. Facilitate product transportation and protection.
4. Assist at-home storage.
5. Aid product consumption.

Source: © Simon Lord/Alamy

Tiffany's brand is defined in part by its iconic Tiffany Blue packaging.

To achieve these objectives and satisfy consumers' desires, marketers must choose the functional and aesthetic components of packaging correctly. Functionally, structural design is crucial. The packaging elements must harmonize with each other and with pricing, advertising, and other parts of the marketing program. Aesthetic considerations relate to a package's size and shape, material, color, text, and graphics.

Color is a particularly important aspect of packaging and carries different meanings in different cultures and market segments. As one expert says, "Color is all-pervasive. It is language-neutral, but loaded with meaning. It's completely overt, yet each person sees color through different eyes, both literally and figuratively."[84]

Color can define a brand, from Tiffany's blue box to Cadbury's purple wrapping and UPS's brown trucks. Orange, the telecom mobile operator, uses color as both its name and its look. Table 13.3 summarizes the beliefs of some visual marketing experts about the role of color in Western culture.

| TABLE 13.3 | The Color Wheel of Branding and Packaging |
| --- | --- |

**Red** symbolizes excitement, energy, passion, courage, and being bold.

**Orange** connotes friendliness and fun. It combines the energy of red and the warmth of yellow.

**Yellow**, as the color of the sun, is equated with warmth, joy, and happiness.

**Green**, as the color of nature, connotes health, growth, freshness, and renewal.

**Blue,** as the color of the sky and sea, is associated with dependability, trust, competence, and integrity.

**Purple** has symbolized nobility, wealth, and wisdom. It combines the stability of blue and the energy of red.

**Pink** is considered to have soft, peaceful, comforting qualities.

**Brown**, as the color of the earth, connotes honesty and dependability.

**Black** is seen as classic, strong, and balanced.

**White** connotes purity, innocence, and cleanliness.

**Sources:** Elisabeth Sullivan, "Color Me Profitable," *Marketing News*, October 15, 2008, p. 8; "Color Meaning," www.color-wheel-pro.com, accessed June 2, 2014; Melissa Stanger, "How Brands Use the Psychology of Color to Manipulate You," *Business Insider*, December 29, 2012; The Logo Company, "Color Emotion Guide," www.thelogocompany. net/blog/infographics/psychology-color-logo-design, January 13, 2013; Lauren Labrecque and George R. Milne, "Exciting Red and Competent Blue: the Importance of Color in Marketing," *Journal of Academy of Marketing Science* 40 (September 2012), pp. 711–27.

Packaging updates and redesigns can occur frequently to keep the brand contemporary, relevant, or practical. Although these changes can have immediate impact on sales, they also can have a downside, as PepsiCo learned for its Tropicana brand.[85]

**TROPICANA**  PepsiCo experienced great success with its Tropicana brand, acquired in 1998. Then in 2009, the company launched a redesigned package to "refresh and modernize" the brand. The goal was to create "emotional attachment by 'heroing' the juice and trumpeting the natural fruit goodness." Arnell Group led the extreme makeover, which led to an entirely new look, downplaying the brand name, highlighting the phrase "100 percent orange pure & natural," and replacing the "straw in an orange" graphic on the front with a close-up of a glass of orange juice. Consumer response was swift and negative. The package was deemed "ugly" or "stupid," and some even confused the product with a store brand. Sales dropped 20 percent. After only two months, PepsiCo management announced it would revert to the old packaging.

After the company designs its packaging, it must test it. *Engineering tests* ensure that the package stands up under normal conditions; *visual tests,* that the script is legible and the colors harmonious; *dealer tests,* that dealers find the packages attractive and easy to handle; and *consumer tests,* that buyers will respond favorably.

Although developing effective packaging may require several months and several hundred thousand dollars, companies must consider growing environmental and safety concerns about excess and wasteful packaging. Fortunately, as discussed above, many firms have gone "green" and are finding creative new ways to package their wares.

Dell introduced bamboo packaging as an alternative to corrugated cardboard, foam, molded paper pulp, and plastic and took other steps to reduce the overall volume of packaging used.[86] Developmental environmentally friendly packaging that also satisfies customers' needs can be challenging, as Frito-Lay found out.[87]

**SUN CHIPS**  Frito-Lay's Sun Chips multigrain snacks, containing 30 percent less fat than potato chips, have succeeded as a healthier, "good for you" snack option. Part of the firm's effort to also support a "healthier planet" was to to run its factory in Modesto on solar power and unveil a novel 100 percent compostable bag made of plant-based materials. Much research went into the development of the bag, and it was launched with fanfare in 2010. Unfortunately, it included polymers that made it "kind of crispy and crunchy" at room temperature, and consumers began to complain about how noisy it was. One Air Force pilot said it was louder than the cockpit of his jet. To prove his point, he squeezed the new Sun Chips bag and recorded a 95-decibel level with a sound meter, considerably more than the 77-decibel level recorded when he squeezed a conventional Tostitos bag. When thousands of people chose to friend a Facebook page called "Sorry But I Can't Hear You Over This Sun Chips Bag"—and with sales sliding—Frito-Lay decided to drop the bag after an 18-month run.

## LABELING

The label can be a simple attached tag or an elaborately designed graphic that is part of the package. It might carry a great deal of information, or only the brand name. Even if the seller prefers a simple label, the law may require more.

A label performs several functions. First, it *identifies* the product or brand—for instance, the name Sunkist stamped on oranges. It might also *grade* the product; canned peaches are grade-labeled A, B, and C. The label might *describe* the product: who made it, where and when, what it contains, how it is to be used, and how to use it safely. Finally, the label might *promote* the product through attractive graphics. Advanced technology allows 360-degree shrink-wrapped labels to surround containers with bright graphics and accommodate more product information, replacing glued-on paper labels.

Labels eventually need freshening up. The label on Ivory soap has been redone at least 18 times since the 1890s, with gradual changes in the size and design of the letters. As Tropicana found out (see above), companies with labels that have become icons need to tread very carefully in order to preserve key branding elements when undertaking a redesign.

A long history of legal concerns surrounds labels and packaging. In 1914, the Federal Trade Commission Act held that false, misleading, or deceptive labels or packages constitute unfair competition. The Fair Packaging and Labeling Act, passed by Congress in 1967, set mandatory labeling requirements, encouraged voluntary industry packaging standards, and allowed federal agencies to set packaging regulations in specific industries.

The Food and Drug Administration (FDA) has required processed-food producers to include nutritional labeling that clearly states the amounts of protein, fat, carbohydrates, and calories contained in products, as well as vitamin and mineral content as a percentage of the recommended daily allowance.[88] The FDA has also taken action against potentially misleading uses of such descriptions as "light," "high fiber," and "low fat."

Not all countries apply such strict definitions. In the United Kingdom, "light" and "lite" do not have an official meaning in law, though "low fat" does—the food product must be less than 3 percent fat to qualify. As a result, some foods branded "light" there have been found to contain up to seven times more fat than those described as "low fat."[89]

## WARRANTIES AND GUARANTEES

All sellers are legally responsible for fulfilling a buyer's normal or reasonable expectations. **Warranties** are formal statements of expected product performance by the manufacturer. Products under warranty can be returned to the manufacturer or designated repair center for repair, replacement, or refund. Whether expressed or implied, warranties are legally enforceable.

Extended warranties and service contracts can be extremely lucrative for manufacturers and retailers. Analysts estimate that warranty sales have accounted for a large percentage of Best Buy's operating profits.[90] Despite evidence that extended warranties do not pay off for them, some consumers value the peace of mind.[91] These warranties still generate multibillion dollars in revenue for electronic goods in the United States, though the total has declined as consumers have become more comfortable seeking solutions to technical problems online or from friends.[92]

Many sellers offer either general or specific guarantees. A company such as Procter & Gamble promises general or complete satisfaction without being more specific—"If you are not satisfied for any reason, return for replacement, exchange, or refund." A. T. Cross guarantees its Cross pens and pencils for life. The customer mails the pen to A. T. Cross (mailers are provided at stores), and the pen is repaired or replaced at no charge.

Guarantees reduce the buyer's perceived risk. They suggest that the product is of high quality and the company and its service performance are dependable. They can be especially helpful when the company or product is not well known or when the product's quality is superior to that of competitors. Hyundai's and Kia's highly successful 10-year or 100,000-mile power train warranty programs were designed in part to assure potential buyers of the quality of the products and the companies' stability.

# Summary

1. Product is the first and most important element of the marketing mix. Product strategy calls for making coordinated decisions on product mixes, product lines, brands, and packaging and labeling.

2. In planning its market offering, the marketer needs to think through the five levels of the product: the core benefit, the basic product, the expected product, the augmented product, and the potential product, which encompasses all the augmentations and transformations the product might ultimately undergo.

3. Products can be nondurable goods, durable goods, or services. In the consumer-goods category are convenience goods (staples, impulse goods, emergency goods), shopping goods (homogeneous and heterogeneous), specialty goods, and unsought goods. The industrial-goods category has three subcategories: materials and parts (raw materials and manufactured materials and parts), capital items (installations and equipment), and supplies and business services (operating supplies, maintenance and repair items, maintenance and repair services, and business advisory services).

4. Brands can be differentiated on the basis of product form, features, performance, conformance, durability, reliability, repairability, style, customization, and design, as well as such service dimensions as ordering ease, delivery, installation, customer training, customer consulting, and maintenance and repair.

5. Design is the totality of features that affect how a product looks, feels, and functions. A well-designed product offers functional and aesthetic benefits to consumers and can be an important source of differentiation.

6. Luxury brands command price premiums and often have a strong lifestyle component. They can require some special considerations in how they are sold.

7. Products and their packaging must be designed to reduce adverse environmental impact as much as possible.

8. Most companies sell more than one product. A product mix can be classified according to width, length, depth, and consistency. These four dimensions are the tools for developing the company's marketing strategy and deciding which product lines to grow, maintain, harvest, and divest. To analyze a product line and decide how many resources to invest in it, product line managers need to look at sales and profits and market profile.

9. A company can change the product component of its marketing mix by lengthening its product via line stretching (down-market, up-market, or both) or line filling, by modernizing its products, by featuring certain products, and by pruning its products to eliminate the least profitable.

10. Brands are often sold or marketed jointly with other brands. Ingredient brands and co-brands can add value, assuming they have equity and are perceived as fitting appropriately.

11. Physical products must be packaged and labeled. Well-designed packages can create convenience value for customers and promotional value for producers. Warranties and guarantees can offer further assurance to consumers.

---

## MyMarketingLab

Go to **mymktlab.com** to complete the problems marked with this icon ⭐ as well as for additional Auto-graded and Assisted-graded writing questions.

---

# Applications

---

## Marketing Debate
### With Products, Is It Form or Function?

The "form vs. function" debate applies in many arenas, including marketing. Some marketers believe product performance is the be-all and end-all. Other marketers maintain that the look, feel, and other design elements of products are what really make the difference.

**Take a position:** Product performance is the key to brand success *versus* Product aesthetics are the key to brand success.

## Marketing Discussion:
### Product and Service Differentiation

⭐ Consider the many means of differentiating products and services. Which ones have the most impact on your choices? Why? Can you think of certain brands that excel on a number of these means of differentiation?

---

## Marketing Excellence

### >> Caterpillar

Caterpillar was founded in 1925 when two California-based tractor companies merged. The name "Caterpillar," however, dates back to the early 1900s when Benjamin Holt, one of the company's founders, designed a tractor crawler with wide, thick tracks instead of wheels. These tracks prevented the machine from sinking into California's deep, rich soil, inspiring one observer to say it "crawled like a caterpillar."

Holt sold the tractor under the Caterpillar brand, and after the merger, the company became the Caterpillar Tractor Company. Caterpillar Inc., or CAT, is now the largest manufacturer of earth-moving equipment and engines in the world, selling hundreds of different machines for eight industries: residential, nonresidential, industrial, infrastructure, mining and quarrying, energy, waste, and forestry. Their distinctive yellow color has helped make the brand a U.S. icon.

How did a small tractor manufacturer become one of the biggest companies in the world? Caterpillar grew steadily at first, hitting a few critical milestones including the use of its trademark farm treads on Army tanks in World Wars I and II. Huge postwar construction contracts and strong overseas demand kept sales strong through the mid-20th century, as did innovations like the diesel tractor and rubber-tired tractors.

Things changed, however, when the early 1980s recession hit Caterpillar hard and international competitors like Japan's Komatsu gained market share. High prices and inflexible bureaucracy nearly sent the company into bankruptcy. In 1982 alone, it lost $6.5 billion, laid off thousands of employees, closed several factories, and suffered a long United Auto Workers strike.

In the 1990s, Caterpillar recognized that it desperately needed to change, and under new leadership it pulled off one of the biggest turnarounds in corporate history. Several factors played a role:

- Caterpillar boldly fought the United Auto Workers and outlasted two strikes and seven years of disagreements.

- The company decentralized and restructured into several business units, each responsible for its own P&L.

- It invested $1.8 billion in automating and streamlining manufacturing with a combination of just-in-time inventory and flexible manufacturing. Caterpillar became more efficient and competitive, though it also was forced to lay off more of its workforce.

- The company made research and development one of its biggest priorities, investing hundreds of millions of dollars in new technologies, products, and machines. As a result, CAT construction trucks became more high-tech, competitive, and environmentally friendly.

Today, Caterpillar ranks first or second in every industry it serves. Its products are unmatched in quality and reliability, and the company remains focused on innovation with a $2.5 billion annual R&D budget. New products are launched every year. Recent innovations include hybrid diesel-electric tractors—the first of their kind—and lower-emission engines with ACERT clean-diesel technology that also improves fuel efficiency.

Caterpillar's product range is immense. From a small 47-horsepower skid steer to an 850-horsepower tractor and a massive 3,370-horsepower mining truck, the firm develops products that serve each market and region's specific needs. In China, for example, a market critical to its future, Caterpillar has divided its product strategy into three segments: World Class, Mid-Tier, and Low-End. The company is focused on innovating high-tech

machinery for the growing World Class segment and leaving the Low-End segment to local competitors that will eventually be consolidated.

Another reason for Caterpillar's dominance is its business model. The company sells it all: machines, services, and support for a wide range of industries. It accomplishes this feat through its extensive Global Dealer Network—specially trained independent CAT dealers who provide services on a local basis, giving the global company a personal feel despite its size.

Feeling local is important considering that 56 percent of Caterpillar's business comes from overseas, making it one of the United States' biggest exporters. The company has been a leader in building roads, bridges, highways, and airports all over the world. In developing cities like Antamin, Peru, for example, which is abundant in copper, large mining companies spend hundreds of millions of dollars on CAT machinery and services each year. As many as 50 different kinds of CAT bulldozers, front loaders, excavators, and special mining trucks help clear roads, clean up spills, and dig for copper. These massive trucks are all manufactured in Decatur, Illinois, shipped in pieces, and assembled at the job site.

Caterpillar maintains more than 500 production facilities and retailer locations in 180 countries and saw sales hit $55.7 billion in 2013. Deere & Co. and Komatsu are its closest competitors, each with about half its sales. As the company moves forward, it remains focused on providing customers with the best products, the best service, and the best value proposition.

## Questions

1. What were some of the key steps that made Caterpillar the industry leader in earth-moving machinery? Explain how Caterpillar's products differ from competitors'.

2. Discuss Caterpillar's future. What should it do next with its product line? Where is the future growth for this company?

**Sources:** Green Rankings, The 2009 List," *Newsweek,* http://greenrankings.newsweek.com; Tim McKeough, "The Caterpillar Self-Driving Dump Truck," *Fast Company,* December 1, 2008; Alex Taylor III, "Caterpillar: Big Trucks, Big Sales, Big Attitude," *Fortune,* August 13, 2007; Tudor Van Hampton, "A New Heavyweight among Hybrids," *New York Times,* January 21, 2010; Steven Pearlstein, "After Caterpillar's Turnaround, a Chance to Reinvent Globalization," *Washington Post,* April 19, 2006; Dale Buss, "CAT Is Back: An Icon That Once Seemed Headed for the Dustbin, Caterpillar Has Made an Impressive Turnaround. Here's How," *Chief Executive,* July 2005; Jessie Scanlon, "Caterpillar Rolls Out Its Hybrid D7E Tractor," *BusinessWeek,* July 20, 2009; Caterpillar, Inc. supporting materials at CLSA Asia USA Forum; Caterpillar 2012 Annual Report; www.cat.com.

## Marketing Excellence

### >> Toyota

The world's largest automaker, Toyota has come a long way in its nearly 80-year history. The company launched its first passenger car, the Model AA, in 1936, copying the body design of Chrysler's landmark Airflow and the engine of a 1933 Chevrolet. Toyota then suffered several challenges, including a financial crisis in 1950. However, when consumers wanted smaller, more fuel-efficient automobiles during the 1973 oil crisis, the company responded. The Toyota Corona and Toyota Corolla offered basic features and acted as the company's new entry-level cars. Toyota also launched the Cressida, with the fuel efficiency consumers desired but space and amenities like air conditioning and AM-FM radio.

During the 1980s and 1990s, Toyota gradually added more models ranging in price, size, and features. In 1982, the company introduced the Camry—a four-door, mid-sized car that offered more space than the Corona and became the best-selling passenger car in North America. The first of the company's popular SUVs, the 4Runner, appeared in 1984 looking and acting much like a pickup truck. It later morphed into more of a passenger vehicle and led the way for the Rav4, Highlander, and LandCruiser. Toyota also introduced a full-sized pickup truck—today's Tundra—and several sporty and affordable cars that targeted young adults.

In 1989, it launched Lexus, its luxury division, promising an unparalleled experience starting with white-glove treatment at the dealership. Toyota understood, however, that each country defines luxury differently. In the United States, it meant comfort, size, and dependability; in Europe, attention to detail and brand heritage. As a result, the company varied its advertising depending on the country and culture.

In 1997, Toyota launched the Prius, the first mass-produced hybrid car, for $19,995—between the Corolla and the Camry. The company's keen focus on developing a clean-energy car was brilliantly timed. Before the second-generation Prius hit showrooms in 2002, dealers had already received 10,000 orders. Over the next decade, Ford, Nissan, GM, and Honda followed the Prius with models of their own.

Toyota also started creating vehicles for specific target groups, like the Scion for young adults. Having learned this market wanted more personalization, the company now builds the car "mono-spec" at the factory, with just one well-equipped trim level, letting customers choose from dozens of customization elements at dealerships. Toyota marketed the Scion at music events and has showrooms where "young people feel comfortable hanging out and not a place where they just go stare at a car," said Scion Vice President Jim Letz.

Another big reason behind Toyota's success is its mastery of lean manufacturing and continuous improvement. Its plants can make as many as eight models at the same time, bringing huge increases in productivity and market responsiveness. The company also relentlessly innovates; a typical Toyota assembly line makes thousands of operational changes in a year. Employees see their purpose as threefold: making cars, making cars better, and teaching everyone how to make cars better. The company encourages problem solving, always looking to improve the process by which it improves all other processes.

Toyota has integrated its assembly plants around the world into a single giant network that can customize cars for local markets and shift production quickly to meet surges in demand from markets worldwide. The company is thus able to fill market niches inexpensively as they emerge, without building whole new assembly operations. "If there's a market or market segment where they aren't present, they go there," said Tatsuo Yoshida, auto analyst at Deutsche Securities Ltd.

Over the years, Toyota automobiles have consistently ranked high in quality and reliability. In 2009 and 2010, however, the company recalled more than 8 million cars for potential perceived problems ranging from sticking accelerator pedals to sudden acceleration to software glitches in the braking system. The Lexus, Prius, Camry, Corolla, and Tundra brands were all affected. Next, Toyota lost billions of dollars when an earthquake and tsunami in Japan destroyed the company's plants and parts suppliers in 2011. TMC President Akio Toyoda said, "We have faced many challenges since 2009, but have learned valuable lessons including the need for Toyota to maintain sustainable growth."

Despite these challenges, Toyota recouped its losses. Its strong focus on hybrid vehicles has proved profitable and helped the company rebound. It sold its 4 millionth unit in 2012 and plans to continue to innovate hybrids, believing "there are many more gains we can achieve with hybrids." Today, Toyota offers a full line of cars for the global market, from family sedans and sport utility vehicles to trucks and minivans. In 2013, the company earned more than 22 trillion yen (or $217 billion) and sold 8.87 million automobiles, edging past General Motors to become the world's largest carmaker.

## Questions

1. Toyota has built a huge manufacturing capacity that can produce millions of cars each year for a wide variety of consumers. Why was it able to become so much bigger than any other auto manufacturer?

2. Has Toyota done the right thing by manufacturing a car brand for everyone? Why or why not?

**Sources:** Martin Zimmerman, "Toyota's First Quarter Global Sales Beat GM's Preliminary Numbers," *Los Angeles Times,* April 24, 2007; Charles Fishman, "No Satisfaction at Toyota," *Fast Company,* December 2006–January 2007, pp. 82–90; Stuart F. Brown, "Toyota's Global Body Shop," *Fortune,* February 9, 2004, p. 120; James B. Treece, "Ford Down; Toyota Aims for No. 1," *Automotive News,* February 2, 2004, p. 1; Brian Bemner and Chester Dawson, "Can Anything Stop Toyota?," *BusinessWeek,* November 17, 2003, pp. 114–22; Tomoko A. Hosaka, "Toyota Counts Rising Costs of Recall Woes," *Associated Press,* March 16, 2010; "World Motor Vehicle Production by Manufacturer," *OICA,* July 2009; Chris Isidore, "Toyota Recall Costs: $2 Billion," http://money.cnn.com, February 4, 2010; Associated Press, "Toyota Sells Most Cars despite China Slump," July 26, 2013; Trefis Team, "Japan Quake, Tsunami Take Heavy Toll On Toyota," *Forbes,* April 8, 2011; Mike Ramsey, "Toyota Calls Hybrids 'Sturdy Bridge' to Automotive Future," *Wall Street Journal,* September 30, 2013; Toyota Motor Corporation 2013 Annual Report; www.toyota.com.

## In This Chapter, We Will Address the Following **Questions**

1. How can services be defined and classified, and how do they differ from goods? (p. 399)

2. What are the new services realities? (p. 406)

3. How can companies achieve excellence in services marketing? (p. 410)

4. How can companies improve service quality? (p. 417)

5. How can goods marketers improve customer-support services? (p. 418)

USAA's legendary quality of service and continual innovation has created strong customer loyalty.

*Source: © Blend Images/Alamy*

MyMarketingLab™

⭐ Improve Your Grade!
Over 10 million students improved their results using the Pearson MyLabs. Visit **mymktlab.com** for simulations, tutorials, and end-of-chapter problems.

# Designing and Managing Services

**As companies find it harder to differentiate their physical products, they turn to** service differentiation, whether that means on-time delivery, better and faster response to inquiries, or quicker resolution of complaints. Top service providers know these advantages well and also how to create memorable customer experiences.[1] One service business that understands how to better satisfy customers' needs is USAA.[2]

 *USAA Insurance sells auto and other insurance products to current and former members of the military and their families. The company has increased its share of each customer's business by launching a consumer bank, issuing credit cards, opening a discount brokerage, and offering no-load mutual funds. Its legendary quality of service has led to the highest customer satisfaction in the industry. USAA subscribers will often relate how the company looks out for them, even counseling them not to take out more insurance than they need. With such levels of trust, the company enjoys high customer loyalty and significant cross-selling opportunities. It cross-trains its call center reps to answer investment queries as well as insurance-related calls, increasing productivity and reducing the need to transfer customers between agents. With servicemen and women needing remote access to financial products earlier and more often than civilians, USAA has become a technological leader in the financial services industry. It was the first bank to allow iPhone deposits for its military customers and to conduct face-to-face video chats with soldiers in the field. Whether a customer is using a tablet, smart phone, or computer or visiting one of its financial centers—located mostly near military bases—USAA is committed to providing exemplary service.*

**Because it is critical to** understand the special nature of services and what that means to marketers, in this chapter we systematically analyze services and how to market them most effectively.

# The Nature of Services

The Bureau of Labor Statistics reports that the service-producing sector will continue to be the dominant employment generator in the future economy, adding about 18 million jobs between 2010 and 2018, or about 88 percent of the expected increase in total employment. By 2020, the goods-producing sector is expected to account for 11.9 percent of total jobs, down from 12.4 percent in 2010 and 16.8 percent in 2000. Manufacturing lost a staggering 5.7 million jobs from 2000 through 2010.[3] These numbers and others have led to a growing interest in the unique opportunities of marketing services.[4]

## SERVICE INDUSTRIES ARE EVERYWHERE

The *government sector,* with its courts, employment services, hospitals, loan agencies, military services, police and fire departments, postal service, regulatory agencies, and schools, is in the service business. The *private nonprofit sector*—museums, charities, churches, colleges, foundations, and hospitals—is in the service business. A good part of the *business sector,* with its airlines, banks, hotels, insurance companies, law firms, management consulting firms, medical practices, motion picture companies, plumbing repair companies, and real estate firms, is in the service business. Many workers in the *manufacturing sector,* such as computer operators, accountants, and legal staff, are really service providers. In fact, they make up a "service factory" providing services to the "goods factory." And those in the *retail sector,* such as cashiers, clerks, salespeople, and customer service representatives, are also providing a service.

A **service** is any act or performance one party can offer to another that is essentially intangible and does not result in the ownership of anything. Its production may or may not be tied to a physical product. Increasingly, manufacturers, distributors, and retailers are providing value-added services, or simply excellent customer service, to differentiate themselves. Many pure service firms are now using the Internet to reach customers; some operate purely online.

## CATEGORIES OF SERVICE MIX

The service component can be a minor or a major part of the total offering. We distinguish five categories of offerings:

1.  *A pure tangible good* such as soap, toothpaste, or salt with no accompanying services.
2.  *A tangible good with accompanying services*, like a car, computer, or cell phone, with a warranty or specialized customer service contract. Typically, the more technologically advanced the product, the greater the need for high-quality supporting services.
3.  *A hybrid* offering, like a restaurant meal, of equal parts goods and services. People patronize restaurants for both the food and its preparation.
4.  *A major service with accompanying minor goods and services*, like air travel with supporting goods such as snacks and drinks. This offering requires a capital-intensive good—an airplane—for its realization, but the primary item is a service.
5.  *A pure service,* primarily an intangible service, such as babysitting, psychotherapy, or massage.

Restaurants are good examples of hybrid offerings combining products and services. One of the more successful restaurant brands is Panera Bread.[5]

**PANERA BREAD** Founded by Ron Shaich as a Boston bakery called the Cookie Jar in 1980, Panera Bread has emerged over time as a leader, with Chipotle, in the "fast casual" restaurant category. Panera combines the speed and convenience of fast food with the quality and menu variety of waiter-service dining. The chain targets "food people who understand and respond to food or those on the verge of that" by selling fresh "real" food at full prices customers are more than willing to pay. An unpretentious atmosphere—no table service, but no time limit—encourages customers to linger. The brand is seen as family-oriented but also sophisticated, offering fresh-baked artisan bread and a full menu of healthy, good-tasting sandwiches, salads, soups, and breakfast foods. Panera has innovated in a number of different ways, infusing a strong social conscience in much that it does. With the slogan "Live Consciously. Eat Deliciously," CMO Michael Simon leads a number of social and community initiatives such as the Panera Bread Foundation, collaborations with Feeding America, and donations to local hunger relief agencies and charities. The company has opened five "pay-what-you-can" Panera Cares stores. In other marketing areas, it has boosted its digital spend and boasts a loyalty program with 14 million members, accounting for almost half its transactions.

The range of service offerings makes it difficult to generalize without a few further distinctions.

- Services are *equipment-based* (automated car washes, vending machines) or *people-based* (window washing, accounting services). People-based services vary by whether unskilled, skilled, or professional workers provide them.
- Service companies can choose among different *processes* to deliver their service. Restaurants offer cafeteria-style, fast-food, buffet, and candlelight service formats.
- Some services need the *client's presence*. Brain surgery requires the client's presence; a car repair does not. If the client must be present, the service provider must be considerate of his or her needs. Thus beauty salon operators will invest in décor, play background music, and engage in light conversation with the client.
- Services may meet a *personal need* (personal services) or a *business need* (business services). Service providers typically develop different marketing programs for these markets.
- Service providers differ in their *objectives* (profit or nonprofit) and *ownership* (private or public). These two characteristics, when crossed, produce four quite different types of organizations. The marketing programs of a private investor hospital will differ from those of a private charity hospital or a Veterans Administration hospital.

A leader in the "fast casual" restaurant category, Panera Bread has also opened some "pay-what-you-can" Panera Cares stores.

Customers typically cannot judge the technical quality of some services even after they have received them. Figure 14.1 shows various products and services according to difficulty of evaluation.[6] At the left are goods high in *search qualities*—that is, characteristics the buyer can evaluate before purchase. In the middle are goods and services high in *experience qualities*—characteristics the buyer can evaluate after purchase. At the right are goods and services high in *credence qualities*—characteristics the buyer normally finds hard to evaluate even after consumption.[7]

Because services are generally high in experience and credence qualities, there is more risk in their purchase, with several consequences. First, service consumers generally rely on word of mouth rather than advertising. Second, they rely heavily on price, provider, and physical cues to judge quality. Third, they are highly loyal to service providers who satisfy them. Fourth, because switching costs are high, consumer inertia can make it challenging to entice business away from a competitor.

Although customer loyalty can be strong with services, in today's modern communications environment, a service failure can be a PR nightmare and undermine that loyalty, as Carnival Cruises found.[8]

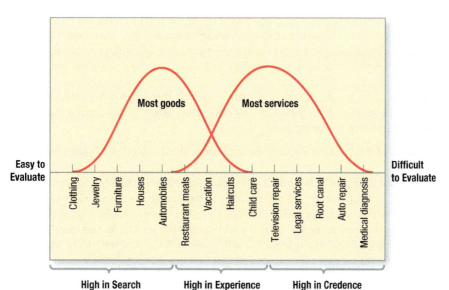

| **Fig. 14.1** |

## Continuum of Evaluation for Different Types of Products

Source: Valarie A. Zeithaml, "How Consumer Evaluation Processes Differ between Goods and Services," James H. Donnelly and William R. George, eds., *Marketing of Services* (Chicago: American Marketing Association, 1981). Reprinted with permission of the American Marketing Association.

An on-board disaster on one of Carnival's cruise ships created longer-term problems for the company.

Source: © Greg Balfour Evans/Alamy

▌CARNIVAL   The Carnival Triumph was on the third day of a four-day cruise from Galveston, Texas, to Mexico when an engine room fire set the boat adrift and disabled, leaving 3,100 passengers with little access to food, water, and toilets. Waste spilled into the hallways, and decks below became insufferably hot. When the boat returned to shore after a long five days, the CEO greeted passengers as they disembarked, given them each $500, a free flight home, a refund for the trip, and credit for another cruise. Nevertheless, given the publicity surrounding what the media called the "poop cruise," the damage had been done. Public opinion of cruises as a whole dropped. Carnival found its bookings declining by a hefty 20 percent, forcing the company to pass along steep discounts to fill boats. To avoid future problems, the cruise line invested $600 million to upgrade its fleet and hired a new VP of Technical Operations to oversee its safety initiatives.

## DISTINCTIVE CHARACTERISTICS OF SERVICES

Four distinctive service characteristics greatly affect the design of marketing programs: *intangibility, inseparability, variability,* and *perishability.*[9]

**INTANGIBILITY**   Unlike physical products, services cannot be seen, tasted, felt, heard, or smelled before they are bought. A person getting cosmetic surgery cannot see the results before the purchase, and the patient in the psychiatrist's office cannot know the exact outcome of treatment. To reduce uncertainty, buyers will look for evidence of quality by drawing inferences from the place, people, equipment, communication material, symbols, and price. Therefore, the service provider's task is to "manage the evidence," to "tangibilize the intangible."[10]

Service companies can try to demonstrate their service quality through *physical evidence* and *presentation.*[11] Suppose a supermarket wants to position itself as the "fast" supermarket. It could make this positioning strategy tangible through any number of marketing tools:

1.  *Place*—The layout of the checkout area and the traffic flow should be planned carefully. Waiting lines should not get overly long.
2.  *People*—Checkout staff should be busy, but there should be a sufficient number to manage the workload.
3.  *Equipment*—UPC scanners, credit card readers, and electronic registers should all be state of the art.
4.  *Communication material*—signage and brochures—text and photos—should suggest efficiency and speed.
5.  *Symbols*—The supermarket's name and symbol could suggest fast service, for instance, "Speedy Shop."
6.  *Price*—The supermarket could advertise a $10 rebate if customers have to wait in line more than five minutes.

Disney is a master at "tangibilizing the intangible" and creating magical fantasies in its theme parks; so are retailers such as Toys "R" Us and Bass Pro Shops.[12] Table 14.1 measures brand experiences along sensory, affective, behavioral, and intellectual dimensions. Applications to services are clear.

| TABLE 14.1 | Dimensions of Brand Experience |
| --- | --- |

**Sensory**

- This brand makes a strong impression on my visual sense or other senses.
- I find this brand interesting in a sensory way.
- This brand does not appeal to my senses.

**Affective**

- This brand induces feelings and sentiments.
- I do not have strong emotions for this brand.
- This brand is an emotional brand.

**Behavioral**

- I engage in physical actions and behaviors when I use this brand.
- This brand results in bodily experiences.
- This brand is not action-oriented.

**Intellectual**

- I engage in a lot of thinking when I encounter this brand.
- This brand does not make me think.
- This brand stimulates my curiosity and problem solving.

**Source:** Joško Brakus, Bernd H. Schmitt, and Lia Zarantonello, "Brand Experience: What Is It? How Is It Measured? Does It Affect Loyalty?," *Journal of Marketing* 73 (May 2009), pp. 52–68.

Because there is no physical product, the service provider's facilities—its primary and secondary signage, environmental design and reception area, employee apparel, collateral material, and so on—are especially important. All aspects of the service delivery process can be branded, which is why Allied Van Lines is concerned about the appearance of its drivers and laborers, why UPS has developed such strong equity with its brown trucks, and why Doubletree by Hilton hotels offers fresh-baked chocolate chip cookies to symbolize care and friendliness.

Service providers often choose brand elements—logos, symbols, characters, and slogans—to make the service and its key benefits more tangible—for example, the "friendly skies" of United, the "good hands" of Allstate, and the "bullish" nature of Merrill Lynch.

**INSEPARABILITY** Whereas physical goods are manufactured, then inventoried, then distributed, and later consumed, services are typically produced and consumed simultaneously.[13] A haircut can't be stored—or produced without the barber. The provider is part of the service. Because the client is also often present, provider–client interaction is a special feature of services marketing. Buyers of entertainment and professional services are very interested in the specific provider. It's not the same concert if Taylor Swift is indisposed and replaced by Beyoncé or if a corporate legal defense is supplied by an intern because antitrust expert David Boies is unavailable. When clients have strong provider preferences, the provider can raise its price to ration its limited time.

Several strategies exist for getting around the limitations of inseparability. The service provider can work with larger groups. Some psychotherapists have moved from one-on-one therapy to small-group therapy to groups of more than 300 people in a large hotel ballroom. The service provider can work faster—the psychotherapist can spend 30 more efficient minutes with each patient instead of 50 less-structured minutes and thus see more patients. The service organization can train more service providers and build up client confidence, as H&R Block has done with its national network of trained tax consultants.

**VARIABILITY** Because the quality of services depends on who provides them, when and where, and to whom, services are highly variable. Some doctors have an excellent bedside manner; others are less empathetic. Service firms know that variability in their performance puts them at risk. Hilton initiated a major program to create more uniformity in guest experiences.[14]

Source: © StockImages/Alamy

Hilton's H360 program created higher and more uniform service standards for its properties all over the world.

**HILTON HOTELS** Between 1964 when Hilton Hotels sold its foreign licensee Hilton International Co. and 2006 when it bought it back, the two companies operated largely independently, and as a result, the Hilton brand was no longer providing customers with a uniform high-quality experience. Nomura research analyst Harry Curtis said, "The brand standards in Europe were always very different from those in the U.S. I think they were, quite frankly, a bit slacker in Europe." Chris Nassetta, appointed CEO in 2008, initiated H360, a project to review everything from breakfast fare to bath amenities, the décor of lobbies, Wi-Fi service, hotel architecture, and handling of customer complaints at all the company's hotels. Nassetta said, "There was a huge amount of inconsistency in the granular standards that travelers care about." As a result of H360, independent owners of Hilton-branded hotels in the United States and abroad have been forced to upgrade to Hilton standards where necessary or be dropped from the Hilton system. Protecting the brand seems to have served the company well—by 2010, the company had the highest brand equity of nearly 40 hotel chains.

Service buyers are aware of potential variability and often talk to others or go online to collect information before selecting a specific service provider. To reassure customers, some firms offer *service guarantees* that may reduce consumer perceptions of risk.[15] Here are three steps service firms can take to increase quality control.

1. *Invest in good hiring and training procedures.* Recruiting the right employees and giving them excellent training are crucial, whether they are highly skilled professionals or low-skilled workers. Better-trained people exhibit six characteristics that improve service quality: competence, courtesy, credibility, reliability, responsiveness, and communication skill.

2. *Standardize the service-performance process throughout the organization.* A *service blueprint* can map out the service process, the points of customer contact, and the evidence of service from the customer's point of view.[16] Figure 14.2 shows a service blueprint for an overnight guest at a hotel.[17] Behind the scenes, the hotel must skillfully help the guest move from one step to the next. Service blueprints can be helpful in identifying potential "pain points" for customers, developing new services, supporting a zero-defects culture, and devising service recovery strategies.

3. *Monitor customer satisfaction.* Employ suggestion and complaint systems, customer surveys, and third-party comparison shopping. Customer needs may vary in different areas, allowing firms to develop region-specific customer satisfaction programs.[18] Firms can also develop customer information databases and systems for more personalized service, especially online.[19]

Service firms can also design marketing communication and information programs so consumers learn more about the brand than what their subjective experience alone tells them.

**PERISHABILITY** Services cannot be stored, so their perishability can be a problem when demand fluctuates. To accommodate rush-hour demand, public transportation companies must own more equipment than if demand was even throughout the day. Some doctors charge patients for missed appointments because the service value (the doctor's availability) exists only at the time of the appointment.

Demand or yield management is critical—the right services must be available to the right customers at the right places at the right times and right prices to maximize profitability. Several strategies can produce a better match between service demand and supply.[20] On the demand (customer) side:

- *Differential pricing* will shift some demand from peak to off-peak periods. Examples include low matinee movie prices and weekend discounts for car rentals.[21]
- *Nonpeak demand* can be cultivated. McDonald's pushes breakfast service, and hotels promote minivacation weekends.

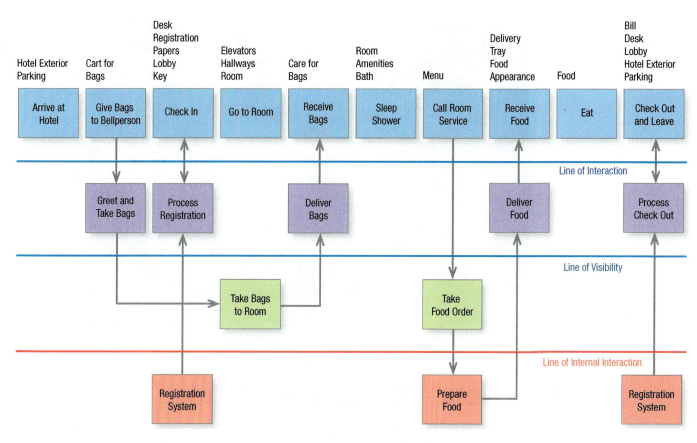

**| Fig. 14.2 |**

Blueprint for Overnight Hotel Stay

Source: Valarie Zeithaml, Mary Jo Bitner, and Dwayne D. Gremler, *Services Marketing: Integrating Customer Focus across the Firm*, 4th ed. (New York: McGraw-Hill, 2006).

- **Complementary services** can provide alternatives to waiting customers, such as cocktail lounges in restaurants and automated teller machines in banks.
- **Reservation systems** are a way to manage the demand level. Airlines, hotels, and physicians employ them extensively.

On the supply side:

- **Part-time employees** can serve peak demand. Colleges add part-time teachers when enrollment goes up; stores hire extra clerks during holiday periods.
- **Peak-time efficiency routines** can allow employees to perform only essential tasks during peak periods. Paramedics assist physicians during busy periods.
- **Increased consumer participation** frees service providers' time. Consumers fill out their own medical records or bag their own groceries.
- **Shared services** can improve offerings. Several hospitals can share medical-equipment purchases.
- **Facilities for future expansion** can be a good investment. An amusement park might buy surrounding land for later development.

For fast-food chains, drive-through windows are a way to expand selling opportunities beyond sit-down meals. An impressive 70 percent of revenue for the fast-food industry comes via drive-through windows. According to *QSR* magazine, Taco Bell operates some of the fastest and most accurate drive-through windows. The company aims for 3 minutes and 30 seconds per order and is constantly looking at ways to shave seconds and cut costs.[22]

A huge source of revenue for fast food chains, Taco Bell has excelled in its drive-through speed and accuracy.

Source: Taco Bell Corp.

# The New Services Realities

Service firms once lagged behind manufacturers in their understanding and use of marketing because they were small or they faced large demand or little competition. This has certainly changed. Some of the most skilled marketers now are service firms. One that wins consistent praise for its brand-building success is Singapore Airlines.[23]

**SINGAPORE AIRLINES**   Singapore Airlines (SIA) has been consistently recognized as the world's "best" airline, in large part due to its stellar marketing. The carrier wins so many awards, it has to update its Web site monthly to keep up to date. Famous for pampering passengers, it continually strives to create a "wow effect" and surpass customers' expectations. SIA was the first to launch on-demand entertainment systems in all classes, Dolby sound systems, and a book-the-cook service that allows business- and first-class passengers to order meals before boarding. Thanks to a first-of-its-kind $1 million simulator the airline built to mimic the air pressure and humidity inside a plane, it found that taste buds change in the air and that, among other things, it needed to cut back on spices in its food. New SIA recruits receive four months of training, twice the industry average, and existing staff get nearly three weeks of refresher training a year (costing $70 million). With its stellar reputation, the carrier attracts some of the best local graduates and staffs each flight with more attendants and other cabin crew members than other airlines. SIA applies a 40–30–30 rule: 40 percent of resources go to training and motivating staff, 30 percent to reviewing process and procedures, and 30 percent to creating new product and service ideas.

## A SHIFTING CUSTOMER RELATIONSHIP

Because U.S. consumers generally have high expectations about service delivery, they often feel their needs are not being adequately met. A 2013 Forrester study asked consumers to rate 154 companies on how well they met their needs and how easy and enjoyable they were to do business with. Almost two-thirds of the companies were rated only "OK," "poor," or "very poor." Retail and hotel companies were rated the highest on average, and Internet, health service, and television service providers were rated the worst. The highest-ranking companies were Marshalls, USAA (bank), Amazon.com, Kohl's, Target, Courtyard by Marriott, Sam's Club, Rite Aid, Costco, Lowe's, TJ Maxx, JCPenney, and Marriott Hotels & Resorts.[24]

Service providers receive low marks for many reasons. Customers complain about inaccurate information; unresponsive, rude, or poorly trained workers; and long waits. Even worse, many find their complaints never reach

Singapore's exemplary service quality starts with its famed flight attendants.

a human ear because of slow or faulty phone or online reporting systems. They say companies mishandle online complaints by responding selectively or inconsistently (or not at all) and by "cutting and running," appearing insincere, or attempting to just "bribe" the consumer.[25]

It doesn't have to be that way. Fifty-five operators on Butterball Turkey's 800 number handle 100,000 calls a year about how to prepare, cook, and serve turkeys; 12,000 people call on Thanksgiving Day alone. Trained at Butterball University, the operators have all cooked turkeys dozens of different ways and can handle any queries that come their way, including why you shouldn't stash turkeys in snow banks and how to tell when the turkey is done.[26]

Savvy services marketers are recognizing the new services realities, such as the importance of the newly empowered customer, customer coproduction, and the need to engage employees as well as customers.

**CUSTOMER EMPOWERMENT** The digital era has clearly altered customer relationships. Customers are becoming more sophisticated about buying product-support services and are pressing for "unbundled services" and the right to select the elements they want. They increasingly dislike having to deal with a multitude of service providers handling different types of products or equipment. With that in mind, some third-party service organizations now service a greater range of equipment. A plumbing business may also service air conditioners, furnaces, and other components of a household infrastructure.

Most importantly, the Internet has empowered customers by letting them send their comments around the world with a mouse click. A person who has a good customer experience is more likely to talk about it, but someone who has a bad experience will talk to more people.[27] Ninety percent of angry customers reported sharing their story with a friend; now, they can share it with strangers too. At PlanetFeedback.com shoppers can send a complaint, compliment, suggestion, or question directly to a company, with the option to post comments publicly on the site as well. Online sites such as Angie's List, Yelp, Google Places, and Urbanspoon are other popular means to spread the word on customer service adventures.

Even more challenging for firms, unhappy customers may choose to download a damaging video to share their customer service miseries with others. "Marketing Memo: Lights! Camera! Customer Service Disasters!" describes some notable customer service disasters brought to light with online videos.

When a customer complains, most companies now respond quickly. Comcast allows contact 24/7 by phone and e-chat but also reaches out to customers and monitors blogs, Web sites, and social media. If employees see a customer report a problem on a blog, they get in touch and offer help. Clear, helpful e-mail replies to customers' queries can be effective too.[28] Delta Airlines introduced Delta Assist to monitor customer Twitter tweets and Facebook posts around the clock with a 10-person team and to provide real-time replies to any queries or problems.[29]

More important than simply responding to a disgruntled customer, however, is preventing dissatisfaction from occurring in the future. That may mean simply taking the time to nurture customer relationships with attention from a real person. Solving a customer's problem quickly and easily goes a long way toward winning long-term loyal customers.[30]

**CUSTOMER COPRODUCTION** The reality is that customers do not merely purchase and use a service; they play an active role in its delivery. Their words and actions affect the quality of their service experiences and those of others as well as the productivity of frontline employees.[31]

## marketing memo

## Lights! Cameras! Customer Service Disasters!

The explosion of videos online has posed many challenges to firms. Not only customers but also employees can damage the firm's reputation, and the Internet greatly magnifies the impact.

Many fast-food chains have had to deal with unflattering or inappropriate behavior their employees capture on video as a prank. Online clips have shown a Wendy's worker with his mouth wide open under a Frosty machine, a Domino's employee putting cheese up his nose and mucus on food meant for delivery, and a Taco Bell employee licking a stack of empty taco shells.

Any service organization may pay the price for a service breakdown. When Canadian singer Dave Carroll faced $1,200 in damages to his $3,000 Gibson guitar after a United flight, he put his creative energy to good use and launched a humorous YouTube video, *United Breaks Guitars*, with this catchy refrain:

"United, you broke my Taylor guitar. United, some big help you are. You broke it, you should fix it. You're liable, just admit it. I should have flown with someone else or gone by car 'cuz United breaks guitars."

Carroll's follow-up video about his frustrating efforts to get United to pay for the damage was viewed more than 5 million times. The airline got the message and donated a check for $1,200 to a charity Carroll designated. It now uses the incident to train baggage handlers and customer-service representatives.

After a security camera caught a FedEx driver delivering a computer monitor by throwing it over a six-foot fence instead of ringing the doorbell, the 21-second YouTube video placed by the irate customer received millions of views and heaps of negative publicity. FedEx cut a YouTube apology of its own, titled "Absolutely, Positively Unacceptable"—a play on its old advertising slogan, though with only a fraction of the views. FedEx not only replaced the customer's computer monitor free of charge, it also has shared the video internally with employees.

Critics credit the companies for attempting to deal with their problems quickly and forcefully, while often faulting them too for their hiring and training practices and for not creating a stronger, brand-supportive climate with employees.

**Sources:** "Bruce Horovitz, "Wendy's Is Latest to See Gross Photo Go Viral," *USA Today*, June 13, 2013; Bruce Horovitz, "Photo of Taco Bell Worker Licking Shells Sends Shudders," *USA Today*, June 3, 2013; Chad Brooks, "Caught on Video: Employees Behaving Badly," *Business News*, March 28, 2012; Chunka Mui, "The 5 Most Brand-Damaging Viral Videos of 2011," *Forbes*, December 28, 2011; Laurent Belsie, "FedEx Delivery Video: Package Thrown. FedEx Apologizes on YouTube," *Christian Science Monitor*, December 23, 2011; Dan Reed, "United Makeover Aims to Refresh and Renew," *USA Today*, September 17, 2009, pp. 1B–2B; Elisabeth Sullivan, "Happy Endings Lead to Happy Returns," *Marketing News*, October 30, 2009, p. 20.

Customers often feel they derive more value, and feel a stronger connection to the service provider, if they are actively engaged in the service process. This coproduction can put stress on employees, however, and reduce their satisfaction, especially if they differ from customers culturally or in other ways.[32] Moreover, one study estimated that one-third of all service problems are caused by the customer.[33] The growing shift to self-service technologies will likely increase this percentage.

Preventing service failures is crucial because recovery is always challenging. One of the biggest problems is attribution—customers often feel the firm is at fault or, even if not, that it is still responsible for righting any wrongs. Unfortunately, although many firms have well-designed and executed procedures to deal with their own failures, they find managing *customer* failures—when a service problem arises from a customer's mistake or lack of understanding—much more difficult. Solutions come in all forms, as these examples show:[34]

1. *Redesign processes and redefine customer roles to simplify service encounters.* Staples transformed its business with its "Easy" program to take the hassle out of ordering office supplies.
2. *Incorporate the right technology to aid employees and customers.* Comcast, the largest U.S. cable operator, introduced software to identify network glitches before they affected service and to better inform call-center operators about customer problems. Repeat service calls dropped 30 percent as a result.
3. *Create high-performance customers by enhancing their role clarity, motivation, and ability.* USAA reminds enlisted policyholders to suspend their car insurance when they are stationed overseas.
4. *Encourage "customer citizenship" so customers help each other.* At golf courses, players can not only follow the rules by playing and behaving appropriately, they can encourage others to do so.

**SATISFYING EMPLOYEES AS WELL AS CUSTOMERS** Excellent service companies know that positive employee attitudes will strengthen customer loyalty.[35] Instilling a strong customer orientation in employees can also increase their job satisfaction and commitment, especially if they have high customer contact. Employees thrive in customer-contact positions when they have an internal drive to (1) pamper customers, (2) accurately read their needs, (3) develop a personal relationship with them, and (4) deliver high-quality service to solve customers' problems.[36]

Consistent with this reasoning, Sears found a high correlation between customer satisfaction, employee satisfaction, and store profitability. The downside of not treating employees right is significant. A survey of 10,000 employees from the largest 1,000 companies found that 40 percent of workers cited "lack of recognition" as a key reason for leaving a job.[37]

Given the importance of positive employee attitudes to customer satisfaction, service companies must attract the best employees they can find. They need to market a career rather than just a job. They must design a sound training program and provide support and rewards for good performance. They can use an intranet, internal newsletters, daily reminders, and employee roundtables to reinforce customer-centered attitudes. Finally, they must audit employee job satisfaction regularly.

The Panda Express restaurant chain has management turnover that's half the industry average, due in part to a combination of ample bonuses and health benefits with a strong emphasis on worker self-improvement through meditation, education, and hobbies. Special wellness seminars and get-to-know-you events outside work help create a caring, nurturing atmosphere.[38]

Zappos has built a customer-focused organization admired by many.[39]

Source: Zappos.com Inc

▌ **ZAPPOS**  Online retailer Zappos was cofounded by Tony Hsieh in 1999 with superior customer service at the core of its culture. With free shipping and returns, 24/7 customer service, and fast turnaround on the numerous products offered on the site from thousands of brands, the company works hard to create repeat customers. Unlike many other companies, it has not outsourced its Zappos.com call centers, and half the interview process is devoted to finding out whether job candidates are sufficiently outgoing, open-minded, and creative to be a good cultural fit. Zappos empowers its customer service reps to solve problems. When a customer called to complain that a pair of boots was leaking after a year of use, the rep sent a new pair even though the company's policy is that only unworn shoes are returnable. Every employee has a chance each year to contribute to the company's Culture Book, about life at Zappos and how each department implements superior customer service from selling to warehousing, delivery, pricing, and billing. Bought by Amazon.com in 2009 for a reported $850 million but still run separately, the company now also sells clothing, handbags, and accessories. Thanks to its success, it even offers two-day seminars to business executives eager to learn the secrets behind Zappos's unique corporate culture and approach to customer service.

Founder Tony Hsieh's customer service practices at online retailer Zappos are widely-admired and studied.

# Achieving Excellence In Services Marketing

The increased importance of the service industry has sharpened the focus on what it takes to excel in the marketing of services.[40] Here are some guidelines.

## MARKETING EXCELLENCE

Marketing excellence in services requires excellence in three broad areas: external, internal, and interactive marketing (see Figure 14.3).[41]

- **External marketing** describes the normal work of preparing, pricing, distributing, and promoting the service to customers.

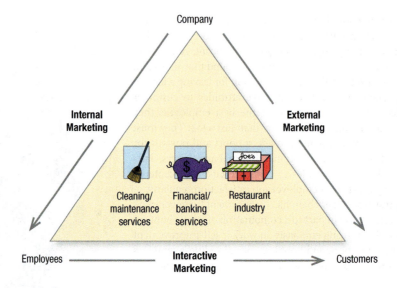

- *Internal marketing* describes training and motivating employees to serve customers well. Arguably the most important contribution the marketing department can make is to be "exceptionally clever in getting everyone else in the organization to practice marketing."[42]
- *Interactive marketing* describes the employees' skill in serving the client. Clients judge service not only by its *technical quality* (Was the surgery successful?), but also by its *functional quality* (Did the surgeon show concern and inspire confidence?).[43] In interactive marketing, teamwork is often key. Delegating authority to frontline employees can allow for greater service flexibility and adaptability because it promotes better problem solving, closer employee cooperation, and more efficient knowledge transfer.[44]

A good example of a service company achieving marketing excellence is Charles Schwab.[45]

**CHARLES SCHWAB**  Charles Schwab, one of the nation's largest discount brokerage houses, uses the telephone, Internet, and wireless devices to create an innovative combination of high-tech and high-touch services. One of the first major brokerage houses to provide online trading, the company today serves more than 8 million individual and institutional accounts. It offers account information and proprietary research from retail brokers, real-time quotes, an after-hours trading program, the Schwab learning center, live events, online chats with customer service representatives, a global investing service, and market updates delivered by e-mail. It has also been adding a slew of mobile capabilities to satisfy its customer on the go. Schwab grew during the financial crisis by offering new products for sophisticated investors, such as managed portfolio ETFs and fixed income funds. Besides the discount brokerage, the firm offers mutual funds, annuities, bond trading, and now mortgages through its Charles Schwab Bank. Its success has been driven by its efforts to lead in three areas: superior service (online, via phone, and in local branch offices), innovative products, and low prices. Its long-running "Talk to Chuck" marketing campaign reinforces how the firm is always there to help its customers.

## TECHNOLOGY AND SERVICE DELIVERY

Technology is changing the rules of the game for services in a very fundamental way. Banking, for instance, is being transformed by the ability to bank online and via mobile apps—some customers rarely see a bank lobby or interact with an employee anymore.[46] Technology also has great power to make service workers more productive. When USAirways deployed handheld scanners to better track baggage, mishandled baggage decreased almost 50 percent. The new technology paid for itself in the first year and helped contribute to a 35 percent drop in complaints.[47]

Sometimes new technology has unanticipated benefits. When BMW introduced Wi-Fi to its dealerships to help customers pass the time more productively while their cars were being serviced, more chose to wait rather than use loaner cars, an expensive item for dealers to maintain.[48]

Companies must avoid pushing technological efficiency so hard, however, that they reduce perceived quality.[49] Some methods lead to too much standardization, but service providers must deliver "high touch" as well as "high tech."[50] Amazon has some of the most innovative technology in online retailing, but it also keeps customers extremely satisfied when a problem arises even if they don't actually talk to an Amazon employee.[51] More companies are introducing "live chat" features to blend technology with a human voice.[52]

As Chapter 5 reviewed, the Internet lets firms improve their service offerings and strengthen their relationships with customers by allowing for true interactivity, customer-specific and situational personalization, and real-time adjustments of the firm's offerings. But as companies collect, store, and use more information about customers, they have also raised concerns about security and privacy. Companies must incorporate the proper safeguards and reassure customers about their efforts.

## BEST PRACTICES OF TOP SERVICE COMPANIES

Well-managed service companies that achieve marketing excellence have in common a strategic concept, a history of top-management commitment to quality, high standards, profit tiers, and systems for monitoring service performance and customer complaints.

**STRATEGIC CONCEPT** Top service companies are "customer obsessed." They have a clear sense of their target customers and their needs and have developed a distinctive strategy for satisfying them. At the Four Seasons luxury hotel chain, employees must pass four interviews before being hired. Each hotel also employs a "guest historian" to track guest preferences. With more than 10,000 branches in the United States, more than any other brokerage firm, Edward Jones stays close to customers by assigning a single financial advisor and one administrator to each office. Although costly, maintaining such small teams fosters personal relationships.[53]

**TOP-MANAGEMENT COMMITMENT** Companies such as Marriott, Disney, and Ace Hardware have a thorough commitment to service quality. Their managers look monthly not only at financial performance, but also at service performance. Ray Kroc of McDonald's insisted on continually measuring each McDonald's outlet on its conformance to QSCV: quality, service, cleanliness, and value. Some companies insert a reminder along with employees' paychecks: "Brought to you by the customer." Sam Walton of Walmart required the following employee pledge: "I solemnly swear and declare that every customer that comes within 10 feet of me, I will smile, look them in the eye, and greet them, so help me Sam." Allstate, Dunkin' Brands, Oracle, and USAA have high-level senior executives with titles such as Chief Customer Officer, Chief Client Officer, or Chief Experience Officer who have the power and authority to improve customer service across every customer interaction.[54]

Edward Jones has invested in an extensive branch network to foster closer customer relationships.

*Source: © ZUMA Press, Inc./Alamy*

**HIGH STANDARDS** The best service providers set high quality standards. In the highly regulated banking industry, Citibank still aims to answer customer phone calls within 10 seconds and letters within two days; it has been an industry leader in using social media for customer service.[55] The standards must be set *appropriately* high. A 98 percent accuracy standard may sound good, but it would result in 64,000 lost FedEx packages a day; six misspelled words on each page of a book; 400,000 incorrectly filled prescriptions daily; 3 million lost piece of USPS mail each day; no phone, Internet, or electricity for eight days per year or 29 minutes per day; 1,000 mislabeled or (mispriced) products at a supermarket; and 6 million people unaccounted for in a U.S. census.

**PROFIT TIERS** Firms have decided to coddle big spenders to retain their patronage as long as possible. Customers in high-profit tiers get special discounts, promotional offers, and lots of special service; those in lower-profit tiers who barely pay their way may get more fees, stripped-down service, and voice messages to process their inquiries.

When the recent recession hit, Zappos decided to stop offering complimentary overnight shipping to first-time buyers and offer it to repeat buyers only. The money saved was invested in a new VIP service for the company's most loyal customers.[56] Companies that provide differentiated levels of service must be careful about claiming superior service, however—customers who receive lesser treatment will bad-mouth the company and injure its reputation. Delivering services that maximize both customer satisfaction and company profitability can be challenging.

**MONITORING SYSTEMS** Top firms audit service performance, both their own and competitors', on a regular basis. They collect *voice of the customer (VOC) measurements* to probe customer satisfiers and dissatisfiers and use comparison shopping, mystery or ghost shopping, customer surveys, suggestion and complaint forms, service-audit teams, and customers' letters.

We can judge services on *customer importance* and *company performance. Importance-performance analysis* rates the various elements of the service bundle and identifies required actions. Table 14.2 shows how customers rated 14 service elements or attributes of an automobile dealer's service department on importance and performance. For example, "Job done right the first time" (attribute 1) received a mean importance rating of 3.83 and a

| TABLE 14.2 | Customer Importance and Performance Ratings for an Auto Dealership |

| Number Attribute | Attribute Description | Mean Importance Rating[a] | Mean Performance Rating[b] |
|---|---|---|---|
| 1 | Job done right the first time | 3.83 | 2.63 |
| 2 | Fast action on complaints | 3.63 | 2.73 |
| 3 | Prompt warranty work | 3.60 | 3.15 |
| 4 | Able to do any job needed | 3.56 | 3.00 |
| 5 | Service available when needed | 3.41 | 3.05 |
| 6 | Courteous and friendly service | 3.41 | 3.29 |
| 7 | Car ready when promised | 3.38 | 3.03 |
| 8 | Perform only necessary work | 3.37 | 3.11 |
| 9 | Low prices on service | 3.29 | 2.00 |
| 10 | Clean up after service work | 3.27 | 3.02 |
| 11 | Convenient to home | 2.52 | 2.25 |
| 12 | Convenient to work | 2.43 | 2.49 |
| 13 | Courtesy buses and cars | 2.37 | 2.35 |
| 14 | Send out maintenance notices | 2.05 | 3.33 |

[a] Ratings obtained from a four-point scale of "extremely important" (4), "important" (3), "slightly important" (2), and "not important" (1).

[b] Ratings obtained from a four-point scale of "excellent" (4), "good" (3), "fair" (2), and "poor" (1). A "no basis for judgment" category was also provided.

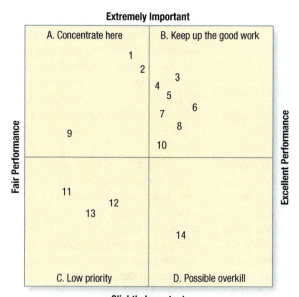

**| Fig. 14.4 |**

Importance-
Performance Analysis

mean performance rating of 2.63, indicating that customers felt it was highly important but not performed well. The ratings of the 14 elements are divided into four sections in Figure 14.4.

- Quadrant A in the figure shows important service elements that are not being performed at the desired levels; they include elements 1, 2, and 9. The dealer should concentrate on improving the service department's performance on these elements.
- Quadrant B shows important service elements that are being performed well; the company needs to maintain this high performance.
- Quadrant C shows minor service elements that are being delivered in a mediocre way but do not need any attention.
- Quadrant D shows that a minor service element, "Send out maintenance notices," is being performed in an excellent manner.

Perhaps the company should spend less on sending out maintenance notices and use the savings to improve performance on important elements. Management can enhance its analysis by checking on competitors' performance levels on each element.[57]

**SATISFYING CUSTOMER COMPLAINTS** On average, 40 percent of customers who suffer through a bad service experience stop doing business with the company.[58] But if those customers are willing to complain first, they actually offer the company a gift if the complaint is handled well.

Companies that encourage disappointed customers to complain—and also empower employees to remedy the situation on the spot—have been shown to achieve higher revenues and greater profits than companies without a systematic approach for addressing service failures.[59] Frontline employees who adopt *extra-role behaviors* and who advocate the interests and image of the firm to consumers, as well as taking initiative and engaging in conscientious behavior in dealing with customers, can be a critical asset in handling complaints.[60] Customers evaluate complaint incidents in terms of the outcomes they receive, the procedures used to arrive at those outcomes, and the nature of interpersonal treatment during the process.[61]

Companies also are increasing the quality of their *call centers* and their *customer service representatives* (CSRs). "Marketing Insight: Improving Company Call Centers" illustrates what top companies are doing.

# DIFFERENTIATING SERVICES

Finally, customers who view a service as fairly homogeneous care less about the provider than about the price. Marketing excellence requires service marketers to continually differentiate their brands so they are not seen as a commodity. Consider how JetBlue and Southwest Airlines have succeeded through differentiation.[62]

## marketing insight

# Improving Company Call Centers

Many firms have learned the hard way that empowered customers will not put up with poor service. After Sprint and Nextel merged, they set out to run their call centers as cost centers, rather than a means to enhance customer loyalty. Employee rewards were based on keeping customer calls short, and when management started to monitor even bathroom trips, morale sank. With customer churn spinning out of control, Sprint Nextel adopted a plan to emphasize service over efficiency. The company appointed its first chief service officer and started rewarding operators for solving problems on a customer's first call rather than for keeping their calls short. After a year, the average customer was contacting customer service only four times instead of eight.

Some firms, such as AT&T, JPMorgan Chase, and Expedia, have established call centers in the Philippines rather than India because Filipinos speak lightly accented English and are more steeped in U.S. culture than Indians, who speak British-style English and may use unfamiliar idioms. Others are getting smarter about the type of calls they send to off-shore call centers, *homeshoring* by directing more complex calls to highly trained domestic customer service reps. These work-at-home reps often provide higher-quality service at less cost with lower turnover.

Firms have to decide how many customer service reps they need. One study showed that cutting just four reps at a call center of three dozen sent the number of customers put on hold for four minutes or more from zero to eighty. Firms can also try to reasonably get more from each rep. Marriott and other firms such as KeyBank and Ace Hardware have consolidated call center operations into fewer locations, allowing them to maintain their number of reps in the process.

Hiring and training are influential too. An extensive study by Xerox demonstrated that a good call-center worker with a high probability to stay the six months necessary to recoup the company's $5,000 investment was likely to have a creative rather than an inquisitive personality. Rather than emphasizing prior experience in hiring for its roughly 50,000 call-center jobs, Xerox now factors in answers to questions like "I ask more questions than most people do" and "People tend to trust what I say."

Some firms are taking advantage of Big Data capabilities to match individual customers with the call center agent best suited to meet their needs. Using something like the methods of online dating sites, advanced analytics technology mines transaction and demographic information about customers (products or services they've purchased, contract terms and expiration date, record of complaints or average call wait time) and call center agents (average call handling time and sales efficiency) to identify optimal matches in real time.

Finally, keeping call center reps happy and motivated is obviously a key to boosting their ability to offer excellent customer service. American Express lets call center reps choose their own hours and swap shifts without a supervisor's approval.

**Sources:** Claudia Jasmand, Vera Blazevic, and Ko de Ruyter, "Generating Sales while Providing Service: A Study of Customer Service Representatives' Ambidextrous Behavior," *Journal of Marketing* 76 (January 2012), pp. 20–37; Kimmy Wa Chan and Echo Wen Wan, "How Can Stressed Employees Deliver Better Customer Service? The Underlying Self-Regulation Depletion Mechanism," *Journal of Marketing* 76 (January 2012), pp. 119–37; Joseph Walker, "Meet the New Boss: Big Data," *Wall Street Journal*, September 20, 2012; Vikas Bajaj, "A New Capital of Call Centers," *New York Times*, November 25, 2011; Michael Shroeck, "Why the Customer Call Center Isn't Dead," *Forbes*, March 15, 2011; Michael Sanserino and Cari Tuna, "Companies Strive Harder to Please Customers," *Wall Street Journal*, July 27, 2009, p. B4; Spencer E. Ante, "Sprint's Wake-Up Call," *BusinessWeek*, March 3, 2008, pp. 54–57; Jena McGregor, "Customer Service Champs," *BusinessWeek*, March 5, 2007.

**JETBLUE AND SOUTHWEST AIRLINES**  In an industry often characterized by bankruptcies and unhappy customers, two exceptions are JetBlue and Southwest Airlines. The companies have followed very different paths on their way to financial and marketplace success. Southwest, the older of the two, developed an unusual business model for an airline: short hauls only, no travel agents, no meals, no gates at major airports, and no fees. Although the carrier has changed some of those practices, it remains determined to avoid the bag, ticket change, and other fees adopted by competing airlines, believing it would lose $1 billion in revenue from lost bookings otherwise. A true discount airline, Southwest has been able to offer low fares by virtue of a disciplined cost structure that keeps planes in the air and seats filled, all with an informal, friendly style. The company hires employees with outgoing personalities who like to work with people and empowers them to do so. JetBlue also started with a very different business model, primarily targeting leisure travelers at its JFK hub in New York City. Another discount carrier with a low-cost structure, the company had the advantage of offering comfy seats, live TV, and choice of snacks. It is building a $25 million lodge at JetBlue University in Orlando to foster culture and camaraderie among employees and exploring options for business travelers, including fancier, more expensive seating on its transcontinental routes.

**PRIMARY AND SECONDARY SERVICE OPTIONS** Marketers can differentiate their service offerings in many ways, through people and processes that add value. What the customer expects is called the *primary*

Although they have very different business models, discount airlines JetBlue and Southwest Airlines have both experienced great marketplace success.

*service package.* Vanguard, one of the world's largest no-load mutual fund company, has a unique client ownership structure that lowers costs and permits better fund returns. Strongly differentiated from many competitors, the brand grew through word of mouth, PR, and viral marketing.[63]

The provider can also add *secondary service features* to the package. In the hotel industry, various chains have introduced such secondary service features as merchandise for sale, free breakfast buffets, and loyalty programs. Seaside Luxe has transformed sleepy gift shops into profitable revenue generators for various resorts by making them a more engaging shopping experience that reflects their particular customers and locale.[64]

Many companies are using the Internet to offer primary or secondary service features that were never possible before. Salesforce.com uses cloud computing—centralized computing services delivered over the Internet—to run customer-management databases for companies. Häagen-Dazs estimated it would have had to spend $65,000 for a custom-designed database to stay in contact with its retail franchises across the country. Instead, the company spent only $20,000 to set up an account with Salesforce.com and pays $125 per month for 20 users to remotely monitor franchises via the Internet.[65]

The service company that regularly introduces innovations can intrigue customers and stay a step ahead of any competitors.[66] Sometimes it can even reinvent a service category, as Cirque du Soleil did.[67]

**CIRQUE DU SOLEIL** In its more than 25-year history, Cirque du Soleil (French for "circus of the sun") has repeatedly broken loose from circus convention. The company takes traditional ingredients such as trapeze artists, clowns, muscle men, and contortionists and places them in a nontraditional setting with lavish costumes, new age music, and spectacular stage designs. And it eliminates other common circus elements—there are no animals. Each production is loosely tied together with a theme such as "a tribute to the nomadic soul" (Varekai) or "a phantasmagoria of urban life" (Saltimbanco). The group has grown from its Quebec street-performance roots to become a half-billion-dollar global enterprise, with 3,000 employees on four continents entertaining audiences of millions annually. Part of its success comes from a company culture that encourages artistic creativity and innovation and carefully safeguards the brand. One new production is created each year—always in-house—and is unique: There are no duplicate touring companies. In addition to Cirque's mix of media and local promotion, an extensive interactive e-mail program to its million-plus-member Cirque Club creates an online community of fans—20 percent to 30 percent of all ticket sales come from club members. Generating $800 million in revenue annually, the Cirque du Soleil brand has expanded to encompass a record label, a retail operation, and resident productions in Las Vegas (five in all), Orlando, Tokyo, and other cities.

**INNOVATION WITH SERVICES** Innovation is as vital in services as in any industry.[68] After years of losing customers to its Hilton and Marriott hotel competitors, Starwood decided to invest $1.7 billion in its Sheraton chain of 400 properties worldwide to give them fresher décor and brighter colors, as well as more enticing lobbies, restaurants, and cafés. In explaining the need for the makeover, one hospitality industry expert noted, "There was a time when Sheraton was one of the leading brands. But it lagged in introducing new design and service concepts and developed a level of inconsistency."[69]

Cirque du Soleil defied conventions to create a totally unique and non-traditional circus experience.

On the other hand, consider how these relatively new service categories emerged and how, in some cases, organizations found creative solutions in existing categories.

- **Online travel.** Online travel agents such as Expedia and Travelocity offer customers the opportunity to conveniently book travel at discount prices. However, they make money only when visitors go to their Web sites and book travel. Kayak successfully entered the category later by applying the Google business model of collecting money on a per-click basis. Kayak's marketing emphasis is on building a better search engine by offering more alternatives, flexibility, and airlines. Hipmunk is a newer online travel agency that tries to make things even simpler for the savvy traveler by fitting all search results on one easy-to-navigate page—with fewer ads—ranking flights on an "agony algorithm" that factors in price, duration, and number of stops and offering information about and discounts on nearby hotels.[70]

- **Retail health clinics.** One of the hardest areas in which to innovate is health care. But whereas the current health care system is designed to treat a small number of complex cases, retail health clinics address a large number of simple cases. Retail health clinics such as Quick Care, RediClinic, and MinuteClinic are often found in drugstores and other retail chain stores such as Target and Walmart. They typically use nurse practitioners to handle minor illnesses and injuries such as colds, flu, and ear infections; offer various health and wellness services such as physicals and exams for high school sports; and administer vaccinations. They seek to offer convenient, predictable service and transparent pricing, without an appointment, seven days (and evenings) a week. Most visits take no more than 15 minutes, and costs vary from $25 to $100.[71]

- **Private aviation.** Initially, private aviation was restricted to those who could own or charter a private plane. Fractional ownership, pioneered by NetJets, allowed customers to pay a percentage of the cost of a private plane plus maintenance and a direct hourly cost, making it more affordable for a broader customer base. Marquis Jets came up with the simple idea of prepaid time on the world's largest, best-maintained fleet, offering the consistency and benefits of fractional ownership without the long-term commitment. The two companies merged in 2010. Along with competitor Flight Options, private aviation firms are capitalizing on business executives' increasing dissatisfaction with commercial airline service and need for efficient travel options.[72]

New service categories are constantly being introduced to satisfy unmet needs and wants: Examples include drybar, the new "blow-dry bar" salon concept created around the simple promise "No Cuts. No Color. Just Blowouts for Only $40"; Reddit, a giant online digital bulletin board with tens of thousands of active forums where registered users can post content or links; and online start-up Carelinx, which functions as a matchmaking site for families with at-home elderly and nonmedical caregivers who can provide home care.[73]

Innovation in existing services can also have big payoffs. When Ticketmaster introduced interactive seat maps that allowed customers to pick their own seats instead of being given one by a "best seat available" function, the conversion rate from potential to actual buyers increased by 25 percent to 30 percent. Persuading a ticket buyer to add an "I'm going…" message to Facebook adds an extra $5 in ticket sales on average; adding reviews of a show on the site doubles the conversion rate.[74]

New service categories are always being created as with drybar, a blow-dry only chain of salons founded by Alli Webb.

*Source: Getty/The Washington Post*

# Managing Service Quality

The service quality of a firm is tested at each service encounter. If employees are bored, cannot answer simple questions, or are visiting each other while customers are waiting, customers will think twice about doing business there again. Wells Fargo has succeeded in the banking industry by focusing on its customers and delivering superior service.[75]

**WELLS FARGO** Through acquisitions and steady growth, Wells Fargo has become the largest U.S. bank. Marketing has also played a key role. The company's stagecoach symbol reinforces heritage and experience, but it's the way Wells Fargo operates that ensures continued success, beginning with a customer-focused corporate culture that aims to "treat the customer right." The bank also sees a financial benefit to its customer focus. As its values handbook notes:

> The core of our vision and our strategy is "cross-selling." ...The more we give our customers what they need, the more we know about them. The more we know about their other financial needs, the easier it is for them to bring us more of their business. The more business they do with us, the better value they receive, the more loyal they are.

Given the diverse nature of its customer base in California, Wells Fargo actively seeks and trains a diverse workforce. The average customer uses 5.2 different bank products, roughly twice the industry average, thanks in part to the teamwork of the company's highly motivated staff. Wells Fargo's market share declined from 2003 to 2006, but because it also avoided issuing risky mortgages, its stock has delivered a 25 percent return over the past 10 years, comparable to Goldman Sachs and better than many other large banks.

Service outcome and customer loyalty are influenced by a host of variables. One study identified more than 800 critical behaviors that cause customers to switch services; see the eight categories of those behaviors in Table 14.3.[76] A more recent study honed in on the service dimensions customers would most like companies to measure. Knowledgeable frontline workers and the ability to achieve one-call-and-done rose to the top.[77]

Flawless service delivery is the ideal output for any service organization. "Marketing Memo: Recommendations for Improving Service Quality" offers a comprehensive set of guidelines to which top service marketing organizations can adhere. Two top activities are managing customer expectations and incorporating self-service technologies.

| TABLE 14.3 | Factors Leading to Customer Switching Behavior |
|---|---|

**Pricing**
- High price
- Price increases
- Unfair pricing
- Deceptive pricing

**Inconvenience**
- Location/hours
- Wait for appointment
- Wait for service

**Core Service Failure**
- Service mistakes
- Billing errors
- Service catastrophe

**Service Encounter Failures**
- Uncaring
- Impolite
- Unresponsive
- Unknowledgeable

**Response to Service Failure**
- Negative response
- No response
- Reluctant response

**Competition**
- Found better service

**Ethical Problems**
- Cheat
- Hard sell
- Unsafe
- Conflict of interest

**Involuntary Switching**
- Customer moved
- Provider closed

**Source:** Susan M. Keaveney, "Customer Switching Behavior in Service Industries: An Exploratory Study," *Journal of Marketing* (April 1995), pp. 71–82. Reprinted with permission from *Journal of Marketing*, published by the American Marketing Association.

## MANAGING CUSTOMER EXPECTATIONS

Customers form service expectations from many sources, such as past experiences, word of mouth, and advertising. In general, they compare perceived and expected service. If the perceived service falls below the expected service, customers are disappointed. Successful companies add benefits to their offering that not only satisfy customers but surprise and delight them by exceeding expectations.[78] One company that has built its business around exceeding customer expectations is American Express.[79]

**AMERICAN EXPRESS**   Under the direction of Executive VP Jim Bush, American Express has embraced a relationship-building approach in which customer service reps are judged in part on whether customers say they would recommend the brand to friends or family (NPS or Net Promoter Score; see Chapter 5). Reps—called customer care professionals—can see all kinds of relevant data on their screen when a customer calls, including name, age, address, and buying and payment habits. Whether a cardmember loses a wallet or purse while traveling or needs assistance finding a missing child in a foreign country, American Express has empowered its customer care professionals to do whatever it takes to help. This exemplary customer service brings financial benefits too. Cardmembers designated promoters on the basis of NPS score increase their AmEx card spending 10 percent to 15 percent and are four to five times more likely to remain customers, increasing shareholder value. Not least, because of its strong service culture and support, American Express boasts some of the highest employee retention rates in the industry.

The service-quality model in Figure 14.5 highlights the main requirements for delivering high service quality.[80] It identifies five gaps that prevent successful delivery:

1. *Gap between consumer expectation and management perception*—Management does not always correctly perceive what customers want. Hospital administrators may think patients want better food, but patients may be more concerned with nurse responsiveness.

Pioneers in conducting academic service research, Berry, Parasuraman, and Zeithaml offer 10 lessons they maintain are essential for improving service quality across service industries.

1. *Listening*—Service providers should understand what customers really want through continuous learning about the expectations and perceptions of customers and noncustomers (for instance, by means of a service-quality information system).

2. *Reliability*—Reliability is the single most important dimension of service quality and must be a service priority.

3. *Basic service*—Service companies must deliver the basics and do what they are supposed to do—keep promises, use common sense, listen to customers, keep customers informed, and be determined to deliver value to customers.

4. *Service design*—Service providers should take a holistic view of the service while managing its many details.

5. *Recovery*—To satisfy customers who encounter a service problem, service companies should encourage customers to complain (and make it easy for them to do so), respond quickly and personally, and develop a problem-resolution system.

6. *Surprising customers*—Although reliability is the most important dimension in *meeting* customers' service expectations, process dimensions such as assurance, responsiveness, and empathy are most important in *exceeding* customer expectations, for example, by surprising them with uncommon swiftness, grace, courtesy, competence, commitment, and understanding.

7. *Fair play*—Service companies must make special efforts to *be* fair, and to *demonstrate* fairness, to customers and employees.

8. *Teamwork*—Teamwork is what enables large organizations to deliver service with care and attentiveness by improving employee motivation and capabilities.

9. *Employee research*—Marketers should conduct research with employees to reveal why service problems occur and what companies must do to solve problems.

10. *Servant leadership*—Quality service comes from inspired leadership throughout the organization; from excellent service-system design; from the effective use of information and technology; and from a slow-to-change, invisible, all-powerful, internal force called corporate culture.

**Sources:** Leonard L. Berry, A. Parasuraman, and Valarie A. Zeithaml, "Ten Lessons for Improving Service Quality," *MSI Reports Working Paper Series, No.03-001* (Cambridge, MA: Marketing Science Institute, 2003), pp. 61–82. See also Leonard L. Berry, Venkatesh Shankar, Janet Parish, Susan Cadwallader, and Thomas Dotzel, "Creating New Markets through Service Innovation," *Sloan Management Review* (Winter 2006), pp. 56–63; and Leonard L. Berry, Kathleen Seiders, and Dhruv Grewal, "Understanding Service Convenience," *Journal of Marketing* (July 2002), pp. 1–17.

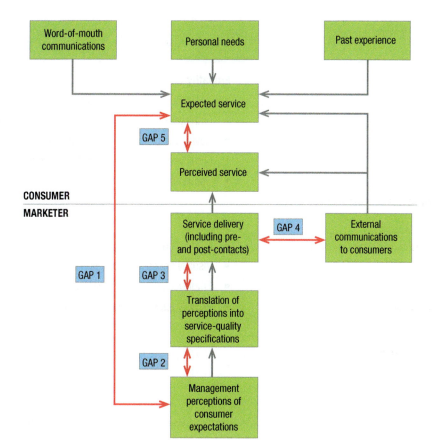

| Fig. 14.5 |

## Service-Quality Model

Sources: A. Parasuraman, Valarie A. Zeithaml, and Leonard L. Berry, "A Conceptual Model of Service Quality and Its Implications for Future Research," *Journal of Marketing* (Fall 1985), p. 44. The model is more fully discussed or elaborated in Valarie Zeithaml, Mary Jo Bitner, and Dwayne D. Gremler, *Services Marketing: Integrating Customer Focus across the Firm*, 6th ed. (New York: McGraw-Hill/Irwin, 2013).

2. ***Gap between management perception and service-quality specification***—Management might correctly perceive customers' wants but not set a performance standard. Hospital administrators may tell the nurses to give "fast" service without specifying speed in minutes.

3. ***Gap between service-quality specifications and service delivery***—Employees might be poorly trained or incapable of or unwilling to meet the standard; they may be held to conflicting standards, such as taking time to listen to customers and serving them fast.

4. ***Gap between service delivery and external communications***—Consumer expectations are affected by statements made by company representatives and ads. If a hospital brochure shows a beautiful room but the patient finds it cheap and tacky-looking, external communications have distorted the customer's expectations.

5. ***Gap between perceived and expected service***—The consumer may misperceive the service quality. The physician may keep visiting the patient to show care, but the patient may interpret this as an indication that something is really wrong.

Based on this service-quality model, researchers identified five determinants of service quality, in descending order of importance:[81]

1. ***Reliability***—The ability to perform the promised service dependably and accurately.
2. ***Responsiveness***—The willingness to help customers and provide prompt service.
3. ***Assurance***—The knowledge and courtesy of employees and their ability to convey trust and confidence.
4. ***Empathy***—The provision of caring, individualized attention to customers.
5. ***Tangibles***—The appearance of physical facilities, equipment, staff, and communication materials.

Based on these five factors, the researchers developed the 21-item SERVQUAL scale (see Table 14.4).[82] They also note there is a *zone of tolerance,* or a range in which a service dimension would be deemed satisfactory, anchored by the minimum level consumers are willing to accept and the level they believe can and should be delivered.

| TABLE 14.4 | SERVQUAL Attributes |
|---|---|

**Reliability**
- Providing service as promised
- Dependability in handling customers' service problems
- Performing services right the first time
- Providing services at the promised time
- Maintaining error-free records
- Employees who have the knowledge to answer customer questions

**Empathy**
- Giving customers individual attention
- Employees who deal with customers in a caring fashion
- Having the customer's best interests at heart
- Employees who understand the needs of their customers
- Convenient business hours

**Responsiveness**
- Keeping customer informed as to when services will be performed
- Prompt service to customers
- Willingness to help customers
- Readiness to respond to customers' requests

**Tangibles**
- Modern equipment
- Visually appealing facilities
- Employees who have a neat, professional appearance
- Visually appealing materials associated with the service

**Assurance**
- Employees who instill confidence in customers
- Making customers feel safe in their transactions
- Employees who are consistently courteous

**Source:** A. Parasuraman, Valarie A. Zeithaml, and Leonard L. Berry, "A Conceptual Model of Service Quality and Its Implications for Future Research," *Journal of Marketing* (Fall 1985), pp. 41–50. Reprinted by permission of the American Marketing Association.

Subsequent research has extended the service-quality model. One *dynamic process model* of service quality was based on the premise that customer perceptions and expectations of service quality change over time, but at any one point they are a function of prior expectations about what *will* and what *should* happen during the service encounter, as well as the *actual* service delivered during the last contact.[83] Tests of the dynamic process model reveal that the two different types of expectations have opposite effects on perceptions of service quality.

1. *Increasing* customer expectations of what the firm *will* deliver can lead to improved perceptions of overall service quality.
2. *Decreasing* customer expectations of what the firm *should* deliver can also lead to improved perceptions of overall service quality.

Much work has validated the role of expectations in consumers' interpretations and evaluations of the service encounter and in the relationship they adopt with a firm over time.[84] Consumers are often forward-looking with respect to their decision to keep or drop a service relationship in terms of their likely behavior and interactions with a firm. Any marketing activity that affects current or expected future usage can help to solidify a service relationship.

With continuously provided services, such as public utilities, health care, financial and computing services, insurance, and other professional, membership, or subscription services, customers have been observed to mentally calculate their *payment equity*—the perceived economic benefits in relationship to the economic costs. In other words, customers ask themselves, "Am I using this service enough, given what I pay for it?" A negative response will lead to change in behavior and possible termination of an account.

Long-term service relationships can have a dark side. An ad agency client may feel that over time the agency is losing objectivity, becoming stale in its thinking, or beginning to take advantage of the relationship.[85]

## INCORPORATING SELF-SERVICE TECHNOLOGIES (SSTS)

Consumers value convenience in services,[86] and many person-to-person service interactions are being replaced by self-service technologies (SSTs) intended to provide that convenience. To traditional vending machines we can add automated teller machines (ATMs), self-pumping at gas stations, self-checkout at hotels, and a variety of activities on the Internet, such as ticket purchasing, investment trading, and customization of products.

Chili's is installing tabletop computer screens in its restaurants so customers can order directly and pay by credit card. The restaurant found users of the service spend more per check, in part because they buy more desserts and coffee when the screen is present.[87] You can add an app like WaitAway to your cell phone and be contacted by text message when your table is ready at a restaurant—and monitor the length of the line in the process.[88] OpenTable lets you easily book the reservation ahead of time.[89]

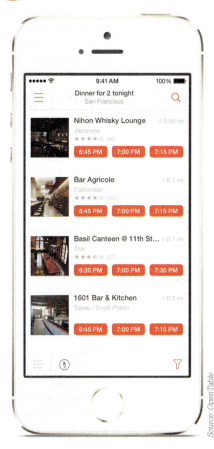

**OPENTABLE** OpenTable has become the world's largest online reservation system, letting users book a reservation on its Web site or with its smart-phone app at thousands of restaurants around the world. A new deal with Facebook allows users to book on a restaurant's Facebook page. For a fairly modest setup charge and monthly fee—$249 a month for software to manage bookings plus $1 for every diner seated through the Web site—a restaurant can tap into OpenTable's vast customer base. With half of all restaurants in North America signed up and more than 15 million people seated monthly via the Web site, the service has been adding functionality. For instance, the acquisition of Foodspotting for $10 million allows users to search menu images by dish. Now more than 40 percent of its reservations are booked via phone or tablet, OpenTable is beefing up its mobile strategy and adding payment services with a new app. Its new priority is to take the massive amounts of data it has collected on users' dining preferences to offer customized dining recommendations.

OpenTable, the market leader in online restaurant reservations, is investing heavily in its mobile offerings.

*Source: OpenTable*

Not all SSTs improve service quality, but they can make service transactions more accurate, convenient, and faster. Obviously, they can also reduce costs. One technology firm, Comverse, estimates the cost to answer a query through a call center at $7, but online at only 10 cents. One of Comverse's clients was able to direct 200,000 calls a week through online self-service support, saving $52 million a year.[90]

Every company needs to think about improving its service using SSTs. Comcast can offer less customer service because 40 percent of its installations are done by the customer and 31 percent of customers now manage their accounts completely online.[91]

Successfully integrating technology into the workforce thus requires a comprehensive reengineering of the front office to identify what people do best, what machines do best, and how to deploy them separately and together.[92] Some companies have found the biggest obstacle is not the technology itself, but convincing customers to use it, especially for the first time.

Customers must have a clear sense of their roles in the SST process, must see a clear benefit, and must feel they can actually use it.[93] SST is not for everyone. Although some automated voices are actually popular with customers—the unfailingly polite and chipper voice of Amtrak's "Julie" has been generally well-received by callers—many can incite frustration and even rage.[94]

# Managing Product-Support Services

No less important than service industries are product-based industries that must provide a service bundle.[95] Manufacturers of equipment—small appliances, office machines, tractors, mainframes, airplanes—all must provide *product-support services,* now a battleground for competitive advantage. Many product companies also have a stronger online presence than before and must ensure they offer adequate—if not superior—service online as well.

Chapter 13 described how products could be augmented with key service differentiators—ordering ease, delivery, installation, customer training, customer consulting, maintenance, and repair. Some equipment companies, such as Caterpillar Tractor and John Deere, make a significant percentage of their profits from these services.[96] In the global marketplace, companies that make a good product but provide poor local service support are seriously disadvantaged.

## IDENTIFYING AND SATISFYING CUSTOMER NEEDS

Traditionally, customers have had three specific worries about product service:[97]

- They worry about reliability and *failure frequency.* A farmer may tolerate a combine that will break down once a year, but not one that goes down two or three times a year.
- They worry about *downtime.* The longer the downtime, the higher the cost. The customer counts on the seller's *service dependability*—the ability to fix the machine quickly or at least provide a loaner.
- They worry about *out-of-pocket costs.* How much does the customer have to spend on regular maintenance and repair costs?

A buyer takes all these factors into consideration and tries to estimate the **life-cycle cost,** which is the product's purchase cost plus the discounted cost of maintenance and repair less the discounted salvage value. A one-computer office will need higher product reliability and faster repair service than an office where other computers are available if one breaks down. An airline needs 100 percent reliability in the air. Where reliability is important, manufacturers or service providers can offer guarantees to promote sales.

To provide the best support, a manufacturer must identify the services customers value most and their relative importance. For expensive equipment, manufacturers offer *facilitating services* such as installation, staff training, maintenance and repair services, and financing. They may also add *value-augmenting services* that extend beyond the functioning and performance of the product itself. Johnson Controls reached beyond its climate control equipment and components business to manage integrated facilities, offering products and services that optimize energy use and improve comfort and security.

A manufacturer can offer, and charge for, product-support services in different ways. One specialty organic-chemical company provides a standard offering plus a basic level of services. If the customer wants additional services, it can pay extra or increase its annual purchases to a higher level. Many companies offer *service contracts* (also called *extended warranties*), in which sellers agree to provide maintenance and repair services for a specified period of time at a specified contract price.

Product companies must understand their strategic intent and competitive advantage in developing services. Are service units supposed to support and protect existing product businesses or grow as an independent platform? Are the sources of competitive advantage based on economies of scale (size) or economies of skill (smarts)?[98]

## POSTSALE SERVICE STRATEGY

The quality of customer service departments varies greatly. At one extreme are those that simply transfer customer calls to the appropriate person for action with little follow-up. At the other extreme are departments eager to receive customer requests, suggestions, and even complaints and handle them expeditiously. Some firms even proactively contact customers to provide service after the sale is complete.[99]

**CUSTOMER-SERVICE EVOLUTION** Manufacturers usually start by running their own parts-and-service departments. They want to stay close to the equipment and know its problems. They also find it expensive and time consuming to train others and discover they can make good money from parts and service if they are the only supplier and can charge a premium price. In fact, many equipment manufacturers price their equipment low and compensate by charging high prices for parts and service.

Over time, manufacturers switch more maintenance and repair service to authorized distributors and dealers. These intermediaries are closer to customers, operate in more locations, and can offer quicker service. Still later, independent service firms emerge and offer a lower price or faster service. A significant percentage of auto-service work is now done outside franchised automobile dealerships by independent garages and chains such as Midas Muffler and Sears. Independent service organizations handle mainframes, telecommunications equipment, and a variety of other equipment lines.

**THE CUSTOMER-SERVICE IMPERATIVE** Customer-service choices are increasing rapidly, however, and equipment manufacturers increasingly must figure out how to make money on their equipment, independent of service contracts. Some new-car warranties now cover 100,000 miles before customers have to pay for servicing. The increase in disposable or never-fail equipment makes customers less inclined to pay 2 percent to 10 percent of the purchase price every year for service. A company with several hundred laptops, printers, and related equipment might find it cheaper to have its own service people on-site.

# Summary

1. A service is any act or performance that one party can offer to another that is essentially intangible and does not result in the ownership of anything. It may or may not be tied to a physical product.

2. Services are intangible, inseparable, variable, and perishable. Each characteristic poses challenges and requires certain strategies. Marketers must find ways to give tangibility to intangibles, to increase the productivity of service providers, to increase and standardize the quality of the service provided, and to match the supply of services with market demand.

3. Marketing of services faces new realities in the 21st century due to customer empowerment, customer coproduction, and the need to satisfy employees as well as customers.

4. Achieving excellence in service marketing calls not only for external marketing but also for internal marketing to motivate employees, as well as interactive marketing to emphasize the importance of both "high tech" and "high touch."

5. Top service companies adopt a strategic concept, have a history of top-management commitment to quality, commit to high standards, establish profit tiers, and pay attention to their systems for monitoring service performance and customer complaints. They also differentiate their brands through

primary and secondary service features and continual innovation.

6. Superior service delivery requires managing customer expectations and incorporating self-service technologies. Customers' expectations play a critical role in their service experiences and evaluations. Companies must manage service quality by understanding the effects of each service encounter.

7. Even product-based companies must provide post-purchase service. To offer the best support, a manufacturer must identify the services customers value most and their relative importance. The service mix includes both presale services (facilitating and value-augmenting services) and postsale services (customer service departments, repair and maintenance services).

## MyMarketingLab

Go to **mymktlab.com** to complete the problems marked with this icon ⭐ as well as for additional Auto-graded and Assisted-graded writing questions.

# Applications

## Marketing Debate
### Is Service Marketing Different from Product Marketing?

Some service marketers maintain that service marketing is fundamentally different from product marketing and relies on different skills. Some traditional product marketers disagree, saying "good marketing is good marketing."

**Take a position:** Product and service marketing are fundamentally different *versus* Product and service marketing are highly related.

## Marketing Discussion
### Educational Institutions

⭐ Colleges, universities, and other educational institutions can be classified as service organizations. How can you apply the marketing principles developed in this chapter to your school? Do you have any advice for how it could become a better service marketer?

## Marketing Excellence

### >> The Ritz-Carlton

Few brands attain such a high standard of customer service as the Ritz-Carlton. This luxury hotel chain began with the original Ritz-Carlton Boston, which revolutionized the way U.S. travelers experienced customer service in a hotel. It was the first of its kind to provide a private bath in each guest room, fresh flowers throughout the hotel, and an entire staff dressed in formal white tie, black tie, or morning-coat attire.

In 1983, hotelier Horst Schulze and a four-person development team acquired the rights to the Ritz-Carlton name and created the concept by which it is known today, with its company-wide concentration on both the personal and the functional side of service. The five-star hotel provides impeccable facilities but also takes customer service extremely seriously. Its credo is "We are Ladies and Gentlemen serving Ladies and Gentlemen." According to the company's Web site, The Ritz-Carlton "pledge(s) to provide the finest personal service and facilities for our guests who will always enjoy a warm, relaxed, yet refined ambience."

The Ritz-Carlton fulfills this promise by providing impeccable training for its employees and executing its Three Steps of Service and 12 Service Values. The Three Steps of Service state that employees must use a warm and sincere greeting always using the guest's name, anticipate and fulfill each guest's needs, and give a warm good-bye, again using the guest's name. Every manager carries a laminated card with the 12 Service

Values, which include bullets such as number 3: "I am empowered to create unique, memorable and personal experiences for our guests," and number 10: "I am proud of my professional appearance, language and behavior." Simon Cooper, president and chief operating officer, explained, "It's all about people. Nobody has an emotional experience with a thing. We're appealing to emotions." The Ritz-Carlton's 35,000 employees in 29 countries go out of their way to create unique and memorable experiences for their guests.

Not only is the company known for training its employees to provide impeccable customer service, but it also reinforces its mission and values with them on a daily basis. Each day, managers gather their employees for a 15-minute "line up" to check in, resolve any impending problems, and read and discuss what The Ritz-Carlton calls "wow stories." These true stories, read to every employee around the world, recognize an individual employee for his or her outstanding customer service and also highlight one of the 12 Service Values.

One family staying at The Ritz-Carlton, Bali, needed a particular type of egg and milk for their son who suffered from food allergies. Employees could not find the appropriate items in town, but the executive chef at the hotel remembered a store in Singapore that sold them. He contacted his mother-in-law, who purchased the items and personally flew them more than 1,000 miles to Bali for the family. This example showcased Service Value 6: "I own and immediately resolve guests' problems."

In another instance, a waiter overheard a man telling his wheelchair-bound wife that it was too bad he couldn't get her down to the beach. The waiter told the maintenance crew, and by the next day they had constructed a wooden walkway to the beach and pitched a tent at the far end where the couple had dinner.

Wow stories can also be as simple as an employee's remembering how a guest prefers coffee and then preparing it that way without asking for the rest of his or her stay. According to Cooper, the daily wow story is "the best way to communicate what we expect from our ladies and gentlemen around the world. Every story reinforces the actions we are looking for and demonstrates how each and every person in our organization contributes to our service values." Each employee is empowered to spend as much as $2,000 without management approval to help deliver a guest's anticipated need or desire, supporting the company's intention to build lifelong positive relationships with each customer.

Ritz-Carlton measures the success of its customer service efforts through Gallup phone interviews, which ask both functional and emotional questions. Functional questions include: "How was the meal?" or "Was your bedroom clean?" while emotional questions reveal the customer's sense of well-being. The hotel uses these findings as well as day-to-day experiences to continually enhance and improve the experience for its guests.

In less than three decades, Ritz-Carlton has grown from one U.S. location to 87 in 29 countries; the company plans to expand further throughout Europe, Africa, Asia, the Middle East, and the Americas. It has also earned two Malcolm Baldrige Quality Awards—the only company ever to win the prestigious award twice.

## Questions

1. How does The Ritz-Carlton match up to competing hotels? What are the key differences?

2. Discuss the importance of the "wow stories" in maintaining top-quality customer service for a luxury hotel like The Ritz-Carlton.

**Sources:** Robert Reiss, "How Ritz-Carlton Stays at Top," *Forbes,* October 30, 2009; Carmine Gallo, "Employee Motivation the Ritz-Carlton Way," *BusinessWeek,* February 29, 2008; Carmine Gallo, "How Ritz-Carlton Maintains Its Mystique," *BusinessWeek,* February 13, 2007; Jennifer Robison, "How The Ritz-Carlton Manages the Mystique," *Gallup Management Journal,* December 11, 2008; Kelly Kearsley, "Taking a Cue from Ritz-Carlton's Customer Service," *Wall Street Journal,* March 1, 2013; Micah Solomon, "How Four Seasons and Ritz-Carlton Empower Employees and Uphold Customer Service Standards," *Forbes,* October 28, 2013; Micah Solomon, "A Great Customer Experience (Ritz-Carlton Caliber) Requires More than Just Empowered Employees," *Forbes,* September 18, 2013; *The Ritz-Carlton,* www.RitzCarlton.com.

# Marketing Excellence

## >> Mayo Clinic

Mayo Clinic was the first and now the largest integrated not-for-profit medical group practice in the world. William and Charles Mayo founded the clinic more than 100 years ago as a small outpatient facility pioneering the medical group practice, a model widely used today.

Mayo Clinic provides exceptional medical care and leads the nation in many specialties such as cancer, heart disease, respiratory disorders, and urology. The organization consistently ranks at the top of *U.S. News & World Report*'s Best Hospitals list and enjoys 85 percent brand recognition among U.S. adults. It has reached this level of success by taking a different approach from most clinics and hospitals and putting a relentless focus on the patient's experience. Two interrelated core values that trace back to its founders are at the heart of all the organization does: placing the patient's interests above all others and practicing teamwork.

Every aspect of the patient's experience is considered at Mayo Clinic's three campuses in Rochester, MN; Scottsdale, AZ; and Jacksonville, FL. From the moment a patient arrives, he or she experiences something entirely different.

It all starts with greeters who welcome new patients into the building and walk them through the administrative process. Returning patients are greeted by name and with a warm smile. The buildings and facilities themselves are designed with patients' needs in mind. One architect explained that the buildings are meant to make "patients feel a little better before they see their doctors." For example, the lobby of the Mayo Clinic hospital in Scottsdale has an indoor waterfall and a wall of windows overlooking mountains.

The 21-story Gonda Building in Rochester is Mayo Clinic's headquarters of sorts; people come for medical help from around the world. The building has spectacular wide-open spaces and huge windows and hosts a Center for Innovation, whose mission is "transforming the delivery and experience of health care." To help accomplish this goal, employees observe patients, interview families, and conduct research as well as test and model possible solutions.

For example, when Mayo Clinic decided on a major room innovation, the Center for Innovation built prototype exam rooms in a flexible space so employees and patients could test new layouts and identify the most efficient and patient-friendly environment. The resulting design featured "Jack and Jill rooms," an exam space in the middle separated from two conversation spaces on either side with room for family members. Physicians also preferred not having furniture in the exam room.

The other significant difference in serving patients is Mayo Clinic's concept of teamwork. When a patient arrives, a team is assembled that can include any blend of medical professionals, including the primary physician, surgeons, radiation oncologists, radiologists, nurses, residents, and other specialists with the appropriate skill, experience, and knowledge. Team members work together to diagnose each patient's medical problems, including analyzing and debating test results for hours if necessary to achieve the most accurate diagnosis and identify the best treatments. Once consensus has been reached, the team leader meets with the patient and discusses his or her options. If surgery is necessary, the procedure will often take place within 24 hours, a dramatic difference from the long wait patients experience at many hospitals. Mayo Clinic's doctors understand that those who seek their care want action as soon as possible.

The clinic's doctors earn a salary instead of being paid by the number of patients they see or tests they order. As a result, patients receive more individualized attention and care, and physicians work together instead of against each other. As one pediatrician explained, "We're very comfortable with calling colleagues for what I call 'curbside consulting.' I don't have to make a decision about splitting a fee or owing someone something. It's never a case of quid pro quo."

Mayo Clinic is a not-for-profit organization, so all its operating income is invested back into its research and education programs. Breakthrough research is quickly implemented into the quality care of the patients. The clinic offers educational programs through its five medical schools, and many of its physicians come up through these programs with its philosophies engrained in their heads, including the motto, "The best interest of the patient is the only interest to be considered."

Mayo Clinic has been recognized countless times for its independent thinking, outstanding service and performance, and core focus on patient care and satisfaction. CEO Dr. John Noseworthy stated, "Sometimes we have to make decisions that don't make a lot of sense from a business standpoint, but they're the right thing for the patient." Perhaps that is why more than 1.1 million patients come to Mayo Clinic each year, including several U.S. presidents and foreign heads of state.

### Questions

1. Explain why Mayo Clinic is exceptional at customer service. What are the key differentiating points from other hospitals or medical facilities?

2. Is there a conflict between wanting to make your patient happy and providing the best medical care possible? Why or why not?

**Sources:** Avery Comarow, "America's Best Hospitals," *U.S. News & World Report*, July 15, 2009; Chen May Yee, "Mayo Clinic Reports 2007 Revenue Grew 10%," *Star Tribune*, March 17, 2008; Leonard L. Berry and Kent D. Seltman, *Management Lessons from Mayo Clinic* (New York: McGraw-Hill, 2008); Leonard L. Berry, "Leadership Lessons from Mayo Clinic," *Organizational Dynamics* 33 (August 2004), pp. 228–42; Leonard L. Berry and Neeli Bendapudi, "Clueing in Customers," *Harvard Business Review*, February 2003, pp. 100–6; John La Forgia, Kent Seltman, and Scott Swanson, "Mayo Clinic: Sustaining a Legacy Brand and Leveraging Its Equity in the 21st-Century Market," Presentation at the Marketing Science Institute's Conference on Brand Orchestration, Orlando, FL, December 4–5, 2003; Paul Roberts, "The Agenda—Total Teamwork," *Fast Company*, March 31, 1999; Max Nissen, "Mayo Clinic CEO: Here's Why We've Been the Leading Brand in Medicine for 100 Years," *Business Insider*, February 23, 2013; Jack Nicas, "Mayo Clinic's Upmarket Move," *Wall Street Journal*, April 22, 2013; mayoclinic.com.

## In This Chapter, We Will Address the Following **Questions**

1. How can new products be categorized? (p. 429)

2. What challenges does a company face in developing new products and services? (p. 431)

3. What organizational structures and processes do managers use to oversee new-product development? (p. 434)

4. What are the main stages in developing new products and services? (p. 436)

5. What is the best way to manage the generation of new ideas? (p. 438)

6. What is the best way to manage concept and strategy development? (p. 445)

7. What is the best way to manage the commercialization of new products? (p. 450)

8. What factors affect the rate of diffusion and consumer adoption of newly launched products and services? (p. 454)

The unique features of General Motors' innovative OnStar in-car communication system are highly valued by GM's customers.

*Source: General Motors, LLC 2011*

# **15** Introducing New Market Offerings

**New-product development shapes the company's future.** Improved or replacement products and services can maintain or build sales; new-to-the-world products and services can transform industries and companies and change lives. Companies that challenge industry norms and apply imaginative solutions will delight and engage consumers, as General Motors has done with OnStar.[1]

 *Technology has always played an important role in the automobile industry, and breakthrough innovations can have enormous payoffs. General Motors has found a real winner in its OnStar technology, a creative blend of cellular technology, Bluetooth, GPS, speakers, and, most importantly, human operators. The in-car communication system provides both safety and convenience benefits, including hands-free calling, turn-by-turn navigation, stolen vehicle location assistance, and an Automatic Crash Response System that contacts the driver immediately if airbags have been activated and sends emergency medical assistance if needed. Two thousand advisers staff the call center 24 hours a day and can help drivers if they have a flat tire, run out of gas, need to find the nearest bank or pizza parlor, or just want the weather report or a phone number. An OnStar adviser can even unlock a car via satellite. More than 4.5 million GM owners were so satisfied with the service, which is backed by a strong ad campaign, that they signed up to pay for it after their six-month free trial expired. OnStar FMV ("for my vehicle") expands many of these benefits to non-GM cars for a sign-up fee and monthly charge by replacing the existing rear view mirror with a special OnStar mirror.*

**Marketers play a key role** in new-product development by identifying and evaluating ideas and working with R&D and other areas in every stage of development. This chapter provides a detailed analysis of the new-product development process. Much of the discussion is equally relevant to new products, services, or business models.

## New-Product Options

There are a variety of types of new products and ways to create them.[2]

### MAKE OR BUY

A company can add new products through acquisition or development. When acquiring, the company can buy other companies, buy patents from other companies, or buy a license or franchise from another company. Swiss food giant Nestlé has increased its presence in North America by acquiring a variety of different brands such as Carnation, Stouffer's, Ralston Purina, Dreyer's Ice Cream, Jenny Craig, Gerber, Poland Springs, and PowerBar.[3]

But firms can successfully make only so many acquisitions. At some point, they need *organic growth*—the development of new products from within. Praxair, worldwide provider of industrial gases, achieved an ambitious goal of $200 million per year of double-digit new annual sales growth only through a healthy dose of organic growth and a large number of smaller but significant $5 million projects.[4]

For product development, the company can create new products in its own laboratories, or it can contract with independent researchers or new-product development firms to develop specific new products or new technology.[5] Firms such as Samsung, GE, Diageo, Hershey, and USB have engaged new-product consulting boutiques to provide fresh insights and points of view.

# TYPES OF NEW PRODUCTS

New products range from new-to-the-world items that create an entirely new market to minor improvements or revisions of existing products. Most new-product activity is devoted to improving existing products. Some recent product launches in the supermarket were brand extensions, such as Tide To Go Stain Eraser, Gillette Fusion ProGlide Styler, Dawn Power Clean, Crest 3D White Glamorous White Toothpaste, and Coconut Delight Oreo Fudge Cremes.[6] At Sony, modifications of established products accounted for more than 80 percent of new-product activity.

It is increasingly difficult to identify blockbuster products that will transform a market, but continuous innovation can broaden the brand meaning and also force competitors to play catch-up.[7] Armstrong World Industries moved from selling floor coverings to selling ceilings to decorating all interior surfaces. Once a running-shoe manufacturer, Nike now competes with makers of all types of athletic shoes, clothing, and equipment. Its innovative FuelBand measures a person's energy output during the day and allows it to be shared with others online; its sock-like Flyknit Racer shoes are environmentally friendly and create a wholly different running experience.[8]

Fewer than 10 percent of all new products are truly innovative and new to the world.[9] These products incur the greatest cost and risk. And while radical innovations can hurt the company's bottom line in the short run, if they succeed they can improve the corporate image, create a greater sustainable competitive advantage than ordinary products, and produce significant financial rewards.[10]

Keurig pioneered the one-cup-at-a-time pod-style brewing system that has swept homes and offices alike. For the speed, convenience, and variety offered, users are willing to pay 10 times the cost of a traditionally brewed cup of coffee, helping Keurig sales approach $4 billion and its sales based revenue market share exceed 40 percent.[11] Another innovative new product that commands a premium is Beats by Dr. Dre headphones.[12]

Beats by Dre's innovative features and design permits the brand to command a premium price in the marketplace.

**■ BEATS BY DRE**  Born Andrew Young and a founding member of N.W.A and famed rap producer, Dr. Dre had made an indelible mark on the music scene before becoming an entrepreneur. His Beats by Dre headphones, launched in 2006 with music mogul Jimmy Iovine, have become a must for many music lovers despite costing $300, nearly 10 times what ordinary ear buds sell for. Their appeal is in the thumping bass-heavy sound and sleek look, even if the reviews among audiophiles are somewhat mixed. With strong adoption among celebrity musicians and athletes—the headphones were seen everywhere at the 2012 Summer Olympic Games in London—Beats became as fashionable as they were practical and an essential modern lifestyle item. Beats by Dre has partnered with firms like Chrysler, HP, and HTC to build its sound technology in their cars, computers, and smart phones and has also introduced its own version of ear buds and other products. The company was acquired by Apple for $3 billion in August 2014.

Companies typically must create a strong R&D and marketing partnership to pull off a radical innovation.[13] The right corporate culture is another crucial determinant; the firm must prepare to cannibalize existing products, tolerate risk, and maintain a future market orientation.[14] A keen understanding of customers is also paramount.[15]

Few reliable techniques exist for estimating demand for radical innovations.[16] Focus groups can provide perspective on customer interest and need, but marketers may need a probe-and-learn approach based on observation and feedback of early users' experiences and other means such as online chats or product-focused blogs.

High-tech firms in telecommunications, computers, consumer electronics, biotech, and software in particular seek radical innovation.[17] They face a number of product-launch challenges: high technological

Source: © epa european pressphoto agency b.v./Alamy

Google co-founder Sergey Brin is a strong supporter of innovative new products such as Google Glass.

uncertainty, high market uncertainty, fierce competition, high investment costs, short product life cycles, and scarce funding sources for risky projects.[18] Successes abound, however. Goggle has launched a number of path-breaking products and is looking for more.[19]

**GOOGLE** Since its beginnings as the quintessential search engine, Google has launched a wide variety of products that earned its reputation as one of the most innovative companies and amassed a market cap exceeding $300 billion. The company has introduced a series of related online products—notably gmail e-mail, Google+ social networking, and the Google Chrome enhanced browser. It has made a strong entry in the mobile market with its Andrioid operating system and its acquisition of Motorola Mobility for $12.5 billion. But not all new products are hits; some that seemed to miss their mark were Google Answers, Dodgeball, and Lively. Perhaps one of Google's most ambitious new products is Google Glass, a computer worn like eyewear with an optical display that allows the user to answer calls, record video, and take photos with voice activation, connect to a smart phone, post to social media, and perform Google searches, among other things. The company has been beta-testing the product with thousands of Glass Explorers, who are paying $1,500 each for the opportunity to be an early adopter and pass along feedback. Google X, the internal group that developed Google Glass, is looking into other "out of this world" products, like self-driving cars and balloons that can transmit broadband Internet to remote regions from 12 miles in the air.

# Challenges in New-Product Development

In retailing, consumer goods, electronics, autos, and other industries, the time to bring a product to market has been cut in half.[20] For instance, luxury leather-goods maker Louis Vuitton has implemented a new factory format dubbed Pégase so it could ship fresh collections to its boutiques every six weeks—more than twice as frequently as in the past—giving customers more new looks to choose from.[21]

Through different policies and processes, W.L. Gore has created an innovative culture that has produced numerous new product successes.

# THE INNOVATION IMPERATIVE

In an economy of rapid change, continuous innovation is a necessity. Companies that fail to develop new products leave themselves vulnerable to changing customer needs and tastes, shortened product life cycles, increased domestic and foreign competition, and especially new technologies. Google, Dropbox, and Box update their software daily.[22]

Highly innovative firms are able to repeatedly identify and quickly seize new market opportunities. They create a positive attitude toward innovation and risk taking, routinize the innovation process, practice teamwork, and allow their people to experiment and even fail. One such firm is W. L. Gore.[23]

**W. L. GORE**   Best known for its GORE-TEX high-performance fabrics, W. L. Gore has introduced breakthrough versions of guitar strings, dental floss, medical devices, and fuel cells—while constantly reinventing the uses of the polymer polytetrafluoroethylene (PTFE). Several principles guide the company's new-product development. First, it works with potential customers. Its thoracic graft, designed to combat heart disease, was developed in close collaboration with physicians. Second, Gore has a distinctly egalitarian culture; it lets employees choose projects and appoints few product leaders and teams. The company likes to nurture "passionate champions" who convince others a project is worth their time and commitment, and leaders have positions of authority because they have followers. The development of the fuel cell rallied more than 100 of Gore's 9,000 research associates. Third, all research associates spend 10 percent of their work hours on "dabble time," developing their own ideas. Promising ideas are judged according to a "Real, Win, Worth" exercise: Is the opportunity real? Can we win? Can we make money? Fourth, Gore knows when to let go, though dead ends in one area can spark innovation in another: Elixir acoustic guitar strings were the result of a failed venture into bike cables. Even successful ventures may need to move on. Glide shred-resistant dental floss was sold to Procter & Gamble because Gore knew retailers want to deal with a company selling a family of health care products. The 10,000-person private company now has operations in dozens of countries around the globe and revenue of more than $3 billion.

Innovation is about "creating new choices" the competition doesn't have access to, says IDEO's CEO Tim Brown. It isn't about brilliant people spontaneously generating new ideas, he argues, but about finding hidden assumptions and ignored processes that can change the way a company does business.[24]

# NEW-PRODUCT SUCCESS

Most established companies focus on *incremental innovation*, entering new markets by tweaking products for new customers, using variations on a core product to stay one step ahead of the market, and creating interim solutions for industry-wide problems. With the widespread adoption of smart phones, mobile apps are becoming a lucrative business, as the creators of Angry Birds video game have found, securing their leadership with continual innovation.[25]

Mobile app Angry Birds is so popular that there are even themed activity parks in some different countries.

Source: Sarkanniemi Adventure Park

....................................................................................................................................................................

**ANGRY BIRDS**  A spectacular success, Angry Birds has transcended its origins as a mobile app to become a cultural phenomenon and entrenched brand franchise. Created in Finland by Niklas Hed and commercialized by Rovio Entertainment, the video game uses a slingshot to hurl brightly colored birds at green pigs trying to take shelter. It scored 50 million downloads in its first year while becoming the top seller at the Apple App Store, spawning a series of sequels, RIO Seasons and Space, and two subsequent releases tied to *Star Wars*. Rovio has kept users interested in existing titles by continually adding new levels to the games—Angry Birds had 63 levels when it began, which grew to more than 360. Taking a page from Disney, the brand has been successfully extended within and outside entertainment, with toys, games, backpacks, fruit snacks, underwear, and more that have reached $650 million in sales. Rovio— Finnish for "bonfire"—is worth an estimated $9 billion. There is an Angry Birds television show, comic book series, and planned 3-D movie; its YouTube site has had more than 1 billion views. The brand has more than 400 partners, from Coca-Cola to Intel to Kraft. Rovio has also opened up retail stores in China and themed activity parks in Finland, China, and the United Kingdom.

....................................................................................................................................................................

Newer companies create *disruptive technologies* that are cheaper and more likely to alter the competitive space. Established companies can be slow to react or invest in these disruptive technologies because they threaten their investment. Then they suddenly find themselves facing formidable new competitors, and many fail.[26] To avoid this trap, incumbent firms must carefully monitor the preferences of both customers and noncustomers and uncover evolving, difficult-to-articulate customer needs.[27]

What else can a company do? In a classic study of industrial products, new-product specialists Cooper and Kleinschmidt found that the number-one success factor is a unique, superior product. Such products succeed 98 percent of the time, compared with products with a moderate advantage (58 percent success) or minimal advantage (18 percent success). Another key factor is a well-defined product concept. The company carefully defines and assesses the target market, product requirements, and benefits before proceeding. Other success factors are technological and marketing synergy, quality of execution in all stages, and market attractiveness. Products designed with other countries and a global perspective in mind also tended to fare better.[28]

## NEW-PRODUCT FAILURE

New products continue to fail at rates estimated as high as 50 percent or even 95 percent in the United States and 90 percent in Europe.[29] The reasons are many: ignored or misinterpreted market research; overestimates of market size; high development costs; poor design or ineffectual performance; incorrect positioning, advertising, or price; insufficient distribution support; competitors who fight back hard; and inadequate ROI or payback. Some additional drawbacks new-product launches face are:

- **Fragmented markets.** Companies must aim their new products at smaller market segments than before, which can mean lower sales and profits for each product.
- **Social, economic, and governmental constraints.** New products must satisfy consumer safety and environmental concerns and stringent production constraints.
- **Cost of development.** A company typically must generate many ideas to find just one worthy of development and thus often faces high R&D, manufacturing, and marketing costs.
- **Capital shortages.** Some companies with good ideas cannot raise the funds to research and launch them.
- **Shorter required development time.** Companies must learn to compress development time with new techniques, strategic partners, early concept tests, and advanced marketing planning.
- **Poor launch timing.** New products are sometimes launched too late, after the category has already taken off, or too early for sufficient interest to have gathered.
- **Shorter product life cycles.** Rivals are quick to copy success. At one time, Sony enjoyed a three-year lead on its new products, but Matsushita and others learned to copy them within six months, leaving Sony with barely time to recoup its investment.
- **Lack of organizational support.** The new product may not mesh with the corporate culture or receive the financial or other support it needs.

But failure comes with the territory, and truly innovative firms accept it as part of what's necessary to be successful. Silicon Valley marketing expert Seth Godin maintains, "It is not just OK to fail; it's imperative to fail."[30] Many Internet companies are the result of failed earlier ventures and experience numerous setbacks as their services evolve. Dogster.com, a social network site for dog lovers, emerged after the spectacular demise of Pets.com.[31]

Failure is not always the end of an idea. Recognizing that 90 percent of experimental drugs are unsuccessful, Eli Lilly looks at failure as an inevitable part of discovery and encourages its scientists to find new uses for compounds that fail at any stage in a human clinical trial. Evista, a failed contraceptive, became a $1 billion-a-year drug for osteoporosis. Strattera was unsuccessful as an antidepressant but became a top seller for attention deficit/hyperactivity disorder.[32]

# Organizational Arrangements

Many companies use *customer-driven engineering* to develop new products, incorporating customer preferences in the final design. Some, such as SAP, have relied on organizational changes to help develop more successful new products.[33]

> **SAP**  After a series of high-profile acquisitions of firms such as SuccessFactors, Sybase, and Ariba, business software leader SAP set out to create internal start-ups to pursue new business ideas in adjacent markets or just in markets where large companies typically did not operate. Hiring entrepreneurs from inside and outside its ranks, the company treated every project much like a typical start-up, making funding decisions like an investor at each stage of the new-product development process. In formulating their business ideas, the start-ups had to be cognizant of SAP's global footprint and the need to satisfy regulatory requirements around the world, but they could also tap into its strong relationships with clients. One success was the development of HANA, the company's real-time database analysis technology. HANA was designed to be a powerful computing platform, so SAP also enlisted the developer community to discover applications that could be part of that platform.

New-product development requires senior management to define business domains, product categories, and specific criteria. One company established the following acceptance criteria:

- The product can be introduced within five years.
- The product has a market potential of at least $50 million and a 15 percent growth rate.
- The product can provide at least 30 percent return on sales and 40 percent on investment.
- The product can achieve technical or market leadership.

## BUDGETING FOR NEW-PRODUCT DEVELOPMENT

R&D outcomes are so uncertain that it is difficult to use normal investment criteria when budgeting for new-product development. Some companies simply finance as many projects as possible, hoping to achieve a few winners. Others apply a conventional percentage-of-sales figure or spend what the competition spends. Still others decide how many successful new products they need and work backward to estimate the required investment.

| TABLE 15.1 | Cost of Finding One Successful New Product (Starting with 64 New Ideas) | | | |
|---|---|---|---|---|
| **Stage** | **Number of Ideas** | **Pass Ratio** | **Cost per Product Idea** | **Total Cost** |
| 1. Idea screening | 64 | 1:4 | $ 1,000 | $ 64,000 |
| 2. Concept testing | 16 | 1:2 | 20,000 | 320,000 |
| 3. Product development | 8 | 1:2 | 200,000 | 1,600,000 |
| 4. Test marketing | 4 | 1:2 | 500,000 | 2,000,000 |
| 5. National launch | 2 | 1:2 | 5,000,000 | 10,000,000 |
| | | | $5,721,000 | $13,984,000 |

Table 15.1 shows how a company might calculate the cost of new-product development. The new-products manager at a large consumer packaged-goods company reviewed 64 ideas. Sixteen passed the screening stage and cost $1,000 each to review at this point. Half, or eight, survived the concept-testing stage, at a cost of $20,000 each. Four survived the product-development stage, at a cost of $200,000 each. Two did well in the test market, costing $500,000 each. When they were launched, at a cost of $5 million each, one was highly successful. Thus, this one successful idea cost the company $5,721,000 to develop, while 63 others fell by the wayside for a total development cost of $13,984,000. Unless the company can improve its pass ratios and reduce costs at each stage, it will need to budget nearly $14 million for each successful new idea it hopes to find.

Hit rates vary. Inventor Sir James Dyson claims he made 5,127 prototypes of his bagless, transparent vacuum cleaner over a 14-year period before getting it right, resulting in the best-selling vacuum cleaner by revenue in the United States with more than 20 million sold and annual revenue of more than $1.5 billion. He doesn't lament his failures, though: "If you want to discover something that other people haven't, you need to do things the wrong way...watching why that fails can take you on a completely different path." His latest successes: the Airblade, an energy-efficient hand drier for public restrooms, and the Air Multiplier, a bladeless table fan.[34]

## ORGANIZING NEW-PRODUCT DEVELOPMENT

Companies handle the organizational aspect of new-product development in several ways. Many assign responsibility to *product managers*. But product managers are often busy managing existing lines and may lack the skills and knowledge to develop and critique new products.

Inventor Sir James Dyson acknowledges that he has endured many unsuccessful new product ideas on his way to finding a few successful ones.

Source: © Adrian Sherratt/Alamy

Kraft and Johnson & Johnson have employed *new-product managers* who report to category managers. Westinghouse has used *growth leaders*—a full-time job for its most creative and successful managers.[35] Intuit uses a team of *innovation catalysts*—design-thinking coaches—to help mangers work on initiatives throughout the organization.[36] Some companies have a *high-level management committee* charged with reviewing and approving proposals.

Large companies often establish a *new-product department* headed by a manager with substantial authority, access to top management, and responsibility for generating and screening new ideas, working with the R&D department, and carrying out field testing and commercialization. Eli Lilly put every department engaged in the process of turning molecules into medicine—from R&D staff to the team who seek FDA approval—under one roof to improve efficiency and cut development time.[37]

Some firms open innovation centers in new geographical locations to better design new products for those regions. Diageo, purveyor of premium spirits, beers, and wine, opened such a center in Singapore to support the company's Asian growth initiatives.[38]

**CROSS-FUNCTIONAL TEAMS** 3M, Dow, and General Mills have assigned new-product development to **venture teams,** cross-functional groups charged with developing a specific product or business. These "intrapreneurs" are relieved of other duties and given a budget, time frame, and "skunkworks" setting.

**Skunkworks** are informal workplaces, sometimes garages, where intrapreneurial teams work to develop new products. As it transforms itself from a PC company to a solutions company in the cyber-security and data center design and management business, Dell has established separate headquarters for its new units with marching orders to think entrepreneurially.[39]

**Communities of practice** are often housed on internal Web sites where employees from different departments are encouraged to share knowledge and skills with others.[40] Japanese pharmaceutical maker Esai Co. has formed more than 400 innovation communities. One helped develop a jelly-like medication for Alzheimer's patients that is easy to swallow. Of the 29 innovation community projects commissioned by grocery retailer Supervalu, 22 were implemented over a 10-year period.[41]

Cross-functional teams can collaborate and use concurrent new-product development to push new products to market.[42] Concurrent product development resembles a rugby match, with team members passing the new product back and forth as they head toward the goal. Using this system, Allen-Bradley Corporation (a maker of industrial controls) was able to develop a new device in just two years, down from six under its old system. Cross-functional teams help ensure that engineers are not driven to create a "better mousetrap" when potential customers don't need or want one.

**CROWDSOURCING** The Internet lets companies engage external participants in the new-product development process in rich and meaningful ways. Through **crowdsourcing,** these paid or unpaid outsiders can offer needed expertise or a different perspective on a task or project that might otherwise be overlooked.

Companies such as Edison Nation and the Big Idea Group have sprung up to tap into crowdsourcing's possibilities.[43] Quirky combines its own design, branding, engineering, and sales teams with 864,000 online participants, forming a community for devising new products. The company sifts through thousands of submissions weekly to identify eight to ten ideas that merit greater scrutiny. For the chosen ideas, it will design, manufacture, and sell the product. Inventors and any members of the community who contribute to the design and branding get a cut.[44]

As another example, P&G wanted to create a dishwashing detergent "smart enough" to reveal when the right amount of soap has been added to a sink full of dirty plates. With its formidable in-house research and development team stumped, the company went to InnoCentive, a spin-off of Eli Lilly, which handed the problem over to its global network of volunteer tinkerers—professionals, retired scientists, students, and others. As it happened, an Italian chemist working from her home laboratory had pioneered a new kind of dye that turns dishwater blue when a certain amount of soap is added. For $30,000 in prize money, P&G had a solution.[45]

**STAGE-GATE SYSTEMS** Many top companies use the *stage-gate system* to divide the innovation process into stages, with a gate or checkpoint at the end of each.[46] The project leader, working with a cross-functional team, must bring a set of known deliverables to each gate before the project can pass to the next stage. To move from the business plan stage into product development requires a convincing market research study of consumer needs and interest, a competitive analysis, and a technical appraisal. Senior managers review the criteria at each gate to make one of four decisions: *go, kill, hold,* or *recycle.*

For example, at Tata Steel, initial ideas generated by "trend scouting" become future pipeline developments and then, in turn, priority product and process developments and finally product and process implementations. About 50 to 100 ideas are generated for every one that makes it to implementation, and at any point in time, 50 to 70 priority product or process development projects are in the pipeline before the final-phase gate.[47]

The stages in the new-product development process are shown in Figure 15.1. Many firms have parallel sets of projects working through the process, each at a different stage.[48] Think of the process as a *funnel:* A large number

Quirky uses crowdsourcing with a large online consumer panel and its own experts to help develop new products.

*Source: Quirky*

of initial new-product ideas and concepts are winnowed down to a few high-potential products that are ultimately launched. But the process is not always linear. Many firms use a *spiral development process* that recognizes the value of returning to an earlier stage to make improvements before moving forward.[49]

Stage-gate systems make the innovation process visible to all and clarify the project leader's and team's responsibilities at each stage.[50] The gates or controls should not be so rigid, however, that they inhibit learning and the development of novel products.[51] These systems have evolved over the years as users have made them more flexible, adaptive, and scalable; built in better governance; integrated portfolio management; incorporated accountability and continuous improvement; and adapted the process to include *open innovation* and input from sources outside the company at different stages.[52]

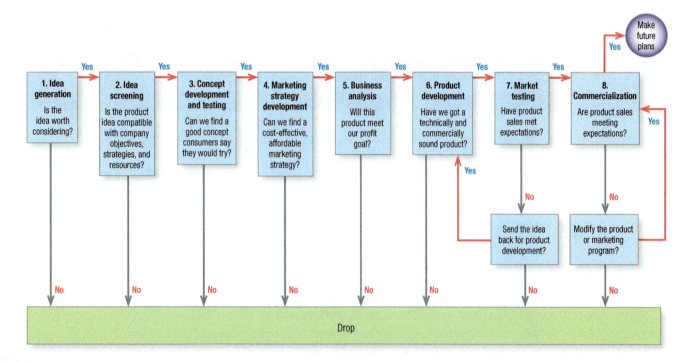

| **Fig. 15.1** |

The New-Product Development Decision Process

# Managing the Development Process: Ideas

## GENERATING IDEAS

The new-product development process starts with the search for ideas. Some marketing experts believe we find the greatest opportunities and highest leverage for new products by uncovering the best possible set of unmet customer needs or technological innovation.[53] New-product ideas can in fact come from interacting with various groups and using creativity-generating techniques.[54] (See "Marketing Memo: Ten Ways to Find Great New-Product Ideas.")

**INTERACTING WITH EMPLOYEES** Employees can be a source of ideas for improving production, products, and services.[55] Consider what these three firms have done:

- Toyota reports its employees submit 2 million ideas annually (about 35 suggestions per employee), more than 85 percent of which are implemented.[56]
- LinkedIn launched an in-house incubator that allows any employee to organize a team and pitch a project to a group of executives. The company has also created "hackdays"—one Friday a month when employees work on creative projects.57
- Pricewaterhouse Coopers set up an *American Idol*–style innovation competition dubbed "PowerPitch," in which the winning team received $100,000 and the opportunity to implement their proposal for a new line of business that could eventually be worth $100 million in revenue. Live chats and an online platform for discussion and voting led up to a five-team finale televised internally from the company's New York City headquarters.[58]

Top management can be another major source of ideas. Some company leaders, such as former CEO Andy Grove of Intel, take personal responsibility for technological innovation in the firm. New-product ideas can come from a variety of outside sources, as discussed below, however, their chances of receiving serious attention often depend on having an employee in the organization take the role of product champion.

**INTERACTING WITH OUTSIDERS** Encouraged by the open innovation movement, many firms are going outside their bounds to tap external sources of new ideas, including customers, scientists, engineers, patent attorneys, university and commercial laboratories, industrial consultants and publications, channel members, marketing and advertising agencies, and even competitors.[59] "Marketing Insight: P&G's Connect + Develop Approach to Innovation" describes how P&G has made new-product development more externally focused.

## marketing memo — Ten Ways to Find Great New-Product Ideas

1. Run informal sessions where groups of customers meet with company engineers and designers to discuss problems and needs and brainstorm potential solutions.
2. Allow time off—scouting time—for technical people to putter on their own pet projects. Google has allowed 20 percent time off; 3M 15 percent; and Rohm & Haas 10 percent.
3. Make a customer brainstorming session a standard feature of plant tours.
4. Survey your customers: Find out what they like and dislike in your and competitors' products.
5. Undertake "fly-on-the-wall" or "camping out" research with customers, as do Fluke and Hewlett-Packard.
6. Use iterative rounds: a group of customers in one room, focusing on identifying problems, and a group of your technical people in the next room, listening and brainstorming solutions. Immediately test proposed solutions with the group of customers.
7. Set up a keyword search that routinely scans trade publications in multiple countries for new-product announcements.
8. Treat trade shows as intelligence missions, where you view all that is new in your industry under one roof.
9. Have your technical and marketing people visit your suppliers' labs and spend time with their technical people—find out what's new.
10. Set up an idea vault, and make it open and easily accessed. Allow employees to review the ideas and add constructively to them.

**Source:** Adapted from Robert G. Cooper, *Product Leadership: Creating and Launching Superior New Products* (New York: Perseus Books, 1998). Adapted with permission from the author. See also Robert G. Cooper and Scott J. Edgett, "Ideation for Product Innovation: What are the Best Methods?," *PDMA Visions*, March 2008, pp. 12–17.

Source: © Mark Peterson 2011

## marketing insight

## P&G'S Connect + Develop Approach to Innovation

In the first decade of the 21st century, one of the corporations with the fastest-growing revenue and profit was Procter & Gamble. Fueling its growth were successful new products such as Olay Regenerist, Swiffer, Mr. Clean Magic Eraser, Pulsonic toothbrushes, and Actonel, prescribed for osteoporosis. Many of these reflected innovation in what then-CEO A. G. Lafley called "the core"—core markets, categories, brands, technologies, and capabilities.

To more effectively develop its core, P&G has adopted a "Connect + Develop" model that emphasizes the pursuit of outside innovation. The firm collaborates with organizations and individuals around the world, searching for proven technologies, packages, and products it can improve, scale up, and market on its own or in partnership with other companies. It has strong relationships with external designers, distributing product development around the world to increase what it calls "consumer sensing."

P&G identifies the top 10 customer needs, closely related products that could leverage or benefit from existing brand equity, and "game boards" that map the adoption of technology across different product categories. It may consult government and private labs as well as academic and other research institutions, venture capital firms, individual entrepreneurs, and suppliers, retailers, competitors, and development and trade partners, using online networks to reach thousands of experts worldwide.

P&G's three core requirements for a successful Connect + Develop strategy are:

1. *Never assume that "ready to go" ideas found outside are truly ready to go.* There will always be development work to do, including risky scale-up.

2. *Don't underestimate the internal resources required.* A full-time, senior executive will need to run any connect-and-develop initiative.

3. *Never launch without a mandate from the CEO.* Connect-and-develop cannot succeed if it's cordoned off in R&D. It must be a top-down, company-wide strategy.

P&G vets 4,000 submissions annually and actively solicits innovation ideas from a larger network of individuals and businesses with a past history of working with the company. Through Connect + Develop—and improvements in product cost, design, and marketing—P&G increased R&D productivity nearly 60 percent during the decade. The innovation success rate has more than doubled, and costs have fallen.

**Sources:** www.pgconnectdevelop.com; Lydia Dishman, "How Outsiders Get Their Products to the Innovation Big League at Proctor & Gamble," *Fast Company*, July 13, 2012; Bruce Brown and Scott D. Anthony, "How P&G Tripled Its Innovation Success Rate," *Harvard Business Review*, June 2011, pp. 64–72; A.G. Lafley and Ram Charan, *The Game Changer: How You Can Drive Revenue and Profit Growth Through Innovation* (New York: Crown Business, 2009); Larry Huston and Nabil Sakkab, "Connect and Develop: Inside Procter & Gamble's New Model for Innovation," *Harvard Business Review,* March 2006, pp. 58–66.

---

Customer needs and wants are the logical place to start the search.[60] Griffin and Hauser suggest that conducting 10 to 20 in-depth experiential interviews per market segment often uncovers the vast majority of customer needs.[61] But other approaches can be profitable (see "Marketing Memo: Seven Ways to Draw New Ideas from Your Customers"). One marketer-sponsored café in Tokyo tests products of all kinds with affluent, influential young Japanese women.[62]

## marketing memo

## Seven Ways to Draw New Ideas from Your Customers

1. *Observe how customers are using your product.* Medtronic, a medical device company, has salespeople and market researchers regularly observe spine surgeons who use their products and competitive products to learn how theirs can be improved. After living with lower-middle-class families in Mexico City, Procter & Gamble researchers devised Downy Single Rinse, a fabric softener that removed an arduous step from the partly manual laundry process there.

2. *Ask customers about their problems with your products.* Komatsu Heavy Equipment sent a group of engineers and designers to the United States for six months to ride with equipment drivers and learn how to make products better. Procter & Gamble, recognizing consumers were frustrated that potato chips break and are difficult to save after opening the bag, designed Pringles to be uniform in size and encased in a protective tennis-ball-type can.

3. *Ask customers about their dream products.* Ask your customers what they want your product to do, even if the ideal sounds impossible. One 70-year-old camera user told Minolta he would like the camera to make his subjects look better and not show their wrinkles and aging. In response, Minolta produced a camera with two lenses, one for rendering softer images of the subjects.

4. *Use a customer advisory board to comment on your company's ideas.* Levi Strauss uses youth panels to discuss lifestyles, habits, values, and brand engagements; Cisco runs Customer Forums to improve its offerings; and Harley-Davidson solicits product ideas from its one million H.O.G. (Harley Owners Group) members.

5. *Use Web sites for new ideas.* Companies can use specialized search engines such as Technorati to find blogs and postings relevant to their businesses. P&G's corporate global Web site has a *Share Your Thoughts* section to gain advice and feedback from customers.

6. *Form a brand community of enthusiasts who discuss your product.* Harley-Davidson and Apple have strong brand enthusiasts and advocates; Sony engaged in collaborative dialogues with consumers to codevelop its PlayStation products. LEGO draws on kids and influential adult enthusiasts for feedback on new-product concepts in early stages of development.

7. *Encourage or challenge your customers to change or improve your product.* Salesforce.com wants its users to develop and share new software applications using simple programming tools; International Flavors & Fragrances gives a toolkit to its customers to modify specific flavors, which IFF then manufactures; LSI Logic Corporation also provides customers with do-it-yourself toolkits so customers can design their own specialized chips; and BMW posted a toolkit on its Web site to let customers develop ideas using telematics and in-car online services.

**Source:** From an unpublished paper, Philip Kotler, "Drawing New Ideas from Your Customers," 2013.

The traditional company-centric approach to product innovation is giving way to a world in which companies cocreate products with consumers. At BlankLabel.com, you can design your own unique shirt by specifying the cut, size, collar, buttons, cuffs, and pockets you want.[63]

As noted above, companies are also increasingly turning to crowdsourcing to generate new ideas. One form of crowdsourcing invites the online community to help create content or software, often with prize money or a moment of glory as an incentive.[64] When Baskin-Robbins ran an online contest to pick its next flavor, 40,000 consumers entered. The winning entry—from a 62-year-old grandmother of four—combined chocolate, nuts, and caramel and was launched as Toffee Pecan Crunch.[65] One recent convert to crowdsourcing is Cisco.[66]

**CISCO**    The Cisco Internet of Things (IoT) Grand Challenge (formerly the Cisco I-Prize) is a worldwide initiative, aiming to bring the industry together and accelerate the adoption of breakthrough technologies and products that will contribute to the growth and evolution of the Internet of Things. Awards of U.S. $250,000 in cash prizes are to be shared among three winners, and can be used to jump-start ventures. Cisco also provides winners with mentoring, training, and access to business expertise from Cisco and other supporting organizations. From the inception of I-Prize, Cisco's rationale for these challenges—which drew 2,500 entrepreneurs from 104 countries in its first iteration—was simple: "In many parts of the world, you have incredibly smart people with incredibly great ideas who have absolutely no access to capital to take a great idea and turn it into a business."

In the first year, high-potential technology start-ups aimed to meet five main criteria with their submissions: (1) Does it address a real pain point? (2) Will it appeal to a big enough market? (3) Is the timing right? (4) If we pursue the idea, will we be good at it? and (5) Can we exploit the opportunity for the long term? The public judged the entries online, where Cisco found the detailed comments even more useful than the actual votes. The winning entry in the first competition was a plan for a sensor-enabled smart-electricity grid. The second competition drew 3,000 participants from more than 156 countries. The winning entry was from a team of five university students from Mexico and based on the idea of a "Life Account" that gathered information about users through connected devices in the physical world and online data from the virtual world. The next two IoT Grand Challenges targeted Russia where Cisco has massive investment plans. One of the winning Russian IoT Grand Challenge teams developed a system that uses a mobile phone as a mediator for transmitting data from sensors to healthcare systems and is compatible with all major mobile phone platforms, as well as more than 40 medical devices.

As the Cisco I-Prize has evolved into the form of the Cisco IoT Grand Challenge, submissions are now entered into one of six categories: Applications and Application Enablement, Analytics, Management, Networking, Security or Things. Each submission must map to one of a variety of industries Education, Energy, Healthcare, Manufacturing, Oil and Gas, Retail, Smart Cities, Sports and Entertainment or Transportation.

Besides producing new and better ideas, cocreation can help customers feel closer to the company and create favorable word of mouth.[67] Getting the right customers engaged in the right way, however, is critical.[68]

Lead users can be a good source of input, even when they innovate products without the consent or knowledge of the companies that produce them. Mountain bikes developed as a result of youngsters taking their bikes to the top of a mountain and riding down. When the bikes broke, the youngsters began building more durable bikes and adding motorcycle brakes, improved suspension, and accessories. They, not bike companies, developed these innovations.

Some companies, particularly those that want to appeal to younger, leading-edge consumers, bring their lead users into their product-design process. Technical companies can learn a great deal by studying customers who make the most advanced use of the company's products and who recognize the need for improvements before other customers do.[69] In a business-to-business market, collecting information from distributors and retailers who are not usually in close contact can provide more diverse insights and information.[70]

Not everyone believes a customer focus helps create better new products.[71] As Henry Ford famously said, "If I'd asked people what they wanted, they would have said a faster horse." Some still caution that being overly focused on consumers who may not really know what they want, or what could be possible, can result in shortsighted product development and miss real potential breakthroughs.[72] Apple and IKEA have reputations for incorporating user input with some caution, and others believe focusing on lead users leads to incremental and not breakthrough innovation.[73]

**STUDYING COMPETITORS** Companies can find good ideas by researching the products and services of competitors and other companies. They can find out what customers like and dislike about competitors' products. They can buy their competitors' products, take them apart, and build better ones. They can ask their own sales representatives and intermediaries for ideas. These groups have firsthand exposure to customers and are often the first to learn about competitive developments. Electronic retailer Best Buy even checks with venture capitalists to find out what start-ups are working on.

*Source: Cisco I-Prize (now referred to IoT Challenge) Moscow Team*

Cisco's I-Prize innovation competition, now called IoT, draws entries from around the world, like this winning team from Russia, and has generated numerous new product ideas.

To establish the optimal brand positioning for the new product and the right points-of-parity and points-of-differences, marketers need a thorough understanding of the competition. Consider how the fierce video game console battle among Microsoft, Sony, and Nintendo has spurred innovation as each firm attempts to break loose from the pack.[74]

> **VIDEO GAME CONSOLES**   Makers of video game consoles fight tooth-and-nail for the minds and hearts of the 1 billion gamers worldwide, 220 million of whom live in the United States. For the 2013 holiday season, Microsoft's new Xbox One went head to head with Sony's new PS4. Although the two game consoles both added many new features—from motion-detection cameras to allow gamers to play using gestures to technology linking the gaming console to a smart phone or tablet—the Xbox One was priced $100 higher than the PS4's $399 list price. Microsoft also lost the early PR battle when it announced policies that angered customers, such as restrictions on the process of gaming and sharing games. And the company had a tough act to follow. Its earlier model, the Xbox 360, brought significant power and online functionality to gamers, introducing Achievements and the gamer score to facilitate competition. With sales of more than 75 million units, Xbox 360 also drew more than 40 million users into Microsoft's Xbox Live connected gaming service. The third major player, Nintendo, found great success in 2006 with its Wii gaming system. Bucking industry trends, it chose a cheaper, lower-power chip with fewer graphics capabilities, creating a totally different style of play based on physical gestures. A sleek white design and motion-sensitive wireless controller also made Wii much more engaging and interactive, and Nintendo's decision to embrace outside software developers meant new titles quickly became available. Its collaborative nature made Wii a hit with non-gamers drawn by its capabilities and with hard-core players seeking to master its many intriguing games. The 2012 follow-up, the Wii U, did not attract the same interest, putting Nintendo in a tough spot against its two chief competitors.

**ADOPTING CREATIVITY TECHNIQUES**  Internal brainstorming sessions also can be quite effective—if conducted correctly. "Marketing Memo: How to Run a Successful Brainstorming Session" provides some guidelines.

## marketing memo
## How to Run a Successful Brainstorming Session

If done correctly, group brainstorming sessions can create insights, ideas, and solutions that would have been impossible without everyone's participation. If done incorrectly, they are a painful waste of time that can frustrate and antagonize participants. To ensure success, experts recommend the following:

1. A trained facilitator should guide the session, and the right physical environment must be used.

2. The right participants must be chosen. Sometimes it is useful to have a real mixture with many different points of view.

3. Participants must see themselves as collaborators working toward a common goal.

4. Rules need to be set up and followed so conversations don't get off track. Some structure is needed, though flexibility is desired too.

5. Participants must be given proper background preparation and materials so they can get into the task quickly.

6. Individual sessions before and after the brainstorming can be useful for thinking and learning about the topic ahead of time and for reflecting afterward on what happened.

7. During the session, each participant must be encouraged to participate and think freely and constructively. It may be useful to give participants time to think and gather their thoughts based on what they have heard.

8. To help stimulate thinking, participants may be told to identify and challenge existing assumptions, role-play some aspect of the situation they are analyzing, or consider borrowing ideas from other firms, even outside the industry.

9. Brainstorming sessions must lead to a clear plan of action and implementation so the ideas that materialize can provide tangible value.

10. Brainstorming can do more than just generate ideas—it should help build teams and leave participants better informed and energized.

**Sources:** Anne Fisher, "Why Most Brainstorming Sessions Fail," *Fortune*, August 23, 2013; "7 Ways to Enliven Your Next Brainstorming Session," *Forbes*, March 18, 2013; Natalie Peace, "Why Most Brainstorming Sessions Are Useless," *Forbes*, April 9, 2012; Linda Tischler, "Be Creative: You Have 30 Seconds," *Fast Company*, May 2007, pp. 47–50; Michael Myser, "When Brainstorming Goes Bad," *Business 2.0*, October 2006, p. 76; Robert I. Sutton, "Eight Rules to Brilliant Brainstorming," *BusinessWeek IN Inside Innovation*, September 2006, pp. 17–21.

Creativity is mostly about making connections in ways that are not obvious. Here is a sampling of techniques for stimulating creativity in individuals and groups.[75]

- *Attribute listing.* List the attributes of an object, such as a screwdriver. Then modify each attribute, such as replacing the wooden handle with plastic, providing torque power, adding different screw heads, and so on.
- *Forced relationships.* List several ideas and consider each in relationship to each of the others. In designing new office furniture, for example, consider a desk, bookcase, and filing cabinet as separate ideas. Then imagine a desk with a built-in bookcase or a desk with built-in files or a bookcase with built-in files.
- *Morphological analysis.* Start with a problem, such as "getting something from one place to another via a powered vehicle." Now think of dimensions, such as the type of platform (cart, chair, sling, bed), the medium (air, water, oil, rails), and the power source (compressed air, electric motor, magnetic fields). By listing every possible combination, you can generate many new solutions.
- *Reverse-assumption analysis.* List all the normal assumptions about an entity and then reverse them. Instead of assuming that a restaurant has menus, charges for food, and serves food, reverse each assumption. The new restaurant may decide to serve only what the chef bought that morning, provide some food but charge for the time the person sits at the table, or design an exotic atmosphere and rent the space to people who bring their own food and beverages.
- *New contexts.* Take familiar processes, such as people-helping services, and put them into a new context. Imagine helping dogs and cats with day care service, stress reduction, psychotherapy, funerals, and so on. Instead of sending hotel guests to the front desk to check in, greet them at curbside and use a wireless device to register them.
- *Mind mapping.* Start with an idea, such as a car, then think of the next idea that comes up (say Mercedes) and link it to car, then think of the next association (Germany), and do this with all associations that come up with each new word. Perhaps a whole new idea will materialize.

New-product ideas can arise from *lateral marketing* that combines two product concepts or ideas to create a new offering.[76] Cereal bars are a successful combination of cereal and snacking. Kinder Surprise combined candy with a toy.

## USING IDEA SCREENING

In screening ideas, the company must avoid two types of errors. A *DROP-error* occurs when the company dismisses a good idea. It is extremely easy to find fault with other people's ideas (Figure 15.2). Some companies shudder when they look back at ideas they dismissed or breathe sighs of relief when they realize how close they came to dropping what eventually became a huge success. Consider the hit television show *Friends*.[77]

**FRIENDS** The NBC situation comedy *Friends* enjoyed a 10-year run from 1994 to 2004 as a perennial ratings powerhouse. But the show almost didn't see the light of the day. According to an internal NBC research report, the pilot episode was described as "not very entertaining, clever, or original" and was given a failing grade, scoring 41 of a possible 100. Ironically, the pilot for an earlier hit sitcom, *Seinfeld,* was also rated "weak," though the pilot for the medical drama *ER* scored a healthy 91. Courteney Cox's Monica was the *Friends* character who scored best with test audiences, while characters portrayed by Lisa Kudrow and Matthew Perry were deemed to have marginal appeal, and the Rachel, Ross, and Joey characters scored even lower. Adults 35 and older in the sample found the characters as a whole "smug, superficial, and self-absorbed."

The purpose of screening is to drop poor ideas as early as possible. The rationale is that product-development costs rise substantially at each successive development stage. Most companies require new-product ideas to be described on a standard form for a committee's review. The description states the product idea, the target market, and the competition and roughly estimates market size, product price, development time and costs, manufacturing costs, and rate of return.

The executive committee then reviews each idea against a set of criteria. Does the product meet a need? Would it offer superior value? Can it be distinctively advertised or promoted? Does the company have the necessary know-how and capital? Will the new product deliver the expected sales volume, sales growth, and profit? Consumer input may be necessary too.[78]

"I've got a great idea!"

"It won't work here."

"We've tried it before."

"This isn't the right time."

"It can't be done."

"It's not the way we do things."

"We've done all right without it."

"It will cost too much."

"Let's discuss it at our next meeting."

**| Fig. 15.2 |**

## Forces Fighting New Ideas

Source: With permission of Jerold Panas, Young & Partners Inc.

A research study almost killed one of the all-time successful TV sitcoms, *Friends*, reinforcing the fact that research must be interpreted and used carefully.

Source: © Pictorial Press Ltd/Alamy

Management can rate the surviving ideas using a weighted-index method like that in Table 15.2. The first column lists factors required for successful product launches, and the second column assigns importance weights. The third column scores the product idea on a scale from 0 to 1.0, with 1.0 the highest score. The final step multiplies each factor's importance by the product score to obtain an overall rating. In this example, the product idea scores 0.69, which places it in the "good idea" level. The purpose of this basic rating device is to promote systematic evaluation and discussion, not to make the decision for management.

As the idea moves through development, the company will need to constantly revise its estimate of the product's overall probability of success, using the following formula:

| Overall probability of success | = | Probability of technical completion | × | Probability of commercialization given technical completion | × | Probability of economic success given commercialization |

| TABLE 15.2 | Product–Idea Rating Device | | |
|---|---|---|---|
| **Product Success Requirements** | **Relative Weight (a)** | **Product Score (b)** | **Product Rating (c = a × b)** |
| Unique or superior product | .40 | .8 | .32 |
| High performance-to-cost ratio | .30 | .6 | .18 |
| High marketing dollar support | .20 | .7 | .14 |
| Lack of strong competition | .10 | .5 | .05 |
| Total | 1.00 | | .69 |

[a] Rating scale: .00–.30 poor; .31–.60 fair; .61–.80 good. Minimum acceptance rate: .61

For example, if the three probabilities are estimated at 0.50, 0.65, and 0.74, respectively, the overall probability of success is 0.24. The company then must judge whether this probability is high enough to warrant continued development.

# Managing the Development Process: Concept to Strategy

Attractive ideas must be refined into testable product concepts. A *product idea* is a possible product the company might offer to the market. A *product concept* is an elaborated version of the idea expressed in consumer terms.

## CONCEPT DEVELOPMENT AND TESTING

Concept development is a necessary but not sufficient step for new-product success. Marketers must also distinguish winning concepts from losers by testing.

**CONCEPT DEVELOPMENT** Imagine a large food-processing company gets the idea of producing a powder to add to milk to increase its nutritional value and taste. This is a product *idea*, but consumers don't buy product ideas; they buy product *concepts*.

A product idea can be turned into several concepts. The first question is: Who will use this product? It can be aimed at infants, children, teenagers, young or middle-aged adults, or older adults. Second, what primary benefit should this product provide—taste, nutrition, refreshment, or energy? Third, when will people consume this drink—at breakfast, midmorning, for lunch, midafternoon, with dinner, late evening? By answering these questions, a company can form several concepts:

- *Concept 1.* An instant drink for adults who want a quick nutritious breakfast without preparation.
- *Concept 2.* A tasty snack for children to drink as a midday refreshment.
- *Concept 3.* A health supplement for older adults to drink in the late evening before bed.

Each concept represents a *category concept* that defines the product's competition. An instant breakfast drink would compete against bacon and eggs, breakfast cereals, coffee and pastry, and other breakfast alternatives. A snack drink would compete against soft drinks, fruit juices, sports drinks, and other thirst quenchers.

Suppose the instant-breakfast-drink concept looks best. The next task is to show where this powdered product would stand in relationship to other breakfast products via perceptual mapping. Figure 15.3(a) uses the two dimensions of cost and preparation time to create a *product-positioning map* for the breakfast drink, which offers low cost and quick preparation. Its nearest competitors are cold cereal and breakfast bars; its most distant is bacon and eggs. These contrasts can help communicate and promote the concept to the market.

Next, the product concept becomes a *brand concept.* Figure 15.3(b) is a *brand-positioning map*, a perceptual map showing the current positions of three existing brands of instant breakfast drinks (A–C) as seen by consumers. As Chapter 10 described, it can also be useful to overlay current or desired consumer preferences on to the map. Figure 15.3(b) also shows four segments of consumers (1–4) whose preferences are clustered around the points on the map.

The brand-positioning map helps the company decide how much to charge and how calorific to make its drink. Three segments (1–3) are well served by existing brands (A–C). The company would not want to position itself next to one of those existing brands, unless that brand is weak or inferior or market demand was high enough to be shared. As it turns out, the new brand would be distinctive in the medium-price, medium-calorie market or in the high-price, high-calorie market. There is also a segment of consumers (4) clustered fairly near the medium-price, medium-calorie market, suggesting this may offer the greatest opportunity.

**CONCEPT TESTING** Concept testing means presenting the product concept to target consumers, physically or symbolically, and getting their reactions. The more the tested concepts resemble the final product or experience, the more dependable concept testing is. Concept testing of prototypes can help avoid costly mistakes, but it may be especially challenging with radically different, new-to-the-world products.[79] Visualization techniques can help respondents match their mental state with what might occur when they are actually evaluating or choosing the new product.[80]

**(a) Product-positioning Map (Breakfast Market)**

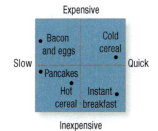

**(b) Brand-positioning Map (Instant Breakfast Market)**

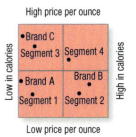

| **Fig. 15.3** |

Product and Brand Positioning

In the past, creating physical prototypes was costly and time consuming, but today firms can use *rapid prototyping* to design products on a computer and then produce rough models to show potential consumers for their reactions. Firms developing big-ticket items such as orthopedic devices for knee replacements or electric cars use rapid prototyping in new-product development to save time and money.[81] In response to a short-term oversupply of wine in the marketplace, the makers of Kendall-Jackson developed two new brands by using rapid prototyping to quickly bring their ideas to life, selling 100,000 cases of each brand, 10 times more than expected, in the process.[82]

Companies are also using *virtual reality* to test product concepts. Virtual reality programs use computers and sensory devices (such as gloves or goggles) to simulate reality. Lockheed Martin uses virtual reality to develop its GPS satellites for the U.S. Air Force.[83] Supercomputers allow for elaborate product testing to assess changes in performance and supplement consumer input. Kenworth used to test new truck designs with clay models and wind tunnels. Using supercomputer analysis, it can now make more accurate estimates of how much drag and fuel use it can eliminate with new trimmed and tapered mud flaps (answer: $400 of a typical truck's annual gas bill).[84]

Concept testing presents consumers with an elaborated version of the concept. Here is the elaboration of concept 1 in our milk example:

> Our product is a powdered mixture added to milk to make an instant breakfast that gives all the day's needed nutrition along with good taste and high convenience. The product comes in three flavors (chocolate, vanilla, and strawberry) and individual packets, six to a box, at $2.49 a box.

After receiving this information, researchers measure product dimensions by having consumers respond to questions like these:

1. **Communicability and believability**—"Are the benefits clear to you and believable?" If the scores are low, the concept must be refined or revised.
2. **Need level**—"Do you see this product solving a problem or filling a need for you?" The stronger the need, the higher the expected consumer interest.
3. **Gap level**—"Do other products currently meet this need and satisfy you?" The greater the gap, the higher the expected consumer interest. Marketers can multiply the need level by the gap level to produce a *need-gap score.* A high score means the consumer sees the product as filling a strong need not satisfied by available alternatives.
4. **Perceived value**—"Is the price reasonable in relationship to value?" The higher the perceived value, the higher is expected consumer interest.
5. **Purchase intention**—"Would you (definitely, probably, probably not, definitely not) buy the product?" Consumers who answered the first three questions positively should answer "Definitely" here.
6. **User targets, purchase occasions, purchasing frequency**—"Who would use this product, when, and how often?"

Respondents' answers indicate whether the concept has a broad and strong consumer appeal, what products it competes against, and which consumers are the best targets. The need-gap levels and purchase-intention levels can

A in-depth conjoint analysis helped to design the Courtyard by Marriott hotel chain.

be checked against norms for the product category to see whether the concept appears to be a winner, a long shot, or a loser. One food manufacturer rejects any concept that draws a definitely-would-buy score lower than 40 percent.

**CONJOINT ANALYSIS** Consumer preferences for alternative product concepts can be measured with **conjoint analysis,** a method for deriving the utility values that consumers attach to varying levels of a product's attributes.[85] Conjoint analysis has become one of the most popular concept-development and testing tools. For example, Marriott used it to design its Courtyard hotel concept.[86]

With conjoint analysis, respondents see different hypothetical offers formed by combining varying levels of the attributes and rank them. Management can then identify the most appealing offer and its estimated market share and profit. In a classic illustration, academic research pioneers Green and Wind used this approach in connection with developing a new spot-removing, carpet-cleaning agent for home use.[87] Suppose the new-product marketer is considering five design elements:

- Three package designs (A, B, C—see Figure 15.4)
- Three brand names (K2R, Glory, Bissell)
- Three prices ($1.19, $1.39, $1.59)
- A possible Good Housekeeping seal (yes, no)
- A possible money-back guarantee (yes, no)

Although the researcher can form 108 possible product concepts with these five elements ($3 \times 3 \times 3 \times 2 \times 2$), it would be too much to ask consumers to rank them all from most to least preferred. A sample of, say, 18 contrasting product concepts is feasible.

The marketer now uses a statistical program to derive the consumer's utility functions for each of the five attributes (see Figure 15.5). Utility ranges between zero and one; the higher the utility, the stronger the consumer's preference for that level of the attribute. Looking at packaging, package B is the most favored, followed by C and then A (A has hardly any utility). The preferred names are Bissell, K2R, and Glory in that order. The consumer's utility varies inversely with price. A Good Housekeeping seal is preferred, but it does not add that much utility and may not be worth the effort to obtain it. A money-back guarantee is strongly preferred.

The consumer's most desired offer is package design B, brand name Bissell, priced at $1.19, with a Good Housekeeping seal and a money-back guarantee. We can also determine the relative importance to this consumer of each attribute—the difference between the highest and lowest utility level for that attribute. The greater the

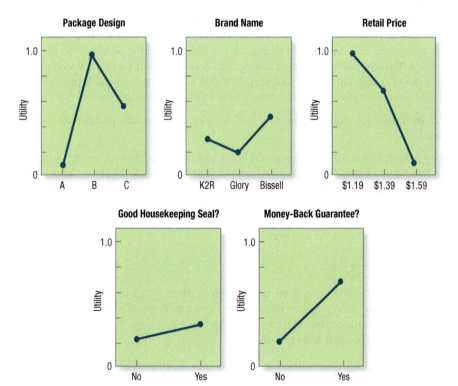

**| Fig. 15.5 |**

Utility Functions Based on Conjoint Analysis

difference, the more important the attribute. Clearly, this consumer sees price and package design as the most important attributes, followed by money-back guarantee, brand name, and a Good Housekeeping seal.

Preference data from a sufficient sample of target consumers help to estimate the market share any specific offer is likely to achieve, given any assumptions about competitive response. Still, the company may not launch the market offer that promises to gain the greatest market share because of cost considerations. The most customer-appealing offer is not always the most profitable offer to make.

Under some conditions, researchers will collect the data by presenting not a full-profile description of each offer, but two factors at a time. For example, respondents may see a table with three price levels and three package types and indicate which of the nine combinations they would like best, second-best, and so on. Another table consists of trade-offs between two other variables. This trade-off approach may be easier to use when there are many variables and possible offers. However, it is less realistic in that respondents are focusing on only two variables at a time. Adaptive conjoint analysis (ACA) is a "hybrid" data collection technique that combines self-stated or explicated importance ratings of attributes with pair-wise trade-off tasks comparing two options.[88]

## MARKETING STRATEGY DEVELOPMENT

Following a successful concept test, the new-product manager will develop a preliminary three-part strategy plan for introducing the new product into the market. The first part describes the target market's size, structure, and behavior; the planned brand positioning; and the sales, market share, and profit goals sought in the first few years:

> The target market for the instant breakfast drink is families with children who are receptive to a new, convenient, nutritious, and inexpensive form of breakfast. The company's brand will be positioned at the higher-price, higher-quality end of the instant-breakfast-drink category. The company will aim initially to sell 500,000 cases or 10 percent of the market, with a loss in the first year not exceeding $1.3 million. The second year it will aim for 700,000 cases or 14 percent of the market, with a planned profit of $2.2 million.

The second part outlines the planned price, distribution strategy, and marketing budget for the first year:

> The product will be offered in chocolate, vanilla, and strawberry, in individual packets of six to a box, at a retail price of $2.49 a box. There will be 48 boxes per case, and the case price to distributors will be $24. For the first two months, dealers will be offered one case free for every four cases bought, plus cooperative-advertising allowances. Free samples will be distributed in stores. Coupons for 50 cents off will appear in newspapers and online. The total sales promotional budget will be $2.9 million. An advertising budget of $6 million will be split 50:50 between national and local. Two-thirds will go into television and one-third into online. Advertising copy will emphasize the benefit concepts of nutrition and convenience. The advertising-execution concept will revolve around a small boy who drinks instant breakfast and grows strong. During the first year, $100,000 will be spent on marketing research to buy store audits and consumer-panel information to monitor market reaction and buying rates.

The third part of the marketing strategy plan describes the long-run sales and profit goals and marketing-mix strategy over time:

> The company intends to win a 25 percent market share and realize an after-tax return on investment of 12 percent. To achieve this return, product quality will start high and be improved over time through technical research. Price will initially be set at a high level and gradually drop to expand the market and meet competition. The total promotion budget will be boosted about 20 percent each year, with the initial advertising–sales promotion split of 65:35 eventually evolving to 50:50. Marketing research will be reduced to $60,000 per year after the first year.

## BUSINESS ANALYSIS

After management develops the product concept and marketing strategy, it can evaluate the proposal's business attractiveness. Management needs to prepare sales, cost, and profit projections to determine whether they satisfy company objectives. If they do, the concept can move to the development stage. As new information comes in, the business analysis will undergo revision and expansion.

**ESTIMATING TOTAL SALES** Total estimated sales are the sum of estimated first-time sales, replacement sales, and repeat sales. Sales-estimation methods depend on whether the product is purchased once (such as an engagement ring or retirement home), infrequently, or often. For one-time products, sales rise at the beginning, peak, and approach zero as the number of potential buyers becomes exhausted [see Figure 15.6(a)]. If new buyers keep entering the market, the curve will not go to zero.

Infrequently purchased products—such as automobiles, microwaves, and industrial equipment—exhibit replacement cycles dictated by physical wear or obsolescence associated with changing styles, features, and performance. Sales forecasting for this product category calls for estimating first-time sales and replacement sales separately [see Figure 15.6(b)].

Frequently purchased products, such as consumer and industrial nondurables, have product life-cycle sales resembling Figure 15.6(c). The number of first-time buyers initially increases and then decreases as fewer buyers are left (assuming a fixed population). Repeat purchases occur soon, providing the product satisfies some buyers. The sales curve eventually falls to a plateau representing a level of steady repeat-purchase volume; by this time, the product is no longer a new product.

In estimating sales, the manager's first task is to estimate first-time purchases of the new product in each period. To estimate replacement sales, management researches the product's *survival-age distribution*—that is, the number of units that fail in year one, two, three, and so on. The low end of the distribution indicates when the first replacement sales will take place. Because replacement sales are difficult to estimate before the product is in use, some manufacturers base the decision to launch a new product on their estimate of first-time sales alone.

For a frequently purchased new product, the seller estimates repeat sales as well as first-time sales. A high rate of repeat purchasing means customers are satisfied; sales are likely to stay high even after all first-time purchases take place. Some products and brands are bought a few times and dropped. Colgate's Wisp disposable toothbrush received much trial, but repeat sales slowed considerably after that.[89]

**ESTIMATING COSTS AND PROFITS** Costs are estimated by the R&D, manufacturing, marketing, and finance departments. Table 15.3 illustrates a five-year projection of sales, costs, and profits for the instant breakfast drink.

*Row 1* shows projected sales revenue over the five-year period. The company expects to sell $11,889,000 (approximately 500,000 cases at $24 per case) in the first year. Behind this projection is a set of assumptions about the rate of market growth, the company's market share, and the factory-realized price. *Row 2* shows the cost of goods sold, which hovers around 33 percent of sales revenue. We find this cost by estimating the average cost of labor, ingredients, and packaging per case. *Row 3* shows the expected gross margin, the difference between sales revenue and cost of goods sold.

*Row 4* shows anticipated development costs of $3.5 million, including product-development cost, marketing research costs, and manufacturing development costs. *Row 5* shows the estimated marketing costs over the five-year period to cover advertising, sales promotion, and marketing research and an amount allocated for sales force coverage and marketing administration. *Row 6* shows the allocated overhead to this new product to cover its share of the cost of executive salaries, heat, light, and so on.

*Row 7*, the gross contribution, is gross margin minus the preceding three costs. *Row 8*, supplementary contribution, lists any change in income to other company products caused by the new-product introduction. *Dragalong income* is additional income to them, and *cannibalized income* is reduced income.[90] Table 15.3 assumes no supplementary contributions. *Row 9* shows net contribution, which in this case is the same as gross contribution. *Row 10* shows discounted contribution—that is, the present value of each future contribution discounted at 15 percent per annum. For example, the company will not receive $4,716,000 until the fifth year. This amount is worth only $2,346,000 today if the company can earn 15 percent on its money through other investments.[91]

Finally, *row 11* shows the cumulative discounted cash flow, the accumulation of the annual contributions in row 10. Two points are of central interest. First is the maximum investment exposure, the highest loss the project can create. The company will be in a maximum loss position of $4,613,000 in year 1. The second is the payback period, the time when the company recovers all its investment, including the built-in return of 15 percent. The payback period here is about three and a half years. Management must decide whether to risk a maximum investment loss of $4.6 million and a possible payback period of three and a half years. As part of their financial analysis, firms may conduct a breakeven or risk analysis.

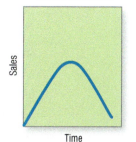
**(a) One-time Purchased Product**

**(b) Infrequently Purchased Product**

**(c) Frequently Purchased Product**

| Fig. 15.6 |

Product Life-Cycle Sales for Three Types of Products

| TABLE 15.3 | Projected Five-Year Cash Flow Statement (in thousands of dollars) | | | | | |
|---|---|---|---|---|---|---|
| | **Year 0** | **Year 1** | **Year 2** | **Year 3** | **Year 4** | **Year 5** |
| 1. Sales revenue | $0 | $11,889 | $15,381 | $19,654 | $28,253 | $32,491 |
| 2. Cost of goods sold | 0 | 3,981 | 5,150 | 6,581 | 9,461 | 10,880 |
| 3. Gross margin | 0 | 7,908 | 10,231 | 13,073 | 18,792 | 21,611 |
| 4. Development costs | −3,500 | 0 | 0 | 0 | 0 | 0 |
| 5. Marketing costs | 0 | 8,000 | 6,460 | 8,255 | 11,866 | 13,646 |
| 6. Allocated overhead | 0 | 1,189 | 1,538 | 1,965 | 2,825 | 3,249 |
| 7. Gross contribution | −3,500 | −1,281 | 2,233 | 2,853 | 4,101 | 4,716 |
| 8. Supplementary contribution | 0 | 0 | 0 | 0 | 0 | 0 |
| 9. Net contribution | −3,500 | −1,281 | 2,233 | 2,853 | 4,101 | 4,716 |
| 10. Discounted contribution (15%) | −3,500 | −1,113 | 1,691 | 1,877 | 2,343 | 2,346 |
| 11. Cumulative discounted cash flow | −3,500 | −4,613 | −2,922 | −1,045 | 1,298 | 3,644 |

# Managing the Development Process: Development to Commercialization

Up to now, the product has existed only as a word description, a drawing, or a prototype. The next step represents a jump in investment that dwarfs the costs incurred so far. The company will determine whether the product idea can translate into a technically and commercially feasible product. If not, the accumulated project cost will be lost, except for any useful information gained in the process.

## PRODUCT DEVELOPMENT

The job of translating target customer requirements into a working prototype is helped by a set of methods known as *quality function deployment* (QFD). The methodology takes the list of desired *customer attributes* (CAs) generated by market research and turns them into a list of *engineering attributes* (EAs) that engineers can use. For example, customers of a proposed truck may want a certain acceleration rate (CA). Engineers can turn this into the required horsepower and other engineering equivalents (EAs). A major contribution of QFD is improved communication between marketers, engineers, and manufacturing people.[92]

**PHYSICAL PROTOTYPES** The goal of the R&D department is to find a prototype that embodies the key attributes in the product-concept statement, performs safely under normal use and conditions, and can be produced within budgeted manufacturing costs. Sophisticated virtual reality technology and the Internet now permit rapid prototyping and flexible development processes.

R&D must also decide how consumers will react to different colors, sizes, and weights. Historically, a yellow mouthwash supported an "antiseptic" claim (Listerine), red a "refreshing" claim (Lavoris), and green or blue a "cool" claim (Scope). Marketers need to supply R&D with information about what attributes consumers seek and how they judge whether these are present.

Firms rigorously test product prototypes internally. Vibram, which makes its own FiveFingers line as well as soles for all types of shoes—such as for skateboarding, cycling, rock climbing, and fly fishing—employs a team of product testers. The company puts its products into the most extreme conditions by executing tests directly in the field and employing a series of procedures:[93]

> If our chemist creates a new compound targeted towards road running applications, first we perform a battery of lab tests to understand the compound's physical properties. Next, we bring natural environments and surfaces into the laboratory and calculate information. Then lastly shoes are distributed to our tester team who will document things like weather/temp, distance, location, and running surfaces, etc. They'll comment on the differences in the grip of the soles. We then compile the results and make a decision on validation.

**CUSTOMER TESTS** When the prototypes are ready, they must be put through rigorous functional and customer tests before they enter the marketplace. *Alpha testing* tests the product within the firm to see how it performs in different applications. After refining the prototype further, the company moves to *beta testing* with customers.

Consumer testing can bring consumers into a laboratory or give them samples to use at home. Procter & Gamble has on-site labs such as a diaper-testing center where dozens of mothers bring their babies to be studied. To develop its Cover Girl Outlast all-day lip color, P&G invited 500 women to come to its labs each morning to apply the lipstick, record their activities, and return eight hours later so it could measure remaining lip color, resulting in a product that came with a tube of glossy moisturizer that women could apply on top of their color without looking at a mirror. In-home placement tests are common for products from ice cream flavors to new appliances.

## MARKET TESTING

After management is satisfied with functional and psychological performance, the product is ready to be branded with a name, logo, and packaging and go into a market test, if desired.

Not all companies undertake market testing. A company officer at Revlon stated: "In our field—primarily higher-priced cosmetics not geared for mass distribution—it would be unnecessary for us to market test. When we develop a new product, say an improved liquid makeup, we know it's going to sell because we're familiar with the field. And we've got 1,500 demonstrators in department stores to promote it."

One problem is that many managers find it difficult to kill a project that attracted much effort and attention, even if they *should* do so based on market testing. The result is an unfortunate (and typically unsuccessful) escalation of commitment.[94]

Many companies, however, believe market testing, if done correctly, can yield valuable information about buyers, dealers, marketing program effectiveness, and market potential. The main issues are: How much market testing should be done, and what kind(s)?

Vibram has professional product testers who put the soles it makes for shoes through extreme conditions to see how they hold up.

The amount of testing is influenced by the investment cost and risk on the one hand and time pressure and research cost on the other. High-investment–high-risk products, whose chance of failure is high, must be market tested; the cost will be an insignificant percentage of total project cost. High-risk products that create new-product categories (the first instant-breakfast drink) or have novel features (the first gum-strengthening toothpaste) warrant more market testing than modified products (another toothpaste brand).

**CONSUMER-GOODS MARKET TESTING** Consumer-products tests seek to estimate four variables: *trial*, *first repeat*, *adoption*, and *purchase frequency*. Many consumers may try the product but not rebuy it, or it might achieve high permanent adoption but low purchase frequency (like gourmet frozen foods).

Here are four major methods of consumer-goods market testing, from least to most costly.

*Sales-Wave Research* Consumers who initially try the product at no cost are reoffered it, or a competitor's product, at slightly reduced prices. The offer may be made as many as five times (sales waves), while the company notes how many customers select it again and their reported level of satisfaction.

Sales-wave research can be implemented quickly, conducted with a fair amount of security, and carried out without final packaging and advertising. However, because customers are preselected, it does not indicate trial rates the product would achieve with different sales incentives, nor does it indicate the brand's power to gain distribution and favorable shelf position.

*Simulated Test Marketing* Thirty to 40 qualified shoppers are asked about brand familiarity and preferences in a specific product category and attend a brief screening of both well-known and new TV or print ads. One ad advertises the new product but is not singled out for attention. Consumers receive a small amount of money and are invited into a store where they may buy any items. The company notes how many consumers buy the new brand and competing brands. This provides a measure of the ad's relative effectiveness against competing ads in stimulating trial. Consumers are asked the reasons for their purchases or nonpurchases. Those who did not buy the new brand are given a free sample. Some weeks later, they are contacted to ascertain product attitudes, usage, satisfaction, and repurchase intention and are offered an opportunity to repurchase any products.

This method can give some surprisingly accurate results about advertising effectiveness and trial rates (and repeat rates if extended) in a much shorter time and at a fraction of the cost of using real test markets, making it especially appealing to marketers of fast-moving consumer goods.[95] As media and channels have grown more fragmented, however, it has become harder to truly simulate market conditions with only traditional approaches.

***Controlled Test Marketing*** The company with the new product specifies the number of stores and geographic locations it wants to test. A research firm delivers the product to a panel of participating stores and controls shelf position, pricing, and number of facings, displays, and point-of-purchase promotions. Electronic scanners measure sales at checkout. The company can also evaluate the impact of local advertising and promotions and interview a sample of customers later to get their impressions of the product. It does not have to use its own sales force, give trade allowances, or "buy" distribution. However, controlled test marketing provides no information about how to sell the trade on carrying the new product. It also exposes the product and its features to competitors' scrutiny.

***Test Markets*** The ultimate way to test a new consumer product is to put it into full-blown test markets. The company chooses a few representative cities and puts on a full marketing communications campaign, and the sales force tries to sell the trade on carrying the product and giving it good shelf exposure. Test marketing also measures the impact of alternative marketing plans by implementing them in different cities. A full-scale test can cost more than $1 million, depending on the number of test cities, the test duration, and the amount of data the company wants to collect.

In designing a test market, management faces several decisions: (1) How many test cities? (2) Which test cities? (3) Length of the test? (4) Which information to collect? and (5) What action to take? A number of considerations come into play for each decision. Columbus, Ohio, is a popular location for testing new fast-food products: The city is reasonably representative demographically of the rest of the nation, with a healthy dose of college-aged students, and is a contained media market with reasonable ad rates.[96]

Many major global consumer goods makers such as L'Oréal, Philips, and Nikon like to test in South Korea because its demanding but fair consumers and well-developed marketing infrastructure help ensure that products are in good enough shape to enter other global markets.[97] Gucci likes to test its luxury products in China because it feels consumers there indicate where the luxury market is heading.[98]

Many companies today skip test marketing despite its benefits and rely on faster and more economical testing methods. Starbucks regularly launches products before they have been deemed "perfect," based on this philosophy espoused by chief digital officer, Adam Brotman: "We don't think it is okay if things aren't perfect, but we're willing to innovate and have speed to market trump a 100% guarantee that it's be perfect." The company's mobile payments app had a number of flaws and corrections in its first six months after launch, but it now generates 3 million mobile transactions a week.[99] General Mills prefers to launch new products in 25 percent of the country, an area too large for rivals to disrupt. Managers review retail scanner data, which tells them within days how the product is doing and what corrective fine-tuning to do.

Some companies like to test their new products in South Korea because of the open-minded attitude of consumers who live there and the marketing infrastructure that exists.

**BUSINESS-GOODS MARKET TESTING** Business goods can also benefit from market testing. Expensive industrial goods and new technologies will normally undergo alpha and beta testing.[100] During beta testing, the company's technical people observe how customers use the product, a practice that often exposes unanticipated problems of safety and servicing and alerts the company to customer training and servicing requirements. The company can also observe how much value the equipment adds to the customer's operation, as a clue to subsequent pricing.

Companies must interpret beta test results carefully because only a small number of test customers are used, they are not randomly drawn, and tests are somewhat customized to each site. Another risk is that testers unimpressed with the product may leak unfavorable reports about it. Square doesn't employ beta testing—preferring to test at its own internally controlled locations—because it feels it should never put out an unfinished product.[101]

At trade shows the company can observe how much interest buyers show in the new product, how they react to various features and terms, and how many express purchase intentions or place orders. In distributor and dealer display rooms, products may stand next to the manufacturer's other products and possibly competitors' products, yielding preference and pricing information in the product's normal selling atmosphere. However, customers who come in might not represent the target market, or they might want to place early orders that cannot be filled.

Industrial manufacturers come close to using full test marketing when they give a limited supply of the product to the sales force to sell in a limited number of areas that receive promotion support and printed catalog sheets.

# COMMERCIALIZATION

Commercialization incurs the company's highest costs to date.[102] Too often companies are so focused on developing a new product that they neglect to spend adequate time developing a winning marketing launch program.[103] The firm will need to contract for manufacture, or it may build or rent a full-scale manufacturing facility. Most new-product campaigns also require a sequenced mix of market communication tools to build awareness and ultimately preference, choice, and loyalty.[104]

To introduce a major new consumer packaged good into the national market can cost $25 million to $100 million in advertising, promotion, and other communications in the first year. For new food products, marketing expenditures typically represent 57 percent of first-year sales.

To raise funds, some inventors who don't have the backing of a major corporation are relying on crowdfunding and companies like Kickstarter.[105] With **crowdfunding,** individuals or start-ups fund their projects by using social media and other means to generate interest and contributions from the general public.

**WHEN (TIMING)** Suppose a company has almost completed the development work on its new product and learns a competitor is nearing the end of its development work. The company faces three choices:

1. *First entry*—The first firm entering a market usually enjoys the "first mover advantages" of locking up key distributors and customers and gaining leadership. But if rushed to market before it has been thoroughly debugged, the first entry can backfire.
2. *Parallel entry*—The firm might time its entry to coincide with the competitor's entry. The market may pay more attention when two companies are advertising the new product.[106]
3. *Late entry*—The firm might delay its launch until after the competitor has borne the cost of educating the market, and its product may reveal flaws the late entrant can avoid. The late entrant can also learn the size of the market.

If a new product replaces an older product, the company might delay until the old product's stock has been drawn down. If the product is seasonal, it might wait until the season arrives; often a product waits for a "killer application" to occur. Many companies are now encountering competitive "design-arounds"—rivals are making their own versions just different enough to avoid patent infringement and royalties.[107]

**WHERE (GEOGRAPHIC STRATEGY)** Most companies will develop a planned market rollout over time. In choosing rollout markets, the major criteria are market potential, the company's local reputation, the cost of filling the pipeline, the cost of communication media, the influence of the area on other areas, and competitive penetration. Small companies select an attractive city and put on a blitz campaign, entering other cities one at a time. Large companies introduce their product into a whole region and then move to the next. Companies with national distribution networks, such as auto companies, launch new models nationally.

With the Internet connecting far-flung parts of the globe, competition is more likely to cross national borders. Companies are increasingly rolling out new products simultaneously across the globe. However, masterminding a global launch poses challenges, as Chapter 8 described, and a sequential rollout across countries may still be the best option.[108]

**TO WHOM (TARGET-MARKET PROSPECTS)** Within the rollout markets, the company must target initial distribution and promotion to the best prospect groups. Ideally these should be early adopters, heavy users, and opinion leaders it can reach at low cost. Few groups include all these, so the company should rate prospects and target the best group. The aim is to generate strong sales as soon as possible to attract further prospects.

**HOW (INTRODUCTORY MARKET STRATEGY)** Because new-product launches often take longer and cost more than expected, many potentially successful offerings suffer from underfunding. It's important to allocate sufficient time and resources—yet not overspend—as the new product gains traction in the marketplace.[109]

To coordinate the many tasks in launching a new product, management can use network-planning techniques such as **critical path scheduling (CPS)**, which develops a master chart showing the simultaneous and sequential activities that must take place. By estimating how much time each activity takes, planners estimate completion time for the entire project. Any delay in any activity on the critical path—the shortest route to completion—will delay the project. If the launch must be completed sooner, the planner searches for ways to reduce time along the critical path.[110]

# The Consumer-Adoption Process

**Adoption** is an individual's decision to become a regular user of a product and is followed by the *consumer-loyalty process*. New-product marketers typically aim at early adopters and use the theory of innovation diffusion and consumer adoption to identify them.

## STAGES IN THE ADOPTION PROCESS

An **innovation** is any good, service, or idea that someone *perceives* as new, no matter how long its history. Everett Rogers defines the **innovation diffusion process** as "the spread of a new idea from its source of invention or creation to its ultimate users or adopters."[111] The **consumer-adoption process** is the mental steps through which an individual passes from first hearing about an innovation to final adoption.[112] They are:

1. *Awareness*—The consumer becomes aware of the innovation but lacks information about it.
2. *Interest*—The consumer is stimulated to seek information about the innovation.
3. *Evaluation*—The consumer considers whether to try the innovation.
4. *Trial*—The consumer tries the innovation to improve his or her estimate of its value.
5. *Adoption*—The consumer decides to make full and regular use of the innovation.

The new-product marketer should facilitate movement through these stages. A water filtration system manufacturer might discover that many consumers are stuck in the interest stage; they do not buy because of their uncertainty and the large investment cost.[113] But these same consumers would be willing to use a water filtration system at home on a trial basis for a small monthly fee. The manufacturer should consider offering a trial-use plan with option to buy.

## FACTORS INFLUENCING THE ADOPTION PROCESS

Marketers recognize the following characteristics of the adoption process: differences in individual readiness to try new products, the effect of personal influence, differing rates of adoption, and differences in organizations' readiness to try new products. Some researchers are focusing on use-diffusion processes as a complement to adoption process models to see how consumers actually use new products.[114]

**READINESS TO TRY NEW PRODUCTS AND PERSONAL INFLUENCE** Everett Rogers defines a person's level of innovativeness as "the degree to which an individual is relatively earlier in adopting new ideas than the other members of his social system." Some people are the first to adopt new clothing fashions or new appliances; some doctors are the first to prescribe new medicines.[115] See the adopter categories in Figure 15.7. After a slow start, an increasing number of people adopt the innovation, the number reaches a peak, and then it diminishes as fewer nonadopters remain.

The five adopter groups differ in their value orientations and their motives for adopting or resisting the new product.[116]

- *Innovators* are technology enthusiasts; they are venturesome and enjoy tinkering with new products and mastering their intricacies. In return for low prices, they are happy to conduct alpha and beta testing and report on early weaknesses.

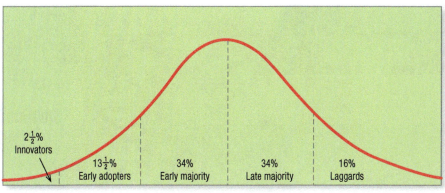

Source: Tungsten, http://en.wikipedia.org/wiki/Everett_Rogers. Based on E. Rogers, *Diffusion of Innovations* (London: Free Press, 1962).

**| Fig. 15.7 |**

Adopter Categorization on the Basis of Relative Time of Adoption of Innovations

• *Early adopters* are opinion leaders who carefully search for new technologies that might give them a dramatic competitive advantage. They are less price sensitive and are willing to adopt the product if given personalized solutions and good service support.
• *Early majority* are deliberate pragmatists who adopt the new technology when its benefits have been proven and a lot of adoption has already taken place. They make up the mainstream market.
• *Late majority* are skeptical conservatives who are risk averse, technology shy, and price sensitive.
• *Laggards* are tradition-bound and resist the innovation until the status quo is no longer defensible.

Each group requires a different type of marketing if the firm wants to move its innovation through the full product life cycle. In addition to or instead of targeting opinions leaders, some experts advocate targeting *revenue leaders* with a new product—those customers with higher customer lifetime-values—to accelerate the path to profitability.[117]

**Personal influence,** the effect one person has on another's attitude or purchase probability, has greater significance in some situations and for some individuals than others, and it is more important in evaluation than in the other stages. It has more power over late than early adopters and in risky situations.

Companies often target innovators and early adopters with product rollouts. When Nike entered the skateboarding market, it recognized an anti-establishment, big-company bias from the target market that could present a sizable challenge. To gain "street cred" with teen skaters, it sold exclusively to independent shops, advertised nowhere but skate magazines, and gained sponsorships from admired pro riders by engaging them in product design.[118]

**CHARACTERISTICS OF THE INNOVATION** Some products catch on immediately (roller blades), whereas others take a long time to gain acceptance (diesel engine autos). One new-product concept that quickly took hold was StubHub online ticket reselling service.[119]

**STUBHUB** The cofounders of StubHub, Jeff Fluhr and Eric Barker, came up with the idea for their site when they were Stanford MBA students. Realizing there were far too many unused tickets for sporting events, theater events, and concerts, they decided to set up an "eBay for tickets" where sellers could set a price higher or lower than face value depending on demand. StubHub would take a 10 percent cut from the buyer and a 15 percent cut from the seller on every purchase. The service had to negotiate state laws restricting ticket reselling, but by 2006 it was making $100 million in revenue, split between sports (75 percent), concerts (20 percent), and theater (5 percent) in a market estimated to be worth $4 billion in the United States. StubHub was sold to eBay for $310 million in 2007. Original-ticket seller Ticketmaster and its Live Nation parent have fought the company from the start, threatening legal action, introducing paperless tickets that limit reselling, and launching the TicketExchange service to compete. StubHub has sets its sights on being more than a ticket seller and becoming a multiplatform e-commerce site. A brand-building multimedia campaign launched in 2012 was designed to add emotional components to the company's functional message, including the idea of tickets "growing on trees." With 40 percent of primary tickets going unsold, StubHub is also emphasizing helping consumers discover events and attend more of them.

StubHub, a leader in online ticket reselling, is considering other e-commerce options while adding a more emotional component to its core business.

Five characteristics influence an innovation's rate of adoption. We consider them for digital video recorders (DVRs) for home use, as exemplified by TiVo.[120]

1.  *Relative advantage*—the degree to which the innovation appears superior to existing products. The greater the perceived relative advantage of using a DVR, say, for easily recording favorite shows, pausing live TV, or skipping commercials, the more quickly it was adopted.
2.  *Compatibility*—the degree to which the innovation matches consumers' values and experiences. DVRs are highly compatible with the preferences of avid television watchers.
3.  *Complexity*—the degree to which the innovation is difficult to understand or use. DVRs are somewhat complex and therefore took a slightly longer time to penetrate into home use.
4.  *Divisibility*—the degree to which the innovation can be tried on a limited basis. This provided a sizable challenge for DVRs—sampling could occur only in a retail store or perhaps a friend's house.
5.  *Communicability*—the degree to which the benefits of use are observable or describable to others. The fact that DVRs have some clear advantages helped create interest and curiosity.

Other characteristics that influence the rate of adoption are cost, risk and uncertainty, scientific credibility, and social approval. The new-product marketer must research all these factors and give the key ones maximum attention in designing the product and its marketing program.

**ORGANIZATIONS' READINESS TO ADOPT INNOVATIONS** The creator of a new teaching method would want to identify innovative schools. The producer of a new piece of medical equipment would want to identify innovative hospitals. Adoption is associated with variables in the organization's environment (community progressiveness, community income), the organization itself (size, profits, pressure to change), and the administrators (education level, age, sophistication). Other forces come into play in trying to get a product adopted into organizations that receive the bulk of their funding from the government, such as public schools. A controversial or innovative product can be squelched by negative public opinion.

# Summary

1.  Once a company has segmented the market, chosen its target customer groups and identified their needs, and selected its desired market positioning, it is ready to develop and launch appropriate new products and services. Marketing should participate with other departments in every stage of new-product development.

2.  Successful new-product development requires the company to establish an effective organization for managing the development process. Companies can choose product managers or new-product managers, committees, departments, or venture teams. Increasingly, they are adopting cross-functional teams, connecting to individuals and organizations outside the company through crowd-sourcing and other means, and developing multiple product concepts.

3.  Eight stages define the new-product development process: idea generation, screening, concept development and testing, marketing strategy development, business

analysis, product development, market testing, and commercialization. At each stage, the company must decide whether to drop the idea or move to the next stage.

4. The consumer-adoption process is the process by which customers learn about new products, try them, and adopt or reject them. Today many marketers are targeting heavy users and early adopters of new products because both groups can be reached by specific media and tend to be opinion leaders. The consumer-adoption process is influenced by many factors beyond the marketer's control, including consumers' and organizations' willingness to try new products, personal influences, and the characteristics of the new product or innovation.

## MyMarketingLab

Go to mymktlab.com to complete the problems marked with this icon ★ as well as for additional Auto-graded and Assisted-graded writing questions.

# Applications

## Marketing Debate
### Whom Should You Target with New Products?

Some new-product experts maintain that getting close to customers through intensive research is the only way to develop successful new products. Other experts disagree and say customers can't possibly provide useful feedback on what they don't know and can't provide insights that will lead to breakthrough products.

**Take a position:** Consumer research is critical to new-product development *versus* Consumer research may not be all that helpful in new-product development.

## Marketing Discussion
### Product Innovativeness

★ Think about the last new product you bought. How do you think its success will be affected by the five characteristics of an innovation: relative advantage, compatibility, complexity, divisibility, and communicability?

## Marketing Excellence

### >> Apple

Apple has transformed the way people listen to music, play video games, talk on the phone, and even read books. The company's revolutionary product innovations include the iPod, the iMac, the iPhone, and the iPad. They are the reason the company topped *Fortune*'s Most Admired Companies list every year from 2008 to 2014.

The iPod introduced many consumers to Apple and initiated a series of monumental product innovations. It exemplified Apple's innovative design skills and looked, felt, and operated like no other device. To the delight of Apple (and the chagrin of competitor Sony), the revolutionary MP3 player became "the Walkman of the 21st century," and the launch of the iTunes online music store helped drive iPod sales through the roof.

The iPod was also central in changing the way people listened to and used music. According to musician John Mayer, people felt like they were "walking through musicology" when they used their iPods, leading them to listen to more music and with more passion. The iPod has gone through a series of re-generations, adding features like photo, video, and radio capabilities along the way.

Apple reached its impressive market domination through a combination of shrewd product innovation and clever marketing. The marketing effort appealed to both Apple fans and people new to the brand. To reach such a broad base, the company had to shift its channel strategies. It added "mass electronic" retailers such as Best Buy and Circuit City (now defunct) to its existing channels, which quadrupled its number of outlets.

Besides this enhanced "push" effort, Apple also developed memorable, creative "pull" advertising that helped drive the popularity of the iPod. The Silhouettes campaign featured silhouettes of people listening to and dancing with their iPods and appeared all over the world. This simple message worked across cultures, portraying the iPod as cool but not beyond the reach of anyone who enjoyed music.

As the iPod's popularity grew, a halo effect helped increase Apple's share in its other markets. In fact, in 2007 the company officially changed its name from Apple Computer Inc. to Apple Inc. to help communicate its focus on non-computer products.

Apple's next-largest product launch after the iPod was the iPhone, its 2007 entry to the cell phone industry. With its touch-screen pad, virtual keyboard, and Internet and e-mail capabilities, the iPhone launched to huge consumer excitement; people lined up for hours to be among the first to buy one. Investment analysts initially feared that Apple's two-year contract with AT&T and the iPhone's high price would hinder its success. But 74 days after the product's debut, 1 million units had been sold. It had taken the iPod two years to reach the cumulative sales ($1.1 million) the iPhone had reached after just its first quarter. In fact, half the iPhones' buyers switched to AT&T, incurring fees to break their contracts with other carriers, just to have a chance to own an iPhone.

Over the next few years, Apple dropped the price of the iPhone significantly and added impressive picture and video capabilities, video game features, a faster processor, and access to millions of additional applications. The iPhone had become yet another game-changing technological invention. When the iPhone 4 launched in 2010, showcasing FaceTime video calling, Steve Jobs declared it "the most successful product launch in Apple's history." Jobs died in 2011 and didn't get to witness the success of the iPhone 5 launch in 2012. Apple received more than 2 million preorders of the iPhone 5 within the first 24 hours, far exceeding sales of any preceding iPhone launch. When the phone officially hit the shelves on September 21, 2012, the company couldn't keep up with the initial demand.

The launch of the iPad also created media frenzy in 2013. The multitouch device combined the look and feel of the iPhone with the power of a MacBook and gave consumers access to music, books, movies, pictures, video games, documents, and hundreds of thousands of applications at the touch of a finger without mouse or keyboard. Apple followed up with the launch of the iPad mini, a smaller version of the original, and the iPad Air, accompanied by a powerful marketing campaign that inspired consumers to do anything with their iPad, including creating movies, building wind turbines, studying coral reefs, and making mountain climbing safer.

In recent years, Apple has faced more serious competition for its smart phones, tablets, and other handheld devices, especially from Samsung and HTC. Investment in research and development is just one way the company remains a leader in this cutthroat industry. It spent $2.4 billion in R&D in 2011, $3.4 billion in 2012, and $4.5 billion in 2013. Creating, producing, and launching new products is a top priority for Apple. With creative marketing support behind them, these products are the reason consumers and analysts stay on their toes awaiting Apple's latest product news.

## Questions

1. Apple's product launches over the past decade have been monumental. What makes the company so good at innovation? Is anyone comparable to Apple in this respect?

2. How important was the iPod to Apple's current success? Discuss the significance of the iPhone and iPad launches to Apple's new-product development strategy.

3. It has been a few years since Apple's last epic innovation. What's next for Apple?

**Sources:** Matt Vella, "Apples' Latest Ad Is Probably Going to Give You the Chills," *Time*, January 13, 2014; www.apple.com; 2013 Apple Annual Report; "iPhone4: The 'Most Successful Product Launch' in Apple's History," *Independent*, June 28, 2010; Joseph De Avila, "Why Some Apple Fans Won't Buy the iPhone," *Wall Street Journal*, September 12, 2007, p. D3; Nick Wingfield, "Apple Businesses Fuel Each Other; Net Jumps as Mac Sales Top PC-Industry Growth Rate; iPhones, iPods Also Thrive," *Wall Street Journal*, October 23, 2007; Terril Yue Jones, "How Long Can the iPod Stay on Top?," *Los Angeles Times*, March 5, 2006; Beth Snyder Bulik, "Grab an Apple and a Bag of Chips," *Advertising Age*, May 23, 2005; Jay Parsons, "A Is for Apple on iPod," *Dallas Morning News*, October 6, 2005; Peter Burrows, "Rock On, iPod," *BusinessWeek*, June 7, 2004, pp. 130–31; Jay Lyman, "Mini iPod Moving Quickly, Apple Says," *TechNewsWorld*, February 26, 2004; Steven Levy, "iPod Nation," *Newsweek*, July 25, 2004; "Apple Computer: iPod Silhouettes," New York Marketing Association; Steven Levy, "iPod Nation," *Newsweek*, July 25, 2004; Effie Worldwide, www.effie.org.

# Marketing Excellence

## >> Salesforce.com

Salesforce.com was founded by former Oracle executive Marc Benioff in 1999. Benioff believed software should be free of troublesome installations, maintenance issues, and continuous upgrades. His vision was "to make software easier to purchase, simpler to use, and more democratic." With that in mind, Benioff led a start-up company called Salesforce.com that offered software-as-a-service (SaaS), or cloud computing.

SaaS differs from old-school software technology because companies pay for the product per use each month, much like a utility bill. Salesforce.com uses the Internet or "cloud" to host its customer relationship management (CRM) applications and to deliver them directly to customers, who can access the software from any device just by logging on to a Web site. They don't have to invest in servers or software licensing, install the software, or store the data themselves. With this innovative concept, Salesforce.com turned the software industry upside down and created an entirely new multibillion-dollar industry.

From the start, Salesforce.com wanted its products to be everything traditional software wasn't. Its first product had an extremely user-friendly sales interface that organized contacts, accounts, and opportunities. The company welcomed customer feedback, and as a result it could develop new features to fit users' needs. Today, The Sales Cloud is Salesforce.com's key product. It lets companies track leads, change forecasts, collaborate with colleagues, and access real-time customer information, improving productivity and closing more sales.

Salesforce.com next launched The Service Cloud, a CRM solution that changed the way companies connect with their customers. This product provides companies with a call-center view of each customer and the ability to track each case on an individual basis. Users can communicate with customers through every media channel, escalate complaints, and plug into conversations on social networking sites, ultimately resulting in better overall customer service.

From 2010 to 2012, Salesforce.com acquired 19 companies in order to expand its product offerings. In 2011, it purchased Radian6, which allowed it to launch The Marketing Cloud, with which customers can listen to and engage in conversations taking place on public social media sites like Twitter and Facebook. In addition, The Marketing Cloud enables companies to monitor their brand and products across the Internet and analyze their sales leads.

Salesforce.com transitioned into the platform-as-a-service or PaaS category with the launch of Force.com. PaaS provides customers with tools to build their own applications rather than supplying the application already built. For example, a university might develop an application for its student body that includes campus maps, bus routes, and school events, while a clothing store can customize sale discounts and product offerings for each customer based on previous purchase patterns. By 2014, more than 4 million customers had created their own applications using the Force.com platform.

A first mover, Salesforce.com is also the market leader with 14 percent market share. The company spends 7 percent of revenues on research and development and an astonishing 53 percent on marketing to help generate leads and new customers. Cloud computing has become a competitive, rapidly evolving industry, inhabited by big players like Oracle, IBM, and Workday as well as niche companies that focus on specific industries such as health care and hospitality.

Over the years, Salesforce.com has won numerous awards for its products and services. *Forbes* ranked it the most innovative company in the world from 2011 to 2014. With $3 billion in sales, it has expanded into 16 different languages and has more than 100,000 customers and more than 2.1 million subscribers.

### Questions

1. Why has Salesforce.com been so successful? What did the company do well when it created and expanded its product offerings?

2. What are some of the challenges Salesforce.com faces in the near future?

3. What other products and services might Salesforce.com offer next? Why?

**Sources**: Spencer E. Ante, "New Cloud-Software Firms Take Off," *Wall Street Journal*, March 5, 2014, p. B5; Salesforce.com; 2013 Salesforce.com Annual Report; David Trainer, "Salesforce.com Has Insider Selling, Valuation in the Clouds," *Forbes*, December 16, 2013; blogs.salesforce.com/company/2013/03/how-to-turn-a-simple-idea-into-a-high-growth-company, accessed June 2, 2014; Vauhini Vara, "Business Technology: An Early Adopter's New Idea; Salesforce.com Sees Future Built on 'Platforms,'" *Wall Street Journal*, January 22, 2008, p. B3; Floyd Norris, "First Insiders Sold Their Shares Privately, then Salesforce.com Filed to Go Public," *New York Times*, May 14, 2004, p. C1.

Ryanair's revolutionary pricing strategy charges a nominal airfare—or even nothing—for the seat, but also charges a fee for almost everything else involved in the flight.

*Source: © Alex Segre/Alamy*

## In This Chapter, We Will Address the Following **Questions**

1. How do consumers process and evaluate prices? (p. 461)

2. How should a company set prices initially for products or services? (p. 467)

3. How should a company adapt prices to meet varying circumstances and opportunities? (p. 482)

4. When and how should a company initiate a price change? (p. 485)

5. How should a company respond to a competitor's price change? (p. 487)

# 16 Developing Pricing Strategies and Programs

**Price is the one element of the marketing mix that produces revenue; the other elements** produce costs. Price also communicates the company's intended value positioning of its product or brand. A well-designed and marketed product can still command a price premium and reap big profits. But new economic realities have caused many consumers to reevaluate what they are willing to pay for products and services, and companies have had to carefully review their pricing strategies as a result. One that has caught the attention of consumers and businesses is Ryanair, with an unusual pricing strategy.[1]

*Profits for discount European air carrier Ryanair have been sky-high thanks to its revolutionary business model. The secret? Founder Michael O'Leary thinks like a retailer, charging passengers for almost everything—except their seat. A quarter of Ryanair's seats are free, and O'Leary wants to double that within five years, with the ultimate goal of making all seats free. Passengers currently pay only taxes and fees of about $10 to $24, with an average one-way fare of roughly $52. Everything else is extra: checked luggage ($9.50 per bag), snacks ($5.50 for a hot dog, $4.50 for chicken soup, $3.50 for water), and bus or train transportation into town from the far-flung airports Ryanair uses ($24). Flight attendants sell a variety of merchandise, including digital cameras ($137.50) and iPocket MP3 players ($165). Onboard gambling and cell phone service are projected new revenue sources. Other strategies cut costs or generate outside revenue. Seats don't recline, window shades and seat-back pockets have been removed, and there is no entertainment. Seat-back trays carry ads, and the exteriors of the planes are giant revenue-producing billboards for Vodafone Group, Jaguar, Hertz, and others. More than 99 percent of tickets are sold online. The Web site also offers travel insurance, hotels, ski packages, and car rentals. Only Boeing 737-800 jets are flown to reduce maintenance costs, and flight crews buy their own uniforms. O'Leary has even discussed the possibility of pay toilets and 10 rows of standing room with handrails like a New York City subway car (to squeeze 30 more passengers aboard), though both suggestions drew much public concern and skepticism. Although his ideas may seem unconventional, the formula works for Ryanair's customers; the airline flies 58 million people to more than 150 airports each year. All the extras add up to 20 percent of revenue. Ryanair enjoys net margins of 25 percent, more than three times Southwest's 7 percent. Some industry pundits even refer to Ryanair as "Walmart with wings"!*

**Pricing decisions are complex** and must take into account many factors—the company, the customers, the competition, and the marketing environment. Holistic marketers know their pricing decisions must also be consistent with the firm's marketing strategy and its target markets and brand positions. In this chapter, we provide concepts and tools to facilitate the setting of initial prices and adjusting prices over time and markets.

# Understanding Pricing

Price is not just a number on a tag. It comes in many forms and performs many functions. Rent, tuition, fares, fees, rates, tolls, retainers, wages, and commissions are all the price you pay for some good or service. Price also has many components. If you buy a new car, the sticker price may be adjusted by rebates and dealer incentives. Some firms allow customers to pay through multiple forms, such as $150 plus 25,000 frequent flier miles for a flight.[2]

Throughout most of history, prices were set by negotiation between buyers and sellers. Bargaining is still a sport in some areas. Setting one price for all buyers is a relatively modern idea that arose with the development of large-scale retailing at the end of the nineteenth century. F. W. Woolworth, Tiffany & Co., John Wanamaker, and others advertised a "strictly one-price policy," efficient because they carried so many items and supervised so many employees.

## PRICING IN A DIGITAL WORLD

Traditionally, price has operated as a major determinant of buyer choice. Consumers and purchasing agents who have access to price information and price discounters put pressure on retailers to lower their prices. Retailers in turn put pressure on manufacturers to lower their prices. The result can be a marketplace characterized by heavy discounting and sales promotion.

Downward price pressure from a changing economic environment coincided with some longer-term trends in the technological environment. For some years now, the Internet has been changing the way buyers and sellers interact. Here is a short list of how the Internet allows sellers to discriminate between buyers and buyers to discriminate between sellers.

Buyers can:

- *Get instant price comparisons from thousands of vendors.* Customers can compare the prices offered by multiple retailers by clicking mySimon.com. Intelligent shopping agents ("bots") take price comparison a step further and seek out products, prices, and reviews from hundreds if not thousands of merchants.
- *Check prices at the point of purchase.* Customers can use smart phones to make price comparisons in stores before deciding whether to purchase, pressure the retailer to match or better the price, or buy elsewhere.
- *Name their price and have it met.* On Priceline.com, customers state the price they want to pay for an airline ticket, hotel, or rental car, and the site looks for any seller willing to meet that price.[3] Volume-aggregating sites combine the orders of many customers and press the supplier for a deeper discount.
- *Get products free.* Open source, the free software movement that started with Linux, will erode margins for just about any company creating software. The biggest challenge confronting Microsoft, Oracle, IBM, and virtually every other major software producer is: How do you compete with programs that can be had for free? "Marketing Insight: Giving It All Away" describes how firms have been successful with essentially free offerings.

Sellers can:

- *Monitor customer behavior and tailor offers to individuals.* GE Lighting, which gets 55,000 pricing requests a year from its B-to-B customers, has Web programs that evaluate 300 factors going into a pricing quote, such as past sales data and discounts, so it can reduce processing time from up to 30 days to six hours.
- *Give certain customers access to special prices.* Ruelala is a members-only Web site that sells upscale women's fashion, accessories, and footwear through limited-time sales, usually two-day events. Other business market-ers are already using extranets to get a precise handle on inventory, costs, and demand at any given moment in order to adjust prices instantly.

Both buyers and sellers can:

- *Negotiate prices in online auctions and exchanges or even in person.* Want to sell hundreds of excess and slightly worn widgets? Post a sale on eBay. Want to purchase vintage baseball cards at a bargain price? Go to www.baseball-cards.com. According to *Consumer Reports*, more than half of U.S. adults reported bargain-ing for a better deal on everyday goods and services in the past three years; almost 90 percent were success-ful at least once. Some successful tactics included: told salesperson I'd check competitor's prices (57 percent of respondents); looked for lower prices at a walk-in store (57 percent); chatted with salesperson to make a personal connection (46 percent); used other store circulars or coupons as leverage (44 percent); and checked user reviews to see what others paid (39 percent).[4]

## A CHANGING PRICING ENVIRONMENT

Pricing practices have changed significantly, thanks in part to a severe recession in 2008–2009, a slow recovery, and rapid technological advances. But the new millennial generation also brings new attitudes and values to con-sumption. Often burdened by student loans and other financial demands, members of this group (born between about 1977 and 1994) are reconsidering just what they really need to own. Renting, borrowing, and sharing are valid options to many.

# marketing insight

## Giving It All Away

Giving away products for free via sampling has been a successful marketing tactic for years. Estée Lauder gave free samples of cosmetics to celebrities, and organizers at awards shows lavish winners with plentiful free items or gifts known as "swag." Other manufacturers, such as Gillette and HP, built their business model around selling the host product essentially at cost and making money on the sale of necessary supplies, such as razor blades and printer ink.

Software companies adopted similar practices. Adobe gave away its Adobe Reader for free in 1994, as did Macromedia with its Shockwave player in 1995. Their software became the industry standard, but the firms really made their money selling their authoring software. More recently, start-ups such as Blogger Weblog and Skype have succeeded with a "freemium" strategy—free online services with a premium component.

Chris Anderson, former editor-in-chief of *Wired*, believes that in a digital marketplace companies can make money with free products. As evidence, he offers revenue models relying on cross-subsidies (giving away a DVR to sell cable service) and freemiums (offering the Flickr online photo management and sharing application for free to everyone while selling the superior Flickr Pro to more committed users).

Some online firms have successfully moved "from free to fee" and begun charging for services. Under a new participative-pricing mechanism that lets consumers decide on the price they feel is warranted, buyers often choose to pay more than zero, and even enough for sellers' revenues to increase over what a fixed price would have yielded.

Red Hat successfully applied a "freemium" model. A pioneer with open source Linux software, the company offers its business customers stability and dependability. Every few years it freezes a version of the constantly evolving software and sells a long-term support edition with customized applications, backdated updates from later versions of Linux, and customer support, all for a subscription fee. Red Hat also works with developers and programmers for its free version of Linux via its Fedora program. Thanks to these moves, Red Hat is now a billion-dollar company serving 80 percent of the *Fortune* 500 companies.

**Sources:** Ashlee Vance, "Red Hat Sees Lots of Green," *Bloomberg Businessweek*, March 29, 2012; Jon Brodkin, "How Red Hat Killed Its Core Product—and Became a Billion-Dollar Business," www.arstechnica.com, February 28, 2012; Chris Anderson, *Free: The Future of a Radical Price* (New York: Hyperion, 2009); Ju-Young Kim, Martin Natter, and Martin Spann, "Pay What You Want: A New Participative Pricing Mechanism," *Journal of Marketing* 73 (January 2009), pp. 44–58; Koen Pauwels and Allen Weiss, "Moving from Free to Fee: How Online Firms Market to Change Their Business Model Successfully," *Journal of Marketing* 72 (May 2008), pp. 14–31.

Source: ASSOCIATED PRESS

Champion of open source Linux software, Red Hat complements its free offerings with valuable fee-based services.

Some say these new behaviors are creating a **sharing economy** in which consumers share bikes, cars, clothes, couches, apartments, tools, and skills and extracting more value from what they already own. As one sharing-related entrepreneur noted, "We're moving from a world where we're organized around ownership to one organized around access to assets." In a sharing economy, someone can be both a consumer and a producer, reaping the benefits of both roles.[5]

Trust and a good reputation are crucial in any exchange, but imperative in a sharing economy. Most platforms that are part of a sharing-related business have some form of self-policing mechanism such as public profiles and community rating systems, sometimes linked with Facebook. Let's look at bartering and renting, two pillars of a sharing economy.

**BARTERING** Bartering, one of the oldest ways of acquiring goods, is making a comeback through transactions estimated to total $12 billion annually in the United States. Trade exchange companies like Florida Barter and Web sites like www.swap.com connect people and businesses seeking win-win solutions. One financial analyst has traded financial plans to clients in return for a tutorial in butter churning and trapeze and fire-breathing lessons. ThredUP allows parents to swap kids' outgrown and unused clothing and toys with other parents in similar situations all over the United States. Zimride is a ride-sharing social network for college campuses.[6]

Experts advise using barter only for goods and services that someone would be willing to pay for anyway. The founders of a Web site for swapping sporting goods and outdoor gear drew up these criteria for sharable objects: cost more than $100 but less than $500, easily transportable, and infrequently used.[7]

**RENTING** The sector of the new sharing economy that is really exploding is rentals. RentTheRunway offers affordable rentals of designer dresses. Customers are sent two different sizes of the dress they choose—to ensure better fit—at a cost of $50 to $300, or about 10 percent of retail value. The site is adding 100,000 customers a month, typically 15 to 35 years old.[8] One of the pioneers in the rental economy is Airbnb.[9]

**AIRBNB** Rhode Island School of Design graduates Brian Chesky and Joe Gebbia came upon the idea of making a little extra money by launching www.airbedandbreakfast.com and renting out air mattresses to attendees at an industrial design conference in San Francisco. Emboldened by their success at attracting three very different guests for a week, the two shortened the name of their venture to Airbnb, hired a tech expert, and set out to extend their "couch-surfing" business by adding features such as escrow payments and professional photography so the potential rental properties looked their best. Around-the-clock customer service for guests and a $1 million insurance policy for hosts provided each party with valuable peace of mind. All kinds of spaces were included—not just rooms, apartments, and houses but also driveways, treehouses, igloos, and even castles. Airbnb applied a broker's model to generate revenues: 3 percent from the host and 6 percent to 12 percent from the guest, depending on the property price. Although it now operates in 190 countries and 28,000 cities, books millions of spaces annually, and has seen its valuation approach $10 billion, it faces several significant challenges, including government intervention in the form of taxes, disputes over illegal subletting, and the imposition of safety and other hospitality-related regulation.

Even big companies are getting in on the act. German car maker Daimler introduced its Car2Go service for customers who want to rent a car for a short period of time—even at the spur of the moment. In about half its stores, Home Depot has a unit that rents out all kinds of products such as drills and saws that it also sells.[10]

## HOW COMPANIES PRICE

In small companies, the boss often sets prices. In large companies, division and product line managers do. Even here, top management sets general pricing objectives and policies and often approves lower management's proposals.

Where pricing is a key competitive factor (aerospace, railroads, oil companies), companies often establish a pricing department to set or assist others in setting appropriate prices. This department reports to the marketing department, finance department, or top management. Others who influence pricing include sales managers, production managers, finance managers, and accountants. In B-to-B settings, research suggests that pricing performance improves when pricing authority is spread horizontally across the sales, marketing, and finance units and when there is a balance in centralizing and delegating that authority between individual salespeople and teams and central management.[11]

Many companies do not handle pricing well and fall back on "strategies" such as: "We calculate our costs and add our industry's traditional margins." Other common mistakes are not revising price often enough to capitalize on market changes; setting price independently of the rest of the marketing program rather than as an intrinsic element of market-positioning strategy; and not varying price enough for different product items, market segments, distribution channels, and purchase occasions.

For any organization, effectively designing and implementing pricing strategies requires a thorough understanding of consumer pricing psychology and a systematic approach to setting, adapting, and changing prices.

## CONSUMER PSYCHOLOGY AND PRICING

Many economists traditionally assumed that consumers were "price takers" who accepted prices at face value or as a given. Marketers, however, recognize that consumers often actively process price information, interpreting it from the context of prior purchasing experience, formal communications (advertising, sales calls, and brochures), informal communications (friends, colleagues, or family members), point-of-purchase or online resources, and other factors.[12]

Purchase decisions are based on how consumers perceive prices and what they consider the current actual price to be—*not* on the marketer's stated price. Customers may have a lower price threshold, below which prices signal inferior or unacceptable quality, and an upper price threshold, above which prices are prohibitive and the product appears not worth the money. Different people interpret prices in different ways. Consider the consumer psychology involved in buying a simple pair of jeans and a T-shirt.[13]

For even something as simple as a black t-shirt and a pair of jeans or pants, consumers may choose to pay as little as $50 or hundreds of dollars instead.

Source: ©Peshkov Daniil/Shutterstock

**JEANS AND A T-SHIRT** Why does a black T-shirt for women that looks pretty ordinary cost $275 from Armani but only $14.90 from the Gap and $7.90 from Swedish discount clothing chain H&M? Customers who purchase the Armani T-shirt are paying for a more stylishly cut T-shirt made of 70 percent nylon, 25 percent polyester, and 5 percent elastane with a "Made in Italy" label from a luxury brand known for suits, handbags, and evening gowns that sell for thousands of dollars. The Gap and H&M shirts are made mainly of cotton. For pants to go with that T-shirt, choices abound. Gap sells its "Original Khakis" for $44.50, though Abercrombie & Fitch's classic button-fly chinos cost $70. But that's a comparative bargain compared to Michael Bastian's plain khakis for $480 or Giorgio Armani's for $595. High-priced designer jeans may use expensive fabrics such as cotton gabardine and require hours of meticulous hand-stitching to create a distinctive design, but equally important are an image and a sense of exclusivity.

Understanding how consumers arrive at their perceptions of prices is an important marketing priority. Here we consider three key topics—reference prices, price–quality inferences, and price endings.

**REFERENCE PRICES** Although consumers may have fairly good knowledge of price ranges, surprisingly few can accurately recall specific prices.[14] When examining products, however, they often employ **reference prices,** comparing an observed price to an internal reference price they remember or an external frame of reference such as a posted "regular retail price."[15]

All types of reference prices are possible (see Table 16.1), and sellers often attempt to manipulate them. For example, a seller can situate its product among expensive competitors to imply that it belongs in the same class. Department stores will display women's apparel in separate departments differentiated by price; dresses in the more expensive department are assumed to be of better quality.[16] Marketers also encourage reference-price thinking by stating a high manufacturer's suggested price, indicating that the price was much higher originally, or by pointing to a competitor's high price.[17]

When consumers evoke one or more of these frames of reference, their perceived price can vary from the stated price.[18] Research has found that unpleasant surprises—when perceived price is lower than the stated price—can have a greater impact on purchase likelihood than pleasant surprises.[19] Consumer expectations can also play a

| TABLE 16.1 | Possible Consumer Reference Prices |
|---|---|

- "Fair Price" (what consumers feel the product should cost)
- Typical Price
- Last Price Paid
- Upper-Bound Price (reservation price or the maximum most consumers would pay)
- Lower-Bound Price (lower threshold price or the minimum most consumers would pay)
- Historical Competitor Prices
- Expected Future Price
- Usual Discounted Price

**Source:** Adapted from Russell S. Winer, *Pricing*, MSI Relevant Knowledge Series (Cambridge, MA: Marketing Science Institute, 2006).

key role in price response. On Internet auction sites such as eBay, when consumers know similar goods will be available in future auctions, they will bid less in the current auction.[20]

Clever marketers try to frame the price to signal the best value possible. For example, a relatively expensive item can look less expensive if the price is broken into smaller units, such as a $500 annual membership for "under $50 a month," even if the totals are the same.[21]

**PRICE-QUALITY INFERENCES** Many consumers use price as an indicator of quality. Image pricing is especially effective with ego-sensitive products such as perfumes, expensive cars, and designer clothing. A $100 bottle of perfume might contain $10 worth of scent, but gift givers pay $100 to communicate their high regard for the receiver.

Price and quality perceptions of cars interact. Higher-priced cars are perceived to possess high quality. Higher-quality cars are likewise perceived to be higher priced than they actually are. When information about true quality is available, price becomes a less significant indicator of quality. When this information is not available, price acts as a signal of quality.

Some brands adopt exclusivity and scarcity to signify uniqueness and justify premium pricing. Luxury-goods makers of watches, jewelry, perfume, and other products often emphasize exclusivity in their communication messages and channel strategies. For luxury-goods customers who desire uniqueness, demand may actually increase price because they then believe fewer other customers can afford the product.[22]

To maintain its air of exclusivity, Ferrari deliberately curtailed sales of its iconic, $200,000-or-more Italian sports car to below 7,000 despite growing demand in China, the Middle East, and the United States. But even exclusivity and status can vary by customer. Brahma beer is a no-frills light brew in its home market of Brazil but has thrived in Europe, where it is seen as "Brazil in a bottle." Pabst Blue Ribbon is a retro favorite among U.S. college students, but its sales have exploded in China where an upgraded bottle and claims of being "matured in a precious wooden cask like a Scotch whiskey" allow it to command a $44 price tag.[23]

**PRICE ENDINGS** Many sellers believe prices should end in an odd number. Customers perceive an item priced at $299 to be in the $200 rather than the $300 range; they tend to process prices "left to right" rather than by rounding.[24] Price encoding in this fashion is important if there is a mental price break at the higher, rounded price.

Another explanation for the popularity of "9" endings is that they suggest a discount or bargain, so if a company wants a high-price image, it should probably avoid the odd-ending tactic.[25] One study showed that demand actually increased one-third when the price of a dress *rose* from $34 to $39 but was unchanged when it rose from $34 to $44.[26]

Prices that end with 0 and 5 are also popular and are thought to be easier for consumers to process and retrieve from memory. "Sale" signs next to prices spur demand, but only if not overused: Total category sales are highest when some, but not all, items in a category have sale signs; past a certain point, sale signs may cause total category sales to fall.[27]

Pricing cues such as sale signs and prices that end in 9 are more influential when consumers' price knowledge is poor, when they purchase the item infrequently or are new to the category, and when product designs vary over time, prices vary seasonally, or quality or sizes vary across stores.[28] They are less effective the more they are used. Limited availability (for example, "three days only") also can spur sales among consumers actively shopping for a product.[29]

Source: © Ian Shaw/Alamy

Despite booming demand, Ferrari limits production and the number of sports cars that it sells to maintain the brand's exclusivity.

# Setting the Price

A firm must set a price for the first time when it develops a new product, when it introduces its regular product into a new distribution channel or geographical area, and when it enters bids on new contract work. The firm must decide where to position its product on quality and price.

Most markets have three to five price points or tiers. Marriott Hotels is good at developing different brands or variations of brands for different price points: Marriott Vacation Club—Vacation Villas (highest price), Marriott Marquis (high price), Marriott (high-medium price), Renaissance (medium-high price), Courtyard (medium price), TownePlace Suites (medium-low price), and Fairfield Inn (low price). Firms devise their branding strategies to help convey the price-quality tiers of their products or services to consumers.[30]

Having a range of price points allows a firm to cover more of the market and to give any one consumer more choices. "Marketing Insight: Trading Up, Down, and Over" describes how consumers have been shifting their spending in recent years.

The firm must consider many factors in setting its pricing policy.[31] Table 16.2 summarizes the six steps in the process.

## STEP 1: SELECTING THE PRICING OBJECTIVE

The company first decides where it wants to position its market offering. The clearer a firm's objectives, the easier it is to set price. Five major objectives are: survival, maximum current profit, maximum market share, maximum market skimming, and product-quality leadership.

| TABLE 16.2 | Steps in Setting a Pricing Policy |
|---|---|

1. Selecting the Pricing Objective
2. Determining Demand
3. Estimating Costs
4. Analyzing Competitors' Costs, Prices, and Offers
5. Selecting a Pricing Method
6. Selecting the Final Price

## marketing insight

# Trading Up, Down, And Over

Michael Silverstein and Neil Fiske, the authors of *Trading Up*, have observed a number of middle-market consumers periodically "trading up" to what they call "New Luxury" products and services "that possess higher levels of quality, taste, and aspiration than other goods in the category but are not so expensive as to be out of reach." The authors identify three main types of New Luxury products:

- *Accessible super-premium products*, such as Victoria's Secret underwear and Kettle gourmet potato chips, carry a significant premium over middle-market brands, yet consumers can readily trade up to them because they are relatively low-ticket items in affordable categories.

- *Old Luxury brand extensions* extend historically high-priced brands down-market while retaining their cachet, such as the Mercedes-Benz C-class and the American Express Blue card.

- *Masstige goods*, such as Kiehl's skin care and Kendall-Jackson wines, are priced between average middle-market brands and super-premium Old Luxury brands. They are "always based on emotions, and consumers have a much stronger emotional engagement with them than with other goods."

To trade up to brands that offer these emotional benefits, consumers often "trade down" by shopping at discounters such as Walmart and Costco for staple items or goods that confer no emotional benefit but still deliver quality and functionality. As one consumer explained in rationalizing why her kitchen boasted a Sub-Zero refrigerator, a state-of-the-art Fisher & Paykel dishwasher, and a $900 warming drawer but a giant 12-pack of Bounty paper towels from a warehouse discounter: "When it comes to this house, I didn't give in on anything. But when it comes to food shopping or cleaning products, if it's not on sale, I won't buy it."

The recent economic downturn increased the prevalence of trading down, as many found themselves unable to sustain their lifestyles. Consumers began to buy more from need than desire and to trade down more frequently in price. They shunned conspicuous consumption, and sales of some luxury goods suffered. Even purchases that had never been challenged before were scrutinized. Almost 1 million U.S. patients became "medical tourists" in 2010 and traveled overseas for medical procedures at lower costs, sometimes at the urging of U.S. health insurance companies.

As the economy improved and consumers tired of putting off discretionary purchases, retail sales picked up, benefiting luxury products in the process. Trading up and down has persisted, however, along with "trading over" or switching spending from one category to another,

buying a new home theater system, say, instead of a new car. Often this meant setting priorities and making a decision not to buy in some categories in order to buy in others.

**Sources:** Cotten Timberlake, "U.S. 2 Percenters Trade Down with Post-Recession Angst," www.bloomberg.com, May 15, 2013; Anna-Louise Jackson and Anthony Feld, "Frugality Fatigue Spurs Americans to Trade Up," www.bloomberg.com, April 13, 2012; Walker Smith, "Consumer Behavior: From Trading Up to Trading Off," *Branding Strategy Insider,* January 26, 2012; Sbriya Rice, "'I Can't Afford Surgery in the U.S.,' Says Bargain Shopper," www.cnn.com, April 26, 2010; Bruce Horovitz, "Sale, Sale, Sale: Today Everyone Wants a Deal," *USA Today*, April 21, 2010, pp. 1A–2A; Michael J. Silverstein, *Treasure Hunt: Inside the Mind of the New Consumer* (New York: Portfolio, 2006); Michael J. Silverstein and Neil Fiske, *Trading Up: The New American Luxury* (New York: Portfolio, 2003).

*Source: Digital Vision/Getty Images*

Some consumers are trading up to buy expensive luxury products like Sub-Zero refrigerators, but also trading down to buy basic staples and more functional products.

**SURVIVAL** Companies pursue *survival* as their major objective if they are plagued with overcapacity, intense competition, or changing consumer wants. As long as prices cover variable costs and some fixed costs, the company stays in business. Survival is a short-run objective; in the long run, the firm must learn how to add value or face extinction.

**MAXIMUM CURRENT PROFIT** Many companies try to set a price that will *maximize current profits*. They estimate the demand and costs associated with alternative prices and choose the price that produces maximum current profit, cash flow, or rate of return on investment. This strategy assumes the firm knows its demand and cost functions; in reality, these are difficult to estimate. In emphasizing current performance, the company may sacrifice long-run performance by ignoring the effects of other marketing variables, competitors' reactions, and legal restraints on price.

**MAXIMUM MARKET SHARE** Some companies want to *maximize their market share.* They believe a higher sales volume will lead to lower unit costs and higher long-run profit, so they set the lowest price, assuming the market is price sensitive. Texas Instruments famously practiced this **market-penetration pricing** for years. The company would build a large plant, set its price as low as possible, win a large market share, experience falling costs, and cut its price further as costs fell.

The following conditions favor adopting a market-penetration pricing strategy: (1) The market is highly price sensitive and a low price stimulates market growth; (2) production and distribution costs fall with accumulated production experience; and (3) a low price discourages actual and potential competition.

**MAXIMUM MARKET SKIMMING** Companies unveiling a new technology favor setting high prices to *maximize market skimming.* Sony has been a frequent practitioner of **market-skimming pricing,** in which prices start high and slowly drop over time. When Sony introduced the world's first high-definition television (HDTV) to the Japanese market in 1990, it was priced at $43,000. So that Sony could "skim" the maximum amount of revenue from the various segments of the market, the price dropped steadily through the years—a 28-inch Sony HDTV cost just over $6,000 in 1993, but a 42-inch Sony LED HDTV cost only $579 20 years later in 2013.

This strategy can be fatal, however, if a worthy competitor decides to price low. When Philips, the Dutch electronics manufacturer, priced its videodisc players to make a profit on each, Japanese competitors priced low and rapidly built their market share, which in turn pushed down their costs substantially.

Moreover, consumers who buy early at the highest prices may be dissatisfied if they compare themselves with those who buy later at a lower price. When Apple dropped the early iPhone's price from $600 to $400 only two months after its introduction, public outcry caused the firm to give initial buyers a $100 credit toward future Apple purchases.[32]

Market skimming makes sense under the following conditions: (1) A sufficient number of buyers have a high current demand; (2) the unit costs of producing a small volume are high enough to cancel the advantage of charging what the traffic will bear; (3) the high initial price does not attract more competitors to the market; and (4) the high price communicates the image of a superior product.

**PRODUCT-QUALITY LEADERSHIP** A company might aim to be the *product-quality leader* in the market.[33] Many brands strive to be "affordable luxuries"—products or services characterized by high levels of perceived quality, taste, and status with a price just high enough not to be out of consumers' reach. Brands such as Starbucks, Aveda, Victoria's Secret, BMW, and Viking have positioned themselves as quality leaders in their categories, combining quality, luxury, and premium prices with an intensely loyal customer base. Grey Goose and Absolut carved out a superpremium niche in the essentially odorless, colorless, and tasteless vodka category through clever on-premise and off-premise marketing that made the brands seem hip and exclusive.

**OTHER OBJECTIVES** Nonprofit and public organizations may have other pricing objectives. A university aims for *partial cost recovery,* knowing that it must rely on private gifts and public grants to cover its remaining costs. A nonprofit hospital may aim for full cost recovery in its pricing. A nonprofit theater company may price its productions to fill the maximum number of seats. A social service agency may set a service price geared to client income.

Whatever the specific objective, businesses that use price as a strategic tool will profit more than those that simply let costs or the market determine their pricing. For art museums, which earn an average of only 5 percent of their revenues from admission charges, pricing can send a message that affects their public image and the amount of donations and sponsorships they receive.

**| Fig. 16.1 |**

Inelastic and Elastic
Demand

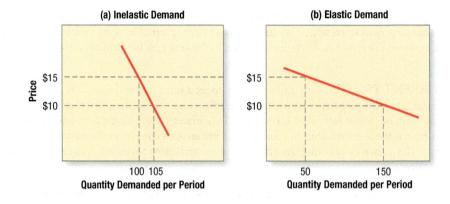

STEP 2: DETERMINING DEMAND

Each price will lead to a different level of demand and have a different impact on a company's market-ing objectives. The normally inverse relationship between price and demand is captured in a demand curve (see Figure 16.1): The higher the price, the lower the demand. For prestige goods, the demand curve sometimes slopes upward. Some consumers take the higher price to signify a better product. However, if the price is too high, demand may fall.

PRICE SENSITIVITY The demand curve shows the market's probable purchase quantity at alternative prices, summing the reactions of many individuals with different price sensitivities. The first step in estimating demand is to understand what affects price sensitivity. Generally speaking, customers are less price sensitive to low-cost items or items they buy infrequently. They are also less price sensitive when (1) there are few or no substitutes or competitors; (2) they do not readily notice the higher price; (3) they are slow to change their buying habits; (4) they think the higher prices are justified; and (5) price is only a small part of the total cost of obtaining, operating, and servicing the product over its lifetime.

A seller can successfully charge a higher price than competitors if it can convince customers that it offers the lowest *total cost of ownership* (TCO). Marketers often treat the service elements in a product offering as sales incentives rather than as value-enhancing augmentations for which they can charge. In fact, pricing expert Tom Nagle believes the most common mistake manufacturers have made in recent years is to offer all sorts of services to differentiate their products without charging for them.[34]

Of course, companies prefer customers who are less price-sensitive. Table 16.3 lists some characteristics associ-ated with decreased price sensitivity. On the other hand, the Internet has the potential to *increase* price sensitivity. In some established, fairly big-ticket categories, such as auto retailing and term insurance, consumers pay lower prices as a result of the Internet. Car buyers use the Internet to gather information and borrow the negotiating

| TABLE 16.3 | Factors That Reduce Price Sensitivity |
|---|---|

- The product is more distinctive.
- Buyers are less aware of substitutes.
- Buyers cannot easily compare the quality of substitutes.
- The expenditure is a smaller part of the buyer's total income.
- The expenditure is small compared to the total cost of the end product.
- Part of the cost is borne by another party.
- The product is used in conjunction with assets previously bought.
- The product is assumed to have more quality, prestige, or exclusiveness.
- Buyers cannot store the product.

**Source:** Based on information from Thomas T. Nagle, John E. Hogan, and Joseph Zale, *The Strategy and Tactics of Pricing,* 5th ed. (Upper Saddle River, NJ: Pearson, 2011). Printed and electronically reproduced by permission of Pearson Education, Inc., Upper Saddle River, New Jersey.

clout of an online buying service.[35] But customers may have to visit multiple sites to realize possible savings, and they don't always do so. Targeting only price-sensitive consumers may in fact be "leaving money on the table."

**ESTIMATING DEMAND CURVES** Most companies attempt to measure their demand curves using several different methods.

- *Surveys* can explore how many units consumers would buy at different proposed prices. Although consumers might understate their purchase intentions at higher prices to discourage the company from pricing high, they also tend to actually exaggerate their willingness to pay for new products or services.[36]
- *Price experiments* can vary the prices of different products in a store or of the same product in similar territories to see how the change affects sales. Online, an e-commerce site could test the impact of a 5 percent price increase by quoting a higher price to every 40th visitor to compare the purchase response. However, it must do this carefully and not alienate customers or be seen as reducing competition in any way (thus violating the Sherman Antitrust Act).[37]
- *Statistical analysis* of past prices, quantities sold, and other factors can reveal their relationships. The data can be longitudinal (over time) or cross-sectional (from different locations at the same time). Building the appropriate model and fitting the data with the proper statistical techniques call for considerable skill, but sophisticated price optimization software and advances in database management have improved marketers' abilities to optimize pricing.

One large retail chain was selling a line of "good-better-best" power drills at $90, $120, and $130, respectively. Sales of the least and most expensive drills were fine, but sales of the midpriced drill lagged. Based on a price optimization analysis, the retailer dropped the price of the midpriced drill to $110. Sales of the low-priced drill dropped 4 percent because it seemed less of a bargain, but sales of the midpriced drill increased 11 percent. Profits rose as a result.[38]

In measuring the price-demand relationship, the market researcher must control for various factors that will influence demand.[39] The competitor's response will make a difference. Also, if the company changes other aspects of the marketing program besides price, the effect of the price change itself will be hard to isolate.

**PRICE ELASTICITY OF DEMAND** Marketers need to know how responsive, or elastic, demand is to a change in price. Consider the two demand curves in Figure 16.1. In demand curve (a), a price increase from $10 to $15 leads to a relatively small decline in demand from 105 to 100. In demand curve (b), the same price increase leads to a substantial drop in demand from 150 to 50. If demand hardly changes with a small change in price, we say it is *inelastic*. If demand changes considerably, it is *elastic*.

The higher the elasticity, the greater the volume growth resulting from a 1 percent price reduction. If demand is elastic, sellers will consider lowering the price to produce more total revenue. This makes sense as long as the costs of producing and selling more units do not increase disproportionately.

Price elasticity depends on the magnitude and direction of the contemplated price change. It may be negligible with a small price change and substantial with a large price change. It may differ for a price cut than for a price increase, and there may be a *price indifference band* within which price changes have little or no effect.

Finally, long-run price elasticity may differ from short-run elasticity. Buyers may continue to buy from a current supplier after a price increase but eventually switch suppliers. Here demand is more elastic in the long run than in the short run, or the reverse may happen: Buyers may drop a supplier after a price increase but return later. The distinction between short-run and long-run elasticity means that sellers will not know the total effect of a price change until time passes.

Research has shown that consumers tend to be more sensitive to prices during tough economic times, but that is not true across all categories.[40] One comprehensive review of a 40-year period of academic research on price elasticity yielded interesting findings:[41]

- The average price elasticity across all products, markets, and time periods studied was −2.62. In other words, a 1 percent decrease in prices led to a 2.62 percent increase in sales.
- Price elasticity magnitudes were higher for durable goods than for other goods and higher for products in the introduction/growth stages of the product life cycle than in the mature/decline stages.
- Inflation led to substantially higher price elasticities, especially in the short run.
- Promotional price elasticities were higher than actual price elasticities in the short run (though the reverse was true in the long run).
- Price elasticities were higher at the individual item or SKU level than at the overall brand level.

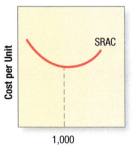

(a) Cost Behavior in
a Fixed-Size Plant

SRAC

Cost per Unit

1,000

**Quantity Produced per Day**

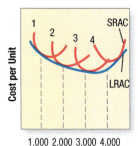

(b) Cost Behavior over
Different-Size Plants

SRAC

LRAC

Cost per Unit

1,000 2,000 3,000 4,000

**Quantity Produced per Day**

**| Fig. 16.2 |**

Cost per Unit at
Different Levels of
Production per Period

# STEP 3: ESTIMATING COSTS

Demand sets a ceiling on the price the company can charge for its product. Costs set the floor. The company wants to charge a price that covers its cost of producing, distributing, and selling the product, including a fair return for its effort and risk. Yet when companies price products to cover their full costs, profitability isn't always the net result.

**TYPES OF COSTS AND LEVELS OF PRODUCTION** A company's costs take two forms, fixed and variable. **Fixed costs,** also known as **overhead,** are costs that do not vary with production level or sales revenue. A company must pay bills each month for rent, heat, interest, salaries, and so on, regardless of output.

**Variable costs** vary directly with the level of production. For example, each tablet computer produced by Samsung incurs the cost of plastic and glass, microprocessor chips and other electronics, and packaging. These costs tend to be constant per unit produced, but they're called *variable* because their total varies with the number of units produced.

**Total costs** consist of the sum of the fixed and variable costs for any given level of production. **Average cost** is the cost per unit at that level of production; it equals total costs divided by production. Management wants to charge a price that will at least cover the total production costs at a given level of production.

To price intelligently, management needs to know how its costs vary with different levels of production. Take the case in which a company such as Samsung has built a fixed-size plant to produce 1,000 tablet computers a day. The cost per unit is high if few units are produced per day. As production approaches 1,000 units per day, the average cost falls because the fixed costs are spread over more units. Short-run average cost *increases* after 1,000 units, however, because the plant becomes inefficient: Workers must line up for machines, getting in each other's way, and machines break down more often [see Figure 16.2(a)].

If Samsung believes it can sell 2,000 units per day, it should consider building a larger plant. The plant will use more efficient machinery and work arrangements, and the unit cost of producing 2,000 tablets per day will be lower than the unit cost of producing 1,000 per day. This is shown in the long-run average cost curve (LRAC) in Figure 16.2(b). In fact, a 3,000-capacity plant would be even more efficient according to Figure 16.2(b), but a 4,000-daily production plant would be less so because of increasing diseconomies of scale: There are too many workers to manage, and paperwork slows things down. Figure 16.2(b) indicates that a 3,000-daily production plant is the optimal size if demand is strong enough to support this level of production.

There are more costs than those associated with manufacturing. To estimate the real profitability of selling to different types of retailers or customers, the manufacturer needs to use activity-based cost (ABC) accounting instead of standard cost accounting, as described in Chapter 5.

**ACCUMULATED PRODUCTION** Suppose Samsung runs a plant that produces 3,000 tablet computers per day. As the company gains experience producing tablets, its methods improve. Workers learn shortcuts, materials flow more smoothly, and procurement costs fall. The result, as Figure 16.3 shows, is that average cost

**| Fig. 16.3 |**

Cost per Unit
as a Function
of Accumulated
Production: The
Experience Curve

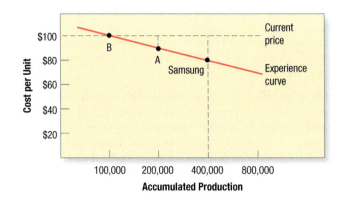

falls with accumulated production experience. Thus the average cost of producing the first 100,000 tablets is $100 per tablet. When the company has produced the first 200,000 tablets, the average cost has fallen to $90. After its accumulated production experience doubles again to 400,000, the average cost is $80. This decline in the average cost with accumulated production experience is called the **experience curve** or **learning curve.**

Now suppose three firms compete in this particular tablet market, Samsung, A, and B. Samsung is the lowest-cost producer at $80, having produced 400,000 units in the past. If all three firms sell the tablet for $100, Samsung makes $20 profit per unit, A makes $10 per unit, and B breaks even. The smart move for Samsung would be to lower its price to $90. This will drive B out of the market, and even A may consider leaving. Samsung will pick up the business that would have gone to B (and possibly A). Furthermore, price-sensitive customers will enter the market at the lower price. As production increases beyond 400,000 units, Samsung's costs will drop still further and faster, more than restoring its profits, even at a price of $90.

*Experience-curve pricing* nevertheless carries major risks. Aggressive pricing might give the product a cheap image. It also assumes competitors are weak followers. The strategy leads the company to build more plants to meet demand, but a competitor may choose to innovate with a lower-cost technology. The market leader is now stuck with the old technology.

Most experience-curve pricing has focused on manufacturing costs, but all costs can be improved on, including marketing costs. If three firms are each investing a large sum of money in marketing, the firm that has used it longest might achieve the lowest costs. This firm can charge a little less for its product and still earn the same return, all other costs being equal.[42]

**TARGET COSTING** Costs change with production scale and experience. They can also change as a result of a concentrated effort by designers, engineers, and purchasing agents to reduce them through **target costing.** Market research establishes a new product's desired functions and the price at which it will sell, given its appeal and competitors' prices. This price less desired profit margin leaves the target cost the marketer must achieve.

The firm must examine each cost element—design, engineering, manufacturing, sales—and bring down costs so the final cost projections are in the target range. When ConAgra Foods decided to increase the list prices of its Banquet frozen dinners to cover higher commodity costs, the average retail price of the meals increased from $1 to $1.25. When sales dropped significantly, management vowed to return to a $1 price, which necessitated cutting $250 million in other costs through a variety of methods, such as centralizing purchasing and shipping, using less expensive ingredients, and designing smaller portions.[43]

Cost cutting cannot go so deep as to compromise the brand promise and value delivered. Despite the early success of the PT Cruiser, Chrysler chose to squeeze out more profit by avoiding certain redesigns and cutting costs with cheaper radios and inferior materials. Once a best-selling car, the PT Cruiser was eventually discontinued.[44] Apparel makers tweak clothing designs to cut costs but are careful to avoid overly shallow pants pockets, waistbands that can roll over, and buttons that crack.[45] "Marketing Memo: How to Cut Costs" describes how firms are successfully cutting costs to improve profitability.

Overly aggressive cost-cutting actions resulted in declines in perceived quality for the PT Cruiser, helping to contribute to the brand's demise.

Source: © Tom Hanslien Photography/Alamy

Prices inevitably have to reflect the cost structure of the products and services. Rising commodity costs and a highly competitive post-recession environment have put pressure on many firms to manage their costs carefully and decide what cost increases, if any, to pass along to consumers in the form of higher prices. When calf-skin prices surged due to a shortage, pressure was placed on those luxury goods makers that need fine leather. Similarly, when steel and other input prices soared by as much as 20 percent, Whirlpool and Electrolux raised their own prices 8 percent to 10 percent.

Companies can cut costs in many ways. For General Mills, it was as simple as reducing the number of varieties of Hamburger Helper from 75 to 45 and the number of pasta shapes from 30 to 10. Dropping multicolored Yoplait lids saved $2 million a year. Other firms are attempting to shrink their products and packages while holding price and hoping consumers don't notice or care. Canned vegetables dropped to 13 or 14 ounces from 16, boxes of baby wipes hold 72 instead of 80, and sugar is sold in 4-pound instead of 5-pound bags.

The cost savings from minor shrinkage can be significant. When the size of a Scott 1000 toilet paper sheet dropped from 4.5 by 3.7 inches to 4.1 by 3.7 inches, the height of a four-pack package decreased from 9.2 to 8 inches, resulting in a 12 percent to 17 percent increase in the amount of product Scott can fit in a truck and a drop of 345,000 gallons in the gasoline needed for shipping because of the resulting fewer trucks on the road.

Some marketers attempt to justify packaging changes on environmental grounds (smaller packages are "greener") or to address health concerns (smaller packages have "fewer calories"), though consumers may not be duped. Others add other benefits in the process ("even stronger" or "new look"). Some companies are applying what they learned from making affordable products with scarce resources in developing countries such as India to the task of cutting costs in developed markets. Cisco blends teams of U.S. software engineers with Indian supervisors.

Supermarket giant Aldi takes advantage of its global scope. It stocks only about 1,000 of the most popular everyday grocery and household items, compared with more than 20,000 at a traditional grocer such as Royal Ahold's Albert Heijn. Almost all the products carry Aldi's own exclusive label. Because it sells so few items, Aldi can exert strong control over quality and price and simplify shipping and handling, leading to high margins. With more than 8,200 stores worldwide currently, Aldi brings in almost $60 billion in annual sales.

**Sources:** Richard Alleyne, "Household Brands Slash Size of Goods in 'Hidden Price Hikes,'" *The Telegraph,* March 21, 2013; Andrew Roberts, "Getting a Handle on the Steep Price of Leather," *Bloomberg Businessweek,* September 19, 2011; Stephanie Clifford and Catherine Rampell, "Inflation Looms, but Is Stealthily Disguised in Packaging," *New York Times,* March 28, 2011; "Everyday Higher Prices," *The Economist,* February 26, 2011; Beth Kowitt, "When Less Is . . . Less," *Fortune,* November 15, 2010, p. 21; Reena Jane, "From India, the Latest Management Fad," *Bloomberg BusinessWeek,* December 14, 2009, p. 57; "German Discounter Aldi Aims to Profit from Belt-Tightening in US," www.dw-world.de, January 15, 2009; Mina Kimes, "Cereal Cost Cutters," *Fortune,* November 10, 2008, p. 24.

## STEP 4: ANALYZING COMPETITORS' COSTS, PRICES, AND OFFERS

Within the range of possible prices identified by market demand and company costs, the firm must take competitors' costs, prices, and possible reactions into account. If the firm's offer contains features not offered by the nearest competitor, it should evaluate their worth to the customer and add that value to the competitor's price. If the competitor's offer contains some features not offered by the firm, the firm should subtract their value from its own price. Now the firm can decide whether it can charge more, the same, or less than the competitor.[46]

**VALUE-PRICED COMPETITORS** Companies offering the powerful combination of low price and high quality are capturing the hearts and wallets of consumers all over the world.[47] Value players, such as Aldi, E*TRADE Financial, JetBlue Airways, Southwest Airlines, Target, and Walmart, are transforming the way consumers of nearly every age and income level purchase groceries, apparel, airline tickets, financial services, and other goods and services.

Traditional players are right to feel threatened. Upstart firms often rely on serving one or a few consumer segments, providing better delivery or just one additional benefit, and matching low prices with highly efficient operations to keep costs down. They have changed consumer expectations about the trade-off between quality and price.

One school of thought is that companies should set up their own low-cost operations to compete with value-priced competitors only if: (1) their existing businesses will become more competitive as a result and (2) the new business will derive some advantages it would not have gained if independent.[48]

Creating a successful low cost marketing entry is not easy—United is one of many airlines who failed to do so.

Low-cost operations set up by HSBC, ING, Merrill Lynch, and Royal Bank of Scotland—First Direct, ING Direct, ML Direct, and Direct Line Insurance, respectively—succeed in part thanks to synergies between the old and new lines of business. Major airlines have also introduced their own low-cost carriers. But Continental's Lite, KLM's Buzz, SAS's Snowflake, and United's Shuttle have all been unsuccessful, due in part to a lack of synergies. The low-cost operation must be designed and launched as a moneymaker in its own right, not just as a defensive play.

## STEP 5: SELECTING A PRICING METHOD

Given the customers' demand schedule, the cost function, and competitors' prices, the company is now ready to select a price. Figure 16.4 summarizes the three major considerations in price setting: Costs set a floor to the price. Competitors' prices and the price of substitutes provide an orienting point. Customers' assessment of unique features establishes the price ceiling.

Companies select a pricing method that includes one or more of these three considerations. We will examine seven price-setting methods: markup pricing, target-return pricing, perceived-value pricing, value pricing, EDLP, going-rate pricing, and auction-type pricing.

**MARKUP PRICING** The most elementary pricing method is to add a standard **markup** to the product's cost. Construction companies submit job bids by estimating the total project cost and adding a standard markup for profit. Lawyers and accountants typically price by adding a standard markup on their time and costs.

| | |
|---|---|
| *Variable cost per unit* | $10 |
| *Fixed costs* | $300,000 |
| *Expected unit sales* | 50,000 |

Suppose a toaster manufacturer has the following costs and sales expectations:
The manufacturer's unit cost is given by:

$$\text{Unit cost} = \text{variable cost} + \frac{\text{fixed cost}}{\text{unit sales}} = \$10 + \frac{\$300,00}{50,000} = \$16$$

Now assume the manufacturer wants to earn a 20 percent markup on sales. The manufacturer's markup price is given by:

$$\text{Markup price} = \frac{\text{unit cost}}{(1 - \text{desired return on sales})} = \frac{\$16}{1 - 0.2} = \$20$$

The manufacturer will charge dealers $20 per toaster and make a profit of $4 per unit. If dealers want to earn 50 percent on their selling price, they will mark up the toaster 100 percent to $40. Markups are generally higher on seasonal items (to cover the risk of not selling), specialty items, slower-moving items, items with high storage and handling costs, and demand-inelastic items, such as prescription drugs.

High Price

(No possible demand at this price)

Ceiling price

Customers' assessment of unique product features

Orienting point

Competitors' prices and prices of substitutes

Costs

Floor price

Low Price

(No possible profit at this price)

| **Fig. 16.4** |

The Three Cs Model for Price Setting

Does the use of standard markups make logical sense? Generally, no. Any pricing method that ignores current demand, perceived value, and competition is not likely to lead to the optimal price. Markup pricing works only if the marked-up price actually brings in the expected level of sales. Consider what happened at Parker Hannifin.[49]

**PARKER HANNIFIN**    When Don Washkewicz took over as CEO of Parker Hannifin, maker of 800,000 industrial parts for the aerospace, transportation, and manufacturing industries, pricing was done one way: Calculate how much it costs to make and deliver a product and then add a flat percentage (usually 35 percent). Even though this method was historically well received, Washkewicz set out to get the company to think more like a retailer and charge what customers were willing to pay. Encountering initial resistance from some of the company's 115 different divisions, Washkewicz assembled a list of the 50 most commonly given reasons why the new pricing scheme would fail and announced he would listen only to arguments that were not on the list. The new pricing scheme put Parker Hannifin's products into one of four categories depending on how much competition existed. About one-third fell into niches where Parker offered unique value, there was little competition, and higher prices were appropriate. Each division now has a pricing guru or specialist who assists in strategic pricing. The division making industrial fittings reviewed 2,000 different items and concluded that 28 percent were priced too low, raising prices anywhere from 3 percent to 60 percent. As a result of the higher margins from this new strategic pricing approach, Parker estimates it has added $1 billion in profit during the fiscal years 2005–2011.

Still, markup pricing remains popular. First, sellers can determine costs much more easily than they can estimate demand. By tying the price to cost, sellers simplify the pricing task. Second, when all firms in the industry use this pricing method, prices tend to be similar and price competition is minimized. Third, many people feel cost-plus pricing is fairer to both buyers and sellers. Sellers do not take advantage of buyers when the latter's demand becomes acute, and sellers earn a fair return on investment.

**TARGET-RETURN PRICING**    In **target-return pricing,** the firm determines the price that yields its target rate of return on investment. Public utilities, which need to make a fair return on investment, often use this method.

Suppose the toaster manufacturer has invested $1 million in the business and wants to set a price to earn a 20 percent ROI, specifically $200,000. The target-return price is given by the following formula:

$$\text{Target-return price} = \text{unit cost} + \frac{\text{desired return} \times \text{invested capital}}{\text{unit sales}}$$

$$= \$16 + \frac{.20 \times \$1,000,000}{50,000} = \$20$$

The manufacturer will realize this 20 percent ROI provided its costs and estimated sales turn out to be accurate. But what if sales don't reach 50,000 units? The manufacturer can prepare a break-even chart to learn what would happen at other sales levels (see Figure 16.5). Fixed costs are $300,000 regardless of sales volume. Variable costs, not shown in the figure, rise with volume. Total costs equal the sum of fixed and variable costs. The total revenue curve starts at zero and rises with each unit sold.

| Fig. 16.5 |

Break-Even Chart for Determining Target-Return Price and Break-Even Volume

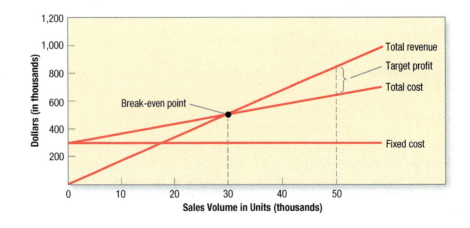

The total revenue and total cost curves cross at 30,000 units. This is the break-even volume. We can verify it by the following formula:

$$\text{Break-even volume} = \frac{\text{fixed cost}}{(\text{price} - \text{variable cost})} = \frac{\$300,000}{\$20 - \$10} = 30,000$$

The manufacturer, of course, is hoping the market will buy 50,000 units at $20, in which case it earns $200,000 on its $1 million investment, but much depends on price elasticity and competitors' prices. Unfortunately, target-return pricing tends to ignore these considerations. The manufacturer needs to consider different prices and estimate their probable impacts on sales volume and profits.

The manufacturer should also search for ways to lower its fixed or variable costs because lower costs will decrease its required break-even volume. Taiwan's Acer gained share in the tablet market through rock-bottom prices made possible by its bare-bones cost strategy. Acer sells only via retailers and other outlets and outsources all manufacturing and assembly, reducing its overhead to 8 percent of sales versus 14 percent at Dell and 15 percent at HP.[50]

**PERCEIVED-VALUE PRICING** An increasing number of companies now base their price on the customer's **perceived value.** Perceived value is made up of a host of inputs, such as the buyer's image of the product performance, the channel deliverables, the warranty quality, customer support, and softer attributes such as the supplier's reputation, trustworthiness, and esteem. Companies must deliver the value promised by their value proposition, and the customer must perceive this value. Firms use the other marketing program elements, such as advertising, sales force, and the Internet, to communicate and enhance perceived value in buyers' minds.

Caterpillar uses perceived value to set prices on its construction equipment. It might price its tractor at $100,000, though a similar competitor's tractor might be priced at $90,000. When a prospective customer asks a Caterpillar dealer why he should pay $10,000 more for the Caterpillar tractor, the dealer answers:

| | |
|---|---|
| $90,000 | is the tractor's price if it is only equivalent to the competitor's tractor |
| $7,000 | is the price premium for Caterpillar's superior durability |
| $6,000 | is the price premium for Caterpillar's superior reliability |
| $5,000 | is the price premium for Caterpillar's superior service |
| $2,000 | is the price premium for Caterpillar's longer warranty on parts |
| $110,000 | is the normal price to cover Caterpillar's superior value |
| − $10,000 | discount |
| $100,000 | final price |

The Caterpillar dealer is able to show that although the customer is asked to pay a $10,000 premium, he is actually getting $20,000 extra value! The customer chooses the Caterpillar tractor because he is convinced its lifetime operating costs will be lower.

Ensuring that customers appreciate the total value of a product or service offering is crucial. Consider the experience of PACCAR.[51]

**PACCAR** PACCAR Inc., maker of Kenworth and Peterbilt trucks, is able to command a 10 percent premium through its relentless focus on all aspects of the customer experience to maximize total value. Contract Freighters trucking company, a loyal PACCAR customer for 20 years, justified ordering another 700 new trucks, despite their higher price, because of their higher perceived quality—greater reliability, higher trade-in value, even the superior plush interiors that might attract better drivers. PACCAR bucks the commoditization trend by custom-building its trucks to individual specifications. The company invests heavily in technology and can prototype new parts in hours rather than days and weeks, allowing more frequent upgrades. It was the first to roll out hybrid vehicles in the fuel-intensive commercial trucking industry (and sell at a premium). A $1 billion, multiyear program to design and develop the highest-quality, most efficient trucks in the industry resulted in successful launches of the Kenworth T680, the Peterbilt Model 579, and the DAF XF Euro 6 lines of trucks. The company generated $1.17 billion of net income on $17.21 billion of revenue in 2013—its 74th consecutive year of profitability—bolstered by an expanded geographic footprint and a thriving business in aftermarket parts.

By maximizing total value and all aspects of the customer experience, PACCAR is able to command a significant price premium for its trucks.

Source: Kenworth T680 Lineup Courtesy of Kenworth Truck Company.

Even when a company claims its offering delivers more total value, not all customers will respond positively. Some care only about price. But there is also typically a segment that cares about quality. Umbrellas are essential during the three months of near-nonstop monsoon rain in Indian cities such as Mumbai, and the makers of Stag umbrellas there found themselves in a bitter price war with cheaper Chinese competitors. After realizing they were sacrificing quality too much, Stag's managers decided to increase quality with new colors, designs, and features such as built-in high-power flashlights and prerecorded music. Despite higher prices, sales of the improved Stag umbrellas actually increased.[52]

The key to perceived-value pricing is to deliver more unique value than competitors and to demonstrate this to prospective buyers. Thus, a company needs to fully understand the customer's decision-making process. For example, Goodyear found it hard to command a price premium for its more expensive new tires despite innovative new features to extend tread life. Because consumers had no reference price to compare tires, they tended to gravitate toward the lowest-priced offerings. Goodyear's solution was to price its models on expected miles of wear rather than their technical product features, making product comparisons easier.[53]

The company can try to determine the value of its offering in several ways: managerial judgments within the company, value of similar products, focus groups, surveys, experimentation, analysis of historical data, and conjoint analysis.

**VALUE PRICING** Companies that adopt value pricing win loyal customers by charging a fairly low price for a high-quality offering. **Value pricing** is thus not a matter of simply setting lower prices; it is a matter of reengineering the company's operations to become a low-cost producer without sacrificing quality to attract a large number of value-conscious customers.

Among the best practitioners of value pricing are IKEA, Target, and Southwest Airlines. In the early 1990s, Procter & Gamble created quite a stir when it reduced prices on supermarket staples such as Pampers and Luvs diapers, liquid Tide detergent, and Folgers coffee. To value-price these products, P&G redesigned the way it developed, manufactured, distributed, priced, marketed, and sold them to deliver better value at every point in the supply chain.[54] Its acquisition of Gillette in 2005 for $57 billion (a record five times its sales) brought another brand into its fold that has also traditionally adopted a value pricing strategy.

Value pricing can change the way a company sets prices too. One company that sold and maintained switch boxes in a variety of sizes for telephone lines found that the probability of failure—and thus the level of maintenance costs—was proportional to the number of switches customers had in their boxes rather than to the dollar value of the installed boxes. The number of switches per box could vary, though. Therefore, rather than charging customers based on the total spent on installation, the company began charging based on the total number of switches that needed servicing.[55]

**EDLP** A retailer using **everyday low pricing (EDLP)** charges a constant low price with little or no price promotion or special sales. Constant prices eliminate week-to-week price uncertainty and the high-low pricing of promotion-oriented competitors. In **high-low pricing,** the retailer charges higher prices on an everyday basis but runs frequent promotions with prices temporarily lower than the EDLP level.[56]

These two strategies have been shown to affect consumer price judgments—deep discounts (EDLP) can lead customers to perceive lower prices over time than frequent, shallow discounts (high-low), even if the price actually averages to the same level.[57] In recent years, high-low pricing has given way to EDLP at such widely different venues as Toyota Scion car dealers and upscale department stores such as Nordstrom, but the king of EDLP is surely Walmart, which practically defined the term. Except for a few sale items every month, Walmart promises everyday low prices on major brands.

The most important reason retailers adopt EDLP is that constant sales and promotions are costly and have eroded consumer confidence in everyday shelf prices. Some consumers also have less time and patience for past traditions like watching for supermarket specials and clipping coupons.

Yet promotions and sales do create excitement and draw shoppers, so EDLP does not guarantee success and is not for everyone.[58] JC Penney learned that lesson the hard way.[59]

........................................................................................................................................................................

**❚ JC PENNEY** When JC Penney hired Apple's retailing guru Ron Johnson as CEO, there was much anticipation as to how he would transform the venerable department store giant. When Johnson found that the company had held 590 sales events the previous year and that almost three-quarters of sales revenue was from merchandise marked down 50 percent or more, he decided to embark on a simplified pricing strategy. Coupons and sales were eliminated and replaced by across-the-board price decreases of 40 percent. The everyday low pricing plan turned out to be a disaster, however, and with sales and stock price plunging, Johnson was quickly shown the door. A number of reasons have been suggested for the program's failure. Competitors like Macy's and Sears continued to offer sales and discounts, giving the perception of good deals. Penney's customers missed the coupons and weekly sales events. Everyday low prices are thought to be more effective with more functional products, but they may actually harm more image-oriented products like fashion, an important category for JC Penney. One commentator might have said it best when he stated, "At the end of the day, people don't want a fair price. They want a great deal."

........................................................................................................................................................................

**GOING-RATE PRICING** In **going-rate pricing,** the firm bases its price largely on competitors' prices. In oligopolistic industries that sell a commodity such as steel, paper, or fertilizer, all firms normally charge the same price. Smaller firms "follow the leader," changing their prices when the market leader's prices change rather than when their own demand or costs change. Some may charge a small premium or discount, but they preserve the difference. Thus, minor gasoline retailers usually charge a few cents less per gallon than the major oil companies, without letting the difference increase or decrease.

Going-rate pricing is quite popular. Where costs are difficult to measure or competitive response is uncertain, firms feel it is a good solution because they believe it reflects the industry's collective wisdom.

JC Penny's move from high-low pricing to everyday low pricing was disastrous.

Source: ASSOCIATED PRESS

**AUCTION-TYPE PRICING** Auction-type pricing is growing more popular, especially with scores of electronic marketplaces selling everything from pigs to used cars as firms dispose of excess inventories or used goods. These are the three major types of auctions and their separate pricing procedures:[60]

- *English auctions (ascending bids)* have one seller and many buyers. On sites such as eBay and Amazon.com, the seller puts up an item and bidders raise their offer prices until the top price is reached. The highest bidder gets the item. English auctions are used today for selling antiques, cattle, real estate, and used equipment and vehicles. Kodak and Nortel sold hundreds of patents for wireless and digital imaging via auctions, raising hundreds of millions of dollars.[61]
- *Dutch auctions (descending bids)* feature one seller and many buyers or one buyer and many sellers. In the first kind, an auctioneer announces a high price for a product and then slowly decreases the price until a bidder accepts. In the other, the buyer announces something he or she wants to buy, and potential sellers compete to offer the lowest price. Ariba—acquired by SAP in 2012—runs business-to-business auctions to help companies acquire low-priced items as varied as steel, fats, oils, name badges, pickles, plastic bottles, solvents, cardboard, and even legal and janitorial work.[62]
- *Sealed-bid auctions* let would-be suppliers submit only one bid; they cannot know the other bids. The U.S. and other governments often use this method to procure supplies or to grant licenses. A supplier will not bid below its cost but cannot bid too high for fear of losing the job. The net effect of these two pulls is the bid's *expected profit.*[63]

To buy equipment for its drug researchers, Pfizer uses reverse auctions online in which suppliers submit the lowest price they are willing to be paid. If the increased savings a buying firm obtains in an online auction translate into decreased margins for an incumbent supplier, however, the supplier may feel the firm is opportunistically squeezing out price concessions. Online auctions with a large number of bidders, higher economic stakes, and less visibility in the specific prices involved result in greater overall satisfaction for both parties, more positive future expectations, and fewer perceptions of opportunism.[64]

# STEP 6: SELECTING THE FINAL PRICE

Pricing methods narrow the range from which the company must select its final price. In selecting that price, the company must consider additional factors, including the impact of other marketing activities, company pricing policies, gain-and-risk-sharing pricing, and the impact of price on other parties.

**IMPACT OF OTHER MARKETING ACTIVITIES** The final price must take into account the brand's quality and advertising relative to the competition. In a classic study, Paul Farris and David Reibstein examined the relationships among relative price, relative quality, and relative advertising for 227 consumer businesses and found the following:[65]

- Brands with average relative quality but high relative advertising budgets could charge premium prices. Consumers were willing to pay higher prices for known rather than for unknown products.
- Brands with high relative quality and high relative advertising obtained the highest prices. Conversely, brands with low quality and low advertising charged the lowest prices.
- For market leaders, the positive relationship between high prices and high advertising held most strongly in the later stages of the product life cycle.

These findings suggest that in many cases price may not be necessarily as important as quality and other benefits.

**COMPANY PRICING POLICIES** The price must be consistent with company pricing policies. Yet companies are not averse to establishing pricing penalties under certain circumstances.

Airlines charge $200 to buyers of discount tickets who change their reservations. Banks charge fees for too many withdrawals in a month or early withdrawal of a certificate of deposit. Dentists, hotels, car rental companies, and other service providers charge penalties for no-shows. Although these policies are often justifiable, marketers must use them judiciously and not unnecessarily alienate customers. (See "Marketing Insight: Stealth Price Increases.")

Many companies set up a pricing department to develop policies and establish or approve decisions. The aim is to ensure salespeople quote prices that are reasonable to customers and profitable to the company.

**GAIN-AND-RISK-SHARING PRICING** Buyers may resist accepting a seller's proposal because they perceive a high level of risk, such as in a big computer hardware purchase or a company health plan. The seller then has the option of offering to absorb part or all the risk if it does not deliver the full promised value.

# marketing insight

## Stealth Price Increases

With consumers resisting higher prices, companies trying to increase revenue in other ways often resort to adding fees for once-free features. Although some consumers abhor "nickel-and-dime" pricing strategies, small additional charges can add up to a substantial source of revenue.

The numbers can be staggering. U.S. airlines collected a massive $3.35 billion in baggage fees and $2.81 billion in reservation change/cancellation fees in 2013. The telecommunications industry has been aggressive in adding fees for setup, change-of-service, service termination, directory assistance, regulatory assessment, number portability, and cable hookup and equipment, costing consumers billions of dollars. Fees for consumers who pay bills online, bounce checks, or use automated teller machines bring banks billions of dollars annually. Credit card companies responded to restrictions on certain of their pricing practices by adopting rate floors for variable rate cards, higher penalties for overdue payments at lower balance thresholds, and inactivity fees for unused cards.

This explosion of fees has a number of implications. Given that list prices stay fixed, they may understate the degree of price inflation. They also make it harder for consumers to compare competitive offerings. Although various citizens' groups have tried to pressure companies to roll back some fees, they don't always get a sympathetic ear from state and local governments, which use their own array of fees, fines, and penalties to raise necessary revenue.

Companies justify the extra fees as the only fair and viable way to cover expenses without losing customers. Many argue that it makes sense to charge a premium for added services that cost more to provide and that only some customers use. Thus, basic costs can stay low. Companies also use fees to weed out unprofitable customers or get them to change their behavior.

Ultimately, the viability of extra fees will be decided in the marketplace and by the willingness of consumers to vote with their wallets and pay the fees or vote with their feet and move on.

**Sources:** Katia Hetter, "Airlines Collect $6 Billion in Fees," www.cnn.com, May 15, 2013; Alexis Leondis and Jeff Plungis, "The Latest Credit Card Tricks," *Bloomberg Businessweek*, December 28, 2009, and January 4, 2010, p. 95; Brian Burnsed, "A New Front in the Credit Card Wars," *BusinessWeek*, November 9, 2009, p. 60.

Source: ©Brian A Jackson /Shutterstock

Airlines generate billions of dollars in baggage fees as a source of extra income.

---

Baxter Healthcare, a leading medical products firm, was able to secure a contract for an information management system from Columbia/HCA, a leading health care provider, by guaranteeing the firm several million dollars in savings over an eight-year period. An increasing number of companies, especially B-to-B marketers, may have to stand ready to guarantee any promised savings but also participate in the upside if the gains are much greater than expected.

**IMPACT OF PRICE ON OTHER PARTIES** How will distributors and dealers feel about the contemplated price?[66] If they don't make enough profit, they may choose not to bring the product to market. Will the sales force be willing to sell at that price? How will competitors react? Will suppliers raise their prices when they see the company's price? Will the government intervene and prevent this price from being charged?

U.S. legislation states that sellers must set prices without talking to competitors: Price-fixing is illegal. Twenty-one airlines, including British Airways, Korean Air and Air France-KLM, were fined a total of $1.7 billion for artificially inflating passenger prices and cargo fuel surcharges between 2000 and 2006.[67] Many federal and state statutes protect consumers against deceptive pricing practices. For example, it is illegal for a company to set artificially high "regular" prices, then announce a "sale" at prices close to previous everyday prices.

# Adapting the Price

Companies usually do not set a single price but rather develop a pricing structure that reflects variations in geographical demand and costs, market-segment requirements, purchase timing, order levels, delivery frequency, guarantees, service contracts, and other factors. As a result of discounts, allowances, and promotional support, a company rarely realizes the same profit from each unit of a product that it sells. Here we will examine several price-adaptation strategies: geographical pricing, price discounts and allowances, promotional pricing, and differentiated pricing.

## GEOGRAPHICAL PRICING (CASH, COUNTERTRADE, BARTER)

In geographical pricing, the company decides how to price its products to different customers in different locations and countries. Should the company charge higher prices to distant customers to cover higher shipping costs or a lower price to win additional business? How should it account for exchange rates and the strength of different currencies?

Another question is how to get paid. This issue is critical when buyers lack sufficient hard currency to pay for their purchases. Many want to offer other items in payment, a practice known as **countertrade,** and U.S. companies are often forced to accept if they want the business. Countertrade may account for 15 percent to 20 percent of world trade and takes several forms:[68]

- *Barter.* The buyer and seller directly exchange goods, with no money and no third party involved.
- *Compensation deal.* The seller receives some percentage of the payment in cash and the rest in products. A British aircraft manufacturer sold planes to Brazil for 70 percent cash and the rest in coffee.
- *Buyback arrangement.* The seller sells a plant, equipment, or technology to a company in another country and agrees to accept as partial payment products manufactured with the supplied equipment. A U.S. chemical company built a plant for an Indian company and accepted partial payment in cash and the remainder in chemicals manufactured at the plant.
- *Offset.* The seller receives full payment in cash for a sale overseas but agrees to spend a substantial amount of the money in that country within a stated time period. In the Gorbachev era, PepsiCo sold its cola syrup to the government of the Soviet Union for rubles and agreed to buy Russian vodka at a certain rate for sale in the United States.[69]

## PRICE DISCOUNTS AND ALLOWANCES

Most companies will adjust their list price and give discounts and allowances for early payment, volume purchases, and off-season buying (see Table 16.4).[70] Companies must do this carefully or find their profits much lower than planned.[71]

In the early days of its entry into the Russian market, PepsiCo used an offset agreement with the Russian government involving a swap of cola syrup for vodka.

Source: AFP/Getty Images

| TABLE 16.4 | Price Discounts and Allowances |
|---|---|
| Discount: | A price reduction to buyers who pay bills promptly. A typical example is "2/10, net 30," which means payment is due within 30 days and the buyer can deduct 2 percent by paying within 10 days. |
| Quantity Discount: | A price reduction to those who buy large volumes. A typical example is "$10 per unit for fewer than 100 units; $9 per unit for 100 or more units." Quantity discounts must be offered equally to all customers and must not exceed the cost savings to the seller. They can be offered on each order placed or on the number of units ordered over a given period. |
| Functional Discount: | Discount (also called *trade discount*) offered by a manufacturer to trade-channel members if they perform certain functions, such as selling, storing, and record keeping. Manufacturers must offer the same functional discounts within each channel. |
| Seasonal Discount: | A price reduction to those who buy merchandise or services out of season. Hotels, motels, and airlines offer seasonal discounts in slow selling periods. |
| Allowance: | An extra payment designed to gain reseller participation in special programs. *Trade-in allowances* are granted for turning in an old item when buying a new one. *Promotional allowances* reward dealers for participating in advertising and sales support programs. |

Discount pricing has become the modus operandi of a surprising number of companies offering both products and services. Salespeople in particular are quick to give discounts to close a sale. But word can get around fast that the company's list price is "soft," and discounting becomes the norm, undermining the perceived value of the offerings. Some product categories self-destruct by always being on sale.

Some companies with overcapacity are tempted to give discounts or even begin to supply a retailer with a store-brand version of their product at a deep discount. Because the store brand is priced lower, however, it may start making inroads on the manufacturer's brand. Manufacturers should consider the implications of supplying retailers at a discount because they may end up losing long-run profits in an effort to meet short-run volume goals.

Only people with higher incomes and higher product involvement willingly pay more for features, customer service, quality, added convenience, and the brand name. So it can be a mistake for a strong, distinctive brand to plunge into price discounting as a response to low-price attacks. At the same time, discounting can be a useful tool if the customer will give concessions in return, such as signing a longer contract, ordering electronically, or buying larger quantities.

Sales management needs to monitor the proportion of customers receiving discounts, the average discount, and any tendency for salespeople to over-rely on discounting. Upper management should conduct a **net price analysis** to arrive at the "real price" of the offering. The real price is affected not only by discounts but by other expenses that reduce the realized price (see "Promotional Pricing" below). Suppose the company's list price is $3,000. The average discount is $300. The company's promotional spending averages $450 (15 percent of the list price). Retailers are given co-op advertising money of $150 to back the product. The company's net price is $2,100, not $3,000.

## PROMOTIONAL PRICING

Companies can use several pricing techniques to stimulate early purchase:

- *Loss-leader pricing.* Supermarkets and department stores often drop the price on well-known brands to stimulate additional store traffic. This pays if the revenue on the additional sales compensates for the lower margins on the loss-leader items. Manufacturers of loss-leader brands typically object because this practice can dilute the brand image and bring complaints from retailers who charge the list price. Manufacturers have tried to keep intermediaries from using loss-leader pricing by lobbying for retail-price-maintenance laws, but these laws have been revoked.
- *Special event pricing.* Sellers will establish special prices in certain seasons to draw in more customers. Every August, there are back-to-school sales.

- *Special customer pricing.* Sellers will offer special prices exclusively to certain customers. Members of Road Runner Sports' Run America Club get "exclusive" online offers with price discounts twice those given to regular customers.[72]
- *Cash rebates.* Auto companies and other consumer-goods companies offer cash rebates to encourage purchase of the manufacturers' products within a specified time period. Rebates can help clear inventories without cutting the stated list price.
- *Low-interest financing.* Instead of cutting its price, the company can offer low-interest financing. Automakers have used no-interest financing to try to attract more customers.
- *Longer payment terms.* Sellers, especially mortgage banks and auto companies, stretch loans over longer periods and thus lower the monthly payments. Consumers often worry less about the cost (the interest rate) of a loan and more about whether they can afford the monthly payment.
- *Warranties and service contracts.* Companies can promote sales by adding a free or low-cost warranty or service contract.
- *Psychological discounting.* This strategy sets an artificially high price and then offers the product at substantial savings; for example, "Was $359, now $299." Discounts from normal prices are a legitimate form of promotional pricing; the Federal Trade Commission and Better Business Bureau fight illegal discount tactics.

Promotional-pricing strategies are often a zero-sum game. If they work, competitors copy them and they lose their effectiveness. If they don't work, they waste money that could have been put into other marketing tools, such as building up product quality and service or strengthening product image through advertising.

## DIFFERENTIATED PRICING

Companies often adjust their basic price to accommodate differences among customers, products, locations, and so on. Lands' End creates men's shirts in many different styles, weights, and levels of quality. In March 2014, a men's white button-down shirt could cost as little as $19.99 or as much as $70.00.[73]

**Price discrimination** occurs when a company sells a product or service at two or more prices that do not reflect a proportional difference in costs. In first-degree price discrimination, the seller charges a separate price to each customer depending on the intensity of his or her demand.

In second-degree price discrimination, the seller charges less to buyers of larger volumes. With certain services such as cell phone service, however, tiered pricing results in consumers actually paying *more* with higher levels of usage. With the iPhone, 3 percent of users accounted for 40 percent of the traffic on AT&T's network, resulting in costly network upgrades to AT&T and causing the firm to set higher prices for those users.[74]

In third-degree price discrimination, the seller charges different amounts to different classes of buyers, as in the following cases:[75]

- *Customer-segment pricing.* Different customer groups pay different prices for the same product or service. For example, museums often charge a lower admission fee to students and senior citizens.
- *Product-form pricing.* Different versions of the product are priced differently, but not in proportion to their costs. Evian prices a 2-liter bottle of its mineral water as low as $1 but 5 ounces of the same water in a moisturizer spray for as much as $12.
- *Image pricing.* Some companies price the same product at two different levels based on image differences. A perfume manufacturer can put a scent in one bottle, give it a name and image, and price it at $10 an ounce. The same scent in another bottle with a different name and image can sell for $30 an ounce.
- *Channel pricing.* Coca-Cola carries a different price depending on whether the consumer purchases it from a fine restaurant, a fast-food restaurant, or a vending machine.
- *Location pricing.* The same product is priced differently at different locations even though the cost of offering it at each location is the same. A theater varies its seat prices according to audience preferences for different locations.
- *Time pricing.* Prices vary by season, day, or hour. Restaurants charge less to "early bird" customers, and some hotels charge less on weekends. Retail prices for roses increase by as much as 200 percent in the lead-up to Valentine's Day.[76]

The airline and hospitality industries use yield management systems and **yield pricing,** by which they offer discounted but limited early purchases, higher-priced late purchases, and the lowest rates on unsold inventory just before it expires. Airlines charge different fares to passengers on the same flight, depending on the seating class; the time of day (morning or night coach); the day of the week (workday or weekend); the season; the person's employer, past business, or status (youth, military, senior citizen); and so on. That's why on a flight from New York City to Miami you might pay $200 and sit across from someone who paid $1,290.

The phenomenon of offering different pricing schedules to different consumers and dynamically adjusting prices is exploding. Merchants are adjusting process based on inventory levels, item velocity or how fast it sells, competitor's pricing, and advertising. Even sports teams are adjusting ticket prices to reflect the popularity of the competitor and the timing of the game.[77]

Many companies are using software to make real-time controlled tests of actual consumer response to different pricing schedules. Online merchants selling their products on Amazon.com are changing their prices on an hourly or even minute-by-minute basis, in part so they can secure the top spot on search results.[78]

Constant price variation can be tricky, however, where consumer relationships are concerned. Research shows it's most effective when there's no bond between the buyer and the seller. One way to make it work is to offer customers a unique bundle of products and services to meet their needs precisely, making it harder to make price comparisons. The tactic most companies favor is to use variable prices as a reward rather than a penalty. Shipping company APL rewards customers who can better predict how much cargo space they'll need with cheaper rates for booking early.

Customers are getting savvier about how to avoid overpaying, changing their buying behavior to accommodate the new realities of dynamic pricing. But most are probably not even aware of the degree to which they are the targets of discriminatory pricing. Retailers like Staples, Office Depot, and Home Depot vary their online and in-store prices on a host of factors related to costs of doing business and consumer sensitivity to prices. Some firms use computer IP addresses to deduce people's zip codes and use their proximity to a competitor's store to adjust their prices.

When online travel agency Orbitz found that people using Apple Mac computers spent as much as 30 percent more a night on hotels, it began to show them different, and sometimes costlier, travel options than Windows users saw. Orbitz also considers a user's location and history on the site as a well as a hotel's overall popularity and promotions.[79]

Although some forms of price discrimination are illegal (such as offering different prices to different customers within the same trade group), the practice is legal if the seller can prove its costs are different when selling different volumes or different qualities of the same product to different retailers. Predatory pricing—selling below cost with the intention of destroying competition—is unlawful, though.

For price discrimination to work, certain conditions must exist. First, the market must be segmentable and the segments must show different intensities of demand. Second, members in the lower-price segment must not be able to resell the product to the higher-price segment. Third, competitors must not be able to undersell the firm in the higher-price segment. Fourth, the cost of segmenting and policing the market must not exceed the extra revenue derived from price discrimination. Fifth, the practice must not breed customer resentment and ill will. Sixth, of course, the particular form of price discrimination must not be illegal.[80]

# Initiating and Responding to Price Changes

Companies often need to cut or raise prices.

## INITIATING PRICE CUTS

Several circumstances might lead a firm to cut prices. One is *excess plant capacity*: The firm needs additional business and cannot generate it through increased sales effort, product improvement, or other measures. Companies sometimes initiate price cuts in a *drive to dominate the market through lower costs*. Either the company starts with lower costs than its competitors, or it initiates price cuts in the hope of gaining market share and lower costs.

Cutting prices to keep customers or beat competitors often encourages customers to demand price concessions, however, and trains salespeople to offer them.[81] A price-cutting strategy can lead to other possible traps:

- *Low-quality trap.* Consumers assume quality is low.
- *Fragile-market-share trap.* A low price buys market share but not market loyalty. The same customers will shift to any lower-priced firm that comes along.
- *Shallow-pockets trap.* Higher-priced competitors match the lower prices but have longer staying power because of deeper cash reserves.
- *Price-war trap.* Competitors respond by lowering their prices even more, triggering a price war.[82]

Customers often question the motivation behind price changes.[83] They may assume the item is about to be replaced by a new model, the item is faulty and is not selling well, the firm is in financial trouble, the price will come down even further, or the quality has been reduced. The firm must monitor these attributions carefully.

## INITIATING PRICE INCREASES

A successful price increase can raise profits considerably. If the company's profit margin is 3 percent of sales, a 1 percent price increase will increase profits by 33 percent if sales volume is unaffected. This situation is illustrated in Table 16.5. The assumption is that a company charged $10 and sold 100 units and had costs of $970, leaving a profit of $30, or 3 percent on sales. By raising its price by 10 cents (a 1 percent price increase), it boosted its profits by 33 percent, assuming the same sales volume.

A major circumstance provoking price increases is *cost inflation*. Rising costs unmatched by productivity gains squeeze profit margins and lead companies to regular rounds of price increases. Companies often raise their prices by more than the cost increase, in anticipation of further inflation or government price controls, in a practice called *anticipatory pricing*.

Another factor leading to price increases is *overdemand*. When a company cannot supply all its customers, it can raise its prices, ration supplies, or both. It can increase price in the following ways, each of which has a different impact on buyers.

- *Delayed quotation pricing.* The company does not set a final price until the product is finished or delivered. This pricing is prevalent in industries with long production lead times, such as industrial construction and heavy equipment.
- *Escalator clauses.* The company requires the customer to pay today's price plus all or part of any inflation increase that takes place before delivery. Escalator clauses base price increases on some specified price index. They are found in contracts for major industrial projects, such as aircraft construction and bridge building.
- *Unbundling.* The company maintains its price but removes or prices separately one or more elements that were formerly part of the offer, such as delivery or installation. Car companies sometimes add higher-end audio entertainment systems or GPS navigation systems to their vehicles as separately priced extras.
- *Reduction of discounts.* The company instructs its sales force not to offer its normal cash and quantity discounts.

Although there is always a chance a price increase can carry some positive meanings to customers—for example, that the item is "hot" and represents an unusually good value—consumers generally dislike higher prices. In passing price increases on to them, the company must avoid looking like a price gouger.[84] Coca-Cola's proposed smart vending machines that would raise prices as temperatures rose and Amazon.com's dynamic pricing experiment that varied prices by purchase occasion both became front-page news. The more similar the products or offerings from a company, the more likely consumers are to interpret any pricing differences as unfair. Product customization and differentiation and communications that clarify differences are thus critical.[85]

Several techniques help consumers avoid sticker shock and a hostile reaction when prices rise: One is maintaining their sense of fairness, such as by giving them advance notice so they can do forward buying or shop around. Sharp price increases also need to be explained in understandable terms. Making low-visibility price moves first is also a good technique: Eliminating discounts, increasing minimum order sizes, and curtailing production of low-margin products are examples, and contracts or bids for long-term projects should contain escalator clauses based on such factors as increases in recognized national price indexes.[86]

## ANTICIPATING COMPETITIVE RESPONSES

The introduction or change of any price can provoke a response from customers, competitors, distributors, suppliers, and even government. Competitors are most likely to react when the number of firms is few, the product is homogeneous, and buyers are highly informed.

| TABLE 16.5 | Profits before and after a Price Increase | | |
|---|---|---|---|
| | **Before** | **After** | |
| Price | $10 | $10.10 | (a 1% price increase) |
| Units sold | 100 | 100 | |
| Revenue | $1,000 | $1,010 | |
| Costs | −970 | −970 | |
| Profit | $30 | $40 | (a 33 1/3% profit increase) |

Consumers had a hostile reaction when they heard reports that Coca-Cola was considering introducing smart vending machines which would adjust prices according to the temperature outside.

*Source: AFP/Getty Images*

How can a firm anticipate a competitor's reactions? One way is to assume the competitor reacts in the standard way to a price being set or changed. Another is to assume the competitor treats each price difference or change as a fresh challenge and reacts according to self-interest at the time. Now the company will need to research the competitor's current financial situation, recent sales, customer loyalty, and corporate objectives. If the competitor has a market share objective, it is likely to match price differences or changes.[87] If it has a profit-maximization objective, it may react by increasing its advertising budget or improving product quality.

The problem is complicated because the competitor can put different interpretations on lowered prices or a price cut: that the company is trying to steal the market, that it is doing poorly and trying to boost its sales, or that it wants the whole industry to reduce prices to stimulate total demand. When Walmart began to run ads claiming lower prices than Publix, the regional supermarket chain dropped its prices below Walmart's on roughly 500 essential items and began its own advertising campaign in retaliation.[88]

## RESPONDING TO COMPETITORS' PRICE CHANGES

How should a firm respond to a competitor's price cut? It depends on the situation. The company must consider the product's stage in the life cycle, its importance in the company's portfolio, the competitor's intentions and resources, the market's price and quality sensitivity, the behavior of costs with volume, and the company's alternative opportunities.

In markets characterized by high product homogeneity, the firm can search for ways to enhance its augmented product. If it cannot find any, it may need to meet the price reduction. If the competitor raises its price in a homogeneous product market, other firms might not match it if the increase will not benefit the industry as a whole. Then the leader will need to roll back the increase.

In nonhomogeneous product markets, a firm has more latitude. It needs to consider the following: (1) Why did the competitor change the price? To steal the market, to utilize excess capacity, to meet changing cost conditions, or to lead an industry-wide price change? (2) Does the competitor plan to make the price change temporary or permanent? (3) What will happen to the company's market share and profits if it does not respond? Are other companies going to respond? (4) What are the competitors' and other firms' likely responses to each possible reaction?

Market leaders often face aggressive price cutting by smaller firms trying to build market share. Using price, Fuji has attacked Kodak, Schick has attacked Gillette, and AMD has attacked Intel. Brand leaders also face lower-priced store brands. Three possible responses to low-cost competitors are: (1) further differentiate the product or service, (2) introduce a low-cost venture, or (3) reinvent as a low-cost player.[89] The right strategy depends on the ability of the firm to generate more demand or cut costs.

An extended analysis of alternatives may not always be feasible when the attack occurs. The company may have to react decisively within hours or days, especially where prices change with some frequency and it is important to react quickly, such as in the meatpacking, lumber, or oil industries. It would make better sense to anticipate possible competitors' price changes and prepare contingent responses.

# Summary

1. Price is the only marketing element that produces revenue; the others produce costs. Pricing decisions have become more challenging in a changing economic and technological environment.

2. In setting pricing policy, a company follows a six-step procedure. It selects its pricing objective. It estimates the demand curve, the probable quantities it will sell at each possible price. It estimates how its costs vary at different levels of output, at different levels of accumulated production experience, and for differentiated marketing offers. It examines competitors' costs, prices, and offers. It selects a pricing method, and it selects the final price.

3. Companies usually set a pricing structure that reflects variations in geographical demand and costs, market-segment requirements, purchase timing, order levels, and other factors. Several price-adaptation strategies are available: (1) geographical pricing, (2) price

discounts and allowances, (3) promotional pricing, and (4) discriminatory pricing.

4. A price decrease might be brought about by excess plant capacity, declining market share, a desire to dominate the market through lower costs, or economic recession. A price increase might be brought about by cost inflation or overdemand. Companies must carefully manage customer perceptions when raising prices.

5. Companies must anticipate competitor price changes and prepare contingent responses, including maintaining or changing price or quality.

6. The firm facing a competitor's price change must try to understand the competitor's intent and the likely duration of the change. A market leader attacked by lower-priced competitors can seek to better differentiate itself, introduce its own low-cost competitor, or transform itself more completely.

## MyMarketingLab

Go to **mymktlab.com** to complete the problems marked with this icon ⭐ as well as for additional Auto-graded and Assisted-graded writing questions.

# Applications

## Marketing Debate
### Is the Right Price a Fair Price?

Prices are often set to satisfy demand or to reflect the premium consumers are willing to pay for a product or service. Some critics shudder, however, at the thought of $2 bottles of water, $150 running shoes, and $500 concert tickets.

**Take a position:** Prices should reflect the value consumers are willing to pay *versus* Prices should reflect only the cost of making a product or delivering a service.

## Marketing Discussion
### Pricing Methods

⭐ Think about the pricing methods described in this chapter—markup pricing, target-return pricing, perceived-value pricing, value pricing, EDLP, going-rate pricing, and auction-type pricing. As a consumer, which do you prefer? Why? If the average price were to stay the same, which would you prefer a firm to do: (1) set one price and not deviate or (2) employ slightly higher prices most of the year but offer slightly discounted prices or specials for certain occasions?

## Marketing Excellence

### >> eBay

In 1995, Pierre Omidayar, a French-Iranian immigrant, wrote the code for an auction Web site where everyone would have equal access to a single global marketplace. Omidayar couldn't believe it when a collector bought the first item, a broken laser pointer, for $14.83.* Soon the site grew into a broader auction site where consumers could sell collectibles ranging from baseball cards to Barbie dolls. The momentum continued when individuals and small businesses discovered that eBay was an efficient way to reach new customers and other businesses, and large companies began using it as a means of selling their bulk lots of unsold inventory. The company grew from 250,000 auctions in 1996 to 2,000,000 auctions in 1997. In 1998, it hired Meg Whitman as CEO, and she helped take eBay public later that year.

eBay's success created a pricing revolution because it allowed buyers to decide what they would pay for an item. The result pleased both sides; customers gained control and received the best possible price for the item, while sellers made good margins due to the site's efficiency and wide reach.

For years, buyers and sellers also used eBay as an informal guide to market value. Even a company with a new-product design that wanted to know the going price for anything from a copier to a new DVD player checked on eBay. The online marketplace was fascinating to economists as well, who used it to analyze pricing theories and compare them with actual buying and selling behaviors.

eBay itself doesn't buy any inventory or own the products on its site. It earns its revenue by collecting fees: an insertion fee for each listing plus a final-value fee based on the auction or fixed price. For example, if an item sells for $60.00, the seller pays 8.75 percent on the first $25.00 ($2.19) plus 3.5 percent on the remaining $35.00 ($1.23). Therefore, the final-value fee for the sale is $3.42. This pricing structure was developed to attract high-volume sellers and deter those who list only a few low-priced items. With eBay's expansion into a wide range of other categories—from boats, cars, and travel to health and beauty and home and garden—collectibles now make up only a small percentage of sales.

eBay now offers more pricing options, including a fixed-price "buy it now" option to those who don't want to wait for an auction and are willing to pay the seller's price. Sellers can also use the fixed-price format with a "best offer" option that allows them to counteroffer, reject, or accept an offer.

The company's business model is based on connecting individuals who otherwise would not be in touch. It was the first example of online social networking, years before Twitter and Facebook existed, and consumer trust is a key element of its success. While skeptics initially questioned whether consumers would buy products from strangers, Omidayar believed people are innately good, and eBay's originators did two things well: They built a strong online community, and they developed tools to help reinforce trust between strangers. The company tracks and publishes the reputations of both buyers and sellers on the basis of feedback from each transaction. It now has four seller criteria: items as described, communication, shipping time, and shipping and handling rate. The ratings are anonymous but are visible to buyers. Sellers with the highest rankings appear at the top of search results.

Over the years, eBay has expanded its capabilities, services, and partnerships to continue building its community and connecting people around the world. For instance, the company acquired PayPal, an online payment service, in 2002 after eBay members made it clear that PayPal was the preferred method of payment. The acquisition gave consumers a safe way to transfer money, lowered currency and language barriers, and helped merchants sell their products around the world.

Although eBay was a darling in the dot-com boom and has achieved tremendous success since then, it has had its fair share of challenges. These include a worldwide recession, increased competition from Google and Amazon.com, and difficulties expanding globally into markets such as China.

Meg Whitman retired in 2008 after leading the company for 10 years and was replaced by John Donahoe. Under Donahoe, eBay has made 34 acquisitions—primarily e-commerce and payments businesses such as Shopping.com, StubHub, and Bill Me Later but also businesses offering back-end technologies. Donahoe is moving the company toward a business model that can compete with Amazon.com, including expanding its online marketplace to include many returnable goods at fixed prices. Only 30 percent of eBay's sales now come from auctions. The company has also been promoting eBay Now, which partners with big retailers like Macy's, Target, Home Depot, and Toys "R"

*Some believe eBay was created to help Omidayar's girlfriend collect Pez candy dispensers. However, that story was invented by an employee to help generate initial interest in the company.

Us to deliver orders in about an hour for a minimum charge.

Today, people can buy and sell virtually any product or service on the world's largest online marketplace. From appliances and computers to cars and real estate, sellers can list anything as long as it is not illegal and does not violate eBay's rules and policies.

The impact of eBay's global reach is significant. In 2014, the online marketplace had almost 150 million active users and more than 500 million items listed. A pair of shoes is sold there every two seconds, a man's necktie every 23 seconds, a major appliance every 26 seconds, and an LCD television every six minutes. With its high volume, its acquisitions, and consumers' increased use of mobile devices, Donahoe hopes to double eBay's active-user count to more than 200 million by 2015 and increase revenue from $14 billion to $23 billion.

**Questions**

1 Why has eBay succeeded as an online auction marketplace while so many others have failed?

2 Evaluate eBay's fee structure. Is it optimal, or could it be improved? Why? How?

3 Discuss Donahoe's vision for eBay. Is moving away from online auctions sustainable for the company?

**Sources:** Douglas MacMillan, "Can eBay Get Its Tech Savvy Back?," *BusinessWeek*, June 22, 2009, pp. 48–49; Catherine Holahan, "eBay's New Tough Love CEO," *BusinessWeek*, February 4, 2008, pp. 58–59; Adam Lashinsky, "Building eBay 2.0," *Fortune*, October 16, 2006, pp. 161–64; Matthew Creamer, "A Million Marketers," *Advertising Age*, June 26, 2006, pp. 1, 71; Clive Thompson, "eBay Heads East," *Fast Company*, July–August 2006, pp. 87–89; Glen L. Urban, "The Emerging Era of Customer Advocacy," *MIT Sloan Management Review* (Winter 2004): 77–82; Greg Bensinger, "EBay's New Goal: Double Its Users," *Wall Street Journal*, March 29, 2013, p. B.5; Elizabeth Harris, "After Carriers Falter, Questions for Web Shopping," *New York Times*, December 27, 2013, p. B.1; Jeff Himmelman, "eBay's Strategy for Taking on Amazon," *New York Times*, December 19, 2013; www.ebay.com.

## Marketing Excellence

## >> Southwest Airlines

Southwest Airlines debuted in 1971 with little money but lots of personality. Marketing itself as the LUV airline, the company featured a bright red heart logo and relied on outrageous antics to generate word of mouth and new business. Flight attendants in red-orange hot pants served Love Bites (peanuts) and Love Potions (drinks). Today, it is *Fortune's* seventh-most admired company in the world.

How did a small-budget airline accomplish so much? Southwest's business model is based on streamlining its operations, which results in low fares and satisfied, loyal consumers. The company uses a point-to-point routing system, flying thousands of shuttle trips between different pairs of airports or "points" and carrying more passengers per plane than any other airline. Each aircraft averages 6.25 flights a day, flying for almost 12 hours. Southwest can accomplish such a feat because it avoids the traditional hub-and-spoke system and has extremely fast turnaround. In its early years, it turned planes around in less than 10 minutes. Today it averages 30 minutes—half the industry average.

Southwest's unique boarding process also helps expedite departure. Instead of getting assigned seating, passengers are put in one of three groups (A, B, C) and given a number when they check in. Group A boards first and in numerical order (for example, A1–A30). Once on board, passengers may sit anywhere they like.

Southwest also saves by flying only Boeing 737-700s and 737-800s. This simplifies the training process for pilots, flight attendants, and mechanics and lets management substitute aircraft, reschedule flight crews, and transfer mechanics quickly and effortlessly.

One of Southwest's biggest cost savings techniques is its strategy of purchasing fuel options years in advance. Jet fuel is an airline's largest expense and now accounts for 35 percent of operating costs versus 13 percent just a little more than a decade ago. Many of Southwest's long-term contracts allowed the airline to purchase fuel at $51 per barrel, a significant savings especially during the 1990s and 2000s when oil spiked past $100 per barrel. Analysts estimate it has saved more than $2 billion this way.

Southwest also improves its fuel efficiency by making its planes lighter. Crew members power-wash the jet engines each night to remove dirt, planes carry less water in bathrooms, and seats have been replaced with lighter models. Because the airline consumes approximately 1.5 billion gallons of jet fuel each year, every minor change adds up.

Southwest has expanded by entering new markets other airlines overprice and underserve. These usually include secondary cities with smaller airports, whose lower gate fees and reduced congestion promote faster turnaround and lower fares. The company believes it can reduce fares by one-third to one-half whenever it enters a new market, and it expands every market it serves by making flying affordable for more people. Southwest acquired Air Tran in 2011 for $1.4 billion, expanding its consumer base and adding new destinations like Richmond, Memphis, and cities in Mexico and Puerto Rico, its first international locations.

Southwest has pioneered unique services and pricing programs such as same-day freight service, senior discounts, Fun Fares, and Ticketless Travel. The airline was the first with a Web site, the first to deliver live updates on ticket deals, and the first to post a blog. In recent years, it has added revenue through premium ticketing features like premium boarding positions at the gate and early bird check-in, which automatically assigns the best seat possible.

Throughout Southwest's history, its advertising has focused on low fares, frequent flights, on-time arrivals, and a top safety record. The company uses humor to convey its warm, friendly personality. Its tagline, "Ding! You are now free to move around the country," was a parody of in-flight announcements. The lighthearted attitude carries over to entertaining on-board messages, crews who burst into song in the terminal, and several personalized aircrafts, including three painted like flying orca whales.

Despite its no-frills service, Southwest wins the hearts of customers. The company consistently ranks at the top in customer service for airlines and has the lowest ratio of complaints per passenger. It has been *Fortune* magazine's most admired U.S. airline since 1994 and one of its five best places to work. Southwest's financial results also shine; the company has been profitable for 41 straight years, with no layoffs despite a travel slump created by the slow economy and fears of terrorism. When other airlines started charging for baggage, drinks, and snacks, Southwest went against the tide with a "bags fly free" policy.

Although the hot pants are long gone, Southwest's NYSE stock symbol is LUV, and red hearts are found across the company, embodying the idea of employees "caring about themselves, each other, and Southwest's customers." "Our fares can be matched; our airplanes and routes can be copied. But we pride ourselves on our customer service," said Sherry Phelps, director of corporate employment. In fact, having a sense of humor is a selection criterion for hiring. As one employee explained, "We can train you to do any job, but we can't give you the right spirit."

## Questions

1   Southwest has mastered the low-price model and has the financial results to prove it. Why don't other airlines copy Southwest's model?

2   What risks does Southwest face? Can it continue to thrive as a low-cost airline when tough economic times hit or other airlines mimic its business model?

**Sources:** Barney Gimbel, "Southwest's New Flight Plan," *Fortune*, May 16, 2005, pp. 93–98; Melanie Trottman, "Destination: Philadelphia," *Wall Street Journal*, May 4, 2004; Andy Serwer, "Southwest Airlines: The Hottest Thing in the Sky," *Fortune*, March 8, 2004; Colleen Barrett, "Fasten Your Seat Belts," *Adweek*, January 26, 2004, p. 17; Jeff Bailey, "Southwest Airlines Gains Advantage by Hedging on Long-Term Oil Contracts." *New York Times,* November 28, 2007; Michelle Maynard, "To Save Fuel, Airlines Find No Speck Too Small," *New York Times,* June 11, 2008; Daniel B. Honigan, "Fred Taylor Leads Southwest Airlines' Customers to New Heights of Customer Satisfaction," *Marketing News*, May 1, 2008, pp. 24–26; Matthew Malone, "In for a Landing," *Condé Nast Portfolio*, August 2008, pp. 91–93; Hugo Martin, "Is Southwest Airlines Losing the Luv?," *Los Angeles Times,* February 9, 2013; Danielle Schlanger, "How Southwest Keeps Making Money in a Brutal Airline Industry," *BusinessInsider,* June 13, 2012; Southwest Annual Report 2012; www.southwest.com.

L.L. Bean has expanded beyond its famed catalog to sell online and through its own stores.

*Source: L.L.Bean*

# In This Chapter, We Will Address the Following **Questions**

1.   What is a marketing channel system and value network? (p. 494)

2.   What work do marketing channels perform? (p. 499)

3.   How should channels be designed? (p. 503)

4.   What decisions do companies face in managing their channels? (p. 508)

5.   How should companies integrate channels? (p. 512)

6.   What are the key channel issues in e-commerce? (p. 514)

7.   What are the key channel issues in m-commerce? (p. 516)

8.   How should companies manage channel conflict? (p. 518)

MyMarketingLab™

⭐ **Improve Your Grade!**
Over 10 million students improved their results using the Pearson MyLabs. Visit mymktlab.com for simulations, tutorials, and end-of-chapter problems.

# 17 Designing and Managing Integrated Marketing Channels

**Successful value creation needs successful value delivery. Instead of limiting their** focus to their immediate suppliers, distributors, and customers, holistic marketers are examining the whole supply chain as a value network, including their suppliers' suppliers upstream and their distributors' customers downstream. They are also looking at how technology is changing the way customers shop and retailers sell and finding new and different means to distribute and service their offerings. Consider how L.L.Bean develops strong customer ties with a well-executed channel strategy.[1]

*L.L.Bean's founder Leon Leonwood (L.L.) Bean returned from a Maine hunting trip in 1911 with cold, damp feet—and a revolutionary idea for stitching leather uppers to workmen's rubber boots to create a comfortable, functional boot. To a mailing list of hunters, Bean sent a three-page flier describing the benefits of his new Maine Hunting Shoe and backing it with a complete guarantee. The shoe was not an initial success. Of the first 100 pairs ordered, 90 were returned when the tops and bottoms separated. True to his word, Bean refunded the purchase price and fixed the problem. L.L.Bean quickly became known as a trusted source for reliable outdoor equipment and expert advice. The company's guarantee of 100 percent satisfaction is still at the core of its business, as is its original Golden Rule, "Sell good merchandise at a reasonable profit, treat your customers like human beings, and they will always come back for more." Today, it is a $1.5 billion company, selling through its famous catalogs as well as online and in retail stores. L.L Bean has also expanded globally, with stores in Japan and China. To better meet its U.S. customers' needs, the company launched free shipping in 2011. Online it has opened up to customer ratings and reviews, given customers the opportunity to chat and e-mail with customer service, and introduced a "click to call" system that triggers a customer service call within two minutes. Ranked #1 in customer service by Bloomberg Businessweek, L.L.Bean monitors customer feedback closely. When one of its customer-favorite products, Supima Cotton Fitted Sheets, began to be criticized in online reviews, the company quickly pulled the product from its Web site to investigate. It turned out that a wrinkle-resistance treatment mistakenly added by a contractor was causing the cotton fabric to tear or shred. L.L.Bean immediately offered new sheets to the 6,300 customers who had purchased the defective set and destroyed the remaining faulty products.*

**With the advent of e-commerce** (selling online) and m-commerce (selling via mobile phones and tablets), customers are buying in ways they never have before. Companies today must build and manage a continuously evolving and increasingly complex channel system and value network. In this chapter, we consider strategic and tactical issues in integrating marketing channels and developing value networks. We will examine marketing channel issues from the perspective of retailers, wholesalers, and physical distribution agencies in Chapter 18.

# Marketing Channels and Value Networks

Most producers do not sell their goods directly to the final users; between them stands a set of intermediaries performing a variety of functions. These intermediaries constitute a marketing channel (also called a trade channel or distribution channel). Formally, **marketing channels** are sets of interdependent organizations participating in the process of making a product or service available for use or consumption. They are the set of pathways a product or service follows after production, culminating in purchase and consumption by the final end user.[2]

Some intermediaries—such as wholesalers and retailers—buy, take title to, and resell the merchandise; they are called *merchants*. Others—brokers, manufacturers' representatives, sales agents—search for customers and may negotiate on the producer's behalf but do not take title to the goods; they are called *agents*. Still others—transportation companies, independent warehouses, banks, advertising agencies—assist in the distribution process but neither take title to goods nor negotiate purchases or sales; they are called *facilitators*.

Channels of all types play an important role in the success of a company and affect all other marketing decisions. Marketers should judge them in the context of the entire process by which their products are made, distributed, sold, and serviced. We consider all these issues in the following sections.

## THE IMPORTANCE OF CHANNELS

A **marketing channel system** is the particular set of marketing channels a firm employs, and decisions about it are among the most critical ones management faces. In the United States, channel members as a group have historically earned margins that account for 30 percent to 50 percent of the ultimate selling price. In contrast, advertising typically has accounted for less than 5 percent to 7 percent of the final price.[3] One of the chief roles of marketing channels is to convert potential buyers into profitable customers. Marketing channels must not just *serve* markets, they must also *make* them.[4]

The channels chosen affect all other marketing decisions. The company's pricing depends on whether it uses online discounters or high-quality boutiques. Its sales force and advertising decisions depend on how much training and motivation dealers need. In addition, channel decisions include relatively long-term commitments with other firms as well as a set of policies and procedures. When an automaker signs up independent dealers to sell its automobiles, it cannot buy them out the next day and replace them with company-owned outlets. But at the same time, channel choices themselves depend on the company's marketing strategy with respect to segmentation, targeting, and positioning. Holistic marketers ensure that marketing decisions in all these different areas are made to maximize value overall.

In managing its intermediaries, the firm must decide how much effort to devote to push and to pull marketing. A **push strategy** uses the manufacturer's sales force, trade promotion money, or other means to induce intermediaries to carry, promote, and sell the product to end users. This strategy is particularly appropriate when there is low brand loyalty in a category, brand choice is made in the store, the product is an impulse item, and product benefits are well understood.

In a **pull strategy** the manufacturer uses advertising, promotion, and other forms of communication to persuade consumers to demand the product from intermediaries, thus inducing the intermediaries to order it. This strategy is particularly appropriate when there is high brand loyalty and high involvement in the category, when consumers are able to perceive differences between brands, and when they choose the brand before they go to the store.

Top marketing companies such as Apple, Coca-Cola, and Nike skillfully employ both push *and* pull strategies. A push strategy is more effective when accompanied by a well-designed and well-executed pull strategy that activates consumer demand. On the other hand, without at least some consumer interest, it can be very difficult to gain much channel acceptance and support, and vice versa for that matter.

## MULTICHANNEL MARKETING

Today's successful companies typically employ **multichannel marketing**, using two or more marketing channels to reach customer segments in one market area. HP uses its sales force to sell to large accounts, outbound telemarketing to sell to medium-sized accounts, direct mail with an inbound phone number to sell to small accounts, retailers to sell to still smaller accounts, and the Internet to sell specialty items. Each channel can target a different segment of buyers, or different need states for one buyer, to deliver the right products in the right places in the right way at the least cost.

When this doesn't happen, channel conflict, excessive cost, or insufficient demand can result. Launched in 1976, Dial-a-Mattress successfully grew for three decades by selling mattresses directly over the phone and later online. A major expansion into 50 brick-and-mortar stores in major metro areas was a failure, however. Secondary locations, chosen because management considered prime locations too expensive, could not generate enough customer traffic. The company eventually declared bankruptcy.[5]

On the other hand, when a major catalog and Internet retailer invested significantly in brick-and-mortar stores, different results emerged. Customers near the store purchased through the catalog less frequently, but their online purchases were unchanged. As it turned out, customers who liked to spend time browsing were happy to either use a catalog or visit the store; those channels were interchangeable. Customers who shopped online, on the other hand, were more transaction-focused and interested in efficiency, so they were less affected by the introduction of stores. Returns and exchanges at the stores were found to increase because of ease and accessibility, but extra purchases made by customers returning or exchanging at the store offset any revenue deficit.[6]

Research has shown that multichannel customers can be more valuable to marketers.[7] Nordstrom found that its multichannel customers spend four times as much as those who only shop through one channel, though some academic research suggests that this effect is stronger for hedonic products (apparel and cosmetics) than for functional products (office and garden supplies).[8]

## INTEGRATING MULTICHANNEL MARKETING SYSTEMS

Most companies today have adopted multichannel marketing. Disney sells its videos through multiple channels: movie rental merchants such as Netflix and Redbox, Disney Stores (now owned and run by The Children's Place), retail stores such as Best Buy, online retailers such as Disney's own online stores and Amazon.com, and the Disney Club catalog and other catalog sellers. This variety affords Disney maximum market coverage and enables it to offer its videos at a number of price points.[9] Here are some of the channel options for leather-goods maker Coach.[10]

**COACH** Coach markets a high-end line of luxury handbags, briefcases, luggage, and accessories. In its 2013 fiscal year 10-K, the company describes its multichannel global distribution model as follows: "Coach products are available in image-enhancing locations globally wherever our consumer chooses to shop including: retail stores and factory outlets, directly operated shop-in-shops, online, and department and specialty stores. This allows Coach to maintain a dynamic balance as results do not depend solely on the performance of a single channel or geographic area." The North America segment consists of direct-to-consumer and indirect channels and includes sales to consumers through 351 company-operated retail stores, including the Internet, and sales to wholesale customers and distributors. Coach began as a U.S. wholesaler and still sells to 1,000 U.S. department-store locations, such as Macy's (including Bloomingdale's), Dillard's, Nordstrom, Saks Fifth Avenue, and Lord & Taylor, often within a tightly controlled shop-within-a-shop, as well as on some of those retailer's Web sites. This segment represented approximately 69 percent of the company's total net sales in fiscal 2013. The International segment sells to consumers online and through company-operated stores in Japan and mainland China, Hong Kong, Macau, Singapore, Taiwan, Malaysia, and Korea and to wholesale customers and distributors. Coach also has store-in-store offerings in Japan and China inside major department stores. The International segment represented approximately 31 percent of total net sales in fiscal 2013. Finally, Coach has licensing relationships with Movado (watches), Jimlar (footwear), and Marchon (eyewear). These licensed products are sometimes sold in other channels such as jewelry stores, high-end shoe stores, and optical retailers as Coach continues to broaden its meaning from a "bag brand" to a whole lifestyle brand.

Source: © Jeff Greenberg "0 people images" / Alamy

Coach uses a broad range of channels to better sell its expanding product lines.

Companies are increasingly employing digital distribution strategies, selling directly online to customers or through e-merchants who have their own Web sites. In doing so, these companies are seeking to achieve **omnichannel marketing**, in which multiple channels work seamlessly together and match each target customer's preferred ways of doing business, delivering the right product information and customer service regardless of whether customers are online, in the store, or on the phone.

An **integrated marketing channel system** is one in which the strategies and tactics of selling through one channel reflect the strategies and tactics of selling through one or more other channels. Adding more channels gives companies three important benefits. The first is increased market coverage. Not only are more customers able to shop for the company's products in more places, as noted above, but those who buy in more than one channel are often more profitable than single-channel customers.[11] The second benefit is lower channel cost—selling online or by catalog and phone is cheaper than using personal selling to reach small customers. The third is the ability to do more customized selling—such as by adding a technical sales force to sell complex equipment.

There is a trade-off, however. New channels typically introduce conflict and problems with control and cooperation. Two or more may end up competing for the same customers.[12] Clearly, companies need to think through their channel architecture and determine which channels should perform which functions.[13] Figure 17.1 shows a simple grid to help make channel architecture decisions. It consists of major marketing channels (as rows) and the major channel tasks to be completed (as columns).[14]

The grid illustrates why using only one channel is typically not efficient. Consider a direct sales force. A salesperson would have to find leads, qualify them, presell, close the sale, provide service, and manage account growth. With an integrated multichannel approach, however, the company's marketing department could run a preselling campaign informing prospects about the company's products through advertising, direct mail, and e-mails; generate leads through telemarketing, more e-mails, and trade shows; and qualify leads as hot, warm, or cool. The salesperson enters when the prospect is ready to talk business and invests his or her costly time primarily in closing the sale. This multichannel architecture optimizes coverage, customization, and control while minimizing cost and conflict.

Companies should use different sales channels for different-sized business customers—a direct sales force for large customers, a digital strategy or telemarketing for midsize customers, and distributors for small customers—but be alert for conflict over account ownership. For example, territory-based sales representatives may want credit for all sales in their territories, regardless of the marketing channel used.

Multichannel marketers also need to decide how much of their product to offer in each of the channels. Patagonia views the Web as the ideal channel for showing off its entire line of goods, given that its 88 retail

**Demand-generation Tasks**

Marketing Channels and Methods — VENDOR

| | Gather relevant information | Develop & disseminate communications | Reach price agreements | Place orders | Acquire funds for inventories | Assume risks | Facilitate product storage & movement | Facilitate payment | Oversee ownership transfer |
|---|---|---|---|---|---|---|---|---|---|
| Internet | | | | | | | | | |
| National account management | | | | | | | | | |
| Direct sales | | | | | | | | | |
| Telemarketing | | | | | | | | | |
| Direct mail | | | | | | | | | |
| Retail stores | | | | | | | | | |
| Distributors | | | | | | | | | |
| Dealers and value-added resellers | | | | | | | | | |

CUSTOMER

| **Fig. 17.1** |

## The Hybrid Grid

Source: Adapted from Rowland T. Moriarty and Ursula Moran, "Marketing Hybrid Marketing Systems," *Harvard Business Review*, November–December, 1990, p. 150.

Outdoor equipment supplier REI is known for its seamless blending of online and offline channels.

locations are limited by space to offering a selection only, and even its catalog promotes less than 70 percent of its total merchandise.[15] Other marketers prefer to limit their online offerings, theorizing that customers look to Web sites and catalogs for a "best of" array of merchandise and don't want to have to click through dozens of pages. Here's a company that has carefully managed its multiple channels.[16]

**REI** Outdoor equipment supplier REI has been lauded by industry analysts for the seamless integration of its retail store, Web site, Internet kiosks, mail-order catalogs, value-priced outlets, mobile app, and toll-free order number. If an item is out of stock in the store, all customers need to do is tap into the store's Internet kiosk to order it from REI's Web site. Less Internet-savvy customers can have clerks place the order for them at the checkout counters. And REI not only generates store-to-Internet traffic, it also sends online shoppers into its stores. If a customer browses REI's site and stops to read an REI "Learn and Share" article on backpacking, the site might highlight an in-store promotion on hiking boots. To create a more common experience across channels, the specific icons and information used in ratings and reviews on REI.com also appear on in-store product displays. Like many retailers, REI has found that dual-channel shoppers spend significantly more than single-channel shoppers, and tri-channel shoppers spend even more. For example, one of every three people who buy something online will spend an additional $90 in the store when they come to pick that purchase up.

## VALUE NETWORKS

A supply chain view of a firm sees markets as destination points and amounts to a linear view of the flow of ingredients and components through the production process to their ultimate sale to customers. The company should first think of the target market, however, and then design the supply chain backward from that point. This strategy has been called **demand chain planning**.[17]

A broader view sees a company at the center of a **value network**—a system of partnerships and alliances that a firm creates to source, augment, and deliver its offerings. A value network includes a firm's suppliers and its suppliers' suppliers and its immediate customers and their end customers. It also incorporates valued relationships with others such as university researchers and government approval agencies.

A company needs to orchestrate the work of these parties to deliver superior value to the target market. Oracle relies on 15 million developers—the largest developer community in the world.[18] Apple Developer—where folks create iPhone apps for the Apple operating system—has 275,000 registered iOS members. Developers keep 70 percent of any revenue their products generate; Apple gets 30 percent. After releasing more than 850,000 apps that were downloaded 45 billion times in the first five years, Apple has paid out almost $9 billion.[19]

Demand chain planning yields several insights.[20] First, the company can estimate whether more money is made upstream or downstream, in case it can integrate backward or forward. Second, the company is more aware of disturbances anywhere in the supply chain that might change costs, prices, or supplies. Third, companies can go online with their business partners to speed communications, transactions, and payments; reduce costs; and increase accuracy. Ford not only manages numerous supply chains but also sponsors many B-to-B Web sites and exchanges.

Managing a value network means making increasing investments in information technology (IT) and software. Firms have introduced supply chain management (SCM) software and invited such software firms as SAP and Oracle to design comprehensive *enterprise resource planning* (ERP) systems to manage cash flow, manufacturing, human resources, purchasing, and other major functions within a unified framework. They hope to break up departmental silos—in which each department acts only in its own self-interest—and carry out core business processes more seamlessly. Most, however, are still a long way from truly comprehensive ERP systems.

Marketers, for their part, have traditionally focused on the side of the value network that looks toward the customer, adopting customer relationship management (CRM) software and practices. In the future, they will increasingly participate in and influence their companies' upstream activities and become network managers, not just product and customer managers.

## THE DIGITAL CHANNELS REVOLUTION

The digital revolution is profoundly transforming distribution strategies. With customers—both individuals and businesses—becoming more comfortable buying online and the use of smart phones exploding, traditional brick-and-mortar channel strategies are being modified or even replaced.

Online retail sales (or e-commerce) have been growing at a double-digit rate; apparel and accessories, consumer electronics, and computer hardware are the three fastest-growing categories. Skeptics initially felt apparel wouldn't sell well online, but easy returns, try-on tools, and customer reviews have helped counter the inability to try clothes on in the store.

As brick-and-mortar retailers promote their online ventures and other companies bypass retail activity by selling online, they all are embracing new practices and policies. As in all marketing, customers hold the key. Customers want the advantages both of digital—vast product selection, abundant product information, helpful customer reviews and tips—and of physical stores—highly personalized service, detailed physical examination of products, an overall event and experience. They expect seamless channel integration so they can:[21]

- Enjoy helpful customer support in a store, online, or on the phone
- Check online for product availability at local stores before making a trip
- Find out in-store whether a product that is unavailable can be purchased and shipped from another store to home
- Order a product online and pick it up at a convenient retail location
- Return a product purchased online to a nearby store of the retailer
- Receive discounts and promotional offers based on total online and offline purchases

Retailers and manufacturers are responding. Consider some of the changes being made by retail giant Walmart.[22]

**WALMART**   With a huge investment in brick-and-mortar stores, many entrenched executives, and long-established policies, Walmart was slow to embrace online and mobile technology and had online operations accounting for less than 2 percent of its global sales. Then the company decided to make its digital strategy a priority, giving customers anytime, anywhere access to Walmart by combining mobile, online, and physical stores. After acquiring social-media start-up Kosmix, known for its strong expertise in search and analytics, it established its @WalmartLabs group in Silicon Valley, leading to company innovations such as smart-phone payment technology, mobile shopping applications, and Twitter-influenced product selection for stores. Walmart found that many of its core customer group who made $30,000 to $60,000 a year were shopping from its Web site in large numbers and often on smart phones rather than computers. Always a wizard with logistics, Walmart adopted a "ship from store" practice that uses its more than 4,000 U.S. stores as warehouses to fulfill online orders quickly. The company is also exploring same-day shipping. It improved the search engine on its Web site, increasing its "browsers to buyers" conversion by as much as 15 percent; launched its Shopycat gift recommendation app, which uses social media to suggest gifts; introduced its Scan and Go app so customers can automatically apply coupons when checking out; and added an in-aisle mobile-scanning system to speed check-out. A top priority for Walmart is its smart-phone app. Users of the app spend more and frequent the store twice as often as non-users. When near a store, the app flips into "store mode" to help locate items on a shopping list and make additional recommendations, provide a digital version of the latest circulars, and highlight new products available in the store.

Retailers and manufacturers are assembling massive amounts of social, mobile, and location (SoMoLo) information they can mine to learn about their customers. They are using software that closely monitors what's selling where and at what price in order to adjust their offerings and prices.[23] The goal for many marketers is to develop a

Source: © IanDagnall Computing/Alamy

By skillfully combining mobile, online, and physical stores, Walmart's goal is to give customers access to its merchandise anytime, anywhere.

customized "next best offer" (NBO) that takes into account customers' attitudes and behavior, purchase (product or service), and shopping channel (in store or online) and the marketer's goal with respect to those consumers, whether it is to increase sales, say, or build loyalty.[24]

# The Role of Marketing Channels

Why does a producer delegate some of the selling job to intermediaries, relinquishing control over how and to whom its products are sold? Through their contacts, experience, specialization, and scale of operation, intermediaries make goods widely available and accessible to target markets, offering more effectiveness and efficiency than the selling firm could achieve on its own.[25]

Source: © michael going/Alamy

Many manufacturers would find it cost prohibitive to open up their own stores—their best options are to tap into established dealer and retailer networks.

| TABLE 17.1 | Channel Member Functions |
|---|---|

- Gather information about potential and current customers, competitors, and other actors and forces in the marketing environment.
- Develop and disseminate persuasive communications to stimulate purchasing.
- Negotiate and reach agreements on price and other terms so that transfer of ownership or possession can be affected.
- Place orders with manufacturers.
- Acquire the funds to finance inventories at different levels in the marketing channel.
- Assume risks connected with carrying out channel work.
- Provide for the successive storage and movement of physical products.
- Provide for buyers' payment of their bills through banks and other financial institutions.
- Oversee actual transfer of ownership from one organization or person to another.

Many producers lack the financial resources and expertise to sell directly on their own. The William Wrigley Jr. Company would not find it practical to establish small retail gum shops throughout the world or to sell gum online or by mail order. It is easier to work through the extensive network of privately owned distribution organizations. Even Ford would be hard-pressed to replace all the tasks done by its almost 8,500 dealer outlets worldwide.[26]

## CHANNEL FUNCTIONS AND FLOWS

A marketing channel performs the work of moving goods from producers to consumers. It overcomes the time, place, and possession gaps that separate goods and services from those who need or want them. Members of the marketing channel perform a number of key functions (see Table 17.1).

Some of these functions (storage and movement, title, and communications) constitute a *forward flow* of activity from the company to the customer; others (ordering and payment) constitute a *backward flow* from customers to the company. Still others (information, negotiation, finance, and risk taking) occur in both directions. Five flows are illustrated in Figure 17.2 for the marketing of forklift trucks. If these flows were superimposed in one diagram, we would see the tremendous complexity of even simple marketing channels.

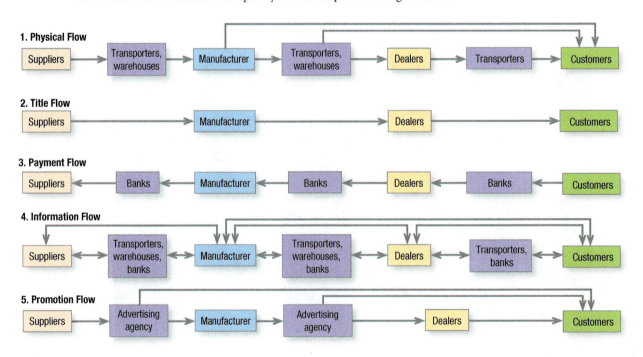

| Fig. 17.2 |

Five Marketing Flows in the Marketing Channel for Forklift Trucks

A manufacturer selling a physical product and services might require three channels: a *sales channel,* a *delivery channel,* and a *service channel.* To sell its Bowflex fitness equipment, the Nautilus Group historically has emphasized direct marketing via television infomercials and ads, inbound/outbound call centers, response mailings, and the Internet as sales channels; UPS ground service as the delivery channel; and local repair people as the service channel. Reflecting shifting consumer buying habits, Nautilus now also sells Bowflex through regional and national retailers such as Sears and Dick's Sporting Goods as well as through online merchants such as Amazon.com.

The question for marketers is not *whether* various channel functions need to be performed—they must be—but, rather, *who* is to perform them. All channel functions have three characteristics in common: They use up scarce resources; they can often be performed better through specialization; and they can be shifted among channel members. Shifting some functions to intermediaries lowers the producer's costs and prices, but the intermediary must add a charge to cover its work. If the intermediaries are more efficient than the manufacturer, prices to consumers should be lower. If consumers perform some functions themselves, they should enjoy even lower prices. Changes in channel institutions thus largely reflect the discovery of more efficient ways to combine or separate the economic functions that provide assortments of goods to target customers.

## CHANNEL LEVELS

The producer and the final customer are part of every channel. We will use the number of intermediary levels to designate the length of a channel. Figure 17.3(a) illustrates several consumer-goods marketing channels of different lengths.

A **zero-level channel**, also called a **direct marketing channel**, consists of a manufacturer selling directly to the final customer. The major examples are mail order, online selling, TV selling, telemarketing, door-to-door sales, home parties, and manufacturer-owned stores. Traditionally, Franklin Mint sold collectibles through mail order; Red Envelope sold gifts online; Time-Life sold music and video collections through TV commercials or longer "infomercials"; nonprofits and political organizations and candidates use the telephone to raise funds; Avon sales representatives sold cosmetics door to door; Tupperware sold its containers via in-home parties; and Apple sold computers and other consumer electronics through its own stores. Many of these firms now sell directly to customers online and via catalogs. Even traditional consumer-product firms are considering adding direct-to-consumer e-commerce sites to their channel mix. Kimberly-Clark launched an online Kleenex Shop in the United Kingdom.[27]

A *one-level channel* contains one selling intermediary, such as a retailer. A *two-level channel* contains two intermediaries, typically a wholesaler and a retailer, and a *three-level channel* contains three. In the meatpacking industry, wholesalers sell to **jobbers**, essentially small-scale wholesalers, who sell to small retailers. In Japan, food distribution may include as many as six levels. Obtaining information about end users and exercising control become more difficult for the producer as the number of channel levels increases.

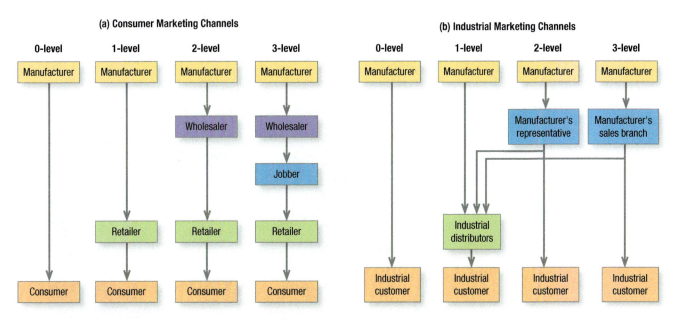

| **Fig. 17.3** |

Consumer and Industrial Marketing Channels

Figure 17.3(b) shows channels commonly used in B-to-B marketing. An industrial-goods manufacturer can use its sales force to sell directly to industrial customers, or it can sell to industrial distributors who sell to industrial customers, or it can sell through manufacturer's representatives or its own sales branches directly to industrial customers or indirectly to industrial customers through industrial distributors. Zero-, one-, and two-level marketing channels are quite common.

Channels normally describe a forward movement of products from source to user, but *reverse-flow channels* are also important (1) to reuse products or containers (such as refillable chemical-carrying drums), (2) to refurbish products for resale (such as circuit boards or computers), (3) to recycle products, and (4) to dispose of products and packaging. Reverse-flow intermediaries include manufacturers' redemption centers, community groups, trash-collection specialists, recycling centers, trash-recycling brokers, and central processing warehousing.

## SERVICE SECTOR CHANNELS

Many of the most successful new banks, insurance and travel companies, and stock brokerages have emerged with strictly or largely online operations, such as Ally banking, Esurance insurance, Expedia travel, and E*TRADE investments. Marketing channels also keep changing for "person marketing." Besides providing live and programmed entertainment, entertainers, musicians, and other artists can reach prospective and existing fans online in many ways—through their own Web sites, on social community sites such as Facebook and Twitter, and through third-party Web sites. Politicians also must choose a mix of channels—mass media, rallies, coffee hours, spot TV ads, direct mail, billboards, faxes, e-mail, blogs, podcasts, Web sites, and social networking sites—for delivering their messages to voters.

Nonprofit service organizations such as schools develop education-dissemination systems and hospitals develop health-delivery systems. These institutions must figure out agencies and locations for reaching a far-flung population.[28]

**CLEVELAND CLINIC**   One of the largest and most highly respected hospitals in the country, Cleveland Clinic provides medical care in a variety of ways and settings. Its main campus in Cleveland, 50 buildings on 166 acres, is its hub for patient care, research, and education. The clinic also operates 16 full-service Family Health Centers in the suburbs, while eight hospitals extend its reach in Northeast Ohio. Community outreach programs in all these areas provide patient education and free health screenings. Cleveland Clinic also offers major medical care in Florida, Toronto, and manages a Mubadala Development Company medical campus in Abu Dhabi, United Arab Eimireates, scheduled to begin seeing patients in 2015. It has a suite of secure online health services for both patients and physicians and is developing partnerships with Google and Microsoft to extend its online capabilities.

Cleveland Clinic has a comprehensive health-delivery system to provide different kinds of medical care to different markets.

Source: © Philip Scalia/Alamy

# Channel-Design Decisions

To design a marketing channel system, marketers analyze customer needs and wants, establish channel objectives and constraints, and identify and evaluate major channel alternatives.

## ANALYZING CUSTOMER NEEDS AND WANTS

Consumers may choose the channels they prefer based on price, product assortment, and convenience as well as their own shopping goals (economic, social, or experiential).[29] Channel segmentation exists, and marketers must be aware that different consumers have different needs during the purchase process.

Even the same consumer, though, may choose different channels for different reasons.[30] As Chapter 16 described, some consumers are willing to "trade up" to retailers offering higher-end goods such as TAG Heuer watches or Callaway golf clubs and "trade down" to discount retailers for private-label paper towels, detergent, or vitamins.[31] Others may browse a catalog before visiting a store or test-drive a car at a dealership before ordering online. "Marketing Insight: Understanding the Showrooming Phenomena" describes some of the new ways customers are using multiple channels as they make their purchases.

Channels produce five service outputs:

1. ***Desired lot size***—The number of units the channel permits a typical customer to purchase on one occasion. In buying cars for its fleet, Hertz prefers a channel from which it can buy a large lot size; a household wants a channel that permits a lot size of one.

## Understanding the Showrooming Phenomena

Consumers have always shopped around to get the best deal or broaden their options, and now e-commerce and m-commerce (selling via mobile phone and tablet) offer them a new twist. **Showrooming** lets them physically examine a product and collect information in a store but make their actual purchase from the retailer later online or, in the store's least desirable outcome, from a different retailer altogether, typically to secure a lower price.

Showrooming has been given a boost by smart phones. Thanks to their mobile devices, consumers in stores have never been better equipped to decide whether they should buy. One study showed that more than half of U.S. mobile phone users, especially younger ones, have used their phones to ask for purchase advice from a friend or family member or to look for reviews or lower prices while shopping.

Retailers used to worry about getting consumers into the store, but experts note they now need to worry instead about selling to consumers who are bringing other stores in with them. Amazon's Price Check phone app, for instance, allows shoppers to instantly compare prices while in a brick-and-mortar store. Online retailers that mobile users can tap offer traditional brick-and-mortar chains serious competition because of their wide selections, lower prices (often with no taxes), and 24/7 convenience.

Mobile has become a top priority for many retailers as a means to combat showrooming. Target has expanded its use of mobile media, incorporating QR codes, text-to-buy features, and new checkout scanners to make mobile coupon redemption easier and faster. Forty percent of PetSmart's Web traffic comes from smart phones and tablets. eBay observed that 60 percent of e-mails sent by its retail clients were opened on mobile devices and more than half the time were transitioned to other devices to make the transaction.[32]

Addressing showrooming head-on, Best Buy and Target announced they would permanently match the prices of online retailers. Others have more closely linked their stores and Web sites in response to the trend. Walmart, Macy's, and Best Buy allow in-store pickup of online orders and returns of online purchases.

Many retailers are making the in-store experience more informative and rewarding. Guess, PacSun, and Aéropostale are equipping in-store sales staff with iPads or tablets for collecting more in-depth product information to share with shoppers. Shoppers enrolled in loyalty programs can also quickly download their purchase histories, product preferences, and other useful background.

The main goal of all these efforts is to hold on to the customer. One study found that 70 percent of a showrooming audience was more likely to buy from retailers with well-designed Web sites and apps, strong multichannel support, and price comparisons via QR codes. Shifting sales from a store to online can actually be more profitable for a retailer if it prevents the customer from buying elsewhere.

**Sources:** "Showrooming Threat Hits Major Chains," www.warc.com, March 1, 2013; "'Showrooming' Grows in U.S.," www.warc.com, February 4, 2013; "Showrooming to Shape U.S. Holiday Sales," www.warc.com, November 16, 2012; Hadley Malcolm, "Smartphones to Play Bigger Role in Shopping," *USA Today*, November 15, 2012; Maribel Lopez, "Can Omni-Channel Retail Combat Showrooming," *Forbes*, October 22, 2012; Australian School of Business, "Stop Customers Treating Your Business as a Showroom," www.smartcompany.com.au, October 8, 2012.

2. ***Waiting and delivery time***—The average time customers wait for receipt of goods. Customers increasingly prefer faster delivery channels.
3. ***Spatial convenience***—The degree to which the marketing channel makes it easy for customers to purchase the product. Toyota offers greater spatial convenience than Lexus because there are more Toyota dealers, helping customers save on transportation and search costs in buying and repairing an automobile.
4. ***Product variety***—The assortment provided by the marketing channel. Normally, customers prefer a greater assortment because more choices increase the chance of finding what they need, though too many choices can sometimes create a negative effect.[33]
5. ***Service backup***—Add-on services (credit, delivery, installation, repairs) provided by the channel. The more service backup, the greater the benefit provided by the channel.

Providing more service outputs also means increasing channel costs and raising prices. The success of discount stores such as Walmart and Target and extreme examples like Dollar General and Family Dollar indicates that many consumers are willing to accept less service if they can save money.

## ESTABLISHING OBJECTIVES AND CONSTRAINTS

Marketers should state their channel objectives in terms of the service output levels they want to provide and the associated cost and support levels. Under competitive conditions, channel members should arrange their functional tasks to minimize costs and still provide desired levels of service. Usually, planners can identify several market segments based on desired service and choose the best channels for each.

Channel objectives vary with product characteristics. Bulky products, such as building materials, require channels that minimize the shipping distance and the amount of handling. Nonstandard products such as custom-built machinery are sold directly by sales representatives. Products requiring installation or maintenance services, such as heating and cooling systems, are usually sold and maintained by the company or by franchised dealers. High-unit-value products such as generators and turbines are often sold through a company sales force rather than intermediaries.

Marketers must adapt their channel objectives to the larger environment. When economic conditions are depressed, producers want to move goods to market using shorter channels and without services that add to the final price. Legal regulations and restrictions also affect channel design. U.S. law looks unfavorably on channel arrangements that substantially lessen competition or create a monopoly.

In entering new markets, firms often closely observe what other firms are doing. French retailer Auchan considered the presence of its French rivals Leclerc and Casino in Poland as key to its decision to also enter that market.[34] Apple's channel objective of creating a dynamic retail experience for consumers was not being met by existing channels, so it chose to open it own stores.[35]

**APPLE STORES**   When Apple launched its stores in 2001, many questioned their prospects; *BusinessWeek* published an article titled "Sorry Steve, Here's Why Apple Stores Won't Work." Just five years later, the company was celebrating the launch of its spectacular Manhattan showcase. By the end of 2013, it had taken in global sales of $16 billion from more than 400 stores in North America, Europe, and Asia, about 20 percent of total corporate revenue. Roughly 30,000 of Apple's 43,000 U.S. employees work in its stores. Annual sales per square foot were estimated to be $4,406 in 2011—the Fifth Avenue location reportedly earns a staggering $35,000 per square foot—compared with Tiffany's $3,070, Coach's $1,776, and Best Buy's $880. Any way you look at them, Apple Stores have also been an unqualified success in fueling excitement for the brand. They let people see and touch the products—and experience what Apple can do for them—making it more likely they'll become customers. They target tech-savvy customers with in-store product presentations and workshops; a full line of Apple products, software, and accessories; and a "Genius Bar" staffed by specialists who provide technical support, often free of charge. Apple's meticulous attention to detail is reflected in the preloaded music and photos on demo devices, innovative touches such as roving credit-card swipers to minimize checkout lines, and hours invested in employee training. Employees receive no sales commissions and have no sales quotas. They are told their mission is to "help customers solve problems." Although the stores initially upset existing Apple retailers, the company worked hard to smooth relationships, in part justifying its decision as a natural evolution of its online sales channel.

Although some predicted it would fail, Apple Stores have become an unqualified success both financially and as a brand builder.

Source: © Trevor Mogg/Alamy

# IDENTIFYING MAJOR CHANNEL ALTERNATIVES

Each channel—from sales forces to agents, distributors, dealers, direct mail, telemarketing, and the Internet—has unique strengths and weaknesses. Sales forces can handle complex products and transactions, but they are expensive. The Internet is inexpensive but may not be as effective for complex products. Distributors can create sales, but the company loses direct contact with customers. Several clients can share the cost of manufacturers' reps, but the selling effort is less intense than company reps provide.

Channel alternatives differ in three ways: the types of intermediaries, the number needed, and the terms and responsibilities of each. Let's look at these factors.

**TYPES OF INTERMEDIARIES** Consider the channel alternatives identified by a consumer electronics company that produces satellite radios. It could sell its players directly to automobile manufacturers to be installed as original equipment, auto dealers, rental car companies, or satellite radio specialist dealers through a direct sales force or through distributors. It could also sell its players through company stores, online retailers, mail-order catalogs, or mass merchandisers such as Best Buy.

Sometimes a company chooses a new or unconventional channel because of the difficulty, cost, or ineffectiveness of working with the dominant channel. When video rental stores were rapidly declining, Coinstar successfully introduced the Redbox chain of conveniently located DVD- and game-rental kiosks.[36] Netflix is quickly moving away from the revolutionary channel that brought it much success—direct mail—to capitalize on a new one.[37]

NETFLIX    Convinced that DVDs were the home video medium of the future, Netflix founder Reed Hastings came up with a new form of rental distribution via mail order in 1997. The company quickly developed strong customer loyalty and positive word of mouth with its modest subscription fees (as low as $9 a month), usually overnight delivery, and extensive library of thousands of movies and television episodes with no late fees. The service also had proprietary software that let customers search for obscure films and discover new ones. To improve the quality of its searches, Netflix sponsored a well-publicized million-dollar contest that drew thousands of entrants; the winning solution was expected to make its recommendation algorithm twice as effective. With new competition from thousands of Redbox rental kiosks and Amazon.com's download services, Netflix began emphasizing streaming videos and instantaneous delivery mechanisms. After an initial misstep, the firm split the two businesses and charges roughly $8 a month each for physical DVDs and for a streaming download plan. It is now the single-largest source of download traffic in North America, making up more than a third of the total, but it still anticipates growth in DVD rentals from its more than 40 million subscribers. Netflix's success has also captured Hollywood's attention. The company's online communities of customers who read and post reviews and feedback can be an important source of fans for films. Netflix is also creating its own award-winning television programming and has moved into international markets in Canada, Europe, and Latin America.

NUMBER OF INTERMEDIARIES  Three strategies based on the number of intermediaries are exclusive, selective, and intensive distribution.

**Exclusive distribution** severely limits the number of intermediaries. It's appropriate when the producer wants to ensure more knowledgeable and dedicated efforts by the resellers, and it often requires a closer partnership with them. Exclusive distribution is used for new automobiles, some major appliances, and some women's apparel brands.

Exclusive distribution often includes *exclusive dealing* arrangements, especially in markets increasingly driven by price. When the legendary Italian designer label Gucci found its image severely tarnished by overexposure from licensing and discount stores, it decided to end contracts with third-party suppliers, control its distribution, and open its own stores to bring back some of the luster.[38]

**Selective distribution** relies on only some of the intermediaries willing to carry a particular product. Whether established or new, the company does not need to worry about having too many outlets; it can gain adequate market coverage with more control and less cost than intensive distribution. STIHL is a good example of successful selective distribution.[39]

Stihl has successfully adopted a selective distribution strategy that bypasses mass merchants, catalogs and the Internet.

**STIHL**   STIHL manufactures handheld outdoor power equipment. All its products are branded under one name, and it does not make private labels for other companies. Best known for its chain saws, the company has expanded into string trimmers, blowers, hedge trimmers, and cut-off machines. It sells exclusively to six independent U.S. distributors and six company-owned marketing and distribution centers, which sell to a nationwide network of more than 8,000 independent retail dealers offering service. STIHL also exports to 80 countries and is one of the few outdoor-power-equipment companies not selling through mass merchants, catalogs, or the Internet. It even ran an ad campaign called "Why" that touted the strength and support of its independent dealers with headlines such as "Why is the World's No. 1-selling brand of chain saw not sold at Lowe's or The Home Depot?" and "What makes this handblower too powerful to be sold at Lowe's or The Home Depot?"

**Intensive distribution** places the goods or services in as many outlets as possible. This strategy serves well for snack foods, soft drinks, newspapers, candies, and gum—products consumers buy frequently or in a variety of locations. Convenience stores such as 7-Eleven and Circle K and gas-station outlets like ExxonMobil's On the Run survive by providing simple location and time convenience.

Manufacturers are constantly tempted to move from exclusive or selective distribution to more intensive distribution to increase coverage and sales. This strategy may help in the short term, but if not done properly, it can hurt long-term performance by encouraging retailers to compete aggressively. Price wars can then erode profitability, dampening retailer interest and harming brand equity. Some firms do not want to be sold everywhere. After Sears acquired discount chain Kmart, Nike pulled all its products from Sears to make sure Kmart could not carry the brand.[40]

## TERMS AND RESPONSIBILITIES OF CHANNEL MEMBERS

Each channel member must be treated respectfully and be given the opportunity to be profitable. The main elements in the "trade relations mix" are price policies, conditions of sale, territorial rights, and specific services to be performed by each party.

- *Price policy* calls for the producer to establish a price list and schedule of discounts and allowances that intermediaries see as equitable and sufficient.
- *Conditions of sale* refers to payment terms and producer guarantees. Most producers grant cash discounts to distributors for early payment. They might also offer a guarantee against defective merchandise or price declines, creating an incentive to buy larger quantities.
- *Distributors' territorial rights* define the distributors' territories and the terms under which the producer will enfranchise other distributors. Distributors normally expect to receive full credit for all sales in their territory, whether or not they did the selling.
- *Mutual services and responsibilities* must be carefully spelled out, especially in franchised and exclusive-agency channels. McDonald's provides franchisees with a building, promotional support, a record-keeping system, training, and general administrative and technical assistance. In turn, franchisees are expected to satisfy company standards for the physical facilities, cooperate with new promotional programs, furnish requested information, and buy supplies from specified vendors, as well as pay monthly franchisee fees.

## EVALUATING MAJOR CHANNEL ALTERNATIVES

Each channel alternative needs to be evaluated against economic, control, and adaptive criteria.

**ECONOMIC CRITERIA** Every channel member will produce a different level of sales and costs. Figure 17.4 shows how six different sales channels stack up in terms of the value added per sale and the cost per transaction. For example, in the sale of industrial products costing between $2,000 and $5,000, the cost per transaction has been estimated at $500 (field sales), $200 (distributors), $50 (telesales), and $10 (Internet). A Booz Allen Hamilton study showed that at one time the average transaction at a full-service branch cost a bank $4.07, a phone transaction $.54, and an ATM transaction $.27, but a typical online transaction cost only $.01.[41]

Clearly, sellers try to replace high-cost channels with low-cost channels as long as the value added per sale is sufficient. Consider the following situation:

> A North Carolina furniture manufacturer wants to sell its line to retailers on the West Coast. One alternative is to hire 10 new sales representatives to operate out of a sales office in San Francisco and receive a base salary plus commissions. The other alternative is to use a San Francisco manufacturer's sales agency that has extensive contacts with retailers. Its 30 sales representatives would receive a commission based on their sales.

The first step is to estimate the dollar volume of sales each alternative will likely generate. A company sales force will concentrate on the company's products, be better trained to sell them, be more aggressive, and be more successful because many customers will prefer to deal directly with the company. The sales agency has 30 representatives, however, not just 10; it may be just as aggressive, depending on the commission level; customers may appreciate its independence; and it may have extensive contacts and market knowledge. The marketer needs to evaluate all these factors in formulating a demand function for the two different channels.

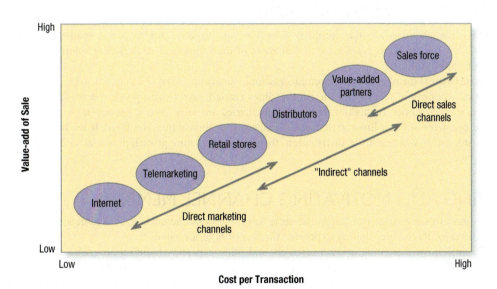

| **Fig. 17.4** |

The Value-Adds versus Costs of Different Channels

Source: Oxford Associates, adapted from Dr. Rowland T. Moriarty. Cubex Corp.

**| Fig. 17.5 |**

Break-Even Cost Chart for the Choice between a Company Sales Force and a Manufacturer's Sales Agency

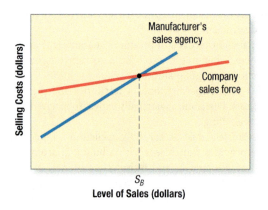

The next step is to estimate the costs of selling different volumes through each channel. The cost schedules are shown in Figure 17.5. Engaging a sales agency is less expensive, but costs rise faster because sales agents get larger commissions.

The final step is comparing sales and costs. As Figure 17.5 shows, there is one sales level ($S_B$) at which selling costs for the two channels are the same. The sales agency is thus the better channel for any sales volume below $S_B$, and the company sales branch is better at any volume above $S_B$. Given this information, it is not surprising that sales agents tend to be used by smaller firms or by large firms in smaller territories where the volume is low.

**CONTROL AND ADAPTIVE CRITERIA** Using a sales agency can pose a control problem. Agents may concentrate on the customers who buy the most, not necessarily those who buy the manufacturer's goods. They might not master the technical details of the company's product or handle its promotion materials effectively.

To develop a channel, members must commit to each other for a specified period of time. Yet these commitments invariably reduce the producer's ability to respond to change and uncertainty. The producer needs channel structures and policies that provide high adaptability.

# Channel-Management Decisions

After a company has chosen a channel system, it must select, train, motivate, and evaluate intermediaries for each channel. It must also modify channel design and arrangements over time, including the possibility of expansion into international markets.

## SELECTING CHANNEL MEMBERS

To customers, the channels are the company. Consider the negative impression customers would get of McDonald's, Shell Oil, or Mercedes-Benz if one or more of their outlets or dealers consistently appeared dirty, inefficient, or unpleasant.

To facilitate channel member selection, producers should determine what characteristics distinguish the better intermediaries—number of years in business, other lines carried, growth and profit record, financial strength, cooperativeness, and service reputation. If the intermediaries are sales agents, producers should evaluate the number and character of other lines carried and the size and quality of the sales force. If the intermediaries are department stores that want exclusive distribution, their locations, future growth potential, and type of clientele will matter.

## TRAINING AND MOTIVATING CHANNEL MEMBERS

A company needs to view its intermediaries the same way it views its end users. It should determine their needs and wants and tailor its channel offering to provide them with superior value.

Carefully implemented training, market research, and other capability-building programs can motivate and improve intermediaries' performance. The company must constantly communicate that intermediaries are crucial partners in a joint effort to satisfy end users of the product. Microsoft requires its third-party service engineers to complete a set of courses and take certification exams. Those who pass are formally recognized as Microsoft Certified Professionals and can use this designation to promote their own business. Other firms use customer surveys rather than exams.

**CHANNEL POWER** Producers vary greatly in their skill in managing distributors. **Channel power** is the ability to alter channel members' behavior so they take actions they would not have taken otherwise.[42] Manufacturers can draw on the following types of power to elicit cooperation:

- *Coercive power.* A manufacturer threatens to withdraw a resource or terminate a relationship if intermediaries fail to cooperate. This power can be effective, but its exercise produces resentment and can lead the intermediaries to organize countervailing power.
- *Reward power.* The manufacturer offers intermediaries an extra benefit for performing specific acts or functions. Reward power typically produces better results than coercive power, but intermediaries may come to expect a reward every time the manufacturer wants a certain behavior to occur.
- *Legitimate power.* The manufacturer requests a behavior that is warranted under the contract. As long as the intermediaries view the manufacturer as a legitimate leader, legitimate power works.
- *Expert power.* The manufacturer has special knowledge the intermediaries value. Once the intermediaries acquire this expertise, however, expert power weakens. The manufacturer must continue to develop new expertise so intermediaries will want to continue cooperating.
- *Referent power.* The manufacturer is so highly respected that intermediaries are proud to be associated with it. Companies such as IBM, Caterpillar, and Hewlett-Packard have high referent power.[43]

Coercive and reward power are objectively observable; legitimate, expert, and referent power are more subjective and depend on the ability and willingness of parties to recognize them.

Most producers see gaining intermediaries' cooperation as a huge challenge. They often use positive motivators, such as higher margins, special deals, premiums, cooperative advertising allowances, display allowances, and sales contests. At times they will apply negative sanctions, such as threatening to reduce margins, slow down delivery, or terminate the relationship. The weakness of this approach is that the producer is using crude, stimulus-response thinking.

In many cases, retailers hold the power. One estimate is that manufacturers offer the nation's supermarkets between 150 and 250 new items each week, of which store buyers reject more than 70 percent. Manufacturers need to know the acceptance criteria buyers, buying committees, and store managers use. ACNielsen interviews found that store managers were most influenced by strong evidence of consumer acceptance, a well-designed advertising and sales promotion plan, and generous financial incentives.

**CHANNEL PARTNERSHIPS** More sophisticated companies try to forge a long-term partnership with distributors.[44] The manufacturer clearly communicates what it wants from its distributors in the way of market coverage, inventory levels, marketing development, account solicitation, technical advice and services, and marketing information and may introduce a compensation plan for adhering to the policies.

To streamline the supply chain and cut costs, many manufacturers and retailers have adopted *efficient consumer response (ECR) practices* to organize their relationships in three areas: (1) *demand-side management,* or collaborative practices to stimulate consumer demand by promoting joint marketing and sales activities, (2) *supply-side management,* or collaborative practices to optimize supply (with a focus on joint logistics and supply chain activities), and (3) *enablers and integrators,* or collaborative information technology and process improvement tools to support joint activities that reduce operational problems, allow greater standardization, and so on.

Research has shown that although ECR has a positive impact on manufacturers' economic performance and capability development, manufacturers may also feel they are inequitably sharing the burdens of adopting it and not getting as much as they deserve from retailers.[45]

## EVALUATING CHANNEL MEMBERS

Producers must periodically evaluate intermediaries' performance against such standards as sales-quota attainment, average inventory levels, customer delivery time, treatment of damaged and lost goods, and cooperation in promotional and training programs. A producer will occasionally discover it is overpaying particular intermediaries for what they are actually doing. One manufacturer compensating a distributor for holding inventories found its goods were being held in a public warehouse at its own expense. Producers should set up functional discounts in which they pay specified amounts for the trade channel's performance of each agreed-upon service. Underperformers need to be counseled, retrained, motivated, or terminated.

## MODIFYING CHANNEL DESIGN AND ARRANGEMENTS

No channel strategy remains effective over the whole product life cycle. In competitive markets with low entry barriers, the optimal channel structure will inevitably change over time. New technologies have created digital channels undreamed of years ago. The change could mean adding or dropping individual market channels or channel members or developing a totally new way to sell goods. When new competition from Best Buy and Costco forced one-third of Leica's U.S. dealers to close, the high-end camera maker decided to open its own stylish stores to appeal to serious photographers.[46]

**CHANNEL EVOLUTION** A new firm typically starts as a local operation selling in a fairly circumscribed market, using a few existing intermediaries. Identifying the best channels might not be a problem; the problem is often to convince the available intermediaries to handle the firm's line.

If the firm is successful, it might branch into new markets with different channels. In smaller markets, it might sell directly to retailers; in larger markets, through distributors. In rural areas, it might work with general-goods merchants; in urban areas, with limited-line merchants. It may choose to create its own online store to sell directly to customers. It might grant exclusive franchises or sell through all willing outlets. In one country, the firm might use international sales agents; in another, it might partner with a local firm.

Early buyers might be willing to pay for high-value-added channels, but later buyers will switch to lower-cost channels. Small office copiers were first sold by manufacturers' direct sales forces, later through office equipment dealers, still later through mass merchandisers, and now by mail-order firms and Internet marketers. In short, the channel system evolves as a function of local opportunities and conditions, emerging threats and opportunities, and company resources and capabilities.

## CHANNEL MODIFICATION DECISIONS

A producer must periodically review and modify its channel design and arrangements.[47] The distribution channel may not work as planned, consumer buying patterns change, the market expands, new competition arises, innovative distribution channels emerge, and the product moves into later stages in the product life cycle.[48]

To add or drop individual channel members, the company needs to make an incremental analysis. Customer databases and sophisticated analysis tools can provide guidance.[49] A basic question is: What would the firm's sales and profits look like with and without this intermediary? Perhaps the most difficult decision is whether to revise the overall channel strategy.[50] Avon's door-to-door system for selling cosmetics was modified as more women left the house and entered the paid workforce.

## GLOBAL CHANNEL CONSIDERATIONS

International markets pose distinct challenges, including variations in customers' shopping habits and the need to gain social acceptance or legitimacy among others, but opportunities do exist.[51] U.S. retailers such as The Limited and the Gap have become globally prominent. Dutch retailer Ahold and Belgian retailer Delhaize earn almost two-thirds and three-quarters of their sales, respectively, in nondomestic markets. Among foreign-based global retailers in the United States are Italy's Benetton, Sweden's IKEA home furnishings stores, and Japan's UNIQLO casual apparel retailer.

Developing markets have become a target for many retailers. Franchised companies such as Subway sandwich shops have experienced double-digit growth overseas, especially in Brazil and Central and Eastern Europe. In some cases, *master franchisees* pay a significant fee to acquire a territory or country where they operate as "mini-franchisers" in their own right. More knowledgeable about local laws, customs, and consumer needs than foreign companies, they sell and oversee franchises and collect royalties.[52]

In India, sales from "organized retail"—hypermarkets, supermarkets, and department stores—make up only a small percentage of the huge market. As Chapter 8 noted, most shopping still takes place in millions of independent grocery stores or *kirana* shops, which are run by their owners and are popular because they extend credit and deliver even small orders. India's complex regulations, poor infrastructure, and expensive real estate also make it a difficult market for retail chains to enter.[53]

China has similar logistical challenges, though a growing middle class offers opportunity and firms such as Best Buy, Coach, and the Gap are meeting with some success.[54] But many pitfalls exist in global expansion. The world's top three retailers—U.S.-based Walmart, UK-based Tesco, and France-based Carrefour—all have struggled to enter certain overseas markets. Consider the plight of Tesco.[55]

Despite much consumer research and a sizable investment, British retailing giant Tesco's entry into the U.S. market, Fresh & Easy neighborhood markets, ultimately failed.

Source: © TJP/Alamy

**TESCO**   Tesco introduced its Fresh & Easy gourmet mini-supermarkets into California after much research that included spending time with U.S. families and videotaping the contents of their refrigerators. Fresh & Easy's 200 or so stores were roughly 10,000 square feet, about one-fifth the size of a standard U.S. supermarket but much bigger than a convenience store, with a focus on fresh-food offerings. Yet, after five unprofitable years and more than $1.6 billion in losses, Tesco decided to exit the market in 2013. A host of problems plagued the retailer. Its U.S. customers were unaccustomed to British-style ready meals, self-service cash registers, and unorthodox store layouts. Other complaints were that the product range was too narrow, there was no bakery and an underwhelming flower department, and the stores were physically too cold. The United States was not the only trouble spot for Tesco. The company had exited Japan the preceding year and was finding trouble in Central and Eastern Europe. While it focused on geographical expansion, its core supermarket business in the United Kingdom was neglected. Stores weren't properly staffed, fresh food was not properly maintained, and new private-label products were not introduced. The attempt to add non-grocery items like clothing and electronics proved difficult in a recession, and entry into new areas like banking and telephony was a distraction. After enduring six consecutive quarters of same-store sales declines in its home market, Tesco announced a $1.7 billion program to refresh its UK stores and a pull-back of its global ambitions.

The problems Tesco courted in the United Kingdom are a common downside of overly aggressive global expansion. Selling everything from food to televisions, Carrefour, the world's second-biggest retailer, has also encountered stiff competition at home, from smaller supermarkets for groceries and from specialist retailers such as IKEA for other goods. Although strong in some parts of Europe and Asia, Carrefour (which means "crossroads" in French) has been forced to cease operations in Japan, South Korea, Mexico, Czech Republic, Slovakia, Switzerland, and Portugal.[56]

The first step in global channel planning, as so often in marketing, is to get close to customers. To adapt its clothing lines to European tastes, Philadelphia-based Urban Outfitters set up a separate design and merchandising unit in London before it opened its first store in Europe. Although it increased costs, the distinctive blend of U.S. and European looks helped the retailer stand out, and it was one of the few fashion retailers to build strength during the recent recession.[57]

A good retail strategy that offers customers a positive shopping experience and unique value, if properly adapted, is likely to find success in more than one market. Take Topshop, for instance.[58]

Urban Outfitters carefully studied the European market to ensure its blend of fashion merchandise would appeal to consumer tastes there.

Source: © Loop Images Ltd/Alamy

**TOPSHOP**    Founded by Sir Richard Green in 1994, British clothing retailer Topshop is a chain of more than 300 UK stores and 130 franchise stores in 37 countries that commands intense loyalty from its trendy, style-obsessed customer base. Selling primarily women's party clothes, accessories, and daywear, the chain blends English street fashion, reasonable prices, and fun services. A higher-end, quirkier version of fast-fashion chains H&M and Zara, it allows middle-market consumers to dress trendily and affordably, in punk-inspired pinafores or ladylike tweed. New products are flown in two to three times a week, and store selections are updated multiple times in a day. Partnering with style icons Kate Moss, Stella Vine, and Celia Birtwell to create the latest designs, Topshop offers style advisors, Topshop-to-Go (a Tupperware-type party that brings a style advisor to a customer's home with outfits for as many as 10 people), and Topshop Express (an express delivery service via Vespa scooters for fashion "emergencies"). The company's Topman chain caters to a male audience. It seeks prime locations for its stores and complements them with an online store. The 60,000-square-foot store on Broadway in New York City is Topshop's second biggest and the first flagship store outside the United Kingdom. It has shop-in-shop locations in Nordstrom department stores throughout the United States and in the Karstadt department store chain in Germany.

# Channel Integration and Systems

Distribution channels don't stand still. We'll look at the recent growth of vertical, horizontal, and multichannel marketing systems. After considering some e-commerce and m-commerce issues, we next examine how these systems cooperate, conflict, and compete.

## VERTICAL MARKETING SYSTEMS

A **conventional marketing channel** consists of an independent producer, wholesaler(s), and retailer(s). Each is a separate business seeking to maximize its own profits, even if this goal reduces profit for the system as a whole. No channel member has complete or substantial control over other members.

A **vertical marketing system (VMS)**, by contrast, includes the producer, wholesaler(s), and retailer(s) acting as a unified system. One channel member, the *channel captain,* sometimes called a *channel steward,* owns or franchises the others or has so much power that they all cooperate. Stewards accomplish channel coordination without issuing commands or directives by persuading channel partners to act in the best interest of all.[59]

A channel steward might be the maker of the product or service (Procter & Gamble or American Airlines), the maker of a key component (microchip maker Intel), the supplier or assembler (Dell or Arrow Electronics), or the distributor (W.W. Grainger) or retailer (Walmart). Within a company, stewardship might rest with the CEO, a top manager, or a team of senior managers.

Channel stewardship has two important outcomes. First, it expands value for the steward's customers, enlarging the market or increasing existing customers' purchases through the channel. Second, it creates a more tightly woven and yet adaptable channel in which valuable members are rewarded and the less valuable are weeded out.

VMSs arose from strong channel members' attempts to control channel behavior and eliminate conflict over independent members pursuing their own objectives. These systems achieve economies through size, bargaining power, and elimination of duplicated services. Business buyers of complex products and systems value the extensive exchange of information they can offer.[60] VMSs have become the dominant mode of distribution in the U.S. consumer marketplace, serving 70 percent to 80 percent of the market. There are three types: corporate, administered, and contractual.

**CORPORATE VMS** A *corporate VMS* combines successive stages of production and distribution under single ownership. For years, Sears obtained more than half the goods it sells from companies it partly or wholly owned. Sherwin-Williams makes paint but also owns and operates 3,500 retail outlets.

**ADMINISTERED VMS** An *administered VMS* coordinates successive stages of production and distribution through the size and power of one of the members. Manufacturers of dominant brands can secure strong trade cooperation and support from resellers. Thus, Frito-Lay, Procter & Gamble, and Campbell Soup command high levels of cooperation from their resellers in the matter of displays, shelf space, promotions, and price policies. The most advanced supply-distributor arrangement for administered VMSs relies on **distribution programming**, which builds a planned, professionally managed, vertical marketing system that meets the needs of both manufacturer and distributors.

**CONTRACTUAL VMS** A *contractual VMS* consists of independent firms at different levels of production and distribution integrating their programs on a contractual basis to obtain more economies or sales impact than they could achieve alone.[61] Sometimes thought of as "value-adding partnerships" (VAPs), contractual VMSs come in three types:

1. *Wholesaler-sponsored voluntary chains*—Wholesalers organize voluntary chains of independent retailers to help standardize their selling practices and achieve buying economies in competing with large chain organizations.
2. *Retailer cooperatives*—Retailers take the initiative and organize a new business entity to carry on wholesaling and possibly some production. Members concentrate their purchases through the retailer co-op and plan their advertising jointly, sharing in profits in proportion to their purchases. Nonmember retailers can also buy through the co-op but do not share in the profits.
3. *Franchise organizations*—A channel member called a *franchisor* might link several successive stages in the production-distribution process. Franchising has been the fastest-growing retailing development in recent years.

Although the basic idea is an old one, some forms of franchising are quite new. The traditional system is the *manufacturer-sponsored retailer franchise*. Ford licenses independent businesspeople to sell its cars who agree to meet specified conditions of sales and services. Another system is the *manufacturer-sponsored wholesaler franchise*. Coca-Cola licenses bottlers (wholesalers) in various markets that buy its syrup concentrate and then carbonate, bottle, and sell it to retailers in local markets. A newer system is the *service-firm-sponsored retailer franchise*, organized by a service firm to bring its service efficiently to consumers. We find examples in auto rental (Hertz and Avis), fast food (McDonald's and Burger King), and the motel business (Howard Johnson and Ramada Inn). In a dual distribution system, firms use both vertical integration (the franchisor actually owns and runs the units) and market governance (the franchisor licenses the units to other franchisees).[62]

**THE NEW COMPETITION IN RETAILING** Many independent retailers that have not joined VMSs have developed specialty stores serving special market segments. The result is a polarization in retailing between large vertical marketing organizations and independent specialty stores, which creates a problem for manufacturers. They are strongly tied to independent intermediaries but must eventually realign themselves with the high-growth vertical marketing systems on less attractive terms. Furthermore, vertical marketing systems constantly threaten to bypass large manufacturers and set up their own manufacturing. The new competition in retailing is no longer between independent business units but between whole systems of centrally programmed networks (corporate, administered, and contractual), competing against one another to achieve the best cost economies and customer response.

## HORIZONTAL MARKETING SYSTEMS

Another channel development is the **horizontal marketing system**, in which two or more unrelated companies put together resources or programs to exploit an emerging marketing opportunity. Each company lacks the capital, know-how, production, or marketing resources to venture alone, or it is afraid of the risk. The companies might work together on a temporary or permanent basis or create a joint venture company.

For example, many supermarket chains have arrangements with local banks to offer in-store banking. Citizens Bank has more than 500 branches in supermarkets, making up roughly one-third of its branch network. Citizens's staff members in these locations are more sales oriented, younger, and more likely to have some retail sales background than staff in the traditional brick-and-mortar branches.[63]

# E-Commerce Marketing Practices

**E-commerce** uses a Web site to transact or facilitate the sale of products and services online. Online retail sales have exploded, and it is easy to see why. Online retailers can predictably provide convenient, informative, and personalized experiences for vastly different types of consumers and businesses. By saving the cost of retail floor space, staff, and inventory, they can also profitably sell low-volume products to niche markets.

While consumers often go online to try to find lower prices,[64] online retailers in fact compete in three key aspects of a transaction: (1) customer interaction with the Web site, (2) delivery, and (3) ability to address problems when they occur.[65]

We can distinguish between **pure-click** companies, those that have launched a Web site without any previous existence as a firm, and **brick-and-click** companies, existing companies that have added an online site for information or e-commerce.

## PURE-CLICK COMPANIES

There are several kinds of pure-click companies: search engines, Internet service providers (ISPs), commerce sites, transaction sites, content sites, and enabler sites. Commerce sites sell all types of products and services, notably books, music, toys, insurance, stocks, clothes, financial services, and so on. They use various strategies to compete: AutoNation is a leading metamediary of car buying and related services; Hotels.com is the information leader in hotel reservations; Buy.com leads on price.

**E-COMMERCE SUCCESS FACTORS** Companies must set up and operate their e-commerce Web sites carefully. Customer service is critical. Online shoppers may select an item for purchase but fail to complete the transaction. Worse, only 2 percent to 3 percent of visits to online retailers lead to sales, compared with 5 percent of visits to department stores.[66]

To improve conversion rates, firms should make the Web site fast, simple, and easy to use. Something as simple as enlarging product images on screen can increase perusal time and the amount customers buy.[67] Some of the larger e-commerce firms such as eBay and Amazon are offering same-day delivery in major markets.[68] A good return policy is also crucial.[69] To drive traffic to a site, many firms employ affiliate marketing, paying online content providers to drive business to their brands' sites.[70]

Consumer surveys suggest that the most significant inhibitors of online shopping are the absence of pleasurable experiences, social interaction, and personal consultation with a company representative.[71] Firms have responded. Many now offer live online chat to give potential customers immediate advice about products and suggest additional items. When a representative is active in the sale, the average dollar amount per order is typically higher. B-to-B marketers also need to put a human face on their e-commerce presence, and some are taking advantage of technologies such as virtual environments, blogs, online videos, and click-to-chat.

To increase customer satisfaction and the entertainment and information value of online shopping experiences, some firms are employing *avatars,* animated characters that act as company representatives, personal shopping assistants, Web site guides, or conversation partners. Avatars can enhance the effectiveness of an online sales channel, especially if they are seen as expert or attractive.[72]

Ensuring security and privacy online remains important. Customers must find the Web site trustworthy, even if it represents an already highly credible offline firm. Investments in Web site design and security can help reassure customers sensitive to online risk.[73]

**B-TO-B E-COMMERCE** Although business-to-consumer (B-to-C) Web sites have attracted much attention in the media, even more activity is being conducted on business-to-business (B-to-B) sites, which are changing the supplier–customer relationship in profound ways.

In the past, buyers exerted a lot of effort to gather information about worldwide suppliers. B-to-B sites make markets more efficient, giving buyers easy access to a great deal of information from (1) supplier Web sites; (2) *infomediaries,* third parties that add value by aggregating information about alternatives; (3) *market makers,* third parties that link buyers and sellers; and (4) *customer communities*, where buyers can swap stories about suppliers' products and services.[74]

Firms are using B-to-B auction sites, spot exchanges, online product catalogs, barter sites, and other online resources to obtain better prices. Ironically, the largest of the B-to-B market makers is Alibaba, homegrown in China where businesses have faced decades of Communist hostility to private enterprise.[75]

**ALIBABA**   The brainchild of Jack Ma, Alibaba began in 1999 and has grown through the years to become the world's largest online marketplace, allowing people and businesses to buy and sell any type of product—from Fuji apples to Boeing 737s. Its numbers are staggering. The $15 billion company has 500 million registered users on nine platforms in 220 countries and regions and enjoys about 80 percent of the Chinese e-commerce market. On Singles' Day on November 11, 2012—a local twist on Valentine's Day and China's biggest online shopping day—Taoboa (a consumer-to-consumer marketplace) and Tmall (a business-to-consumer marketplace), Alibaba's two main platforms, topped $5.75 billion in sales from 400 million unique visitors in 24 hours. More than 10 million of the 16 million parcels delivered in China each day originate from Taobao and Tmall, so logistics providers are crucial (there are no UPS or FedEx counterparts). A cross between Amazon.com, eBay, Rackspace, and PayPal, Alibaba makes money primarily from commissions and from advertising by buyers and sellers exchanging goods. To establish customer trust, the company set up TrustPass, in which users pay Alibaba a fee to hire a third party that verifies them. Users must have five people vouch for them and provide a list of all their certificates/business licenses. Anyone who has done business with a user is encouraged to comment, in the same way buyers comment on sellers in Amazon.com's or eBay's marketplace. The company is valued at more than $120 billion, making Yahoo's 24 percent stake in it a very wise investment.

The effect of these B-to-B mechanisms is to make prices more transparent. For undifferentiated products, price pressure will increase. For highly differentiated products, buyers will gain a better picture of the items' true value. Suppliers of superior products will be able to offset price transparency with value transparency; suppliers of undifferentiated products will need to drive down their costs in order to compete.

## BRICK-AND-CLICK COMPANIES

Although many brick-and-mortar companies once hesitated to open an e-commerce channel for fear of conflict with their channel partners, most have added the Internet after seeing how much business was generated online.[76] Even Procter & Gamble, which used traditional physical channels of distribution exclusively for years, is selling some big brands such as Tide, Pampers, and Olay online via its P&G e-store, in part to be able to examine consumer shopping habits more closely.[77] One study showed that more than a third of Internet users have made purchases directly from brand Web sites.[78]

Managing the online and offline channels has thus become a priority for many firms.[79] There are at least three strategies for trying to gain acceptance from intermediaries. One, offer different brands or products online and offline. Two, offer offline partners higher commissions to cushion the negative impact on sales. Three, take orders on the Web site but have retailers deliver and collect payment. Harley-Davidson decided to tread carefully before going online.[80]

**HARLEY-DAVIDSON**   Given that Harley-Davidson sells more than $1 billion worth of parts and accessories and general merchandise to its loyal followers—generating roughly one-quarter of its annual revenue—an online venture to reach even more customers was an obvious next step. The company needed to be careful, however, to avoid the wrath of its 850 dealers who benefit from high margins on their sales. Its solution was to prompt online customers to select a participating Harley dealer from which to purchase, ensuring that the dealer remains the focal point of the customer experience. Dealers, in turn, agreed to a number of standards, such as checking for orders twice a day and shipping promptly. In-store pickup is also an option, and some products are available only in-store.

Harley-Davidson made sure to not anger its loyal dealer network when it expanded online distribution for its parts and accessories and general merchandise.

Source: © picturesbyrob/Alamy

# M-Commerce Marketing Practices

Mobile channels and media can keep consumers as connected and interacting with a brand as they choose. By mid-2013, more than half of all online U.S. buyers had made a purchase on a mobile device, and m-commerce accounted for more than 11 percent of all e-commerce.[81] Tablets are expected to overtake smart phones for mobile shopping, and one estimate says tablets will make up more than 70 percent of mobile retail sales by 2017.[82]

In some parts of the world, m-commerce is very well established. Asian consumers use their mobile phones as their main computers and benefit from a well-developed mobile infrastructure. Mobile ads are well accepted by consumers and relatively inexpensive for firms. In South Korea, Tesco created virtual subway stores for commuters traveling on Seoul's underground transportation system. Interactive, lifelike store aisles with a wide range of product and brand images were superimposed on walls. Consumers could order products for home delivery by simply snapping photos with their phones.[83]

Millions of Japanese teenagers carry DOCOMO phones available from NTT (Nippon Telephone and Telegraph), the country's largest mobile service provider with an ultra-high-speed LTE network. They can also use their phones to order goods. Each month, subscribers receive a bill from NTT listing the monthly subscriber fee, usage fee, and cost of all m-commerce transactions.[84]

M-commerce is well-established in South Korea where virtual stores have been introduced into underground subway stations.

Source: ASSOCIATED PRESS

In the United States, mobile marketing is becoming more prevalent and taking all forms. It is easy to understand how entertainment, travel, sporting events, and other time-sensitive categories can benefit from mobile phone apps, but the impact of m-commerce extends far beyond these. Consumers and companies are adapting.[85] Look at Dunkin' Donuts.[86]

**DUNKIN' DONUTS** An early mobile marketer, Dunkin' Donuts has refined its DD Perks program as part of its corporate goal to lead in digital mobility in the QSR (Quick Serve Restaurant) industry. The DD program was integrated into the company's unified point-of-sales and mobile app to reward loyal customers and encourage them to visit more often and spend more on each visit. The mobile app received 3.5 million downloads in the first year alone. By constructing a purchase history and profile for customers, Dunkin' Donuts can offer more customized and geographically targeted offers that change as customers go from market to market. The app includes a store locator feature and lets customers pay for drinks and meals with a bar code scanned at the point of sale. The company also uses Twitter to run quick, fun promotions and sweepstakes for its on-the-go customers.

## CHANGES IN CUSTOMER AND COMPANY BEHAVIOR

Consumers are fundamentally changing the way they shop in stores, increasingly using a cell phone to text a friend or relative about a product while shopping in stores. Fifty percent of all Google searches are done on mobile phones.[87] Women may use smart phones more than men in all phases of the shopping experience, making shopping lists and product wish lists, collecting coupons, and sharing photos of their purchases.[88]

Companies are trying to give their customers more control over their shopping experiences by bringing Web technologies into the store, especially via mobile apps. Consider these two examples:

- Although Nordstrom expected its app to be used remotely, many customers launched it while shopping in a store rather than approaching a salesperson. As one executive noted, "A lot of customers like to touch and feel and try on the merchandise, but they also want the information they get online." Nordstrom has added Wi-Fi to almost all its stores, in part so its app will work fast.[89]
- American Express launched its "Link-Like-Love" social commerce program, which sends cardmembers couponless personalized offers from merchants based on their Facebook "likes" and Facebook Places check-ins that are automatically redeemed through card use. Via a partnership with Foursquare, cardmembers could also automatically receive and redeem promotional offers from merchants based on their Foursquare activity.[90]

## M-COMMERCE MARKETING PRACTICES

Marketers are using a number of new and traditional practices in m-marketing.

**ADVERTISING AND PROMOTION** Understanding how consumers want to use their smart phones is critical to understanding the role of advertising. Given the small screen and fleeting attention paid, fulfilling advertising's traditional role of informing and persuading is more challenging for m-commerce marketers. On the plus side, consumers are more engaged and attentive with their smart phones than when they are online.[91] Nevertheless, a number of m-commerce companies are eliminating ads to allow consumers to make purchases with as few clicks as possible.[92]

*Source: Dunkin' Donuts*

Dunkin' Donuts is determined to be a market leader in digital mobility for its products and brands.

Outdoor supplier North Face targets customers with mobile promotions at parks and ski resorts as well as near its stores.

Promotions are a different story. Consumers often use their smart phones to find deals or capitalize on them: the redemption rate for mobile coupons (10 percent) far exceeds that of paper coupons (1 percent).[93] For retailers, research has shown that mobile promotions can get consumers to travel greater distances within a store and make more unplanned purchases.[94]

**GEOFENCING** The idea of *geofencing* is to target customers with a mobile promotion when they are within a defined geographical space, typically near or in a store. The local-based service requires just an app and GPS coordinates, but consumers have to opt in. Consider these applications: [95]

- Neiman-Marcus is piloting geofencing in its stores so its salespeople know when their more valuable customers are on the premises and can look at their purchase history to provide more personalized service.
- Outdoor supplier North Face uses geofences around parks and ski resorts in addition to its stores.
- Cosmetics brand retailer Kiehl's uses geofencing around its free-standing stores and kiosks within other stores. It advertises the alerts at its cash register and on social media pages and e-mails list, and it offers customers a free lip balm for enrolling. Thousands have done so, but the company limits it texts to three per month to avoid being intrusive.

## PRIVACY

The fact that a company can pinpoint a customer's or employee's location with GPS technology raises privacy issues. Like so many new technologies, such location-based services have potential for good and harm and will ultimately warrant public scrutiny and regulation.

Many consumers are happy to tolerate cookies, profiles, and other online tools that let e-commerce businesses know who they are and when and how they shop, but they are nevertheless concerned when such tracking occurs in the store. When Nordstrom informed customers it was testing new technology to track customers' movements by following the Wi-Fi signals from their smart phones, some consumers objected, leading Nordstrom to drop the experiment.[96]

# Conflict, Cooperation, and Competition

No matter how well channels are designed and managed, there will be some conflict, if only because the interests of independent business entities do not always coincide. **Channel conflict** is generated when one channel member's actions prevent another channel member from achieving its goal. Software giant Oracle Corp., plagued by conflict between its high-powered sales force and its vendor partners, has tried a number of solutions, including rolling out new

"All Partner Territories" where all deals except for specific strategic accounts go through select Oracle partners and allowing partners to secure bigger $1 billion-plus accounts.[97]

**Channel coordination** occurs when channel members are brought together to advance the goals of the channel instead of their own potentially incompatible goals.[98] Here we examine three questions: What types of conflict arise in channels? What causes conflict? What can marketers do to resolve it?

## TYPES OF CONFLICT AND COMPETITION

Suppose a manufacturer sets up a vertical channel consisting of wholesalers and retailers hoping for channel cooperation and greater profits for each member. Yet horizontal, vertical, and multichannel conflict can occur.

- *Horizontal channel conflict* occurs between channel members at the same level. Some Pizza Inn franchisees complained about others cheating on ingredients, providing poor service, and hurting the overall brand image.
- *Vertical channel conflict* occurs between different levels of the channel. When Estée Lauder set up a Web site to sell its Clinique and Bobbi Brown brands, the department store Dayton Hudson reduced the space it gave the company's products.[99] Greater retailer consolidation—the 10 largest U.S. retailers account for more than 80 percent of the average manufacturer's business—has led to increased price pressure and influence from retailers.[100] Walmart, for example, is the principal buyer for many manufacturers, including Disney, Procter & Gamble, and Revlon, and is able to command reduced prices or quantity discounts from these and other suppliers.[101]
- *Multichannel conflict* exists when the manufacturer has established two or more channels that sell to the same market.[102] It's likely to be especially intense when the members of one channel get a lower price (based on larger-volume purchases) or work with a lower margin. When Goodyear began selling its popular tire brands through Sears, Walmart, and Discount Tire, it angered its independent dealers and eventually placated them by offering exclusive tire models not sold in other retail outlets.

## CAUSES OF CHANNEL CONFLICT

Some causes of channel conflict are easy to resolve; others are not. Conflict may arise from:

- **Goal incompatibility.** The manufacturer may want to achieve rapid market penetration through a low-price policy. Dealers, in contrast, may prefer to work with high margins and pursue short-run profitability.
- **Unclear roles and rights.** HP may sell laptops to large accounts through its own sales force, but its licensed dealers may also be trying to sell to large accounts. Territory boundaries and credit for sales often produce conflict.
- **Differences in perception.** The manufacturer may be optimistic about the short-term economic outlook and want dealers to carry higher inventory, while the dealers may be pessimistic. In the beverage category, it is not uncommon for disputes to arise between manufacturers and their distributors about the optimal advertising strategy.
- **Intermediaries' dependence on the manufacturer.** The fortunes of exclusive dealers, such as auto dealers, are profoundly affected by the manufacturer's product and pricing decisions. This situation creates a high potential for conflict.

## MANAGING CHANNEL CONFLICT

Some channel conflict can be constructive and lead to better adaptation to a changing environment, but too much is dysfunctional.[103] The challenge is not to eliminate all conflict, which is impossible, but to manage it better. Verbal reprimands, fines, withheld bonuses, and other remedies can punish a firm in violation and deter others.[104] Table 17.2 lists some mechanisms for effective conflict management that we discuss next.[105]

***Strategic Justification*** In some cases, a convincing strategic justification that they serve distinctive segments and do not compete as much as they might think can reduce potential for conflict among channel members. Developing special versions of products for different channel members—branded variants as described in Chapter 11—is a clear way to demonstrate that distinctiveness.[106]

***Dual Compensation*** Dual compensation pays existing channels for sales made through new channels. When Allstate started selling insurance online, it agreed to pay agents a 2 percent commission for face-to-face service to customers who got their quotes online. Although lower than the agents' typical 10 percent commission for offline transactions, it did reduce tensions.[107]

| TABLE 17.2 | Strategies to Manage Channel Conflict |
|---|---|
| Strategic justification | |
| Dual compensation | |
| Superordinate goals | |
| Employee exchange | |
| Joint memberships | |
| Co-optation | |
| Diplomacy, mediation, or arbitration | |
| Legal recourse | |

*Superordinate Goals* Channel members can come to an agreement on the fundamental or superordinate goal they are jointly seeking, whether it is survival, market share, high quality, or customer satisfaction. They usually do this best when the channel faces an outside threat, such as a more efficient competing channel, an adverse piece of legislation, or a shift in consumer desires.

*Employee Exchange* A useful step is to exchange persons between two or more channel levels. GM's executives might agree to work for a short time in some dealerships, and some dealership owners might work in GM's dealer policy department. Thus participants can grow to appreciate each other's point of view.

*Joint Memberships* Similarly, marketers can encourage joint memberships in trade associations. Good cooperation between the Grocery Manufacturers of America and the Food Marketing Institute, which represents most of the food chains, led to the development of the universal product code (UPC). The associations can consider issues between food manufacturers and retailers and resolve them in an orderly way.

*Co-optation* Co-optation is an effort by one organization to win the support of the leaders of another by including them in advisory councils, boards of directors, and the like. If the organization treats invited leaders seriously and listens to their opinions, co-optation can reduce conflict, but the initiator may need to compromise its policies and plans to win outsiders' support.

*Diplomacy, Mediation, and Arbitration* When conflict is chronic or acute, the parties may need to resort to stronger means. **Diplomacy** takes place when each side sends a person or group to meet with its counterpart to resolve the conflict. **Mediation** relies on a neutral third party skilled in conciliating the two parties' interests. In **arbitration**, two parties agree to present their arguments to one or more arbitrators and accept their decision.

Sometimes channel conflicts have to be settled by legal recourse as with Coca-Cola and its dispute with Walmart over Powerade.

Source: Getty Images News

*Legal Recourse* If nothing else proves effective, a channel partner may choose to file a lawsuit.[108] When Coca-Cola decided to distribute Powerade thirst quencher directly to Walmart's regional warehouses, 60 bottlers complained the practice would undermine their core direct-store-distribution (DSD) duties and filed suit. A settlement allowed for the mutual exploration of new service and distribution systems to supplement the DSD system.[109]

## DILUTION AND CANNIBALIZATION

Marketers must be careful not to dilute their brands through inappropriate channels, particularly luxury brands whose images often rest on exclusivity and personalized service. Calvin Klein and Tommy Hilfiger both took a hit when they sold too many of their products in discount channels.

Given the lengths to which they go to pamper customers in their stores—with doormen, glasses of champagne, and extravagant surroundings—luxury brands have had to work hard to provide a high-quality digital experience. They aren't forgetting their stores, though, and are increasingly blending the two. Gucci partnered with Samsung Electronics to create an immersive in-store experience for its timepieces and jewelry that combines physical and mobile commerce. Stores feature transparent displays that show images on the screen without obscuring the products behind them and a digital shop-in-shop section where customers can use tablet computers to browse.[110] To reach affluent customers who work long hours and have little time to shop, many high-end fashion brands such as Dior, Louis Vuitton, and Fendi have unveiled e-commerce sites for researching items before visiting a store—and a means to combat fakes sold online.

## LEGAL AND ETHICAL ISSUES IN CHANNEL RELATIONS

Companies are generally free to develop whatever channel arrangements suit them. The law seeks to prevent only exclusionary tactics that might keep competitors from using a channel. Here we briefly consider the legality of certain practices, including exclusive dealing, exclusive territories, tying agreements, and dealers' rights.

We saw earlier that in *exclusive distribution*, only certain outlets are allowed to carry a seller's products, and that requiring these dealers not to handle competitors' products is called *exclusive dealing*. Both channel partners benefit from exclusive arrangements: The seller obtains more loyal and dependable outlets, and the dealer gets a steady supply of special products and stronger seller support. Exclusive arrangements are legal as long as they do not substantially lessen competition or tend to create a monopoly and as long as both parties enter into them voluntarily.

Exclusive dealing often includes exclusive territorial agreements. The producer may agree not to sell to other dealers in a given area, or the buyer may agree to sell only in its own territory. The first practice increases dealer enthusiasm and commitment. It is also perfectly legal—a seller has no legal obligation to sell through more outlets than it wishes. The second practice, whereby the producer tries to keep a dealer from selling outside its territory, has become a major legal issue.

Producers of a strong brand sometimes sell it to dealers only if they will take some or all of the rest of the line. This practice is called *full-line forcing*. Such **tying agreements** are not necessarily illegal, but they do violate U.S. law if they tend to lessen competition substantially.

Producers are free to select their dealers, but their right to terminate them is somewhat restricted. In general, sellers can drop dealers "for cause," but not if, for example, a dealer refuses to cooperate in a doubtful legal arrangement, such as exclusive dealing or tying agreements.

# Summary

1. Most producers do not sell their goods directly to final users. Between producers and final users stands one or more marketing channels, a host of marketing intermediaries performing a variety of functions.

2. Marketing channel decisions are among the most critical decisions facing management. The company's chosen channel(s) profoundly affect all other marketing decisions.

3. Companies use intermediaries when they lack the financial resources to carry out direct marketing, when direct marketing is not feasible, and when they can earn more by doing so. The most important functions performed by intermediaries are information, promotion, negotiation, ordering, financing, risk taking, physical possession, payment, and title.

4. Manufacturers have many alternatives for reaching a market. They can sell direct or use one-, two-, or three-level channels. Deciding which type(s) of channel to use calls for analyzing customer needs, establishing channel objectives, and identifying and evaluating the major alternatives, including the types and numbers of intermediaries involved in the channel.

5. Effective channel management calls for selecting intermediaries and training and motivating them. The goal is to build a long-term partnership that will be profitable for all channel members.

6. Marketing channels are characterized by continuous and sometimes dramatic change. Three of the most important trends are the growth of vertical marketing systems, horizontal marketing systems, and multichannel marketing systems.

7. E-commerce has become firmly established as more companies have adopted "brick-and-click" channel systems. M-commerce (selling via smart phones and tablets) is also gaining in importance. Some consumers engage in showrooming by which they shop in stores to inspect products but buy online later to seek a lower price.

8. Channel integration must recognize the distinctive strengths of online, offline, and mobile selling and maximize their joint contributions.

9. All marketing channels have the potential for conflict and competition resulting from goal incompatibility, poorly defined roles and rights, perceptual differences, and interdependent relationships. Companies can try to manage conflict through dual compensation, superordinate goals, employee exchange, co-optation, and other means.

10. Channel arrangements are up to the company, but certain legal and ethical issues to be considered include exclusive dealing or territories, tying agreements, and dealers' rights.

---

## MyMarketingLab

Go to **mymktlab.com** to complete the problems marked with this icon ⭐ as well as for additional Auto-graded and Assisted-graded writing questions.

---

# Applications

## Marketing **Debate**
### Does It Matter Where You Sell?

Some marketers feel that the image of the particular channel in which they sell their products does not matter—all that matters is that the right customers shop there and the product is displayed in the right way. Others maintain that channel images—such as a retail store—can be critical and must be consistent with the image of the product.

**Take a position:** Channel images do not much affect the brand images of the products they sell *versus* Channel images must be consistent with the brand image.

## Marketing **Discussion**
### Channel Integration

⭐ Think of your favorite retailers. How have they integrated their channel system? How would you like their channels to be integrated? Do you use multiple channels from them? Why?

---

## Marketing **Excellence**

### >> Amazon.com

Founded by Jeff Bezos in 1995, Amazon.com started as the "world's largest bookstore" and, ironically, owned no books. Bezos promised to revolutionize retailing, however, and over the years he has blazed a trail of e-commerce innovations that many executives have studied and companies have followed.

Amazon initially set out to create personalized storefronts for each customer by providing more useful information and more choices than found in a neighborhood bookstore. Readers could review books and evaluate them on a one- to five-star rating scale, while fellow browsers could rate the reviews for helpfulness. The company's personal recommendation service aggregated buying-pattern data to infer who might like which book. Amazon also introduced its revolutionary one-click shopping, which allowed buyers to make purchases effortlessly with a single click.

Amazon started to diversify its product line in the late 1990s, first with DVDs and videos and then with consumer electronics, games, toys, software, video games, and gifts. The company continued to expand its product offerings and in 2007 launched Amazon Video On Demand, allowing consumers to rent or purchase films and television shows to watch on their computers or televisions. Later that year, it introduced Amazon MP3, which competed directly with Apple's iTunes and had participation from all the major music labels.

Amazon's most successful product launch was the Kindle, its branded electronic book reader that delivered hundreds of thousands of books, magazines, blogs, and newspapers in a matter of seconds. As thin as a magazine and light as a paperback, the device has been the company's best-selling product since 2009. Today, you can find virtually anything you want on Amazon.com. The company has successfully established itself as the biggest online retailer in the world by enabling merchants of all kinds to sell items on the site.

In addition to its core business, Amazon also runs an "Associates" program that allows independent sellers and businesses to receive commissions for referring customers to the site in a variety of ways, including direct links and banner ads as well as Amazon Widgets, mini-applications that feature the company's wide selection of products. Associates can create an Amazon-operated online store easily, with low risk and no additional cost or programming knowledge. Fulfillment by Amazon (FBA) takes care of picking, packing, and shipping the merchant's products to its customers.

One consistent key to Amazon's success is its willingness to invest in the latest technology to make shopping online faster, easier, and more personally rewarding for its customers and third-party merchants. During peak season in 2012, the company sold approximately 306 items per second, or 26 million items per day. Small wonder that it continually looks for ways to improve delivery. For a $99 annual fee, Amazon Prime provides unlimited free express shipping for millions of items. While free shipping and price cuts are sometimes unpopular with investors, Bezos believes they build customer satisfaction, loyalty, and frequency of purchase orders.

In 2013, Amazon.com announced a partnership with the U.S. Postal Service to begin delivering orders on Sundays. Bezos also predicted on *60 Minutes* that the company may use drones in the near future to make same-day delivery of lightweight products within short distances of distribution warehouses. (Critics find this unlikely for many reasons, though.)

Amazon has also maintained competitive and low prices throughout its product expansion. The company understands how important it is to keep its prices low in order to drive the volume it needs to remain a market leader and expand geographically. Amazon's practice of selling books at heavily discounted prices, however, has upset some of its channel partners in publishing, as have its attempts to become a publisher in its own right.

From the beginning, Bezos has said that even though he started an online bookstore, he eventually wanted to sell *everything to everyone* through Amazon.com. The company continues to invest significantly in technology, is focused on the long term, and has successfully positioned itself as a technology company with its wide range of Amazon Web Services. This growing collection of infrastructure applications meets the retailing needs of companies of virtually all sizes. Amazon has successfully reinvented itself time and again and created a critical channel for merchants around the world who are able to reach more than 244 million customers worldwide.

## Questions

1. Why has Amazon succeeded online when so many other companies have failed?

2. Will the Kindle revolutionize the book industry? Why or why not?

3. What's next for Amazon? Where else can it grow?

**Sources:** "Click to Download," *Economist*, August 19, 2006, pp. 57–58; Robert D. Hof, "Jeff Bezos' Risky Bet," *BusinessWeek*, November 13, 2006; Erick Schonfield, "The Great Giveaway," *Business 2.0*, April 2005, pp. 80–86; Elizabeth West, "Who's Next?," *Potentials*, February 2004, pp. 7–8; Robert D. Hof, "The Wizard of Web Retailing," *BusinessWeek*, December 20, 2004, p. 18; Chris Taylor, "Smart Library," *Time*, November 17, 2003, p. 68; Deborah Solomon, "Questions for Jeffrey P. Bezos," *New York Times*, December 2, 2009; Patrick Seitz, "Amazon.com Whiz Jeff Bezos Keeps Kindling Hot Concepts," *Investors' Daily Business*, December 31, 2009; Alistair Barr, "Amazon Starts Sunday Delivery with U.S. Postal Service," *USA Today*, November 25, 2013; Adam Lashinsky, "Amazon's Jeff Bezos: The Ultimate Disrupter," *Fortune*, November 16, 2012; Michael Wolf, "Here's Why Amazon Drone Package Delivery May Never Happen," *Forbes*, December 2, 2013; Holman Jenkins Jr., "Jeff Bezos's Mysterious Amazon," *Wall Street Journal*, December 6, 2013; "Amazon's Jeff Bezos Looks to the Future," *60 Minutes*, CBS.com, December 1, 2013; Amazon 2012 Annual Report; George Parker, "Cheap Words," *New Yorker*, February 17, 2014.

## >> Costco

Costco's mission is "to continually provide our members with quality goods and services at the lowest possible prices." With more than 75 million card-carrying members and $110 billion in sales, it is the largest warehouse club chain in the United States and the third-largest retailer in the United States after Walmart and Kroger. The company's success comes from years of building consumer loyalty through its dedicated merchandising and pricing strategy, combined with no-frills, cost-cutting policies.

Costco's merchandising strategy focuses on offering a broad range of brand-name and private-label merchandise at extremely low prices. But unlike a grocery store that carries 40,000 SKUs or a Walmart that can carry up to 150,000, the company offers about 3,750 SKUs—only the fastest-selling flavors, sizes, models, and colors from a single vendor in each category. For example, it sells four brands of toothpaste compared with Walmart's 60. This efficient product sourcing results in several outcomes: high volume of sales, rapid inventory turnover, extremely low prices, and better product manageability.

Costco buys its merchandise directly from the manufacturer. Products are shipped directly to the company's warehouses or to a depot, which reallocates the shipments to warehouses within 24 hours. This process eliminates several steps such as using a distributor and other intermediaries, which avoids costs associated with storage, additional freight, and handling. At the warehouse, shipments are often taken directly to the floor, unwrapped, and left on the pallet, ready to sell.

Over the years, Costco has expanded its products and services from simple boxed items such as cereal and paper products to fresh produce and flowers, which must be displayed attractively and managed more closely. Today, the company sells dairy, baked goods, seafood, clothing, books, computer software, vacuums, home appliances, electronics, jewelry, tires, art, wine, liquor, hot tubs, and furniture. Its service departments include pharmacies, optometrists, photo processors, food courts, and gas stations. Costco's private label, Kirkland Signature, offers high-quality products at lower prices than the comparable branded item, ranging from diapers and bed sheets to coffee and makeup.

Of the 4,000 products sold, 3,000 are staples found at Costco week after week, while the remaining 1,000

rotate as part of the company's "treasure hunt." These special items are offered only temporarily and can be as exotic as Coach bags, Waterford crystal, and expensive jewelry. Costco believes its treasure hunt offerings create excitement and increase consumer loyalty, bringing bargain hunters back again and again.

The company's pricing strategy is transparent: It limits the markup of any branded item to 14 percent and any private-label item to 15 percent. (In comparison, supermarkets and department stores mark up anywhere from 25 percent to 50 percent.) If a manufacturer's price is too high, Costco will not restock the item. Founder and former CEO Jim Sinegal explained, "The traditional retailer will say: 'I'm selling this for $10. I wonder whether I can get $10.50 or $11.' We say: 'We're selling it for $9. How do we get it down to $8?'" One staple is the $1.50 hotdog and fountain drink combo, priced the same since 1985. In 2013, Costco sold about $168 million worth of the combo in the United States alone.

Costco's cost-saving tactics extend to the interiors its 634 warehouse-style stores around the world. Most average 143,000 square feet, with floor plans designed to optimize selling space, the handling of merchandise, and the control of inventory. Decor is simple: concrete floors, bare-bones signage, and product displays that consist of pallets right off the truck. Central skylights and day-lighting controls hold down energy usage, and the company also saves by not supplying shopping bags. Instead, consumers use their own bags or leftover boxes and crates stacked near cash registers. Costco spends little on marketing and promotions, except for the occasional direct mail to prospective new members and coupons to regular members.

The one area Costco does not cut costs is in its workforce. Employees earn an average of $17 per hour, 42 percent higher than Sam's Club salaries. In addition, 85 percent have health insurance, more than twice the percentage at Target or Walmart. As a result, employee turnover and employee theft are extremely low, and employees are better trained and dedicated to the company. Costco's loyal consumer base appreciates the fact that its deep discounts come from strategic business planning and are not at the workers' expense.

Costco's customers are not only loyal; many are affluent. Their average household income is $74,000; 31 percent earn more than $100,000 per year. Membership starts at $55 a year and can be upgraded to Executive levels that provide additional benefits. Costco accepts only debit cards, cash, checks, and

American Express. While consumers need membership to shop at the warehouse locations, nonmembers can shop online without it and pay an additional 5 percent fee for any purchase.

Costco's success has come from focusing on a handful of business practices: sell a limited number of items, keep costs down, rely on high volume, pay workers well, require consumers to buy memberships, and target upscale consumers and business owners. This vision has led to many achievements, including ranking number 22 in the *Fortune* 500 and number 23 on *Fortune*'s Most Admired list. Costco also was the first company to grow from zero to $3 billion in sales in less than six years.

**Questions**

1. What is unique about Costco's channel management process? Which of its channel practices can other retailers borrow or implement?

2. Where can Costco improve? Should it offer more products or advertise more? Why or why not?

**Sources:** Matthew Boyle, "Why Costco Is So Addictive," *Fortune,* October 25, 2006; Steven Greenhouse, "How Costco Became the Anti-Walmart," *New York Times,* July 17, 2005; Ashley Lutz, "The Formula That Made Costco the Anti-Walmart," *BusinessInsider,* November 27, 2012; Jessica Wohl, "Costco CEO's Legacy Continues as He Steps Down," *Reuters,* September 1, 2011; Lori Gordon Logan and Michael Beyman, "Costco: Breaking All the Retail Rules," *CNBC.com,* April 25, 2012; Costco.com; Costco 2013 Annual Report; Angel Gonzalez, "Costco Shareholder Proposals Fall Short; Hot-Dog Sales Do Not," *Seattle Times,* January 30, 2014.

## In This Chapter, We Will Address the Following **Questions**

1. What major types of marketing intermediaries occupy this sector? (p. 527)

2. What major changes are occurring in the modern retail marketing environment with respect to competitive market structure and technology? (p. 532)

3. What marketing decisions do marketing intermediaries make? (p. 535)

4. What does the future hold for private label brands? (p. 541)

5. What are some of the important issues in wholesaling? (p. 543)

6. What are some important issues in logistics? (p. 545)

With an unconventional marketing strategy blending fashion, value, customer experience, and social responsibility, Warby Parker has made a splash in the staid eyewear category.

*Source: Courtesy of Warby Parker. Photographer: Collin Hughes.*

# Managing Retailing, Wholesaling, and Logistics

**In the preceding chapter, we examined marketing intermediaries primarily from the** viewpoint of manufacturers that want to build and manage marketing channels. In this chapter, we view these intermediaries—retailers, wholesalers, and logistical organizations—as requiring and forging their own marketing strategies in a rapidly changing world. Intermediaries also strive for marketing excellence and can reap the benefits like any other type of company. Consider the runaway success of Warby Parker.[1]

 *Started by four Wharton MBA graduates while they were still in school, lifestyle brand Warby Parker is challenging eyewear mammoth Luxottica with a marketing strategy that cleverly combines fashion, value, customer experience, and social responsibility. The company designs its own glasses with a hip if nerdy chic and a fashion ethic that promises, "We will not develop anything that you will be embarrassed to wear in 20 years." With material for frames from a family-owned Italian company, assembly in China, and no middleman, it promises quality comparable to that of well-known designers at a fraction of the cost. Warby Parker eyeglasses start at $95, with free shipping, free exchanges, and free returns. To assess fit, customers can use a virtual try-on tool employing facial recognition technology, have up to five sample pairs shipped to try on in person (free of charge), or visit a retail location. Promoting "eyewear with a purpose," Warby Parker works with a non-profit partner to distribute one pair for every pair sold. To expand reach and engagement beyond its stylish and easy-to-use Web site, the company has launched shops within shops in selected cities, a flagship store in the SoHo area of New York City, and several retail locations across the country. Word of mouth is critical for the brand—50 percent of Web site traffic comes from recommendations by friends and family.*

**The retail market can be unforgiving.** While innovative retailers such as Zappos, Sweden's H&M, Spain's Zara and Mango, and Britain's Topshop have thrived in recent years, others such as former U.S. stalwarts JCPenney, Kohl's, and Kmart have struggled. The more successful use strategic planning, state-of-the-art technology, advanced information systems, and sophisticated marketing tools. They segment their markets, improve their market targeting and positioning, and connect with their customers through memorable experiences, relevant and timely information, and of course the right products and services. In this chapter, we consider marketing excellence in retailing, wholesaling, and logistics.

# Retailing

**Retailing** includes all the activities in selling goods or services directly to final consumers for personal, nonbusiness use. A **retailer** or **retail store** is any business enterprise whose sales volume comes primarily from retailing.

Any organization selling to final consumers—whether it is a manufacturer, wholesaler, or retailer—is doing retailing. It doesn't matter *how* the goods or services are sold (in person, by mail, by telephone, by vending machine, or online) or *where* (in a store, on the street, or in the consumer's home).

Retailing is a fast-moving, challenging industry. Consider the plight of Sears.[2]

**SEARS**  Sears is a classic U.S. company. It was one of the first to sell goods through a mail-order catalog, and for more than 100 years, it was one of the strongest department store brands, associated with high-quality merchandise and responsive customer service. However, in the early 2000s, the company began facing financial difficulties, and to keep its earnings stable, it started aggressively selling assets and cutting costs. Customers began complaining about inattentive sales associates, disorganized sales racks, and stores in disrepair. Sears was spending only $2 to $3 per square foot in annual maintenance and repair of its stores, far less than the $6 to $8 per square foot spent by competitors Target and Walmart. "[T]hey weren't keeping [their] promise. Consumers are pretty sophisticated, and they walked into these stores and it was the same old place…without the freshness, the excitement or the interactivity of the experience." According to the ACS index of customer satisfaction, in 2012, Sears ranked 10th among 11 Department and Discount Stores. Given that same-store sales have declined for so many years, many feel Sears' disillusioned customers may not be coming back.

At the same time, there are many retailing success stories. "Marketing Memo: Innovative Retail Organizations" highlights four examples of innovative retail organizations that have experienced market success in recent years. After reviewing the different types of retailers and some important characteristics of the modern retail marketing environment, we examine in detail the marketing decisions retailers make.

## TYPES OF RETAILERS

Consumers today can shop for goods and services at store retailers, nonstore retailers, and retail organizations.

**STORE RETAILERS**  Perhaps the best-known type of store retailer is the department store. Japanese department stores such as Takashimaya and Mitsukoshi attract millions of shoppers each year and feature art galleries, restaurants, cooking classes, fitness clubs, and children's playgrounds. The most important types of major store retailers are summarized in Table 18.1.

Different formats of store retailers will have different competitive and price dynamics. Discount stores, for example, historically have competed much more directly with each other than with other formats, though that is

Sears has struggled to stay competitive in the dynamic, constantly changing world of retail.

Source: © Helen Sessions/Alamy

## marketing memo

### Innovative Retail Organizations

*GameStop.* Video game and entertainment software retailer GameStop has more than 6,600 convenient locations in malls and shopping strips all over the United States, staffed by hard-core gamers who like to connect with customers. The company boasts a trade-in policy that gives credit for an old game exchanged for a new one. To keep track of the activities of its 25 million customers, it also has a successful data-driven loyalty program, PowerUp Rewards, which offers reward points and allows members to manage their gaming interests with the online Game Library to showcase games members have had in the past, that they currently have, and that they wish they had.

*Dick's Sporting Goods.* Dick's Sporting Goods has grown from a single bait-and-tackle store in Binghamton, New York, into the largest U.S.-based full-line sporting goods retailer, with approximately 574 stores in 44 states. Part of its success springs from the interactive features of its stores. Customers can test golf clubs in indoor ranges, sample shoes on its footwear track, and shoot bows in its archery range. With an advertising tag line of "Every Season Starts at Dick's," the retailer is also emphasizing the fundamental goal of sports achievement and improvement to establish a stronger emotional connection with customers.

*Lumber Liquidators.* Lumber Liquidators is the largest hardwood flooring specialty retailer in the United States, with more than 345 locations. The company buys excess wood directly from lumber mills at a discount and stocks almost 350 kinds of flooring, about the same as Lowe's and Home Depot. It sells at lower prices because it keeps operating costs down by cutting out the middlemen and locating stores in inexpensive locations. Lumber Liquidators also knows a lot about its customers, such as the fact that shoppers who request product samples have a 30 percent likelihood of buying within a month and that most tend to renovate one room at a time, not the entire home at once.

*Net-a-Porter.* London-based Net-a-Porter is an online luxury clothing and accessories retailer whose Web site combines the style of an fashion magazine with the thrill of a chic boutique. Seen by its loyal customers as an authoritative fashion voice, the company publishes its interactive magazine weekly and stocks more than 300 international brands, including Jimmy Choo, Alexander McQueen, Stella McCartney, Givenchy, and Marc Jacobs, as well as many up-and-comers. It ships to 170 countries and offers same-day delivery in London and Manhattan; the average order is $250. A new site, Mr. Porter, targets men.

**Sources:** *GameStop:* Steve Peterson, "GameStop Sees Targeted Marketing on the Rise," www.thealistdaily.com, September 26, 2013; Jeanine Poggi, "GameStop Revamps Business to Ensure Success in a Digital Future," *Advertising Age,* April 9, 2012; Chris Daniels, "GameStop CMO Sees CRM as Key," *Direct Marketing News,* October 2011; Devin Leonard, "GameStop Racks Up the Points," *Fortune,* June 9, 2008, pp. 109–22; *Dick's Sporting Goods:* "Brand Genius: Lauren Hobart, Chief Marketing Officer, Dick's Sporting Goods," *Adweek,* September 23, 2013; Matt Townsend, "Dick's Channels 'Rudy' in New Branding Strategy," www.bloomberg.com, March 1, 2012; "Dick's Sporting Goods Details Growth Strategy to Reach $10 Billion in Sales and 10.5% Operating Margin by the End of Fiscal 2017," *PR Newswire,* August 3, 2013; *Lumber Liquidators:* Mark Heschmeyer, "Lumber Liquidators Planning to Spruce Up Retail Image, www.costar.com, January 30, 2013; Marilyn Much, "Lumber Liquidators' New CEO Helps Drive Sales Surge," *Investor's Business Daily,* May 17, 2012; Helen Coster, "Hardwood Hero," *Forbes,* November 30, 2009, pp. 60–62; *Net-a-Porter:* David Moth, "How Net-a-Porter Plans to Build on Its Mobile Success in 2013," www.econsultancy.com, March 18, 2013; Christina Binkley, "Finding an Audience for Edgy Runway Styles," *Wall Street Journal,* March 28, 2012; Paul Sonne, "Richemont to Buy Net-a-Porter," *Wall Street Journal,* April 2, 2010; John Brodie, "The Amazon of Fashion," *Fortune,* September 14, 2009, pp. 86–95.

changing, as we'll see below.[3] Retailers also meet widely different consumer preferences for service levels and specific services. Specifically, they position themselves as offering one of four levels of service:

1. *Self-service*—Self-service is the cornerstone of all discount operations. Many customers are willing to carry out their own "locate-compare-select" process to save money.
2. *Self-selection*—Customers find their own goods, though they can ask for assistance.
3. *Limited service*—These retailers carry more shopping goods and services such as credit and merchandise-return privileges. Customers need more information and assistance.
4. *Full service*—Salespeople are ready to assist in every phase of the "locate-compare-select" process. Customers who like to be waited on prefer this type of store. The high staffing cost and many services, along with the higher proportion of specialty goods and slower-moving items, result in high-cost retailing.

**NONSTORE RETAILING** Although the overwhelming bulk of goods and services is sold through stores, *nonstore retailing* has been growing much faster than store retailing, especially given e-commerce and m-commerce

| TABLE 18.1 | Major Types of Store Retailers |
|---|---|

**Specialty store:** Narrow product line. The Limited, The Body Shop.

**Department store:** Several product lines. JCPenney, Bloomingdale's.

**Supermarket:** Large, low-cost, low-margin, high-volume, self-service store designed to meet total needs for food and household products. Kroger, Safeway.

**Convenience store:** Small store in residential area, often open 24/7, limited line of high-turnover convenience products plus takeout. 7-Eleven, Circle K.

**Drug store:** Prescription and pharmacies, health and beauty aids, other personal care, small durable, miscellaneous items. CVS, Walgreens.

**Discount store:** Standard or specialty merchandise; low-price, low-margin, high-volume stores. Walmart, Kmart.

**Extreme value or hard-discount store:** A more restricted merchandise mix than discount stores but at even lower prices. Aldi, Lidl, Dollar General, Family Dollar.

**Off-price retailer:** Leftover goods, overruns, irregular merchandise sold at less than retail. Factory outlets; independent off-price retailers such as TJ Maxx; warehouse clubs such as Costco.

**Superstore:** Huge selling space, routinely purchased food and household items, plus services (laundry, shoe repair, dry cleaning, check cashing). Category killer (deep assortment in one category) such as Staples; combination store such as Jewel-Osco; hypermarket (huge stores that combine supermarket, discount, and warehouse retailing) such as Carrefour in France.

**Catalog showroom:** Broad selection of high-markup, fast-moving, brand-name goods sold by catalog at a discount. Customers pick up merchandise at the store. Inside Edge Ski and Bike.

as Chapter 17 outlined. Nonstore retailing falls into four major categories: direct marketing (which includes telemarketing and online selling), direct selling, automatic vending, and buying services:

1. *Direct marketing* has roots in direct-mail and catalog marketing (Lands' End, L.L.Bean); it includes *telemarketing* (1-800-FLOWERS), *television direct-response marketing* (HSN, QVC), and *online shopping* (Amazon.com, Autobytel.com). People are ordering a greater variety of goods and services from a wider range of Web sites. In the United States, online sales were estimated to be $225 billion in 2012, approaching 6 percent of total retail sales.[4]

2. *Direct selling,* also called *multilevel selling* and *network marketing,* is a multibillion-dollar industry, with companies selling door to door or through at-home sales parties. Well-known in such one-to-one selling are Avon, Electrolux, and Southwestern Company of Nashville (Bibles). Tupperware and Mary Kay Cosmetics are sold one-to-many: A salesperson goes to the home of a host who has invited friends; the salesperson demonstrates the products and takes orders. Pioneered by Amway, the multilevel (network) marketing sales system works by recruiting independent businesspeople who act as distributors. The distributor's compensation includes a percentage of sales made by those he or she recruits as well as earnings on his or her own direct sales to customers. These direct-selling firms, now finding fewer consumers at home, are developing multi-distribution strategies.

3. *Automatic vending* offers a variety of merchandise, including impulse goods such as soft drinks, coffee, candy, newspapers, magazines, and other products such as hosiery, cosmetics, hot food, and paperbacks. Vending machines are found in factories, offices, large retail stores, gasoline stations, hotels, restaurants, and many other places. They offer 24-hour selling, self-service, and merchandise that is stocked to be fresh. With more than 5 million units, Japan has the highest per-capita coverage of vending machines in the world. You can buy everything from fresh eggs to pet rhinoceros beetles. Coca-Cola has close to 1 million machines there and annual vending sales of $50 billion—twice its U.S. figures.[5]

4. *Buying service* is a storeless retailer serving a specific clientele—usually employees of large organizations—who are entitled to buy from a list of retailers that have agreed to give discounts in return for membership.

Without question, online nonstore retailing has been exploding and is taking many different forms. Consider the success of flash-sales Web sites such as Gilt.[6]

**GILT** During the recent recession, many designer brands found themselves with excess inventory they badly needed to move. Third-party "flash-sales" sites, offering deep discounts for luxury products and other goods for only a short period of time each day, allowed them to do so in a controlled manner less likely to hurt their brands. Modeled in part after France's flash-sales pioneer Vente-Privée, Gilt was launched in November 2007 to sell fashionable women's clothing from top designer labels for up to 60 percent off, but on a limited-time basis and only to those who joined the online site. Members were alerted of deals and their deadlines via e-mails that conveyed a sense of immediacy and urgency. Adding luxury brands such as Theory and Louis Vuitton, the firm grew to more than 8 million members and an estimated value of $1 billion. As the recession wound down, however, Gilt found itself challenged by dwindling inventory, growing competition from other sites, and its own aggressive expansion strategy, which included men's clothes, kids' products, home products, travel packages, and food. The company responded by focusing more on its core strength in women's fashion and developing tighter relationships with customers via personalized e-mails to announce its sales.

## CORPORATE RETAILING AND FRANCHISING

Although many retail stores are independently owned, an increasing number are part of a **corporate retailing** organization. These organizations achieve economies of scale, greater purchasing power, wider brand recognition, and better-trained employees than independent stores can usually gain alone. The major types of corporate retailing—corporate chain stores, voluntary chains, retailer and consumer cooperatives, franchises, and merchandising conglomerates—are described in Table 18.2.

Franchise businesses such as Hampton, Jiffy-Lube, Subway, Supercuts, 7-Eleven, and many others account for more than 10 percent of businesses with paid employees in the 295 industries for which franchising data are collected by the U.S. Census Bureau.[7]

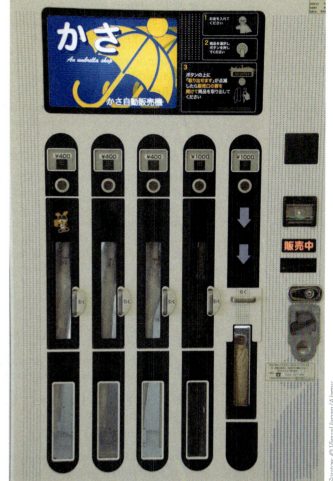

*Source: © VisualJapan/Alamy*

Vending machines can be found almost anywhere in Japan, selling almost any kind of merchandise, including umbrellas.

| TABLE 18.2 | Major Types of Corporate Retail Organizations |
|---|---|

**Corporate chain store:** Two or more outlets owned and controlled, employing central buying and merchandising, and selling similar lines of merchandise. Gap, Pottery Barn.

**Voluntary chain:** A wholesaler-sponsored group of independent retailers engaged in bulk buying and common merchandising. Independent Grocers Alliance (IGA).

**Retailer cooperative:** Independent retailers using a central buying organization and joint promotion efforts. Unified Grocers, ACE Hardware.

**Consumer cooperative:** A retail firm owned by its customers. Members contribute money to open their own store, vote on its policies, elect a group to manage it, and receive dividends. Local cooperative grocery stores can be found in many markets.

**Franchise organization:** Contractual association between a franchisor and franchisees, popular in a number of product and service areas. Dunkin' Donuts, Marriott, H&R Block, and The UPS Store.

**Merchandising conglomerate:** A corporation that combines several diversified retailing lines and forms under central ownership, with some integration of distribution and management. Federated Department Stores renamed itself after one of its best-known retailers, Macy's, but also owns other retailers such as Bloomingdale's.

In a franchising system, individual *franchisees* are a tightly knit group of enterprises whose systematic operations are planned, directed, and controlled by the operation's innovator, called a *franchisor*. Franchises are distinguished by three characteristics:

1. The franchisor owns a trade or service mark and licenses it to franchisees in return for royalty payments.
2. The franchisee pays for the right to be part of the system. Start-up costs include rental and lease equipment and fixtures and usually a regular license fee. McDonald's franchisees typically invest about $1.5 million in total start-up costs and fees. The franchisee then pays McDonald's a certain percentage of sales plus a monthly rent.[8]
3. The franchisor provides its franchisees with a system for doing business. McDonald's requires franchisees to attend "Hamburger University" in Oak Brook, Illinois, for two weeks to learn how to manage the business. Franchisees must follow certain procedures in buying materials.[9]

Franchising benefits both parties. Franchisors gain the motivation and hard work of employees who are entrepreneurs rather than "hired hands," the franchisees' familiarity with local communities and conditions, and the enormous purchasing power of being a franchisor. Franchisees benefit from buying into a business with a well-known and accepted brand name. They find it easier to borrow money for their business from financial institutions, and they receive support in areas ranging from marketing and advertising to site selection and staffing.

Franchisees do walk a fine line between independence and loyalty to the franchisor. Some franchisors are giving their franchisees freedom to run their own operations, from personalizing store names to adjusting offerings and price. Great Harvest Bread believes in a "freedom franchise" approach that encourages its franchisee bakers to create new items for their store menus and to share with other franchisees if they are successful.[10]

# THE MODERN RETAIL MARKETING ENVIRONMENT

The retail marketing environment is dramatically different today from what it was just a decade or so ago. Here we focus on two areas that have seen enormous change: competitive retail market structure and the role of technology.

**COMPETITIVE RETAIL MARKET STRUCTURE** The retail market is very dynamic, and a number of new types of competitors and competition have emerged in recent years. Here are five important developments (see Table 18.3 for a summary).

- *New Retail Forms and Combinations.* To better satisfy customers' need for convenience, a variety of new retail forms have emerged. Bookstores feature coffee shops. Gas stations include food stores. Loblaw's Supermarkets have fitness clubs. Shopping malls and bus and train stations have peddlers' carts in their aisles. Retailers are also experimenting with "pop-up" stores that let them promote brands to seasonal shoppers for a few weeks in busy areas. Pop-up stores are designed to create buzz often through interactive experiences. Internet companies such as Amazon.com and Google use pop-up stores as an easy way to establish a physical presence during holiday shopping seasons.[11]
- *Growth of Giant Retailers.* Through their superior information systems, logistical systems, and buying power, giant retailers such as Walmart are able to deliver good service and immense volumes of product to masses of consumers at appealing prices. They are crowding out smaller manufacturers that cannot deliver enough quantity and often dictate to the most powerful ones what to make, how to price and promote it, when and how to ship, and even how to improve production and management. Without these accounts, manufacturers would lose 10 percent to 30 percent of the market.

  Some giant retailers are *category killers* that concentrate on one product category, such as pet food (PETCO), home improvement (Home Depot), or office supplies (Staples). Others are *supercenters* that combine grocery items with a huge selection of nonfood merchandise (Walmart). With their broad product assortments, reasonable prices, and convenient service, category killers wiped out many smaller specialty

| TABLE 18.3 | Recent Retail Developments |
| --- | --- |

- New Retail Forms and Combinations
- Growth of Giant Retailers
- Growth of Intertype Competition
- Emergence of Fast Retailing
- Decline of Middle-Market Retailers

Many firms set up temporary pop-up stores to create special shopping experiences, especially at Christmas.

Source: © Daily Mail/Rex/Alamy

retailers. The rise of Amazon.com and other online retailers has nullified their advantages, however, and some category killers such as Borders, Circuit City, and Tweeter have even gone out of business.[12]

- *Growth of Intertype Competition.* One consequence of the growth of the supercenters is that department stores can't worry just about other department stores—discount chains such as Walmart and Tesco are expanding into product areas such as clothing, health, beauty, and electrical appliances.[13] Supermarkets also have to worry about these supercenters. Grocery products accounted for 56 percent of Walmart's U.S. sales in 2012, up from 41 percent just six years ago. The reality is that different types of stores can all compete for the same consumers by carrying the same type of merchandise.

- *Emergence of Fast Retailing.* An important trend in fashion retailing in particular, but with broader implications, is the emergence of fast retailing. Here retailers develop completely different supply chain and distribution systems to allow them to offer consumers constantly changing product choices. Fast retailing requires thoughtful decisions in a number of areas, including new product development, sourcing, manufacturing, inventory management, and selling practices. As Chapter 12 described, consumers have been attracted to fast-fashion retailers such as H&M, Zara, Uniqlo, Top Shop, and Forever 21 because of the novelty, value, and fashion sense of their offerings and have made them successful. Critics, however, pan fast fashion for its planned obsolescence and the resulting disposability and waste.[14]

- *Decline of Middle-Market Retailers.* We can characterize the retail market today as hourglass or dog-bone shaped: Growth seems to be centered at the top (with luxury offerings from retailers such as Tiffany and Neiman Marcus) and at the bottom (with discount pricing from retailers such as Walmart and Dollar General). As discount retailers improve their quality and image, consumers have been willing to trade down. Target offers Phillip Lim, Jason Wu, and Missoni designs, and Kmart sells an extensive line of Joe Boxer underwear and sleepwear. At the other end of the spectrum, Coach converted 40 of its nearly 300 stores to a more upscale format that offers higher-priced bags and concierge services. Opportunities are scarcer in the middle, where once-successful retailers like JCPenney, Kohl's, Sears, CompUSA, RadioShack, and Montgomery Ward have struggled or even gone out of business. Supermarket chains like Supervalu and Safeway have found themselves caught in the middle between the affluent appeal of chains like Whole Foods and the discount appeal of Aldi and Walmart. Compounding problems is the plight of the middle class—the 40 percent of U.S. consumers with annual incomes between $50,000 and $140,000—who have seen their buying power shrink due to slumping housing prices and stagnating incomes.[15]

**ROLE OF TECHNOLOGY** Technology is profoundly affecting the way retailers conduct virtually every facet of their business. Almost all now use technology to produce forecasts, control inventory costs, and order from suppliers, reducing the need to discount and run sales to clear out languishing products.

Technology is also directly affecting the consumer shopping experience inside the store. Electronic shelf labeling allows retailers to change price levels instantaneously at need.[16] In-store programming on plasma TVs can run continual demonstrations or promotional messages. Retailers are experimenting with virtual shopping screens, audio/video presentations, and QR code integration.

For flagship stores in Taipei, Hong Kong, London, and Chicago, Burberry made "virtual rain" with a 360° film, as part of its digital "Burberry World Live" program showcasing its rain gear. The UK's Marks & Spencer installed

# marketing insight

## The Growth of Shopper Marketing

Buoyed by research suggesting that as many as 70 percent to 80 percent of purchase decisions are made inside the store, firms are increasingly recognizing the importance of influencing consumers at the point of purchase. **Shopper marketing** is the way manufacturers and retailers use stocking, displays, and promotions to affect consumers actively shopping for a product.

Where and how a product is displayed and sold can have a significant effect on sales. A strong proponent of shopper marketing, Procter & Gamble calls the store encounter the "first moment of truth" (product use and consumption are the second). P&G observed the power of displays in a Walmart project designed to boost sales of premium diapers such as Pampers. By creating the first baby center in which infant products—previously spread across the store—were united in a single aisle, the new shelf layout encouraged parents to linger longer and spend more money, increasing Pampers sales. Another successful promotion, this one for P&G's Cover Girl cosmetics brand, tapped into a fashion trend for a "smoky eye" look by developing kits for Walmart and connecting with potential customers on Facebook with instructions, blogs, and a photo gallery.

Retailers are also using technology to influence customers as they shop. Some supermarkets are employing mobile phone apps or "smart shopping carts" that help customers locate items in the store, find out about sales and special offers, and pay more easily. One academic research study found that real-time spending feedback from a smart shopping cart stimulated budget shoppers to spend more (by buying more national brands) but led non-budget shoppers to spend less (by replacing national brands with store brands).

Kraft Foods spinoff Mondelēz uses "smart shelf" technology by putting sensors on shelves near check-out that can detect the age and sex of a consumer and, by virtue of advanced analytics, target them with ads and promotions for a likely snack candidate on a video screen.[18]

Technology is also playing a crucial research role in the design of shopper marketing programs. Some retailers outfit their aisles with sensors or use video from security cameras or other means to monitor shoppers' movements. Others use infrared goggles or wearable video cameras to record what test customers actually see. One finding was that many shoppers ignored products at eye level—the optimal location was between waist and chest level.

Other academic research found that unplanned purchases increased the more a product is touched, the longer a purchase is considered, the closer a customer is to the shelf, the fewer the shelf displays in sight, and the more quickly shoppers can reference external information. To capitalize on these findings, researchers recommend that retailers put Quick Response (QR) codes next to products to be scanned with smart phones. Even the simple act of touching a product on a tablet screen has been shown in research to increase purchase intent.

**Sources:** Megan Woolhouse, "Tablets Facilitate Impulse Shopping for Many," *Boston Globe*, December 18, 2013; Elizabeth Dwoskin and Greg Bensinger, "Tracking Technology Sheds Light on Shopper Habits," *Wall Street Journal*, December 9, 2013; S. Adam Brasel and Jim Gips, "Tablets, Touchscreens, and Touchpads: How Varying Touch Interfaces Trigger Psychological Ownership and Endowment" *Journal of Consumer Psychology* 24 (April 2014), pp. 226–33; Koert van Ittersum, Brian Wansink, Joost M. E. Pennings, and Daniel Sheehan, "Smart Shopping Carts: How Real-Time Feedback Influences Spending," *Journal of Marketing* 77 (November 2013), pp. 21–36; Barry Silverstein, "Will Mondelez's 'Smart Shelves' Change Retail or Just Add to Privacy Woes," www.brandchannel.com, October 13, 2013; Noreen O'Leary, "Shopper Marketing Goes Mainstream," *Adweek*, May 20, 2013, p. 19; Yanliu Huang, Sam K. Hui, J. Jeffrey Inman, and Jacob A. Suher, "Capturing the 'First Moment of Truth': Understanding Point-of-Purchase Drivers of Unplanned Consideration and Purchase," MSI Report 12-101, www.msi.org, 2012; Pat Lenius, "P&G Leverages Facebook to Enhance Promotions in Walmart," www.cpgmatters.com, November 2011; Venkatesh Shankar, "Shopper Marketing: Current Insights, Emerging Trends, and Future Directions," *MSI Relevant Knowledge Series Book*, www.msi.org, 2011; Anthony Dukes and Yunchuan Liu, "In-Store Media and Distribution Channel Coordination," *Marketing Science* 29 (January–February 2010), pp. 94–107; Richard Westlund, "Bringing Brands to Life: The Power of In-Store Marketing," Special Advertising Supplement to *Adweek*, January 2010; Pierre Chandon, J. Wesley Hutchinson, Eric T. Bradlow, and Scott H. Young, "Does In-Store Marketing Work? Effects of the Number and Position of Shelf Facings on Brand Attention and Evaluation at the Point of Purchase," *Journal of Marketing Research* 73 (November 2009), pp. 1–17; Michael C. Bellas, "Shopper Marketing's Instant Impact," *Beverage World*, November 2007, p. 18; Michael Freedman, "The Eyes Have It," *Forbes*, September 4, 2006, p. 70.

Smart shopping carts are just one of the technological innovations transforming supermarkets.

Source: ASSOCIATED PRESS

virtual mirrors in some of its stores so that, just as on its Web site, customers can see what an eye shadow or lipstick would look like for them without having to physically put it on.[17]

After encountering problems measuring store traffic in the aisles—GPS on shopping carts didn't work because consumers tended to abandon their carts, and thermal imaging couldn't tell the difference between babies and turkeys—bidirectional infrared sensors sitting on store shelves have proven successful. "Marketing Insight: The Growth of Shopper Marketing" describes the important role technology is taking in the aisles.

Retailers are also developing fully integrated digital communication strategies with well-designed Web sites, e-mails, search strategies, and social media campaigns. Social media are especially important for retailers during the holiday season when shoppers are seeking information and sharing successes. For the 2013 holiday season, Toys "R" Us focused on YouTube; Sears used Instagram and hosted holiday parties on Twitter; Target used Pinterest as well as six or seven other social media options.[19] Beyond the holidays, many retailers are linking to customer photos supporting their brands on Instagram, Pinterest, and other sites to create social engagement.[20]

## MARKETING DECISIONS

With this new retail environment as a backdrop, we now examine retailers' marketing decisions in some key areas: target market, channels, product assortment, procurement, prices, services, store atmosphere, store activities and experiences, communications, and location. We discuss private labels in the next section.

**TARGET MARKET** Until it defines and profiles the target market, the retailer cannot make consistent decisions about product assortment, store decor, advertising messages and media, price, and service levels. Whole Foods has succeeded by offering a unique shopping experience to a customer base interested in organic and natural foods.[21]

**WHOLE FOODS MARKET** In 284 stores in North America and the United Kingdom, Whole Foods creates celebrations of food. Its markets are bright and well staffed, and food displays are colorful, bountiful, and seductive. Whole Foods is the largest U.S. organic and natural foods grocer, offering more than 2,400 items in four lines of private-label products that add up to 11 percent of sales: the premium Whole Foods Market, Whole Kitchen, and Whole Market lines and the low-priced 365 Everyday Value line. Whole Foods also offers lots of information about its food. If you want to know, for instance, whether the chicken in the display case lived a happy, free-roaming life, you can get a 16-page booklet and an invitation to visit the farm in Pennsylvania where it was raised. For other help, you have only to ask a knowledgeable and easy-to-find employee. A typical Whole Foods has more than 200 employees, almost twice as many as Safeway. The company works hard to create an inviting store atmosphere with prices scrawled in chalk, cardboard boxes and ice everywhere, and other creative display touches to make the shopper feel at home. Its approach is working, especially for consumers who view organic and artisanal food as an affordable luxury. From 1991 to 2009, sales grew at a 28 percent compounded annual growth rate (CAGR). Although the recession hit the retailer hard, it did emerge with more double-digit growth.

*Source: Courtesy of Whole Foods Market. "Whole Foods Market" is a registered trademark of Whole Foods Market IP, L.P.*

Whole Foods selects merchandise and creates a homey in-store atmosphere to appeal to organic and natural foods lovers.

Mistakes in choosing target markets can be costly. When historically mass-market jeweler Zales decided to chase upscale customers, it replaced one-third of its merchandise, dropping inexpensive, low-quality diamond jewelry for high-margin, fashionable 14-karat gold and silver pieces and shifting its ad campaign in the process. The move was a disaster. Zales lost many of its traditional customers without winning over the new customers it hoped to attract.[22]

To better hit their targets, retailers are slicing the market into ever-finer segments and introducing new lines of stores to exploit niche markets with more relevant offerings: Gymboree launched Janie and Jack, selling apparel and gifts for babies and toddlers; Hot Topic introduced Torrid, selling fashions for plus-sized teen girls; and Limited Brand's Tween Brands began to sell lower-priced fashion to tween girls through its Justice stores and tween boys through its BROTHER shops.

**CHANNELS** Based on a target market analysis and other considerations we reviewed in Chapter 17, retailers must decide which channels to employ to reach their customers. Increasingly, the answer is multiple channels. Staples sells through its traditional retail brick-and-mortar channel, a direct-response Internet site, virtual malls, and thousands of links on affiliated sites.

As Chapter 17 also explained, channels should be designed to work together effectively. Although some experts predicted otherwise, catalogs have actually grown in an Internet world as more firms have revamped them to use them as branding devices and to complement online activity.[23] Victoria's Secret's integrated multichannel approach of retail stores, catalog, and Internet has played a key role in its brand development.[24]

**VICTORIA'S SECRET** Victoria's Secret, purchased by Limited Brands in 1982, has become one of the most identifiable brands in retailing through skillful marketing of women's clothing, lingerie, and beauty products. Most U.S. women a generation ago did their underwear shopping in department stores and owned few items that could be considered "lingerie." After witnessing women buying expensive lingerie as fashion items from small boutiques in Europe, Limited Brands founder Leslie Wexner felt a similar store model could work on a mass scale in the United States, though such a store format was unlike anything the average shopper would have encountered amid the bland racks at department stores. Wexner, however, had reason to believe U.S. women would relish the opportunity to have a European-style lingerie shopping experience with soft pink wallpaper, inviting fitting rooms, and attractive and attentive staff. "Women need underwear, but women want lingerie," he observed. Wexner's assumption proved correct: A little more than a decade after he bought the business, Victoria's Secret's average customer bought eight to 10 bras per year, compared with the national average of two. To enhance its upscale reputation and glamorous appeal, the brand is endorsed by high-profile supermodels in ads and televised fashion show extravaganzas. Victoria's Secret sells through its stores, Web site, and catalog, mailing 325 million U.S. catalogs a year at a cost of $200 million. Web and catalog sales account for 25 percent of the company's $5 billion in revenue. Overseas expansion is being led by "store within a store" beauty boutiques to reduce risk.

**PRODUCT ASSORTMENT** The retailer's product assortment must match the target market's shopping expectations in *breadth* and *depth*.[25] A restaurant can offer a narrow and shallow assortment (small lunch counters), a narrow and deep assortment (delicatessen), a broad and shallow assortment (cafeteria), or a broad and deep assortment (large restaurant).

**Destination categories** may play a particularly important role because they have the greatest impact on where households choose to shop and how they view a particular retailer. A supermarket could be known for the freshness of its produce or for the variety and deals its offers in soft drinks and snacks.[26]

Identifying the right product assortment can be especially challenging in fast-moving industries such as technology or fashion. At one point, Urban Outfitters ran into trouble when it strayed from its "hip but not too hip" formula, embracing new styles too quickly.[27] On the other hand, active and casual apparel retailer Aéropostale has succeeded by carefully matching its product assortment to its young teen needs.[28]

**AÉROPOSTALE** Fourteen- to 17-year-olds, especially those on the young end, often want to look like other teens. So while Abercrombie and American Eagle might reduce the number of cargo pants on the sales floor, Aéropostale embraces this key reality of its target market and will keep an ample supply on hand at an affordable price. Staying on top of the right trends isn't easy, but the company is among the most diligent of teen retailers when it comes to consumer research. In addition to running high-school focus groups and in-store product tests, it launched an online program that seeks the input of 10,000 of its best customers in creating new styles. An average of 3,500 participate in each of 20 tests a year. Aéropostale maintains control over its proprietary brands by designing, sourcing, marketing, and selling all its own merchandise. The company's products can be purchased only in its own stores and online. Aéropostale has gone from a lackluster performer with only 100 stores to a powerhouse with more than 1,000 outlets in the United States, Puerto Rico, and Canada. One hundred new P.S. from Aéropostale stores target 4- to 12-year-olds with a strong value emphasis. Net sales totaled more than $2.6 billion in 2012, with net sales from e-commerce contributing more than $180 billion.

Apparel retailer Aeropostale studies its young teen market carefully as it strives to stock and display the right product assortment.

Source: © Kumar Sriskandan/Alamy

The real challenge begins after defining the store's product assortment, when the retailer must develop a product-differentiation strategy. Here are some possibilities:

- *Feature exclusive national brands not available at competing retailers.* Saks might get exclusive rights to carry the dresses of a well-known international designer.
- *Feature mostly private-label merchandise.* Benetton and Gap design most of the clothes carried in their stores. Many supermarket and drug chains carry private-label merchandise.
- *Feature blockbuster distinctive-merchandise events.* Bloomingdale's ran a month-long celebration for the Barbie doll's 50th anniversary.
- *Feature surprise or ever-changing merchandise.* Off-price apparel retailer TJ Maxx offers surprise assortments of distress merchandise (goods the owner must sell immediately because it needs cash), overstocks, and closeouts sourced from more than 16,000 vendors and priced 20 percent to 60 percent below department and specialty store regular prices online and at its 1000-plus stores.
- *Feature the latest or newest merchandise first.* Zara excels in and profits from being first to market with appealing new looks and designs.
- *Offer merchandise-customizing services.* Harrods of London will make custom-tailored suits, shirts, and ties for customers in addition to ready-made menswear.
- *Offer a highly targeted assortment.* Lane Bryant carries goods for the larger woman. Brookstone offers unusual tools and gadgets for the person who wants to shop in a "toy store for grown-ups."

Merchandise may also vary by geographical market. Macy's and Ross Stores employ *micro-merchandising* and let managers select a significant percentage of store assortments.[29]

PROCUREMENT  After deciding on the product-assortment strategy, the retailer must establish merchandise sources, policies, and practices. In the corporate headquarters of a supermarket chain, specialist buyers (sometimes called *merchandise managers*) are responsible for developing brand assortments and listening to presentations from their suppliers' salespeople.

Retailers are rapidly improving their skills in demand forecasting, merchandise selection, stock control, space allocation, and display. They use sophisticated software to track inventory, compute economic order quantities, order goods, and analyze dollars spent on vendors and products. Supermarket chains use scanner data to manage their merchandise mix on a store-by-store basis.

Some stores are using radio frequency identification (RFID) systems made up of "smart" tags—microchips attached to tiny radio antennas—and electronic readers to facilitate inventory control and product replenishment. The smart tags can be embedded on products or stuck on labels, and when the tag is near a reader, it transmits a unique identifying number to its computer database. Coca-Cola and Gillette have used them to monitor inventory and track goods in real time as they move from factories to supermarkets to shopping baskets.[30]

Trader Joe's unique procurement strategy emphasizes a constantly rotating group of select private label branded products.

*Source: © ZUMA Press, Inc./Alamy*

Stores are using **direct product profitability (DPP)** to measure a product's handling costs (receiving, moving to storage, paperwork, selecting, checking, loading, and space cost) from the time it reaches the warehouse until a customer buys it in the retail store. Sometimes they find that a product's gross margin bears little relationship to the direct product profit. Some high-volume products may have such high handling costs that they are less profitable and deserve less shelf space than low-volume products, at least unless customers buy enough other, more profitable products to justify the loss involved in pushing the high-volume products.

Trader Joe's has differentiated itself on its innovative procurement strategy.[31]

*Source: ASSOCIATED PRESS*

Target's "mass with class" assortment and pricing strategy features designers like popular entertainer Gwen Stefani.

**TRADER JOE'S**  Los Angeles–based Trader Joe's has carved out a special niche as a "gourmet food outlet discount warehouse hybrid," selling a constantly rotating assortment of unique upscale specialty food and wine at lower-than-average prices at its 400 stores. Roughly 80 percent of what the company stocks sells under private labels (compared with only 16 percent at most supermarkets), from Belgian butter waffle cookies to Thai lime-and-chili cashews. For procurement, it has adopted a "less is more" philosophy. Every store carries only 2,000 to 3,000 products, compared with 55,000 at a conventional supermarket, and only what it can buy and sell at a good price, even if that means changing stock weekly. Trader Joe's expert buyers go directly to hundreds of suppliers, not to intermediaries, and about a quarter of these suppliers are overseas. Always thinking about what customers want and engaging them in the process, the company introduces as many as 20 products a week to replace unpopular items. With thousands of vendor relationships all around the world, it has built a success formula that's difficult to copy. Experts praise its ability to be a storyteller and create uniquely friendly experiences. As one expert says, "It really comes down to the small formats, well-edited assortments and value pricing of unique private brand products."

**PRICES**  Prices are a key positioning factor and must be set in relationship to the target market, product-and-service assortment mix, and competition.[32] All retailers would like high *turns × earns* (high volumes and high gross margins), but the two don't usually go together. Most retailers fall into the *high-markup, lower-volume* group (fine specialty stores) or the *low-markup, higher-volume* group (mass merchandisers and discount stores). Within each of these groups are further gradations.

At one end of the price spectrum is by-appointment-only Bijan on Rodeo Drive in Beverly Hills, known as the most expensive store in the world. The original cost of its cologne was $1,500 for six ounces, and its suits are priced at $25,000, ties at $1,200, and socks at $100.[33] At the other end of the scale, Target has skillfully combined a hip image with discount prices to offer customers a strong value proposition. It first introduced a line of products from world-renowned designers such as Michael Graves, Isaac Mizrahi, and Liz Lange and has continued to add high-profile names, such as singer Gwen Stefani to sell hip children's clothes.[34]

Most retailers will put low prices on some items to serve as traffic builders (or loss leaders) or to signal their pricing policies.[35] They will run storewide sales. They will plan markdowns on slower-moving merchandise. Shoe retailers, for example, expect to sell 50 percent of their shoes at the normal markup, 25 percent at a 40 percent markup, and the remaining 25 percent at cost. A store's average price level and discounting policies will affect its price image with consumers, but non-price-related factors such as store atmosphere and levels of service also matter.[36]

As Chapter 16 noted, some retailers such as Walmart have abandoned "sale pricing" in favor of everyday low pricing (EDLP). EDLP can lead to lower advertising costs, greater pricing stability, a stronger image of fairness and reliability, and higher retail profits. Supermarket chains practicing everyday low pricing can be more profitable than those practicing high–low sale pricing, but only in certain circumstances, such as when the market is characterized by many "large basket" shoppers who tend to buy many items on any one trip.[37]

All retailers are seeking to cut costs to improve margins. Some do so in an environmentally friendly way. Walmart has cut energy use by more than 50 percent and maintenance by more than 30 percent by painting store roofs white to reflect sunlight and reduce the use of air conditioning; capturing rain in storage tanks for flushing toilets and other uses that do not require drinking-quality water; and installing LED lights in parking lots.[38]

**SERVICES** Another differentiator is unerringly reliable customer service, whether face to face, across phone lines, or via online chat. Retailers must decide on the *services mix* to offer customers:

- *Prepurchase services* include accepting telephone and mail orders, advertising, window and interior display, fitting rooms, shopping hours, fashion shows, and trade-ins.
- *Postpurchase services* include shipping and delivery, gift wrapping, adjustments and returns, alterations and tailoring, installations, and engraving.
- *Ancillary services* include general information, check cashing, parking, restaurants, repairs, interior decorating, credit, rest rooms, and baby-attendant service.

Due to consumer complaints, many retailers have loosened up their returns policies in recent years. To reduce any possible impediment to sales and to improve their image with consumers, these firms are also eliminating restocking fees and extending return periods. Some policies have necessarily stayed in place, though, to combat frauds such as "wardrobing"—the practice of wearing and then returning clothing items.[39] Gift cards remain another popular service offering; consumers spend more than $100 billion on cards annually.[40]

**STORE ATMOSPHERE** Every store has a look and a physical layout that makes it hard or easy to move around (see "Marketing Memo: Helping Stores to Sell"). Kohl's floor plan is modeled after a racetrack loop and is designed to convey customers smoothly past all the merchandise in the store. It includes a middle aisle that hurried shoppers can use as a shortcut and yields higher spending levels than many competitors.[41]

Retailers must consider all the senses in shaping the customer's experience. Varying the tempo of music affects average time and dollars spent in the supermarket—slow music can lead to higher sales. Bloomingdale's uses different essences or scents in different departments: baby powder in the baby store; suntan lotion in the bathing suit area; lilacs in lingerie; and cinnamon and pine scent during the holiday season. Other retailers such as Victoria's Secret and Juicy Couture use their own distinctive branded perfumes, which they also sell.[42]

**STORE ACTIVITIES AND EXPERIENCES** The growth of e-commerce has forced traditional brick-and-mortar retailers to respond. In addition to their natural advantages, such as products that shoppers can actually see, touch, and test; real-life customer service; and no delivery lag time for most purchases, stores also provide a shopping experience as a strong differentiator.

The store atmosphere should match shoppers' basic motivations—if customers are likely to be in a task-oriented and functional mind-set, then a simpler, more restrained in-store environment may be better.[43] On the other hand, some retailers of experiential products are creating in-store entertainment to attract customers who want fun and excitement.[44] REI, seller of outdoor gear and clothing products, allows consumers to test climbing equipment on 25-foot or even 65-foot walls in the store and to try GORE-TEX raincoats under a simulated rain shower. Bass Pro Shops also offers rich customer experiences.[45]

**BASS PRO SHOPS** Bass Pro Shops, a retailer of outdoor sports equipment, caters to hunters, campers, fisherman, boaters, and outdoors fans of any type. Its Outdoor World superstores feature 200,000 square feet or more of giant aquariums, waterfalls, trout ponds, archery and rifle ranges, fly-tying demonstrations, indoor driving range and putting greens, and classes in everything from ice fishing to conservation—all free. Every department is set up to replicate the corresponding outdoor experience in support of product demonstrations and testing. During the summer, parents can bring their kids to the free in-store Family Summer Camp with a host of activities in all departments. Bass Pro Shops builds a strong connection to its loyal customers from the moment they enter the store—through a turnstile designed to highlight that "they are entering an attraction, not just a retail space"—and are greeted by the irreverent sign saying "Welcome Fishermen, Hunters, and Other Liars." One hundred and sixteen million people shopped at a Bass Pro Shop in 2012; the average customer drove more than 50 miles and stayed for more than two hours. The showroom in Missouri—the first and largest—is the number-one tourist destination in the state.

**COMMUNICATIONS** Retailers use a wide range of communication tools to generate traffic and purchases. They place ads, run special sales, issue money-saving coupons, send e-mail promotions, and run frequent-shopper-reward programs, in-store food sampling, and coupons on shelves or at check-out points. They work with manufacturers to design point-of-sale materials that reflect both their images. They time the arrival of their e-mails and design them with attention-grabbing subject lines and animation and personalized messages and advice.

Retailers are also using interactive and social media to pass on information and create communities around their brands. They study the way consumers respond to their e-mails, not only where and how messages are opened but

## marketing memo

### Helping Stores to Sell

In pursuit of higher sales volume, retailers are studying their store environments for ways to improve the shopper experience. Paco Underhill is a pioneer in that field and managing director of the retail consultant Envirosell, whose clients include McDonald's, Starbucks, Estée Lauder, Gap, Burger King, CVS, and Wells Fargo. Using a combination of in-store video recording and observation tracking of as many as 40 different behaviors, Underhill and his colleagues study 50,000 people each year as they shop. He offers the following advice for fine-tuning retail space:

- *Attract shoppers and keep them in the store.* The amount of time shoppers spend in a store is perhaps the single most important factor in determining how much they buy. To increase shopping time, give shoppers a sense of community; recognize them in some way; make them comfortable, such as by providing chairs in convenient locations for spouses, children, or bags; and make the environment both familiar and fresh each time they come in.

- *Honor the "transition zone."* On entering a store, people need to slow down and sort out the stimuli, which means they will likely be moving too fast to respond positively to signs, merchandise, or sales clerks in the zone they cross before making that transition. Make sure there are clear sight lines. Create a focal point for information within the store. Most right-handed people turn right upon entering a store.

- *Avoid overdesign.* Store fixtures, point-of-sales information, packaging, signage, and flat-screen televisions can combine to create a visual riot. Use crisp and clear signage—"Our Best Seller" or "Our Best Student Computer"—located where people feel comfortable stopping and facing the right way. Window signs, displays, and mannequins communicate best when angled 10 to 15 degrees to face the direction in which people are moving.

- *Don't make them hunt.* Put the most popular products up front to reward busy shoppers and encourage leisurely shoppers to look more. At Staples, ink cartridges are one of the first products shoppers encounter after entering.

- *Make merchandise available to the reach and touch.* It is hard to overemphasize the importance of customers' hands. A store can offer the finest, cheapest, sexiest goods, but if the shopper cannot reach them or pick them up, much of their appeal can be lost.

- *Make kids welcome.* If kids feel welcome, parents will follow. Take a 3-year-old's perspective and make sure there are engaging sights at eye level. A virtual hopscotch pattern or dinosaur on the floor can turn a boring shopping trip for a child into a friendly experience.

- *Note that men do not ask questions.* Men always move faster than women do through a store's aisles. In many settings, it is hard to get them to look at anything they had not intended to buy. Men also do not like asking where things are. If a man cannot find the section he is looking for, typically he will wheel about once or twice, then leave the store without ever asking for help.

- *Remember women need space.* A shopper, especially a woman, is far less likely to buy an item if her body is brushed, even lightly, by another customer when she is looking at a display. Keeping aisles wide and clear is crucial. With women playing an increasingly more significant buying role than men, designing retail experiences to satisfy them is crucial. Cleanliness, control, safety, and consideration are among the important retail decision factors for women.

- *Make check-out easy.* Be sure to have the right high-margin goods near cash registers to satisfy impulse shoppers. People love to buy candy when they check out—so satisfy their sweet tooth.

**Sources:** Paco Underhill, *What Women Want: The Science of Female Shopping* (New York: Simon & Schuster, 2011); Paco Underhill, *Call of the Mall: The Geography of Shopping* (New York: Simon & Schuster, 2004); Paco Underhill, *Why We Buy: The Science of Shopping* (New York: Simon & Schuster, 1999). See also Gloria Moss, "Time for Gatherers to Have More Clout in the Boardroom!," *Huffington Post*, June 3, 2012; Brian Tarren, "Watchman," *Research*, July 17, 2012; Susan Berfield, "Getting the Most Out of Every Shopper, *BusinessWeek*, February 9, 2009, pp. 45–46; Kenneth Hein, "Shopping Guru Sees Death of Detergent Aisle," *Brandweek*, March 27, 2006, p. 11.

also which words and images led to a click. Macy's segments customers into more than a dozen groups and sends different e-mails for different products.[46] Casual dining chain Houlihan's social network site, HQ, gains immediate, unfiltered feedback from 10,500 invitation-only "Houlifan" customers in return for insider information about recipes and redesigns.[47]

With 15 percent of a retailer's most loyal customers accounting for as much as half its sales, reward programs are becoming increasingly sophisticated. Consumers who choose to share personal information can receive discounts, secret or advance sales, exclusive offers, and store credits. CVS has 70 million loyalty club members who can use in-store coupon centers and receive coupons with their sales receipts.[48]

Many retailers are using Twitter to connect with customers and send ads to targeted groups.[49] Some local retailers are using digital daily-deal services from Groupon, LivingSocial, and others, although recently many have soured on the approach due to a lack of profitability.[50]

**LOCATION** The three keys to retail success are often said to be "location, location, and location." Department store chains, oil companies, and fast-food franchisers exercise great care in selecting regions of the country in which to open outlets, then particular cities, and then particular sites. Retailers can place their stores in the following locations:

- *Central business districts.* The oldest and most heavily trafficked city areas, often known as "downtown"
- *Regional shopping centers.* Large suburban malls containing 40 to 200 stores, typically featuring one or two nationally known anchor stores, such as Macy's or Lord & Taylor or a combination of big-box stores such as PETCO, Payless Shoes, or Bed Bath & Beyond, and a great number of smaller stores, many under franchise operation.[51]
- *Community shopping centers.* Smaller malls with one anchor store and 20 to 40 smaller stores
- *Shopping strips.* A cluster of stores, usually in one long building, serving a neighborhood's needs for groceries, hardware, laundry, shoe repair, and dry cleaning
- *A location within a larger store.* Smaller concession spaces taken by well-known retailers like McDonald's, Starbucks, Nathan's, and Dunkin' Donuts within larger stores, airports, or schools or "store-within-a-store" specialty retailers located within a department store such as with Gucci within Neiman Marcus
- *Stand-alone stores.* Some retailers such as Kohl's and JCPenney are avoiding malls and shopping centers in favor of freestanding storefronts so they are not connected directly to other retail stores.

In view of the relationship between high traffic and high rents, retailers must decide on the most advantageous locations for their outlets, using traffic counts, surveys of consumer shopping habits, and analysis of competitive locations.

Bass Pro Shops brings outdoor experiences into different departments of its stores.

# Private Labels

A **private-label brand** (also called a reseller, store, house, or distributor brand) is a brand that retailers and wholesalers develop. Benetton, The Body Shop, and Marks & Spencer carry mostly own-brand merchandise. In grocery stores in Europe and Canada, store brands account for as much as 40 percent of the items sold. In Britain, roughly half of what Sainsbury and Tesco, the largest food chains, sell is store-label goods. Germany and Spain are also European markets with a high percentage of private-label sales.[52]

For many manufacturers, retailers are both collaborators and competitors. According to the Private Label Manufacturers' Association, store brands now account for one of every five items sold in U.S. supermarkets, drug chains, and mass merchandisers. In one study, seven of 10 shoppers believed the private-label products they bought were as good as, if not better than, their national-brand counterparts, and virtually every household purchases private-label brands from time to time.[53] The stakes in private-label marketing are high. A one-percentage-point shift from national brands to private labels in food and beverages is estimated to add $5.5 billion in revenue for supermarket chains.[54]

Private labels are rapidly gaining ground in a way that has many manufacturers of name brands running scared. Recessions increase private-label sales, and once some consumers switch to a private label, they don't always go back.[55] But some experts believe 50 percent is the natural limit on how much private-label volume to carry because (1) consumers prefer certain national brands, and (2) many product categories are not feasible or attractive on a private-label basis. In supermarkets, private labels are big sellers in milk and cheese, bread and baked goods, medications and remedies, paper products, fresh produce, and packaged meats.[56]

## ROLE OF PRIVATE LABELS

Why do intermediaries sponsor their own brands?[57] First, these brands can be more profitable. Intermediaries may be able to use manufacturers with excess capacity that will produce private-label goods at low cost. Other costs, such as research and development, advertising, sales promotion, and physical distribution, are also much lower, so private labels can generate a higher profit margin.[58] Retailers also develop exclusive store brands to differentiate themselves from competitors. Many price-sensitive consumers prefer store brands in certain categories. These preferences give retailers increased bargaining power with marketers of national brands.

We should distinguish private-label or store brands from generics. **Generics** are unbranded, plainly packaged, less expensive versions of common products such as spaghetti, paper towels, and canned peaches. They offer standard or lower quality at a price that may be as much as 20 percent to 40 percent lower than nationally advertised brands and 10 percent to 20 percent lower than the retailer's private-label brands. The lower price is made possible by lower-cost labeling and packaging and minimal advertising and sometimes lower-quality ingredients.

Generics can be found in a wide range of different products, even medicines. Pharma giant Novartis is one of the world's top five makers of branded drugs, with such successes as Diovan for high blood pressure and Gleevec for cancer, but it has also become the world's second-largest maker of generic drugs following its acquisition of Sandoz, HEXAL, Eon Labs, and others.[59]

## PRIVATE-LABEL SUCCESS FACTORS

In the battle between manufacturers' and private labels, retailers have increasing market power. Because shelf space is scarce, many supermarkets charge a *slotting fee* for accepting a new brand to cover the cost of listing and stocking it. Retailers also charge for special display space and in-store advertising space. They typically give more prominent display to their own brands and make sure they are well stocked.

Retailers are building better quality into their store brands and emphasizing attractive, innovative packaging. Supermarket retailers are adding premium store-brand items. When Kroger's switched to new vendors to supply better-quality cheeses, meats, and veggies for its upscale private-label pizza, sales soared; the supermarket chain now owns 60 percent of the premium pizza market in its stores.[60] One of the most successful supermarket retailers with private labels is Canada's Loblaw.[61]

**LOBLAW**  Since 1984, when its President's Choice line of foods made its debut, the term *private label* has brought Loblaw instantly to mind. The Toronto-based company's Decadent Chocolate Chip Cookie quickly became a Canadian leader and showed how innovative store brands could compete effectively with national brands by matching or even exceeding their quality. A finely tuned brand strategy for its premium President's Choice line and its no-frills, yellow-labeled No Name line (which the company relaunched with a vengeance during the recent recession) has helped differentiate its stores and built Loblaw into a powerhouse in Canada and the United States. The President's Choice line has become so successful that Loblaw is licensing it to noncompetitive retailers in other countries. To complete a "good, better, best" brand portfolio, Loblaw has also introduced an "affordable luxury" line of more than 200 President's Choice food products under a distinctive "Black Label" design. Each one—from eight-year-old cheddar and ginger-spiced chocolate sauce to bacon marmalade—is marketed with a story about where it's from, who produces it, and why it was chosen. To capitalize on the overall strength of its private labels, Loblaw launched a Food Network reality TV show, *Recipe to Riches*, where contestants compete to have their homemade recipes developed into an actual President's Choice product available to purchase the very next day at Loblaw's stores.

Although retailers get credit for the success of private labels, the growing power of store brands has also benefited from the weakening of national brands. Many consumers have become more price sensitive, a trend reinforced by the continuous barrage of coupons and price specials that has trained a generation to buy on price. Competing manufacturers and national retailers copy and duplicate the quality and features of the best brands in

## marketing insight

## Manufacturer's Response to the Private-Label Threat

To stay a step ahead of store brands, leading brand marketers are investing significantly in R&D to bring out new brands, line extensions, features, and quality improvements. They are also investing in strong "pull" advertising programs to maintain high brand recognition and consumer preference and to overcome the in-store marketing advantage private labels can enjoy.

Top-brand marketers also are seeking to partner with major mass distributors in a joint search for logistical economies and competitive strategies that produce savings for both sides. Cutting all unnecessary costs allows national brands to command a price premium, though price can't exceed consumers' perception of value.

Creating strong consumer demand is crucial. When Walmart decided to pull Hefty and Glad food bags from its shelves, selling just Ziploc and its own Great Value brand, Hefty and Glad stood to lose because the retail giant accounted for a third of their sales. When consumers complained about the loss of these and other brands and switched some of their shopping to other stores, Walmart relented and put them back on the shelves.

Effective positioning is crucial. Despite holding a hefty 60 percent price premium over its private-label competitors, Pepto-Bismol gained market share during the recession. A clever advertising campaign portraying the product as an effective multipurpose "insurance policy" for gastrointestinal maladies struck a chord with value-minded consumers.

University of North Carolina's Jan-Benedict E. M. Steenkamp and London Business School's Nirmalya Kumar offer four strategic recommendations for manufacturers to compete against or collaborate with private labels.

- *Fight selectively* when manufacturers can win against private labels and add value for consumers, retailers, and shareholders. This typically occurs when the brand is number one or two in the category or occupying a premium niche position. Procter & Gamble rationalized its portfolio, selling off various brands such as Sunny Delight juice drink, Jif peanut butter, and Crisco shortening, in part so it could concentrate on strengthening its 20-plus brands with more than $1 billion in sales.

- *Partner effectively* by seeking win-win relationships with retailers through strategies that complement the retailer's private labels. Estée Lauder created four brands (American Beauty, Flirt, Good Skin, and Grassroots) exclusively for Kohl's to help the retailer generate volume and protect its more prestigious brands in the process. Manufacturers selling through hard discounters such as Lidl and Aldi have increased sales by finding new customers who have not previously bought the brand.

- *Innovate brilliantly* with new products to help beat private labels. Continuously launching incrementally new products keeps the manufacturer brands looking fresh, but the firm must also periodically launch radically new products and protect the intellectual property of all brands. Kraft doubled its number of patent lawyers to make sure its innovations were legally protected as much as possible.

- *Create winning value propositions* by imbuing brands with symbolic imagery as well as functional quality that beats private labels. Too many manufacturer brands have let private labels equal and sometimes better them on functional quality. In addition, to have a winning value proposition, marketers need to monitor pricing and ensure that perceived benefits equal the price premium.

**Sources:** Tony Fanin, "Brands Still Mean Something at Walmart," www.bebranded. wordpress.com, March 22, 2010; Parija Kavilanz, "Dumped! Brand Names Fight to Stay in Stores," *USA Today,* February 16, 2010; Jan-Benedict E. M. Steenkamp and Nirmalya Kumar, "Don't Be Undersold," *Harvard Business Review,* December 2009, p. 91; Jack Neff, "Pepto Beats Private Label despite 60% Price Premium," *Wall Street Journal,* September 21, 2009; Nirmalya Kumar and Jan-Benedict E. M. Steenkamp, *Private Label Strategy: How to Meet the Store-Brand Challenge* (Boston: Harvard Business School Press, 2007); Nirmalya Kumar, "The Right Way to Fight for Shelf Domination," *Advertising Age,* January 22, 2007; James A. Narus and James C. Anderson, "Contributing as a Distributor to Partnerships with Manufacturers," *Business Horizons* (September–October 1987).

a category, reducing physical product differentiation. Moreover, by cutting marketing communication budgets, some firms have made it harder to create any intangible differences in brand image. A steady stream of brand extensions and line extensions has blurred brand identity at times and led to a confusing amount of product proliferation.

Bucking these trends, many manufacturers or national brands are fighting back. "Marketing Insight: Manufacturer's Respond to the Private-Label Threat," describes the strategies and tactics being taken to compete more effectively with private labels.[62]

# Wholesaling

**Wholesaling** includes all the activities in selling goods or services to those who buy for resale or business use. It excludes manufacturers and farmers because they are engaged primarily in production, and it excludes retailers. The major types of wholesalers are described in Table 18.4.

| TABLE 18.4 | Major Wholesaler Types |
|---|---|

**Merchant wholesalers:** Independently owned businesses that take title to the merchandise they handle. They are full-service and limited-service jobbers, distributors, and mill supply houses.

**Full-service wholesalers:** Carry stock, maintain a sales force, offer credit, make deliveries, provide management assistance. Wholesale merchants sell primarily to retailers: Some carry several merchandise lines, some carry one or two lines, others carry only part of a line. Industrial distributors sell to manufacturers and also provide services such as credit and delivery.

**Limited-service wholesalers:** *Cash and carry wholesalers* sell a limited line of fast-moving goods to small retailers for cash. *Truck wholesalers* sell and deliver a limited line of semiperishable goods to supermarkets, grocery stores, hospitals, restaurants, and hotels. *Drop shippers* serve bulk industries such as coal, lumber, and heavy equipment. They assume title and risk from the time an order is accepted to its delivery. *Rack jobbers* serve grocery retailers in nonfood items. Delivery people set up displays, price goods, and keep inventory records; they retain title to goods and bill retailers only for goods sold to the end of the year. *Producers' cooperatives* assemble farm produce to sell in local markets. *Mail-order wholesalers* send catalogs to retail, industrial, and institutional customers; orders are filled and sent by mail, rail, plane, or truck.

**Brokers and agents:** Facilitate buying and selling, on commission of 2 percent to 6 percent of the selling price; limited functions; generally specialize by product line or customer type. *Brokers* bring buyers and sellers together and assist in negotiation; they are paid by the party hiring them—food brokers, real estate brokers, insurance brokers. *Agents* represent buyers or sellers on a more permanent basis. Most manufacturers' agents are small businesses with a few skilled salespeople: Selling agents have contractual authority to sell a manufacturer's entire output; purchasing agents make purchases for buyers and often receive, inspect, warehouse, and ship merchandise; commission merchants take physical possession of products and negotiate sales.

**Manufacturers' and retailers' branches and offices:** Wholesaling operations conducted by sellers or buyers themselves rather than through independent wholesalers. Separate branches and offices are dedicated to sales or purchasing. Many retailers set up purchasing offices in major market centers.

**Specialized wholesalers:** Agricultural assemblers (buy the agricultural output of many farms), petroleum bulk plants and terminals (consolidate the output of many wells), and auction companies (auction cars, equipment, etc., to dealers and other businesses).

Wholesalers (also called *distributors*) differ from retailers in a number of ways. First, wholesalers pay less attention to promotion, atmosphere, and location because they are dealing with business customers rather than final consumers. Second, wholesale transactions are usually larger than retail transactions, and wholesalers usually cover a larger trade area than retailers. Third, wholesalers and retailers are subject to different legal regulations and taxes.

Why do manufacturers not sell directly to retailers or final consumers? Why use wholesalers at all? In general, wholesalers can more efficiently perform one or more of the following functions:

- *Selling and promoting.* Wholesalers' sales forces help manufacturers reach many small business customers at a relatively low cost. They have more contacts, and buyers often trust them more than they trust a distant manufacturer.
- *Buying and assortment building.* Wholesalers are able to select items and build the assortments their customers need, saving them considerable work.
- *Bulk breaking.* Wholesalers achieve savings for their customers by buying large carload lots and breaking the bulk into smaller units.
- *Warehousing.* Wholesalers hold inventories, thereby reducing inventory costs and risks to suppliers and customers.
- *Transportation.* Wholesalers can often provide quicker delivery to buyers because they are closer to the buyers.
- *Financing.* Wholesalers finance customers by granting credit and finance suppliers by ordering early and paying bills on time.

- *Risk bearing.* Wholesalers absorb some risk by taking title and bearing the cost of theft, damage, spoilage, and obsolescence.
- *Market information.* Wholesalers supply information to suppliers and customers regarding competitors' activities, new products, price developments, and so on.
- *Management services and counseling.* Wholesalers often help retailers improve their operations by training sales clerks, helping with store layouts and displays, and setting up accounting and inventory-control systems. They may help industrial customers by offering training and technical services.

## TRENDS IN WHOLESALING

Wholesaler-distributors have faced mounting pressures in recent years from new sources of competition, demanding customers, new technologies, and more direct-buying programs by large industrial, institutional, and retail buyers. Manufacturers' major complaints against wholesalers are: They don't aggressively promote the manufacturer's product line and they act more like order takers; they don't carry enough inventory and therefore don't fill customers' orders fast enough; they don't supply the manufacturer with up-to-date market, customer, and competitive information; they don't attract high-caliber managers to bring down their own costs; and they charge too much for their services.

Savvy wholesalers have rallied to the challenge and adapted their services to meet their suppliers' and target customers' changing needs. They recognize that they must add value to the channel. Arrow Electronics has done just that.[63]

**ARROW ELECTRONICS**   Arrow Electronics is a global provider of products, services, and solutions to the electronic component and computer product industries. It serves as a supply-channel partner for more than 100,000 original-equipment manufacturers, contract manufacturers, and commercial customers through a global network of 470 locations in 55 countries and territories. With huge contract manufacturers buying more parts directly from suppliers, however, distributors like Arrow are being squeezed out. To better compete, the company has embraced services, providing financing, on-site inventory management, parts-tracking software, and chip programming. Services helped quadruple its share price over a five-year stretch, and the company topped $21.4 billion in sales in 2013.

Wholesalers have worked to increase asset productivity by better managing inventories and receivables. They're also reducing operating costs by investing in more advanced materials-handling technology, information systems, and the Internet. Finally, they're improving their strategic decisions about target markets, product assortment and services, price, communications, and distribution.

Academic experts Jim Narus and Jim Anderson interviewed leading industrial distributors and identified four ways they strengthened their relationships with manufacturers:[64]

1. They sought a clear agreement with their manufacturers about their expected functions in the marketing channel.
2. They gained insight into the manufacturers' requirements by visiting their plants and attending manufacturer association conventions and trade shows.
3. They fulfilled their commitments to the manufacturer by meeting the volume targets, paying bills promptly, and feeding back customer information to their manufacturers.
4. They identified and offered value-added services to help their suppliers.

The wholesaling industry remains vulnerable to one of the most enduring trends—fierce resistance to price increases and the winnowing out of suppliers based on cost and quality. The trend toward vertical integration, in which manufacturers try to control or own their intermediaries, is still strong.

# Market Logistics

Physical distribution starts at the factory. Managers choose a set of warehouses (stocking points) and transportation carriers that will deliver the goods to final destinations in the desired time or at the lowest total cost. Physical distribution has now been expanded into the broader concept of **supply chain management (SCM)**. Supply chain management starts before physical distribution and includes strategically procuring the right inputs (raw materials, components, and capital equipment), converting them efficiently into finished products, and dispatching them to the final destinations. An even broader perspective looks at how the company's suppliers themselves obtain their inputs.

The supply chain perspective can help a company identify superior suppliers and distributors and then help it improve productivity and reduce costs. Firms with top supply chains include Apple, McDonald's, Amazon.com, Unilever, Intel, Procter & Gamble, Cisco Systems, and Samsung Electronics.[65] Some companies choose to partner with and outsource to third-party logistics specialists for help with transportation planning, distribution center management, and other valued-added services that go beyond shipping and storing.[66]

Getting the supply chain right can have huge payoffs. In 2005, Whirlpool found itself with a hodgepodge of warehouses, transport depots, and factory-distribution centers. After a four-year, $600 million investment in a new state-of-the-art distribution system built from scratch, the company reduced its annual inventory by about $250 million a year and now realizes a savings of $100 million a year in increased efficiency while being able to deliver products in 48 to 72 hours.[67]

**Market logistics** includes planning the infrastructure to meet demand, then implementing and controlling the physical flows of materials and final goods from points of origin to points of use to meet customer requirements at a profit. Market logistics planning has four steps:[68]

1. Deciding on the company's value proposition to its customers. (What on-time delivery standard should we offer? What levels should we attain in ordering and billing accuracy?)
2. Selecting the best channel design and network strategy for reaching the customers. (Should the company serve customers directly or through intermediaries? What products should we source from which manufacturing facilities? How many warehouses should we maintain, and where should we locate them?)
3. Developing operational excellence in sales forecasting, warehouse management, transportation management, and materials management
4. Implementing the solution with the best information systems, equipment, policies, and procedures

Studying market logistics leads managers to find the most efficient way to deliver value. For example, a software company traditionally produced and packaged software disks and manuals, shipped them to wholesalers, which shipped them to retailers, which sold them to customers, who brought them home to download onto their PCs. Market logistics offered two superior delivery systems. The first let the customer download the software directly onto his or her computer. The second allowed the computer manufacturer to download the software onto its products. Both solutions eliminated the need for printing, packaging, shipping, and stocking millions of disks and manuals and have quickly become the norm of the industries.

## INTEGRATED LOGISTICS SYSTEMS

The market logistics task calls for **integrated logistics systems (ILS)**, which include materials management, material flow systems, and physical distribution, aided by information technology (IT). Information systems play a critical role in managing market logistics, especially via computers, point-of-sale terminals, uniform product bar codes, satellite tracking, electronic data interchange (EDI), and electronic funds transfer (EFT). These developments have shortened the order-cycle time, reduced clerical labor, reduced errors, and provided improved control of operations. They have enabled companies to promise "the product will be at dock 25 at 10:00 AM tomorrow" and to deliver on that promise.

Market logistics encompass several activities. The first is sales forecasting, on the basis of which the company schedules distribution, production, and inventory levels. Production plans indicate the materials the purchasing department must order. These materials arrive through inbound transportation, enter the receiving area, and are stored in raw-material inventory. Raw materials are converted into finished goods. Finished-goods inventory is the link between customer orders and manufacturing activity. Customers' orders draw down the finished-goods inventory level, and manufacturing activity builds it up. Finished goods flow off the assembly line and pass through packaging, in-plant warehousing, shipping-room processing, outbound transportation, field warehousing, and delivery and service.

Management has become concerned about the total cost of market logistics, which can amount to as much as 30 to 40 percent of the product's cost. In the U.S. grocery business, waste or "shrink" affects 8 to 10 percent of perishable goods, costing $20 billion annually. Stop & Shop, a $16 billion grocery chain, discovered that large, mountainous displays of fruits and veggies and other perishables don't necessarily equal more sales. Instead it often led to spoilage on the shelf, displeasing customers and requiring more staff to sort out the perished items. After an analysis of the perishable departments, Stop & Shop cut the number of foods on display—8 avocados instead of 24, 4 salmon filets instead of 12, for example—and saved an estimated annual $100 million by reducing shrink and improving customer satisfaction.[69]

By cutting the number of perishable fruits and vegetables on display, Stop & Shop saves an estimated $100 million annually.

Source: Stop & Shop

Many experts call market logistics "the last frontier for cost economies," and firms are determined to wring every unnecessary cost out of the system: In 1982, logistics represented 14.5 percent of U.S. GDP; by 2012, the share had dropped to about 8.5 percent.[70] Lowering these costs yields lower prices, higher profit margins, or both. Even though the cost of market logistics can be high, a well-planned program can be a potent tool in competitive marketing.

Many firms are embracing **lean manufacturing**, originally pioneered by Japanese firms such as Toyota, to produce goods with minimal waste of time, materials, and money. CONMED's disposable devices are used by a hospital somewhere in the world every 90 seconds to insert and remove fluid around joints during orthoscopic surgery.[71]

**CONMED** To streamline production, medical manufacturer CONMED set out to link its operations as closely as possible to the ultimate buyer of its products, applying lean manufacturing and Six Sigma philosophies to boost productivity, improve its use of floor space, and cut inventory. Rather than moving manufacturing to China, which might have lowered labor costs but could have also risked long lead times, inventory buildup, and unanticipated delays, the firm put new production processes into place to assemble its disposable products only after hospitals placed orders. Some 80 percent of orders were predictable enough that demand forecasts updated every few months could set hourly production targets. As proof of CONMED's new efficiency, the assembly area for fluid-injection devices went from covering 3,300 square feet and stocking $93,000 worth of parts to 650 square feet and $6,000 worth of parts. Output per worker increased 21 percent. Similarly, its shaver blade factory increased production while decreasing costs by as much as 30 percent in some cases.

Lean manufacturing must be implemented thoughtfully and monitored closely. Toyota's crisis in product safety, which resulted in extensive product recalls, has been attributed in part to the fact that some aspects of lean manufacturing—eliminating overlap by using common parts and designs across multiple product lines and reducing the number of suppliers to procure parts with greater economies of scale—can backfire when quality-control issues arise.[72]

## MARKET-LOGISTICS OBJECTIVES

Many companies state their market-logistics objective as "getting the right goods to the right places at the right time for the least cost." Unfortunately, this objective provides little practical guidance. No system can simultaneously maximize customer service and minimize distribution cost. Maximum customer service implies large inventories, premium transportation, and multiple warehouses, all of which raise market-logistics costs.

Nor can a company achieve market-logistics efficiency by asking each market-logistics manager to minimize his or her own logistics costs. Market-logistics costs interact and are often negatively related. For example:

- The traffic manager favors rail shipment over air shipment because rail costs less. However, because the railroads are slower, rail shipment ties up working capital longer, delays customer payment, and might send customers to competitors who offer faster service.
- The shipping department uses cheap containers to minimize shipping costs. Cheaper containers lead to a higher rate of damaged goods and customer ill will.
- The inventory manager favors low inventories. This increases stock-outs, back orders, paperwork, special production runs, and high-cost, fast-freight shipments.

Given these trade-offs, managers must make decisions on a total-system basis. The starting point is to study what customers require and what competitors are offering. Customers are interested in on-time delivery, help meeting emergency needs, careful handling of merchandise, and quick return and replacement of defective goods.

The wholesaler must then research the relative importance of these service outputs. For example, service-repair time is very important to buyers of copying equipment. Xerox developed a service delivery standard that "can put a disabled machine anywhere in the continental United States back into operation within three hours after receiving the service request." It then designed a service division of technicians, parts, and locations to deliver on this promise.

The company must also consider competitors' service standards. It will normally want to match or exceed these, but the objective is to maximize profits, not sales. Some companies offer less service and charge a lower price; other companies offer more service and charge a premium price.

The company ultimately must establish some promise it makes to the market. Some companies define standards for each service factor. One appliance manufacturer promises to deliver at least 95 percent of the dealer's orders within seven days of order receipt, to fill them with 99 percent accuracy, to deal with inquiries about order status within three hours, and to ensure that merchandise damaged in transit does not exceed 1 percent.

## MARKET-LOGISTICS DECISIONS

The firm must make four major decisions about its market logistics: (1) How should we handle orders (order processing)? (2) Where should we locate our stock (warehousing)? (3) How much stock should we hold (inventory)? and (4) How should we ship goods (transportation)?

**ORDER PROCESSING**  Most companies today are trying to shorten the *order-to-payment cycle*—that is, the time between an order's receipt, delivery, and payment. This cycle has many steps, including order transmission by the salesperson, order entry and customer credit check, inventory and production scheduling, order and invoice shipment, and receipt of payment. The longer this cycle takes, the lower the customer's satisfaction and the lower the company's profits.

**WAREHOUSING**  Every company must store finished goods until they are sold because production and consumption cycles rarely match. More stocking locations mean goods can be delivered to customers more quickly, but warehousing and inventory costs are higher. To reduce these costs, the company might centralize its inventory in one place and use fast transportation to fill orders. To better manage inventory, many department stores such as Nordstrom and Macy's now ship online orders from individual stores.[73]

Some warehouses are now taking on activities formerly done in the plant, including product assembly, packaging, and construction of promotional displays. Moving these activities to the warehouse can save costs and match the offerings more closely to demand.

**INVENTORY**  Salespeople would like their companies to carry enough stock to fill all customer orders immediately. However, this is not cost effective. Inventory cost increases at an accelerating rate as the customer-service level approaches 100 percent. Management needs to know how much sales and profits would increase as a result of carrying larger inventories and promising faster order fulfillment times and then make a decision.

As inventory draws down, management must know at what stock level to place a new order. This stock level is called the *order (or reorder) point*. An order point of 20 means reordering when the stock falls to 20 units. The order point should balance the risks of stock-out against the costs of overstock. The other decision is how much to order. The larger the quantity ordered, the less frequently an order needs to be placed.

The company needs to balance order-processing costs and inventory-carrying costs. *Order-processing costs* for a manufacturer consist of *setup costs* and *running costs* (operating costs when production is running) for the item. If setup costs are low, the manufacturer can produce the item often, and the average cost per item is stable and

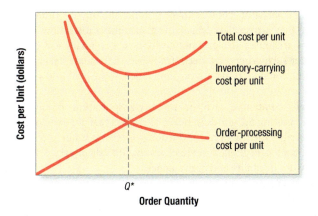

| Fig. 18.1 |

Determining Optimal
Order Quantity

equal to the running costs. If setup costs are high, however, the manufacturer can reduce the average cost per unit by producing a long run and carrying more inventory.

Order-processing costs must be compared with *inventory-carrying costs,* which include storage charges, cost of capital, taxes and insurance, and depreciation and obsolescence. Carrying costs might run as high as 30 percent of inventory value and are higher the larger the average stock carried. This means marketing managers who want to carry larger inventories need to show that incremental gross profits will exceed incremental carrying costs.

We can determine the optimal order quantity by observing how order-processing costs and inventory-carrying costs add up at different order levels. Figure 18.1 shows that the order-processing cost per unit decreases as the number of units ordered increases because the order costs are spread over more units. Inventory-carrying charges per unit increase with the number of units ordered because each unit remains longer in inventory. We sum the two cost curves vertically into a total-cost curve and project the lowest point of the total-cost curve on the horizontal axis to find the optimal order quantity $Q^*$.[74]

Companies are reducing their inventory costs by treating inventory items differently, keeping slow-moving items in a central location and carrying fast-moving items in warehouses closer to customers. Managers are also considering inventory strategies that give them flexibility should anything go wrong, as it often does, whether a dock strike in California, an earthquake in Japan, or political turmoil in North Africa and the Middle East. In an interconnected world, one weak link, if not properly managed, can bring down the entire supply chain.[75]

The ultimate answer to carrying *near-zero inventory* is to build for order, not for stock. Sony calls it SOMO, "Sell one, make one." Dell's inventory strategy for years has been to get the customer to order a computer and pay for it in advance. Then Dell uses the customer's money to pay suppliers to ship the necessary components. As long as customers do not need the item immediately, everyone can save money. Some retailers are unloading excess inventory on eBay where, by cutting out the liquidator middleman, they can make 60 to 80 cents on the dollar as opposed to 10 cents.[76] And some suppliers are snapping up excess inventory to create opportunity.[77]

Cameron Hughes buys excess juice to make and sell affordable, high quality wines to select merchants.

*Source: Cameron Hughes Wine*

❚ CAMERON HUGHES "If a winery has an eight-barrel lot, it may only use five barrels for its customers," says Cameron Hughes, a wine *négociant* who buys excess juice from high-end wineries and wine brokers in France, Italy, Spain, Argentina, South Africa, and California and combines it to make limited-edition, premium blends that taste much more expensive than their price tags. A $100 California Cabernet may sell for $25 a bottle or less under his Lot 500 Napa Valley Cabernet Savignon label. *Négociants* have been around a long time, first as intermediaries who sold or shipped wine as wholesalers, but the profession has expanded as opportunists such as Hughes began making their own wines. Hughes doesn't own any grapes, bottling machines, or trucks. He outsources the bottling, and he sells directly to retailers such as Costco, Sam's Club, and Safeway, eliminating intermediaries and multiple markups. Hughes never knows which lots of wine he will have or how many, but he's turned uncertainty to his advantage—he creates a new product with every batch. Rapid turnover is part of Costco's appeal for him. The discount store's customers love the idea of finding a rare bargain, and Hughes promotes his wines through in-store wine tastings and insider e-mails about his upcoming numbered lots, which sell out quickly. One thing customers won't find out is exactly where the wine comes from. In signing deals Hughes typically has to accept non-disclosure agreements prohibiting him from naming his sources, though the Cameron Confidential flyer that accompanies each wine may hint at it.

**TRANSPORTATION** Transportation choices affect product pricing, on-time delivery performance, and the condition of the goods when they arrive, all of which affect customer satisfaction.

In shipping goods to its warehouses, dealers, and customers, a company can choose rail, air, truck, waterway, or pipeline. Shippers consider such criteria as speed, frequency, dependability, capability, availability, traceability, and cost. For speed, the prime contenders are air, rail, and truck. If the goal is low cost, then the choice is water or pipeline.

Shippers are increasingly combining two or more transportation modes, thanks to containerization. **Containerization** consists of putting the goods in boxes or trailers that are easy to transfer between two transportation modes. *Piggyback* describes the use of rail and trucks; *fishyback*, water and trucks; *trainship*, water and rail; and *airtruck*, air and trucks. Each coordinated mode offers specific advantages. For example, piggyback is cheaper than trucking alone yet provides flexibility and convenience.

Shippers can choose private, contract, or common carriers. If the shipper owns its own truck or air fleet, it becomes a *private carrier*. A *contract carrier* is an independent organization selling transportation services to others on a contract basis. A *common carrier* provides services between predetermined points on a scheduled basis and is available to all shippers at standard rates. Some contract carriers are investing and innovating to create strong value propositions.[78]

**CONTRACT CARRIERS** With so many transportation options available, firms in those industries are constantly competing to cut costs, improve services, and offer even more value to their shipping customers. After 10 years and billions of dollars in investment, including $2.5 billion in 2010 alone, Union Pacific saw on-time delivery on its railroads increase from 30 percent to roughly 90 percent. Improving reliability is also important in ocean shipping. Copenhagen-based Maersk Group is the world's largest global shipper, with around 550 container ships and 225 tankers. To improve efficiency, the firm in 2014 commissioned 20 of the largest ships ever built. Costing $185 million each, these giant ships can cost-effectively carry 18,000 containers, also emitting 50 percent less $CO_2$ in the process. Schneider, one of the country's largest full-truckload freight haulers with more than $3 billion in revenue, developed a fleet-wide "tactical simulator" that has saved the company tens of millions of dollars. Besides helping in the crucial day-to-day route scheduling for drivers, the simulator has also helped with specific decisions ranging from when to raise prices for certain customers to how many drivers to hire (and where). Little changes can make big differences for shippers. Global logistics leader UPS calculated that by having its drivers use a fob instead of a key to operate its trucks, it is cutting out on average 1.7 seconds per stop, or 6.5 minutes per day, saving an estimated $70 million a year in the process.

Union Pacific has invested billions to improve its on-time delivery.

Source: © Stephen Jonas/Alamy

Global shipping leader Maersk commissioned 20 of the largest, efficient ships ever built.

*Source: A.P. Møller-Maersk A/S*

To reduce costly handing at arrival, some firms are putting items into shelf-ready packaging so they don't have to unpack them from a box and place them individually on a shelf. In Europe, P&G has used a three-tier logistic system to schedule deliveries of fast- and slow-moving goods, bulky items, and small items in the most efficient way.[79] To reduce damage in shipping, the size, weight, and fragility of the item must be reflected in the crating technique used and the density of foam cushioning.[80] With logistics, every little detail must be reviewed to see how it might be changed to improve productivity and profitability.

# Summary

1. Retailing includes all the activities in selling goods or services directly to final consumers for personal, non-business use. Retailers can be store retailers, nonstore retailers, and retail organizations.

2. Retailers pass through stages of growth and decline. As existing stores offer more services to remain competitive, costs and prices go up, which opens the door to new retail forms that offer merchandise and services at lower prices. The major types of retail stores are specialty stores, department stores, supermarkets, convenience stores, discount stores, extreme value or hard-discount store, off-price retailers, superstores, and catalog showrooms.

3. Nonstore retailing is growing and includes direct selling (one-to-one selling, one-to-many party selling, and multilevel network marketing), direct marketing (which includes e-commerce and Internet retailing), automatic vending, and buying services.

4. Retail organizations achieve many economies of scale, greater purchasing power, wider brand recognition, and better-trained employees. The major types of corporate retailing are corporate chain stores, voluntary chains, retailer cooperatives, consumer cooperatives, franchise organizations, and merchandising conglomerates.

5. As new retail forms have emerged, competition between them has increased, the rise of giant retailers has been matched by the decline of middle-market retailers, investment in technology has grown, and shopper marketing inside stores has become a priority.

6. Like all marketers, retailers must prepare marketing plans that include decisions about target markets, channels, product assortment and procurement, prices, services, store atmosphere, store activities and experiences, communications, and location.

7. Wholesaling includes all the activities in selling goods or services to those who buy for resale or business use. Wholesalers can perform functions better and more cost-effectively than the manufacturer can. These functions include selling and promoting, buying and assortment building, bulk breaking, warehousing, transportation, financing, risk bearing, dissemination of market information, and provision of management services and consulting.

8. There are four types of wholesalers: merchant wholesalers; brokers and agents; manufacturers' and retailers' sales branches, sales offices, and purchasing offices; and miscellaneous wholesalers such as agricultural assemblers and auction companies.

9. Like retailers, wholesalers must decide on target markets, product assortment and services, price, promotion, and place. The most successful are those that adapt their services to meet suppliers' and target customers' needs.

10. Producers of physical products and services must decide on market logistics—the best way to store and move goods and services to market destinations and to coordinate the activities of suppliers, purchasing agents, manufacturers, marketers, channel members, and customers. Major gains in logistical efficiency have come from advances in information technology.

---

## MyMarketingLab

Go to **mymktlab.com** to complete the problems marked with this icon ⭐ as well as for additional Auto-graded and Assisted-graded writing questions.

---

# Applications

## Marketing Debate
### Should National-Brand Manufacturers Also Supply Private-Label Brands?

Ralston-Purina, Borden, ConAgra, and Heinz have all admitted at some point to supplying products—sometimes lower in quality—to be used for private labels. Other marketers, however, criticize this "if you can't beat them, join them" strategy, maintaining that these actions, if revealed, may create confusion or even reinforce a perception by consumers that all brands in a category are essentially the same.

**Take a position:** Manufacturers should feel free to sell private labels as a source of revenue *versus* National manufacturers should never supply private labels.

## Marketing Discussion
### Retail Customer Loyalty

⭐ Think of your favorite stores. What do they do that encourages your loyalty? What do you like about the in-store experience? What further improvements could these stores make?

---

## Marketing Excellence

### >> Zara

Zara, the Spanish-based company, is Europe's leading apparel retailer, providing consumers with current, high-fashion styles at reasonable prices. With more than $14.5 billion in sales and more than 2,000 stores, the company has succeeded by breaking virtually every traditional rule in the retailing industry.

The first Zara store opened in 1975. By the 1980s, founder Amancio Ortega was working with computer programmers on a new distribution model to reduce the time from design to distribution to just two weeks—a groundbreaking difference from the industry average of six to nine months. As a result, the company now makes between 10,000 and 20,000 different items a year, approximately triple the number made by Gap or H&M. With this revolutionary step, Zara was able to introduce "fast fashion" at affordable prices.

Zara's business model is keenly focused on four strategic elements:

**Design and Production.** Zara employs hundreds of designers at its headquarters in Spain. Thus, new styles are constantly being created and put into production while others are tweaked with various colors or patterns. The firm enforces the speed at which it puts these designs into production by locating half its production facilities nearby in Spain, Portugal, and Morocco. It produces only a small quantity of each collection and is willing to experience occasional shortages to preserve an image of exclusivity. Clothes with a longer shelf life, like T-shirts, are outsourced to lower-cost suppliers in Asia and Turkey. With tight control on its manufacturing process, Zara can move more rapidly than any of its competitors and continues to deliver fresh styles to its stores every week.

**Logistics.** Zara distributes all its merchandise, regardless of origin, from Spain. Its distribution process is designed so that the time from receipt of an order to delivery in the store averages 24 hours in Europe and 48 hours in the United States and Asia. Having 50 percent of its production facilities nearby is key to the success of this model. All Zara stores receive new shipments twice a week, and the small quantities of each collection entice consumers not only to return frequently but also to make purchase decisions more quickly. Because of its logistics and inventory policy, while an average shopper in Spain visits a main street store three times a year, shoppers to a Zara store average 17 trips. Some fans know exactly what day new shipments arrive and show up early to be the first in line, keeping the company's sales strong throughout the year and even during slow economic times. The company also sells more products at full price—85 percent of its merchandise versus the industry average of 60 percent.

**Customers.** Everything revolves around Zara's customers. The retailer monitors customers' changing needs, trends, and tastes through daily reports from shop managers about which products and styles have sold and which haven't. Managers earn as much as 70 percent of their salaries from commission, so they have a strong incentive to stay on top of things. Zara's designers don't have to predict what fashion trends will be in the future. They react to customer feedback—good and bad—and if an idea fails, the line is withdrawn immediately. Zara cuts its losses and the impact is minimal due to the small quantities of each style produced.

**Stores.** Zara does not run advertising campaigns. The retailer's stores, in prestigious high-traffic locations around the world, are its key advertising element, featuring stylish and constantly changing window displays. Other retailers spend 3 percent to 4 percent of revenues on big brand-building campaigns, while Zara spends just 0.3 percent. The company has said it would rather use a percentage of revenue to open new stores than to advertise.

Zara's success comes from having complete control over all the parts of its business—design, production, and distribution. Louis Vuitton's fashion director, Daniel Piette, described the company as "possibly the most innovative and devastating retailer in the world." It has expanded aggressively throughout Europe as well as into emerging markets such as Asia, the Americas, and the Middle East, making sure it honors local tastes in each region. Zara was a latecomer to the Internet and launched its first online store only in 2011. However, the company now uses its Web site to test the waters before entering potential markets like China, Russia, and Canada with retail storefronts.

While Zara has experience record sales as of late, it faces unique challenges ahead, including what to do in the United States, where obesity rates are much higher than in the rest of the world and roomy clothes are preferred to the slim fits and high fashion the company offers. It also needs to decide how to maintain its tight control on manufacturing as it expands throughout the world.

**Questions**

1. Would Zara's model work for other retailers? Why or why not?

2. What can Zara do to ensure successful growth around the world while maintaining the same level of speed and instant fashion?

**Sources:** Rachel Tiplady, "Zara: Taking the Lead in Fast-Fashion," *BusinessWeek*, April 4, 2006; enotes.com, Inditex overview; "Zara: A Spanish Success Story," *CNN*, June 15, 2001; "Fashion Conquistador," *BusinessWeek*, September 4, 2006; Caroline Raux, "The Reign of Spain," *The Guardian*, October 28, 2002; Kerry Capell, "Zara Thrives by Breaking All the Rules," *BusinessWeek*, October 20, 2008, p. 66; Christopher Bjork, "Zara Is to Get Big Online Push," *Wall Street Journal*, September 17, 2009, p. B8; "Best Global Brands 2013," *Interbrand*; Walter Loeb, "Zara's Secret to Success: The New Science of Retailing," *Forbes*, October 14, 2013; Jessica Sheft-Ason, "Zara to Launch Online Shopping in September," *Forbes*, August 3, 2011; Zara.com; Inditex 2012 Annual Report.

## Marketing Excellence

### >> Best Buy

Best Buy is the world's largest multichannel consumer electronics retailer, with $45 billion in sales in fiscal 2013. Sales boomed in the 1980s as the company expanded nationally and made some risky business decisions, like putting its sales staff on salary instead of commission. This decision created a more consumer-friendly, low-pressure shopping atmosphere and resulted in an instant spike in overall revenues. In the 1990s, Best Buy ramped up its computer product offerings, and by 1995 it was the biggest seller of home PCs, a powerful market position during the Internet boom.

At the turn of the 21st century, Best Buy faced new retail competitors, including Costco, Walmart, and Target, which boosted their electronics divisions and product offerings and often priced lower than Best Buy. The company believed the best way to differentiate itself from the competition was to emphasize customer service by selling product warranties and offering personal services like home delivery and installation. Its purchase of Geek Squad, a 24-hour computer service company, proved profitable and strategically wise as home and small-office networks became more complex and the need for personal computing attention increased. By 2004, Best Buy had placed a Geek Squad station in each of its stores, providing consumers with personal computing services in multiple channels: in the stores, online, on the phone, and at home.

Best Buy also segmented its broad customer base into a handful of specific targets such as the affluent tech geek, the busy suburban mom, the young gadget enthusiast, and the price-conscious dad. It used extensive research to determine which segments were the most abundant and lucrative in each market and configured its stores and trained its employees to target those shoppers. For example, stores targeting affluent tech geeks offered a separate home theatre department with knowledgeable salespeople on location. Stores with a high volume of suburban mom shoppers offered personal shopping assistants to help Mom get in and out as quickly as possible with the exact items she needed.

Sometimes a store experienced a new type of lucrative customer. For example, in the coastal town of Baytown, Texas, the local Best Buy observed frequent visits from Eastern European workers coming off cargo ships and oil tankers. These men and women used their precious free time to race over to the store and search the aisles for Apple's iPods and laptops, which were cheaper in the United States than in Europe. To cater to this unique consumer, the store rearranged its layout, moving iPods, MacBooks, and their accessories from the back to the front, and added signage in simple English. The result: Sales from these European workers increased 67 percent.

Best Buy is hailed for growing into a $50 billion company virtually through one channel. However, in recent years, the company has struggled to maintain its retailing dominance. One reason is that consumers no longer have the same interest in large television sets, computers, or entertainment centers that took up so much retail space in years past. In addition, "showrooming" has become a problem, in which consumers visit stores to look, touch, and test out the products but leave empty-handed and purchase online instead. In fact, online retailers like Amazon.com have become Best Buy's biggest competitors in recent years. The company's overall market share in electronics and appliances is 16 percent, but it has only a 7 percent market share online. In comparison, Amazon's overall market share in electronics/appliances is 4 percent, but it is the market leader online, with a 21 percent market share.

Best Buy has acknowledged that it was slow to respond to category and channel shifts and was too focused on a single channel strategy when consumers' behaviors were changing. As a result, sales slipped, customer satisfaction declined, and stock value went with it. To turn things around, the company hired a new CEO who implemented a strategic initiative in 2013. "Renew Blue" was developed to reinvigorate and rejuvenate the customer experience. Online, Best Buy put a huge emphasis on improving the consumer's experience with faster and easier navigation tools, more competitive pricing, and relevant product offerings. The company also started shipping many of its online orders directly from nearby store locations, which improved delivery time and inventory turns.

Within its 1,477 domestic retail stores, Best Buy integrated a new optimization layout, which allocated additional space to growing and more profitable products like smart phones and reduced space for declining categories like entertainment. The company also plans to decrease the number of large stores it operates and increase the number of smaller, mobile stores.

As Best Buy evolves from a single-channel to a multichannel retailer, it faces many opportunities to grow its business even further. The U.S. consumer electronics and appliance market is a $228 billion industry, and the company is making changes to compete better and capture more market share. With so many storefronts across the nation, Best Buy has a competitive advantage and can leverage these assets as it expands into more channels.

**Questions**

1. What were the keys to Best Buy's success? What are the challenges it faces in today's retail environment?

2. How else can Best Buy compete against retail competitors like Walmart and Costco as well as online competitors like Amazon.com?

**Sources:** Jena McGregor, "At Best Buy, Marketing Goes Micro," *Businessweek,* May 15, 2008; Matt Richtel, "Last Man Standing," *The New York Times,* July 17, 2009; Matthew Boyle, "Best Buy's Giant Gamble," *Fortune,* March 29, 2006; Millstein, "Best Buy's Quest to Master Customer Centricity," *Chain Store Age,* December 2007; Ann Zimmerman, "Best Buy Plays Web Hardball," *Wall Street Journal,* October 12, 2012; Walter Loeb, "Best Buy in Turmoil, Will It Survive?," *Forbes,* August 22, 2012; Paula Rosenblum, "Can Best Buy Survive and Are Its Problems Really All about Amazon?," *Forbes,* August 12, 2013; Margaret Bogenrief, "Best Buy Is Pulling Off an Incredible Turnaround," *BusinessInsider,* July 30, 2013; NPD, Nielsen, Stevenson Traqline, Best Buy internal analysis, "Renew Blue," Best Buy Analyst and Investor Day presentation, November 12, 2012; BestBuy.com, 2012 Annual Report.

YOU CAN STILL DUNK IN THE DARK

## In This Chapter, We Will Address the Following **Questions**

1. What is the role of marketing communications? (p. 558)

2. What is the marketing communications mix? (p. 559)

3. How do marketing communications work? (p. 561)

4. What are the major steps in developing effective communications? (p. 564)

5. How should the communications mix be set and evaluated? (p. 573)

6. What is an integrated marketing communications program? (p. 577)

Oreo has become a truly global brand by creatively communicating its message of "togetherness" and "milk's favorite cookie" in markets around the world.

*Source: ASSOCIATED PRESS*

MyMarketingLab™

⭐ **Improve Your Grade!**
Over 10 million students improved their results using the Pearson MyLabs. Visit mymktlab.com for simulations, tutorials, and end-of-chapter problems.

# 19 Designing and Managing Integrated Marketing Communications

**Modern marketing calls for more than developing a good product, pricing it attractively,** and making it accessible. Companies must also communicate with present and potential stakeholders and the general public. For most marketers, therefore, the question is not *whether* to communicate but rather *what* to say, *how* and *when* to say it, to *whom*, and *how often*. Consumers can turn to hundreds of cable and satellite TV channels, thousands of magazines and newspapers, and millions of Internet pages, and they are actively deciding what communications they want to receive. To effectively reach and influence target markets, holistic marketers are creatively employing multiple forms of communications. Consider what Mondelēz International has done in building a global cookie brand.[1]

*Oreo's global brand positioning focuses on "milk's favorite cookie" and "moments of togetherness" using different communications in different countries. In the United States, the highly successful "Celebrate the Kid Inside" campaign was buoyed by celebrations of the brand's 100th anniversary. Ads and in-store contests created a birthday party atmosphere and focused on the "twist, lick, and dunk" method of eating Oreos with milk. The 100-day "Daily Twist" promotion paired the brand in online and print ads with various cultural images, icons, and events, such as Elvis Presley week, the Mars Rover, Gay Pride week, and Bastille Day. The Oreo birthday page on Facebook received 25 million likes, and U.S. sales increased 25 percent. When a power outage darkened the stadium during the Super Bowl in February 2013 for more than half an hour, a tweet for the brand was quickly sent—"Power Out? No problem. You can still dunk in the dark."—that became the social media talk of the game. In India, launch ads featured a father and son in the "twist, lick, and dunk" ritual. Parents there used social media to sign an "Oreo Togetherness Pledge" promising to spend more quality time with their children. An Oreo Togetherness Bus roamed the country providing a platform for parents and children to catch fun family moments. Through these various comunications in different markets, Oreo is establishing a strong global positioning.*

**Done right, marketing communications can** have a huge payoff. This chapter describes how they work and what they can do for a company. It also addresses how holistic marketers combine and integrate marketing communications. Chapter 20 examines mass communications including advertising, sales promotion, and public relations, Chapter 21 looks at digital communications like online, social media, and mobile marketing, and Chapter 22 explores personal communications including direct and database marketing and personal selling.

# The Role of Marketing Communications

**Marketing communications** are the means by which firms attempt to inform, persuade, and remind consumers—directly or indirectly—about the products and brands they sell. In a sense, they represent the voice of the company and its brands; they are a means by which the firm can establish a dialogue and build relationships with consumers. By strengthening customer loyalty, they can contribute to customer equity.

Marketing communications also work by showing consumers how and why a product is used, by whom, where, and when. Consumers can learn who makes the product and what the company and brand stand for, and they can become motivated to try or use it. Marketing communications allow companies to link their brands to other people, places, events, brands, experiences, feelings, and things. They can contribute to brand equity—by establishing the brand in memory and creating a brand image—as well as drive sales and even affect shareholder value.[2]

## THE CHANGING MARKETING COMMUNICATIONS ENVIRONMENT

Technology and other factors have profoundly changed the way consumers process communications, and even whether they choose to process them at all. The rapid diffusion of powerful smart phones, broadband and wireless Internet connections, and ad-skipping digital video recorders (DVRs) have eroded the effectiveness of the mass media. In 1960, a company could reach 80 percent of U.S. women with one 30-second commercial aired simultaneously on three TV networks: ABC, CBS, and NBC. Today, the same ad would have to run on 100 channels or more to achieve this marketing feat. "Marketing Insight: Don't Touch That Remote" describes some developments in television advertising.

---

**marketing insight**

## Don't Touch That Remote

That consumers have more power in the marketplace is perhaps nowhere more evident than in television broadcasting, where digital video recorders (DVRs) allow viewers to watch shows when they want and to skip past ads with a push of the fast-forward button. More than half the U.S. adults who subscribe to a multichannel video service have a DVR, and of viewers who use them, between 60 percent and 70 percent fast-forward through commercials (the others either like ads, don't mind them, or can't be bothered to skip them).

Is that all bad? Surprisingly, research shows that while focusing on an ad in order to fast-forward through it, consumers actually retain and recall a fair amount of information. The most successful ads in fast-forward mode were those consumers had already seen, that used familiar characters, and that didn't have lots of scenes. It also helped to have brand-related information in the center of the screen, where viewers' eyes focus while skipping through. Although consumers are still more likely to recall an ad the next day if they've watched it live, some brand recall occurs even after an ad is deliberately skipped.

Another challenge marketers have long faced is viewers' tendency to switch channels during commercial breaks. Recently, however, Nielsen, which handles television program ratings, has begun to offer ratings for specific ads. Before, advertisers had to pay for air time based on the rating of the program, even if as many as 5 percent to 15 percent of consumers temporarily tuned away. Now they can pay based on the size of the actual audience available when their ad is shown. To increase viewership during commercial breaks, the major broadcast and cable networks are shortening breaks and delaying them until viewers are more likely to be engaged in a program.

A newer challenge for marketers is the time-shifted viewing DVRs permit as more consumers put themselves in charge of their TV schedule. Nielsen now includes Live+3 and Live+7 ratings to capture viewing that occurs three or seven days after initial airing. For some programs and time slots, adding in delayed viewership can make a big difference in the size of the audience.

**Sources:** Merrill Barr, "In a World of DVR Monsters, Do Time Slots Still Matter?," *Forbes*, November 1, 2013; "Over Half of Multi-Channel Video Households Have a DVR," www.leichtmanresearch.com, November 30, 2012; Andrew O'Connell, "Advertisers: Learn to Love the DVR," *Harvard Business Review*, April 2010, p. 22; Erik du Plesis, "Digital Video Recorders and Inadvertent Advertising Exposure," *Journal of Advertising Research* 49 (June 2009); S. Adam Brasel and James Gips, "Breaking Through Fast-Forwarding: Brand Information and Visual Attention," *Journal of Marketing* 72 (November 2008), pp. 31–4; Kenneth C. Wilbur, "How Digital Video Recorder Changes Traditional Television Advertising," *Journal of Advertising* 37 (Summer 2008), pp. 143–49.

Source: imago sportfotodienst/Newscom

Heineken and its digital ad agency AKQA have worked together to leverage their UEFA Champions League soccer sponsorship.

But even as some marketers flee traditional media, they still encounter challenges. Commercial clutter is rampant. The average city dweller is exposed to an estimated 3,000 to 5,000 ad messages a day. Short-form video content and ads appear at gas stations, grocery stores, doctors' offices, and big-box retailers.

Marketing communications in almost every medium and form have been on the rise, and some consumers feel they are increasingly invasive. Marketers must be creative in using technology but not intrude in consumers' lives. One agency that has proven to be a master at building brands and driving sales for its clients in this new digital era is AKQA.[3]

**AKQA**   Established in 2001, AKQA (standing for "All Known Questions Answered") has emerged as one of the premier digital ad agencies by virtue of its creative strategies for clients like Visa, Xbox, Clorox, and others. An online ad for Audi took the visual point of view of the dashboard of a car on Halloween night to show the value of the Audi A6's "thermal imaging night vision assistant" as a safety feature that helped drivers avoid hard-to-see trick-or-treaters. The ad was so well received online that it also ran on prime-time network TV. For Heineken, AKQA created the award-winning Star Player game, which leveraged the brand's UEFA Champions League soccer sponsorship. Using a smart phone or the brand's Facebook page, soccer fans could simultaneously watch a televised match, play the game in real time to predict what would happen next in the match, and publish their results on Twitter and Facebook. For its long-time client Nike, AKQA has created a variety of apps and games, such as one to help launch Nike+ Kinect for home fitness training. The agency also produced an attention-getting online short featuring singer Ellie Golding and her song "Run into the Light" to promote the performance and social benefits of running with Nike+.

# Marketing Communications Mix

In this new communication environment, although advertising is often a central element of a marketing communications program, it is usually not the only one—or even the most important one—for sales and building brand and customer equity. Mondelēz International is partnering with nine digital start-ups to gain an advantage in that area, committing to spend 10 percent of its marketing budget on mobile.[4] To engage its diverse audience, GE uses an in-house content marketing and social media team to play the role of "storyteller" and explain the company's activities on a variety of online platforms.[5]

Ocean Spray—an agricultural cooperative of cranberry growers—has used a variety of communication vehicles to turn sales around.[6]

Ocean Spray's fully integrated "Straight from the Bog" communication program showcased miniature bogs in big cities.

**OCEAN SPRAY** Facing stiff competition, adverse consumer trends, and nearly a decade of declining sales, Ocean Spray COO Ken Romanzi and Arnold Worldwide decided to reintroduce the cranberry as the "surprisingly versatile little fruit that supplies modern-day benefits," through a true 360-degree campaign that used all facets of marketing communications to reach consumers in a variety of settings. The intent was to support the full range of products—cranberry sauce, fruit juices, and dried cranberries in different forms—and leverage the fact that the brand was born in the cranberry bogs and remained there still. The agency decided to tell an authentic, honest, and perhaps surprising story dubbed "Straight from the Bog." The campaign was designed to also reinforce two key brand benefits—that Ocean Spray products tasted good and were good for you. PR played a crucial role. Miniature bogs were brought to Manhattan and featured on an NBC *Today* morning segment. A "Bogs across America Tour" brought the experience to Los Angeles and Chicago. Television and print advertising featured two growers (depicted by actors) standing waist-deep in a bog and talking, often humorously, about what they did. The campaign also included a Web site, in-store displays, and events for consumers and for members of the growers' cooperative itself. Product innovation was crucial too; new flavor blends were introduced, along with a line of 100 percent juices, diet and light versions, and Craisins sweetened dried cranberries. Since then, famed chef Ming Tsai appeared in a pop-up restaurant in New York's Rockefeller Center, and a leap year promotion urged consumers to "leap" to Craisins. The campaign hit the mark, lifting sales an average of 10 percent in its first five years despite continued decline in the fruit juice category.

The **marketing communications mix** consists of eight major modes of communication:[7]

1. *Advertising*—Any paid form of nonpersonal presentation and promotion of ideas, goods, or services by an identified sponsor via print media (newspapers and magazines), broadcast media (radio and television), network media (telephone, cable, satellite, wireless), electronic media (audiotape, videotape, videodisk, CD-ROM, Web page), and display media (billboards, signs, posters).

2. *Sales promotion*—A variety of short-term incentives to encourage trial or purchase of a product or service including consumer promotions (such as samples, coupons, and premiums), trade promotions (such as advertising and display allowances), and business and sales force promotions (contests for sales reps).

3. *Events and experiences*—Company-sponsored activities and programs designed to create daily or special brand-related interactions with consumers, including sports, arts, entertainment, and cause events as well as less formal activities.

4. *Public relations and publicity*—A variety of programs directed internally to employees of the company or externally to consumers, other firms, the government, and media to promote or protect a company's image or its individual product communications.

5. *Online and social media marketing*—Online activities and programs designed to engage customers or prospects and directly or indirectly raise awareness, improve image, or elicit sales of products and services.

6. *Mobile marketing*—A special form of online marketing that places communications on consumer's cell phones, smart phones, or tablets.

7. *Direct and database marketing*—Use of mail, telephone, fax, e-mail, or Internet to communicate directly with or solicit response or dialogue from specific customers and prospects.

8. *Personal selling*—Face-to-face interaction with one or more prospective purchasers for the purpose of making presentations, answering questions, and procuring orders.

Table 19.1 lists examples of these platforms, but company communication goes beyond these. The product's styling and price, the shape and color of the package, the salesperson's manner and dress, the store décor, and the company's stationery all communicate something to buyers. Every *brand contact* delivers an impression that can strengthen or weaken a customer's view of a company.[8]

As Chapter 1 noted, communication options appear in paid media (traditional outlets such as TV, print, direct mail), owned media (company-controlled options such as Web sites, blogs, mobile apps, social media) and earned media (virtual or real-world word of mouth, press coverage).

| TABLE 19.1 | Examples of the Eight Common Communication Platforms | | | | | | |
|---|---|---|---|---|---|---|---|
| **Advertising** | **Sales Promotion** | **Events and Experiences** | **Public Relations and Publicity** | **Online and Social Media Marketing** | **Mobile Marketing** | **Direct and Database Marketing** | **Personal Selling** |
| Print and broadcast ads | Contests, games, sweepstakes, lotteries | Sports | Press kits | Web sites | Text messages | Catalogs | Sales presentations |
| Packaging–outer | Premiums and gifts | Entertainment | Speeches | E-mail | Online marketing | Mailings | Sales meetings |
| Packaging inserts | Sampling | Festivals | Seminars | Search ads | Social media marketing | Telemarketing | Incentive programs |
| Cinema | Fairs and trade shows | Arts | Annual reports | Display ads | | Electronic shopping | Samples |
| Brochures and booklets | Exhibits | Causes | Charitable donations | Company blogs | | TV shopping | Fairs and trade shows |
| Posters and leaflets | Demonstrations | Factory tours | Publications | Third-party chat rooms, forums, and blogs | | Fax | |
| Directories | Coupons | Company museums | Community relations | Facebook and Twitter messages, YouTube channels and videos | | Catalogs | |
| Reprints of ads | Rebates | Street activities | Lobbying | | | | |
| Billboards | Low-interest financing | | Identity media | | | | |
| Display signs | Trade-in allowances | | Company magazine | | | | |
| Point-of-purchase displays | Continuity programs | | | | | | |
| DVDs | Tie-ins | | | | | | |

# How Do Marketing Communications Work?

Marketing communication activities in every medium contribute to brand equity and drive sales in many ways: by creating brand awareness, forging brand image in consumers' memories, eliciting positive brand judgments or feelings, and strengthening consumer loyalty. The way brand associations are formed does not matter. Whether a consumer has a strong, favorable, and unique brand association of Subaru with "outdoors," "active," and "rugged" because of a TV ad that shows the car driving over rough terrain or because Subaru sponsors ski, kayak, and mountain bike events, the impact in terms of Subaru's brand equity should be identical.

But marketing communications activities must be integrated to deliver a consistent message and achieve the strategic positioning. The starting point in planning them is a *communication audit* that profiles all interactions customers in the target market may have with the company and all its products and services. For example, someone interested in purchasing a new smart phone might talk to friends and family members, see television ads, read articles, look for information online, and look at smart phones in a store.

To implement the right communications programs and allocate dollars efficiently, marketers need to assess which experiences and impressions will have the most influence at each stage of the buying process. Armed with these insights, they can judge marketing communications according to their ability to affect experiences and impressions, build customer loyalty and brand equity, and drive sales. For example, how well does a proposed ad campaign contribute to awareness or to creating, maintaining, or strengthening brand associations? Does a sponsorship improve consumers' brand judgments and feelings? Does a promotion encourage consumers to buy more of a product? At what price premium?

In building brand equity, marketers should be "media neutral" and evaluate *all* communication options on effectiveness (how well does it work?) and efficiency (how much does it cost?). Chrysler's gamble with an unconventional campaign for Dodge Durango is one marketing communication program that appeared to pay off.[9]

---

**▌ DODGE DURANGO** To promote its 2013 Dodge Durango, Chrysler chose actor Will Ferrell in character as Ron Burgundy to create an ad coinciding with the release of Ferrell's *Anchorman* sequel. Paramount Productions, Wieden + Kennedy ad agency, and Funny or Die's Web site production company collaborated to shoot dozens of commercials for TV and short films for the Internet of the classy but clueless 1970s-era anchorman admiring the modern features of the new Durango. In one spot, Burgundy touts the glove box as being "comfortable enough to hold two turkey sandwiches or 70 packs of gum." A tongue-in-cheek "Hands on Ron Burgundy" online promotion rewarded those consumers who could "touch" Ron Burgundy by following a moving circle with their cursor or smart-phone button. After the campaign was launched, Web traffic shot up 80 percent with each video earning millions of views. Purchase intent rose 100 percent, and sales increased by almost 60 percent.

---

## THE COMMUNICATIONS PROCESS MODELS

Marketers should understand the fundamental elements of effective communications. Two models are useful: a macromodel and a micromodel.

**MACROMODEL OF THE COMMUNICATIONS PROCESS** Figure 19.1 shows a macromodel with nine key factors in effective communication. Two represent the major parties—*sender* and *receiver*. Two represent the

An unconventional marketing communication campaign for Dodge Durango featuring actor Will Ferrell helped increase sales.

Source: ASSOCIATED PRESS

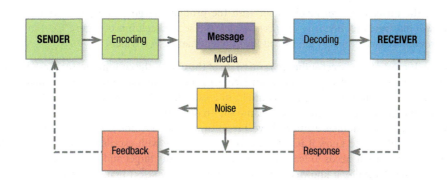

| **Fig. 19.1** |

Elements in the
Communications
Process

major tools—*message* and *media.* Four represent major communication functions—*encoding, decoding, response,* and *feedback.* The last element in the system is *noise,* random and competing messages that may interfere with the intended communication.

Senders must know what audiences they want to reach and what responses they want to get. They must encode their messages so the target audience can successfully decode them. They must transmit the message through media that reach the target audience and develop feedback channels to monitor the responses. The more the sender's field of experience overlaps that of the receiver, the more effective the message is likely to be. Note that selective attention, distortion, and retention processes—first introduced in Chapter 6—may be operating.

**MICROMODEL OF CONSUMER RESPONSES** Micromodels of marketing communications concentrate on consumers' specific responses to communications.[10] Figure 19.2 summarizes four classic *response hierarchy models.*

All these models assume the buyer passes through cognitive, affective, and behavioral stages in that order. This "learn-feel-do" sequence is appropriate when the audience has high involvement with a product category perceived to have high differentiation, such as an automobile or house. An alternative sequence, "do-feel-learn," is relevant when the audience has high involvement but perceives little or no differentiation within the product category, such as airline tickets or personal computers. A third sequence, "learn-do-feel," is relevant when the audience has low involvement and perceives little differentiation, such as with salt or batteries. By choosing the right sequence, the marketer can do a better job of planning communications.

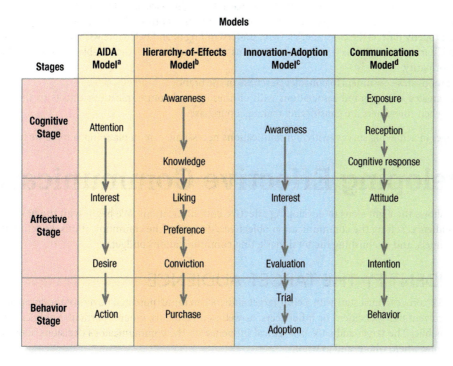

| **Fig. 19.2** |

Response Hierarchy
Models

Sources: [a]E. K. Strong, *The Psychology of Selling* (New York: McGraw-Hill, 1925), p. 9; [b]Robert J. Lavidge and Gary A. Steiner, "A Model for Predictive Measurements of Advertising Effectiveness," *Journal of Marketing* (October 1961), p. 61; [c]Everett M. Rogers, *Diffusion of Innovation* (New York: Free Press, 1962), pp. 79–86; [d]various sources.

Let's assume the buyer has high involvement with the product category and perceives high differentiation within it. We will illustrate the *hierarchy-of-effects model* (the second column of Figure 19.2) in the context of a marketing communications campaign for a small Iowa college named Pottsville:

- *Awareness.* If most of the target audience is unaware of the object, the communicator's task is to build awareness. Suppose Pottsville seeks applicants from Nebraska but has no name recognition there, though 30,000 Nebraska high school juniors and seniors could be interested in it. The college might set the objective of making 70 percent of these students aware of its name within one year.
- *Knowledge.* The target audience might have brand awareness but not know much more. Pottsville may want its target audience to know it is a private four-year college with excellent programs in English, foreign languages, and history. It needs to learn how many people in the target audience have little, some, or much knowledge about Pottsville. If knowledge is weak, Pottsville may select brand knowledge as its communications objective.
- *Liking.* Given target members know the brand, how do they feel about it? If the audience looks unfavorably on Pottsville College, the communicator needs to find out why. In the case of real problems, Pottsville will need to fix these and then communicate its renewed quality. Good public relations calls for "good deeds followed by good words."
- *Preference.* The target audience might like the product but not prefer it to others. The communicator must then try to build consumer preference by comparing quality, value, performance, and other features to those of likely competitors.
- *Conviction.* A target audience might prefer a particular product but not develop a conviction about buying it. The communicator's job is to build conviction and intent to apply among students interested in Pottsville College.
- *Purchase.* Finally, some members of the target audience might have conviction but not quite get around to making the purchase. The communicator must lead these consumers to take the final step, perhaps by offering the product at a low price, offering a premium, or letting them try it out. Pottsville might invite selected high school students to visit the campus and attend some classes, or it might offer partial scholarships to deserving students.

To see how fragile the communication process is, assume the probability of *each* of the six steps being successfully accomplished is 50 percent. The laws of probability suggest that the likelihood of *all* six steps occurring successfully, assuming they are independent events, is $.5 \times .5 \times .5 \times .5 \times .5 \times .5$, which equals 1.5625 percent. If the probability of each's occurring were, on average, a more likely 10 percent, then the joint probability of all six events occurring drops to 0.0001 percent—or only 1 chance in 1,000,000!

To increase the odds of success for a communications campaign, marketers must attempt to increase the likelihood that *each* step occurs. For example, the ideal ad campaign would ensure that:

1. The right consumer is exposed to the right message at the right place and at the right time.
2. The ad causes the consumer to pay attention but does not distract from the intended message.
3. The ad properly reflects the consumer's level of understanding of and behaviors with the product and the brand.
4. The ad correctly positions the brand in terms of desirable and deliverable points-of-difference and points-of-parity.
5. The ad motivates consumers to consider purchase of the brand.
6. The ad creates strong brand associations with all these stored communications effects so they can have an impact when consumers are considering making a purchase.

The challenges in achieving success with communications necessitate careful planning, a topic we turn to next.

# Developing Effective Communications

Figure 19.3 shows the eight steps in developing effective communications. We begin with the basics: identifying the target audience, setting the communication objectives, designing the communications, selecting the communication channels, and establishing the total marketing communications budget.

**| Fig. 19.3 |**

**Steps in Developing Effective Communications**

Identify target audience

Determine objectives

Design communications

Select channels

Establish budget

Decide on media mix

Measure results

Manage integrated marketing communications

## IDENTIFY THE TARGET AUDIENCE

The process must start with a clear target audience in mind: potential buyers of the company's products, current users, deciders, or influencers, as well as individuals, groups, particular publics, or the general public. The target audience is a critical influence on the communicator's decisions about what to say, how, when, where, and to whom.

Though we can profile the target audience in terms of any of the market segments identified in Chapter 9, it's often useful to do so in terms of usage and loyalty. Is the target new to the category or a current user? Is the target loyal to the brand, loyal to a competitor, or someone who switches between brands? If a brand user, is he or she a heavy or light user? Communication strategy will differ depending on the answers. We can also conduct *image analysis* by profiling the target audience in terms of brand knowledge.

## SET THE COMMUNICATIONS OBJECTIVES

As we showed with Pottsville College, marketers can set communications objectives at any level of the hierarchy-of-effects model. John Rossiter and Larry Percy identify four possible objectives:[11]

1. ***Establish need for category***—Establishing a product or service category as necessary for removing or satisfying a perceived discrepancy between a current motivational state and a desired motivational state. A new-to-the-world product such as electric cars will always begin with a communications objective of establishing category need.
2. ***Build brand awareness***—Fostering the consumer's ability to recognize or recall the brand in sufficient detail to make a purchase. Recognition is easier to achieve than recall—consumers asked to think of a brand of frozen entrées are more likely to recognize Stouffer's distinctive orange packages than to recall the brand. Brand recall is important outside the store; brand recognition is important inside the store. Brand awareness provides a foundation for brand equity.
3. ***Build brand attitude***—Helping consumers evaluate the brand's perceived ability to meet a currently relevant need. Relevant brand needs may be negatively oriented (problem removal, problem avoidance, incomplete satisfaction, normal depletion) or positively oriented (sensory gratification, intellectual stimulation, or social approval). Household cleaning products often use problem solution; food products, on the other hand, often use sensory-oriented ads emphasizing appetite appeal.
4. ***Influence brand purchase intention***—Moving consumers to decide to purchase the brand or take purchase-related action. Promotional offers like coupons or two-for-one deals encourage consumers to make a mental commitment to buy. But many consumers do not have an expressed category need and may not be in the market when exposed to an ad, so they are unlikely to form buy intentions. In any given week, only about 20 percent of adults may be planning to buy detergent, only 2 percent to buy a carpet cleaner, and only 0.25 percent to buy a car.

The most effective communications can achieve multiple objectives. Consider what Jockey did.[12]

.................................................................................................................................

**JKY BY JOCKEY** Like many heritage brands with an aging customer base, Jockey suffered under the image of being "your father's" or maybe even "your grandfather's" underwear. To be viable long-term, the brand needed a youthful infusion. Research revealed that women ages 18 to 34 make almost half of all underwear purchases, aligning well with retailer Target's predominantly younger female audience. So in 2012, Jockey launched an integrated, retailer-specific program with Target to change brand perceptions. A new line of underwear and undershorts for men, JKY by Jockey, was introduced with the positioning that the right underwear or undershorts can change the way men look and feel. Research also revealed that women like to see and feel the product, so sleek, attractive packaging was introduced with a see-through box that allowed easy inspection. Color-coding and clean graphics helped buyers find the right sizes and figure out which styles were best for different types of men's clothing. A strong call to action appeared on large in-store ceiling banners with the clever headline "It's Time to Change Your Underwear." The slogan also appeared on the back wall of the store and in cards inserted into the back pockets of men's jeans sold in the store. A Facebook microsite was also launched to promote the line. The campaign achieved its objectives, changing both attitudes and behavior. The average JKY buyer was 32 years old, more than 20 years younger than the core Jockey customer, and the sales success of the line resulted in Target's asking Jockey to create a JKY line for women.

.................................................................................................................................

## DESIGN THE COMMUNICATIONS

Formulating the communications to achieve the desired response requires answering three questions: what to say (message strategy), how to say it (creative strategy), and who should say it (message source).

Careful consumer research helped Jockey successfully craft an integrated communication campaign to launch its JKY underwear and undershorts line sold at Target.

**MESSAGE STRATEGY** In selecting message strategy, management searches for appeals, themes, or ideas that will tie in to the brand positioning and help establish points-of-parity or points-of-difference. Some of these appeals or ideas may relate directly to product or service performance (the quality, economy, or value of the brand); others may relate to more extrinsic considerations (the brand as being contemporary, popular, or traditional).

Researcher John C. Maloney felt buyers expected one of four types of reward from a product: rational, sensory, social, or ego satisfaction.[13] They might visualize these rewards from results-of-use experience, product-in-use experience, or incidental-to-use experience. Crossing the four types of rewards with the three types of experience generates 12 types of messages. For example, the appeal "gets clothes cleaner" is a rational-reward promise following results-of-use experience. The phrase "real beer taste in a great light beer" is a sensory-reward promise connected with product-in-use experience.

**CREATIVE STRATEGY** Communications effectiveness depends on how well a message is expressed as well as on its content. If a communication is ineffective, it may mean the wrong message was used or the right one was poorly expressed. *Creative strategies* are the way marketers translate their messages into a specific communication. We can broadly classify them as either **informational** or **transformational** appeals.[14]

*Informational Appeals* An *informational appeal* elaborates on product or service attributes or benefits. Examples in advertising are problem-solution ads (Aleve offers the longest-lasting relief for aches and pains), product demonstration ads (Thompson Water Seal can withstand intense rain, snow, and heat), product comparison ads (AT&T offers the largest 4G mobile network), and testimonials from unknown or celebrity endorsers (NBA phenomenon LeBron James pitching McDonald's, Nike, Samsung, Sprite, and others). Informational appeals assume strictly rational processing of the communication on the consumer's part. Logic and reason rule.

Carl Hovland's research at Yale has shed much light on informational appeals and their relationship to such issues as conclusion drawing, one-sided versus two-sided arguments, and order of argument presentation. Some early experiments supported stating conclusions for the audience. Subsequent research, however, indicates that the best ads ask questions and allow readers and viewers to form their own conclusions.[15]

You might expect one-sided presentations that praise a product to be more effective than two-sided arguments that also mention shortcomings. Yet two-sided messages may be more appropriate, especially when negative associations must be overcome.[16] Two-sided messages are more effective with more educated audiences and those who are initially opposed.[17] Chapter 6 described how Domino's took the drastic step of admitting to its pizza's taste problems to try to change the minds of consumers with negative perceptions.

Finally, the order in which arguments are presented is important.[18] In a one-sided message, presenting the strongest argument first arouses attention and interest, important in media where the audience often does not attend to the whole message. With a captive audience, a climactic presentation might be more effective.

To be seen as more modern and up-to-date, Radio Shack ran a Super Bowl ad spoofing its old image.

Source: RadioShack

For a two-sided message, if the audience is initially opposed, start with the other side's argument and conclude with your strongest argument. In a widely watched and admired Super Bowl ad in 2014, Radio Shack poked fun at its old-fashioned image by featuring a host of 1980s icons who wanted their store back, ending with an appeal to check out the chain's newly redesigned stores.

**Transformational Appeals** A *transformational appeal* elaborates on a nonproduct-related benefit or image. It might depict what kind of person uses a brand (VW advertised to active, youthful people with its famed "Drivers Wanted" campaign) or what kind of experience results from use (Pringles advertised "Once You Pop, the Fun Don't Stop" for years). Transformational appeals often attempt to stir up emotions that will motivate purchase.[19]

Communicators use negative appeals such as fear, guilt, and shame to get people to do things (brush their teeth, have an annual health checkup) or stop doing things (smoking, abusing alcohol, overeating). Fear appeals work best when they are not too strong, when source credibility is high, and when the communication promises, in a believable and efficient way, that the product or service will relieve the fear it arouses. Messages are most persuasive when they moderately disagree with audience beliefs. Stating only what the audience already believes at best just reinforces beliefs, while messages too much at variance with those beliefs will be rejected.[20]

Communicators also use positive emotional appeals such as humor, love, pride, and joy. Motivational or "borrowed interest" devices—such as cute babies, frisky puppies, popular music, and provocative sex appeals—are often employed to attract attention and raise involvement with an ad. These techniques are thought necessary in the tough new media environment of low-involvement processing and competing messages. Attention-getting tactics may also detract from comprehension, however, or wear out their welcome fast or overshadow the product. Thus, one challenge is figuring out how to break through the clutter *and* deliver the intended message.

Even highly entertaining and creative means of expression must retain the appropriate consumer perspective, as Toys "R" Us found out.[21]

**TOYS "R" US**   Before the 2013 holiday shopping season, Toys "R" Us filmed a prankish video showing a busload of schoolchildren on a nature field trip. As the guide on the bus explains their plans, the children look obviously bored. When the guide rips off his park ranger outfit to reveal a Toys "R" Us uniform, however, and announces they are going to a Toys "R" Us store instead, the children explode with excitement. Many parents, educators, and others objected online to the video's portrayal of science education and nature as boring and the reinforcement of materialistic values instead.

The magic of advertising is to bring abstract concepts to life in the minds of the consumer target. In a print ad, the communicator must decide on headline, copy, illustration, and color.[22] For a radio message, the communicator must choose words, voice qualities, and vocalizations. The sound of an announcer promoting a used automobile should be different from one promoting a new luxury car. If the message is to be carried on television or in person, all these elements plus body language must be planned. For the message to go online, layout, fonts, graphics, and other visual and verbal information must be laid out.

**MESSAGE SOURCE** Research has shown that the source's credibility is crucial to a message's acceptance. The three most often identified sources of credibility are expertise, trustworthiness, and likability.[23] *Expertise* is the specialized knowledge the communicator possesses to back the claim. *Trustworthiness* describes how objective and honest the source is perceived to be. Friends are trusted more than strangers or salespeople, and people who are not paid to endorse a product are viewed as more trustworthy than people who are paid. *Likability* describes the source's attractiveness, measured in terms of candor, humor, and naturalness.

The most credible source will score high on all three dimensions—expertise, trustworthiness, and likability. Pharmaceutical companies want doctors to testify about product benefits because doctors have high credibility. Charles Schwab became the centerpiece of ads for his $4 billion-plus discount brokerage firm via the "Talk to Chuck" and "Own Your Tomorrow" corporate advertising campaigns.

Messages delivered by attractive or popular sources can achieve higher attention and recall, which is why some advertisers use celebrities as spokespeople. "Marketing Memo: Celebrity Endorsements as a Strategy" focuses on the proper use of testimonials.

On the other hand, some marketers are using ordinary people in the their ads to give them more realism and overcome consumer skepticism. Ford featured actual customers being thrust into a press conference to describe their vehicles. Red Lobster used chefs from its restaurants to extol the virtues of its menu.[24]

If a person has a positive attitude toward a source and a message or a negative attitude toward both, a state of *congruity* is said to exist. But what happens if a consumer hears a likable celebrity praise a brand she dislikes? Charles Osgood and Percy Tannenbaum believe attitude change will take place that increases the amount of congruity between the two evaluations.[25] The consumer will end up respecting the celebrity somewhat less or the brand somewhat more. If she encounters the same celebrity praising other disliked brands, she will eventually develop a negative view of the celebrity and maintain negative attitudes toward the brands. The **principle of congruity** implies that communicators can use their good image to reduce some negative feelings toward a brand but in the process might lose some esteem with the audience.

## SELECT THE COMMUNICATIONS CHANNELS

Selecting an efficient means to carry the message becomes more difficult as channels of communication become more fragmented and cluttered. Communications channels may be personal and nonpersonal. Within each are many subchannels.

**PERSONAL COMMUNICATIONS CHANNELS** **Personal communications channels** let two or more persons communicate face to face or person to audience through a phone, surface mail, or e-mail. They derive their effectiveness from individualized presentation and feedback and include direct marketing, personal selling, and word of mouth.

We can draw a further distinction between advocate, expert, and social communications channels. *Advocate channels* consist of company salespeople contacting buyers in the target market. *Expert channels* consist of independent experts making statements to target buyers. *Social channels* consist of neighbors, friends, family members, and associates talking to target buyers.

A study by Burson-Marsteller and Roper Starch Worldwide found that one influential person's word of mouth tends to affect the buying attitudes of two other people, on average. That circle of influence, however, jumps to eight online. Word about good companies travels fast; word about bad companies travels even faster. Reaching the right people is key.

Personal influence carries especially great weight (1) when products are expensive, risky, or purchased infrequently, and (2) when products suggest something about the user's status or taste. People often ask others to recommend a doctor, plumber, hotel, lawyer, accountant, architect, insurance agent, interior decorator, or financial consultant. If we have confidence in the recommendation, we normally act on the referral. Service providers clearly have a strong interest in building referral sources.

Even business-to-business marketers can benefit from strong word of mouth. To give loyal customers and others a voice in product development, John Deere created its own chat show, "You're On," with a mobile production studio called "Chatterbox" built to resemble a local radio station. The award-winning campaign was launched at the world's largest construction show, ConExpo, and also featured daily blogs and real-time texts to engage others outside the event in the design of the 2012 product lineup.[26]

Consumers use *word of mouth* to talk about dozens of brands each day, from media and entertainment products such as movies, TV shows, and publications to food products, travel services, and retail stores. Companies are acutely aware of its power. Hush Puppies shoes, Krispy Kreme doughnuts, and, more recently, Crocs shoes were built through strong word of mouth, as were companies such as Red Bull, Starbucks, and Amazon.com.

# marketing memo

## Celebrity Endorsements as a Message Strategy

A well-chosen celebrity can draw attention to a product or brand—as Priceline found when it picked *Star Trek* icon William Shatner to star in campy ads reinforcing its low-price image. The quirky campaigns have run for more than a decade, and Shatner's decision to receive stock options as compensation reportedly netted him millions of dollars for his work. The right celebrity can also lend his or her image to a brand. To reinforce its high status and prestige image, American Express has used movie legends Robert De Niro and Martin Scorsese in ads.

Celebrities are likely to be effective when they are credible or personify a key product attribute. Statesman-like Dennis Haysbert for State Farm insurance, rugged Brett Favre for Wrangler jeans, and popular singer and actress Jennifer Hudson for Weight Watchers' weight loss program have all been praised by consumers as good fits. Celine Dion, however, failed to add glamour—or sales—to Chrysler, and even though she was locked into a three-year, $14 million deal, she was let go. Ozzy Osbourne seems an odd choice to advertise "I Can't Believe It's Not Butter" given his seemingly perpetual confusion.

A celebrity should have high recognition, high positive affect, and high "fit" with the product. Paris Hilton, Howard Stern, and Donald Trump have high recognition but negative affect among many groups. Johnny Depp has high recognition and high positive affect but might not seem relevant, for example, to a new financial service. Tom Hanks and Oprah Winfrey could successfully advertise a large number of products because they have extremely high ratings for familiarity and likability (known as the Q factor in the entertainment industry).

Celebrities can play a more strategic role too, not only endorsing but also helping to design, position, and sell merchandise and services. Nike often brings its elite athletic endorsers in on product design. Tiger Woods, Paul Casey, and Stewart Cink have helped to design, prototype, and test new golf clubs and balls at Nike Golf's Research & Development facility. Beyoncé (Pepsi), will.i.am (Intel), Justin Timberlake (Bud Light Platinum), Alicia Keys (BlackBerry), and Taylor Swift (Diet Coke) have all been designated "ambassadors" for their brands with various creative duties and responsibilities.

Some celebrities lend their talents to brands without directly using their fame. A host of movie and TV stars do uncredited commercial voice-overs, including Jon Hamm (Mercedes-Benz), Morgan Freeman (Visa), Matt Damon (TD Ameritrade), Jeff Bridges (Duracell), and George Clooney (Budweiser). Although advertisers assume some viewers will recognize the voices, the main rationale for using them is the actors' incomparable voice talent and skill.

Using celebrities poses certain risks. The celebrity might hold out for a larger fee at contract renewal or withdraw. And just like movies and album releases, celebrity campaigns can be expensive flops. The celebrity might lose popularity or, even worse, get caught in a scandal or embarrassing situation, as did Tiger Woods in a heavily publicized 2009 episode. Besides carefully checking endorsers' backgrounds, some marketers are choosing to use more than one to lessen their brand's exposure to any single person's flaws.

Another solution is for marketers to create their own brand celebrities. Dos Equis beer, imported from Mexico, grew U.S. sales by more than 20 percent during the recent recession by riding on the popularity of its "Most Interesting Man in the World" ad campaign. Suave and debonair, with an exotic accent and a silver beard, the character has hundreds of thousands of Facebook friends despite being completely fictitious. Videos of his exploits log millions of views on YouTube. Dos Equis has made it possible for customers to "call" him and listen to a series of automated voicemail messages.

Source: Planet Photos/ZUMAPRESS/Newscom

Jennifer Hudson was seen as a highly credible spokesperson for Weight Watchers.

**Sources:** Lauren Yapalater, "19 Commercials You May Not Have Realized Were Voiced by Famous Actors," www.buzzfeed.com, August 6, 2013; Natalie Zmuda and Rupal Parekh, "More than a Pitchman: Why Stars Are Getting Marketing Titles," *Advertising Age*, February 10, 2013; Tim Nudd, "Dos Equis Invites You to Call the Most Interesting Voicemail in the World," *Adweek*, November 9, 2012; Lucia Moses, "Get Real," *Adweek*, April 30, 2102; Linda Massarella, "Shatner's Singing a Happy Tune," *Toronto Sun*, May 2, 2010; "Nike Golf Celebrates Achievements and Successes of Past Year," www.worldgolf.com, January 2, 2009; Piet Levy, "Keeping It Interesting," *Marketing News*, October 30, 2009, p. 8; Irving Rein, Philip Kotler, and Martin Scoller, *The Making and Marketing of Professionals into Celebrities* (Chicago: NTC Business Books, 1997).

Positive word of mouth sometimes happens organically with little advertising, but as Chapter 21 discusses, it can also be managed and facilitated.[27] Without question, more advertisers now seek greater earned media—unsolicited professional commentary, personal blog entries, social network discussion—as a result of their paid media and owned media efforts. Choosing a unique event can also be helpful, as Volkswagen found out with its Shark Week promotion.[28]

**VOLKSWAGEN AND SHARK WEEK**    Discovery Channel's Shark Week is a cultural TV phenomenon that spans more than 25 years and always generates high ratings. To boost brand affinity among men for its newly redesigned VW Beetle, Volkswagen and its agency partners formed a sponsorship for Shark Week and created a diving cage that was plunged into shark-infested waters. The Shark Observation Cage, as it was called, was a fully operational Beetle. Stunning images showed the car driving on the ocean floor with sharks swirling around. The campaign featured VW-branded videos that ran on air and online, supported by much social media, PR, and traditional print and out-of-home ads. The campaign was liked on Facebook 1.8 million times, and sales increased 50 percent; male buyers went from 20 percent to 40 percent.

Word of mouth can be particularly effective for smaller businesses, with whom customers may feel a more personal relationship. Many are investing in various forms of social media to get the word out instead of newspapers, radio, and Yellow Pages. Southern Jewelz, started by a recent college grad, found sales doubling over six months after it began to actively use Facebook, Twitter, and e-commerce software.[29]

**NONPERSONAL (MASS) COMMUNICATIONS CHANNELS** Nonpersonal channels are communications directed to more than one person and include advertising, sales promotions, events and experiences, and public relations. Much recent growth has taken place through events and experiences. Events marketers who once favored sports events are now using other venues such as art museums, zoos, and ice shows to entertain clients and employees. AT&T and IBM sponsor symphony performances and art exhibits, Visa is an active sponsor of the Olympics, and Harley-Davidson sponsors annual motorcycle rallies. Citibank found a novel way to promote its corporate brand by sponsoring a unique service.[30]

Source: © Steve Hamblin/Alamy

Citibank's bike sponsorship in New York City has paid many different kinds of dividends for the company.

**CITI BIKES**    One growth area in big cities is bike-sharing programs that let members pick up and drop off rented bikes at street-side stations. In New York City, Citibank struck a $41 million, six-year deal to sponsor 10,000 cobalt-blue Citi Bikes at 600 stations across the city. Riders pay a membership fee and a usage fee based on time. The program has been wildly successful; millions of rides were taken in the first year alone. Observers noted that in New York's sea of billboards and ads, Citi Bikes cut through the visual clutter. They also improved consumer perceptions of Citi as "innovative," "socially responsible," and "a company for me." With bike stations often located near retail bank branches, Citi also experienced an uptick in business and credit card applications.

Companies are searching for better ways to quantify the benefits of sponsorship and demanding greater accountability from event owners and organizers. They are also creating their own events designed to surprise the public and create a buzz. Many efforts amount to guerrilla marketing tactics. "Marketing Insight: Playing Tricks to Build a Brand" describes some clever marketing promotions that are out of the ordinary.

Events can create attention, though whether they have a lasting effect on brand awareness, knowledge, or preference will vary considerably depending on the quality of the product, the event itself, and its execution.

## Playing Tricks to Build a Brand

Some marketers are taking advantage of viral videos and other digital forms of expression to develop creative stunts or "reality pranks" to promote their brands. The successful ones capture the public's imagination while reinforcing the brand positioning in the process. Here are two examples.

To demonstrate the picture quality of its Ultra HD TVs, with resolution up to four times greater than regular HD TVs, LG shot a hidden-camera prank commercial in Chile. In an office in a high-rise building, the company replaced the large window overlooking the city with one of its Ultra HD TVs showing the same scene. Then it filmed unsuspecting job seekers responding to interview questions from an actor posing as an employer. All is well until the middle of the interview when a large meteor is shown crashing into the city with a monstrous dust cloud rushing toward the building. The interviewees all try to remain calm until the realistic images eventually overwhelm them and they react in panic.

To demonstrate the eye-tracking feature of its new Galaxy S4 smart phone, Samsung ran a "Stare Down" challenge contest. The concept was simple. Anyone who could sustain eye contact with an S4 handset for a full hour in a busy public setting would win the phone free. The phone was placed at eye level, but as time went on, increasingly attention-getting distractions would appear: Police holding back a barking German shepherd, a one-man band roaming around playing loud music, a motorcycle crashing into a flower stand, and so on. There was a consolation prize too. The longer a participant was able to stare at the S4, the bigger the discount for purchasing one.

Both videos became viral sensations with millions of views, entertainingly reinforcing key benefits that made up the brand positioning.

**Sources:** Will Burns, "Samsung 'Stare Down' the Latest Great Reality Prank," *Forbes*, May 31, 2013; "An Eye to Eye Phone Competition," www.feishmanhillard.com, accessed March 30, 2014; Will Burns, "LG Ultra HDTV: A Product Demo for the Ages," *Forbes*, September 5, 2013; Salvador Rodriguez, "LG Hidden-Camera Prank Ad for Its Ultra HD TV Goes Viral," *Los Angeles Times*, September 7, 2013.

*Source: LG Electronics Chile*

LG's reality prank with scared job interviewees vividly demonstrated the picture quality of its Ultra HD TVs.

**INTEGRATION OF COMMUNICATIONS CHANNELS** Although personal communication is often more effective than mass communication, mass media might be the major means of stimulating it. Mass communications affect personal attitudes and behavior through a two-step process. Ideas often first flow from radio, television, and print to opinion leaders or consumers highly engaged with media and then from these influencers to less media-involved population groups.[31]

This two-step flow has several implications. First, the influence of mass media on public opinion is not as direct, powerful, and automatic as marketers have supposed. It is mediated by opinion leaders and media mavens, people who track new ideas and whose opinions others seek or who carry their opinions to others. Second, the two-step flow challenges the notion that consumption styles are primarily influenced by a "trickle-down" or "trickle-up" effect from mass media. People interact primarily within their own social groups and acquire ideas from others in their groups. Third, mass communicators should direct messages specifically to opinion leaders and others engaged with media if possible and let them carry the message to others.

# ESTABLISH THE TOTAL MARKETING COMMUNICATIONS BUDGET

One of the most difficult marketing decisions is choosing how much to spend on marketing communications. John Wanamaker, the department store magnate, once said, "I know that half of my advertising is wasted, but I don't know which half."

Industries and companies vary considerably in how much they spend on marketing communications. Expenditures might be 40 percent to 45 percent of sales in the cosmetics industry, but only 5 percent to 10 percent in the industrial-equipment industry. Within a given industry, there are low- and high-spending companies.

How do companies set their communications budgets? We will describe four common methods: the affordable method, the percentage-of-sales method, the competitive-parity method, and the objective-and-task method.

**AFFORDABLE METHOD** Some companies set the communications budget at what they think they can afford. The affordable method completely ignores the role of marketing communications as an investment and their immediate impact on sales volume. It leads to an uncertain annual budget, which makes long-range planning difficult.

**PERCENTAGE-OF-SALES METHOD** Some companies set communication expenditures at a specified percentage of current or anticipated sales or of the sales price. Automobile companies typically budget a fixed percentage based on the planned car price. Oil companies appropriate a fraction of a cent for each gallon of gasoline sold under their own label.

The percentage-of-sales method has little to justify it. It views sales as the determiner of communications rather than as the result. It leads to a budget set by the availability of funds rather than by market opportunities. It discourages experimentation with countercyclical communication or aggressive spending. Dependence on year-to-year sales fluctuations interferes with long-range planning. There is no logical basis for choosing the specific percentage, except what has been done in the past or what competitors are doing. Finally, it does not encourage building the communications budget by identifying what each product and territory deserves.

**COMPETITIVE-PARITY METHOD** Some companies set their communications budgets to achieve share-of-voice parity with competitors. This approach is also problematic. There are no grounds for believing competitors know better. Company reputations, resources, opportunities, and objectives differ so much that communications budgets are hardly a guide. And there is no evidence that budgets based on competitive parity discourage communication wars.

**OBJECTIVE-AND-TASK METHOD** The most defensible approach, the objective-and-task method, calls upon marketers to develop communications budgets by defining specific objectives, identifying the tasks that must be performed to achieve these objectives, and estimating the costs of performing them. The sum of these costs is the proposed communications budget.

Suppose Dr. Pepper Snapple wants to introduce a new natural energy drink, called Sunburst, for the casual athlete.[32] Its objectives might be as follows:

1. *Establish the market share goal.* The company estimates 50 million potential users and sets a target of attracting 8 percent of the market—that is, 4 million users.
2. *Select the percentage of the market that should be reached by advertising.* The advertiser hopes to reach 80 percent of the market (40 million prospects) with its advertising message.
3. *Estimate the percentage of aware prospects who should be persuaded to try the brand.* The advertiser would be pleased if 25 percent of aware prospects (10 million) tried Sunburst. It estimates that 40 percent of all triers, or 4 million people, will become loyal users. This is the market share goal.
4. *Calculate the number of advertising impressions per 1 percent trial rate.* The advertiser estimates that 40 advertising impressions (exposures) for every 1 percent of the population will bring about a 25 percent trial rate.
5. *Find the number of gross rating points to be purchased.* A gross rating point is one exposure to 1 percent of the target population. Because the company wants to achieve 40 exposures to 80 percent of the population, it will want to buy 3,200 gross rating points.
6. *Calculate the necessary advertising budget on the basis of the average cost of buying a gross rating point.* Suppose it costs an average of $3,277 to expose 1 percent of the target population to one impression. Then 3,200 gross rating points will cost $10,486,400 (= $3,277 × 3,200) in the introductory year.

The objective-and-task method has the advantage of requiring management to spell out its assumptions about the relationship among dollars spent, exposure levels, trial rates, and regular usage.

COMMUNICATIONS BUDGET TRADE-OFFS How much weight should marketing communications receive compared to alternatives such as product improvement, lower prices, or better service? The answer depends on where the company's products are in their life cycles, whether they are commodities or highly differentiable products, whether they are routinely needed or must be "sold," and other considerations. Marketing communications budgets tend to be higher when there is low channel support, the marketing program changes greatly over time, many customers are hard to reach, customer decision making is complex, products are differentiated and customer needs are nonhomogeneous, and purchases are frequent and quantities small.[33]

In theory, marketers should establish the total communications budget so the marginal profit from the last communication dollar just equals the marginal profit from the last dollar in the best noncommunication use. Implementing this economic principle can be a challenge, however.

# Selecting the Marketing Communications Mix

Companies must allocate their marketing communications budget over the eight major modes of communication—advertising, sales promotion, events and experiences, public relations and publicity, online and social media marketing, mobile marketing, direct and database marketing, and the sales force. Within the same industry, companies can differ considerably in their media and channel choices. Avon concentrates its promotional funds on personal selling, whereas Revlon spends heavily on advertising. Electrolux spent heavily on a door-to-door sales force for years, whereas Hoover relied more on advertising. Table 19.2 forecasts spending on some major forms of communication.

| TABLE 19.2 | Advertising and Digital Marketing Communications Forecast for 2016 |
|---|---|
| **Share of Global Adspend by Medium—2016** | **(%)** |
| Cinema | 0.5% |
| Desktop Internet | 17.9% |
| Magazines | 7.9% |
| Mobile Internet | 2.7% |
| Newspapers | 17.0% |
| Outdoor | 6.9% |
| Radio | 6.9% |
| Television | 40.2% |

**Source:** *Executive Summary: Advertising Expenditure Forecasts December 2013*, ZenithOptimedia, www.zenithoptimedia.com.

| **U.S. Digital Marketing Communications—2016** | |
|---|---|
| Display Advertising | 26.4% |
| Email Marketing | 2.4% |
| Mobile Marketing | 25.5% |
| Search Marketing | 37.5% |
| Social Media | 8.2% |

**Source:** Data from Forrester Research Online Display Advertising Forecast, 2014 to 2019 (US), May 21, 2014; Forrester Research Search Engine Marketing Forecast, 2014 to 2019 (US), May 8, 2014; Forrester Research Mobile Advertising Forecast, 2014 to 2019 (US), May 5, 2014; Forrester Research Social Media Forecast, 2014 to 2019 (US), April 4, 2014; Forrester Research Email Marketing Forecast, 2013 to 2018 (US), July 8, 2013.

Companies are always searching for ways to gain efficiency by substituting one communications tool for others. Many are replacing some field sales activity with ads, direct mail, and telemarketing. One auto dealer dismissed his five salespeople and cut prices, and sales exploded. Substitutability among communications tools explains why marketing functions need to be coordinated.

# CHARACTERISTICS OF THE MARKETING COMMUNICATIONS MIX

Each communication tool has its own unique characteristics and costs. We briefly review them here and discuss them in more detail in Chapters 20, 21, and 22.

**ADVERTISING** Advertising reaches geographically dispersed buyers. It can build up a long-term image for a product (Coca-Cola ads) or trigger quick sales (a Macy's ad for a weekend sale). Certain forms of advertising such as TV can require a large budget, whereas other forms such as newspaper do not. The mere presence of advertising might have an effect on sales: Consumers might believe a heavily advertised brand must offer "good value."[34] Because of the many forms and uses of advertising, it's risky to make generalizations about it.[35] Yet a few observations are worthwhile:

1. *Pervasiveness*—Advertising permits the seller to repeat a message many times. It also allows the buyer to receive and compare the messages of various competitors. Large-scale advertising says something positive about the seller's size, power, and success.
2. *Amplified expressiveness*—Advertising provides opportunities for dramatizing the company and its brands and products through the artful use of print, sound, and color.
3. *Control*—The advertiser can choose the aspects of the brand and product on which to focus communications.

**SALES PROMOTION** Companies use sales promotion tools—coupons, contests, premiums, and the like—to draw a stronger and quicker buyer response, including short-run effects such as highlighting product offers and boosting sagging sales. Sales promotion tools offer three distinctive benefits:

1. *Ability to be attention-getting*—They draw attention and may lead the consumer to the product.
2. *Incentive*—They incorporate some concession, inducement, or contribution that gives value to the consumer.
3. *Invitation*—They include a distinct invitation to engage in the transaction now.

**EVENTS AND EXPERIENCES** Events and experiences offer many advantages as long as they have the following characteristics:

1. *Relevant*—A well-chosen event or experience can be seen as highly relevant because the consumer is often personally invested in the outcome.
2. *Engaging*—Given their live, real-time quality, events and experiences are more actively engaging for consumers.
3. *Implicit*—Events are typically an indirect soft sell.

**PUBLIC RELATIONS AND PUBLICITY** Marketers tend to underuse public relations, yet a well-thought-out program coordinated with the other communications-mix elements can be extremely effective, especially if a company needs to challenge consumers' misconceptions. The appeal of public relations and publicity is based on three distinctive qualities:

1. *High credibility*—News stories and features are more authentic and credible to readers than ads.
2. *Ability to reach hard-to-find buyers*—Public relations can reach prospects who prefer to avoid mass media and targeted promotions.
3. *Dramatization*—Public relations can tell the story behind a company, brand, or product.

**ONLINE AND SOCIAL MEDIA MARKETING** Online marketing and messages can take many forms to interact with consumers when they are in active search mode or just browsing and surfing online for something to do. They share three characteristics:

1. *Rich*—Much information or entertainment can be provided—as much or as little as a consumer might want.
2. *Interactive*—Information can be changed or updated depending on the person's response.
3. *Up to date*—A message can be prepared very quickly and diffused through social media channels.

**MOBILE MARKETING** Increasingly, online marketing and social media rely on mobile forms of communication and smart phones or tablets. Three distinguishing characteristics of mobile marketing are:

1. *Timely*—Mobile communications can be very time-sensitive and reflect when and where a consumer is.
2. *Influential*—Information received or obtained via a smart phone can reach and influence consumers as they are making a purchase decision.
3. *Pervasive*—Consumers typically carry their smart phones everywhere, so mobile communications are at their fingertips.

**DIRECT AND DATABASE MARKETING** The advent of "Big Data" has given marketers the opportunity to learn even more about consumers and develop more personal and relevant marketing communications. Three noteworthy characteristics of direct and database marketing are:

1. *Personal*—Personal facts, opinions, and experiences can be stored in massive databases and incorporated into personal messages.
2. *Proactive*—A direct marketing piece can create attention, inform consumers, and include a call to action.
3. *Complementary*—Product information can be provided that helps other marketing communications, especially in terms of e-commerce. A good catalog might spur online shopping.

**PERSONAL SELLING** Personal selling is the most effective tool at later stages of the buying process, particularly in building up buyer preference, conviction, and action. It has three notable qualities:

1. *Customized*—The message can be designed to appeal to any individual.
2. *Relationship-oriented*—Personal selling relationships can range from a matter-of-fact selling relationship to a deep personal friendship.
3. *Response-oriented*—The buyer is often given personal choices and encouraged to directly respond.

# FACTORS IN SETTING THE MARKETING COMMUNICATIONS MIX

Companies must consider several factors in developing their communications mix: type of product market, consumer readiness to make a purchase, and stage in the product life cycle.

**TYPE OF PRODUCT MARKET** Consumer marketers tend to spend comparatively more on sales promotion and advertising; business marketers tend to spend comparatively more on personal selling. In general, personal selling is used more with complex, expensive, and risky goods and in markets with fewer and larger sellers (hence, business markets).

Although marketers rely more on sales calls in business markets, advertising still plays a significant role:

- Advertising can provide an introduction to the company and its products.
- If the product has new features, advertising can explain them.
- Reminder advertising is more economical than sales calls.
- Advertisements offering brochures and carrying the company's phone number or Web address are an effective way to generate leads for sales representatives.
- Sales representatives can use copies of the company's ads to legitimize their company and products.
- Advertising can remind customers how to use the product and reassure them about their purchase.

Advertising combined with personal selling can increase sales over personal selling alone. Corporate advertising can improve a company's reputation and improve the sales force's chances of getting a favorable first hearing and early adoption of the product. IBM's recent corporate marketing effort is a notable success.[36]

........................................................................................................................................................

**IBM SMARTER PLANET** Working with long-time ad agency Ogilvy & Mather, IBM launched "Smarter Planet" in 2008 as a business strategy and multiplatform communications program to promote the way in which IBM technology and expertise help government as well as transportation, energy, education, health care, and other businesses work better and "smarter." The point was that technology has evolved so far that many of the world's problems are now fixable. The campaign began internally to inform and inspire IBM employees about how they could

IBM's "Smarter Planet" corporate ad campaign improved the company's image and drove sales.

contribute to building a "Smarter Planet." It was then rolled out with unconventional long-form, content-rich print ads, targeted TV ads, and detailed online interactive ads. A "Smarter Cities" tour hosted major events at which IBM and other experts discussed and debated challenges all cities face: transportation, energy, health care, education, and public safety. The success of the campaign was evident in the significant improvements in IBM's image as a company that was "making the world better" and "known for solving its clients' most challenging problems." Despite a recession, significant increases occurred in new business opportunities and the number of companies interested in doing business with IBM, and the company's stock price soared from $80 at the start of the campaign to more than $200 five years later.

On the flip side, personal selling can also make a strong contribution in consumer-goods marketing. Some consumer marketers use the sales force mainly to collect weekly orders from dealers and to see that sufficient stock is on the shelf. Yet an effectively trained company sales force can make four important contributions:

1. *Increase stock position*—Sales reps can persuade dealers to take more stock and devote more shelf space to the company's brand.
2. *Build enthusiasm*—Sales reps can build dealer enthusiasm by dramatizing planned advertising and communications support for the company's brand.
3. *Conduct missionary selling*—Sales reps can sign up more dealers.
4. *Manage key accounts*—Sales reps can take responsibility for growing business with the most important accounts.

**BUYER-READINESS STAGE** Communication tools vary in cost-effectiveness at different stages of buyer readiness. Figure 19.4 shows the relative cost-effectiveness of three communication tools. Advertising and publicity play the most important roles in the awareness-building stage. Customer comprehension is primarily affected by advertising and personal selling. Customer conviction is influenced mostly by personal selling. Personal selling and sales promotion are most helpful in closing the sale. Reordering is also affected mostly by personal selling and sales promotion and somewhat by reminder advertising. Note too that online activities can affect virtually any stage.

| **Fig. 19.4** |

Cost-Effectiveness of Three Different Communication Tools at Different Buyer-Readiness Stages

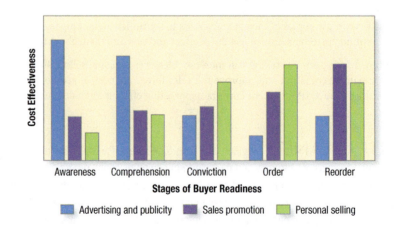

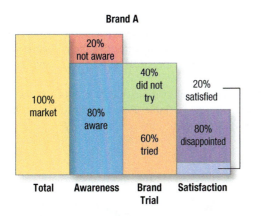

| **Fig. 19.5** |

Current
Consumer States
for Two Brands

**PRODUCT LIFE-CYCLE STAGE** In the introduction stage of the product life cycle, advertising, events and experiences, and publicity have the highest cost-effectiveness, followed by personal selling to gain distribution coverage and sales promotion and direct marketing to induce trial. In the growth stage, demand has its own momentum through word of mouth and interactive marketing. Advertising, events and experiences, and personal selling all become more important in the maturity stage. In the decline stage, sales promotion continues strong, other communication tools are reduced, and salespeople give the product only minimal attention.

## MEASURING COMMUNICATION RESULTS

Senior managers want to know the *outcomes* and *revenues* resulting from their communications investments. Too often, however, their communications directors supply only *inputs* and *expenses:* press clipping counts, numbers of ads placed, or media costs. In fairness, communications directors try to translate inputs into intermediate outputs such as reach and frequency (the percentage of target market exposed to a communication and the number of exposures), recall and recognition scores, persuasion changes, and cost-per-thousand calculations. Ultimately, though, behavior-change measures capture the real payoff.

After implementing the communications plan, the communications director must measure its impact. Members of the target audience are asked whether they recognize or recall the message, how many times they saw it, what points they recall, how they felt about the message, and what are their previous and current attitudes toward the product and the company. The communicator should also collect behavioral measures of audience response, such as how many people bought the product, liked it, and talked to others about it.

Figure 19.5 provides an example of good feedback measurement. We find 80 percent of the consumers in the total market are aware of brand A, 60 percent have tried it, and only 20 percent who tried it are satisfied. This indicates that the communications program is effective in creating awareness, but the product fails to meet consumer expectations. In contrast, 40 percent of the consumers in the total market are aware of brand B and only 30 percent have tried it, but 80 percent of them are satisfied. In this case, the communications program needs to be strengthened to take advantage of the brand's potential power.

# Managing the Integrated Marketing Communications Process

The American Marketing Association defines **integrated marketing communications (IMC)** as "a planning process designed to assure that all brand contacts received by a customer or prospect for a product, service, or organization are relevant to that person and consistent over time." When done well, this planning process evaluates the strategic roles of a variety of communications disciplines and combines them seamlessly to provide clarity, consistency, and maximum impact of messages.

The wide range of communication tools, messages, and audiences available to marketers makes it imperative that companies move toward integrated marketing communications. They must adopt a 360-degree view of consumers to fully understand all the different ways communications can affect behavior.[37]

To facilitate one-stop shopping for marketers, media companies and ad agencies have acquired promotion agencies, public relations firms, package-design consultancies, Web site developers, social media experts, and direct-mail houses. They are redefining themselves as *communications companies* that help clients improve their overall communications effectiveness by offering strategic and practical advice on many forms of communication.

These expanded capabilities make it easier for marketers to assemble various media properties—as well as related marketing services—in an integrated communication program. Table 19.3 lists the different lines of businesses for marketing and advertising services giant WPP, for example.

| TABLE 19.3 | WPP's Lines of Businesses |
| --- | --- |
| **Advertising** | |
| Global, national, and specialist advertising services from a range of top international and specialist agencies, among them Bates CHI & Partners, Grey, JWT, Ogilvy & Mather, United Network, and Y&R | |
| **Media Investment Management** | |
| Above- and below-the-line media planning and buying and specialist sponsorship and branded entertainment services from GroupM companies MediaCom, MEC, Mindshare, Maxus, plus tenthavenue and others | |
| **Consumer Insight** | |
| WPP's Kantar companies, including TNS, Millward Brown, The Futures Company, and many other specialists in brand, consumer, media, and marketplace insight, work with clients to generate and apply great insights | |
| **Public Relations & Public Affairs** | |
| Corporate, consumer, financial, and brand-building services from PR and lobbying firms Burson-Marsteller, Cohn & Wolfe, Hill+Knowlton Strategies, Ogilvy Public Relations Worldwide, RLM Finsbury, and others | |
| **Branding & Identity** | |
| Consumer, corporate, and employee branding and design services, covering identity, packaging, literature, events, training, and architecture from Addison Group, Brand Union, FITCH, Lambie-Nairn, Landor Associates, The Partners, and others | |
| **Direct, Promotion, & Relationship Marketing** | |
| The full range of general and specialist customer, channel, direct, field, retail, promotional, and point-of-sale services from AKQA, Geometry Global, OgilvyOne, RTC Relationship Marketing, VML, Wunderman, and others | |
| **Health Care Communications** | |
| GCI Health, ghg, Ogilvy CommonHealth Worldwide, Sudler & Hennessey, and others provide integrated health care marketing solutions from advertising to medical education and online marketing | |
| **Specialist Communications** | |
| A comprehensive range of specialist services, from custom media and multicultural marketing to event, sports, youth, and entertainment marketing; corporate and business-to-business; media, technology, and production services | |
| **WPP Digital** | |
| Through WPP Digital, WPP companies and their clients have access to a portfolio of digital experts including 24/7 Media, Blue State Digital, and POSSIBLE | |

**Source:** Adapted from WPP, "What We Do," www.wpp.com/wpp/about/whatwedo, as of June 28, 2014.

## COORDINATING MEDIA

Media coordination can occur across and within media types, but marketers should combine personal and nonpersonal communications channels through *multiple-vehicle, multiple-stage campaigns* to achieve maximum impact and increase message reach and impact.

Promotions and online solicitations can be more effective when combined with advertising, for example.[38] The awareness and attitudes created by advertising campaigns can increase the success of more direct sales pitches. Advertising can convey the positioning of a brand and benefit from online display advertising or search engine marketing that sends a stronger call to action.[39]

Most companies are coordinating their online and offline communications activities. Web addresses in ads (especially print ads) and on packages allow people to more fully explore a company's products, find store locations, and get more product or service information. Even if consumers don't order online, marketers can use Web sites in ways that drive them into stores to buy.

## IMPLEMENTING IMC

Many international clients such as IBM (Ogilvy), Colgate (WPP's Red Fuse), and GE (BBDO) have opted to place a substantial portion of their communications work with one full-service agency. The result is integrated and more effective marketing communications at a much lower total cost.

Integrated marketing communications can produce stronger message consistency and help build brand equity and create greater sales impact.[40] It forces management to think about every way the customer comes in contact with the company, how the company communicates its positioning, the relative importance of each vehicle, and timing issues. It gives someone the responsibility—where none existed before—to unify the company's brand images and messages as they are sent through thousands of company activities. IMC should improve the company's ability to reach the right customers with the right messages at the right time and in the right place.[41] "Marketing Memo: How Integrated Is Your IMC Program?" provides some guidelines.

---

## marketing memo

### How Integrated Is Your IMC Program?

In assessing the collective impact of an IMC program, the marketer's overriding goal is to create the most effective and efficient communications program possible. The following "six Cs" criteria can help determine whether communications are truly integrated.

- *Coverage.* Coverage is the proportion of the audience reached by each communication option employed as well as the amount of overlap among those options. In other words, to what extent do different communication options reach the designated target market and the same or different consumers making up that market?

- *Contribution.* Contribution is the inherent ability of a marketing communication to create the desired response and communication effects from consumers in the absence of exposure to any other communication option. How much does a communication affect consumer processing and build awareness, enhance image, elicit responses, and induce sales?

- *Commonality.* Commonality is the extent to which *common* associations are reinforced across communication options; that is, the extent to which different communication options share the same meaning. The consistency and cohesiveness of the brand image are important because they determine how easily existing associations and responses can be recalled and how easily additional associations and responses can become linked to the brand in memory.

- *Complementarity.* Communication options are often more effective when used in tandem. Complementarity relates to the extent to which *different* associations and linkages are emphasized across communication options. For effective positioning, brands typically need to establish multiple brand associations. Different marketing communication options may be better suited to establishing a particular brand association; for example, sponsorship of a cause may improve perceptions of a brand's trust and credibility, but TV and print advertising may be needed to communicate its performance advantages.

- *Conformability.* In any integrated communication program, the message will be new to some consumers and not to others. Conformability refers to the extent to which a marketing communication option works for such different groups of consumers. The ability to work at two levels—effectively communicating to consumers who have and have *not* seen other communications—is critically important.

- *Cost.* Marketers must evaluate marketing communications on all these criteria against their cost to arrive at the most effective *and* most efficient communications program.

**Source:** Adapted from Kevin Lane Keller, *Strategic Brand Management*, 4th ed. (Upper Saddle River, NJ: Pearson, 2013).

# Summary

1. Modern marketing calls for more than developing a good product, pricing it attractively, and making it accessible to target customers. Companies must also communicate with present and potential stakeholders and with the general public.

2. The marketing communications mix consists of eight major modes of communication: advertising, sales promotion, public relations and publicity, events and experiences, online and social media marketing, mobile marketing, direct and database marketing, and personal selling.

3. The communications process consists of nine elements: sender, receiver, message, media, encoding, decoding, response, feedback, and noise. To get their messages through, marketers must take into account how the target audience usually decodes messages. They must also transmit the message through efficient media that reach the target audience and develop feedback channels to monitor response to the message.

4. Developing effective communications requires eight steps: (1) identify the target audience, (2) choose the communications objectives, (3) design the communications, (4) select the communications channels, (5) set the total communications budget, (6) choose the communications mix, (7) measure the communications results, and (8) manage the integrated marketing communications process.

5. In identifying the target audience, the marketer needs to close any gap that exists between current public perception and the image sought. Communications objectives can be to create a need for the category, brand awareness, brand attitude, or brand purchase intention.

6. Designing the communication requires answering three questions: what to say (message strategy), how to say it (creative strategy), and who should say it (message source). Communications channels can be personal (advocate, expert, and social channels) or nonpersonal (media, atmospheres, and events).

7. Although other methods exist, the objective-and-task method of setting the communications budget, which calls upon marketers to develop their budgets by defining specific objectives, is typically most desirable.

8. In choosing the marketing communications mix, marketers must examine the distinct advantages and costs of each communication tool and the company's market rank. They must also consider the type of product market in which they are selling, how ready consumers are to make a purchase, and the product's stage in the company, brand, and product life cycle.

9. Measuring the effectiveness of the marketing communications mix requires asking members of the target audience whether they recognize or recall the communication, how many times they saw it, what points they recall, how they felt about the communication, and what are their previous and current attitudes toward the company, brand, and product.

10. Managing and coordinating the entire communications process calls for integrated marketing communications (IMC): marketing communications planning that recognizes the added value of a comprehensive plan to evaluate the strategic roles of a variety of communications disciplines and that combines these disciplines to provide clarity, consistency, and maximum impact through the seamless integration of discrete messages.

## MyMarketingLab

Go to **mymktlab.com** to complete the problems marked with this icon ⭐ as well as for additional Auto-graded and Assisted-graded writing questions.

# Applications

## Marketing Debate
### Has TV Advertising Lost Its Power?

Long deemed the most successful marketing medium, television advertising is increasingly criticized for being too expensive and, even worse, less effective than it once was. Critics maintain that consumers tune out too many ads and that it is difficult to make a strong impression. The future, claim some, is with online advertising. Supporters of TV advertising disagree, contending that the multisensory experience of TV is unsurpassed and that no other media option offers the same potential impact.

**Take a position:** TV advertising has largely become unimportant *versus* TV advertising is still the most powerful advertising medium.

## Marketing Discussion
### Communications Audit

⭐ Pick a brand and go to its Web site. Locate as many forms of communication as you can find. Conduct an informal communications audit. What do you notice? How consistent are the different communications?

## Marketing Excellence

### >> Red Bull

Red Bull's integrated marketing communications mix has been so successful that the company has created an entirely new billion-dollar drink category—energy drinks. In addition, Red Bull has become a multibillion-dollar beverage brand among fierce competition from beverage kings like Coca-Cola, Pepsi, and Anheuser-Busch. To date, the company has sold more than 40 billion cans of energy drinks across 166 countries. How? Red Bull became the energy drink market leader by skillfully connecting with youth around the globe and doing it differently than anyone else.

Dietrich Mateschitz founded Red Bull with a single product in Austria in 1987. By 1997, the slender silver-and-blue can was available in 25 markets globally, including Western and Eastern Europe, New Zealand, and South Africa. Its size and style immediately signaled to consumers that its contents were different from traditional soft drinks. Red Bull's ingredients—amino acid taurine, B-complex vitamins, caffeine, and carbohydrates—were specifically formulated to make the drink highly caffeinated and energizing. In fact, some users have referred to it as "liquid cocaine" or "speed in a can." Over the past decade, the company introduced other products and flavors, many of which did not succeed. Today, Red Bull offers the original Red Bull Energy Drink, Red Bull Total Zero, Red Bull Sugar Free, and special editions infused with berry, lime, and cranberry flavors.

As the company continued to expand worldwide, it developed an integrated marketing communications plan that reached its target audience on many different levels and built its brand image of authenticity, originality, and community. First, Red Bull focused on pre-marketing, sponsoring events like the Red Bull Snowthrill of Chamonix ski contest in France to help build word-of-mouth excitement around the brand. Once the company entered a new market, it built buzz through its "seeding program," micro-targeting trendy shops, clubs, bars, and stores. This enabled the cultural elite to access Red Bull's product first and influence other consumers. As one Red Bull executive explained, "We go to on-premise accounts first, because the product gets a lot of visibility and attention. It goes faster to deal with individual accounts, not big chains and their authorization process." The company also targeted opinion leaders likely to influence consumers' purchases, including action sports athletes and entertainment celebrities.

Once Red Bull gained some momentum in bars, it moved into gyms, health food stores, restaurants, convenience stores near colleges, and eventually supermarkets. The company's primary point-of-purchase tool has always been its refrigerated sales units, prominently displaying the Red Bull logo. These set the brand apart from other beverages and ensure a prominent location in every retail environment. To guarantee consistency and quality in its point-of-purchase displays, the company hired teams of delivery van drivers whose sole responsibility was stocking Red Bull.

Another essential aspect of Red Bull's marketing communication mix is product trial. Whereas traditional beverage marketers attempt to reach the maximum number of consumers with sampling, the company seeks to reach consumers only in ideal usage occasions, namely when they feel fatigue and need a boost of energy. As a result, its sampling campaigns take place at concerts, parties, festivals, sporting events, beaches, highway rest areas (for tired drivers), and college libraries and in limos before award shows.

Red Bull also aligns itself with a wide variety of extreme sports, athletes, and teams and artists in music, dance, and film. From motor sports to mountain biking, snowboarding to surfing, rock concerts to extreme sailing, there is no limit to the craziness of a Red Bull event or sponsorship. A few company-sponsored events are notorious for taking originality and extreme sporting to the limit. For example, at the annual Flugtag, contestants build homemade flying machines that must weigh less than 450 pounds, including the pilot. Teams launch their contraptions off a specially designed Red Bull–branded ramp, 30 feet above a body of water. Crowds of as many as 300,000 young consumers cheer as the contestants and their craft try to stay true to the brand's slogan: "Red Bull gives you wings!"

Red Bull uses traditional advertising once the market has grown mature and the company needs to reinforce the brand to its consumers. As one executive explained, "Media is not a tool that we use to establish the market. It is a critical part. It's just later in the development."

Red Bull's "anti-marketing" marketing communications strategy has been extremely successful connecting with its young consumers. It falls directly in line with the company's mission to be seen as unique, original, and rebellious—just as its Generation Y consumers want to be viewed.

**Questions**

1. What are Red Bull's greatest strengths as more companies (like Coca-Cola, Pepsi, and Monster) enter the energy drink category and gain market share? What are the risks of competing against such powerhouses?

2. Discuss the pros and cons of Red Bull's nontraditional marketing tactics. Should the company do more traditional advertising? Why or why not?

3. Discuss the effectiveness of Red Bull's sponsorships. Where should the company draw the line in terms of novelty and risk?

**Sources:** Kevin Lane Keller, "Red Bull: Managing a High-Growth Brand," *Best Practice Cases in Branding*, 3rd ed. (Upper Saddle River, NJ: Prentice Hall, 2008); Peter Ha, "Red Bull Stratos: Man Will Freefall from Earth's Stratosphere," *Time*, January 22, 2010; "Red Bull to Go on Sale in U.S. with Fruity Flavors," *Businessweek*, October 8, 2012; www.redbull.com.

## Marketing Excellence

### >> Target

In the mid-1980s, then-dominant Kmart and up-and-coming Walmart were both communicating their low-price promise, but their merchandise was perceived as cheap and low quality. Target, founded in 1962, sensed a gap in the market for "cheap chic" mass retail and set out to distinguish itself from the other big-box retailers by building an up-market cachet for its brand without losing its relevance for price-conscious consumers. Through careful merchandising and a strategic marketing communications plan, the company successfully positioned itself as a high-fashion brand with trendy styles and quality merchandise at affordable low prices.

Target has fulfilled this brand promise in many ways. In the mid-2000s, for instance, the company introduced Europe's "fast fashion" strategy to the United States, gaining a strong competitive advantage in the process. Its merchandisers travel the world; once they have identified a trending style, product, or color scheme, they rush it to the stores' shelves faster than any other retailer. This speed-to-market approach also keeps the company's product selection fresh, leading to more frequent shopper visits.

Target has also partnered with world-renowned designers to deliver stylish and exclusive merchandise lines, including fashion from Mossimo Giannulli, maternity from Liz Lange, cosmetics from Sonia Kashuk, handbags from Anya Hindmarch, shoes from Siegerson Morrison, and beauty from Petra Strand. These items are either staples in Target locations or part of the Go International line, a special design collection available for only a few months at a time.

Target's collection of designer lines is just one part of its integrated marketing communications plan for communicating its "cheap chic" positioning. For instance, the company continuously works to improve every department's appearance and performance. It uses strategically placed low shelves, halogen and track lighting, cleanly styled fixtures and signage, and wide aisles to avoid visual clutter. The shopping carts have a slick plastic design with hundreds of holes resembling Target's bull's-eye logo. Checkout lines are intended to be efficient, clean, speedy, and pleasant. Even the roofs of Target stores near airports display a large red bull's-eye, attracting air passengers' attention.

Target's traditional advertising includes television ads, direct mailers, print ads, radio, and circulars. All prominently display its tagline, "Expect More, Pay Less," and feature hip young customers, a variety of strong name-brand products, and a lighthearted tone. The company also reaches specific demographic groups by aligning itself with a variety of events, sports, athletes, and museums through corporate sponsorships. These range from Target Field, home of the Minnesota Twins in Minneapolis, to Target NASCAR and Indy racing teams, Olympic snowboarder Shaun White, and major awards shows such as the Oscars, Emmys, Grammys, and Golden Globes.

Target reinforces its positive brand image by contributing 5 percent of its annual income, or more than $4 million a week, to community programs that focus on education, the arts, social service, and volunteerism. Employees also use company time to volunteer hundreds of thousands of hours in surrounding communities each year.

Target continuously updates its product mix to match customers' shopping behaviors and needs. For example, during the 2008–2009 recession, when consumers shied away from discretionary items like clothing and home accessories, the company tweaked its marketing message and merchandising strategy by adding perishables to its inventory, which proved highly successful. In 2012, it expanded with a new small-store format called CityTarget located in large cities and targeting urban consumers.

CityTarget stocked its shelves with fresh food, apartment-appropriate household items, trendy fashions, and the company's latest designer collections.

As a result of its highly integrated marketing communications plan, Target has attracted many shoppers who would not otherwise shop at a discount retailer. Its customers are younger, more affluent, and more highly educated than typical Walmart or other discount shoppers. In addition, 97 percent of U.S. consumers recognize the bull's-eye logo. Target is the third-largest retailer in the United States (after Walmart and Kroger) with $73 billion in sales. The company continuously ranks as one of *Fortune*'s "Most Admired Companies" and has also received awards for being innovative, ethical, and environmentally friendly. Its successful marketing communications have resonated so well with consumers that they often jokingly pronounce the company's name "Tar-*Zhay*" as if it were an upscale boutique.

### Questions

1. Describe Target's marketing communications strategy. What has the company done well over the years?

2. How does Target compete against mammoth Walmart, which has four times the revenue? What are the distinct differences in their marketing communications strategies?

3. What are the risks and challenges associated with Target's marketing communications mix? Have these changed over the years? Explain.

**Sources:** "Value for Money Is Back—Target Does Marketing Right," *The Marketing Doctor*, October 2, 2006; Ben Steverman, "Target vs. Wal-Mart: The Next Phase," *BusinessWeek*, August 18, 2009; Ann Zimmerman, "Staying on Target," *Wall Street Journal*, May 7, 2007; Mya Frazier, "The Latest European Import: Fast Fashion," *Advertising Age*, January 9, 2006, p. 6; Julie Schlosser, "How Target Does It," *Fortune*, October 18, 2004, p. 100; Michelle Conlin, "Look Who's Stalking Wal-Mart," *BusinessWeek*, December 7, 2009, pp. 30–36; Wikinvest, www.wikinvest.com; www.target.com; Target 2012 Annual Report.

## In This Chapter, We Will Address the Following **Questions**

1. What steps are required in developing an advertising program? (p. 586)

2. How should marketers choose advertising media and measure their effectiveness? (p. 593)

3. How should sales promotion decisions be made? (p. 600)

4. What are the guidelines for effective brand-building events and experiences? (p. 604)

5. How can companies exploit the potential of public relations? (p. 607)

Backed by a fully-integrated communications program, P&G's "Thank You Mom" Olympic sponsorship has connected with customers and improved sales worldwide.

*Source: Xin yu tj-Imaginechina*

# 20 Managing Mass Communications: Advertising, Sales Promotions, Events and Experiences, and Public Relations

**Despite the enormous increase in marketers' use of personal communications due to** the pervasive nature of the Internet, mass media are still a vitally important component of most marketing communications programs. The old days in which "If you build a great ad, they will come" are long gone, however. To generate consumer interest and sales, mass media must often be supplemented and carefully integrated with other communications. P&G has struck gold with its fully integrated Olympic-themed "Thank You Mom" campaign.[1]

 *After its sponsorship of the U.S. national team at the 2010 Winter Olympics in Vancouver led to an estimated $100 million in increased revenue, Procter & Gamble signed up to be an official Olympic sponsor for the next five Summer and Winter Games from 2012 to 2020. Targeting women in their roles as "caregivers and family anchors," the company backed its sponsorship with the multimedia "Thank You Mom" global marketing campaign. The "Best Job" online and broadcast ad campaign for the 2012 Summer Olympics in London emotionally portrayed the crucial roles played by mothers whose children went on to become Olympic champions. Each ad finished by showing the P&G corporate logo and some of its billion-dollar-plus brands, such as Pampers, Gillette, Duracell, and Bounty. More than 70 million U.S. viewers watched at least one digital ad or video during the fully integrated campaign. It also combined promotions, PR, cause marketing, and other communications to "immerse the consumer with the brands and the message at every level, on every platform, from smartphones to stores in 204 international markets." P&G marketers estimated the firm received $200 million in added sales from the campaign. For the 2014 Winter Olympics in Sochi, Russia, it launched the "Pick Them Back Up" campaign, which "paid homage to moms of athletes from across the globe, bringing to life the daily lessons all mom teach…and the unconditional love moms give kids no matter what." Additional online videos told the real-life stories of Olympians from different countries.*

**Although P&G clearly has** found great success with its multimedia Olympics campaign, other marketers are trying to come to grips with how to best use mass media in the new—and still changing—communication environment.[2] In this chapter, we examine the nature and use of four mass-communication tools—advertising, sales promotion, events and experiences, and public relations and publicity.

# Developing and Managing an Advertising Program

**Advertising** can be a cost-effective way to disseminate messages, whether to build a brand preference or to educate people. Even in today's challenging media environment, good ads can pay off. GEICO has succeeded by keeping both its ad campaigns and their executions fresh.[3]

**GEICO**    GEICO has spent hundreds of millions of dollars on TV advertising. Has it been worth it? Warren Buffet, chairman and CEO of GEICO's parent company Berkshire Hathaway, thinks so. GEICO has more than quintupled its revenue over the past decade, from slightly under $3 billion in 1998 to more than $17 billion in 2013—making it the fastest-growing auto insurance company in the United States. The company sells directly to consumers with a basic message, "15 Minutes Could Save You 15% or More on Your Car Insurance." Partnering with The Martin Agency, GEICO has run a series of highly creative and award-winning ad campaigns to emphasize different aspects of the brand. Four ran concurrently in 2014. TV ads featuring the Cockney-speaking Gecko lizard spokes-character reinforce GEICO's brand image as credible and accomplished. The "Happier Than" campaign comes up with exaggerated situations to describe how happy GEICO customers are, such as a camel on Wednesday (hump day) or Dracula volunteering at a blood drive. A third campaign featuring Maxwell, a talking pig, focuses on specific products and service features. The fourth campaign, "Did You Know," starts with a person commenting on the company's famous 15-minute slogan to a companion, who replies, "Everyone knows that." The first speaker then tries to save face with a twist on some other conventional wisdom, such as that Pinocchio was a poor motivational speaker or Old McDonald was a really bad speller. The multiple campaigns complement each other and build on each other's success; the company dominates the TV airwaves with so many varied car insurance messages that competitors' ads are lost.

In developing an advertising program, marketing managers must always start by identifying the target market and buyer motives. Then they can make the five major decisions known as "the five Ms":

1. *Mission:* What are our advertising objectives?
2. *Money:* How much can we spend and how do we allocate our spending across media types?
3. *Message:* What should the ad campaign say?

Fast-growing auto insurance provider Geico runs multiple ad campaigns at the same time, each emphasizing different aspects of its brand and service.

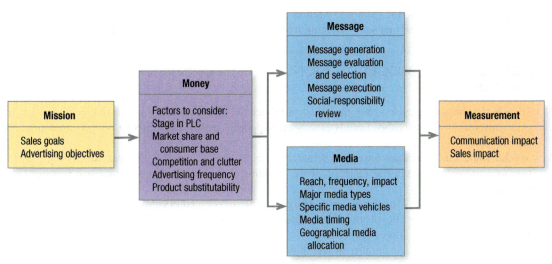

| **Fig. 20.1** |

The Five Ms
of Advertising

4. *Media:* What media should we use?
5. *Measurement:* How should we evaluate the results?

These decisions are summarized in Figure 20.1 and described in the following sections.

## SETTING THE ADVERTISING OBJECTIVES

Advertising objectives must flow from earlier decisions about target market, brand positioning, and the marketing program. An **advertising objective** (or goal) is a specific communications task and achievement level to be accomplished with a specific audience in a specific period of time:[4]

> To increase among 30 million homemakers who own automatic washers the number who identify brand X as a low-sudsing detergent, and who are persuaded that it gets clothes cleaner, from 10 percent to 40 percent in one year.

We classify advertising objectives according to whether they aim to inform, persuade, remind, or reinforce. These goals correspond to stages in the *hierarchy-of-effects* model discussed in Chapter 19.

- *Informative advertising* aims to create brand awareness and knowledge of new products or new features of existing products.[5] Consumer packaged goods companies like Colgate, General Mills, and Unilever will often focus on key product benefits.
- *Persuasive advertising* aims to create liking, preference, conviction, and purchase of a product or service. Some persuasive advertising is comparative advertising, which explicitly compares the attributes of two or more brands, such as the Chrysler TV ad for the Dodge Ram that asks, "What if you were to take away horsepower, torque and warranty coverage from a Ram? Well, you'd end up with a Ford F-150."[6] Comparative advertising works best when it elicits cognitive and affective motivations simultaneously and when consumers are processing advertising in a detailed, analytical mode.[7]
- *Reminder advertising* aims to stimulate repeat purchase of products and services. Expensive, four-color Coca-Cola ads in magazines remind people to purchase Coca-Cola.
- *Reinforcement advertising* aims to convince current purchasers they made the right choice. Automobile ads often depict satisfied customers enjoying special features of their new car.

The advertising objective should emerge from a thorough analysis of the current marketing situation. If the product class is mature, the company is the market leader, and brand usage is low, the objective is to stimulate more usage. If the product class is new, the company is not the market leader, and the brand is superior to the leader, the objective is to convince the market of the brand's superiority.

## DECIDING ON THE ADVERTISING BUDGET

How does a company know it's spending the right amount? Although advertising is treated as a current expense, part of it is really an investment in building brand equity and customer loyalty. When a company spends $5 million on capital equipment, it can call the equipment a five-year depreciable asset and write off only one-fifth of the cost in the first year. When it spends $5 million on advertising to launch a new product, however, it must write off the entire cost in the first year, reducing its reported profit, even if the benefits will persist for many years to come.

**FACTORS AFFECTING BUDGET DECISIONS** Here are five specific factors to consider when setting the advertising budget:[8]

1. *Stage in the product life cycle*—New products typically merit large advertising budgets to build awareness and gain consumer trial. Established brands usually are supported by lower advertising budgets, measured as a ratio to sales.
2. *Market share and consumer base*—High-market-share brands usually require less advertising expenditure as a percentage of sales to maintain share. Building share by increasing market size requires larger expenditures.
3. *Competition and clutter*—In a market with a large number of competitors and high advertising spending, a brand must advertise more heavily to be heard. Even advertisements not directly competitive to the brand create clutter and a need for heavier advertising.
4. *Advertising frequency*—The number of repetitions needed to put the brand's message across to consumers has an obvious impact on the advertising budget.
5. *Product substitutability*—Brands in less-differentiated or commodity-like product classes (beer, soft drinks, banks, and airlines) require heavy advertising to establish a unique image.

**ADVERTISING ELASTICITY** The predominant response function for advertising is often concave but can be S-shaped. When it is S-shaped, some positive amount of advertising is necessary to generate any sales impact, but sales increases eventually flatten out.[9]

One classic study found that increasing the TV advertising budget had a measurable effect on sales only half the time. The success rate was higher for new products and line extensions than for established brands and when there were changes in copy or in media strategy (such as an expanded target market). When advertising increased sales, its impact lasted up to two years after peak spending. Long-term incremental sales were approximately double those in the first year of an advertising spending increase.[10]

Other research reinforces these conclusions. In a 2004 IRI study of 23 brands, advertising often didn't increase sales for mature brands or categories in decline. A review of academic research found that advertising elasticities were estimated to be higher for new (.3) than for established (.1) products.[11] Research has also found that what you say (ad copy) is more important than the number of times you say it (ad frequency).[12]

# DEVELOPING THE ADVERTISING CAMPAIGN

Advertisers employ both art and science to develop the *message strategy* or positioning of an ad—*what* it attempts to convey about the brand—and its *creative strategy*—*how* it expresses the brand claims. They use three steps: message generation and evaluation, creative development and execution, and social-responsibility review.

**MESSAGE GENERATION AND EVALUATION** Advertisers are always seeking "the big idea" that connects with consumers rationally and emotionally, distinguishes the brand from competitors, and is broad and flexible enough to translate to different media, markets, and time periods. Fresh insights are important for creating unique appeals and position.[13]

---

**GOT MILK?** After a 20-year decline in milk consumption among Californians, in 1993 milk processors from across the state formed the California Milk Processor Board (CMPB) with one goal in mind: to get people to drink more milk. The ad agency commissioned by the CMPB, Goodby, Silverstein & Partners, developed a novel approach to pitching milk's benefits. Research had shown most consumers already believed milk was good for them. So the campaign reminded them of the inconvenience of running out of it, which became known as the "milk deprivation" strategy. The "got milk?" tagline reminded consumers to make sure they had enough milk in their refrigerators. A year after the launch, sales volume had increased 1.07 percent. In 1995, the "got milk?" campaign was licensed to the National Dairy Board. In 1998, the National Fluid Milk Processor Education Program, which had been using the "milk mustache" campaign since 1994 to boost sales, bought the rights to the "got milk?" tagline, which it used for the next 15 years. The "got milk?" campaign paid strong dividends by halting the decline in sales of milk in California, even more than a decade after its launch.

---

A good ad normally focuses on one or two core selling propositions. As part of refining the brand positioning, the advertiser should conduct market research to determine which appeal works best with its target audience and then prepare a *creative brief,* typically one or two pages. This is an elaboration of the positioning strategy and includes considerations such as key message, target audience, communications objectives (to do, to know, to believe), key brand benefits, supports for the brand promise, and media.

How many ad themes should the advertiser create before choosing one? The more themes explored, the higher the probability of finding an excellent one. Fortunately, an ad agency's creative department can inexpensively compose many alternatives in a short time by drawing still and video images from computer files. Marketers can also cut the cost of creative dramatically by using consumers as their creative team, a strategy sometimes called "open sourcing" or "crowdsourcing."[14]

## CONSUMER-GENERATED ADVERTISING
One of the first major marketers to feature consumer-generated ads was Converse, whose award-winning campaign "Brand Democracy" used films created by consumers in a series of TV and Web ads. H. J. Heinz ran a "Top This TV Challenge," inviting the public to create the next commercial for its Heinz Ketchup brand and win $57,000. More than 6,000 submissions and 10 million online views resulted, and sales rose more than 13 percent year over year. In addition to creating ads, consumers can help disseminate advertising. A UK "Life's for Sharing" ad for T-Mobile in which 400 people break into a choreographed dance routine in the Liverpool Street Station was shown exactly once on the *Celebrity Big Brother* television show, but it was watched more than 15 million times online when word about it spread via e-mail messages, blogs, and social networks. McDonald's similarly ran a popular user-generated campaign for its 2012 London Olympics sponsorship. Academic researchers have shown that consumer-generated ads can create more emotional and personal appeal, be deemed more credible and authentic, and lead to higher levels of brand loyalty and purchase intentions among viewers than company-produced ads, at least as long as consumers are not overly skeptical.

Although entrusting consumers with a brand's marketing effort can be pure genius, it can also be a regrettable failure. When Kraft sought a hip name for a new flavor of its iconic Vegemite product in Australia, it labeled the first 3 million jars "Name Me" to enlist consumer support. From 48,000 entries, however, the marketer selected one that was thrown in as a joke—iSnack 2.0—and sales plummeted. The company had to pull iSnack jars from the shelves and start from scratch in a more conventional fashion, choosing the new name Cheesybite.[15]

**CREATIVE DEVELOPMENT AND EXECUTION** The ad's impact depends not only on what it says but, often more important, on *how* it says it. Creative execution can be decisive.[16] Every advertising medium has advantages and disadvantages. Here, we briefly review television, print, and radio advertising media.

*Television Ads* Television is generally acknowledged as the most powerful advertising medium and reaches a broad spectrum of consumers at low cost per exposure. TV advertising has two particularly important strengths. First, it can vividly demonstrate product attributes and persuasively explain their corresponding consumer benefits. Second, it can dramatically portray user and usage imagery, brand personality, and other intangibles.

Because of the fleeting nature of the ad, however, and the distracting creative elements often found in it, product-related messages and the brand itself can be overlooked. Moreover, the high volume of nonprogramming material on television creates clutter that makes it easy for consumers to ignore or forget ads. Nevertheless, properly designed and executed TV ads can still be a powerful marketing tool that improves brand equity, sales, and profits. In the highly competitive insurance category, advertising can help a brand to stand out.[17]

## AFLAC
Aflac, the largest supplier of supplemental insurance, was relatively unknown until a highly creative ad campaign made it one of the most recognized brands in recent history. (Aflac stands for American Family Life Assurance Company.) Created by the Kaplan Thaler ad agency, the lighthearted campaign features an irascible duck incessantly squawking the company's name, "Aflac!" while consumers or celebrities discuss its products. The duck's frustrated bid for attention appealed to consumers. Sales were up 28 percent in the first year the duck aired, and name recognition went from 13 percent to 91 percent. Aflac has stuck with the duck in its advertising, even incorporating it into its corporate logo in 2005. Social media have allowed marketers to further develop the duck's personality—it has 515,000 Facebook fans and counting. The Aflac duck is not just a U.S. phenomenon. It also stars in Japanese TV ads—with a somewhat brighter disposition—where it has been credited with helping drive sales in Aflac's biggest market.

Source: SMI/Newscom

The success of the Aflac duck has led to the character being incorporated into the brand's logo and appearing in many different communications like its sponsorship of NASCAR driver Carl Edwards.

**Print Ads** Print media offer a stark contrast to broadcast media. Because readers consume them at their own pace, magazines and newspapers can provide detailed product information and effectively communicate user and usage imagery. At the same time, the static nature of the visual images in print media makes dynamic presentations or demonstrations difficult, and print media can be fairly passive.

The two main print media—magazines and newspapers—share many advantages and disadvantages. Although newspapers are timely and pervasive, magazines are typically more effective at building user and usage imagery. Newspapers are popular for local—especially retailer—advertising. On an average day, roughly one-half to three-quarters of U.S. adults read a newspaper, though increasingly online. Print advertising has steadily declined in recent years.[18] Although advertisers have some flexibility in designing and placing newspaper ads, relatively poor reproduction quality and short shelf life can diminish the impact.

Researchers report that the *picture, headline,* and *copy* in print ads matter in that order. The picture must draw attention. The headline must reinforce the picture and lead the person to read the copy. The copy must be engaging and the brand's name prominent. Even then, less than 50 percent of the exposed audience will notice even a really outstanding ad. About 30 percent might recall the headline's main point, 25 percent register the advertiser's name, and fewer than 10 percent read most of the body copy. Ordinary ads don't achieve even these results.

Some clear managerial implications emerge, as summarized in "Marketing Memo: Print Ad Evaluation Criteria." A print ad should be clear, consistent, and well branded. In an award-winning campaign, ads for the iPad Mini on the back covers of *Time* and *The New Yorker* compared the actual sizes of the device and the magazine.[19] To celebrate its 75th anniversary, Ray-Ban's award-winning "Never Hide" print ad campaign featured seven ads showing how Ray-Ban wearers flouted convention and stood out from the crowd through seven different decades.[20]

**Radio Ads** Radio is a pervasive medium: Ninety-three percent of all U.S. citizens age 12 and older listen daily and for about 20 hours a week on average, numbers that have held steady in recent years. Much radio listening occurs in the car and out of home. To be successful, radio networks are going multi-platform with a strong digital presence to allow listeners to tune in anytime, anywhere.

## marketing memo    Print Ad Evaluation Criteria

In judging the effectiveness of a print ad, marketers should be able to answer *yes* to the following questions about its execution:

1. Is the message clear at a glance? Can you quickly tell what the ad is all about?
2. Is the benefit in the headline?
3. Does the illustration support the headline?
4. Does the first line of the copy support or explain the headline and illustration?
5. Is the ad easy to read and follow?
6. Is the product easily identified?
7. Is the brand or sponsor clearly identified?

**Source:** Adapted from Scott C. Purvis and Philip Ward Burton, *Which Ad Pulled Best,* 9th ed. (Lincolnwood, IL: NTC Business Books, 2002).

Source: Luxottica

The Bronx, 1956

NEVER HIDE  Ray-Ban

Magazine advertising can be
an effective way to build or
reinforce user imagery for
a brand, as with Ray-Ban's
"Never Hide" campaign.

Perhaps radio's main advantage is flexibility—stations are very targeted, ads are relatively inexpensive to produce and place, and short closings for scheduling them allow for quick response. Radio can engage listeners through a combination of popular brands, local presence, and strong personalities.[21] It is a particularly effective medium in the morning; it can also let companies achieve a balance between broad and localized market coverage.

Radio's obvious disadvantages are its lack of visual images and the relatively passive nature of the consumer processing that results. Nevertheless, radio ads can be extremely creative. Clever use of music, sound, and other creative devices can tap into the listener's imagination to create powerfully relevant images. Here is an example:[22]

**MOTEL 6**  Motel 6, the nation's largest budget motel chain, was founded in 1962 when the "6" stood for $6 a night. After its business fortunes hit bottom in 1986 with an occupancy rate of only 66.7 percent, the company made a number of marketing changes, including the launch of humorous 60-second radio ads featuring folksy writer Tom Bodett delivering the clever tagline "We'll Leave the Light on for You." Named one of *Advertising Age's* Top 100 Ad Campaigns of the Twentieth Century, the campaign continues to receive awards, including the 2009 Radio Mercury Awards grand prize for an ad called "DVD." In this ad, Bodett introduces the "DVD version" of his latest commercial, utilizing his trademark self-deprecating style to provide "behind the scenes" commentary on his own performance. Still going strong, the campaign is credited with a rise in occupancy and a revitalization of the brand that continues to this day.

**LEGAL AND SOCIAL ISSUES**  To break through clutter, some advertisers believe they have to push the boundaries of what advertising consumers are used to seeing. They must be sure, however, not to overstep social and legal norms or offend the general public or ethnic, racial, or special-interest groups.

A substantial body of U.S. laws and regulations governs advertising. Advertisers must not make false claims, use false demonstrations, or create ads with the capacity to deceive, even if no one is actually deceived. A floor wax advertiser can't say the product gives six months' protection unless it does so under typical conditions, and a diet bread baker can't say its product has fewer calories simply because its slices are thinner. The challenge is telling the difference between deception and "puffery"—simple exaggerations that are not meant to be believed and that *are* permitted by law. "Marketing Insight: Off-Air Ad Battles" describes a few recent legal disputes about what should be permissible in a brand's advertising.

Sellers in the United States are legally obligated to avoid bait-and-switch advertising that attracts buyers under false pretenses. Suppose a seller advertises a sewing machine at $149. When consumers try to buy the advertised machine, the seller cannot then refuse to sell it, downplay its features, show a faulty one, or promise unreasonable delivery dates in order to switch the buyer to a more expensive machine.[23]

## Off-Air Ad Battles

In a highly competitive environment, perhaps it is not surprising that not everyone sees eye to eye on what is suitable advertising. Here are two notable recent disputes.

### Splenda

Splenda's tagline for its artificial sweetener was "Made from sugar, so it tastes like sugar," with "but it's not sugar" in small writing almost as an afterthought. McNeil Nutritionals, Splenda's manufacturer, does begin production of Splenda with pure cane sugar but burns it off in the manufacturing process.

Merisant, maker of Equal, claimed that Splenda's advertising confused consumers who were likely to conclude that a product "made from sugar" is healthier than one made from aspartame, Equal's main ingredient. A document from McNeil's own files and used in court says consumers' perception of Splenda as "not an artificial sweetener" was one of the biggest triumphs of the company's marketing campaign, which began in 2003.

Splenda became the runaway leader in the sugar-substitute category with 60 percent of the market, leaving roughly 14 percent each to Equal and Sweet'N Low. Although McNeil eventually agreed to settle the lawsuit and pay Merisant an undisclosed but "substantial" award (and change its advertising), it may have been too late to change consumers' perception of Splenda as something sugary *and* sugar-free.

### POM Wonderful

In May 2012, the Federal Trade Commission (FTC) issued a "cease-and-desist" order against POM Wonderful, saying the company had spread deceptive claims in print publications and billboards and online that its POM pomegranate juice could treat or prevent erectile dysfunction, prostate cancer, and heart disease. The ruling came after two years of legal back and forth. Oddly, however, POM appeared to declare victory, running a full-page ad in the *New York Times* lauding the fact that the ruling did not force it to seek re-approval from the Food and Drug Administration (as drug companies must do). A later appeal was rejected as the FTC continued to rule against POM ads using headlines such as "Cheat Death" without stronger evidence.

POM was not the only one to run into trouble over pomegranates. Welch's settled two class-action suits for $30 million because labels on its 100% Juice White Grape Pomegranate Flavored 3 Juice Blend claimed more pomegranate than it really had—only 1 ounce in a 64-ounce bottle.

**Sources:** Sarah Hills, "McNeil and Sugar Association Settle Splenda Dispute," *Food Navigator-usa.com*, www.foodnavigator-usa.com, November 18, 2008; James P. Miller, "Bitter Sweets Fight Ended," *Chicago Tribune*, May 12, 2007; Avery Johnson, "How Sweet It Isn't: Maker of Equal Says Ads for J&J's Splenda Misled; Chemistry Lesson for Jurors," *Wall Street Journal*, April 6, 2007; "In Lawsuit Brought by POM Wonderful, a Federal Jury Finds Juice Maker Welch's Intentionally Misled Consumers," *Reuters*, September 15, 2010; Ily Goyanes, "Welch's Lies about Its Juice, Pays $30 Million and No One Notices," *Miami New Times*, February 24, 2011; Charlie Minato, "POM Wonderful Is Bragging about Loss to FTC in Full Page Ads in the NY Times," *Business Insider*, May 24, 2012; Alicia Mundy, "FTC Bars Pom Juice's Health Claims," *Wall Street Journal*, January 16, 2013. For a discussion of the possible role of corrective advertising, see Peter Darke, Laurence Ashworth, and Robin J. B. Ritchie, "Damage from Corrective Advertising: Causes and Cures," *Journal of Marketing* 72 (November 2008), pp. 81–97.

Source: © Presselect/Alamy

POM Wonderful has tangled with the FTC over its ad claims.

Advertising can play a more positive broader social role. The Ad Council is a nonprofit organization that uses top-notch industry talent to produce and distribute public service announcements for nonprofits and government agencies. From its early origins with "Buy War Bonds" posters, the Ad Council has tackled innumerable pressing social issues through the years, from drunk driving to AIDS prevention to its current focus on domestic violence.

# CHOOSING MEDIA

After choosing the message, the advertiser's next task is to select media to carry it. The steps here are deciding on desired reach, frequency, and impact; choosing among major media types; selecting specific media vehicles; and setting media timing and geographical allocation. Then the marketer evaluates the results of these decisions.

**REACH, FREQUENCY, AND IMPACT** **Media selection** is finding the most cost-effective media to deliver the desired number and type of exposures to the target audience. What do we mean by the desired number of exposures? The advertiser seeks a specified advertising objective and response from the target audience—for example, a target level of product trial. This level depends on, among other things, level of brand awareness. Suppose the rate of product trial increases at a diminishing rate with the level of audience awareness, as shown in Figure 20.2(a). If the advertiser seeks a product trial rate of $T^*$, it will be necessary to achieve a brand awareness level of $A^*$.

The next task is to find out how many exposures, $E^*$, will produce a level of audience awareness of $A^*$. The effect of exposures on audience awareness depends on the exposures' reach, frequency, and impact:

- **Reach (R).** The number of different persons or households exposed to a particular media schedule at least once during a specified time period
- **Frequency (F).** The number of times within the specified time period that an average person or household is exposed to the message
- **Impact (I).** The qualitative value of an exposure through a given medium (thus, a food ad should have a higher impact in *Bon Appetit* than in *Fortune* magazine)

Figure 20.2(b) shows the relationship between audience awareness and reach. Audience awareness will be greater the higher the exposures' reach, frequency, and impact. There are important trade-offs here. Suppose the planner has an advertising budget of $1,000,000 and the cost per thousand exposures of average quality is $5. This means 200,000,000 exposures ($1,000,000 ÷ [$5/1,000]). If the advertiser seeks an average exposure frequency of 10, it can reach 20,000,000 people (200,000,000 ÷ 10) with the given budget. But if the advertiser wants higher-quality media costing $10 per thousand exposures, it will be able to reach only 10,000,000 people unless it is willing to lower the desired exposure frequency.

The relationship between reach, frequency, and impact is captured in the following concepts:

- **Total number of exposures (E).** This is the reach times the average frequency; that is, $E = R \times F$, also called the *gross rating points* (GRP). If a given media schedule reaches 80 percent of homes with an average exposure frequency of 3, the media schedule has a GRP of 240 (80 × 3). If another media schedule has a GRP of 300, it has more weight, but we cannot tell how this weight breaks down into reach and frequency.
- **Weighted number of exposures (WE).** This is the reach times average frequency times average impact, that is $WE = R \times F \times I$.

Reach is most important when launching new products, flanker brands, extensions of well-known brands, and infrequently purchased brands or when going after an undefined target market. Frequency is most important where there are strong competitors, a complex story to tell, high consumer resistance, or a frequent-purchase cycle.[24]

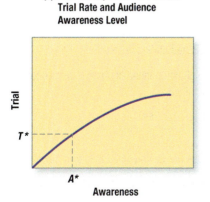

(a) Relationship between Product Trial Rate and Audience Awareness Level

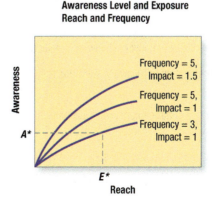

(b) Relationship between Audience Awareness Level and Exposure Reach and Frequency

| **Fig. 20.2** |

Relationship among Trial, Awareness, and the Exposure Function

A key reason for repetition is forgetting. The higher the forgetting rate associated with a brand, product category, or message, the higher the warranted level of repetition. However, advertisers should not coast on a tired ad but insist on fresh executions by their ad agency.[25]

**CHOOSING AMONG MAJOR MEDIA TYPES** The media planner must know the capacity of the major advertising media types to deliver reach, frequency, and impact. The major advertising media along with their costs, advantages, and limitations are profiled in Table 20.1. Media planners make their choices by considering factors such as target audience media habits, product characteristics, message requirements, and cost.

**PLACE ADVERTISING OPTIONS** **Place advertising,** or out-of-home advertising, is a broad category including many creative and unexpected forms to grab consumers' attention where they work, play, and, of course, shop. Popular options include billboards, public spaces, product placement, and point of purchase.

*Billboards* Billboards use colorful, digitally produced graphics, backlighting, sounds, movement, and unusual—even 3D—images.[26] In New York, manhole covers have been reimagined as steaming cups of Folgers coffee; in Belgium, eBay posted "Moved to eBay" stickers on empty storefronts; and in Germany, imaginary workers toiling inside vending machines, ATMs, and photo booths were justification for a German job-hunting Web site to proclaim, "Life Is Too Short for the Wrong Job."[27]

New "Eyes On" measurement techniques allow marketers to better understand who has seen their outdoor ads.[28] A strong creative message can make all the difference. Chang Soda in Bangkok had enough money in its budget for only one digital billboard. To maximize impact, it built a giant bubbling bottle onto the billboard to illustrate the product's carbonation. Word-of-mouth buzz quintupled bottle sales from 200,000 to 1 million.[29]

*Public Spaces* Ads are appearing in such unconventional places as movie screens, airplane bodies, and fitness equipment, as well as in classrooms, sports arenas, office and hotel elevators, and other public places.[30] Transit ads on buses, subways, and commuter trains have become a valuable way to reach working women. "Street furniture"—bus shelters, kiosks, and public areas—is another fast-growing option.

| TABLE 20.1 | Profiles of Major Media Types | |
|---|---|---|
| **Medium** | **Advantages** | **Limitations** |
| Newspapers | Flexibility; timeliness; good local market coverage; broad acceptance; high believability | Short life; poor reproduction quality; small "pass-along" audience |
| Television | Combines sight, sound, and motion; appealing to the senses; high attention; high reach | High absolute cost; high clutter; fleeting exposure; less audience selectivity |
| Direct mail | Audience selectivity; flexibility; no ad competition within the same medium; personalization | Relatively high cost; "junk mail" image |
| Radio | Mass use; high geographic and demographic selectivity; low cost | Audio presentation only; lower attention than television; nonstandardized rate structures; fleeting exposure |
| Magazines | High geographic and demographic selectivity; credibility and prestige; high-quality reproduction; long life; good pass-along readership | Long ad purchase lead time; some waste in circulation |
| Outdoor | Flexibility; high repeat exposure; low cost; low competition | Limited audience selectivity; creative limitations |
| Yellow Pages | Excellent local coverage; high believability; wide reach; low cost | High competition; long ad purchase lead time; creative limitations |
| Newsletters | Very high selectivity; full control; interactive opportunities; relative low costs | Costs could run away |
| Brochures | Flexibility; full control; can dramatize messages | Overproduction could lead to runaway costs |
| Telephone | Many users; opportunity to give a personal touch | Relative high cost; increasing consumer resistance |

Advertisers can buy space in stadiums and arenas and on garbage cans, bicycle racks, parking meters, airport luggage carousels, elevators, gasoline pumps, the bottom of golf cups and swimming pools, airline snack packages, and supermarket produce in the form of tiny labels on apples and bananas. They can even buy space in toilet stalls and above urinals, which office workers visit an average of three to four times a day for roughly four minutes per visit.[31]

**Product Placement** Marketers pay $100,000 to $500,000 so their products will make cameo appearances in movies and on television.[32] Sometimes such product placements are the result of a larger network advertising deal, but small product-placement shops also maintain ties with prop masters, set designers, and production executives.

Some firms get product placement at no cost. Nike does not pay to be in movies but often supplies shoes, jackets, bags, and so on. Increasingly, products and brands are being woven directly into the story, as when a new iPad for the gadget-loving dad of *Modern Family* became the story arc of a whole episode. In some cases, however, brands pay for the rights to appear in a movie, as with *Skyfall*.[33]

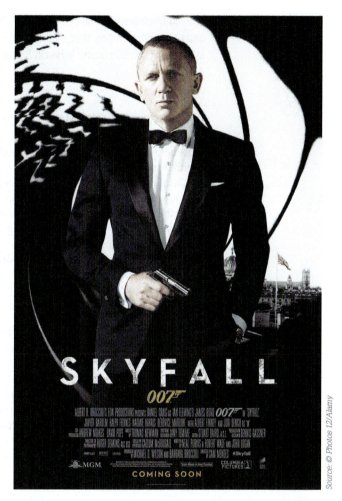

Source: © Photos 12/Alamy

**SKYFALL**  With *Skyfall*, the 23rd film in the franchise, Heineken reportedly paid almost $40 million for the rights to have James Bond drink its beer instead of his traditional vodka martini, covering a third of the film's estimated production budget. Marketers with the most on-screen presence beyond Heineken's in the film included Adidas, Aston Martin, Audi, Omega, Sony, and Tom Ford. One research firm estimated that brands in the film received more than $7.6 million worth of exposure during its opening weekend. Some brands featured their movie promotion off-screen too. Heineken shot an extravagant 90-second ad featuring an inventive chase on a train that ended with a cameo appearance by Daniel Craig, the British actor currently playing Bond. More than 22 million people viewed the campaign online, and Heineken's "Crack the Case" promotion invited consumers in major cities to demonstrate their Bond-like skills in a game.

Heineken was a big sponsor of the popular James Bond film *Skyfall*, using product placement, ads, and a promotion as support.

Product placement is not immune to criticism; lawmakers fault its stealth nature, threatening to force more explicit disclosure of participating advertisers.[34]

**Point of Purchase** Chapter 18 discussed shopper marketing and in-store marketing efforts. The appeal of point-of-purchase advertising is that consumers make many brand decisions in the store—74 percent according to one study.[35]

There are many ways to communicate at the **point of purchase (P-O-P),** including ads on shopping carts, cart straps, aisles, and shelves and in-store demonstrations, live sampling, and instant coupon machines.[36] Some supermarkets are selling floor space for company logos and experimenting with talking shelves. Mobile marketing reaches consumers via smart phones when in store. P-O-P radio provides FM-style programming and commercial messages to thousands of food stores and drugstores nationwide. Video screens in some stores, such as Walmart, play TV-type ads.[37]

**WALMART SMART NETWORK**  Walmart, an in-store advertising pioneer, replaced its original program with a new SMART network in 2008 playing on 27,000 individual screens in its 2,700 stores nationwide. Programming reaches 160 million viewers every four weeks with large welcome screens at the entrance of the store, a category screen in departments, and endcap screens on each aisle. Advertisers pay $325,000 for 30-second spots per two-week cycle in the grocery section and $650,000 per four-week run in the health and beauty department. Five-second ads running every two minutes for two weeks on the welcome screens are $80,000, and 10-second spots running twice every six minutes on the full network cost $50,000 per week. By linking the time when ads were shown and when product sales were made, Walmart can estimate how much ads increase sales by department (from 7 percent in Electronics to 28 percent in Health & Beauty) and by product type (mature items increase 7 percent, seasonal items 18 percent).

**EVALUATING ALTERNATE MEDIA** Nontraditional media can often reach a very precise and captive audience in a cost-effective manner, with ads anywhere consumers have a few seconds to notice them. The message must be simple and direct. Outdoor advertising, for example, is often called the "15-second sell." It's more effective at enhancing brand awareness or brand image than at creating new brand associations.

Unique ad placements designed to break through clutter may also be perceived as invasive and obtrusive, however, especially in traditionally ad-free spaces such as in schools, on police cruisers, and in doctors' waiting rooms. Nevertheless, perhaps because of their sheer pervasiveness, some consumers seem less bothered by nontraditional media now than in the past. "Marketing Insight: Playing Games with Brands" describes the how brands have become infused in gaming.

The challenge for nontraditional media is demonstrating its reach and effectiveness through credible, independent research. But there will always be room for creativity, as when Intel struck a five-year deal with the famed FC Barcelona soccer team to place its Intel Inside logo on the *inside* of players' jerseys, so when they lifted their shirts after scoring a goal, a customary gesture, the logo would appear.[38]

**SELECTING SPECIFIC MEDIA VEHICLES** The media planner must choose the most cost-effective vehicles within each chosen media type. The advertiser who decides to buy 30 seconds of advertising on network television can pay $75,000 for a new show, $350,000 for a popular prime-time show such as *Sunday Night Football, The Big Bang Theory,* or *The Voice,* or almost $4 million for the Super Bowl.[39] These choices are critical: The average cost to produce a national 30-second television commercial is about $300,000,[40] so it can cost as much to run an ad once on network TV as to create and produce it to start with! "Marketing Memo: Winning The Super Bowl of Advertising" describes how marketers approach the biggest event on the U.S. sports scene.

Media planners rely on measurement services that estimate audience size, composition, and media cost and then calculate the cost per thousand persons reached. A full-page, four-color ad in *Sports Illustrated* cost approximately $412,500 in 2014. If *Sports Illustrated*'s estimated readership was 3 million people, the cost of exposing the ad to 1,000 persons was $13.75. The same ad in *People* cost approximately $337,400 and reached 3.475

## Playing Games with Brands

More than half of U.S. adults and virtually all teens (97 percent) play video games, and about one in five play every day or almost every day. About 40 percent of gamers are women, who prefer puzzles and collaborative games, whereas men seem more attracted to competitive or simulation games. Given this explosive popularity, many advertisers have gotten on board.

A top-notch "advergame" can cost between $100,000 and $500,000 to develop. The game can be played on the sponsor's corporate homepage, on gaming portals, or even at public locations such as restaurants. Apple Jacks has an advergame on its Web site called *Race to the Bowl Rally* that targets kids and gives point bonuses for picking up Apple Jacks on the race course. In the M&M Chocolate Factory game, users help the M&M characters make their way through 12 different game levels inside a candy factory and can share content via Facebook and Twitter. Marketers collect valuable customer data

upon registration and often seek permission to send e-mail. Among players of a game sponsored by Ford Escape SUV, 54 percent signed up for e-mail.

Marketers are also starring in popular games. Gatorade appears in *NBA 2k13*, AXE body spray in *Splinter Cell: Chaos Theory*, and White Castle in *Homefront*. Mainstream marketers such as Apple, Procter & Gamble, Toyota, and Visa have all developed games. By integrating branded structures into a city-building game called *We City* for mobile devices, Century 21 increased brand awareness with key 25- to 34-year-old targets.

Research suggests gamers are fine with ads and the way they affect the game experience. One study showed 70 percent of gamers felt dynamic in-game ads "contributed to realism," "fit the games" in which they served, and looked "cool."

**Sources:** Lauren Johnson, "Mars Ups Brand-Building Efforts through Mobile Game," *Mobile Marketer*, December 12, 2012; Molly Soat, "Virtual Development," *Marketing News*, May 31, 2103; Michelle Kung, "We Interrupt This Video Game for a Word from Our Sponsor," *Wall Street Journal*, June 13, 2011; www.applejacks.com/games/race-to-the-rally; Amanda Lenhart, "Video Games: Adults Are Players Too," Pew Internet & American Life Project, www.pewresearch.org, December 7, 2008; Erika Brown, "Game On!" *Forbes*, July 24, 2006, pp. 84–86.

## marketing memo

## Winning The Super Bowl of Advertising

The Super Bowl attracts the largest audience on television; 111 million viewers watched Fox's broadcast in 2014. With an audience that large, a 30-second ad slot sold for a pricey $4 million.

From the first game in 1975, Super Bowl advertising has grown in importance as football has become more popular. Apple's iconic "1984" spot launching Macintosh computers featured a futuristic Orwellian world shot by famed film director Ridley Scott and ushered in a new world of Super Bowl advertising. Appearing just once during a one-sided victory by the Los Angeles Raiders over the Washington Redskins, the ad became the talk of the game, and marketers and ad agencies began to look at advertising in the game in a more ambitious way.

The introduction of the *USA Today* ad meter in 1989 focused even more consumer attention on the ads and their entertainment value. While the normal rate of audience tune-out during a commercial is 4 percent, Super Bowl ads average less than 1 percent. They have been shown to be more memorable and likable than typical ads and can even give a firm's stock price a bump.

Many Super Bowl ads now have a new purpose: to create curiosity and interest so consumers will go online and engage in social media and word of mouth to uncover more detailed information. The most popular—like a Honda CR-V ad with Matthew Broderick spoofing his Ferris Bueller film role and a VW ad with a young kid playing Darth Vader—drew tens of millions of YouTube views. Increasingly, ads are released online before the game as firms attempt to maximize their social media and PR power.

Given the large and diverse audience, many Super Bowl advertisers try to please as many people as possible, employing cute babies, playful animals, and slapstick humor. But Paul Venables, a Super Bowl ad veteran, recommends being as clear as possible about the strategic goal sought. Is it to generate social media buzz, online product searches, or store or dealer visits? As he says, "There are a million metrics and you have to decide what you are measuring." Another agency leader, Brad Kay, advocates a holistic approach, leveraging the high-profile TV spot to create more conversion opportunities online.

**Sources:** Ellen Killoran, "Super Bowl Ads 2014: What Does $4 Million Really Buy You?," *International Business Times*, January 30, 2014; Jin-Woo Kim, Traci H. Freling, and Douglas B. Grisaffe, "The Secret Sauce for Super Bowl Advertising," *Journal of Advertising Research* 53 (June 2013), pp. 134–49; Noreen O'Leary, "How to Win the Super Bowl," *Adweek*, January 28, 2013; Lucia Moses, "Ad Play," *Adweek*, January 28, 2013; Alex Konrad, "5 Ways the Super Bowl Ad Playbook Has Changed," www.tech .fortune.cnn.com, February 2, 2012; Michael Learmonth, "How USA Today's Ad Meter Broke Super Bowl Advertising," *Advertising Age*, January 30, 2012; Bruce Horovitz, "Super Bowl Marketers Go All Out to Create Hype, Online Buzz," *USA Today*, February 8, 2010.

*Source: © Tribune Content Agency LLC/Alamy*

The Super Bowl is a media extravaganza that many advertisers covet, even its halftime shows as with Super Bowl XLVIII in 2014 featuring Bruno Mars and special guests Red Hot Chili Peppers.

SELECTING MEDIA TIMING AND ALLOCATION

million people—at a lower cost-per-thousand of $9.71.[41] Magazines often put together a "reader profile" for their advertisers, describing average readers' age, income, residence, marital status, and leisure activities.

Marketers need to adjust the cost-per-thousand measure. First, consider *audience quality*. For a baby lotion ad, a magazine read by 1 million young parents has an exposure value of 1 million; if read by 1 million teenagers, it has an exposure value of almost zero. Second, look at *audience-attention probability*. Readers of *Vogue* may pay more attention to ads than do readers of *Sports Illustrated*. Third is the medium's *editorial quality*, meaning its prestige and believability. People are more likely to believe a TV or radio ad when it appears within a program they like. Fourth, consider the value of *ad placement policies and extra services*, such as regional or occupational editions and lead-time requirements for magazines.

Media planners are using more sophisticated measures of effectiveness and employing them in mathematical models to arrive at the best media mix.[42] Many advertising agencies use software programs to select the initial media and make improvements based on subjective factors.

**SELECTING MEDIA TIMING AND ALLOCATION** In choosing media, the advertiser makes both a macroscheduling and a microscheduling decision. The *macroscheduling decision* relates to seasons and the business cycle. Suppose 70 percent of a product's sales occur between June and September. The firm can vary its advertising expenditures to follow the seasonal pattern, to oppose the seasonal pattern, or to be constant throughout the year.

The *microscheduling decision* calls for allocating advertising expenditures within a short period to obtain maximum impact. Suppose the firm decides to buy 30 radio spots in September. The left side of Figure 20.3 shows that advertising messages for the month can be concentrated ("burst" advertising), dispersed continuously throughout the month, or dispersed intermittently. The top side shows they can be beamed with a level, rising, falling, or alternating frequency.

The chosen pattern should meet the marketer's communications objectives and consider three factors. *Buyer turnover* expresses the rate at which new buyers enter the market; the higher this rate, the more continuous the advertising should be. *Purchase frequency* is the number of times the average buyer buys the product during the period; the higher the purchase frequency, the more continuous the advertising should be. The *forgetting rate* is the rate at which the buyer forgets the brand; the higher the forgetting rate, the more continuous the advertising should be.

In launching a new product, the advertiser must choose among continuity, concentration, flighting, and pulsing.

- *Continuity* means exposures appear evenly throughout a given period. Generally, advertisers use continuous advertising in expanding markets, with frequently purchased items, and in tightly defined buyer categories.
- *Concentration* calls for spending all the advertising dollars in a single period. This makes sense for products with one selling season or related holiday.
- *Flighting* calls for advertising during a period, followed by a period with no advertising, followed by a second period of advertising activity. It is useful when funding is limited, the purchase cycle is relatively infrequent, or items are seasonal.

| Fig. 20.3 |

## Classification of Advertising Timing Patterns

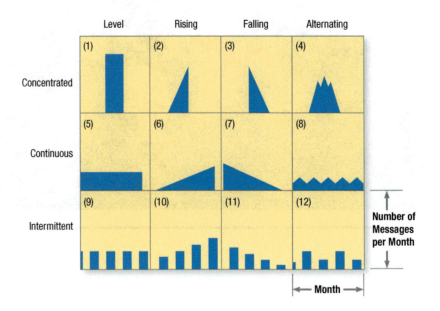

- *Pulsing* is continuous advertising at low levels, reinforced periodically by waves of heavier activity. It draws on the strengths of continuous advertising and flights to create a compromise scheduling strategy. Those who favor pulsing believe the audience will learn the message more thoroughly and at a lower cost to the firm.[43]

A company must allocate its advertising budget over space as well as over time. It makes "national buys" when it places ads on national TV networks or in nationally circulated magazines. It makes "spot buys" when it buys TV time in just a few markets or in regional editions of magazines. These markets are called *areas of dominant influence* (ADIs) or *designated marketing areas* (DMAs). The company makes "local buys" when it advertises in local newspapers, radio, or outdoor sites.

## EVALUATING ADVERTISING EFFECTIVENESS

Most advertisers try to measure the communication effect of an ad—that is, its potential impact on awareness, knowledge, or preference. They would also like to measure its sales effect.

**COMMUNICATION-EFFECT RESEARCH** **Communication-effect research,** called *copy testing,* seeks to determine whether an ad is communicating effectively. Marketers should perform this test both before an ad is put into media and after it is printed or broadcast. Table 20.2 describes some specific advertising pretest research techniques.

Pretest critics maintain that agencies can design ads that test well but may not necessarily perform well in the marketplace. Proponents maintain that useful diagnostic information can emerge and that pretests should not be used as the sole decision criterion anyway. Widely acknowledged as one of the best advertisers around, Nike is known for doing very little ad pretesting.

Many advertisers use posttests to assess the overall impact of a completed campaign. If a company hoped to increase brand awareness from 20 percent to 50 percent and succeeded in increasing it to only 30 percent, then it is not spending enough, its ads are poor, or it has overlooked some other factor.

**SALES-EFFECT RESEARCH** What sales are generated by an ad that increases brand awareness by 20 percent and brand preference by 10 percent? The fewer or more controllable other factors such as features and price are, the easier it is to measure advertising's effect on sales. The sales impact is easiest to measure in direct marketing situations and hardest in brand or corporate image-building advertising.

Companies want to know whether they are overspending or underspending on advertising. One way to answer this question is to work with the formulation shown in Figure 20.4. A company's *share of advertising expenditures* produces a *share of voice* (proportion of company advertising of that product to all advertising of that product) that earns a *share of consumers' minds and hearts* and, ultimately, a *share of market.*

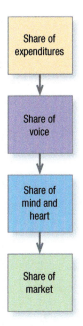

| **Fig. 20.4** |

Formula for Measuring Different Stages in the Sales Impact of Advertising

| TABLE 20.2 | Advertising Pretest Research Techniques |
|---|---|

**FOR PRINT ADS**

Starch and Gallup & Robinson Inc. are two widely used print pretesting services. Test ads are placed in magazines, which are then circulated to consumers. These consumers are contacted later and interviewed. Recall and recognition tests are used to determine advertising effectiveness.

**FOR BROADCAST ADS**

*In-home tests:* A video is taken or downloaded into the homes of target consumers, who then view the commercials.

*Trailer tests:* In a trailer in a shopping center, shoppers are shown the products and given an opportunity to select a series of brands. They then view commercials and are given coupons to be used in the shopping center. Redemption rates indicate commercials' influence on purchase behavior.

*Theater tests:* Consumers are invited to a theater to view a potential new television series along with some commercials. Before the show begins, consumers indicate preferred brands in different categories; after the viewing, consumers again choose preferred brands. Preference changes measure the commercials' persuasive power.

*On-air tests:* Respondents are recruited to watch a program on a regular TV channel during the test commercial or are selected based on their having viewed the program. They are asked questions about commercial recall.

Researchers can measure sales impact with the *historical approach,* which uses advanced statistical techniques to correlate past sales to past advertising expenditures.[44] Other researchers use *experimental data* to measure advertising's sales impact. A growing number of researchers measure the sales effect of advertising expenditures instead of settling for communication-effect measures.[45] Millward Brown International has conducted tracking studies for years to help advertisers decide whether their advertising is benefiting their brand.[46]

# Sales Promotion

**Sales promotion,** a key ingredient in marketing campaigns, consists of a collection of incentive tools, mostly short term, designed to stimulate quicker or greater purchase of particular products or services by consumers or the trade.[47] Whereas advertising offers a *reason* to buy, sales promotion offers an *incentive.*

## ADVERTISING VERSUS PROMOTION

Although sales promotion expenditures increased as a percentage of budget expenditure for a number of years, their growth has recently slowed. Consumers began to tune out promotions: Coupon redemption peaked in 1992 at 7.9 billion coupons but dropped to 2.9 billion by 2013.[48] Incessant price reductions, coupons, deals, and premiums can also devalue the product in buyers' minds. Having turned to 0 percent financing, hefty cash rebates, and special lease programs during sluggish economic times, auto manufacturers have found it difficult to wean consumers from discounts ever since.[49]

Some sales promotion tools are *consumer franchise building.* They impart a selling message along with the deal, such as free samples, frequency awards, coupons with a selling message, and premiums related to the product. Sales promotion tools that are typically *not* brand building include price-off packs, consumer premiums not related to a product, contests and sweepstakes, consumer refund offers, and trade allowances.

Sales promotions in markets of high brand similarity can produce a high sales response in the short run but little permanent gain over the longer term. In markets with high brand dissimilarity, they may be able to alter market shares permanently. In addition to brand switching, consumers may engage in stockpiling—purchasing earlier than usual (purchase acceleration) or buying extra quantities. But sales may then hit a post-promotion dip.[50]

Price promotions also may not build permanent total-category volume. One study of more than 1,000 promotions concluded that only 16 percent paid off.[51] Small-share competitors may benefit from sales promotion because they cannot match market leaders' advertising budgets, nor can they obtain shelf space without offering trade allowances or stimulate consumer trial without offering incentives. Dominant brands offer deals less frequently because most deals subsidize only current users.

Consumer franchise-building promotions can offer the best of both worlds—building brand equity while moving product. McDonald's, Dunkin' Donuts, and Starbucks have given away millions of samples of their new products because consumers like them and they often lead to higher long-term sales for quality products.[52] Gain's "Love at First Sniff" campaign used direct mail and in-store scented tear-pads and ShelfVision TV to entice consumers to smell the product, resulting in an almost 500 percent increase in shipments over the goal.[53]

The fastest-growing area in sales promotions is digital coupons, redeemed via smart phone or downloaded to a consumer's printer. Digital coupons eliminate printing costs, reduce paper waste, are easily updatable, and have higher redemption rates. Coupons.com gets 620,000 unique daily visitors looking for money-saving deals, and CoolSavings.com gets 120,000 seeking money-saving coupons and offers from name brands as well as helpful tips and articles, newsletters, free recipes, sweepstakes, free trials, free samples, and more. Many retailers are now offering customized coupons based on consumer purchase histories.[54] One firm has devised a very different way for firms to offer discounts.[55]

GROUPON   Groupon launched in 2008 to help businesses leverage the Internet and e-mail to use promotions as a form of advertisement. Specifically, the company sends its large base of subscribers a humorously worded daily deal—a specific percentage or dollar amount off the regular price—for a specific client's branded product or service. Through these e-mailed discounts, Groupon offers client firms three benefits: increased consumer exposure to the brand, the ability to price discriminate, and the creation of a "buzz factor." Groupon takes 40 percent to 50 percent of the revenues in each deal in the process. Many promotions are offered on behalf of local retailers such as spas, fitness centers, and restaurants, but Groupon also manages deals on behalf of some national brands. Some businesses have complained that Groupon attracts only deal-seekers and is not as effective in converting regular customers. One study found that 32 percent of companies lost money and 40 percent said they would not utilize such a promotion again, with restaurants faring the worst among service businesses and spas and salons being the most successful. Groupon has tried to innovate in several ways. Leveraging its massive sales force to sell Groupon Now, the company enlists local businesses to offer time- and location-specific deals via the Web or smart phones. The iPhone app for the new service has two buttons, "I'm Bored" and "I'm Hungry," to trigger deals in real time. For businesses, the service is a way to boost traffic at otherwise slow times. Even a popular restaurant might still consider some midday and midweek discounts knowing it is rarely full then. After a heavily hyped IPO, its stock has not performed well as Groupon struggles to find the right business formula.

## MAJOR DECISIONS

In using sales promotion, a company must establish its objectives, select the tools, develop the program, implement and control it, and evaluate the results.

**ESTABLISHING OBJECTIVES** Sales promotion objectives derive from communication objectives, which derive from basic marketing objectives for the product.

- For *consumers*, objectives include encouraging more frequent purchases or purchase of larger-sized units among users, building trial among nonusers, and attracting switchers away from competitors' brands. If some of the brand switchers would not have otherwise tried the brand, promotion can yield long-term increases in market share.[56] Ideally, consumer promotions have short-run sales impact and long-run brand equity effects.[57]
- For *retailers*, objectives include persuading retailers to carry new items and more inventory, encouraging off-season buying, encouraging stocking of related items, offsetting competitive promotions, building brand loyalty, and gaining entry into new retail outlets.
- For the *sales force*, objectives of promotion include encouraging their support of a new product or model, encouraging more prospecting, and stimulating off-season sales.

**SELECTING CONSUMER PROMOTION TOOLS** The promotion planner should take into account the type of market, sales promotion objectives, competitive conditions, and each tool's cost-effectiveness. The main consumer promotion tools are summarized in Table 20.3. *Manufacturer promotions* in the auto industry, for instance, are rebates, gifts to motivate test-drives and purchases, and high-value trade-in credit. *Retailer promotions* include price cuts, feature advertising, retailer coupons, and retailer contests or premiums.[58]

**SELECTING TRADE PROMOTION TOOLS** Manufacturers use a number of trade promotion tools (see Table 20.4).[59] They award money to the trade (1) to persuade the retailer or wholesaler to carry the brand; (2) to persuade the retailer or wholesaler to carry more units than the normal amount; (3) to induce retailers to promote the brand by featuring, display, and price reductions; and (4) to stimulate retailers and their sales clerks to push the product.

The growing power of large retailers has increased their ability to demand trade promotion.[60] The manufacturer's sales force and its brand managers are often at odds here. The sales force says local retailers will not keep the company's products on the shelf unless they receive more trade promotion money, whereas brand managers want to spend their limited funds on consumer promotion and advertising.

Manufacturers often find it difficult to police retailers to make sure they are doing what they agreed to do and increasingly insist on proof of performance before paying any allowances. Manufacturers face several challenges in managing trade promotions.

- Some retailers are doing *forward buying*—that is, buying a greater quantity during the deal period than they can immediately sell. The manufacturer must then schedule more production than planned and bear the costs of extra work shifts and overtime.
- Some retailers are *diverting*, buying more than needed in a region where the manufacturer offers a deal and shipping the surplus to their stores in non-deal regions.

Manufacturers handle forward buying and diverting by limiting the amount they will sell at a discount or by producing and delivering less than the full order in an effort to smooth production.[61]

Ultimately, many manufacturers feel trade promotion has become a nightmare. It contains layers of deals, is complex to administer, and often leads to lost revenues.

| TABLE 20.3 | Major Consumer Promotion Tools |
|---|---|

**Samples:** Offer of a free amount of a product or service delivered door to door, sent in the mail, picked up in a store, attached to another product, or featured in an advertising offer.

**Coupons:** Certificates entitling the bearer to a stated saving on the purchase of a specific product: mailed, enclosed in other products or attached to them, inserted in magazine and newspaper ads, or emailed or made available online.

**Cash Refund Offers (rebates):** Provide a price reduction after purchase rather than at the retail shop: Consumer sends a specified "proof of purchase" to the manufacturer who "refunds" part of the purchase price by mail.

**Price Packs (cents-off deals):** Offers to consumers of savings off the regular price of a product, flagged on the label or package. A *reduced-price pack* is a single package sold at a reduced price (such as two for the price of one). A *banded pack* is two related products banded together (such as a toothbrush and toothpaste).

**Premiums (gifts):** Merchandise offered at a relatively low cost or free as an incentive to purchase a particular product. A *with-pack premium* accompanies the product inside or on the package. A *free in-the-mail premium* is mailed to consumers who send in a proof of purchase, such as a box top or UPC code. A *self-liquidating premium* is sold below its normal retail price to consumers who request it.

**Frequency Programs:** Programs providing rewards related to the consumer's frequency and intensity in purchasing the company's products or services.

**Prizes (contests, sweepstakes, games):** *Prizes* are offers of the chance to win cash, trips, or merchandise as a result of purchasing something. A *contest* calls for consumers to submit an entry to be examined by a panel of judges who will select the best entries. A *sweepstakes* asks consumers to submit their names in a drawing. A *game* presents consumers with something every time they buy—bingo numbers, missing letters—which might help them win a prize.

**Patronage Awards:** Values in cash or in other forms that are proportional to patronage of a certain vendor or group of vendors.

**Free Trials:** Inviting prospective purchasers to try the product without cost in the hope that they will buy.

**Product Warranties:** Explicit or implicit promises by sellers that the product will perform as specified or that the seller will fix it or refund the customer's money during a specified period.

**Tie-in Promotions:** Two or more brands or companies team up on coupons, refunds, and contests to increase pulling power.

**Cross-Promotions:** Using one brand to advertise another noncompeting brand.

**Point-of-Purchase (P-O-P) Displays and Demonstrations:** P-O-P displays and demonstrations take place at the point of purchase or sale.

| TABLE 20.4 | Major Trade Promotion Tools |
|---|---|

**Price-Off (off-invoice or off-list):** A straight discount off the list price on each case purchased during a stated time period.

**Allowance:** An amount offered in return for the retailer's agreeing to feature the manufacturer's products in some way. An *advertising allowance* compensates retailers for advertising the manufacturer's product. A *display allowance* compensates them for carrying a special product display.

**Free Goods:** Offers of extra cases of merchandise to intermediaries who buy a certain quantity or who feature a certain flavor or size.

| TABLE 20.5 | Major Business and Sales Force Promotion Tools |
|---|---|

**Trade Shows and Conventions:** Industry associations organize annual trade shows and conventions. These are a multibillion-dollar business, and business marketers may spend as much as 35 percent of their annual promotion budget on them. Attendance can top 70,000 for large shows held by the restaurant or hotel-motel industries. The International Consumer Electronics Show is one of the largest in the world, with more than 150,000 attendees in 2013. Participating vendors can generate new sales leads, maintain customer contacts, introduce new products, meet new customers, sell more to present customers, and educate customers with publications, videos, and other audiovisual materials.

**Sales Contests:** A sales contest aims at inducing the sales force or dealers to increase sales results over a stated period, with prizes (money, trips, gifts, or points) going to those who succeed.

**Specialty Advertising:** Specialty advertising consists of useful, low-cost items bearing the company's name and address, and sometimes an advertising message, that salespeople give to prospects and customers. Common items are ballpoint pens, calendars, key chains, flashlights, tote bags, and memo pads.

**SELECTING BUSINESS AND SALES FORCE PROMOTION TOOLS** Companies spend billions of dollars on business and sales force promotion tools (see Table 20.5) to gather leads, impress and reward customers, and motivate the sales force.[62] They typically develop budgets for tools that remain fairly constant from year to year. For many new businesses that want to make a splash to a targeted audience, especially in the B-to-B world, trade shows are an important tool, but the cost per contact is the highest of all communication options.

**DEVELOPING THE PROGRAM** In planning sales promotion programs, marketers are increasingly blending several media into a total campaign concept, such as the following award-winning promotion.[63]

**SAMSUNG** To promote its pricy ($450) Galaxy camera brand, Samsung developed a clever mobile and social campaign, "Life's a Photo: Take It." A two-month contest asked 32 of the most popular Instagram influencers from eight international markets to trade their favorite camera phone app for the Samsung Galaxy camera. Their task was to use the new camera to showcase their city on Instagram and Tumblr to prove it was the most photogenic. Each week a different feature of the camera was showcased and fans voted on their favorite photos. A video outlining the campaign was viewed 1.3 million times, brand awareness of the Galaxy camera improved 58 percent, and purchase intent increased 115 percent.

In deciding to use a particular incentive, marketers must first determine its *size*. A certain minimum discount is necessary if the promotion is to succeed. Second, the marketing manager must establish *conditions* for participation. Incentives might be offered to everyone or to select groups. Third, the marketer must decide on the *duration* of the promotion. Fourth, the marketer must choose a *distribution vehicle*. A 50-cents-off coupon can be distributed in the product package, in stores, by mail, online, or in advertising. Fifth, the marketing manager must establish the *timing* of promotion and, finally, the *total sales promotion budget*. The cost of a particular promotion consists of the administrative cost (printing, mailing, and promoting the deal) and the incentive cost (cost of premium or cents-off, including redemption costs), multiplied by the expected number of units sold. The cost of a coupon deal recognizes that only a fraction of consumers will redeem the coupons.

**IMPLEMENTING AND EVALUATING THE PROGRAM** Marketing managers' implementation and control plans must cover lead time and sell-in time for each individual promotion. *Lead time* is the time necessary to prepare the program prior to launching it. *Sell-in time* begins with the promotional launch and ends when approximately 95 percent of the deal merchandise is in the hands of consumers.

Manufacturers can evaluate the program using sales data, consumer surveys, and experiments.

- *Sales (scanner) data* help analyze the types of people who took advantage of the promotion, what they bought before the promotion, and how they behaved later toward the brand and other brands. Sales promotions are most successful when they attract competitors' customers who then switch.

- *Consumer surveys* can uncover how many consumers recall the promotion, what they thought of it, how many took advantage of it, and how it affected later brand-choice behavior.[64]
- *Experiments* vary such attributes as incentive value, duration, and distribution media. For example, coupons can be sent to half the households in a consumer panel. Scanner data can track whether they led more people to buy the product and when.

Additional costs include the risk that promotions might decrease long-run brand loyalty or be more expensive than they appear. Some are inevitably distributed to the wrong consumers. Special production runs, extra sales force effort, and handling requirements bring other costs. Finally, certain promotions irritate retailers, who may demand extra trade allowances or refuse to cooperate.

# Events and Experiences

The IEG Sponsorship Report estimated that marketers spent $19.8 billion on sponsorships in North America during 2013, with 70 percent going to sports; another 10 percent to entertainment tours and attractions; 4 percent to festivals, fairs, and annual events; 4 percent to the arts; 3 percent to associations and membership organizations; and 9 percent to cause marketing.[65] Becoming part of a personally relevant moment in consumers' lives through sponsored events and experiences can broaden and deepen a company's or brand's relationship with the target market.

Daily encounters with brands may also affect consumers' brand attitudes and beliefs. *Atmospheres* are "packaged environments" that create or reinforce leanings toward product purchase. Law offices decorated with Oriental rugs and oak furniture communicate "stability" and "success."[66] A five-star hotel will use elegant chandeliers, marble columns, and other tangible signs of luxury.

## EVENTS OBJECTIVES

Marketers report a number of reasons to sponsor events:

1. **To identify with a particular target market or lifestyle**—Customers can be targeted geographically, demographically, psychographically, or behaviorally according to events. Old Spice sponsors college sports—including its college basketball Old Spice Classic in late November—to highlight product relevance and sample among its target audience of 16- to 24-year-old males.
2. **To increase salience of company or product name**—Sponsorship offers sustained exposure for a brand, a necessary condition for reinforcing brand salience. Top-of-mind awareness for soccer World Cup sponsors Emirates, Hyundai, Kia, and Sony benefited from the repeated brand and ad exposure over the month-long tournament.
3. **To create or reinforce perceptions of key brand image associations**—Events themselves have associations that help to create or reinforce brand associations.[67] To toughen its image and appeal to the heartland, Toyota Tundra sponsors B.A.S.S. fishing tournaments and has sponsored Brooks & Dunn country music tours.

Major sporting events like the FIFA World Cup in soccer attract enormous sponsorship dollars.

4. **To enhance corporate image**—Sponsorship can improve perceptions that the company is likable and prestigious. Although Visa views its long-standing Olympic sponsorship as a means of enhancing international brand awareness and increasing usage and volume, it also engenders patriotic goodwill and taps into the emotional Olympic spirit.

5. **To create experiences and evoke feelings**—The feelings engendered by an exciting or rewarding event may indirectly link to the brand. Audi models featured prominently in the 2010 blockbuster *Iron Man 2*, including main character Tony Stark's personal R8 Spyder and the A8, Q5 and Q7 SUVs, and A3 hatchback. After a month-long marketing blitz, positive word of mouth doubled for the brand.[68]

6. **To express commitment to the community or on social issues**—Cause-related marketing sponsors nonprofit organizations and charities. Firms such as Timberland, Stonyfield Farms, Home Depot, Starbucks, American Express, and Tom's of Maine have made their support of causes an important cornerstone of their marketing programs.

7. **To entertain key clients or reward key employees**—Many events include lavish hospitality tents and other special services or activities only for sponsors and their guests. These perks engender goodwill and establish valuable business contacts. From an employee perspective, events can also build participation and morale or serve as an incentive. BB&T Corp., a major banking and financial services player in the South and Southeast United States, used its NASCAR Busch Series sponsorship to entertain business customers and its minor league baseball sponsorship to generate excitement among employees.[69]

8. **To permit merchandising or promotional opportunities**—Many marketers tie contests or sweepstakes, in-store merchandising, direct response, or other marketing activities with an event. Ford and Coca-Cola have used their sponsorship of the popular TV show *American Idol* in this way.

Despite these potential advantages, the result of an event can still be unpredictable and beyond the sponsor's control. And although many consumers credit sponsors for providing the financial assistance to make an event possible, some may resent its commercialization.

## MAJOR SPONSORSHIP DECISIONS

Making sponsorships successful requires choosing the appropriate events, designing the optimal sponsorship program, and measuring the effects of sponsorship.[70]

**CHOOSING EVENTS** Because of the number of sponsorship opportunities and their huge cost, many marketers are becoming more selective. The event must meet the marketing objectives and communication strategy defined for the brand. It must have sufficient awareness, possess the desired image, and be able to create the desired effects. The audience must match the target market and make favorable attributions for the sponsor's engagement. An ideal event is also unique but not encumbered with many sponsors, lends itself to ancillary marketing activities, and reflects or enhances the sponsor's brand or corporate image.[71]

**DESIGNING SPONSORSHIP PROGRAMS** Many marketers believe the marketing program accompanying an event sponsorship ultimately determines its success. At least two to three times the amount of the sponsorship expenditure should be spent on related marketing activities.

*Event creation* is a particularly important skill in publicizing fund-raising drives for nonprofit organizations. Fund-raisers have developed a large repertoire of special events, including anniversary celebrations, art exhibits, auctions, benefit evenings, book sales, cake sales, contests, dances, dinners, fairs, fashion shows, phonathons, rummage sales, tours, and walkathons.

More firms are now using their names to sponsor arenas, stadiums, and other venues that hold events, spending billions of dollars for naming rights to major North American sports facilities. But as with any sponsorship, the most important consideration is the additional marketing activities.

**MEASURING SPONSORSHIP ACTIVITIES** It's a challenge to measure the success of events. "Marketing Memo: Measuring High-Performance Sponsorship Programs" offers some guidelines from industry experts IEG.

**Supply-side methods** for measuring an event's success assess the media coverage, for example, the number of seconds the brand is clearly visible on a television screen or the column inches of press clippings that mention it. These potential "impressions" can translate into the dollar cost of actually advertising in the particular vehicle. Some industry consultants estimate that 30 seconds of logo exposure during a televised event can be worth 6 percent, 10 percent, or as much as 25 percent of a 30-second TV ad spot.

Although supply-side methods provide quantifiable measures, equating media coverage with advertising exposure ignores the content of the respective communications. The advertiser uses media space and time to

## marketing memo

### Measuring High-Performance Sponsorship Programs

1.  *Measure outcomes, not outputs.* Focus on what a sponsorship actually produced rather than what a sponsor got or did—rather than focus on 5,000 people sampled at an event, how many of those people would be classified as members of the target market and what is the likely conversion rate between their trial and future behaviors?

2.  *Define and benchmark objectives on the front end.* Specific objectives help to identify what measures should be tracked. An objective of motivating the sales force and distributors suggests different measures than one of building brand image and key brand benefits. Contrast measures in terms of sponsorship effects and what might have happened if the sponsorship had not occurred.

3.  *Measure return for each objective against prorated share of rights and activation fees.* Rank and rate objectives by importance and allocate the total sponsorship budget against each of those objectives.

4.  *Measure behavior.* Conduct a thorough sales analysis to identify shifts in marketplace behavior as a result of the sponsorship.

5.  *Apply the assumptions and ratios used by other departments within the company.* Applying statistical methods used by other departments makes it easier to gain acceptance for any sponsorship analysis.

6.  *Research the emotional identities of customers and measure the results of emotional connections.* In what ways does a sponsorship psychologically affect consumers and facilitate and deepen long-term loyalty relationships?

7.  *Identify group norms.* How strong of a community exists around the sponsored event or participants? Are their formal groups that share interests that will be impacted by the sponsorship?

8.  *Include cost savings in ROI calculations.* Contrast expenses that a firm has typically incurred in the past achieving a particular objective from those expenses allocated to achieve the objective as part of the sponsorship.

9.  *Slice the data.* Sponsorship affects market segments differently. Breaking down a target market into smaller segments can better identify sponsorship effects.

10. *Capture normative data.* Develop a core set of evaluation criteria that can be applied across all different sponsorship programs.

**Source:** "Measuring High Performance Sponsorship Programs," IEG Executive Brief, IEG Sponsorship Consulting, www.sponsorship.com, 2009.

communicate a strategically designed message. Media coverage and telecasts only expose the brand and don't necessarily embellish its meaning in any direct way. Although some public relations professionals maintain that positive editorial coverage can be worth five to 10 times the equivalent advertising value, sponsorship rarely provides such favorable treatment.

The **demand-side method** identifies the sponsorship's effect on consumers' brand knowledge. Marketers can survey spectators to measure their recall of the event and their resulting attitudes and intentions toward the sponsor.

## CREATING EXPERIENCES

A large part of local, grassroots marketing is *experiential marketing*, which not only communicates features and benefits but also connects a product or service with unique and interesting experiences. "The idea is not to sell something, but to demonstrate how a brand can enrich a customer's life."[72] Many firms are creating their own events and experiences to create consumer and media interest and involvement.

Consumers seem to appreciate that effort. In one survey, four of five respondents found participating in a live event was more engaging than all other forms of communication. The vast majority also felt experiential marketing gave them more information than other forms of communication and would make them more likely to tell others about the experience and be receptive to other marketing for the brand.[73]

Companies can even create a strong image by inviting prospects and customers to visit their headquarters and factories.[74] Ben & Jerry's, Boeing, Crayola, and Hershey's all sponsor excellent company tours that draw millions of visitors a year. Hallmark, Kohler, and Beiersdorf (maker of NIVEA) have built corporate museums at or near their headquarters that display their history and the drama of producing and marketing their products. Many firms are also creating off-site product and brand experiences. There are the World of Coca-Cola in Atlanta and Las Vegas and M&M's World in Times Square in New York City.

# Public Relations

Not only must the company relate constructively to customers, suppliers, and dealers, it must also relate to a large number of interested publics. A **public** is any group that has an actual or potential interest in or impact on a company's ability to achieve its objectives. **Public relations (PR)** includes a variety of programs to promote or protect a company's image or individual products.

The wise company takes concrete steps to manage successful relationships with its key publics. Most have a public relations department that monitors the attitudes of the organization's publics and distributes information and communications to build goodwill. The best PR departments counsel top management to adopt positive programs and eliminate questionable practices so negative publicity doesn't arise in the first place. They perform the following five functions:

1. *Press relations*—Presenting news and information about the organization in the most positive light
2. *Product publicity*—Sponsoring efforts to publicize specific products
3. *Corporate communications*—Promoting understanding of the organization through internal and external communications
4. *Lobbying*—Dealing with legislators and government officials to promote or defeat legislation and regulation
5. *Counseling*—Advising management about public issues as well as company positions and image during good times and bad

## MARKETING PUBLIC RELATIONS

Many companies are turning to **marketing public relations (MPR)** to support corporate or product promotion and image making. MPR, like financial PR and community PR, serves a special constituency, the marketing department.

The old name for MPR was **publicity,** the task of securing editorial space—as opposed to paid space—in print and broadcast media to promote or hype a product, service, idea, place, person, or organization. MPR goes beyond simple publicity and plays an important role in the following tasks:

- *Launching new products.* The amazing one-time commercial success of toys such as LeapFrog, Beanie Babies, and Silly Bandz owes a great deal to strong publicity.
- *Repositioning mature products.* In a classic PR case study, New York City had extremely bad press in the 1970s until the "I Love New York" campaign.
- *Building interest in a product category.* Companies and trade associations have used MPR to rebuild interest in declining commodities such as eggs, milk, beef, and potatoes and to expand consumption of such products as tea, pork, and orange juice.
- *Influencing specific target groups.* McDonald's sponsors special neighborhood events in Latino and African American communities to build goodwill.
- *Defending products that have encountered public problems.* PR professionals must be adept at managing crises, such as those weathered by such well-established brands as Tylenol, Toyota, and BP in recent years.
- *Building the corporate image in a way that reflects favorably on its products.* The late Steve Jobs's heavily anticipated Macworld keynote speeches helped to create an innovative, iconoclastic image for Apple Corporation.

As the power of mass advertising weakens, marketing managers are turning to MPR to build awareness and brand knowledge for both new and established products. MPR is also effective in blanketing local communities and reaching specific groups, and it can be more cost-effective than advertising. Increasingly, MPR takes place online, but it must be planned jointly with advertising and other marketing communications.[75]

Clearly, creative public relations can affect public awareness at a fraction of the cost of advertising. The company doesn't pay for media space or time but only for a staff to develop and circulate stories and manage certain events. An interesting story picked up by the media can be worth millions of dollars in equivalent advertising. Some experts say consumers are five times more likely to be influenced by editorial copy than by advertising. The following is an example of an award-winning PR campaign.[76]

----

**MEOW MIX** A heritage brand, Meow Mix Cat Food decided to tap into its roots and bring back one of its most identifiable brand elements—a jingle with repetitive meow refrain that had been off the air for 16 years. Marketers chose singer and TV reality coach CeeLo Green and his Persian cat Purrfect to do the honors. The video with Green singing

Source: © AF archive/Alamy

Meow Mix cat food reintroduced its famous ad jingle in a comprehensive PR campaign featuring singer CeeLo Green and his Persian cat Purrfect.

a remixed version of the jingle in a duet with Purrfect garnered attention from all kinds of outlets. The story received 1,200 media placements and 535 million media impressions, including exclusives with AP and *Access Hollywood*. Web traffic for the brand rose 150 percent, and more than 10,000 fans downloaded the song or ringtone. For each download, a pound of Meow Mix was donated to a local pet charity in Los Angeles.

## MAJOR DECISIONS IN MARKETING PR

In considering when and how to use MPR, management must establish the marketing objectives, choose the PR messages and vehicles, implement the plan, and evaluate the results. The main tools of MPR are described in Table 20.6.

**ESTABLISHING OBJECTIVES** MPR can build *awareness* by placing stories in the media to bring attention to a product, service, person, organization, or idea. It can build *credibility* by communicating the message in an editorial context. It can help boost sales force and dealer *enthusiasm* with stories about a new product before it is launched. It can hold down *promotion cost* because MPR costs less than direct-mail and media advertising.

A good MPR campaign can achieve multiple objectives. With its reputation slipping, Cisco launched "The Comeback Kid Initiative" to rebuild faith in its corporate vision and leadership. Raising the profile of key global executives, creating two timely global research studies, and showcasing some of its own technological products and solutions contributed to a 25 percent increase in stock valuation, an 11 percent increase in sales revenue, and a 15 percent boost in employee confidence.[77]

**CHOOSING MESSAGES AND VEHICLES** Suppose a relatively unknown college wants more visibility. The MPR practitioner will search for stories. Are any faculty members working on unusual projects? Are any new and unusual courses being taught? Are any interesting events taking place on campus? If there are no interesting stories, the MPR practitioner should propose newsworthy events the college could sponsor. Here the challenge is to create meaningful news. PR ideas include hosting major academic conventions, inviting expert or celebrity speakers, and developing news conferences. Each event and activity is an opportunity to develop a multitude of stories directed at different audiences.

| TABLE 20.6 | Major Tools in Marketing PR |
| --- | --- |

**Publications:** Companies rely extensively on published materials to reach and influence their target markets. These include annual reports, brochures, articles, company newsletters and magazines, and audiovisual materials.

**Events:** Companies can draw attention to new products or other company activities by arranging and publicizing special events such as news conferences, seminars, outings, trade shows, exhibits, contests and competitions, and anniversaries that will reach the target publics.

**Sponsorships:** Companies can promote their brands and corporate name by sponsoring and publicizing sports and cultural events and highly regarded causes.

**News:** One of the major tasks of PR professionals is to find or create favorable news about the company, its products, and its people and to get the media to accept press releases and attend press conferences.

**Speeches:** Increasingly, company executives must field questions from the media or give talks at trade associations or sales meetings, and these appearances can build the company's image.

**Public Service Activities:** Companies can build goodwill by contributing money and time to good causes.

**Identity Media:** Companies need a visual identity that the public immediately recognizes. The visual identity is carried by company logos, stationery, brochures, signs, business forms, business cards, buildings, uniforms, and dress codes.

Whereas PR practitioners reach their target publics through the mass media, MPR is increasingly borrowing the techniques and technology of online and direct-response marketing to reach target-audience members one on one.

**IMPLEMENTING THE PLAN AND EVALUATING RESULTS** MPR's contribution to the bottom line is difficult to measure because MPR is used along with other promotional tools. The easiest gauge of its effectiveness is the number of *exposures* carried by the media. Publicists supply their client with a clippings book showing all the media that carried news about the product and a summary statement such as the following:

> Media coverage included 3,500 column inches of news and photographs in 350 publications with a combined circulation of 79.4 million; 2,500 minutes of air time on 290 radio stations and an estimated audience of 65 million; and 660 minutes of air time on 160 television stations with an estimated audience of 91 million. If this time and space had been purchased at advertising rates, it would have amounted to $1,047,000.[78]

This measure is not very satisfying because it contains no indication of how many people actually read, heard, or recalled the message and what they thought afterward; nor does it contain information about the net audience reached because publications overlap in readership. It also ignores the effects of electronic media. Publicity's goal is reach, not frequency, so it would be more useful to know the number of unduplicated exposures across all media types.

A better measure is the *change in product awareness, comprehension, or attitude* resulting from the MPR campaign (after accounting for the effect of other promotional tools as well as possible). For example, how many people recall hearing the news item? How many told others about it (a measure of word of mouth)? How many changed their minds after hearing it?

# Summary

-------------------------------------------------------------------------------------------------------------------------

1. Advertising is any paid form of nonpersonal presentation and promotion of ideas, goods, or services by an identified sponsor. Advertisers include not only business firms but also charitable, nonprofit, and government agencies.

2. Developing an advertising program is a five-step process: (1) set advertising objectives, (2) establish a budget, (3) choose the advertising message and creative strategy, (4) decide on the media, and (5) evaluate communication and sales effects.

3. Sales promotion consists of mostly short-term incentive tools, designed to stimulate quicker or greater purchase of particular products or services by consumers or the trade.

4. In using sales promotion, a company must establish its objectives, select the tools, develop the program, implement and control it, and evaluate the results.

5. Events and experiences are a means to become part of special and more personally relevant moments in consumers' lives. Events can broaden and deepen the sponsor's relationship with its target market, but only if managed properly.

6. Public relations (PR) includes a variety of programs designed to promote or protect a company's image or its individual products. Marketing public relations (MPR), to support the marketing department in corporate or product promotion and image making, can affect public awareness at a fraction of the cost of advertising and is often much more credible. The main tools of PR are publications, events, news, community affairs, identification media, lobbying, and social responsibility.

MyMarketingLab

Go to **mymktlab.com** to complete the problems marked with this icon ⭐ as well as for additional Auto-graded and Assisted-graded writing questions.

# Applications

## Marketing Debate
### Should Marketers Test Advertising?

Advertising creatives believe ad pretesting inhibits their creative process and results in too much sameness in commercials. Marketers, on the other hand, believe it ensures the ad campaign will connect with consumers and be well received in the marketplace.

**Take a position:** Ad pretesting is often an unnecessary waste of marketing dollars *versus* Ad pretesting provides an important diagnostic for marketers as to the likely success of an ad campaign.

## Marketing Discussion
### Television Advertising

⭐ What are some of your favorite TV ads? Why? How effective are the message and creative strategies? How are they creating consumer preference and loyalty and building brand equity?

## Marketing Excellence

### >> Coca-Cola

When it comes to mass marketing, perhaps no one does it better than Coca-Cola. Coke is the most popular and best-selling product in the world. With an annual marketing budget of $3 billion and annual sales exceeding $30 billion, the brand tops the Interbrand ranking of the best brands year after year. Today, the company reaches consumers in more than 200 countries and has a brand value of $79 billion. In fact, it is such a global phenomenon that its name is the second-most understood word in the world (after *okay*).

The history of Coke's success is impressive from any perspective. The drink was invented in 1886 by Dr. John S. Pemberton, who mixed a syrup of his own invention with carbonated water to cure headaches. The company's first president turned the product into a pop culture phenomenon by distributing it to pharmacists around the world and engaging consumers through Coca-Cola–branded clocks, posters, and other paraphernalia.

Coca-Cola believed early on that to gain worldwide acceptance, the brand needed to accomplish two things: connect emotionally and socially with the masses and ensure that it was "within arm's-length of desire." So the company focused on gaining extensive distribution and making the product beloved by all. In World War II, it proclaimed, "every man in uniform gets a bottle of Coca-Cola for 5 cents, wherever he is, and whatever it costs the company." This strategy helped introduce the soft drink around the world as well as connecting consumers emotionally with a positive message during a time of turmoil.

How did Coca-Cola become *so much* bigger than any of its competitors? The company not only creates uplifting global campaigns better than anyone; it also translates them brilliantly across different countries, languages, and cultures. Coke's advertising has primarily focused on its ability to quench thirst and connect people no matter who they are or how they live. One of Coca-Cola's most memorable and successful commercials was called "Hilltop" and featured the song, "I'd like to buy the world a Coke." Launched in 1971, the ad featured young adults from all over the world sharing a happy moment and a common bond (holding a Coke) on a hillside in Italy. It touched so many consumers that the song became a top-10 hit single later that year.

Coca-Cola's television commercials still convey the message of universal connection over a Coke. The company's 2014 Super Bowl ad featured "America the Beautiful" sung in nine different languages—English, Spanish, Tagalog, Mandarin, Hindi, Hebrew, Keres (a language of the Pueblo people), French, and Arabic—showing that people of different ethnicities can connect through their love for the United States and Coca-Cola. Other commercials take a lighthearted tone to appeal to a younger audience. In one spot, a group of young adults sit around a campfire laughing, playing the guitar, and passing around a bottle of Coke. The bottle reaches a slimy, one-eyed alien who takes a sip and passes the bottle along. When the next drinker wipes the slime off in disgust, the music stops and the group stares at him in disappointment. The man hands the bottle back to the alien to get re-slimed and then drinks from it, and the music and the party continue in perfect harmony.

Jonathan Mildenhall, Coca-Cola's global head of content and advertising, explained the continued importance of TV ads: "The role of TV will never go from the Coca-Cola company; TV has a unique set of attributes in a marketing campaign that other media just cannot give us but I just don't think it should be the starting point." The company's mass communications strategy thus mixes a wide range of media including television, radio, print, social, in-store, digital, billboard, public relations, events, paraphernalia, and even its own museum. Its target audience and reach are so massive that choosing the right media and marketing message is critical, despite having a $3 billion marketing budget.

Coca-Cola uses big events to hit huge audiences; it has sponsored the Olympics since 1928 and advertises during the Super Bowl. The company targets younger consumers through efforts like 1.3 million tweets each quarter and strategic product placements including the judges' red Coke or Diet Coke cups placed front and center during *American Idol*. And it spends more than $1 billion a year on sports sponsorships such as NASCAR and the World Cup.

The delicate balance between Coca-Cola's local and global marketing is crucial; the campaigns must be relevant and translate well on a local scale. In China, for example, the company has given its regional managers control over advertising so they can include appropriate cultural messages. One executive explained, "Creating effective marketing at a local level in the absence of global scale can lead to huge inefficiencies." In 2006,

for example, Coca-Cola ran two campaigns during the FIFA World Cup as well as several local campaigns. In 2010, it ran a single World Cup campaign in more than 100 markets. Company executives estimated that the latter, global, strategy's efficiency saved it more than $45 million.

Despite its unprecedented success, Coca-Cola is not infallible. In 1985, in perhaps the worst product launch ever, the company introduced New Coke—a sweeter concoction of the original secret formula. Consumers instantly rejected it, and sales plummeted. Three months later, Coca-Cola relaunched the original formula under the name Coca-Cola Classic, to the delight of customers everywhere. Then-CEO Roberto Goizueta stated, "The simple fact is that all the time and money and skill poured into consumer research on the new Coca-Cola could not measure or reveal the deep and abiding emotional attachment to original Coca-Cola felt by so many people."

Coca-Cola's success at marketing a product on such a global, massive scale is unique. Despite the ups and downs of soft-drink trends over the years, no brand is so universally available, universally accepted, and universally loved as Coca-Cola.

## Questions

1. What does Coca-Cola stand for? Does it mean the same thing to everyone? Explain.

2. Coca-Cola has successfully marketed to billions of people around the world. Why is it so successful?

3. Can Pepsi or any other company ever surpass Coca-Cola? Why or why not? What are Coca-Cola's greatest risks?

**Sources:** Natalie Zmuda, "Coca-Cola Lays Out Its Vision for the Future at 2010 Meeting," *Advertising Age,* November 22, 2009; Natalie Zmuda, "Coke's 'Open Happiness' Keeps It Simple for Global Audience," *Advertising Age,* January 21, 2009; John Greenwald, "Will Teens Buy It?," *Time,* June 24, 2001; "Coca-Cola Still Viewed as Most Valuable Brand," *USA Today,* September 18, 2009; Edward Rothstein, "Ingredients: Carbonated Water, High-Fructose Corniness…," *New York Times,* July 30, 2007; Brad Cook, "Coca-Cola: A Classic," *Brandchannel,* December 2, 2002; Natalie Zmuda, "Coca-Cola Boosts Media Spending as Demand Slows," *Advertising Age,* February 18, 2014; Paul McIntyre, "Coke's Local Advertising Campaign a Worldwide Success," *Financial Review,* March 25, 2013; Coca-Cola Company 2012 Annual Report.

## Marketing Excellence

### >> Gillette

Gillette knows men. Not only does the company understand what products men desire for their grooming needs; it understands how to market to men in different countries, cultures, and languages around the world. Today, Gillette holds a commanding lead in the shaving and razor business with a 70 percent global market share and $8 billion in annual sales. More than 800 million men use Gillette products, helping to generate a brand value of $22.9 billion. Gillette's mass appeal is a result of several factors, including high-quality innovation, extensive consumer research, and successful mass communications.

Since the invention of the safety razor by King C. Gillette in 1901, Gillette has made a number of breakthrough product innovations. These include the Trac II, the first twin-blade shaving system in 1971, a razor with a pivoting head called the Atra in 1977, and the first razor with spring-mounted twin blades dubbed the Sensor in 1989. In 1998, Gillette introduced the first triple-blade system, Mach3, which became a billion-dollar brand surpassed only by the 2006 launch of the six-blade Fusion, promoted as "the best shave on the planet." Today, the Fusion and Fusion ProGlide account for approximately 45 percent of men's razors sold in the United States.

While Gillette has launched high-quality products, the company's impressive marketing knowledge and mass marketing campaigns have helped it achieve international success. Traditionally, it uses one global marketing message rather than individual targeted messages for each country or region. This message is backed by a wide spectrum of advertising support, including athletic sponsorships, television campaigns, in-store promotions, print ads, online advertising, and direct marketing.

Perhaps the most critical element is sports marketing. Gillette ads have featured baseball heroes such as Hank Aaron, Mickey Mantle, and Honus Wagner since 1910, and the company's sponsorship of Major League Baseball dates to 1939. The brand's natural fit with baseball and tradition has helped the company connect emotionally and literally with its core audience. Tim Brosnan, EVP for Major League Baseball, explains, "Gillette is a sports marketing pioneer that paved the way for modern day sports sponsorship and endorsements." Gillette has formed strong ties to football as well. The company has sponsored the Orange Bowl, Sugar Bowl, Cotton Bowl, and Rose Bowl. Today, it spends $7 million annually to sponsor Gillette Stadium, home of the New England Patriots, and is a corporate sponsor of the NFL.

Gillette has also sponsored boxing matches, NCAA Basketball, NCAA Football, NASCAR, PGA Tour, Champions Tour, LPGA Tour, and the National Hockey League. Internationally, the company has sponsored events such as the FIFA World Cup, the UK Tri-Nations rugby tournament, the Gillette Cup in Cricket, and Formula One racing. Greg Via, Global Director of Sports Marketing, explains, "We have an 18-month cycle that starts with a brand strategy. We produce a lot of products on a global basis, and we try to holistically leverage our major partnerships. That requires a lot of planning and work. We're not a company that is going to leverage a partnership with one commercial and one SKU. We wrap our arms around a partnership with TV, digital, social media and in-store promotions." The company often integrates creativity into its sponsorships as well. For example, it transformed Zambonis into giant Fusion razors at NHL games to create the illusion that a Gillette razor had just given the ice a perfectly smooth shave.

Gillette also partners with individual athletes to communicate its marketing messages and reflect the brand's image. In 2004, the company signed soccer star David Beckham to appear in its advertising and promotional campaigns around the world. In 2007, it launched the Gillette Champions program, highlighting the athletic accomplishments of Roger Federer, Thierry Henry, and Tiger Woods. It has featured baseball superstar Derek Jeter, soccer star Park Ji-Sung, motorcycle champion Kenan Sofuoglu, cricketer Rahul Dravid, and several NFL players.

While sports marketing is a critical element of Gillette's marketing strategy, the brand aims to reach every man and therefore also aligns with musical acts, video games, and movies. In one James Bond film, *Goldfinger*, a Gillette razor contained a homing device.

Gillette's advertising has resonated well with consumers over the years and left behind some of the most familiar taglines in advertising history. Two of the best known are "Look Sharp, Feel Sharp" and the current "The Best a Man Can Get."

When Procter & Gamble acquired Gillette in 2005 for $57 billion (a record 5-times sales), it aimed to gain more than sales and profit. P&G, an expert on marketing to women, wanted to learn about marketing to men on a global scale, and no one tops Gillette. Today, shaving and grooming make up 9 percent of P&G's total revenues, and razors are one of its most profitable businesses, with operating margins of 31 percent.

## Questions

1. Gillette has successfully convinced the world that "more is better" in terms of number of blades and other razor features. How did it do it? Why has that worked in the past? Will it continue to work in the future? Why or why not?

2. Explain why Gillette's sports marketing partnerships have been so successful.

3. Some of Gillette's spokespeople such as Derek Jeter and Tiger Woods have run into controversy after becoming endorsers for the brand. Does this hurt Gillette's brand equity or marketing message? Explain.

4. Will Gillette ever become as successful at marketing to women as to men? Why or why not?

**Sources:** Gillette press release, "Gillette Launches New Global Brand Marketing Campaign," July 1, 2009; Major League Baseball press release, "Major League Baseball Announces Extension of Historic Sponsorship with Gillette Dating Back to 1939," April 16, 2009; Gillette, *2009 Annual Report*; Jeremy Mullman and Rich Thomaselli, "Why Tiger Is Still the Best Gillette Can Get," *Advertising Age*, December 7, 2009; Louise Story, "Procter and Gillette Learn from Each Other's Marketing Ways," *New York Times*, April 12, 2007; Dan Beucke, "A Blade Too Far," *BusinessWeek*, August 14, 2006; Jenn Abelson, "And Then There Were Five," *Boston Globe*, September 15, 2005; Jack Neff, "Six-Blade Blitz," *Advertising Age*, September 19, 2005, pp. 3, 53; Editorial, "Gillette Spends Smart on Fusion," *Advertising Age*, September 26, 2005, p. 24; "World's Most Valuable Brands," *Fortune*, November 2013; "Five Questions: Greg Via, Gillette Global Director of Sports Marketing," IEG Sponsorship Report, November 18, 2013; "Gillette Enlists Top NFL Players and Sport Science's John Brenkus to Highlight the Importance of Precision in Football and Shaving," P&G corporate press release, September 3, 2013; P&G 2013 Annual Report.

## In This Chapter, We Will Address the Following Questions

1. What are the pros and cons of online marketing? (p. 615)

2. How can companies carry out effective social media campaigns? (p. 620)

3. What are some tips for enjoying positive word of mouth? (p. 623)

4. What are important guidelines for mobile marketing? (p. 628)

With its "Crash the Super Bowl" contest, Frito-Lay gives participants a chance to win $1 million and have their home-made ad aired during the game broadcast.

*Source: Used with permission of Daved Wilkins (talent) and Frito-Lay, Inc.*

# Managing Digital Communications: Online, Social Media, and Mobile

**In the face of the Internet revolution, marketing communications today increasingly** occur as a kind of personal dialogue between the company and its customers. Companies must ask not only "How should we reach our customers?" but also "How should our customers reach us?" and "How can our customers reach each other?" New technologies have encouraged companies to move from mass communication to more targeted, two-way communications. As a result, consumers can now play a much more participatory role in the marketing process. Consider how PepsiCo has engaged the consumer in marketing communications for its various brands.[1]

 *PepsiCo has been an early champion of digital marketing. For its Mountain Dew soft drink, its first "Dewmocracy" contest had consumers go online to determine the flavor, color, packaging, and name of a new Mountain Dew product. The winning flavor, Voltage, generated several hundred million dollars in revenue for the company in its first year. The second contest, Dewmocracy 2, expanded voting through Facebook, Twitter, and a private online Dew Labs Community and crowned White Out as the winner. For its Doritos brand, PepsiCo runs the "Crash the Super Bowl" contest every year, giving contestants a chance to develop an ad to be run during the game broadcast and receive $1 million in the process. In 2014, anyone from Dorito's 35 global markets was allowed to enter the competition, resulting in more than 3,000 submissions. The winning ad, "Time Machine," had a man humor a small kid by taking a ride in the kid's cardboard time machine—with unexpected results. It cost only $200 to make and one day to film, but it was one of the most positively received Super Bowl ads by viewers that year. During the contest, Doritos always enjoys a healthy uptick in Twitter, Facebook, and other social media activity.*

**The newest and fastest-growing** channels for communicating and selling directly to customers are digital. The Internet provides marketers and consumers with opportunities for much greater interaction and individualization. Very few marketing programs can be considered complete without a meaningful digital component. In this chapter, we consider how marketers can use online marketing, social media, and mobile marketing to create loyal customers, build strong brands, and generate profits. We also consider the broader topic of word-of-mouth marketing.

# Online Marketing

As described in Chapter 1, marketers distinguish paid and owned media from earned (or free) media. *Paid media* includes company-generated advertising, publicity, and other promotional efforts. *Earned media* is all the PR and word-of-mouth benefits a firm receives without having directly paid for anything—all the news stories, blogs, and social network conversations that deal with a brand.[2] Social media play a key role in earned media. A large part of *owned media* consists of online marketing communications, which we review next.

Estee Lauder has always relied on word of mouth to build its brands but now has added a sizable digital component.

*Source: Weng lei-Imaginechina*

# ADVANTAGES AND DISADVANTAGES OF ONLINE MARKETING COMMUNICATIONS

Four of the main categories of online marketing communications, which we discuss here, are: (1) Web sites, (2) search ads, (3) display ads, and (4) e-mail. The variety of online communication options means companies can offer or send tailored information or messages that engage consumers by reflecting their special interests and behavior.

Online marketing communications have other advantages. Marketers can easily trace their effects by noting how many unique visitors or "UVs" click on a page or ad, how long they spend with it, what they do on it, and where they go afterward.[3] The Internet also offers the advantage of *contextual placement,* which means marketers can buy ads on sites related to their own offerings. They can also place advertising based on keywords customers type into search engines to reach people when they've actually started the buying process.

Going online has disadvantages too. Consumers can effectively screen out most messages. Marketers may think their ads are more effective than they really are if bogus clicks are generated by software-powered Web sites.[4] Advertisers also lose some control over their online messages, which can be hacked or vandalized.

But the pros clearly can outweigh the cons, and the Internet is attracting marketers of all kinds. Beauty pioneer Estée Lauder, who, in a reflection of times gone by, famously said she relied on three means of communication to build her multimillion-dollar cosmetics business— "telephone, telegraph, and tell a woman"—would now have to add the Internet, where the company's official site describes new and old products, announces special offers and promotions, and helps customers locate stores where they can buy Estée Lauder products.

Marketers must go where the customers are, and increasingly that's online. Of the time U.S. consumers spend with all media, almost half is spent online (see Figure 21.1).[5] Customers define the rules of engagement, however, and insulate themselves with the help of agents and intermediaries if they so choose. They define what information they need, what offerings they're interested in, and what they're willing to pay.[6]

| Fig. 21.1 |

## Share of Time Spent per Day with Major Media by U.S. Adults, 2014 (hrs:mins)

Source: eMarketer, April 2014, accessed at http://www.emarketer.com/Article/Digital-Set-Surpass-TV-Time-Spent-with-US-Media/1010096.

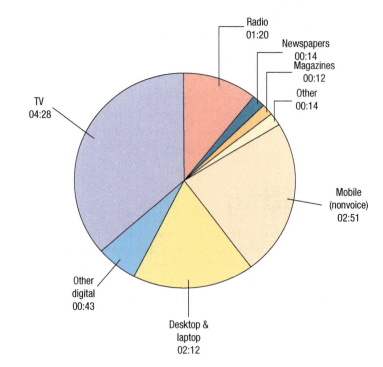

Source: © David Buzzard/Alamy

Tough Mudder used only Facebook advertising and word of mouth to launch its brand.

Digital advertising continues to show much more rapid growth than traditional media. In fact, total digital ad spending in 2013 was estimated to have grown to $42.8 billion, which meant it surpassed TV advertising (at $40.1 billion) for the first time. Search ads made up 43 percent of the total at $18.4 billion; display-related advertising was 30 percent with $12.8 billion; mobile 17 percent with $7.1 billion; and digital video 7 percent with $2.8 billion.[7] More brands are being built by online means. Consider Tough Mudder.[8]

**▌TOUGH MUDDER** Tough Mudder is a challenging obstacle race for teams, designed in the spirit of British Special Forces, that features 29 different obstacles with such creative names as the Devil's Beard, Shocks on the Rocks, and Funky Monkey. Competitors encounter hazards such as walls, 15-foot planks, ice baths, nightmare monkey bars, greased halfpipes, and electrified army crawls. Funded with $20,000 in seed capital in 2010, Tough Mudder spent its entire $8,000 communication budget at launch on Facebook advertising, which generated plenty of word of mouth. The first race was a hit, and word quickly spread. By 2013, more than 750,000 competitors were participating in 53 scheduled events. With entry fees of about $155 per person, the company's margin is about 48 percent.

## ONLINE MARKETING COMMUNICATION OPTIONS

A company chooses which forms of online marketing will be most cost-effective in achieving communication and sales objectives.[9] The options include Web sites, search ads, display ads, and e-mail.

**WEB SITES** Companies must design Web sites that embody or express their purpose, history, products, and vision and that are attractive on first viewing and interesting enough to encourage repeat visits.[10] Jeffrey Rayport and Bernard Jaworski propose that effective sites feature seven design elements they call the 7Cs (see Figure 21.2).[11] To encourage repeat visits, companies must pay special attention to context and content factors and embrace another "C"—constant change.[12]

Visitors will judge a site's performance on ease of use and physical attractiveness.[13] *Ease of use* means: (1) The site downloads quickly, (2) the first page is easy to understand, and (3) it is easy to navigate to other pages that open quickly. *Physical attractiveness* is ensured when: (1) Individual pages are clean and not crammed with content, (2) typefaces and font sizes are very readable, and (3) the site makes good use of color (and sound). J. D. Power found that consumers who were "delighted" with an automotive manufacturer's Web site were more likely to test drive one of its vehicles as a result.[14]

As we describe in more detail below, firms such as comScore and Nielsen Online track where consumers go online through measures like number of page views, number of unique visitors, length of visit, and so on.[15]

**| Fig. 21.2 |**

## Seven Key Design Elements of an Effective Web Site

Source: Jeffrey F. Rayport and Bernard J. Jaworski, *e-commerce* (New York: McGraw-Hill, 2001), p. 116.

- *Context.* Layout and design
- *Content.* Text, pictures, sound, and video the site contains
- *Community.* How the site enables user-to-user communication
- *Customization.* Site's ability to tailor itself to different users or to allow users to personalize the site
- *Communication.* How the site enables site-to-user, user-to-site, or two-way communication
- *Connection.* Degree that the site is linked to other sites
- *Commerce.* Site's capabilities to enable commercial transactions

Companies must also be sensitive to online security and privacy-protection issues. One set of researchers recommends transforming various "touch points" related to privacy on the Web site into a positive customer experience by: (1) developing user-centric privacy controls to give customer control, (2) avoiding multiple intrusions, and (3) preventing human intrusion by using automation whenever possible.[16]

Besides their Web sites, companies may employ **microsites,** individual Web pages or clusters of pages that function as supplements to a primary site. They're particularly relevant for companies selling low-interest products. People rarely visit an insurance company's Web site, for example, but the company can create a microsite on used-car sites that offers advice for buyers of used cars and a good insurance deal at the same time.

**SEARCH ADS** An important component of online marketing is **paid search** or **pay-per-click ads.** Thirty-five percent of all searches are reportedly for products or services.

In paid search, marketers bid in a continuous auction on search terms that serve as a proxy for the consumer's product or consumption interests. When a consumer searches for any of the words with Google, Yahoo!, or Bing, the marketer's ad may appear above or next to the results, depending on the amount the company bids and an algorithm the search engines use to determine an ad's relevance to a particular search.[17]

Advertisers pay only if people click on the links, but marketers believe consumers who have already expressed interest by engaging in search are prime prospects. Average click-through in terms of the percentage of consumers who click on a link is about 2 percent, much more than for comparable online display ads, which range from .08 for standard banner ads with graphics and images to .14 for rich media (expandable banners) ads that incorporate audio and/or video.[18]

The cost per click depends on how highly the link is ranked on the page and the popularity of the keyword. The ever-increasing popularity of paid search has increased competition among keyword bidders, significantly raising search ad prices and putting a premium on choosing the best possible keywords, bidding on them strategically, and monitoring the results for effectiveness and efficiency.

*Search engine optimization (SEO)* describes activities designed to improve the likelihood that a link for a brand is as high as possible in the rank order of all nonpaid links when consumers search for relevant terms. SEO is a crucial part of marketing given the large amount of money marketers are spending on search. A number of guidelines have been suggested as part of SEO as well as paid search.[19]

- Broader search terms ("MP3 player" or "iPod") are useful for general brand building; more specific ones identifying a particular product model or service ("Apple iPod classic 160GB") are useful for generating and converting sales leads.
- Search terms need to be spotlighted on the appropriate pages of the marketer's Web site so search engines can easily identify them.
- Any one product can usually be identified by means of multiple keywords, but marketers must bid on each keyword according to its likely return on revenue. It also helps to have popular sites link back to the marketer's Web site.
- Data can be collected to track the effects of paid search.

Any size business can benefit from a well-executed search strategy. The owner of River Pools and Spas in Virginia and Maryland turned around his floundering business by posting question-and-answer articles that were picked up easily by search engines and drove traffic to the company's Web site.[20]

Consumers are also influenced by the online opinions and recommendations of other consumers. The informal social networks that arise among consumers complement the product networks set up by the company.[21] Online "influentials" who are one of a few or maybe even the only person to influence certain consumers are particularly important and valuable to companies.[22]

**DISPLAY ADS** **Display ads** or **banner ads** are small, rectangular boxes containing text and perhaps a picture that companies pay to place on relevant Web sites.[23] The larger the audience, the higher the cost. In the early days of the Internet, viewers clicked on 2 percent to 3 percent of the banner ads they saw, but as noted previously, that percentage has quickly plummeted, and advertisers have explored other forms of communication.

Given that Internet users spend only 5 percent of their time online actually searching for information, display ads still hold great promise compared to popular search ads. But ads need to be more attention-getting and influential, better targeted, and more closely tracked.[24]

**Interstitials** are advertisements, often with video or animation, that pop up between page changes within a Web site or across Web sites. For example, ads for Johnson & Johnson's Tylenol headache reliever would pop up on brokers' Web sites whenever the stock market fell by 100 points or more. Because consumers find such pop-up ads intrusive and distracting, many use software to block them.

**E-MAIL** E-mail allows marketers to inform and communicate with customers at a fraction of the cost of a d-mail, or direct mail, campaign. E-mails can be very productive selling tools. The rate at which they prompt purchase has been estimated to be at least three times that of social media ads, and the average order value is thought to be 17 percent higher.[25] Firms such as Kellogg, Whirlpool, and Nissan are emphasizing both e-mail and search marketing.[26]

Consumers are besieged by e-mails, though, and many employ spam filters to halt the flow. Privacy concerns are also growing—almost half of British survey respondents said they would refuse to share any personal details with brands even if doing so would bring them better-targeted offers and discounts.[27] Some firms are asking consumers to say whether and when they would like to receive e-mails. FTD, the flower retailer, allows customers to choose whether to receive e-mail reminders to send flowers for virtually any holiday as well as specific birthdays and anniversaries.[28]

E-mails must be timely, targeted, and relevant. The Gilt Groupe sends more than 3,000 variations of its daily e-mail for its flash-sale site based on recipient's past click-throughs, browsing history, and purchase history.[29] "Marketing Memo: How to Maximize the Marketing Value of E-mails" provides some important guidelines for launching productive e-mail campaigns.

With a customer's permission, flower retailer FTD sends email reminders for important events.

*Source: FTD*

## How to Maximize the Marketing Value of E-mails

- *Give the customer a reason to respond.* Offer powerful incentives for reading e-mail pitches and online ads, such as trivia games, scavenger hunts, and instant-win sweepstakes.

- *Personalize the content of your e-mails.* Williams-Sonoma reported a tenfold increase in response rates when it adopted personalized e-mail offerings based on individuals' on-site and catalog shopping behavior. An engaging subject line is especially critical. One expert notes, "You really have about five seconds to grab them or they are clicking out."

- *Offer something the customer can't get via direct mail.* Because e-mail campaigns can be carried out quickly, they can offer time-sensitive information. Travelocity sends frequent e-mails pitching last-minute cheap airfares, and Club Med pitches unsold vacation packages at a discount.

- *Make it easy for customers to opt in as well as unsubscribe.* Run controlled split tests to explore how location, color, and other factors affect "Sign Up Now" messages. Controlled split tests assemble online matched samples of consumers with one sample given a test message that manipulates one factor and the other being a status quo control. Online customers also demand a positive exit experience. Dissatisfied customers leaving on a sour note are more likely to spread their displeasure to others.

- *Combine e-mail with other communications such as social media.* Southwest Airlines found the highest number of reservations occurred after an e-mail campaign followed by a social media campaign. Papa John's was able to add 45,000 fans to its Facebook page through an e-mail campaign inviting customers to participate in a "March Madness" NCAA basketball tournament contest.

To increase the effectiveness of e-mails, some researchers are employing "heat mapping," which tracks eye movements with cameras to measure what people read on a computer screen. One study showed that clickable graphic icons and buttons that linked to more details of a marketing offer increased click-through rates by 60 percent over links that used just an Internet address.

**Sources:** Nora Aurfreiter, Julien Boudet, and Vivien Weng, "Why Marketers Keep Sending You E-Mails," *McKinsey Quarterly*, January 2014; "Email Marketing Central for U.S. Retailers," www.warc.com, December 20, 2012; Richard Westlund, "Success Stories in eMail Marketing," *Adweek Special Advertising Section*, February 16, 2010; Suzanne Vranica, "Marketers Give E-mail Another Look," *Wall Street Journal*, July 17, 2006.

# Social Media

An important component of digital marketing is social media. **Social media** are a means for consumers to share text, images, audio, and video information with each other and with companies, and vice versa.

Social media allow marketers to establish a public voice and presence online. They can cost-effectively reinforce other communication activities. Because of their day-to-day immediacy, they can also encourage companies to stay innovative and relevant. Marketers can build or tap into online communities, inviting participation from consumers and creating a long-term marketing asset in the process.

After reviewing the different social media platforms, we consider how to use social media and how social media can promote the flow of word of mouth. We then delve into more detail on how word of mouth is formed and travels. To start our discussion, consider how one company cleverly used social media to build its brand.[30]

**DOLLAR SHAVE CLUB** E-commerce startup Dollar Shave Club sells a low-priced monthly supply of razors and blades online according to three different plans. The key to the company's launch was an online video. Dubbed the "best startup video ever" by some and the winner of multiple awards, the 90-second Dollar Shave Club video garnered millions of views on YouTube and gained thousands of social media followers in the process. In the quirky, irreverent video, CEO Michael Dubin rides a forklift, plays tennis, and dances with a fuzzy bear while touting the quality, convenience, and price of the company's razors and blades. Dubin has observed, "We are presenting a new business, a good idea, a funny video and tapped the pain point for a lot of consumers." While it was securing several hundred thousand customers, the company was also able to raise more than $20 million in venture capital.

CEO Michael Dubin's online video to launch Dollar Shave Club was an Internet sensation.

Source: Dollar Shave Club

## SOCIAL MEDIA PLATFORMS

There are three main platforms for social media: (1) online communities and forums, (2) blogs (individual blogs and blog networks such as Sugar and Gawker), and (3) social networks (like Facebook, Twitter, and YouTube).

**ONLINE COMMUNITIES AND FORUMS** Online communities and forums come in all shapes and sizes. Many are created by consumers or groups of consumers with no commercial interests or company affiliations. Others are sponsored by companies whose members communicate with the company and with each other through postings, text messaging, and chat discussions about special interests related to the company's products and brands. These online communities and forums can be a valuable resource for companies and fill multiple functions by both collecting and conveying key information.

A key for success in online communities is to create individual and group activities that help form bonds among community members. Apple hosts a large number of discussion groups organized by product lines and type of user (consumer or professional). These groups are customers' primary source of product information after warranties expire.

Information flow in online communities and forums is two-way and can provide companies with useful, hard-to-get customer information and insights. When GlaxoSmithKline prepared to launch its first weight-loss drug, Alli, it sponsored a weight-loss community. The firm felt the feedback it gained was more valuable than what it could have received from traditional focus groups.

Research has shown, however, that firms should avoid too much democratization of innovation. One risk is that groundbreaking ideas can be replaced by lowest-common-denominator solutions.[31]

**BLOGS** *Blogs*, regularly updated online journals or diaries, have become an important outlet for word of mouth. There are millions in existence, and they vary widely, some personal for close friends and families, others designed to reach and influence a vast audience. One obvious appeal of blogs is that they bring together people with common interests.

Blog networks such as Gawker Media offer marketers a portfolio of choices. Online celebrity gossip blog PopSugar has spawned a family of breezy blogs on fashion (FabSugar), beauty (BellaSugar), and romance and culture (TrèsSugar), attracting women ages 18 to 49.

Corporations are creating their own blogs and carefully monitoring those of others.[32] Popular blogs are creating influential opinion leaders. At the TreeHugger site—"the leading media outlet dedicated to driving sustainability mainstream"—a team of bloggers tracks green consumer products for 5 million unique visitors per month, offering an up-to-the minute blog, weekly and daily newsletters, and regularly updated Twitter and Facebook pages.[33]

Because many consumers examine product information and reviews contained in blogs, the Federal Trade Commission has also taken steps to require bloggers to disclose their relationship with marketers whose products they endorse. At the other extreme, some consumers use blogs and videos as a means of getting retribution for a company's bad service or faulty products. Some customer retaliations are legendary.

Dell's customer-service shortcomings were splashed all over the Internet through a series of blistering "Dell Hell" postings. AOL took some heat when a frustrated customer recorded and broadcast online a service representative's emphatic resistance to his wish to cancel his service. Comcast was embarrassed when a video surfaced of one of its technicians sleeping on a customer's couch.[34]

SOCIAL NETWORKS    Social networks have become an important force in both business-to-consumer and business-to-business marketing.[35] Major ones include Facebook, one of the world's biggest; LinkedIn, which focuses on career-minded professionals; and Twitter, with its 140-character messages or "tweets." Different networks offer different benefits to firms. For example, Twitter can be an early warning system that permits rapid response, whereas Facebook allows deeper dives to engage consumers in more meaningful ways.[36]

Marketers are still learning how to best tap into social networks and their huge, well-defined audiences.[37] Given networks' noncommercial nature—users are generally there looking to connect with others—attracting attention and persuading are more challenging. Also, given that users generate their own content, ads may find themselves appearing beside inappropriate or even offensive material.[38]

Advertising is only one avenue, however. Like any individual, companies can also join social groups and actively participate. Having a Facebook page has become a virtual prerequisite for many companies.[39] Twitter can benefit even the smallest firm. To create interest in its products and the events it hosted, small San Francisco bakery Mission Pie began to send tweet alerts, quickly gaining 1,000 followers and a sizable uptick in business. "Follow Me on Twitter" signs are appearing on doors and windows of more small shops.[40]

And although major social networks offer the most exposure, niche networks provide a more targeted market that may be more likely to spread the brand message, as CafeMom did for Playskool.[41]

**CAFEMOM**    Started in 2006, CafeMom has 20 million users across its flagship CafeMom site and other properties such as The Stir (an "all-day, every day content destination for Moms") and Mamás Latinas (the first bilingual site for Latina moms). Users can participate in 70,000 different group forums for moms. When the site started a forum for discussing developmentally appropriate play activities, toymaker Playskool sent toy kits to more than 5,000 members and encouraged them to share their experiences with each other, resulting in 11,600 posts at Playskool Preschool Playgroup. "The great thing is you get direct feedback from actual moms," says the director of media at Hasbro, Playskool's parent company. This kind of feedback can be invaluable in the product-development process as well. The site's sweet spot is young, middle-class women with kids who love the opportunity to make friends and seek support, spending an average of 44 minutes a day on the site.

## USING SOCIAL MEDIA

Social media allow consumers to become engaged with a brand at perhaps a deeper and broader level than ever before. Marketers should do everything they can to encourage willing consumers to engage productively. But as useful as they may be, social media are rarely the sole source of marketing communications for a brand.[42]

- Social media may not be as effective in attracting new users and driving brand penetration.
- Research by DDB suggests that brands and products vary widely in how social they are online. Consumers are most likely to engage with media, charities, and fashion and least likely to engage with consumer goods.[43]
- Although consumers may use social media to get useful information or deals and promotions or to enjoy interesting or entertaining brand-created content, a much smaller percentage want use social media to engage in two-way "conversations" with brands.

In short, marketers must recognize that when it comes to social media, only *some* consumers want to engage with *some* brands, and, even then, only *some* of the time.

Embracing social media, harnessing word of mouth, and creating buzz also require companies to take the good with the bad. When Frito-Lay's "Do Us a Flavor" contest invited U.S. fans to suggest new potato chip flavors for a chance to win a huge cash prize, the Facebook app for submissions crashed the first day due to high traffic. The promotion got back on track, though, with the winner, Cheesy Garlic Bread–flavored chips, joining earlier winners from other countries such as Caesar salad–flavored chips in Australia and shrimp chips in Egypt.[44]

The Frito-Lay example shows the power and speed of social media, but also the challenges they pose to companies. The reality, however, is that whether a company chooses to engage in social media or not, the Internet will always permit scrutiny, criticism, and even "cheap shots" from consumers and organizations.

By using social media and the Internet in a constructive, thoughtful way, firms at least have a means to create a strong online presence and to better offer credible alternative points of view if negative feedback occurs.[45] And if the firm has built a strong online community, members of that community will often rush to defend the brand and play a policing role over inaccurate or unfair characterizations.

Frito-Lay used a social media campaign for new consumer-created flavors it introduced.

*Source: Invision for Frito-Lay*

# Word of Mouth

Social media are one example of online word of mouth. Word of mouth (WOM) is a powerful marketing tool. AT&T found it was one of the most effective drivers of its sales, along with unaided advertising awareness. Some brands have been built almost exclusively by word of mouth.[46]

| **SODASTREAM**  SodaStream, a product that allows consumers to carbonate regular tap water at home to replace store-bought sodas, was built with minimal media spend due to the power of word of mouth. To help promote conversations about the brand, the company has sampled liberally, used product placement, and engaged with affinity groups that might be interested in home carbonation because of its environmental advantages, including various "green" organizations, or because it offers the convenience of not having to store bottles and cans, which appeals to boat and RV owners. CEO Daniel Birnbaum notes, "I would much rather invest in PR than in advertising, because with PR it's not me talking—it's someone else." One of SodaStream's most successful marketing activities is "The Cage." The company calculates the average number of cans and bottles thrown away by a family in a year in a given country and then fills a giant cage-like box to hold them, placing it in high-traffic locations like airports to draw attention to it. After deciding to target Coke and Pepsi head on, SodaStream did purchase advertising time in the 2013 and 2014 Super Bowls. Ironically, with this decision the company still benefited from PR and word of mouth because the networks banned its initial ads for being too aggressive. The banned ads received more attention than the ones that actually ran, racking up millions of views online and a barrage of media coverage. Purchased for $6 million in 2007, SodaStream had a 2014 market cap of more than $1 billion.

SodaStream benefited from PR and word of mouth in launching its brand.

*Source: Photo courtesy of SodaStream*

## FORMS OF WORD OF MOUTH

Contrary to popular opinion, most word of mouth is *not* generated online. In fact, research and consulting firm Keller Fay notes that 90 percent occurs offline, specifically 75 percent face to face and 15 percent over the phone. Keller Fay also notes how advertising and WOM are inextricably linked: "WOM has proven to be highly credible and linked to sales; advertising has proven to help spark conversation."[47] Others note how well offline word of mouth works with social media. Consumers "start conversations in one channel, continue them in a second and finish them in a third. When the communication is happening in so many channels, it becomes almost impossible to separate online and offline."[48]

**Viral marketing** is a form of online word of mouth, or "word of mouse," that encourages consumers to pass along company-developed products and services or audio, video, or written information to others online.[49] With user-generated content sites such as YouTube, Vimeo, and Google Video, consumers and advertisers can upload ads and videos to be shared by millions of people.[50] Online videos can be cost-effective—they can be made for as little as $50,000 to $200,000—and marketers can take more freedom with them, as Blendtec has done.[51]

▌**BLENDTEC**    Utah-based Blendtec used to be known primarily for its commercial blenders and food mills. The company wasn't really familiar to the general public until it launched a hilarious series of "Will It Blend?" online videos to promote some of its commercial products for home use. The videos feature founder and CEO Tom Dickson wearing a white lab coat and pulverizing objects ranging from golf balls and pens to beer bottles, all in a genial but deadpan manner. The genius of the videos (www.willitblend.com) is that they tie into current events. As soon as the iPhone was launched with huge media fanfare, Blendtec aired a video in which Dickson smiled and said, "I love my iPhone. It does everything. But will it blend?" After the blender crushed the iPhone to bits, Dickson lifted the lid on the small pile of black dust and said simply, "iSmoke." The clip drew more than 3.5 million views on YouTube. Dickson has appeared on *Today* and other network television shows and has had a cameo in a Weezer video. One of the few items *not* to blend: A crowbar!

Outrageousness is a two-edged sword. The Blendtec Web site clearly puts its comic videos in the "*Don't* try this at home" category and developed another set showing how to grind up vegetables for soup, for instance, in the "*Do* try this at home" category.

## CREATING WORD-OF-MOUTH BUZZ

Products don't have to be outrageous or edgy to generate word-of-mouth buzz. Although more interesting brands are more likely to be talked about online, whether a brand is seen as novel, exciting, or surprising has little effect on whether it is discussed in face-to-face, oral communications.[52] Brands discussed offline are often those that are salient and visible and come easily to mind.[53]

Blendtec built its consumer brand in part with a series of clever "Will It Blend" online videos.

*Source: Blendtec*

Research has shown that consumers tend to generate positive WOM themselves and share information about their *own* positive consumption experiences. They tend to only transmit negative WOM and pass on information they heard about *others'* negative consumption experiences.[54]

It's worth remembering that much online content is not necessarily naturally shared and does not go viral. One study found that only 4 percent of content "cascaded" to more than one person beyond the initial recipient.[55] In deciding whether to contribute to social media, consumers can be motivated by intrinsic factors such as whether they are having fun or learning, but more often they are swayed by extrinisic factors such as social and self-image considerations.[56]

Harvard Business School viral video expert Thales Teixeira offers this advice for getting a viral ad shared: Utilize brand pulsing so the brand is not too intrusive within the video; open with joy or surprise to hook those fickle viewers who are easily bored; build an emotional roller coaster within the ad to keep viewers engaged throughout; and surprise but don't shock—if an ad makes viewers too uncomfortable, they are unlikely to share it.[57]

Companies can help create buzz for their products or services, and media and advertising are not always necessary for it to occur. Proctor & Gamble (P&G) has enrolled more than half a million mothers in Vocalpoint, a group built on the premise that certain highly engaged individuals want to learn about products, receive samples and coupons, share their opinions with companies, and, of course, talk up their experiences with others. P&G chooses well-connected people—the Vocalpoint moms have big social networks and generally speak to 25 to 30 other women during the day, compared to an average of five for other moms—and their messages carry a strong reason to share product information with a friend. A campaign for P&G's Secret Clinical Strength Deodorant resulted in 42,000 click-throughs to an opt-in coupon redemption and 50,000 strong product reviews on the brand's Web site.

Some agencies exist solely to help clients create buzz. BzzAgent is one.[58]

---

**BZZAGENT** Boston-based BzzAgent has assembled an international word-of-mouth media network powered by 1 million demographically diverse—but essentially ordinary—people who volunteer to talk up products they deem worth promoting. The company pairs consumers with its clients' products, information, and digital tools to activate widespread opinion-sharing throughout its own social media site, called BzzScapes, and within each member's personal social circles. BzzAgent believes this unique combination of people and platform accelerates measurable word of mouth and fosters sustained brand advocacy. As one senior executive at the firm notes: "The bar is pretty low to be a fan and pretty high to be an advocate." The company claims the buzz is honest because being in the network requires just enough work that few people enroll solely for freebies, and members don't talk up products they don't like. Members are also supposed to disclose they're connected to BzzAgent. After being acquired by Dunhumby, BzzAgent launched its analytics dashboard Pulse, which combines social media information with actual sales data to trace the impact of word-of-mouth buzz. The company has completed hundreds of projects. For Hasbro, it helped launch the Nerf FireVision toys—which appear to glow in the dark when viewed with special glasses—by sampling the product among members of its panel who have younger children. For Green Mountain Coffee, it sent samples and information to 10,000 carefully chosen members to spread the word about the client's commitment to Fair Trade Coffee as one component of a bigger marketing program. More than 1.8 million messages were shared about Green Mountain's Fair Trade program, increasing customers' understanding of Fair Trade certification by 61 percent and sales of the coffee by 14 percent.

---

Viral marketing tries to create a splash in the marketplace to showcase a brand and its noteworthy features. Some believe viral marketing efforts are driven more by the rules of entertainment than by the rules of selling. Consider these examples: Quicksilver puts out surfing videos and surf-culture books for teens, Johnson & Johnson and Pampers both have popular Web sites with parenting advice; Walmart places videos with money-saving tips on YouTube; Grey Goose vodka has an entire entertainment division; Mountain Dew has a record label; and Hasbro is joining forces with Discovery to create a TV channel.[59]

Ultimately, however, the success of any viral or word-of-mouth buzz campaign depends on the willingness of consumers to talk to other consumers.[60] Customer reviews can be especially influential.[61] A recent Nielsen survey found that online customer reviews were the second-most trusted source of brand information (after recommendations from friends and family).[62] Many review sites are now using a Facebook login that attaches a review posted by someone to their Facebook profile. By attaching their review to their Facebook page, users can find out what friends or noteworthy celebrities deem positive or negative about a brand.[63]

As Chapter 5 noted, however, online reviews can be biased or just plain fake.[64] Research has shown that social influence can lead to disproportionally positive online ratings, and subsequent raters are more likely to be influenced by previous positive ratings than negative ones. Consumers posting reviews are susceptible to conformity pressures and adopting norms of others.[65] On the other hand, positive online reviews or ratings are often not as influential or valued as much as negative ones.[66]

Companies can try to stimulate personal influence channels to work on their behalf. U.S. women's specialty retailer Chico's increased its revenue per visitor and average order value for its three brands after adding ratings, reviews, questions, and answers to the brands' sites.[67] "Marketing Memo: How to Start a Buzz Fire" describes some techniques to increase word of mouth.

A customer's value to a company depends in part on his or her ability and likelihood of making referrals and engaging in positive word of mouth.[69] As useful as earning positive word of mouth from a consumer can be, though, getting consumers to directly engage with the company and provide it with feedback and suggestions can

---

## marketing memo

### How to Start a Buzz Fire

In analyzing the online success of different songs, media researcher Duncan Watts found their popularity was "incredibly unpredictable." The key to setting a song on the path to popularity was to achieve some early downloads—a phenomenon Watts dubs "cumulative advantage." Although many word-of-mouth effects are beyond marketers' control—as Watts' work suggests—certain steps can improve the likelihood of starting positive buzz:

- *Identify influential individuals and companies and devote extra effort to them.* In technology, influencers might be large corporate customers, industry analysts and journalists, selected policy makers, and early adopters. Companies can trace online activity to identify more influential users who may function as opinion leaders.

- *Supply key people with product samples.* Chevrolet selected about 900 people with a Klout online influence score of more than 50 (of a possible 100) and gave them a free three-day rental of the Chevy Volt, resulting in 46,000 tweets and more than 20.7 million largely positive blog posts about the electric car.

- *Work through community influentials.* Ford's prelaunch "Fiesta Movement" campaign invited 100 handpicked young Millennials to live with the Fiesta car for six months. Drivers were chosen based on their online experience with blogging and size and quality of their online social network as well as a video they submitted about their desire for adventure. After the six months of trial usage, the campaign had drawn 4.3 million YouTube views, more than 500,000 Flickr views, more than 3 million Twitter impressions (the number of times a tweet is read), and 50,000 potential customers, 97 percent of whom were not already Ford owners.[68]

- *Develop word-of-mouth referral channels to build business.* Professionals will often encourage clients to recommend their services. Weight Watchers found that word-of-mouth referrals from someone in the program had a huge impact on business.

- *Provide compelling information that customers want to pass along.* Companies shouldn't communicate with customers in terms better suited for a press release. Make it easy and desirable for a customer to borrow elements from an e-mail message or blog. Information should be original and useful. Originality increases the amount of word of mouth, but usefulness determines whether it will be positive or negative.

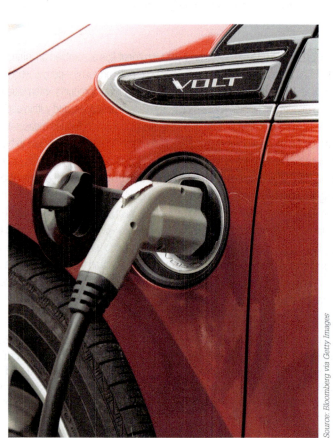

*Source: Bloomberg via Getty Images*

To fuel buzz for its Chevy Volt electric car, Chevrolet gave 900 influential consumers a free three-day rental.

**Sources:** Beth Saulnier, "It's Complicated," *Cornell Alumni Magazine*, September/October 2013, pp. 45-49; Olga Kharif, "Finding a Haystack's Most Influential Needles," *Bloomberg Businessweek*, October 22, 2012; Michael Trusov, Anand V. Bodapati, and Randolph E. Bucklin, "Determining Influential Users in Internet Social Networks," *Journal of Marketing Research* 47 (August 2010), pp. 643–58; Matthew Dolan, "Ford Takes Online Gamble with New Fiesta," *Wall Street Journal*, April 8, 2009; Sarit Moldovan, Jacob Goldenberg, and Amitava Chattopadhyay, "What Drives Word of Mouth? The Roles of Product Originality and Usefulness," *MSI Report No. 06-111* (Cambridge, MA: Marketing Science Institute, 2006); Karen J. Bannan, "Online Chat Is a Grapevine That Yields Precious Fruit," *New York Times*, December 25, 2006.

## Tracking Online Buzz

Marketers have to decide *what* they are going to track online as well as *how* they are going to track it.

**What to track.** DuPont employs measures of online word of mouth such as scale (how far the campaign reached), speed (how fast it spread), share of voice in that space, share of voice in that speed, whether it achieved positive lift in sentiment, whether the message was understood, whether it was relevant, whether it had sustainability (and was not a one-shot deal), and how far it moved from its source.

Other researchers focus more on characterizing the source of word of mouth. For example, one group seeks to evaluate blogs according to three dimensions: relevance, sentiment, and authority. Academic researchers Hoffman and Fodor advocate measuring the various types of investments customers make in engaging with brands in terms of their activity with blogs, microblogging (e.g., Twitter), cocreation (e.g., NIKEiD), forums and discussion boards, product reviews, social networks, and video and photo sharing.

**How to track it.** More firms are setting up technologically advanced central locations to direct their online tracking efforts. To monitor the Gatorade brand on social networks around the clock, Gatorade created a "Mission Control Center"—set up like a broadcast television control room—in the middle of the marketing department in its Chicago headquarters. Mission Control is staffed 24/7 by a cross-function of Gatorade digital, media, and social agencies, with six big monitors providing data visualizations and dashboards.

The Gatorade team reviews blog conversations and tracks sentiment and feedback. The team also has to decide when it is appropriate to intervene in an online conversation and when it is not. Any post that includes a query directly about the brand or that reflects a misunderstanding is usually an opportunity for the team to weigh in, but as one team member notes, "If they want to talk about working out, we let them have that conversation."

Gatorade is just one of many firms that recognize the importance of keeping a finger on the digital pulse of the brand. Consider these efforts.

- Nestlé's Digital Acceleration Team is a 24/7 monitoring center that tracks real-time sentiment about its 2,000 brands.

- Dell's social media ground control and command center in Round Rock, Texas, has 70 employees and processes 25,000 daily social media events in 11 different languages, responding to most queries and complaints within 24 hours.

- Wells Fargo's social media command center tracks 2,000 to 4,000 mentions a day. The team monitors and posts to social media channels such as Facebook, Twitter, LinkedIn, Pinterest, and YouTube. When a rumor started that the bank was going to institute a new $5 fee on domestic direct deposits, the command center was able to quickly squash it.

**Sources:** Wendy W. Moe and David A. Schweidel, *Social Media Intelligence* (New York: Cambridge University Press, 2014); Cotton Dello, "Wells Fargo Command Center to Handle Surge of Social Content," *Advertising Age*, April 8, 2014; Ryan Holmes, "NASA-Style Mission Control Centers for Social Media Are Taking Off," www.tech.fortune.cnn.com, October 25, 2012; Lionel Menchaca, "Dell's Next Step: The Social Media Listening Command Center," www.en.community.dell.com/dell-blogs, December 8, 2010; Donna L. Hoffman and Marek Fodor, "Can You Measure the ROI of Your Social Media Marketing," *MIT Sloan Management Review*, Fall 2010, pp. 41–49; "Valerie Bauerlin, "Gatorade's 'Mission': Sell More Drinks," *Wall Street Journal*, September 13, 2010; Adam Ostrow, "Inside Gatorade's Social Media Command Center," www.mashable.com, June 15, 2010; Rick Lawrence, Prem Melville, Claudia Perlich, Vikas Sindhwani, Steve Meliksetian, Pei-Yun Hsueh, and Yan Liu, "Social Media Analytics," *OR/MS Today*, February 2010, pp. 26–30; "Is There a Reliable Way to Measure Word-of-Mouth Marketing?" *Marketing NPV* 3 (2006), www.marketingnpv.com, pp. 3–9.

Source: The Gatorade Company

Gatorade's HQ-based Mission Control Center tracks brand buzz 24/7.

lead to even greater loyalty and sales.[70] Huba and McConnell describe the following rungs on the customer loyalty ladder (in ascending order):[71]

1. *Satisfaction*—Sticks with your organization as long as expectations are met.
2. *Repeat purchase*—Returns to your company to buy again.
3. *Word of mouth/buzz*—Puts his or her reputation on the line to tell others about you.
4. *Evangelism*—Convinces others to purchase/join.
5. *Ownership*—Feels responsible for the continued success of your organization.

## MEASURING THE EFFECTS OF WORD OF MOUTH

Many marketers concentrate on the online effects of word of mouth, given the ease of tracking them through advertising, PR, and digital agencies. Through demographic information or proxies for that information and cookies, firms can monitor when customers blog, comment, post, share, link, upload, friend, stream, write on a wall, or update a profile. With these tracking tools it is possible, for example, for movie advertisers to target "1 million American women between the ages of 14 and 24 who had uploaded, blogged, rated, shared, or commented on entertainment in the previous 24 hours."[72] "Marketing Insight: Tracking Online Buzz" describes some company efforts there.

# Mobile Marketing

Given the presence of smart phones and tablets everywhere and marketers' ability to personalize messages based on demographics and other consumer behavior characteristics, the appeal of mobile marketing as a communication tool is obvious.

## THE SCOPE OF MOBILE MARKETING

Wharton's David Bell notes four distinctive characteristics of a mobile device: (1) It is uniquely tied to one user; (2) it is virtually always "on" given it is typically carried everywhere; (3) it allows for immediate consumption because it is in effect a channel of distribution with a payment system; and (4) it is highly interactive given it allows for geotracking and picture and video taking.[73]

Six of every 10 U.S. consumers owned a smart phone in 2014, creating a major opportunity for advertisers to reach consumers on the "third screen" (TV and the computer are the first and second).[74] Perhaps not surprisingly, U.S. consumers spend a considerable amount of time on mobile—more than on radio, magazines, and newspapers combined (an average of two hours and 51 minutes versus one hour and 46 minutes).[75]

Mobile ad spending was almost $18 billion worldwide in 2013. With the increased capabilities of smart phones, however, mobile ads can be more than just a display medium using static "mini-billboards." Much recent interest has been generated in **mobile apps**—bite-sized software programs that can be downloaded to smart phones. Apps can perform useful functions—adding convenience, social value, incentives, and entertainment and making consumers' lives a little or a lot better.[76]

In a short period of time, thousands of apps have been introduced by companies large and small. Many companies are adding apps to their marketing toolkit. VW chose to launch its GTI in the United States with an iPhone app, which was downloaded 2 million times in three weeks. In Europe, it launched the VW Tiguan with a mobile app as well as text messages and an interstitial Web site.[77] A mobile app became an important part of a Bank of America campaign for one of its Merrill Lynch products.[78]

**MERRILL EDGE'S "FACE RETIREMENT" APP**   One challenge for many financial services firms is to motivate younger customers to think about their financial needs, especially in terms of retirement. A recent academic study found that aged-progressed renderings of themselves helped younger people better imagine their future selves and adopt a longer-term financial planning perspective. Based in part on this research, Bank of America developed the "Face Retirement" program for its Merrill Edge low-cost financial planning platform. Initially using the brand's Web site and later an app, the Face Retirement tool allowed users to snap pictures of themselves and, with the use of 3D "virtual makeover" imaging technology, see what they might look like when they were 47, 57, or even 107! Accompanying the photos was information about the expected prices of different items in those future years (bread, a gallon of gas, utilities) to provide additional context and motivation. Also present was a link to more information about investing for retirement. Almost 1 million individuals used the app, with 60 percent seeking more information. Many found the photos so intriguing they posted them on Facebook or shared them on Twitter.

To motivate younger consumers to consider investing in retirement, Merrill Edge's "Face Retirement" program created a virtual makeover of consumers to show how they might look at progressively older ages.

Smart phones are also conducive to boosting loyalty programs in which customers can track their visits to and purchases from a merchant and receive rewards. By tracking the whereabouts of receptive customers who opt in to receive communications, retailers can send them location-specific promotions when they are near shops or outlets.[79] Sonic Corp. used GPS data and proximity to cell towers in Atlanta to identify when those customers who had signed up for company communications were near one of roughly 50 Sonic restaurants in the area. When that was the case, the company sent customers a text message with a discount offer or an ad to entice them to visit the restaurant.[80]

Because traditional coupon redemption rates have been declining for years, the ability of mobile to make more relevant and timely offers to consumers at or near the point of purchase has piqued the interest of many marketers. These new coupons can take all forms, and digital in-store signs can dispense them to smart phones.[81]

Although the cookies that allow firms to track online activity don't typically work in wireless applications, technological advances are making it easier to track users across their smart phones and tablets too. With user privacy safeguards in place, marketers' greater knowledge of cross-screen identities (online and mobile) can permit more relevant, targeted ads.[82]

New measurement techniques are also aiding the adoption of mobile marketing. Nielsen has added consumers' viewing of television programing on mobile devices to its Live+3 TV ratings system, which combines average live commercial ratings with three days of time-shifted viewing.[83]

## DEVELOPING EFFECTIVE MOBILE MARKETING PROGRAMS

Even with newer-generation smart phones, the Web experience can be very different for users given smaller screen sizes, longer download times, and the lack of some software capabilities. Marketers are wise to design simple, clear, and clean sites, paying even greater attention than usual to user experience and navigation.[84]

Experts point out that being concise is critical with mobile messaging, offering the following advice:[85]

- Mobile ad copy should occupy only 50 percent of the screen, avoiding complex viewing experiences that may take a toll on consumers' battery and data availability as well as on their time.
- Brands should limit their ads to a pair of phrases—the offer and the tagline.
- Brands should place their logo in the corner of the mobile ad frame.
- Ads should use at least one bright color, but no more than two. Calls to action should be highlighted with a bright color.

## MOBILE MARKETING ACROSS MARKETS

Although a growing population segment uses smart phones and tablets for everything from entertainment to banking, different people have different attitudes toward and experiences with mobile technology. U.S. marketers can learn much about mobile marketing by looking overseas.

Marketers like Coca-Cola are learning much about mobile marketing in China and other Asian countries given the high smart phone penetration and usage there.

*Source: Weng lei-Imaginechina*

In developed Asian markets such as Hong Kong, Japan, Singapore, and South Korea, mobile marketing is fast becoming a central component of customer experiences.[86] In developing markets, high smart-phone penetration also makes mobile marketing attractive. A pioneer in China, Coca-Cola created a national campaign asking Beijing residents to send text messages guessing the high temperature in the city every day for just over a month for a chance to win a one-year supply of Coke products. The campaign attracted more than 4 million messages over the course of 35 days.[87]

As marketers learn more about effective mobile campaigns from all over the world, they are figuring out how to adapt these programs to work in their markets. There is no question that successful marketing in the coming years will involve a healthy dose of mobile marketing.

# Summary

1. Online marketing provides marketers with opportunities for much greater interaction and individualization through well-designed and executed Web sites, search ads, display ads, and e-mails.

2. Social media come in many forms: online communities and forums, blogs, and social networks such as Facebook, Twitter, and YouTube.

3. Social media offer marketers the opportunity to have a public voice and presence online for their brands and reinforce other communications. Marketers can build or tap into online communities, inviting participation from consumers and creating a long-term marketing asset in the process. Social media are rarely the sole source of marketing communications for a brand.

4. Word-of-mouth marketing finds ways to engage customers so they will choose to talk positively with others about products, services, and brands. Viral marketing encourages people to exchange online information related to a product or service.

5. Mobile marketing is an increasingly important form of interactive marketing by which marketers can use text messages, software apps, and ads to connect with consumers via their smart phones and tablets.

# Applications

## Marketing Debate
### What Is the Value of Buzz?

One of the classic debates in the popular press is whether all buzz or word of mouth—positive *and* negative—is good for a brand. Some feel that "any press is good press" and that as long as people are talking, that is a good thing. Others challenge that notion and say the content of the dialogue is what really matters.

**Take a position:** "All news is good news" and any buzz is helpful for a brand *versus* The content of buzz can make or break a brand.

## Marketing Discussion
### Corporate Web Sites

⭐ Pick one of your favorite brands and go to its Web site. How would you evaluate the Web site? How well does it score on the 7Cs of design elements: context, content, community, customization, communication, connection, and commerce?

## Marketing Excellence

### >> Facebook

Facebook was founded in 2004 by Mark Zuckerberg, a Harvard University student at the time. Zuckerberg recalls, "I just thought that being able to have access to different people's profiles would be interesting. Obviously, there's no way you can get access to that stuff unless people are throwing up profiles, so I wanted to make an application that would allow people to do that, to share as much information as they wanted while having control over what they put up."

Within 24 hours of its launch, nearly 1,500 Harvard students had registered on the site. A month later, half the campus had joined. Initially, only Harvard students could view and use the site, which had relatively simple profile and navigation tools at first. The early momentum was tremendous, though, and Facebook soon expanded to include students throughout the Ivy League and then other colleges. The initial decision to keep the site exclusive to college students was critical to its early success. It gave Facebook a sense of privacy, unity, and exclusivity that social media competitors like MySpace did not offer. In 2006, the site opened its doors to everyone.

Today, Facebook is the most popular social networking Web site in the world, with more than 1.3 billion active users. It allows users to create customized personal profiles with information such as their hometown, work experience, educational background, and relationship status as well as an unlimited number of photos and albums. To interact with each other, users send messages, "poke" each other, and "tag" or label people in their photos. They can post comments on friends' "walls," join groups, upload and view albums, plan group events, and create status updates viewable by everyone. In summary, Facebook is on its way to fulfilling its mission: *Give people the power to share and make the world more open and connected.*

Facebook is not only an important part of many people's lives but also a critical marketing component for just about any brand and company. Its pages provide a way to personally interact and communicate with consumers no matter the size of the company. In fact, Facebook is a great way for smaller companies to build strong, long-lasting one-to-one relationships with their initial consumer base and listen to consumer feedback. Even politicians use the site to push their campaigns and communicate with supporters on a local, personal level.

Facebook provides companies a place to expand their personalities in an inviting and nonthreatening environment where they can show a softer side than they might in traditional marketing media. Marketers can launch videos and trailers, unveil promotions, run contests, upload images, and post news. Some companies tie into charitable causes through Facebook. Pacific Bioscience Laboratories, maker of Clarisonic face brushes, pledged to donate $1 to charity each time a Facebook user clicked the "Like" button on its page and raised $30,000 for women suffering from cancer. Burt's Bee's uses Facebook to introduce new products to its loyal consumer base first and hear their immediate feedback. Old Spice has successfully used the site to take its humorous commercials viral. The brand has millions of fans and believes Facebook was one of the key factors in revitalizing a 70-plus-year-old product among young consumers.

Facebook also offers highly targeted advertising opportunities with personalized messages. Ads—the company's major source of income—can target individuals by demographic or keywords based on the demographic and interest information they have placed in their profiles. Many ads include an interactive element such as polls or opportunities to comment or invite friends to an event. Facebook can include "social context" with the advertiser's marketing message, which highlights a friend's connection with that particular brand.

In one survey, college students named Facebook the second-most popular thing in their undergraduate world, tied only with beer. The site offers a unique opportunity to engage consumers on a personal, meaningful level and even reach new ones through its targeted advertising options.

**Questions**

1. Why is Facebook unique in the world of personal marketing? What are Facebook's greatest strengths?

2. Who are Facebook's biggest competitors? What are the greatest risks it faces in the future?

3. What does a company gain by having a Facebook page or advertising through Facebook? What would you think if a brand or company were not on Facebook?

**Sources:** John Cassidy, "Me Media," *New Yorker*, May 15, 2006; "Survey: College Kids Like iPods Better than Beer," *Associated Press*, June 8, 2006; Peter Corbett, "Facebook Demographics and Statistics Report 2010," I Strategy Labs, www.istrategylabs.com; Brian Womack, "Facebook Sees Fourfold Jump in Number of Advertisers since 2009," *BusinessWeek*, June 2, 2010; Kermit Pattison, "How to Market Your Business with Facebook," *New York Times*, November 11, 2009; Allen Adamson, "No Contest: Twitter and Facebook Both Play a Role in Branding," *Forbes*, May 6, 2009; Eilene Zimmerman, "Small Retailers Open Up Storefronts on Facebook Pages," *New York Times*, July 26, 2012; Andrew Adam Newman, "Online a Cereal Maker Takes an Inclusive Approach," *New York Times*, July 24, 2013; "20 Best Company Facebook Pages," *Inc.com;* www.facebook.com; Facebook 2012 Annual Report.

## Marketing Excellence

### >> Unilever (Axe and Dove)

Unilever—manufacturer of several home care, food, and personal care brands—uses personal marketing communications strategies to target specific age groups, demographics, and lifestyles. The company has developed some of the most successful brands in the world, including Axe, a male grooming brand, and Dove, a personal care brand aimed at women.

The Axe brand launched in 1983, was introduced in the United States in 2002, and is now the most popular male grooming brand in the world, sold in more than 70 different countries. It offers young male consumers a wide range of personal care products such as body sprays, body gel, deodorant, and shampoo in a variety of scents. It effectively broke through the clutter by finding the right target group and delivering personal marketing messages that touched home.

The biggest opportunity existed with males who might have felt a need for help in attracting the opposite sex and could easily be persuaded to buy products to help their appearance. Most Axe ads use humor and sex, often featuring skinny, average guys attracting beautiful girls by the dozen, hundreds, or even thousands after dousing themselves with Axe. The result: The brand is aspirational and approachable, and the lighthearted tone appeals to young men.

Axe has won numerous advertising awards not only for its creativity but also for its effective use of unconventional media channels. From edgy online videos to video games, mating game tool kits, chat rooms, and mobile apps, the Axe brand engages young adult males at relevant times, locations, and environments. In Colombia, for example, a female Axe Patrol scopes out the bar and club scene and sprays men with Axe body sprays. Unilever Marketing Director Kevin George explained, "This is all about going beyond the 30-second TV commercial to create a deeper bond with our guy."

Axe knows where to reach its consumers. It advertises only on male-dominated networks such as MTV, ESPN, Spike, and Comedy Central. It partners with the NBA and NCAA, which draw young male audiences, and runs ads during big sporting events. After Axe's Super Bowl commercial ran in February 2014, it was viewed on YouTube.com more than 100 million times. Print ads appear in *Playboy*, *Rolling Stone*, *GQ*, and *Maxim*. Axe's online efforts via Facebook and Twitter help drive consumers back to its Web site, TheAxeEffect.com.

Unilever understands that it must keep the brand fresh, relevant, and cool in order to stay current with its fickle young audience. As a result, the company launches a new fragrance every year and refreshes its online and advertising communications constantly, realizing that new young males enter and exit the target market each year. Axe's success in personal marketing has lifted the brand to become the leader in what many had thought was the mature deodorant category.

On the other side of the personal marketing spectrum, Unilever's Dove brand speaks to women with a different tone and message. In 2003, Dove shifted away from its historical advertising, which touted the brand's benefit of one-quarter moisturizing cream, and launched the "Real Beauty" campaign. "Real Beauty" celebrated "real" women and spoke personally to the target market about the notion that beauty comes in all shapes, sizes, ages, and colors. The campaign arose from research revealing that only 4 percent of women worldwide think they are beautiful.

The first phase of the "Real Beauty" campaign featured nontraditional female models and asked viewers to judge their looks online and decide whether they were "Wrinkled or Wonderful" or "Oversized or Outstanding." The personal questions shocked many but created such a large PR buzz that Dove continued the campaign. The second phase featured candid and confident images of curvy, full-bodied women. Again, the brand smashed stereotypes about what should appear in advertising and touched many women worldwide. The third phase, "Pro-Age," featured older, nude women and asked questions like, "Does beauty have an age limit?" Immediately, the company heard positive feedback from its older consumers. Dove also started a Self-Esteem Fund, aimed at helping women feel better about their looks.

In addition, Dove released a series of short Dove Films, one of which, *Evolution*, won both a Cyber and a film Grand Prix at the International Advertising Festival in Cannes in 2007. The film shows a rapid-motion view of an ordinary-looking woman transformed by makeup artists, hairdressers, lighting, and digital retouching to end up looking like a billboard supermodel. The end tagline is: "No wonder our perception of beauty is distorted." The film became an instant viral hit.

Dove followed up with *Onslaught*, a short film that showed a fresh-faced young girl being bombarded with images of sexy, half-dressed women and promises of products to make her look "smaller," "softer," "firmer," and "better." Dove's 2013 film called *Sketches* featured a police sketch artist who drew two pictures of the same woman. For one, the woman described herself to the sketch artist from behind a curtain, and for the other, a total stranger described her. The difference in language and descriptions revealed how women are often their harshest beauty critics. The ad ended with the tagline "You are more beautiful than you think." The *Sketches* film has become the most watched video advertisement of all time and had more than 175 million views in its first year alone.

Dove's latest effort to change the attitudes of women and promote positive self-esteem was called the Ad Makeover. The campaign appeared only on Facebook and gave women the power to replace negative ads (such as for plastic surgery or weight-loss products) on their friends' Facebook pages with positive messages from Dove like "Hello Beautiful" and "The Perfect Bum Is the One You Are Sitting On." Unilever in effect bought the ad space from Facebook for the positive ads to appear on the friend's site, effectively squeezing out the negative ads. During the first week the Ad Makeover app was launched, 171 million banners with negative messages were replaced.

Although the Axe and the Dove campaigns have both sparked much controversy and debate, they couldn't be more different. Yet both have effectively targeting their consumer base with personal marketing strategies and spot-on messages. In fact, in the 10 years that Dove has focused on changing women's attitudes and promoting positive self-esteem, sales have jumped from $2.5 billion to $4 billion. Axe is not only the most popular male grooming brand in the world, but also Unilever's best-selling brand.

## Questions

1. What makes personal marketing work? Why are Dove and Axe so successful at it?

2. Can a company take personal marketing too far? Explain.

3. Is there a conflict of interests in the way Unilever markets to women and young men? Is it undoing all the good that might be done in the "Campaign for Real Beauty" by making women sex symbols in Axe ads? Discuss.

**Sources:** Jack Neff, "Dove's 'Real Beauty' Pics Could Be Big Phonies," *Advertising Age*, May 7, 2008; Catherine Holahan, "Raising the Bar on Viral Web Ads," *BusinessWeek*, July 23, 2006; Randall Rothenberg, "Dove Effort Gives Packaged-Goods Marketers Lessons for the Future," *Advertising Age*, March 5, 2007; Laura Petrecca, "Amusing or Offensive, Axe Ads Show That Sexism Sells," *USA Today*, April 18, 2007; Kim Bhasin, "How Axe Became the Top-Selling Deodorant by Targeting Nerdy Losers," *Business Insider*, October 10, 2011; https://blogs.monash.edu/presto/2013/04/07/dove-flies-high-with-social-media-ii/; Jonathan Salem Baskin, "The Opportunity for Dove to Get Real with Its Branding," *Forbes*, March 7, 2013; Danielle Kurtzleben, "Unilever Faces Criticism for Real Beauty Ad Campaign," *U.S. News*, April 18, 2013; Jack Neff, "Campaign Has Won Lots of Awards, Sold Heap of Product. But Has It Changed Perceptions?" *Ad Age*, January 22, 2014; Dove, www.campaignforrealbeauty.com; www.unilever.com; Unilever 2013 Annual Report.

In This Chapter, We Will Address
the Following **Questions**

1.  How can companies conduct direct marketing for competitive advantage? (p. 635)

2.  What are the pros and cons of database marketing? (p. 640)

3.  What decisions do companies face in designing a sales force? (p. 642)

4.  What are the challenges of managing a sales force? (p. 647)

5.  How can salespeople improve their selling, negotiating, and relationship marketing skills? (p. 651)

Breaking new ground with database marketing helped propel President Barack Obama to re-election in 2012.

*Source: © epa european pressphoto agency b.v./Alamy*

MyMarketingLab™

⭐ **Improve Your Grade!**
Over 10 million students improved their results using the Pearson MyLabs. Visit mymktlab.com for simulations, tutorials, and end-of-chapter problems.

# 22 Managing Personal Communications: Direct and Database Marketing and Personal Selling

**Although mass and digital communications provide many benefits, there are times** personal communications are needed to be relevant and close a sale—or perhaps even to elect a president! Many political pundits credit savvy database marketing as a crucial factor in the reelection of U.S. President Barack Obama in 2012.[1]

 *After database marketing proved a key to winning the presidential election in 2008, the Obama campaign team vowed to exploit it even more during his 2012 reelection campaign. By merging the main Democratic voter files with information from pollsters, fund-raisers, field workers, and customer databases, as well as social media and mobile contacts, they created one comprehensive database. Sophisticated data analytics helped raise $1 billion and fine-tune the use of TV ads, phone calls, direct mail, door-to-door campaigning, and social media, especially in critical swing states. Much of the $690 million raised online resulted from carefully targeted and tested e-mails. Every day, the campaign used small groups of supporters to test as many as 18 different versions of e-mails varying in subject line, amounts requested, and sender. The winning combination went to the broad base of tens of millions of supporters. Campaign analysts found that a casual tone (such as the word hey) was often effective in subject lines and that supporters seemed to never tire of the e-mails. The campaign also broke new ground with a Facebook campaign in which people who downloaded an app were sent messages with pictures of their friends in swing states and asked to click a button to automatically urge those targeted voters to register to vote or get to the polls. As a result of all these efforts, 1.25 million more 18- to 24-year-old voters supported Obama in 2012 than 2008.*

**Personalizing communications** and saying and doing the right thing for the right person at the right time are critical for marketing effectiveness. In this chapter, we consider how companies personalize their marketing communications to have more impact. We begin by evaluating direct and database marketing, then move on to consider personal selling and the sales force.

## Direct Marketing

Today, many marketers build long-term relationships with customers. They send birthday cards, information materials, or small premiums. Airlines, hotels, and other businesses adopt frequency reward programs and club programs.[2] **Direct marketing** is the use of consumer-direct (CD) channels to reach and deliver goods and services to customers without using marketing middlemen.

Direct marketers can use a number of channels to reach individual prospects and customers: direct mail, catalog marketing, telemarketing, interactive TV, kiosks, Web sites, and mobile devices. They often seek a measurable response, typically a customer order, through **direct-order marketing.**

Direct marketing has been a fast-growing avenue, partly in response to the high and increasing costs of reaching business markets through a sales force. Sales produced through traditional direct marketing channels (catalogs, direct mail, and telemarketing) have been growing rapidly, along with direct-mail sales, which include sales to the consumer market, B-to-B, and fund-raising by charitable institutions. Direct marketing has been outpacing U.S. retail sales. It produced $2.05 trillion in sales in 2012, accounting for approximately 8.7 percent of GDP.[3]

## THE BENEFITS OF DIRECT MARKETING

*Market demassification* has resulted in an ever-increasing number of market niches. Consumers short of time and tired of traffic and parking headaches appreciate toll-free phone numbers, always-open Web sites, next-day delivery, and direct marketers' commitment to customer service. In addition, many chain stores have dropped slower-moving specialty items, creating an opportunity for direct marketers to promote these to interested buyers instead.

Sellers benefit from demassification as well. Direct marketers can buy a list containing the names of almost any group: left-handed people, overweight people, or millionaires. They can customize and personalize messages and build a continuous relationship with each customer. New parents will receive periodic mailings describing new clothes, toys, and other goods as their child grows.

Direct marketing can reach prospects at the moment they want a solicitation and therefore be noticed by more highly interested prospects. It lets marketers test alternate media and messages to find the most cost-effective approach. Direct marketing also makes the company's offer and strategy less visible to competitors. Finally, direct marketers can measure responses to their campaigns to decide which have been the most profitable.

Direct marketing must be integrated with other communications and channel activities.[4] Eddie Bauer, Lands' End, and the Franklin Mint made fortunes building their brands in the direct marketing mail-order and phone-order business and then opened retail stores. They cross-promote their stores, catalogs, and Web sites, for example, by putting their Internet addresses on their shopping bags.

Successful direct marketers view a customer interaction as an opportunity to up-sell, cross-sell, or just deepen a relationship. They make sure they know enough about each customer to customize and personalize offers and messages and develop a plan for lifetime marketing to each valuable customer, based on their knowledge of life events and transitions. They also carefully orchestrate each element of their campaigns. Here is an award-winning campaign that did just that.[5]

**TIP TOP ICE CREAM**   New Zealand loves ice cream—the country has one of the highest per-capita consumption rates in the world. With fierce competition among brands, local brand Tip Top needed a way to maintain its leadership over its well-financed rivals. The "Feel Tip Top" campaign was a clever way to engage its customers. A Facebook app allowed people to nominate friends and family to receive ice cream delivered personally in the company's new truck. The happy reactions of some lucky recipients were captured on film for ads and viral videos. Winner of the Direct Marketing Association's Diamond Echo Award for 2013, the campaign generated 2,000 nominations in 24 hours, rising eventually to 30,000. Sales increased 5 percent.

New Zealand's Tip Top ice cream used social media and video to connect its brand with customers to retain its market leadership.

Source: Fonterra

We next consider some of the key issues that characterize different direct marketing channels.

# DIRECT MAIL

Direct-mail marketing means sending an offer, announcement, reminder, or other item to an individual consumer. Using highly selective mailing lists, direct marketers send out millions of mail pieces each year—letters, fliers, foldouts, and other "salespeople with wings."

Direct mail is a popular medium because it permits target market selectivity, can be personalized, is flexible, and allows early testing and response measurement. Although the cost per thousand is higher than for mass media, the people reached are much better prospects. The success of direct mail, however, has also become its liability—so many marketers are sending out direct-mail pieces that mailboxes are becoming stuffed, leading some consumers to disregard the blizzard of solicitations they receive.

In constructing an effective direct-mail campaign, direct marketers must choose their objectives, target markets and prospects, offer elements, means of testing the campaign, and measures of campaign success.

**OBJECTIVES** Most direct marketers judge a campaign's success by the response rate, measured in customer orders. An order-response rate for letter-sized direct mail averages 3.4 percent to an internal company list and 1.3 percent to a general public list. Although that can vary with product category, price, and the nature of the offering, it is much higher than e-mails' average response rates of 0.12 percent and 0.03 percent, respectively.[6] Direct mail can also produce prospect leads, strengthen customer relationships, inform and educate customers, remind customers of offers, and reinforce recent customer purchase decisions.

**TARGET MARKETS AND PROSPECTS** Most direct marketers apply the RFM (*recency, frequency, monetary amount*) formula to select customers according to how much time has passed since their last purchase, how many times they have purchased, and how much they have spent since becoming a customer.[7] Suppose the company is offering a leather jacket. It might make this offer to the most attractive customers—those who made their last purchase between 30 and 60 days ago, who make three to six purchases a year, and who have spent at least $100 since becoming customers. Points are established for varying RFM levels; the more points, the more attractive the customer.[8]

Marketers also identify prospects on the basis of age, sex, income, education, previous mail-order purchases, and occasion. College freshmen will buy laptop computers, backpacks, and compact refrigerators; newlyweds look for housing, furniture, appliances, and bank loans. Another useful variable is consumer lifestyle or "passions" such as electronics, cooking, and the outdoors.

Dun & Bradstreet provides a wealth of data for B-to-B direct marketing. Here the prospect is often not an individual but a group or committee of both decision makers and decision influencers. Each member needs to be treated differently, and the timing, frequency, nature, and format of contact must reflect the member's status and role.

The company's best prospects are customers who have bought its products in the past. The direct marketer can also buy lists of names from list brokers, but these lists often have problems, including name duplication, incomplete data, and obsolete addresses. Better lists include overlays of demographic and psychographic information. Direct marketers typically buy and test a sample before buying more names from the same list. They can build their own lists by advertising a promotional offer and collecting responses.

**OFFER ELEMENTS** The offer strategy has five elements—the *product,* the *offer,* the *medium,* the *distribution method,* and the *creative strategy.*[9] Fortunately, all can be tested. The direct-mail marketer also must choose five components of the mailing itself: the outside envelope, sales letter, circular, reply form, and reply envelope. A common direct marketing strategy is to follow up direct mail with an e-mail.

**TESTING ELEMENTS** One of the great advantages of direct marketing is the ability to test, under real marketplace conditions, different elements of an offer strategy, such as products, product features, copy platform, mailer type, envelope, prices, or mailing lists. The Teaching Company mails 50 million catalogs and sends 25 million e-mails to sell educational DVDs of lectures and courses. Every element of the offer is tested. Changing the color and location of an "Add to Cart" button on its Web site (from pale green to orange and from side to bottom) increased sales almost 6 percent. Replacing an image of Michelangelo's God's hand with one depicting the ruins of Petra improved sales more than 20 percent.[10]

Response rates typically understate a campaign's long-term impact. Suppose only 2 percent of the recipients who receive a direct-mail piece advertising Samsonite luggage place an order. A much larger percentage became aware of the product (direct mail has high readership), and some percentage may have formed an intention to buy at a later date (either by mail or at a retail outlet). Some may mention Samsonite luggage to others as a result of the direct-mail piece. To better estimate a promotion's impact, some companies measure the impact of direct marketing on awareness, intention to buy, and word of mouth.

**MEASURING CAMPAIGN SUCCESS: LIFETIME VALUE**  By adding up the planned campaign costs, the direct marketer can determine the needed break-even response rate. This rate must be net of returned merchandise and bad debts. A specific campaign may fail to break even in the short run but can still be profitable in the long run if we factor in customer lifetime value (see Chapter 5) by calculating the average customer longevity, average customer annual expenditure, and average gross margin, minus the average cost of customer acquisition and maintenance (discounted for the opportunity cost of money).[11]

## CATALOG MARKETING

In catalog marketing, companies may send full-line merchandise catalogs, specialty consumer catalogs, and business catalogs, usually in print form but also as DVDs or online. In 2010, three of the top B-to-C catalog sellers were Dell ($52 billion), Staples ($9.8 billion), and CDW ($8.8 billion). Three top B-to-B catalog sellers were Thermo Fisher Scientific lab and research supplies ($10.8 billion), Henry Schien dental, medical, and vet supplies ($7.5 billion), and WESCO International electrical and industry maintenance supplies ($5.0 billion).[12] Thousands of small businesses also issue specialty catalogs. Many direct marketers find combining catalogs and Web sites an effective way to sell.

Catalogs are a huge business—the Internet and catalog retailing industry includes 20,000 companies with combined annual revenue of $350 billion.[13] Successfully marketing a catalog business depends on managing customer lists carefully to avoid duplication or bad debts, controlling inventory, offering good-quality merchandise so returns are low, and projecting a distinctive image. Some companies add literary or information features, send swatches of materials, operate a special online or telephone hotline to answer questions, send gifts to their best customers, and donate a percentage of profits to good causes. Putting their entire catalog online also provides business marketers with better access to global consumers than ever before, saving printing and mailing costs.

## TELEMARKETING

**Telemarketing** is the use of the telephone and call centers to attract prospects, sell to existing customers, and provide service by taking orders and answering questions. It helps companies increase revenue, reduce selling costs, and improve customer satisfaction. Companies use call centers for *inbound telemarketing*—receiving calls from customers—and *outbound telemarketing*—initiating calls to prospects and customers.

As Chapter 4 noted, because of the establishment of the National Do Not Call Registry in 2003, consumer telemarketing has lost much of its effectiveness. Business-to-business telemarketing is increasing, however.

Raleigh Bicycles used telemarketing to cuts costs and drive sales.

TV infomercials have been used with great success to sell the George Foreman grill, backed by the former heavyweight boxing champion.

Source: HORST OSSINGER/EPA/Newscom

Raleigh Bicycles used telemarketing to reduce the personal selling costs of contacting its dealers. In the first year, sales force travel costs dropped 50 percent and sales in a single quarter went up 34 percent. As it improves with the use of video conferencing, telemarketing will increasingly replace, though never eliminate, more expensive field sales calls.

## OTHER MEDIA FOR DIRECT-RESPONSE MARKETING

Direct marketers use all the major media. Newspapers and magazines carry ads offering books, clothing, appliances, vacations, and other goods and services that individuals can order via toll-free numbers. Radio ads present offers 24 hours a day. Some companies prepare 30- and 60-minute *infomercials* to combine the selling power of television commercials with the draw of information and entertainment. Infomercials promote products that are complicated or technologically advanced or that require a great deal of explanation. Some of the most successful are for Proactiv acne system, P90X workout DVDs, and the George Foreman grill. At-home shopping channels are dedicated to selling goods and services through a toll-free number or via the Internet for delivery within 48 hours.

## PUBLIC AND ETHICAL ISSUES IN DIRECT MARKETING

Direct marketers and their customers usually enjoy mutually rewarding relationships. Occasionally, however, a darker side emerges:

- *Irritation.* Many people don't like hard-sell direct marketing solicitations. Firms have been popping up to help block unwanted junk mail.[14]
- *Unfairness.* Some direct marketers take advantage of impulsive or less sophisticated buyers or prey on the vulnerable, especially the elderly.
- *Deception and fraud.* Some direct marketers design mailers and write copy intended to mislead or exaggerate product size, performance claims, or the "retail price." The Federal Trade Commission receives thousands of complaints each year about fraudulent investment scams and phony charities.
- *Invasion of privacy.* It seems that almost every time consumers order products by mail or telephone, apply for a credit card, or take out a magazine subscription, their names, addresses, and purchasing behavior may be added to several company databases. As Chapters 3 and 5 discussed, critics worry that marketers may know too much about consumers' lives and that they may use this knowledge to take unfair advantage.[15]

People in the direct marketing industry know that, left unattended, such problems will lead to increasingly negative consumer attitudes, lower response rates, and calls for greater state and federal regulation. Most direct marketers want the same thing consumers want: honest and well-designed marketing offers targeted only to those who appreciate hearing about them.

# Customer Databases and Database Marketing

To conduct direct marketing, marketers must know their customers.[16] And to do that, they must collect information and store it in a database from which to conduct database marketing. A **customer database** is an organized collection of comprehensive information about individual customers or prospects that is current, accessible, and actionable for lead generation, lead qualification, sale of a product or service, or maintenance of customer relationships. **Database marketing** is the process of building, maintaining, and using customer databases and other databases (of products, suppliers, or resellers) to contact, transact, and build customer relationships.

Chapter 3 reviewed "Big Data" and the analysis of massive data sets. Here we consider some additional issues in building customer databases and conducting database marketing.

## CUSTOMER DATABASES

Many companies confuse a customer mailing list with a customer database. A **customer mailing list** is simply a set of names, addresses, and telephone numbers. A customer electronic mailing or e-mail list may literally be just names and e-mail addresses. A customer database, however, contains much more information, accumulated through customer transactions, registration information, telephone queries, cookies, and every customer contact. Ideally, a customer database also contains the consumer's past purchases, demographics (age, income, family members, birthdays), psychographics (activities, interests, and opinions), mediagraphics (preferred media), and other useful information.

A typical **business database** contains business customers' past purchases; past volumes, prices, and profits; buyer team members' names (and ages, birthdays, hobbies, and favorite foods); status of current contracts; the supplier's estimated share of the customer's business; competitive suppliers; assessment of competitive strengths and weaknesses in selling and servicing the account; and relevant customer buying practices, patterns, and policies. A Latin American unit of the Swiss pharmaceutical firm Novartis keeps data on 100,000 of Argentina's farmers, knows their crop protection chemical purchases, groups them by value, and treats each group differently.

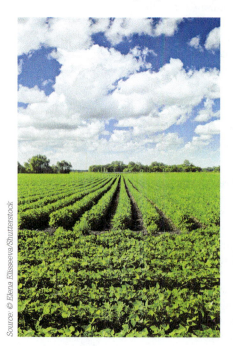

*Source: © Elena Elisseeva/Shutterstock*

In Argentina, Novartis keeps a detailed data base on its farmer customers so that it can market more effectively to them.

## DATA WAREHOUSES AND DATA MINING

Savvy companies capture information every time a customer contacts any of their departments, whether via purchase, a service call, an online query, or a mail-in rebate card.[17] Banks and credit card companies, telephone companies, catalog marketers, and many other companies have a great deal of information about their customers, including transaction history and enhanced data on age, family size, income, and other demographics.

These data are collected by the company's contact center and organized into a **data warehouse** where marketers can capture, query, and analyze them to draw inferences about an individual customer's needs and responses. Customer service reps inside the company can respond to customer inquiries based on a complete picture of the customer relationship, and customized marketing activities can be directed to individual customers. Some firms provide specialized help to support database marketing.[18]

**DUNNHUMBY** British research firm Dunnhumby has increased the profitability of retailers and other firms by gleaning insights from their loyalty program data and credit card transactions. The firm has helped British supermarket giant Tesco manage every aspect of its business: creating new shop formats, arranging store layouts, developing private label products, and tailoring coupons and special discounts to its loyalty card shoppers. Tesco decided against dropping a poor-selling type of bread after Dunnhumby's analysis revealed it was a "destination product" for a loyal cohort that would shop elsewhere if it disappeared. U.S. clients of Dunnhumby have included Coca-Cola, Kroger, Macy's, and Home Depot. Based on data from

350 million people in 28 countries, Dunnhumby's insights have aided decisions about product range, availability, space planning, and new-product innovations. For a major European catalog company, Dunnhumby found that not only did shoppers with different body types prefer different clothing styles, they also shopped at different times of the year: Slimmer consumers tended to buy early in a new season, whereas larger folks tended to take fewer risks and wait until later in the season to see which styles proved popular.

Through **data mining,** marketing statisticians can extract from the mass of data useful information about individuals, trends, and segments. Data mining uses sophisticated statistical and mathematical techniques such as cluster analysis, automatic interaction detection, predictive modeling, and neural networking.

Some observers believe a proprietary database can provide a company with a significant competitive advantage.[19] In general, companies can use their databases in five ways:

1. *To identify prospects*—Many companies generate sales leads by advertising their product or service and including a response feature, such as a link to a home page, a business reply card, or a toll-free phone number, and building a database from customer responses. The company sorts through the database to identify the best prospects, then contacts them by mail, e-mail, or phone to try to convert them into customers.

2. *To decide which customers should receive a particular offer*—Companies interested in selling, up-selling, and cross-selling set up criteria describing the ideal target customer for a particular offer. Then they search their customer databases for those who most closely resemble the ideal. By noting response rates, a company can improve its targeting precision. Following a sale, it can set up an automatic sequence of activities: One week later e-mail a thank-you note; five weeks later e-mail a new offer; 10 weeks later (if the customer has not responded) e-mail an offer of a special discount.

3. *To deepen customer loyalty*—Companies can build interest and enthusiasm by remembering customer preferences and sending appropriate gifts, discount coupons, and interesting reading material.

4. *To reactivate customer purchases*—Automatic mailing programs (automatic marketing) can send out birthday or anniversary cards, holiday shopping reminders, or off-season promotions. The database can help the company make attractive or timely offers.

5. *To avoid serious customer mistakes*—A major bank confessed to a number of mistakes it had made by not using its customer database well. In one case, the bank charged a customer a penalty for late payment on his mortgage, failing to note he headed a company that was a major depositor in this bank. The customer quit the bank. In a second case, two different staff members of the bank phoned the same mortgage customer offering a home equity loan at different prices. Neither knew the other had made the call. In a third case, the bank gave a premium customer only standard service in another country.

Source: © Alex Segre/Alamy

Tesco uses insights gained from a massive customer data base to help make all kinds of business and marketing decisions.

## THE DOWNSIDE OF DATABASE MARKETING

Database marketing is most frequently used by business marketers and service providers that routinely collect masses of customer data, like hotels, banks, airlines, and insurance, credit card, and phone companies. Other types of companies that invest in database marketing are those that favor cross-selling and up-selling (such as GE and Amazon.com) or whose customers have highly differentiated needs and are of highly differentiated value to the company. Although packaged-goods retailers and consumer packaged-goods companies use database marketing less frequently, many (such as Kraft, Quaker Oats, Ralston Purina, and Nabisco) are building databases for certain brands.

Having covered the upside of database marketing, we also need to cover the downside. Five main problems can prevent a firm from effectively using database marketing.

1. **Some situations are just not conducive to database marketing.** Building a customer database may not be worthwhile when: (1) the product is a once-in-a-lifetime purchase (a grand piano); (2) customers show little loyalty to a brand (there is a lot of customer churn); (3) the unit sale is very small (a candy bar) so customer lifetime value is low; (4) the cost of gathering information is too high; and (5) there is no direct contact between the seller and ultimate buyer.

2. **Building and maintaining a customer database require a large investment.** Computer hardware, database software, analytical programs, communication links, and skilled staff can be costly. It's difficult to collect the right data, especially to capture all the occasions of company interaction with individual customers. Deloitte Consulting found 70 percent of firms experienced little or no improvement from implementing customer relationship management (CRM) because the system was poorly designed, it became too expensive, users didn't make much use of it or report much benefit, and collaborators ignored it. Sometimes companies mistakenly concentrate on customer contact processes without making corresponding changes in internal structures and systems.[20]

3. **Employees may resist becoming customer-oriented and using the available information.** Employees find it far easier to carry on traditional transaction marketing than to practice CRM. Effective database marketing requires managing and training employees as well as dealers and suppliers.

4. **Not all customers want a relationship with the company.** Some may resent knowing the company has collected that much personal information about them. Online companies should explain their privacy policies and give consumers the right not to have their information stored. European countries do not look favorably on database marketing and are protective of consumers' private information. The European Union passed a law handicapping the growth of database marketing in its 28 member countries.

5. **The assumptions behind CRM may not always hold true.**[21] High-volume customers often know their value to a company and can leverage it to extract premium service and/or price discounts, so it may not cost the firm less to serve them. Loyal customers may also be jealous of attention lavished on other customers. When eBay began to chase big corporate customers such as IBM, Disney, and Sears, some mom-and-pop businesses that helped build the brand felt abandoned.[22] Loyal customers also may not necessarily be the best ambassadors for the brand. One study found those who scored high on behavioral loyalty and bought a lot of a company's products were less active word-of-mouth marketers than customers who scored high on attitudinal loyalty and expressed greater commitment to the firm.[23]

When it works, a data warehouse yields more than it costs, but the data must be in good condition, and the discovered relationships must be valid and acceptable to consumers.

# Designing the Sales Force

The original and oldest form of direct marketing is the field sales call. To locate prospects, develop them into customers, and grow the business, most industrial companies rely heavily on a professional sales force or hire manufacturers' representatives and agents. Many consumer companies such as Allstate, Amway, Avon, Mary Kay, Merrill Lynch, and Tupperware use a direct-selling force.

U.S. firms spend more than a trillion dollars annually on sales forces and sales force materials—more than on any other promotional method. In 2012, more than 10 percent of the total workforce worked full time in sales occupations, both nonprofit and for profit.[24] Hospitals and museums, for example, use fund-raisers to contact donors and solicit donations. In asserting that selling is the core function of every company, Boston Beer founder Jim Koch notes, "Without sales, there is no business to manage."[25] For many firms, sales force performance is critical.[26]

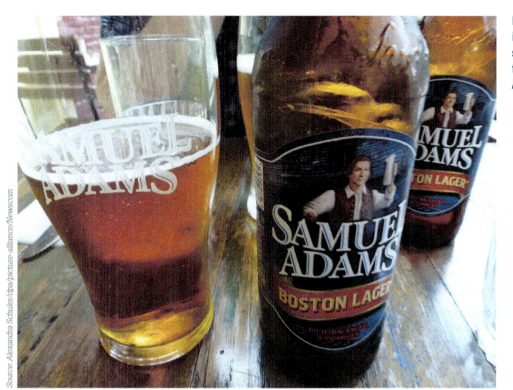

Source: Alexandra Schuler/dpa/picture-alliance/Newscom

Boston Beer founder Jim Koch is a firm believer that the selling function is essential to the success of its Samuel Adams brand.

**SOBE** John Bello, founder of SoBe nutritionally enhanced teas and juices, has given much credit to his sales force for the brand's successful ascent. Bello claims that the superior quality and consistent sales effort from the 150 salespeople the company had at its peak was directed toward one simple goal: "SoBe won in the street because our salespeople were there more often and in greater numbers than the competition, and they were more motivated by far." SoBe's sales force operated at every level of the distribution chain: At the distributor level, steady communication gave SoBe disproportionate focus relative to the other brands; at the trade level, most senior salespeople had strong personal relationships with retailers such as 7-Eleven, Costco, and Safeway; and at the individual store level, the SoBe team was always at work setting and restocking shelves, cutting in product, and putting up point-of-sale displays. According to Bello, bottom-line success in any entrepreneurial endeavor depends on sales execution.

Although no one debates the importance of the sales force in marketing programs, companies are sensitive to the high and rising costs of maintaining one, including salaries, commissions, bonuses, travel expenses, and benefits. Not surprisingly, companies are trying to increase sales force productivity through better selection, training, supervision, motivation, and compensation.[27]

The term *sales representative* covers six positions, ranging from the least to the most creative types of selling:[28]

1. *Deliverer*—A salesperson whose major task is the delivery of a product (water, fuel, oil).
2. *Order taker*—An inside order taker (standing behind the counter) or outside order taker (calling on the supermarket manager).
3. *Missionary*—A salesperson not permitted to take an order but expected rather to build goodwill or educate the actual or potential user (the medical "detailer" representing an ethical pharmaceutical house).
4. *Technician*—A salesperson with a high level of technical knowledge (the engineering salesperson who is primarily a consultant to client companies).
5. *Demand creator*—A salesperson who relies on creative methods for selling tangible products (vacuum cleaners, cleaning brushes, household products) or intangibles (insurance, advertising services, or education).
6. *Solution vendor*—A salesperson whose expertise is solving a customer's problem, often with a system of the company's products and services (for example, computer and communications systems).

| Fig. 22.1 |

Designing a
Sales Force

Salespeople are the company's personal link to its customers. In designing the sales force, the company must develop sales force objectives, strategy, structure, size, and compensation (see Figure 22.1).

## SALES FORCE OBJECTIVES AND STRATEGY

The days when all the sales force did was "sell, sell, and sell" are long gone. Sales reps need to know how to diagnose a customer's problem and propose a solution that can help improve the customer's profitability. The best salespeople even go beyond the customer's stated problems to offer fresh insights into the customer's business model and identify unrecognized needs and unstated problems.[29]

In performing their jobs, salespeople complete one or more specific tasks:

- *Prospecting.* Searching for prospects or leads
- *Targeting.* Deciding how to allocate their time among prospects and customers
- *Communicating.* Communicating information about the company's products and services
- *Selling.* Approaching, presenting, answering questions, overcoming objections, and closing sales
- *Servicing.* Providing various services to the customers—consulting on problems, rendering technical assistance, arranging financing, expediting delivery
- *Information gathering.* Conducting market research and doing intelligence work
- *Allocating.* Deciding which customers will get scarce products during product shortages

To manage costs, most companies are choosing a *leveraged sales force* that focuses reps on selling the company's more complex and customized products to large accounts and uses inside salespeople and online ordering for low-end selling. Salespeople handle fewer accounts and are rewarded for key account growth; lead generation, proposal writing, order fulfillment, and postsale support are turned over to others. This is far different from expecting salespeople to sell to every possible account, the common weakness of geographically based sales forces.[30]

Companies must deploy sales forces strategically so they call on the right customers at the right time in the right way, acting as "account managers" who arrange fruitful contact between people in the buying and selling organizations. Selling increasingly calls for teamwork and the support of others, such as *top management,* especially when national accounts or major sales are at stake; *technical people,* who supply information and service before, during, and after product purchase; *customer service representatives,* who provide installation, maintenance, and other services; and *office staff,* consisting of sales analysts, order expediters, and assistants.[31]

To maintain a market focus, salespeople should know how to analyze sales data, measure market potential, gather market intelligence, and develop marketing strategies and plans. Especially at the higher levels of sales management, they need analytical marketing skills. Marketers believe sales forces are more effective in the long run if they understand and appreciate marketing as well as selling.

Too often marketing and sales are in conflict: the sales force complains marketing isn't generating enough leads, and marketers complain the sales force isn't converting them (see Figure 22.2). Improved collaboration and communication between these two can increase revenues and profits.[32]

---

*Sales:* I need leads, but marketing never sends me any good leads. How am I supposed to get new business with no good leads?

*Marketing:* We deliver tons of leads, and they just sit in the system. Why won't sales call on any of them?

*Sales:* I have nothing new to sell. What is marketing doing? Why can't they figure out what customers want before they give it to us? Why don't they give me anything that's easy to sell?

*Marketing:* Why won't sales get out and sell my new programs? How do they expect customers to place orders without sales contacts?

*Sales:* My people spend too much time on administration and paperwork. I need them out selling.

*Marketing:* We need information to get new ideas. How long does it take to type in a few words? Don't they know their own customers?

*Sales:* How am I going to hit my number? Marketing is a waste of time. I'd rather have more sales reps.

*Marketing:* How am I going to hit my number? Sales won't help, and I don't have enough people to do it myself.

---

| Fig. 22.2 |

## A Hypothetical (Dysfunctional) Sales Marketing Exchange

Source: Based on a talk by Scott Sanderude and Jeff Standish, "Work Together, Win Together: Resolving Misconceptions between Sales and Marketing," talk given at Marketing Science Institute's *Marketing, Sales, and Customers* conference, December 7, 2005.

Ford CMO Jim Farley believes that it is highly beneficial that he is in charge of both marketing and sales.

Jim Farley, CMO at Ford, notes that "the coolest thing about my job at Ford is that I'm in charge of both marketing and sales" and maintains that it is a mistake to have separate people in charge. He sees the best salespeople at Ford as a cross between *problem solvers*, who help explain and customize all the sophisticated automobile electronics, and *concierges*, who help with all the steps in the complicated process of buying a car.[33] To improve mutual understanding, Honeywell moves marketers into sales and vice versa when appropriate, as well as getting them together for joint meetings throughout the year.[34]

Once the company chooses its strategy, it can use a direct or a contractual sales force. A **direct (company) sales force** consists of full- or part-time paid employees who work exclusively for the company. Inside sales people conduct business from the office and receive visits from prospective buyers, and field sales people travel and visit customers. A **contractual sales force** consists of manufacturers' reps, sales agents, and brokers who earn a commission based on sales.

## SALES FORCE STRUCTURE

The sales force strategy also has implications for its structure. A company that sells one product line to one end-using industry with customers in many locations would use a territorial structure. A company that sells many products to many types of customers might need a product or market structure.

Some companies need a more complex structure and adopt some combination of four types of sales force: (1) a strategic market sales force assigned to major accounts (see below); (2) a geographic sales force calling on customers in different territories; (3) a distributor sales force calling on and coaching distributors; and (4) an inside sales force marketing and taking orders online and via phone.

Established companies need to revise their sales force structures as market and economic conditions change. SAS, seller of business intelligence software, reorganized its sales force into industry-specific groups to serve such customers as banks, brokerages, and insurers and saw revenue soar by 14 percent.[35] "Marketing Insight: Major Account Management" discusses a specialized form of sales force structure.

## Major Account Management

Marketers typically single out for attention major accounts (also called key accounts, national accounts, global accounts, or house accounts). These are important customers with multiple divisions in many locations that use uniform pricing and coordinated service for all divisions. A major account manager (MAM) usually reports to the national sales manager and supervises field reps calling on customer plants within their territories. The average company manages about 75 key accounts. If a company has several such accounts, it's likely to organize a major account management division, in which the average MAM handles nine accounts.

Large accounts are often handled by a strategic account management team with cross-functional members who integrate new-product development, technical support, supply chain, marketing activities, and multiple communication channels to cover all aspects of the relationship. Procter & Gamble has a strategic account management team of 300 staffers to work with Walmart in its Bentonville, Arkansas, headquarters, with more stationed at Walmart headquarters in Europe, Asia, and Latin America. P&G has credited this relationship with saving the company billions of dollars.

Major account management is growing. As buyer concentration increases through mergers and acquisitions, fewer buyers are accounting for a larger share of sales. Many are centralizing their purchases of certain items, gaining more bargaining power. And as products become more complex, more groups in the buyer's organization participate in the purchase process. The typical salesperson alone might not have the skill, authority, or coverage to sell effectively to the large buyer.

In selecting major accounts, companies look for those that purchase a high volume (especially of more profitable products), purchase centrally, require a high level of service in several geographic locations, may be price sensitive, and want a long-term partnership. Major account managers act as the single point of contact, develop and grow customer business, understand customer decision processes, identify added-value opportunities, provide competitive intelligence, negotiate sales, and orchestrate customer service.

Many major accounts look for added value more than a price advantage. They appreciate having a single point of dedicated contact, single billing, special warranties, EDI links, priority shipping, early information releases, customized products, and efficient maintenance, repair, and upgraded service. And there's the value of goodwill. Personal relationships with people who value the major account's business and have a vested interest in its success are compelling reasons for remaining a loyal customer.

**Sources:** Noel Capon, Dave Potter, and Fred Schindler, *Managing Global Accounts: Nine Critical Factors for a World-Class Program*, 2nd ed. (Bronxville, NY: Wessex Press, 2008); Peter Cheverton, *Global Account Management: A Complete Action Kit of Tools and Techniques for Managing Key Global Customers* (London, UK: Kogan Page, 2008); Malcolm McDonald and Diana Woodburn, *Key Account Management: The Definitive Guide*, 2nd ed. (Oxford, UK: Butterworth-Heinemann, 2007); Jack Neff, "Bentonville or Bust," *Advertising Age*, February 24, 2003. More information can be obtained from SAMA (Strategic Account Management Association) and the *Journal of Selling and Major Account Management*.

## SALES FORCE SIZE

Sales representatives are one of the company's most productive and expensive assets. Increasing their number increases both sales and costs. Once the company establishes the number of customers it wants to reach, it can use a *workload approach* to establish sales force size. This method has five steps:

1. Group customers into size classes according to annual sales volume.
2. Establish desirable call frequencies (number of calls on an account per year) for each customer class.
3. Multiply the number of accounts in each size class by the corresponding call frequency to arrive at the total workload for the country, in sales calls per year.
4. Determine the average number of calls a sales representative can make per year.
5. Divide the total annual calls required by the average annual calls made by a sales representative to arrive at the number of sales representatives needed.

Suppose the company estimates it has 1,000 A accounts and 2,000 B accounts. A accounts require 36 calls a year, and B accounts require 12, so the company needs a sales force that can make 60,000 sales calls (36,000 + 24,000) a year. If the average full-time rep can make 1,000 calls a year, the company needs 60 reps.

## SALES FORCE COMPENSATION

To attract top-quality reps, the company must develop an attractive compensation package. Sales reps want income regularity, extra reward for above-average performance, and fair pay for experience and longevity. Management wants control, economy, and simplicity. Some of these objectives will conflict. No wonder compensation plans vary tremendously among and even within industries.

The company must quantify four components of sales force compensation. The *fixed amount,* a salary, satisfies the need for income stability. The *variable amount,* whether commissions, bonus, or profit sharing, serves to stimulate and reward effort.[36] *Expense allowances* enable sales reps to meet the costs of travel and entertaining on the company's behalf. *Benefits,* such as paid vacations, sickness or accident benefits, pensions, and health and life insurance, provide security and job satisfaction.

Fixed compensation is common in jobs with a high ratio of nonselling to selling duties and jobs where the selling task is technically complex and requires teamwork. Variable compensation works best where sales are cyclical or depend on individual initiative. Fixed and variable compensation give rise to three basic types of compensation plans—straight salary, straight commission, and combination salary and commission. One survey revealed that more than half of sales reps receive 40 percent or more of their compensation in variable pay.[37]

Straight-salary plans provide a secure income, encourage reps to complete nonselling activities, and reduce incentive to overstock customers. For the firm, these plans deliver administrative simplicity and lower turnover. When semiconductor company Microchip dropped commissions for its sales force, sales actually increased.[38] Straight-commission plans attract higher performers, provide more motivation, require less supervision, and control selling costs. On the negative side, they emphasize getting the sale over building the relationship. Combination plans feature the benefits of both plans while limiting their disadvantages.

Plans that combine fixed and variable pay link the variable portion to a wide variety of strategic goals. One current trend deemphasizes sales volume in favor of gross profitability, customer satisfaction, and customer retention. Other companies reward reps partly on sales team or even company-wide performance, motivating them to work together for the common good.

# Managing the Sales Force

Various policies and procedures guide the firm in recruiting, selecting, training, supervising, motivating, and evaluating sales representatives to manage its sales force (see Figure 22.3).

## RECRUITING AND SELECTING REPRESENTATIVES

At the heart of any successful sales force are appropriately selected representatives. One survey revealed that the top 25 percent of the sales force brought in more than 52 percent of the sales. It's a great waste to hire the wrong people. The average annual turnover rate of sales reps for all industries is almost 20 percent. Sales force turnover leads to lost sales, the expense of finding and training replacements, and often pressure on existing salespeople to pick up the slack.[39]

Studies have not always shown a strong relationship between sales performance on one hand and background and experience variables, current status, lifestyle, attitude, personality, and skills on the other. More effective predictors of high performance in sales are composite tests and assessment centers that simulate the working environment and assess applicants in an environment similar to the one in which they would work.[40]

Although scores from formal tests are only one element in a set that includes personal characteristics, references, past employment history, and interviewer reactions, they have been weighted quite heavily by companies such as IBM, Prudential, and Procter & Gamble. Gillette claims tests have reduced turnover and scores have correlated well with the progress of new reps.

## TRAINING AND SUPERVISING SALES REPRESENTATIVES

Today's customers expect salespeople to have deep product knowledge, add ideas to improve operations, and be efficient and reliable. These demands have required companies to make a much greater investment in sales training.

New reps may spend a few weeks to several months in training. The median training period is 28 weeks in industrial-products companies, 12 in service companies, and 4 in consumer-products companies. Training time varies with the complexity of the selling task and the type of recruit. New methods of training are continually emerging, such as the use of programmed learning, distance learning, and videos. Some firms use role playing and sensitivity or empathy training to help reps identify with customers' situations and motives.

Reps paid mostly on commission generally receive less supervision. Those who are salaried and must cover definite accounts are likely to receive substantial supervision. With multilevel selling, which Avon, Sara Lee, Virgin, and others use, independent distributors are also in charge of their own sales force selling company products. These independent contractors or reps are paid a commission not only on their own sales but also on the sales of people they recruit and train.

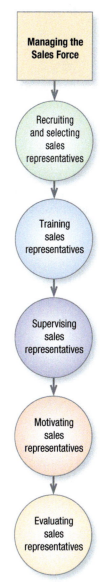

| **Fig. 22.3** |

Managing the Sales Force

Avon was an early pioneer in multilevel selling, using women as sales reps to sell to other women.

Source: ASSOCIATED PRESS

## SALES REP PRODUCTIVITY

How many calls should a company make on a particular account each year? Some research suggests today's sales reps spend too much time selling to smaller, less profitable accounts instead of focusing on larger, more profitable ones.[41]

**NORMS FOR PROSPECT CALLS** Left to their own devices, many reps will spend most of their time with current customers, who are known quantities. Reps can depend on them for some business, whereas a prospect might never deliver any. Companies therefore often specify how much time reps should spend prospecting for new accounts.[42] Spector Freight wants its sales representatives to spend 25 percent of their time prospecting and stop after three unsuccessful calls. Some companies rely on a missionary sales force to create new interest and open new accounts.

**USING SALES TIME EFFICIENTLY** In the course of a day, reps plan, travel, wait, sell, and perform administrative tasks (writing reports and billing, attending sales meetings, and talking to others in the company about production, delivery, billing, and sales performance). It's no wonder face-to-face selling accounts for as little as 29 percent of total working time![43] The best sales reps manage their time efficiently. *Time-and-duty analysis* and hour-by-hour breakdowns of activities help them understand how they spend their time and how they might increase their productivity.

Companies constantly try to improve sales force productivity.[44] To cut costs, reduce time demands on their outside sales force, and leverage technological innovations, many have increased the size and responsibilities of their inside sales force.

Inside selling is less expensive and growing faster than in-person selling. Each contact made by an inside salesperson might cost a company $25 to $30 compared with $300 to $500 for a field staff person with travel expenses. Virtual meeting software such as WebEx, communication tools such as Skype, and social media sites such as LinkedIn, Facebook, and Twitter make it easier to sell with few if any face-to-face meetings. And inside sellers don't even need to be in the office—a growing percentage work at home.[45]

The inside sales force frees outside reps to spend more time selling to major accounts, identifying and converting new major prospects, and obtaining more blanket orders and systems contracts. Inside salespeople spend more time checking inventory, following up orders, and phoning smaller accounts. They typically earn a salary or salary-plus-bonus pay.

**SALES TECHNOLOGY** The salesperson today has truly gone electronic. Not only is sales and inventory information transferred much more quickly, but specific computer-based decision support systems have been created for sales managers and sales representatives. Going online with a tablet or laptop, salespeople can prime themselves on backgrounds of clients, call up prewritten sales letters, transmit orders and resolve customer-service issues on the spot, and send samples, pamphlets, brochures, and other materials to clients.

One of the most valuable digital tools for the sales rep is the company Web site. It can help define the firm's relationships with individual accounts and identify those whose business warrants a personal sales call. It provides an introduction to self-identified potential customers and a way to contact the seller; it might even receive the initial order.

Social media are another valuable digital selling tool. Social networking is useful in "front end" prospecting and lead qualification as well as in "back end" relationship building and management. When one B-to-B sales rep for virtual-meetings company PGi was monitoring Twitter tweets for various keywords, he noticed that someone from a company tweeted about dissatisfaction with "web conferencing." The sales rep got in touch with the company's CEO and was able to quickly convince him of the merits of PGi's products, securing an agreement within a few hours.[46]

## MOTIVATING SALES REPRESENTATIVES

The majority of sales representatives require encouragement and special incentives, especially those in the field who encounter daily challenges.[47] Most marketers believe that the higher the salesperson's motivation, the greater the effort and the resulting performance, rewards, and satisfaction—all of which in turn further increase motivation.

**INTRINSIC VERSUS EXTRINSIC REWARDS** Marketers reinforce intrinsic and extrinsic rewards of all types. One research study found the employee reward with the highest value was pay, followed by promotion, personal growth, and sense of accomplishment.[48] Least valued were liking and respect, security, and recognition. In other words, salespeople are highly motivated by pay and the chance to get ahead and satisfy their intrinsic needs, and they may be less motivated by compliments and security. Some firms use sales contests to increase sales effort.[49]

Compensation plans may even need to vary depending on the type of salespersons: stars, core or solid performers, and laggards.[50] *Stars* benefit from no ceiling or caps on commissions, overachievement commissions for exceeding quotas, and prize structures that allow multiple winners.[51] *Core performers* benefit from multi-tier targets that serve as stepping stones for achievement and sales contests with prizes that vary in nature and value. *Laggards* respond to consistent quarterly bonuses and social pressure.[52]

**SALES QUOTAS** Many companies set annual sales quotas, developed from the annual marketing plan, for dollar sales, unit volume, margin, selling effort or activity, or product type. Compensation is often tied to degree of quota fulfillment. The company first prepares a sales forecast that becomes the basis for planning production, workforce size, and financial requirements. Management then establishes quotas for regions and territories, which typically add up to more than the sales forecast to encourage managers and salespeople to perform at their best. Even if they fail to make their quotas, the company nevertheless may reach its sales forecast.

Conventional wisdom says profits are maximized by sales reps focusing on the more important products and more profitable products. Reps are unlikely to achieve their quotas for established products when the company is launching several new products at the same time. The company may need to expand its sales force for new-product launches.

Setting sales quotas can create problems. If the company underestimates and the sales reps easily achieve their quotas, it has overpaid them. If it overestimates sales potential, the salespeople will find it very hard to reach their quotas and be frustrated or quit. Another downside is that quotas can drive reps to get as much business as possible—often ignoring the service side of the business. The company gains short-term results at the cost of long-term customer satisfaction. For these reasons, some companies are dropping quotas. Even hard-driving Oracle has changed its approach to sales compensation.[53]

**ORACLE** Finding sales flagging and customers griping, Oracle, the second-largest software company in the world, decided to overhaul its sales department and practices. Its rapidly expanding capabilities, with diverse applications such as human resources, supply chain, and CRM, meant one rep could no longer be responsible for selling all Oracle products to certain customers. Reorganization let reps specialize in a few particular products. To tone down the sales force's reputation as overly aggressive, Oracle changed the commission structure from a range of 2 percent to 12 percent to a flat 4 percent to 6 percent and adopted guidelines on how to "play nice" with channels, independent software vendors (ISVs), resellers, integrators, and value-added resellers (VARs). Six principles instructed sales staff to identify and work with partners in accounts and respect their positions and the value they add in order to address partner feedback that Oracle should be more predictable and reliable.

# EVALUATING SALES REPRESENTATIVES

We have been describing the *feed-forward* aspects of sales supervision—how management communicates what the sales reps should be doing and motivates them to do it. But good feed-forward requires good *feedback,* which means getting regular information about reps to evaluate their performance.

**SOURCES OF INFORMATION** The most important source of information about reps is sales reports. Additional information comes through personal observation, salesperson self-reports, customer letters and complaints, customer surveys, and conversations with other reps.

Sales reports are divided between *activity plans* and *write-ups of activity results.* The best example of the former is the salesperson's work plan, which reps submit a week or month in advance to describe intended calls and routing. This report forces sales reps to plan and schedule their activities and inform management of their whereabouts. It provides a basis for comparing their plans and accomplishments, or their ability to "plan their work and work their plan."

Many companies require representatives to develop an annual territory-marketing plan in which they outline their program for developing new accounts and increasing business from existing accounts. Sales managers study these plans, make suggestions, and use them to develop sales quotas. Sales reps write up completed activities on *call reports.* They also submit expense reports, new-business reports, lost-business reports, and reports on local business and economic conditions.

These reports provide raw data from which sales managers can extract key indicators of sales performance: (1) average number of sales calls per salesperson per day, (2) average sales call time per contact, (3) average revenue per sales call, (4) average cost per sales call, (5) entertainment cost per sales call, (6) percentage of orders per hundred sales calls, (7) number of new customers per period, (8) number of lost customers per period, and (9) sales force cost as a percentage of total sales.

**FORMAL EVALUATION** The sales force's reports along with other observations supply the raw materials for evaluation. One type of evaluation compares current with past performance. An example is shown in Table 22.1.

The sales manager can learn many things about rep John Smith from this table. Total sales increased every year (line 3). This does not necessarily mean Smith is doing a better job. The product breakdown shows he has been able to push the sales of product B further than the sales of product A (lines 1 and 2), though A is more profitable for the company. Given his quotas for the two products (lines 4 and 5), Smith could be increasing product B sales at the expense of product A sales. Although he increased total sales by $1,100 between 2013 and 2014 (line 3), gross profits on total sales actually decreased by $580 (line 8).

Sales expense (line 9) shows a steady increase, though total expense as a percentage of total sales seems to be under control (line 10). The upward trend in total dollar expense does not seem to be explained by any increase in the number of calls (line 11), though it might be related to success in acquiring new customers (line 14). Perhaps in prospecting for new customers, this rep is neglecting present customers, as indicated by an upward trend in the annual number of lost accounts (line 15).

The last two lines show the level and trend in sales and gross profits per customer. These figures become more meaningful when compared with overall company averages. If Smith's average gross profit per customer is lower than the company's average, he could be concentrating on the wrong customers or not spending enough time with each customer. A review of annual number of calls (line 11) shows he might be making fewer annual calls than the average

| TABLE 22.1 | Form for Evaluating Sales Representative's Performance | | | |
|---|---|---|---|---|
| **Territory: Midland Sales Representative: John Smith** | **2011** | **2012** | **2013** | **2014** |
| 1. Net sales product A | $251,300 | $253,200 | $270,000 | $263,100 |
| 2. Net sales product B | 423,200 | 439,200 | 553,900 | 561,900 |
| 3. Net sales total | 674,500 | 692,400 | 823,900 | 825,000 |
| 4. Percent of quota product A | 95.6 | 92.0 | 88.0 | 84.7 |
| 5. Percent of quota product B | 120.4 | 122.3 | 134.9 | 130.8 |
| 6. Gross profits product A | $50,260 | $50,640 | $54,000 | $52,620 |
| 7. Gross profits product B | 42,320 | 43,920 | 55,390 | 56,190 |
| 8. Gross profits total | 92,580 | 94,560 | 109,390 | 108,810 |
| 9. Sales expense | $10,200 | $11,100 | $11,600 | $13,200 |
| 10. Sales expense to total sales (%) | 1.5 | 1.6 | 1.4 | 1.6 |
| 11. Number of calls | 1,675 | 1,700 | 1,680 | 1,660 |
| 12. Cost per call | $6.09 | $6.53 | $6.90 | $7.95 |
| 13. Average number of customers | 320 | 24 | 328 | 334 |
| 14. Number of new customers | 13 | 14 | 15 | 20 |
| 15. Number of lost customers | 8 | 10 | 11 | 14 |
| 16. Average sales per customer | $2,108 | $2,137 | $2,512 | $2,470 |
| 17. Average gross profit per customer | $289 | $292 | $334 | $326 |

salesperson. If distances in the territory are similar to those in other territories, he might not be putting in a full work-day, might be poor at sales planning and routing, or might be spending too much time with certain accounts.

Even if effective in producing sales, the rep may not rate highly with customers. Success may come because competitors' salespeople are inferior, the rep's product is better, or new customers are always found to replace those who dislike the rep. Managers can glean customer opinions of the salesperson, product, and service by mail questionnaires or telephone calls. Sales reps can analyze the success or failure of a sales call and how they would improve the odds on subsequent calls. Their performance could be related to internal factors (effort, ability, and strategy) and/or external factors (task and luck).[54]

# Principles of Personal Selling

Personal selling is an ancient art. Effective salespeople today have more than instinct, however. Companies now spend hundreds of millions of dollars each year to train them in methods of analysis and customer management and to transform them from passive order takers into active order getters. Reps are taught the SPIN method to build long-term relationships by asking prospects several types of questions:[55]

1. *Situation questions*—These ask about facts or explore the buyer's present situation. For example, "What system are you using to invoice your customers?"
2. *Problem questions*—These deal with problems, difficulties, and dissatisfactions the buyer is experiencing. For example, "What parts of the system create errors?"
3. *Implication questions*—These ask about the consequences or effects of a buyer's problems, difficulties, or dissatisfactions. For example, "How does this problem affect your people's productivity?"
4. *Need-payoff questions*—These ask about the value or usefulness of a proposed solution. For example, "How much would you save if our company could help you reduce errors by 80 percent?"

Most sales training programs agree on the major steps in any effective sales process. We show these steps in Figure 22.4 and discuss their application to industrial selling next.[56] Note that application of these selling practices can vary in different parts of the world. Pfizer has to sell very differently in Latin America than in North America.[57]

## THE SIX STEPS

**PROSPECTING AND QUALIFYING** The first step in selling is to identify and qualify prospects. More companies are taking responsibility for finding and qualifying leads so salespeople can use their expensive time doing what they do best: selling. IBM qualifies leads according to the BANT acronym: Does the customer have the necessary *budget,* the *authority* to buy, a compelling *need* for the product or service, and a *timeline* for delivery that aligns with what is possible?

Marketers these days are going beyond BANT and getting increasingly sophisticated in their pursuit of qualified leads. One software firm, Infer, uses 150 different signals—including dozens of online data feeds—to rate customer leads. Using inputs as diverse as prospects' hiring practices, job boards, and sample tweets from customers and employees, the company's software classifies prospects as worth a call or offer—or not.[58]

**PREAPPROACH** The salesperson needs to learn as much as possible about the prospect company (what it needs, who takes part in the purchase decision) and its buyers (personal characteristics and buying styles). How is the purchasing process conducted at the company? How is it structured? Many purchasing departments in larger companies have been elevated to strategic supply departments with more professional practices. Centralized purchasing may put a premium on having larger suppliers able to meet all the company's needs. At the same time, some companies are also decentralizing purchasing for smaller items such as coffeemakers, office supplies, and other inexpensive necessities.

The sales rep must thoroughly understand the purchasing process in terms of who, when, where, how, and why in order to set call objectives: to qualify the prospect, gather information, or make an immediate sale. Another task is to choose the best contact approach—a personal visit, phone call, e-mail, or letter. The right approach is crucial given that it has become harder for sales reps to get into the offices of purchasing agents, physicians, and other time-starved and Internet-enabled potential customers. Finally, the salesperson should plan an overall sales strategy for the account.

**PRESENTATION AND DEMONSTRATION** The salesperson tells the product "story" to the buyer, using a *features, advantages, benefits,* and *value* (FABV) approach. Features describe physical characteristics of a market offering, such as chip processing speeds or memory capacity. Advantages describe why the features give the

| **Fig. 22.4** |

Major Steps in Effective Selling

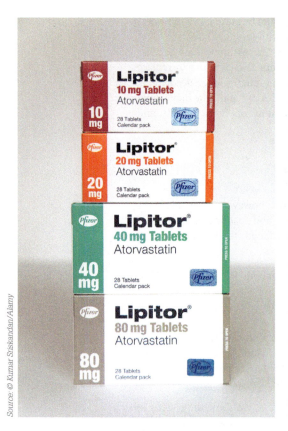

Pharma giant Pfizer sells its drug brands differently in different parts of the world.

customer an edge. Benefits describe the economic, technical, service, and social pluses delivered. Value describes the offering's worth (often in monetary terms).

Salespeople often spend too much time on product features (a product orientation) and not enough time stressing benefits and value (a customer orientation), especially when selling individualized or premium-priced products and in highly competitive markets.[59] The pitch to a prospective client must be highly relevant, engaging, and compelling—there is always another company waiting to take that business.[60]

**OVERCOMING OBJECTIONS** Customers typically pose objections. *Psychological resistance* includes resistance to interference, preference for established supply sources or brands, apathy, reluctance to give up something, unpleasant associations created by the sales rep, predetermined ideas, dislike of making decisions, and a neurotic attitude toward money. *Logical resistance* might be objections to the price, delivery schedule, or product or company characteristics.

To handle these objections, the salesperson maintains a positive approach, asks the buyer to clarify the objection, questions in such a way that the buyer answers his own objection, denies the validity of the objection, or turns it into a reason for buying. Although price is the most frequently negotiated issue—especially in tight economic times—others include contract completion time, quality of goods and services offered, purchase volume, product safety, and responsibility for financing, risk taking, promotion, and title.

Salespeople sometimes give in too easily when customers demand a discount. One company recognized this problem when sales revenues went up 25 percent but profit remained flat. The company decided to retrain its salespeople to "sell the price" rather than "sell through price." Salespeople were given richer information about each customer's sales history and behavior. They received training to recognize value-adding opportunities rather than price-cutting opportunities. As a result, the company's sales revenues climbed and so did its margins.[61]

**CLOSING** Closing signs from the buyer include physical actions, statements or comments, and questions. Reps can ask for the order, recapitulate the points of agreement, offer to help write up the order, ask whether the buyer wants A or B, get the buyer to make minor choices such as color or size, or indicate what the buyer will lose by not placing the order now. The salesperson might offer specific inducements to close, such as an additional service, an extra quantity, or a token gift.

If the client still isn't budging, perhaps the salesperson is not interacting with the right executive—a more senior person may have the necessary authority. The salesperson also may need to find other ways to reinforce the value of the offering and how it alleviates financial or other pressures the client faces.[62]

**FOLLOW-UP AND MAINTENANCE** Follow-up and maintenance are necessary to ensure customer satisfaction and repeat business. Immediately after closing, the salesperson should cement any necessary details about delivery time, purchase terms, and other matters important to the customer. He or she should schedule a follow-up call after delivery to ensure proper installation, instruction, and servicing and to detect any problems, assure the buyer of his or her interest, and reduce any cognitive dissonance. The salesperson should develop a maintenance and growth plan for the account.

## RELATIONSHIP MARKETING

The principles of personal selling and negotiation are largely transaction-oriented because their purpose is to close a specific sale. But in many cases the company seeks not an immediate sale but rather a long-term supplier–customer relationship. Today's customers prefer suppliers who can sell and deliver a coordinated set of products and services to many locations, who can quickly solve problems in different locations, and who can work closely with customer teams to improve products and processes.[63]

Salespeople working with key customers must do more than email or call only when they think customers might be ready to place orders. They should get in touch at other times and make useful suggestions about the business to create value. They should monitor key accounts, know customers' problems, and be ready to serve them in a number of ways, adapting and responding to different customer needs or situations.[64]

Relationship marketing is not effective in all situations. But when it is the right strategy and is properly implemented, the organization will focus as much on managing its customers as on managing its products.

# Summary

1. Direct marketing is an interactive marketing system that uses one or more media to effect a measurable response or transaction at any location. Direct marketing, especially electronic marketing, is showing explosive growth.

2. Direct marketers plan campaigns by deciding on objectives, target markets and prospects, offers, and prices. Next, they test and establish measures to determine the campaign's success.

3. Major channels for direct marketing include face-to-face selling, direct mail, catalog marketing, telemarketing, interactive TV, kiosks, Web sites, and mobile devices.

4. Customer relationship management often requires building a customer database and data mining to detect trends, segments, and individual needs. A number of significant risks also exist, so marketers must proceed thoughtfully.

5. What are the pros and cons of database marketing?

6. Salespeople serve as a company's link to its customers. The sales rep *is* the company to many of its customers, and it is the rep who brings back to the company much-needed information about the customer.

7. Designing the sales force requires choosing objectives, strategy, structure, size, and compensation. Objectives may include prospecting, targeting, communicating, selling, servicing, information gathering, and allocating. Selecting strategy requires choosing the most effective mix of selling approaches. Structuring the sales force entails dividing territories by geography, product, or market (or some combination of these). To estimate how large the sales force needs to be, the firm estimates the total workload and how many sales hours (and hence salespeople) will be needed. Compensating reps requires identifying the types of salaries, commissions, bonuses, expense accounts, and benefits to give and how much weight customer satisfaction should have in determining total compensation.

8. There are five steps in managing the sales force: (1) recruiting and selecting sales representatives; (2) training the representatives in sales techniques and in the company's products, policies, and customer-satisfaction orientation; (3) supervising the sales force and helping reps to use their time efficiently; (4) motivating the sales force and balancing quotas, monetary rewards, and supplementary motivators; and (5) evaluating individual and group sales performance.

9. Effective salespeople are trained in methods of analysis and customer management as well as the art of sales professionalism. No single approach works best in all circumstances, but most trainers agree that selling has six steps: prospecting and qualifying customers, preapproach, presentation and demonstration, overcoming objections, closing, and follow-up and maintenance.

## MyMarketingLab

Go to **mymktlab.com** to complete the problems marked with this icon ⭐ as well as for additional Auto-graded and Assisted-graded writing questions.

# Applications

## Marketing Debate
### Are Great Salespeople Born or Made?

One debate in sales is about the impact of training versus selection in developing an effective sales force. Some observers maintain the best salespeople are born that way and are effective due to their personalities and interpersonal skills developed over a lifetime. Others contend that application of leading-edge sales techniques can make virtually anyone a sales star.

**Take a position:** The key to developing an effective sales force is selection *versus* The key to developing an effective sales force is training.

## Marketing Discussion
### Role of the Salesperson

⭐ Think about the last time you went to make a major purchase in a store. How important was the salesperson in that decision? What did he or she do that you liked or didn't like?

# Marketing Excellence

## >> Progressive

Progressive Corporation is among the largest providers of auto, motorcycle, boat, and RV insurance in the United States. The company was founded in 1937 and is considered one of the most innovative in the industry. From the beginning, its philosophy has been to approach auto insurance "like no other company had."

Progressive attracts new customers through its unique product offerings and services. For example, it was the first insurance company to offer a drive-thru claim service, a 24-hour claim service, and reduced rates for low-risk drivers. In 1994, it introduced comparison insurance shopping service, encouraging customers to call 800-AUTO-PRO (now 800-PROGRESSIVE) and receive a Progressive quote as well as comparison quotes from three other competitors. The company extended this service when it launched comparison rate shopping on the Internet. It was also the first insurance company to offer the Immediate Response Vehicle (IRV), a special vehicle that brought trained claims professionals to wherever customers needed them, including the scene of an accident. Today, Progressive has thousands of IRVs located across the country.

The insurance industry has changed a lot over the years as consumers have become more educated, more cost-conscious, and less likely to use an agent during the buying process. Jonathan Beamer, marketing strategy and innovation business leader at Progressive, explained the company's media strategy: "As a company, we've always had the belief that customers should be able to interact with us in their channel of choice. In the past, that was by phone, online, or through an agent. Social media is another means for customers to engage with our brand." The company has a network of 35,000 independent agents but also gives customers the opportunity to interact with it via the Internet or mobile devices. It offers consumers several options to manage their service claims as well. Policyholders can bring their damaged vehicle to a Progressive service center, or they can call Progressive for roadside assistance to take care of problems ranging from flat tires to locksmith needs.

Consumers have responded positively Progressive's marketing campaigns in recent years thanks to the company's iconic character Flo, a quirky, witty employee dressed in a white uniform and white apron bearing the company's logo. Flo commercials are often set in an imaginary insurance superstore and aimed at consumers who are considering getting a new insurance policy or changing insurers. The company has found that using a person to represent the brand helps consumers envision the intangible act of buying and selling insurance as a tangible one. Its ads also often feature a large white-and-blue "insurance" package, again reinforcing the idea that Progressive sells something concrete rather than abstract. In every commercial, Flo goes out of her way to help customers and their businesses. She works alongside plumbers, lugs shrubbery with landscapers, and finds stranded cars and drivers in pouring rain. Flo, her packages of insurance, and the Progressive supercenters have all helped differentiate Progressive in a competitive industry.

Flo is now one of the most recognized advertising icons, and as Chief Marketing Officer Jeff Charney explained, "Flo has made us a household name." However, Progressive's marketing team is careful to keep her modern and relevant. She appears across all screens, including TV, the Internet, mobile devices, smartphone apps, video games like Sims Social, and animated YouTube videos, and she even has her own Facebook page (along with millions of fans). The company's marketing has also won multiple awards, including *Adweek's* "Brand Genius: Marketer of the Year Award" in 2011 and an Effie award for marketing efficiency.

Progressive has experienced impressive growth over the past two decades thanks to its innovative and affordable insurance solutions and direct marketing campaigns. Between 1996 and 2005, the company grew an average of 17 percent per year, from $3.4 billion to $14 billion. In 2013, it wrote 17.3 billion policies and earned $18.2 billion in revenue.

### Questions

1. What has Progressive done well over the years to attract new insurance customers?

2. Discuss Progressive's direct marketing campaign, which primarily revolves around the character Flo. Why does it resonant so well with consumers?

3. What else should Progressive be doing to ensure it stays top of mind in the competitive industry of insurance?

**Sources:** Avi Dan, "How Progressive's CMO Jeff Charney Made 'Flo' More Loveable than Ducks and Geckos," *Forbes*, May 3, 2012; Giselle Abramovich, "How Progressive Got Its Social Flow," CMO.com, December 11, 2013; Stuart Elliott, "A Nomadic Insurance Pitchman, Luring New Consumers," *New York Times*, November 30, 2010; Gary Strauss, "Progressive CEO Calls Flo 'Essential' to Its Marketing Plan," *USA Today*, July 26, 2012; E. J. Schultz, "Progressive Goes Flo-less in Corporate Image Campaign," *Ad Age*, September 23, 2013; "BtoB's Best—Integrated Campaign (more than $200,000): Progressive Commercial," *Ad Age*, October 8, 2013; E. J. Schultz, "Flo Gets More Company as Progressive Rolls Out 'The Box,'" *Ad Age*, December 5, 2012; Progressive.com; Progressive Insurance 2013 Annual Report.

**Marketing** Excellence

## >> Victoria's Secret

Victoria's Secret is the largest retailer of lingerie in the United States. Roy Raymond founded the company in 1977 because he thought retailers offered only "racks of terry-cloth robes and ugly floral-print nylon nightgowns." In 1982, Raymond sold the company to Leslie Wexner, creator of Limited Stores Inc., for $1 million. At the time, Victoria's Secret had expanded to four stores and a catalog business. The company wasn't profitable, but Wexner recalled its attraction: "There wasn't erotic lingerie, but there was very sexy lingerie, and I hadn't seen anything like it in the U.S." Although Wexner knew nothing about lingerie at the time, he saw an opportunity to look at the market in a new light. He explained, "Most of the women that I knew wore underwear most of the time, and most of the women that I knew I thought would rather wear lingerie most of the time, but there were no lingerie stores. I thought if we could develop price points and products that have a broader base of customer, it could be something big."

The market during the 1970s and early 1980s in fact offered women very few options for lingerie shopping. At one end, women could buy Fruit of the Loom, Hanes, or Jockey cotton underwear in three-pair packages just as men did. Department stores offered little in terms of design and style. And lacy lingerie could be found only in stores like Frederick's of Hollywood, whose products were considered provocative, not for daily wear, and often embarrassing to shop for.

Wexner took several steps to revamp Victoria's Secret. First, he realized the company should target female consumers who buy for themselves, rather than male customers who shop for their significant others. As a result, Victoria's Secret launched a range of new products in stylish colors, textiles, and patterns that made women feel sexy and glamorous in a tasteful manner. The company focused on consistency of fit, which helped create customer loyalty, and stores were reconfigured to appeal to female shoppers. Bra displays and fitting rooms were moved to the back, for instance, to provide customers with more privacy.

Next, Wexner reinforced the brand image of style and sophistication by evoking a European look and feel throughout the stores and catalogs. Catalogs bore a fake London address (the company was really headquartered in Columbus, Ohio), while storefronts resembled 19th-century England, complete with soft classical music and romantic-style details throughout. Within five years, Victoria's Secret had expanded from a handful of stores to 346 and a growing catalog business.

Victoria's Secret's catalog business is considered one of the most successful in the retail industry. When Wexner bought the company in 1982, each catalog cost a hefty $3 to produce and distribute. Its customer database grew significantly over the next 20 years and peaked at 400 million mailings in 1998. Today, Victoria's Secret spends approximately $220 million a year and mails 390 million catalogs worldwide. Its catalog business has been so successful because it accomplishes several things a retail store cannot. Most importantly, catalogs allow consumers to browse and shop for lingerie in the comfort and privacy of their homes. To accommodate them, Victoria's Secret takes telephone orders 24 hours a day. Before the Internet, this was a critical key to the company's success. Catalogs also provide the opportunity to extend and test different product offerings, including bathing suits, sweaters, and dresses.

Another milestone in Victoria's Secret's marketing strategy was its shift to include supermodel fashion shows and television commercials in the 1990s. In 1999, the company's steamy 30-second Super Bowl ad resulted in millions of visits to the company's Web site. Each year, millions more tune in to watch the world's top supermodels, including Victoria's Secret Angels, strut down the runway in diamond-studded lingerie, high heels, and the company's signature angel wings. Erika Maschmeyer, an analyst at Robert W. Baird & Co., explained that the TV show "is essentially an hour-long commercial.... There are a lot of places to buy intimate apparel, but there's no other place that has such a strong brand connotation to it, and I think the fashion show is definitely a part of that."

Victoria's Secret has accomplished what no company has: It took an intimate product and made it stylish, trendy, acceptable, and accessible through innovative and pitch-perfect direct marketing. The company recently expanded with the launch of Pink, a lingerie line targeted at 15- to 22-year-old women. The hope is that Pink consumers remain loyal to the Victoria's Secret brand as they grow older.

Today, Victoria's Secret sells its products through alluring catalogs, through its Web site, and in more than 1,075 stores located primarily in shopping malls throughout the United States, Canada, and the United Kingdom. Annual sales topped $6 billion in 2013, and the company continues to grow the business, making lingerie trendy and stylish for women of all ages.

### Questions

1. Why has Victoria's Secret been so successful? How does the company reach its target audience?

2. What do you think are Victoria's Secret's biggest challenges?

3. What's next for Victoria's Secret? How does the company grow?

**Sources:** Carlye Adler, "How Victoria's Secret Made Lingerie Mainstream," *Newsweek*, June 9, 2010; Carlye Adler, "Victoria's Secret's Secret—The Man behind the Company That Made Lingerie Mainstream and Mall-friendly," *Newsweek*, October 15, 2012; Sapna Maheshwari, "Victoria's Secret Marketing Goes Own Way," SFgate.com, November 12, 2013; Ashley Lutz, "How Victoria's Secret Gets Way with Marketing to Teenagers," *Business Insider*, November 15, 2013; VictoriasSecret.com; 2013 Limited Brands Annual Report.

# DON'T BUY THIS JACKET

It's Black Friday, the day in the year retail turns from red to black and starts to make real money. But Black Friday, and the culture of consumption it reflects, puts the economy of natural systems that support all life firmly in the red. We're now using the resources of one-and-a-half planets on our one and only planet.

Because Patagonia wants to be in business for a good long time – and leave a world inhabitable for our kids – we want to do the opposite of every other business today. We ask you to buy less and to reflect before you spend a dime on this jacket or anything else.

Environmental bankruptcy, as with corporate bankruptcy, can happen very slowly, then all of a sudden. This is what we face unless we slow down, then reverse the damage. We're running short on fresh water, topsoil, fisheries, wetlands – all our planet's natural systems and resources that support business, and life, including our own.

The environmental cost of everything we make is astonishing. Consider the R2® Jacket shown, one of our best sellers. To make it required 135 liters of

**COMMON THREADS INITIATIVE**

**REDUCE**
WE make useful gear that lasts a long time
YOU don't buy what you don't need

**REPAIR**
WE help you repair your Patagonia gear
YOU pledge to fix what's broken

**REUSE**
WE help find a home for Patagonia gear
you no longer need
YOU sell or pass it on*

**RECYCLE**
WE will take back your Patagonia gear
that is worn out
YOU pledge to keep your stuff out of
the landfill and incinerator

**REIMAGINE**
TOGETHER we reimagine a world where we take
only what nature can replace

water, enough to meet the daily needs (three glasses a day) of 45 people. Its journey from its origin as 60% recycled polyester to our Reno warehouse generated nearly 20 pounds of carbon dioxide, 24 times the weight of the finished product. This jacket left behind, on its way to Reno, two-thirds its weight in waste.

And this is a 60% recycled polyester jacket, knit and sewn to a high standard; it is exceptionally durable, so you won't have to replace it as often. And when it comes to the end of its useful life we'll take it back to recycle into a product of equal value. But, as is true of all the things we can make and you can buy, this jacket comes with an environmental cost higher than its price.

There is much to be done and plenty for us all to do. Don't buy what you don't need. Think twice before you buy anything. Go to patagonia.com/CommonThreads or scan the QR code below. Take the Common Threads Initiative pledge, and join us in the fifth "R," to reimagine a world where we take only what nature can replace.

## patagonia®
patagonia.com

TAKE THE PLEDGE

* If you sell your used Patagonia product on eBay® and take the Common Threads Initiative pledge, we will co-list your product on patagonia.com for no additional charge.
© 2011 Patagonia, Inc.

## In This Chapter, We Will Address the Following **Questions**

1. What are important trends in marketing practices? (p. 657)

2. What are the keys to effective internal marketing? (p. 658)

3. How can companies be socially responsible marketers? (p. 663)

4. What tools are available to help companies monitor and improve their marketing activities? (p. 675)

5. What do marketers need to do to succeed in the future? (p. 680)

Environmental concerns impacts all that outdoor clothing and equipment provider Patagonia does, leading to some fairly unconventional advertising!

*Source: Patagonia, Inc.*

# 23  Managing a Holistic Marketing Organization for the Long Run

**Healthy long-term growth for a brand requires holistic marketers to engage in a host of** carefully planned, interconnected marketing activities and satisfy a broad set of constituents and objectives. Marketers must also consider a wide range of short- and long-term effects of their actions. Corporate social responsibility and sustainability have become priorities for many. Some firms fully embrace this vision of corporate enlightenment.[1]

*Patagonia, maker of high-end outdoor clothing and equipment, has always put environmental issues at the core of what it does. Company founder Yvon Chouinard, also the author of* The Responsible Company, *actively promotes a post-consumerist economy in which goods are "high quality, recyclable and repairable." Under Chouinard's leadership, Patagonia even ran a full-page ad in the New York Times headlined "Don't Buy This Jacket." Below a photo of the retailer's R2 jacket was text explaining that despite its many positive features—"60% recyclable polyester, knit and sewn to high standards, and exceptionally durable"—the jacket still imposed many environmental costs (using 135 liters of water and 20 pounds of carbon dioxide to manufacture). The ad concluded by promoting the Common Threads Initiative asking consumers to engage in five behaviors: (1) reduce (what you buy); (2) repair (what you can); (3) reuse (what you have); (4) recycle (everything else); and (5) reimagine (a sustainable world). With $575 million in annual sales, privately held Patagonia is always trying to find better environmental solutions for everything it does and makes, such as offering the first wetsuits made from plant-based material as an alternative to neoprene.*

**Brands such as** Ben & Jerry's, Odwalla, Stonyfield Farm, Whole Foods, and Seventh Generation have embraced similar philosophies and practices. Successful holistic marketing requires effective relationship marketing, integrated marketing, internal marketing, and performance marketing. In this chapter, we consider internal and performance marketing and how to conduct them responsibly. We begin by examining changes in the way companies conduct marketing today.

## Trends in Marketing Practices

With globalization, deregulation, market fragmentation, consumer empowerment, environmental concerns, and all the remarkable developments in communication technology, the world has unquestionably become a very different place for marketers.[2] Table 23.1 summarizes some important shifts in marketing realities.

In making all these shifts in marketing and business practices, firms also face ethical dilemmas and perplexing trade-offs. Consumers may value convenience, but how can they justify disposable products or elaborate packaging in a world trying to minimize waste? Increasing material aspirations can defy the need for sustainability. Smart companies are creatively designing with energy efficiency, carbon footprints, toxicity, and disposability in mind. There have been some successes.[3]

| TABLE 23.1 | Important Shifts in Marketing and Business Practices |
|---|---|

- *Reengineering.* Appointing teams to manage customer-value-building processes and break down walls between departments
- *Outsourcing.* Buying more goods and services from outside domestic or foreign vendors
- *Benchmarking.* Studying "best practice companies" to improve performance
- *Supplier partnering.* Partnering with fewer but better value-adding suppliers
- *Customer partnering.* Working more closely with customers to add value to their operations
- *Merging.* Acquiring or merging with firms in the same or complementary industries to gain economies of scale and scope
- *Globalizing.* Increasing efforts to "think global" and "act local"
- *Flattening.* Reducing the number of organizational levels to get closer to the customer
- *Focusing.* Determining the most profitable businesses and customers and focusing on them
- *Justifying.* Becoming more accountable by measuring, analyzing, and documenting the effects of marketing actions
- *Accelerating.* Designing the organization and setting up processes to respond more quickly to changes in the environment
- *Empowering.* Encouraging and empowering personnel to produce more ideas and take more initiative
- *Broadening.* Factoring the interests of customers, employees, shareholders, and other stakeholders into the activities of the enterprise
- *Monitoring.* Tracking what is said online and elsewhere and studying customers, competitors, and others to improve business practices
- *Uncovering.* Using data mining and other analytical methods to develop deep insights into customers and how they behave

**TOYOTA PRIUS**   Some auto experts scoffed when Toyota predicted sales of 300,000 cars within five years of launching its gas-and-electric Prius hybrid sedan in 2001. But by 2004, the Prius had a six-month waiting list. Toyota's winning formula consists of a powerful electric motor and the ability to quickly switch power sources—resulting in 55 miles per gallon for city and highway driving—with the roominess and power of a family sedan and an eco-friendly design and look for a little more than $20,000. Some consumers also liked that the Prius's distinctive design allowed them to make a visible statement about their commitment to the environment. The lesson? Functionally successful products that consumers see as also being good for the environment can offer enticing options. In both 2012 and 2013, *Consumer Reports* rated the Toyota Prius as best overall value for the automotive dollar. Toyota is now rolling out hybrids throughout its auto lineup, and U.S. automakers have followed suit.

Now more than ever, marketers must think holistically and use creative win-win solutions to balance conflicting demands. They must develop fully integrated marketing programs and meaningful relationships with a range of constituents.[4] They must do all the right things inside their company and consider the broader consequences in the marketplace, topics we turn to next.

# Internal Marketing

Traditionally, marketers played the role of intermediary, charged with understanding customers' needs and transmitting their voice to various functional areas.[5] But in a networked enterprise, *every* functional area can interact directly with customers. Marketing no longer has sole ownership of customer interactions; it now must integrate all the customer-facing processes so customers see a single face and hear a single voice when they interact with the firm.[6]

*Internal marketing* requires that everyone in the organization accept the concepts and goals of marketing and engage in identifying, providing, and communicating customer value. Only when *all* employees realize their job is to create, serve, and satisfy customers does the company become an effective marketer.[7] "Marketing Memo: Characteristics of Company Departments That Are Truly Customer Driven" presents a tool that evaluates which company departments excel at being customer-centric.

Let's look at how marketing departments are being organized, how they can work effectively with other departments, and how firms can foster a creative marketing culture across the organization.[8]

## marketing memo
### Characteristics of Company Departments that Are Truly Customer Driven

**R&D** 
___ They spend time meeting customers and listening to their problems.
___ They welcome the involvement of marketing, manufacturing, and other departments on each new project.
___ They benchmark competitors' products and seek "best of class" solutions.
___ They solicit customer reactions and suggestions as the project progresses.
___ They continuously improve and refine the product on the basis of market feedback.

**Purchasing**
___ They proactively search for the best suppliers rather than choose only from those who solicit their business.
___ They build long-term relationships with fewer but more reliable high-quality suppliers.
___ They do not compromise quality for price savings.

**Manufacturing**
___ They invite customers to visit and tour their plants.
___ They visit customer factories to see how customers use the company's products.
___ They willingly work overtime when it is important to meet promised delivery schedules.
___ They continuously search for ways to produce goods faster, at lower costs, and with fewer adverse environmental consequences.
___ They continuously improve product quality, aiming for zero defects.
___ They meet customer requirements for "customization" where this can be done profitably.

**Marketing**
___ They study customer needs and wants in well-defined market segments.
___ They allocate marketing effort in relationship to the long-run profit potential of the targeted segments.
___ They develop winning offerings for each target segment.
___ They measure company image and customer satisfaction and loyalty on a continuous basis.
___ They continuously gather and evaluate ideas for new products, product improvements, and services to meet customers' needs.
___ They influence all company departments and employees to be customer-centered in their thinking and practice.

**Sales**
___ They acquire specialized knowledge of the customer's industry.
___ They strive to give the customer "the best solution" but make only promises they can keep.
___ They feed customers' needs and ideas back to those in charge of product development.
___ They serve the same customers for a long period of time.

**Logistics**
___ They set a high standard for service delivery time and meet it consistently.
___ They operate a knowledgeable and friendly customer service department that can answer questions, handle complaints, and resolve problems in a satisfactory and timely manner.

**Accounting**
___ They prepare periodic profitability reports by product, market segment, sales territory, order size, and individual customers.
___ They prepare invoices tailored to customer needs and answer customer queries courteously and quickly.

**Finance**
___ They understand and support marketing investments (like image advertising) that produce long-term customer preference and loyalty.
___ They tailor the financial package to the customers' financial requirements.
___ They make quick decisions on customer creditworthiness.

**Public Relations**
___ They disseminate favorable news about the company and handle damage control for unfavorable news.
___ They act as an internal customer and public advocate for better company policies and practices.

**Other Customer-Contact Employees**
___ They are competent, courteous, cheerful, credible, reliable, and responsive.

# ORGANIZING THE MARKETING DEPARTMENT

Modern marketing departments can be organized in a number of different, sometimes overlapping ways: functionally, geographically, by product or brand, by market, or in a matrix.

**FUNCTIONAL ORGANIZATION** In the most common form of marketing organization, functional specialists report to a marketing vice president who coordinates their activities. Figure 23.1 shows five specialists. Others might include a customer service manager, a marketing planning manager, a market logistics manager, a direct marketing manager, and a digital marketing manager.

The main advantage of a functional marketing organization is its administrative simplicity. It can be quite a challenge for the departments to develop smooth working relationships, however. This form also can result in inadequate planning as the number of products and markets increases and each functional group vies for budget and status. The marketing vice president constantly weighs competing claims and faces a difficult coordination problem.

**GEOGRAPHIC ORGANIZATION** A company selling in a national market often organizes its sales force (and sometimes its marketing) along geographic lines.[9] The national sales manager may supervise four regional sales managers, who each supervise six zone managers, who in turn supervise eight district sales managers, who each supervise 10 salespeople.

Some companies are adding *area market specialists* (regional or local marketing managers) to support sales efforts in high-volume markets. One such market might be Miami-Dade County, Florida, where almost two-thirds of households are Hispanic.[10] The Miami specialist would know Miami's customer and trade makeup, help marketing managers at headquarters adjust their marketing mix for Miami, and prepare local annual and long-range plans for selling all the company's products there. Some companies must develop different marketing programs in different parts of the country because geography alters their brand development so much, as noted in Chapter 8.

**PRODUCT- OR BRAND-MANAGEMENT ORGANIZATION** Companies producing a variety of products and brands often establish a product- (or brand-) management organization. This does not replace the functional organization but serves as another layer of management. A group product manager supervises product category managers, who in turn supervise specific product and brand managers.

A product-management organization makes sense if the company's products are quite different or there are more than a functional organization can handle. This form is sometimes characterized as a **hub-and-spoke system.** The brand or product manager is figuratively at the center, with spokes leading to various departments representing working relationships (see Figure 23.2). The manager may:

- Develop a long-range and competitive strategy for the product.
- Prepare an annual marketing plan and sales forecast.
- Work with advertising, digital, and merchandising agencies to develop copy, programs, and campaigns.
- Increase support of the product among the sales force and distributors.
- Gather continuous intelligence about the product's performance, customer and dealer attitudes, and new problems and opportunities.
- Initiate product improvements to meet changing market needs.

The product-management organization lets the product manager concentrate on developing a cost-effective marketing program and react more quickly to new products in the marketplace; it also gives the company's smaller brands a product advocate. However, it has disadvantages too:

- Product and brand managers may lack authority to carry out their responsibilities.
- They become experts in their product area but rarely achieve functional expertise.

| **Fig. 23.1** |

Functional
Organization

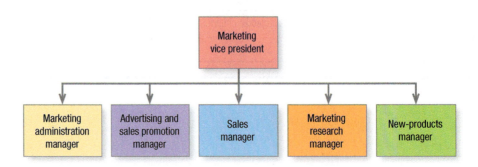

| **Fig. 23.2** |

## The Product Manager's Interactions

(a) Vertical Product Team

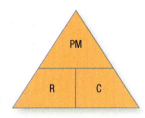

(b) Triangular Product Team

(c) Horizontal Product Team

PM = product manager
APM = associate product manager
PA = product assistant
R = market researcher
C = communication specialist
S = sales manager
D = distribution specialist
F = finance/accounting specialist
E = engineer

- The system often proves costly. One person is appointed to manage each major product or brand, and soon more are appointed to manage even minor products and brands.
- Brand managers normally manage a brand for only a short time. Short-term involvement leads to short-term planning and fails to build long-term strengths.
- The fragmentation of markets makes it harder to develop a national strategy. Brand managers must please regional and local sales groups, transferring power from marketing to sales.
- Product and brand managers focus the company on building market share rather than customer relationships.

A second alternative in a product-management organization is *product teams*. There are three types: vertical, triangular, and horizontal (see Figure 23.3). The triangular and horizontal product-team approaches let each major brand be run by a **brand-asset management team (BAMT)** consisting of key representatives from functions that affect the brand's performance. The company consists of several BAMTs that periodically report to a BAMT directors committee, which itself reports to a chief branding officer. This is quite different from the way brands have traditionally been handled.

A third alternative is to eliminate product manager positions for minor products and assign two or more products to each remaining manager. This is feasible when two or more products appeal to a similar set of needs. A cosmetics company doesn't need product managers for each product because cosmetics serve one major need—beauty. A toiletries company needs different managers for headache remedies, toothpaste, soap, and shampoo because these products differ in use and appeal.

In a fourth alternative, *category management*, a company focuses on product categories to manage its brands. Procter & Gamble (P&G), a pioneer of the brand-management system, and other top packaged-goods firms have made a major shift to category management, as have firms outside the grocery channel.[11] Diageo's shift to category management was seen as a means to better manage the development of premium brands. It also helped the firm address the plight of under-performing brands.[12]

P&G cited a number of advantages to its shift to category management. By fostering internal competition among brand managers, the traditional brand-management system had created strong incentives to excel, but also internal competition for resources and a lack of coordination. The new scheme was designed to ensure adequate resources for all categories.

Another rationale is the increasing power of the retail trade, which has thought of profitability in terms of product categories. P&G felt it only made sense to deal along similar lines. Retailers and regional grocery chains such as Walmart and Dominick's embrace category management as a means to define a particular product category's strategic role within the store and address logistics, the role of private-label products, and the trade-offs between product variety and inefficient duplication.[13]

| **Fig. 23.3** |

## Three Types of Product Teams

Source: © Jeff Greenberg "0 people images" / Alamy

Sales in the dairy aisle increased once marketers for General Mills' Yoplait Yogurt became category advisors to a number of major retailers.

In fact, in some packaged-goods firms, category management has evolved into aisle management and encompasses multiple related categories typically found in the same sections of supermarkets and grocery stores. General Mills' Yoplait Yogurt has served as category advisor to the dairy aisle for 24 major retailers, boosting the yogurt base footprint four to eight feet at a time and increasing sales of yogurt by 9 percent and category sales in dairy by 13 percent nationwide.[14]

**MARKET-MANAGEMENT ORGANIZATION** Canon sells printers to consumer, business, and government markets. Nippon Steel sells to the railroad, construction, and public utility industries. When customers fall into different user groups with distinct buying preferences and practices, a **market-management organization** is desirable. Market managers supervise several market-development managers, market specialists, or industry specialists and draw on functional services as needed. Market managers of important markets might even have functional specialists reporting to them.

Market managers are staff (not line) people, with duties like those of product managers. They develop long-range and annual plans for their markets and are judged by their market's growth and profitability. Because this system organizes marketing activity to meet the needs of distinct customer groups, it shares many advantages and disadvantages of product-management systems. Many companies are reorganizing along market lines and becoming **market-centered organizations.** Xerox converted from geographic selling to selling by industry, as did IBM and Hewlett-Packard.

When a close relationship is advantageous, such as when customers have diverse and complex requirements and buy an integrated bundle of products and services, a **customer-management organization,** which deals with individual customers rather than the mass market or even market segments, should prevail.[15] One study showed that companies organized by customer groups reported much higher accountability for the overall quality of relationships and greater employee freedom to take actions to satisfy individual customers.[16]

**MATRIX-MANAGEMENT ORGANIZATION** Companies that produce many products for many markets may adopt a matrix organization employing both product and market managers. The rub is that it's costly and often creates conflicts. There's the cost of supporting all the managers and questions about where authority and responsibility for marketing activities should reside—at headquarters or in the division?[17] Some corporate marketing groups assist top management with overall opportunity evaluation, provide divisions with consulting assistance on request, help divisions that have little or no marketing, and promote the marketing concept throughout the company.

## RELATIONSHIPS WITH OTHER DEPARTMENTS

Under the marketing concept, all departments need to "think customer" and work together to satisfy customer needs and expectations. Yet departments define company problems and goals from their own viewpoints, so conflicts of interest and communications problems are unavoidable. The marketing vice president or the CMO must usually work through persuasion rather than through authority to coordinate the company's internal marketing activities and coordinate marketing with finance, operations, and other company functions to serve the customer.[18]

Many companies now focus on key processes rather than on departments because departmental organization can be a barrier to smooth performance. They appoint process leaders, who manage cross-disciplinary teams that include marketing and salespeople. Marketers thus may have a solid-line responsibility to their teams and a dotted-line responsibility to the marketing department.

Given the goal of providing positive customer experiences from start to finish, all areas of the organization need to work effectively together. In particular, because of the growing importance of "Big Data," marketers must work closely with those in the IT department to gain critical insights and updates.

## BUILDING A CREATIVE MARKETING ORGANIZATION

Many companies realize they're not yet really market and customer driven—they are product and sales driven. Transforming into a true market-driven company requires, among other actions: (1) developing a company-wide passion for customers; (2) organizing around customer segments instead of products; and (3) understanding customers through qualitative and quantitative research.

## The Marketing CEO

What steps can a CEO take to create a market- and customer-focused company?

1. **Convince senior management of the need to become customer focused.** The CEO personally exemplifies strong customer commitment and rewards those in the organization who do likewise. Former CEOs Jack Welch of GE and Lou Gerstner of IBM famously spent 100 days a year visiting customers in spite of their many strategic, financial, and administrative burdens.

2. **Appoint a senior marketing officer and marketing task force.** The marketing task force should include the CEO; C-level executives from sales, R&D, purchasing, manufacturing, finance, and human resources; and other key individuals.

3. **Get outside help and guidance.** Consulting firms have considerable experience helping companies adopt a marketing orientation.

4. **Change the company's reward measurement and system.** As long as purchasing and manufacturing are rewarded for keeping costs low, they will resist accepting some costs required to serve customers better. As long as finance focuses on short-term profit, it will oppose major investments designed to build satisfied, loyal customers.

5. **Hire strong marketing talent.** The company needs a strong chief marketing officer who not only manages the marketing department but also gains respect from and influence with the other C-level executives. A multidivisional company will benefit from establishing a strong corporate marketing department.

6. **Develop strong in-house marketing training programs.** The company should design well-crafted marketing training programs for corporate management, divisional general managers, marketing and sales personnel, manufacturing personnel, R&D personnel, and others. Many companies such as GE, Unilever, and Accenture have centralized training facilities to run such programs.

7. **Install a modern marketing planning system.** The planning format will require managers to think about the marketing environment, opportunities, competitive trends, and other forces. These managers then prepare strategies and sales-and-profit forecasts for specific products and segments and are accountable for performance.

8. **Establish an annual marketing excellence recognition program.** Business units that believe they've developed exemplary marketing plans should submit a description of their plans and results. Winning teams should be rewarded at a special ceremony and the plans disseminated to the other business units as "models of marketing thinking." Procter & Gamble, SABMiller, and Becton, Dickinson and Company follow this strategy.

9. **Shift from a department focus to a process-outcome focus.** After defining the fundamental business processes that determine its success, the company should appoint process leaders and cross-disciplinary teams to reengineer and implement these processes.

10. **Empower the employees.** Progressive companies encourage and reward their employees for coming up with new ideas and empower them to settle customer complaints to save the customer's business. IBM lets frontline employees spend as much as $5,000 to solve a customer problem on the spot.

---

The task is not easy, but the payoffs can be considerable. See "Marketing Insight: The Marketing CEO" for concrete actions a CEO can take to improve marketing capabilities.

Although it's *necessary* to be customer oriented, it's not *enough*. The organization must also be creative.[19] Companies today copy each others' advantages and strategies with increasing speed, making differentiation harder to achieve and lowering margins as firms become more alike. The only answer is to build a capability in strategic innovation and imagination. This capability comes from assembling tools, processes, skills, and measures that let the firm generate more and better new ideas than its competitors.[20] Companies also try to put together inspiring work spaces that help to stimulate new ideas and foster imagination.

Companies must watch trends and be ready to capitalize on them. Nestlé was late seeing the trend toward coffeehouses such as Starbucks. Coca-Cola was slow to pick up beverage trends toward fruit-flavored drinks such as Snapple, energy drinks such as Gatorade, and designer water brands. Market leaders can miss trends when they are risk averse, obsessed about protecting their existing markets and physical resources, and more interested in efficiency than innovation.[21]

# Socially Responsible Marketing

Effective internal marketing must be matched by a strong sense of ethics, values, and social responsibility.[22] Taking a more active, strategic role in corporate social responsibility is thought to benefit not just customers, employees, community, and the environment but also shareholders. Firms feel they also benefit in different ways, as Figure 23.4 illustrates.

**| Fig. 23.4 |**

## Rationale for Investing in Corporate Social Responsibility

Rationale for Investing in Corporate Social Responsibility

- Companies need to differentiate themselves. Companies with civic virtues will be preferred.
- Companies need a decision framework for facing daily requests for sponsorships, improved health coverage, injury prevention, environmental protection, and community contributions.
- Corporate heads and boards need to understand the social pressures and opportunities facing their companies.
- Companies need to build a bank of public goodwill to offset potential criticisms.
- Employees, investors, and partners will be more motivated and loyal.

The most admired—and most successful—companies in the world abide by high standards of business and marketing conduct that dictate serving people's interests, not only their own. Procter & Gamble has made "brand purpose" a key component of the company's marketing strategies. The company has launched a number of award-winning cause programs to support its brands, such as with Downy fabric softener's "Touch of Comfort," Tide laundry detergent's "Loads of Hope," and Secret deodorant's "Mean Stinks."[23] P&G is not alone, as the following demonstrates. [24]

## FIRMS OF ENDEARMENT

Researchers Raj Sisodia, David Wolfe, and Jag Sheth believe humanistic companies make great companies. They see "Firms of Endearment" as those with a culture of caring that serve the interests of their stakeholders, who are defined by the acronym SPICE: Society, Partners, Investors, Customers, and Employees. Sisodia and colleagues believe Firms of Endearment create a love affair with stakeholders. Their senior managers run an open-door policy, are passionate about customers, and earn modest compensation. They pay their employees more, relate more closely to a smaller group of excellent suppliers, and give back to the communities in which they work. They actually spend less on marketing as a percentage of sales yet earn greater profits because customers who love the company do most of the marketing. The authors see the 21st-century marketing paradigm as creating value for all stakeholders and becoming a beloved firm. Table 23.2 lists firms receiving top marks as Firms of Endearment from a sample of thousands of customers, employees, and suppliers.

## CORPORATE SOCIAL RESPONSIBILITY

Raising the level of socially responsible marketing calls for making a three-pronged attack that relies on proper legal, ethical, and social responsibility behavior. One company that puts social responsible marketing squarely at the center of all it does is Stonyfield Farm.[25]

| TABLE 23.2 | Top Firms of Endearment | | |
|---|---|---|---|
| Best Buy | BMW | CarMax | Caterpillar |
| Commerce Bank | Container Store | Costco | eBay |
| Google | Harley-Davidson | Honda | IDEO |
| IKEA | JetBlue | Johnson & Johnson | Jordan's Furniture |
| L.L.Bean | New Balance | Patagonia | Progressive Insurance |
| REI | Southwest | Starbucks | Timberland |
| Toyota | Trader Joe's | UPS | Wegmans |
| Whole Foods | | | |

**Source:** Raj Sisodia, David B. Wolfe, and Jag Sheth, *Firms of Endearment: How World-Class Companies Profit from Passion and Purpose* (Upper Saddle River, NJ: Wharton School Publishing, 2007), p. 16, © 2007. Printed and electronically reproduced by permission of Pearson Education, Inc., Upper Saddle River, New Jersey.

Procter & Gamble has embraced cause marketing programs, such as Tide laundry detergent's "Loads of Hope," to help its brands achieve their brand purposes.

**STONYFIELD FARM**   Stonyfield Farm was cofounded in 1983 by long-time "CE-Yo" Gary Hirshberg on the belief that there was a business opportunity in selling all-natural organic dairy products while "restoring the environment." The company's suppliers avoid the productivity practices of agribusiness, including the use of antibiotics, growth hormones, pesticides, and fertilizers. After calculating the amount of energy used to run its plant, Stonyfield decided to make an equivalent investment in environmental projects such as reforestation, wind farms, and the company's own anaerobic wastewater digester. The company has modified the plastic lids on its yogurt, saving about a million pounds of plastic a year, and added on-package messages about global warming, the perils of hormones, and genetically modified foods. It has also added cultures or dietary supplements to help the immune system fight off illness and makes low-fat versions of its products. Stonyfield donates 10 percent of profits "to efforts that help protect and restore the Earth." Although premium-priced, the brand still lacks the margins for big budget advertising campaigns and relies on sampling (such as at the Boston marathon), PR, word of mouth, and guerilla tactics instead. Its progressive business practices have not hurt its financial performance. Stonyfield is the number-three yogurt brand in the United States and has added smoothies, milk, frozen yogurt, and ice cream. Hirshberg, now just chairman of the company, has also launched a nonprofit foundation called "Climate Counts" that scores companies annually on the basis of their voluntary actions to reverse climate change. The goal is to spur corporate responsibility and inform consumers about which companies are more engaged.

## One New Apple Product Your Family Doesn't Need.

Just say "know" to
## genetically engineered apples.

Join millions in calling for national labeling of GMOs: www.justlabelit.org

**JUST LABEL IT!**
We have the right to know • justlabelit.org

Stonyfield Farm co-founder Gary Hirshberg is leading the charge in labeling products which use genetically modified organism (GMO) ingredients.

**LEGAL BEHAVIOR** Organizations must ensure every employee knows and observes relevant laws.[26] For example, it's illegal for salespeople to lie to consumers or mislead them about the advantages of buying a product. They may not offer bribes to purchasing agents or others influencing a B-to-B sale. Their statements must match advertising claims, and they may not obtain or use competitors' technical or trade secrets through bribery or industrial espionage. They must not disparage competitors or their products by suggesting things that are not true. Managers must make sure every sales representative knows the law and acts accordingly.

**ETHICAL BEHAVIOR**  Business practices come under attack because business situations routinely pose ethical dilemmas: It's not easy to draw a clear line between normal marketing practice and unethical behavior. Some issues can generate controversy or sharply divide critics, such as acceptable marketing to children.[27]

## ▌REGULATING FOOD AND BEVERAGE MARKETING TO CHILDREN

Amid pressure from regulators and the threat of lawsuits, food and beverage manufacturers have cut back on marketing their least healthful products to kids; developed new recipes to reduce calories, sodium, sugar, and fat in thousands of products; and made changes to place nutrition information on the front of the package. Some watch groups feel that is still not enough, and with childhood obesity an administration priority being addressed by First Lady Michelle Obama's "Let's Move!" and other programs, tight new government standards to further limit advertising to children and teens take effect in 2016. These standards require food marketed toward children ages 2 to 17 to make a "meaningful contribution" to a healthy diet by providing a certain amount of healthy items (fruits, vegetables, whole grains) and limiting unhealthy items (sodium, sugar, and saturated fat). Later regulation was proposed to ban in-school advertising for foods high in sugar, fat, and salt and to eliminate the tax deductions of advertising and marketing expenses for food and marketing companies if the products are of "poor nutritional quality" and marketed to kids. Although proposed regulations often change a great deal before taking effect, there will be increased government scrutiny of the way food and beverages are marketed to children.

Of course, certain business practices are clearly unethical or illegal. These include bribery, theft of trade secrets, false and deceptive advertising, exclusive dealing and tying agreements, quality or safety defects, false warranties, inaccurate labeling, price-fixing or undue discrimination, and barriers to entry and predatory competition.

Companies must adopt and disseminate a written code of ethics, build a company tradition of ethical behavior, and hold their people fully responsible for observing ethical and legal guidelines. In the past, a disgruntled customer might bad-mouth an unethical or poorly performing firm to 12 other people; today, via the Internet, he or she can reach thousands. The general distrust of companies among U.S. consumers is evident in research showing the percentage of those who view corporations unfavorably is almost 40 percent.[28]

**SOCIAL RESPONSIBILITY BEHAVIOR**  Marketers must exercise their social conscience in specific dealings with customers and stakeholders. Some top-rated companies for corporate social responsibility are Whole Foods, Walt Disney, Coca-Cola, Johnson & Johnson, and Google.[29]

Increasingly, people want information about a company's record on social and environmental responsibility to help them decide which companies to buy from, invest in, and work for.[30] Communicating corporate social responsibility can be a challenge. Once a firm touts an environmental initiative, it can become a target for criticism. Often, the more committed a company is to sustainability and environmental protection, the more dilemmas can arise, as Green Mountain Coffee Roasters has found.[31]

Source: ASSOCIATED PRESS

A firm that prides itself on its sustainability efforts, Green Mountain Coffee Roasters is committed to reducing any adverse environmental impact of its popular K-cups.

## ▌GREEN MOUNTAIN COFFEE ROASTERS

Vermont-based Green Mountain Coffee Roasters prides itself on sustainability efforts that have helped it become one of the fastest-selling coffee brands around. The company supports local and global communities by offsetting 100 percent of its greenhouse gas emissions, investing in sustainably grown coffee, and allocating at least 5 percent of its pre-tax profits to social and environmental projects. Through its C.A.F.E. Time or Community Action for Employees programs, employees are encouraged to volunteer as many as 52 hours annually of company-paid service to give back to local organizations and communities. All these activities help Green Mountain fulfill its purpose statement to "create the ultimate coffee experience in every life we touch, from tree to cup—transforming the way the world views business." The firm's 2006 purchase of Keurig and its popular single-cup brewing system posed a quandary, though: The K-Cups used with the Keurig brewing system were made of totally nonrecyclable plastic and foil. Although disposal makes up only about 5 percent of their total environmental impact—more significant effects are related to brewer use, coffee cultivation, and product packaging—Green Mountain has engaged in extensive R&D and explored numerous partnerships to find a more environmentally sound solution, vowing to make K-Cup packs recyclable by 2020 while also addressing their other environmental effects in different ways.

Corporate philanthropy also can pose dilemmas. Merck, DuPont, Walmart, and Bank of America have each donated $100 million or even more to charities in a year. Yet good deeds can be overlooked—even resented—if the company is seen as exploitive or fails to live up to a "good guys" image. Some critics worry that cause marketing or "consumption philanthropy" may replace virtuous actions with less thoughtful consumer buying, reduce emphasis on real solutions, or deflect attention from the fact that markets may create many social problems to begin with.[32]

SUSTAINABILITY *Sustainability*—the ability to meet humanity's needs without harming future generations—now tops many corporate agendas. Major corporations outline in great detail how they are trying to improve the long-term impact of their actions on communities and the environment. Coca-Cola, AT&T, and DuPont have even installed Chief Sustainability Officers.[33]

As one sustainability consultant put it, "There is a triple bottom line—people, planet, and profit—and the people part of the equation must come first. Sustainability means more than being eco-friendly, it also means you are in it for the long haul."[34] Corporate actions toward achieving sustainability take all forms. For example, Whole Foods, Wegmans, Target, and Walmart no longer sell fish caught in areas subject to overfishing or in a manner likely to harm other marine life or habitats.[35]

Sustainability ratings exist, but there is no consistent agreement about what metrics are appropriate.[36] One comprehensive study used 11 factors to assemble a list of the top 100 sustainable corporations in the world: energy, water, $CO_2$, and waste productivity; leadership diversity; CEO-to-average-worker pay; taxes paid; sustainability leadership; sustainability pay link; innovation capacity; and transparency. Some notable global firms in the top 10 include Statoil (Norway), Adidas (Germany), and Westpac Banking (Australia).[37]

Some feel companies that score well on sustainability exhibit high-quality management in that "they tend to be more strategically nimble and better equipped to compete in the complex, high-velocity, global environment."[38] Consumer interest is also creating market opportunities, such as for organic products (see "Marketing Insight: The Rise of Organic").

---

**marketing insight**

# The Rise of Organic

Organic and natural products have become a strong presence in many food and beverage categories. Caster & Pollux's success with organic and natural pet foods led to its distribution in major specialty retail chains such as PETCO. All-organic Honest Tea grew 50 percent a year after its founding in 1998; the firm sold 40 percent of the business to Coca-Cola in 2008. Annie's Home Grown started as an organic farm in Connecticut in 1989, went public in 2012 with an IPO raising $95 million, and was bought by General Mills for $820 million in 2014.

Many organic and natural products ground their brand positioning in sustainability and social values. Started in 1990 by avid cyclist Gary Erickson and named to honor his father, CLIF Bar set out to offer a better-tasting energy bar with wholesome, organic ingredients. CLIF Bar relies on biodiesel-powered vehicles, supports the construction of farmer- and Native American–owned wind farms through carbon offsets, and is active in its local community.

Given their premium prices and profitability, organic food and beverage products have also become big business. Erickson turned down a $120 million offer from Quaker Oats in 2000 so his firm could remain private, in part so he could continue its focus on eco-friendly practices. Other small firms have not followed suit, however, and major corporations like Cargill, ConAgra, Kraft, and M&M Mars now control much of the nation's organic food industry. Farms with annual sales of $500,000 or more account for nearly 80 percent of all organic sales, even though such farms make up only 12.5 percent of all farms.

Many nonfood companies are embracing organic ingredients to avoid chemicals and pesticides. Apparel and other nonfood items make up the second-fastest-growing category of the organic products industry. Organic nonfood grew to $2.8 billion in 2013—now 8 percent of the $35.1 billion organic products industry. Organic cotton grown by farmers who fight boll weevils with ladybugs, weed crops by hand, and use manure for fertilizer has become a hot product at retail.

**Sources:** Liz Webber, "USDA Survey Reveals Extent of Big Organic," *Supermarket News*, October 18, 2012; Stephanie Strom, "Has 'Organic' Been Oversized?," *New York Times*, July 7, 2012; George Avalos, "Annie's CEO Aims to Make Profit on Organic Mission," *Oakland Tribune*, June 24, 2012; Michelle Wu, "A Company Fueled by Athletes' Sweat," *Wall Street Journal*, March 22, 2010; Jessica Shambora, "The Honest Tea Guys Look Back," *Fortune*, July 26, 2010; Megan Johnston, "Hard Sell for a Soft Fabric," *Forbes*, October 30, 2006, pp. 73–80. See also Ram Bezawada and Koen Pauwels, "What Is Special about Marketing Organic Products? How Organic Assortment, Price, and Promotions Drive Retailer Performance," *Journal of Marketing* 77 (January 2013), pp. 31–51.

Timberland has adopted practices to protect the environment across a broad range of its corporate activities.

Heightened interest in sustainability has also unfortunately resulted in *greenwashing,* which gives products the appearance of being environmentally friendly without living up to that promise. One study revealed that half the labels on allegedly green products focus on an eco-friendly benefit (such as recycled content) while omitting information about significant environmental drawbacks (such as manufacturing intensity or transportation costs).[39] Stonyfield Farm's cofounder Gary Hirshberg is leading the charge with the "Just Label It!" campaign to provide more useful information on labels about the use of GMO (genetically modified organism) ingredients.[40]

Because insincere firms have jumped on the green bandwagon, consumers bring a healthy skepticism to environmental claims. They are also unwilling to sacrifice product performance and quality, nor are they necessarily willing to pay a price premium for green products.[41] Unfortunately, green products can be more expensive because ingredients are costly and transportation costs are higher for lower shipping volumes. As Chapter 3 described, when the recession hit, sales of many green household products slid. Sales of the premium-priced Clorox Green Works line, for example, dropped from more than $100 million in 2008 to $60 million five years later.[42]

## SOCIALLY RESPONSIBLE BUSINESS MODELS

Companies that innovate solutions and values in a socially responsible way are most likely to succeed.[43] Consider Timberland.[44]

**TIMBERLAND**   Timberland, the maker of rugged boots, shoes, clothing, and gear, targets individuals who live, work, and play outdoors, so it only makes sense to do whatever it takes to protect the environment. The company's actions have blazed trails for green companies around the world. Its revolutionary initiatives include putting a "nutrition label" on its shoeboxes, measuring the brand's environmental footprint—from renewable energy used in its facilities to recycled, organic, and renewable materials in its products to trees planted around the globe. Timberland also introduced a new line of shoes called Earthkeepers, which incorporates organic cotton, recycled PET, and recycled rubber (for the soles) and later expanded across multiple Timberland product categories. Outside of product, the brand has made a major commitment to reforestation, with nearly five million trees planted worldwide. With sales topping $1.6 billion in 2013, its business accomplishments prove that socially and environmentally responsible companies can be successful.

Companies such as The Body Shop, Working Assets, and Smith & Hawken are also giving social responsibility a more prominent role, as has Newman's Own. Late actor Paul Newman's homemade salad dressing grew into a huge business. Newman's Own brand also includes pasta sauce, salsa, popcorn, and lemonade and is now sold in 15 overseas markets. The company has given away all its profits and royalties after tax—more than $400 million so far—to thousands of educational and charitable programs worldwide, including the Hole in the Wall Gang camps Newman created for children with serious illnesses.[45]

Corporate philanthropy as a whole is on the rise. After years of steady growth, even during a recession, $16.8 billion in cash and in-kind support was given in 2013.[46] In addition to these contributions, more firms are coming to believe corporate social responsibility in the form of cause marketing and employee volunteerism programs is not just the "right thing" but also the "smart thing to do."[47]

## CAUSE-RELATED MARKETING

Many firms blend corporate social responsibility initiatives with marketing activities.[48] **Cause-related marketing** links the firm's contributions toward a designated cause to customers' engaging directly or indirectly in revenue-producing transactions with the firm. Cause marketing is part of *corporate societal marketing (CSM),* which Minette Drumwright and Patrick Murphy define as marketing efforts "that have at least one noneconomic objective related to social welfare and use the resources of the company and/or of its partners."[49] Drumwright and Murphy also include traditional and strategic philanthropy and volunteerism in CSM.

One study showed that 90 percent of U.S. consumers have a more positive image of, are more loyal to, and trust more a company that supports a cause, and 54 percent have bought a product because it was associated with a cause.[50] After describing Dawn's successful cause marketing program, we next review pros and cons of such programs and some important guidelines that apply to them.[51]

**DAWN** Procter & Gamble's Dawn, the top dishwashing liquid in the United States, has an unusual side benefit—it can clean birds caught in oil spills. A report by the U.S. Fish and Wildlife Service called Dawn "the only bird-cleaning agent that is recommended because it removes oil from feathers; is non-toxic; and does not leave a residue." A Web site launched in 2006, www.DawnSavesWildlife.com, drew 130,000 people who formed virtual groups to encourage friends and others to stop gas and oil leaks from their cars. After the catastrophic BP oil spill in 2010, P&G donated thousands of bottles of Dawn as well as placing a code on bottles and donating $1 to Gulf wildlife causes for each code customers activated, eventually totaling $500,000. To date, the company has donated more than 50,000 bottles of Dawn to help rescue and release 75,000 animals harmed by oil pollution. Teaming up with the Marine Mammal Center and International Bird Rescue, P&G pledged $1 million for 2014, also launching the premiere of a seven-part documentary series narrated by actor Rob Lowe.

**CAUSE-MARKETING BENEFITS AND COSTS** A successful cause-marketing program can improve social welfare, create differentiated brand positioning, build strong consumer bonds, enhance the company's public image, create a reservoir of goodwill, boost internal morale and galvanize employees, drive sales, and increase the firm's market value.[52] Consumers may develop a strong, unique bond with the firm that transcends normal marketplace transactions.

Specifically, from a branding point of view, cause marketing can (1) build brand awareness, (2) enhance brand image, (3) establish brand credibility, (4) evoke brand feelings, (5) create a sense of brand community, and (6) elicit brand engagement.[53] It has a particularly interested audience in socially minded 18- to 34-year-old Millennial consumers who, not surprisingly, are more likely than the general population to use social media to learn about cause activities and engage with companies about them.[54]

Cause-related marketing could backfire, however, if consumers question the link between the product and the cause or see the firm as self-serving and exploitive.[55] Problems can also arise if consumers do not think a company is consistent and sufficiently responsible in all its behavior, as happened to KFC.[56]

**KFC** KFC's "Buckets for the Cure" program was to donate 50 cents to the Susan G. Komen for the Cure Foundation for every $5 "pink" bucket of fried chicken purchased over a one-month period. It was slotted to be the single biggest corporate donation ever to fund breast cancer research—more than $8.5 million. One problem: At virtually the same time, KFC also launched its Double Down sandwich with two pieces of fried chicken, bacon, and cheese. Critics immediately pointed out that KFC was selling a food item with excessively high calories, fat, and sodium that contributed to obesity. On the Susan G. Komen site, being overweight was flagged for increasing the risk of breast cancer by 30 percent to 60 percent in postmenopausal women, also leaving the foundation open to criticism over the partnership.

Source: © National Geographic Image Collection/Alamy

P&G has created a series of cause-related activities around its Dove dishwashing liquid, taking advantage of its unusual side benefit to clean birds caught in oil spills.

U2's Bono has been the spokesperson for the PRODUCT(RED) partnership, whereby major brands donate proceeds from sales of designated "red" products to fight HIV/AIDS in Africa.

To avoid backlash, some firms take a soft-sell approach to their cause marketing.[57] One interesting recent cause program is the PRODUCT(RED) campaign.[58]

**PRODUCT(RED)**   The highly publicized launch of PRODUCT(RED) in 2006, championed by U2 singer and activist Bono and Bobby Shriver, chairman of DATA, raised awareness and money for the Global Fund by teaming with some of the world's most iconic brands—American Express cards, Motorola phones, Converse sneakers, Gap T-shirts, Apple iPods, and Emporio Armani sunglasses—to produce (RED)-branded products. As much as 50 percent of the profits from sales of these products go to the Global Fund to help women and children affected by HIV/AIDS in Africa. Each company that becomes PRODUCT(RED) places its logo in the "embrace" signified by the parentheses and is "elevated to the power of red." Although some critics felt the PRODUCT(RED) project was either misguided or overmarketed, more than $275 million has been donated to date, an enormous increase over donations to the Global Fund prior before the program launch. Many well-known brands have joined the cause since then, such as Bank of America, Beats by Dr. Dre, Microsoft, and Starbucks.

**DESIGNING A CAUSE PROGRAM**  Firms must make a number of decisions in designing and implementing a cause-marketing program, such as how many and which cause(s) to choose and how to brand the cause program. "Marketing Memo: Making a Difference: Top 10 Tips for Cause Branding" provides some tips from a top cause-marketing firm.

Some experts believe the positive impact of cause-related marketing is diluted if a company is only occasionally engaged in a number of causes. Cathy Chizauskas, Gillette's director of civic affairs, states: "When you're spreading out your giving in fifty-dollar to one-thousand-dollar increments, no one knows what you are doing.... It doesn't make much of a splash."[59] Many companies focus on one or a few main causes to simplify execution and maximize impact. McDonald's has focused on children and family health and well-being through three major programs:[60]

- Ronald McDonald Houses in 35 countries and regions offer more than 8,000 rooms each night to families needing support while their child is in the hospital, saving them a total of $657 million annually in hotel costs.
- Ronald McDonald Family Rooms in 23 countries help 4,000 families each day with a place to rest and regroup at the hospital next to their sick child.
- Fifty-two Ronald McDonald Care Mobiles in nine countries provide neighborhood on-site medical care for children.

Limiting support to a single cause, however, may limit the pool of consumers or other stakeholders who can transfer positive feelings from the cause to the firm. Many popular causes also already have numerous corporate sponsors. More than 130 companies, including American Airlines, Dell, Ford, Georgia Pacific, Merck, Samsung, and Walgreens, have become corporate partners of Susan G. Komen for the Cure.[61] Thus, a brand may find itself overlooked in a sea of symbolic pink ribbons.

## marketing memo

# Making a Difference: Top 10 Tips for Cause Branding

Cone, a Boston-based strategic communications agency specializing in cause branding and corporate responsibility, offers these tips for developing authentic and substantive programs:

1. *Select a focus area that aligns with your mission, goals, and organization.*

2. *Evaluate your institutional "will" and resources.* If you, your employees, and other allies don't believe or invest in your organization's cause, neither will your audience.

3. *Analyze your competitors' cause positioning.* There are few remaining wide, open spaces, but this may help you locate a legitimate societal need or an untapped element within a more crowded space that you can own.

4. *Choose your partners carefully.* Look for alignment in values, mission, and will. Carefully outline roles and responsibilities. Set your sights on a multiyear, sustainable relationship with annual measurement of accomplishments for both partners.

5. *Don't underestimate the name of your program—it's key to the identity of your campaign.* Develop a few words that say exactly what you do and create a visual identity that is simple yet memorable. The Avon Breast Cancer Crusade, American Heart Association's Go Red for Women, and Target Take Charge of Education are good examples.

6. *To create a sustainable and effective program, start by developing a cross-functional strategy team.* Include representatives from the office of the CEO, public affairs, human resources, marketing, public and community relations, research/measurement, and volunteer and program management, among others. If you're in silos, you will spend too much valuable time building bridges to other departments to get the real work done.

7. *Leverage both your assets and those of your partner(s) to bring the program to life.* Assets may include volunteers, cash and in-kind donations, special events, in-store presence, partner resources, and marketing/advertising support. And, remember, emotion is one of your greatest assets. It can help you to connect with your audience and differentiate your organization in a crowded marketplace.

8. *Communicate through every possible channel.* Craft compelling words *and* visuals because stirring images can penetrate the heart. Then take your messages beyond traditional media outlets and become multidimensional! Think special events, Web sites, workshops, PSAs, expert spokespersons, and even celebrity endorsements.

9. *Go local.* National programs reach the "grass tops," but true transformation begins at the grassroots. Engage citizens/volunteers through hands-on activities at local events, cause promotions, and fund-raisers.

10. *Innovate.* True cause leaders constantly evolve their programs to add energy, new engagement opportunities, and content to remain relevant and to build sustainability.

**Sources:** Carol C. Cone, "Top 10 Tips for Cause Branding," www.coneinc.com/10-tips-cause-branding; see also Carol L. Cone, Mark A. Feldman, and Alison T. DaSilva, "Cause and Effects," *Harvard Business Review*, July 2003, 95–101.

Source: Richard Sennott/ZUMAPRESS/Newscom

McDonald's has focused its cause marketing efforts on Ronald McDonald House Charities which includes its Ronald McDonald Care Mobiles to provide local medical care for children.

Opportunities may be greater with "orphan causes"—diseases that afflict fewer than 200,000 people.[62] Another option is overlooked diseases; pancreatic cancer is the fourth-deadliest form of cancer behind skin, lung, and breast yet has received little or no corporate support. Diabetes is linked to the deaths of many more people than breast cancer but receives significantly less funding support. Even major killers such as prostate cancer for men and heart disease for women have been relatively neglected compared to breast cancer, though some firms have begun to fill the void. The American Heart Association launched a "Go Red for Women" program, with a red dress symbol and a national "Wear Red Day" sponsored by Macy's, to draw attention from corporations and others to a disease that kills roughly 12 times as many women a year as breast cancer.[63]

Most firms choose causes that fit their corporate or brand image and matter to their employees and shareholders.[64] LensCrafters' Give the Gift of Sight program—rebranded OneSight after the company was purchased by the Italian firm Luxottica—is a family of charitable vision-care programs providing free vision screenings, eye exams, and glasses to millions of needy people in North America and developing countries around the world. Luxottica pays most of the overhead, so more than 90 percent of all donations goes directly to fund programming.[65] Barnum's Animal Crackers launched a campaign to raise awareness of endangered species and help protect the Asian tiger. Issuing special edition packaging and collaborating with the World Wildlife Fund, the Nabisco brand saw a "healthy lift in sales."[66] Here is an example of a firm that used cause marketing in part to successfully build a new business.[67]

**TOMS**  Although Blake Mycoskie did not win the reality show contest *Amazing Race*, his return trip to Argentina in 2006 sparked a desire to start a business to help the scores of kids he saw who suffered for one simple reason—they lacked shoes. Shoeless children incur a health risk but are also disadvantaged by often being barred from school. Thus was born TOMS shoes, named to suggest "a better tomorrow," with a pledge to donate a pair of shoes to a needy child for each pair sold. Picked up by stores like Whole Foods, Nordstrom, and Neiman Marcus and also sold online, TOMS shoes are based on the rope-soled, canvas-topped *alpargata* footwear of Argentina and can now be found on the feet of more than 1 million kids in developing countries. The donations were good marketing too. The firm has garnered heaps of publicity, and AT&T and American Express even featured Mycoskie in a commercial. TOMS also sponsored "A Day Without Shoes" promotion to help people imagine what life would be like shoeless. Some critics feel the brand is treating a symptom but not really addressing the root economic problem and that it could even be undermining the local shoe economy. Nevertheless, it has moved into eyewear with the same business model and is estimated to earn $250 million in revenues annually while giving away literally millions of shoes and now eyeglasses.

## SOCIAL MARKETING

Cause-related marketing supports a cause. **Social marketing** by nonprofit or government organizations *furthers* a cause, such as "say no to drugs" or "exercise more and eat better."[68] Some notable global social marketing successes are:

- A mass media campaign to promote oral rehydration therapy in Honduras significantly decreased deaths from diarrhea in children under 5.

TOMS shoes puts cause marketing at the core of what it does, donating a pair of shoes to underprivileged children in developing countries for each pair it sells.

*Source: Handout/MCT/Newscom*

- Social marketers created booths in marketplaces where Ugandan midwives sold contraceptives at affordable prices.
- Population Communication Services created and promoted two extremely popular songs in Latin America, "Stop" and "When We Are Together," to help young adults learn sexual responsibility.
- The National Heart, Lung, and Blood Institute successfully raised awareness in the U.S. about cholesterol and high blood pressure, which helped significantly reduce deaths.

Different types of organizations conduct social marketing in the United States. Government agencies include the Centers for Disease Control and Prevention, Departments of Health, Social, and Human Services, Department of Transportation, and the U.S. Environmental Protection Agency. The literally hundreds of nonprofit organizations include the American Red Cross, the United Way, and the American Cancer Society.

Choosing the right goal or objective for a social marketing program is critical. Should a family-planning campaign focus on abstinence or birth control? Should a campaign to fight air pollution focus on ride sharing or mass transit? Table 23.3 illustrates the range of possible objectives.

While social marketing uses a number of different tactics to achieve its goals, the planning process follows many of the same steps as for traditional products and services (see Table 23.4).[69] Some key success factors for changing behavior include:[70]

- Choose target markets that are most ready to respond.
- Promote a single, doable behavior in clear, simple terms.
- Explain the benefits in compelling terms.
- Make it easy to adopt the behavior.
- Develop attention-grabbing messages and media.
- Consider an education-entertainment approach.

One organization that has accomplished many of these goals through the application of modern marketing practices is the World Wildlife Fund.[71]

........................................................................................................................

## ▌WORLD WILDLIFE FUND   The World Wildlife Fund (WWF) is a Washington, D.C.-based nonprofit

with 1.2 million members in the United States and 5 million globally. Its annual budget does not allow for lavish marketing, so it relies primarily on creative direct marketing to solicit contributions. The organization sends about 36 million pieces of eco-friendly mail in the United States each year, garnering 65 percent of its membership revenue in the process. It has an award-winning Web site, is active on Facebook and Twitter, and earns revenue through partnerships with a host of firms including Avon, Disney, The Gap, and Build-A-Bear Workshop. Partnerships sometimes include joint marketing programs; Coca-Cola donated $2 million for a campaign to help create safe areas for polar bears in Canada and other Arctic regions. WWF also tackles important wildlife issues head on, as with its multimedia anti-poaching campaign, which used billboards, print ads, public service announcements, and online posters with the tagline "Stop Wildlife Crime—It's Dead Serious."

........................................................................................................................

| TABLE 23.3 | Some Possible Social Marketing Program Objectives |
|---|---|

**Cognitive Campaigns**

- Explain the nutritional values of different foods.
- Demonstrate the importance of conservation.

**Action Campaigns**

- Attract people for mass immunization.
- Motivate people to vote "yes" on a certain issue.
- Inspire people to donate blood.
- Motivate women to receive a Pap test.

**Behavioral Campaigns**

- Demotivate cigarette smoking.
- Demotivate use of hard drugs.
- Demotivate excessive alcohol consumption.

**Value Campaigns**

- Alter ideas about abortion.
- Change attitudes of bigoted people.

| TABLE 23.4 | The Social Marketing Planning Process |
|---|---|

**Where Are We?**

- Choose program focus
- Identify campaign purpose
- Conduct an analysis of strengths, weaknesses, opportunities, and threats (SWOT)
- Review past and similar efforts

**Where Do We Want to Go?**

- Select target audiences
- Set objectives and goals
- Analyze target audiences and the competition

**How Will We Get There?**

- Product: Design the market offering
- Price: Manage costs of behavior change
- Distribution: Make the product available
- Communications: Create messages and choose media

**How Will We Stay on Course?**

- Develop a plan for evaluation and monitoring
- Establish budgets and find funding sources
- Complete an implementation plan

Social marketing programs are complex; they take time and may require phased programs or actions. There were many steps involved in curbing the prevalence of smoking: release of cancer reports, labeling of cigarettes as harmful, bans on cigarette advertising, education about secondary smoke effects, bans on smoking in restaurants and planes, increased taxes on cigarettes to pay for antismoking campaigns, and states' suits against tobacco companies.

Social marketing organizations should evaluate program success in terms of their objectives, measuring criteria like incidence of adoption, speed of adoption, continuance of adoption, low cost per unit of adoption, and absence of counterproductive consequences.

In addition to its popular Christmas ads featuring playful animated polar bears, Coca-Cola also partners with the World Wildlife Fund to protect real polar bears in their native regions.

Source: ASSOCIATED PRESS

# Marketing Implementation and Control

Table 23.5 summarizes the characteristics of a great marketing company, great not for what it is but for what it does. Great marketing companies know the best marketers thoughtfully and creatively devise marketing plans and then bring them to life. Marketing implementation and control are critical to making sure marketing plans have their intended results year after year.

## MARKETING IMPLEMENTATION

**Marketing implementation** is the process that turns marketing plans into action assignments and ensures they accomplish the plan's stated objectives.[72] A brilliant strategic marketing plan counts for little if not implemented properly. Strategy addresses the *what* and *why* of marketing activities; implementation addresses the *who, where, when,* and *how.* They are closely related: One layer of strategy implies certain tactical implementation assignments at a lower level. For example, top management's strategic decision to "harvest" a product must be translated into specific actions and assignments.

Companies today are striving to make their marketing operations more efficient and their return on marketing investment more measurable (see Chapter 4). Marketing costs can amount to as much as a quarter of a company's total operating budget. Marketers need better templates for marketing processes, better management of marketing assets, and better allocation of marketing resources.

Marketing resource management (MRM) software provides a set of Web-based applications that automate and integrate project management, campaign management, budget management, asset management, brand management, customer relationship management, and knowledge management. The knowledge management component consists of process templates, how-to wizards, and best practices. Software packages can provide what some have called *desktop marketing,* giving marketers information and decision structures on computer dashboards. MRM software lets marketers improve spending and investment decisions, bring new products to market more quickly, and reduce decision time and costs.

## MARKETING CONTROL

*Marketing control* is the process by which firms assess the effects of their marketing activities and programs and make necessary changes and adjustments. Table 23.6 lists four types of needed marketing control: annual-plan control, profitability control, efficiency control, and strategic control.

| TABLE 23.5 | Characteristics of a Great Marketing Company |
|---|---|

- The company selects target markets in which it enjoys superior advantages and exits or avoids markets where it is intrinsically weak.
- Virtually all the company's employees and departments are customer- and market-minded.
- There is a good working relationship between marketing, R&D, and manufacturing.
- There is a good working relationship between marketing, sales, and customer service.
- The company has installed incentives designed to lead to the right behaviors.
- The company continuously builds and tracks customer satisfaction and loyalty.
- The company manages a value delivery system in partnership with strong suppliers and distributors.
- The company is skilled in building its brand name(s) and image.
- The company is flexible in meeting customers' varying requirements.

| TABLE 23.6 | Types of Marketing Control | | |
| --- | --- | --- | --- |
| **Type of Control** | **Prime Responsibility** | **Purpose of Control** | **Approaches** |
| I. Annual-plan control | Top management<br>Middle management | To examine whether the planned results are being achieved | • Sales analysis<br>• Market share analysis<br>• Sales-to-expense ratios<br>• Financial analysis<br>• Market-based scorecard analysis |
| II. Profitability control | Marketing controller | To examine where the company is making and losing money | Profitability by:<br>• product<br>• territory<br>• customer<br>• segment<br>• trade channel<br>• order size |
| III. Efficiency control | Line and staff management<br>Marketing controller | To evaluate and improve the spending efficiency and impact of marketing expenditures | Efficiency of:<br>• sales force<br>• advertising<br>• sales promotion<br>• distribution |
| IV. Strategic control | Top management<br>Marketing auditor | To examine whether the company is pursuing its best opportunities with respect to markets, products, and channels | • Marketing effectiveness rating instrument<br>• Marketing audit<br>• Marketing excellence review<br>• Company ethical and social responsibility review |

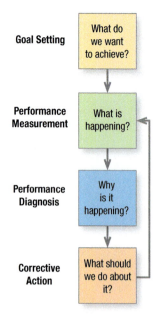

| Fig. 23.5 |

The Control Process

**ANNUAL-PLAN CONTROL** Annual-plan control ensures the company achieves the sales, profits, and other goals established in its annual plan. At its heart is management by objectives (see Figure 23.5). First, management sets monthly or quarterly goals. Second, it monitors performance in the marketplace. Third, management determines the causes of serious performance deviations. Fourth, it takes corrective action to close gaps between goals and performance.

This control model applies to all levels of the organization. Top management sets annual sales and profit goals; each product manager, regional district manager, sales manager, and sales rep is committed to attaining specified levels of sales and costs. Each period, top management reviews and interprets the results. Marketers today have better marketing metrics for measuring the performance of marketing plans (see Table 23.7 for some samples).[73] Four tools for the purpose are sales analysis, market share analysis, marketing expense-to-sales analysis, and financial analysis. The chapter appendix outlines them in detail.

**PROFITABILITY CONTROL** Companies should measure the profitability of their products, territories, customer groups, segments, trade channels, and order sizes to help determine whether to expand, reduce, or eliminate any products or marketing activities. The chapter appendix shows how to conduct and interpret a marketing profitability analysis.

**EFFICIENCY CONTROL** Suppose a profitability analysis reveals the company is earning poor profits in certain products, territories, or markets. Are there more efficient ways to manage the sales force, advertising, sales promotion, and distribution?

Some companies have established a *marketing controller* position to work out of the controller's office but specialize in improving marketing efficiency. These marketing controllers examine adherence to profit plans, help prepare brand managers' budgets, measure the efficiency of promotions, analyze media

| TABLE 23.7 | Marketing Metrics |
| --- | --- |

**Sales Metrics**

- Sales growth
- Market share
- Sales from new products

**Customer Readiness to Buy Metrics**

- Awareness
- Preference
- Purchase intention
- Trial rate
- Repurchase rate

**Customer Metrics**

- Customer complaints
- Customer satisfaction
- Ratio of promoters to detractors
- Customer acquisition costs
- New-customer gains
- Customer losses
- Customer churn
- Retention rate
- Customer lifetime value
- Customer equity
- Customer profitability
- Return on customer

**Distribution Metrics**

- Number of outlets
- Share in shops handling
- Weighted distribution
- Distribution gains
- Average stock volume (value)
- Stock cover in days
- Out-of-stock frequency
- Share of shelf
- Average sales per point of sale

**Communication Metrics**

- Spontaneous (unaided) brand awareness
- Top-of-mind brand awareness
- Prompted (aided) brand awareness
- Spontaneous (unaided) advertising awareness
- Prompted (aided) advertising awareness
- Effective reach
- Effective frequency
- Gross rating points (GRP)
- Response rate

production costs, evaluate customer and geographic profitability, and educate marketing staff on the financial implications of marketing decisions.

**STRATEGIC CONTROL** Each company should periodically reassess its strategic approach to the marketplace with a good marketing audit. Companies can also perform marketing excellence reviews and ethical/social responsibility reviews.

***The Marketing Audit*** The average U.S. corporation loses half its customers in five years, half its employees in four years, and half its investors in less than one year. Clearly, this points to some weaknesses. Companies that discover weaknesses should undertake a thorough study known as a marketing audit.[74]

A **marketing audit** is a comprehensive, systematic, independent, and periodic examination of a company's or business unit's marketing environment, objectives, strategies, and activities, with a view to determining problem areas and opportunities and recommending a plan of action to improve the company's marketing performance.

Let's examine the marketing audit's four characteristics:

1. ***Comprehensive***—The marketing audit covers all the major marketing activities of a business, not just a few trouble spots as in a functional audit. Although functional audits are useful, they sometimes mislead management. Excessive sales force turnover, for example, could be a symptom not of poor sales force training or compensation but of weak company products and promotion. A comprehensive marketing audit usually is more effective in locating the real source of problems.

2. ***Systematic***—The marketing audit is an orderly examination of the organization's macro- and micromarketing environments, marketing objectives and strategies, marketing systems, and specific activities. It identifies the most-needed improvements and incorporates them into a corrective-action plan with short- and long-run steps.

3. *Independent*—Self-audits, in which managers rate their own operations, lack objectivity and independence. The 3M Company has made good use of a corporate auditing office, which provides marketing audit services to divisions on request.[75] Usually, however, outside consultants bring the necessary objectivity, broad experience in a number of industries, familiarity with the industry being audited, and undivided time and attention.

4. *Periodic*—Firms typically initiate marketing audits only after failing to review their marketing operations during good times, with resulting problems. A periodic marketing audit can benefit companies in good health as well as those in trouble.

A marketing audit starts with agreement between the company officer(s) and the marketing auditor(s) on the audit's objectives and time frame and a detailed plan of who is to be asked what questions. The cardinal rule for marketing auditors is: Don't rely solely on company managers for data and opinions. Ask customers, dealers, and other outside groups. Many companies don't really know how their customers and dealers see them, nor do they fully understand customer needs.

The marketing audit examines six major components of the company's marketing situation. Table 23.8 lists the major questions.

| TABLE 23.8 | Components of a Marketing Audit |
|---|---|

**Part I. Marketing Environment Audit**
**Macroenvironment**

| A. Demographic | What major demographic developments and trends pose opportunities or threats to this company? What actions has the company taken in response to these developments and trends? |
|---|---|
| B. Economic | What major developments in income, prices, savings, and credit will affect the company? What actions has the company been taking in response to these developments and trends? |
| C. Environmental | What is the outlook for the cost and availability of natural resources and energy needed by the company? What concerns have been expressed about the company's role in pollution and conservation, and what steps has the company taken? |
| D. Technological | What major changes are occurring in product and process technology? What is the company's position in these technologies? What major generic substitutes might replace this product? What are the digital implications of how the company conducts its business and its marketing? |
| E. Political | What changes in laws and regulations might affect marketing strategy and tactics? What is happening in the areas of sustainability, equal employment opportunity, product safety, advertising, price control, and so forth, that affects marketing strategy? |
| F. Cultural | What is the public's attitude toward business and toward the company's products? What changes in customer lifestyles and values might affect the company? |

**Task Environment**

| A. Markets | What is happening to market size, growth, geographical distribution, and profits? What are the major market segments? |
|---|---|
| B. Customers | What are the customers' needs and buying processes? How do customers and prospects rate the company and its competitors on reputation, product quality, service, sales force, and price? How do different customer segments make their buying decisions? |
| C. Competitors | Who are the major competitors? What are their objectives, strategies, strengths, weaknesses, sizes, and market shares? What trends will affect future competition and substitutes for the company's products? |
| D. Distribution and Dealers | What are the main trade channels for bringing products to customers? What are the efficiency levels and growth potentials of the different trade channels? |
| E. Suppliers | What is the outlook for the availability of key resources used in production? What trends are occurring among suppliers? |
| F. Facilitators and Marketing Firms | What is the cost and availability outlook for transportation services, warehousing facilities, and financial resources? How effective are the company's advertising agencies and marketing research firms? |

| TABLE 23.8 | (Continued) |
|---|---|

| G. Publics | Which publics represent particular opportunities or problems for the company? What steps has the company taken to deal effectively with each public? |

**Part II. Marketing Strategy Audit**

| A. Business Mission | Is the business mission clearly stated in market-oriented terms? Is it feasible? |
|---|---|
| B. Marketing Objectives and Goals | Are the company and marketing objectives and goals stated clearly enough to guide marketing planning and performance measurement? Are the marketing objectives appropriate, given the company's competitive position, resources, and opportunities? |
| C. Strategy | Has the management articulated a clear marketing strategy for achieving its marketing objectives? Is the strategy convincing? Is the strategy appropriate to the stage of the product life cycle, competitors' strategies, and the state of the economy? Is the company using the best basis for market segmentation? Does it have clear criteria for rating the segments and choosing the best ones? Has it developed accurate profiles of each target segment? Has the company developed an effective positioning and marketing mix for each target segment? Are marketing resources allocated optimally to the major elements of the marketing mix? Are enough resources or too many resources budgeted to accomplish the marketing objectives? |

**Part III. Marketing Organization Audit**

| A. Formal Structure | Does the marketing vice president or CMO have adequate authority and responsibility for company activities that affect customers' satisfaction? Are the marketing activities optimally structured along functional, product, segment, end user, and geographical lines? |
|---|---|
| B. Functional Efficiency | Are there good communication and working relations between marketing and sales? Is the product-management system working effectively? Are product managers able to plan profits or only sales volume? Are there any groups in marketing that need more training, motivation, supervision, or evaluation? |
| C. Interface Efficiency | Are there any problems between marketing and manufacturing, R&D, IT, purchasing, finance, accounting, and/or legal that need attention? |

**Part IV. Marketing Systems Audit**

| A. Marketing Information System | Is the marketing information system producing accurate, sufficient, and timely information about marketplace developments with respect to customers, prospects, distributors and dealers, competitors, suppliers, and various publics? Are company decision makers asking for enough marketing research, and are they using the results? Is the company employing the best methods for market measurement and sales forecasting? |
|---|---|
| B. Marketing Planning System | Is the marketing planning system well conceived and effectively used? Do marketers have decision support systems available? Does the planning system result in acceptable sales targets and quotas? |
| C. Marketing Control System | Are the control procedures adequate to ensure that the annual-plan objectives are being achieved? Does management periodically analyze the profitability of products, markets, territories, and channels of distribution? Are marketing costs and productivity periodically examined? |
| D. New-Product Development System | Is the company well organized to gather, generate, and screen new-product ideas? Does the company do adequate concept research and business analysis before investing in new ideas? Does the company carry out adequate product and market testing before launching new products? |

**Part V. Marketing Productivity Audit**

| A. Profitability Analysis | What is the profitability of the company's different products, markets, territories, and channels of distribution? Should the company enter, expand, contract, or withdraw from any business segments? |
|---|---|
| B. Cost-Effectiveness Analysis | Do any marketing activities seem to have excessive costs? Can cost-reducing steps be taken? |

*(Continued)*

| TABLE 23.8 | (Continued) |
|---|---|

**Part VI. Marketing Function Audits**

| A. Products | What are the company's product line objectives? Are they sound? Is the current product line meeting the objectives? Should the product line be stretched or contracted upward, downward, or both ways? Which products should be phased out? Which products should be added? What are the buyers' knowledge and attitudes toward the company's and competitors' product quality, features, styling, brand names, and so on? What areas of product and brand strategy need improvement? |
|---|---|
| B. Price | What are the company's pricing objectives, policies, strategies, and procedures? To what extent are prices set on cost, demand, and competitive criteria? Do the customers see the company's prices as being in line with the value of its offer? What does management know about the price elasticity of demand, experience-curve effects, and competitors' prices and pricing policies? To what extent are price policies compatible with the needs of distributors and dealers, suppliers, and government regulation? |
| C. Distribution | What are the company's distribution objectives and strategies? Is there adequate market coverage and service? How effective are distributors, dealers, manufacturers' representatives, brokers, agents, and others? Should the company consider changing its distribution channels? |
| D. Marketing Communications | Is the company making enough use of mass, digital, and personal communications? What are the organization's communication objectives? Are they sound? Is the right amount being spent on communications? What do customers and the public think about the communications? Are media well chosen? Is the internal communications staff adequate? Is the communication budget adequate? |
| E. Sales Force | What are the sales force's objectives? Is the sales force large enough to accomplish the company's objectives? Is the sales force organized along the proper principles of specialization (territory, market, product)? Are there enough (or too many) sales managers to guide the field sales representatives? Do the sales compensation level and structure provide adequate incentive and reward? Does the sales force show high morale, ability, and effort? Are the procedures adequate for setting quotas and evaluating performance? How does the company's sales force compare to competitors' sales forces? |

*The Marketing Excellence Review* The three columns in Table 23.9 distinguish among poor, good, and excellent business and marketing practices. The profile management creates from indicating where it thinks the business stands on each line can highlight where changes could help the firm become a truly outstanding player in the marketplace.

# The Future of Marketing

Top management recognizes that marketing requires more accountability than in the past. "Marketing Memo: Major Marketing Weaknesses" summarizes companies' major deficiencies in marketing and how to find and correct them.

To succeed in the future, marketing must be more holistic and less departmental. Marketers must achieve wider influence in the company, continuously create new ideas, and strive for customer insight by treating customers differently but appropriately. They must build their brands more through performance than promotion. They must go electronic and win through building superior information and communication systems.

The coming years will see:

- The demise of the marketing department and the rise of holistic marketing
- The demise of free-spending marketing and the rise of ROI marketing
- The demise of marketing intuition and the rise of marketing science
- The demise of manual marketing and the rise of both automated *and* creative marketing
- The demise of mass marketing and the rise of precision marketing

| TABLE 23.9 | The Marketing Excellence Review: Best Practices | |
|---|---|---|
| **Poor** | **Good** | **Excellent** |
| Product driven | Market driven | Market driving |
| Mass-market oriented | Segment-oriented | Niche-oriented and customer-oriented |
| Product offer | Augmented product offer | Customer solutions offer |
| Average product quality | Better than average | Legendary |
| Average service quality | Better than average | Legendary |
| End-product oriented | Core-product oriented | Core-competency oriented |
| Function oriented | Process oriented | Outcome oriented |
| Reacting to competitors | Benchmarking competitors | Leapfrogging competitors |
| Supplier exploitation | Supplier preference | Supplier partnership |
| Dealer exploitation | Dealer support | Dealer partnership |
| Price driven | Quality driven | Value driven |
| Average speed | Better than average | Legendary |
| Hierarchy | Network | Teamwork |
| Vertically integrated | Flattened organization | Strategic alliances |
| Stockholder driven | Stakeholder driven | Societally driven |

## marketing memo

# Major Marketing Weaknesses

A number of "deadly sins" signal that the marketing program is in trouble. Here are 10 deadly sins, the signs, and some solutions.

**Deadly Sin #1: The company is not sufficiently market focused and customer driven.**

*Signs:* There is evidence of poor identification of market segments, poor prioritization of market segments, no market segment managers, employees who think it is the job of marketing and sales to serve customers, no training program to create a customer culture, and no incentives to treat the customer especially well. *Solutions:* Use more advanced segmentation techniques, prioritize segments, specialize the sales force, develop a clear hierarchy of company values, foster more "customer consciousness" in employees and company agents, and make it easy for customers to reach the company and respond quickly to any communication.

**Deadly Sin #2: The company does not fully understand its target customers.**

*Signs:* The latest study of customers is three years old; customers are not buying your product like they once did; competitors' products are selling better; and there is a high level of customer returns and complaints. *Solutions:* Do more sophisticated consumer research, use more analytical techniques, establish customer and dealer panels, use customer relationship software, and do data mining.

**Deadly Sin #3: The company needs to better define and monitor its competitors.**

*Signs:* The company focuses on near competitors, misses distant competitors and disruptive technologies, and has no system for gathering and distributing competitive intelligence. *Solutions:* Establish an office for competitive intelligence, hire competitors' people, watch for technology that might affect the company, and prepare offerings like those of competitors.

*(Continued)*

**Deadly Sin #4: The company does not properly manage relationships with stakeholders.**

*Signs:* Employees, dealers, and investors are not happy; and good suppliers do not come.
*Solutions:* Move from zero-sum thinking to positive-sum thinking; and do a better job of managing employees, supplier relations, distributors, dealers, and investors.

**Deadly Sin #5: The company is not good at finding new opportunities.**

*Signs:* The company has not identified any exciting new opportunities for years, and the new ideas the company has launched have largely failed.
*Solutions:* Set up a system for stimulating the flow of new ideas.

**Deadly Sin #6: The company's marketing planning process is deficient.**

*Signs:* The marketing plan format does not have the right components, there is no way to estimate the financial implications of different strategies, and there is no contingency planning.
*Solutions:* Establish a standard format including situational analysis, SWOT, major issues, objectives, strategy, tactics, budgets, and controls; ask marketers what changes they would make if they were given 20 percent more or less budget; and run an annual marketing awards program with prizes for best plans and performance.

**Deadly Sin #7: Product and service policies need tightening.**

*Signs:* There are too many products and many are losing money; the company is giving away too many services; and the company is poor at cross-selling products and services.
*Solutions:* Establish a system to track weak products and fix or drop them; offer and price services at different levels; and improve processes for cross-selling and up-selling.

**Deadly Sin #8: The company's brand-building and communications skills are weak.**

*Signs:* The target market does not know much about the company; the brand is not seen as distinctive; the company allocates its budget to the same marketing tools in about the same proportion each year; and there is little evaluation of the ROI impact of marketing communications and activities.
*Solutions:* Improve brand-building strategies and measurement of results; shift money into effective marketing instruments; and require marketers to estimate the ROI impact in advance of funding requests.

**Deadly Sin #9: The company is not organized for effective and efficient marketing.**

*Signs:* Staff lacks 21st-century marketing skills, and there are bad vibes between marketing/sales and other departments.
*Solutions:* Appoint a strong leader and build new skills in the marketing department, and improve relationships between marketing and other departments.

**Deadly Sin #10: The company has not made maximum use of technology.**

*Signs:* There is evidence of minimal use of the Internet, an outdated sales automation system, no market automation, no decision-support models, and no marketing dashboards.
*Solutions:* Use the Internet more, improve the sales automation system, apply market automation to routine decisions, and develop formal marketing decision models and marketing dashboards.

**Source:** Philip Kotler, *Ten Deadly Marketing Sins: Signs and Solutions* (Hoboken, NJ: Wiley, 2004). © Philip Kotler.

To accomplish these changes and become truly holistic, marketers need a new set of skills and competencies in:

- Customer relationship management (CRM)
- Partner relationship management (PRM)
- Database marketing and data mining
- Contact center management and telemarketing
- Digital marketing and social media
- Public relations marketing (including event and sponsorship marketing)
- Brand-building and brand-asset management
- Experiential marketing
- Integrated marketing communications
- Profitability analysis by segment, customer, and channel

The benefits of successful 21st-century marketing are many, but they will come only with hard work, insight, and inspiration. New rules and practices are emerging, and it is an exciting time. The words of 19th-century U.S. author Ralph Waldo Emerson have perhaps never been more true: "This time like all times is a good one, if we but know what to do with it."

# Summary

1. The modern marketing department has evolved through the years from a simple sales department to an organizational structure where marketers work mainly on cross-disciplinary teams.

2. Some companies are organized by functional specialization; others focus on geography and regionalization, product and brand management, or market-segment management. Some companies establish a matrix organization consisting of both product and market managers.

3. Effective modern marketing organizations are marked by customer focus within and strong cooperation among marketing, R&D, engineering, purchasing, manufacturing, operations, finance, accounting, and credit.

4. Companies must practice social responsibility through their legal, ethical, and social words and actions. Cause marketing can be a means for companies to productively link social responsibility to consumer marketing programs. Social marketing is done by a nonprofit or government organization to directly address a social problem or cause.

5. A brilliant strategic marketing plan counts for little unless implemented properly, including recognizing and diagnosing a problem, assessing where the problem exists, and evaluating results.

6. The marketing department must monitor and control marketing activities continuously. Marketing plan control ensures the company achieves the sales, profits, and other goals in its annual plan. The main tools are sales analysis, market share analysis, marketing expense-to-sales analysis, and financial analysis of the marketing plan. Profitability control measures and controls the profitability of products, territories, customer groups, trade channels, and order sizes. Efficiency control finds ways to increase the efficiency of the sales force, advertising, sales promotion, and distribution. Strategic control periodically reassesses the company's strategic approach to the marketplace using marketing effectiveness and marketing excellence reviews as well as marketing audits.

7. Achieving marketing excellence in the future will require a new set of skills and competencies.

## MyMarketingLab

Go to mymktlab.com to complete the problems marked with this icon ⭐ as well as for additional Auto-graded and Assisted-graded writing questions.

# Applications

## Marketing Debate
### Is Marketing Management an Art or a Science?

Some observers maintain that good marketing is mostly an art and does not lend itself to rigorous analysis and deliberation. Others contend it is a highly disciplined enterprise that shares much with other business disciplines.

**Take a position:** Marketing management is largely an artistic exercise and therefore highly subjective *versus* Marketing management is largely a scientific exercise with well-established guidelines and criteria.

## Marketing Discussion
### Cause Marketing

⭐ How does cause or corporate societal marketing affect your personal consumer behavior? Do you ever buy or not buy any products or services from a company because of its environmental policies or programs? Why or why not?

## Marketing Excellence

### >> Starbucks

Starbucks opened in Seattle in 1971, when coffee consumption in the United States had been declining for a decade and rival brands used cheaper beans to compete on price. The company's founders decided to try a new concept: selling only the finest imported coffee beans and coffee-brewing equipment. (The original store didn't sell coffee by the cup, only beans.)

Howard Schultz came to Starbucks in 1982. While in Milan on business, he had walked into an Italian coffee bar and had an epiphany: "There was nothing like this in America. It was an extension of people's front porch. It was an emotional experience." To bring this concept to the United States, Schultz set about creating an environment that would blend Italian elegance with U.S. informality. He envisioned Starbucks as a "personal treat" for its customers, a comfortable, sociable gathering spot bridging the workplace and home.

Starbucks' expansion throughout the United States was carefully planned. All stores were company-owned and operated, ensuring complete control over the product and an unparalleled image of quality. Starbucks used a "hub" strategy; coffeehouses entered a new market in a clustered group. Although this deliberate saturation often cannibalized 30 percent of one store's sales, any drop in revenue was offset by efficiencies in marketing and distribution costs and the enhanced image of convenience. A typical customer stopped by Starbucks 18 times a month. No U.S. retailer had a higher frequency rate of customer visits.

Starbucks' success is often attributed to its high-quality products and services and its relentless commitment to providing consumers the richest possible sensory experience. However, another critical component is its commitment to social responsibility.

***Community***: Starbucks gives back to its community in many ways starting with employees, called partners. Schultz believed that to exceed customers' expectations, the company must first exceed those of employees. Since 1990, it has provided comprehensive health care to all employees, including part-timers. (Health insurance now costs the company more each year than coffee.) A stock option plan allows employees to participate in the firm's financial success, and the company has committed to hiring 10,000 veterans and military spouses over the next five years. In 2013, employees donated 630,000 hours of community service; the company hopes to top 1 million hours by the end of 2015.

Starbucks created The Starbucks Foundation in 1997 to "create hope, discovery, and opportunity in communities," mainly by supporting literacy programs for children and families in the United States and Canada and charities worldwide. In 2013, the foundation gave $8.7 million to 144 nonprofit organizations around the world. Starbucks has donated more than $11 million to the Global Fund through its partnership with PRODUCT(RED), a global initiative to help stop the spread of HIV in Africa.

***Ethical Sourcing***: Starbucks collaborates with Conservation International (CI), a nongovernmental organization, and follows Coffee and Farmer Equity (C.A.F.E.) Practices, a comprehensive coffee-buying program, to purchase high-quality coffee from farmers who meet social, economic, and environmental standards. Of 396 million pounds of coffee Starbucks purchased in 2013, 95 percent was ethically sourced. The company also works continuously with farmers to improve responsible methods of farming, such as by planting trees along rivers and using shade-growing techniques to help preserve forests. Over the years, Starbucks has invested more than $70 million in collaborative farmer programs and activities.

***Environment***: Starbucks is considered a leader in green initiatives, building new LEED-certified green buildings, reducing waste, and improving water conservation. The world's first recycled beverage cup made of 10 percent postconsumer fiber, 10 years in the making, and a new hot-cup paper sleeve that requires fewer materials to make conserve approximately 100,000 trees a year. Now the team is working to ensure that customers recycle. Jim Hanna, Starbucks's director of environmental impact, explained, "[Starbucks] defines a recyclable cup not by what the cup is made out of but by our customers actually having access to recycling services." Starbucks's goal: to make 100 percent of its cups recycled or reused by 2015.

Howard Schultz stepped down as CEO in 2000 but returned as CEO, president, and chairman in 2008 to help restore growth and excitement to the powerhouse chain. Today, more than 3 billion customers visit Starbucks' 20,000 stores in 65 countries annually. The company has more than 200,000 employees and brought in $14.9 billion in revenue in 2013. To achieve its international growth goals, Schultz believes Starbucks must retain a passion for coffee and a sense of humanity and continue to prove that the company "stands for something more than just profitability."

### Questions

1.  Starbucks makes business decisions that are both ethical and responsible. Has it done a good job communicating its efforts to consumers? Do consumers believe Starbucks is a socially responsible company? Why or why not?

2. Where does a company like Starbucks draw the line on supporting socially responsible programs? How much of its annual budget should go toward these programs? How much time should employees focus on them? Which programs should it support?

3. How do you measure the results of Starbucks's socially responsible programs?

**Sources:** Howard Schultz, "Dare to Be a Social Entrepreneur," *Business 2.0*, December 2006, p. 87; Edward Iwata, "Owner of Small Coffee Shop Takes on Java Titan Starbucks," *USA Today*, December 20, 2006; "Staying Pure: Howard Schultz's Formula for Starbucks," *Economist*, February 25, 2006, p. 72; Diane Anderson, "Evolution of the Eco Cup," *Business 2.0*, June 2006, p. 50; Bruce Horovitz, "Starbucks Nation," *USA Today*, May 19, 2006; Theresa Howard, "Starbucks Takes Up Cause for Safe Drinking Water," *USA Today*, August 2, 2005; Howard Schultz and Dori Jones Yang, *Pour Your Heart into It: How Starbucks Built a Company One Cup at a Time* (New York: Hyperion, 1997); "At MIT-Starbucks Symposium, Focus on Holistic Approach to Recycling," *MIT*, www.mit.edu, May 12, 2010; Starbucks Global Responsibility Report 2013; Starbucks 2013 Annual Report.

## Marketing Excellence

### >> Virgin Group

Virgin roared onto the British stage in the 1970s with the innovative Virgin Records, the brainchild of entrepreneur Richard Branson, a high school dropout who signed unknown artists and began a marathon of publicity that continues to this day. The flamboyant Briton sold Virgin Records in 1992 and has gone on to launch more than 400 companies worldwide whose combined revenues exceeded $24 billion in 2012.

The Virgin name—the third most respected brand in Britain—and the Branson personality help sell the company's diverse portfolio of branded air travel, railroads, financial services, music, mobile phones, cars, wine, publishing, and medical devices. The Virgin Group looks for new opportunities in markets with underserved, overcharged customers and complacent competition. Branson explained, "Wherever we find them, there is a clear opportunity area for Virgin to do a much better job than the competition. We introduce trust, innovation, and customer friendliness where they don't exist."

Some marketing and financial critics have pointed out that Branson dilutes the brand and covers too many businesses. There have been some fumbles: Virgin Cola, Virgin Cosmetics, Virgin Vodka, and Virgin Brides have all but disappeared. But despite the diversity, all Virgin Group's brands stand for quality, innovation, and fun.

Branson is a master of the strategic publicity stunt and knows photographers will turn up if he gives them a good reason. When he took on stodgy British Airways in 1984, he wore World War I–era flying gear to announce the formation of Virgin Atlantic. The first Virgin flight took off laden with celebrities, media, a brass band in full swing, waiters from Maxim's dressed in white tie and tails, and free-flowing champagne. The airborne party enjoyed international press coverage and millions of dollars' worth of free publicity.

When Branson launched Virgin Cola in the United States in 1998, he steered an army tank down New York's Fifth Avenue and blew up a Coca-Cola sign, garnering interviews on network TV news shows the next morning. In 2002, he plunged into Times Square from a crane to announce his new mobile phone business. In 2004, he appeared at a New York City nightclub wearing flesh-colored tights and a strategically placed portable CD player to introduced a line of hip techie gadgets called Virgin Pulse. Branson has attended press conferences dressed in an astronaut's suit and angel's wings, driven across the English Channel in an amphibious car, and even bared his bottom to the press when Virgin Atlantic landed in Canada for the first time. His good-natured humor and flamboyant personality attract media attention and customer admiration around the globe. Reports say Virgin's press coverage equates to $1.6 billion in media value per year.

Although Branson avoids traditional market research, he stays in touch through constant customer contact. When he first set up Virgin Atlantic, he called 50 customers every month to chat and get their feedback. He appeared in airports to rub elbows with customers, and if a plane was delayed, he handed out gift certificates to a Virgin Megastore or discounts on future travel.

Virgin Unite is a nonprofit foundation that tackles global, social, and environmental problems with an entrepreneurial approach. A team of scientists, entrepreneurs, and environmental enthusiasts work with Virgin to reinvent the way "we live and work to help make people's lives better." Virgin Green Fund is a private equity firm investing in renewable energy and resource efficiency sectors. Virgin established the Earth Challenge in 2007 to award $25 million to any person or group who develops a safe, long-term, commercially viable way to remove greenhouse gases from the atmosphere. Submissions are being reviewed by a team of scientists, professors, and environmental professionals.

Now knighted by the Queen of England, Sir Richard never does anything small and quiet. He once said, "Lavish praise on people and people will flourish; criticize and they shrivel up." This philosophy has led him to many successes both in business and in life. Whether looking for a new business, generating publicity in his characteristic style, or encouraging research to help the planet, Branson does it with a bang.

**Questions**

1. How is Virgin unique in its quest to be a socially responsible and sustainable company?

2. Discuss the contradiction between Virgin's negative environmental impact (via air and rail) and the green message and communication efforts behind endeavors such as the Earth Challenge.

**Sources:** Peter Elkind, "Branson Gets Grounded," *Fortune*, February 5, 2007, pp. 13–14; Alan Deutschman, "The Enlightenment of Richard Branson," *Fast Company*, September 2006, p. 49; Andy Serwer, "Do Branson's Profits Equal His *Joie de Vivre?*," *Fortune*, October 17, 2005, p. 57; Kerry Capell with Wendy Zellner, "Richard Branson's Next Big Adventure," *BusinessWeek*, March 8, 2004, pp. 44–45; Melanie Wells, "Red Baron," *Forbes*, July 3, 2000, pp. 151–60; Sam Hill and Glenn Rifkin, *Radical Marketing* (New York: HarperBusiness, 1999); "Branson Pledges Three Billion Dollars to Develop Cleaner Energy," *Terra Daily*, September 21, 2006; Richard Wachman, "Virgin Brands: What Does Richard Branson Really Own?," *The Guardian*, January 7, 2012; Carmine Gallo, "The Key to a Lasting Relationship in Business and in Marriage," *Forbes*, April 10, 2014; Virgin, www.virgin.com.

# Appendix

## TOOLS FOR MARKETING CONTROL

In this appendix, we provide detailed guidelines and insights about how to best conduct several marketing control procedures.

## ANNUAL PLAN CONTROL

Four sets of analyses can be useful for annual plan control.

**SALES ANALYSIS** **Sales analysis** measures and evaluates actual sales in relationship to goals. Two specific tools make it work.

**Sales-variance analysis** measures the relative contribution of different factors to a gap in sales performance. Suppose the annual plan called for selling 4,000 widgets in the first quarter at $1 per widget, for total revenue of $4,000. At quarter's end, only 3,000 widgets were sold at $.80 per widget, for total revenue of $2,400. How much of the sales performance gap is due to the price decline, and how much to the volume decline? This calculation answers the question:

$$
\begin{array}{lll}
\text{Variance due to price decline: } (\$1.00 - \$.80)\,(3{,}000) = \$\ \ 600 & 37.5\% \\
\text{Variance due to volume decline: } (\$1.00)(4{,}000 - 3{,}000) = \$1{,}000 & 62.5\% \\
\hline
= \$1{,}600 & 100.0\%
\end{array}
$$

Almost two-thirds of the variance is due to failure to achieve the volume target. The company should look closely at why it failed to achieve expected sales volume.

**Microsales analysis** looks at specific products, territories, and so forth, that failed to produce expected sales. Suppose the company sells in three territories, and expected sales were 1,500 units, 500 units, and 2,000 units, respectively. Actual volumes were 1,400 units, 525 units, and 1,075 units, respectively. Thus, territory 1 showed a 7 percent shortfall in terms of expected sales; territory 2, a 5 percent improvement over expectations; and territory 3, a 46 percent shortfall! Territory 3 is causing most of the trouble. Maybe the sales rep in territory 3 is underperforming, a major competitor has entered this territory, or business is in a recession there.

**MARKET SHARE ANALYSIS** Company sales don't reveal how well the company is performing relative to competitors. For this, management needs to track its market share in one of three ways.

**Overall market share** expresses the company's sales as a percentage of total market sales. **Served market share** is sales as a percentage of the total sales to the market. The **served market** is all the buyers able and willing to buy the product, and served market share is always larger than overall market share. A company could capture 100 percent of its served market and yet have a relatively small share of the total market. **Relative market share** is market share in relationship to the largest competitor. A relative market share of exactly 100 percent means the company is tied for the lead; more than 100 percent indicates a market leader. A rise in relative market share means a company is gaining on its leading competitor.

Conclusions from market share analysis, however, are subject to qualifications:

- *The assumption that outside forces affect all companies in the same way is often not true.* The U.S. Surgeon General's report on the harmful consequences of smoking depressed total cigarette sales, but not equally for all companies.
- *The assumption that a company's performance should be judged against the average performance of all companies is not always valid.* A company's performance is best judged against that of its closest competitors.
- *If a new firm enters the industry, every existing firm's market share might fall.* A decline in market share might not mean the company is performing any worse than other companies. Share loss depends on the degree to which the new firm hits the company's specific markets.
- *Sometimes a market share decline is deliberately engineered to improve profits.* For example, management might drop unprofitable customers or products.
- *Market share can fluctuate for many minor reasons.* For example, it can be affected by whether a large sale occurs on the last day of the month or at the beginning of the next month. Not all shifts in market share have marketing significance.[76]

A useful way to analyze market share movements is in terms of four components:

$$\begin{matrix} Overall \\ market \\ share \end{matrix} = \begin{matrix} Customer \\ penetration \end{matrix} \times \begin{matrix} Customer \\ loyalty \end{matrix} \times \begin{matrix} Customer \\ selectivity \end{matrix} \times \begin{matrix} Price \\ selectivity \end{matrix}$$

where:

| | |
|---|---|
| *Customer penetration* | Percentage of all customers who buy from the company |
| *Customer loyalty* | Purchases from the company by its customers as a percentage of their total purchases from all suppliers of the same products |
| *Customer selectivity* | Size of the average customer purchase from the company as a percentage of the size of the average customer purchase from an average company |
| *Price selectivity* | Average price charged by the company as a percentage of the average price charged by all companies |

Now suppose the company's dollar market share falls during the period. The overall market share equation provides four possible explanations: The company lost some customers (lower customer penetration); existing customers are buying less from the company (lower customer loyalty); the company's remaining customers are smaller in size (lower customer selectivity); or the company's price has slipped relative to competition (lower price selectivity).

**MARKETING EXPENSE-TO-SALES ANALYSIS**  Annual-plan control requires making sure the company isn't overspending to achieve sales goals. The key ratio to watch is *marketing expense-to-sales.* In one company, this ratio was 30 percent and consisted of five component expense-to-sales ratios: sales force-to-sales (15 percent), advertising-to-sales (5 percent), sales promotion-to-sales (6 percent), marketing research-to-sales (1 percent), and sales administration-to-sales (3 percent).

Fluctuations outside the normal range are cause for concern. Management needs to monitor period-to-period fluctuations in each ratio on a *control chart* (see Figure 23.6). This chart shows the advertising expense-to-sales ratio normally fluctuates between 8 percent and 12 percent, say 99 of 100 times. In the 15th period, however, the ratio exceeded the upper control limit. Either (1) the company still has good expense control and this situation represents a rare chance event, or (2) the company has lost control over this expense and should find the cause. If there is no investigation, the risk is that some real change might have occurred, and the company will fall behind.

Managers should make successive observations even within the upper and lower control limits. Note in Figure 23.6 that the level of the expense-to-sales ratio rose steadily from the 8th period onward. The probability of encountering six successive increases in what should be independent events is only 1 in 64.[77] This unusual pattern should have led to an investigation sometime before the 15th observation.

**FINANCIAL ANALYSIS**  Marketers should analyze the expense-to-sales ratios in an overall financial framework to determine how and where the company is making its money. They can, and are increasingly, using financial analysis to find profitable strategies beyond building sales.

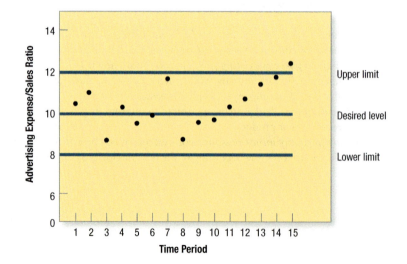

**| Fig. 23.6 |**

The Control-
Chart Model

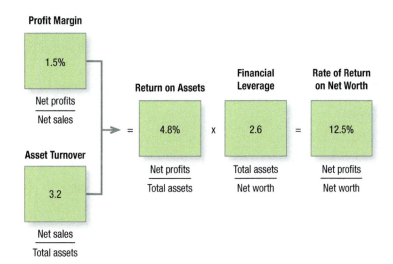

**| Fig. 23.7 |**

Financial Model of Return on Net Worth

Management uses financial analysis to identify factors that affect the company's *rate of return on net worth*.[78] The main factors are shown in Figure 23.7, along with illustrative numbers for a large chain-store retailer. The retailer is earning a 12.5 percent return on net worth. The return on net worth is the product of two ratios, the company's *return on assets* and its *financial leverage*. To improve its return on net worth, the company must increase its ratio of net profits to assets or increase the ratio of assets to net worth. The company should analyze the composition of its assets (cash, accounts receivable, inventory, and plant and equipment) to see whether it can improve its asset management.

The return on assets is the product of two ratios, the *profit margin* and the *asset turnover*. The profit margin in Figure 23.7 seems low, whereas the asset turnover is more normal for retailing. The marketing executive can seek to improve performance in two ways: (1) increase the profit margin by increasing sales or cutting costs, and (2) increase the asset turnover by increasing sales or reducing assets (inventory, receivables) held against a given level of sales.

# PROFITABILITY CONTROL

**MARKETING PROFITABILITY ANALYSIS** We will illustrate the steps in marketing profitability analysis with the following example: The marketing vice president of a lawn mower company wants to determine the profitability of selling through three types of retail channels: hardware stores, garden supply shops, and department stores. The company's profit-and-loss statement is shown in Table 23.10.

| TABLE 23.10 | A Simplified Profit-and-Loss Statement | |
|---|---|---|
| Sales | | $60,000 |
| Cost of goods sold | | 39,000 |
| Gross margin | | $21,000 |
| Expenses | | |
| Salaries | $9,300 | |
| Rent | 3,000 | |
| Supplies | 3,500 | |
| | | 15,800 |
| Net profit | | $ 5,200 |

| TABLE 23.11 | Mapping Natural Expenses into Functional Expenses | | | | |
|---|---|---|---|---|---|
| Natural Accounts | Total | Selling | Advertising | Packing and Delivery | Billing and Collecting |
| Salaries | $ 9,300 | $5,100 | $1,200 | $1,400 | $1,600 |
| Rent | 3,000 | — | 400 | 2,000 | 600 |
| Supplies | 3,500 | 400 | 1,500 | 1,400 | 200 |
| | $15,800 | $5,500 | $3,100 | $4,800 | $2,400 |

**Step 1: Identifying Functional Expenses** Assume the expenses listed in Table 23.10 are incurred to sell the product, advertise it, pack and deliver it, and bill and collect for it. The first task is to measure how much of each expense was incurred in each activity.

Suppose most of the salary expense went to sales representatives and the rest to an advertising manager, packing and delivery help, and an office accountant. Let the breakdown of the $9,300 be $5,100, $1,200, $1,400, and $1,600, respectively. Table 23.11 shows the allocation of the salary expense to these four activities.

Table 23.11 also shows the rent account of $3,000 allocated to the four activities. Because the sales reps work away from the office, none of the building's rent expense is assigned to selling. Most of the expenses for floor space and rented equipment are for packing and delivery. The supplies account covers promotional materials, packing materials, fuel purchases for delivery, and home office stationery. The $3,500 in this account is reassigned to functional uses of the supplies.

**Step 2: Assigning Functional Expenses to Marketing Entities** The next task is to measure how much functional expense was associated with selling through each type of channel. Consider the selling effort, indicated by the number of sales in each channel. This number is in the selling column of Table 23.12. Altogether, 275 sales calls were made during the period. Because the total selling expense amounted to $5,500 (see Table 23.12), the selling expense averaged $20 per call.

We can allocate advertising expense according to the number of ads addressed to different channels. Because there were 100 ads altogether, the average ad cost $31.

The packing and delivery expense is allocated according to the number of orders placed by each type of channel. This same basis was used for allocating billing and collection expense.

| TABLE 23.12 | Bases for Allocating Functional Expenses to Channels | | | |
|---|---|---|---|---|
| Channel Type | Selling | Advertising | Packing and Delivery | Billing and Collecting |
| Hardware stores | 200 | 50 | 50 | 50 |
| Garden supply shops | 65 | 20 | 21 | 21 |
| Department stores | 10 | 30 | 9 | 9 |
| | 275 | 100 | 80 | 80 |
| Functional expense ÷ No. of units | $5,500 | $3,100 | $4,800 | $2,400 |
| | 275 | 100 | 80 | 80 |
| equals | $ 20 | $ 31 | $ 60 | $ 30 |

*Step 3: Preparing a Profit-and-Loss Statement for Each Marketing Entity* We can now prepare a profit-and-loss statement for each type of channel (see Table 23.13). Because hardware stores accounted for half of total sales ($30,000 out of $60,000), charge this channel with half the cost of goods sold ($19,500 out of $39,000). This leaves a gross margin from hardware stores of $10,500. From this we deduct the proportions of functional expenses hardware stores consumed.

According to Table 23.12, hardware stores received 200 of 275 total sales calls. At an imputed value of $20 a call, hardware stores must bear a $4,000 selling expense. Table 23.12 also shows hardware stores were the target of 50 ads. At $31 an ad, the hardware stores are charged with $1,550 of advertising. The same reasoning applies in computing the share of the other functional expenses. The result is that hardware stores gave rise to $10,050 of the total expenses. Subtracting this from gross margin, we find the profit of selling through hardware stores is only $450.

Repeat this analysis for the other channels. The company is losing money in selling through garden supply shops and makes virtually all its profits through department stores. Notice that gross sales is not a reliable indicator of the net profits for each channel.

**DETERMINING CORRECTIVE ACTION** It would be naive to conclude the company should drop garden supply shops and hardware stores to concentrate on department stores. We need to answer the following questions first:

- To what extent do buyers buy on the basis of type of retail outlet versus brand?
- What trends affect the relative importance of these three channels?
- How good are the company's marketing strategies for the three channels?

Using the answers, marketing management can evaluate five alternatives:

1. Establish a special charge for handling smaller orders.
2. Give more promotional aid to garden supply shops and hardware stores.
3. Reduce sales calls and advertising to garden supply shops and hardware stores.
4. Ignore the weakest retail units in each channel.
5. Do nothing.

Marketing profitability analysis indicates the relative profitability of different channels, products, territories, or other marketing entities. It does not prove the best course of action is to drop unprofitable marketing entities or capture the likely profit improvement of doing so.

**TABLE 23.13** Profit-and-Loss Statements for Channels

| | Hardware Stores | Garden Supply Shops | Dept. Stores | Whole Company |
|---|---|---|---|---|
| Sales | $30,000 | $10,000 | $20,000 | $60,000 |
| Cost of goods sold | 19,500 | 6,500 | 13,000 | 39,000 |
| Gross margin | $10,500 | $ 3,500 | $ 7,000 | $21,000 |
| Expenses | | | | |
| Selling ($20 per call) | $ 4,000 | $ 1,300 | $ 200 | $ 5,500 |
| Advertising ($31 per advertisement) | 1,550 | 620 | 930 | 3,100 |
| Packing and delivery ($60 per order) | 3,000 | 1,260 | 540 | 4,800 |
| Billing ($30 per order) | 1,500 | 630 | 270 | 2,400 |
| Total expenses | $10,050 | $ 3,810 | $ 1,940 | $15,800 |
| Net profit or loss | $ 450 | $ (310) | $ 5,060 | $ 5,200 |

**DIRECT VERSUS FULL COSTING** Like all information tools, marketing profitability analysis can lead or mislead, depending on how well marketers understand its methods and limitations. The lawn mower company chose bases somewhat arbitrarily for allocating the functional expenses to its marketing entities. It used "number of sales calls" to allocate selling expenses, generating less record keeping and computation, when in principle "number of sales working hours" is a more accurate indicator of cost.

A far more serious decision is whether to allocate full costs or only direct and traceable costs in evaluating a marketing entity's performance. The lawn mower company sidestepped this problem by assuming only simple costs that fit with marketing activities, but we cannot avoid the question in real-world analyses of profitability. We distinguish three types of costs:

1. Direct costs—We can assign direct costs directly to the proper marketing entities. Sales commissions are a direct cost in a profitability analysis of sales territories, sales representatives, or customers. Advertising expenditures are a direct cost in a profitability analysis of products to the extent that each advertisement promotes only one product. Other direct costs for specific purposes are sales force salaries and traveling expenses.
2. Traceable common costs—We can assign traceable common costs only indirectly, but on a plausible basis, to the marketing entities. In the example, we analyzed rent this way.
3. Nontraceable common costs—Common costs whose allocation to the marketing entities is highly arbitrary are nontraceable common costs. To allocate "corporate image" expenditures equally to all products would be arbitrary because all products don't benefit equally. To allocate them proportionately to the sales of the various products would be arbitrary because relative product sales reflect many factors besides corporate image making. Other examples are top management salaries, taxes, interest, and other overhead.

No one disputes the inclusion of direct costs in marketing cost analysis. There is some controversy about including traceable common costs, which lump together costs that would and would not change with the scale of marketing activity. If the lawn mower company drops garden supply shops, it would probably continue to pay the same rent. Its profits would not rise immediately by the amount of the present loss in selling to garden supply shops ($310).

The major controversy is about whether to allocate the nontraceable common costs to the marketing entities. Such allocation is called the *full-cost approach*, and its advocates argue that all costs must ultimately be imputed in order to determine true profitability. However, this argument confuses the use of accounting for financial reporting with its use for managerial decision making. Full costing has three major weaknesses:

1. The relative profitability of different marketing entities can shift radically when we replace one arbitrary way to allocate nontraceable common costs by another.
2. The arbitrariness demoralizes managers, who feel their performance is judged adversely.
3. The inclusion of nontraceable common costs could weaken efforts at real cost control.

Operating management is most effective in controlling direct costs and traceable common costs. Arbitrary assignments of nontraceable common costs can lead managers to spend their time fighting cost allocations instead of managing controllable costs well.

Companies show growing interest in using marketing profitability analysis or its broader version, activity-based cost accounting (ABC), to quantify the true profitability of different activities.[79] Managers can then reduce the resources required to perform various activities, make the resources more productive, acquire them at lower cost, or raise prices on products that consume heavy amounts of support resources. The contribution of ABC is to refocus management's attention away from using only labor or material standard costs to allocate full cost and toward capturing the actual costs of supporting individual products, customers, and other entities.

# Appendix

# The Marketing Plan: An Introduction

As a marketer, you'll need a good marketing plan to provide direction and focus for your brand, product, or company. With a detailed plan, any business will be better prepared to launch an innovative new product or increase sales to current customers. Nonprofit organizations also use marketing plans to guide their fund-raising and outreach efforts. Even government agencies put together marketing plans for initiatives such as building public awareness of proper nutrition and stimulating area tourism.

## The Purpose and Content of a Marketing Plan

A marketing plan has a more limited scope than a business plan, which offers a broad overview of the entire organization's mission, objectives, strategy, and resource allocation. The marketing plan documents how the organization's strategic objectives will be achieved through specific marketing strategies and tactics, with the customer as the starting point. It is also linked to the plans of other organizational departments. Suppose a marketing plan calls for selling 200,000 units annually. The production department must gear up to make that many units, finance must arrange funding to cover the expenses, human resources must be ready to hire and train staff, and so on. Without the appropriate level of organizational support and resources, no marketing plan can succeed.

Although the exact length and layout vary from company to company, a marketing plan usually contains the sections described in Chapter 2. Smaller businesses may create shorter or less formal marketing plans, whereas corporations generally require highly structured marketing plans. To guide implementation effectively, every part of the plan must be described in considerable detail. Sometimes a company will post its marketing plan on an internal Web site so managers and employees in different locations can consult specific sections and collaborate on additions or changes.

## The Role of Research

To develop innovative products, successful strategies, and action programs, marketers need up-to-date information about the environment, the competition, and the selected market segments. Often, analysis of internal data is the starting point for assessing the current marketing situation, supplemented by marketing intelligence and research investigating the overall market, the competition, key issues, threats, and opportunities. As the plan is put into effect, marketers use research to measure progress toward objectives and to identify areas for improvement if results fall short of projections.

Finally, marketing research helps marketers learn more about their customers' requirements, expectations, perceptions, satisfaction, and loyalty. This deeper understanding provides a foundation for building competitive advantage through well-informed segmenting, targeting, and positioning decisions. Thus, the marketing plan should outline what marketing research will be conducted and when, as well as how, the findings will be applied.

## The Role of Relationships

Although the marketing plan shows how the company will establish and maintain profitable customer relationships, it also affects both internal and external relationships. First, it influences how marketing personnel work with each other and with other departments to deliver value and satisfy customers. Second, it affects how the company works with suppliers, distributors, and partners to achieve the plan's objectives. Third, it influences the company's dealings with other stakeholders, including government regulators, the media, and the community at large. All these relationships are important to the organization's success and must be considered when developing a marketing plan.

## From Marketing Plan to Marketing Action

Most companies create yearly marketing plans, though some plans cover a longer period. Marketers start planning well in advance of the implementation date to allow time for marketing research, analysis, management review, and coordination between departments. Then, after each action program begins, marketers monitor ongoing results, investigate any deviation from the projected outcome, and take corrective steps as needed. Some marketers also prepare contingency plans for implementation if certain conditions emerge. Because of inevitable and sometimes unpredictable environmental changes, marketers must be ready to update and adapt marketing plans at any time.

For effective implementation and control, the marketing plan should define how progress toward objectives will be measured. Managers typically use budgets, schedules, and marketing metrics for monitoring and evaluating results. With budgets, they can compare planned expenditures with actual expenditures for a given period. Schedules allow management to see when tasks were supposed to be completed and when they were actually completed. Marketing metrics track the actual outcomes of marketing programs to see whether the company is moving forward toward its objectives.

# Sample Marketing Plan for Sonic

This section takes you inside the sample marketing plan for Sonic, a hypothetical start-up company. The company's first product is the Sonic 1000, a state-of-the-art, fully loaded multimedia smart phone. Sonic will be competing with Apple, Samsung, LG, Motorola, HTC, and other well-established rivals in a crowded, fast-changing marketplace where smart phones have many communication and entertainment capabilities. The annotations explain more about what each section of the plan should contain.

## 1.0 Executive Summary

This section summarizes market opportunities, marketing strategy, and marketing and financial objectives for senior managers who will read and approve the marketing plan.

Sonic is preparing to launch a major new state-of-the-art multimedia smart phone, the Sonic 1000, in a mature market. We can effectively compete with many types of smart phones because our product offers a unique combination of advanced features and functionality at a very competitive value-added price. We are targeting specific segments in the consumer and business markets, taking advantage of the growing interest in a single powerful but affordable device with extensive communication, organization, and entertainment benefits.

The primary marketing objective is to achieve first-year U.S. market share of 1 percent with unit sales of 800,000. The primary financial objectives are to achieve first-year sales revenues of $200 million, keep first-year losses to less than $40 million, and break even early in the second year.

## 2.0 Situation Analysis

The situation analysis describes the market, the company's capability to serve targeted segments, and the competition.

Sonic, founded 18 months ago by two well-known entrepreneurs with telecommunications experience, is about to enter the highly competitive smart-phone market. Multifunction cell phones are increasingly popular for both personal and professional use, with more than 968 million smart phones sold worldwide in 2013. Competition is increasingly intense even as technology evolves, industry consolidation continues, and pricing pressures squeeze profitability. To gain market share in this dynamic environment, Sonic must carefully target specific segments with valued features and plan for a next-generation product to keep brand momentum going.

Market summary includes size, needs, growth, and trends. Describing the targeted segments in detail provides context for marketing strategies and programs discussed later in the plan.

**2.1 MARKET SUMMARY** Sonic's market consists of consumers and business users who prefer to use a powerful but affordable single device for fully functional communication, information storage and exchange, organization, and entertainment on the go. Specific segments being targeted during the first year include professionals, corporations, students, entrepreneurs, and medical users. Exhibit A.1 shows how the Sonic 1000 addresses some of the most basic needs of targeted consumer and business segments in a cost-effective manner. The additional communication and entertainment benefits of the product just enhance its appeal to those segments.

# Needs and Corresponding Features/Benefits of Sonic Smart Phone

| Targeted Segment | Customer Need | Corresponding Feature/Benefit |
|---|---|---|
| Professionals (consumer market) | ■ Stay in touch while on the go | ■ Wireless e-mail to conveniently send and receive messages from anywhere; cell phone capability for voice communication from anywhere |
| | ■ Record information while on the go | ■ Voice recognition for no-hands recording |
| Students (consumer market) | ■ Perform many functions without carrying multiple gadgets | ■ Compatible with numerous applications and peripherals for convenient, cost-effective functionality |
| | ■ Express style and individuality | ■ Case wardrobe of different colors and patterns allows users to make a fashion statement |
| Corporate users (business market) | ■ Input and access critical data on the go | ■ Compatible with widely available software |
| | ■ Use for proprietary tasks | ■ Customizable to fit diverse corporate tasks and networks |
| Entrepreneurs (business market) | ■ Organize and access contacts, schedule details | ■ No-hands, wireless access to calendar and address book to easily check appointments and connect with contacts |
| Medical users (business market) | ■ Update, access, and exchange medical records | ■ No-hands, wireless recording and exchange of information to reduce paperwork and increase productivity |

Smart-phone purchasers can choose between models based on several different operating systems. The biggest-selling smart-phone operating system is Android. Android's smaller rivals include BlackBerry OS, iOS, and the Windows Phone OS. Storage capacity (hard drive or flash drive) is an expected feature, so Sonic is equipping its first product with an ultra-fast 64-gigabyte drive that can be supplemented by extra storage. Technology costs are decreasing even as capabilities are increasing, which makes value-priced models more appealing to consumers and to business users with older smart phones who want to trade up to new, high-end multifunction units.

**2.2 STRENGTHS, WEAKNESSES, OPPORTUNITIES, AND THREAT ANALYSIS** Sonic has several powerful strengths on which to build, but our major weakness is lack of brand awareness and image. The major opportunity is demand for multifunction communication, organization, and entertainment devices that deliver a number of valued benefits at a lower cost. We also face the threat of ever-higher competition and downward pricing pressure.

*Strengths* Sonic can build on three important strengths:

1. *Innovative product*—The Sonic 1000 offers a combination of features that are hard to find in single devices, with extensive telecommunications capabilities and highest-quality digital video/music/TV program storage/playback.
2. *Security*—Our smart phone uses a Linux-based operating system that is less vulnerable to hackers and other security threats that can result in stolen or corrupted data.
3. *Pricing*—Our product is priced lower than competing smart phones—none of which offer the same bundle of features—which gives us an edge with price-conscious customers.

*Weaknesses* By waiting to enter the smart-phone market until considerable consolidation of competitors has occurred, Sonic has learned from the successes and mistakes of others. Nonetheless, we have two main weaknesses:

1. *Lack of brand awareness*—Sonic has no established brand or image, whereas Samsung, Apple, Motorola, and others have strong brand recognition. We will address this issue with aggressive promotion.
2. *Heavier and thicker unit*—The Sonic 1000 is slightly heavier and thicker than most competing models because it incorporates so many telecommunication and multimedia features. To counteract this weakness, we will emphasize our product's benefits and value-added pricing, two compelling competitive strengths.

> Strengths are internal capabilities that can help the company reach its objectives.

> Weaknesses are internal elements that may interfere with the company's ability to achieve its objectives.

*Opportunities*  Sonic can take advantage of two major market opportunities:

1.  *Increasing demand for state-of-the-art multimedia devices with a full array of communication functions*—The market for cutting-edge multimedia, multifunction devices is growing rapidly. Smart phones are already commonplace in public, work, and educational settings; in fact, users who bought entry-level models are now trading up.
2.  *Lower technology costs*—Better technology is now available at a lower cost than ever before. Thus, Sonic can incorporate advanced features at a value-added price that allows for reasonable profits.

*Threats*  We face three main threats at the introduction of the Sonic 1000:

1.  *Increased competition*—More companies are offering devices with some but not all of the features and benefits provided by the Sonic 1000. Therefore, Sonic's marketing communications must stress our clear differentiation and value-added pricing.
2.  *Downward pressure on pricing*—Increased competition and market share strategies are pushing smart-phone prices down. Still, our objective of breaking even with second-year sales of the original model is realistic, given the lower margins in the smart-phone market.
3.  *Compressed product life cycle*—Smart phones are reaching the maturity stage of their life cycle more quickly than earlier technology products. Because of this compressed life cycle, we plan to introduce an even greater-enhanced media-oriented second product during the year following the Sonic 1000's launch.

**2.3 COMPETITION**  The emergence of well-designed multifunction smart phones, including the Apple iPhone, has increased competitive pressure. Competitors are continually adding features and sharpening price points. Key competitors:

*   *Apple:* The leader in smart-phone market share, Apple takes pride in being forward thinking, innovative, and consumer-centric. Its latest iPhone 5s features an impressively thin and lightweight metallic design, fingerprint identity sensor, dual LED flash, and CPU power up to two times faster than the previous generation.
*   *Samsung*: A strong competitor in the smart-phone industry, Samsung ranks as a top 10 global brand and has plans to reach $400 billion in revenue by 2020. The Galaxy S5 features a whopping 16-megapixel camera and the first-ever built-in heart rate monitor.
*   *LG*: Founded in 1958, LG Electronics strives to be a worldwide leader in the digital market and in 2014 ranked third in total smart-phone subscribers, behind Apple and Samsung. Its G2 smart phone features a large 5.2-inch full HD IPS display and ergonomically positioned rear key control on the back.
*   *Motorola*: Motorola pioneered the mobile communications industry and invented the first mobile phone in 1973. Today, the company prides itself on creating value with comfortable, approachable, and powerful devices. The Moto X is first smart phone to be designed, engineered, and assembled entirely in the United States.
*   *HTC*: Founded in 1997, HTC is a relatively new competitor to the industry but still ranks fifth in smart-phone market share. HTC built its reputation on providing high-quality products that garnered recommendations and referrals from both retailers and consumers. Its HTC One (M8) smart phone comes with a 5.0-inch full HD 1080p display and is curved to fit in the palm of the hand.

Despite strong competition, Sonic can carve out a definitive image and gain recognition among targeted segments. Our appealing combination of state-of-the-art features and low price is a critical point of differentiation for competitive advantage. Our second product will be even more media-oriented to appeal to segments where we will have strong brand recognition. Exhibit A.2 shows a sample of competitive products and prices.

**2.4 PRODUCT OFFERINGS**  The Sonic 1000 offers the following standard features:

*   Voice recognition for hands-free operation
*   Full array of apps
*   Complete organization functions, including linked calendar, address book, synchronization

## Selected Smart-Phone Products and Pricing

|  | Apple<br>iPhone 5s | Samsung<br>Galaxy S5 | LG G2 | Motorola<br>Moto X | HTC One (M8) |
|---|---|---|---|---|---|
| Built-in Storage | 64 GB | 32 GB, micro SD up<br>to 128 GB | 32 GB | 16 GB | 32 GB, micro SD up<br>to 128 GB |
| Display | 4" IPS LCD | 5.1" Super AMOLED | 5.2" IPS LCD | 4.7" AMOLED | 5.0" IPS LCD |
| Camera | 8.0 MP | 16 MP | 13 MP | 10 MP | 4 MP |
| Price | $399.99 | $199.99 | $399.99 | $399.99 | $199.99 |

- Digital music/video/television recording, wireless downloading, and instant playback
- Wireless Web and e-mail, text messaging, instant messaging
- Four-inch high-quality color touch screen
- Ultra-fast 64-gigabyte drive and expansion slots
- Integrated 12-megapixel camera with flash and photo editing/sharing tools

First-year sales revenues are projected to be $200 million, based on sales of 800,000 of the Sonic 1000 model at a wholesale price of $250 each. Our second-year product will be the Sonic All Media 2000, stressing enhanced multimedia communication, networking, and entertainment functions. The Sonic All Media 2000 will include Sonic 1000 features plus additional features such as:

- Built-in media beaming to share music, video, and television files with other devices
- Webcam for instant video capture and uploading to popular video Web sites
- Voice-command access to popular social networking Web sites

**2.5 DISTRIBUTION** Sonic-branded products will be distributed through a network of retailers in the top 50 U.S. markets. Among the most important channel partners being contacted are:

- *Office supply superstores.* Office Depot and Staples will all carry Sonic products in stores, in catalogs, and online.
- *Computer stores.* Independent computer retailers will carry Sonic products.
- *Electronics specialty stores.* Best Buy will feature Sonic smart phones in its stores, online, and in its media advertising.
- *Online retailers.* Amazon.com will carry Sonic smart phones and, for a promotional fee, will give Sonic prominent placement on its homepage during the introduction.

> Distribution explains each channel for the company's products and mentions new developments and trends.

Distribution will initially be restricted to the United States, with appropriate sales promotion support. Later, we plan to expand into Canada and beyond.

# 3.0 Marketing Strategy

> Objectives should be defined in specific terms so management can measure progress and take corrective action to stay on track.

**3.1 OBJECTIVES** We have set aggressive but achievable objectives for the first and second years of market entry.

- *First-Year Objectives.* We are aiming for a 1 percent share of the U.S. smart-phone market through unit sales volume of 800,000.
- *Second-Year Objectives.* Our second-year objective is to achieve break-even on the Sonic 1000 and launch our second model.

**3.2 TARGET MARKETS** Sonic's strategy is based on a positioning of product differentiation. Our primary consumer target for the Sonic 1000 is middle- to upper-income professionals who need one fully loaded device to coordinate their busy schedules, stay in touch with family and

> All marketing strategies start with segmentation, targeting, and positioning.

colleagues, and be entertained on the go. Our secondary consumer target is high school, college, and graduate students who want a multimedia, dual-mode device. This segment can be described demographically by age (16–30) and education status. Our Sonic All Media 2000 will be aimed at teens and twentysomethings who want a device with features to support social networking and heavier, more extensive entertainment media consumption.

The primary business target for the Sonic 1000 is mid- to large-sized corporations that want to help their managers and employees stay in touch and input or access critical data when out of the office. This segment consists of companies with more than $25 million in annual sales and more than 100 employees. A secondary target is entrepreneurs and small business owners. Also we will target medical users who want to update or access patients' medical records.

Each of the marketing-mix strategies conveys Sonic's differentiation to these target market segments.

**3.3 POSITIONING** Using product differentiation, we are positioning the Sonic smart phone as the most versatile, convenient, value-added model for personal and professional use. Our marketing will focus on the value-priced multiple communication, entertainment, and information capabilities differentiating the Sonic 1000.

| |
|---|
| Positioning identifies the brand, benefits, points-of-difference, and points-of-parity for the product or line. |

**3.4 STRATEGIES**

*Product* The Sonic 1000, including all the features described in the earlier Product Offerings section and more, will be sold with a one-year warranty. We will introduce the Sonic All Media 2000 during the following year, after we have established our Sonic brand. The brand and logo (Sonic's distinctive yellow thunderbolt) will be displayed on our products and packaging as well as in all marketing campaigns.

*Pricing* The Sonic 1000 will be introduced at a $250 wholesale price and a $300 estimated retail price per unit. We expect to lower the price of this model when we expand the product line by launching the Sonic All Media 2000, to be priced at $350 wholesale per unit. These prices reflect a strategy of (1) attracting desirable channel partners and (2) taking share from established competitors.

*Distribution* Our channel strategy is to use selective distribution, marketing Sonic smart phones through well-known stores and online retailers. During the first year, we will add channel partners until we have coverage in all major U.S. markets and the product is included in the major electronics catalogs and Web sites. We will also investigate distribution through cell-phone outlets maintained by major carriers such as Verizon Wireless. In support of channel partners, we will provide demonstration products, detailed specification handouts, and full-color photos and displays featuring the product. Finally, we plan to arrange special payment terms for retailers that place volume orders.

*Marketing Communications* By integrating all messages in all media, we will reinforce the brand name and the main points of product differentiation. Research about media consumption patterns will help our advertising agency choose appropriate media and timing to reach prospects before and during product introduction. Thereafter, advertising will appear on a pulsing basis to maintain brand awareness and communicate various differentiation messages. The agency will also coordinate public relations efforts to build the Sonic brand and support the differentiation message. To generate buzz, we will host a user-generated video contest on our Web site. To attract, retain, and motivate channel partners for a push strategy, we will use trade sales promotions and personal selling. Until the Sonic brand has been established, our communications will encourage purchases through channel partners rather than from our Web site.

Product strategy includes decisions about product mix and lines, brands, packaging and labeling, and warranties.

Pricing strategy covers decisions about setting initial prices and adapting prices in response to opportunities and competitive challenges.

Distribution strategy includes selection and management of channel relationships to deliver value to customers.

Marketing communications strategy covers all efforts to communicate to target audiences and channel members.

**3.5 MARKETING MIX** The Sonic 1000 will be introduced in February. Here are summaries of action programs we will use during the first six months to achieve our stated objectives.

The marketing mix includes tactics and programs that support product, pricing, distribution, and marketing communications strategy.

- *January.* We will launch a $200,000 trade sales promotion campaign and participate in major industry trade shows to educate dealers and generate channel support for the product launch in February. Also, we will create buzz by providing samples to selected product reviewers, opinion leaders, influential bloggers, and celebrities. Our training staff will work with retail sales personnel at major chains to explain the Sonic 1000's features, benefits, and advantages.

- *February.* We will start an integrated print/radio/Internet/social media campaign targeting professionals and consumers. The campaign will show how many functions the Sonic smart phone can perform and emphasize the convenience of a single, powerful handheld device. This multimedia campaign will be supported by point-of-sale signage as well as online-only ads and video tours.
- *March.* As the multimedia advertising campaign continues, we will add consumer sales promotions such as a contest in which consumers post videos to our Web site, showing how they use the Sonic in creative and unusual ways. We will also distribute new point-of-purchase displays to support our retailers.
- *April.* We will hold a trade sales contest offering prizes for the salesperson and retail organization that sell the most Sonic smart phones during the four-week period.
- *May.* We plan to roll out a new national advertising campaign this month. The radio ads will feature celebrity voices telling their Sonic smart phones to perform functions such as initiating a phone call, sending an e-mail, playing a song or video, and so on. The stylized print and online ads will feature avatars of these celebrities holding their Sonic smart phones. We plan to repeat this theme for next year's product launch.
- *June.* Our radio campaign will add a new voice-over tagline promoting the Sonic 1000 as a graduation gift. We will exhibit at the semiannual electronics trade show and provide retailers with new competitive comparison handouts as a sales aid. In addition, we will analyze the results of customer satisfaction research for use in future campaigns and product development efforts.

**3.6 MARKETING RESEARCH** Using research, we will identify specific features and benefits our target market segments value. Feedback from market tests, surveys, and focus groups will help us develop and fine-tune the Sonic All Media 2000. We are also measuring and analyzing customers' attitudes toward competing brands and products. Brand awareness research will help us determine the effectiveness and efficiency of our messages and media. Finally, we will use customer satisfaction studies to gauge market reaction.

# 4.0 Financials

Total first-year sales revenue for the Sonic 1000 is projected at $200 million, with an average wholesale price of $250 per unit and variable cost per unit of $150 for unit sales volume of 800,000. We anticipate a first-year loss of as much as $40 million. Break-even calculations indicate that the Sonic 1000 will become profitable after the sales volume exceeds 267,500 during the product's second year. Our break-even analysis assumes per-unit wholesale revenue of $250 per unit, variable cost of $150 per unit, and estimated first-year fixed costs of $26,750,000. With these assumptions, the break-even calculation is:

$$\frac{26,750,000}{\$250 - \$150} = 267,500 \text{ units}$$

# 5.0 Controls

Controls are being established to cover implementation and the organization of our marketing activities.

**5.1 IMPLEMENTATION** We are planning tight control measures to closely monitor quality and customer service satisfaction. This will enable us to react very quickly in correcting any problems that may occur. Other early warning signals that will be monitored for signs of deviation from the plan include monthly sales (by segment and channel) and monthly expenses.

**5.2 MARKETING ORGANIZATION** Sonic's chief marketing officer, Jane Melody, holds overall responsibility for all of the company's marketing activities. Exhibit A.3 shows the structure of the eight-person marketing organization. Sonic has hired Worldwide Marketing to handle national sales campaigns, digital, trade and consumer sales promotions, and public relations efforts.

Programs should coordinate with the resources and activities of other departments that contribute to customer value for each product.

This section shows how marketing research will support the development, implementation, and evaluation of marketing strategies and programs.

Financials include budgets and forecasts to plan for marketing expenditures, scheduling, and operations.

Controls help management measure results and identify any problems or performance variations that need corrective action.

The marketing department may be organized by function, as in this sample, or by geography, product, customer, or some combination of these.

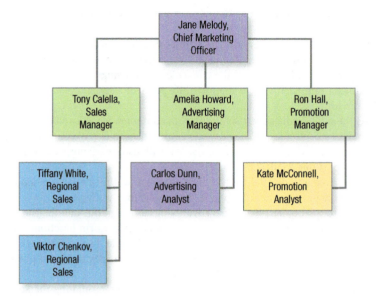

# Sonic Marketing Plan Chapter Assignments

## Chapter 2: Developing Marketing Strategies and Plans

As an assistant to Jane Melody, Sonic's chief marketing officer, you've been assigned to draft a mission statement for top management's review.[1] This should cover the competitive spheres within which the firm will operate and your recommendation of an appropriate generic competitive strategy. Using your knowledge of marketing, the information you have about Sonic, and library or Internet resources, answer the following questions.

- What should Sonic's mission be?
- In what competitive spheres (industry, products and applications, competence, market-segment, vertical, and geographic) should Sonic operate?
- Which of Porter's generic competitive strategies would you recommend Sonic follow in formulating overall strategy?

As your instructor directs, enter your answers and supporting information in a written marketing plan to document your ideas.

## Chapter 3: Collecting Information and Forecasting Demand

Jane Melody asks you to scan Sonic's external environment for early warning signals of new opportunities and emerging threats that could affect the success of the Sonic 1000 smart phone. Using Internet or library sources (or both), locate information to answer three questions about key areas of the macroenvironment.

- What demographic changes are likely to affect Sonic's targeted segments?
- What economic trends might influence buyer behavior in Sonic's targeted segments?
- How might the rapid pace of technological change alter Sonic's competitive situation?

Enter your answers about Sonic's environment in the appropriate sections of a written marketing plan to record your comments.

# Chapter 4: Conducting Market Research

Your next task is to consider how marketing research can help Sonic support its marketing strategy. Jane Melody also asks you how Sonic can measure results after the marketing plan is implemented. She wants you to answer the following three questions.

- What surveys, focus groups, observation, behavioral data, or experiments will Sonic need to support its marketing strategy? Be specific about the questions or issues that Sonic needs to resolve using marketing research.
- Where can you find suitable secondary data about total demand for smart phones over the next two years? Identify at least two sources (online or offline), describe what you plan to draw from each source, and indicate how the data would be useful for Sonic's marketing planning.
- Recommend three specific marketing metrics for Sonic to apply in determining marketing effectiveness and efficiency.

Enter this information in the marketing plan you've been writing to document your responses.

# Chapter 5: Creating Long-Term Loyalty Relationships

Sonic has decided to focus on total customer satisfaction as a way of encouraging brand loyalty in a highly competitive marketplace. With this in mind, you've been assigned to analyze three specific issues as you continue working on Sonic's marketing plan.

- How (and how often) should Sonic monitor customer satisfaction?
- Would you recommend that Sonic use the Net Promoter method? Explain your reasoning.
- Which customer touch points should Sonic pay particularly close attention to, and why?

Consider your answers in the context of Sonic's current situation and the objectives it has set. Then enter your latest decisions in the written marketing plan.

# Chapter 6: Analyzing Consumer Markets

You're responsible for researching and analyzing the consumer market for Sonic's smart-phone product. Look again at the data you've already entered about the company's current situation and macroenvironment, especially the market being targeted. Now answer these questions about the market and buyer behavior.

- What cultural, social, and personal factors are likely to most influence consumer purchasing of smart phones? What research tools would help you better understand the effect on buyer attitudes and behavior?
- Which aspects of consumer behavior should Sonic's marketing plan emphasize, and why?
- What marketing activities should Sonic plan to coincide with each stage of the consumer buying process?

After you've analyzed these aspects of consumer behavior, consider the implications for Sonic's marketing efforts to support the launch of its smart phone. Finally, document your findings and conclusions in the written marketing plan.

# Chapter 7: Analyzing Business Markets

You've been learning more about the business market for Sonic's smart phone. Jane Melody has defined this market as mid- to large-sized corporations that want their employees to stay in touch and be able to input or access data from any location. Respond to the following three questions based on your knowledge of Sonic's current situation and business-to-business marketing.

- What types of businesses appear to fit Melody's market definition? How can you research the number of employees and find other data about these types of businesses?
- What type of purchase would a Sonic smart phone represent for these businesses? Who would participate in and influence this type of purchase?
- Would demand for smart phones among corporate buyers tend to be inelastic? What are the implications for Sonic's marketing plan?

Your answers to these questions will affect how Sonic plans marketing activities for the business segments to be targeted. Take a few minutes to note your ideas in the written marketing plan.

## Chapter 8: Tapping into Global Markets

As Jane Melody's assistant, you're researching how to market the Sonic 1000 smart-phone product outside the United States within a year. You've been asked to answer the following questions about Sonic's use of global marketing.

- As a start-up company, should Sonic use indirect or direct exporting, licensing, joint ventures, or direct investment to enter the Canadian market next year? To enter other markets? Explain your answers.
- If Sonic starts marketing its smart phone in other countries, which of the international product strategies is most appropriate? Why?
- Although some components are made in Asia, Sonic's smart phones will be assembled in Mexico through a contractual arrangement with a local factory. How are country-of-origin perceptions likely to affect your marketing recommendations?

Think about how these global marketing issues fit into Sonic's overall marketing strategy. Now document your ideas in the marketing plan you've been writing.

## Chapter 9: Identifying Market Segments and Targets

Identifying suitable market segments and selecting targets are critical to the success of any marketing plan. As Jane Melody's assistant, you're responsible for market segmentation and targeting. Look back at the market information, buyer behavior data, and competitive details you previously gathered as you answer the following questions.

- Which variables should Sonic use to segment its consumer and business markets?
- How can Sonic evaluate the attractiveness of each identified segment? Should Sonic market to one consumer segment and one business segment or target more than one in each market? Why?
- Should Sonic pursue full-market coverage, market specialization, product specialization, selective specialization, or single-segment concentration? Why?

Next, consider how your decisions about segmentation and targeting will affect Sonic's marketing efforts. Depending on your instructor's directions, summarize your conclusions in the written marketing plan.

## Chapter 10: Crafting the Brand Positioning

As before, you're working with Jane Melody on Sonic's marketing plan for launching a new smart phone. Now you're focusing on Sonic's brand positioning by answering three specific questions.

- In a sentence or two, what is an appropriate brand positioning for the Sonic 1000 smart phone?
- Create a perceptual map to diagram points-of-parity and points-of-difference between Sonic and its competitors. Are there any opportunities based on your findings?
- How can Sonic create differentiation from competitors using emotional branding?

Document your ideas in the written marketing plan. Note any additional research you may need to determine how to proceed after the Sonic 1000 has been launched.

## Chapter 11: Creating Brand Equity

Sonic is a new brand with no prior brand associations, which presents a number of marketing opportunities and challenges. Jane Melody has given you responsibility for making recommendations about three brand equity issues that are important to Sonic's marketing plan.

- What brand elements would be most useful for differentiating the Sonic brand from competing brands?
- How can Sonic sum up its brand promise for the new smart phone?
- Should Sonic add a brand for its second product or retain the Sonic name?

Be sure your brand ideas are appropriate in light of what you've learned about your targeted segments and the competition. Then add this information to your written marketing plan.

## Chapter 12: Addressing Competition and Driving Growth

Knowing that the smart-phone market is likely to remain highly competitive, Jane Melody wants you to look ahead at how Sonic can develop new products outside the smart-phone market. Review the competitive situation and the market situation before you continue working on the Sonic marketing plan.

- List three new-product ideas that build on Sonic's strengths and the needs of its various target segments. What criteria should Sonic use to screen these ideas?
- Develop the most promising idea into a product concept, and explain how Sonic can test this concept. What particular dimensions must be tested?
- Assume that the most promising idea tests well. Now develop a marketing strategy for introducing it, including a description of the target market; the product positioning; the estimated sales, profit, and market share goals for the first year; your channel strategy; and the marketing budget you will recommend for this new-product introduction. If possible, estimate Sonic's costs and conduct a break-even analysis.

Document all the details of your new-product development ideas in the written marketing plan.

## Chapter 13: Setting Product Strategy

Introducing a new product entails a variety of decisions about product strategy, including differentiation, ingredient branding, packaging, labeling, warranty, and guarantee. Your next task is to answer the following questions about Sonic's product strategy.

- Which aspect of product differentiation would be most valuable in setting Sonic apart from its competitors, and why?
- Should Sonic use ingredient branding to tout the Linux-based operating system that it says makes its smart phone more secure than smart phones based on some other operating systems?
- How can Sonic use packaging and labeling to support its brand image and help its channel partners sell the smart-phone product more effectively?

Once you've answered these questions, incorporate your ideas into the marketing plan you've been writing.

## Chapter 14: Designing and Managing Services

You're planning customer support services for Sonic's new smart-phone product. Review what you know about your target market and its needs; also think about what Sonic's competitors are offering. Then respond to these three questions about designing and managing services.

- What support services are buyers of smart-phone products likely to want and need?
- How can Sonic manage gaps between perceived service and expected service to satisfy customers?
- What postsale service arrangements must Sonic make, and how would you expect these to affect customer satisfaction?

Consider how your service strategy will support Sonic's overall marketing efforts. Summarize your recommendations in the written marketing plan to document your ideas.

## Chapter 15: Introducing New Market Offerings

Sonic is a new entrant in an established industry characterized by competitors with relatively high brand identity and strong market positions. Use research and your knowledge of how to deal with competitors to consider three issues that will affect the company's ability to successfully introduce its first product:

- What factors will you use to determine Sonic's strategic group?
- Should Sonic select a class of competitor to attack on the basis of strength versus weakness, closeness versus distance, or good versus bad? Why is this appropriate in the smart-phone market?
- As a start-up company, what competitive strategy would be most effective as Sonic introduces its first product?

Take time to analyze how Sonic's competitive strategy will affect its marketing strategy and tactics. Now summarize your ideas in the written marketing plan.

## Chapter 16: Developing Pricing Strategies and Programs

You're in charge of pricing Sonic's product for its launch early next year. Review the SWOT analysis you previously prepared as well as Sonic's competitive environment, targeting strategy, and product positioning. Now continue working on your marketing plan by responding to the following questions.

- What should Sonic's primary pricing objective be? Explain your reasoning.
- Are smart-phone customers likely to be price sensitive? What are the implications for your pricing decisions?
- What price adaptations (such as discounts, allowances, and promotional pricing) should Sonic include in its marketing plan?

Make notes about your answers to these questions and then document the information in the written marketing plan.

## Chapter 17: Designing and Managing Integrated Marketing Channels

At Sonic, you have been asked to develop a marketing channel system for the new Sonic 1000 smart phone. Based on what you know about designing and managing integrated marketing channels, answer the three questions that follow.

- Do you agree with Jane Melody's decision to use a push strategy for the new product? Explain your reasoning.
- How many channel levels are appropriate for Sonic's targeted consumer and business segments?
- In determining the number of channel members, should you use exclusive, selective, or intensive distribution? Why?

Be sure your marketing channel ideas support the product positioning and are consistent with the goals that have been set. Record your recommendations in the written marketing plan.

## Chapter 18: Managing Retailing, Wholesaling, and Logistics

At this point, you need to make more specific decisions about managing the marketing intermediaries for Sonic's first product. Formulate your ideas by answering the following questions.

- What types of retailers would be most appropriate for distributing Sonic's smart phone? What are the advantages and disadvantages of selling through these types of retailers?

- What role should wholesalers play in Sonic's distribution strategy? Why?
- What market-logistics issues must Sonic consider for the launch of its first smart phone?

Summarize your decisions about retailing, wholesaling, and logistics in the marketing plan you've been writing.

# Chapter 19: Designing and Managing Integrated Marketing Communications

Jane Melody has assigned you to plan integrated marketing communications for Sonic's new-product introduction. Review the data, decisions, and strategies you previously documented in your marketing plan before you answer the next three questions.

- What communications objectives are appropriate for Sonic's initial campaign?
- How can Sonic use personal communications channels to influence its target audience?
- Which communication tools would you recommend using after Sonic's initial product has been in the market for six months? Why?

Confirm that your marketing communications plans make sense in light of Sonic's overall marketing efforts. Now, as your instructor directs, summarize your thoughts in the written marketing plan.

# Chapter 20: Managing Mass Communications: Advertising, Sales Promotions, Events and Experiences, and Public Relations

Mass communications will play a key role in Sonic's product introduction. After reviewing your earlier decisions and thinking about the current situation (especially your competitive circumstances), respond to the following questions to continue planning Sonic's marketing communications strategy.

- Once Sonic begins to use consumer advertising, what goals would be appropriate?
- Should Sonic continue consumer and trade sales promotion after the new product has been in the market for six months? Explain your reasoning.
- Jane Melody wants you to recommend an event sponsorship possibility that would be appropriate for the new-product campaign. What type of event would you suggest, and what objectives would you set for the sponsorship?

Record your ideas about mass communications in the marketing plan you've been writing.

# Chapter 21: Managing Digital Communications: Online, Social Media, and Mobile

Digital communications strategies will be essential to Sonic's marketing plan as brand awareness can be generated quickly through online channels, social media, and word of mouth. Jane Melody is especially interested in your answers to the following questions.

- How should Sonic use word of mouth to generate brand awareness and encourage potential buyers to visit retailers to see the new smart phone in person?
- Which social media platforms and networks should Sonic pursue based on their target audiences? Explain your reasoning.
- Is mobile marketing a viable strategy for Sonic's smart phone? Why or why not?

Consider your overall marketing objectives as you compile your answers. Document your ideas in your marketing plan.

# Chapter 22: Managing Personal Communications: Direct and Database Marketing and Personal Selling

Sonic needs a strategy for managing personal communications during its new-product launch. This is the time to look at direct marketing, database marketing, and personal selling. Answer these three questions as you consider Sonic's personal communications strategy.

- Which forms of direct marketing are appropriate for Sonic, given its objectives, mass communications arrangements, and channel decisions?
- Should Sonic use database marketing to identify and cultivate prospects? What are the opportunities and potential downsides of this approach?
- Does Sonic need a direct sales force or can it sell through agents and other outside representatives?

Look back at earlier decisions and ideas before you document your comments about personal communications in your written marketing plan.

# Chapter 23: Managing a Holistic Marketing Organization for the Long Run

With the rest of the marketing plan in place, you're ready to make recommendations about how to manage Sonic's marketing activities. Here are some specific questions Jane Melody wants you to consider.

- How can Sonic drive customer-focused marketing and strategic innovation throughout the organization?
- What role should social responsibility play in Sonic's marketing?
- How can Sonic evaluate its marketing? Suggest several specific steps the company should take.

To complete your written marketing plan, enter your answers to these questions. Finally, draft the executive summary of the plan's highlights.

# Endnotes

## Chapter 1

1. "'Captain Planet,' The HBR Interview: Unilever CEO Paul Polman," *Harvard Business Review*, June 2012; "Unilever Reframes Marketing," February 8, 2012, www.warc.com; "Unilever Gets Back to Basics," www.warc.com, September 11, 2012; "Unilever Confident on China," www.warc.com, September 17, 2012; Geoffrey Precourt, "Engaging with Media and Markets: Unilever's Prowl for Experiential Improvement," *WARC Events Report: 4A's Transformation*, March 2011; "Unilever Targets Russia," www.warc.com, October 4, 2012; "Unilever Adopts 'Reverse Engineering,'" www.warc.com, October 1, 2012; "Unilever Seeks New Way Forward," www.warc.com, October 23, 2012; "Unilever Prioritises Emerging Markets," www.warc.com, October 31, 2012.

2. Philip Kotler, "Marketing: The Underappreciated Workhorse," *Market Leader* Quarter 2 (2009), pp. 8–10.

3. Marc de Swan Arons and Frank van den Driest, *The Global Brand CEO: Building the Ultimate Marketing Machine* (New York: Airstream, 2010).

4. Peter C. Verhoef and Peter S. H. Leeflang, "Understanding the Marketing Department's Influence within the Firm," *Journal of Marketing* 73 (March 2009), pp. 14–37; Pravin Nath and Vijay Mahajan, "Marketing in the C-Suite: A Study of Chief Marketing Officer Power in Firm's Top Management Teams," *Journal of Marketing*, 75 (January 2012), pp. 60–77; Christian Schulze, Bernd Skiera, and Thorsten Weisel, "Linking Customer and Financial Metrics to Shareholder Value: The Leverage Effect in Customer-Based Valuation," *Journal of Marketing*, 76 (March 2012), pp. 17–32.

5. "How We See It: Three Senior Executives on the Future of Marketing," *McKinsey Quarterly*, July 2011; "American Express Open: Small Business Saturday," *Jay Chiat Strategic Excellence Awards: Gold 2012*, www.warc.com, accessed November 5, 2012; John Tozzi, "Black Friday's Younger Cousin Grows Up," *Bloomberg Businessweek*, December 3, 2012, pp. 54–55; Christine Birker, "AmEx's Small Business Saturday a Big Marketing Hit," *Marketing News*, January 2013, p. 4.

6. Alex Webb, "BMW Courts Bloggers for $100 Million Online Boost: Cars," www.bloomberg.com, June 11, 2012.

7. Geoffrey Precourt, "How Corning Broke the Rules in Online Video—and Won," www.warc.com, July 2012.

8. American Marketing Association, "Definition of Marketing," www.marketingpower.com/AboutAMA/ Pages/DefinitionofMarketing.aspx, 2007; Lisa Keefe, "Marketing Defined," *Marketing News*, January 15, 2008, pp. 28–29.

9. Robert F. Lusch and Frederick E. Webster Jr., "A Stakeholder-Unifying, Cocreation Philosophy for Marketing," *Journal of Macromarketing* 31,no. 2, 2011, 129–34. See also Robert F. Lusch and Frederick E. Webster Jr., "Elevating Marketing: Marketing Is Dead! Long Live Marketing!," *Journal of Academy of Marketing Science* 41 (January 2013), pp. 389–99.

10. Peter Drucker, *Management: Tasks, Responsibilities, Practices* (New York: Harper and Row, 1973), pp. 64–65.

11. Lisa Mataloni and Andrew Hodge, "Gross Domestic Product: First Quarter 2012 (Second Estimate)," *Bureau of Economic Analysis*, May 31, 2012.

12. Irving J. Rein, Philip Kotler, Michael Hamlin, and Martin Stoller, *High Visibility*, 3rd ed. (New York: McGraw-Hill, 2006).

13. Philip Kotler, Christer Asplund, Irving Rein, and Donald H. Haider, *Marketing Places in Europe: Attracting Investments, Industries, Residents, and Visitors to European Cities, Communities, Regions, and Nations* (London: Financial Times Prentice Hall, 1999); Philip Kotler, Irving J. Rein, and Donald Haider, *Marketing Places: Attracting Investment, Industry, and Tourism to Cities, States, and Nations* (New York: Free Press, 1993).

14. Emily Glazer and Melissa Korn, "Marketing Pros: Big Brands on Campus," *Wall Street Journal*, August 5, 2012.

15. http://thomsonreuters.com/about/, accessed October 1, 2012.

16. Jena McGregor, Matthew Boyle, and Peter Burrows, "Your New Customer: The State," *BusinessWeek*, March 23 and 30, 2009, p. 66.

17. Nikolaus Franke, Peter Keinz, and Christoph J. Steger, "Testing the Value of Customization: When Do Customers Really Prefer Products Tailored to Their Preferences?" *Journal of Marketing* 73 (September 2009), pp. 103–21.

18. Sean Corcoran, "Defining Earned, Owned and Paid Media," *Forrester Blogs*, December 16, 2009. For an empirical examination, see Andrew T. Stephen and Jeff Galak, "The Effects of Traditional and Social Earned Media on Sales: A Study of a Microlending Marketplace," *Journal of Marketing Research* 49 (October 2012), pp. 624–39.

19. Jim Edwards, "How Chipotle's Business Model Depends on NEVER Running TV Ads," *Business Insider*, March 16, 2012; Dan Klamm, "How Chipotle Uses Social Media to Cultivate a Better World," *Spredfast*, March 21, 2012; Danielle Sacks, "For Exploding All the Rules; Chipotle: The World's 50 Most Innovative Companies in 2012," *Fast Company*, October 2012; Leslie Patton, "Chipotle, Growth Slowing, Looks at Fast Food Future," *Bloomberg BusinessWeek*, October 25, 2012.

20. "Three Screen Report: Media Consumption and Multi-tasking Continue to Increase across TV, Internet and Mobile," *NielsenWire*, December 18, 2009; Felix Gillette, "For Bravo, One Screen Isn't Enough," *Bloomberg BusinessWeek*, November 8, 2010; "Global Online Consumers and Multi-Screen Media: Today and Tomorrow," *A Nielsen Report*, May 2012.

21. Jonathan D. Rockoff and Joann S. Lublin, "J&J Recruits Bayer Executive, *Wall Street Journal*, September 14, 2012.

22. Jessi Hempel, "Is Pinterest the Next Facebook?," *Fortune*, April 9, 2012, pp. 109–14; "Can Ben Silberman Turn Pinterest into the World's Greatest Shopfront?," *Fast Company*, September 2012; Pui-Wing Tam, "Pinterest Raises $100 Million with $1.5 Billion Valuation," *Wall Street Journal*, May 17, 2012; "Pinterest Holds Major Promise for Brands," www.warc.com, October 18, 2012; Laura Schlereth, "Marketers' Interest in Pinterest," *Marketing News*, April 30, 2012, p. 8.

23. Geoffrey Precourt, "Engaging with Media and Markets: Unilever's Prowl for Experiential Improvement," *WARC Events Report: 4A's Transformation*, March 2011; "Facebook Hits 1bn Users," www.warc.com, October 5, 2012; "African Consumers Get Online," www.warc.com, October 5, 2012.

24. "Digital Focus Vital for Brands," www.warc.com, January 30, 2012.

25. Jessi Hempel, "Don Draper Goes to the Data Center," *Fortune*, July 23, 2012.

26. "P&G Uses Real-Time Approach," www.warc.com, October 15, 2012; "Procter & Gamble Taps New Tech Trends," www.warc.com, September 19, 2012; Quentin Hardy, "The Matrix of Soap," *Forbes*, August 22, 2011. For broader discussion, see David Kiron, Pamela Kirk Prentice, and Renee Boucher Ferguson, "Innovating with Analytics," *MIT Sloan Management Review*, Fall 2012, pp. 47–52.

27. David Kirkpatrick, "Social Power and the Coming Corporate Revolution," *Forbes*, September 26, 2011.

28. David Kiron, Doug Palmer, Anh Nguyen Phillips and Nina Kruschwitz, "What Managers Really Think about Social Business," *Sloan Management Review*, Summer 2012, pp. 51–60.

29. Alex Knapp, "Hair Extensions," *Forbes*, April 20, 2012, p. 60.

30. Peter Mansell, "Pharma Sales and the Digital Rep," *Eye for Pharma*, May 28, 2012.

31. Yuval Atsmon, Peter Child, Richard Dobbs, and Laxman Narasimhan, "Winning the $30 Trillion Decathalon: Going for Gold in Emerging Marketing Markets," *McKinsey Quarterly*, August 2012.

32. "Brands Must Serve New Consumers," www.warc.com, October 22, 2012.

33. "Multicultural Shoppers Attract U.S. Brands," www.warc.com, October 8, 2012.

34. Vijay Govindarajan and Chris Trimble, *Reverse Innovation: Create Far from Home, Win Everywhere* (Boston: Harvard Business School Publishing, 2012).

35. Rajendra Sisodia, David Wolfe, and Jagdish Sheth, *Firms of Endearment: How World-Class Companies Profit from Passion* (Upper Saddle River, NJ: Wharton School Publishing, 2007).

36. Jeffrey Hollender and Stephen Fenichell, *What Matters Most* (New York: Basic Books, 2004), p. 168. But CSR efforts may not work well for all types of brands, e.g., luxury brands; see Carlos J. Torelli, Alokparna Basu Monga, and Andrew M. Kaikati, "Doing Poorly by Doing Good: Corporate Social Responsibility and Brand Concepts," *Journal of Consumer Research* 38 (February 2012), pp. 948–63.

37. "Older Consumers Go Social in Germany," www.warc.com, September 10, 2012; "Digital Media Booms in Germany," www.warc.com, October 26, 2012; "German Firms See Social Payback," www.warc.com, November 2, 2012; "German Web Users Willing to Spend More," www.warc.com, November 15, 2012; "Tablet Uptake Rises in Germany," www.warc.com, November 20, 212, "Mobile Web Gains Ground in Germany," www.warc.com, November 23, 2012; "German Firms Focus on Social Media," www.warc.com, December 11, 2012.

38. Dana Garrett, "Progressive Settles with Accident Victim's Family after Tale Went Viral," www.money.cnn.com, August 17, 2012; Erik Holm, "On Twitter, Over 1,000 Claim They've Already Dropped Progressive," *Wall Street Journal*, August 20, 2012; Brian Patrick Eha, "Progressive Robo-Tweets Spark Social Media Crisis," www.money.cnn.com, August 14, 2012.

39. "'Showrooming Is Not a Worry for Retailers," www.warc.com, October 8, 2012.

40. "Smartphones Shape Habits in Europe," www.warc.com, October 8, 2012.

41. Allen Tsai, "A Second Chance for Sprint and Dan Hesse," www.mobiledia.com, October 18, 2012.

42. Gina Trapini, "What Business Card? Just Scan My QR Code," *Fast Company*, March 17, 2010; for a description of alternative technology, see Jason Feifer, "To Catch a Customer," *Fast Company*, February 2012, p. 36.

43. Greg Stuart, "Why Consumers Hate Advertising and What They Are Doing About It," Market Research Report, *Vizu Answers*, September 2008.

44. "New Directions: Consumer Goods Companies Honea Cross-Channel Approach to Consumer Marketing," *The Economist Intelligence Unit Special Report*, February 2012.

45. Bruce Horovitz, "In Trend toward Vanity Food, It's Getting Personal," *USA Today*, August 9, 2006; J. P. Gownder, "Why Large-Scale Product Customization Is Finally Viable for Business," www.mashable.com, April 13, 2011.

46. http://info.cvscaremark.com/our-company/cvs-caremark-facts, accessed February 16, 2014.

47. Antonio Gonsalves, "Dell Makes $3 Million from Twitter-Related Sales," *InformationWeek*, June 12, 2009; Lionel Menchaca, "Expanding Connections with Customers through Social Media," www.Direct2Dell.com, December 8, 2009.

48. Mark Schaefer, "The 10 Best Corporate Blogs in the World," www.businessesgrow.com, January 5, 2011; Roger Yu, "More Companies Quit Blogging, Go with Facebook Instead," *USA Today*, April 20, 2012

49. David Kirkpatrick, "Social Power and the Coming Corporate Revolution," *Forbes*, September 26, 2011.

50. "Intranet Case Study: GM's mySocrates," www.communitelligence.com, accessed February 16, 2014.

51. David Kirkpatrick, "Social Power and the Coming Corporate Revolution," *Forbes*, September 26, 2011.

52. Byron Acohido, "Social-Media Tools Can Boost Productivity," *USA Today*, August 12, 2012.

53. "Privatisation in the 21st Century: Recent Experiences of OECD Countries," white paper, Organisation for Economic Co-operation and Development, January 2009, p. 10.

54. "Hindustan Unilever Empowers Staff," www.warc.com, July 19, 2012.

55. Rachel Dodes, "Twitter Goes to the Movies," *Wall Street Journal*, August 3, 2012; Dave Roos, "How Movie Marketing Works," www.howstuffworks.com, September 25, 2008; Ryan McKee, "The 7 Best Viral Marketing Campaigns in Movie History," www.moviefone.com, June 7, 2011; Mallory Russell, "13 Really Strange Movie Marketing Campaigns," www.businessinsider.com, February 12, 2012.

56. Theodore Levitt, "Marketing Myopia," *Harvard Business Review*, July–August 1960, p. 50.

57. "1100100 and Counting," *The Economist*, June 11, 2011; Spencer Ante, "As Economy Cools, IBM Furthers Focus on Marketers," *Wall Street Journal*, July 17, 2012.

58. "Case Study: Promote Iceland," www.warc.com, 2012; "How to Use a Volcanic Eruption to Your Advantage in Marketing," ICCA Best Marketing Award Entry 2010; Marc Springate and George Bryant, "Promote Iceland: Inspired by Iceland," www.warc.com, 2012.

59. For a discussion of the conditions when consumers are most likely to prefer fair-trade products, see Katherine White, Rhiannon MacDonnell, and John H. Ellard, "Belief in a Just World: Consumer Intentions and Behaviors Toward Ethical Products," *Journal of Marketing* 76 (January 2012), pp. 103–18.

60. "Many Shoppers Support Regulation," www.warc.com, July 10, 2012.

61. E. Jerome McCarthy and William D. Perreault, *Basic Marketing: A Global-Managerial Approach*, 14th ed. (Homewood, IL: McGraw-Hill/Irwin, 2002).

# Chapter 2

1. Ben Worthen and Shara Tibken, "H-P to Book $8 Billion Charge," *Wall Street Journal*, August 8, 2012; Ben Worthen, "H-P Tries On a Sleeker Look," *Wall Street Journal*, September 17, 2012; Ben Worthen, "H-P, Dell Struggle as Buyers Shun PCs," *Wall Street Journal*, August 22, 2012; Aaron Ricadela, "Why Hewlett-Packard Impulse Buy Didn't Pay Off," *Bloomberg Businessweek*, December 3, 2012, pp. 35–36.

2. Nirmalya Kumar, *Marketing as Strategy: The CEO's Agenda for Driving Growth and Innovation* (Boston: Harvard Business School Press, 2004).

3. Michael E. Porter, *Competitive Advantage: Creating and Sustaining Superior Performance* (New York: Free Press, 1985).

4. For an academic treatment of benchmarking, see Douglas W. Vorhies and Neil A. Morgan, "Benchmarking Marketing Capabilities for Sustained Competitive Advantage," *Journal of Marketing* 69 (January 2005), pp. 80–94.

5. Michael Hammer and James Champy, *Reengineering the Corporation: A Manifesto for Business Revolution* (New York: Harper Business, 1993).

6. Ibid.; Jon R. Katzenbach and Douglas K. Smith, *The Wisdom of Teams: Creating the High-Performance Organization* (Boston: Harvard Business School Press, 1993). Matias G. Enz and Douglas M. Lambert, "Using Cross-Functional, Cross-Firm Teams to Co-Create Value: The Role of Financial Measures," *Industrial Marketing Management*, 41 (April 2012), pp. 495–507.

7. "Ford Targets 30% Water Reduction per Vehicle," *Manufacturing Close-Up*, January 10, 2012.

8. Agneta Larsson, Mats Johansson, Fredrik Bååth, and Sanna Neselius, "Reducing Throughput Time in a Service Organization by Introducing Cross-Functional Teams," *Production Planning & Control* 23 (July 2012), pp. 571–80.

9. George S. Day, "Closing the Marketing Capabilities Gap," *Journal of Marketing* 75 (July 2011), p. 183–95.

10. George S. Day and Paul J. H. Schoemaker, *Peripheral Vision: Detecting the Weak Signals That Will Make or Break Your Company* (Cambridge, MA: Harvard Business School Press, 2006); Paul J. H. Schoemaker and George S. Day, "How to Make Sense of Weak Signals," *MIT Sloan Management Review* (Spring 2009), pp. 81–89.

11. "Peabody Energy Announces Global Business Realignment," www.bizjournals.com, March 7, 2012.

12. Kana Inagaki and Juro Osawa, "Panasonic Beats a Retreat as Green Energy Bets Flop," *Wall Street Journal*, October 31, 2012; "Panasonic to Close Czech LCD Panel Plant," *Industry Week*, October 31, 2012; Jonathan Soble, "Panasonic Warns of Second $10bn Loss," *Financial Times*, November 1, 2012; Daisuke Wakabayashi, "Panasonic Returns to Profit," *Wall Street Journal*, July 31, 2012.

13. Peter Drucker, *Management: Tasks, Responsibilities and Practices* (New York: Harper and Row, 1973), chapter 7.

14. James R. Hagerty, "Office Furniture in the Age of Smartphones," *Wall Street Journal*, August 7, 2012.

15. Kawasaki also humorously suggests checking out comic strip character Dilbert's mission statement generator first if one has to be developed by the organization: Dilbert.com.

16. www.americanapparel.net/aboutus/verticalint/, accessed October 20, 2012.

17. Peter Freedman, "The Age of the Hollow Company," *TimesOnline*, April 25, 2004; www.metro.lu/about/metro_facts, accessed October 20, 2012.

18. This section is based on Robert M. Grant, *Contemporary Strategy Analysis*, 8th ed. (New York: John Wiley & Sons, 2013), chapter 5.

19. Diane Mermigas, "ESPN Could Be Digital Sports Nirvana," www.mediapost.com, January 14, 2011; www.worldofespn.com, accessed February 20, 2014.

20. "Merck: Acquisitions & Divestments," www.merckgroup.com, October 23, 2010.

21. Jesse Eisinger, "The Marriage from Hell," *Condé Nast Portfolio*, February 2008, pp. 84–88, 132.

22. Peter Svensson, "Sprint's Nextel to Be Shut Off as Early as June 2013," www.huffingtonpost.com, May 29, 2012.

23. Susan Carey, "United's CEO Apologizes for Service Woes," *Wall Street Journal*, July 26, 2012; Drake Bennett, "Marriage at 30,000 Feet," *Bloomberg BusinessWeek*, February 6, 2012; Becky Quick, "A Sticky (Notes) Problem: Mergers and Consumers," *Fortune*, October 8, 2012, p. 75.

24. Curious George (Movie), www.rottentomatoes.com; The Adventures of Curious George, www.universalstudioshollywood.com; Curious George (TV Show), www.pbskids.org; all accessed October 20, 2012.

25. "AIG to Divest Runoff Businesses," Zacks Equity Research Analyst Blog, www.zacks.com, June 28, 2012.

26. Beth Snyder Bulik, "Customer Service Playing Bigger Role as Marketing Tool," *Advertising Age*, November 7, 2011.

27. Reckitt Benckiser (RB) New Product Review, Invention & New Product Exposition, www.inpex.com, accessed October 20, 2012.

28. "About Krka," www.krka.si, accessed October 20, 2012.

29. Paul J. H. Shoemaker, "Scenario Planning: A Tool for Strategic Thinking," *Sloan Management Review* (Winter 1995), pp. 25–40.

30. Ronald Grover, "Hollywood Ponders a Post-DVD Future, *BusinessWeek*, March 2, 2009, p. 56; Brooks Barnes, "Movie Studios See a Threat in Growth of Redbox," *New York Times*, September 7, 2009; Ben Fritz, "Warner's Approach to Video Games Is Paying Off," *Los Angeles Times*, October 18, 2011; Dan Sabbagh, "Hollywood in Turmoil as DVD Sales Drop and Downloads Steal the Show," www.guardian.co.uk, May 4, 2011.

31. Philip Kotler, *Kotler on Marketing* (New York: Free Press, 1999).

32. Ibid.

33. Phaedra Hise, "Was It Time to Go Downmarket?" *Inc*., September 2006, p. 47; Patrick J. Sauer, "Returning to Its Roots," *Inc.*, November 2007; www.loanbright.com, accessed February 20, 2014.

34. Dominic Dodd and Ken Favaro, "Managing the Right Tension," *Harvard Business Review*, December 2006, pp. 62–74.

35. Michael E. Porter, *Competitive Strategy: Techniques for Analyzing Industries and Competitors* (New York: Free Press, 1980), chapter 2.

36. Michael E. Porter, "What Is Strategy?" *Harvard Business Review*, November–December 1996, pp. 61–78.

37. "Member Airlines, Travel the World with the Star Alliance Network," www.staralliance.com, accessed October 20, 2012.

38. "VIBE Announces Partnership with Hoop It Up," *Business Wire*, March 14, 2011

39. Kerry Capell, "Vodafone: Embracing Open Source with Open Arms," *BusinessWeek*, April 20, 2009, pp. 52–53; "Call the Carabiniere," *The Economist*, May 16, 2009, p. 75; *Vodafone Annual Report*, www.vodfone.com, March 31, 2012.

40. Sonya Misquitta and Cecilie Rohwedder, "Kraft Covets Cadbury's Know-How in India," *Wall Street Journal*, September 10, 2009; Scott Moeller, "Case Study: Kraft's Takeover of Cadbury," *Financial Times*, January 9, 2012.

41. Robin Cooper and Robert S. Kalpan, "Profit Priorities from Activity-Based Costing," *Harvard Business Review*, May–June 1991, pp. 130–135.

42. See Robert S. Kaplan and David P. Norton, *The Balanced Scorecard: Translating Strategy into Action* (Boston: Harvard Business School Press, 1996) as a tool for monitoring stakeholder satisfaction.

43. Thomas J. Peters and Robert H. Waterman Jr., *In Search of Excellence: Lessons from America's Best-Run Companies* (New York: Harper and Row, 1982), pp. 9–12.

44. John P. Kotter and James L. Heskett, *Corporate Culture and Performance* (New York: Free Press, 1992).

45. An excellent hands-on guide to developing a marketing plan can be found with Alexander Chernev, *The Marketing Plan Handbook* (Chicago, IL: Cerebellum Press, 2011), on which some of the discussion in this section is built. See also Marian Burk Wood, *The Marketing Plan: A Handbook*, 4th ed. (Upper Saddle River, NJ: Pearson, 2011); Tim Calkins, *Breakthrough Marketing Plans: How to Stop Wasting Time and Start Driving Growth* (New York: Palgrave MacMillan, 2008).

46. Donald R. Lehmann and Russell S. Winer, *Product Management*, 3rd ed. (Boston: McGraw-Hill/Irwin, 2001).

# Chapter 3

1. David Welch, "Campbell Looks Way Beyond the Tomato," *Bloomberg BusinessWeek*, August 13, 2012; Candice Choi, "Campbell Soup Tries to Reinvent Itself," *Huffington Post*, September 7, 2012; Karl Greenberg, "Campbell's Go Soups Add Zing for Millennial Palates," *Marketing Daily*, November 13, 2012; Craig Torres and Anthony Field, "Campbell's Quest for Productivity," *Bloomberg BusinessWeek*, November 29, 2012; Jenna Goudreau, "Kicking the Can," *Forbes*, December 24, 2012, pp. 46–51.

2. Susan Warren, "Pillow Talk: Stackers Outnumber Plumpers; Don't Mention Drool," *Wall Street Journal*, January 8, 1998.

3. Dan Buckley, "Sweet Teeth Serve Irish Well in Chocoholics League," *Irish Examiner*, June 27, 2012; "Health Statistics: Tobacco: Cigarette Consumption (Most Recent) by Country," www.nationmaster.com, accessed November 7, 2012; "Global Beer Consumption by Country in 2010," *Kirin Institute of Food and Lifestyle Report* 33 (December 21, 2011); "Per Capita Wine Consumption by Country," 2010, *Trade Data and Analysis*, www.wineinstitute.org.

4. Ronald D. Michman, Edward M. Mazze, and Alan J. Greco, *Lifestyle Marketing: Reaching the New American Consumer* (Westport: Praeger, 2008); Scarlett Lindeman, "Jell-O Love: A Guide to Mormon Cuisine," *The Atlantic*, March 24, 2010; Julie Zeveloff, "These Cities Love Ice Cream the Most," *Business Insider*, July 20, 2012; Jim Farber, "New York is the King of Country," *Daily News*, August 9, 2012; "About Seattle," www.depts.washington.edu/uwsp/tsa/seattle.html, accessed February 7, 2014.

5. William Holstein, "The Dot Com within Ford," *BusinessWeek*, January 30, 2000.

6. For some thought-provoking academic perspectives on the challenges of Big Data, see George S. Day, "Closing the Marketing Capabilities Gap," *Journal of Marketing* 75 (July 2011), pp. 183–95.

7. Leonard M. Fuld, "Staying a Step Ahead of the Rest," *Chief Executive* 218 (June 2006), p. 32.

8. "Spies, Lies & KPMG," *BusinessWeek*, February 26, 2007.

9. Jennifer Esty, "Those Wacky Customers!" *Fast Company,* January 2004, p. 40.

10. Helen Coster, "Shopping Cart Psychology," *Forbes,* September 7, 2009, pp. 64–65.

11. Sara Steindorf, "Shoppers Spy on Those Who Serve," *Christian Science Monitor,* May 28, 2002; Edward F. McQuarrie, *Customer Visits: Building a Better Market Focus,* 3rd ed. (Newbury Park, CA: Sage Press, 2008).

12. "Customer Service Is Key: SavOn Convenience Stores Score Exceptionally High on Mystery Shop Reviews for Its Customer Service Skills," *Convenience Store Decisions,* June 6, 2012.

13. Heather Green, "It Takes a Web Village," *Business Week,* September 4, 2006, p. 66.

14. www.claritas.com/sitereports/default.jsp, accessed November 7, 2012.

15. www.attensity.com/products/, accessed February 5, 2014.

16. "More Younger Homemakers Rate Their Cooking Skills as Very Good Than Do Older Age Groups, Reports NPD," www.npd.com, November 29, 2011.

17. www.nielsen-online.com/products_buzz.jsp?section=pro_buzz#1, accessed February 7, 2014.

18. Alex Wright, "Mining the Web for Feelings, Not Facts," *New York Times,* August 24, 2009; Sarah E. Needleman, "For Companies, a Tweet in Time Can Avert PR Mess, *Wall Street Journal,* August 3, 2009, p. B6.

19. See *BadFads Museum,* www.badfads.com, for examples of fads and collectibles through the years.

20. Katy McLaunghlin, "Macaroni Grill's Order: Cut Calories, Keep Customers," *Wall Street Journal,* September 16, 2009, p. B6.

21. John Naisbitt and Patricia Aburdene, *Megatrends 2000* (New York: Avon Books, 1990).

22. World POPClock Projection, U.S. Census Bureau, www.census.gov, 2011; Statistical Abstract of the United States 2011, U.S. Census Bureau.

23. See Donella H. Meadows, Dennis L. Meadows, and Jorgen Randers, *Beyond Limits* (White River Junction, VT: Chelsea Green, 1993) for some commentary; see also Matt Rosenberg, "If The World Were a Village…," www.geography.about.com, August 19, 2011.

24. "World Development Indicators Database," *World Bank,* http://site_resources.worldbank.org/DATASTATISTICS/Resources/POP.pdf, September 15, 2009; "World Population Growth," www.worldbank.org/depweb/english/beyond/beyondco/beg_03.pdf.

25. For an academic examination of some relevant consumer behavior issues, see Kelly D. Martin and Ronald Paul Hill, "Life Satisfaction, Self-Determination, and Consumption Adequacy at the Bottom of the Pyramid," *Journal of Consumer Research* 38 (April 2012), pp. 1155–68.

26. "Facts and Statistics," U.S. Census Bureau, November 30, 2011.

27. Christine Birker, "The Census and the New American Consumer, *Marketing News,* May 15, 2011.

28. Queena Sook Kim, "Fisher-Price Reaches for Hispanics," *Wall Street Journal,* November 1, 2004.

29. "Census: Asian-Indian Population Explodes across U.S.," www.newamericamedia.org, May 13, 2011; Dan Ouellette, "Spice Market," *Adweek,* May 12, 2008;

30. Mark R. Forehand and Rohit Deshpandé, "What We See Makes Us Who We Are: Priming Ethnic Self-Awareness and Advertising Response," *Journal of Marketing Research* 38 (August 2001), pp. 336–48.

31. *The Central Intelligence Agency's World Factbook,* www.cia.gov/library/publications/the-world-factbook, June 25, 2012.

32. www.census.gov/newsroom/releases/archives/facts_for_features_special_editions/cb11-ff15.html; Richard Pérez-Peña, "U.S. Bachelor Degree Rate Passes Milestone," www.nytimes.com, February 23, 2012.

33. Sabrina Tavernise, "Married Couples Are No Longer a Majority, Census Finds," *The New York Times,* May 26, 2011; D'Vera Cohn, Jeffrey Passel, Wendy Wang and Gretchen Livingston, "Barely Half of U.S. Adults Are Married—A Record Low," www.pewsocialtrends.org, December 14, 2011.

34. Susan Donaldson James, "Gay Americans Make Up 4 Percent of Population," www.abcnews.go.com, April 8, 2011.

35. Lucia Moses, "Data Point: Modern Families," *Adweek,* August 20, 2012.

36. Nanette Byrnes, "Secrets of the Male Shopper," *BusinessWeek,* September 4, 2006, p. 44.

37. For a data-rich examination of the post-recession consumer, see John Gerzema and Michael D'Antonio, *Spend Shift: How the Post-Crisis Values Revolution Is Changing the Way We Buy, Sell and Live.* (San Francisco: Jossey-Bass, 2011).

38. Elisabeth Sullivan, "The Age of Prudence," *Marketing News,* April 15, 2009, pp. 8–11; Steve Hamm, "The New Age of Frugality," *BusinessWeek,* October 20, 2008, pp. 55–60; Jessica Deckler, "Never Pay Retail Again," CNNMoney.com, May 30, 2008.

39. Richard K. Miller and Kelli Washington, *Consumer Behavior 2011,* Richard K. Miller & Associates, chapter 11, pp. 63–74.

40. Michael Barnett, "They're Shopping, but Not As We Know It," *Marketing Week,* June 14, 2012.

41. Peter Wise, "Austerity Set to Increase Inequality in Portugal," *Financial Times,* December, 2011.

42. Julie Schlosser, "Infosys U.," *Fortune,* March 20, 2006, pp. 41–42; "Q1 Earnings: Five Things to Watch Out For from Infosys-TCS Double Header," *Economic Times,* July 12, 2012.

43. "Clearing House Suit Chronology," *Associated Press,* January 26, 2001; Paul Wenske, "You Too Could Lose $19,000!" *Kansas City Star,* October 31, 1999.

44. Laura Zinn, "Teens: Here Comes the Biggest Wave Yet," *BusinessWeek,* April 11, 2004, pp. 76–86.

45. Chris Taylor (ed.), "Go Green. Get Rich." *Business 2.0,* January/February 2007, pp. 68–79.

46. Philip Kotler, "Reinventing Marketing to Manage the Environmental Imperative," *Journal of Marketing* 75 (July 2011), pp. 132–35; Subhabrata Bobby Banerjee, Easwar S. Iyer, and Rajiv K Kashyap, "Corporate Enviromentalism: Antecedents and Influence of Industry Type," *Journal of Marketing* 67 (April 2003), pp. 106–22.

47. Apple quarterly press releases, culminating in "Apple Reports Fourth Quarter Results," www.apple.com, October 25, 2012.

48. David DiSalvo, "10 Big Science and Technology Advances to Watch," *Forbes,* July 29, 2011.

49. Allison Lim, "The U.S Is Still No. 1 in R&D Spending, but…," www.nbcnews.com, August 17, 2012; Martin Grueber and Tim Studt, *R&D,* December 16, 2011.

50. www.fda.gov/AboutFDA, accessed February 7, 2014; Henry I. Miller, "The FDA's Imprudent Caution," *Policy Review,* June/July 2010, pp. 73–85; John A. Vernon and Joseph H. Golec, "The Case for *Less,* not More, US FDA Regulation," *Pharmaeconomics 2011* 29, no. 8, pp. 637–40.

51. Schumpter: Beyond Economics, "Businesspeople Need to Think Harder about Political Risk," February 12, 2011.

52. See Dorothy Cohen, *Legal Issues in Marketing Decision Making* (Cincinnati: South-Western, 1995).

53. Paul Ohm, "Don't Build a Database of Ruin," *HBR Blog Network,* August 23, 2012.

54. Mark Sullivan, "Data Snatchers! The Booming Market for Your Online Identity," *PC World,* June 26, 2012.

55. Conference Summary, "Excelling in Today's Multimedia World," Economist Conferences' Fourth Annual Marketing Roundtable, Landor, March 2006.

56. For a good discussion and illustration, see Roger J. Best, *Market-Based Management,* 6th ed. (Upper Saddle River, NJ: Prentice Hall, 2013).

57. For further discussion, see Gary L. Lilien, Philip Kotler, and K. Sridhar Moorthy, *Marketing Models* (Upper Saddle River, NJ: Prentice Hall, 1992); Gary L. Lilien, "Bridging the Academic-Practitioner Divide in Marketing Decision Models," *Journal of Marketing* 75 (July 2011), pp. 196–210.

58. www.naics.com, accessed February 7, 2010; www.census.gov/epcd/naics02, December 9, 2010.

59. Stanley F. Slater and Eric M. Olson, "Mix and Match," *Marketing Management,* July–August 2006, pp. 32–37; Brian Sternthal and Alice M. Tybout, "Segmentation and Targeting," Dawn Iacobucci, ed., *Kellogg on Marketing* (New York: John Wiley & Sons, 2001), pp. 3–30.

60. Stephanie Clifford, "Measuring the Results of an Ad Right Down to the City Block," *New York Times,* August 5, 2009.

61. For an excellent overview of market forecasting, see Scott Armstrong, ed., *Principles of Forecasting: A Handbook for Researchers and Practitioners* (Norwell, MA: Kluwer Academic Publishers, 2001) and his Web site: www.forecastingprinciples.com; also see Roger J. Best, "An Experiment in Delphi Estimation in Marketing Decision Making," *Journal of Marketing Research* 11 (November 1974), pp. 447–52; Norman Dalkey and Olaf Helmer, "An Experimental Application of the Delphi Method to the Use of Experts," *Management Science,* April 1963, pp. 458–67.

# Chapter 4

1. "Twitter Buzz Informs TV Ads," www.warc.com, October 24, 2012; Josh Lowensohn, "Samsung Slams iPhone 5 Linegoers in New Attack Ad," *CNET News,* September 19, 2012; Salvador Rodriguez, "Samsung Pokes Fun at People Waiting in Line for iPhone 5," *Los Angeles Times,* September 19, 2012.

2. www.marketingpower.com/AboutAMA, accessed February 16, 2014.

3. See Robert Schieffer, *Ten Key Customer Insights: Unlocking the Mind of the Market* (Mason, OH: Thomson, 2005) for a comprehensive, in-depth discussion of how to generate customer insights to drive business results.

4. David Kiley, "Walmart Is Out to Change Its Story with New Ads," *Bloomberg Businessweek,* September 13, 2007.

5. Jessica Shambora, "Wanted: Fearless Marketing Execs," *Fortune,* August 15, 2011, p. 27.

6. Ellen Byron, "Wash Away Bad Hair Days," *Wall Street Journal,* June 30, 2010.

7. Natalie Zmuda, "Tropicana Line's Sales Plunge 20% Post-Rebranding," *Advertising Age,* April 2, 2009.

8. "2012 Global Market Research Report," *Esomar,* accessed February 16, 2014.

9. www.pgjobs.com, accessed February 16, 2014.

10. www.innovationchallenge.com, accessed February 16, 2014.

11. Christine Birkner, "High Impact Research on a Small-Business Budget," *Marketing News,* May 30, 2011.

12. Scott Martin, "Custom Research Easier in Digital Era," *USA Today,* August 28, 2012. For an interesting academic application, see Rex Yuxing Du and Wagner Kamakura, "Quantitative Trendspotting," *Journal of Marketing Research* 49 (August 2012), pp. 514–36.

13. Stephanie L. Gruner, "Spies Like Us," *Inc.,* August 1, 1998; Darren Dahl, "10 Tips on How to Research Your Competition," *Inc.,* May 11, 2011.

14. Michael Fielding, "Special Delivery: UPS Conducts Surveys to Help Customers Export to China," *Marketing News,* February 1, 2007, pp. 13–14.

15. Brad Smith, "Figure Out the Customer," *Bloomberg BusinessWeek,* April 12, 2012.

16. Adapted from Arthur Shapiro, "Let's Redefine Market Research," *Brandweek,* June 21, 2004, p. 20; Kevin Ohannessian, "Star Wars: Thirty Years of Success," *Fast Company,* May 29, 2007.

17. Ned Levi, "What's the Future for U.S. Airline Inflight Entertainment?," www.consumertraveler.com, April 9, 2012.

18. Fiona Blades, "Real-time Experience Tracking Gets Closer to the Truth," *International Journal of Market Research* 54, no. 2 (2012), pp. 283–85; Emma K. Macdonald, Hugh N. Wilson and Umut Konus, "Better Consumer Insight—in Real Time," *Harvard Business Review,* September 2012, pp. 102–108; Lynda Andrews, Rebekah Russell

Bennett, and Judy Drennan, "Capturing Affective Experiences Using the SMS Experience Sampling (SMS-ES) Method," *International Journal of Market Research* 53, no. 4 (2011), pp. 479–506.

19. Ashley Lutz and Matt Townsend, "Big Brother Has Arrived at a Store Near You, *Bloomberg Businessweek,* December 19, 2011.

20. For a detailed review of some relevant academic work, see Eric J. Arnould and Amber Epp, "Deep Engagement with Consumer Experience," Rajiv Grover and Marco Vriens, eds., *Handbook of Marketing Research* (Thousand Oaks, CA: Sage Publications, 2006). For a range of academic discussion, see the following special issue: "Can Ethnography Uncover Richer Consumer Insights?" *Journal of Advertising Research* 46 (September 2006). For some practical tips, see Richard Durante and Michael Feehan, "Leverage Ethnography to Improve Strategic Decision Making," *Marketing Research* (Winter 2005).

21. Eric J. Arnould and Linda L. Price, "Market-Oriented Ethnography Revisited," *Journal of Advertising Research* 46 (September 2006), pp. 251–62; Eric J. Arnould and Melanie Wallendorf, "Market-Oriented Ethnography: Interpretation Building and Marketing Strategy Formulation," *Journal of Marketing Research* 31 (November 1994), pp. 484–504.

22. Michael V. Copeland, "Intel's Cultural Anthropologist," *Fortune,* September 27, 2010.

23. Helen Coster, "Shopping Cart Psychology," *Forbes,* September 7, 2009, pp. 64–65.

24. "Smith & Nephew Launches ALLEVYN Life," www.smith-nephew.com, July 20, 2012.

25. Richard J. Harrington and Anthony K. Tjan, "Transforming Strategy One Customer at a Time," *Harvard Business Review,* March 2008, pp. 62–72; Stanley Reed, "The Rise of a Financial Data Powerhouse," *BusinessWeek,* May 15, 2007; Stanley Reed, "Media Giant or Media Muddle?" *BusinessWeek,* May 1, 2008.

26. Piet Levy, "In with the Old, in Spite of the New," *Marketing News,* May 30, 2009, p. 19.

27. William Grimes, "When Businesses Can't Stop Asking, 'How Am I Doing,'" *New York Times,* March 16, 2012.

28. Catherine Marshall and Gretchen B. Rossman, *Designing Qualitative Research,* 4th ed. (Thousand Oaks, CA: Sage Publications, 2006); Bruce L. Berg, *Qualitative Research Methods for the Social Sciences,* 6th ed. (Boston: Allyn & Bacon, 2006); Norman K. Denzin and Yvonna S. Lincoln, eds., *The Sage Handbook of Qualitative Research,* 3rd ed. (Thousand Oaks, CA: Sage Publications, 2005); Linda Tischler, "Every Move You Make," *Fast Company,* April 2004, pp. 73–75.

29. Paula Andruss, "Keeping Both Eyes on Quality," *Marketing News,* September 15, 2008, pp. 22–23.

30. Evan Ramstead, "Big Brother, Now at the Mall," *Wall Street Journal,* October 8, 2012; Natasha Singer, "Face Recognition Makes the Leap From Sci-Fi," *The New York Times,* November 13, 2011; Emily Glazer, "The Eyes Have It: Marketers Now Track Shoppers' Retinas," *Wall Street Journal,* July 12, 2012; Lessley Anderson, "A Night on the Town with SceneTap," *The Verve,* May 29, 2012; Kashmir Hill, "SceneTap Wants to One Day Tell You the Weights, Heights, Races and Income Levels of the Crowd at Every Bar," www.forbes.com, September 25, 2012.

31. Laurie Burkitt, "Battle for the Brain," *Forbes,* November 16, 2009, pp. 76–77.

32. Emily Steel, "Does Shopping Stress You Out Too Much?," *Wall Street Journal,* November 23, 2011. For an academic application of some of these techniques, see Thales Teixeira, Michel Wedel, and Rik Pieters, "Emotion-Induced Engagement in Internet Video Advertisements," *Journal of Marketing Research* 49 (April 2012), pp. 144–59.

33. For a comprehensive and informative review of the topic, see Hilke Plassmann, Thomas Zoëga Ramsøy, and Milica Milosavljevic, "Branding the Brain: A Critical Review and Outlook," *Journal of Consumer Psychology* 22 (2012), pp. 18–36, as well as other articles in that special issue.

34. Jon Evans, "In Five Years, Most Africans Will Have Smart Phones," www.techcrunch.com, June 9, 2012.

35. Bradley Johnson, "Forget Phone and Mail: Online's the Best Place to Administer Surveys," *Advertising Age,* July 17, 2006, p. 23.

36. Emily Steel, "The New Focus Groups: Online Networks Proprietary Panels Help Consumer Companies Shape Products, Ads," *Wall Street Journal*, January 14, 2008.

37. Scott Martin, "Custom Research Easier in Digital Era," *USA TODAY*, August 28, 2012.

38. Neil Swidey, "Cambridge's Bluefin Labs Decodes Social Media Chatter," *Boston Globe*, November 25, 2012.

39. For an interesting examination of consumer candidness, see David Gal and Derek D. Rucker, "Answering the Unasked Question: Response Substitution in Consumer Surveys," *Journal of Marketing Research* 48 (February 2011), pp. 185–95.

40. Jon Brodkin, "119 Million Americans Lack Broadband Internet, FCC Reports," www.arstechnica.com, August 21, 2012.

41. Deborah L. Vence, "Global Consistency: Leave It to the Experts," *Marketing News,* April 28, 2003, p. 37. For some scaling issues, see Bart de Langhe, Stefano Puntoni, Daniel Fernandes, and Stijn M. J. Van Osselaer, "The Anchor Contraction Effect in International Marketing Research," *Journal of Marketing Research* 48 (April 2011), pp. 366–80.

42. Kevin J. Clancy and Peter C. Krieg, *Counterintuitive Marketing: How Great Results Come from Uncommon Sense* (New York: Free Press, 2000).

43. *The Advertising Research Foundation*, www.thearf.org/assets/ogilvy-09, accessed February 16, 2014.

44. John D. C. Little, "Decision Support Systems for Marketing Managers," *Journal of Marketing* 43 (Summer 1979), p. 11.

45. *Marketing News* can be found at www.marketingpower.com.

46. Karen V. Beaman, Gregory R. Guy, and Donald E. Sexton, "Managing and Measuring Return on Marketing Investment," The Conference Board Research Report R-1435-08-RR, 2008.

47. Paul Farris, Neil T. Bendle, Phillip E. Pfeifer, and David J. Reibstein, *Marketing Metrics: 50+ Metrics Every Executive Should Master* (Upper Saddle River, NJ: Pearson Education, 2006); John Davis, *Magic Numbers for Consumer Marketing: Key Measures to Evaluate Marketing Success* (Singapore: John Wiley & Sons, 2005).

48. Elisabeth Sullivan, "Measure Up," *Marketing News*, May 30, 2009, pp. 8–11.

49. Michael Krauss, "Which Metrics Matter Most?" *Marketing News*, February 28, 2009, p. 20.

50. Tim Ambler, *Marketing and the Bottom Line: The New Methods of Corporate Wealth,* 2nd ed. (London: Pearson Education, 2003).

51. Kusum L. Ailawadi, Donald R. Lehmann, and Scott A. Neslin, "Revenue Premium as an Outcome Measure of Brand Equity," *Journal of Marketing* 67 (October 2003), pp. 1–17.

52. Tim Ambler, *Marketing and the Bottom Line: The New Methods of Corporate Wealth,* 2nd ed. (London: Pearson Education, 2003).

53. Gerard J. Tellis, "Modeling Marketing Mix," Rajiv Grover and Marco Vriens, eds., *Handbook of Marketing Research* (Thousand Oaks, CA: Sage Publications, 2006).

54. David J. Reibstein, "Connect the Dots," *CMO Magazine*, May 2005.

55. For insightful discussion of the design and implementation of marketing dashboards, see Koen Pauwels, *It's Not the Size of the Data, It's How You Use It: Smarter Marketing with Analytics and Dashboards* (New York: AMACOM: 2014) and consult the resources at www.marketdashboards.com.

56. Robert S. Kaplan and David P. Norton, *The Balanced Scorecard* (Boston: Harvard Business School Press, 1996).

## Chapter 5

1. Seth Fiegerman, "Pandora Now Has 200 Million Registered Users," www.mashable.com, April 9, 2013; Drake Baer, "What You Can Learn from Pandora's Near-Death Experience," *Fast Company*, April 4, 2013; Tyler Gray, "Pandora Pulls Back the Curtain on Its Magic Music Machine," *Fast Company*, January 21, 2011; Rob Medich, "Pandora Goes Local," *Adweek*, February 14, 2011; Charlie White, "Music Services Compared," www.mashable.com, February 13, 2013.

2. For discussion of some of the issues involved, see Glen Urban, *Don't Just Relate—Advocate* (Upper Saddle River, NJ: Pearson Education Wharton School Publishing, 2005).

3. "Customer Reviews Drive 196% Increase in Paid Search Revenue for Office Depot," *Bazaarvoice,* September 15, 2008.

4. Steven Burke, "Dell's vs. HP's Value," *CRN*, May 15, 2006, p. 46; David Kirkpatrick, "Dell in the Penalty Box," *Fortune*, September 18, 2006, p. 70.

5. 2012—US Mid-Year Rankings, www.brandindex.com.

6. Irwin P. Levin and Richard D. Johnson, "Estimating Price–Quality Tradeoffs Using Comparative Judgments," *Journal of Consumer Research* 11 (June 1984), pp. 593–600. Customer-perceived value can be measured as a difference or as a ratio. If total customer value is $20,000 and total customer cost is $16,000, then the customer-perceived value is $4,000 (measured as a difference) or 1.25 (measured as a ratio). Ratios that are used to compare offers are often called *value–price ratios.*

7. Alex Taylor, "Caterpillar: Big Trucks, Big Sales, Big Attitude," *Fortune*, August 20, 2007, pp. 48–53; Tim Kelly, "Squash the Caterpillar," *Forbes*, April 21, 2008, pp. 136–41; Jeff Borden, "Eat My Dust," *Marketing News*, February 1, 2008, pp. 20–22; Geoff Colvin, "Caterpillar Is Absolutely Crushing It," *Fortune*, May 23, 2011, pp. 136–44; Jon Birger, "10 Best Stocks for 2012," *Fortune*, December 26, 2011, pp. 100–7; Simon Montlake, "Cat Scammed," *Forbes*, March 4, 2013, pp. 36–38.

8. For an interesting approach to assess customer product perceptions and market structure online, see Thomas Y. Lee and Eric T. Bradlow, "Automated Marketing Research Using Online Customer Reviews," *Journal of Marketing Research* 48 (October 2011), pp. 881–94.

9. Gary Hamel, "Strategy as Revolution," *Harvard Business Review,* July–August 1996, pp. 69–82.

10. Vikas Mittal, Eugene W. Anderson, Akin Sayrak, and Pandu Tadilamalla, "Dual Emphasis and the Long-Term Financial Impact of Customer Satisfaction," *Marketing Science* 24 (Fall 2005), pp. 544–55.

11. Michael Tsiros, Vikas Mittal, and William T. Ross Jr., "The Role of Attributions in Customer Satisfaction: A Reexamination," *Journal of Consumer Research* 31 (September 2004), pp. 476–83. For a succinct review, see Richard L. Oliver, "Customer Satisfaction Research," Rajiv Grover and Marco Vriens, eds., *Handbook of Marketing Research* (Thousand Oaks, CA: Sage Publications, 2006), pp. 569–87; for in-depth discussion, see Richard L. Oliver, *Satisfaction: A Behavioral Perspective on the Consumer* (Armonk, NY: M. E. Sharpe, 2010).

12. For some provocative analysis and discussion, see Praveen K. Kopalle and Donald R. Lehmann, "Setting Quality Expectations when Entering a Market: What Should the Promise Be?," *Marketing Science* 25 (January–February 2006), pp. 8–24; Susan Fournier and David Glenmick, "Rediscovering Satisfaction," *Journal of Marketing* 63 (October 1999), pp. 5–23.

13. Jennifer Aaker, Susan Fournier, and S. Adam Brasel, "When Good Brands Do Bad," *Journal of Consumer Research* 31 (June 2004), pp. 1–16; Pankaj Aggrawal, "The Effects of Brand Relationship Norms on Consumer Attitudes and Behavior," *Journal of Consumer Research* 31 (June 2004), pp. 87–101; Florian Stahl, Mark Heitmann, Donald R. Lehmann, and Scott A. Neslin, "The Impact of Brand Equity on Customer Acquisition, Retention, and Profit Margin," *Journal of Marketing* 76 (July 2012), pp. 44–63.

14. Vikas Mittal, William T. Ross and Patrick M. Baldasare, "The Asymmetric Impact of Negative and Positive Attribute-Level Performance on Overall Satisfaction and Repurchase Intentions," *Journal of Marketing* 62 (January 1998), pp. 333–347.

15. For an interesting analysis of the effects of different types of expectations, see William Boulding, Ajay Kalra, and Richard Staelin, "The Quality Double Whammy," *Marketing Science* 18 (April 1999), pp. 463–84.

16. Neil A. Morgan, Eugene W. Anderson, and Vikas Mittal, "Understanding Firms' Customer Satisfaction Information Usage," *Journal of Marketing* 69 (July 2005), pp. 131–51.

17. Although for moderating factors, see Kathleen Seiders, Glenn B. Voss, Dhruv Grewal, and Andrea L. Godfrey, "Do Satisfied Customers Buy More? Examining Moderating Influences in a Retailing Context," *Journal of Marketing* 69 (October 2005), pp. 26–43.

18. See, for example, Christian Homburg, Nicole Koschate, and Wayne D. Hoyer, "Do Satisfied Customers Really Pay More? A Study of the Relationship between Customer Satisfaction and Willingness to Pay," *Journal of Marketing* 69 (April 2005), pp. 84–96.

19. Thomas O. Jones and W. Earl Sasser Jr., "Why Satisfied Customers Defect," *Harvard Business Review,* November–December 1995, pp. 88–99.

20. Companies should also note that managers and salespeople can manipulate customer satisfaction ratings. They can be especially nice to customers just before the survey. They can also try to exclude unhappy customers. Another danger is that if customers know the company will go out of its way to please them, some may express high dissatisfaction in order to receive more concessions.

21. Timothy L. Keiningham, Lerzan Aksoy, Alexander Buoye, and Bruce Cooil, "Customer Loyalty Isn't Enough. Grow Your Share of Wallet," *Harvard Business Review*, October 2011, pp. 29–31.

22. Eugene W. Anderson and Claes Fornell, "Foundations of the American Customer Satisfaction Index," *Total Quality Management* 11 (September 2000), pp. S869–82; Claes Fornell, Michael D. Johnson, Eugene W. Anderson, Jaesung Cha, and Barbara Everitt Bryant, "The American Customer Satisfaction Index: Nature, Purpose, and Findings," *Journal of Marketing* 60 (October 1996), pp. 7–18.

23. For a thorough and insightful review, see Vikas Mittal and Carly Frenna, "Customer Satisfaction: A Strategic Review and Guidelines for Managers," *Fast Forward Series*, (Cambridge, MA: Marketing Science Institute, 2010). See also Claes Fornell, Sunil Mithas, Forrest V. Morgeson III, and M. S. Krishnan, "Customer Satisfaction and Stock Prices: High Returns, Low Risk," *Journal of Marketing* 70 (January 2006), pp. 3–14. See also Thomas S. Gruca and Lopo L. Rego, "Customer Satisfaction, Cash Flow, and Shareholder Value," *Journal of Marketing* 69 (July 2005), pp. 115–30; Eugene W. Anderson, Claes Fornell, and Sanal K. Mazvancheryl, "Customer Satisfaction and Shareholder Value," *Journal of Marketing* 68 (October 2004), pp. 172–85.

24. For an empirical comparison of different methods to measure customer satisfaction, see Neil A. Morgan and Lopo Leotto Rego, "The Value of Different Customer Satisfaction and Loyalty Metrics in Predicting Business Performance," *Marketing Science* 25 (September–October 2006), pp. 426–39.

25. James C. Ward and Amy L. Ostrom, "Complaining to the Masses: The Role of Protest Framing in Customer-Created Complaint Sites," *Journal of Consumer Research* 33 (September 2006), pp. 220–30; Kim Hart, "Angry Customers Use Web to Shame Firms," *Washington Post,* July 5, 2006.

26. "Basic Concepts," ASQ, www.asq.org/glossary/q.html, January 16, 2014. For a thorough conceptual discussion, see Peter N. Golder, Debanjan Mitra, and Christine Moorman, "What Is Quality? An Integrative Framework of Processes and States," *Journal of Marketing* 76 (July 2012), pp. 1–23.

27. For influential, classic research, see Robert D. Buzzell and Bradley T. Gale, "Quality Is King," *The PIMS Principles: Linking Strategy to Performance* (New York: Free Press, 1987), pp. 103–34. (PIMS stands for Profit Impact of Market Strategy.)

28. "Home Depot CEO: Sorry We Let You Down," *MSN Money*, www.moneycentral.msn.com, March 13, 2007; Jena McGregor, "Putting Home Depot's House in Order," *BusinessWeek*, May 14, 2009; Dhanya Skariachan, "Home Depot Raises Outlook; Eclipses Lowe's," www.reuters.com, August 16, 2011; Jeff Williams, "Home Depot: Customer Service Initiatives Increase Revenues," www.seekingalpha.com, April 11, 2012; Katie Benner, "The Other Side of Home Improvement," *Fortune*, October 29, 2012.

29. Lerzan Aksoy, Timothy L. Keiningham, and Terry G. Vavra, "Nearly Everything You Know about Loyalty Is Wrong," *Marketing News,* October 1, 2005, pp. 20–21; Timothy L. Keiningham, Terry G. Vavra, Lerzan Aksoy, and Henri Wallard, *Loyalty Myths* (Hoboken, NJ: John Wiley & Sons, 2005).

30. Don Pepper and Martha Rogers, "Return on Customer: How Marketing Creates Value," *Marketing Review St. Gallen* 28 (June 2011), pp. 14–19.

31. Werner J. Reinartz and V. Kumar, "The Impact of Customer Relationship Characteristics on Profitable Lifetime Duration," *Journal of Marketing* 67 (January 2003), pp. 77–99; Werner J. Reinartz and V. Kumar, "On the Profitability of Long-Life Customers in a Noncontractual Setting: An Empirical Investigation and Implications for Marketing," *Journal of Marketing* 64 (October 2000), pp. 17–35.

32. Rakesh Niraj, Mahendra Gupta, and Chakravarthi Narasimhan, "Customer Profitability in a Supply Chain," *Journal of Marketing* 65 (July 2001), pp. 1–16.

33. Thomas M. Petro, "Profitability: The Fifth 'P' of Marketing," *Bank Marketing*, September 1990, pp. 48–52; "Who Are Your Best Customers?," *Bank Marketing*, October 1990, pp. 48–52.

34. "Easier Than ABC," *Economist*, October 25, 2003, p. 56; Robert S. Kaplan and Steven R. Anderson, *Time-Driven Activity Based Costing* (Boston MA: Harvard Business School Press, 2007); "Activity-Based Accounting" *Economist*, June 29, 2009. See also Morten Holm, V. Kumar, and Carsten Rohde, "Measuring Customer Profitability in Complex Environments: An Interdisciplinary Contingency Framework," *Journal of the Academy of Marketing Science* 40 (May 2012) pp. 387–401.

35. V. Kumar, "Customer Lifetime Value," Rajiv Grover and Marco Vriens, eds., *Handbook of Marketing Research* (Thousand Oaks, CA: Sage Publications, 2006), pp. 602–27; Sunil Gupta, Donald R. Lehmann, and Jennifer Ames Stuart, "Valuing Customers," *Journal of Marketing Research* 61 (February 2004), pp. 7–18; Rajkumar Venkatesan and V. Kumar, "A Customer Lifetime Value Framework for Customer Selection and Resource Allocation Strategy," *Journal of Marketing* 68 (October 2004), pp. 106–25.

36. V. Kumar, "Profitable Relationships," *Marketing Research* 18 (Fall 2006), pp. 41–46.

37. For some recent analysis and discussion, see Michael Haenlein, Andreas M. Kaplan, and Detlef Schoder, "Valuing the Real Option of Abandoning Unprofitable Customers when Calculating Customer Lifetime Value," *Journal of Marketing* 70 (July 2006), pp. 5–20; Teck-Hua Ho, Young-Hoon Park, and Yong-Pin Zhou, "Incorporating Satisfaction into Customer Value Analysis: Optimal Investment in Lifetime Value," *Marketing Science* 25 (May–June 2006), pp. 260–77; and Peter S. Fader, Bruce G. S. Hardie, and Ka Lok Lee, "RFM and CLV: Using Iso-Value Curves for Customer Base Analysis," *Journal of Marketing Research* 62 (November 2005), pp. 415–30; V. Kumar, Rajkumar Venkatesan, Tim Bohling, and Denise Beckmann, "The Power of CLV: Managing Customer Lifetime Value at IBM," *Marketing Science* 27 (2008), pp. 585–99.

38. Louis Columbus, "Lessons Learned in Las Vegas: Loyalty Programs Pay," *CRM Buyer*, July 29, 2005; Oskar Garcia, "Harrah's Broadens Customer Loyalty Program; Monitors Customer Behavior," *Associated Press*, September 27, 2008; Dan Butcher, "Harrah's Casino Chain Runs Mobile Coupon Pilot," *Mobile Marketer*, November 19, 2009; Michael Bush, "Why Harrah's Loyalty Effort Is Industry's Gold Standard," *Advertising Age*, October 5, 2009, p. 8; Emily Steel, "Marketers Find Web Chat Can Be Inspiring," *Wall Street Journal*, November 23, 2009; Liz Benston, "MGM Mirage, Harrah's Finding Revenue in Rewards Programs," *Las Vegas Sun*, May 10, 2010; Karl Taro Greenfield, "How to Survive in Vegas," *Bloomberg Businessweek*, August 9, 2010, pp. 70–75.

39. Michael Lewis, "Customer Acquisition Promotions and Customer Asset Value," *Journal of Marketing Research* 63 (May 2006), pp. 195–203; see also Romana Khan, Michael Lewis, and Vishal Singh, "Dynamic Customer Management and the Value of One-to-One Marketing," *Marketing Science* 28 (November–December 2009), pp. 1063–79.

40. V. Kumar and Bharath Rajan, "The Perils of Social Coupon Campaigns," *MIT Sloan Management Review* 53 (Summer 2012), pp. 13–14; Karen E. Klein, "Small Businesses See Red over Daily Deals," *Bloomberg Businessweek*, December 3, 2012, pp. 53–54.

41. Hamish Pringle and Peter Field, "Why Customer Loyalty Isn't as Valuable as You Think," *Advertising Age*, March 23, 2009, p. 22.

42. Werner Reinartz, Jacquelyn S. Thomas, and V. Kumar, "Balancing Acquisition and Retention Resources to Maximize Customer Profitability," *Journal of Marketing* 69 (January 2005), pp. 63–79.

43. "Service Invention to Increase Retention," *CMO Council*, August 3, 2009, www.cmocouncil.org.

44. Frederick F. Reichheld, "Learning from Customer Defections," *Harvard Business Review,* March–April 1996, pp. 56–69.

45. Frederick F. Reichheld, *Loyalty Rules* (Boston: Harvard Business School Press, 2001); Frederick F. Reichheld, *The Loyalty Effect* (Boston: Harvard Business School Press, 1996).

46. Michael D. Johnson and Fred Selnes, "Diversifying Your Customer Portfolio," *MIT Sloan Management Review* 46 (Spring 2005), pp. 11–14; Crina O. Tarasi, Ruth N. Bolton, Michael D. Hutt, and Beth A. Walker, "Balancing Risk and Return in a Customer Portfolio," *Journal of Marketing* 75 (May 2011), pp. 1–17.

47. Wendy Liu and David Gal, "Bringing Us Together or Driving Us Apart: The Effect of Soliciting Consumer Input on Consumers' Propensity to Transact with an Organization," *Journal of Consumer Research* 38 (August 2011), pp. 242–59.

48. Tom Ostenon, *Customer Share Marketing* (Upper Saddle River, NJ: Prentice Hall, 2002); Alan W. H. Grant and Leonard A. Schlesinger, "Realize Your Customer's Full Profit Potential," *Harvard Business Review*, September–October 1995, pp. 59–72.

49. Denish Shah and V. Kumar, "The Dark Side of Cross-Selling," *Harvard Business Review*, December 2012, pp. 21–23; Denish Shah, V. Kumar, Yingge Qu, and Sylia Chen, "Unprofitable Cross-buying: Evidence from Consumer and Business Markets," *Journal of Marketing* 76 (May 2012), pp. 78–95.

50. Gail McGovern and Youngme Moon, "Companies and the Customers Who Hate Them," *Harvard Business Review*, June 2007, pp. 78–84.

51. Elisabeth A. Sullivan, "Just Say No," *Marketing News*, April 15, 2008, p. 17.

52. Sunil Gupta and Carl F. Mela, "What Is a Free Customer Worth," *Harvard Business Review*, November 2008, pp. 102–9.

53. Leonard L. Berry and A. Parasuraman, *Marketing Services: Computing through Quality* (New York: Free Press, 1991), pp. 136–42. For an academic examination in a business-to-business context, see Robert W. Palmatier, Srinath Gopalakrishna, and Mark B. Houston, "Returns on Business-to-Business Relationship Marketing Investments: Strategies for Leveraging Profits," *Marketing Science* 25 (September–October 2006), pp. 477–93. See also Irit Nitzan and Barak Libai, "Social Effects on Customer Retention," *Journal of Marketing* 75 (November 2011), pp. 24–38.

54. Adam M. Grant, "How Customers Can Rally Troops," *Harvard Business Review*, June 2011, pp. 96–103.

55. Frederick F. Reichheld, "Learning from Customer Defections," *Harvard Business Review,* March 3, 2009, pp. 56–69.

56. Mike White and Teresa Siles, e-mail message, July 14, 2008.

57. Ben McConnell and Jackie Huba, "Learning to Leverage the Lunatic Fringe," *Point*, July–August 2006, pp. 14–15; Michael Krauss, "Work to Convert Customers into Evangelists," *Marketing News*, December 15, 2006, p. 6; "Ask Maxine Clark," *Inc.*, July 1, 2008; "How Maxine Clark Built Build-a-Bear," *Fortune*, March 19, 2012.

58. Utpal M. Dholakia, "How Consumer Self-Determination Influences Relational Marketing Outcomes: Evidence from Longitudinal Field Studies," *Journal of Marketing Research* 43 (February 2006), pp. 109–20.

59. Joseph C. Nunes and Xavier Drèze, "Feeling Superior: The Impact of Loyalty Program Structure on Consumers' Perception of Status," *Journal of Consumer Research* 35 (April 2009), pp. 890–905; Joseph C. Nunes and Xavier Drèze, "Your Loyalty Program Is Betraying You," *Harvard Business Review*, April 2006, pp. 124–31.

60. Peter Burrows, "Apple vs. Google," *BusinessWeek*, January 25, 2010, pp. 28–34.

61. James H. McAlexander, John W. Schouten, and Harold F. Koenig, "Building Brand Community," *Journal of Marketing* 66 (January 2002), pp. 38–54. For some notable examinations of brand communities, see René Algesheimer, Uptal M. Dholakia, and Andreas Herrmann, "The Social Influence of Brand Community: Evidence from European Car Clubs," *Journal of Marketing* 69 (July 2005), pp. 19–34; Albert M. Muniz Jr. and Hope Jensen Schau, "Religiosity in the Abandoned Apple Newton Brand Community," *Journal of Consumer Research* 31 (2005), pp. 412–32; Robert Kozinets, "Utopian Enterprise: Articulating the Meanings of *Star Trek*'s Culture of Consumption," *Journal of Consumer Research* 28 (June 2001), pp. 67–87; John W. Schouten and James H. McAlexander, "Subcultures of Consumption: An Ethnography of New Bikers," *Journal of Consumer Research* 22 (June 1995), pp. 43–61.

62. Albert M. Muniz Jr. and Thomas C. O'Guinn, "Brand Community," *Journal of Consumer Research* 27 (March 2001), pp. 412–32.

63. Susan Fournier and Lara Lee, "The Seven Deadly Sins of Brand Community 'Management,'" Marketing Science Institute Special Report 08-208, 2008; see also Mark Bubula, "The Myth about Brand Communities," *Admap*, November 2012.

64. Harley-Davidson USA, www.hog.com, accessed May 20, 2014; Joseph Weber, "Harley Just Keeps on Cruisin'," *BusinessWeek*, November 6, 2006, pp. 71–72; Robert Klara, "Tweeters of the Pack," *Adweek*, March 5, 2012, p. 12; "Harley Davidson Tackles Stereotypes in New Advertising Campaign," *PRNewswire*, March 1, 2012; Raine Devries, "Harley-Davidson Embraces Social Media to Tackle Stereotypes," www.examiner.com, March 1, 2012; Robert Klara, "A Whole Different Hog," *Adweek*, July 23, 2012, p. 40.

65. Christina Chaey, "How to Create Community," *Fast Company*, February 2012, p. 16.

66. http://growyourbiz.kodak.com/growyourbiz/, accessed May 20, 2014.

67. www.pb.com/social/user-forums-and-user-groups/index.shtml.

68. Puneet Manchanda, Grant Packard, and Adithya Pattabhiramaiah, "Social Dollars: The Economic Impact of Consumer Participation in a Firm-Sponsored Online Community," working paper, January 2012, University of Michigan.

69. Scott A. Thompson and Rajiv K. Sinha, "Brand Communities and New Product Adoption: The Influence and Limits of Oppositional Loyalty," *Journal of Marketing* 72 (November 2008), pp. 65–80.

70. Susan Fournier and Lara Lee, "Getting Brand Communities Right," *Harvard Business Review*, April 2009, pp. 105–11.

71. Mavis T. Adjei, Charles H. Noble, and Stephanie M. Noble, "Enhancing Relationships with Customers through Online Brand Communities," *MIT Sloan Management Review*, Summer 2012, pp. 22–24.

72. Jacquelyn S. Thomas, Robert C. Blattberg, and Edward J. Fox, "Recapturing Lost Customers," *Journal of Marketing Research* 61 (February 2004), pp. 31–45.

73. Werner Reinartz and V. Kumar, "The Impact of Customer Relationship Characteristics on Profitable Lifetime Duration," *Journal of Marketing* 67 (January 2003), pp. 77–99; Werner Reinartz and V. Kumar, "The Mismanagement of Customer Loyalty," *Harvard Business Review*, July 2002, pp. 86–97.

74. For a comprehensive set of articles from a variety of perspectives on brand relationships, see Deborah J. MacInnis, C. Whan Park, and Joseph R. Preister, eds., *Handbook of Brand Relationships* (Armonk, NY: M. E. Sharpe, 2009).

75. For a study of the processes involved, see Werner Reinartz, Manfred Kraft, and Wayne D. Hoyer, "The Customer Relationship Management Process: Its Measurement and Impact on Performance," *Journal of Marketing Research* 61 (August 2004), pp. 293–305. For a thorough examination of the practical issues involved, see Peter Fader, *Customer Centricity: Focus on the Right Customers for Strategic Advantage* (Philadelphia, PA: Wharton Digital Press, 2012).

76. Peter C. Verhoef and Katherine N. Lemon, "Customer Value Management: Optimizing the Value of the Customer's Base," *Fast Forward Series* (Cambridge, MA: Marketing Science Institute, 2011).

77. Nora A. Aufreiter, David Elzinga, and Jonathan W. Gordon, "Better Branding," *The McKinsey Quarterly* 4 (2003), pp. 29–39.

78. Joe Light, "With Customer Service, Real Person Trumps Text," *Wall Street Journal*, April 25, 2011. See also Wagner A. Kamakura, Vikas Mittal, Fernando de Rosa, and Jose Afonso Mazzon "Assessing the Service-Profit Chain," *Marketing Science* 21 (Summer 2002), pp. 294–317.

79. Nancy Trejos, "British Airways Gets More Personal," *USA Today*, July 8, 2012; "Know Your Customers: Case Studies from BA, The Guardian, and Milka," *MarketingWeek*, July 11, 2012; Tim Hume, "BA Googles Passengers: Friendlier Flights or Invasion of Privacy," www.cnn.com, August 22, 2012; Kashmir Hill, "British Airways Won't Be Google Image Stalking You Unless You're a V.I.P.," *Forbes*, July 9, 2012; Alex Williams, "British Airways Borders on Creepy With 'Know Me' Google Identity Check," www.techcrunch.com, July 5, 2012. See also Robert McGarvey, "Mind Readers," *Executive Travel Magazine*, November/December 2012, pp. 60–65.

80. Joann Muller, "The Bespoke Auto: BMW's Push for Made-to-Order Cars," *Forbes*, September 27, 2010.

81. Jennifer Cirillo, "Custom Made," *Beverage World*, June 2012, pp. 14–15.

82. Seth Godin, *Permission Marketing: Turning Strangers into Friends, and Friends into Customers* (New York: Simon & Schuster, 1999). See also Susan Fournier, Susan Dobscha, and David Mick, "Preventing the Premature Death of Relationship Marketing," *Harvard Business Review*, January–February 1998, pp. 42–51.

83. Rob Walker, "Amateur Hour, Web Style," *Fast Company*, October 2007, p. 87.

84. Doc Searls, "The Customer as a God," *Wall Street Journal*, July 20, 2012.

85. Martin Mende, Ruth N. Bolton, and Mary Jo Bitner, "Decoding Customer–Firm Relationships: How Attachment Styles Help Explain Customers' Preferences for Closeness, Repurchase Intentions, and Changes in Relationship Breadth," *Journal of Marketing Research* 50 (February 2013), pp. 125–42.

86. Carolyn Heller Baird and Gautam Parasnis, *From Social Media to Social CRM*, (Somers, NY: IBM Corporation, 2011).

87. Christine Birkner, "How I Do It: Christine Birkner," *Marketing News*, September 15, 2011, p. 46. For some behavioral perspectives on recommendations and reviews, see Min Zhao and Jinhong Xie, "Effects of Social and Temporal Distance on Consumers' Responses to Peer Recommendations," *Journal of Marketing Research* 48 (May 2011), pp. 486–96 and Rebecca Walker Naylor, Cait Poynor Lamberton, and David A. Norton, "Seeing Ourselves in Others: Reviewer Ambiguity, Egocentric Anchoring, and Persuasion," *Journal of Marketing Research* 48 (May 2011), pp. 617–31.

88. Amy Farley, "Hotel Handbook," *Travel + Leisure*, June 2012, p. 168; "Wyndham Worldwide's CEO Discusses Q1 2012 Results—Earnings Call Transcript," www.seekingalpha.com, April 25, 2012.

89. "300 Million People View TripAdvisor Content on Sites Other than TripAdvisor Each Month," *PRNewswire*, December 13, 2012; "TripAdvisor," www.crunchbase.com, January 2, 2013; "TripAdvisor," www.wikipedia.com, January 2, 2013; Josh Constine, "Lost among Its 60 Million Travel Tips? TripAdvisor Highlights Reviews by Friends of Friends," www.techcrunch.com, April 11, 2012; Josh Constine, "TripAdvisor Aims to Beat Yelp with Social, Revives Restaurant 'Local Picks' Facebook App," www.techcrunch.com, June 20, 2012; Jordan Crook, "TripAdvisor Acquires Wanderfly to Continue Social Travel Push," www.techcrunch.com, October 2, 2012.

90. Jonah Bloom, "The New Realities of a Low Trust Marketing World," *Advertising Age*, February 13, 2006.

91. Mylene Mangalindan, "New Marketing Style: Clicks and Mortar," *Wall Street Journal*, December 21, 2007, p. B5.

92. Shrihari Sridhar and Raj Srinivasan, "Social Influence Effect in Online Product Ratings," *Journal of Marketing* 76 (September 2012), pp. 70–88.

93. Shelley Banjo, "Firms Take Online Reviews to Heart," *Wall Street Journal*, July 29, 2012.

94. Noah Davis, "Leading the Conversation," *Fast Company*, July/August 2012, p. 33-37.

95. Ron Lieber, "At Angie's List, the Reviews Are Real (So Is Angie)," *New York Times*, March 2, 2012.

96. Nick Wingfield, "High Scores Matter to Game Makers, Too," *Wall Street Journal*, September 20, 2007, p. B1; see also Yubo Chen, Yong Liu and Jurui Zhang, "When Do Third-Party Product Reviews Affect Firm Value and What Can Firms Do? The Case of Media Critics and Professional Movie Reviews," *Journal of Marketing* 75 (September 2011), pp. 116–34.

97. Candice Choi, "Bloggers Serve Up Opinions," *Associated Press*, March 23, 2008.

98. Elisabeth Sullivan, "Consider Your Source," *Marketing News*, February 15, 2008, pp. 16–19; Mylene Mangalindan, "Web Stores Tap Product Reviews," *Wall Street Journal*, September 11, 2007; Jonah Berger, Alan T. Sorensen, and Scott J. Rasmussen, "Positive Effects of Negative Publicity: When Negative Reviews Increase Sales," *Marketing Science* 29, no. 5 (2010), pp. 815–27; Venessa Wong, "How to Cope with a Terrible Review," *Bloomberg Businessweek*, November 16, 2012.

99. Piyush Sharma, Roger Marshall, Peter Alan Reday, and WoonBong Na, "Complainers vs. Non-Complainers: A Multi-National Investigation of Individual and Situational Influences on Customer Complaint Behaviour," *Journal of Marketing Management* 26 (February 2010), pp. 163–80.

100. Stephen S. Tax and Stephen W. Brown, "Recovering and Learning from Service Failure," *Sloan Management Review* 40 (Fall 1998), pp. 75–88.

101. Andrew McMains, "Airline Lost Your Luggage? Tell It to Twitter," *Adweek*, February 20, 2012, p. 12.

102. Christian Homburg and Andreas Fürst, "How Organizational Complaint Handling Drives Customer Loyalty: An Analysis of the Mechanistic and the Organic Approach," *Journal of Marketing* 69 (July 2005), pp. 95–114.

103. Philip Kotler, *Kotler on Marketing* (New York: Free Press, 1999), pp. 21–22; Jochen Wirtz, "How to Deal with Customer Shakedowns," *Harvard Business Review*, April 2011, p. 24.

104. Lea Dunn and Darren W. Dahl, "Self-threat and Product Failure: How Internal Attributions of Blame Impact Consumer Complaining Behavior," *Journal of Marketing Research* 49 (October 2012), pp. 670–81.

105. Julie Jargon, Emily Steel, and Joann S. Lublin, "Taco Bell Makes Spicy Retort to Suit," *Wall Street Journal*, January 31, 2011.

106. Felix Gillette, "It's Getting Tougher to Bully Brands," *Bloomberg Businessweek*, August 6, 2012, pp. 20–22.

## Chapter 6

1. Seth Stevenson, "Like Cardboard," *Slate*, January 11, 2010; Ashley M. Heher, "Domino's Comes Clean with New Pizza Ads," *Associated Press*, January 11, 2010; Bob Garfield, "Domino's Does Itself a Disservice by Coming Clean about Its Pizza," *Advertising Age*, January 11, 2010; *Domino's Pizza*, www.pizzaturnaround.com, accessed May 20, 2014; Anna-Louise Jackson and Anthony Feld, "Domino's 'Brutally Honest' Ads Offset Slow Consumer Spending," *Bloomberg Businessweek*, October 17, 2011; Mark Brandau, "A Look behind Domino's Marketing Strategies," *Nation's Restaurant News*, January 13, 2012.

2. Michael R. Solomon, *Consumer Behavior: Buying, Having, and Being*, 10th ed. (Upper Saddle River, NJ: Prentice Hall, 2013).

3. Leon G. Schiffman and Leslie Lazar Kanuk, *Consumer Behavior*, 10th ed. (Upper Saddle River, NJ: Prentice Hall, 2010).

4. For some classic perspectives, see Richard P. Coleman, "The Continuing Significance of Social Class to Marketing," *Journal of Consumer Research* 10 (December 1983), pp. 265–80; Richard P. Coleman and Lee P. Rainwater, *Social Standing in America: New Dimension of Class* (New York: Basic Books, 1978).

5. Leon G. Schiffman and Leslie Lazar Kanuk, *Consumer Behavior*, 10th ed. (Upper Saddle River, NJ: Prentice Hall, 2010).

6. Michael Trusov, Anand Bodapati, and Randolph E. Bucklin, "Determining Influential Users in Internet Social Networks," *Journal of Marketing Research* 47 (August 2010), pp. 643–58.

7. Jacqueline Johnson Brown, Peter M. Reingen, and Everett M. Rogers, *Diffusion of Innovations*, 4th ed. (New York: Free Press, 1995); Peter

H. Riengen and Jerome B. Kernan, "Analysis of Referral Networks in Marketing: Methods and Illustration," *Journal of Marketing Research* 23 (November 1986), pp. 37–78; Laura J. Kornish and Qiuping Li, "Optimal Referral Bonuses with Asymmetric Information: Firm-Offered and Interpersonal Incentives," *Marketing Science* 29 (January–February 2010), pp. 108–21.

8. Malcolm Gladwell, *The Tipping Point: How Little Things Can Make a Big Difference* (Boston: Little, Brown & Company, 2000).

9. Terry McDermott, "Criticism of Gladwell Reaches Tipping Point," *Columbia Journalism Review*, November 17, 2009; Clive Thompson, "Is the Tipping Point Toast?," *Fast Company*, February 1, 2008; Duncan Watts, *Six Degrees: The Science of a Connected Age* (New York: W. W. Norton, 2003).

10. Douglas Atkin, *The Culting of Brands: When Customers Become True Believers* (New York: Penguin, 2004); Marian Salzman, Ira Matathia, and Ann O'Reilly, *Buzz: Harness the Power of Influence and Create Demand* (New York: Wiley, 2003).

11. Bob Greenberg, "A Platform for Life," *Adweek NEXT*, September 14, 2009, p. 38.

12. Natasha Singer, "Secret E-Scores Chart Consumers' Buying Power," *New York Times*, August 18, 2012; Erin Griffin, "A Million Little Klouts," *Adweek*, December 12, 2011, p. 18; Jon Swartz, "Klout Says Scoring Parameters Enhanced," *USA Today*, August 15, 2012.

13. Ed Keller, "How Influence Works," *Admap*, December 2012.

14. Dave Balter and John Butman, "Clutter Cutter," *Marketing Management* (July–August 2006), pp. 49–50; "Is There a Reliable Way to Measure Word-of-Mouth Marketing?," *Marketing NPV* 3 (2006), pp. 3–9; Michael Trusov, Randolph E. Bucklin, and Koen Pauwels, "Effects of Word-of-Mouth versus Traditional Marketing: Findings from an Internet Social Networking Site," *Journal of Marketing* 73 (September 2009), pp. 90–102.

15. Elizabeth S. Moore, William L. Wilkie, and Richard J. Lutz, "Passing the Torch: Intergenerational Influences as a Source of Brand Equity," *Journal of Marketing* 66 (April 2002), pp. 17–37.

16. Kay M. Palan and Robert E. Wilkes, "Adolescent-Parent Interaction in Family Decision Making," *Journal of Consumer Research* 24 (March 1997), pp. 159–69; Sharon E. Beatty and Salil Talpade, "Adolescent Influence in Family Decision Making: A Replication with Extension," *Journal of Consumer Research* 21 (September 1994), pp. 332–41.

17. Scott I. Rick, Deborah A. Small, and Eli J. Finkel, "Fatal (Fiscal) Attraction: Spendthrifts and Tightwads in Marriage," *Journal of Marketing Research* 48 (April 2011), pp. 228–37.

18. Valentyna Melnyk, Stijn M. J. van Osselaer, and Tammo H. A. Bijmolt, "Are Women More Loyal Customers than Men? Gender Differences in Loyalty to Firms and Individual Service Providers," *Journal of Marketing* 73 (July 2009), pp. 82–96.

19. "YouthPulse: The Definitive Study of Today's Youth Generation," *Harris Interactive*, www.harrisinteractive.com, January 29, 2010.

20. Deborah Roedder John, "Consumer Socialization of Children: A Retrospective Look at Twenty-Five Years of Research," *Journal of Consumer Research* 26 (December 1999), pp. 183–213; Lan Nguyen Chaplin and Deborah Roedder John, "The Development of Self-Brand Connections in Children and Adolescents," *Journal of Consumer Research* 32 (June 2005), pp. 119–29; Lan Nguyen Chaplin and Deborah Roedder John, "Growing Up in a Material World: Age Differences in Materialism in Children and Adolescents," *Journal of Consumer Research* 34 (December 2007), pp. 480–93; Lan Nguyen Chaplin and Tina M. Lowrey, "The Development of Consumer-Based Consumption Constellations in Children," *Journal of Consumer Research* 36 (February 2010), pp. 757–77.

21. "Families and Living Arrangements," *U.S. Census Bureau*, www. census.gov/population/www/ socdemo/hh-fam.html, January 29, 2010; "U.S. Census Bureau Reports Men and Women Wait Longer to Marry," *Newsroom*, www.census.gov, November 10, 2010.

22. Rex Y. Du and Wagner A. Kamakura, "Household Life Cycles and Lifestyles in the United States," *Journal of Marketing Research* 48 (February 2006), pp. 121–32.

23. Brooks Barnes, "Disney Looking into Cradle for Customers," *New York Times*, February 6, 2011; Lisa Yorgey Lester, "Expectant Parents: Tap into the Baby Boom," *Target Marketing*, September 2008; Melanie Linder and Lisa LaMotta, "How to Market to the Modern Mom," *Forbes*, January 8, 2009.

24. Stephanie Clifford, "Even Marked Up, Luxury Goods Fly Off Shelves," *The New York Times*, August 3, 2011; "Recession, Reschmession: Let Them Eat Cake, Buy Prada," www.cmn.com, March 19, 2012; "Gucci Performance Withstands Recession," *The New York Times*, November 9, 2009.

25. Harold H. Kassarjian and Mary Jane Sheffet, "Personality and Consumer Behavior: An Update," Harold H. Kassarjian and Thomas S. Robertson, eds., *Perspectives in Consumer Behavior* (Glenview, IL: Scott Foresman, 1981), pp. 160–80.

26. Jennifer Aaker, "Dimensions of Measuring Brand Personality," *Journal of Marketing Research* 34 (August 1997), pp. 347–56.

27. Jennifer L. Aaker, Veronica Benet-Martinez, and Jordi Garolera, "Consumption Symbols as Carriers of Culture: A Study of Japanese and Spanish Brand Personality Constructs," *Journal of Personality and Social Psychology* 81 (March 2001), pp. 492–508.

28. Yongjun Sung and Spencer F. Tinkham, "Brand Personality Structures in the United States and Korea: Common and Culture-Specific Factors," *Journal of Consumer Psychology* 15 (December 2005), pp. 334–50.

29. Lucia Malär, Harley Krohmer, Wayne D. Hoyer, and Bettina Nyffenegger, "Emotional Brand Attachment and Brand Personality: The Relative Importance of the Actual and the Ideal Self," *Journal of Marketing* 75 (July 2011), pp. 35–52.

30. Timothy R. Graeff, "Image Congruence Effects on Product Evaluations: The Role of Self-Monitoring and Public/Private Consumption," *Psychology & Marketing* 13 (August 1996), pp. 481–99.

31. Jennifer L. Aaker, "The Malleable Self: The Role of Self-Expression in Persuasion," *Journal of Marketing Research* 36 (February 1999), pp. 45–57.

32. Chip Conley, *The Rebel Rules* (New York: Fireside, 2001); Tom Osborne, "What Is Your Band Personality," *Viget Inspire*, www.viget.com, February 2, 2009; Alice Z. Cuneo, "Magazines as Muses: Hotelier Finds Inspiration in Titles Such as *Wired*," *Advertising Age*, November 6, 2006, p. 10.

33. Kavita Daswani, "Multitasking BB Skin Creams Becoming Popular in U.S.," *Los Angeles Times*, July 15, 2012.

34. Anne D'Innocenzio, "Frugal Times: Hamburger Helper, Kool-Aid in Advertising Limelight," *Associated Press, Seattle Times*, April 29, 2009; Julie Jargon, "Velveeta Shows Its Sizzle against Hamburger Helper," *Wall Street Journal*, December 29, 2011.

35. Thomas J. Reynolds and Jerry C. Olson, *Understanding Consumer Decision-Making: The Means-Ends Approach to Marketing and Advertising* (Mahwah, NJ: Lawrence Erlbaum, 2001); Brian Wansink, "Using Laddering to Understand and Leverage a Brand's Equity," *Qualitative Market Research* 6 (2003).

36. Ernest Dichter, *Handbook of Consumer Motivations* (New York: McGraw-Hill, 1964).

37. "Retail Therapy: How Ernest Dichter, an Acolyte of Sigmund Freud, Revolutionised Marketing," *The Economist*, December 17, 2011.

38. Clotaire Rapaille, "Marketing to the Reptilian Brain," *Forbes,* July 3, 2006; Clotaire Rapaille, *The Culture Code* (New York: Broadway Books, 2007); Douglas Gantebein, "How Boeing Put the Dream in Dreamliner," *Air and Space*, September 2007; Tom Otley, "The Boeing Dreamliner: A Sneak Preview," *Business Traveller*, June 3, 2009.

39. Abraham Maslow, *Motivation and Personality* (New York: Harper & Row, 1954), pp. 80–106. For an interesting business application, see Chip Conley, *Peak: How Great Companies Get Their Mojo from Maslow* (San Francisco: Jossey Bass 2007).

40. See Frederick Herzberg, *Work and the Nature of Man* (Cleveland: William Collins, 1966); Thierry and Koopman-Iwema, "Motivation and Satisfaction," P. J. D. Drenth, H. Thierry, P. J. Willems, and C. J. de

Wolff, eds., *A Handbook of Work and Organizational Psychology* (East Sussex, UK: Psychology Press, 1984), pp. 141–42.

41. Bernard Berelson and Gary A. Steiner, *Human Behavior: An Inventory of Scientific Findings* (New York: Harcourt Brace Jovanovich, 1964), p. 88.

42. Florida's Chris Janiszewski has conducted fascinating research looking at preconscious processing effects. See Chris Janiszewski, "Preattentive Mere Exposure Effects," *Journal of Consumer Research* 20 (December 1993), pp. 376–92, as well as some of his earlier and subsequent research. For more foundational perspectives, see also John A. Bargh and Tanya L. Chartrand, "The Unbearable Automaticity of Being," *American Psychologist* 54 (1999), pp. 462–79; and Gráinne M. Fitzsimons, Tanya L. Chartrand, and Gavan J. Fitzsimons, "Automatic Effects of Brand Exposure on Motivated Behavior: How Apple Makes You 'Think Different,'" *Journal of Consumer Research* 35 (June 2008), pp. 21–35, as well as the research programs of both authors.

43. See Timothy E. Moore, "Subliminal Advertising: What You See Is What You Get," *Journal of Marketing* 46 (Spring 1982), pp. 38–47 for an early classic discussion; and Andrew B. Aylesworth, Ronald C. Goodstein, and Ajay Kalra, "Effect of Archetypal Embeds on Feelings: An Indirect Route to Affecting Attitudes?," *Journal of Advertising* 28 (Fall 1999), pp. 73–81 for additional discussion.

44. Jonah Lerner, "The Buzz on Buzz," *Wall Street Journal,* October 16, 2010.

45. Jack Neff, "Creativity Marks This Spot: K-C Thrives in Tiny Neenah," *Advertising Age*, June 6, 2011; "U by Kotex Creates a Social Movement,"*Adweek*, November 22, 2011.

46. Ed Keller, "Showing Emotion Is the New Black,' www. mediabizbloggers.com, October 6, 2011; Jonah Berger and Katherine L. Milkman, "What Makes Online Content Viral?," *Journal of Marketing Research* 49 (April 2012), pp. 192–205.

47. Jason Feifer, "Axe's Highly Scientific, Typically Outrageous and Totally Irresistible Selling of Lust," *Fast Company*, September 2012, pp. 104–9; Bruce Horovitz, "Axe Showerpool Promo Raises Eyebrows," *USA Today*, September 17, 2012; "Axe Turns Up the Heat to Marketing to Young Men," *ABC News Radio*, March 25, 2011; Martin Lindstrom, "Can a Commercial Be Too Sexy for Its Own Good? Ask Axe," *The Atlantic*, October 2011.

48. Scott Berinato, "The Demographics of Cool," *Harvard Business Review*, December 2011, pp. 136–37; Steve Stoute, *The Tanning of America: How Hip-Hop Created a Culture That Rewrote the Rules of the New Economy* (New York: Gotham, 2012).

49. For additional discussion, see John G. Lynch Jr. and Thomas K. Srull, "Memory and Attentional Factors in Consumer Choice: Concepts and Research Methods," *Journal of Consumer Research* 9 (June 1982), pp. 18–36; and Joseph W. Alba, J. Wesley Hutchinson, and John G. Lynch Jr., "Memory and Decision Making," Harold H. Kassarjian and Thomas S. Robertson, eds., *Handbook of Consumer Theory and Research* (Englewood Cliffs, NJ: Prentice Hall, 1992), pp. 1–49.

50. Leonard M. Lodish, Magid Abraham, Stuart Kalmenson, Jeanne Livelsberger, Beth Lubetkin, Bruce Richardson, and Mary Ellen Stevens, "How T.V. Advertising Works: A Meta-Analysis of 389 Real World Split Cable T.V. Advertising Experiments," *Journal of Marketing Research* 32 (May 1995), pp. 125–39.

51. Malcolm Faulds, "Five Tips for Driving Word-of-Mouth—No Matter What Your Product Is," *Advertising Age*, November 28, 2011, p. 17; Jonah Berger and Eric M. Schwartz, "What Drives Immediate and Ongoing Word of Mouth?," *Journal of Marketing Research* 48 (October 2011), pp. 869–80.

52. Marketing scholars have developed several models of the consumer buying process through the years. See Mary Frances Luce, James R. Bettman, and John W. Payne, *Emotional Decisions: Tradeoff Difficulty and Coping in Consumer Choice* (Chicago: University of Chicago Press, 2001); James F. Engel, Roger D. Blackwell, and Paul W. Miniard, *Consumer Behavior,* 8th ed. (Fort Worth, TX: Dryden, 1994); and John A. Howard and Jagdish N. Sheth, *The Theory of Buyer Behavior* (New York: John Wiley & Sons, 1969).

53. For a comprehensive treatment of how consumers make purchase decisions in the modern marketing environment, see Todd Powers, Dorothy Advincula, Manila S. Austin, Stacy Graiko, and Jasper Snyder, "Digital and Social Media in the Purchase Decision Process: A Special Report from the Advertising Research Foundation," *Journal of Advertising Research*, December 2012, pp. 479–89.

54. Ellen Byron, "In-Store Sales Begin at Home," *Wall Street Journal*, April 25, 2011; Lauren Coleman-Lochner, "Social Networking Takes Center Stage at P&G," *Bloomberg Businessweek*, March 29, 2012; Giselle Tsirulnik, "P&G's CoverGirl Targets Women with Mobile Ads for LashBlast Mascara," *Mobile Marketer*, September 2, 2009; Jack Neff, "CoverGirl: An America's Hottest Brands Study," *Advertising Age*, November 16, 2009.

55. For a recent academic examination, see Gerald Häubl, Benedict G. C. Dellaert, and Bas Donkers, "Tunnel Vision: Local Behavioral Influences on Consumer Decisions in Product Search," *Marketing Science* 29 (May–June 2012), pp. 438–55.

56. Geoffrey Precourt, "How Unilever Uses Online Data to Map the Path to Purchase," www.warc.com, April 2012.

57. Janet Schwartz, Mary Frances Luce, and Dan Ariely, "Are Consumers Too Trusting? The Effects of Relationships with Expert Advisers," *Journal of Marketing Research* 48 (Special Issue 2011), pp. S163–S174.

58. Min Ding, John R. Hauser, Songting Dong, Daria Dzyabura, Zhilin Yang, Chenting Su, and Steven Gaskin, "Unstructured Direct Elicitation of Decision Rules," *Journal of Marketing Research* 48 (February 2011), pp. 116–27; Michaela Draganska and Daniel Klapper, "Choice Set Heterogeneity and the Role of Advertising: An Analysis with Micro and Macro Data," *Journal of Marketing Research* 48 (August 2011), pp. 653–69; John R. Hauser, Olivier Toubia, Theodoros Evgeniou, Rene Befurt, and Daria Dzyabura, "Disjunctions of Conjunctions, Cognitive Simplicity and Consideration Sets," *Journal of Marketing Research* 47 (June 2010), pp. 485–96; Erjen Van Nierop, Bart Bronnenberg, Richard Paap, Michel Wedel, and Philip Hans Franses, "Retrieving Unobserved Consideration Sets from Household Panel Data," *Journal of Marketing Research* 47 (February 2010), pp. 63–74. For some behavioral perspectives, see Jeffrey R. Parker and Rom Y. Schrift, "Rejectable Choice Sets: How Seemingly Irrelevant No-Choice Options Affect Consumer Decision Processes," *Journal of Marketing Research* 48 (October 2011), pp. 840–54.

59. Benedict G. C. Dellaert and Gerald Häubl, "Searching in Choice Mode: Consumer Decision Processes in Product Search with Recommendations," *Journal of Marketing Research* 49 (April 2012), pp. 277–88. See also Jun B. Kim, Paulo Albuquerque, and Bart J. Bronnenberg, "Mapping Online Consumer Search," *Journal of Marketing Research* 48 (February 2011), pp. 13–27.

60. Paul E. Green and Yoram Wind, *Multiattribute Decisions in Marketing: A Measurement Approach* (Hinsdale, IL: Dryden, 1973), chapter 2; Richard J. Lutz, "The Role of Attitude Theory in Marketing," H. Kassarjian and T. Robertson, eds., *Perspectives in Consumer Behavior* (Lebanon, IN: Scott Foresman, 1981), pp. 317–39.

61. This expectancy-value model was originally developed by Martin Fishbein, "Attitudes and Prediction of Behavior," Martin Fishbein, ed., *Readings in Attitude Theory and Measurement* (New York: John Wiley & Sons, 1967), pp. 477–92; for a critical review, see Paul W. Miniard and Joel B. Cohen, "An Examination of the Fishbein-Ajzen Behavioral-Intentions Model's Concepts and Measures," *Journal of Experimental Social Psychology* (May 1981), pp. 309–39.

62. Michael R. Solomon, *Consumer Behavior: Buying, Having, and Being*, 10th ed. (Upper Saddle River, NJ: Prentice Hall, 2013).

63. For an advanced measurement technique to assess consumers use of decision heuristics, see Daria Dzyabura and John R. Hauser, "Active Machine Learning for Consideration Heuristics," *Marketing Science* 30 (September–October 2011), pp. 801–19.

64. Richard H. Thaler and Cass R. Sunstein, *Nudge: Improving Decisions about Health, Wealth, and Happiness* (New York: Penguin, 2009); Michael Krauss, "A Nudge in the Right Direction," *Marketing News*, March 30, 2009, p. 20.

65. Martin Fishbein, "Attitudes and Prediction of Behavior," M. Fishbein, ed., *Readings in Attitude Theory and Measurement* (New York: John Wiley & Sons, 1967), pp. 477–92.

66. For a fascinating examination of the use of *Consumer Reports*, see Uri Simonsohn, "Lessons from an 'Oops' at *Consumer Reports*: Consumers Follow Experts and Ignore Invalid Information," *Journal of Marketing Research* 48 (February 2011), pp. 1–12.

67. Tom Long, "'Ted' Least Expected Hero of the Summer," *The Detroit News*, August 11, 2012; Ben Fritz, "'Ted' Marketing Campaign Balances Raunch with Heart," *Los Angeles Times*, June 22, 2012; Rachel Dodes, "Twitter Goes to the Movies," *Wall Street Journal*, August 3, 2012.

68. Margaret C. Campbell and Ronald C. Goodstein, "The Moderating Effect of Perceived Risk on Consumers' Evaluations of Product Incongruity: Preference for the Norm," *Journal of Consumer Research* 28 (December 2001), pp. 439–49; Grahame R. Dowling, "Perceived Risk," Peter E. Earl and Simon Kemp, eds., *The Elgar Companion to Consumer Research and Economic Psychology* (Cheltenham, UK: Edward Elgar, 1999), pp. 419–24; James R. Bettman, "Perceived Risk and Its Components: A Model and Empirical Test," *Journal of Marketing Research* 10 (May 1973).

69. Richard L. Oliver, "Customer Satisfaction Research," Rajiv Grover and Marco Vriens, eds., *Handbook of Marketing Research* (Thousand Oaks, CA: Sage Publications, 2006), pp. 569–87.

70. Albert O. Hirschman, *Exit, Voice, and Loyalty* (Cambridge, MA: Harvard University Press, 1970).

71. John D. Cripps, "Heuristics and Biases in Timing the Replacement of Durable Products," *Journal of Consumer Research* 21 (September 1994), pp. 304–18.

72. Andrea Rothman and Susanna Ray, "Final Destination: The Cotswolds," *Bloomberg Businessweek*, March 5, 2012, pp. 24–25; Ben Paytner, "From Trash to Cash," *Fast Company*, February 2009, p. 44.

73. Richard E. Petty, *Communication and Persuasion: Central and Peripheral Routes to Attitude Change* (New York: Springer-Verlag, 1986); Richard E. Petty and John T. Cacioppo, *Attitudes and Persuasion: Classic and Contemporary Approaches* (New York: McGraw-Hill, 1981).

74. For an overview of some issues involved, see James R. Bettman, Mary Frances Luce, and John W. Payne, "Constructive Consumer Choice Processes," *Journal of Consumer Research* 25 (December 1998), pp. 187–217; and Itamar Simonson, "Getting Closer to Your Customers by Understanding How They Make Choices," *California Management Review* 35 (Summer 1993), pp. 68–84. For examples of some classic studies in this area, see some of the following: Rom Y. Schrift, Oded Netzer, and Ran Kivetz, "Complicating Choice," *Journal of Marketing Research* 48 (April 2011), pp. 308–26; Dan Ariely and Ziv Carmon, "Gestalt Characteristics of Experiences: The Defining Features of Summarized Events," *Journal of Behavioral Decision Making* 13 (April 2000), pp. 191–201; Ravi Dhar and Klaus Wertenbroch, "Consumer Choice between Hedonic and Utilitarian Goods," *Journal of Marketing Research* 37 (February 2000), pp. 60–71; Itamar Simonson and Amos Tversky, "Choice in Context: Tradeoff Contrast and Extremeness Aversion," *Journal of Marketing Research* 29 (August 1992), pp. 281–95; Itamar Simonson, "The Effects of Purchase Quantity and Timing on Variety-Seeking Behavior," *Journal of Marketing Research* 27 (May 1990), pp. 150–62.

75. Leon Schiffman and Leslie Kanuk, *Consumer Behavior*, 10th ed. (Upper Saddle River, NJ: Prentice Hall, 2010); Wayne D. Hoyer, Deborah J. MacInnis, and Rik Pieters, *Consumer Behavior*, 6th ed. (Mason, OH: South-Western College Publishing, 2013).

76. For a detailed review of the practical significance of consumer decision making, see Itamar Simonson, "Get Close to Your Customers by Understanding How They Make Their Choices," *California Management Review* 35 (Summer 1993), pp. 78–79.

77. For some recent research investigations of framing effects, see Eesha Sharma and Adam L. Alter, "Financial Deprivation Prompts Consumers to Seek Scarce Goods," *Journal of Consumer Research* 39 (October 2012), pp. 545–60.

78. Mario Pandelaere, Barbara Briers, and Christophe Lembregts, "How to Make a 29% Increase Look Bigger: The Unit Effect in Option Comparisons," *Journal of Consumer Research* 38 (August 2011), pp. 308–22.

79. Mark Scott, "A Stairway to Marketing Heaven," *Bloomberg BusinessWeek*, October 30, 2009. p. 17.

80. See Richard H. Thaler, "Mental Accounting and Consumer Choice," *Marketing Science* 4 (Summer 1985), pp. 199–214 for a seminal piece; and Richard Thaler, "Mental Accounting Matters," *Journal of Behavioral Decision Making* 12 (September 1999), pp. 183–206 for additional perspectives. For some diverse applications of the theory, see Robin L. Soster, Ashwani Monga, and William O. Bearden, "Tracking Costs of Time and Money: How Accounting Periods Affect Mental Accounting," *Journal of Consumer Research* 37 (December 2010), pp. 712–21; Jonathan Levav and A. Peter McGraw, "Emotional Accounting: How Feelings about Money Influence Consumer Choice," *Journal of Marketing Research* 46 (February 2009), pp. 66–80; John Godek and Kyle B. Murray, "The Effect of Spikes in the Price of Gasoline on Behavioral Intentions: A Mental Accounting Explanation," *Journal of Behavioral Decision Making* 25 (July 2012), pp. 295–302.

81. Gary L. Gastineau and Mark P. Kritzman, *Dictionary of Financial Risk Management*, 3rd ed. (New York: John Wiley & Sons, 1999).

82. Example adapted from Daniel Kahneman and Amos Tversky, "Prospect Theory: An Analysis of Decision under Risk," *Econometrica* 47 (March 1979), pp. 263–91.

83. For some recent academic research, see Abigail B. Sussman and Adam L. Alter, "The Exception Is the Rule: Underestimating and Overspending on Exceptional Expenses," *Journal of Consumer Research* 39 (December 2012), pp. 800–14.

## Chapter 7

1. Ian Simpson, "Number of U.S. Business Fell in 2010: Census Bureau," www.reuters.com, June 26, 2012.

2. Quentin Hardy, "Chambers Challenged," *Forbes*, March 14, 2011, pp. 30–32; Rich Karlgaard, "Cisco's Disruptive (and Cooler) Rival," *Forbes*, July 18, 2011, p. 21; Rich Karlgaard, "Driving Change: Cisco's Chambers," *Forbes*, February 13, 2012; "Charlie Rose Talks to Cisco's John Chambers," *Bloomberg Businessweek*, April 23, 2012, p. 41.

3. For a comprehensive review of the topic, see James C. Anderson and James A. Narus, *Business Market Management: Understanding, Creating, and Delivering Value*, 3rd ed. (Upper Saddle River, NJ: Prentice Hall, 2009); and Gary L. Lilien and Rajdeep Grewal, eds., *Handbook of Business-to-Business Marketing* (Northampton, MA: Edward Elgar Publishing, 2012).

4. Frederick E. Webster Jr. and Yoram Wind, *Organizational Buying Behavior* (Upper Saddle River, NJ: Prentice Hall, 1972), p. 2; for a review of some academic literature on the topic, see Håkan Håkansson and Ivan Snehota, "Marketing in Business Markets," Bart Weitz and Robin Wensley, eds., *Handbook of Marketing* (London: Sage Publications, 2002), pp. 513–26; Mark Glynn and Arch Woodside, eds., *Business-to-Business Brand Management: Theory, Research, and Executive Case Study Exercises in Advances in Business Marketing & Purchasing* series, volume 15 (Bingley, UK: Emerald Group Publishing, 2009).

5. Shoe Material, www.bata.com, accessed May 20, 2014. See also www.shoeguide.org/Shoe_Anatomy, accessed May 20, 2014.

6. Philip Kotler and Waldemar Pfoertsch, *B2B Brand Management* (Berlin, Germany: Springer, 2006).

7. Anita Raghavan, "No More Excuses," *Forbes*, April 27, 2009, pp. 121–22; Richard Weiss and Benedikt Kammel, "How Siemens Got Its *Geist* Back," *Bloomberg Businessweek*, January 31, 2011, pp. 18–20; Piet Levy, "The Right Answer," *Marketing News*, September 15, 2011, pp. 19–22.

8. Fred Wiersema, "The B2B Agenda: The Current State of B2B Marketing and a Look Ahead," *Institute for the Study of Business Markets*, http://isbm.smeal.psu.edu, accessed February 20, 2014.

9. Susan Avery, *Purchasing* 135 (November 2, 2006), p. 36; "PPG Honors Seven Excellent Suppliers," www.ppg.com, July 11, 2012.

10. Michael Collins, "Breaking into the Big Leagues," *American Demographics,* January 1996, p. 24.

11. Patrick J. Robinson, Charles W. Faris, and Yoram Wind, *Industrial Buying and Creative Marketing* (Boston: Allyn & Bacon, 1967).

12. Michele D. Bunn, "Taxonomy of Buying Decision Approaches," *Journal of Marketing* 57 (January 1993), pp. 38–56.

13. Ashlee Vance, "EMC Wants R-E-S-P-E-C-T," *Bloomberg BusinessWeek*, January 24, 2011, pp. 33–34; Justin Kern, "EMC Kicks Up Content Management with Update, Acquisition," *Information Management*, May 22, 2012.

14. Sheridan Prasso, "Oracle's Bold Moves," *Fortune*, April 11, 2011, p. 27; Adam Lashinsky, "The Enforcer," *Fortune*, September 28, 2009, pp. 117–24; Steve Hamm, "Oracle Faces Its Toughest Deal Yet," *BusinessWeek*, May 4, 2009, p. 24; Steve Hamm and Aaron Ricadela, "Oracle Has Customers over a Barrel," *BusinessWeek*, September 21, 2009, pp. 52–55.

15. Jeffrey E. Lewin and Naveen Donthu, "The Influence of Purchase Situation on Buying Center Structure and Involvement: A Select Meta-Analysis of Organizational Buying Behavior Research," *Journal of Business Research* 58 (October 2005), pp. 1381–90; R. Venkatesh and Ajay K. Kohli, "Influence Strategies in Buying Centers," *Journal of Marketing* 59 (October 1995), pp. 71–82.

16. Frederic E. Webster and Yoram Wind, *Organizational Buying Behavior* (Upper Saddle River, NJ: Prentice Hall, 1972), p. 6.

17. James C. Anderson and James A. Narus, *Business Market Management: Understanding, Creating, and Delivering Value*, 3rd ed. (Upper Saddle River, NJ: Prentice Hall, 2009); Frederick E. Webster Jr. and Yoram Wind, "A General Model for Understanding Organizational Buying Behavior," *Journal of Marketing* 36 (April 1972), pp. 12–19.

18. Allison Enright, "It Takes a Committee to Buy into B-to-B," *Marketing News*, February 15, 2006, pp. 12–13.

19. Frederick E. Webster Jr. and Kevin Lane Keller, "A Roadmap for Branding in Industrial Markets," *Journal of Brand Management* 11 (May 2004), pp. 388–402.

20. Scott Ward and Frederick E. Webster Jr., "Organizational Buying Behavior," Tom Robertson and Hal Kassarjian, eds., *Handbook of Consumer Behavior* (Upper Saddle River, NJ: Prentice Hall, 1991), chapter 12, pp. 419–58.

21. Bob Donath, "Emotions Play Key Role in Biz Brand Appeal," *Marketing News*, June 1, 2006, p. 7.

22. Piet Levy, "Reeling in the Hungry Fish," *Marketing News*, May 30, 2009, p. 6; Stephen Baker, Timken Plots a Rust Belt Resurgence," *BusinessWeek*, October 15, 2009; Matt McClellan, "Rolling Along," *Smart Business Akron/Canton*, October 2008; Robert Wang, "Timken Co. Had Record Revenue in 2011," www.cantonrep.com, January 26, 2012; "Strong Energy Market to Propel Timken," *Metal Bulletin Daily*, January 27, 2012, p. 64.

23. Frederic E. Webster and Yoram Wind, *Organizational Buying Behavior* (Saddle River, NJ: Prentice Hall, 1972), p. 6.

24. Victoria Barret, "SAP Gets a Pit Bull," *Forbes*, February 13, 2012, pp. 38–40.

25. Michael Fielding, "Shift the Focus," *Marketing News*, September 1, 2006, pp. 18–20.

26. James C. Anderson and Marc Wouters, "What You Can Learn from Your Customer's Customer," *MIT Sloan Management Review*, Winter 2013, pp. 75–82.

27. James C. Anderson, James A. Narus, and Wouter van Rossum, "Customer Value Proposition in Business Markets," *Harvard Business Review*, March 2006, pp. 2–10; James C. Anderson, "From Understanding to Managing Customer Value in Business Markets," H. Håkansson, D. Harrison, and A. Waluszewski, eds., *Rethinking Marketing: New Marketing Tools* (London: John Wiley & Sons, 2004), pp. 137–59.

28. "Case Studies: Rio Tinto," *Quadrem*, www.quadrem.com, February 6, 2010.

29. "Best Practices of the Best-Run Sales Organizations: Sales Opportunity Blueprinting," *SAP*, http://download.sap.com, February 6, 2010.

30. Cliff Hocker, "The Critical Link: The 40 Best Companies for Diversity," Black Enterprise, July 2012; "About McDonald's: Supplier Diversity," www.aboutmcdonalds.com, accessed February 14, 2013.

31. Patrick J. Robinson, Charles W. Faris, and Yoram Wind, *Industrial Buying and Creative Marketing* (Boston, MA: Allyn & Bacon, 1967).

32. Geri Smith, "Hard Times Ease for a Cement King," *BusinessWeek*, November 9, 2009, p. 28; Nicole Skibola, "CEMEX Blazes the Social Innovation Trail," *Forbes*, November 12, 2010.

33. *Ritchie Bros Auctioneers,* www.rbauction.com, accessed May 20, 2014.

34. "2009–10 B2B Marketing Benchmark Report," *Marketing Sherpa*, www.sherpastore.com, February 6, 2010.

35. Allison Enright, "It Takes a Committee to Buy into B-to-B," *Marketing News,* February 15, 2006, pp. 12–13.

36. Daniel E. Flint, Robert B. Woodruff, and Sarah Fisher Gardial, "Exploring the Phenomenon of Customers' Desired Value Change in a Business-to-Business Context," *Journal of Marketing* 66 (October 2002), pp. 102–17.

37. Ruth N. Bolton and Matthew B. Myers, "Price-Based Global Market Segmentation for Services," *Journal of Marketing* 67 (July 2003), pp. 108–28.

38. Wolfgang Ulaga and Werner Reinartz, "Hybrid Offerings: How Manufacturing Firms Combine Goods and Services Successfully," *Journal of Marketing* 75 (November 2011), pp. 5–23.

39. Wolfgang Ulaga and Andreas Eggert, "Value-Based Differentiation in Business Relationships: Gaining and Sustaining Key Supplier Status," *Journal of Marketing* 70 (January 2006), pp. 119–36.

40. Christopher Palmeri, "Serving Two (Station) Masters," *BusinessWeek,* July 24, 2006, p. 46.

41. David Kiley, "Small Print Jobs for Peanuts," *BusinessWeek,* July 17, 2006, p. 58.

42. Nirmalya Kumar, *Marketing as Strategy: Understanding the CEO's Agenda for Driving Growth and Innovation* (Boston: Harvard Business School Press, 2004).

43. Ibid.

44. See www.lincolnelectric.com/knowledge/custsolutions/gcr.asp, accessed February 22, 2014; William Atkinson, "Now That's Value Added," *Purchasing*, December 11, 2003, p. 26; James A. Narus and James C. Anderson, "Turn Your Industrial Distributors into Partners," *Harvard Business Review*, March–April 1986, pp. 66–71.

45. "Case Study: Automotive Vendor Managed Inventory, Plexco (Australia)," www.marciajedd.com, accessed February 22, 2014.

46. Maria Jobin, "Bringing a Brand to Life: Driving Preference Across Cultures," talk given in Lugano, Switzerland, December 6, 2012.

47. Britt Dionne, "Behind the Scenes with NetApp," *The Hub*, July/August 2009; "Close-up with Jay Kidd, CMO, NetApp," *BtoB Magazine*, January 20, 2010; Piet Levy, "It's Alive! Alive!" *Marketing News*, April 30, 2009, p. 8; Ben Burrowes, "NetApp Rides on Social Media Success," www.marketing-interactive.com, December 14, 2009; Caroline Donnelly, "NetApp Hails Mid-Market Success," www.channelweb.co.uk, March 24, 2011.

48. Michael Krauss, "Warriors of the Heart," *Marketing News,* February 1, 2006, p. 7; Brian Hindo, "Emerson Electric's Innovation Metrics," *BusinessWeek*, June 5, 2008; Kate Maddox, "BtoB's Best Marketers: Kathy Button Bell," *B to B*, October 11, 2010.

49. Bob Lamons, "Branding, B-to-B Style," *Sales and Marketing Management* 157 (September 2005), pp. 46–50; David A. Kaplan, "No. 1 SAS," in "The 100 Best Companies to Work For," *Fortune*, February 8, 2010, pp. 56–64; "Study Shows SAS Dominates Global Advanced Analytics Market," *Reuters*, July 9, 2012.

50. Elisabeth Sullivan, "A Worthwhile Investment," *Marketing News*, December 30, 2009, p. 10.

51. Josh Bernoff, "Why B-to-B Ought to Love Social Media," *Marketing News*, April 15, 2009, p. 20; Elisabeth Sullivan, "A Long Slog," *Marketing News*, February 28, 2009, pp. 15–18.

52. Elisabeth Sullivan, "One to One," *Marketing News*, May 15, 2009, pp. 10–12.

53. Christine Birkner, "10 Minutes with Kirsten Watson," *Marketing News*, January 2013, pp. 52–58.

54. Christine Birkner, "Success by Association," *Marketing News*, April 30, 2012, pp. 14–18; Geoffrey Precourt, "How Xerox Tapped Unlikely B2B Emotions," *Advertising Week*, September 2009.

55. Elizabeth Woyke, "A Sexier Office Phone," *Forbes*, September 13, 2010, pp. 42–43.

56. Ashlee Vance, "EMC Wants R-E-S-P-E-C-T," *Bloomberg Businessweek*, January 24, 2011, pp. 33–34.

57. "Per Ardua," *The Economist*, February 5, 2011; "Rolls-Royce Celebrates 50th Anniversary of Power by the Hour," October 30, 2012, www.rolls-royce.com.

58. Kevin Kelleher, "Will Adobe's New Cloud Strategy Pay Off?," *Fortune*, December 24, 2012, pp. 29–33.

59. "Ready, Set, Grow," *The Economist*, March 5, 2011, p. 72.

60. For foundational material, see Lloyd M. Rinehart, James A. Eckert, Robert B. Handfield, Thomas J. Page Jr., and Thomas Atkin, "An Assessment of Buyer–Seller Relationships," *Journal of Business Logistics* 25 (2004), pp. 25–62; F. Robert Dwyer, Paul Schurr, and Sejo Oh, "Developing Buyer–Supplier Relationships," *Journal of Marketing* 51 (April 1987), pp. 11–28. For an important caveat, see Christopher P. Blocker, Mark B. Houston, and Daniel J. Flint, "Unpacking What a 'Relationship' Means to Commercial Buyers: How the Relationship Metaphor Creates Tension and Obscures Experience," *Journal of Consumer Research* 38 (February 2012), pp. 886–908.

61. Arnt Buvik and George John, "When Does Vertical Coordination Improve Industrial Purchasing Relationships?," *Journal of Marketing* 64 (October 2000), pp. 52–64.

62. Das Narayandas, "Building Loyalty in Business Markets," *Harvard Business Review*, September 2005, pp. 131–39; V. Kumar, S. Sriram, Anita Luo, and Pradeep K. Chintagunta, "Assessing the Effect of Marketing Investments in a Business Marketing Context," *Marketing Science* 30 (September–October 2011), pp. 924–40; Anita Luo and V. Kumar, "Recovering Hidden Buyer–Seller Relationship States to Measure the Return on Marketing Investment in Business-to-Business Markets," *Journal of Marketing Research* 50 (February 2013), pp. 143–60.

63. Michal Lev-Ram, "Inside SAP's Radical Makeover," *Fortune*, April 9, 2012.

64. Das Narayandas and V. Kasturi Rangan, "Building and Sustaining Buyer–Seller Relationships in Mature Industrial Markets," *Journal of Marketing* 68 (July 2004), pp. 63–77.

65. Robert W. Palmatier, Rajiv P. Dant, Dhruv Grewal, and Kenneth R. Evans, "Factors Influencing the Effectiveness of Relationship Marketing: A Meta-Analysis," *Journal of Marketing* 70 (October 2006), pp. 136–53; Jean L. Johnson, Ravipreet S. Sohli, and Rajdeep Grewal, "The Role of Relational Knowledge Stores in Interfirm Partnering," *Journal of Marketing* 68 (July 2004), pp. 21–36; Fred Selnes and James Sallis, "Promoting Relationship Learning," *Journal of Marketing* 67 (July 2003), pp. 80–95.

66. Joseph P. Cannon and William D. Perreault Jr., "Buyer–Seller Relationships in Business Markets," *Journal of Marketing Research* 36 (November 1999), pp. 439–60.

67. Jan B. Heide and Kenneth H. Wahne, "Friends, Businesspeople, and Relationship Roles: A Conceptual Framework and Research Agenda," *Journal of Marketing* 70 (July 2006), pp. 90–103.

68. Joseph P. Cannon and William D. Perreault Jr., "Buyer–Seller Relationships in Business Markets," *Journal of Marketing Research* 36 (November 1999), pp. 439–60.

69. Thomas G. Noordewier, George John, and John R. Nevin, "Performance Outcomes of Purchasing Arrangements in Industrial Buyer–Vendor Arrangements," *Journal of Marketing* 54 (October 1990), pp. 80–93; Buvik and John, "When Does Vertical Coordination Improve Industrial Purchasing Relationships?," pp. 52–64.

70. Corine S. Noordhoff, Kyriakos Kyriakopoulos, Christine Moorman, Pieter Pauwels, and Benedict G. C. Dellaert, "The Bright Side and Dark Side of Embedded Ties in Business-to- Business Innovation," *Journal of Marketing* 75 (September 2011), pp. 34–52.

71. Akesel I. Rokkan, Jan B. Heide, and Kenneth H. Wathne, "Specific Investment in Marketing Relationships: Expropriation and Bonding Effects," *Journal of Marketing Research* 40 (May 2003), pp. 210–24.

72. Kenneth H. Wathne and Jan B. Heide, "Relationship Governance in a Supply Chain Network," *Journal of Marketing* 68 (January 2004), pp. 73–89; Douglas Bowman and Das Narayandas, "Linking Customer Management Effort to Customer Profitability in Business Markets," *Journal of Marketing Research* 61 (November 2004), pp. 433–47; Mrinal Ghosh and George John, "Governance Value Analysis and Marketing Strategy," *Journal of Marketing* 63 (Special Issue, 1999), pp. 131–45.

73. Janet Bercovitz, Sandy D. Jap, and Jackson Nickerson, "The Antecedents and Performance Implications of Cooperative Exchange Norms," *Organization Science* 17, no. 6 (2006), pp. 724–40; Sandy Jap, "Pie Expansion Effects: Collaboration Processes in Buyer–Seller Relationships," *Journal of Marketing Research* 36 (November 1999), pp. 461–75.

74. Buvik and John, "When Does Vertical Coordination Improve Industrial Purchasing Relationships?," pp. 52–64.

75. Kenneth H. Wathne and Jan B. Heide, "Opportunism in Interfirm Relationships: Forms, Outcomes, and Solutions," *Journal of Marketing* 64 (October 2000), pp. 36–51.

76. Mark Vandenbosch and Stephen Sapp, "Opportunism Knocks," *MIT Sloan Management Review*, October 1, 2010.

77. Mark B. Houston and Shane A. Johnson, "Buyer–Supplier Contracts versus Joint Ventures: Determinants and Consequences of Transaction Structure," *Journal of Marketing Research* 37 (February 2000), pp. 1–15.

78. Aksel I. Rokkan, Jan B. Heide, and Kenneth H. Wathne, "Specific Investment in Marketing Relationships: Expropriation and Bonding Effects," *Journal of Marketing Research* 40 (May 2003), pp. 210–24.

79. Paul King, "Purchasing: Keener Competition Requires Thinking Outside the Box," *Nation's Restaurant News,* August 18, 2003, p. 87; www.aramark.com, accessed May 20, 2014.

80. Peter Burrows, "Investors Fret as Cisco Scales Back Forecasts," *Bloomberg Businessweek*, November 22, 2010, pp. 49–50.

81. "The Next Battle," *Bloomberg Government Insider*, Fall 2011, www.bgov.com.

82. Jeanne Sahedi, "Cutting Washington Could Hit Main Street," www.money.cnn.com, July 23, 2012.

83. Elizabeth Woyke, "The Other Motorola," *Forbes*, November 7, 2011, pp. 52–54.

84. Bill Gormley, "The U.S. Government Can Be Your Lifelong Customer," *Washington Business Journal*, January 23, 2009; Chris Warren, "How to Sell to Uncle Sam," *BNET Crash Course*, www.bnet.com, February 6, 2010.

85. Matthew Swibel and Janet Novack, "The Scariest Customer," *Forbes,* November 10, 2003, pp. 96–97.

86. Laura M. Litvan, "Selling to Uncle Sam: New, Easier Rules," *Nation's Business* (March 1995), pp. 46–48.

87. Gormley, "The U.S. Government Can Be Your Lifelong Customer."

## Chapter 8

1. Alex Taylor III, "Hyundai Smokes the Competition," *Fortune*, January 18, 2010, pp. 62–71; Moon Ihlwan and David Kiley, "Hyundai Gains with Marketing Blitz, *BusinessWeek*, September 17, 2009; Christoph Rauwald, "Hyundai Tracks Silver Arrow through Europe's 'Green Hell,'" www.bloomberg.com, February 13, 2013; Henry Foy and

Hyunjoo Jin, "Hyundai's Focus on Quality Risks Emerging Market Share," www.reuters.com, November 11, 2012.

2. Jack Schofield, "Samsung Tipped to Lead China's Mobile Phone Market," www.ZDnet.com, July 13, 2012.

3. Alexandra Berzon, "Starwood CEO Moves to China to Grow Brand," *Wall Street Journal*, June 6, 2011.

4. Michael Arndt, "Invasion of the Guatemalan Chicken," *Bloomberg BusinessWeek*, March 22 and 29, 2010, pp. 72–73; Steven Thompson, "Dallas' Pollo Campero Tests New Concept Model," *Dallas Business Journal*, June 29, 2012; "Pollo Campero Opens in Lawrence, Massachusetts," *QSR Magazine*, June 14, 2012.

5. Matthew Eyring, "Learning from Tata Motors' Nano Mistakes," *Harvard Business Review Blog*, January 11, 2011; Mahendra Ramsinghani, "The Trouble with India's People Car," *Technology Review*, December 6, 2011; Drew Guarini, "Tata Nano: $3,000 Car Coming to U.S.," *Huffington Post*, October 15, 2012; Kartika Trehan, "Tata Motors Likely to Launch 800cc Nano in 2013," *Economic Times*, December 26, 2012.

6. Michael E. Porter, *Competitive Strategy* (New York: Free Press, 1980), p. 275.

7. Trade in Services, National Bureau of Asian Research, www.nbr.org, retrieved February 15, 2013; "Understanding the WTO—Members," www.wto.org, retrieved February 15, 2013.

8. Joshua Cooper Ramo, "Globalism Goes Backward," *Fortune*, November 20, 2102, pp. 135–40.

9. For a comprehensive treatment, see Philip R. Cateora, Mary C. Gilly, and John L. Graham, *International Marketing* (New York: McGraw-Hill/Irwin, 2009).

10. Leslie Kwoh, "Cinnabon Finds Sweet Success in Russia, Mideast," *Wall Street Journal*, December 25, 2012.

11. "US Export Fact Sheet," *International Trade Administration,* www.trade.gov, February 8, 2013.

12. Jan Johanson and Finn Wiedersheim-Paul, "The Internationalization of the Firm," *Journal of Management Studies* 12 (October 1975), pp. 305–22.

13. Michael R. Czinkota and Ilkka A. Ronkainen, *International Marketing,* 9th ed. (Cincinnati, OH: South-Western Cengage Learning, 2010).

14. For a thorough review of academic research on global marketing, see Johny K. Johansson, "Global Marketing: Research on Foreign Entry, Local Marketing, Global Management," Bart Weitz and Robin Wensley, eds., *Handbook of Marketing* (London: Sage, 2002), pp. 457–83. Also see Johny K. Johansson, *Global Marketing,* 5th ed. (New York: McGraw-Hill, 2009). For some global marketing research issues, see C. Samuel Craig and Susan P. Douglas, *International Marketing Research,* 3rd ed. (Chichester, UK: John Wiley & Sons, 2005).

15. Marc Gunther, "The World's New Economic Landscape," *Fortune,* July 26, 2010, pp. 105–6; Sheila Shayon, "Microsoft Unleashes Global Marketing Blitz for Windows 8, New Devices," www.brandchannel.com, October 25, 2012; Bill Rigby, "Windows 8 Sales Steady, Hit 60 Million since October Launch," *Reuters,* January 8, 2013.

16. Michael J. Silverstein, Abheek Singhi, Carol Liao, and David Michael, *The $10 Trillion Prize: Captivating the Newly Affluent in China and India* (Boston: Harvard Business School Publishing, 2012).

17. Karen Cho, "KFC China's Recipe for Success," *Forbes India,* October 28, 2009; *Staying the Course: Yum! Annual Report 2012,* ; Diane Brady, "KFC's Big Game of Chicken," *Bloomberg Businessweek,* March 29, 2012; Drew Hinshaw, "As KFC Goes to Africa It Lacks Only One Thing: Chickens," *Wall Street Journal,* February 8, 2013; Laurie Burkitt, "Yum Brands Apologizes amid Chicken Probe, *Wall Street Journal,* January 10, 2013.

18. Johny K. Johansson, "Global Marketing: Research on Foreign Entry, Local Marketing, Global Management," Bart Weitz and Robin Wensley, eds., *Handbook of Marketing* (London: Sage, 2002), pp. 457–83.

19. Bernard Condon, "Babble Rouser," *Forbes,* August 11, 2008, pp. 72–77; Elenoa Baselala, Digicel's New Look," *Fiji Times,* November 4, 2010; "About Digicel," www.digicel.com, accessed April 17, 2013.

20. According to the *CIA World Factbook* (www.cia.gov/library/publications/the-world-factbook/ index.html), there are 34 developed countries: Andorra, Australia, Austria, Belgium, Bermuda, Canada, Denmark, Faroe Islands, Finland, France, Germany, Greece, Holy See, Iceland, Ireland, Israel, Italy, Japan, Liechtenstein, Luxembourg, Malta, Monaco, Netherlands, New Zealand, Norway, Portugal, San Marino, South Africa, Spain, Sweden, Switzerland, Turkey, United Kingdom, and United States. They note that DCs are similar to the new International Monetary Fund (IMF) term *advanced economies* that adds Hong Kong, South Korea, Singapore, and Taiwan but drops Malta, South Africa, and Turkey.

21. "Key Emerging Markets Offer Growth," www.warc.com, October 24, 2012.

22. Sapna Agrawal, "Kraft Aims to Be among Top Food Firms in India," *Mint,* June 30, 2010; Matthew Boyle, "In Emerging Markets, Unilever Finds a Passport to Profit," *Bloomberg Businessweek,* January 3, 2013.

23. "World Population to Exceed 9 Billion by 2050," press release, *United Nations,* www.un.org, March 11, 2009; "2012 World Population Data Sheet," www.PRB.org, retrieved February 15, 2013.

24. Seth Kugel, "Marketing to Brazil's Emerging Middle Class," *Global Post,* March 30, 2010; Paulo Prada, "For Brazil, It's Finally Tomorrow," *Wall Street Journal,* March 29, 2010; Laura Snoad, "Breaking into Brazil," *Marketing Week,* February 9, 2012; Claudia Penteado, "Rio Slums Undergo a Marketplace Makeover," *Advertising Age,* June 11, 2012, p. 18; David Biller and Katerina Petroff, "In Brazil's Favelas, A Middle Class Arises," *Bloomberg Businessweek,* December 24, 2012.

25. Lyubov Pronina, "Dreams of an iPad Economy for Russia," *Bloomberg Businessweek,* February 7, 2011; "A Bridge to Asia," *The Economist,* September 8, 2012; Julia Ioffe, "In Russia, Facebook Is More than a Social Network," *Bloomberg Businessweek,* January 3, 2011; "Facebook Aims for Russian Growth," www.warc.com, October 8, 2012.

26. "Unfinished Journey," *The Economist,* March 24, 2012; Nikhil Gulati and Rumman Ahmed, "India Has 1.2 Billion People but Not Enough Drink Coke," *Wall Street Journal,* July 13, 2012; Vijay Govindrajan and Gunjan Bagla, "Watch Out for India's Consumer Market Pitfalls," *HBR Blog Network,* October 19, 2012; "The Other Asian Giant," *The Economist,* August 6, 2011; Naazneen Karmali, "Rough and Ready," *Forbes,* May 9, 2011; "India Brands Go Mobile," www.warc.com, May 7, 2012.

27. "The Mystery of the Chinese Consumer," *The Economist,* July 2011, pp. 59–60; Laurie Birkett, "PepsiCo Chips Away at China," *Wall Street Journal,* July 10, 2012; Tom Doctoroff, "What the Chinese Want," *Wall Street Journal,* May 18, 2012; Helen H. Wang, "Five Things Starbucks Did to Get China Right," *Forbes,* August 10, 2012; Julie Cruz, "Playing Catch-Up in Luxe's Promised Land," *Bloomberg Businessweek,* April 16, 2012; April Rabkin, "The Tao of the Sea Turtle," *Fast Company,* February 2012; Douglas A. McIntyre, "The Most Popular American Companies in China," www.247wallst.com, January 3, 2012.

28. "The Price of Freedom: A Special Report on South Africa," *Economist,* June 5, 2010; Frank Aquilla, "Africa's Biggest Score: A Thriving Economy," *BusinessWeek,* June 28, 2010; "Continental Shift," Special Advertising Section, *Bloomberg Businessweek,* May 23, 2011; Emma Hall, "Telecoms Vodafone, MTN Fill Banking Breach in Africa," *Advertising Age,* June 11, 2012; Susan Caminiti "Africa's Moment," Special Advertising Section, *Fortune,* July 23, 2012; "A Continent Goes Shopping," *The Economist,* August 18, 2012; Damian Hattingh, Bill Russo, Ade Sun-Basorun, and Arend Van Wamelen, "The Rise of the African Consumer," *McKinsey Quarterly,* November 2012; "Nestlé Positive on Africa," www.warc.com , December 7, 2012; "GM Takes New Approach in Africa," www.warc.com, January 11, 2013; "Innovation Drives Mobile Use in Africa," www.warc.com, February 22, 2103. *All: CIA World Factbook,* www.cia.gov.

29. Louise Lavabre, "Talking with Our Thumbs: Twitter in Indonesia," *Jakarta Post,* September 22, 2010; Peter Geiling, "Will Indonesia Make It BRICI?," *GlobalPost,* July 7, 2009; Arief Budiman, Heang Chhor, Rohit Razdan, and Ajay Sohoni, "The New Indonesian Consumer,"

white paper, www.mckinsey.com, December 2012; "Branding Key in Indonesia," www.warc.com, December 24, 2012; "L'Oréal Targets Indonesia," www.warc.com, November 7, 2012.

30. Jagdish N. Sheth, "Impact of Emerging Markets on Marketing: Rethinking Existing Perspectives and Practices," *Journal of Marketing* 75 (July 2011), pp. 166–82; Yuval Atsmon, Peter Child, Richard Dobbs, and Laxman Narasimhan, "Winning the $30 Trillion Decathlon: Going for Gold in Emerging Markets," *McKinsey Quarterly*, August 2012.

31. Adapted from Vijay Mahajan, Marcos V. Pratini De Moraes, and Jerry Wind, "The Invisible Global Market," *Marketing Management* (Winter 2000), pp. 31–35. See also Joseph Johnson and Gerard J. Tellis, "Drivers of Success for Market Entry into China and India," *Journal of Marketing* 72 (May 2008), pp. 1–13; Tarun Khanna and Krishna G. Palepu, "Emerging Giants: Building World-Class Companies in Developing Countries," *Harvard Business Review*, October 2006, pp. 60–69.

32. Bart J. Bronnenberg, Jean-Pierre Dubé, and Sanjay Dhar, "Consumer Packaged Goods in the United States: National Brands, Local Branding," *Journal of Marketing Research* 44 (February 2007), pp. 4–13; Bart J. Bronnenberg, Jean-Pierre Dubé, and Sanjay Dhar, "National Brands, Local Branding: Conclusions and Future Research Opportunities," *Journal of Marketing Research* 44 (February 2007), pp. 26–28; Bart J. Bronnenberg, Sanjay K. Dhar, and Jean-Pierre Dubé, "Brand History, Geography, and the Persistence of CPG Brand Shares," *Journal of Political Economy* 117 (February 2009), pp. 87–115.

33. Schumpter, "Mammon's New Monarch's," *The Economist*, January 5, 2013.

34. Tom Doctoroff, *What Chinese Want: Culture, Communism and China's Modern Consumer* (New York: Palgrave Macmillan, 2012).

35. Boyle, "In Emerging Markets, Unilever Finds a Passport to Profit."

36. Erik Simanis, "Reality Check at the Bottom of the Pyramid," *Harvard Business Review*, June 2012, pp. 120–25.

37. Manjeet Kripalani, "Finally, Coke Gets It Right," *BusinessWeek,* February 10, 2003, p. 47; Manjeet Kripalani, "Battling for Pennies in India's Villages," *BusinessWeek,* June 10, 2002, p. 22.

38. Carlos Niezen and Julio Rodriguez, "Distribution Lessons from Mom and Pop," *Harvard Business Review*, April 2008; Jose Hector Darlington, "Uniqueness of Kirana Stores Will Keep Them Relevant," *Financial Express*, January 26, 2012; Sagar Malviya and Maulik Vyas, "Modern Retailing Outgrowing Kirana Stores in India," *The Economic Times*, June 16, 2011.

39. Clayton M. Christensen, Stephen Wunker, and Hari Nair, "Innovation vs. Poverty," *Forbes*, October 13, 2008; Nomaswazi Nkosi, "Nokia Still Top SA Choice," *Sowetan Live*, August 15, 2012; Kevin Kwang, "Nokia's Grip on Asia Weakens," www.ZDnet.com, July 10, 2012.

40. "Digital Media Leads in Emerging Markets," www.warc.com, March 6, 2013.

41. For an award-winning analysis, see Amitava Chattopadhyay, Rajeev Batra, and Aysegul Ozsomer, *The New Emerging Market Multinationals: Four Strategies for Disrupting Markets and Building Brands* (New York: McGraw-Hill, 2012).

42. For a thorough examination of the topic, see Nirmalya Kumar and Jan-Benedict E. M. Steenkamp, *Brand Breakout: How Emerging Market Brands Will Go Global* (New York: Palgrave Macmillan, 2013).

43. Beth Hirschler, "Emerging Market Companies Buy Up the World," www.reuters.com, January 27, 2011.

44. Peter J. Williamson and Ming Zeng, "Value for Money Strategies for Recessionary Times," *Harvard Business Review*, March 2009, pp. 66–74; Vikram Skula, "Business Basics at the Base of the Pyramid," *Harvard Business Review*, June 2008, pp. 53–57.

45. Jenny Mero, "John Deere's Farm Team," *Fortune*, April 14, 2008, pp. 119–24; ENS Economic Bureau, "John Deere India to Ramp Up Tractor Production," *New Indian Express*, April 26, 2011; Bryan Gruley and Shruit Daté Singh, "Big Green Profit Machine," *Bloomberg Businessweek*, July 5, 2012.

46. "Volkswagen and GAZ Sign Agreement for Contract Manufacturing in Russia," *Targeted News Service*, June 14, 2011.

47. John Letzing, "Toshiba, Hitachi Reported Consolidating Factories," *MarketWatch*, www.wsj.com, May 13, 2009.

48. "Top 100 Global Franchises 2012," www.franchisedirect.com, retrieved February 24, 2013.

49. Claudia H. Deutsch, "The Venturesome Giant," *New York Times*, October 5, 2007.

50. Vikram Mahidhar, Craig Giffi, and Ajit Kambil with Ryan Alvanos, "Rethinking Emerging Market Strategies," *Deloitte Review* no. 4 (2009).

51. E. J. Schultz, "SABMiller Thinks Globally, but Gets 'Intimate' Locally," *Advertising Age*, October 4, 2010; Clementine Fletcher, "This Bud's for You, Emerging Markets," *Bloomberg Businessweek*, October 3, 2011; Clementine Fletcher, "SABMiller Tries Selling African Home-Brew," *Bloomberg Businessweek*, March 19, 2012; Michael Barnett, "Why Global Brands Must Be Part of Local Cultures," *MarketingWeek*, April 12, 2012; Jonathan Buck, "Master Brewer Buys a Round," *Barron's*, October 20, 2012.

52. Johny K. Johansson, "Global Marketing: Research on Foreign Entry, Local Marketing, Global Management," Bart Weitz and Robin Wensley, eds., *Handbook of Marketing* (London: Sage, 2002), pp. 457–83.

53. Patti Waldmeir, "Oreo Takes the Biscuit for Its China Reinvention," *Financial Times*, 7 March 2012; Bruce Einhorn, "Want Some Milk with Your Green Tea Oreos?," *Bloomberg Businessweek*, May 7, 2012; Sanette Tanaka, "What's Selling Where?: Oreo Cookies," *Wall Street Journal*, August 29, 2012.

54. Gail Edmondson, "Skoda Means Quality. Really," *BusinessWeek*, October 1, 2007, p. 46. Other more popular jokes from the past include: "How do you double the value of a Skoda? Fill up the gas tank" and "What do you call a Skoda with a sunroof? A dumpster."

55. For some research method issues in adapting surveys to different cultures, see Martijn G. de Jong, Jan-Benedict E. M. Steenkamp, and Bernard P. Veldkamp, "A Model for the Construction of Country-Specific yet Internationally Comparable Short-Form Marketing Scales," *Marketing Science* 28 (July–August 2009), pp. 674–89.

56. "Field Listing: Median Age," *CIA World Factbook*, www.cia.gov, retrieved February 18, 2013.

57. Barnett, "Why Global Brands Must Be Part of Local Cultures."

58. Nigel Hollis, *The Global Brand* (New York: Palgrave Macmillan, 2008); Nigel Hollis, "Going Global? Better Think Local Instead," *Brandweek*, December 1, 2008, p. 14.

59. "How People Spend Their Time Online," www.Go-Gulf.com, February 2, 2012.

60. For some recent examples, see Ana Valenzuela, Barbara Mellers, and Judi Stebel, "Pleasurable Surprises: A Cross-Cultural Study of Consumer Responses to Unexpected Incentives," *Journal of Consumer Research* 36 (February 2010), pp. 792–805; Tuba Üstüner and Douglas B. Holt, "Toward a Theory of Status Consumption in Less Industrialized Countries," *Journal of Consumer Research* 37 (June 2010), pp. 37–56; Praveen K. Kopalle, Donald R. Lehmann, and John U. Farley, "Consumer Expectations and Culture: The Effect of Belief in Karma in India," *Journal of Consumer Research* 37 (August 2010), pp. 251–63; Carlos J. Torelli, Aysegül Özsomer, Sergio W. Carvalho, Hean Tat Keh, and Natalia Maehle, "Brand Concepts as Representations of Human Values: Do Cultural Congruity and Compatibility Between Values Matter?," *Journal of Marketing* 76 (July 2012), pp. 92–108.

61. Geert Hofstede, *Culture's Consequences* (Beverley Hills, CA: Sage, 1980).

62. For some organizational issues in adaptation, see Julien Cayla and Lisa Peñaloza, "Mapping the Play of Organizational Identity in Foreign Market Adaptation," *Journal of Marketing* 76 (November 2012), pp. 38–54.

63. For some in-depth treatments of branding in Asia in particular, see S. Ramesh Kumar, *Marketing & Branding: The Indian Scenario* (Delhi: Pearson Education, 2007); Martin Roll, *Asian Brand Strategy: How Asia Builds Strong Brands* (New York: Palgrave MacMillan, 2006); Paul Temporal, *Branding in Asia: The Creation, Development, and Management of Asian Brands for the Global Market* (Singapore: John Wiley & Sons, 2001).

64. Michael Arnt, "Knock Knock, It's Your Big Mac," *BusinessWeek*, July 23, 2007, p. 36; Lulu Raghavan, "Lessons from the Maharaja Mac: Five Rules for Entering the Indian Market," *Landor Associates*, www.landor.com, December 2007.

65. Greg Bensinger, "Amazon vs. Netflix: Streaming Battle Heats Up," *Wall Street Journal*, February 1, 2013, Barry Jepson, "Amazon's International Sales Growth Slows," *Financial Times*, July 27, 2012; Ingrid Lunden, "Amazon Expands Its Android Appstore to Nearly 200 Countries; It's All about Scale," www.techcrunch.com, April 17, 2013; Ingrid Lunden, "Amazon Ramps Up Global Expansion, Opens Massive R&D Center in London," www.techcrunch.com, July 23, 2012; Brian Stelter, "A Resurgent Netflix Beats Projections, Even Its Own," *The New York Times*, January 24, 2013; Rip Empson, "With Overseas Subscribers Topping 6M, Netflix Puts a Hold on Expanding into International Markets," www.techcrunch.com, January 23, 2013.

66. Deepa Chandrasekaran and Gerard J. Tellis, "Global Takeoff of New Products: Culture, Wealth, or Vanishing Differences?," *Marketing Science* 27 (September–October 2008), pp. 844–60.

67. Leila Abboud, "Philips Widens Marketing Push in India," *Wall Street Journal*, March 20, 2009; Paul Glader, "Philips's CEO Urges Local Strategies for Emerging Markets," *Wall Street Journal*, August 30, 2010.

68. www.danone.com, accessed May 2014.

69. Walter J. Keegan and Mark C. Green, *Global Marketing*, 4th ed. (Upper Saddle River, NJ: Prentice Hall, 2005); Warren J. Keegan, *Global Marketing Management*, 7th ed. (Upper Saddle River, NJ: Prentice Hall, 2002).

70. Tiffany Hsu, "Dunkin' Donuts to Return to Southland with 150 stores in 2 years," *Los Angeles Times*, January 18, 2013

71. Paulo Prada and Bruce Orwall, "A Certain 'Je Ne Sais Quoi' at Disney's New Park," *Wall Street Journal*, March 12, 2003.

72. Atsmon et al., "Winning the $30 Trillion Decathlon."

73. Anne VanderMey, "What Ever Happened to Tang?," *Fortune*, December 12, 2011.

74. Ralf van der Lans, Joseph A. Cote, Catherine A. Cole, Siew Meng Leong, Ale Smidts, Pamela W. Henderson, Christian Bluemelhuber, Paul A. Bottomley, John R. Doyle, Alexander Fedorikhin, Janakiraman Moorthy, B. Ramaseshan, and Bernd H. Schmitt, "Cross-National Logo Evaluation Analysis: An Individual-Level Approach," *Marketing Science* 28 (September–October 2009), pp. 968–85.

75. F. C. (Frank) Hong, Anthony Pecotich, and Clifford J. Shultz II, "Language Constraints, Product Attributes, and Consumer Perceptions in East and Southeast Asia," *Journal of International Marketing* 10 (June 2002), pp. 29–45.

76. Marc Fetscherin, Ilan Alon, Romie Littrell, and Allan Chan, "In China? Pick Your Brand Name Carefully," *Harvard Business Review*, September 2012, p. 706. See also Valentyna Melnyk, Kristina Klein, and Franziska Völckner, "The Double-Edged Sword of Foreign Brand Names for Companies from Emerging Countries," *Journal of Marketing* 76 (November 2012), pp. 21–37.

77. "Why the Number Four Is Considered Unlucky in Some East Asian Cultures," www.todayifoundout.com, January 20, 2011.

78. Thomas J. Madden, Kelly Hewett, and Martin S. Roth, "Managing Images in Different Cultures: A Cross-National Study of Color Meanings and Preferences," *Journal of International Marketing* 8 (Winter 2000), pp. 90–107; Zeynep Gürhan-Canli and Durairaj Maheswaran, "Cultural Variations in Country-of-Origin Effects," *Journal of Marketing Research* 37 (August 2000), pp. 309–17.

79. Mark Lasswell, "Lost in Translation," *Business 2.0*, August 2004, pp. 68–70; Richard P. Carpenter and the *Globe* Staff, "What They Meant to Say Was...," *Boston Globe*, August 2, 1998.

80. For an interesting distinction based on the concept of global consumer culture positioning, see Dana L. Alden, Jan-Benedict E. M. Steenkamp, and Rajeev Batra, "Brand Positioning through Advertising in Asia, North America, and Europe: The Role of Global Consumer Culture," *Journal of Marketing* 63 (January 1999), pp. 75–87.

81. David A. Kaplan, "General Mills' Global Sweet Spot," *Fortune*, May 23, 2011, pp. 194–201.

82. Geoffrey Fowler, Brian Steinberg, and Aaron O. Patrick, "Globalizing Apple's Ads," *Wall Street Journal*, March 1, 2007; Joan Voight, "Best Campaign of the Year: Apple 'Mac vs. PC,'" *Adweek*, July 17, 2007.

83. Matthew Day, "Swedish Toy Catalogue Goes Gender Neutral," *The Telegraph*, November 26, 2012.

84. Ray A. Smith and Christina Binkley, ""Israel's New Year's Resolution: No Overly Thin Models," *Wall Street Journal*, January 1, 2013.

85. See, for example, Haksin Chan, Lisa C. Wan, and Leo Y. M. Shin, "The Contrasting Effects of Culture on Consumer Tolerance: Interpersonal Face and Impersonal Fate," *Journal of Consumer Research* 36 (August 2009), pp. 292–304.

86. Aradhna Krishna and Rohini Ahluwalia, "Language Choice in Advertising to Bilinguals: Asymmetric Effects for Multinationals versus Local Firms," *Journal of Consumer Research* 35 (December 2008), pp. 692–705.

87. Preeti Khicha, "Building Brands in Rural India," *Brandchannel*, www.brandchannel.com, October 8, 2007.

88. John L. Graham, Alma T. Mintu, and Waymond Rogers, "Explorations of Negotiations Behaviors in Ten Foreign Cultures Using a Model Developed in the United States," *Management Science* 40 (January 1994), pp. 72–95.

89. Price perceptions may differ too, see Lisa E. Bolton, Hean Tat Keh, and Joseph W. Alba, "How Do Price Fairness Perceptions Differ Across Culture?," *Journal of Marketing Research* 47 (June 2010), pp. 564–76.

90. David Pierson, "Beijing Loves IKEA—But Not for Shopping," *Los Angeles Times*, August 25, 2009; Mei Fong, "IKEA Hits Home in China: The Swedish Design Giant, Unlike Other Retailers, Slashes Prices for the Chinese," *Wall Street Journal*, March 3, 2006, p. B1; Helen H. Wang, "Why Home Depot Struggles and IKEA Thrives in China?," www.forbes.com, February 10, 2011.

91. Brian Wingfield, "U.S. Boosts Import Duties on Chinese Wind-Energy Firms," www.bloomberg.com, December 19, 2012.

92. Christopher Weaver, Jeanne Whalen, and Benoît Faucon, "Drug Distributor Is Tied to Imports of Fake Avastin," *Wall Street Journal*, March 7, 2012.

93. David Blanchard, "Just in Time—How to Fix a Leaky Supply Chain," *IndustryWeek*, May 1, 2007.

94. Kersi D. Antia, Mark E. Bergen, Shantanu Dutta, and Robert J. Fisher, "How Does Enforcement Deter Gray Market Incidence?," *Journal of Marketing* 70 (January 2006), pp. 92–106; Matthew B. Myers and David A. Griffith, "Strategies for Combating Gray Market Activity," *Business Horizons* 42 (November–December 1999), pp. 2–8.

95. David Rocks and Nick Leiber, "Made in China? Not Worth the Trouble," *Bloomberg Businessweek*, June 25, 2012, pp. 49-50.

96. Brian Grow, Chi-Chu Tschang, Cliff Edwards, and Brian Burnsed, "Dangerous Fakes," *BusinessWeek*, October 8, 2008; Brian Burnsed, "The Most Counterfeited Products," *Businessweek*, October 8, 2008.

97. "US Seizes Counterfeit Goods Worth $1.26 Billion in 2012," www.worldipreview.com, January 22, 2013.

98. "Egypt Olympic Team Gets 'Fake' Nike Kit," www.aljazeera.com, July 27, 2012; Martha C. White, "Nike Donating Outfits to Egyptian Team, Replacing Counterfeit Gear," www.nbcnews.com, August 3, 2012.

99. Steve Hargreaves, "Counterfeit Goods Becoming More Dangerous," www.money.cnn.com, September 27, 2012.

100. Douglas A. McIntyre, "The Most Popular American Companies in China," www.247wallst.com, January 3, 2012.

101. Eric Shine, "Faking Out the Fakers," *BusinessWeek*, June 4, 2007, pp. 76–80.

102. Deborah Kong, "Smart Tech Fights Fakes," *Business 2.0*, March 2007, p. 30.

103. David Arnold, "Seven Rules of International Distribution," *Harvard Business Review*, November–December 2000, pp. 131–37; Rajdeep Grewal, Alok Kumar, Girish Mallapragada, and Amit Saini, "Marketing Channels in Foreign Markets: Control Mechanisms and the Moderating Role of Multinational

Corporation Headquarters–Subsidiary Relationship," *Journal of Marketing Research* 50 (June 2013), pp. 378–98.

104. Zhilin Yang, Chenting Su, and Kim-Shyan Fam, "Dealing with Institutional Distances in International Marketing Channels: Governance Strategies That Engender Legitimacy and Efficiency," *Journal of Marketing* 76 (May 2012), pp. 41–55.

105. Katrijn Gielens, Linda M. Van De Gucht, Jan-Benedict E.M. Steenkamp, and Marnik G. Dekimpe, "Dancing with a Giant: The Effect of Wal-Mart's Entry into the United Kingdom on the Performance of European Retailers," *Journal of Marketing Research* 45 (October 2008), pp. 519–34.

106. Miguel Bustillo, "After Early Errors, Wal-Mart Thinks Locally to Act Globally," *Wall Street Journal*, August 14, 2009; Holman W. Jenkins Jr., "Wal-Mart Innocents Abroad," *Wall Street Journal*, April 25, 2012.

107. Noreen O'Leary, "Infiniti Plays Up Japanese Heritage in Global Campaign," *Brandweek*, February 15, 2010, p. 5.

108. A. Pawlowski, "Hobbit Fever Heats Up New Zealand Tourism," www.NBCnews.com, November 14, 2012; Brooks Barnes and Michael Cieply, "New Zealand's Hobbit Trail," *New York Times*, October 5, 2012.

109. James Kilner, "Borat 'Has Given Kazakhstan Tourist Boost,'" *The Telegraph*, April 23, 2012; "Borat Still Boosting Kazakhstan Tourism," *Huffington Post*, April 23, 2012.

110. Joanna Kakissis, "Vacationers Rethink Greece amid Debt Crisis," *National Public Radio*, www.npr.org, June 22, 2010; Elena Becatoros, "Greece's Tourism Industry under Threat," *MSNBC*, www.msnbc.com, June 15, 2010.

111. Gurhan-Canli and Maheswaran, "Cultural Variations in Country-of-Origin Effects," pp. 309–17. For some different related issues, see also Lily Dong and Kelly Tian, "The Use of Western Brands in Asserting Chinese National Identity," *Journal of Consumer Research* 36 (October 2009), pp. 504–23; Yinlong Zhang and Adwait Khare, "The Impact of Accessible Identities on the Evaluation of Global versus Local Products," *Journal of Consumer Research* 36 (October 2009), pp. 524–37; Rohit Varman and Russell W. Belk, "Nationalism and Ideology in an Anticonsumption Movement," *Journal of Consumer Research* 36 (December 2009), pp. 686–700.

112. Ellen Byron, "P&G's Global Target: Shelves of Tiny Stores," *Wall Street Journal*, July 16, 2007; "Not So Fizzy," *Economist*, February 23, 2002, pp. 66–67.

113. Douglas B. Holt, John A. Quelch, and Earl L. Taylor, "How Global Brands Compete," *Harvard Business Review* 82, September 2004, pp. 68–75; Jan-Benedict E. M. Steenkamp, Rajeev Batra, and Dana L. Alden, "How Perceived Brand Globalness Creates Brand Value," *Journal of International Business Studies* 34 (January 2003), pp. 53–65.

114. Gürhan-Canli and Maheswaran, "Cultural Variations in Country-of-Origin Effects"; Johny K. Johansson, "Global Marketing: Research on Foreign Entry, Local Marketing, Global Management," Barton A. Weitz and Robin Wensley, eds., *Handbook of Marketing* (London: Sage, 2002), pp. 457–83.

115. Consumer Reports, "How to Decipher 'Made in the USA' Claims," *Boston Globe*, April 7, 2013.

116. Kimberly Weisul, "Why More Are Buying into 'Buy Local,'" *Bloomberg BusinessWeek*, March 1, 2010, pp. 57–60.

117. Jathon Sapsford and Norihiko Shirouzo, "Mom, Apple Pie and…Toyota?," *Wall Street Journal*, May 11, 2006.

118. Joel Backaler, "Haier: A Chinese Company That Innovates," *China Tracker*, www.forbes.com, June 17, 2010; Zhang Ruimin, "Voices from China," *Forbes*, September 28, 2009; Ariel Tung, "Home Appliance Maker Haier. Taking on America," *China Daily*, August 3, 2012; Ron Gluckman, "Appliances for Everyone," *Forbes*, May 7, 2012; Patti Waldmeir, "Haier Seeks to Boost European Sales," *Financial Times*, June 18, 2012; Atsmon et al., "Winning the $30 Trillion Decathlon."

119. For additional discussion, see "Strengthening Brand America," *The Burghard Group*, www.strengtheningbrandamerica.com, December 9, 2010.

# Chapter 9

1. E. B. Boyd, "After LinkedIn's IPO, What Will It Have to Do to Earn Its $4.3 Billion Valuation," *Fast Company*, May 19, 2011; Evelyn M. Rusli, "LinkedIn Earnings: Profit Soars, but Shares Fall on Weak Outlook," *Wall Street Journal*, May 2, 2013; Sam Grobart, "Why LinkedIn Is Buying Newsreader App Pulse," *Bloomberg Businessweek*, April 18, 2013; Alexandra Chang, "LinkedIn Revamps Mobile Apps to Focus on Stories, Updates," *Wired*, April 18, 2013.

2. Dale Buss, "Brands in the 'Hood," *Point*, December 2005, pp. 19–24.

3. By visiting the company's sponsored site, MyBestSegments.com, you can enter in a zip code and discover the top five clusters for that area. Note that another leading supplier of geodemographic data is ClusterPlus (Strategic Mapping). For background, see Becky Ebenkamp, "Urban America Redefined," *Brandweek*, October 6, 2003, pp. 12–13.

4. "The PRIZM's Use in Target Marketing," www.bizCovering.com, June 8, 2012

5. Max Chafkin, "Star Power," *Fast Company*, December 2012/January 2013, pp. 91–96, 126; Rolfe Winkler, "Is It Time Local Site Called for Yelp?," *Wall Street Journal*, January 17, 2013; "How Yelp's Business Works," *Business Insider*, March 2012; Karen Weise, "A Lie Detector Test for Online Reviews," *Bloomberg Businessweek*, September 29, 2011.

6. "YouthPulse: The Definitive Study of Today's Youth Generation," *Harris Interactive*, 2009, www.harrisinteractive.com.

7. Gina Chon, "Car Makers Talk 'Bout G-G-Generations," *Wall Street Journal*, May 9, 2006.

8. Cathy Lynn Grossman, "Only Just Begun to Owe," *USA Today*, August 10, 2012, pp. 1B–2B.

9. Brooks Barnes and Monica M. Clark, "Tapping into the Wedding Industry to Sell Broadway Seats," *Wall Street Journal*, July 3, 2006.

10. Eric Klinenberg, "The Solo Economy," *Fortune*, February 6, 2012.

11. For some consumer behavior findings on gender, see Kristina M. Durante, Vladas Griskevicius, Sarah E. Hill, Carin Perilloux, and Norman P. Li, "Ovulation, Female Competition, and Product Choice: Hormonal Influences on Consumer Behavior," *Journal of Consumer Research* 37 (April 2011), pp. 921–34; Valentyna Melnyk, Stijn M.J. van Osselaer, and Tammo H. A. Bijmolt, "Are Women More Loyal Customers than Men? Gender Differences in Loyalty to Firms and Individual Service Providers," *Journal of Marketing* 73 (July 2009), pp. 82–96; Jane Cunningham and Philippa Roberts, "What Women Want," *Brand Strategy*, December 2006–January 2007, pp. 40–41; Robert J. Fisher and Laurette Dube, "Gender Differences in Responses to Emotional Advertising: A Social Desirability Perspective," *Journal of Consumer Research* 31 (March 2005), pp. 850–58.

12. Dawn Klingensmith, "Marketing Gurus Try to Read Women's Minds," *Chicago Tribune*, April 19, 2006; Elisabeth Sullivan, "The Mother Lode," *Marketing News*, July 15, 2008, p. 28; Claire Cain Miller, "Advertising Woman to Woman, Online," *New York Times*, August 13, 2008; Eric Newman, "The Mook Industrial Complex," *Brandweek*, January 14, 2008, pp. 21–24.

13. Eric Spitznagel, "It's Pinterest For Dudes!," *Bloomberg Businessweek*, April 29, 2013.

14. Molly Soat, "Tide Equips Mr. Mom," *Marketing News Exclusives*, January 17, 2013; Jack Neff, "Ogilvyism for New Era? Consumer Is Not a Moron. He Is Your Husband," *Advertising Age*, October 17, 2011; Heather Chaet, "The Manscape," *Adweek*, September 24, 2012.

15. "Gillette, Olay Co-Brand Razor," *Chain Drug Review*, February 27, 2012, www.gillettevenus.com/en_US/about_venus/index.jsp, accessed May 4, 2013; Jenn Abelson, "Gillette Sharpens Its Focus on Women," *Boston Globe*, January 4, 2009; A. G. Lafley, interview, "It Was a No-Brainer," *Fortune*, February 21, 2005, p. 96; Naomi Aoki, "Gillette Hopes to Create a Buzz with Vibrating Women's Razor," *Boston Globe*, December 17, 2004; Chris Reidy, "The Unveiling of a New Venus," *Boston Globe*, November 3, 2000.

16. Charles D. Schewe and Geoffrey Meredith, "Segmenting Global Markets by Generational Cohort: Determining Motivations by Age," *Journal of Consumer Behavior* 4 (October 2004), pp. 51–63; Geoffrey E. Meredith and Charles D. Schewe, *Managing by Defining Moments: America's 7 Generational Cohorts, Their Workplace Values, and Why Managers Should Care* (New York: Hungry Minds, 2002); Geoffrey E. Meredith, Charles D. Schewe, and Janice Karlovich, *Defining Markets Defining Moments* (New York: Hungry Minds, 2001).

17. Burt Helm, "PNC Lures Gen Y with Its 'Virtual Wallet' Account," *BusinessWeek*, November 26, 2008; *Virtual Wallet by PNC Leading the Way*, www.pncvirtualwallet.com, January 26, 2010; Jeremy Quittner, "At PNC, Wallet Is Virtual Only to a Point," *American Banker*, March 4, 2011; Daniel Wolfe, "How a Blog Helped PNC Fine-Tune Its Virtual Wallet, *American Banker*, June 12, 2012.

18. Christine Barton, Jeff Fromm, and Chris Egan, "The Millennial Consumer: Debunking Stereotypes," white paper, *Boston Consulting Group*, April 2012.

19. Josh T. Saunders, "Vans Sponsors U.S. Open," *Surfer*, February 7, 2013; Natasha Singer, "On Campus, It's One Big Commercial," *New York Times*, September 10, 2011; Piet Levy, "The Quest for Cool," *Marketing News*, February 28, 2009, p. 6; Michelle Conlin, "Youth Quake," *BusinessWeek*, January 21, 2008, pp. 32–36.

20. Karen E. Klein, "The ABCs of Selling to Generation X," *BusinessWeek*, April 15, 2004; M. J. Stephey, "Gen-X: The Ignored Generation?," *Time*, April 16, 2008; Tamara Erickson, "Don't Treat Them Like Baby Boomers," *BusinessWeek*, August 25, 2008, p. 64.

21. Amy Chozick, "Television's Senior Moment," *Wall Street Journal*, March 9, 2011.

22. Judann Pollack, "Boomers Don't Want Your Pity, but They Do Demand Your Respect," *Advertising Age*, October 8, 2007, p. 24.

23. Michelle Barnhart and Lisa Peñaloza, "Who Are You Calling Old? Negotiating Old Age Identity in the Elderly Consumption Ensemble," *Journal of Consumer Research* 39 (April 2013), pp. 1133–53.

24. Mark Dolliver, "Marketing to Today's 65-plus Consumers," *Adweek*, July 27, 2009.

25. Stuart Elliott, "The Older Audience Is Looking Better than Ever," *New York Times*, April 19, 2009.

26. Stephanie Schomer, "Bring on the Boomers," *Fast Company*, February 2011, pp. 47–51.

27. Marissa Miley, "Don't Bypass African-Americans," *Advertising Age*, February 2, 2009.

28. Jim Farley, "Lessons from the Leader: Ford," *Advertising Age's In Plain Sight: The Black Consumer Opportunity*, April 23, 2012, p. 21.

29. "Hispanics Will Top All U.S. Minority Groups for Purchasing Power by 2007," *Selig Center of Economic Growth, Terry College of Business, University of Georgia*, www.selig.uga.edu, September 1, 2004; Jeffrey M. Humphreys, "The Multicultural Economy 2008," *Selig Center of Economic Growth, Terry College of Business, University of Georgia*, 2008.

30. Jeff Bercovi, "Latino Love," *Forbes*, August 6, 2012, pp. 66–73.

31. Julie Liesse, "Univision: One for All," *Special Advertising Supplement to Advertising Age*, April 1, 2013, pp. C1–C4; Jeff Koyen, "The Truth about Hispanic Consumers," *Hispanic Advertising: Special Advertising Section to Adweek*, March 11, 2012, pp. H1–H4.

32. Stuart Feil, "The Best of Both Worlds," *Hispanic Advertising: Special Advertising Section to Adweek*, March 11, 2012, pp. H11–H14.

33. Laurel Wentz, "With an Ever-Growing Population of 'Fusionistas,' Consistency Is Key," *Advertising Age*, October 17, 2011, p. 28.

34. Glenny Brock, "Hispanics Check In," *Hispanic Advertising: Special Advertising Section to Adweek*, October 17, 2011, pp. H1–H4. See also Cynthia Rodriguez Cano and David J. Ortinau, "Digging for Spanish 'Gold': How to Connect with Hispanic Consumers," *Journal of Advertising Research* 52 (September 2012), pp. 322–32.

35. Barbara De Lollis, "At Goya, It's All in La Familia," *USA Today*, March 24, 2008, pp. 1B–2B; Erin Carlyle, "Goya Foods Secret Sauce," *Forbes*, May 27, 2013, p. 50.

36. Elaine Wong, "Why Bounty Is a Hit with U.S. Hispanics," *Brandweek*, August 17, 2009, p. 6.

37. Jeff Bercovi, "Latino Love," *Forbes*, August 6, 2012, pp. 66–73; Liesse, "Univision: One for All," pp. C1–C4.

38. Charlenne Gonzalez, "U.S. Hispanic Consumer: Marketing to the World's Ninth Largest Economy," independent study, May 2013, Tuck School of Business at Dartmouth College.

39. Piet Levy, "Artistic Expression," *Marketing News*, May 15, 2011, p. 10.

40. Laurel Wentz, "Clorox Fraganzia Launch Targets U.S. Hispanic Consumers," *Advertising Age*, July 16, 2012.

41. Elisabeth A. Sullivan, "Speak Our Language," *Marketing News*, March 15, 2008, pp. 20–22; Edward Lewine and Malia Wollan, "Latin Lovers," *Fast Company*, July–August 2011, pp. 55–62.

42. Rita Chang, "Mobile Marketers Target Receptive Hispanic Audience," *Advertising Age*, January 26, 2009, p. 18.

43. Brock, "Hispanics Check In," pp. H1–H4.

44. Vicky Uhland, "Marketing to Asian-American Customers," *Natural Food Merchandiser*, March 2012, p. 62.

45. "The 'Invisible' Market," *Brandweek*, January 30, 2006.

46. http://stateofthemedia.org/2010/ethnic-summary-essay/asian-american, accessed May 20, 2014.

47. Bill Imada, "How Wells Fargo Became a Banking Leader in the Asian-American Market," *Advertising Age*, July 26, 2010.

48. "Marketing to Asian-Americans," Special Supplement to *Brandweek*, May 26, 2008.

49. Adele Lassere, "The Marketing Corner: Marketing to African-American Consumers," *Epoch Times*, November 27, 2009; Michael A. Fletcher, "Advertisers Aren't Tapping into Strong African American Market, Report Says," *Washington Post*, September 21, 2012.

50. Lisa Sanders, "How to Target Blacks? First You Gotta Spend," *Advertising Age*, July 3, 2006, p. 19; Pepper Miller and Herb Kemp, *What's Black about It? Insights to Increase Your Share of a Changing African-American Market* (Ithaca, NY: Paramount Market Publishing, 2005); *Advertising Age's In Plain Sight: The Black Consumer Opportunity*, April 23, 2012.

51. Fletcher, "Advertisers Aren't Tapping into Strong African American Market, Report Says." For broader discussion, see Pepper Miller, *Black Still Matters in Marketing: Why Increasing Your Cultural IQ about Black America Is Critical to Your Company and Brand* (Ithaca, NY: Paramount Market Publishing, 2012).

52. Rieva Lesonsky, "How to Reach African-American Consumers," www.networksolutions.com, March 4, 2013.

53. Marissa Fabris, "Special Report on Multicultural Marketing: Market Power," *Target Marketing*, , May 2008.

54. Robert Klara, "Brands New Way of Thinking," *Adweek*, November 12, 2012.

55. Sonya A. Grier and Shiriki K. Kumanyika, "The Context for Choice: Health Implications of Targeted Food and Beverage Marketing to African-Americans," *American Journal of Public Health* 98 (September 2008), pp. 1616–29.

56. Kate Rockwood, "Partnering with Pride," *Fast Company*, November 2009, pp. 21–28.

57. Molly Soat, "Brands From JCPenney to NHL Aim to Be More Fan Friendly," *Marketing News Exclusives*, April 18, 2013.

58. *Prime Access, Inc*, www.primeaccess.net.

59. www.strategicbusinessinsights.com/vals/presurvey.shtml, accessed May 20, 2014.

60. Daniel Yankelovich and David Meer, "Rediscovering Market Segmentation," *Harvard Business Review*, February 2006, pp. 1–11; Sharon E. Beatty, Pamela M. Homer, and Lynn R. Kahle "Problems with VALS in International Marketing Research: An Example from an Application of the Empirical Mirror Technique," *Advances in Consumer Research*, volume 15, Michael J. Houston, ed. (Provo, UT: Association for Consumer Research, 1988), pp. 375–80.

61. Andrew Kaplan, "A Fruitful Mix," *Beverage World*, May 2006, pp. 28–36.

62. Jenni Romaniuk, "Are You Blinded by the Heavy (Buyer)…Or Are You Seeing the Light?," *Journal of Advertising Research*, 51 (December 2011), pp. 561–63.

63. This classification was adapted from George H. Brown, "Brand Loyalty: Fact or Fiction?," *Advertising Age*, June 1952–January 1953, a series. See also Peter E. Rossi, Robert E. McCulloch, and Greg M. Allenby, "The Value of Purchase History Data in Target Marketing," *Marketing Science* 15 (Fall 1996), pp. 321–40.

64. James C. Anderson and James A. Narus, "Capturing the Value of Supplementary Services," *Harvard Business Review*, January–February 1995, pp. 75–83. But also see Frank V. Cespedes, James P. Dougherty, and Ben S. Skinner III, "How to Identify the Best Customers for Your Business," *MIT Sloan Management Review*, Winter 2013, pp. 53–59.

65. For a review of many of the methodological issues in developing segmentation schemes, see William R. Dillon and Soumen Mukherjee, "A Guide to the Design and Execution of Segmentation Studies," Rajiv Grover and Marco Vriens, eds., *Handbook of Marketing Research* (Thousand Oaks, CA: Sage, 2006).

66. Michael E. Porter, *Competitive Strategy* (New York: Free Press, 1980), pp. 22–23.

67. *Estée Lauder*, www.esteelauder.com, accessed June 23, 2013.

68. Barry Silverstein, "Hallmark—Calling Card," www.brandchannel.com, June 15, 2009; Brad van Auken, "Leveraging the Brand: Hallmark Case Study," www.brandstrategyinsider.com, January 11, 2008; www.hallmark.com/card-collections/, accessed May 15, 2013.

69. Jack Nicas, "Allegiant Air: The Tardy, Gas-Guzzling, Most Profitable Airline in America," *Wall Street Journal*, June 4, 2013; Ilene Aleshire, "How Allegiant Air Turned a Profit for 39 Consecutive Quarters," www.skift.com, November 4, 2012; "Heard of Allegiant Air? Why It's the Nation's Most Profitable Airline," *Fast Company*, September 2009; Charisse Jones, "Allegiant Profits from Leisure Fliers," *USA Today*, October 19, 2009.

70. Don Peppers and Martha Rogers, *One-to-One B2B: Customer Development Strategies for the Business-to-Business World* (New York: Doubleday, 2001); Jerry Wind and Arvind Rangaswamy, "Customerization: The Next Revolution in Mass Customization," *Journal of Interactive Marketing* 15 (Winter 2001), pp. 13–32; Itamar Simonson, "Determinants of Customers' Responses to Customized Offers: Conceptual Framework and Research Propositions," *Journal of Marketing* 69 (January 2005), pp. 32–45.

71. James H. Gilmore and B. Joseph Pine II, *Markets of One: Creating Customer-Unique Value through Mass Customization* (Boston: Harvard Business School Press, 2000); B. Joseph Pine II, "Beyond Mass Customization," *Harvard Business Review*, May 2, 2011.

72. Erik Eliason, "3 Reasons Why Mass Customization Is the Future of Consumer Products," *Huffington Post*, March 21, 2012.

73. Scott Davis, "MINI Cooper, Amazon, and McDonald's: Are Customers Lovin' It?," *Forbes*, October 31, 2011.

74. Raquel Laneri, "Mr. Green Jeans," *Forbes*, November 7, 2011, pp. 74–76; Zack O'Malley Greenburg, "Bespoke Unspoken," *Forbes*, November 7, 2011, p. 78.

75. Christopher Steiner, "The Perfect Ski," *Forbes*, February 28, 2011.

76. Elizabeth Dwoskin, "The Like-Me Election," *Bloomberg Businessweek*, September 26, 2011, pp. 37–38.

77. Don Peppers and Martha Rogers, *The One-to-One Manager: Real-World Lessons in Customer Relationship Management* (New York: Doubleday, 1999); Don Peppers, Martha Rogers, and Bob Dorf, *The One-to-One Fieldbook: The Complete Toolkit for Implementing a One-to-One Marketing Program* (New York: Bantam, 1999); among their other publications.

78. Nikolaus Franke, Peter Keinz, and Christoph J. Steger, "Testing the Value of Customization: When Do Customers Really Prefer Products Tailored to Their Preferences," *Journal of Marketing* 73 (September 2009), pp. 103–21.

79. Woo Jin Choi and Karen Page Winterich, "Can Brands Move In from the Outside? How Moral Identity Enhances Out-Group Brand Attitudes," *Journal of Marketing* 77 (March 2013), pp. 96–111; Jennifer E. Escales and James R. Bettman, "Self-Construal, Reference Groups, and Brand Meaning," *Journal of Consumer Research* 32 (December 2005), pp. 378–89.

80. Sarah Jane Glynn, "Families Need More Help to Care for Their Children," white paper, Center for American Progress, August 16, 2012.

81. Caroline E. Mayer, "Nurturing Brand Loyalty; With Preschool Supplies, Firms Woo Future Customers—and Current Parents," *Washington Post*, October 12, 2003.

## Chapter 10

1. Noel Murray, "DirecTV's Ad Campaign Wants to Make You Hate Cable as Much as It Does," www.avclub.com, February 26, 2013; Shalini Ramachandran and Ben Fox Rubin, "DirecTV Profit Rises on Latin America Growth," *Wall Street Journal*, February 14, 2013; Alex Sherman, "DirecTV Profit Lags Estimates after First U.S. Customer Loss," *Bloomberg BusinessWeek*, August 2, 2012; Suzanne Vranica, "DirecTV Plays Offense with NFL Ads," *Wall Street Journal*, July 29, 2010.

2. Al Ries and Jack Trout, *Positioning: The Battle for Your Mind, 20th Anniversary Edition* (New York: McGraw-Hill, 2000).

3. Michael J. Lanning and Lynn W. Phillips, "Building Market-Focused Organizations," Gemini Consulting White Paper, 1991.

4. David A. Aaker, *Brand Portfolio Strategy: Creating Relevance, Differentiation, Energy, Leverage, and Clarity* (New York: Free Press, 2004); Rebecca Wright, "The Next Frontier for Nutrition Bars," *Nutraceuticals World*, January/February 2011.

5. Jeff Bercovi, "Poker Shuffles the Deck," *Forbes*, December 5, 2011.

6. Robert Klara, "The Tough Sell," *Adweek*, July 9, 2012, p. 40.

7. Allan D. Shocker, "Determining the Structure of Product-Markets: Practices, Issues, and Suggestions," Barton A. Weitz and Robin Wensley, eds., *Handbook of Marketing* (London: Sage, 2002), pp. 106–25. See also Bruce H. Clark and David B. Montgomery, "Managerial Identification of Competitors," *Journal of Marketing* 63 (July 1999), pp. 67–83.

8. "What Business Are You In? Classic Advice from Theodore Levitt," *Harvard Business Review*, October 2006, pp. 127–37. See also Theodore Levitt's seminal article, "Marketing Myopia," *Harvard Business Review*, July–August 1960, pp. 45–56.

9. Jeffrey F. Rayport and Bernard J. Jaworski, *e-Commerce* (New York: McGraw-Hill, 2001), p. 53.

10. For discussion of some of the long-term implications of marketing activities, see Koen Pauwels, "How Dynamic Consumer Response, Competitor Response, Company Support, and Company Inertia Shape Long-Term Marketing Effectiveness," *Marketing Science* 23 (Fall 2004), pp. 596–610; Marnik Dekimpe and Dominique Hanssens, "Sustained Spending and Persistent Response: A New Look at Long-term Marketing Profitability," *Journal of Marketing Research* 36 (November 1999), pp. 397–412.

11. Kevin Lane Keller, Brian Sternthal, and Alice Tybout, "Three Questions You Need to Ask about Your Brand," *Harvard Business Review*, September 2002, pp. 80–89.

12. Patrick Barwise, *Simply Better: Winning and Keeping Customers by Delivering What Matters Most* (Cambridge, MA: Harvard Business School Press, 2004). But see Susan M. Broniarczyk and Andrew D. Gershoff, "The Reciprocal Effects of Brand Equity and Trivial Attributes," *Journal of Marketing Research* 40 (May 2003), pp. 161–75; Gregory S. Carpenter, Rashi Glazer, and Kent Nakamoto, "Meaningful Brands from Meaningless Differentiation: The Dependence on Irrelevant Attributes," *Journal of Marketing Research* 31 (August 1994), pp. 339–50.

13. Elaine Wong, "Method Co-Founder Offers Spin on Viral Video," *Adweek*, January 11, 2010; "Champions of Design: Method," *Marketing*, June 15, 2011, p. 18; Stuart Elliott, "Ads for Method Celebrate the Madness," *New York Times*, March 12, 2012; Lindsay Riddell, "Method Sold to Belgium Competitor Ecover," *San Francisco Times*, September 4, 2012.

14. Dan Slater, "She Drives a Cadillac?," *Fast Company*, February 2012, pp. 26–28.

15. "America Is High on Sugar, Down on Splenda," www.marketwatch.com, May 14, 2013.

16. Jennifer Cirillo, "Energy's MVP," *Beverage World*, August 2012, pp. 35–42.

17. Thomas A. Brunner and Michaela Wänke, "The Reduced and Enhanced Impact of Shared Features on Individual Brand Evaluations," *Journal of Consumer Psychology* 16 (April 2006), pp. 101–11.

18. Professor Brian Sternthal, "Miller Lite Case," *Kellogg Graduate School of Management, Northwestern University*; E. J. Schultz, "New Miller Time Spots Unveiled: MillerCoors Explains the Return," *Advertising Age*, March 22, 2012.

19. L. Joshua Sosland, "Dunkin' Donuts' Strategy," *Food Business News*, May 18, 2011; Chris Barth, "Can Dunkin's New Deal Brew Enough Growth to Catch Starbucks," *Forbes*, January 4, 2012.

20. Jim Henry, "BMW Still the Ultimate Driving Machine, Not That It Ever Wasn't," *Forbes*, May 31, 2012; "No Joy Here from BMW Ad Switch," *Automotive News*, April 12, 2010.

21. Michael E. Porter, *Competitive Strategy: Techniques for Analyzing Industries and Competitors* (New York: Free Press, 1980).

22. Makiko Kitamura and David Wainer, "Similar but Not the Same," *Bloomberg Businessweek*, March 25, 2013, pp. 19–20.

23. Francis J. Kelly III and Barry Silverstein, *The Breakaway Brand* (New York: McGraw-Hill, 2005).

24. Jennifer Cirillo, "Lemon-Lime Bubbly Goes Au Naturel," *Beverage World*, January 2011, p. 14.

25. For a classic analysis of perceptual maps, see John R. Hauser and Frank S. Koppelman, "Alternative Perceptual Mapping Techniques: Relative Accuracy and Usefulness," *Journal of Marketing Research* 16 (November 1979), pp. 495–506. For some contemporary perspectives on measurement techniques for positioning, see Sanjay K. Rao, "Data-Based Differentiation," *Marketing Insights*, Spring 2013, pp. 26–32.

26. Brian Sheehan, *Loveworks: How the World's Top Marketers Make Emotional Connections to Win in the Marketplace* (Brooklyn, NY: powerHouse, 2013).

27. Piet Levy, "Express Yourself," *Marketing News*, June 15, 2009, p. 6.

28. Walter Loeb, "Kate Spade Is a Brand Ready to Boom Around the World," *Forbes*, March 22, 2013; Jon Caramanica, "At Jack Spade, Carefully Appearing Not to Care," *New York Times*, September 1, 2010; Meredith Galante, "How Kate Spade New York Uses Social Media to Sell Handbags," *BusinessInsider*, April 17, 2012; Rachel Lamb, "Kate Spade Tries Global Marketing Via New Partnership," *Luxury Daily*, May 20, 2011.

29. James H. Gilmore and B. Joseph Pine II, *Authenticity: What Consumers Really Want* (Cambridge, MA: Harvard Business School Press, 2007); Lynn B. Upshaw, *Truth: The New Rules for Marketing in a Skeptical World* (New York: AMACOM, 2007).

30. Owen Jenkins, "Gimme Some Lovin'," *Marketing News*, May 15, 2009, p. 19.

31. Jack Neff, "Welch's Local-Sourcing Story Core to Outreach," *Advertising Age*, January 24, 2011.

32. Hamish Pringle and Peter Field, "Why Emotional Messages Beat Rational Ones," *Advertising Age*, March 2, 2009, p. 13; Hamish Pringle and Peter Field, *Brand Immortality: How Brands Can Live Long and Prosper* (Philadelphia: Kogan Page, 2009).

33. Scott Bedbury, *A New Brand World* (New York: Viking Press, 2002).

34. Stuart Elliott, "Bank Leaves Child's Play Behind," *New York Times*, September 17, 2010; Dakin Campbell, "Ally's New Campaign Replaces Ads That Showed Bankers as Cheaters," *Bloomberg Business Week*, September 20, 2010; "If Advertising Doesn't Work, then Why Is 'Ally' a Household Word?," www.thefinancialbrand.com, November 12, 2010; "Ally Bank Launches New 'Stages' Ad Campaign," *PR Newswire*, September 4, 2012; Andrew R. Johnson, "Ally Ads Take Aim at Enemies," *Wall Street Journal*, September 4, 2012.

35. Keith Naughton, "Ford's 'Perfect Storm,'" *Newsweek*, September 17, 2001, pp. 48–50; Byron Pope, "Ford Flex Not Minivan Replacement, Marketing Chief Says," *WardsAuto*, April 16, 2007.

36. Kerry Capell, "Thinking Simple at Philips," *BusinessWeek*, December 11, 2006, p. 50; Philips, www.philips.com.

37. Rajendra S. Sisodia, David B. Wolfe, and Jagdish N. Sheth, *Firms of Endearment: How World-Class Companies Benefit Profit from Passion & Purpose* (Upper Saddle River, NJ: Wharton School Publishing, 2007).

38. Melissa Korn, "Wanted: Gurus with Actual Experience," *Wall Street Journal*, July 2, 2013.

39. Randall Ringer and Michael Thibodeau, "A Breakthrough Approach to Brand Creation," *Verse, The Narrative Branding Company*, www.versegroup.com, accessed March 7, 2014.

40. Patrick Hanlon, *Primal Branding: Create Zealots for Your Brand, Your Company, and Your Future* (New York: Free Press, 2006); ThinkTopia, www.thinktopia.com, accessed May 26, 2014.

41. Douglas Holt, *How Brands Become Icons: The Principle of Cultural Branding* (Cambridge, MA: Harvard Business School Press, 2004); Douglas Holt, "Branding as Cultural Activism," www.zibs.com; Douglas Holt, "What Becomes an Icon Most," *Harvard Business Review*, March 2003, pp. 43–49; See also Grant McKracken, *Culture and Consumption II: Markets, Meaning, and Brand Management* (Bloomington, IN: Indiana University Press, 2005).

42. Craig Thompson, "Brands as Culturally Embedded Resources," 43rd AMA Sheth Foundation Doctoral Consortium, University of Missouri, June 6, 2008. See also research by John Sherry and Robert Kozinets, including John F. Sherry Jr., Robert V. Kozinets, Adam Duhachek, Benét DeBerry-Spence, Krittinee Nuttavuthisit and Diana Storm, "Gendered Behavior in a Male Preserve: Role Playing at ESPN Zone Chicago," *Journal of Consumer Psychology* 14, nos. 1 & 2 (2004), pp. 151–58; Stephen Brown, Robert V. Kozinets, and John F. Sherry Jr., "Teaching Old Brands New Tricks: Retro Branding and the Revival of Brand Meaning," *Journal of Marketing* 67 (July 2003), pp. 19–33.

43. Nick Wreden, *Fusion Branding: How to Forge Your Brand for the Future* (Atlanta: Accountability Press, 2002); Fusion Branding, www.fusionbranding.com, accessed May 26, 2014.

44. Ashley Lutz, "Uniqlo's Brilliant Strategy Is to Totally Ignore Fashion," *Business Insider*, October 11, 2012; Lydia Dishman, "Uniqlo's Secret Brick-and-Mortar Expansion Strategy Is E-commerce," *Forbes*, October 22, 2012; Minter Dial, "Uniqlo: A Well Executed Glocal Digital and Social Media Market Strategy," *The Myndset*, February 10, 2013.

45. Ashlee Vance, "It's a Doc in a Box," *Bloomberg Businessweek*, May 7, 2012, pp. 45–47; Victoria Barret, "Software's Boy Wonder," *Forbes*, March 4, 2013; Ashlee Vance and Dina Bass, "Microsoft's New Office Is Finally Up to Speed," *Bloomberg Businessweek*, February 4, p. 201.

46. Daniel Roberts, "The Secrets of See's Candies," *Fortune*, September 3, 2012, pp. 67–72.

47. Jason Ankeny, "Building a Brand on a Budget," *Entrepreneur*, May 2010, pp. 48–51.

48. Jefferson Graham, "How to Ride Facebook's Giant Wave," *USA Today*, May 30, 2013, p. 5B.

49. Roger Yu, "Small Businesses Seek Big Sales from Mobile Ads," *USA Today*, June 10, 2013.

50. Rob Walker, "The Cult of Evernote," *Bloomberg Businessweek*, February 28, 2013.

51. Andrew Ross Sorkin and Andrew Martin, "Coca-Cola Agrees to Buy Vitaminwater," *New York Times*, May 26, 2007.

# Chapter 11

1. Jennifer Haderspeck, "Sports and Protein Drinks Share the Glory," *Beverage Industry*, May 2013; Natalie Zmuda, "Why Gatorade Held Big Play for Second Quarter and Print Is Key to New Push," *Advertising Age*, March 25, 2013; Jason Feifer, "How Gatorade Redefined Its Audience and a Flagging Brand," *Fast Company*, June 2012; Duane Stanford, "Gatorade Goes Back to the Lab," *Bloomberg Businessweek*, November 28, 2010; Kate MacArthur, "Gatorade

Execs Focus on Sales Gains as Powerade Gulps More of Sports Drink Market," *Chicago Business,* May 30, 2011.

2. Kevin Lane Keller, *Strategic Brand Management,* 4th ed. (Upper Saddle River, NJ: Pearson, 2013). For other foundational work on branding, see Jean-Noel Kapferer, *The New Strategic Brand Management,* 5th ed. (London, UK: Kogan Page, 2012); Leslie de Chernatony, *From Brand Vision to Brand Evaluation: The Strategic Process of Growing and Strengthening Brands,* 3rd ed. (Oxford, UK: Butterworth-Heinemann, 2010); David A. Aaker and Erich Joachimsthaler, *Brand Leadership* (New York: Free Press, 2000).

3. Michael J. de la Merced, Nick Bilton, and Nicole Perlroth, "Yahoo to Buy Tumblr for $1.1 Billion," *New York Times,* May 19, 2013; Michael J. de la Merced, "The Tumblr and Instagram Deals: A Tale of the Tape," *New York Times,* May 19, 2013; Eric Savitz, "Why 2013 Is the Year You Need to Get Serious about Tumblr," *Forbes,* January 24, 2013; Jeff Bercovici, "Tumblr: David Karp's $800 Million Art Project," *Forbes,* January 2, 2013; Tomio Geron, "After Backlash, Instagram Changes Back to Original Terms of Service," *Forbes,* December 12, 2012; Dan Primack, "Breaking: Facebook Buying Instagram for $1 Billion," *CNN,* April 9, 2012; www.instagram.com/about/faq, accessed July 20, 2103.

4. Interbrand Group, *World's Greatest Brands: An International Review* (New York: John Wiley & Sons, 1992). See also Karl Moore and Susan Reid, "The Birth of Brand," *Business History* 50 (2008), pp. 419–32.

5. JoAndrea Hoegg and Joseph W. Alba, "Taste Perception: More than Meets the Tongue," *Journal of Consumer Research* 33 (March 2007), pp. 490–98.

6. Rajneesh Suri and Kent B. Monroe, "The Effects of Time Pressure on Consumers' Judgments of Prices and Products," *Journal of Consumer Research* 30 (June 2003), pp. 92–104.

7. Rosellina Ferraro, Amna Kirmani, and Ted Matherly, "Look at Me! Look at Me! Conspicuous Brand Usage, Self-Brand Connection, and Dilution," *Journal of Marketing Research* 50 (August 2013), pp. 477–88; Alexander Chernev, Ryan Hamilton, and David Gal, "Competing for Consumer Identity: Limits to Self-Expression and the Perils of Lifestyle Branding," *Journal of Marketing* 75 (May 2011).

8. Pankaj Aggrawal and Ann L. McGill, "When Brands Seem Human, Do Humans Act Like Brands? Automatic Behavioral Priming Effects of Brand Anthropomorphism," *Journal of Consumer Research* 39 (August 2012), pp. 307–23. For some related research, see Nicolas Kervyn, Susan T. Fiske, and Chris Malone, "Brands as Intentional Agents Framework: How Perceived Intentions and Ability Can Map Brand Perception," *Journal of Consumer Psychology* 22 (2012), pp. 166–76, as well as commentaries on that article published in that issue.

9. Matthew Thomson, Jodie Whelan, and Allison R. Johnson, "Why Brands Should Fear Fearful Consumers: How Attachment Style Predicts Retaliation," *Journal of Consumer Psychology* 22 (2012), pp. 289–98; Shirley Y. Y. Cheng, Tiffany Barnett White, and Lan Nguyen Chaplin, "The Effects of Self-Brand Connections on Responses to Brand Failure: A New Look at the Consumer-Brand Relationship," *Journal of Consumer Psychology* 22 (2012), pp. 280–88.

10. Tilde Heding, Charlotte F. Knudtzen, and Mogens Bjerre, *Brand Management: Research, Theory & Practice* (New York: Routledge, 2009); Rita Clifton and John Simmons, eds., *The Economist on Branding* (New York: Bloomberg Press, 2004); Rik Riezebos, *Brand Management: A Theoretical and Practical Approach* (Essex, UK: Pearson Education, 2003); and Paul Temporal, *Advanced Brand Management: From Vision to Valuation* (Singapore: John Wiley & Sons, 2002).

11. Constance E. Bagley, *Managers and the Legal Environment: Strategies for the 21st Century,* 3rd ed. (Cincinnati, OH: South-Western College/West Publishing, 2005); for a marketing academic point of view of some important legal issues, see Judith Zaichkowsky, *The Psychology behind Trademark Infringement and Counterfeiting* (Mahwah, NJ: LEA Publishing, 2006) and Maureen Morrin, Jonathan Lee, and Greg M. Allenby, "Determinants of Trademark Dilution," *Journal of Consumer Research* 33 (September 2006), pp. 248–57.

12. Joffre Swait and Tulin Erdem, "Brand Effects on Choice and Choice Set Formation under Uncertainty," *Marketing Science* 26 (September–October 2007), pp. 679–97; Tulin Erdem, Joffre Swait, and Ana

Valenzuela, "Brands as Signals: A Cross-Country Validation Study," *Journal of Marketing* 70 (January 2006), pp. 34–49.

13. Scott Davis, *Brand Asset Management: Driving Profitable Growth through Your Brands* (San Francisco: Jossey-Bass, 2000); Mary W. Sullivan, "How Brand Names Affect the Demand for Twin Automobiles," *Journal of Marketing Research* 35 (May 1998), pp. 154–65.

14. The power of branding is not without its critics, however, some of whom reject the commercialism associated with branding activities. See Naomi Klein, *No Logo: Taking Aim at the Brand Bullies* (New York: Picador, 2000).

15. For a discussion of the role of brands across different categories and markets, see Marc Fischer, Franziska Völckner, and Henrik Sattler, "How Important Are Brands? A Cross-Category, Cross-Country Study," *Journal of Marketing Research* 47 (October 2010), pp. 823–39.

16. To read about Morgan Spurlock's documentary on the ubiquity of brands and brand messages, *Pom Wonderful Presents: The Greatest Movie Ever Sold,* see Rick Tetzeli and Ari Karpel, "I'm with the Brand," *Fast Company,* April 2011, pp. 82–92.

17. "Study: Food in McDonald's Wrapper Tastes Better to Kids," *Associated Press,* August 6, 2007.

18. Xueming Luo, Sascha Raithel, and Michael A. Wiles, "The Impact of Brand Rating Dispersion on Firm Value," *Journal of Marketing Research* 50 (June 2013), pp. 399–415.

19. Michael A. Wiles, Neil A. Morgan, and Lopo L. Rego, "The Effect of Brand Acquisition and Disposal on Stock Returns," *Journal of Marketing* 76 (January 2012), pp. 38–58.

20. Natalie Mizik and Robert Jacobson, "Talk about Brand Strategy," *Harvard Business Review,* October 2005, p. 1; Baruch Lev, *Intangibles: Management, Measurement, and Reporting* (Washington, DC: Brookings Institute, 2001). For a detailed examination, see Nigel Hollis, *The Meaningful Brand: How Strong Brands Make More Money* (New York: Palgrave Macmillan, 2013).

21. Danielle Sacks, "The Devil Wears J.Crew," *Fast Company,* May 2013.

22. For an academic discussion of how consumers become so strongly attached to people as brands, see Matthew Thomson, "Human Brands: Investigating Antecedents to Consumers' Stronger Attachments to Celebrities," *Journal of Marketing* 70 (July 2006), pp. 104–19.

23. Lara O'Reilly, "Real Madrid Beat Man U to World's Richest Football Team Spot," *Marketing Week,* April 18, 2013; Agustino Fontevecchia, "The Team to Top: Real Madrid Overtakes ManU to Become the Most Valuable Sports Team in the World," *Forbes,* April 17, 2013; Tony Karon, "Why Real Madrid Can't Beat Barca on The Field, but Leads Comfortably in the Market," *Time,* March 23, 2012.

24. Other approaches are based on economic principles of signaling (e.g., Tulin Erdem, "Brand Equity as a Signaling Phenomenon," *Journal of Consumer Psychology* 7 (1998), pp. 131–57) or more of a sociological, anthropological, or biological perspective (e.g., Grant McCracken, *Culture and Consumption II: Markets, Meaning, and Brand Management* (Bloomington: Indiana University Press, 2005)). For a broad view of consumer psychology perspectives on branding, see Bernd Schmitt, "The Consumer Psychology of Brands," *Journal of Consumer Psychology* 22 (2012), pp. 7–17.

25. For an overview of academic research on branding, see Kevin Lane Keller, "Branding and Brand Equity," Bart Weitz and Robin Wensley, eds., *Handbook of Marketing* (London: Sage Publications, 2002), pp. 151–78; Kevin Lane Keller and Don Lehmann, "Brands and Branding: Research Findings and Future Priorities," *Marketing Science* 25 (November–December 2006), pp. 740–59.

26. Keller, *Strategic Brand Management.*

27. Kusum Ailawadi, Donald R. Lehmann, and Scott Neslin, "Revenue Premium as an Outcome Measure of Brand Equity," *Journal of Marketing* 67 (October 2003), pp. 1–17.

28. Jon Miller and David Muir, *The Business of Brands* (West Sussex, UK: John Wiley & Sons, 2004).

29. Lara O'Reilly, "Virgin America Bids to Banish 'Command Culture,'" *Marketing Week,* September 20, 2012; Joan Voight, "Where's the

Party? At 30,000 Feet Virgin America Marketing Chief: 'What Would Richard Do?,'" *Adweek*, February 5, 2013; Michael Bush, "Virgin America," *Advertising Age*, November 16, 2009, p. 12.

30. Nilofer Merchant, "When TED Lost Control of Its Crowd," *Harvard Business Review*, April 2013, pp. 79–83.

31. Kevin Lane Keller, "Building Customer-Based Brand Equity: A Blueprint for Creating Strong Brands," *Marketing Management* 10 (July–August 2001), pp. 15–19.

32. Natalie Zmuda, "MasterCard's Priceless Evolution," *Advertising Age*, October 11, 2012; Geoffrey Precourt, "How MasterCard Updated 'Priceless' for Post-Crisis Consumers," www.warc.com, October 2012; Matthew de Paula, "MasterCard Puts New Premium on Priceless," *American Banker*, September 1, 2011; Avi Dan, "MasterCard Moves Forward by Going Back," *Forbes*, August 25, 2011.

33. For some academic insights, see Matthew Thomson, Deborah J. MacInnis, and C. W. Park, "The Ties That Bind: Measuring the Strength of Consumers' Emotional Attachments to Brands," *Journal of Consumer Psychology* 15 (2005), pp. 77–91; Alexander Fedorikhin, C. Whan Park, and Matthew Thomson, "Beyond Fit and Attitude: The Effect of Emotional Attachment on Consumer Responses to Brand Extensions," *Journal of Consumer Psychology* 18 (2008), pp. 281–91; Jennifer Edson Escalas, "Narrative Processing: Building Consumer Connections to Brands," *Journal of Consumer Psychology* 14 (1996), pp. 168–79. See also Rajeev Batra, Aaron Ahuvia, and Richard P. Bagozzi, "Brand Love," *Journal of Marketing* 76 (March 2012), pp. 1–16. For some managerial guidelines, see Kevin Roberts, *Lovemarks: The Future beyond Brands* (New York: Powerhouse Books, 2004); and Douglas Atkins, *The Culting of Brands* (New York: Penguin Books, 2004).

34. Paul Rittenberg and Maura Clancey, "Testing the Value of Media Engagement for Advertising Effectiveness," www.knowledgenetworks.com, Spring–Summer 2006, pp. 35–42.

35. M. Berk Ataman, Carl F. Mela, and Harald J. van Heerde, "Building Brands," *Marketing Science* 27 (November–December 2008), pp. 1036–54.

36. Todd Wasserman, "Why Microsoft Chose the Name 'Bing,'" *Brandweek*, June 1, 2009, p. 33.

37. Jefferson Graham, "General Mills Spoons Up Digital Fun on Cereal Boxes," *USA Today*, January 31, 2013.

38. "No Matter How You 'Like' It, 42BELOW Vodka Encourages Everyone to Celebrate National Coming Out Day," *PR Newswire*, October 7, 2011.

39. Alina Wheeler, *Designing Brand Identity* (Hoboken, NJ: John Wiley & Sons, 2003).

40. John R. Doyle and Paul A. Bottomly, "Dressed for the Occasion: Font-Product Congruity in the Perception of Logotype," *Journal of Consumer Psychology* 16 (2006), pp. 112–23; Kevin Lane Keller, Susan Heckler, and Michael J. Houston, "The Effects of Brand Name Suggestiveness on Advertising Recall," *Journal of Marketing* 62 (January 1998), pp. 48–57; for an in-depth examination of how brand names get developed, see Alex Frankel, *Wordcraft: The Art of Turning Little Words into Big Business* (New York: Crown Publishers, 2004).

41. Eric A. Yorkston and Geeta Menon, "A Sound Idea: Phonetic Effects of Brand Names on Consumer Judgments," *Journal of Consumer Research* 31 (June 2004), pp. 43–51; Tina M. Lowery and L. J. Shrum, "Phonetic Symbolism and Brand Name Preference," *Journal of Consumer Research* 34 (October 2007), pp. 406–14.

42. For some interesting theoretical perspectives, see Claudiu V. Dimofte and Richard F. Yalch, "Consumer Response to Polysemous Brand Slogans," *Journal of Consumer Research* 33 (March 2007), pp. 515–22.

43. Eric Dash, "Citi's New Slogan Is Said to Be Second Choice," *New York Times*, May 12, 2008.

44. Darren Booth, "Is Avis 'Trying Hard' Enough with New Slogan?," www.cnbc.com, August 31, 2012.

45. Don Schultz and Heidi Schultz, *IMC: The Next Generation* (New York: McGraw-Hill, 2003).

46. Scott Bedbury, *A New Brand World* (New York: Viking Press, 2002).

47. Diana T. Kurylko, "Goofy Ads, Variants Help Mini Rule Its Own Little World," *Automotive News*, May 20, 2013; Micheline Maynard, "BMW's Bold Plan to Build Lots More Minis," *Forbes*, July 9, 2012; "NOT NORMAL—Start Of New MINI Brand Campaign," *BMW GROUP*, www.m.miniusa.com, September 26, 2012; "Creative Mini Cooper Advertising," www.toxel.com/inspiration, February 16, 2010; Douglas B. Holt and John A. Quelch, "Launching the New Mini," HBS Case# 9-505-020, 2004.

48. Dawn Iacobucci and Bobby Calder, eds., *Kellogg on Integrated Marketing* (New York: John Wiley & Sons, 2003).

49. Cotton Timberlake, "Is the Party Over for UGGs?," *Bloomberg Businessweek*, December 13, 2012; Patricia Odell, "UGG VP Marketing on Tom Brady's Impact on the Brand," *Chief Marketer Network*, November 29, 2012; Giselle Abramovich, "Inside UGG's Content-Marketing Strategy," *Digiday*, August 21, 2012; Alyssa Abkowitz, "Decks Finds Its Footing with UGGs," *Fortune*, August 19, 2009.

50. Eddie Pells, "Despite Numbers, Burton Still Bullish on Boarding," *Bloomberg Businessweek*, February 12, 2013.

51. Scott Davis and Michael Dunn, *Building the Brand-Driven Business* (New York: John Wiley & Sons, 2002).

52. For an interesting application of branding to internal projects, see Karen A. Brown, Richard E. Ettenson, and Nancy Lea Hyer, "Why Every Project Needs a Brand (and How to Create One)," *MIT Sloan Management Review*, Summer 2011, pp. 61–68.

53. Coeli Carr, "Seeking to Attract Top Prospects, Employers Brush Up on Brands," *New York Times*, September 10, 2006.

54. Tom Beaman, "Chevy Dealers Enroll in Mickey Mouse Courses," *Wards Auto*, September 6, 2012; Brooks Barnes, "In Customer Service Consulting, Disney's Small World Is Growing," *New York Times*, April 21, 2012.

55. The principles and examples from this passage are based on Colin Mitchell, "Selling the Brand Inside," *Harvard Business Review*, January 2002, pp. 99–105. For an in-depth discussion of how two organizations, QuikTrip and Wawa, developed stellar internal branding programs, see Neeli Bendapudi and Venkat Bendapudi, "Creating the Living Brand," *Harvard Business Review*, May 2005, pp. 124–32.

56. Dale Buss, "Go Further Brand Message Is Aimed at Ford's Employees, Too," *Forbes*, June 14, 2012.

57. John F. Marshall, "How Starbucks, Walmart And IBM Launch Brands Internally and What You Can Learn from Them," *Forbes*, April 9, 2013.

58. Ibid.

59. Deborah Roedder John, Barbara Loken, Kyeong-Heui Kim, and Alokparna Basu Monga, "Brand Concept Maps: A Methodology for Identifying Brand Association Networks," *Journal of Marketing Research* 43 (November 2006), pp. 549–63.

60. Jennifer Rooney, "Kellogg's Completes Major Brand Overhaul," *Forbes*, May 10, 2012; Mark J. Miller, "Kellogg's Aims to Make Today Great with Refreshed Verbal and Visual Identity," *Brand Channel*, May 14, 2012; "Refreshing an Icon: Kellogg's Updates Brand to Keep Pace with Today's Consumers," www.newsroom.kelloggcompany.com, May 14, 2012.

61. "The Best Global Brands," *BusinessWeek*, October 2, 2012; the article ranks and critiques the 100 best global brands using the valuation method developed by Interbrand. For an academic discussion of valuing brand equity, see V. Srinivasan, Chan Su Park, and Dae Ryun Chang, "An Approach to the Measurement, Analysis, and Prediction of Brand Equity and Its Sources," *Management Science* 51 (September 2005), pp. 1433–48. For an interesting comparison of the Interbrand valuation to a consumer-based brand equity measure, see Johny K. Johansson, Claudiu V. Dimofte, and Sanal K. Mazvancheryl, "The Performance of Global Brands in the 2008 Financial Crisis: A Test of Two Brand Value Measures," *International Journal of Research in Marketing* 29 (September 2012), pp. 235–45.

62. Mark Sherrington, *Added Value: The Alchemy of Brand-Led Growth* (Hampshire, UK: Palgrave Macmillan, 2003).

63. For some discussion of what factors determine long-term branding success, see Allen P. Adamson, *Brand Simple* (New York: Palgrave Macmillan, 2006).

64. Nikhil Bahdur and John Jullens, "New Life for Tired Brands," *Strategy+Business* 50 (Spring 2008).

65. Joshua Brustein, "Even Finns Don't Want Nokia Phones Anymore," *Business Week,* May 29, 2013; Juhana Rossi, "Nokia CEO Sticks to Company's Strategy," *Wall Street Journal,* May 7, 2013; Adam Ewing, "Nokia Declines as New Smartphone Disappoints Investors," *Bloomberg,* May 14, 2013; Seth Fiegerman, "Nokia Thought the iPhone Would Be a Flop because It Couldn't Hold Up to a 5 Foot Drop Test," *Business Insider,* July 19, 2012; Anton Troianovski and Sven Grundberg, "Nokia's Bad Call on Smartphones," *Wall Street Journal,* July 18, 2012; Alexandra Chang, "5 Reasons Why Nokia Lost Its Handset Sales Lead and Got Downgraded to 'Junk,'" *Wired,* April 27, 2012.

66. Natalie Mizik and Robert Jacobson, "Trading Off between Value Creation and Value Appropriation: The Financial Implications of Shifts in Strategic Emphasis," *Journal of Marketing* 67 (January 2003), pp. 63–76.

67. Jessica Dubois-Maahs, "Sears' Failure to Adapt Disillusions Shoppers, Shareholders," *Medill Report,* March 12, 2013; Michael Brush, "Why Sears Is on Its Last Legs," *MSN Money,* April 17, 2012; Chris Morran, "Sears Is Failing because It Spends Next-to-Nothing to Maintain Stores," *Consumerist,* July 30, 2012; Andrea Billups, "Sears, Kmart Failed to Anticipate Their Customers' Needs," *The Washington Times,* December 29, 2011.

68. Larry Light and Joan Kiddon, *Six Rules for Brand Revitalization: Learn How Companies Like McDonald's Can Re-Energize Their Brands* (Wharton School Publishing, 2009).

69. Rick Newman, "Cadillac: An American Luxemobile Comes Roaring Back," *Yahoo! Finance,* June 3, 2013; Jeff Bennett and Joseph B. White, "Can the New Cadillac Catch Up to BMW?," *Wall Street Journal,* March 27, 2013; Matthew de Paula, "Cadillac's Comeback: It's for Real," *Forbes,* April 30, 2011.

70. Jonathan R. Copulsky, *Brand Resilience: Managing Risk and Recovery in a High Speed World* (New York: Palgrave Macmillan, 2011).

71. Evan West, "Smells Like a Billion Bucks," *Fast Company,* May 2009, pp. 44–46.

72. Rebecca J. Slotegraaf and Koen Pauwels, "The Impact of Brand Equity and Innovation on the Long-Term Effectiveness of Promotions," *Journal of Marketing Research* 45 (June 2008), pp. 293–306.

73. John Kotter, "Burberry's Secrets to Successful Brand Reinvention," *Forbes,* February 26, 2013; Angela Ahrendts, "Burberry's CEO on Turning an Aging British Icon into a Global Luxury Brand," *Harvard Business Review,* February 2013; Moira Forbes, "Burberry CEO Proves Tradition Doesn't Prevent Innovation," *Forbes,* March 9, 2012.

74. Yuxin Chen and Tony Haitao Cui, "The Benefit of Uniform Price for Branded Variant," *Marketing Science* 32 (January–February 2013), pp. 36–50.

75. Bradford Wernie, "Ford Licensing Staffer's Job: Protect the Brand," *Automotive News,* June 11, 2012; Dale Buss, "Ford Has Built $1.5B Business Licensing Blue Oval, Products," *Forbes,* May 24, 2012; "Top 100 Global Licensors," *License! Global,* April 1, 2009; Jean Halliday, "Troubled Automakers' Golden Goose," *AutoWeek,* August 14, 2006.

76. Jing Lei, Niraj Dawar, and Jos Lemmink, "Negative Spillover in Brand Portfolios: Exploring the Antecedents of Asymmetric Effects," *Journal of Marketing* 72 (May 2008), pp. 111–23.

77. For comprehensive corporate branding guidelines, see James R. Gregory, *The Best of Branding: Best Practices in Corporate Branding* (New York: McGraw-Hill, 2004). For some international perspectives, see Majken Schultz, Yun Mi Antorini, and Fabian F. Csaba, eds., *Corporate Branding: Purpose, People, and Process* (Denmark: Copenhagen Business School Press, 2005); Mary Jo Hatch and Majken Schultz, *Taking Brand Initative: How Companies Can Align Strategy, Culture, and Identity through Corporate Branding* (San Francisco, CA: Jossey-Bass, 2008). For some B-to-B applications, see Atlee Valentine Pope and Ralph Oliva, "Building Blocks: Ten Key Roles of B-to-B Corporate Marketing," *Marketing Management,* Winter 2012, pp. 23–28.

78. Guido Berens, Cees B. M. van Riel, and Gerrit H. van Bruggen, "Corporate Associations and Consumer Product Responses: The Moderating Role of Corporate Brand Dominance," *Journal of Marketing* 69 (July 2005), pp. 35–48; Zeynep Gürhan-Canli and Rajeev Batra, "When Corporate Image Affects Product Evaluations: The Moderating Role of Perceived Risk," *Journal of Marketing Research* 41 (May 2004), pp. 197–205; Gabriel J. Biehal and Daniel A. Sheinin, "The Influence of Corporate Messages on the Product Portfolio," *Journal of Marketing* 71 (April 2007), pp. 12–25.

79. Vithala R. Rao, Manoj K. Agarwal, and Denise Dalhoff, "How Is Manifest Branding Strategy Related to the Intangible Value of a Corporation?," *Journal of Marketing* 68 (October 2004), pp. 126–41. For an examination of the financial impact of brand portfolio decisions, see Neil A. Morgan and Lopo L. Rego, "Brand Portfolio Strategy and Firm Performance," *Journal of Marketing* 73 (January 2009), pp. 59–74; S. Cem Bahadir, Sundar G. Bharadwaj, and Rajendra K. Srivastava, "Financial Value of Brands in Mergers and Acquisitions: Is Value in the Eye of the Beholder?," *Journal of Marketing* 72 (November 2008), pp. 49–64.

80. "Global Urbanization Is Fueling United Technologies' Growth," *Forbes,* June 3, 2013; Chuck Carnevale, "United Technologies Has Transitioned Itself for Accelerated Growth," *Forbes,* March 22, 2013; William J. Holstein, "The Incalculable Value of Building Brands," *Chief Executive,* April–May 2006, pp. 52–56.

81. Deborah Roedder John, Barbara Loken, and Christopher Joiner, "The Negative Impact of Extensions: Can Flagship Products Be Diluted?," *Journal of Marketing* 62 (January 1998), pp. 19–32.

82. Dan Carney, "Taurus, LaCrosse Mark Return of Detroit Sedan," www.msnbc.com, January 11, 2009.

83. Vanessa Fuhrmans, "Mercedes Pins Hopes on Sleek S-Class," *Wall Street Journal,* May 16, 2013.

84. David A. Aaker, *Brand Portfolio Strategy: Creating Relevance, Differentiation, Energy, Leverage, and Clarity* (New York: Free Press, 2004).

85. Christopher Hosford, "A Transformative Experience," *Sales & Marketing Management* 158 (June 2006), pp. 32–36; Mike Beirne and Javier Benito, "Starwood Uses Personnel to Personalize Marketing," *Brandweek,* April 24, 2006, p. 9; www.starwoodhotels.com, accessed July 21, 2013.

86. Michael Krauss, "The Glamour of B-to-B," *Marketing News,* February 2013, pp. 22–23.

87. Stuart Elliott, "Lipton Goes Back to Basics with a Tea Bag," *New York Times,* January 9, 2013; Heather Landi, "High Tea," *Beverage World,* July 2011, pp. 18–22; Matthew Boyle, "Weak Tea at Unilever Persists amid Innovation at Rivals," *Bloomberg,* October 24, 2012.

88. Nirmalya Kumar, "Kill a Brand, Keep a Customer," *Harvard Business Review,* December 2003, pp. 87–95.

89. Mark Ritson, "Should You Launch a Fighter Brand?," *Harvard Business Review,* October 2009, pp. 87–94.

90. Alan Oshman, "Toyota's Tiny Scion iQ Boosts U.S. by 19 Percent," *Bloomberg Businessweek,* April 25, 2012.

91. Jeff Bennett and Joseph B. White, "GM's New Corvette Begins Brand Update," *Wall Street Journal,* January 13, 2013.

92. Valarie A. Taylor and William O. Bearden, "Ad Spending on Brand Extensions: Does Similarity Matter?," *Journal of Brand Management* 11 (September 2003), pp. 63–74; Sheri Bridges, Kevin Lane Keller, and Sanjay Sood, "Communication Strategies for Brand Extensions: Enhancing Perceived Fit by Establishing Explanatory Links," *Journal of Advertising* 29 (Winter 2000), pp. 1–11.

93. Ralf van der Lans, Rik Pieters, and Michel Wedel, "Competitive Brand Salience," *Marketing Science* 27 (September–October 2008), pp. 922–31.

94. Subramanian Balachander and Sanjoy Ghose, "Reciprocal Spillover Effects: A Strategic Benefit of Brand Extensions," *Journal of Marketing* 67 (January 2003), pp. 4–13.

95. Bharat N. Anand and Ron Shachar, "Brands as Beacons: A New Source of Loyalty to Multiproduct Firms," *Journal of Marketing Research* 41 (May 2004), pp. 135–50.

96. Clementine Fletcher, "With Black Crown, Budweiser Aims to Refresh the Brand," *Bloomberg Businessweek,* January 10, 2013.

97. For consumer processing implications, see Huifung Mao and H. Shanker Krishnan, "Effects of Prototype and Exemplar Fit on Brand Extension Evaluations: A Two-Process Contingency Model," *Journal of Consumer Research* 33 (June 2006), pp. 41–49; Byung Chul Shine, Jongwon Park, and Robert S. Wyer Jr., "Brand Synergy Effects in Multiple Brand Extensions," *Journal of Marketing Research* 44 (November 2007), pp. 663–70.

98. Al Ries and Jack Trout, *Positioning: The Battle for Your Mind, 20th Anniversary Edition* (New York: McGraw-Hill, 2000).

99. David A. Aaker, *Brand Portfolio Strategy: Creating Relevance, Differentiation, Energy, Leverage, and Clarity* (New York: Free Press, 2004).

100. Vanessa Fuhrmans, "Is Porsche Still a Sports Car Maker?," *Wall Street Journal*, May 29, 2013.

101. Mary W. Sullivan, "Measuring Image Spillovers in Umbrella-Branded Products," *Journal of Business* 63 (July 1990), pp. 309–29.

102. See also Franziska Völckner and Henrik Sattler, "Drivers of Brand Extension Success," *Journal of Marketing* 70 (April 2006), pp. 1–17. For some recent research, see Eric A. Yorkston, Joseph C. Nunes, and Shashi Matta, "The Malleable Brand: The Role of Implicit Theories in Evaluating Brand Extensions," *Journal of Marketing* 74 (January 2010), pp. 80–93; Tom Meyvis, Kelly Goldsmith, and Ravi Dhar, "The Importance of the Context in Brand Extension: How Pictures and Comparisons Shift Consumers' Focus from Fit to Quality," *Journal of Marketing Research* 49 (April 2012), pp. 206–17; Alokparna Basu Monga and Zeynep Guhan-Canli, "The Influence of Mating Mind-Sets on Brand Extension Evaluation," *Journal of Marketing Research* 49 (August 2012), pp. 581–93; Susan Spiggle, Hang T. Nguyen, and Mary Caravella, "More than Fit: Brand Extension Authenticity," *Journal of Marketing Research* 49 (December 2012), pp. 967–83; Pragya Mathur, Shailendra P. Jain, and Durairaj Maheswaran, "Consumers' Implicit Theories about Personality Influence Their Brand Personality Judgments," *Journal of Consumer Psychology* 22 (2012), pp. 545–57; Keisha M. Cutright, James R. Bettman, and Gavan J. Fitzsimons, "Putting Brands in Their Place: How a Lack of Control Keeps Brand Contained," *Journal of Marketing Research* 50 (June 2013), pp. 365–77.

103. For more relevant research on extension evaluations, see Alokparna Basu Monga and Deborah Roedder John, "Cultural Differences in Brand Extension Evaluation: The Influence of Analytical versus Holistic Thinking," *Journal of Marketing Research* 33 (March 2007), pp. 529–36; James L. Oakley, Adam Duhachek, Subramanian Balachander, and S. Sriram, "Order of Entry and the Moderating Role of Comparison Brands in Extension Evaluations," *Journal of Consumer Research* 34 (February 2008), pp. 706–12; Junsang Yeo and Jongwon Park, "Effects of Parent-Extension Similarity and Self Regulatory Focus on Evaluations of Brand Extensions," *Journal of Consumer Psychology* 16 (2006), pp. 272–82; Catherine W. M. Yeung and Robert S. Wyer, "Does Loving a Brand Mean Loving Its Products? The Role of Brand-Elicited Affect in Brand Extension Evaluations," *Journal of Marketing Research* 43 (November 2005), pp. 495–506; Huifang Mao and H. Shankar Krishnan, "Effects of Prototype and Exemplar Fit on Brand Extension Evaluations: A Two-Process Contingency Model," *Journal of Consumer Research* 33 (June 2006), pp. 41–49; Rohini Ahluwalia, "How Far Can a Brand Stretch? Understanding the Role of Self-Construal," *Journal of Marketing Research* 45 (June 2008), pp. 337–50.

104. Pierre Berthon, Morris B. Holbrook, James M. Hulbert, and Leyland F. Pitt, "Viewing Brands in Multiple Dimensions," *MIT Sloan Management Review* (Winter 2007), pp. 37–43.

105. Andrea Rothman, "France's Bic Bets U.S. Consumers Will Go for Perfume on the Cheap," *Wall Street Journal*, January 12, 1989.

106. Roland T. Rust, Valerie A. Zeithaml, and Katherine A. Lemon, "Measuring Customer Equity and Calculating Marketing ROI," Rajiv Grover and Marco Vriens, eds., *Handbook of Marketing Research* (Thousand Oaks, CA: Sage Publications, 2006), pp. 588–601.

107. Robert C. Blattberg and John Deighton, "Manage Marketing by the Customer Equity Test," *Harvard Business Review*, July–August 1996, pp. 136–44.

108. Robert C. Blattberg, Gary Getz, and Jacquelyn S. Thomas, *Customer Equity: Building and Managing Relationships as Valuable Assets* (Boston: Harvard Business School Press, 2001).

109. Much of this section is based on Robert Leone, Vithala Rao, Kevin Lane Keller, Man Luo, Leigh McAlister, and Rajendra Srivatstava, "Linking Brand Equity to Customer Equity," *Journal of Service Research* 9 (November 2006), pp. 125–38. This special issue is devoted to customer equity and has a number of thought-provoking articles.

110. Niraj Dawar, "What Are Brands Good For?," *MIT Sloan Management Review* (Fall 2004), pp. 31–37. For an insightful analysis of the relationship between brand equity and CLV, see Florian Stahl, Mark Heitmann, Donald R. Lehmann, and Scott A. Neslin, "The Impact of Brand Equity on Customer Acquisition, Retention, and Profit Margin," *Journal of Marketing* 76 (July 2012), pp. 44–63.

# Chapter 12

1. Vanessa Mock, "UPS to Appeal EU's Blocking of TNT Merger," *Wall Street Journal*, April 7, 2013; Betsy Morris, "UPS, FedEx Escalate Holiday Shipping War," *Wall Street Journal*, December 13, 2012; Bob Sechler, "FedEx, UPS Get a Toehold in China's Express Delivery," *Wall Street Journal*, September 10, 2012; Aaron Karp, "Big Brown's Big Deal," *Air Transport World*. September 2012; Jeff Berman, "UPS, FedEx Receive Limited Domestic Delivery Licenses in China," *Logistics Management*, September 11, 2012; John T. Bowen Jr., "A Spatial Analysis of FedEx and UPS: Hubs, Spokes, and Network Structure," *Journal of Transport Geography*, September, 2012; Rob Martinez, "Forecasting Critical Changes in the Carrier Market," *Multichannel Market*, December 1, 2010; Jennifer Levitz, "UPS Leaves 'Brown' for New Love," *Wall Street Journal*, September 13, 2010.

2. Philip Kotler and Milton Kotler, *Market Your Way to Growth: 8 Ways to Win* (Hoboken, NJ: John Wiley & Sons, 2013).

3. Matt Townsend, "Under Armour Finds Feminine Side to Go Beyond $2 Billion," *Bloomberg*, February 15, 2013; Molly Soat, "Moving Beyond Shrink It & Pink It," *Marketing News*, February 2013, pp. 33–36; John Kell, "Under Armour Arrives on Global Stage," *Wall Street Journal*, June 3, 2012, p. B2; Daniel Roberts, "Under Armour Gets Serious," *Fortune*, October 2011; Jeremy Mullman, "Protecting This Brand while Running Ahead," *Advertising Age*, January 12, 2009, p. 16; Elaine Wong, "Under Armour Makes a Long-Run Calculation," *Brandweek*, January 19, 2009, p. 28; Stephanie N. Mehta, "Under Armour Reboots," *Fortune*, February 2, 2009, pp. 29–33.

4. Evan Hirsh and Kasturi Rangan, "The Grass Isn't Greener," *Harvard Business Review*, January–February 2013, pp. 21–23.

5. David Taylor, *Grow the Core: How to Focus on Your Core Business for Brand Success* (West Sussex, UK: John Wiley & Sons, 2012).

6. Shivani Shinde, "Aegis Eyes Organic Growth to Turn into a $2-bn Company by 2015," *Business Standard*, June 22, 2012; Maiseis McCabe, "Aegis Reports Organic Revenue Growth of 8% in Q1," *Campaign*, April 27, 2012.

7. Robert Stockdill, "Levi's Asian Folly," *Inside Retailing*, October 12, 2012.

8. Alex Letourneau, "Organic Growth to Lead Fortuna Silver Production Higher: President," *Forbes*, October 25, 2012.

9. Juro Osawa, "Lenovo Turns to Phones as PC Industry Declines," *Wall Street Journal*, June 19, 2013.

10. William M. Bulkeley, "Xerox Tries to Go Beyond Copiers," *Wall Street Journal*, February 24, 2009, p. B5; Nanette Byrnes and Roger O. Crockett, "An Historic Succession at Xerox," *BusinessWeek*, June 8, 2009, pp. 18–22; Geoff Colvin, "An Interview with Ursula Burns," *Fortune*, May 3, 2010, pp. 96–102; "Xerox Focuses on Personalization," *Direct Marketing News*, July 12, 2010; Ellen McGirt, "Fresh Copy," *Fast Company*, December 2011/January 2012, pp. 130–38; Christa Carone "Xerox's Brand Repositioning Challenge," *Advertising Age*, March 12, 2013.

11. Starbucks, www.starbucks.com/aboutus/overview.asp, December 1, 2009.

12. "Daimler Takes Balanced Approach," www.warc.com, November 28, 2012.

13. Priya Raghubir and Eric A. Greenleaf, "Ratios in Proportion: What Should the Shape of the Package Be?," *Journal of Marketing* 70 (April 2006), pp. 95–107; and Valerie Folkes and Shashi Matta, "The Effect of Package Shape on Consumers' Judgments of Product Volume: Attention as a Mental Contaminant," *Journal of Consumer Research* 31 (September 2004), pp. 390–401.

14. Sarah Nassaur, "The Psychology of Small Packages," *Wall Street Journal*, April 15, 2013.

15. Andrew Adam Newman, "Too Much Holiday Food? This Campaign's for You," *New York Times*, November 29, 2011.

16. John D. Cripps, "Heuristics and Biases in Timing the Replacement of Durable Products," *Journal of Consumer Research* 21 (September 1994), pp. 304–18.

17. "Creative New Monroe Marketing Campaign Reminds Consumers to Replace Worn Shocks and Struts," www.monroe.com, March 18, 2013. Monroe is a registered trademark of Tenneco Automotive Operating Company Inc.

18. George Stalk Jr. and Rob Lachanauer, "Hardball: Five Killer Strategies for Trouncing the Competition," *Harvard Business Review*, April 2004, pp. 62–71; Richard D'Aveni, "The Empire Strikes Back: Counterrevolutionary Strategies for Industry Leaders," *Harvard Business Review*, November 2002, pp. 66–74.

19. Kyle B. Murray and Gerald Häubl, "Why Dominant Companies Are Vulnerable," *MIT Sloan Management Review*, Winter 2012, pp. 12–14.

20. Nirmalya Kumar, Lisa Sheer, and Philip Kotler, "From Market Driven to Market Driving," *European Management Journal* 18 (April 2000), pp. 129–42.

21. Much of the remaining section on proactive marketing is based on an insightful book by Leonardo Araujo and Rogerio Gava, *The Proactive Enterprise: How to Anticipate Market Changes* (Hampshire, UK: Palgrave Macmillan, 2012).

22. "New Trends Worth $4.5tr," www.warc.com, January 25, 2013.

23. Jonathan Glancey, "The Private World of the Walkman," *Guardian*, October 11, 1999.

24. Kristin Jones, "Lululemon's Product Chief to Exit," *Wall Street Journal*, April 3, 2013; Alli McConnon, "Lululemon's Next Workout," *BusinessWeek*, June 9, 2008, pp. 43–44; Danielle Sacks, "Lululemon's Cult of Selling," *Fast Company*, March 2009; Bryant Urstadt, "Lust for Lulu," *New York Magazine*, July 26, 2009.

25. For some contemporary perspectives on defense strategies, see Timothy Calkins, *Defending Your Brand: How Smart Companies Use Defense Strategy to Deal with Competitive Attacks* (New York: Palgrave Macmillan, 2012).

26. These six defense strategies, as well as the five attack strategies, are taken from some classic work by Philip Kotler and Ravi Singh, "Marketing Warfare in the 1980s," *Journal of Business Strategy* (Winter 1981), pp. 30–41.

27. Kevin P. Coyne, "Predicting Your Competitor's Reactions," *Harvard Business Review*, April 2009, pp. 90–97.

28. Michael E. Porter, *Market Signals, Competitive Strategy: Techniques for Analyzing Industries and Competitors* (New York: Free Press, 1998), pp. 75–87; Jaideep Prabhu and David W. Stewart, "Signaling Strategies in Competitive Interaction: Building Reputations and Hiding the Truth," *Journal of Marketing Research* 38 (February 2001), pp. 62–72.

29. Halah Touryalai, "ATMs Not the Only Things Disappearing at Bank Of America, It's Closed the Most Branches Too," www.forbes.com, July 26, 2012.

30. Yuhong Wu, Sridhar Balasubramanian, and Vijay Mahajan, "When Is a Preannounced New Product Likely to Be Delayed?," *Journal of Marketing* 68 (April 2004), pp. 101–13; Barry L. Bayus, Sanjay Jain, and Ambar G. Rao, "Truth or Consequences: An Analysis of Vaporware and New-Product Announcements," *Journal of Marketing Research* 38 (February 2001), pp. 3–13.

31. Marshall Eckblad, "Sara Lee No More: A Hillshire Is Born," *Wall Street Journal*, June 6, 2012; Emily Bryson York, "Sara Lee to Split into Two Businesses," *Los Angeles Times*, January 28, 2011; Melissa Born and Ilan Brat, "Global Finance: Sara Lee to Split into Two Public Companies," *Wall Street Journal*, January 19, 2011.

32. "P&G Completes Sale of Pringles to Kellogg," *Business Wire*, May 31, 2012.

33. E.J. Schultz, "Kraft's New Grocery Company Plans Marketing Boost in Search of 'Renaissance,'" *Advertising Age*, September 7, 2012; Heidi Stevens, "The Many Meanings of Mondelez," *Chicago Tribune*, May 24, 2012; Candice Choi, "Mondelez, Kraft's New Name, Elicits Jokes from All Corners," *Huffington Post*, May 21, 2012; Paul Ziobro, "Kraft Defends Split," *Wall Street Journal*, September 8, 2011; Duane Stanford and Jeffrey McCracken, "Kraft Foods Chief Rosenfeld Says More Acquisitions Possible after Spinoff," *Bloomberg*, August 4, 2011; Jonathan Burr, "Why the Kraft Split Makes Sense," *Daily Finance*, August 5, 2011.

34. J. Scott Armstrong and Kesten C. Green, "Competitor-Oriented Objectives: The Myth of Market Share," *International Journal of Business* 12 (Winter 2007), pp. 115–34; Stuart E. Jackson, *Where Value Hides: A New Way to Uncover Profitable Growth for Your Business* (New York: John Wiley & Sons, 2006).

35. Nirmalya Kumar, *Marketing as Strategy* (Cambridge, MA: Harvard Business School Press, 2004); Philip Kotler and Paul N. Bloom, "Strategies for High-Market-Share Companies," *Harvard Business Review*, November–December 1975, pp. 63–72.

36. Robert D. Buzzell and Frederick D. Wiersema, "Successful Share-Building Strategies," *Harvard Business Review*, January–February 1981, pp. 135–44.

37. "Fairpoint Meets Broadband Commitment in Maine," *Associated Press*, January 27, 2011; John Downey, "FairPoint Struggles with Merger, Declining Stock," *Charlotte Business Journal*, March 19, 2009; John Downey, FairPoint Faces Enduring Debt, Service Headaches," *Charlotte Business Journal*, September 15, 2009.

38. Neeru Paharia, Anat Keinan, Jill Avery, and Juliet B. Schor, "The Underdog Effect: The Marketing of Disadvantage and Determination through Brand Biography," *Journal of Consumer Research* 37 (February 2011), pp. 775–90; Anat Keinan, Jill Avery, and Neeru Paharia, "Capitalizing on the Underdog Effect," *Harvard Business Review*, November 2010, p. 32.

39. Venkatesh Shankar, Gregory Carpenter, and Lakshman Krishnamurthi, "Late-Mover Advantage: How Innovative Late Entrants Outsell Pioneers," *Journal of Marketing Research* 35 (February 1998), pp. 54–70; Gregory S. Carpenter and Kent Nakamoto, "The Impact of Consumer Preference Formation on Marketing Objectives and Competitive Second-Mover Strategies," *Journal of Consumer Psychology* 5 (1996), pp. 325–58.

40. Adam Morgan, "How Market Leaders Can Become Challenger Brands Once More," *Market Leader*, Fall 2009; Adam Morgan, "Strategies from a New Generation of Challenger Brands," *Market Leader*, Winter 2009.

41. Lance Whitney, "Large Carriers Losing Prepaid Phone Sales to Smaller Players," *CNET News*, November 15, 2012.

42. Michael V. Copeland, "These Boots Really Were Made for Walking," *Business 2.0*, October 2004, pp. 72–74.

43. Katrina Booker, "The Pepsi Machine," *Fortune*, February 6, 2006, pp. 68–72.

44. Theodore Levitt, "Innovative Imitation," *Harvard Business Review*, September–October 1966, p. 63. Also see Steven P. Schnaars, *Managing Imitation Strategies: How Later Entrants Seize Markets from Pioneers* (New York: Free Press, 1994).

45. Amir Efrati, "Clone Wars Roil App World," *Wall Street Journal*, March 4, 2013; Ben Rooney, "Rise of a Cloner Draws VC Fans and Critics," *Wall Street Journal*, May 17, 2012; Brian Caulfield, "The Predator," *Forbes*, March 12, 2012.

46. www.ralstonfoodservice.com/ralstonbrands.html, accessed June 23, 2013.

47. Claire Ruckin, "RLPC-Distressed Debt Investors Eye Spain's Telepizza—Bankers," *Reuters*. March 8, 2013.

48. Felix Gillette, "Inside Big Pharma's Fight against the $75 Billion Counterfeit Drug Business," *Bloomberg Businessweek*, January 17, 2013.

49. "Pretty Profitable Parrots," *The Economist*, May 12, 2012.

50. Meghan Casserly, "Copycat," *Forbes*, February 11, 2013, pp. 74–75.

51. Frank Shyong, "Siracha Hot Sauce Founder Turns Up the Heat," *Los Angeles Times*, April 12, 2103; Caleb Hannan, "Burning Sensation," *Bloomberg Businessweek*, February 21, 2013, pp. 66–69; John T. Edge, "A Chili Sauce to Crow About," *New York Times*, May 19, 2009.

52. Eric K. Clemon, Paul F, Nunes, and Matt Reilly, "Six Strategies for Successful Niche Marketing," *Wall Street Journal*, May 24, 2010.

53. Karsten Strauss, "Sound Judgment," *Forbes*, April 15, 2013, pp. 68–69.

54. Robert Klara, "Burning for You," *Adweek*, May 21, 2012; James R. Hagerty, "Zippo Preps for a Post-Smoker World," *Wall Street Journal*, March 8, 2011; Michael Learmonth, "Zippo Reignites Brand with Social Media, New Products," *Advertising Age*, August 10, 2009, p. 12; Thomas A. Fogarty, "Keeping Zippo's Flame Eternal," *USA Today,* June 24, 2003; www.zippo.com, accessed May 26, 2014.

55. Some authors distinguished additional stages. Wasson suggested a stage of competitive turbulence between growth and maturity. See Chester R. Wasson, *Dynamic Competitive Strategy and Product Life Cycles* (Austin, TX: Austin Press, 1978). Maturity describes a stage of sales growth slowdown and saturation, a stage of flat sales after sales have peaked.

56. John E. Swan and David R. Rink, "Fitting Market Strategy to Varying Product Life Cycles," *Business Horizons*, January–February 1982, pp. 72–76; Gerald J. Tellis and C. Merle Crawford, "An Evolutionary Approach to Product Growth Theory," *Journal of Marketing* 45 (Fall 1981), pp. 125–34.

57. William E. Cox Jr., "Product Life Cycles as Marketing Models," *Journal of Business* (October 1967), pp. 375–84.

58. Jordan P. Yale, "The Strategy of Nylon's Growth," *Modern Textiles Magazine,* February 1964, p. 32. Also see Theodore Levitt, "Exploit the Product Life Cycle," *Harvard Business Review,* November–December 1965, pp. 81–94.

59. Chester R. Wasson, "How Predictable Are Fashion and Other Product Life Cycles?," *Journal of Marketing* 32 (July 1968), pp. 36–43.

60. Ibid.

61. William H. Reynolds, "Cars and Clothing: Understanding Fashion Trends," *Journal of Marketing* 32 (July 1968), pp. 44–49.

62. "Heelys, Inc. Announces Agreement to Be Acquired by Sequential Brands Group, Inc. for $2.25 per Share," www.globalnewswire.com, December 10, 2012; "Heelys Agrees to Sell Operations to Private Buyer," *Bloomberg Businessweek*, October 23, 2012; Jessica Pallay, "New Heelys CEO in Rebuild Mode," *Footwear News*, August 24, 2009.

63. Ryan Perlowin, "Product Line Expansion Will Be Catalyst for Growth at Crocs," www.seekingalpha.com, April 12, 2013; David Englander, "Crocs Strides toward a Comeback," *Barron's*, January 19, 2013; Jennifer Overstreet, "How Crocs Is Building a Brand Bigger than the Clog," *National Retail Federation*, August 29, 2012; Edward Teach, "How Crocs Regained Its Footing," *CFO Magazine*, May 15, 2012.

64. Rajesh J. Chandy, Gerard J. Tellis, Deborah J. MacInnis, and Pattana Thaivanich, "What to Say When: Advertising Appeals in Evolving Markets," *Journal of Marketing Research* 38 (November 2001), pp. 399–414.

65. Brad Tuttle, "Does Selling Out to Avis Represent Success for ZipCar? Failure? Something Else?," *Time*, January 3, 2013; Dennis K. Berman, "Zipcar: Entrepreneurial Genius, Public-Company Failure," *Wall Street Journal,* January 2, 2013; Trefis Team, "Why Zipcar Should Focus on U.S. Growth Rather than International," *Forbes*, April 18, 2012; Mark Clothier, "Can Hertz Outrun Zipcar in Hourly Car Rentals?," *Business Week*, March 29, 2012; Trefis Team, "Hertz, Enterprise Challenge Zipcar's Car Sharing Dominance," *Forbes*, June 8, 2012; Paul Keegan, "The Best New Idea in Business," *Fortune*, September 14, 2009, pp. 42–52; Adam Ashton, "Growth Galore but Profits Are Zip," *BusinessWeek*, September 8, 2008, p. 62; Alex Frankel, "Zipcar Makes the Leap," *Fast Company*, March 2008, pp. 48–50; Mike Beirne, "Temporary Plates," *Brandweek*, July 9, 2007, pp. 30–34.

66. Glen L. Urban et al., "Market Share Rewards to Pioneering Brands: An Empirical Analysis and Strategic Implications," *Management Science* (June 1986), pp. 645–59; William T. Robinson and Claes Fornell, "Sources of Market Pioneer Advantages in Consumer Goods Industries," *Journal of Marketing Research* 22 (August 1985), pp. 305–17.

67. Gregory S. Carpenter and Kent Nakamoto, "Consumer Preference Formation and Pioneering Advantage," *Journal of Marketing Research* 26 (August 1989), pp. 285–98.

68. William T. Robinson and Sungwook Min, "Is the First to Market the First to Fail? Empirical Evidence for Industrial Goods Businesses," *Journal of Marketing Research* 39 (February 2002), pp. 120–28.

69. Kurt A. Carlson, Margaret G. Meloy, and J. Edward Russo, "Leader-Driven Primacy: Using Attribute Order to Affect Consumer Choice," *Journal of Consumer Research* 32 (March 2006), pp. 513–18.

70. Venkatesh Shankar, Gregory S. Carpenter, and Lakshman Krishnamurthi, "Late Mover Advantage: How Innovative Late Entrants Outsell Pioneers," *Journal of Marketing Research* 35 (February 1998), pp. 54–70; Elena Reutskaja and Barbara Fasolo, "It's Not Necessarily Best to Be First," *Harvard Business Review*, January–February 2013, pp. 28–29.

71. Steven P. Schnaars, *Managing Imitation Strategies* (New York: Free Press, 1994). See also Jin K. Han, Namwoon Kim, and Hony-Bom Kin, "Entry Barriers: A Dull-, One-, or Two-Edged Sword for Incumbents? Unraveling the Paradox from a Contingency Perspective," *Journal of Marketing* 65 (January 2001), pp. 1–14.

72. Peter N. Golder, "Historical Method in Marketing Research with New Evidence on Long-term Market Share Stability," *Journal of Marketing Research* 37 (May 2000), pp. 156–72; Peter N. Golder and Gerald J. Tellis, "Pioneer Advantage: Marketing Logic or Marketing Legend?," *Journal of Marketing Research* 30 (May 1993), pp. 34–46. See also Shi Zhang and Arthur B. Markman, "Overcoming the Early Advantage: The Role of Alignable and Nonalignable Differences," *Journal of Marketing Research* 35 (November 1998), pp. 1–15.

73. Peter N. Golder, Julie R. Irwin, and Debanjan Mitra, "Long-term Market Leadership Persistence: Baselines, Economic Conditions, and Category Types," MSI Report 13-110, Marketing Science Institute, 2013.

74. Gerald Tellis and Peter Golder, *Will and Vision: How Latecomers Can Grow to Dominate Markets* (New York: McGraw-Hill, 2001); Rajesh K. Chandy and Gerald J. Tellis, "The Incumbent's Curse? Incumbency, Size, and Radical Product Innovation," *Journal of Marketing Research* 64 (July 2000), pp. 1–17. See also Dave Ulrich and Norm Smallwood, "Building a Leadership Brand," *Harvard Business Review*, July–August 2007, pp. 93–100.

75. Sungwook Min, Manohar U. Kalwani, and William T. Robinson, "Market Pioneer and Early Follower Survival Risks: A Contingency Analysis of Really New versus Incrementally New Product-Markets," *Journal of Marketing* 70 (January 2006), pp. 15–35. See also Raji Srinivasan, Gary L. Lilien, and Arvind Rangaswamy, "First In, First Out? The Effects of Network Externalities on Pioneer Survival," *Journal of Marketing* 68 (January 2004), pp. 41–58.

76. As reported in Joseph T. Vesey, "The New Competitors: They Think in Terms of Speed to Market," *Academy of Management Executive* 5 (May 1991), pp. 23–33; and Brian Dumaine, "How Managers Can Succeed through Speed," *Fortune,* February 13, 1989, pp. 54–59.

77. Tim Higgins, "GM's First Mover Disadvantage," *Bloomberg Businessweek*, October 1, 2012.

78. Marty Bates, Syed S. H. Rizvi, Prashant Tewari, and Dev Vardhan, "How Fast Is Too Fast?," *McKinsey Quarterly* no. 3 (2001); See also Stephen Wunker, "Better Growth Decisions: Early Mover, Fast Follower or Late Follower?," *Strategy & Leadership* 40, no. 2 (2012).

79. Rita Gunther McGrath, "Transient Advantage," *Harvard Business Review*, June 2013, pp. 62–70.

80. Simon Zekaria, "Electrolux Moves to Add Sizzle to Its Brand," *Wall Street Journal*, September 30, 2012; Ola Kinnander and Kim McLaughlin, "Electrolux Wants to Rule the Appliance World," *Bloomberg Businessweek*, March 28, 2011; Trond Riiber Knudsen, "Escaping the Middle-Market Trap: An Interview with CEO of Electrolux," *McKinsey Quarterly* (December 2006), pp. 72–79.

81. Ashlee Vance, "Shutterfly's Improbably Long Lifespan," *Bloomberg Businessweek*, January 7, 2013, pp. 33–34.

82. "The Paper Chase," Special Advertising Section, *Fortune*, January 14, 2013.

83. Emily Glazer, "National Envelope Files for Bankruptcy Protection," *Wall Street Journal*, June 10, 2013; Joann S. Lublin, "Pitney Bowes Readies 21st Century Message," *Wall Street Journal*, June 25, 2013.

84. Jorge Cauz, "Encyclopædia Britannica's President on Killing Off a 244-Year-Old Product," *Harvard Business Review*, March 2013, pp. 39–42.

85. Nick Bunkley, "Pontiac Falls from Muscle Car Glory to Graveyard," *New York Times*, October 29, 2010.

86. Rajan Varadarajan, Mark P. DeFanti, and Paul S. Busch, "Brand Portfolio, Corporate Image, and Reputation: Managing Brand Deletions," *Journal of the Academy of Marketing Science* 34 (Spring 2006), pp. 195–205; Stephen J. Carlotti Jr., Mary Ellen Coe, and Jesko Perrey, "Making Brand Portfolios Work," *McKinsey Quarterly* 4 (2004), pp. 24–36; Nirmalya Kumar, "Kill a Brand, Keep a Customer," *Harvard Business Review*, December 2003, pp. 86–95.

87. Laurence P. Feldman and Albert L. Page, "Harvesting: The Misunderstood Market Exit Strategy," *Journal of Business Strategy* (Spring 1985), pp. 79–85; Philip Kotler, "Harvesting Strategies for Weak Products," *Business Horizons*, August 1978, pp. 15–22.

88. Rob Walker, "Can Ghost Brands…," *International Herald Tribune*, May 17–18, 2008, pp. 17–18; Peter Carbona, "The Rush to Grab Orphan Brands," *BusinessWeek*, August 3, 2009, pp. 47–48.

89. Stuart Elliott, "Those Shelved Brands Start to Look Tempting," *New York Times*, August 21, 2008.

90. Peter N. Golder and Gerard J. Tellis, "Growing, Growing, Gone: Cascades, Diffusion, and Turning Points in the Product Life Cycle," *Marketing Science* 23 (Spring 2004), pp. 207–18.

91. Youngme Moon, "Break Free from the Product Life Cycle," *Harvard Business Review*, May 2005, pp. 87–94.

92. Hubert Gatignon and David Soberman, "Competitive Response and Market Evolution," Barton A. Weitz and Robin Wensley, eds., *Handbook of Marketing* (London, UK: Sage Publications, 2002), pp. 126–47; Robert D. Buzzell, "Market Functions and Market Evolution," *Journal of Marketing* 63 (Special Issue 1999), pp. 61–63.

93. Philip Kotler and John A. Caslione, *Chaotics: The Business and Marketing in the Age of Turbulence* (New York: AMACOM, 2009).

94. Raji Srinivasan, Arvind Rangaswamy, and Gary L. Lilien, "Turning Adversity into Advantage: Does Proactive Marketing During Recession Pay Off?," *International Journal of Research in Marketing* 22 (June 2005), pp. 109–25.

95. Jon Fine, "Why General Mills Marketing Pays Off," *BusinessWeek*, July 27, 2009, pp. 67–68; Matthew Boyle, "Snap, Crackle, Pop at the Food Giants," *BusinessWeek*, October 6, 2008, p. 48.

96. Philip Lay, Todd Hewlin, and Geoffrey Moore, "In a Downturn, Provoke Your Customers," *Harvard Business Review*, March 2009, pp. 48–56.

97. John A. Quelch and Katherine E. Jocz, "How to Market in a Downturn," *Harvard Business Review*, April 2009, pp. 52–62.

98. Maria Bartiromo, "Facetime: Inside a Company Resetting for Recovery," *BusinessWeek*, July 13 and 20, 2009, pp. 15–17.

99. Steve Hamm, "The New Age of Frugality," *BusinessWeek*, October 20, 2008, pp. 55–58.

100. Jane Porter and Burt Heim, "Doing Whatever Gets Them in the Door," *BusinessWeek*, June 30, 2008, p. 60.

101. David Taylor, David Nichols, Diego Kerner, and Anne Charbonneau, "Leading Brands Out of the Recession," *Brandgym Research Paper 2*, www.brandgym.com, September 2009.

102. Todd Wasserman, "Maverick CMOs Try Going without TV," *Brandweek*, January 24, 2009.

103. Maureen Scarpelli, "Dentists Step Up Marketing Efforts as Patients Scrimp by Skipping Visits," *Wall Street Journal*, August 11, 2009.

104. Peter J. Williamson and Ming Zeng, "Value for Money Strategies for Recessionary Times," *Harvard Business Review*, March 2009, pp. 66–74.

105. Burt Heim, "How to Sell Luxury to Penny-Pinchers," *BusinessWeek*, November 10, 2008, p. 60.

106. Lien Lamey, Barbara Deleersnyder, Jan-Benedict E.M. Steenkamp, and Marnik G. Dekimpe, "The Effect of Business-Cycle Fluctuations on Private-Label Share: What Has Marketing Conduct Got to Do with It?," *Journal of Marketing* 76 (January 2012), pp. 1–19.

107. Stuart Elliott, "Trying to Pitch Products to the Savers," *New York Times*, June 3, 2009.

108. Luisa Zargani, "Armani Goes Big in Beijing," *WWD*, May 31, 2012; Luisa Zargani, "Giorgia Armani Sees Profit Climb 23%," *WWD*, May 24, 2012; Alessandra Galloni, "The Future of Armani," *Wall Street Journal*, May 23, 2012.

109. Andrew Martin, "In Tough Times, Spam Is Suddenly Appealing," *Boston Globe*, November 16, 2008; Marshall Ecklbad, "At Hormel, Spam Is Small Part of the Buffet," *Wall Street Journal*, July 31, 2012.

# Chapter 13

1. Michael McCarthy, "Lexus Makes Big 'Move' to Regain Crown," *Advertising Age*, June 24, 2013; "Audi, Lexus and BMW Triumph as Leading High-End Auto Brands by Wealthy U.S. Drivers," *Luxury Institute Press Release*, January 10, 2013; Cheryl Jensen, "Cars More Dependable than Ever, Lexus Tops the Chart while Land Rover Is Least Reliable," *New York Daily News*, April 16, 2013; Matthew de Paula, "Lexus Pursues Hipper Crowd with New Ads for Its LS Sedan," *Forbes*, October 31, 2012.

2. This discussion is adapted from a classic article: Theodore Levitt, "Marketing Success through Differentiation: Of Anything," *Harvard Business Review*, January–February 1980, pp. 83–91. The first level, core benefit, has been added to Levitt's discussion.

3. Andrew D. Gershoff, Ran Kivetz, and Anat Keinan, "Consumer Response to Versioning: How Brands' Production Methods Affect Perceptions of Unfairness," *Journal of Consumer Research* 39 (August 2012), pp. 382–98.

4. Mads Nipper, "Lego Clicks," *The Hub*, July/August 2012, pp. 26–30; Yun Mi Antorini, Albert M. Muñiz Jr., and Tormod Askildsen, "Collaborating with Customer Communities: Lessons from the Lego Group," *MIT Sloan Management Review* 53 (Spring 2012), pp. 73–79; David Robertson and Per Hjuler, "Innovating a Turnaround at LEGO," *Harvard Business Review*, September 2009, pp. 20–21; Kim Hjelmgaard, "Lego, Refocusing on Bricks, Builds on Image," *Wall Street Journal*, December 24, 2009; Paul Grimaldi, "Consumers Design Products Their Way," *Knight Ridder Tribune Business News*, November 25, 2006.

5. For some definitions, see *AMA Dictionary* from the American Marketing Association, www.ama.org/resources/Pages/Dictionary.aspx.

6. Richard McGill Murphy, "Rising Stars," *Fortune*, September 6, 2010, pp. 110–16; since that analyst statement, some legal and cost issues have muddied the water, see Robert Langreth, "Intuitive Surgical Declines on Warning Letter from FDA," *Bloomberg*, July 20, 2013.

7. Some of these bases are discussed in David A. Garvin, "Competing on the Eight Dimensions of Quality," *Harvard Business Review*, November–December 1987, pp. 101–9.

8. Marco Bertini, Elie Ofek, and Dan Ariely, "The Impact of Add-On Features on Product Evaluations," *Journal of Consumer Research* 36 (June 2009), pp. 17–28; Tripat Gill, "Convergent Products: What Functionalities Add More Value to the Base," *Journal of Marketing* 72 (March 2008), pp. 46–62; Robert J. Meyer, Sheghui Zhao, and Jin K. Han, "Biases in Valuation vs. Usage of Innovative Product Features," *Marketing Science* 27 (November–December 2008), pp. 1083–96.

9. Debora Viana Thompson, Rebecca W. Hamilton, and Roland Rust, "Feature Fatigue: When Product Capabilities Become Too Much of a Good Thing," *Journal of Marketing Research* 42 (November 2005), pp. 431–42.

10. Sami Haj-Assaad, "Are German Cars Reliable? The Myth of 'German Engineering,'" www.autoguide.com, May 10, 2012; Cheryl Jensen, "Honda Repeats, Ford Surges and Mercedes Tumbles in 2011 Consumer Reports Study," www.wheels.blogs.nytimes.com, February 28, 2011; Peter Gumbel, "How Dr. Z Plans to Fix Mercedes," www.

money.cnn.com, July 13, 2009; Chris Shunk, "Paradox: As Quality Improves, Mercedes-Benz Dealership Profits Decline," *Automotive News*, January 27, 2009; Gail Edmondson, "Mercedes Gets Back up to Speed," *BusinessWeek*, November 13, 2006, pp. 46–47.

11. David Kesmodel, "No Glass Ceiling for the Best Job in the Universe," *Wall Street Journal*, June 29, 2010.

12. Bernd Schmitt and Alex Simonson, *Marketing Aesthetics: The Strategic Management of Brand, Identity, and Image* (New York: Free Press, 1997).

13. Mark Brohan, "Nike's Web Sales Flourish in Fiscal 2010," *Internet Retailer*, June 30, 2010.

14. Rupal Parekh, "Personalized Products Please but Can They Create Profit," *Advertising Age*, May 20, 2012; www.us.burberry.com/store/bespoke; Paul Sonne, "Mink or Fox? The Trench Gets Complicated," *Wall Street Journal*, November 3, 2011.

15. Stanley Reed, "Rolls-Royce at Your Service," *BusinessWeek*, November 15, 2005, pp. 92–93; *Rolls-Royce*, www.rolls-royce.com/civil/services, accessed March 16, 2014; "Rolls-Royce Engine Support," *Aviation Today*, June 1, 2006.

16. Mohanbir Sawhney, Robert C. Wolcott, and Inigo Arroniz, "The 12 Different Ways for Companies to Innovate," *MIT Sloan Management Review* (April 1, 2006); "Cemex Demand Forecasting, Inventory Management and Route Planning," www.CAvQM.com, September 29, 2010.

17. "Goodyear Launches Tire Services," *Fleet Owner Exclusive Insight*, February 22, 2012.

18. Chris Prentice, "The Washers and Dryers that Talk Back," *Bloomberg Businessweek*, August 9, 2010.

19. Paul McDougall, "Movado Builds Customer Ties with Repair Process," *Informationweek*, September 17, 2012.

20. Karen Talley, "The Holiday-Gift Return Free-for-All," *Wall Street Journal*, December 23, 2012.

21. Beth Teitell, "I Hate It. I'll Never Wear It. But I Won't Return It.," *Boston Globe*, January 1, 2011.

22. J. Andrew Petersen and V. Kumar, "Can Product Returns Make You Money?," *MIT Sloan Management Review* 51 (Spring 2010), pp. 85–89.

23. This section is based on a comprehensive treatment of product returns: James Stock, Thomas Speh, and Herbert Shear, "Managing Product Returns for Competitive Advantage," *MIT Sloan Management Review* (Fall 2006), pp. 57–62. See also J. Andrew Petersen and V. Kumar, "Can Product Returns Make You Money?," *MIT Sloan Management Review* (Spring 2010), pp. 85–89.

24. Dave Blanchard, "Moving Forward in Reverse," *Logistics Today*, July 12, 2005; Kelly Shermach, "Taming CRM in the Retail Sector," *CRM Buyer*, October 12, 2006; www.epinions.com, June 28, 2010.

25. Ravindra Chitturi, Rajagopal Raghunathan, and Vijay Mahajan, "Delight by Design: The Role of Hedonic versus Utilitarian Benefits," *Journal of Marketing* 72 (May 2008), pp. 48–63.

26. Linda Tischler, "The United States of Design," *Fast Company*, October 2011.

27. Levent Ozler, "Winners of 2013 International Design Excellence Awards," *Designer*, July 1, 2013; Megan Rose Dickey, "THE DESIGN 75: The Best Designers in Technology," *Business Insider*, May 7, 2013; "The World's Most Innovative Companies," *Forbes*, August 14, 2013.

28. Haydn Shaughnessy, "How Samsung Competes with Apple In Design," *Forbes*, April 19, 2013; "Samsung Wins 39 iF Design Awards This Year!," *Samsung Tomorrow*, March 25, 2013; Melissa J. Perneson, "An Inside Look at Samsung's Approach to Product Design," *Tech Hive*, January 9, 2013.

29. Virginia Postrel, *The Substance of Style: How the Rise of Aesthetic Value Is Remaking Commerce, Culture, and Consciousness* (New York: HarperCollins, 2003).

30. Elena Bergeron, "Keeping Eyes on the Rides," *Fast Company*, September 2012, p. 34.

31. Joe McKendrick, "Bringing Design Thinking to Information Technology," *ZDNet*, April 29, 2013. See also Ananth Narayanan, Asutosh Padhi, and Jim Williams, "Designing Products for Value," *McKinsey Quarterly*, October 2012.

32. Ulrich R. Orth and Keven Malkewitz, "Holistic Package Design and Consumer Brand Impressions," *Journal of Marketing* 72 (May 2008), pp. 64–81.

33. Todd Wasserman, "Thinking by Design," *Brandweek*, November 3, 2008, pp. 18–21.

34. Rachel Lamb, "How Will Bang & Olufsen's Lower-End Product Line Affect the Brand?," *Luxury Daily*, January 12, 2012; Andrew Cave, "Bang & Olufsen Chief Pumps Up the Volume to Make Another Killing for Denmark," *The Telegraph*, December 2, 2012; Jay Green, "Where Designers Rule," *BusinessWeek*, November 5, 2007, pp. 46–51; Deborah Steinborn, "Talking about Design," *Wall Street Journal*, June 23, 2008, p. R6; www.bang-olufsen.com; note that the BeoLab 8000 was replaced by the BeoLab 8002 in 2010.

35. Andrew Roberts, "Louis Vuitton Tops Hermes as World's Most Valuable Luxury Brand," *Bloomberg Businessweek*, May 21, 2012.

36. Thomas Tochterman and Linda Dauriz, "Luxury Lifestyle: Business Beyond Buzzwords," McKinsey white paper report, www.mckinsey.com, June 2012. For recessionary effects on luxury goods, see Wagner A. Kamakura and Rex Yuxing Du, "How Economic Contractions and Expansions Affect Expenditure Patterns," *Journal of Consumer Research*, 39 (August 2012), pp. 229–47.

37. Stellene Volande, "The Secret to Hermès's Success," *Departures*, November–December 2009, pp. 110–12; Cathy Horyn, "Why So Stodgy, Prada.com?," *New York Times*, December 30, 2009.

38. Tricia Carr, "Sub-Zero Pushes Products via Digital Quiz," *Luxury Daily*, April 4, 2012; "Creative Campaigns from Massage Envy, Sub-Zero and Hoveround," *Direct Marketing News*, May 17, 2010; Beth Snyder Bulik, "Sub-Zero Keeps Its Cool in a Value-Obsessed Economy," *Advertising Age*, May 25, 2009, p. 14.

39. "Patrón Tequila Picks Up Steam, Heads toward 2M Cases," *Shanken News Daily*, April 12, 2012; Elizabeth Behrman, "Staying Ahead, On and Off the Track," *Tampa Bay Times*, March 9, 2012; Christopher Palmeri, "The Barroom Brawl over Patron," *BusinessWeek*, September 17, 2007, p. 72.

40. Ariel Adams, "Montblanc on How to Be a Luxury Brand for Many," *Forbes*, March 14, 2013; Lorna Pappas, "Montblanc CEO Shares Pricing and Brand Marketing Insights," *Retail Touchpoints*, October 19, 2012; Ken Kamen, "Investors Should Take a Page from Montblanc's Successful Strategy," *Forbes*, December 20, 2011.

41. Mignon Reyneke, Alexandra Sorokáčová, and Leyland Pitt, "Managing Brands in Times of Economic Downturn: How Do Luxury Brands Fare?," *Journal of Brand Management* 19 (April 2012), pp. 457–66.

42. Christina Binkley, "Like Our Sunglasses? Try Our Vodka! Brand Extensions Get Weirder, Risking Customer Confusion," *Wall Street Journal*, November 8, 2007.

43. "Luxury Habits Mature in China," www.warc.com, December 21, 2012; "China Becomes Biggest Luxury Market," www.warc.com, December 17, 2012.

44. Andrew Roberts, "Building Luxury Brand Loyalty via Exclusive Experiences," *Businessweek*, January 31, 2013.

45. Brett Berk, "Extreme Test Drive," *Bloomberg Businessweek*, May 14, 2012; www.porsche.com/usa/eventsandracing/sportdrivingschool, accessed June 2, 2014.

46. "Luxury Brands Fall Short on the Web," www.warc.com, January 21, 2103; "Gucci Sees Mobile Success," www.warc.com, March 12, 2013; "Fashion Giants Fail on Digital in China," www.warc.com, March 22, 2013; "Luxury Apps Fall Short," www.warc.com, February 21, 2103.

47. Natalie Zmuda, "How the Recession Changed the Luxury-Advertising Landscape," *Advertising Age*, April 25, 2011.

48. "Levi's Introduces New Waste<Less Jean Using Recycled Materials," *Daily News*, August 21, 2013; Flemmich Webb, "Rubbish Jeans: How Levi's Is Turning Plastic into Fashion," *The Guardian*, April 18, 2013; Herb Weisbaum, "Would You Wear These? Jeans Made from Recycled Plastic Bottles," *Today*, March 13, 2013; Susan Berfield, "Levi's Has a

New Color for Blue Jeans: Green," *Bloomberg Businessweek*, October 18, 2012.

49. For branding advantages of a product system, see Ryan Rahinel and Joseph P. Redden, "Brands as Product Coordinators: Matching Brands Make Joint Consumption Experiences More Enjoyable," *Journal of Consumer Research* 39 (April 2013), pp. 1290–99.

50. In reality, Tide's product line is actually deeper and more complex. There are nine powder products, 17 liquid products, one stain release product, one Tide to Go product, one Tide washing machine cleaner, and nine Tide accessories.

51. A. Yesim Orhun, "Optimal Product Line Design when Consumers Exhibit Choice Set-Dependent Preferences," *Marketing Science* 28 (September–October 2009), pp. 868–86; Robert Bordley, "Determining the Appropriate Depth and Breadth of a Firm's Product Portfolio," *Journal of Marketing Research* 40 (February 2003), pp. 39–53; Peter Boatwright and Joseph C. Nunes, "Reducing Assortment: An Attribute-Based Approach," *Journal of Marketing* 65 (July 2001), pp. 50–63.

52. Ryan Hamilton and Alexander Chernev, "The Impact of Product Line Extensions and Consumer Goals on the Formation of Price Image," *Journal of Marketing Research* 47 (February 2010), pp. 51–62.

53. Adapted from a Hamilton Consultants white paper, December 1, 2000.

54. This illustration is found in Benson P. Shapiro, *Industrial Product Policy: Managing the Existing Product Line* (Cambridge, MA: Marketing Science Institute, 1977), pp. 3–5, 98–101.

55. Tim Higgins, "Mercedes Adds Coupe to U.S. C-Class Line in Bid to Top BMW: Cars," www.bloomberg.com, September 26, 2011.

56. Aner Sela, Jonah Berger, and Wendy Liu, "Variety, Vice and Virtue: How Assortment Size Influences Option Choice," *Journal of Consumer Research* 35 (April 2009), pp. 941–51; Cassie Mogilner, Tamar Rudnick, and Sheena S. Iyengar, "The Mere Categorization Effect: How the Presence of Categories Increases Choosers' Perceptions of Assortment Variety and Outcome Satisfaction," *Journal of Consumer Research* 35 (August 2008), pp. 202–15; John Gourville and Dilip Soman, "Overchoice and Assortment Type: When and Why Variety Backfires," *Marketing Science* 24 (Summer 2005), pp. 382–95.

57. Ellen Byron, "Tide Turns 'Basic' for P&G in Slump," *Wall Street Journal*, August 6, 2009; Dan Sewell, "P&G Ends 'Tide Basic' Test, No Word on Plans," *Bloomberg Businessweek*, June 23, 2010.

58. Timothy B. Heath, Devon DelVecchio, and Michael S. McCarthy, "The Asymmetric Effects of Extending Brands to Lower and Higher Quality," *Journal of Marketing* 75 (July 2011), pp. 3–20.

59. "BMW Group Posts Highest Sales Ever in 2012," *PR Newswire*, January 10, 2013; Alex Taylor III, "Bavaria's Next Top Model," *Fortune*, March 30, 2009, pp. 100–3; Alex Taylor III, "The Ultimate Fairly Inexpensive Driving Machine," *Fortune*, November 1, 2004, pp. 130–40.

60. Steuart Henderson Britt, "How Weber's Law Can Be Applied to Marketing," *Business Horizons*, February 1975, pp. 21–29.

61. Brett R. Gordon, "A Dynamic Model of Consumer Replacement Cycles in the PC Processor Industry," *Marketing Science* 28 (September–October 2009), pp. 846–67; Raghunath Singh Rao, Om Narasimhan, and George John, "Understanding the Role of Trade-Ins in Durable Goods Markets: Theory and Evidence," *Marketing Science* 28 (September–October 2009), pp. 950–67.

62. Scott Cendrowski, "Nike's New Marketing Mojo," *Fortune*, February 13, 2012.

63. Nirmalya Kumar, "Kill a Brand, Keep a Customer," *Harvard Business Review*, December 2003, pp. 86–95.

64. Laurens M. Sloot, Dennis Fok, and Peter Verhoef, "The Short- and Long-Term Impact of an Assortment Reduction on Category Sales," *Journal of Marketing Research* 43 (November 2006), pp. 536–48.

65. Joann Muller, "How Volkswagen Will Rule the World," *Forbes*, April 17, 2013; "Volkswagen Brand Turnaround Drives Q1 Group Profits," *Reuters*, April 29, 2010; Andreas Cremer, "VW in 'Last Attempt' to Save Seat amid Spanish Crisis," *Bloomberg Businessweek*, May 14, 2010; George Rädler, Jan Kubes, and Bohdan Wojnar, "Skoda Auto: From 'No-Class' to World-Class in One Decade," *Critical EYE* 15 (July 2006).

66. Eric T. Anderson and Duncan I. Simester, "Does Demand Fall when Customers Perceive That Prices Are Unfair? The Case of Premium Pricing for Large Sizes," *Marketing Science* 27 (May–June 2008), pp. 492–500.

67. "2014 Subaru Outback Review," www.edmunds.com, accessed August 17, 2013.

68. Ricard Gil and Wesley R. Hartmann, "Empirical Analysis of Metering Price Discrimination: Evidence from Concession Sales at Movie Theaters," *Marketing Science* 28 (November–December 2009), pp. 1046–62.

69. Rick Aristotle Munarriz, "Why Hewlett-Packard Will Never Be Great Again," *Daily Finance*, August 8, 2012; Kevin Kelleher, "HP's Printer Problem," *Fortune*, March 29, 2012; Connie Guglielmo, "Hewlett-Packard Says Printer Business Is 'Healthy,'" *Bloomberg News*, December 22, 2009; "HP Annual Report 2008."

70. R. Venkatesh and Vijay Mahajan, "The Design and Pricing of Bundles: A Review of Normative Guidelines and Practical Approaches," Vithala R. Rao, ed., *Handbook of Pricing Research in Marketing* (Northampton, MA: Edward Elgar Publishing Company, 2009), pp. 232–57.

71. Jerilyn Klein Bier, "Want to Make A Bundle? Try Bundling," *Automotive News*, March 28, 2012.

72. Dilip Soman and John T. Gourville, "Transaction Decoupling: How Price Bundling Affects the Decision to Consume," *Journal of Marketing Research* 38 (February 2001), pp. 30–44; Ramanathan Subramaniam and R. Venkatesh, "Optimal Bundling Strategies in Multiobject Auctions of Complements or Substitutes," *Marketing Science* 28 (March–April 2009), pp. 264–73.

73. Anita Elberse, "Bye-Bye Bundles: The Unbundling of Music in Digital Channels," *Journal of Marketing* 74 (May 2010), pp. 107–23.

74. Tansev Geylani, J. Jeffrey Inman, and Frenkel Ter Hofstede, "Image Reinforcement or Impairment: The Effects of Co-Branding on Attribute Uncertainty," *Marketing Science* 27 (July–August 2008), pp. 730–44; Ed Lebar, Phil Buehler, Kevin Lane Keller, Monika Sawicka, Zeynep Aksehirli, and Keith Richey, "Brand Equity Implications of Joint Branding Programs," *Journal of Advertising Research* 45 (December 2005).

75. Based in part on a talk by Nancy Bailey, "Using Licensing to Build the Brand," Brand Masters Conference, December 7, 2000.

76. Philip Kotler and Waldermar Pfoertsch, *Ingredient Branding: Making the Invisible Visible* (Heidelberg, Germany: Springer-Verlag, 2011).

77. Simon Graj, "Intel, Gore-Tex and Eastman: The Provenance of Ingredient Branding," *Forbes*, July 10, 2013; Anil Jayaraj, "Solving Ingredient Branding Puzzle," *Business Standard*, August 13, 2012.

78. "Facts and Figures," www.vibram.com, accessed August 17, 2013.

79. Kalpesh Kaushik Desai and Kevin Lane Keller, "The Effects of Brand Expansions and Ingredient Branding Strategies on Host Brand Extendibility," *Journal of Marketing* 66 (January 2002), pp. 73–93.

80. Martin Bishop, "Finding Your Nemo: How to Survive the Dangerous Waters of Ingredient Branding," *Chief Executive*, March 15, 2010.

81. "DuPont Receives Corporate Innovation Award," DuPont, www.dupont.com, November 13, 2009.

82. Kevin Lane Keller, *Strategic Brand Management,* 4th ed. (Upper Saddle River, NJ: Prentice Hall, 2013). See also Philip Kotler and Waldemar Pfoertsch, *B2B Brand Management* (New York: Springer, 2006).

83. "New and Improved?," *Consumer Reports*, September 2013, pp. 12–13.

84. Howard Fox, "The Secret Language of Colour," *Brands & Branding*, October 2010, pp. 48–50. See also Lauren Labrecque and George Milne, "Exciting Red and Competent Blue: The Importance of Color in Marketing," *Journal of the Academy of Marketing Science* 40 (September 2012), pp. 711–27; and Niki Hynes, "Colour and Meaning in Corporate Logos: An Empirical Study," *Journal of Brand Management* 16 (July/August 2009), pp. 545–55.

85. Stuart Elliott, "Tropicana Discovers Some Buyers Are Passionate about Packaging," *New York Times*, February 23, 2009; Linda Tischler, "Never Mind! Pepsi Pulls Much-Loathed Tropicana Packaging," *Fast*

*Company,* February 23, 2009; Natalie Zmuda, "Tropicana Line's Sales Plunge 20% Post-Rebranding," *Advertising Age,* April 2, 2009; Kenneth Hein, "Tropicana Squeezes Out Fresh Design with a Peel," *Brandweek,* January 19, 2009, p. 30.

86. John Pflueger, "How Dell Turned Bamboo and Mushrooms into Environmental-Friendly Packaging," *MIT Sloan Management Review,* July 17, 2012; Caroline Lennon, "5 Companies Producing Products with Eco-Friendly Packaging," *One Green Planet,* April 2, 2013.

87. Sarah Skidmore, "SunChips Biodegradable Bag Made Quieter for Critics," *Huffington Post,* February 24, 2011; Bruce Horovitz, "Frito-Lay Sends Noisy, 'Green' SunChips Bag to the Dump," *USA Today,* October 5, 2010; Suzanne Vranica, "Snack Attack: Chip Eaters Make Noise about a Crunchy Bag," *Wall Street Journal,* August 18, 2010.

88. John C. Kozup, Elizabeth H. Creyer, and Scot Burton, "Making Healthful Food Choices: The Influence of Health Claims and Nutrition Information on Consumers' Evaluations of Packaged Food Products and Restaurant Menu Items," *Journal of Marketing* 67 (April 2003), pp. 19–34; Siva K. Balasubramanian and Catherine Cole, "Consumers' Search and Use of Nutrition Information: The Challenge and Promise of the Nutrition Labeling and Education Act," *Journal of Marketing* 66 (July 2002), pp. 112–27.

89. Sean Poulter, "How Food Labels Can Mislead Shoppers about Fat Content," *Daily Mail,* September 1, 2010. For some FDA background, see "Guidance for Industry: A Food Labeling Guide," www.fda.gov/food/GuidanceRegulation, October 2009.

90. Robert Berner, "Watch Out, Best Buy and Circuit City," *BusinessWeek,* November 21, 2005, pp. 46–48.

91. Tao Chen, Ajay Kalra, and Baohung Sun, "Why Do Consumers Buy Extended Service Contracts," *Journal of Consumer Research* 36 (December 2009), pp. 611–23.

92. Chris Serres, "More Electronics Buyers Skip Extended Warranties," *Minneapolis Star Tribune,* July 14, 2007. For an empirical study, see Junhong Chu and Pradeep K. Chintagunta, "Quantifying the Economic Value of Warranties in the U.S. Server Market," *Marketing Science* 28 (January–February 2009), pp. 99–121.

## Chapter 14

1. Leonard L. Berry, *On Great Service: A Framework for Action* (New York: Free Press, 2006), as well as others of his texts.

2. John Adams, "How USAA Innovates Online Banking," *American Banker,* September 1, 2012; David Rohde, "In the Era of Greed, Meet America's Good Bank: USAA," *The Atlantic,* January 27, 2012; Jena McGregor, "USAA's Battle Plan," *Bloomberg BusinessWeek,* March 1, 2010; "Customer Service Champs," *BusinessWeek,* March 5, 2007; Allison Enright, "Serve Them Right," *Marketing News,* May 1, 2006.

3. "Employment by Major Industry Sector, 2000, 2010, and Projected 2020," Bureau of Labor Statistics, www.bls.gov, February 1, 2012.

4. For a thorough review of academic research into services, see Roland T. Rust and Tuck Siong Chung, "Marketing Models of Service and Relationships," *Marketing Science* 25 (November–December 2006), pp. 560–80; and Roland T. Rust and Ming-Hui Huang, *Service Marketing: Insights and Direction,* Fast Forward Series (Cambridge, MA: Marketing Science Institute, 2011).

5. Annie Gasparro, "A New Test for Panera's Pay-What-You-Can," *Wall Street Journal,* June 4, 2013; Brandon Gutman, "Panera Bread Doubles Digital Spend from Last Year," *Forbes,* February 20, 2013; Stuart Elliott, "Selling Products by Selling Shared Values," *New York Times,* February 13, 2013; Ben Fox, "Panera Bread Net up 34% on Same Store Sales Growth," *Wall Street Journal,* February 5, 2013; Beth Kowitt, "A Founder's Bold Gamble on Panera," *Fortune,* August 13, 2012; Jenn Abelson, "Bread and Circumstance," *Boston.com,* February 14, 2010; Kate Rockwood, "Rising Dough," *Fast Company,* October 2009, pp. 69–71.

6. Valarie A. Zeithaml, "How Consumer Evaluation Processes Differ between Goods and Services," J. Donnelly and W. R. George, eds., *Marketing of Services* (Chicago: American Marketing Association, 1981), pp. 186–90.

7. Jin Sun, Hean Tat Keh, and Angela Y. Lee, "The Effect of Attribute Alignability on Service Evaluation: The Moderating Role of

Uncertainty," *Journal of Consumer Research* 39 (December 2012), pp. 831–47.

8. "After Recent Cruise Disasters, Carnival Tries to Right the Ship," *CBS News,* September 3, 2013; Brad Tuttle, "Four Months after the 'Poop Cruise,' the Carnival Triumph Sails Again—and Is Sold Out," *Time,* June 14, 2013; Allan Adamson and Chekitan Dev, "Can Carnival Recover from the Damage to Its Brand?," *Marketing Daily,* April 12, 2013; "Cruise Ship Fire Started with Leaking Fuel-Oil Line," *KTLA 5,* February 19, 2013; Lateef Mungin and Steve Almasy, "Crippled Cruise Ship Returns; Passengers Happy to Be Back," *CNN,* February 15, 2013.

9. For discussion of how the blurring of the line distinguishing products and services changes the meaning of this taxonomy, see Christopher Lovelock and Evert Gummesson, "Whither Services Marketing? In Search of a New Paradigm and Fresh Perspectives," *Journal of Service Research* 7 (August 2004), pp. 20–41; and Stephen L. Vargo and Robert F. Lusch, "Evolving to a New Dominant Logic for Marketing," *Journal of Marketing* 68 (January 2004), pp. 1–17.

10. Theodore Levitt, "Marketing Intangible Products and Product Intangibles," *Harvard Business Review,* May–June 1981, pp. 94–102; Leonard L. Berry, "Services Marketing Is Different," *Business,* May–June 1980, pp. 24–29.

11. B. H. Booms and M. J. Bitner, "Marketing Strategies and Organizational Structures for Service Firms," J. Donnelly and W. R. George, eds., *Marketing of Services* (Chicago: American Marketing Association, 1981), pp. 47–51.

12. Bernd H. Schmitt, *Customer Experience Management* (New York: John Wiley & Sons, 2003); Bernd H. Schmitt, David L. Rogers, and Karen Vrotsos (2003), *There's No Business That's Not Show Business: Marketing in an Experience Culture* (Upper Saddle River, NJ: Prentice Hall Financial Times, 2004).

13. For some emerging research results on the effects of creating time and place service separation, see Hean Tat Keh and Jun Pang, "Customer Reaction to Service Separation," *Journal of Marketing* 74 (March 2010), pp. 55–70.

14. "The Client: Larry Traxler and Dave Horton, Hilton," *Hospitality Style,* November 15, 2012; David Carey, "Cleaning Up at Hilton," *The Deal Magazine,* July 22, 2011; "Hilton Brand Unveils New Lobby Look," *National Real Estate Investor,* April 19, 2011; "Princess Cruises, Hilton Hotels, Southwest Airlines, and Enterprise Rental Cars Rank Highest in Brand Equity by Category: 2010 Harris Poll EquiTrend Results," Harris Interactive, March 23, 2010.

15. Rebecca J. Slotegraaf and J. Jeffrey Inman, "Longitudinal Shifts in the Drivers of Satisfaction with Product Quality: The Role of Attribute Resolvability," *Journal of Marketing Research* 41 (August 2004), pp. 269–80.

16. The material in this paragraph is based in part on Valarie Zeithaml, Mary Jo Bitner, and Dwayne D. Gremler, "Service Innovation and Design," *Services Marketing: Integrating Customer Focus across the Firm,* 6th ed. (New York: McGraw-Hill, 2013), chapter 8.

17. John DeVine, Shyam Lal, and Michael Zea, "The Human Factor in Service Design," *McKinsey Quarterly,* January 2012; G. Lynn Shostack, "Service Positioning through Structural Change," *Journal of Marketing* 51 (January 1987), pp. 34–43.

18. Vikas Mittal, Wagner A. Kamakura, and Rahul Govind, "Geographical Patterns in Customer Service and Satisfaction: An Empirical Investigation," *Journal of Marketing* 68 (July 2004), pp. 48–62.

19. Jeffrey F. Rayport, Bernard J. Jaworski, and Ellie J. Kyung, "Best Face Forward: Improving Companies' Service Interface with Customers," *Journal of Interactive Marketing* 19 (Autumn 2005), pp. 67–80; Asim Ansari and Carl F. Mela, "E-Customization," *Journal of Marketing Research* 40 (May 2003), pp. 131–45.

20. W. Earl Sasser, "Match Supply and Demand in Service Industries," *Harvard Business Review,* November–December 1976, pp. 133–40.

21. Steven M. Shugan and Jinhong Xie, "Advance Selling for Services," *California Management Review* 46 (Spring 2004), pp. 37–54; Eyal Biyalogorsky and Eitan Gerstner, "Contingent Pricing to Reduce Price Risks," *Marketing Science* 23 (Winter 2004), pp. 146–55.

22. Karl Taro Greenfeld, "Fast and Furious," *Bloomberg Businessweek*, May 9, 2011.

23. David Fickling, "Singapore Airlines' Competition Rises," *Bloomberg Businessweek*, May 17, 2012; Loizos Heracleous and Jochen Wirtz, "Singapore Airlines' Balancing Act," *Harvard Business Review*, July/August, 2010; James Wallace, "Singapore Airlines Raises the Bar for Luxury Flying," *Seattle Post Intelligencer*, January 18, 2007; Justin Doebele, "The Engineer," *Forbes,* January 9, 2006, pp. 122–24; www.singaporeair.com.

24. David Roe, "Forrester's Customer Experience Index: The Good, The Bad and the Poor," www.cmswire.com, January 17, 2013; "The Emerging Role of Social Customer Experience in Customer Care," www.lithium.com, May 2013; "The State of Customer Experience, 2012," white paper, Forrester Research, Inc., April 24, 2012; Josh Bernoff, "Numbers Show Marketing Value in Sustaining Good Customer Service," *Advertising Age*, January 17, 2011.

25. Cheryl Conner, "Why Every Organization Needs a Standard Response Time Policy," *Forbes*, August 16, 2013; Cheryl Conner, "The 5 Ways Companies Mishandle Online Complaints," *Forbes*, August 2, 2013. See also Guda van Noort and Lotte M. Willemsen, "Online Damage Control: The Effects of Proactive versus Reactive Webcare Interventions in Consumer-Generated and Brand-Generated Platforms," *Journal of Interactive Marketing* 26 (August 2012), pp. 131–40.

26. "Butterball, LLC," *Hoover's Company Records*, October 15, 2012; Stephanie Warren, "Turkey 911! Butterball's Hotline Saves Your Thanksgiving," *Popular Mechanics*, November 23, 2011.

27. Elisabeth Sullivan, "Happy Endings Lead to Happy Returns," *Marketing News*, October 30, 2009, p. 20.

28. "How to Provide Customer Self-Service Online," *Inc.*, accessed August 17, 2012; Nikki Hopewell, "Moyer Is Committed to Delivering a Comcastic Experience," *Marketing News*, October 15, 2008, pp. 28–30.

29. https://twitter.com/DeltaAssist; "Delta Airlines Tracks the Pulse of Its Customers, Responds with Twitter," *Ragan's PR Daily*, 2012; "Delta Assist Brings Airline Customer Service to Facebook," www.SimpliFlying.com, March 14, 2011; "The Stevie Awards for Sales & Customer Service," www.stevieawards.com, 2013.

30. Matthew Dixon, Karen Freeman, and Nicholas Toman, "Stop Trying to Delight Your Customers," *Harvard Business Review*, July–August 2010, pp. 116–22.

31. Chi Kin (Bennett) Yim, Kimmy Wa Chan, and Simon S. K. Lam, "Do Customers and Employees Enjoy Service Participation? Synergistic Effects of Self- and Other-Efficacy," *Journal of Marketing* 76 (November 2012), pp. 121–40; Zhenfeng Ma & Laurette Dubé, "Process and Outcome Interdependency in Frontline Service Encounters," *Journal of Marketing* 75 (May 2011), pp. 83–98; Stephen S. Tax, Mark Colgate, and David Bowen, "How to Prevent Your Customers from Failing," *MIT Sloan Management Review* (Spring 2006), pp. 30–38.

32. Kimmy Wa Chan, Chi Kin (Bennett) Yim, and Simon S. K. Lam, "Is Customer Participation in Value Creation a Double-Edged Sword? Evidence from Professional Financial Services Across Cultures," *Journal of Marketing* 74 (May 2010), pp. 48–64.

33. Valarie Zeithaml, Mary Jo Bitner, and Dwayne D. Gremler, *Services Marketing: Integrating Customer Focus across the Firm*, 6th ed. (New York: McGraw-Hill, 2013).

34. Rachel R. Chen, Eitan Gerstner, and Yinghui (Catherine) Yang, "Customer Bill of Rights Under No-Fault Service Failure: Confinement and Compensation," *Marketing Science* 31 (January/February 2012), pp. 157–71; Michael Sanserino and Cari Tuna, "Companies Strive Harder to Please Customers," *Wall Street Journal*, July 27, 2009, p. B4.

35. James L. Heskett, W, Earl Sasser Jr., and Joe Wheeler, *Ownership Quotient: Putting the Service Profit Chain to Work for Unbeatable Competitive Advantage* (Boston, MA: Harvard Business School Press, 2008).

36. D. Todd Donovan, Tom J. Brown, and John C. Mowen, "Internal Benefits of Service Worker Customer Orientation: Job Satisfaction, Commitment, and Organizational Citizenship Behaviors," *Journal of Marketing* 68 (January 2004), pp. 128–46.

37. Dan Heath and Chip Heath, "I Love You. Now What?," *Fast Company*, October 2008, pp. 95–96.

38. Evan Hessel, "Kung Pao Chicken for the Soul," *Forbes*, April 21, 2008, pp. 106–7.

39. Jeffrey Hollender, "Lessons We Can All Learn from Zappos CEO Tony Hsieh," *The Guardian*, March 14, 2013; Tricia Morris, "Using Metrics to Create a Zappos-Like Customer Service Culture," *Parature*, November 13, 2012; Mig Pascual, "Zappos: 5 Out-of-the-Box Ideas for Keeping Employees Engaged," *U.S. News*, October 30, 2012; Helen Coster, "A Step Ahead," *Forbes*, June 2, 2008, pp. 78–80; Paula Andruss, "Delivering Wow through Service," *Marketing News*, October 15, 2008, p. 10; Jeffrey M. O'Brien, "Zappos Knows How to Kick It," *Fortune*, February 2, 2009, pp. 55–60; Brian Morrissey, "Amazon to Buy Zappos," *Adweek*, July 22, 2009; Christopher Palmeri, "Now for Sale, the Zappos Culture," *Bloomberg BusinessWeek*, January 11, 2010, p. 57.

40. Frances X. Frei, "The Four Things a Service Business Must Get Right," *Harvard Business Review*, April 2008, pp. 70–80.

41. Christian Gronroos, "A Service-Quality Model and Its Marketing Implications," *European Journal of Marketing* 18 (1984), pp. 36–44.

42. Detelina Marinova, Jun Ye, and Jagdip Singh, "Do Frontline Mechanisms Matter? Impact of Quality and Productivity Orientations on Unit Revenue, Efficiency, and Customer Satisfaction," *Journal of Marketing* 72 (March 2008), pp. 28–45.

43. Christian Gronroos, "A Service-Quality Model and Its Marketing Implications," *European Journal of Marketing* 18 (1984), pp. 36–44.

44. Ad de Jong, Ko de Ruyter, and Jos Lemmink, "Antecedents and Consequences of the Service Climate in Boundary-Spanning Self-Managing Service Teams," *Journal of Marketing* 68 (April 2004), pp. 18–35; Michael D. Hartline and O. C. Ferrell, "The Management of Customer-Contact Service Employees: An Empirical Investigation," *Journal of Marketing* 60 (October 1996), pp. 52–70; Christian Homburg, Jan Wieseke, and Torsten Bornemann, "Implementing the Marketing Concept at the Employee-Customer Interface: The Role of Customer Need Knowledge," *Journal of Marketing* 73 (July 2009), pp. 64–81; Chi Kin (Bennett) Yim, David K. Tse, and Kimmy Wa Chan, "Strengthening Customer Loyalty through Intimacy and Passion: Roles of Customer-Firm Affection and Customer-Staff Relationships," *Journal of Marketing Research* 45 (December 2008), pp. 741–56.

45. "Charles Schwab Launches Brokerage and Schwab Bank Mobile Deposit for iPad," www.markets.on.nytimes.com, September 11, 2011; Sheridan Prasso, "Charles Schwab's Money Moves," *Fortune*, June 13, 2011; Betsy Morris, "Chuck Schwab Is Worried about the Small Investor. Does That Mean We Should Be Worried Too?," *Bloomberg Businessweek*, May 31, 2010; Rob Markey, Fred Reichheld, and Andreas Dullweber, "Closing the Customer Feedback Loop," *Harvard Business Review*, December 2009, pp. 43–47.

46. William Baldwin, "Who Needs Bank Branches?," *Forbes*, August 22, 2011.

47. Michael Sanserino and Cari Tuna, "Companies Strive Harder to Please Customers," *Wall Street Journal*, July 27, 2009, p. B4.

48. Jena McGregor, "When Service Means Survival," *BusinessWeek*, March 2, 2009, pp. 26–30.

49. Roland T. Rust and Ming-Hui Huang, "Optimizing Service Productivity," *Journal of Marketing* 76 (March 2012), pp. 47–66.

50. Linda Ferrell and O.C. Ferrell, "Redirecting Direct Selling: High-touch Embraces High-tech," *Business Horizons* 55 (May 2012), pp. 273–81.

51. Heather Green, "How Amazon Aims to Keep You Clicking," *BusinessWeek*, March 2, 2009, pp. 34–40.

52. Allison Enright, "Live Chat Use Is on the Rise, Survey Says," *Internet Retailer*, May 10, 2011.

53. Gregory Jones, "Jim Weddle Is Positioning Edward Jones to Be the Top of Mind Choice," *Smart Business*, May 31, 2013; www.edwardjones.com/en_US/different/index.html, accessed June 2, 2014;

Jena McGregor, "Customer Service Champs," *BusinessWeek*, March 5, 2007, pp. 52–64.

54. Paul Hagen, "The Rise of the Chief Customer Officer," *Forbes*, February 16, 2011.

55. Suzanne Kapner, "Citi Won't Sleep on Customer Tweets," *Wall Street Journal*, October 4, 2012.

56. Jena McGregor, "When Service Means Survival," *BusinessWeek*, March 2, 2009, pp. 26–30.

57. John A. Martilla and John C. James, "Importance-Performance Analysis," *Journal of Marketing* 41 (January 1977), pp. 77–79.

58. Dave Dougherty and Ajay Murthy, "What Service Customers Really Want," *Harvard Business Review*, September 2009, p. 22; for a contrarian point of view, see Edward Kasabov, "The Compliant Customer," *MIT Sloan Management Review* (Spring 2010), pp. 18–19.

59. Jeffrey G. Blodgett and Ronald D. Anderson, "A Bayesian Network Model of the Customer Complaint Process," *Journal of Service Research* 2 (May 2000), pp. 321–38.

60. Jeroen Schepers, Tomas Falk, Ko de Ruyter, Ad de Jong, and Maik Hammerschmidt, "Principles and Principals: Do Customer Stewardship and Agency Control Compete or Complement when Shaping Frontline Employee Behavior?," *Journal of Marketing* 76 (November 2012), pp. 1–20; James G. Maxham III and Richard G. Netemeyer, "Firms Reap What They Sow: The Effects of Shared Values and Perceived Organizational Justice on Customers' Evaluations of Complaint Handling," *Journal of Marketing* 67 (January 2003), pp. 46–62; Jagdip Singh, "Performance Productivity and Quality of Frontline Employees in Service Organizations," *Journal of Marketing* 64 (April 2000), pp. 15–34.

61. Stephen S. Tax, Stephen W. Brown, and Murali Chandrashekaran, "Customer Evaluations of Service Complaint Experiences: Implications for Relationship Marketing," *Journal of Marketing* 62 (April 1998), pp. 60–76.

62. Brad Tuttle, "One Airline That Stubbornly Refuses to Pile on the Fees (for Now)," *Time*, May 7, 2013; Jennifer Rooney, "Southwest Airlines CMO Kevin Krone Explains What's Behind the New Grown-Up Ads," *Forbes*, April 22, 2013; Brad Tuttle, "Southwest Airlines: We're Not Really about Cheap Flights Anymore," *Time*, March 26, 2013; David Whelan, "All Grown Up," *Forbes*, July 18, 2011. Dan Tracy, "JetBlue Revives Plans for Trainee Hotel at Orlando Airport," *Orlando Sentinel*, August 19, 2013; Justin Bachman, "How JetBlue Aims to Grab Some High-Dollar Traffic," *Bloomberg*, June 13, 2013; Robin Farzad and Justin Bachman, "Once High-Flying, JetBlue Returns to Earth," *Bloomberg Businessweek*, April 5, 2012.

63. Lisa Shidler, "John Bogle Tells the Morningstar Crowd Just Why the Vanguard Group Has a Problem," www.riabiz.com, June 14, 2013; Eric Schurenberg, "How I Did It: John Bogle of the Vanguard Group," *Inc*, September 25, 2012.

64. Sarah Turcotte, "Rousing Hotel Retail," *Fast Company*, December 2012/January 2013, p. 50; Joseph DeAcetis, "Seaside Luxe: Branding the Retail Space to Fit a Resort's Clientele," *Forbes*, May 17, 2012.

65. Jessi Hempel, "Salesforce Hits Its Stride," *Fortune*, March 2, 2009, pp. 29–32.

66. Leonard Berry, Venkatesh Shankar, Janet Turner Parish, Susan Cadwallader, and Thomas Dotzel, "Creating New Markets through Service Innovation," *Sloan Management Review* 47 (Winter 2006), pp. 56–63.

67. Dinah Eng, "The Rise of Cirque du Soleil," *Fortune*, November 7, 2011, pp. 39–42; Matt Krantz, "Tinseltown Gets Glitzy New Star," *USA Today*, August 24, 2009; Linda Tischler, "Join the Circus," *Fast Company*, July 2005, pp. 53–58; "Cirque du Soleil," *America's Greatest Brands* 3 (2004); Geoff Keighley, "The Factory," *Business 2.0*, February 2004, p. 102; Robin D. Rusch, "Cirque du Soleil Phantasmagoria Contorts," Brandchannel.com, December 1, 2003.

68. Thomas Dotzel, Venkatesh Shankar, and Leonard L. Berry, "Service Innovativeness and Firm Value," *Journal of Marketing Research* 50 (April 2013), pp. 259–76.

69. Roger Yu, "Sheraton Has Designs on Fresh Look," *USA Today*, August 26, 2008, p. 4B.

70. Bruce Upbin, "Why Hipmunk Is the World's Best Travel Site," *Forbes*, June 29, 2012; Luke O'Brien, "Travel Search Gets Hip (Again)," *Fast Company*, March 2011, p. 40; Tomio Geron, "Priceline Buying Travel Site Kayak for $1.8 Billion," *Forbes*, November 8, 2012; Geoff Colvin, "Kayak Takes on the Big Dogs," *Fortune*, September 27, 2012; Michael J. De La Merced, "For Kayak Founders, Winding Journey to an I.P.O. Ends," *New York Times*, July 20, 2012.

71. "MinuteClinic Opens Its First Walk-in Medical Clinics Inside CVS/Pharmacy Stores in Cincinnati and Dayton," *PRNewswire*, October 4, 2012; Shelly Banjo, "Wal-Mart's New Health Push," *Wall Street Journal*, August 23, 2012; Peter West, "Retail Medical Clinics Offer Quality Care: Study," *HealthDay*, August 31, 2009; Ellen McGirt, "Fast Food Medicine," *Fast Company*, September 2007, pp. 37–38.

72. Joe Sharkey, "Clearing Skies for Private Jets," *New York Times*, August 20, 2012; Dealbook, "Berkshire Hathaway's NetJets to Buy Marquis Jet," *New York Times*, November 4, 2010; "Kenny Dichter: A Big Idea Takes Off," Special Advertising Supplement, CIT Behind the Business, *Condé Nast Portfolio*, September 2007.

73. Meghan Casserly, "Blow Out," *Forbes*, November 19, 2012, pp. 66–70; George Anders, "What Is Reddit Worth?," *Forbes*, November 19, 2012, pp. 56–60; Nick Leiber, "Elderly Care, A Click Away," *Bloomberg Businessweek*, October 29, 2012.

74. Eric Savitz, "Can Ticketmaster CEO Nathan Hubbard Fix the Ticket Market," *Forbes*, February 18, 2011.

75. Abbey Klaasen, "How Wells Fargo Has Evolved Its Marketing to Fit a Larger Footprint," *Ad Age*, August 20, 2013; Geoff Colvin, "Wells Fargo CEO: Why Americans Are Saving So Much," *Fortune*, November 26, 2012; Steve Denning, "Does Wells Fargo Practice Radical Management?," *Forbes*, January 30, 2012.

76. Susan M. Keaveney, "Customer Switching Behavior in Service Industries: An Exploratory Study," *Journal of Marketing* 59 (April 1995), pp. 71–82.

77. Dave Dougherty and Ajay Murthy, "What Service Customers Really Want," *Harvard Business Review*, September 2009, p. 22.

78. Roland T. Rust and Richard L. Oliver, "Should We Delight the Customer?," *Journal of the Academy of Marketing Science* 28 (December 2000), pp. 86–94.

79. "American Express Ranks Highest in Customer Service for the Seventh Consecutive Year," *Business Wire*, August 22, 2013; Blake Ellis, "America's Favorite Credit Card," *Fortune*, August 22, 2013; Geoff Colvin, "How Can American Express Help You?," *Fortune*, April 30, 2012; "100 Best Companies to Work For," *Fortune*, 2012

80. A. Parasuraman, Valarie A. Zeithaml, and Leonard L. Berry, "A Conceptual Model of Service Quality and Its Implications for Future Research," *Journal of Marketing* 49 (Fall 1985), pp. 41–50. See also Michael K. Brady and J. Joseph Cronin Jr., "Some New Thoughts on Conceptualizing Perceived Service Quality," *Journal of Marketing* 65 (July 2001), pp. 34–49.

81. Leonard L. Berry and A. Parasuraman, *Marketing Services: Competing through Quality* (New York: Free Press, 1991), p. 16.

82. Parasuraman, Zeithaml, and Berry, "A Conceptual Model of Service Quality and Its Implications for Future Research," pp. 41–50.

83. William Boulding, Ajay Kalra, Richard Staelin, and Valarie A. Zeithaml, "A Dynamic Model of Service Quality: From Expectations to Behavioral Intentions," *Journal of Marketing Research* 30 (February 1993), pp. 7–27.

84. Roland T. Rust and Tuck Siong Chung, "Marketing Models of Service and Relationships," *Marketing Science* 25 (November–December 2006), pp. 560–80; Katherine N. Lemon, Tiffany Barnett White, and Russell S. Winer, "Dynamic Customer Relationship Management: Incorporating Future Considerations into the Service Retention Decision," *Journal of Marketing* 66 (January 2002), pp. 1–14.

85. Kent Grayson and Tim Ambler, "The Dark Side of Long-Term Relationships in Marketing Services," *Journal of Marketing Research* 36 (February 1999), pp. 132–41.

86. Leonard L. Berry, Kathleen Seiders, and Dhruv Grewal, "Understanding Service Convenience," *Journal of Marketing* 66 (July 2002), pp. 1–17.

87. Sarah Nassauer, "Chili's to Install Tabletop Computer Screens," *Wall Street Journal*, September 15, 2013.

88. Sarah Turcotte, "The Wait Is Over," *Fast Company*, September 2012.

89. J. J. Colao, "Last Man Sitting," *Forbes*, November 18, 2013, p. 88; Tomio Geren, "Facebook Moves into Local Commerce with OpenTable Restaurant Bookings," *Forbes*, August 12, 2013; Brian X. Chen, "OpenTable Begins Testing Mobile Payments," *New York Times*, July 30, 2013; Brian X. Chen, "OpenTable to Acquire Foodspotting for $10 Million," *New York Times*, January 29, 2013; Richard McGill Murphy, "Your Table Is Waiting at OpenTable," *Fortune*, October 3, 2012.

90. "Help Yourself," *Economist*, July 2, 2009, pp. 62–63.

91. "Comcast Gets By without Providing Customer Service," *SBWire*, August 12, 2013; Dominic Basulto, "Can Silicon Valley Re-Invent Customer Service," *The Washington Post*, April 19, 2013.

92. Jeffrey F. Rayport and Bernard J. Jaworski, *Best Face Forward* (Boston: Harvard Business School Press, 2005); Jeffrey F. Rayport, Bernard J. Jaworski, and Ellie J. Kyung, "Best Face Forward," *Journal of Interactive Marketing* 19 (Autumn 2005), pp. 67–80; Jeffrey F. Rayport and Bernard J. Jaworski, "Best Face Forward," *Harvard Business Review*, December 2004, pp. 47–58.

93. Matthew L. Meuter, Mary Jo Bitner, Amy L. Ostrom, and Stephen W. Brown, "Choosing among Alternative Service Delivery Modes: An Investigation of Customer Trial of Self-Service Technologies," *Journal of Marketing* 69 (April 2005), pp. 61–83.

94. Ian Urbina, "Your Train Will Be Late She Says Cheerily," *New York Times*, November 24, 2004.

95. Venkatesh Shankar, Leonard L. Berry and Thomas Dotzel, "A Practical Guide to Combining Products and Services," *Harvard Business Review*, November 2009, pp. 94–99.

96. Eric Fang, Robert W. Palmatier, and Jan-Benedict E. M. Steenkamp, "Effect of Service Transition Strategies on Firm Value," *Journal of Marketing* 72 (September 2008), pp. 1–14.

97. Mark Vandenbosch and Niraj Dawar, "Beyond Better Products: Capturing Value in Customer Interactions," *MIT Sloan Management Review* 43 (Summer 2002), pp. 35–42.

98. Byron G. Auguste, Eric P. Harmon, and Vivek Pandit, "The Right Service Strategies for Product Companies," *McKinsey Quarterly* 1 (2006), pp. 41–51.

99. Goutam Challagalla, R. Venkatesh, and Ajay K. Kohli, "Proactive Postsales Service: When and Why Does It Pay Off?," *Journal of Marketing* 73 (March 2009), pp. 70–87.

## Chapter 15

1. Joann Muller, "OnStar Mirror: When Only a Human Will Do," *Forbes*, May 3, 2012; "OnStar FMV: Bringing OnStar to Non-GM Vehicles," www.AolAutos.com, September 4, 2012; Carrie Kim, "Testing OnStar's Add-on Kit," *Chicago Tribune*, October 19, 2011; David Pogue, "OnStar for All Who Have the Wherewithal," *New York Times*, August 31, 2011.

2. For some scholarly reviews, see John R. Hauser, Gerald Tellis, and Abbie Griffin, "Research on Innovation: A Review and Agenda for Marketing Science," *Marketing Science*, 25, (November/December 2006), pp. 687–717; Ely Dahan and John R. Hauser, "Product Development: Managing a Dispersed Process," Bart Weitz and Robin Wensley, eds., *Handbook of Marketing* (London: Sage, 2002), pp. 179–222; Dipak Jain, "Managing New-Product Development for Strategic Competitive Advantage," Dawn Iacobucci, ed., *Kellogg on Marketing* (New York: Wiley, 2001), pp. 130–48; for an overview of different industry approaches, see Frank T. Rothaermel and Andrew M. Hess, "Innovation Strategies Combined," *MIT Sloan Management Review* (Spring 2010), pp. 13–15. See also Merle Crawford and Anthony Di Benedetto, *New Products Management*, 10th ed. (New York: McGraw-Hill, 2011).

3. "Brands A–Z, Nestlé," www.nestlé.com, retrieved February 3, 2013.

4. Scott Sanderude, "Growth from Harvesting the Sky: The $200 Million Challenge," talk at Marketing Science Institute Conference: New Frontiers for Growth, Boston, MA, April 2005.

5. Stephen J. Carson, "When to Give Up Control of Outsourced New-Product Development," *Journal of Marketing* 71 (January 2007), pp. 49–66.

6. "2013 Best New Product Awards—Shopping List," www.betterhomesandgardens.com, retrieved February 3, 2013.

7. For some academic discussion of the effects of new-product introductions on markets, see Harald J. Van Heerde, Carl F. Mela, and Puneet Manchanda, "The Dynamic Effect of Innovation on Market Structure," *Journal of Marketing Research* 41 (May 2004), pp. 166–83; and for a contrast with radically different new products, see Khaled Aboulnasr, Om Narasimhan, Edward Blair, and Rajesh Chandy, "Competitive Response to Radical Product Innovations," *Journal of Marketing* 72 (May 2008), pp. 94–110.

8. Austin Carr, "Nike: The No. 1 Most Innovative Company of 2013," *Fast Company*, February 2013.

9. "Enabling Multifaceted Innovation," *IBM Global Business Services*, www-935.ibm.com/services/us/gbs/bus/pdf/g510-6310-executive-brief-enabling-multifaceted.pdf, 2006.

10. Thomas Dotzel, Venkatesh Shankar, and Leonard L. Berry, "Service Innovativeness and Firm Value," *Journal of Marketing Research* 50 (April 2013), pp. 259–76; Michael J. Barone and Robert D. Jewell, "The Innovator's License: A Latitude to Deviate from Category Norms," *Journal of Marketing* 77 (January 2013), pp. 120–34; Christine Moorman, Simone Wies, Natalie Mizik, and Fredrika J. Spencer, "Firm Innovation and the Ratchet Effect among Consumer Packaged Goods Firms," *Marketing Science* 31 (November/December 2012), pp. 934–51; Katrijn Gielens, "New Products: The Antidote to Private Label Growth?," *Journal of Marketing Research* 49 (June 2012), pp. 408–23; Gaia Rubera and Ahmet H. Kirca, "Firm Innovativeness and Its Performance Outcomes: A Meta-Analytic Review and Theoretical Integration," *Journal of Marketing* 76 (May 2012), pp. 130–47; Shuba Srinivasan, Koen Pauwels, Jorge Silva-Risso, and Dominique M. Hanssens, "Product Innovations, Advertising and Stock Returns," *Journal of Marketing* 73 (January 2009), pp. 24–43; Alina B. Sorescu and Jelena Spanjol, "Innovation's Effect on Firm Value and Risk: Insights from Consumer Packaged Goods," *Journal of Marketing* 72 (March 2008), pp. 114–32; Sungwook Min, Manohar U. Kalwani, and William T. Robinson, "Market Pioneer and Early Follower Survival Risks: A Contingency Analysis of Really New versus Incrementally New Product-Markets," *Journal of Marketing* 70 (January 2006), pp. 15–33.

11. Eddie Yoon and Linda Deeken, "Why It Pays to Be a Category Creator," *Harvard Business Review*, March 2013, pp. 21–23.

12. Lydia Dishman, "How Dr. Dre's Burgeoning Headphones Company Stays True to Its Bass-Thumping Roots," *Fast Company*, September 13, 2012; Andrew Das and Andrew Martin, "Tuning Out Olympic Edict," *New York Times*, August 1, 2012; Neil Janowitz, "50 Cent Remixes Beats by Dre with SMS Headphones," *Fast Company*, March 19, 2012; Andrew J. Martin, "Headphones with Swagger (and Lots of Bass)," *New York Times*, November 19, 2011.

13. Stefan Wuyts, Shantanu Dutta, and Stefan Stremersch, "Portfolios of Interfirm Agreements in Technology-Intensive Markets: Consequences for Innovation and Profitability," *Journal of Marketing* 68 (April 2004), pp. 88–100; Aric Rindfleisch and Christine Moorman, "The Acquisition and Utilization of Information in New-Product Alliance: A Strength-of-Ties Perspective," *Journal of Marketing* 65 (April 2001), pp. 1–18. See also Raghunath Singh Rao, Rajesh K. Chandy, and Jaideep C. Prabhu, "The Fruits of Legitimacy: Why Some New Ventures Gain More from Innovation than Others," *Journal of Marketing* 72 (July 2008), pp. 58–75.

14. Rajesh Sethi, Zafar Iqbal, and Anju Sethi, "Developing New-to-the-Firm Products: The Role of Micropolitical Strategies," *Journal of Marketing* 76 (March 2012), pp. 99–115; Gerard J. Tellis, Jaideep C. Prabhu,

and Rajesh K. Chandy, "Radical Innovation across Nations: The Preeminence of Corporate Culture," *Journal of Marketing* 73 (January 2009), pp. 3–23.

15. Jan R. Landwehr, Daniel Wentzel, and Andreas Herrmann, "Product Design for the Long Run: Consumer Responses to Typical and Atypical Designs at Different Stages of Exposure," *Journal of Marketing* 77 (September 2013), pp. 92–107; Ji Hoon Jhang, Susan Jung Grant, and Margaret C. Campbell, "Get It? Got It. Good! Enhancing New Product Acceptance by Facilitating Resolution of Extreme Incongruity," *Journal of Marketing Research* 49 (April 2012), pp. 247–59; Theodore J. Noseworthy and Remi Trudel, "Looks Interesting, but What Does It Do? Evaluation of Incongruent Product Form Depends on Positioning," *Journal of Marketing Research* 48 (December 2011), pp. 1008–19; C. Page Moreau, Arthur B. Markman, and Donald R. Lehmann, "'What Is It?' Category Flexibility and Consumers' Response to Really New Products," *Journal of Consumer Research* 27 (March 2001), pp. 489–98.

16. Steve Hoeffler, "Measuring Preferences for Really New Products," *Journal of Marketing Research* 40 (November 2003), pp. 406–20; Glen Urban, Bruce Weinberg, and John R. Hauser, "Premarket Forecasting of Really New Products," *Journal of Marketing* 60 (January 1996), pp. 47–60.

17. Ashish Sood and Gerard J. Tellis, "Technological Evolution and Radical Innovation," *Journal of Marketing* 69 (July 2005), pp. 152–68.

18. For more discussion, see Jakki Mohr, Sanjit Sengupta, and Stanley Slater, *Marketing of High-Technology Products and Innovations*, 3rd ed. (Upper Saddle River, NJ: Pearson Prentice Hall, 2010).

19. Lillie-Beth Brinkman, "5 Things Google Glass Has Taught Me about Beta Testing," *NewsOK*, July 11, 2013; "Google Gets Deeper into Hardware with New Tablet, TV Gadget," *Reuters*, July 24, 2013; Joe Lazauskas, "How Google Glass Could Transform Marketing and Business," *Forbes*, June 24, 2013; Brad Stone, "Inside the Moonshot Factory," *Bloomberg Businessweek*, May 22, 2103; Sarah Rotman Epps, "Project Glass: Google's Transparent Product Strategy Is Great Marketing, Too," *Forrester*, March 4, 2013; Marcus Moretti, "Presenting: Google's 10 Worst Flops Ever," *Business Insider*, June 27, 2012; Susan Wojcicki, "The Eight Pillars of Innovation," *Google*, July 2011.

20. Steve Hamm, "Speed Demons," *BusinessWeek*, March 27, 2006, pp. 69–76.

21. Christina Passariello, "Brand New Bag: Louis Vuitton Tries Modern Methods on Factory Lines," *Wall Street Journal*, October 9, 2006.

22. Dina Bass, "Microsoft Tries to Pick Up the Pace," *Bloomberg Businessweek*, July 1, 2013.

23. Robert Safian, "Terry Kelly, the 'Un-CEO' of W. L. Gore, on How to Deal with Chaos: Grow Up," *Fast Company*, October 2012; "100 Best Companies to Work For," www.CNNmoney.com, February 6, 2012; Gary Hamel, "W. L. Gore: Lessons from a Management Revolutionary," *Wall Street Journal*, March 18, 2010; "The World's Most Innovative Companies," *Fast Company*, March 2009.

24. Tim Brown, *Change by Design: How Design Thinking Transforms Organizations and Inspires Innovation* (New York: HarperCollins, 2009).

25. Stuart Dredge, "Angry Birds Star Wars II to Launch for iOS, Android, and Windows Phone," *The Guardian*, August 23, 2013; Edmond Lococo, "Angry Birds Maker Rovio Expects Consumer to Drive Sales," *Bloomberg*, May 8, 2013; Brett Molina, "'Angry Birds' Maker Rovio Sees Revenue Soar," *USA Today*, April 3, 2013; Roger Cheng, "Angry Birds and Rovio's Plans for World Domination," *CNET*, December 18, 2012; J. J. McCorvey, "Rovio Takes Flight with 'Angry Birds' but Disney-Sized Success Still Up in the Air," *Fast Company*, November 26, 2012; Cliff Edwards and Ronald Grover, "Even Angry Birds Need an Agent," *Bloomberg Businessweek*, May 30, 2011.

26. Clayton M. Christensen, *Disrupting Class: How Disruptive Innovation Will Change the Way the World Learns* (New York: McGraw-Hill, 2008) and others of his books.

27. Ely Dahan and John R. Hauser, "Product Development: Managing a Dispersed Process," Bart Weitz and Robin Wensley, eds., *Handbook of Marketing* (London: Sage, 2002), pp. 179–222.

28. Robert G. Cooper and Elko J. Kleinschmidt, *New Products: The Key Factors in Success* (Chicago: American Marketing Association, 1990).

29. Elaine Wong, "The Most Memorable Product Launches of 2010," *Forbes*, December 3, 2010; Susumu Ogama and Frank T. Piller, "Reducing the Risks of New-Product Development," *MIT Sloan Management Review* 47 (Winter 2006), pp. 65–71.

30. Steve Hamm, "Speed Demons," *BusinessWeek*, March 27, 2006, pp. 69–76.

31. Tom McNichol, "A Start-Up's Best Friend? Failure," *Business 2.0*, March 2007, pp. 39–41.

32. Thomas N. Burton, "By Learning from Failures Lilly Keeps Drug Pipelines Full," *Wall Street Journal*, April 21, 2004.

33. Ashlee Vance, "SAP Dials It Up to Warp Speed, *Bloomberg Businessweek*, February 25, 2013, pp. 27–28; Chris Kanaracus, "SAP Retools Research Strategy around Internal Startups," *InfoWorld*, December 5, 2012; Kevin Kwang, "SAP Targets Startups to Widen Reach," www.ZDnet.com, September 6, 2012; Alex Williams, "SAP Holding Startup Forums to Develop Ecosystem for HANA—The Company's First Ever Platform Play," www.TechCrunch.com, August 25, 2012.

34. Steve Alexander, "Dyson Likes 'Wrong Thinking,'" *Star Tribune*, October 28, 2012; Virginia Gardiner, "Dyson Airblade," *Dwell*, March 10, 2010; Reena Jana, "Dyson's Air Multiplier: Flaw as Function," *Bloomberg BusinessWeek*, October 12, 2009.

35. Brian Hindo, "Rewiring Westinghouse," *BusinessWeek*, May 19, 2008, pp. 48–49.

36. Roger L. Martin, "The Innovation Catalysts," *Harvard Business Review*, June 2011, pp. 82–87.

37. Arlene Weintraub and Meg Tirrell, "Eli Lilly's Drug Assembly Line," *Bloomberg Businessweek*, March 8, 2010.

38. "Diageo Focuses on Innovation in Asia," www.warc.com, July 31, 2013.

39. Anne VanderMey, "Dell Gets in Touch with Its Inner Entrepreneur," *Fortune*, December 12, 2011.

40. John Bessant, Kathrin Moslein, and Bettina Von Stamm, "In Search of Innovation," *Wall Street Journal*, March 22, 2009.

41. J. C. Spender and Bruce Strong, "Who Has Innovative Ideas? Employees.," *Wall Street Journal*, June 14, 2012.

42. Lisa C. Troy, Tanat Hirunyawipada, and Audhesh K. Paswan, "Cross-Functional Integration and New Product Success: An Empirical Investigation of the Findings," *Journal of Marketing* 72 (September 2008), pp. 132–46; Rajesh Sethi, Daniel C. Smith, and C. Whan Park, "Cross-Functional Product Development Teams, Creativity, and the Innovativeness of New Consumer Products," *Journal of Marketing Research* 38 (February 2001), pp. 73–85.

43. Amy Wallace, "You Bring an Idea, and They'll Do the Rest," *New York Times*, June 11, 2011.

44. J. J. Colao, "Can a Crowdsourcing Invention Company Become the Best Retailer in the World?," *Forbes*, May 9, 2013.

45. Barrett Sheridan, "It's Getting Crowded in Here," *Newsweek*, September 11, 2008.

46. Robert G. Cooper, *Winning at New Products: Accelerating the Process from Idea to Launch* (New York: Perseus Publishing, 2001); see also Robert G. Cooper, "Stage-Gate Systems: A New Tool for Managing New Products," *Business Horizons*, May–June 1990, pp. 44–54.

47. Richard Barrett, "Tata Steel's Cutting Edge," *Metal Bulletin Weekly*, August 13, 2012.

48. Ely Dahan and John R. Hauser, "Product Development: Managing a Dispersed Process," Bart Weitz and Robin Wensley, eds., *Handbook of Marketing* (London: Sage, 2002), pp. 179–222.

49. Another alternative approach to the funnel process advocates "rocketing." See David Nichols, *Return on Ideas* (West Sussex, UK: Wiley, 2007).

50. Robert G. Cooper, *Product Leadership: Creating and Launching Superior New Products* (New York: Perseus Books, 1998).

51. Rajesh Sethi and Zafar Iqbal, "Stage-Gate Controls, Learning Failure, and Adverse Effect on Novel New Products," *Journal of Marketing* 72 (January 2008), pp. 118–34.

52. Robert G. Cooper, "How Companies Are Reinventing Their Idea-to-Launch Methodologies," *Research Technology Management*, March–April 2009, pp. 47–57.

53. John Hauser, Gerard J. Tellis, and Abbie Griffin, "Research on Innovation: A Review and Agenda for Marketing Science," *Marketing Science* 25 (November–December 2006), pp. 687–717.

54. "How Marketers Approach Creativity," *Advertising Age*, June 10, 2013; Byron Acohido, "Microsoft Cultures Creativity in Unique Lab," *USA Today*, July 11, 2007; Erich Joachimsthaler, *Hidden in Plain Sight: How to Find and Execute Your Company's Next Big Growth Strategy* (Boston: Harvard Business School Press, 2007); Subin Im and John P. Workman Jr., "Market Orientation, Creativity, and New-Product Performance in High-Technology Firms," *Journal of Marketing* 68 (April 2004), pp. 114–32.

55. Sharon Machlis, "Innovation and the 20% Solution," *Computerworld*, February 2, 2009.

56. "The World's Fifty Most Innovative Companies," Special Report, *BusinessWeek*, May 9, 2007.

57. Christina Chaey, "LinkedIn Launches an Incubator to Turn Employees into Entrepreneurs," *Fast Company*, December 7, 2012

58. Alison Overholt, "American Idol: Accounting Edition," *Fortune*, October 17, 2011.

59. Andrew King and Karim R. Lakhani, "Using Open Innovation to Identify the Best Ideas," *MIT Sloan Management Review*, Fall 2013, pp. 41–48; Anna S. Cui and Gina O'Connor, "Alliance Portfolio Resource Diversity and Firm Innovation," *Journal of Marketing* 76 (July 2012), pp. 24–43; Néomie Raassens, Stefan Wuyts, and Inge Geyskens, "The Market Valuation of Outsourcing New Product Development," *Journal of Marketing Research* 49 (October 2012), pp. 682–95; Henry Chesbrough, *Open Business Models: How to Thrive in the New-Innovation Landscape* (Boston: Harvard University Press, 2006); Eric Von Hippel, *Democratizing Innovation* (Cambridge, MA: MIT Press, 2005).

60. Ashwin W. Joshi and Sanjay Sharma, "Customer Knowledge Development: Antecedents and Impact on New-Product Performance," *Journal of Marketing* 68 (October 2004), pp. 47–59.

61. Abbie J. Griffin and John Hauser, "The Voice of the Customer," *Marketing Science* 12 (Winter 1993), pp. 1–27. See also Nicole E. Coviello and Richard M. Joseph, "Creating Major Innovations with Customers: Insights from Small and Young Technology Firms," *Journal of Marketing* 76 (November 2012), pp. 87–104.

62. Miho Inada, "Tokyo Café Targets Trend Makers," *Wall Street Journal*, August 24, 2008.

63. Amy Wallace, "Putting Customers in Charge Of Design," *New York Times*, May 15, 2010.

64. Alan MacCormack, Fiona Murray, and Erika Wagner, "Spurring Innovations through Competitions," *MIT Sloan Management Review*, Fall 2013, pp. 25–32.

65. Bruce Horovitz, "Savvy Marketers Let Consumers Call the Shots," *USA Today*, March 24, 2011.

66. Ben Hopkins, "Mobile Medical Platform MedM Wins Cisco I-Prize," www.rusbase.com, September 18, 2013; "Companies Increasingly Use Crowdsourcing Strategically: Cisco's I-Prize," www.yannigroth.com, October 8, 2012; "Cisco Announces Winner of Global I-Prize Innovation Competition," press release, www.cisco.com, June 29, 2010; Guido Jouret, "Inside Cisco's Search for the Next Big Idea," *Harvard Business Review*, September 2009, pp. 43–45; Anya Kamentz, "The Power of the Prize," *Fast Company*, May 2008, pp. 43–45; www.cisco.com/web/solutions/iprize/index.html, accessed June 2, 2014

67. Martin Schreier, Christoph Fuchs, and Darren W. Dahl, "The Innovation Effect of User Design: Exploring Consumers' Innovation Perceptions of Firms Selling Products Designed by Users," *Journal of Marketing* 76 (September 2012), pp. 18–32; Patricia Seybold, *Outside Innovation: How Your Customers Will Codesign Your Company's Future* (New York: Collins, 2006).

68. Christine Raasch and Eric Von Hippel, "Innovation Process Benefits: The Journey as Reward," *MIT Sloan Management Review*, Fall 2013, pp. 33–39; Donna L. Hoffman, Praveen K. Kopalle, and Thomas P. Novak, "The 'Right' Consumers for Better Concepts: Identifying and Using Consumers High in Emergent Nature to Further Develop New Product Concepts," *Journal of Marketing Research* 47 (October 2010), pp. 854–65; Helena Yli-Renko and Ramkumar Janakiraman, "How Customer Portfolio Affects New Product Development in Technology-Based Firms," *Journal of Marketing* 72 (September 2008), pp. 131–48.

69. Eric von Hippel, *Democratizing Innovation* (Cambridge, MA: MIT Press, 2005); Pamela D. Morrison, John H. Roberts, and David F. Midgley, "The Nature of Lead Users and Measurement of Leading Edge Status," *Research Policy* 33 (2004), pp. 351–62.

70. John W. Heinke Jr. and Chun Zhang, "Increasing Supplier-Driven Innovation," *MIT Sloan Management Review* (Winter 2010), pp. 41–46; Eric (Er) Fang, "Customer Participation and the Trade-Off Between New Product Innovativeness and Speed to Market," *Journal of Marketing* 72 (July 2008), pp. 90–104. Note that this research also shows that customer involvement can also slow the development process if a high level of interaction and coordination is required across stages.

71. Jacob Goldenberg, Ronu Horowitz, Amnon Levav, and David Mazursky, "Find Your Innovation Sweet Spot," *Harvard Business Review*, March 2003.

72. Kevin Zheng Zhou, Chi Kin (Bennett) Yim, and David K. Tse, "The Effects of Strategic Orientations on Technology- and Market-Based Breakthrough Innovations," *Journal of Marketing* 69 (April 2005), pp. 42–60.

73. Jens Martin Skibsted and Rasmus Bech Hansen, "User-Led Innovation Can't Create Breakthroughs; Just Ask Apple and Ikea," *Fast Company*, February 15, 2011.

74. Erik Kain, "Xbox One Vs. PS4: Why Sony Is Still the Best Choice for Gamers," *Forbes*, July 25, 2013; "Sony's PS4 Has Fifty Percent Lead over Microsoft's Xbox One Says Survey," *PR Newswire*, July 24, 2013; Ian Sherr, "Sony Boosts Initial Internal Sales Estimates for its PlayStation 4," *Wall Street Journal*, June 11, 2013; Brad Stone, "Nintendo Wii to Add Netflix Service for Streaming Video," *New York Times*, January 13, 2010; Eric A. Taub, "Will Nothing Slow Wii?," *New York Times Bits Blog*, October 17, 2008; John Gaudiosi, "How the Wii Is Creaming the Competition," *Business 2.0*, April 25, 2007; Martin Fackler, "Putting the We Back in Wii," *New York Times*, June 8, 2007.

75. Darren W. Dahl and Page Moreau, "The Influence and Value of Analogical Thinking during New-Product Ideation," *Journal of Marketing Research* 39 (February 2002), pp. 47–60; Michael Michalko, *Cracking Creativity: The Secrets of Creative Genius* (Berkeley, CA: Ten Speed Press, 1998); James M. Higgins, *101 Creative Problem-Solving Techniques* (New York: New Management, 1994).

76. Drew Boyd and Jacob Goldenberg, "Think Inside the Box," *Wall Street Journal*, June 14, 2013; Philip Kotler and Fernando Trias de Bes, *Lateral Marketing: New Techniques for Finding Breakthrough Ideas* (New York: Wiley, 2003).

77. NBC Research, "Friends," *Program Test Report*, May 27, 1994; "NBC's Failing Grade for 'Friends,'" *The Smoking Gun*, May 10, 2004, www.smokinggun.com.

78. Olivier Toubia and Laurent Florès, "Adaptive Idea Screening Using Consumers," *Marketing Science* 26 (May–June 2007), pp. 342–60.

79. David L. Alexander, John G. Lynch Jr., and Qing Wang, "As Time Goes By: Do Cold Feet Follow Warm Intentions for Really New Versus Incrementally New Products," *Journal of Marketing Research* 45 (June 2008), pp. 307–19; Steve Hoeffler, "Measuring Preferences for Really New Products," *Journal of Marketing Research* 40 (November 2003), pp. 406–20.

80. Min Zhao, Steve Hoeffler, and Darren W. Dahl, "The Role of Imagination-Focused Visualization on New Product Evaluation," *Journal of Marketing Research* 46 (February 2009), pp. 46–55; Raquel Castano, Mita Sujan, Manish Kacker, and Harish Sujan, "Managing Customer Uncertainty in the Adoption of New Products: Temporal Distance and Mental Stimulation," *Journal of Marketing Research* 45 (June 2008), pp. 320–36; Darren W. Dahl and C. Page Moreau, "The Influence and Value of Analogical Thinking during New-Product Ideation," *Journal of Marketing Research* 39 (February 2002), pp. 47–60; Michelle L. Roehm and Brian Sternthal, "The Moderating Effect of Knowledge and Resources on the Persuasive Impact of Analogies," *Journal of Consumer Research* 28 (September 2001), pp. 257–72; Darren W. Dahl, Amitava Chattopadhyay, and Gerald J. Gorn, "The Use of Visual Mental Imagery in New-Product Design," *Journal of Marketing Research* 36 (February 1999), pp. 18–28.

81. Eric Fish, "Rapid Prototyping: How It's Done at GM," *Automotive Design & Production*, September/October 2011; Leslie Gordon, "Rapid Prototyping for Orthopedics," *Medical Design News*, October 2009.

82. Steve Hamm, "Speed Demons," *BusinessWeek*, March 27, 2006, pp. 69–76.

83. Leonard David, "Next-Generation GPS Satellites Designed in Virtual Reality," www.NBCnews.com, March 22, 2012; Greg Avery, "Inside Lockheed Martin's Out-of-This-World Virtual-Reality Lab," *Denver Business Journal*, January 24, 2011.

84. Jon Fortt, "Heavy Duty Computing," *Fortune*, March 2, 2009, pp. 34–36.

85. For additional information, also see David Bakken and Curtis L. Frazier, "Conjoint Analysis: Understanding Consumer Decision Making," Rajiv Grover and Marco Vriens, eds., *The Handbook of Marketing Research* (Thousand Oaks, CA: Sage, 2006); Vithala R. Rao and John R. Hauser, "Conjoint Analysis, Related Modeling, and Application," Yoram Wind and Paul E. Green, eds., *Market Research and Modeling: Progress and Prospects: A Tribute to Paul Green* (New York: Springer, 2004), pp. 141–68. For another approach, see Young-Hoon Park, Min Ding, and Vithala R. Rao, "Eliciting Preference for Complex Products: A Web-Based Upgrading Method," *Journal of Marketing Research* 45 (October 2008), pp. 562–74.

86. Jerry Wind, Paul Green, Douglas Shifflet, and Marsha Scarbrough, "Courtyard by Marriott: Designing a Hotel Facility with Consumer-Based Marketing Models," *Interfaces* 19 (January–February 1989), pp. 25–47; for another interesting application, see Paul E. Green, Abba M. Krieger, and Terry Vavra, "Evaluating EZ-Pass: Using Conjoint Analysis to Assess Consumer Response to a New Tollway Technology," *Marketing Research* (Summer 1999), pp. 5–16.

87. The full-profile example was taken from Paul E. Green and Yoram Wind, "New Ways to Measure Consumers' Judgments," *Harvard Business Review*, July–August 1975, pp. 107–17.

88. To learn about some of the new research developments in conjoint, see Olivier Toubia, Theodoros Evgeniou, and John R. Hauser, "Optimization-Based and Machine-Learning Methods for Conjoint Analysis: Estimation and Question Design," A. Gustafsson, A. Herrmann, and F. Huber, eds., *Conjoint Measurement: Methods and Applications*, 4th ed. (New York: Springer, 2008), pp. 231–57; and Oded Netzer, Olivier Toubia, Eric T. Bradlow, Ely Dahan, Theodoros Evgeniou, Fred M. Feinberg, Eleanor M. Feit, Sam K. Hui, Joseph Johnson, John C. Liechty, James B. Orlin, and Vithala R. Rao, "Beyond Conjoint Analysis: Advances in Preference Measurement," *Marketing Letters* 19, no. 3 (2008), pp. 337–54.

89. Peter N. Golder and Gerald J. Tellis, "Will It Ever Fly? Modeling the Takeoff of Really New Consumer Durables," *Marketing Science* 16 (Summer 1997), pp. 256–70.

90. Roger A. Kerin, Michael G. Harvey, and James T. Rothe, "Cannibalism and New-Product Development," *Business Horizons*, October 1978, pp. 25–31.

91. The present value ($V$) of a future sum ($I$) to be received $t$ years from today and discounted at the interest rate ($r$) is given by $V = I_t/(1 + r)t$. Thus $\$4{,}716{,}000/(1.15)^5 = \$2{,}345{,}000$.

92. John Hauser, "House of Quality," *Harvard Business Review*, May–June 1988, pp. 63–73; customer-driven engineering is also called "quality function deployment."

93. Cindy Atoji Keene, "Shoe Tester Puts His Sole into the Job," *Boston Globe*, November 4, 2012.

94. Eyal Biyalogorsky, William Boulding, and Richard Staelin, "Stuck in the Past: Why Managers Persist with New-Product Failures," *Journal of Marketing* 70 (April 2006), pp. 108–21.

95. Jack Neff, "Packaged-Goods Testing Gets a Makeover," *Ad Age*, February 11, 2013; Kevin J. Clancy, Peter C. Krieg, and Marianne McGarry Wolf, *Marketing New Products Successfully: Using Simulated Test Marketing Methodology* (New York: Lexington Books, 2005); Glen L. Urban, John R. Hauser, and Roberta A. Chicos, "Information Acceleration: Validation and Lessons from the Field," *Journal of Marketing Research* 34 (February 1997), pp. 143–53.

96. Karlee Weinmann and Aimee Groth, "New Fast Food Products Get Tested First in Columbus, Ohio," *Business Insider*, November 2, 2011.

97. Su Hyun Lee, "Companies Turn to South Korea for Product Testing," *New York Times*, November 10, 2010.

98. Megan Barnett, "China Is the New Test Market for Luxury," *Fortune*, June 7, 2013.

99. Austin Carr, "Starbucks Leap of Faith," *Fast Company*, June 2013, pp. 46–48.

100. Lora Kolodny, "Startups Get Help Testing Apps before Their Release," *The Wall Street Journal*, April 17, 2013.

101. Tomio Geren, "Square's Early Testing Program Connects with Merchants," *Forbes*, March 21, 2013.

102. Rajesh Chandy, Brigette Hopstaken, Om Narasimhan, and Jaideep Prabhu, "From Invention to Innovation: Conversion Ability in Product Development," *Journal of Marketing Research* 43 (August 2006), pp. 494–508.

103. Joan Schneider and Julie Hall, "Why Most Product Launches Fail," *Harvard Business Review*, April 2011, pp. 21–23.

104. Alicia Barroso and Gerard Llobet, "Advertising and Consumer Awareness of New, Differentiated Products," *Journal of Marketing Research* 49 (December 2012), pp. 773–92; Norris I. Bruce, Natasha Zhang Foutz, and Ceren Kolsarici, "Dynamic Effectiveness of Advertising and Word of Mouth in Sequential Distribution of New Products," *Journal of Marketing Research* 49 (August 2012), pp. 469–86.

105. Rob Trump, "Why Would You Ever Give Money through Kickstarter?," *New York Times*, February 8, 2013; Julianne Pepitone, "Kickstarter's Growing Pains," www.cnn.com, December 18, 2012; Suw Charman-Anderson, "Kickstarter: Dream Maker or Promise Breaker?," *Forbes*, November 30, 2012.

106. Remco Prins and Peter C. Verhoef, "Marketing Communication Drivers of Adoption Timing of a New E-Service among Existing Customers," *Journal of Marketing* 71 (April 2007), pp. 169–83.

107. For further discussion, see Elie Ofek and Özge Turut, "Vaporware, Suddenware, and Trueware: New Product Preannouncements under Market Uncertainty," *Marketing Science* 32 (March/April 2013), pp. 342–55; Feryal Erhun, Paulo Conçalves, and Jay Hopman, "The Art of Managing New Product Transitions," *MIT Sloan Management Review* 48 (Spring 2007), pp. 73–80; Yuhong Wu, Sridhar Balasubramanian, and Vijay Mahajan, "When Is a Preannounced New Product Likely to Be Delayed?," *Journal of Marketing* 68 (April 2004), pp. 101–13; Raji Srinivasan, Gary L. Lilien, and Arvind Rangaswamy, "First In First Out? The Effects of Network Externalities on Pioneer Survival," *Journal of Marketing* 68 (January 2004), pp. 41–58; Barry L. Bayus, Sanjay Jain, and Ambar Rao, "Truth or Consequences: An Analysis of Truth or Vaporware and New-Product Announcements," *Journal of Marketing Research* 38 (February 2001), pp. 3–13.

108. Yvonne van Everdingen, Dennis Folk, and Stefan Stremersch, "Modeling Global Spillover in New Product Takeoff," *Journal of Marketing Research* 46 (October 2009), pp. 637–52; Katrijn Gielens and Jan-Benedict E. M. Steenkamp, "Drivers of Consumer Acceptance of New Packaged Goods: An Investigation across

Products and Countries," *International Journal of Research in Marketing* 24 (June 2007), pp. 97–111; Venkatesh Shankar, Gregory S. Carpenter, and Lakshman Krishnamukthi, "Late Mover Advantages: How Innovative Late Entrants Outsell Pioneers," *Journal of Marketing Research* 35 (February 1998), pp. 54–70.

109. Mark Leslie and Charles A. Holloway, "The Sales Learning Curve," *Harvard Business Review*, July–August 2006, pp. 114–23.

110. For details, see Keith G. Lockyer, *Critical Path Analysis and Other Project Network Techniques* (London: Pitman, 1984); see also Arvind Rangaswamy and Gary L. Lilien, "Software Tools for New-Product Development," *Journal of Marketing Research* 34 (February 1997), pp. 177–84.

111. The following discussion leans heavily on Everett M. Rogers, *Diffusion of Innovations* (New York: Free Press, 1962). Also see his third edition, published in 1983.

112. Karthik Sridhar, Ram Bezawada, and Minakshi Trivedi, "Investigating the Drivers of Consumer Cross-Category Learning for New Products Using Multiple Data Sets," *Marketing Science* 31 (July/August 2012), pp. 668–88; C. Page Moreau, Donald R. Lehmann, and Arthur B. Markman, "Entrenched Knowledge Structures and Consumer Response to New Products," *Journal of Marketing Research* 38 (February 2001), pp. 14–29.

113. John T. Gourville, "Eager Sellers & Stony Buyers," *Harvard Business Review*, June 2006, pp. 99–106.

114. Chuan-Fong Shih and Alladi Venkatesh, "Beyond Adoption: Development and Application of a Use-Diffusion Model," *Journal of Marketing* 68 (January 2004), pp. 59–72. See also Ashish Sood, Gareth M. James, Gerard J. Tellis, and Ji Zhu, "Predicting the Path of Technological Innovation: SAW vs. Moore, Bass, Gompertz, and Kryder," *Marketing Science* 31 (November/December 2012), pp. 964–79.

115. Michal Herzenstein, Steven S. Posavac, and J. Joʻsko Brakuz, "Adoption of New and Really New Products: The Effects of Self-Regulation Systems and Risk Salience," *Journal of Marketing Research* 44 (May 2007), pp. 251–60; Christophe Van den Bulte and Yogesh V. Joshi, "New-Product Diffusion with Influentials and Imitators," *Marketing Science* 26 (May–June 2007), pp 400–21; Steve Hoeffler, "Measuring Preferences for Really New Products," *Journal of Marketing Research* 40 (November 2003), pp. 406–20.

116. Everett M. Rogers, *Diffusion of Innovations* (New York: Free Press, 1962), p. 192; Geoffrey A. Moore, *Crossing the Chasm: Marketing and Selling High-Tech Products to Mainstream Customers* (New York: HarperBusiness, 1999); for an interesting application with services, see Barak Libai, Eitan Muller, and Renana Peres, "The Diffusion of Services," *Journal of Marketing Research* 46 (April 2009), pp. 163–75.

117. Michael Haenlein and Barak Libai, "Targeting Revenue Leaders for a New Product," *Journal of Marketing* 77 (May 2013), pp. 65–80.

118. Jordan Robertson, "How Nike Got Street Cred," *Business 2.0,* May 2004, pp. 43–46.

119. Ted Marzilli, "Fresh Ticket Oak Campaign a Boost for StubHub Perception," *Forbes,* May 23, 2013; Mallory Russell, "Five Questions with StubHub's CMO," *AdAge,* October 23, 2012; Karl Greenberg, "StubHub CMO Ray Elias: We Are Not Just a Ticket Seller," *Marketing Daily,* September 13, 2012; Dinah Eng, "StubHub: Anatomy of a Game-Changing Idea," *Fortune,* July 23, 2012; Rob Golum, "Live Nation Wields 'The Boss' in StubHub Ticket Battle," *Bloomberg,* March 2, 2012.

120. Cliff Edwards, "Will Souping Up TiVo Save It?," *BusinessWeek,* May 17, 2004, pp. 63–64; Cliff Edwards, "Is TiVo's Signal Still Fading?," *BusinessWeek,* September 10, 2001, pp. 72–74.

# Chapter 16

1. "Ryanair Food Costs More than Price of Flight," *The Telegraph*, August 28, 2012; Simon Calder, "Ryanair Unveils Its Latest Plan to Save Money: Remove Toilets from the Plane," *The Independent*, October 12, 2011; Felix Gillette, "Ryanair's O'Leary Mulls One-Euro Toilets, Standing Passengers," www.bloomberg.com, September 2, 2010; Peter J. Howe, "The Next Pinch: Fees to Check Bags," *Boston Globe*, March 8, 2007; Kerry Capel, "'Wal-Mart with Wings,'" *BusinessWeek*, November 27, 2006, pp. 44–45.

2. Xavier Dreze and Joseph C. Nunes, "Using Combined-Currency Prices to Lower Consumers' Perceived Cost," *Journal of Marketing Research* 41 (February 2004), pp. 59–72; Raghuram Iyengar, Kamel Jedidi, and Rajeev Kohli, "A Conjoint Approach to Multipart Pricing," *Journal of Marketing Research* 45 (April 2008), pp. 195–201; Marco Bertini and Luc Wathieu, "Attention Arousal through Price Partitioning," *Marketing Science* 27 (March/April 2008), pp. 236–46.

3. Daniel Fisher, "Cheap Seats," *Forbes*, August 24, 2009, pp. 102–3.

4. "Let's Make a Deal," *Consumer Reports*, August 2013, pp. 15–17.

5. Tomio Geron, "The Share Economy," *Forbes*, February 11, 2013

6. Eric Spitznagel, "Rise of the Barter Economy," *Bloomberg Businessweek*, April 30, 2012, pp. 75–77; Stephanie Schomer, "Dare to Share," *Fast Company*, December 2010/January 2011, pp. 75–84.

7. Tomio Geron, "The Share Economy," *Forbes*, February 11, 2013; Danielle Sacks, "The Sharing Economy," *Fast Company*, May 2011, pp. 88–93, 130–31.

8. Caroline Fairchild, "The Rental Generation Sees No Point in Buying," *Bloomberg Businessweek*, August 13, 2012; Stephanie Schomer, "RentTheRunway Lets You Wear Designer Fashion on the Cheap," *Fast Company*, December 31, 2010.

9. Michael J. De La Merced, "New Capital Could Raise Airbnb Value to $10 Billion," *New York Times*, March 20, 2014; Tomio Geron, "Is Airbnb the Next eBay, Uber the Next Amazon?," *Forbes*, August 7, 2013; Larry Downes, "Airbnb: A Spare Room for Debate," *Harvard Business Review*, June 26, 2013; Mackenzie Yang, "NYC Judge Rules Airbnb Rental Is an 'Illegal Hotel,'" *Time*, May 21, 2013; Tomio Geron, "Airbnb and the Unstoppable Rise of the Share Economy," *Forbes*, January 23, 2013.

10. Sacks, "The Sharing Economy," pp. 88–93, 130–31.

11. Christian Homburg, Ove Jensen, and Alexander Hahn, "How to Organize Pricing? Vertical Delegation and Horizontal Dispersion of Pricing Authority," *Journal of Marketing* 76 (September 2012), pp. 49–69.

12. For a thorough review of pricing research, see Chezy Ofir and Russell S. Winer, "Pricing: Economic and Behavioral Models," Bart Weitz and Robin Wensley, eds., *Handbook of Marketing* (London: Sage Publications, 2002). For a recent sampling of some of the abundant academic research on consumer processing of prices, see Ray Weaver and Shane Frederick, "A Reference Price Theory of the Endowment Effect," *Journal of Marketing Research* 49 (October 2012), pp. 696–707; and Kwanho Suk, Jiheon Lee, and Donald R. Lichtenstein, "The Influence of Price Presentation Order on Consumer Choice," *Journal of Marketing Research* 49 (October 2012), pp. 708–17.

13. Eric Wilson, "Why Does This Pair of Pants Cost $550?," *New York Times*, April 26, 2010; Pia Sarkar, "Which Shirt Costs $275?—Brand Loyalty, Bargain Hunting, and Unbridled Luxury All Play a Part in the Price You'll Pay for a T-Shirt," *Final Edition*, March 15, 2007, p. C1.

14. Hooman Estalami, Alfred Holden, and Donald R. Lehmann, "Macro-Economic Determinants of Consumer Price Knowledge: A Meta-Analysis of Four Decades of Research," *International Journal of Research in Marketing* 18 (December 2001), pp. 341–55.

15. For a comprehensive review, see Tridib Mazumdar, S. P. Raj, and Indrajit Sinha, "Reference Price Research: Review and Propositions," *Journal of Marketing* 69 (October 2005), pp. 84–102. For a different point of view, see Chris Janiszewski and Donald R. Lichtenstein, "A Range Theory Account of Price Perception," *Journal of Consumer Research* 25 (March 1999), pp. 353–68. For business-to-business applications, see Hernan A. Bruno, Hai Che, and Shantanu Dutta, "Role of Reference Price on Price and Quantity: Insights from Business-to-Business Markets," *Journal of Marketing Research* 49 (October 2012), pp. 640–54.

16. For a discussion of how "incidental" prices outside the category can serve as contextual reference prices, see Joseph C. Nunes and Peter Boatwright, "Incidental Prices and Their Effect on Willingness to Pay," *Journal of Marketing Research* 41 (November 2004), pp. 457–66.

17. Ritesh Saini, Raghunath Singh Rao, and Ashwani Monga, "Is the Deal Worth My Time? The Interactive Effect of Relative and Referent Thinking on Willingness to Seek a Bargain," *Journal of Marketing* 74 (January 2010), pp. 34–48.

18. Gurumurthy Kalyanaram and Russell S. Winer, "Empirical Generalizations from Reference-Price Research," *Marketing Science* 14 (Summer 1995), pp. 161–69.

19. Glenn E. Mayhew and Russell S. Winer, "An Empirical Analysis of Internal and External Reference-Price Effects Using Scanner Data," *Journal of Consumer Research* 19 (June 1992), pp. 62–70.

20. Robert Ziethammer, "Forward-Looking Buying in Online Auctions," *Journal of Marketing Research* 43 (August 2006), pp. 462–76.

21. John T. Gourville, "Pennies-a-Day: The Effect of Temporal Reframing on Transaction Evaluation," *Journal of Consumer Research* 24 (March 1998), pp. 395–408. See also Anja Lambrecht and Catherine Tucker, "Paying with Money or Effort: Pricing when Customers Anticipate Hassle," *Journal of Marketing Research* 49 (February 2012), pp. 66–82.

22. Wilfred Amaldoss and Sanjay Jain, "Pricing of Conspicuous Goods: A Competitive Analysis of Social Effects," *Journal of Marketing Research* 42 (February 2005).

23. "Ferrari Focuses on Exclusivity," www.warc.com, May 10, 2013; Roger Bennett, "Gained in Translation," *Bloomberg Businessweek*, April 2, 2012.

24. Mark Stiving and Russell S. Winer, "An Empirical Analysis of Price Endings with Scanner Data," *Journal of Consumer Research* 24 (June 1997), pp. 57–68.

25. Eric T. Anderson and Duncan Simester, "Effects of $9 Price Endings on Retail Sales: Evidence from Field Experiments," *Quantitative Marketing and Economics* 1 (March 2003), pp. 93–110.

26. Eric Anderson and Duncan Simester, "Mind Your Pricing Cues," *Harvard Business Review*, September 2003, pp. 96–103.

27. Anderson and Simester, "Mind Your Pricing Cues," *Harvard Business Review*, September 2003, pp. 96–103.

28. Ibid.

29. Daniel J. Howard and Roger A. Kerin, "Broadening the Scope of Reference-Price Advertising Research: A Field Study of Consumer Shopping Involvement," *Journal of Marketing* 70 (October 2006), pp. 185–204.

30. Katherine N. Lemon and Stephen M. Nowlis, "Developing Synergies between Promotions and Brands in Different Price-Quality Tiers," *Journal of Marketing Research* 39 (May 2002), pp. 171–85; but see also Serdar Sayman, Stephen J. Hoch, and Jagmohan S. Raju, "Positioning of Store Brands," *Marketing Science* 21 (Fall 2002), pp. 378–97.

31. Shantanu Dutta, Mark J. Zbaracki, and Mark Bergen, "Pricing Process as a Capability: A Resource-Based Perspective," *Strategic Management Journal* 24 (July 2003), pp. 615–30.

32. "To All iPhone Customers," Apple Inc., www.apple.com/hotnews/openiphoneletter, September 6, 2007; Gary F. Gebhardt, "Price Skimming's Unintended Consequences," *Marketing Science Institute Working Paper Series*, MSI Report No. 09-109, 2009.

33. Wilfred Amaldoss and Chuan He, "Pricing Prototypical Products," *Marketing Science* 32 (September–October 2013), pp. 733–52.

34. Timothy Aeppel, "Seeking Perfect Prices, CEO Tears Up the Rules," *Wall Street Journal*, March 27, 2007.

35. Florian Zettelmeyer, Fiona Scott Morton, and Jorge Silva-Risso, "How the Internet Lowers Prices: Evidence from Matched Survey and Automobile Transaction Data," *Journal of Marketing Research* 43 (May 2006), pp. 168–81; Jeffrey R. Brown and Austan Goolsbee, "Does the Internet Make Markets More Competitive? Evidence from the Life Insurance Industry," *Journal of Political Economy* 110 (October 2002), pp. 481–507.

36. Joo Heon Park and Douglas L. MacLachlan, "Estimating Willingness to Pay with Exaggeration Bias-Corrected Contingent Valuation Method," *Marketing Science* 27 (July–August 2008), pp. 691–98.

37. Walter Baker, Mike Marn, and Craig Zawada, "Price Smarter on the Net," *Harvard Business Review*, February 2001, pp. 122–27.

38. Brian Bergstein, "The Price Is Right," *Associated Press*, April 29, 2007.

39. Thomas T. Nagle, John E. Hogan, and Joseph Zale, *The Strategy and Tactics of Pricing*, 5th ed. (Upper Saddle River, NJ: Pearson, 2011)

40. Brett R. Gordon, Avi Goldfarb, and Yang Li, "Does Price Elasticity Vary with Economic Growth? A Cross-Category Analysis," *Journal of Marketing Research* 50 (February 2013), pp. 4–23. See also Harald J. Van Heerde, Maarten J. Gijsenberg, Marnik G. Dekimpe, and Jan-Benedict E. M. Steenkamp, "Price and Advertising Effectiveness over the Business Cycle," *Journal of Marketing Research* 50 (April 2013), pp. 177–93.

41. Tammo H. A. Bijmolt, Harald J. Van Heerde, and Rik G. M. Pieters, "New Empirical Generalizations on the Determinants of Price Elasticity," *Journal of Marketing Research* 42 (May 2005), pp. 141–56.

42. William W. Alberts, "The Experience Curve Doctrine Reconsidered," *Journal of Marketing* 53 (July 1989), pp. 36–49.

43. Joseph Weber, "Over a Buck for Dinner? Outrageous," *BusinessWeek*, March 9, 2009, p. 57.

44. Sharon Silkey Carter, "Death of PT Cruiser Seen as a Symbol of Industry's Problem," *USA Today*, July 8, 2010.

45. Chris Burritt, "Why 'Less Is More' Rules Fashion," *Bloomberg Businessweek*, May 30, 2011, pp. 18–19.

46. Marco Bertini, Luc Wathieu, and Sheena S. Iyengar, "The Discriminating Consumer: Product Proliferation and Willingness to Pay for Quality," *Journal of Marketing Research* 49 (February 2012), pp. 39–49.

47. Nirmalya Kumar, "Strategies to Fight Low-Cost Rivals," *Harvard Business Review*, December 2006, pp. 104–12; Robert J. Frank, Jeffrey P. George, and Laxman Narasimhan, "When Your Competitor Delivers More for Less," *McKinsey Quarterly* (Winter 2004), pp. 48–59. See also Jan-Benedict E. M. Steenkamp and Nirmalya Kumar, "Don't Be Undersold," *Harvard Business Review*, December 2009, pp. 90–95.

48. Nirmalya Kumar, "Strategies to Fight Low-Cost Rivals," *Harvard Business Review*, December 2006, pp. 104–12.

49. "2011 Win Strategy Report," www.parker.com/winstrategyreport, 2011; Tom Brennan, "High-Tech Parker Hannifin?," www.cnbc.com, April 29, 2008; Aeppel, "Seeking Perfect Prices, CEO Tears Up the Rules"; Todd Shryock, "Parker Hannifin: Perpetual Motion," *Smart Business Cleveland*, October 1, 2005.

50. Bruce Einhorn, "Acer's Game-Changing PC Offensive," *BusinessWeek*, April 20, 2009, p. 65; Bruce Einhorn and Tim Culpan, "With Dell in the Dust, Acer Chases HP," *Bloomberg Businessweek*, March 8, 2010, pp. 58–59.

51. "PACCAR Announces Fourth Quarter Revenue and Profit: Company Achieves Record Annual Revenue," www.paccar.con, January 31, 2013; Jay Thompson, "The 2010 U.S. Diesel Engine Landscape—Paccar's Approach Will Be Most Changed without Cat," *Gerson Lehrman Group*, www.glgroup.com; Angel Gonzales, "Paccar's Fuel-Saving Hybrid Truck Aimed at Nation's Distribution," *Seattle Times*, July 29, 2008; Michael Arndt, "PACCAR: Built for the Long-Haul," *BusinessWeek*, January 30, 2006.

52. Anupam Mukerj, "Monsoon Marketing," *Fast Company*, April 2007, p. 22.

53. Marco Bertini and Luc Wathieu, "How to Stop Customers from Fixating on Price," *Harvard Business Review*, May 2010, pp. 85–91.

54. Bill Saporito, "Behind the Tumult at P&G," *Fortune*, March 7, 1994, pp. 74–82. For empirical analysis of its effects, see Kusim L. Ailawadi, Donald R. Lehmann, and Scott A. Neslin, "Market Response to a Major Policy Change in the Marketing Mix: Learning from Procter & Gamble's Value Pricing Strategy," *Journal of Marketing* 65 (January 2001), pp. 44–61.

55. Elisabeth Sullivan, "Value Pricing," *Marketing News*, January 15, 2008, p. 08.

56. Michael Tsiros and David M. Hardesty, "Ending a Price Promotion: Retracting It in One Step or Phasing It Out Gradually," *Journal of Marketing* 74 (January 2010), pp. 49–64.

57. Paul B. Ellickson and Sanjog Misra, "Supermarket Pricing Strategies," *Marketing Science* 27 (September–October 2008), pp. 811–28.

58. Paul B. Ellickson, Sanjog Misra, and Harikesh S. Nair, "Repositioning Dynamics and Pricing Strategy," *Journal of Marketing Research* 49 (December 2012), pp. 750–72.

59. Stephanie Clifford and Catherine Rampell, "Sometimes, We Want Price to Fool Us, *New York Times*, April 13, 2013; "Why Walmart Can Pull Off 'Everyday Low Prices' but Everyone Else Keeps Failing," *Business Insider*, September 3, 2012; Alexander Chernev, "Why Everyday Low Pricing Might Not Fit J.C. Penney," www.bloomberg.com, May 17, 2012.

60. For a discussion of some theoretical issues with auctions, see Amar Cheema, Dipankar Chakravarti, and Atanu R. Sinha, "Bidding Behavior in Descending and Ascending Auctions," *Marketing Science* 31 (September–October 2012), pp. 779–800; and Jason Shachat and Lijia Wei, "Procuring Commodities: First-Price Sealed-Bid or English Auctions?," *Marketing Science* 31 (March–April 2012), pp. 317–33.

61. Nick Brown, "Kodak Patent Sale Plan Gets Bankruptcy Court Approval," *Reuters*, January 11, 2013.

62. Eric Savitz, "SAP to Buy Ariba for $4.3B," www.forbes.com, May 22, 2012; Ashlee Vance, "For an Online Marketplace, It's Better Late than Never," *New York Times*, November 20, 2010.

63. Using expected profit for setting price makes sense for the seller that makes many bids. The seller who bids only occasionally or who needs a particular contract badly will not find it advantageous to use expected profit. This criterion does not distinguish between a $1,000 profit with a 0.10 probability and a $125 profit with a 0.80 probability. Yet the firm that wants to keep production going would prefer the second contract to the first.

64. Bernard Condon, "The Haggle Economy," *Forbes*, June 8, 2009, pp. 26–27; Sandy D. Jap, "The Impact of Online Reverse Auction Design on Buyer-Supplier Relationships," *Journal of Marketing* 71 (January 2007), pp. 146–59; Sandy D. Jap, "An Exploratory Study of the Introduction of Online Reverse Auctions," *Journal of Marketing* 67 (July 2003), pp. 96–107.

65. Paul W. Farris and David J. Reibstein, "How Prices, Expenditures, and Profits Are Linked," *Harvard Business Review*, November–December 1979, pp. 173–84.

66. Joel E. Urbany, "Justifying Profitable Pricing," *Journal of Product and Brand Management* 10 (2001), pp. 141–57; Charles Fishman, "The Wal-Mart You Don't Know," *Fast Company*, December 2003, pp. 68–80.

67. Alicia A. Caldwell, "21 Airlines Fined in Price-Fixing Scheme," *Associated Press*, March 5, 2011.

68. P. N. Agarwala, *Countertrade: A Global Perspective* (New Delhi: Vikas, 1991); Michael Rowe, *Countertrade* (London: Euromoney Books, 1989); Christopher M. Korth, ed., *International Countertrade* (New York: Quorum Books, 1987).

69. Anthony Ramirez, "Pepsi Will Be Bartered for Ships and Vodka in Deal with Soviets," *New York Times*, April 9, 1990.

70. For an interesting discussion of a quantity surcharge, see David E. Sprott, Kenneth C. Manning, and Anthony Miyazaki, "Grocery Price Settings and Quantity Surcharges," *Journal of Marketing* 67 (July 2003), pp. 34–46.

71. Kusum L. Ailawadi, Scott A. Neslin, and Karen Gedenk, "Pursuing the Value-Conscious Consumer: Store Brands versus National-Brand Promotions," *Journal of Marketing* 65 (January 2001), pp. 71–89.

72. Raghunath Singh Rao and Richard Schaefer, "Conspicuous Consumption and Dynamic Pricing," *Marketing Science* 32 (September–October 2013), pp. 786–804; Michael J. Barone and Tirthankar Roy, "Does Exclusivity Always Pay Off? Exclusive Price Promotions and Consumer Response," *Journal of Marketing* 74 (March 2010), pp. 121–32.

73. Jay E. Klompmaker, William H. Rogers, and Anthony E. Nygren, "Value, Not Volume," *Marketing Management* (May–June 2003), pp. 45–48; Lands' End, www.landsend.com, June 23, 2013.

74. Peter Burrows and Olga Kharif, "Can AT&T Tame the iHogs," *Bloomberg Businessweek*, December 28, 2009, and January 4, 2010, pp. 21–22.

75. For an illustrative academic application, see Adib Bagh and Hemant K. Bhargava, "How to Price Discriminate when Tariff Size Matters," *Marketing Science* 32 (January–February 2013), pp. 111–26.

76. Matthew Phillips, "We've Only Just Begun (to Spend)," *Bloomberg Businessweek*, February 13, 2012.

77. Andrea Rothman, "Greyhound Taps Airline Pricing Models to Boost Profit," www.bloomberg.com, May 21, 2013; Bill Saporito, "This Offer Won't Last! Why Sellers Are Switching to Dynamic Pricing," *Time*, January 21, 2013, p. 56; Patrick Rishe, "Dynamic Pricing: The Future of Ticket Pricing in Sports," *Forbes*, January 6, 2012.

78. "Increasing Revenue and Reducing Workload Using Yield Management Software," *Globe Newswire*, March 12, 2013; Julia Angwin and Dana Mattioli, "Coming Soon: Toilet Paper Priced Like Airline Tickets," *Wall Street Journal*, September 5, 2012.

79. Dana Mattioli, "On Orbitz, Mac Users Steered to Pricier Hotels," *Wall Street Journal*, August 23, 2012; Christopher Elliott, "Do Travel Companies Raise Prices Based on Who You Are?," *Huffington Post*, September 1, 2013.

80. Felix Salmon, "Why the Internet Is Perfect for Price Discrimination," *Reuters*, September 3, 2013. For more information about

specific types of price discrimination that are illegal, see Henry Cheeseman, *Business Law,* 8th ed. (Upper Saddle River, NJ: Pearson, 2013).

81. Bob Donath, "Dispel Major Myths about Pricing," *Marketing News,* February 3, 2003, p. 10. For an interesting historical account, see Meghan R. Busse, Duncan I. Simester, and Florian Zettelmeyer, "'The Best Price You'll Ever Get': The 2005 Employee Discount Pricing Promotions, in the U.S. Automobile Industry," *Marketing Science* 29 (March–April 2010), pp. 268–90.

82. Harald J. Van Heerde, Els Gijsbrechts, and Koen Pauwels, "Winners and Losers in a Major Price War," *Journal of Marketing Research* 45 (October 2008), pp. 499–518.

83. For a classic review, see Kent B. Monroe, "Buyers' Subjective Perceptions of Price," *Journal of Marketing Research* 10 (February 1973), pp. 70–80. See also Z. John Zhang, Fred Feinberg, and Aradhna Krishna, "Do We Care What Others Get? A Behaviorist Approach to Targeted Promotions," *Journal of Marketing Research* 39 (August 2002), pp. 277–91.

84. Margaret C. Campbell, "Perceptions of Pricing Unfairness: Antecedents and Consequences," *Journal of Marketing Research* 36 (May 1999), pp. 187–99.

85. Lan Xia, Kent B. Monroe, and Jennifer L. Cox, "The Price Is Unfair! A Conceptual Framework of Price Fairness Perceptions," *Journal of Marketing* 68 (October 2004), pp. 1–15; Eric T. Anderson and Duncan Simester, "Does Demand Fall when Customers Perceive That Prices Are Unfair? The Case of Premium Pricing for Larger Sizes," *Marketing Science* 27 (May–June 2008), pp. 492–500.

86. Eric Mitchell, "How Not to Raise Prices," *Small Business Reports,* November 1990, pp. 64–67.

87. Kusum L. Ailawadi, Donald R. Lehmann, and Scott A. Neslin, "Market Response to a Major Policy Change in the Marketing Mix: Learning from Procter & Gamble's Value Pricing Strategy," *Journal of Marketing* 65 (January 2001), pp. 44–61.

88. Laura Heller, "Publix the Walmart Slayer Wins Another Round with Low Prices," *Forbes,* July 30, 2013.

89. Nirmalya Kumar, "Strategies to Fight Low-Cost Rivals," *Harvard Business Review* (December 2006), pp. 104–12. See also Adrian Ryans, *Beating Low Cost Competition: How Premium Brands Can Respond to Cut-Price Rivals* (West Sussex, England: John Wiley & Sons, 2008); Jack Neff, "How the Discounters Hurt Themselves," *Advertising Age,* December 10, 2007, p. 12.

# Chapter 17

1. L.L.Bean, www.llbean.com; Shelley Banjo, "Firms Take Online Reviews to Heart," *Wall Street Journal,* July 29, 2012; Michael Arndt, "L.L. Bean Follows Its Shoppers to the Web," *Bloomberg Businessweek,* February 18, 2010.

2. Anne T. Coughlan, Erin Anderson, Louis W. Stern, and Adel I. El-Ansary, *Marketing Channels,* 7th ed. (Upper Saddle River, NJ: Prentice Hall, 2007).

3. Louis W. Stern and Barton A. Weitz, "The Revolution in Distribution: Challenges and Opportunities," *Long Range Planning* 30 (December 1997), pp. 823–29.

4. For a summary of academic research, see Erin Anderson and Anne T. Coughlan, "Channel Management: Structure, Governance, and Relationship Management," Bart Weitz and Robin Wensley, eds., *Handbook of Marketing* (London: Sage, 2001), pp. 223–47.

5. Sarah E. Needleman, "Dial-a-Mattress Retailer Blames Troubles on Stores, Executive Team," *Wall Street Journal,* July 14, 2009, p. B1.

6. For an academic treatment of related issues, see Elie Ofek, Zsolt Katona, and Miklos Sarvary, "'Bricks and Clicks': The Impact of Product Returns on the Strategies of Multichannel Retailers," *Marketing Science* 30 (January–February 2011), pp. 42–60.

7. V. Kumar and Rajkumar Venkatesan, "Who Are Multichannel Shoppers and How Do They Perform? Correlates of Multichannel Shopping Behavior," *Journal of Interactive Marketing* 19 (Spring 2005), pp. 44–61.

8. Tarun Kushwaha and Venkatesh Shankar, "Are Multichannel Customers Really More Valuable? The Moderating Role of Product Category Characteristics," *Journal of Marketing* 77 (July 2013), pp. 67–85.

9. www.disney.com, December 9, 2010; Joyceann Cooney, "Mooney's Kingdom," *License,* October 1, 2006.

10. Robert Klara, "Coach Trots Out a New Message," *Adweek,* September 30, 2013, p. 15; Cotton Timberlake, "Luxury Brand Coach Moves to Sell Shoes," *Bloomberg Businessweek,* June 13, 2013; Dana Mattioli, "Coach Sales Feel Pressure of Michael Kors," *Wall Street Journal,* January 23, 2013; Coach Inc. Form 10-K filed with SEC on August 2, 2013.

11. Rajkumar Venkatesan, V. Kumar, and Nalini Ravishanker, "Multichannel Shopping: Causes and Consequences," *Journal of Marketing* 71 (April 2007), pp. 114–32.

12. For detailed conceptual model, see Jill Avery, Thomas J. Steenburgh, John Deighton, Mary Caravella, "Adding Bricks to Clicks: Predicting the Patterns of Cross-Channel Elasticities Over Time," *Journal of Marketing* 76 (May 2012), pp. 96–111.

13. Peter C. Verhoef, Scott A. Neslin, and Björn Vroomen, "Multichannel Customer Management: Understanding the Research-Shopper Phenomenon," *International Journal of Research in Marketing* 24, no. 2 (2007), pp. 129–48.

14. Based on Rowland T. Moriarty and Ursula Moran, "Marketing Hybrid Marketing Systems," *Harvard Business Review,* November–December 1990, pp. 146–55.

15. Hugo Martin, "Outdoor Retailer Patagonia Puts Environment Ahead of Sales Growth," *Los Angeles Times,* May 24, 2012.

16. Mary Wagner, "IRCE 2011 Report: Learn It on the Web, Use It Cross-Channel," www.internetretailer.com, June 20, 2011; Monte Burke, "A Conversation with REI Chief Executive, Sally Jewell," *Forbes,* May 19, 2011; Megan Santosus, "Channel Integration: How REI Scaled E-Commerce Mountain," www.cio.com, May 15, 2004.

17. Chekitan S. Dev and Don E. Schultz, "In the Mix: A Customer-Focused Approach Can Bring the Current Marketing Mix into the 21st Century," *Marketing Management* 14 (January–February 2005).

18. www.oracle.com/us/corporate/oracle-fact-sheet-079219.pdf, accessed November 1, 2013.

19. www.apple.com/about/job-creation/, accessed November 1, 2013.

20. Robert Shaw and Philip Kotler, "Rethinking the Chain," *Marketing Management* (July/August 2009), pp. 18–23.

21. "E-commerce Sales to Rise in U.S.," www.warc.com, March 15, 2013; Lucia Moses, "Data Points: Spending It," *Adweek,* April 16, 2012, pp. 24–25; Darrell Rigby, "The Future of Shopping," *Harvard Business Review,* December 2011.

22. Lauren Johnson, "Walmart App Users Spend 40pc More than Average Shopper," *Mobile Commerce Daily,* September 26, 2013; Chantal Tode, "Walmart Boosts Scan & Go Self-Checkout with Mobile Coupons," *Mobile Commerce Daily,* August 2, 2013; Enid Burns, "Walmart's Mobile App Aims for 'Indispensable' Customer Tools," *E-Commerce Times,* May 22, 2013; "Walmart Takes on Amazon," www.warc.com, March 29, 2013; Farhad Manjoo, "Dot Convert," *Fast Company,* December 2012/January 2013; "Showrooming Shoppers Key for Walmart," www.warc.com, November 26, 2012; Shelly Banjo, "Wal-Mart Is Testing Mobile

Checkout," *Wall Street Journal*, September 1, 2012; Matthew Boyle and Douglas MacMillan, "Wal-Mart's Rocky Path from Bricks to Clicks," *Bloomberg Businessweek*, July 25, 2011.

23. Jayne O'Donnell, "As Shoppers Change, So Do Stores," *USA Today*, January 26, 2010.

24. Thomas H. Davenport, Leandro Dalle Mule, and John Lucker, "Know What Your Customers Want Before They Do," *Harvard Business Review*, December 2011, pp. 84–92.

25. Anderson and Coughlan, "Channel Management: Structure, Governance, and Relationship Management," *Handbook of Marketing*, pp. 223–47.

26. "Ford Dealers Are Recognized for Outstanding Contributions to Their Communities with Ford's Salute to Dealers Award," www.media.ford. com, February 3, 2012.

27. "Kimberly-Clark Test Online Retail Site," www.warc.com, March 6, 2013.

28. www.clevelandclinic.org, December 9, 2010; Geoff Colvin, "The Cleveland Clinic's Delos Cosgrove," *Fortune*, March 1, 2010, pp. 38–45.

29. Asim Ansari, Carl F. Mela, and Scott A. Neslin, "Customer Channel Migration," *Journal of Marketing Research* 45 (February 2008), pp. 60–76; Jacquelyn S. Thomas and Ursula Y. Sullivan, "Managing Marketing Communications," *Journal of Marketing* 69 (October 2005), pp. 239–51; Sridhar Balasubramanian, Rajagopal Raghunathan, and Vijay Mahajan, "Consumers in a Multichannel Environment: Product Utility, Process Utility, and Channel Choice," *Journal of Interactive Marketing* 19 (Spring 2005), pp. 12–30; Edward J. Fox, Alan L. Montgomery, and Leonard M. Lodish, "Consumer Shopping and Spending across Retail Formats," *Journal of Business* 77 (April 2004), pp. S25–S60.

30. Sara Valentini, Elisa Montaguti, and Scott A. Neslin, "Decision Process Evolution in Customer Channel Choice," *Journal of Marketing* 75 (November 2011), pp. 72–86.

31. "They're Shopping, but Not as We Know It," *Marketing Week*, June 14, 2012; John Helyar, "The Only Company Wal-Mart Fears," *Fortune*, November 24, 2003, pp. 158–66. See also Michael Silverstein and Neil Fiske, *Trading Up: The New American Luxury* (New York: Portfolio, 2003).

32. Kelly Liyakasa, "Retailers Brace for Holiday Mobile Commerce Crush," www.adexchanger.com, September 25, 2013; Lydia Dishman, "Target's Carwheel to Bridge the Digital and Brick-and-Mortar Divide," *Forbes*, May 9, 2013; "Retailers Begin to Fight Back on Mobile," www.warc. com, November 23, 2012.

33. Susan Broniarczyk, "Product Assortment," Curtis Haugtvedt, Paul Herr, and Frank Kardes, eds., *Handbook of Consumer Psychology* (New York: Lawrence Erlbaum Associates, 2008), pp. 755–79; Alexander Chernev and Ryan Hamilton, "Assortment Size and Option Attractiveness in Consumer Choice among Retailers," *Journal of Marketing Research* 46 (June 2009), pp. 410–20; Richard A. Briesch, Pradeep K. Chintagunta, and Edward J. Fox, "How Does Assortment Affect Grocery Store Choice," *Journal of Marketing Research* 46 (April 2009), pp. 176–89.

34. Katrijn Gielens and Marnik G. Dekimpe, "The Entry Strategies Retail Firms into Transition Economies," *Journal of Marketing* 71 (April 2007), pp. 196–212.

35. David Segal, "Apple's Retail Army, Long on Loyalty but Short on Pay," *The New York Times*, June 23, 2012; Gardiner Morse and Ron Johnson, "Retail Isn't Broken. Stores Are," *Harvard Business Review*, December 2011, pp. 78–82; Yukari Iwatani Kane and Ian Sherr, "Secrets from Apple's Genius Bar: Full Loyalty, No Negativity," *Wall Street Journal*, June 15, 2011; Alex Frankel, "Magic Shop," *Fast Company*, November 2007, pp. 45–49; Jerry Useem, "Simply Irresistible," *Fortune*, March 19, 2007, pp. 107–12; Nick Wingfield, "How Apple's Store Strategy Beat the Odds," *Wall Street Journal*, May 17, 2006.

36. Richard McGill Murphy, "Cashing In on Kiosks," *Fortune*, December 3, 2012; Jessica Mintz, "Redbox Machines Take On Netflix's Red Envelope," *USA Today*, June 22, 2009; Michael Kraus, "How Redbox Is Changing Retail," *Marketing News*, November 15, 2009, p. 23.

37. Janko Roettgers, "Netflix May Ditch DVDs Sooner Rather than Later," *Bloomberg Businessweek*, October 21, 2013; Ashlee Vance, "Netflix, Reed Hastings Survive Missteps to Join Silicon Valley's Elite," *Bloomberg Businessweek*, May 9, 2013; Ronald Grover, Adam Satariano, and Ari Levy, "Honest, Hollywood, Netflix Is Your Friend," *Bloomberg Businessweek*, January 11, 2010, pp. 54–55; Michael V. Copeland, "Tapping Tech's Beautiful Minds," *Fortune*, October 12, 2009, pp. 35–36; Jefferson Graham, "Netflix Is Still Renting Strong," *USA Today*, July 1, 2009, p. 2B; Timothy J. Mullaney, "The Mail Order House That Clobbered Blockbuster," *BusinessWeek*, June 5, 2006, pp. 56–57.

38. "Trouser Suit," *Economist*, November 24, 2001, p. 56.

39. "Why STIHL Chooses Independent Dealers," www.stihlusa.com, accessed November 2, 2013; Ken Waldron, "How Stihl Fulfilled Brand Promise of Superior Product, Customer Service," *Advertising Age*, December 10, 2009; Timothy Appel, "Too Good for Lowe's and Home Depot?," *Wall Street Journal*, July 24, 2006.

40. "Nike Says No to Blue-Light Specials," *Fortune*, May 4, 2005.

41. Robert K. Heady, "Online Bank Offers Best Rates," *South Florida Sun-Sentinel*, November 22, 2004.

42. Anderson and Coughlan, "Channel Management: Structure, Governance, and Relationship Management," *Handbook of Marketing*, pp. 223–47; Michaela Draganska, Daniel Klapper, and Sofia B. Villa-Boas, "A Larger Slice or a Larger Pie? An Empirical Investigation of Bargaining Power in the Distribution Channel," *Marketing Science* 29 (January–February 2010), pp. 57–74.

43. These bases of power were identified in John R. P. French and Bertram Raven, "The Bases of Social Power," Dorwin Cartwright, ed., *Studies in Social Power* (Ann Arbor: University of Michigan Press, 1959), pp. 150–67.

44. Joydeep Srivastava and Dipankar Chakravarti, "Channel Negotiations with Information Asymmetries: Contingent Influences of Communication and Trustworthiness Reputations," *Journal of Marketing Research* 46 (August 2009), pp. 557–72.

45. Daniel Corsten and Nirmalya Kumar, "Do Suppliers Benefit from Collaborative Relationships with Large Retailers? An Empirical Investigation of Efficient Consumer Response Adoption," *Journal of Marketing* 69 (July 2005), pp. 80–94; for some related research, see Ashwin W. Joshi, "Continuous Supplier Performance Improvement: Effects of Collaborative Communication and Control," *Journal of Marketing* 73 (January 2009), pp. 133–50.

46. Cotton Timberlake, "In the iPhone Era, Leica Tries Its Own Stores," *Bloomberg Businessweek*, June 18, 2012.

47. For a detailed case study example, see Jennifer Shang, Tuba Pinar Yildrim, Pandu Tadikamalla, Vikas Mittal, and Lawrence Brown, "Distribution Network Redesign for Marketing Competitiveness," *Journal of Marketing* 73 (March 2009), pp. 146–63.

48. Xinlei Chen, George John, and Om Narasimhan, "Assessing the Consequences of a Channel Switch," *Marketing Science* 27 (May–June 2008), pp. 398–416.

49. Thomas H. Davenport and Jeanne G. Harris, *Competing on Analytics: The New Science of Winning* (Boston: Harvard Business School Press, 2007).

50. Junhong Chu, Pradeep K. Chintagunta, and Naufel J. Vilcassim, "Assessing the Economic Value of Distribution Channels: An Application to the Personal Computer Industry," *Journal of Marketing Research* 44 (February 2007), pp. 29–41.

51. Rajdeep Grewal, Alok Kumar, Girish Mallapragada, and Amit Saini, "Marketing Channels in Foreign Markets: Control Mechanisms and the Moderating Role of Multinational Corporation Headquarters–Subsidiary Relationship," *Journal of Marketing Research* 50 (June 2013), pp. 378–98; Zhilin Yang, Chenting Su, and Kim-Shyan Fam, "Dealing with Institutional Distances in International Marketing Channels: Governance Strategies That Engender Legitimacy and Efficiency," *Journal of Marketing* 76 (May 2012), pp. 41–55.

52. Richard Gibson, "U.S. Franchises Find Opportunities to Grow Abroad," *Wall Street Journal*, August 11, 2009, p. B5.

53. "Send for the Supermarketers," *The Economist*, April 16, 2011, pp. 67–68; "Unshackling the Chain Stores," *The Economist*, May 31, 2008, pp. 69–70.

54. "Coach Taps Chinese Opportunity," www.warc.com, October 25, 2012; Jeffrey Ng and Mariko Sanchanta, "J. Crew Brings Its Brand to China," *Wall Street Journal*, July 31, 2012; Laurie Burkitt and Bob Davis, "Chasing China's Shoppers," *Wall Street Journal*, June 14, 2012; "All Eyes on Chinese Aisles," *The Economist*, May 21, 2011;

55. Paul Sonne and Peter Evans, "The $1.6 Billion Grocery Flop: Tesco Poised to Quit U.S.," *Wall Street Journal*, December 5, 2012; Paul Sonne, "At Tesco Expansion Takes a Back Seat," *Wall Street Journal*, November 7, 2012; Peter Evans, "Britain's Tesco Tries Out New Retail Recipe," *Wall Street Journal*, July 8, 2012; Matthew Boyle and Michael V. Copeland, "Tesco Reinvents the 7-Eleven," *Fortune*, November 26, 2007, p. 34.

56. Christina Passariello, "Carrefour's Makeover Plan: Become Ikea of Groceries," *Wall Street Journal*, September 16, 2010.

57. Harriett Walker, "Bright Sparks: Urban Outfitters," *The Independent*, January 23, 2012; Michael Arndt, "Urban Outfitters Grow-Slow Strategy," *Bloomberg Businessweek*, March 1, 2010, p. 56; Michael Arndt, "How to Play It: Apparel Makers," *Bloomberg Businessweek*, March 1, 2010, p. 61.

58. "Nordstrom to Expand Topshop and Topman Partnership to 28 Additional Stores This Fall," *PRNewswire*, August 27, 2013; "Topshop Confirms German Expansion," *Fashion United*, July 8, 2013; Stephanie Wong and Susan Li, "Billionaire Green Starts Hunt for First Topshop China Stores," *Bloomberg Businessweek*, June 5, 2013; Cara Waters, "Topshop Opens Its Doors in Sydney: Five Secrets to the Retailer's Success in Australia," *Smart Company*, October 4, 2012; Cotton Timberlake, "Nordstrom Tries an Extreme Makeover with Topshop," *Bloomberg Businessweek*, July 12, 2102; Damien Reece, "Topshop's Injection of True Brit Stirs Up the Big Apple," *Daily Telegraph*, April 2, 2009; Jenifer Reingold, "The British (Retail) Invasion," *Fortune*, July 7, 2008, pp. 132–38.

59. V. Kasturi Rangan, *Transforming Your Go-to-Market Strategy: The Three Disciplines of Channel Management* (Boston: Harvard Business School Press, 2006).

60. Stefan Wuyts, Stefan Stremersch, Christophe Van Den Bulte, and Philip Hans Franses, "Vertical Marketing Systems for Complex Products: A Triadic Perspective," *Journal of Marketing Research* 41 (November 2004), pp. 479–87.

61. Arnt Bovik and George John, "When Does Vertical Coordination Improve Industrial Purchasing Relationships," *Journal of Marketing* 64 (October 2000), pp. 52–64

62. Raji Srinivasan, "Dual Distribution and Intangible Firm Value: Franchising in Restaurant Chains," *Journal of Marketing* 70 (July 2006), pp. 120–35.

63. www.citizensbank.com, December 9, 2010.

64. "Low Prices Key to E-commerce," www.warc.com, March 6, 2013.

65. Joel C. Collier and Carol C. Bienstock, "How Do Customers Judge Quality in an E-tailer," *MIT Sloan Management Review* (Fall 2006), pp. 35–40.

66. *Coremetrics Benchmark December US Retail*, www.coremetrics.com/downloads/coremetrics-benchmark-industry-report-2008-12-us.pdf.

67. Jeff Borden, "The Right Tools," *Marketing News*, April 15, 2008, pp. 19–21.

68. Geg Bensinger, "Order It Online, and…Voilá," *Wall Street Journal*, December 3, 2012.

69. Amanda B. Bower and James G. Maxham III, "Return Shipping Policies of Online Retailers: Normative Assumptions and the Long-Term Consequences of Fee and Free Returns," *Journal of Marketing* 76 (September 2012), pp. 110–24.

70. Christine Birkner, "The ABCs of Affiliate Marketing," *Marketing News*, August 31, 2012.

71. Alexis K. J. Barlow, Noreen Q. Siddiqui, and Mike Mannion, "Development in Information and Communication Technologies for Retail Marketing Channels," *International Journal of Retail and Distribution Management* 32 (March 2004), pp. 157–63; G&J Electronic Media Services, *7th Wave of the GfK-Online-Monitor* (Hamburg: GfK Press, 2001).

72. Martin Holzwarth, Chris Janiszewski, and Marcus M. Newmann, "The Influence of Avatars on Online Consumer Shopping Behavior," *Journal of Marketing* 70 (October 2006), pp. 19–36.

73. Ann E. Schlosser, Tiffany Barnett White, and Susan M. Lloyd, "Converting Web Site Visitors into Buyers: How Web Site Investment Increases Consumer Trusting Beliefs and Online Purchase Intentions," *Journal of Marketing* 70 (April 2006), pp. 133–48.

74. Ronald Abler, John S. Adams, and Peter Gould, *Spatial Organizations: The Geographer's View of the World* (Upper Saddle River, NJ: Prentice Hall, 1971), pp. 531–32.

75. "Alibaba Breaks Sales Record amid China Singles-Day Rebate," *Bloomberg*, November 12, 2013; Julianne Pepitone, "Meet Alibaba, Yahoo's Chinese Secret Weapon," *CNNMoney*, October 29, 2013; Danielle Kucera, "How Alibaba Could Underprice Amazon, and Other Things You Should Know," *Bloomberg Businessweek*, October 14, 2013; John Foley, "Why Alibaba Could Be China's Next $100 Billion IPO," *Reuters Breakingviews*, April 26, 2013; Jessica E. Vascellaro, "Alibaba.com Plans U.S Push," *Wall Street Journal*, August 7, 2009.

76. Andrea Chang, "Retailers Fuse Stores with E-commerce," *Los Angeles Times*, June 27, 2010.

77. Anjali Cordeiro, "Procter & Gamble Sees Aisle Expansion on the Web," *Wall Street Journal*, September 2, 2009, p. B6A; Anjali Cordeiro and Ellen Byron, "Procter & Gamble to Test Online Store to Study Buying Habits," *Wall Street Journal*, January 15, 2010.

78. "Brands Gain Ground in Online Retail Race," www.warc.com, February 8, 2013.

79. Xubing Zhang, "Retailer's Multichannel and Price Advertising Strategies," *Marketing Science* 28 (November–December 2009), pp. 1080–94.

80. "2012 Annual Report," www.harley-davidson.com; Rick Barrett, "Store Closings Place Number of U.S. Dealerships at About Same Level as 2002," *Milwaukee Journal Sentinel*, January 29, 2012; Susan Fournier and Lara Lee, "Getting Brand Communities Right," *Harvard Business Review*, April 2009, pp. 105–11; "New Harley Davidson Accessory and Clothing Store," *PRLog*, July 21, 2009; Bob Tedeshi, "How Harley Revved Online Sales," *Business 2.0*, December 2002–January 2003, pp. 44.

81. "How Mobile Coupons Are Driving an Explosion in Mobile Commerce," *Business Insider*, August 12, 2013; "New York Startup Launches First Stand-Alone Mobile Commerce Solution for Small and Medium-Sized Businesses," *PRNewswire*, June 27, 2013.

82. Lucia Moses, "Data Points: Mobile Shopping," *Adweek*, May 20, 2013, pp. 20–21.

83. Christopher Heine, "For Mobile Marketing That Really Works, Just Look to Asia," *Adweek*, February 11, 2013, pp. 19–21.

84. Jon Fingas, "NTT DoCoMo's Xi Gets 10 Million Subscribers on the LTE Bandwagon," www.engadget.com, February 19, 2013.

85. Venkatesh Shankar, Alladi Venkatesh, Charles Hofacker, and Prasad Naik, "Mobile Marketing in the Retailing Environment: Current Insights and Future Research Avenues," special issue, Venkatesh Shankar and Manjit Yadav, eds., *Journal of Interactive Marketing* 24 (May 2010), pp. 111–20; Venkatesh Shankar and Sridhar Balasubramanian, "Mobile Marketing: A Synthesis and Prognosis," *Journal of Interactive Marketing* 23 (2009), pp. 118–29; Herbjørn Nysveen, Per E. Pedersen, Helge Thorbjørnsen, and Pierre Berthon, "Mobilizing the Brand: The Effects of Mobile Services on Brand Relationships and Main Channel Use," *Journal of Service Research* 7 (2005), pp. 257–76; Douglas Lamont, *Conquering the Wireless World: The Age of M-Commerce* (New York: John Wiley & Sons, 2001).

86. Chantal Tode, "Dunkin' Donuts Tries to Best Starbucks in Mobile Loyalty," *Mobile Commerce Daily*, October 28, 2013; Christopher Heine, "Dunkin' Drives to Twitter & Vine," *Adweek*, October 14, 2013, p. 16; Paul Frumkin, "Dunkin' Donuts Taps Eli Manning to Promote App," *Nation's Restaurant News*, September 4, 2013; Lauren Johnson, "Dunkin' Donuts Drills Down on Location to Boost Mobile Payments App," *Mobile Commerce Daily*, August 19, 2013.

87. Jonathan Nelson, "One Screen to Rule Them All," *Adweek*, February 11, 2013.

88. Lucia Moses, "Data Points: Women and Mobile," *Adweek*, October 28, 2013.

89. Stephanie Clifford, "Retailers Add Gadgets for Shoppers at Ease with Technology," *Wall Street Journal*, March 9, 2012.

90. Dr. Paul Marsden, "The Social Commerce Acid Test from Amex," *Social Commerce Today*, July 21, 2011; Shayndi Raice and Robin Sidel, "AmEx Teams Up with Foursquare," *Wall Street Journal*, March 4, 2011.

91. Christopher Heine, "The Top 7 Reasons Mobile Ads Don't Work," *Adweek*, October 17, 2013.

92. Farhan Thawar, "2013: The Breakout Year for Mobile Commerce," *Wired*, March 15, 2013.

93. "How Mobile Coupons Are Driving an Explosion in Mobile Commerce," *Business Insider*, August 12, 2013.

94. Sam K. Hui, J. Jeffrey Inman, Yanliu Huang, and Jacob Suher, "The Effect of In-Store Travel Distance on Unplanned Spending: Applications to Mobile Promotion Strategies," *Journal of Marketing* 77 (March 2013), pp. 1–16.

95. Lauren Brousel, "5 Things You Need to Know about Geofencing," *CIO*, August 28, 2013; Dana Mattioli and Miguel Bustillo, "Can Texting Save Stores?," *Wall Street Journal*, May 8, 2012.

96. Stephanie Clifford, "Attention, Shoppers: Store Is Tracking Your Cell," *New York Times*, July 14, 2013.

97. Rick Whiting, "Oracle Says Recent Initiatives Are Reducing Channel Conflict," www.crn.com, October 14, 2009; Barbara Darow, "Oracle's New Partner Path," *CRN*, August 21, 2006, p. 4.

98. Anne Coughlan and Louis Stern, "Marketing Channel Design and Management," Dawn Iacobucci, ed., *Kellogg on Marketing* (New York: John Wiley & Sons, 2001), pp. 247–69.

99. Nirmalya Kumar, "Some Tips on Channel Management," rediff.com, July 1, 2005.

100. Matthew Boyle, "Brand Killers," *Fortune*, August 11, 2003, pp. 51–56; for an opposing view, see Anthony J. Dukes, Esther Gal-Or, and Kannan Srinivasan, "Channel Bargaining with Retailer Asymmetry," *Journal of Marketing Research* 43 (February 2006), pp. 84–97.

101. Jerry Useem, Julie Schlosser, and Helen Kim, "One Nation under Wal-Mart," *Fortune* (Europe), March 3, 2003. For a more thorough academic examination that shows the benefits to suppliers from Walmart expanding their market, see Qingyi Huang, Vincent R. Nijs, Karsten Hansen, and Eric T. Anderson, "Wal-Mart's Impact on Supplier Profits," *Journal of Marketing Research* 49 (April 2012), pp. 131–43.

102. Sreekumar R. Bhaskaran and Stephen M. Gilbert, "Implications of Channel Structure for Leasing or Selling Durable Goods," *Marketing Science* 28 (September–October 2009), pp. 918–34.

103. For some examples of when conflict can be viewed as helpful, see Anil Arya and Brian Mittendorf, "Benefits of Channel Discord in the Sale of Durable Goods," *Marketing Science* 25 (January–February 2006), pp. 91–96; and Nirmalya Kumar, "Living with Channel Conflict," *CMO Magazine,* October 2004.

104. Danny T. Wang, Flora F. Gu, and Maggie Chuoyan Dong, "Observer Effects of Punishment in a Distribution Network," *Journal of Marketing Research* 50 (October 2013), pp. 627–43.

105. This section draws on Coughlan et al., *Marketing Channels*, chapter 9. See also Jonathan D. Hibbard, Nirmalya Kumar, and Louis W. Stern, "Examining the Impact of Destructive Acts in Marketing Channel Relationships," *Journal of Marketing Research* 38 (February 2001), pp. 45–61; Kersi D. Antia and Gary L. Frazier, "The Severity of Contract Enforcement in Interfirm Channel Relationships," *Journal of Marketing* 65 (October 2001), pp. 67–81; James R. Brown, Chekitan S. Dev, and Dong-Jin Lee, "Managing Marketing Channel Opportunism: The Efficiency of Alternative Governance Mechanisms," *Journal of Marketing* 64 (April 2000), pp. 51–65; Alberto Sa Vinhas and Erin Anderson, "How Potential Conflict Drives Channel Structure: Concurrent (Direct and Indirect) Channels," *Journal of Marketing Research* 42 (November 2005), pp. 507–15.

106. Niraj Dawar and Jason Stornelli, "Rebuilding the Relationship Between Manufacturers and Retailers," *MIT Sloan Management Review*, Winter 2013, pp. 83–90.

107. Nirmalya Kumar, "Living with Channel Conflict," *CMO Magazine,* October 2004.

108. Kersi D. Antia, Xu (Vivian) Zheng, and Gary L. Frazier, "Conflict Management and Outcomes in Franchise Relationships: The Role of Regulation," *Journal of Marketing Research* 50 (October 2013), pp. 577–89.

109. Andrew Kaplan, "All Together Now?," *Beverage World*, March 2007, pp. 14–16.

110. Tricia Carr, "Gucci Combines Physical, Mobile Commerce via Digital Store-in-Store," *Luxury Daily*, June 18, 2012; Christina Passriello, "Fashionably Late? Designer Brands Are Starting to Embrace E-Commerce," *Wall Street Journal*, May 19, 2006.

## Chapter 18

1. Mike O'Toole, "Warby Parker, One Million Eyeglasses, and the Next Generation of Brands," *Forbes,* July 22, 2013; Knowledge@Wharton, "The Consumer Psychology behind Warby Parker's $95 Pricing for Eyeglasses," *Time,* May 23, 2013; Sheila Shayon, "Warby Parker's Long-Term Vision: From the Web to the Street, NYC to the World," *Brandchannel,* September 11, 2012; "Warby Parker Revolutionizes Eyewear Market by Borrowing from Apple, Zappos," *Advertising Age*, November 27, 2011.

2. Mina Kimes, "The Sun Tzu at Sears," *Bloomberg Businessweek*, July 11, 2013; Jessica Dubois-Maahs, "Sears' Failure to Adapt Disillusions Shoppers, Shareholders," *Medill Report*, March 12, 2013; "February 2013 and Historical ACSI Benchmarks," *American Customer Satisfaction Index*, February 26, 2013; Chris Morran, "Sears

Is Failing Because It Spends Next-to-Nothing to Maintain Stores," *Consumerist*, July 30, 2012; Michael Brush, "Why Sears Is on Its Last Legs," *MSN Money*, April 17, 2012; Andrea Billups, "Sears, Kmart Failed to Anticipate Their Customers' Needs," *The Washington Times*, December 29, 2011.

3. Karsten Hansen and Vishal Singh, "Market Structure across Retail Formats," *Marketing Science* 28 (July–August 2009), pp. 656–73.

4. "U.S. E-commerce Sales as Percent of Retail Sales," Census Bureau, September 30, 2013.

5. Jill Becker, "Vending Machines for All Your Needs," www.cnn.com, August 16, 2012; Nick Montano, "Japan's Vending Machine Industry Declines 2%," *Vending Times*, June, 2012; David Meerman Scott, "Should Coca-Cola Unplug Its Vending Machines in Japan to Conserve Scarce Power?," *Huffington Post*, March 22, 2011.

6. Alistair Barr and Scott Martin, "The First 'Flash Sales' Site to Go Public Is…Zulily," *USA Today*, October 8, 2013; Sarah Frier, "Gilt Groupe CEO Seeks to Prove Flash Sales Are No Fad," *Bloomberg Businessweek*, August 1, 2013; Spencer E. Ante, "Are Flash Sales Still 'Fab'ulous?," *Wall Street Journal*, July 19, 2012; Christina Cheddar Berk, "Time for Flash Sales to Adapt or Die," www.cnbc.com, May 25, 2012; Shelley Dubois, "What's Gilt Groupe's Secret Weapon?," *Fortune*, March 5, 2012; Matthew Carroll, "The Rise of Gilt Groupe: The Great Recession Fuels the Perfect Storm," *Forbes*, January 2, 2012; Claire Cain Miller, "Flash-Sale Site Shifts Its Model," *New York Times*, August 14, 2011.

7. "Census Bureau's First Release of Comprehensive Franchise Data Shows Franchises Make Up More than 10 Percent of Employer Businesses," www.census.gov, September 14, 2010.

8. J. J. Colao, "Top 20 Franchises for the Buck," *Forbes*, February 8, 2012.

9. Vivian Giang, "McDonald's Hamburger University: Step Inside the Most Exclusive School in the World," *Business Insider*, April 12, 2012.

10. Raymund Flandez, "New Franchise Idea: Fewer Rules, More Difference," *Wall Street Journal*, September 18, 2007, p. B4; www.greatharvest.com/company/philosophy.html, accessed December 9, 2013.

11. Karma Allen, "How Savvy Retailers Are Reinventing the Pop-Up Model," www.cnbc.com, November 22, 2013; Matt Townsend, "The Staying Power of Pop-Ups," *Bloomberg Businessweek*, November 15, 2010.

12. Brad Stone and David Welch, "The Future Retail Wasteland," *Bloomberg Businessweek*, April 16, 2012.

13. Mark Vroegrijk, Els Gijsbrechts, and Katia Campo, "Close Encounter with the Hard Discounter: A Multiple-Store Shopping Perspective on the Impact of Local Hard-Discounter Entry," *Journal of Marketing Research* 50 (October 2013), pp. 606–26.

14. Jim Zarroli, "In Trendy World of Fast Fashion, Styles Aren't Made to Last," www.npr.org, March 11, 2013; "Zara, H&M Are Top UK Fashion Brands," www.warc.com, December 17, 2012; "Fast Retailing Prioritizes Innovation," www.warc.com, October 15, 2012.

15. Annie Gasparro and Timothy W. Martin, "What's Wrong with America's Supermarkets," *Wall Street Journal*, July 12, 2012; Elizabeth Shell, "Bargain Basement and Top Shelf: What's Driving Growth for Retailers," www.pbs.org, December 23, 2011; Ellen Byron, "As Middle Class Shrinks, P&G Aims High and Low," *Wall Street Journal*, September 12, 2011.

16. Tim Dickey, "Electronic Shelf Labels," *Retail Technology Trends*, February 26, 2010.

17. K. C. Ifeanyi, "Burberry Makes It Rain in Taipei," www.fastcompany.com, April 27, 2012; Barry Silverstein, "The Future of Retail: Reinventing and Preserving the In-Store Experience," www.brandchannel.com, March 22, 2013.

18. Clint Boulton, "Snackmaker Modernizes the Impulse Buy with Sensors, Analytics," *Wall Street Journal*, October 11, 2013.

19. Elizabeth A. Harris, "Retailers Seek Partners in Social Networks," *New York Times*, November 26, 2013.

20. Christopher Heine, "Social Pics Help Retailers Get Real," *Adweek*, September 16, 2013, p. 11.

21. Sam Grobart, "Cracking Whole Foods," *Bloomberg Businessweek*, November 26, 2012; "Forbes Earnings Preview: Whole Foods Market," *Forbes*, November 2, 2012; Leslie Patton and Bryan Gruley, "Walter Robb on Whole Foods' Recession Lessons," *Bloomberg Businessweek*, August 9, 2012; Martin Lindstrom, "How Whole Foods 'Primes' You to Shop," *Fast Company*, September 14, 2011; "Whole Foods Market 2009 Annual Report," www.wholefoodsmarket.com/company/pdfs/ar09.pdf.

22. Ann Zimmerman and Kris Hudson, "Chasing Upscale Customers Tarnishes Mass-Market Jeweler," *Wall Street Journal*, June 26, 2006; Kris Hudson, "Signet Sparkles with Jewelry Strategy," *Wall Street Journal*, June 26, 2006.

23. Jillian Berman, "Retailers Try to Get Creative with Their Catalogs during Tough Times," *USA Today*, July 19, 2010.

24. Ashley Lutz, "Why the Lingerie Industry Can't Compete with Victoria's Secret," *Business Insider*, September 2, 2013; Sapna Maheshwari, "Victoria's Secret Channels Mad Men into Hottest Limited," *Bloomberg Businessweek*, November 12, 2012; Scott Cendrowski and Anne VanderMey, "Victoria's Secret Weapons," *Fortune*, February 6, 2012.

25. Robert P. Rooderkerk, Harald J. van Heerde, and Tammo H. A. Bijmolt, "Optimizing Retail Assortment," *Marketing Science* 32 (September–October 2013), pp. 699–715.

26. Richard A. Briesch, William R. Dillon, and Edward J. Fox, "Category Positioning and Store Choice: The Role of Destination Categories," *Marketing Science* 32 (May–June 2013), pp. 488–509.

27. Jessi Hempel, "Urban Outfitters, Fashion Victim," *BusinessWeek*, July 17, 2006, p. 60.

28. Aeropostale, www.aeropostale.com, accessed December 9, 2013; Jeanine Poggi, "Best in Class: Price Is Right at Aeropostale," *The Street*, June 16, 2009; "Aeropostale, Inc. Seeks New Faces for Fall Ad Campaign with 'Real Teens 2010' Contest," *PR Newswire*, March 15, 2010; Robert Berner, "To Lure Teenager Mall Rats, You Need the Right Cheese," *BusinessWeek*, June 7, 2004, pp. 96–101.

29. Vanessa O'Connell, "Reversing Field, Macy's Goes Local," *Wall Street Journal*, April 21, 2008.

30. Mary Catherine O'Conner, "Gillette Fuses RFID with Product Launch," *RFID Journal*, March 27, 2006; "The End of Privacy?," *Consumer Reports*, June 2006, pp. 33–40; "Radio Silence," *Economist*, June 9, 2007, pp. 20–21; Todd Lewan, "The Chipping of America," *Associated Press*, July 29, 2007.

31. George Anderson, "Why Are the Trader Joe's Customers the Most Satisfied In America?," *Forbes*, July 30, 2013; Tim Linden, "Re-Invention Key to Success at Trader Joe's," *The Produce News*, November 26, 2012; Beth Kowitt, "Inside the Secret World of Trader Joe's," *Fortune*, August 23, 2010; "Trader Joe's Named a Breakaway Brand for 2009," *Supermarket Industry News*, August 17, 2009; Christopher Palmeri. "Trader Joe's Recipe for Success," *BusinessWeek*, February 21, 2008.

32. Venkatesh Shankar and Ruth N. Bolton, "An Empirical Analysis of Determinants of Retailer Pricing Strategy," *Marketing Science* 23 (Winter 2004), pp. 28–49.

33. Nishu Kakkar, "Bijan: The Most Expensive Store by Appointment Only," www.most-expensive.com/store-world, December 14, 2011; Eric Wilson, "Bijan Pakzad, Designer of High Fashion, Dies at 71," *New York Times*, April 18, 2011.

34. Sam Grobart, "Target Practice," *Bloomberg Businessweek*, January 7, 2013; Anne D'Innocenzio, "Target versus Walmart: Haves and Have Nots," *Associated Press*, November 18, 2012; Stuart Feil, "50 Years of Discounting," Special Advertising Section, *Adweek*, June 24, 2012.

35. Paul W. Miniard, Shazad Mustapha Mohammed, Michael J. Barone, and Cecilia M. O. Alvarez, "Retailers' Use of Partially Comparative Pricing: From Across-Category to Within-Category Effects," *Journal of Marketing* 77 (July 2013), pp. 33–48; Jiwoong Shin, "The Role of Selling Costs in Signaling Price Image," *Journal of Marketing Research* 42 (August 2005), pp. 305–12.

36. For a comprehensive framework of the key image drivers of price image formation for retailers, see Ryan Hamilton and Alexander Chernev, "Low Prices Are Just the Beginning: Price Image in Retail Management," *Journal of Marketing* 77 (November 2013), pp. 1–20.

37. David R. Bell and James M. Lattin, "Shopping Behavior and Consumer Preference for Retail Price Format: Why 'Large Basket' Shoppers Prefer EDLP," *Marketing Science* 17 (Spring 1998), pp. 66–68.

38. Ken Belson, "Meccas of Shopping Try Hand at Being Misers of Energy," *New York Times*, April 10, 2012.

39. Cotten Timberlake, "Don't Even Think about Returning This Dress," *Bloomberg Businessweek*, September 26, 2013; Miguel Bustillo, "Retailers Loosen Up on Returns," *Wall Street Journal*, December 27, 2010. See also J. Andrew Peterson and V. Kumar, "Earning a Nice Return on Product Returns," *MIT Sloan Management Review* 51 (Spring 2010), pp. 85–89; and J. Andrew Peterson and V. Kumar, "Are Product Returns a Necessary Evil? Antecedents and Consequences," *Journal of Marketing* 73 (May 2009), pp. 35–51.

40. Christopher Steiner, "Taming the Spread," *Forbes*, February 28, 2011.

41. Ilaina Jones, "Kohl's Looking at Spots in Manhattan," *Reuters*, August 19, 2009; Cametta Coleman, "Kohl's Retail Racetrack," *Wall Street Journal*, March 1, 2000.

42. Robert Klara, "Something in the Air," *Adweek*, March 5, 2012, pp. 25–27.

43. Velitchka D. Kaltcheva and Barton Weitz, "When Should a Retailer Create an Exciting Store Environment?," *Journal of Marketing* 70 (January 2006), pp. 107–18.

44. For more discussion, see B. Joseph Pine II and James H. Gilmore, *The Experience Economy* (Boston: Harvard Business School Press, 1999).

45. Dave Hodges, "Fans Welcome Bass Pro Shops to Town," Tallahassee.com, September 5, 2013; Seth Lubove, "Bass Pro Billionaire Building Megastore with Boats, Guns," *Bloomberg, Businessweek*, June 3, 2013; Michael Sheffield, "Details of Bass Pro Shops Megastore Revealed," *Memphis Business Journal*, February 22, 2013; "Increase Retail Customer Traffic by Learning from Bass Pro Shop," *Infinitee*, June 26, 2012; Thomas Pardee, "Bass Pro Shops," *Advertising Age*, November 15, 2010.

46. Elizabeth Holmes, "Dark Art of Store Emails," *Wall Street Journal*, December 18, 2012.

47. "Social Network Rockets Houlihan Restaurants' Profits," *Fast Company*, March 2010.

48. Elizabeth Holmes, "Why Pay Full Price," *Wall Street Journal*, May 5, 2011.

49. Shira Ovide, "Now on Twitter: Holiday Shopping Deals," *Wall Street Journal*, December 16, 2012.

50. Christopher Heine, "The Daily Deal Gets Squeezed," *Adweek*, March 11, 2013.

51. Carol Tice, "Anchors Away: Department Stores Lose Role at Malls," *Puget Sound Business Journal*, February 13, 2004, p. 1.

52. "Private Label Sales Rise in Europe," www.warc.com, October 19, 2012.

53. E. J. Schultz, "Grocery Shoppers Continue to Spend Less, Embrace Private Label," *Advertising Age*, June 10, 2011; "Store Brands Growing across All Channels," Private Label Manufacturers Association, www.

plma.com, accessed April 3, 2013; Emily Bryson York, "Don't Blame Private Label Gains on the Recession," *Advertising Age*, April 21, 2009.

54. Matthew Boyle, "Even Better than the Real Thing," *Bloomberg Businessweek*, November 28, 2011.

55. Lien Lamey, Barbara Deleersnyder, Jan-Benedict E. M. Steenkamp, and Marnik G. Dekimpe, "The Effect of Business-Cycle Fluctuations on Private-Label Share: What Has Marketing Conduct Got to Do with It?," *Journal of Marketing* 76 (January 2012), pp. 1–19.

56. Kusum Ailawadi and Bari Harlam, "An Empirical Analysis of the Determinants of Retail Margins: The Role of Store-Brand Share," *Journal of Marketing* 68 (January 2004), pp. 147–65.

57. For a detailed analysis of contemporary research on private labels, see Michael R. Hyman, Dennis A. Kopf, and Dongdae Lee, "Review of Literature—Future Research Suggestions: Private Label Brands: Benefits, Success Factors, and Future Research, *Journal of Brand Management* 17 (March 2010), pp. 368–89. See also Kusum Ailawadi, Bari Harlam, Jacques Cesar, and David Trounce, "Retailer Promotion Profitability: The Role of Promotion, Brand, Category, and Market Characteristics," *Journal of Marketing Research* 43 (November 2006), pp. 518–35; Kusum Ailawadi, Koen Pauwels, and Jan-Benedict E. M. Steenkamp, "Private Label Use and Store Loyalty," *Journal of Marketing* 72 (November 2008), pp. 19–30.

58. Anne ter Braak, Marnik G. Dekimpe, and Inge Geyskens, "Retailer Private-Label Margins: The Role of Supplier and Quality-Tier Differentiation," *Journal of Marketing* 77 (July 2013), pp. 86–103.

59. Natasha Singer, "Drug Firms Apply Brand to Generics," *New York Times*, February 16, 2010; Casey Feldman, "Generic Drug Superstars," *Fortune*, August 5, 2009; Mina Kimes, "Teva: The King of Generic Drugs," *Fortune*, August 5, 2009; Jeanne Whalen, "Betting $10 Billion on Generics, Novartis Seeks to Inject Growth," *Wall Street Journal*, May 4, 2006.

60. Boyle, "Even Better than the Real Thing."

61. Grant Surridge, "Brands of the Year: Rediscovering the Loblaw Story," *Strategy*, September 28, 2012; Jeff Beer, "An Even Better Choice?," *Canadian Business*, October 5, 2011; Hollie Shaw, "Loblaws Bets on Black Label to Lure Sales," *Financial Post*, September 13, 2011; Jim Chrizan, "Loblaw's Reverses Private Label Trend," *Packaging World*, January 22, 2010; "Loblaw Launches a New Line of Discount Store Brands," *Store Brand Decisions*, February 16, 2010; John J. Pierce, "Private Label Stimulus," *Private Label*, March/April 2009.

62. For an analytical examination, see Sherif Nasser, Danko Turcic, and Chakravarthi Narasimhan, "National Brand's Response to Store Brands: Throw In the Towel or Fight Back?," *Marketing Science* 32 (July–August 2013), pp. 591–608.

63. Brett Nelson, "Stuck in the Middle," *Forbes*, August 15, 2005, p. 88; "Arrow Company Profile," www.arrow.com, accessed December 12, 2013.

64. James A. Narus and James C. Anderson, "Contributing as a Distributor to Partnerships with Manufacturers," *Business Horizons* (September–October 1987). See also Hlavecek and McCuistion, "Industrial Distributors—When, Who, and How," pp. 96–101.

65. Debra Hoffman, "Gartner Supply Chain Top 25," www.gartner.com, May 30, 2013.

66. "The Supply Chain Evolution," *Fortune*, Special Advertising Section, March 8, 2012.

67. Joe Barrett, "Whirlpool Cleans Up Its Delivery Act," *Wall Street Journal*, September 24, 2009.

68. William C. Copacino, *Supply Chain Management* (Boca Raton, FL: St. Lucie Press, 1997); Robert Shaw and Philip Kotler, "Rethinking the Chain: Making Marketing Leaner, Faster, and Better," *Marketing Management* (July/August 2009), pp. 18–23.

69. Danielle Gould, "Cutting Food Waste Increases Corporate Profits & Consumer Savings, Says Report," *Forbes*, August 30, 2012.

70. Patrick Burnson, ""Slow and Steady: 24th Annual State of Logistics Report," *Logistics Management*, July 2013; "The Logistics and Transportation Industry in the United States," www.selectusa. commerce.gov.

71. Margie Manning, "ConMed Linvatec Takes a 'Lean' Journey," *Tampa Bay Business Journal*, May 17, 2010; Pete Engardio, "Lean and Mean Gets Extreme," *BusinessWeek*, March 23 and 30, 2009, pp. 60–62; Traci Gregory, "ConMed Takes Lean Approach," *Central New York Business Journal*, May 22, 2009.

72. Daisuke Wakabayashi, "How Lean Manufacturing Can Backfire," *Wall Street Journal*, January 30, 2010; for some additional discussion of the downside of lean manufacturing, see Brian Hindo, "At 3M, a Struggle between Efficiency and Creativity," *BusinessWeek*, June 11, 2007.

73. Dana Mattioli, "Macy's Regroups in Warehouse Wars," *Wall Street Journal*, May 14, 2012.

74. The optimal order quantity is given by the formula $Q^* = 2DS/IC$, where $D$ = annual demand, $S$ = cost to place one order, and $I$ = annual carrying cost per unit. Known as the economic-order quantity formula, it assumes a constant ordering cost, a constant cost of carrying an additional unit in inventory, a known demand, and no quantity discounts. For further reading on this subject, see Richard J. Tersine, *Principles of Inventory and Materials Management*, 4th ed. (Upper Saddle River, NJ: Prentice Hall, 1994).

75. "All the Right Moves," *Fortune*, Special Advertising Section, May 2, 2011.

76. Renee DeGross, "Retailers Try eBay Overstocks, Returns for Sale Online," *Atlanta Journal-Constitution*, April 10, 2004.

77. Katie Kelly Bell, "94 Point Brunello for Peanuts? How Wine Negociant Cameron Hughes Finds the Deals," *Forbes*, November 27, 2012; Lettie Teague, "Taking Advantage of the Wine Glut," *Wall Street Journal*, May 7, 2010; Maureen Farrell, "Wine Workout," *Forbes*, March 30, 2009, pp. 64–65.

78. "The Total Package," *Bloomberg Businessweek*, Special Advertising Section, November 28, 2011; Geoff Colvin, "The Trade Tracker," *Fortune*, November 7, 2011; Helen Coster, "Calculus for Truckers," *Forbes*, September 12, 2011; "All the Right Moves," *Fortune*, Special Advertising Section, May 2, 2011.

79. "Manufacturing Complexity," *Economist: A Survey of Logistics*, June 17, 2006, pp. 6–9.

80. Perry A. Trunick, "Nailing a Niche in Logistics," *Logistics Today*, March 4, 2008.

# Chapter 19

1. Tim Nudd, "Inside Oreo's Adorable Triple Play for Father's Day," *Adweek*, June 10, 2013; Jennifer Rooney, "Behind the Scenes of Oreo's Real-Time Super Bowl Slam Dunk," *Forbes*, February 4, 2013; T. L. Stanley, "Brand Genius: Lisa Mann, VP Cookies, Mondelēz International," *Adweek*, October 29, 2012; Stuart Elliott, "For Oreo Campaign Finale, a Twist on Collaboration," *New York Times*, September 24, 2012; Rohit Nautiyal, "Cookie Time," *The Financial Express*, June 28, 2011.

2. Ernst C. Osinga, Peter S. H. Leeflang, Shuba Srinivasan, and Jaap E. Wieringa, "Why Do Firms Invest in Consumer Advertising with Limited Sales Response? A Shareholder Perspective," *Journal of Marketing* 75 (January 2011), pp. 109–24; Xueming Luo and Naveen Donthu, "Marketing's Credibility: A Longitudinal Investigation of Marketing Communication Productivity and Shareholder Value," *Journal of Marketing* 70 (October 2006), pp. 70–91.

3. Gabriel Beltrone, "Agency of the Year (Digital Winner): AKQA," *Adweek*, December 12, 2011; "Digital Agency of the Year: AKQA," *Campaign*, December 11, 2011; Eliza Williams, "Heineken Launches Live Football Game StarPlayer," *Creative Review*, April 27, 2011.

4. "Mondelez Seeks Digital Lead," www.warc.com, January 14, 2013.

5. "Content Drive Works for GE," www.warc.com, August 12, 2013.

6. Alexander Konrad, "Bigger than Craisins," *Forbes*, December 2, 2013; "Ocean Spray Challenges Raisins Fans to Make the Leap to Craisins Dried Cranberries," *Reuters*, February 23, 2012; "Ocean Spray's Pop-Up Restaurant Emerges from 2,000 lbs. of Cranberries Inside a Cranberry Bog in Rockefeller Center," *Business Wire*, September 29, 2011; Ken Romanzi, "Reintroducing the Cranberry to America!," talk at the Tuck School of Business at Dartmouth, January 7, 2010; Francis J. Kelly III and Barry Silverstein, *The Breakaway Brand* (New York: McGraw-Hill, 2005).

7. Some of these definitions are adapted from the *AMA Dictionary* from the American Marketing Association, www.ama.org/resources/Pages/Dictionary.aspx.

8. Tom Duncan, *Principles of Advertising and IMC,* 2nd ed. (New York: McGraw-Hill/Irwin, 2005).

9. Michael McCarthy, "Ron Burgundy's Durango Campaign Helps Dodge Laugh All the Way to the Bank," *Advertising Age*, December 9, 2013; Marissa McNaughton, "Hands On Ron Burgundy Mobile Game Promotes Dodge Durango, Anchorman 2 Movie," *The Realtime Report*, November 21, 2013; Greg Gilman, "How Will Ferrell's Ron Burgundy Became Dodge's Best Car Salesman Ever," *The Wrap*, October 24, 2013.

10. Norris I. Bruce, Kay Peters, and Prasad A. Naik, "Discovering How Advertising Grows Sales and Builds Brands," *Journal of Marketing Research* 49 (December 2012), pp. 793–806.

11. This section is based on the excellent text, John R. Rossiter and Larry Percy, *Advertising and Promotion Management,* 2nd ed. (New York: McGraw-Hill, 1997).

12. Patricia Odell, "Jockey and Target Join to Sell Women on Men's Brief," *Chief Marketer*, August 6, 2012; "Best Retail Promotion: Jockey JKY Right on Target—Gold," Pro Awards 2013, www.chiefmarketer.com; TPN Holdings, "Jockey Right on Target with JKY," www.baalink.com/reggie-case-study, accessed June 23, 2014.

13. James F. Engel, Roger D. Blackwell, and Paul W. Minard, *Consumer Behavior*, 9th ed. (Fort Worth, TX: Dryden, 2001).

14. John R. Rossiter and Larry Percy, *Advertising and Promotion Management,* 2nd ed. (New York: McGraw-Hill, 1997).

15. Roger D. Blackwell, Paul W. Miniard, and James F. Engel, *Consumer Behavior*, 10th ed. (Mason, OH: South-Western Publishing, 2006).

16. Ayn E. Crowley and Wayne D. Hoyer, "An Integrative Framework for Understanding Two-Sided Persuasion," *Journal of Consumer Research* 20 (March 1994), pp. 561–74.

17. C. I. Hovland, A. A. Lumsdaine, and F. D. Sheffield, *Experiments on Mass Communication,* vol. 3 (Princeton, NJ: Princeton University Press, 1949).

18. H. Rao Unnava, Robert E. Burnkrant, and Sunil Erevelles, "Effects of Presentation Order and Communication Modality on Recall and Attitude," *Journal of Consumer Research* 21 (December 1994), pp. 481–90.

19. Gillian Naylor, Susan Bardi Kleiser, Julie Baker, and Eric Yorkston, "Using Transformational Appeals to Enhance the Retail Experience," *Journal of Retailing* 84 (April 2008), pp. 49–57.

20. Michael R. Solomon, *Consumer Behavior,* 10th ed. (Upper Saddle River, NJ: Pearson Prentice Hall, 2013).

21. Will Burns, "Reality Prank from Toys R Us Backfires with Women," *Forbes*, November 6, 2013; Christopher Heine, "Toys R Us' Holiday Ads Employ Prankvertising," *Adweek*, October 21, 2013.

22. Rik Pieters and Michel Wedel, "Attention Capture and Transfer in Advertising: Brand, Pictorial, and Text-Size Effects," *Journal of Marketing* 68 (April 2004), pp. 36–50.

23. Herbert C. Kelman and Carl I. Hovland, "Reinstatement of the Communication in Delayed Measurement of Opinion Change," *Journal of Abnormal and Social Psychology* 48 (July 1953), pp. 327–35.

24. Lucia Moses, "What Do These Real People Think of Ads Starring Real People," *Adweek*, May 1, 2012.

25. C. E. Osgood and P. H. Tannenbaum, "The Principles of Congruity in the Prediction of Attitude Change," *Psychological Review* 62 (January 1955), pp. 42–55.

26. Victoria Clarke, "Campaign of the Month: John Deere Launches Its Own Chat Show," *B2B Marketing*, January 17, 2013; Kay Plantes, "John Deere—Branding and Business Models at Their Best," *WTN News*, December 6, 2012.

27. Robert V. Kozinets, Kristine de Valck, Andrea C. Wojnicki, and Sarah J. S. Wilner, "Networked Narratives: Understanding Word-of-Mouth Marketing in Online Communities," *Journal of Marketing* 74 (March 2010), pp. 71–89; David Godes and Dina Mayzlin, "Firm-Created Word-of-Mouth Communication: Evidence from a Field Test," *Marketing Science* 28 (July–August 2009), pp. 721–39.

28. David Taintor, "Best Use of Branded Content: The Jaws of Opportunity," *Adweek*, August 19, 2013; "MediaCom Wins Adweek Media Plan of the Year for Volkswagen Campaign," *PRNewswire*, August 19, 2013; "Volkswagen, 'The Beetle Shark Cage,'" *Mediacom*, accessed March 26, 2014.

29. Jon Swartz, "Small Firms Dive into Social Media," *USA Today*, July 22, 2010, p. 3B.

30. Edward Skyler, "Citi Bike *Boom*," *The Hub*, March/April 2014; Nick Summers, "How Citibank Bought a City Cheap," *Bloomberg BusinessWeek*, October 31, 2013; Christine Birker, "In Like Schwinn," *Marketing News*, May 15, 2012, p. 7; Anne VanderMey, "By the Numbers: Pushing Pedals," *Fortune*, July 23, 2012; Jon Gertner, "Wheeling and Dealing," *Fast Company*, July/August 2012.

31. Norris I. Bruce, Natasha Zhang Foutz, and Ceren Kolsarici, "Dynamic Effectiveness of Advertising and Word of Mouth in Sequential Distribution of New Products," *Journal of Marketing Research* 49 (August 2012), pp. 469–86. See also Shyam Gopinath, Jacquelyn Thomas, and Lakshman Krishnamurthi, "Investigating the Relationship between the Content of Online Word of Mouth, Advertising and Brand Performance," *Marketing Science* 33 (March–April 2014), pp. 241–58.

32. Adapted from G. Maxwell Ule, "A Media Plan for 'Sputnik' Cigarettes," *How to Plan Media Strategy* (American Association of Advertising Agencies, 1957 Regional Convention), pp. 41–52.

33. Thomas C. Kinnear, Kenneth L. Bernhardt, and Kathleen A. Krentler, *Principles of Marketing*, 6th ed. (New York: HarperCollins, 1995).

34. K. Sridhar Moorthy and Scott A. Hawkins, "Advertising Repetition and Quality Perceptions," *Journal of Business Research* 58 (March 2005), pp. 354–60; Amna Kirmani and Akshay R. Rao, "No Pain, No Gain: A Critical Review of the Literature on Signaling Unobservable Product Quality," *Journal of Marketing* 64 (April 2000), pp. 66–79.

35. Demetrios Vakratsas and Tim Ambler, "How Advertising Works: What Do We Really Know?," *Journal of Marketing* 63 (January 1999), pp. 26–43.

36. Ashlee Vance, "IBM on a Mission to Save the Planet," *Bloomberg Businessweek*, March 15, 2012; "Let's Build a Smarter Planet," *Effie Worldwide*, www.effie.org/winners/showcase/2010/; "IBM Smarter Planet Campaign from Ogilvy & Mather Wins Global Effie," *PRNewswire*, June 9, 2010; Jeffrey M. O'Brien, "IBM's Grand Plan to Save the Planet," *Fortune*, April 21, 2009.

37. Prasad A. Naik and Kalyan Raman, "Understanding the Impact of Synergy in Multimedia Communications," *Journal of Marketing Research* 40 (November 2003), pp. 375–88. See also Prasad A. Naik, Kalyan Raman, and Russell S. Winer, "Planning Marketing-Mix Strategies in the Presence of Interaction Effects," *Marketing Science* 24 (January 2005), pp. 25–34.

38. Scott Neslin, *Sales Promotion*, MSI Relevant Knowledge Series (Cambridge, MA: Marketing Science Institute, 2002).

39. Markus Pfeiffer and Markus Zinnbauer, "Can Old Media Enhance New Media?," *Journal of Advertising Research* (March 2010), pp. 42–49.

40. Sreedhar Madhavaram, Vishag Badrinarayanan, and Robert E. McDonald, "Integrated Marketing Communication (IMC) and Brand Identity as Critical Components of Brand Equity Strategy," *Journal of Advertising* 34 (Winter 2005), pp. 69–80; Mike Reid, Sandra Luxton, and Felix Mavondo, "The Relationship between Integrated Marketing Communication, Market Orientation, and Brand Orientation," *Journal of Advertising* 34 (Winter 2005), pp. 11–23.

41. Don E. Schultz and Heidi Schultz, *IMC, The Next Generation: Five Steps for Delivering Value and Measuring Financial Returns* (New York: McGraw-Hill, 2003).

## Chapter 20

1. Alexander Coolidge, "P&G Aims for Moms' Heart with Latest 'Thank You' Ad," *USA Today*, January 8, 2013; Emma Bazilian, "Ad of the Day: P&G Has a Winner with Latest Big Tearjerker Spot for Moms," *Adweek*, January 7, 2014; "Procter & Gamble Brands Unite to Kick Off Sochi 2014 Olympic Winter Games," www.pg.com, October 28, 2013; "In 2013, Once Again: Marketing Art Meets Science—Best in Show Winners of the Advertising Research Foundation's David Ogilvy Awards," *Journal of Advertising Research* 53, no. 3 (2013); Katy Bachman, "Brought to You by the Moms of the World," *Adweek*, August 19, 2013.

2. Paul F. Nunes and Jeffrey Merrihue, "The Continuing Power of Mass Advertising," *Sloan Management Review* (Winter 2007), pp. 63–69.

3. E. J. Schultz, "Muscling Past Mayhem: Geico Rides Giant Ad Budget Past Allstate," *Advertising Age*, July 8, 2013; Tim Nudd, "You Know the 'Fifteen Minutes' Line by Heart, but Did You Also Know . . . ," *Adweek*, July 1, 2013; Gabriel Beltrone, "Eddie Money Falls Short of Paradise, but the Martin Agency's 'Happier Than' Spots Generally Do the Trick," *Adweek*, August 28, 2012.

4. Russell H. Colley, *Defining Advertising Goals for Measured Advertising Results* (New York: Association of National Advertisers, 1961).

5. Alicia Barroso and Gerard Llobet, "Advertising and Consumer Awareness of New, Differentiated Products," *Journal of Marketing Research* 49 (December 2012), pp. 773–92; Wilfred Amaldoss and Chuan He, "Product Variety, Informative Advertising, and Price Competition," *Journal of Marketing Research* 47 (February 2010), pp. 146–56.

6. Stephen Williams, "Rivals Gang Up on Ford Trucks as Dodge Ram Joins Battering," *Advertising Age*, February 20, 2012.

7. Debora Viana Thompson and Rebecca W. Hamilton, "The Effects of Information Processing Mode on Consumers' Responses to Comparative Advertising," *Journal of Consumer Research* 32 (March 2006), pp. 530–40.

8. Rajesh Chandy, Gerard J. Tellis, Debbie MacInnis, and Pattana Thaivanich, "What to Say When: Advertising Appeals in Evolving Markets," *Journal of Marketing Research* 38 (November 2001); Gerard J. Tellis, Rajesh Chandy, and Pattana Thaivanich, "Decomposing the Effects of Direct Advertising: Which Brand Works, When, Where, and How Long?," *Journal of Marketing Research* 37 (February 2000), pp. 32–46; Peter J. Danaher, André Bonfrer, and Sanjay Dhar, "The Effect of Competitive Advertising," *Journal of Marketing Research* 45 (April 2008), pp. 211–25.

9. Demetrios Vakratsas, Fred M. Feinberg, Frank M. Bass, and Gurumurthy Kalyanaram, "The Shape of Advertising Response Functions Revisited: A Model of Dynamic Probabilistic Thresholds," *Marketing Science* 23 (Winter 2004), pp. 109–19.

10. Leonard M. Lodish, Magid Abraham, Stuart Kalmenson, Jeanne Livelsberger, Beth Lubetkin, Bruce Richardson, and Mary Ellen Stevens, "How T.V. Advertising Works: A Meta-Analysis of 389 Real-World Split Cable T.V. Advertising Experiments," *Journal of Marketing Research* 32 (May 1995), pp. 125–39.

11. For an excellent review, see Greg Allenby and Dominique Hanssens, "Advertising Response," Marketing Science Institute, *Special Report,* No. 05-200, 2005. See also Harald J. Van Heerde, Maarten J. Gijsenberg, Marnik G. Dekimpe, and Jan-Benedict E. M. Steenkamp, "Price and Advertising Effectiveness over the Business Cycle," *Journal of Marketing Research* 50 (April 2013), pp. 177–93; Raj Sethuraman, Gerard J. Tellis, and Richard A. Briesch, "How Well Does Advertising Work? Generalizations from Meta-Analysis of Brand Advertising Elasticities," *Journal of Marketing Research* 48 (June 2011), pp. 457–71.

12. Shyam Gopinath, Jacquelyn S. Thomas, and Lakshman Krishnamurthi, "Investigating the Relationship between the Content of Online Word of Mouth, Advertising, and Brand Performance," *Marketing Science* 33 (March–April 2014), pp. 241–58.

13. Jeff Manning, "Got Milk?," *Associations Now,* July 1, 2006, pp. 56–61; Jeff Manning and Kevin Lane Keller, "Making Advertising Work: How Got Milk? Marketing Stopped a 20-Year Sales Decline," *Marketing Management* (January–February 2003); Jeff Manning, *Got Milk? The Book* (New York: Prima Lifestyles, 1999).

14. Debora V. Thompson and Prashant Malaviya, "Consumer-Generated Ads: Does Awareness of Advertising Co-Creation Help or Hurt Persuasion?," *Journal of Marketing* 77 (May 2013), pp. 33–47; Benjamin Lawrence, Susan Fournier, and Frederic Brunel, "When Companies Don't Make the Ad: A Multi-Method Inquiry into the Differential Effectiveness of Consumer-Generated Advertising," *Journal of Advertising* 42, no. 4 (2013), pp. 292–307; Rosie Baker, "McDonald's Preps Crowdsourced Olympic Ads," *Marketing Week,* August 3, 2012; Eric Pfanner, "When Consumers Help, Ads Are Free," *New York Times,* June 22, 2009, p. B6; Elisabeth Sullivan, "H. J. Heinz: Consumers Sit in the Director's Chair for Viral Effort," *Marketing News,* February 10, 2008, p. 10; Louise Story, "The High Price of Creating Free Ads," *New York Times,* May 26, 2007. See also the Special Issue on the Emergence and Impact of User-Generated Content, *Marketing Science* 31 (May–June 2012).

15. Anat Keinan, Francis Farrelly, and Michael Beverland, "Introducing iSnack 2.0: The New Vegemite," Harvard Business School Case, April 2012; Ruth Lamperd, "Vegemite Product Renamed Vegemite Cheesybite after iSnack 2.0 Was Dumped," *Herald Sun,* October 7, 2009.

16. Werner Reinartz and Peter Saffert, "Creativity in Advertising: When It Works and When It Doesn't," *Harvard Business Review,* June 2013, pp. 107–12.

17. "Ouch! Advertising Icon Can't Duck Injury of His Own," *PR Newswire,* January 8, 2012; Daniel P. Amos, "How I Did It: Aflac's CEO Explains How He Fell for the Duck," *Harvard Business Review,* January–February 2010; Stuart Elliott, "Not Daffy or Donald, but Still Aflac's Rising Star," *New York Times,* April 22, 2009.

18. "Newspapers: By the Numbers," The State of the News Media 2013, www.stateofthemedia.org.

19. "iPad Mini Shows Off Its Size Print Ads in Time, The New Yorker," *Advertising Age,* November 30, 2012.

20. Tim Nudd, "The 2013 Clio Awards Winners," *Adweek,* May 12, 2013.

21. Carol Hanley, "Radio Is …," *Adweek,* October 15, 2012, p. R4.

22. "Motel 6 Ad Earns Grand Prize at Radio Mercury Awards," Motel 6, www.motel6.com, July 1, 2009; "Motel 6 Receives Hermes and Silver GALAXY Awards for 2002 Advertising Campaigns," Business Editors/Travel Writers, *Business Wire,* November 22, 2002.

23. For further reading, see Dorothy Cohen, *Legal Issues in Marketing Decision Making* (Cincinnati, OH: South-Western, 1995).

24. Schultz et al., *Strategic Advertising Campaigns* (Chicago: NTC/Contemporary Publishing Company, September 1994), p. 340.

25. Prashant Malaviya, "The Moderating Influence of Advertising Context on Ad Repetition Effects: The Role of Amount and Type of Elaboration," *Journal of Consumer Research* 34 (June 2007), pp. 32–40.

26. Sam Jaffe, "Easy Riders," *American Demographics,* March 2004, pp. 20–23.

27. Max Chafkin, "Ads and Atmospherics," *Inc.,* February 2007.

28. Stephanie Clifford, "Billboards That Look Back," *New York Times,* May 31, 2008.

29. Abbey Klaassen and Andrew Hampp, "Inside Outdoor's Digital Makeover," *Advertising Age: Creativity,* June 14, 2010, p. 5.

30. Jon Fine, "Where Are Advertisers? At the Movies," *BusinessWeek,* May 25, 2009, pp. 65–66; "Advertisers Go Outside to Play," *AdweekMedia,* March 9, 2009, p. 1; Zack O'Malley Greenburg, "Take Your Brand for a Ride," *Forbes,* March 2, 2009, p. 67.

31. Jeff Pelline, "New Commercial Twist in Corporate Restrooms," *San Francisco Chronicle,* October 6, 1986.

32. Michael A. Wiles and Anna Danielova, "The Worth of Product Placement in Successful Films: An Event Study Analysis," *Journal of Marketing* 73 (July 2009), pp. 44–63; Siva K. Balasubramanian, James Karrh, and Hemant Patwardhan, "Audience Response to Product Placements: An Integrative Framework and Future Research Agenda," *Journal of Advertising* 35 (2006), pp. 115–41.

33. "Grow the Heineken Brand," *Heineken Annual Report 2012;* Guy Lodge, "The Skyfall's the Limit on James Bond Marketing," *The Guardian,* October 23, 2012; Marc Graser, "'Skyfall' a Windfall for Product Placement," *Variety,* November 9, 2012; Oliver Chiang, "iPad, Product Placement Star of ABC's 'Modern Family' Even before Launch," *Forbes,* April 1, 2010.

34. "FCC Opens Inquiry into Stealthy TV Product Placement," *Associated Press,* June 26, 2008.

35. Popai, www.popai.com, accessed August 22, 2010.

36. Ram Bezawada, S. Balachander, P. K. Kannan, and Venkatesh Shankar, "Cross-Category Effects of Aisle and Display Placements: A Spatial Modeling Approach and Insights," *Journal of Marketing* 73 (May 2009), pp. 99–117; Pierre Chandon, J. Wesley Hutchinson, Eric T. Bradlow, and Scott H. Young, "Does In-Store Marketing Work? Effects of the Number and Position of Shelf Facings on Brand Attention and Evaluation at the Point of Purchase," *Journal of Marketing* 73 (November 2009), pp. 1–17.

37. www.walmartsmartnetwork.info, accessed March 27, 2014; Bob Greenberg, "Reinventing Retail; E-commerce Impacts the Brick-and-Mortar Store Experience," *Adweek,* February 15, 2010; Bill Yackey, "Walmart Reveals 18-Month Results for SMART Network," *Digital Signage Today,* February 23, 2010.

38. Matt McFarland, "Intel's Hidden Ad Gamble Pays Off in First Game of Deal with FC Barcelona," *Washington Post,* December 12, 2013.

39. Jeanine Poggi, "TV Ad Prices: Football Is Still King," *Advertising Age,* October 20, 2013.

40. Steve McClellan, "Costs for TV Spots Rocket 7%," *Media Daily News,* January 29, 2013; "4As Television Production Cost Survey," 4As, January 21, 2013

41. "Sports Illustrated Rate Card 2014" and "People Magazine Rate Card 2014"

42. Chen Lin, Sriram Venkataraman, and Sandy Jap, "Media Multiplexing Behavior: Implications," *Marketing Science,* 32 (March–April 2013), pp. 310–24.

43. Marshall Freimer and Dan Horsky, "Periodic Advertising Pulsing in a Competitive Market," *Marketing Science* 31 (July–August 2012), pp. 637–48.

44. David B. Montgomery and Alvin J. Silk, "Estimating Dynamic Effects of Market Communications Expenditures," *Management Science* (June 1972), pp. 485–501; Kristian S. Palda, *The Measurement of Cumulative Advertising Effect* (Upper Saddle River, NJ: Prentice Hall, 1964), p. 87.

45. Peter J. Danaher and Tracey S. Dagger, "Comparing the Relative Effectiveness of Advertising Channels: A Case Study of a Multimedia

Blitz Campaign," *Journal of Marketing Research* 50 (August 2013), pp. 517–34; Gerard J. Tellis, Rajesh K. Chandy, and Pattana Thaivanich, "Which Ad Works, When, Where, and How Often? Modeling the Effects of Direct Television Advertising," *Journal of Marketing Research* 37 (February 2000), pp. 32–46.

46. Nigel Hollis, "The Future of Tracking Studies," *Admap*, October 2004, pp. 151–53.

47. From Robert C. Blattberg and Scott A. Neslin, *Sales Promotion: Concepts, Methods, and Strategies* (Upper Saddle River, NJ: Prentice Hall, 1990). This text provides a detailed, analytical treatment of sales promotion. An comprehensive review of academic work on sales promotions can be found in Scott Neslin, "Sales Promotion," Bart Weitz and Robin Wensley, eds., *Handbook of Marketing* (London: Sage, 2002), pp. 310–38.

48. "2014 Coupon Trends: 2013 Year-End Report," www.inmar.com, March 2014.

49. For a good summary of the research on whether promotion erodes the consumer franchise of leading brands, see Robert C. Blattberg and Scott A. Neslin, "Sales Promotion: The Long and Short of It," *Marketing Letters* 1 (December 2004). For a related topic, see Michael J. Barone and Tirthankar Roy, "Does Exclusivity Pay Off? Exclusive Price Promotions and Consumer Response," *Journal of Marketing* 74 (March 2010), pp. 121–32.

50. Harald J. Van Heerde, Sachin Gupta, and Dick Wittink, "Is 75% of the Sales Promotion Bump due to Brand Switching? No, Only 33% Is," *Journal of Marketing Research* 40 (November 2003), pp. 481–91.

51. Magid M. Abraham and Leonard M. Lodish, "Getting the Most out of Advertising and Promotion," *Harvard Business Review,* May–June 1990, pp. 50–60. See also Shuba Srinivasan, Koen Pauwels, Dominique Hanssens, and Marnik Dekimpe, "Do Promotions Benefit Manufacturers, Retailers, or Both?," *Management Science* 50 (May 2004), pp. 617–29.

52. Emily Bryson York and Natalie Zmuda, "Sampling: The New Mass Media," *Advertising Age,* May 12, 2008, pp. 3, 56.

53. "2010 REGGIE Awards Shopper Marketing: P&G Gain — Project Gainiac," *Promotion Marketing Association,* www.pmalink.org.

54. Rajkumar Venkatesan and Paul W. Farris, "Measuring and Managing Returns from Retailer-Customized Coupon Campaigns," *Journal of Marketing* 76 (January 2012), pp. 76–94.

55. Nathan Vardi, "Groupon and Zynga Are the Worst-Performing Stocks of the Year," *Forbes,* October 8, 2012; Cassie Lancellotti-Young, "Groupon Case," Glassmeyer/McNamee Center for Digital Strategies, Dartmouth College, 2011; Brad Stone and Douglas MacMillan, "Are These Four Words Worth $25 Billion," *Bloomberg BusinessWeek,* March 27, 2011; "Is Groupon a Good Deal?," *Entrepreneur,* March 2011, p. 61. For relevant academic research, see Xueming Luo, Michelle Andrews, Yiping Song, and Jaakko Aspara, "Group-Buying Deal Popularity," *Journal of Marketing* 78 (March 2014), pp. 20–33.

56. Kusum L. Ailawadi, Karen Gedenk, Christian Lutzky, and Scott A. Neslin, "Decomposition of the Sales Impact of Promotion-Induced Stockpiling," *Journal of Marketing Research* 44 (August 2007); Eric T. Anderson and Duncan Simester, "The Long-Run Effects of Promotion Depth on New versus Established Customers: Three Field Studies," *Marketing Science* 23 (Winter 2004), pp. 4–20; Luc Wathieu, A. V. Muthukrishnan, and Bart J. Bronnenberg. "The Asymmetric Effect of Discount Retraction on Subsequent Choice," *Journal of Consumer Research* 31 (December 2004), pp. 652–65.

57. Rebecca J. Slotegraaf and Koen Pauwels, "The Impact of Brand Equity Innovation on the Long-Term Effectiveness of Promotions," *Journal of Marketing Research* 45 (June 2008), pp. 293–306.

58. Kusum L. Ailawadi, Bari A. Harlam, Jacques Cesar, and David Trounce, "Promotion Profitability for a Retailer: The Role of Promotion, Brand, Category, and Store Characteristics," *Journal of Marketing Research* 43 (November 2006), pp. 518–36.

59. Miguel Gomez, Vithala Rao, and Edward McLaughlin, "Empirical Analysis of Budget and Allocation of Trade Promotions in the U.S. Supermarket Industry," *Journal of Marketing Research* 44 (August 2007); Norris Bruce, Preyas S. Desai, and Richard Staelin, "The Better They Are, the More They Give: Trade Promotions of Consumer Durables," *Journal of Marketing Research* 42 (February 2005), pp. 54–66.

60. Kusum L. Ailawadi and Bari Harlam, "An Empirical Analysis of the Determinants of Retail Margins: The Role of Store Brand Share," *Journal of Marketing* 68 (January 2004), pp. 147–66; Kusum L. Ailawadi, "The Retail Power-Performance Conundrum: What Have We Learned?," *Journal of Retailing* 77 (Fall 2001), pp. 299–318; Koen Pauwels, "How Retailer and Competitor Decisions Drive the Long-Term Effectiveness of Manufacturer Promotions," *Journal of Retailing* 83 (2007), pp. 364–90.

61. James Bandler, "The Shadowy Business of Diversion," *Fortune,* August 17, 2009, p. 65.

62. IBIS World USA, www.ibisworld.com; Noah Lim, Michael J. Ahearne, and Sung H. Ham, "Designing Sales Contests: Does the Prize Structure Matter?," *Journal of Marketing Research* 46 (June 2009), pp. 356–71.

63. Christopher Heine, "Best Use of Mobile: Go Ahead, Take a Picture — It Lasts Longer," *Adweek,* August 19, 2013; "Samsung Galaxy Camera's Successful E-commerce Campaign," VanWestMedia, August 26, 2013; "Samsung Galaxy Camera Presents 'Life's a Photo — Take It' Competition," www.venturebeat.com, December 13, 2012.

64. Joe A. Dodson, Alice M. Tybout, and Brian Sternthal, "Impact of Deals and Deal Retraction on Brand Switching," *Journal of Marketing Research* 15 (February 1978), pp. 72–81.

65. "Sponsorship Spending Growth Slows in North America as Marketers Eye Newer Media and Marketing Options," *IEG Sponsorship Report,* January 7, 2014.

66. Philip Kotler, "Atmospherics as a Marketing Tool," *Journal of Retailing* (Winter 1973–1974), pp. 48–64.

67. Bettina Cornwell, Michael S. Humphreys, Angela M. Maguire, Clinton S. Weeks, and Cassandra Tellegen, "Sponsorship-Linked Marketing: The Role of Articulation in Memory," *Journal of Consumer Research* 33 (December 2006), pp. 312–21.

68. "Brands Suit Up for 'Iron Man 2,'" *Adweek,* May 14, 2010.

69. "BB&T Continues Sponsorship with Clint Bowyer, Richard Childress Racing," *SceneDaily,* January 14, 2010; "BB&T Puts Name on New Winston-Salem Ballpark," *Winston-Salem Journal,* February 24, 2010.

70. The Association of National Advertisers has a useful source: *Event Marketing: A Management Guide,* which is available at www.ana.net/bookstore.

71. T. Bettina Cornwell, Clinton S. Weeks, and Donald P. Roy, "Sponsorship-Linked Marketing: Opening the Black Box," *Journal of Advertising* 34 (Summer 2005).

72. B. Joseph Pine and James H. Gilmore, *The Experience Economy: Work Is Theatre and Every Business a Stage* (Cambridge, MA: Harvard University Press, 1999).

73. "2006 Experiential Marketing Study," *Jack Morton,* www.jackmorton.com.

74. www.factorytour.com, accessed June 23, 2014.

75. "Do We Have a Story for You!," *Economist,* January 21, 2006, pp. 57–58; Al Ries and Laura Ries, *The Fall of Advertising and the Rise of PR* (New York: HarperCollins, 2002).

76. "A Purr-fect Fit: CeeLo Green and Purrfect Remix the Meow Mix Cat Food Jingle," PRWeek Awards 2014, www.awards.prweekus.com; Rebecca Cullers, "CeeLo Green Creates a Purrfect Meow Mix Remix with His Cat," *Adweek,* May 10, 2012; Ken Wheaton, "Stop the Presses: CeeLo Green, Purrfect Remix Meow Mix Jingle," *Advertising Age,* May 4, 2012.

77. "The Comeback Kid: Cisco Bounces Back from a Knockdown Punch," PRWeek Awards 2014, www.awards.prweekus.com.

78. Arthur M. Merims, "Marketing's Stepchild: Product Publicity," *Harvard Business Review,* November–December 1972, pp. 111–12.

# Chapter 21

1. Thomas Leskin, "Schuylkill Native Part of Winning Doritos Super Bowl Commercial," *The Morning Call,* February 4, 2014; Jennifer Rooney, "Doritos Again Asks Fans to 'Crash the Super Bowl'—This Time from around the World," *Forbes,* September 12, 2013; Elaine Wong, "What Mountain Dew Learned from 'DEWmocracy,'" *Adweek,* June 16, 2010; Natalie Zmuda, "New Pepsi 'Dewmocracy' Push Threatens to Crowd Out Shops," *Advertising Age,* November 2, 2009;

2. Andrew T. Stephen and Jeff Galak, "The Effects of Traditional and Social Earned Media on Sales: A Study of a Microlending Marketplace," *Journal of Marketing Research* 49 (October 2012), pp. 624–39.

3. For example, see André Bonfrer and Xavier Drèze, "Real-Time Evaluation of E-mail Campaign Performance," *Marketing Science* 28 (March–April 2009), pp. 251–63.

4. Kenneth C. Wilbur and Yi Zhu, "Click Fraud," *Marketing Science* 28 (March–April 2009), pp. 293–308.

5. "Mobile Continues to Steal Share of US Adults' Daily Time Spent with Media," *eMarketer,* April 22, 2014.

6. Asim Ansari and Carl F. Mela, "E-customization," *Journal of Marketing Research* 40 (May 2003), pp. 131–45.

7. "U.S. Digital Adspend Passes TV," www.warc.com, April 11, 2014.

8. Mike Kacsmar, "Tough Mudder CEO Redefines a Successful Race," *Forbes,* March 20, 2014; Matt Gutman, "The Tough Mudder: 'The Toughest Race on the Planet,'" *ABC News,* January 27, 2012; Mike Ozanian, "Tough Mudder Has Created a New Business Model for Sports," *Forbes,* October 26, 2010.

9. Hans Risselada, Peter C. Verhoef, and Tammo H.A. Bijmolt, "Dynamic Effects of Social Influence and Direct Marketing on the Adoption of High-Technology Products," *Journal of Marketing* 78 (March 2014), pp. 52–68; Zsolt Katona, Peter Pal Zubcsek, and Miklos Sarvary, "Network Effects and Personal Influences: The Diffusion of an Online Social Network," *Journal of Marketing Research* 48 (June 2011), pp. 425–43; Allen P. Adamson, *Brand Digital* (New York: Palgrave Macmillan, 2008).

10. John R. Hauser, Glen L. Urban, Guilherme Liberali, and Michael Braun, "Website Morphing," *Marketing Science* 28 (March–April 2009), pp. 202–23; Peter J. Danaher, Guy W. Mullarkey, and Skander Essegaier, "Factors Affecting Web Site Visit Duration: A Cross-Domain Analysis," *Journal of Marketing Research* 43 (May 2006), pp. 182–94; Philip Kotler, *According to Kotler* (New York: American Management Association, 2005).

11. Jeffrey F. Rayport and Bernard J. Jaworski, *e-commerce* (New York: McGraw-Hill, 2001), p. 116.

12. Bob Tedeschi, "E-Commerce Report," *New York Times,* June 24, 2002.

13. Jan-Benedict E. M. Steenkamp and Inge Geyskens, "How Country Characteristics Affect the Perceived Value of Web Sites," *Journal of Marketing* 70 (July 2006), pp. 136–50.

14. "Automotive Brand Websites Drive Trials," www.warc.com, January 31, 2013.

15. Jessi Hempel, "The Online Numbers Game," *Fortune,* September 3, 2007, p. 18.

16. Avi Goldfarb and Catherine Tucker, "Why Managing Consumer Privacy Can Be an Opportunity," *MIT Sloan Management Review,* Spring 2013, pp. 10-12.

17. Emily Steel, "Marketers Take Search Ads beyond Search Engines," *Wall Street Journal,* January 19, 2009.

18. "Paid Search Clickthrough Rates Up Year over Year," *eMarketer,* January 23, 2012; Mike Chapman, What Clicks Worldwide?," *Adweek,* May 31, 2011.

19. Ron Berman and Zsolt Katona, "The Role of Search Engine Optimization in Search Marketing," *Marketing Science* 32 (July–August 2013), pp. 644–51; Oliver J. Rutz, Randolph E. Bucklin, and Garrett P. Sonnier, "A Latent Instrumental Variables Approach to Modeling Keyword Conversion in Paid Search Advertising," *Journal of Marketing Research* 49 (June 2012), pp. 306–19; Oliver J. Rutz and Randolph E. Bucklin, "From Generic to Branded: A Model of Spillover in Paid Search Advertising," *Journal of Marketing Research* 48 (February 2011), pp. 87–102; Paula Andruss, "How to Win the Bidding Wars," *Marketing News,* April 1, 2008, p. 28; Jefferson Graham, "To Drive Traffic to Your Site, You Need to Give Good Directions," *USA Today,* June 23, 2008.

20. Jay Paul, "A Revolutionary Marketing Strategy: Answer Customers' Questions," *New York Times,* February 27, 2013.

21. Jacob Goldenberg, Gal Oestreicher-Singer, and Shachar Reichman, "The Quest for Content: How User-Generated Links Can Facilitate Online Exploration," *Journal of Marketing Research* 49 (August 2012), pp. 452–68.

22. Zsolt Katona, "Competing for Influencers in a Social Network," working paper, Haas School of Business, University of California at Berkeley, 2014; Michael Trusov, Anand V. Bodapati, and Randolph E. Bucklin, "Determining Influential Users in Internet Social Networks," *Journal of Marketing Research* 47 (August 2010), pp. 643–58.

23. Peter J. Danaher, Janghyuk Lee, and Laoucine Kerbache, "Optimal Internet Media Selection," *Marketing Science* 29 (March–April 2010), pp. 336–47; Puneet Manchanda, Jean-Pierre Dubé, Khim Yong Goh, and Pradeep K. Chintagunta, "The Effects of Banner Advertising on Internet Purchasing," *Journal of Marketing Research* 43 (February 2006), pp. 98–108.

24. Glen Urban, Guilherme (Gui) Liberali, Erin Macdonald, Robert Bordley, and John Hauser, "Morphing Banner Advertising," *Marketing Science* 33 (January–February 2014), pp. 27–46; Jan H. Schumann, Florian von Wangenheim, and Nicole Groene, "Targeted Online Advertising: Using Reciprocity Appeals to Increase Acceptance among Users of Free Web Services," *Journal of Marketing* 78 (January 2014), pp. 59–75; Michael Braun and Wendy Moe, "Online Display Advertising: Modeling the Effects of Multiple Creatives and Individual Impression Histories," *Marketing Science* 32 (September/October 2013), pp. 753–67; Anja Lambrecht and Catherine Tucker, "When Does Retargeting Work? Information Specificity in Online Advertising," *Journal of Marketing Research* 50 (October 2013), pp. 561–76.

25. Nora Aufreiter, Julien Boudet and Vivien Weng, "Why Marketers Keep Sending You E-mails," *McKinsey Quarterly,* January 2014.

26. "Email, Search Remain Key for Brands," www.warc.com, January 24, 2013.

27. "Email Advertisers Face Backlash," www.warc.com, January 18, 2013.

28. Natalie Zmuda, "How E-mail Became a Direct-Marketing Rock Star in Recession," *Advertising Age,* May 11, 2009, p. 27.

29. Aurfreiter, Boudet and Weng, "Why Marketers Keep Sending You E-mails."

30. Jessica Naziri, "Dollar Shave Club Co-founder Michael Dubin Had a Smooth Transition," *Los Angeles Times,* August 16, 2013; Emily Glazer, "A David and Gillette Story," *Wall Street Journal,* April 12, 2012, Mark Evans, "Is DollarShaveClub.com Really the Best Launch Video?," www.blog.sysomos.com, March 19, 2012.

31. Paul Dwyer, "Measuring the Value of Word of Mouth and Its Impact in Consumer Communities," *Journal of Interactive Marketing* 21 (Spring 2007), pp. 63–79; Kelly K. Spors, "The Customer Knows Best," *Wall Street Journal,* July 13, 2009, p. R5.

32. For an academic discussion of chat rooms, recommendation sites, and customer review sections online, see Dina Mayzlin, "Promotional Chat on the Internet," *Marketing Science* 25 (March–April 2006), pp. 155–63; and Judith Chevalier and Dina Mayzlin, "The Effect of Word of Mouth on Sales: Online Book Reviews," *Journal of Marketing Research* 43 (August 2006), pp. 345–54.

33. Heather Green, "The Big Shots of Blogdom," *BusinessWeek*, May 7, 2007; TreeHugger, www.treehugger.com/about, accessed April 28, 2014.

34. Kim Hart, "Angry Customers Use Web to Shame Firms," *Washington Post*, July 5, 2006.

35. For a review of some relevant academic literature, see Christophe Van Den Bulte and Stefan Wuyts, *Social Networks and Marketing* (Marketing Science Institute Relevant Knowledge Series, Cambridge, MA, 2007); and for some practical considerations, see "A World of Connections: A Special Report on Social Networking," *Economist*, January 30, 2010.

36. Allen Adamson, "No Contest: Twitter and Facebook Can Both Play a Role in Branding," www.forbes.com, May 6, 2009.

37. Jae Young Lee and David R. Bell, "Neighborhood Social Capital and Social Learning for Experience Attributes of Products," *Marketing Science* 32 (November–December 2013), pp. 960–76.

38. "Profiting from Friendship," *Economist*, January 30, 2010, pp. 9–12.

39. Rebecca Walker Naylor, Cait Poynor Lamberton, and Patricia M. West, "Beyond the 'Like' Button: The Impact of Mere Virtual Presence on Brand Evaluations and Purchase Intentions in Social Media Settings," *Journal of Marketing* 76 (November 2012), pp. 105–20.

40. "A Peach of Opportunity," *Economist*, January 30, 2010, pp. 9–12.

41. "CafeMom Launches The Stir, the All-Day, Every Day Content Destination for Moms," www.prnewswire.com, March 30, 2010; Claire Cain Miller, "The New Back Fence," *Forbes*, April 7, 2008; www.cafemom.com/about, accessed April 26, 2014.

42. David Taylor, "Can Social Media Show You the Money," *Brandgym Research Paper 6*, September 2012.

43. Christian Schulze, Lisa Schöler, and Bernd Skiera, "Not All Fun and Games: Viral Marketing for Utilitarian Products," *Journal of Marketing* 78 (January 2014), pp. 1–19.

44. "Lay's 'Do Us a Flavor' Contest Is Back: Fans Invited to Submit Next Great Potato Chip Flavor Idea for the Chance to Win $1 Million," *PR Newswire*, January 14, 2014; Valeri Reaves, "Facebook's App Crashes during the Lay's 'Do Us a Flavor' Million Dollar Contest," www.examiner.com, July 21, 2012; Bruce Horovitz, "Lay's Goes on Facebook with $1 Million Prize for New Flavor," *USA Today*, July 18, 2012.

45. Stephen Baker, "Beware Social Media Snake Oil," *Bloomberg Businessweek*, December 14, 2009, pp. 48–51.

46. Daniel Birnbaum, "SodaStream's CEO on Turning a Banned Super Bowl Ad into Marketing Gold," *Harvard Business Review*, January–February 2014; Kyle Stock, "The Secret of SodaStream's Success," *Bloomberg Businessweek*, July 31, 2013; Stuart Feil, "Gift for Gab," *Adweek*, December 10, 2012.

47. Ed Keller and Brad Fay, "Word of Mouth Advocacy: A New Key to Advertising Effectiveness," *Journal of Advertising Research*, 52 (December 2012), pp. 459–64.

48. Jeff Koyen, "Mouth Meets Mouse," *Adweek*, November 22, 2011, pp. W1–W5.

49. Barak Libai, Eitan Muller, and Renana Peres, "Decomposing the Value of Word-of-Mouth Seeding Programs: Acceleration Versus Expansion," *Journal of Marketing Research* 50 (April 2013), pp. 161–76, Oliver Hinz, Bernd Skiera, Christian Barrot, and Jan U. Becker, "Seeding Strategies for Viral Marketing: An Empirical Comparison," *Journal of Marketing* 75 (November 2011), pp. 55–71; Ralf van der Lans, Gerrit van Bruggen, Jehoshua Eliashberg, and Berend Wierenga, "A Viral Branching Model for Predicting the Spread of Electronic Word of Mouth," *Marketing Science* 29 (March–April 2010), pp. 348–65.

50. Thales Teixeira, "How to Profit from 'Lean' Advertising," *Harvard Business Review*, June 2013, pp. 23–25.

51. *Will It Blend?* www.willitblend.com; Blendtec, www.blendtec.com; Piet Levy, "I Tube, YouTube," *Marketing News*, March 30, 2009, p. 8;

Phyllis Berman, "Food Fight," *Forbes*, October 13, 2008, p. 110; Rob Walker, "Mixing It Up," *New York Times*, August 24, 2008; Jon Fine, "Ready to Get Weird, Advertisers?," *BusinessWeek*, January 8, 2007, p. 24.

52. Jonah Berger and Raghuram Iyengar, "Communication Channels and Word of Mouth: How the Medium Shapes the Message," *Journal of Consumer Research* 40 (October 2013), pp. 567–79. See also Mitch Lovett, Renana Peres, and Roni Shachar, "On Brands and Word of Mouth," *Journal of Marketing Research* 50 (August 2013), pp. 427–44; Amar Cheema and Andrew M. Kaikati, "The Effect of Need for Uniqueness on Word of Mouth," *Journal of Marketing Research* 47 (June 2010), pp. 553–63.

53. Jonah Berger and Eric M. Schwartz, "What Drives Immediate and Ongoing Word of Mouth?," *Journal of Marketing Research* 48 (October 2011), pp. 869–80.

54. Matteo De Angelis, Andrea Bonezzi, Alessandro M. Peluso, Derek D. Rucker, and Michele Costabile, "On Braggarts and Gossips: A Self-Enhancement Account of Word-of-Mouth Generation and Transmission," *Journal of Marketing Research* 49 (August 2012), pp. 551–63; Sha Yang, Mantian Hu, Russ Winer, Henry Assael, and Xiaohong Chen, "An Empirical Study of Word-of-Mouth Generation and Consumption," *Marketing Science* 31 (November–December 2012), pp. 952–63. See also Yinlong Zhang, Lawrence Feick, and Vikas Mittal, "How Males and Females Differ in Their Likelihood of Transmitting Negative Word of Mouth," *Journal of Consumer Research* 40 (April 2014), pp. 1097–108; David Dubois, Derek D. Rucker, and Zakary L. Tormala, "From Rumors to Facts, and Facts to Rumors: The Role of Certainty Decay in Consumer Communications," *Journal of Marketing Research* 48 (December 2011), pp. 1020–32.

55. Sharad Goel, Duncan J. Watts, and Daniel G. Goldstein, "The Structure of Online Diffusion Networks," *Proceedings of the 13th ACM Conference on Electronic Commerce (EC'12)*, Valencia, Spain, June 4–8, 2012, pp. 623–38.

56. Olivier Toubia and Andrew T. Stephen, "Intrinsic vs. Image-Related Utility in Social Media: Why Do People Contribute Content to Twitter?," *Marketing Science* 32 (May–June 2013), pp. 368–92.

57. Thales Teixeira, "The New Science of Viral Ads," *Harvard Business Review*, March 2012, pp. 25–27; Thales Teixeira, Michel Wedel, and Rik Pieters, "Emotion-Induced Engagement in Internet Video Advertisements," *Journal of Marketing Research* 49 (April 2012), pp. 144–59. See also Jonah Berger and Katherine L. Milkman, "What Makes Online Content Viral?," *Journal of Marketing Research* 49 (April 2012), pp. 192–205.

58. James Peter Rubin, "Where Word-of-Mouth and Shopper Data Meet," *Adweek*, December 10, 2012; Zak Stambor, "For Green Mountain Coffee Roasters a Little Education Goes a Long Way," *Internet Retailer*, July 27, 2012; Stuart Feil, "Gift for Gab," *Adweek*, December 10, 2012; Barbara Kiviat, "Word on the Street," *Time*, April 12, 2007; Dave Balter, "Rules of the Game," *Advertising Age Point*, December 2005, pp. 22–23.

59. Matthew Creamer and Rupal Parekh, "Ideas of the Decade," *Advertising Age*, December 14, 2009.

60. Amar Cheema and Andrew M. Kaikati, "The Effect of Need for Uniqueness on Word of Mouth," *Journal of Marketing Research* 47 (June 2010), pp. 553–63.

61. Stephan Ludwig, Ko de Ruyter, Mike Friedman, Elisabeth C. Brüggen, Martin Wetzels, and Gerard Pfann, "More than Words: The Influence of Affective Content and Linguistic Style Matches in Online Reviews on Conversion Rates," *Journal of Marketing* 77 (January 2013), pp. 87–103; Yi Zhao, Sha Yang, Vishal Narayan, and Ying Zhao, "Modeling Consumer Learning from Online Product Reviews," *Marketing Science* 32 (January–February 2013), pp. 153–69; Rebecca Walker Naylor, Cait Poynor Lamberton, and David A. Norton, "Seeing Ourselves in Others: Reviewer Ambiguity, Egocentric Anchoring, and

Persuasion," *Journal of Marketing Research* 48 (June 2011), pp. 617–31.

62. "Nielsen: Global Consumers' Trust in 'Earned' Advertising Grows in Importance," April 10, 2012. See also Itamar Simonson and Emanuel Rosen, *Added Value* (New York: Harper Collins, 2014).

63. Ekaterina Walter, "When Co-creation Becomes the Beating Heart of Marketing, Companies Win," *Fast Company*, November 29, 2012.

64. Dina Mayzlin, Yaniv Dover, and Judith A. Chevalier, "Promotional Reviews: An Empirical Investigation of Online Review Manipulation," *American Economic Review*, 2014, forthcoming.

65. Sinan Aral, "The Problem with Online Ratings," *MIT Sloan Management Review*, Winter 2014, pp. 47–52. See also Shrihari Sridhar and Raji Srinivasan, "Social Influence Effects in Online Product Ratings," *Journal of Marketing* 76 (September 2012), pp. 70–88; Wendy W. Moe and Michael Trusov, "The Value of Social Dynamics in Online Product Ratings Forums," *Journal of Marketing Research* 48 (June 2011), pp. 444–56. For related research, see Ann Kronrod and Shai Danziger, "Wii Will Rock You! The Use and Effect of Figurative Language in Consumer Reviews of Hedonic and Utilitarian Consumption," *Journal of Consumer Research* 40 (December 2013), pp. 726–39.

66. Zoey Chen and Nicholas Lurie, "Temporal Contiguity and Negativity Bias in the Impact of Online Word of Mouth," *Journal of Marketing Research* 50 (August 2013), pp. 463–76; Yubo Chen, Qi Wang, and Jinhong Xie, "Online Social Interactions: A Natural Experiment on Word of Mouth versus Observational Learning," *Journal of Marketing Research* 48 (April 2011), pp. 238–54.

67. "The Value of Conversation," *Adweek*, May 14, 2012.

68. Keith Barry, "Fiesta Stars in Night of the Living Social Media Campaign," *Wired*, May 21, 2010; Matthew Dolan, "Ford Takes Online Gamble with New Fiesta," *Wall Street Journal*, April 8, 2009.

69. V. Kumar, J. Andrew Petersen, and Robert P. Leone, "How Valuable Is Word of Mouth?," *Harvard Business Review*, October 2007, pp. 139–46.

70. Omar Merlo, Andreas B. Eisingerich, and Seigyoung Auh, "Why Customer Participation Matters," *MIT Sloan Management Review*, Winter 2014, pp. 81–88.

71. Jackie Huba, "From Word of Mouth to Customer Evangelism," *AMA Marketing News*, August 31, 2012; www.churchofthecustomer.com.

72. Adam L. Penenberg, "How Much Are You Worth to Facebook?," *Fast Company*, October 1, 2009.

73. Preethi Chamikuttyl, "Wharton Professor David Bell, on Brand Building in the Offline and Online World," *Your Story*, September 3, 2013.

74. "Mobile Marketing Facts 2014," *Advertising Age*, April 14, 2014.

75. "Mobile Continues to Steal Share of US Adults' Daily Time Spent with Media," *eMarketer*, April 22, 2014.

76. Sunil Gupta, "For Mobile Devices, Think Apps, Not Ads," *Harvard Business Review*, March 2013, pp. 71–75.

77. "VW Set for Launch in 8 Months," WorldCarFans.com, www.worldcarfans.com, March 20, 2007; Eleftheria Parpis, "Volkswagen's Public Polling Pays Off," *Adweek*, May 19, 2008; Andrew Grill, "Volkswagen Tiguan Mobile Advertising Case Study," *London Calling*, www.londoncalling.mobi, May 20, 2009.

78. "New Merrill Edge Mobile App Uses 3D Technology to Put Retirement Planning in Your Hands," www.newsroom.bankofamerica.com, February 26, 2014; Emily Brandon, "An Innovative Way to Face Retirement," www.money.usnews.com, January 14, 2013; Kayla Tausche and Jesse Bergman, "Your 'Face' and Your Retirement at 100," www.cnbc.com, December 19, 2012; Hal E. Hershfield, Daniel G. Goldstein, William F. Sharpe, Jesse Fox, Leo Yeykelis, Laura L. Carstensen, and Jeremy N. Bailenson, "Increasing Saving Behavior through Age-Progressed Renderings of the Future Self," *Journal of Marketing Research* 48 (November 2011), pp. S23–S37.

79. Peter DaSilva, "Cellphone in New Role: Loyalty Card," *New York Times*, May 31, 2010.

80. Diana Ransom, "When the Customer Is in the Neighborhood," *Wall Street Journal*, May 17, 2010.

81. Don Clark and Nick Wingfield, "Intel, Microsoft Offer Smart Sign Technology," *Wall Street Journal*, January 12, 2010; Andrew Lavallee, "Unilever to Test Mobile Coupons in Trial at Supermarket, Cellphones Will Be the Medium for Discount Offers," *Wall Street Journal*, May 29, 2009; Bob Tedeschi, "Phone Smart Cents-Off Coupons and Other Special Deals, via Your Cellphone," *New York Times*, December 17, 2008.

82. Spencer E. Ante, "Online Ads Can Follow You Home," *Wall Street Journal*, April 29, 2013.

83. Paul Heine, "Is This the Long-Awaited Answer to Measuring Video Viewers Everywhere They're Watching?," *Adweek*, March 23, 2104.

84. Piet Levy, "Set Your Sites on Mobile," *Marketing News*, April 30, 2010, p. 6; Tom Lowry, "Pandora: Unleashing Mobile-Phone Ads," *BusinessWeek*, June 1, 2009, pp. 52–53.

85. Christopher Heine, "Agencies And Cannes Judges Say Less Is More for Mobile," *Ad Week*, June 17, 2013.

86. Elisabeth Sullivan, "The Tao of Mobile Marketing," *Marketing News*, April 30, 2010, pp. 16–20.

87. Loretta Chao, "Cell Phone Ads Are Easier Pitch in China Interactive Campaigns," *Wall Street Journal*, January 4, 2007.

## Chapter 22

1. Joshua Green, "The Science behind Those Obama Campaign E-Mails," *Bloomberg Businessweek*, November 29, 2012; Michael Scherer, "Inside the Secret World of the Data Crunchers Who Helped Obama Win," *Time*, November 7, 2012; David Jackson, "How Obama Won Re-Election," *USA Today*, November 9, 2012; Joshua Green, "Corporations Want Obama's Winning Formula," *Bloomberg Businessweek*, November 26, 2012, pp. 37–39.

2. Ran Kivetz and Itamar Simonson, "The Idiosyncratic Fit Heuristic: Effort Advantage as a Determinant of Consumer Response to Loyalty Programs," *Journal of Marketing Research* 40 (November 2003), pp. 454–67; Ran Kivetz and Itamar Simonson, "Earning the Right to Indulge: Effort as a Determinant of Customer Preferences toward Frequency Program Rewards," *Journal of Marketing Research* 39 (May 2002), pp. 155–70.

3. Ira Kalb, "How to Do Direct Marketing That's Not Annoying," *Business Insider*, November 12, 2013.

4. Stan Rapp and Thomas L. Collins, *Maximarketing* (New York: McGraw-Hill, 1987).

5. "Tip Top: Diamond Echo Award," Direct Marketing Association, www.dma.org; "Feel Tip Top: Bronze Winner," www.caples.org; Ben Fahey, "Kiwis Urged to Feel Tip Top This Summer," *Idealog*, October 23, 2012; "Tip Top Delivers Ice Creams to Kiwis' Doors in New Integrated Campaign via Colenso, BBDO NZ," *Campaign Brief*, November 29, 2012.

6. Allison Schiff, "DMA: Direct Response Rates Beat Digital," *Direct Marketing News*, June 14, 2012.

7. For an intriguing variation based on the timing involved with RFM, see Y. Zhang, Eric T. Bradlow, and Dylan S. Small, "Capturing Clumpiness when Valuing Customers: From RFM to RFMC," working paper, 2014, Wharton School of Business.

8. Bob Stone and Ron Jacobs, *Successful Direct Marketing Methods*, 8th ed. (New York: McGraw-Hill, 2007). See also David A. Schweidel and George Knox, "Incorporating Direct Marketing Activity into Latent Attrition Models," *Marketing Science* 32 (May–June 2013), pp. 471–87.

9. Edward L. Nash, *Direct Marketing: Strategy, Planning, Execution*, 4th ed. (New York: McGraw-Hill, 2000).

10. Matt Schifrin, "Master Class," *Forbes*, January 17, 2011, pp. 54–55.

11. The *average customer longevity* (N) is related to the *customer retention rate* (CR). Suppose the company retains 80 percent of its customers each year. Then the average customer longevity is given by: N = 1/(1 – CR) = 1/.2 = 5 years.

12. 2011 MCM 100, *MultiChannel Merchant*, www.multichannelmerchant.com, accessed January 27, 2014.

13. "Internet & Mail-Order Retail Industry Profile," www.firstresearch.com, March 3, 2014.

14. Todd Woody, "War on Junk Mail," *Forbes*, May 7, 2012, pp. 48–49.

15. Steve Kroft," The Data Brokers: Selling Your Personal Information," www.cbsnews.com, March 9, 2014.

16. V. Kumar, Rajkumar Venkatesan, and Werner Reinartz, "Knowing What to Sell, When, and to Whom," *Harvard Business Review*, March 2006, pp. 131–37.

17. Jeff Zabin, "The Importance of Being Analytical," *Brandweek*, July 24, 2006, p. 21; Stephen Baker, "Math Will Rock Your World," *BusinessWeek*, January 23, 2006, pp. 54–62; Michelle Kessler and Byron Acohido, "Data Miners Dig a Little Deeper," *USA Today*, July 11, 2006.

18. www.dunnhumby.com, accessed December 27, 2012; Burt Heim, "Getting inside the Customer's Mind," *BusinessWeek*, September 22, 2008, p. 88; Mike Duff, "Dunnhumby Complicates Outlook for Tesco, Kroger, Wal-Mart," bnet.com, January 13, 2009; Sarah Mahoney, "Macy's Readies New Marketing Strategy, Hires Dunnhumby," *Marketing Daily*, August 14, 2008; Kerry Capell, "Tesco: Wal-Mart's Worst Nightmare," *Bloomberg Businessweek*, December 29, 2008.

19. Christopher R. Stephens and R. Sukumar, "An Introduction to Data Mining," Rajiv Grover and Marco Vriens, eds., *Handbook of Marketing Research* (Thousand Oaks, CA: Sage Publications, 2006), pp. 455–86; Pang-Ning Tan, Michael Steinbach, and Vipin Kumar, *Introduction to Data Mining* (Upper Saddle River, NJ: Addison Wesley, 2005); Michael J. A. Berry and Gordon S. Linoff, *Data Mining Techniques: For Marketing, Sales, and Customer Relationship Management*, 2nd ed. (Hoboken, NJ: Wiley Computer, 2004); James Lattin, Doug Carroll, and Paul Green, *Analyzing Multivariate Data* (Florence, KY: Thomson Brooks/Cole, 2003).

20. Ibid.; George S. Day, "Creating a Superior Customer-Relating Capability," *MSI Report No. 03–101* (Cambridge, MA: Marketing Science Institute, 2003); "Why Some Companies Succeed at CRM (and Many Fail)," *Knowledge at Wharton*, http://knowledge.wharton.upenn.edu, January 15, 2003.

21. Werner Reinartz and V. Kumar, "The Mismanagement of Customer Loyalty," *Harvard Business Review*, July 2002, pp. 86–94; Susan M. Fournier, Susan Dobscha, and David Glen Mick, "Preventing the Premature Death of Relationship Marketing," *Harvard Business Review*, January–February 1998, pp. 42–51.

22. Jon Swartz, "eBay Faithful Expect Loyalty in Return," *USA Today*, July 1, 2002.

23. V. Kumar and Werner J. Reinartz, "The Mismanagement of Customer Loyalty," *Harvard Business Review*, July 2002.

24. "Employment by Major Occupational Group, 2012 and Projected 2022," www.bls.gov/news.release/ecopro.t06.htm.

25. "The View from the Field," *Harvard Business Review*, July–August 2012, pp. 101–9.

26. John Bello, "Sell Like Your Outfit Is at Stake. It Is," *BusinessWeek Online*, February 5, 2004; John Bello, "The Importance of Sales for Entrepreneurs," *USA Today*, February 11, 2004; Jeanine Prezioso, "Lizard King's Story," *Fairfield County Business Journal*, December 10, 2001.

27. Shrihari Sridhar, Murali K. Mantrala, and Sönke Albers, "Personal Selling Elasticities: A Meta-Analysis," *Journal of Marketing Research* 47 (October 2010).

28. Adapted from Robert N. McMurry, "The Mystique of Super-Salesmanship," *Harvard Business Review*, March–April 1961, p. 114. Also see William C. Moncrief III, "Selling Activity and Sales Position Taxonomies for Industrial Sales Forces," *Journal of Marketing Research* 23 (August 1986), pp. 261–70.

29. Brent Adamson, Matthew Dixon, and Nicholas Toman, "The End of Solution Sales," *Harvard Business Review*, July–August 2012, pp. 60–68.

30. Lawrence G. Friedman and Timothy R. Furey, *The Channel Advantage: Going to Marketing with Multiple Sales Channels* (Oxford, UK: Butterworth-Heinemann, 1999).

31. Michael Ahearne, Scott B. MacKenzie, Philip M. Podsakoff, John E. Mathieu, and Son K. Lam, "The Role of Consensus in Sales Team Performance," *Journal of Marketing Research* 47 (June 2010), pp. 458–69.

32. Ashwin W. Joshi, "Salesperson Influence on Product Development: Insights from a Study of Small Manufacturing Organizations," *Journal of Marketing* 74 (January 2010), pp. 94–107; Philip Kotler, Neil Rackham, and Suj Krishnaswamy, "Ending the War between Sales & Marketing," *Harvard Business Review*, July–August 2006, pp. 68–78; Timothy M. Smith, Srinath Gopalakrishna, and Rubikar Chaterjee, "A Three-Stage Model of Integrated Marketing Communications at the Marketing-Sales Interface," *Journal of Marketing Research* 43 (November 2006), pp. 546–79.

33. "The View from the Field," pp. 101–9.

34. Piet Levy, "Sales Support," *Marketing News*, March 30, 2011, pp. 18–23.

35. Michael Copeland, "Hits and Misses," *Business 2.0*, April 2004, p. 142.

36. For distinctions between bonuses and commissions, see Sunil Kishore, Raghunath Singh Rao, Om Narasimhan, and George John, "Bonuses versus Commissions: A Field Study," *Journal of Marketing Research* 50 (June 2013), pp. 317–33.

37. "Sales Performance Benchmarks," *Go-to-Market Strategies*, June 5, 2007. For international tax implications in compensation, see Dominique Rouziès, Anne T. Coughlan, Erin Anderson, and Dawn Iacobucci, "Determinants of Pay Levels and Structures in Sales Organizations," *Journal of Marketing* 73 (November 2009), pp. 92–104.

38. Daniel H. Pink, "A Radical Prescription for Sales," *Harvard Business Review*, July–August 2012, pp. 76–77.

39. Tony Ritigliano and Benson Smith, *Discover Your Sales Strengths* (New York: Random House Business Books, 2004).

40. Sonke Albers, "Sales-Force Management—Compensation, Motivation, Selection, and Training," Bart Weitz and Robin Wensley, eds., *Handbook of Marketing* (London: Sage, 2002), pp. 248–66.

41. Michael R. W. Bommer, Brian F. O'Neil, and Beheruz N. Sethna, "A Methodology for Optimizing Selling Time of Salespersons," *Journal of Marketing Theory and Practice* (Spring 1994), pp. 61–75. See also Lissan Joseph, "On the Optimality of Delegating Pricing Authority to the Sales Force," *Journal of Marketing* 65 (January 2001), pp. 62–70.

42. Gaurav Sabnis, Sharmila C. Chatterjee, Rajdeep Grewal, and Gary L. Lilien, "The Sales Lead Black Hole: On Sales Reps' Follow-up of Marketing Leads," *Journal of Marketing* 77 (January 2013), pp. 52–67.

43. Dartnell Corporation, *30th Sales-Force Compensation Survey* (Chicago: Dartnell Corp., 1999). Other breakdowns show that 12.7 percent is spent in service calls, 16 percent in administrative tasks, 25.1 percent in telephone selling, and 17.4 percent in waiting/traveling. For an analysis of this database, see Sanjog Misra, Anne T. Coughlan, and Chakravarthi Narasimhan, "Salesforce Compensation:

An Analytical and Empirical Examination of the Agency Theoretic Approach," *Quantitative Marketing and Economics* 3 (March 2005), pp. 5–39.

44. Michael Ahearne, Son K. Lam, John E. Mathieu, and Willy Bolander, "Why Are Some Salespeople Better at Adapting to Organizational Change?," *Journal of Marketing* 74 (May 2010), pp. 65–79.

45. Jeff Green, "The New Willy Loman Survives by Staying Home," *Bloomberg Businessweek*, January 14, 2013, pp. 16–17.

46. Barbara Giamanco and Kent Gregoire, "Tweet Me, Friend Me, Make Me Buy," *Harvard Business Review*, July–August 2012, pp. 88–93.

47. Willem Verbeke and Richard P. Bagozzi, "Sales-Call Anxiety: Exploring What It Means when Fear Rules a Sales Encounter," *Journal of Marketing* 64 (July 2000), pp. 88–101. See also Douglas E. Hughes and Michael Ahearne, "Energizing the Reseller's Sales Force: The Power of Brand Identification," *Journal of Marketing* 74 (July 2010), pp. 81–96; Jeffrey P. Boichuk, Willy Bolander, Zachary R. Hall, Michael Ahearne, William J. Zahn, and Melissa Nieves, "Learned Helplessness among Newly Hired Salespeople and the Influence of Leadership," *Journal of Marketing* 78 (January 2014), pp. 95–111.

48. Gilbert A. Churchill Jr., Neil M. Ford, Orville C. Walker Jr., Mark W. Johnston, and Greg W. Marshall, *Sales-Force Management*, 9th ed. (New York: McGraw-Hill/Irwin, 2009). See also Eric G. Harris, John C. Mowen, and Tom J. Brown, "Reexamining Salesperson Goal Orientations: Personality Influencers, Customer Orientation, and Work Satisfaction," *Journal of the Academy of Marketing Science* 33 (Winter 2005), pp. 19–35.

49. Noah Lim, Michael J. Ahearne, and Sung H. Ham, "Designing Sales Contests: Does the Prize Structure Matter?," *Journal of Marketing Research* 46 (June 2009), pp. 356–71.

50. Thomas Steenburgh and Michael Ahearne, "Motivating Salespeople: What Really Works," *Harvard Business Review*, July–August 2012, pp. 70–75.

51. Sanjog Misra and Harikesh Nair, "A Structural Model of Sales-Force Compensation Dynamics: Estimation and Field Implementation," *Quantitative Marketing and Economics* 9 (September 2011), pp. 211–25.

52. Thomas Steenburgh and Michael Ahearne, "Motivating Salespeople: What Really Works," *Harvard Business Review*, July–August 2012, pp. 70–75.

53. Lisa Vaas, "Oracle Teaches Its Sales Force to Play Nice," *eWeek*, July 28, 2004; Lisa Vaas, "Oracle's Sales Force Reorg Finally Bears Fruit," *eWeek*, December 17, 2003; Ian Mount, "Out of Control," *Business 2.0*, August 2002, pp. 38–44.

54. Andrea L. Dixon, Rosann L. Spiro, and Magbul Jamil, "Successful and Unsuccessful Sales Calls: Measuring Salesperson Attributions and Behavioral Intentions," *Journal of Marketing* 65 (July 2001), pp. 64–78; Verbeke and Bagozzi, "Sales-Call Anxiety: Exploring What It Means when Fear Rules a Sales Encounter," pp. 88–101.

55. Neil Rackham, *SPIN Selling* (New York: McGraw-Hill, 1988). Also see his *The SPIN Selling Fieldbook* (New York: McGraw-Hill, 1996); James Lardner, "Selling Salesmanship," *Business 2.0*, December 2002–January 2003, p. 66; Sharon Drew Morgen, *Selling with Integrity: Reinventing Sales through Collaboration, Respect, and Serving* (New York: Berkeley Books, 1999); Neil Rackham and John De Vincentis, *Rethinking the Sales Force* (New York: McGraw-Hill, 1996).

56. Some of the following discussion is based on a classic analysis in W. J. E. Crissy, William H. Cunningham, and Isabella C. M. Cunningham, *Selling: The Personal Force in Marketing* (New York: Wiley, 1977), pp. 119–29. For some contemporary perspective and tips, see Jia Lynn Yang, "How to Sell in a Lousy Economy," *Fortune*, September 29, 2008, pp. 101–6; and Jessi Hempel, "IBM's All-Star Salesman," *Fortune*, September 29, 2008, pp. 110–19.

57. "The View from the Field," pp. 101–9.

58. Ashlee Vance, "Crawling the Web for Sales Leads," *Bloomberg Businessweek*, May 6, 2013.

59. Christian Homburg, Michael Müller, and Martin Klarmann, "When Should the Customer Really Be King? On the Optimum Level of Salesperson Customer Orientation in Sales Encounters," *Journal of Marketing* 75 (March 2011), pp. 55–74.

60. Stephanie Clifford, "Putting the Performance in Sales Performance," *Inc.*, February 2007, pp. 87–95.

61. Joel E. Urbany, "Justifying Profitable Pricing," *Journal of Product & Brand Management* 10 (2001), pp. 141–59.

62. Jia Lynn Yang, "How Can I Keep My Sales Team Productive in a Recession?," *Fortune*, March 2, 2009, p. 22.

63. Brent Adamson, Matthew Dixon, and Nicholas Toman, "Dismantling the Sales Machine," *Harvard Business Review*, November 2013, pp. 103–9.

64. V. Kumar, Rajkumar Venkatesan, and Werner Reinartz, "Performance Implications of Adopting a Customer-Focused Sales Campaign," *Journal of Marketing* 72 (September 2008), pp. 50–68; George R. Franke and Jeong-Eun Park, "Salesperson Adaptive Selling Behavior and Customer Orientation: A Meta-Analysis," *Journal of Marketing Research* 43 (November 2006), pp. 693–702; Richard G. McFarland, Goutam N. Challagalla, and Tasadduq A. Shervani, "Influence Tactics for Effective Adaptive Selling," *Journal of Marketing* 70 (October 2006), pp. 103–17.

## Chapter 23

1. Mat McDermott, "Patagonia's New Wetsuits Will Be Made from Plants," TreeHugger.com, November 19, 2012; Brian Dumaine, "Patagonia Products: Built to Last," www.cnn.com, August 13, 2012; Tim Nudd, "Ad of the Day: Patagonia," *Adweek*, November 28, 2011.

2. For additional analysis and discussion, see Philip Kotler, Hermawan Karatajaya, and Iwan Setiawan, *Marketing 3.0: From Products to Consumers to the Human Spirit* (Hoboken, NJ: Wiley, 2010).

3. Cheryl Jensen, "Prius Tops Consumer Reports List of Best New-Car Values," *New York Times*, December 27, 2012; Dan Neil, "The Fuel-Sipping Prius Gets a Bigger Brother," *Wall Street Journal*, June 18, 2011; Karey Wutkowski, "Car Makers Try to Copy Green Halo of Prius," *Reuters*, April 8, 2008.

4. For some thoughtful academic perspectives on marketing strategy and tactics, see *Kellogg on Marketing*, 2nd ed., Alice M. Tybout and Bobby J. Calder, eds. (New York: Wiley, 2010); and *Kellogg on Integrated Marketing*, Dawn Iacobucci and Bobby Calder, eds. (New York: Wiley, 2003).

5. For a broad historical treatment of marketing thought, see D. G. Brian Jones and Eric H. Shaw, "A History of Marketing Thought," Barton A. Weitz and Robin Wensley, eds., *Handbook of Marketing* (London: Sage, 2002), pp. 39–65; for more specific issues related to the interface between marketing and sales, see Christian Homburg, Ove Jensen, and Harley Krohmer, "Configurations of Marketing and Sales: A Taxonomy," *Journal of Marketing* 72 (March 2008), pp. 133–54.

6. Frederick E. Webster Jr., "Expanding Your Network," *Marketing Management* (Fall 2010), pp. 16–23; Frederick E. Webster Jr., Alan J. Malter, and Shankar Ganesan, "Can Marketing Regain Its Seat at the Table?," *Marketing Science Institute Report No. 03-113* (Cambridge, MA: Marketing Science Institute, 2003); Frederick E. Webster Jr., "The Role of Marketing and the Firm," Barton A. Weitz and Robin Wensley, eds., *Handbook of Marketing* (London: Sage, 2002), pp. 39–65.

7. Jan Wieseke, Michael Ahearne, Son K. Lam, and Rolf van Dick, "The Role of Leaders in Internal Marketing," *Journal of Marketing* 73 (March 2009), pp. 123–45; Hamish Pringle and William Gordon, *Beyond*

*Manners: How to Create the Self-Confident Organisation to Live the Brand* (West Sussex, UK: John Wiley & Sons, 2001); John P. Workman Jr., Christian Homburg, and Kjell Gruner, "Marketing Organization: An Integrative Framework of Dimensions and Determinants," *Journal of Marketing* 62 (July 1998), pp. 21–41.

8. Grant McKracken, *Chief Culture Officer: How to Create a Living Breathing Corporation* (New York: Basic Books, 2009).

9. Todd Guild, "Think Regionally, Act Locally: Four Steps to Reaching the Asian Consumer," *McKinsey Quarterly* 4 (September 2009), pp. 22–30.

10. "State and Country Quick Facts," *U.S. Census Bureau*, http://quickfacts.census.gov/qfd/states/12/12086.html, accessed May 24, 2014.

11. "Category Management Goes beyond Grocery," *Cannondale Associates White Paper*, www.cannondaleassoc.com, February 13, 2007; Laurie Freeman, "P&G Widens Power Base: Adds Category Managers," *Advertising Age*, October 12, 1987.

12. Jane Simms, "Categorically Speaking," *Marketing*, June 16, 2010.

13. For some further historical reading on the origins of brand and category management, see George S. Low and Ronald A. Fullerton, "Brands, Brand Management, and the Brand Manager System: A Critical Historical Evaluation," *Journal of Marketing Research* 31 (May 1994), pp. 173–90.

14. D. Gail Fleenor, "The Next Space Optimizer," *Progressive Grocer*, March 2009.

15. Larry Selden and Geoffrey Colvin, *Angel Customers & Demon Customers* (New York: Portfolio [Penguin], 2003).

16. For an in-depth discussion of issues around implementing a customer-based organization on which much of this paragraph is based, see George S. Day, "Aligning the Organization with the Market," *MIT Sloan Management Review* 48 (Fall 2006), pp. 41–49.

17. Frederick E. Webster Jr., "The Role of Marketing and the Firm," Barton A. Weitz and Robin Wensley, eds., *Handbook of Marketing* (London: Sage, 2002), pp. 39–65.

18. For research on the prevalence of CMOs, see Pravin Nath and Vijay Mahajan, "Chief Marketing Officers: A Study of Their Presence in Firms' Top Management Teams," *Journal of Marketing* 72 (January 2008), pp. 65–81. For more discussion on the importance of CMOs, see David A. Aaker, *Spanning Silos: The New CMO Imperative* (Boston: Harvard Business School Press, 2008).

19. For more on creativity, see Pat Fallon and Fred Senn, *Juicing the Orange: How to Turn Creativity into a Powerful Business Advantage* (Boston: Harvard Business School Press, 2006); Bob Schmetterer, *Leap: A Revolution in Creative Business Strategy* (Hoboken, NJ: Wiley, 2003); Jean-Marie Dru, *Beyond Disruption: Changing the Rules in the Marketplace* (Hoboken, NJ: Wiley, 2002); and all the books by Edward DeBono.

20. Gary Hamel, *Leading the Revolution* (Boston: Harvard Business School Press, 2000).

21. Jagdish N. Sheth, *The Self-Destructive Habits of Good Companies . . . and How to Break Them* (Upper Saddle River, NJ: Wharton School Publishing, 2007).

22. William L. Wilkie and Elizabeth S. Moore, "Marketing's Relationship to Society," Barton A. Weitz and Robin Wensley, eds., *Handbook of Marketing* (London: Sage, 2002), pp. 1–38.

23. David Hessekiel, "Cause Marketing Leaders of the Pack," www.forbes.com, January 31, 2012.

24. Raj Sisodia, David B. Wolfe, and Jag Sheth, *Firms of Endearment: How World-Class Companies Profit from Passion and Purpose* (Upper Saddle River, NJ: Wharton School Publishing, 2007).

25. "Growth on Principle: The Unconventional Leadership of Stonyfield Farm," *Center for Customer Insights*, February 12, 2014; Gary Hirshberg, *Stirring It Up: How to Make Money and Save the World* (New York: Hyperion, 2008); Marc Gunther, "Stonyfield Stirs Up the Yogurt Market," www.money.cnn.com, January 4, 2008; Melanie D. G. Kaplan, "Stonyfield Farm CEO: How an Organic Yogurt Business Can Scale," *SmartPlanet*, www.smartplanet.com, May 17, 2010.

26. Elisabeth Sullivan, "Play by the New Rules," *Marketing News*, November 30, 2009, pp. 5–9; for further reading, see Dorothy Cohen, *Legal Issues in Marketing Decision Making* (Cincinnati, OH: South-Western College Publishing, 1995).

27. E. J. Schultz, "Senators Target Tax Deduction—This Time for the Children," *Advertising Age*, May 16, 2014; Lyndsey Layton, "In a First, Agriculture Dept. Plans to Regulate Food Marketing in Schools," *Washington Post*, February 25, 2014; Janet Adamy, "Tough New Rules Proposed on Food Advertising for Kids," *Wall Street Journal*, April 29, 2011. For relevant academic research, see Tirtha Dhar and Kathy Baylis, "Fast-Food Consumption and the Ban on Advertising Targeting Children: The Quebec Experience," *Journal of Marketing Research* 48 (October 2011), pp. 799–813.

28. Kent Hoover, "Favorability Ratings Up for Both Businesses and Labor Unions," *American Business Daily*, June 27, 2013.

29. "The Harris Poll 2013 RQ® Summary Report," www.harrisinteractive.com, accessed May 21, 2014.

30. Mary Jo Hatch and Majken Schultz, *Taking Brand Initiative: How Companies Can Align Strategy, Culture, and Identity through Corporate Branding* (San Francisco: Jossey-Bass, 2008); Majken Schultz, Yun Mi Antorini, and Fabian F. Csaba, *Corporate Branding: Purpose, People, and Process* (Køge, Denmark: Copenhagen Business School Press, 2005); Ronald J. Alsop, *The 18 Immutable Laws of Corporate Reputation: Creating, Protecting, and Repairing Your Most Valuable Asset* (New York: Free Press, 2004).

31. Monique Oxener, "Sustainability Ambitions: Keurig Green Mountain Commits to a Recyclable K-Cup Pack by 2020," www.csrnewswire.com, April 3, 2014; "Massachusetts Governor Deval Patrick Commends Green Mountain Coffee Roaster Inc. and Keurig on Corporate Social Responsibility," *Business Wire*, July 21, 2011; Scott Kirsner, "An Environmental Quandary Percolates at Green Mountain Coffee Roasters," *Boston Globe*, January 3, 2010; Natalie Zmuda, "Green Mountain Takes on Coffee Giants Cup by Cup," *Advertising Age*, June 1, 2009, p. 38.

32. Angela M. Eikenberry, "The Hidden Cost of Cause Marketing," *Stanford Social Innovation Review* (Summer 2009); Aneel Karnani, "The Case against Corporate Social Responsibility," *Wall Street Journal*, August 23, 2010.

33. Dina Spector, "The Simple Way Stonyfield Farm Cut $18 Million in Expenses," *Business Insider*, February 23, 2012.

34. Sandra O'Loughlin, "The Wearin' o' the Green," *Brandweek*, April 23, 2007, pp. 26–27. For a critical response, see also John R. Ehrenfield, "Feeding the Beast," *Fast Company*, December 2006–January 2007, pp. 42–43.

35. Rachel Tepper, "Whole Foods Seafood Ban: Unsustainable Fish No Longer Sold Include Skate and Atlantic Cod," *Huffington Post*, April 23, 2012.

36. Pete Engardio, "Beyond the Green Corporation," *BusinessWeek*, January 29, 2007, pp. 50–64.

37. Global 100, www.global100.org, accessed May 21, 2014.

38. Pete Engardio, "Beyond the Green Corporation," *BusinessWeek*, January 29, 2007, pp. 50–64.

39. David Roberts, "Another Inconvenient Truth," *Fast Company*, March 2008, p. 70; Melanie Warner, "P&G's Chemistry Test," *Fast Company*, July/August 2008, pp. 71–74.

40. Heather Clancy, "Icon: Gary Hirshberg, Co-Founder and Chairman, Stonyfield Farms," www.smartplanet.com, August 26, 2013.

41. Ying-Ching Lin and Chiu-chi Angela Chang, "Double Standard: The Role of Environmental Consciousness in Green Product Usage," *Journal of Marketing* 76 (September 2012), pp. 125–34; Michael Hopkins, "What the 'Green' Consumer Wants," *MIT Sloan Management Review* (Summer 2009), pp. 87–89. For some related consumer research, see Julie R. Irwin and Rebecca Walker Naylor, "Ethical Decisions and Response Mode Compatibility: Weighting of Ethical Attributes in Consideration Sets Formed by Excluding versus Including Product Alternatives," *Journal of Marketing Research* 46 (April 2009), pp. 234–46.

42. Stephanie Clifford and Andrew Martin, "As Consumers Cut Spending, 'Green' Products Lose Allure," *New York Times*, April 21, 2011.

43. John A. Quelch and Nathalie Laidler-Kylander, *The New Global Brands: Managing Non-Government Organizations in the 21st Century* (Mason, OH: South-Western, 2006); Philip Kotler and Nancy Lee, *Corporate Social Responsibility: Doing the Most Good for Your Company and Your Cause* (New York: Wiley, 2005); Lynn Upshaw, *Truth: The New Rules for Marketing in a Skeptical World* (New York: AMACOM, 2007).

44. www.timberland.com/en/about-timberland, accessed May 21, 2014; Mark Borden and Anya Kamentz, "The Prophet CEO," *Fast Company*, September 2008, pp. 126–29; Tara Weiss, "Special Report: Going Green," Forbes.com, July 3, 2007; Matthew Grimm, "Progressive Business," *Brandweek*, November 28, 2005, pp. 16–26; Kate Galbraith, "Timberland's New Footprint: Recycled Tires," *New York Times*, April 3, 2009; Aman Singh, "Timberland's Smoking Ban: Good Corporate Citizenship or Overkill?," *Forbes*, June 3, 2010; Amy Cortese, "Products; Friend of Nature? Let's See Those Shoes," *New York Times*, March 6, 2007.

45. Newman's Own Foundation, www.newmansown foundation.org, accessed May 17, 2014; Paul Newman and A. E. Hotchner, *Shameless Exploitation in Pursuit of the Common Good: The Madcap Business Adventure by the Truly Oddest Couple* (Waterville, ME: Thorndike Press, 2003).

46. "Giving USA: Charitable Donations Grew in 2012, but Slowly, Like the Economy," www.philanthropy.iupui.edu, June 18, 2013.

47. Daniel Korschun, C.B. Bhattacharya, and Scott D. Swain, "Corporate Social Responsibility, Customer Orientation, and the Job Performance of Frontline Employees," *Journal of Marketing* 78 (May 2014), pp. 20–37.

48. Larry Chiagouris and Ipshita Ray, "Saving the World with Cause-Related Marketing," *Marketing Management* 16 (July–August 2007), pp. 48–51; Hamish Pringle and Marjorie Thompson, *Brand Spirit: How Cause-Related Marketing Builds Brands* (New York: Wiley, 1999); Sue Adkins, *Cause-Related Marketing: Who Cares Wins* (Oxford, UK: Butterworth-Heinemann, 1999); "Marketing, Corporate Social Initiatives, and the Bottom Line," Marketing Science Institute Conference Summary, *MSI Report No. 01-106*, 2001.

49. Minette Drumwright and Patrick E. Murphy, "Corporate Societal Marketing," Paul N. Bloom and Gregory T. Gundlach, eds., *Handbook of Marketing and Society* (Thousand Oaks, CA: Sage, 2001), pp. 162–83.

50. "2013 Cone Communications Social Impact Study: The Next Cause Evolution," www.conecomm.com.

51. "How Dawn Saves Wildlife," www.dawnsaveswildlife.com, accessed May 17, 2014; www.dawn-dish.com/us/dawn/savingwildlife, accessed May 17, 2014; "Dawn Expands 40-Year Commitment to Wildlife Rescue with $1 Million Donation and New Documentary Series Featuring Rob Lowe," *Business Wire*, July 16, 2013.

52. Christian Homburg, Marcel Stierl, and Torsten Bornemann, "Corporate Social Responsibility in Business-to-Business Markets: How Organizational Customers Account for Supplier Corporate Social Responsibility Engagement," *Journal of Marketing* 77 (November 2013), pp. 54–72; Sean Blair and Alexander Chernev, "Doing Well by Doing Good: The Benevolent Halo of Social Goodwill," Marketing Science Institute Report 12-103, 2011, www.msi.org; Xueming Luo and C. B. Bhattacharya, "Corporate Social Responsibility, Customer Satisfaction, and Market Value," *Journal of Marketing* 70 (October 2006), pp. 1–18; C. B. Bhattacharya and Sankar Sen, "Consumer-Company Identification: A Framework for Understanding Consumers' Relationships with Companies," *Journal of Marketing* 67 (April 2003), pp. 76–88; Sankar Sen and C. B. Bhattacharya, "Does Doing Good Always Lead to Doing Better? Consumer Reactions to Corporate Social Responsibility," *Journal of Marketing Research* 38 (May 2001), pp. 225–44.

53. Paul N. Bloom, Steve Hoeffler, Kevin Lane Keller, and Carlos E. Basurto, "How Social-Cause Marketing Affects Consumer Perceptions," *MIT Sloan Management Review* (Winter 2006), pp. 49–55; Carolyn J. Simmons and Karen L. Becker-Olsen, "Achieving Marketing Objectives through Social Sponsorships," *Journal of Marketing* 70 (October 2006), pp. 154–69; Guido Berens, Cees B. M. van Riel, and Gerrit H. van Bruggen, "Corporate Associations and Consumer Product Responses: The Moderating Role of Corporate Brand Dominance," *Journal of Marketing* 69 (July 2005), pp. 35–48; Donald R. Lichtenstein, Minette E. Drumwright, and Bridgette M. Braig, "The Effect of Social Responsibility on Customer Donations to Corporate-Supported Nonprofits," *Journal of Marketing* 68 (October 2004), pp. 16–32; Stephen Hoeffler and Kevin Lane Keller, "Building Brand Equity through Corporate Societal Marketing," *Journal of Public Policy and Marketing* 21 (Spring 2002), pp. 78–89. See also Special Issue: Corporate Responsibility, *Journal of Brand Management* 10, nos. 4–5 (May 2003).

54. "2013 Cone Communications Social Impact Study: The Next Cause Evolution," www.conecomm.com; C. B. Bhattacharya, Sankar Sen, and Daniel Korschun, "Using Corporate Social Responsibility to Win the War for Talent," *MIT Sloan Management Review* 49 (January 2008), pp. 37–44.

55. Mark R. Forehand and Sonya Grier, "When Is Honesty the Best Policy? The Effect of Stated Company Intent on Consumer Skepticism," *Journal of Consumer Psychology* 13 (2003), pp. 349–56. See also Aradhna Krishna, "Can Supporting a Cause Decrease Donations and Happiness?: The Cause Marketing Paradox," *Journal of Consumer Psychology* 21 (July 2011), pp. 338–45.

56. Susan Perry, "KFC-Komen 'Buckets for the Cure' Campaign Raises Questions," MinnPost.com, www.minnpost.com, April 20, 2010; Chuck English, "Cause Splash vs. Cause Marketing," *Doing Good for Business*, www.doinggoodforbusiness.wordpress.com, May 17, 2010; Nancy Schwartz, "Busted Nonprofit Brand: Anatomy of a Corporate Sponsorship Meltdown (Case Study)," *Getting Attention!*, www.gettingattention.org, April 28, 2010.

57. For some related research, see Ann Kronrod, Amir Grinstein, and Luc Wathieu, "Go Green! Should Environmental Messages Be So Assertive?," *Journal of Marketing* 76 (January 2012), pp. 95–102; Katherine White, Rhiannon MacDonnell, and John H. Ellard, "Belief in a Just World: Consumer Intentions and Behaviors toward Ethical Products," *Journal of Marketing* 76 (January 2012), pp. 103–18.

58. Kevin Lane Keller and Lowey Bundy Sichol, "(Product) Red: Building a Social Marketing Brand," *Best Practice Cases in Brand Management* (Upper Saddle River, NJ: Pearson Prentice Hall, 2015); www.red.org, accessed May 21, 2014; Mya Frazier, "Costly Red Campaign Reaps Meager $18 Million," *Advertising Age*, March 5, 2007; Viewpoint: Bobby Shriver, "CEO: Red's Raised Lots of Green," *Advertising Age*, March 12, 2007; Michelle Conlin, "Shop (in the Name of Love)," *BusinessWeek*, October 2, 2006, p. 9.

59. Ronald J. Alsop, *The 18 Immutable Laws of Corporate Reputation: Creating, Protecting, and Repairing Your Most Valuable Asset* (New York: Free Press, 2004), p. 125.

60. Ronald McDonald House Charities, www.rmhc.org, accessed May 17, 2014.

61. http://ww5.komen.org/CorporatePartners.aspx, accessed May 17, 2014.

62. Christine Bittar, "Seeking Cause and Effect," *Brandweek*, November 11, 2002, pp. 18–24.

63. www.goredforwomen.org/home/about-go-red, accessed May 17, 2014.

64. Stefanie Rosen Robinson, Caglar Irmak, and Satish Jayachandran, "Choice of Cause in Cause-Related Marketing," *Journal of Marketing* 76 (July 2012), pp. 126–39.

65. One Sight, www.onesight.org, accessed May 17, 2014.

66. www.worldwildlife.org/partnerships, accessed May 24, 2014.

67. Jeff Chu, "The Cobbler's Conundrum," *Fast Company*, July/August 2013; Christina Binkley, "Charity Gives Shoe Brand Extra Shine," *Wall Street Journal*, April 1, 2010; "How I Got Started . . . Blake Mycoskie, Founder of TOMS Shoes," *Fortune*, March 22, 2010, p. 72; Dan Heath and Chip Heath, "An Arms Race of Goodness," *Fast Company*,

October 2009, pp. 82–83; Toms, www.toms.com/movement-one-for-one, accessed May 22, 2014.

68. Philip Kotler, David Hessekiel, and Nancy Lee, *Good Works: Marketing and Corporate Initiatives That Build a Better World…and the Bottom Line* (Hoboken, NJ: John Wiley & Sons, 2012); Philip Kotler and Nancy Lee, *Social Marketing: Influencing Behaviors for Good* (Thousand Oaks, CA: Sage, 2008); Alan Andreasen, *Social Marketing in the 21st Century* (Thousand Oaks, CA: Sage, 2006).

69. For an application, see Sekar Raju, Priyali Rajagopal, and Timothy J. Gilbride, "Marketing Healthful Eating to Children: The Effectiveness of Incentives, Pledges, and Competitions," *Journal of Marketing* 74 (May 2010), pp. 93–106.

70. For some relevant academic research on developing social marketing programs, see Deborah A. Small and Nicole M. Verrochi, "The Face of Need: Facial Emotion Expression on Charity Advertisements," *Journal of Marketing Research* 46 (December 2009), pp. 777–87; Katherine White and John Peloza, "Self-Benefit versus Other-Benefit Marketing Appeals: Their Effectiveness in Generating Charitable Support," *Journal of Marketing* 73 (July 2009), pp. 109–24; Merel Van Diepen, Bas Donkers, and Philip Hans Franses, "Dynamic and Competitive Effects of Direct Mailings: A Charitable Giving Application," *Journal of Marketing Research* 46 (February 2009), pp. 120–33; Jen Shang, Americus Reed II, and Rachel Croson, "Identity Congruency Effects on Donations," *Journal of Marketing Research* 45 (June 2008), pp. 351–61.

71. www.wwf.org, "Current Partners," accessed May 14, 2014; Andrew Adam Newman, "Avoiding Violent Images for an Anti-Poaching Campaign," *New York Times*, February 19, 2013; Mike DeSouza, "Coke Cans Turning White to Protect Polar Bears," *Edmonton Journal*, October 26, 2011; Mindy Charski, "World Wildlife Fund Roars as the King of the Direct Marketing Jungle," *Deliver*, December 12, 2011.

72. For more on developing and implementing marketing plans, see H. W. Goetsch, *Developing, Implementing, and Managing an Effective Marketing Plan* (Chicago: NTC Business Books, 1993). See also Thomas V. Bonoma, *The Marketing Edge: Making Strategies Work* (New York: Free Press, 1985). Much of this section is based on Bonoma's work.

73. For other examples, see Paul W. Farris, Neil T. Bendle, Phillip E. Pfeifer, and David J. Reibstein, *Marketing Metrics: 50+ Metrics Every Executive Should Master* (Upper Saddle River, NJ: Wharton School Publishing, 2006).

74. Philip Kotler, William Gregor, and William Rodgers, "The Marketing Audit Comes of Age," *Sloan Management Review* 30 (Winter 1989), pp. 49–62; Frederick Reichheld, *The Loyalty Effect* (Boston: Harvard Business School Press, 1996) discusses attrition of the figures.

75. Kotler, Gregor, and Rodgers, "The Marketing Audit Comes of Age," pp. 49–62.

76. Alfred R. Oxenfeldt, "How to Use Market-Share Measurement," *Harvard Business Review*, January–February 1969, pp. 59–68.

77. There is a one-half chance that a successive observation will be higher or lower. Therefore, the probability of finding six successively higher values is given by 1/2 to the sixth power, or 1/64.

78. Alternatively, companies need to focus on factors affecting shareholder value. The goal of marketing planning is to increase shareholder value, which is the present value of the future income stream created by the company's present actions. Rate-of-return analysis usually focuses on only one year's results. See Alfred Rapport, *Creating Shareholder Value*, rev. ed. (New York: Free Press, 1997).

79. Robin Cooper and Robert S. Kaplan, "Profit Priorities from Activity-Based Costing," *Harvard Business Review*, May–June 1991, pp. 130–35; for a recent application to shipping, see Tom Kelley, "What Is the *Real* Cost: How to Use Lifecycle Cost Analysis for an Accurate Comparison," *Beverage World*, January 2010, pp. 50–51.

## Appendix

1. Background information and market data adapted from Sascha Seagan and Eugene Kim, "Which Is the Best Next-Gen Android Smartphone?," *PC Magazine*, May 2014, pp. 55–62; smart-phone specs: www.phonearena.com; "Smartphone Subscriber Market Share Report," June 4, 2014, www.comscore.com; "Gartner Says Annual Smartphone Sales Surpassed Sales of Feature Phones for the First Time in 2013," Feb. 13, 2014, www.gartner.com; company history: www.apple.com, www.samsung.com, www.lg.com, www.motorola.com, www.htc.com.

# Glossary

**activity-based costing (ABC)** accounting procedures that can quantify the true profitability of different activities by identifying their actual costs.

**adoption** an individual's decision to become a regular user of a product.

**advertising** any paid form of nonpersonal presentation and promotion of ideas, goods, or services by an identified sponsor.

**advertising objective** a specific communications task and achievement level to be accomplished with a specific audience in a specific period of time.

**anchoring and adjustment heuristic** when consumers arrive at an initial judgment and then make adjustments of their first impressions based on additional information.

**arbitration** to resolve a conflict, when two parties agree to present their arguments to one or more arbitrators and accept their decision.

**arm's-length price** the price charged by other competitors for the same or a similar product.

**aspirational groups** groups a person hopes or would like to join.

**associative network memory model** a conceptual representation that views memory as consisting of a set of nodes and interconnecting links where nodes represent stored information or concepts and links represent the strength of association between this information or concepts.

**attitude** a person's enduring favorable or unfavorable evaluation, emotional feeling, and action tendencies toward some object or idea.

**augmented product** a product that includes features that go beyond consumer expectations and differentiate the product from competitors.

**available market** the set of consumers who have interest, income, and access to a particular offer.

**availability heuristic** when consumers base their predictions on the quickness and ease with which a particular example of an outcome comes to mind.

**average cost** the cost per unit at a given level of production; it is equal to total costs divided by production.

**backward invention** reintroducing earlier product forms that can be well adapted to a foreign country's needs.

**banner ads** (Internet) small, rectangular boxes containing text and perhaps a picture to support a brand.

**basic product** what specifically the actual product is.

**belief** a descriptive thought that a person holds about something.

**brand** a name, term, sign, symbol, or design, or a combination of them, intended to identify the goods or services of one seller or group of sellers and to differentiate them from those of competitors.

**brand architecture** *see* branding strategy.

**brand-asset management team (BAMT)** key representatives from functions that affect the brand's performance.

**brand associations** all brand-related thoughts, feelings, perceptions, images, experiences, beliefs, attitudes, and so on, that become linked to the brand node.

**brand audit** a consumer-focused exercise that involves a series of procedures to assess the health of the brand, uncover its sources of brand equity, and suggest ways to improve and leverage its equity.

**brand community** a specialized community of consumers and employees whose identification and activities focus around the brand.

**brand contact** any information-bearing experience a customer or prospect has with the brand, the product category, or the market that relates to the marketer's product or service.

**brand development index (BDI)** the index of brand sales to category sales.

**brand dilution** when consumers no longer associate a brand with a specific product or highly similar products or start thinking less favorably about the brand.

**brand elements** those trademarkable devices that serve to identify and differentiate the brand such as a brand name, logo, or character.

**brand equity** the added value endowed to products and services.

**brand equity drivers** the three main ways you build brand equity through choice of brand elements, marketing programs and activities and leveraging secondary associations.

**brand extension** a company's use of an established brand to introduce a new product.

**brand knowledge** all the thoughts, feelings, images, experiences, beliefs, and so on, that become associated with the brand.

**brand line** all products, original as well as line and category extensions, sold under a particular brand name.

**brand mix** the set of all brand lines that a particular seller makes available to buyers.

**brand personality** the specific mix of human traits that may be attributed to a particular brand.

**brand portfolio** the set of all brands and brand lines a particular firm offers for sale to buyers in a particular category.

**brand promise** the marketer's vision of what the brand must be and do for consumers.

**brand-tracking studies** quantitative data collected from consumers over time to provide consistent, baseline information about how brands and marketing program are performing.

**brand valuation** an estimate of the total financial value of the brand.

**brand value chain** a structured approach to assessing the sources and outcomes of brand equity and the manner in which marketing activities create brand value.

**branded variants** specific brand lines uniquely supplied to different retailers or distribution channels.

**branding** endowing products and services with the power of a brand.

**branding strategy** the number and nature of common and distinctive brand elements applied to the different products sold by the firm.

**brick-and-click** existing companies that have added an online site for information and/or e-commerce.

**business database** complete information about business customers' past purchases, past volumes, prices, and profits.

**business market** all the organizations that acquire goods and services used in the production of other products or services that are sold, rented, or supplied to others.

# C

**capital items** long-lasting goods that facilitate developing or managing the finished product.

**captive products** products that are necessary to the use of other products, such as razor blades or film.

**category extension** using the parent brand to brand a new product outside the product category currently served by the parent brand.

**category membership** the products or sets of products with which a brand competes and that function as close substitutes.

**cause-related marketing** marketing that links a firm's contributions to a designated cause to customers' engaging directly or indirectly in revenue-producing transactions with the firm.

**channel conflict** when one channel member's actions prevent the channel from achieving its goal.

**channel coordination** when channel members are brought together to advance the goals of the channel as opposed to their own potentially incompatible goals.

**channel power** the ability to alter channel members' behavior so that they take actions they would not have taken otherwise.

**club membership programs** programs open to everyone who purchases a product or service or limited to an affinity group of those willing to pay a small fee.

**co-branding** (also **dual branding** or **brand bundling**) two or more well-known brands are combined into a joint product or marketed together in some fashion.

**cohorts** groups of individuals born during the same time period who travel through life together.

**communication adaptation** changing marketing communications programs for each local market.

**communication-effect research** determining whether an ad is communicating effectively.

**communities of practice** often housed on internal Web sites, when employees from different departments are encouraged to share knowledge and skills with others

**company demand** the company's estimated share of market demand at alternative levels of company marketing effort in a given time period.

**company sales forecast** the expected level of company sales based on a chosen marketing plan and an assumed marketing environment.

**company sales potential** the sales limit approached by company demand as company marketing effort increases relative to that of competitors.

**competitive advantage** a company's ability to perform in one or more ways that competitors cannot or will not match.

**competitive frame of reference** closely linked to target market decisions, defines which other brands a brand competes with and which should thus be the focus of competitive analysis. Decisions about the competitive frame of reference are closely linked to target market decisions

**company sales potential** the sales limit approached by company demand as company marketing effort increases relative to that of competitors.

**conformance quality** the degree to which all the produced units are identical and meet the promised specifications.

**conjoint analysis** a method for deriving the utility values that consumers attach to varying levels of a product's attributes.

**conjunctive heuristic** the consumer sets a minimum acceptable cutoff level for each attribute and chooses the first alternative that meets the minimum standard for all attributes.

**consumer-adoption process** the mental steps through which an individual passes from first hearing about an innovation to final adoption

**consumer behavior** the study of how individuals, groups, and organizations elect, buy, use, and dispose of goods, services, ideas, or experiences to satisfy their needs and wants.

**consumer involvement** the level of engagement and active processing undertaken by the consumer in responding to a marketing stimulus.

**consumerist movement** an organized movement of citizens and government to strengthen the rights and powers of buyers in relation to sellers.

**containerization** putting the goods in boxes or trailers that are easy to transfer between two transportation modes.

**contractual sales force** manufacturers' reps, sales agents, and brokers who are paid a commission based on sales.

**convenience goods** goods the consumer purchases frequently, immediately, and with a minimum of effort.

**conventional marketing channel** an independent producer, wholesaler(s), and retailer(s).

**co-optation** an effort by one organization to win the support of the leaders of another by including them in advisory councils, boards of directors, and the like

**core benefit** the service or benefit the customer is really buying.

**core competency** attribute that (1) is a source of competitive advantage in that it makes a significant contribution to perceived customer benefits, (2) has applications in a wide variety of markets, and (3) is difficult for competitors to imitate.

**core values** the belief systems that underlie consumer attitudes and behavior and that determine people's choices and desires over the long term.

**corporate culture** the shared experiences, stories, beliefs, and norms that characterize an organization.

**corporate retailing** corporately owned retailing outlets that achieve economies of scale, greater purchasing power, wider brand recognition, and better-trained employees.

**countertrade** offering other items in payment for purchases.

**critical path scheduling (CPS)** network planning techniques to coordinate the many tasks in launching a new product.

**crowdfunding** individuals or start-ups fund their projects by using social media and other means to generate interest and contributions from the general public.

**crowdsourcing** paid or unpaid outsiders who can offer needed expertise or a different perspective on a task or project such as with new product development.

**cues** stimuli that determine when, where, and how a person responds.

**culture** the fundamental determinant of a person's wants and behavior.

**customer-based brand equity** the differential effect that brand knowledge has on a consumer response to the marketing of that brand.

**customer churn** high customer defection.

**customer consulting** data, information systems, and advice services that the seller offers to buyers.

**customer database** an organized collection of comprehensive information about individual customers or prospects that is current, accessible, and actionable for marketing purposes.

**customer equity** the sum of lifetime values of all customers.

**customer lifetime value (CLV)** the net present value of the stream of future profits expected over the customer's lifetime purchases.

**customer mailing list** a set of names, addresses, and telephone numbers.

**customer-management organization** deals with individual customers rather than the mass market or even market segments.

**customer-perceived value (CPV)** the difference between the prospective customer's evaluation of all the benefits and all the costs of an offering and the perceived alternatives.

**customer-performance scorecard** how well the company is doing year after year on particular customer-based measures.

**customer profitability analysis (CPA)** a means of assessing and ranking customer profitability through accounting techniques such as activity-based costing (ABC).

**customer relationship management (CRM)** the process of carefully managing detailed information about individual customers and all customer "touch points" to maximize loyalty.

**customer training** training the customer's employees to use the vendor's equipment properly and efficiently.

**customer value analysis** report of the company's strengths and weaknesses relative to various competitors.

**customer-value hierarchy** five product levels that must be addressed by marketers in planning a market offering: core benefit; basic product; expected product; augmented product; and potential product.

**customer value management (CVM)** the analysis of individual data on prospects and customers to develop marketing strategies to acquire and retain customers and drive customer behavior.

# D

**data mining** the extracting of useful information about individuals, trends, and segments from the mass of data.

**data warehouse** a collection of current data captured, organized, and stored in a company's contact center.

**database marketing** the process of building, maintaining, and using customer databases and other databases for the purpose of contacting, transacting, and building customer relationships.

**deep metaphors** basic frames or orientations that consumers have toward the world around them.

**delivery** how well the product or service is delivered to the customer.

**demand chain planning** the process of designing the supply chain based on adopting a target market perspective and working backward.

**demand-side method** identifying the effect sponsorship has on consumers' brand knowledge.

**design** the totality of features that affect how a product looks, feels, and functions to a consumer.

**destination categories** product categories that have the greatest impact on where households choose to shop and how they view a particular retailer

**diplomacy** when each side sends a person or group to meet with its counterpart to resolve a conflict

**direct (company) sales force** full- or part-time paid employees who work exclusively for the company.

**direct marketing** the use of consumer-direct (CD) channels to reach and deliver goods and services to customers without using marketing middlemen.

**direct-order marketing** marketing in which direct marketers seek a measurable response, typically a customer order.

**direct product profitability (DDP)** a way of measuring a product's handling costs from the time it reaches the warehouse until a customer buys it in the retail store.

**discrimination** the process of recognizing differences in sets of similar stimuli and adjusting responses accordingly.

**display ads** small, rectangular boxes containing text and perhaps a picture to support a brand online.

**dissociative groups** those groups whose values or behavior an individual rejects.

**distribution programming** building a planned, professionally managed, vertical marketing system that meets the needs of both manufacturer and distributors.

**drive** a strong internal stimulus impelling action.

**dual adaptation** adapting both the product and the communications to the local market.

**dumping** situation in which a company charges either less than its costs or less than it charges in its home market in order to enter or win a market.

**durability** a measure of a product's expected operating life under natural or stressful conditions.

**durable goods** tangible goods that normally survive many uses by consumers, require more personal selling and service, command a higher margin, and require more seller guarantees

# E

**e-commerce** a company or site offers to transact or facilitate the selling of products and services online.

**elimination-by-aspects heuristic** situation in which the consumer compares brands on an attribute selected probabilistically and brands are eliminated if they do not meet minimum acceptable cutoff levels.

**environmental threat** a challenge posed by an unfavorable trend or development that would lead to lower sales or profit.

**ethnographic research** a particular observational research approach that uses concepts and tools from anthropology and other social science disciplines to provide deep cultural understanding of how people live and work.

**everyday low pricing (EDLP)** in retailing, a constant low price with few or no price promotions and special sales.

**exclusive distribution** severely limiting the number of intermediaries in order to maintain control over the service level and outputs offered by resellers.

**expectancy-value model** consumers evaluate products and services by combining their brand beliefs—positive and negative—according to their weighted importance.

**expected product** a set of attributes and conditions buyers normally expect when they purchase this product.

**experience curve (learning curve)** a decline in the average cost with accumulated production experience.

**experimental research** the most scientifically valid research designed to capture cause-and-effect relationships by eliminating competing explanations of the observed findings.

# F

**fad** a craze that is unpredictable, short-lived, and without social, economic, and political significance.

**family brand** situation in which the parent brand is already associated with multiple products through brand extensions.

**family of orientation** parents and siblings.

**family of procreation** spouse and children.

**features** things that enhance the basic function of a product.

**fixed costs (overhead)** costs that do not vary with production or sales revenue.

**flexible market offering** (1) a naked solution containing the product and service elements that all segment members value, and (2) discretionary options that some segment members value.

**focus group** a gathering of 6 to 10 people who are carefully selected based on certain demographic, psychographic, or other considerations and brought together to discuss various topics of interest.

**forecasting** the art of anticipating what buyers are likely to do under a given set of conditions.

**form** the size, shape, or physical structure of a product.

**forward invention** creating a new product to meet a need in another country.

**frequency programs (FPs)** designed to provide rewards to customers who buy frequently and in substantial amounts.

# G

**generics** unbranded, plainly packaged, less expensive versions of common products such as spaghetti, paper towels, and canned peaches.

**global firm** a firm that operates in more than one country and captures R&D, production, logistical, marketing, and financial advantages in its costs and reputation that are not available to purely domestic competitors.

**global industry** an industry in which the strategic positions of competitors in major geographic or national markets are fundamentally affected by their overall global positions.

**goal formulation** the process of developing specific goals for the planning period.

**going-rate pricing** price based largely on competitors' prices.

**gray market** branded products diverted from normal or authorized distribution channels in the country of product origin or across international borders.

# H

**hedonic bias** when people have a general tendency to attribute success to themselves and failure to external causes.

**heuristics** rules of thumb or mental shortcuts in the decision process.

**high-low pricing** charging higher prices on an everyday basis but then running frequent promotions and special sales.

**holistic marketing** a concept based on the development, design, and implementation of marketing programs, processes, and activities that recognizes their breadth and interdependencies.

**horizontal marketing system** two or more unrelated companies put together resources or programs to exploit an emerging market opportunity.

**hub-and-spoke system** product-management organization where brand or product manager is figuratively at the center, with spokes leading to various departments representing working relationships.

# I

**industry** a group of firms that offer a product or class of products that are close substitutes for one another.

**informational appeal** elaborates on product or service attributes or benefits.

**ingredient branding** a special case of co-branding that involves creating brand equity for materials, components, or parts that are necessarily contained within other branded products.

**innovation** any good, service, or idea that is perceived by someone as new.

**innovation diffusion process** the spread of a new idea from its source of invention or creation to its ultimate users or adopters.

**installation** the work done to make a product operational in its planned location.

**institutional market** schools, hospitals, nursing homes, prisons, and other institutions that must provide goods and services to people in their care.

**integrated logistics systems (ILS)** materials management, material flow systems, and physical distribution, abetted by information technology (IT).

**integrated marketing** mixing and matching marketing activities to maximize their individual and collective efforts.

**integrated marketing channel system** the strategies and tactics of selling through one channel reflect the strategies and tactics of selling through one or more other channels.

**integrated marketing communications (IMC)** a concept of marketing communications planning that recognizes the added value of a comprehensive plan.

**intensive distribution** the manufacturer placing the goods or services in as many outlets as possible.

**internal branding** activities and processes that help to inform and inspire employees.

**internal marketing** an element of holistic marketing; the task of hiring, training, and motivating able employees who want to serve customers well.

**interstitials** advertisements, often with video or animation, that pop up between changes on a Web site.

## J

**jobbers** small-scale wholesalers who sell to small retailers.

**joint venture** a company in which multiple investors share ownership and control.

## L

**lean manufacturing** producing goods with minimal waste of time, materials, and money.

**learning** changes in an individual's behavior arising from experience.

**lexicographic heuristic** a consumer choosing the best brand on the basis of its perceived most important attribute.

**licensed product** one whose brand name has been licensed to other manufacturers who actually make the product.

**life-cycle cost** the product's purchase cost plus the discounted cost of maintenance and repair less the discounted salvage value.

**life stage** a person's major concern, such as going through a divorce, going into a second marriage, taking care of an older parent, deciding to cohabit with another person, deciding to buy a new home, and so on.

**lifestyle** a person's pattern of living in the world as expressed in activities, interests, and opinions.

**line extension** the parent brand is used to brand a new product that targets a new market segment within a product category currently served by the parent brand.

**line stretching** a company lengthens its product line beyond its current range.

**long-term memory (LTM)** a permanent repository of information.

**loyalty** a commitment to rebuy or repatronize a preferred product or service.

## M

**maintenance and repair** the service program for helping customers keep purchased products in good working order.

**market** various groups of customers.

**market-buildup method** identifying all the potential buyers in each market and estimating their potential purchases.

**market-centered organizations** companies that are organized along market lines.

**market demand** the total volume of a product that would be bought by a defined customer group in a defined geographical area in a defined time period in a defined marketing environment under a defined marketing program.

**market forecast** the market demand corresponding to the level of industry marketing expenditure.

**market logistics** planning the infrastructure to meet demand, then implementing and controlling the physical flows or materials and final goods from points of origin to points of use to meet customer requirements at a profit.

**market-management organization** a market manager supervising several market-development managers, market specialists, or industry specialists and drawing on functional services as needed.

**market-penetration index** a comparison of the current level of market demand to the potential demand level.

**market-penetration pricing** pricing strategy where prices start low to drive higher sales volume from price-sensitive customers and produce productivity gains.

**market potential** the limit approached by market demand as industry marketing expenditures approach infinity for a given marketing environment.

**market share** a higher level of selective demand for a product.

**market-skimming pricing** pricing strategy where prices start high and are slowly lowered over time to maximize profits from less price-sensitive customers.

**marketer** someone who seeks a response (attention, a purchase, a vote, a donation) from another party, called the prospect.

**marketing** the activity, set of institutions, and processes for creating, communicating, delivering, and exchanging offerings that have value for customers, clients, partners, and society at large.

**marketing audit** a comprehensive, systematic, independent, and periodic examination of a company's or business unit's marketing environment, objectives, strategies, and activities.

**marketing channel system** the particular set of marketing channels employed by a firm.

**marketing channels** sets of interdependent organizations involved in the process of making a product or service available for use or consumption.

**marketing communications** the means by which firms attempt to inform, persuade, and remind consumers—directly or indirectly—about products and brands that they sell.

**marketing communications mix** advertising, sales promotion, events and experiences, public relations and publicity, direct marketing, and personal selling.

**marketing concept** holds that the key to achieving organizational goals is being more effective than competitors in creating, delivering, and communicating superior customer value to target markets.

**marketing dashboards** a structured way to disseminate the insights gleaned from marketing metrics and marketing-mix modeling.

**marketing decision support system (MDSS)** a coordinated collection of data, systems, tools, and techniques with supporting software and hardware by which an organization gathers and interprets relevant information from business and the environment and turns it into a basis for marketing action.

**marketing funnel** identifies the percentage of the potential target market at each stage in the decision process, from merely aware to highly loyal.

**marketing implementation** the process that turns marketing plans into action assignments and ensures that such assignments are executed in a manner that accomplishes the plan's stated objectives.

**marketing information system (MIS)** people, equipment, and procedures to gather, sort, analyze, evaluate, and distribute information to marketing decision makers.

**marketing insights** diagnostic information about how and why certain effects are observed in the marketplace and what that means to marketers.

**marketing intelligence system** a set of procedures and sources managers use to obtain everyday information about developments in the marketing environment.

**marketing management** the art and science of choosing target markets and getting, keeping, and growing customers through creating, delivering, and communicating superior customer value.

**marketing metrics** the set of measures that helps firms to quantify, compare, and interpret their marketing performance.

**marketing network** the company and its supporting stakeholders, with whom it has built mutually profitable business relationships.

**marketing opportunity** an area of buyer need and interest in which there is a high probability that a company can profitably satisfy that need.

**market opportunity analysis (MOA)** system used to determine the attractiveness and probability of success.

**market partitioning** the process of investigating the hierarchy of attributes consumers examine in choosing a brand if they use phased decision strategies.

**marketing plan** written document that summarizes what the marketer has learned about the marketplace, indicates how the firm plans to reach its marketing objectives, and helps direct and coordinate the marketing effort.

**marketing public relations (MPR)** publicity and other activities that build corporate or product image to facilitate marketing goals.

**markup** pricing an item by adding a standard increase to the product's cost.

**mass customization** the ability of a company to meet each customer's requirements

**master brand** situation in which the parent brand is already associated with multiple products through brand extensions.

**materials and parts** goods that enter the manufacturer's product completely.

**media selection** finding the most cost-effective media to deliver the desired number and type of exposures to the target audience.

**mediation** when a neutral third party skilled in conciliating two parties' interests is brought in to resolve a dispute.

**megatrend** a large social, economic, political, or technological change that is slow to form and, once in place, has an influence for seven to ten years or longer.

**membership groups** groups having a direct influence on a person.

**memory encoding** how and where information gets into memory.

**memory retrieval** how and from where information gets out of memory.

**mental accounting** the manner by which consumers code, categorize, and evaluate financial outcomes of choices.

**microsales analysis** examination of specific products and territories that fail to produce expected sales.

**microsite** a limited area on the Web managed and paid for by an external advertiser/company.

**mission statement** a statement that an organization develops to share with managers, employees, and (in many cases) customers.

**mixed bundling** the seller offers goods both individually and in bundles.

**mobile apps** bite-sized software programs that can be downloaded to smart phones

**motive** a need aroused to a sufficient level of intensity to drive us to act.

**multichannel marketing** a single firm uses two or more marketing channels to reach one or more customer segments.

**multitasking** doing two or more things at the same time.

# N

**net price analysis** analysis that encompasses company list price, average discount, promotional spending, and co-op advertising to arrive at net price.

**Neuromarketing** brain research on the effect of marketing stimuli.

**noncompensatory models** in consumer choice, when consumers do not simultaneously consider all positive and negative attribute considerations in making a decision.

**nondurable goods** tangible goods purchased frequently and normally consumed in one or a few uses.

# O

**omnichannel marketing** when multiple channels work seamlessly together and match each target customer's preferred ways of doing business, regardless of whether customers are online, in the store, or on the phone.

**opinion leader** the person in informal, product-related communications who offers advice or information about a specific product or product category.

**ordering ease** how easy it is for the customer to place an order with the company.

**organization** a company's structures, policies, and corporate culture.

**organizational buying** the decision-making process by which formal organizations establish the need for purchased products and services and identify, evaluate, and choose among alternative brands and suppliers.

**overall market share** the company's sales expressed as a percentage of total market sales.

# P

**packaging** all the activities of designing and producing the container for a product.

**paid search** marketers bid on search terms, when a consumer searches for those words using Google, Yahoo!, or Bing, the marketer's ad will appear on the results page, and advertisers pay only if people click on links.

**parent brand** an existing brand that gives birth to a brand extension.

**partner relationship management (PRM) activities** the firm undertakes to build mutually satisfying long-term relations with key partners such as suppliers, distributors, ad agencies, and marketing research suppliers.

**pay-per-click ads** *see* paid search.

**penetrated market** the set of consumers who are buying a company's product.

**perceived value** the value promised by the company's value proposition and perceived by the customer.

**perception** the process by which an individual selects, organizes, and interprets information inputs to create a meaningful picture of the world.

**performance quality** the level at which the product's primary characteristics operate.

**personal communications channels** two or more persons communicating directly face to face, person to audience, over the telephone, or through e-mail.

**personal influence** the effect one person has on another's attitude or purchase probability.

**personality** a set of distinguishing human psychological traits that lead to relatively consistent responses to environmental stimuli.

**place advertising** (also **out-of-home advertising**) ads that appear outside of home and where consumers work and play.

**point-of-purchase (P-O-P)** the location where a purchase is made, typically thought of in terms of a retail setting.

**points-of-difference (PODs)** attributes or benefits that consumers strongly associate with a brand, positively evaluate, and believe they could not find to the same extent with a competitive brand.

**points-of-parity (POPs)** attribute or benefit associations that are not necessarily unique to the brand but may in fact be shared with other brands.

**positioning** the act of designing a company's offering and image to occupy a distinctive place in the minds of the target market.

**potential market** the set of consumers who profess a sufficient level of interest in a market offer.

**potential product** all the possible augmentations and transformations the product or offering might undergo in the future.

**price discrimination** a company sells a product or service at two or more prices that do not reflect a proportional difference in costs.

**price escalation** an increase in the price of a product due to added costs of selling it in different countries.

**primary groups** groups with which a person interacts continuously and informally, such as family, friends, neighbors, and coworkers.

**principle of congruity** psychological mechanism that states that consumers like to see seemingly related objects as being as similar as possible in their favorability.

**private-label brand** brand that retailers and wholesalers develop and market.

**product** anything that can be offered to a market to satisfy a want or need, including physical goods, services, experiences, events, person, places, properties, organizations, information, and ideas.

**product adaptation** altering the product to meet local conditions or preferences.

**product assortment** the set of all products and items a particular seller offers for sale.

**product concept** proposes that consumers favor products offering the most quality, performance, or innovative features.

**product invention** creating something new via product development or other means.

**product map** competitors' items that are competing against company X's items.

**product mix** *see* product assortment.

**product mix pricing** the firm searches for a set of prices that maximizes profits on the total mix.

**product-penetration percentage** the percentage of ownership or use of a product or service in a population.

**product system** a group of diverse but related items that function in a compatible manner.

**production concept** holds that consumers prefer products that are widely available and inexpensive.

**profitable customer** a person, household, or company that over time yields a revenue stream that exceeds by an acceptable amount the company's cost stream of attracting, selling, and servicing that customer.

**prospect** a purchase, a vote, or a donation by a prospective client.

**prospect theory** when consumers frame decision alternatives in terms of gains and losses according to a value function.

**psychographics** the science of using psychology and demographics to better understand consumers.

**public** any group that has an actual or potential interest in or impact on a company's ability to achieve its objectives.

**public relations (PR)** a variety of programs designed to promote or protect a company's image or its individual products.

**publicity** the task of securing editorial space—as opposed to paid space—in print and broadcast media to promote something.

**pull strategy** when the manufacturer uses advertising and promotion to persuade consumers to ask intermediaries for the product, thus inducing the intermediaries to order it.

**purchase probability scale** a scale to measure the probability of a buyer making a particular purchase.

**pure bundling** a firm only offers its products as a bundle.

**pure-click** companies that have launched a Web site without any previous existence as a firm.

**push strategy** when the manufacturer uses its sales force and trade promotion money to induce intermediaries to carry, promote, and sell the product to end users.

## Q

**quality** the totality of features and characteristics of a product or service that bear on its ability to satisfy stated or implied needs.

**questionnaire** a set of questions presented to respondents.

## R

**reference groups** all the groups that have a direct or indirect influence on a person's attitudes or behavior.

**reference prices** pricing information a consumer retains in memory that is used to interpret and evaluate a new price.

**relative market share** market share in relation to a company's largest competitor.

**reliability** a measure of the probability that a product will not malfunction or fail within a specified time period.

**repairability** a measure of the ease of fixing a product when it malfunctions or fails.

**representativeness heuristic** when consumers base their predictions on how representative or similar an outcome is to other examples.

**retailer (or retail store)** any business enterprise whose sales volume comes primarily from retailing.

**retailing** all the activities in selling goods or services directly to final consumers for personal, nonbusiness use.

**risk analysis** a method by which possible rates of returns and their probabilities are calculated by obtaining estimates for uncertain variables affecting profitability.

**role** the activities a person is expected to perform.

## S

**sales analysis** measuring and evaluating actual sales in relation to goals.

**sales budget** a conservative estimate of the expected volume of sales, used for making current purchasing, production, and cash flow decisions.

**sales promotion** a collection of incentive tools, mostly short term, designed to stimulate quicker or greater purchase of particular products or services by consumers or the trade.

**sales quota** the sales goal set for a product line, company division, or sales representative.

**sales-variance analysis** a measure of the relative contribution of different factors to a gap in sales performance.

**satisfaction** a person's feelings of pleasure or disappointment resulting from comparing a product's perceived performance or outcome in relation to his or her expectations.

**scenario analysis** developing plausible representations of a firm's possible future that make different assumptions about forces driving the market and include different uncertainties.

**secondary groups** groups that tend to be more formal and require less interaction than primary groups, such as religious, professional, and trade-union groups.

**selective attention** the mental process of screening out certain stimuli while noticing others.

**selective distortion** the tendency to interpret product information in a way that fits consumer perceptions.

**selective distribution** the use of more than a few but less than all of the intermediaries who are willing to carry a particular product.

**selective retention** good points about a product that consumers like are remembered and good points about competing products are forgotten.

**selling concept** holds that consumers and businesses, if left alone, won't buy enough of the organization's products.

**served market** all the buyers who are able and willing to buy a company's product.

**served market share** a company's sales expressed as a percentage of the total sales to its served market.

**service** any act or performance that one party can offer to another that is essentially intangible and does not result in the ownership of anything.

**share-penetration index** a comparison of a company's current market share to its potential market share.

**sharing economy** when consumers share bikes, cars, clothes, couches, apartments, tools, and skills and extract more value from what they already own.

**shopper marketing** the way manufacturers and retailers use stocking, displays, and promotions to affect consumers actively shopping for a product.

**shopping goods** goods that the consumer, in the process of selection and purchase, characteristically compares on such bases as suitability, quality, price, and style.

**short-term memory (STM)** a temporary repository of information.

**showrooming** when consumers physically examine a product and collect information in a store but make their actual purchase from the retailer later online, or from a different retailer altogether, typically to secure a lower price

**skunkworks** informal workplaces, sometimes garages, where intrapreneurial teams work to develop new products

**social classes** homogeneous and enduring divisions in a society, which are hierarchically ordered and whose members share similar values, interests, and behavior.

**social marketing** marketing done by a nonprofit or government organization to further a cause, such as "say no to drugs."

**social media** a means for consumers to share text, images, audio, and video information with each other and with companies and vice versa.

**specialty goods** goods with unique characteristics or brand identification for which enough buyers are willing to make a special purchasing effort.

**stakeholder-performance scorecard** a measure to track the satisfaction of various constituencies who have a critical interest in and impact on the company's performance.

**status** one's position within his or her own hierarchy or culture.

**straight extension** introducing a product in a foreign market without any change in the product.

**strategic business units (SBUs)** a single business or collection of related businesses that can be planned separately from the rest of the company, with its own set of competitors and a manager who is responsible for strategic planning and profit performance.

**strategic group** firms pursuing the same strategy directed to the same target market.

**strategic marketing plan** laying out the target markets and the value proposition that will be offered, based on analysis of the best market opportunities.

**strategy** a company's game plan for achieving its goals.

**style** a product's look and feel to the buyer.

**sub-brand** a new brand combined with an existing brand.

**subcultures** groups with shared values, beliefs, preferences, and behaviors emerging from their special life experiences or circumstances, such as with nationalities, religions, racial groups, and geographical regions.

**subliminal perception** receiving and processing subconscious messages that affect behavior.

**supersegment** a set of segments sharing some exploitable similarity.

**supplies and business services** short-term goods and services that facilitate developing or managing the finished product.

**supply chain management (SCM)** procuring the right inputs (raw materials, components, and capital equipment), converting them efficiently into finished products, and dispatching them to the final destinations.

**supply-side methods** approximating the amount of time or space devoted to media coverage of an event, for example, the number of seconds the brand is clearly visible on a television screen or the column inches of press clippings that mention it.

## T

**tactical marketing plan** marketing tactics, including product features, promotion, merchandising, pricing, sales channels, and service.

**target costing** deducting the desired profit margin from the price at which a product will sell, given its appeal and competitors' prices.

**target market** the part of the qualified available market the company decides to pursue.

**target-return pricing** determining the price that would yield the firm's target rate of return on investment (ROI).

**telemarketing** the use of telephone and call centers to attract prospects, sell to existing customers, and provide service by taking orders and answering questions.

**total costs** the sum of the fixed and variable costs for any given level of production.

**total customer benefit** the perceived monetary value of the bundle of economic, functional, and psychological benefits customers expect from a given market offering because of the product, service, people, and image.

**total customer cost** the bundle of costs customers expect to incur in evaluating, obtaining, using, and disposing of the given market offering, including monetary, time, energy, and psychic costs.

**total market potential** the maximum sales available to all firms in an industry during a given period, under a given level of industry marketing effort and environmental conditions.

**transfer price** the price a company charges another unit in the company for goods it ships to foreign subsidiaries.

**transformational appeal** elaborates on a nonproduct-related benefit or image.

**trend** a direction or sequence of events that has some momentum and durability.

**two-part pricing** a fixed fee plus a variable usage fee.

**tying agreements** agreement in which producers of strong brands sell their products to dealers only if dealers purchase related products or services, such as other products in the brand line.

## U

**unsought goods** those the consumer does not know about or does not normally think of buying, like smoke detectors.

## V

**value chain** a tool for identifying ways to create more customer value.

**value delivery network (supply chain)** a company's supply chain and how it partners with specific suppliers and distributors to make products and bring them to markets.

**value delivery system** all the expectancies the customer will have on the way to obtaining and using the offering.

**value network** a system of partnerships and alliances that a firm creates to source, augment, and deliver its offerings.

**value pricing** winning loyal customers by charging a fairly low price for a high-quality offering.

**value proposition** the whole cluster of benefits the company promises to deliver customers.

**variable costs** costs that vary directly with the level of production.

**venture team** a cross-functional group charged with developing a specific product or business.

**vertical marketing system (VMS)** producer, wholesaler(s), and retailer(s) acting as a unified system.

**viral marketing** using the Internet to create word-of-mouth effects to support marketing efforts and goals.

## W

**warranties** formal statements of expected product performance by the manufacturer.

**wholesaling** all the activities in selling goods or services to those who buy for resale or business use.

## Y

**yield pricing** situation in which companies offer (1) discounted but limited early purchases, (2) higher-priced late purchases, and (3) the lowest rates on unsold inventory just before it expires.

## Z

**zero-level channel (direct marketing channel)** a manufacturer selling directly to the final customer.

# Index

## Company, Brand, and Organization